BUSINESS

BUSINESS

3rd Edition

WILLIAM M. PRIDE
Texas A & M University

ROBERT J. HUGHES
Dallas County Community College

JACK R. KAPOOR
College of DuPage

Houghton Mifflin Company   Boston

Dallas   Geneva, Illinois   Palo Alto   Princeton, New Jersey

To   Nancy, Allen, and Michael Pride

To   Peggy Hughes

To   My parents, Ram and Sheela; my wife, Theresa; and my children, Karen, Kathy, and Dave

CREDITS

Cover   Painting by Francis M. Celentano, *Spira R Harmonic* (detail). Copyright Francis M. Celentano. All rights reserved.

Line Art   Rossi & Associates

Photos

Chapter 1
Part 1 opener page M. Burnside/AllStock, Inc. 2 Michael Melford. 4 The Walt Disney Company. 7 Peter Zeray. 8 The Granger Collection, New York. 12 The Granger Collection, New York. 13 © 1990 Mary Beth Camp/Matrix. 18 Pepsi-Cola Company, Division of PepsiCo Inc. 23 The Bettmann Archive. 24 © Jeff Zaruba/After Image. 28 Courtesy: Echlin Inc. Photo: Gary Gladstone.

Chapter 2
34 A. Tannenbaum/Sygma. 36 Mike Mathers/Black Star. 38 Diego Goldberg/Sygma. 39 © 1989 by Marianne Barcellona. 42 Advertisement reprinted courtesy of NYNEX Corporation. 43 International Museum of Photography at George Eastman House. 49 Peter Freed. 58 Lance M. Tucker. 60 Courtesy of Walgreen Co.

(Credits continued on p. C1)

Printed in the U.S.A.

Library of Congress Catalog Card Number: 90-83039

ISBN: 0-395-47308-X

ABCDEFGHIJ—D—9876543210

BRIEF CONTENTS

■CONTENTS

6   Creating the Organization   160

PART 4 / MARKETING   315

11 An Overview of Marketing   316

INSIDE BUSINESS   Catering to Customers   318

BUSINESS JOURNALS
Marketing with
Computers 322
Telemarketing: A Tool
for the 1990s 330

PART 6 / FINANCE AND INVESTMENT   519

17 Money, Banking, and Credit   520

18 Financial Management   552

19 Securities Markets   **584**

PREFACE

*T*he American system of business is no mere abstraction. It's a network of real people—millions of individuals seeking challenges, opportunities, and excitement through participation in business. Professors and students of business are an important part of this network. The time they invest jointly in examining the business system today bears directly on the success of the business system tomorrow.

Accordingly, we believe that professors and students deserve the best textbook available, one that is current, dynamic, and interesting—just like business itself. We have developed *Business, Third Edition*, to meet this challenge. Along with its comprehensive instructional package, *Business* provides instructors with the opportunity to present business fundamentals effectively and efficiently. For their part, students will enjoy the *Business* experience and will be well prepared for further study in a variety of business fields.

The third edition of *Business* covers new topics, presents expanded coverage of important issues, focuses on small as well as large businesses, provides thorough career information, and contains numerous pedagogical aids. The comprehensive ancillary package includes a computerized study guide and the *Video Resource Manual*, which accompanies *Business Video File*, a free series of twenty-four videos—one for each chapter and the Appendix. Here are several distinctive features of *Business, Third Edition*, and the instructional package that accompanies it.

Broad Coverage of Contemporary Issues

Students value currentness; instructors have limited time for monitoring trends. In the revised edition of *Business*, therefore, we emphasize broad, up-to-date coverage of contemporary issues facing business people today. We've given particular attention to topics requested by business professors through surveys. Topics with expanded coverage include

Measuring economic performance

Competing through quality improvement

Business ethics

Codes of ethics

Strategic alliances

Developing a business plan

Franchising

Demassing

Home-based businesses

Pay-for-performance compensation systems

Sexual harassment

Employee stock ownership plans

Consumer demographic changes

Telemarketing

Branding strategies

Superstores

Specialty advertising

Data-base management

Generally Accepted Accounting Principles

The savings and loan crisis

Insider trading

Takeovers and mergers

Investment firms

Arbitration contracts

Deregulation

European Community 1992

Importance of international business

These issues are integrated into the basic text and are also featured in vignettes that open each chapter, in boxed inserts, and in cases. All revisions are based on the most current information available in contemporary business literature.

Focus on Small Business

Because small companies in the United States outnumber large firms by about nine to one, it follows that many students will either work in small businesses or start their own businesses after leaving college. The third edition of *Business*, therefore, spotlights small business operations. We devote an entire chapter to small business in Part 1 of the text, and we illustrate numerous other concepts throughout the text with examples, opening vignettes, and cases drawn from real-life small businesses.

Two supplements—*Entrepreneur: A Business Simulation*, and *Opening a Business*, a project manual—support the text materials on small businesses and provide opportunities for further study.

Effective Pedagogical Aids

We have worked to make *Business, Third Edition*, the most interesting and most pedagogically effective of any introductory business text available. Many of the following pedagogical features in the text have been evaluated and recommended by reviewers with years of teaching experience.

Part Introductions

Each of the text's seven parts begins with a concise description of the materials to follow. From the outset of each part, a student not only is made aware of what's in each part but also has a better understanding of how the chapters in that part fit with the chapters in the rest of the text.

Learning Objectives

A student with a purpose will learn more effectively than a student wandering aimlessly through the text. Therefore, each chapter of *Business* contains clearly stated learning objectives that signal important concepts to be mastered. Together, the chapter previews and learning objectives enable the student to see where each chapter is going. To aid instructors, questions in the *Test Bank* are keyed to the learning objectives.

Chapter Previews

Each chapter is introduced with a preview—a capsule summary of what to expect in the chapter. The student can grasp quickly the major topics in the chapter and the sequence in which they are covered. Each chapter preview also serves as a useful reminder of that chapter's contents when the student is ready to review.

Inside Business

Chapter opening vignettes, entitled Inside Business, bring business concepts alive for students. With Inside Business we introduce the theme of each chapter, focusing on pertinent activities of a real organization, including Exxon, Burger King, Merrill Lynch, Disney, and Mazda. The decisions and activities of these and other familiar organizations not only demonstrate what companies are actually doing but also make the materials in each chapter relevant and absorbing for students.

Business Journal

Business Journal—a series of boxed essays running throughout the text— explores a wide range of organizations and current topics. Technology, international businesses, small businesses, and social issues are covered in the Business Journals, as well as information students can use right now. Students will find the Business Journals to be both interesting and enlightening. Sample titles include

- ▶ The Best Competitors
- ▶ Codes of Ethics
- ▶ Small Business Failures: Knowing the Warning Signs
- ▶ The Intrapreneur—Going Out on a High Wire . . . with a Safety Net
- ▶ Moving Up Through the Glass Ceiling
- ▶ Keep Your Hands, Comments, and Jokes to Yourself!
- ▶ The Name of the Game is the Brand Name
- ▶ Attention, K mart Shoppers!
- ▶ Is Accounting Information Accurate?

> ▶ My Bank Just Failed!
> ▶ Turn Your Computer Into an Investment Tool
> ▶ What Happens in a Tax Audit?
> ▶ Ronald McDonald in Pushkin Square

Margin Notes

Two types of margin notes help students understand and retain important concepts. First, to aid the student in building a basic business vocabulary, the definition of each key term (in contrasting color) is placed in the margin near the introduction of the term in the text. Second, each learning objective is positioned near the beginning of the section in which that objective is emphasized. This easy reference to terms and objectives reinforces the learning of business fundamentals.

Stimulating Writing Style

One of our major objectives in *Business, Third Edition*, is to communicate to students our enthusiasm for business in a direct, engaging manner. Throughout the book we have used a lucid writing style that builds interest and facilitates students' understanding of the concepts discussed. To ensure that the text is stimulating and easy for students to use, we have given special attention to word choice, sentence structure, and the presentation of business language.

Real-World Examples and Illustrations

Numerous real-world examples drawn from familiar organizations and recognizable products are used in each chapter. How does Federal Express utilize computerized technology to handle an average of 650,000 packages a night? Why does Shell Oil Company donate more than $11 million annually to educational programs? How was McDonald's franchise in Tokyo able to break McDonald's world record for one-day sales? Examples such as these from today's business world catch students' attention and enable them to apply the concepts and issues of each chapter.

Complete End-of-Chapter Materials

Each end-of-chapter summary brings important ideas together for the student. A list of key terms and complete set of review questions reinforces the learning of definitions and concepts. Discussion questions and exercises encourage independent thinking about the issues presented in the chapter.

Cases

Each chapter ends with two cases, based on recognizable organizations. These descriptions of current business issues and activities allow students to make real-world applications of the concepts they've covered in the chapter. Questions suitable for class discussion or individual assignments are provided for each case. Sample case titles include

- Business Philosophy at the J. M. Smucker Company
- Ownership Feud at U-Haul
- Caterpillar Streamlines Its Production Plants
- United Parcel Service Runs a Tight Ship
- Eastern Airlines and the IAM
- Mrs. Fields: The Cookie Crumbles?
- Of Cigarettes and Science: MR FIT Study
- Polaroid v. Kodak

Glossary

A glossary containing 700 fundamental business terms appears at the end of our text. The glossary serves as a convenient reference tool to reinforce students' learning the basic business vocabulary.

Useful Guides to Career Planning

Sooner or later, every student who takes an introductory business course will be faced with career choices. Therefore, we have included thorough coverage of career information for many fields of business.

The Appendix in our text provides information useful for planning a career, including career preparation, resumé writing, and interviewing. Additional career information follows each of the text's seven parts. We outline briefly the career path of a successful business person whose skills are particularly relevant to issues discussed in the preceding part. We also discuss specific jobs associated with business activities covered in that part. Finally, we include a useful independent project manual, *Toward a Career in Business*, as part of our instructional package.

Complete Package of Support Materials

Accompanying the third edition of *Business* is a full array of supplementary materials—instructional tools that both augment learning for students and increase the effectiveness of instructors.

Business Video File

The *Business Video File* (which is free to adopters) contains twenty-four videotapes—one for each chapter and the Appendix on careers. These videos, many developed by business organizations, provide unique insights into real-world companies and products. Examples of organizations featured in the *Business Video File* include Intel, McDonald's, Federal Reserve, *Wall Street Journal*, GTE, and Ernst & Young. Through these videos, students can see ideas in action in today's business world.

Video Resource Manual

This manual is designed to help instructors integrate the content of the chapters in the text with the videos in the *Business Video File*. For each chapter video, the title, topic, organization, and length are given. Suggested uses, an overview of the video, teaching objectives, and a chapter integration section are then provided to help instructors understand how the content of a specific video corresponds to chapter coverage. Discussion questions as well as class and individual experiential exercises are also included in the *Video Resource Manual*.

Instructor's Resource Manual

The *Instructor's Resource Manual* is in two volumes in the third edition. It includes the following items for each chapter:

▶ Note from the authors

▶ Brief chapter outline

▶ Guide for using transparency acetates

▶ Information about chapter video

▶ Learning objectives

▶ Comprehensive lecture outline

▶ Supplemental lecture

▶ Controversial issue

▶ Answers to the review questions

▶ Answers to the discussion questions

▶ Answers to the case questions

▶ Two chapter quizzes with answer keys

The Teaching Idea Exchange is a new addition to the *Instructor's Resource Manual*. Over fifty introduction-to-business instructors from around the country have contributed teaching ideas for teaching the introduction-to-business course.

The *Instructor's Resource Manual* also includes an extensive listing, by chapter, of suggested films and videos for classroom use; instructions for using the student enrichment project manuals; and approximately 100 transparency masters.

Test Bank

The *Test Bank* for *Business* contains essay, true/false, and multiple-choice questions—more than 3,000 items in all. About 70 percent of the items are multiple-choice questions. The final multiple-choice questions in each chapter refer to the chapter video. An item-information column in the *Test Bank* specifies details about each question. Specific information appears in the introduction to the *Test Bank*.

Microcomputerized Test Generator

This computerized version of the *Test Bank* contains more than 3,000 test items in the form of essay, true/false, and multiple-choice questions. The microcomputerized test generator is available on diskette for use on IBM-compatible personal computers.

Instructor's Presentation Software

This software package contains detailed lecture files, key terms, and illustrations for every chapter in the text. With this program, instructors can present "electronic transparencies" or customize the lecture outlines provided in ASCII format. For use with IBM PC and compatible computers equipped with Kodak Datashow or other computer-driven LCD panel used with overhead projectors. The program is provided free to adopters of Pride/Hughes/Kapoor, *Business, Third Edition.*

Transparencies

The instructional package for *Business* includes 150 color transparencies. One-half of the transparencies reproduce figures that appear in the text, while the other half are illustrations not found in the text.

Microcomputerized Study Guide

The microcomputerized study guide is a computer-aided instructional program for students that helps them review and assess their knowledge of concepts, issues, and applications discussed in each chapter of the text.

The microcomputerized study guide gives students the opportunity for active, not passive, learning. For each chapter, there is a summary; learning objectives; and multiple choice, true/false, and matching questions. In the case of the multiple-choice questions, after the student responds to each question, the easy-to-use program provides reinforcement for correct answers and reasons why incorrect answers are inappropriate.

Study Guide

Written by Kathryn Hegar of Mountain View College the *Study Guide* is a self-help tool for students to use in learning definitions, concepts, and relationships in each chapter. The exercises and questions are especially useful for self-evaluation and review purposes. For each chapter in the text, the *Study Guide* provides the following:

- ▶ Chapter overview
- ▶ Chapter summary using learning objectives
- ▶ Key terms and other important terms
- ▶ Exercises
- ▶ Matching questions
- ▶ True/false questions
- ▶ Multiple-choice questions
- ▶ Completion questions
- ▶ Essay questions
- ▶ Mini-case with questions
- ▶ Answer key

Entrepreneur: A Business Simulation

This business simulation, written by Jerald R. Smith and Peggy Golden of the University of Louisville, allows student players to make business decisions through simulated real-world experiences. *Entrepreneur* involves the planning, start-up, and continuing operation of a retail store. Acting as management teams, students encounter many factors as they make decisions for each phase of the business. Additional support materials are provided for instructors.

Student Enrichment Project Manuals

Written by Kathryn Hegar of Mountain View College, the three project manuals are entitled *Toward a Career in Business*, *Investing in Business*, and *Opening a Business*. At the discretion of the instructor, the manuals can serve as independent, self-paced projects for students or can be used as exercises for class assignments. Instructors' resource materials for each project are included in the *Instructor's Manual*.

Toward a Career in Business guides students through the four stages of getting a job: self-assessment, occupational search, employment tools, and success techniques. This manual supplements the Appendix and the Career Profiles in the text.

Investing in Business helps students learn how to invest money and how to maximize returns on their investments. Students who use *Investing in Business* should become familiar with the advantages and disadvantages of various investment instruments and should develop skills in acquiring financial information.

Opening a Business introduces students to the details of starting a company. Part One guides students through the process of gathering and analyzing essential information about business ownership. Part Two contains worksheets for students to complete based on their findings in Part One. After completing this project, students should be able to evaluate their skills as entrepreneurs and managers, calculate the capital needed to start a business, determine applicable state and federal regulations, and begin the planning process.

Business Careers

Business Careers, by Robert Luke, compiles information about salary, career ladders, and getting ahead in the fields of marketing, management, accounting, entrepreneurship, and finance in an informal style that students will find enjoyable.

William M. Pride
Robert J. Hughes
Jack R. Kapoor

Acknowledgments

We wish to express a great deal of appreciation to Kathryn Hegar, Mountain View College, for developing the *Study Guide* and the three student involvement projects. For creating *Entrepreneur: A Business Simulation*, we wish to thank Jerald R. Smith and Peggy Golden, University of Louisville. For her assistance in editing and manuscript development, we are indebted to Diane Dowdell. Finally, we wish to thank the following people for technical assistance: Marty Butler, Amy Flanagan, Neil Herndon, Dale Hoelscher, Dave Kapoor, Kathryn Kapoor, Emily Kays, Linda Limbaugh, Wendy Reed, Marissa Salinas, Debbie Thorne, and Jimmy Whitling.

We appreciate the assistance and helpful suggestions of numerous individuals who have contributed to the development of this text and instructional package. For the generous giving of their time and their thoughtful and useful comments and suggestions, we are indebted to the following reviewers:

Harold Amsbaugh
North Central Technical College

Carole Anderson
Clarion University

James O. Armstrong, II
John Tyler Community College

Xenia P. Balabkins
Middlesex County College

Charles Bennett
Tyler Junior College

Robert W. Bitter
Southwest Missouri State University

Stewart Bonem
Cincinnati Technical College

James Boyle
Glendale Community College

Lyle V. Brenna
Pikes Peak Community College

Tom Brinkman
Cincinnati Technical College

Harvey S. Bronstein
Oakland Community College

Edward Brown
Sinclair Community College

Joseph Brum
Fayetteville Technical Institute

Clara Buitenbos
Pan American University

Robert Carrel
Vincennes University

Richard M. Chamberlain
Lorain County Community College

Bruce H. Charnov
Hofstra University

William Clarey
Bradley University

J. Michael Cicero
Highline Community College

Robert Coiro
LaGuardia Community College

Don Coppa
Chabot College

Rex Cutshall
Vincennes University

John Daily
St. Edward's University

Harris D. Dean
Lansing Community College

Wayne H. Decker
Memphis State University

William M. Dickson
Green River Community College

M. Dougherty
Madison Area Technical College

Robert Elk
Seminole Community College

Carleton S. Everett
Des Moines Area Community College

Frank M. Falcetta
Middlesex County College

Thomas Falcone
Indiana University of Pennsylvania

Coe Fields
Tarrant County Junior College

Eduardo F. Garcia
Laredo Junior College

Arlen Gastineau
Valencia Community College

Edwin Giermak
College of DuPage

R. Gillingham
Vincennes University

Robert Googins
Shasta College

Joseph Gray
Nassau Community College

Ricky W. Griffin
Texas A & M University

Stephen W. Griffin
Tarrant County Junior College

Roy Grundy
College of DuPage

John Gubbay
Moraine Valley Community College

Rick Guidicessi
Des Moines Area Community College

Ronald Hadley
St. Petersburg Junior College

Carnella Hardin
Glendale Community College

Richard D. Hartley
Solano Community College

Sanford Helman
Middlesex County College

Victor B. Heltzer
Middlesex County College

Leonard Herzstein
Skyline College

Donald Hiebert
Northern Oklahoma College

Nathan Himelstein
Essex Community College

L. Duke Hobbs
Texas A&M University

Marie R. Hodge
Bowling Green State University

Joseph Hrebenak
Community College of Allegheny County, Allegheny Campus

James L. Hyek
Los Angeles Valley College

Sally Jefferson
Western Illinois University

Marshall Keyser
Moorpark College

Betty Ann Kirk
Tallahassee Community College

Edward Kirk
Vincennes University

Patrick Kroll
University of Minnesota, General College

Clyde Kobberdahl
Cincinnati Technical College

Robert Kreitner
Arizona State University

R. Michael Lebda
DeVry Institute of Technology

George Leonard
St. Petersburg Junior College

Melvin Levine
Orange County Community College

Chad Lewis
Everett Community College

William M. Lindsay
Northern Kentucky University

James Londrigan
Mott Community College

Fritz Lotz
Southwestern College

Robert C. Lowery
Brookdale Community College

Sheldon A. Mador
*Los Angeles Trade and Technical
College*

John Martin
*Mt. San Antonio Community
College*

John F. McDonough
Menlo College

L. J. McGlamory
North Harris County College

Charles Meiser
Lake Superior State University

Edwin Miner
Phoenix College

Charles Morrow
Cuyahoga Community College

W. Gale Mueller
Spokane Community College

C. Mullery
Humboldt State University

Robert J. Mullin
*Orange County Community
College*

James Nead
Vincennes University

Jerry Novak
Alaska Pacific University

Jerry O'Bryan
Danville Area Community College

Dennis Pappas
Columbus Technical Institute

Roberta F. Passenant
Berkshire Community College

Clarissa M. H. Patterson
Bryant College

Donald Pettit
*Suffolk County Community
College*

Norman Petty
*Central Piedmont Community
College*

Gloria D. Poplawsky
University of Toledo

Kenneth Robinson
Wesley College

John Roisch
Clark County Community College

Karl C. Rutkowski
Pierce Junior College

P. L. Sandlin
East Los Angeles College

Jon E. Seely
Tulsa Junior College

John E. Seitz
Oakton Community College

J. Gregory Service
*Broward Community College,
North Campus*

Richard Shapiro
Cuyahoga Community College

Anne Smevog
Cleveland Technical College

John Spence
*University of Southwestern
Louisiana*

Nancy Z. Spillman
*President, Economic Education
Enterprises*

Richard J. Stanish
Tulsa Junior College

J. Stauffer
Ventura College

W. Sidney Sugg
Lakeland Community College

Robert E. Swindle
Glendale Community College

Raymond D. Tewell
American River College

George Thomas
Johnston Technical College

Judy Thompson
Briar Cliff College

Jay Todes
North Lake College

Theodore F. Valvoda
Lakeland Community College

Frederick A. Viohl
Troy State University

C. Thomas Vogt
Allan Hancock College

Loren K. Waldman
Franklin University

Stephen R. Walsh
Providence College

Jerry E. Wheat
Indiana University, Southeast Campus

Larry Williams
Palomar College

Gregory J. Worosz
Schoolcraft College

For sharing their pedagogical suggestions in the Teaching Idea Exchange section of the *Instructor's Resource Manual*, we thank the following contributors:

Stephen R. Ahrens
L.A. Pierce College

Dave Aiken
Hocking Technical College

Frederick J. Bartelheim
Truckee Meadow Community College

Catherine Ann Beegan
Winona State University

Mary Jo Boehms
Jackson State Community College

Sanford Boswell
Coastal Carolina Community College

Roy K. Boutwell
Midwestern State University

Sallie Branscom
Virginia Western Community College

John Buckley
Orange County Community College

Michael Cicero
Highline Community College

Thomas F. Collins
Central Florida Community College

Allen Commander
University of Houston, Downtown

Bruce L. Conners
Kaskaskia College

Nancy Copeland
Eastern Michigan University

Robert J. Cox
Salt Lake Community College

Rex R. Cutshall
Vincennes University

John DeNisco
Buffalo State College

James Eason
Coastal Carolina College

Pat Ellebracht
Northeast Missouri State University

Elinor Garely
Rus Hotels

Martin Gerber
Kalamazoo Valley Community College

Wynell Goddard
Tyler Junior College

Patricia A. Green
Nassau Community College

Donald Gren
Salt Lake Community College

Gene E.A. Johnson
Clark College

Ted Johnson
Tarrant County Junior College, NE

Jim Kennedy
Angelina College

Edward J. Kirk
Vincennes University

Chad Lewis
Everett Community College

Ann Maddox
Angelo State University

Normand Martin
Oklahoma State University

T.D. McConnell
Manchester Community College

D. Dwain McInnis
Palo Alto College

John Q. McMillian
Walters State Community College

Robert R. Meyer
Brookhaven College

Sylvia Meyer
Scottsdale Community College

Rebecca W. Mihelcic
Howard Community College

James Miles
Anoka-Ramsey Community College

Charles A. Miller
L.A. Southwest College

Craig Miller
Normandale Community College

Robert A. Moore
South Utah State College

Lewis J. Neisner
SUNY College at Buffalo

Fred D. Pragasam
State University of New York

Larry J. Seibert
Purdue University, North Central

Dennis G. Shine
Fresno City College

Lee Sutherland
Suffolk University

Laura Turano
Mohegan Community College

H.R. Werrell
Rose State College

Diane Williams
Baker College

Blaine R. Wilson
Central Washington University

Lance Wrzesinski
South Puget Sound Community College

Nancy Zeliff
Northwest Missouri State University

BUSINESS

AMERICAN BUSINESS TODAY

This introductory part of *Business* is an overview of American business. We begin with an examination of the American business system, its basis, and its function within our society. Then we discuss the responsibilities of business as part of that society. Next we move to an important and very practical aspect of business: how businesses are owned and by whom. Finally, because the vast majority of businesses are small, we look at American small business in some detail. Included in this part are:

Chapter 1 Foundations of Business

Chapter 2 Ethics and Social Responsibility

Chapter 3 The Forms of Business Ownership

Chapter 4 Small Business, Entrepreneurship, and Franchises

FOUNDATIONS OF BUSINESS

1 **Understand the definition of business and its risks and rewards**

2 **Recognize the four main ingredients of laissez-faire capitalism**

3 **Know how the three basic economic questions—what, how, and for whom—are answered in free-market and planned economies**

4 **Comprehend how supply and demand determine price in competitive markets**

5 **Become aware of the origins and development of our modified capitalist business system**

6 **Identify the roles that households, businesses, and governments play in our business system**

In this chapter, we look briefly at what business is and how it got that way. First we define business, noting how business systems differ in free-market, socialist, and communist economies. We emphasize especially how the three basic economic questions—what, how, and for whom—are answered in a free-market economy. Then our focus shifts to the four degrees of business competition— pure competition, monopolistic competition, oligopoly, and monopoly. We also describe the role of supply and demand in competition. Next we look back into American history to see how events have shaped the American economic system. We conclude this chapter with a discussion of today's mixed economy and the challenges it faces in the future.

INSIDE BUSINESS

Walt Disney Company: The Magic Is Back

The stories of Bambi, Cinderella, and Snow White are familiar to all of us and, thanks to the animation genius of Walt Disney, they remain a wonderful and vivid piece of childhood that stays with us as we grow older. But the era during which these films were produced ended with the death of Walt Disney in 1966, and the Walt Disney Company lost much of its sparkle. The creative drive behind Disney seemed to fizzle out. The company produced only three or four new movies a year, and these were not highly successful. Until the mid-1980s, Disney depended on its theme parks and its real estate holdings for the majority of its revenues.

Then in 1984 Michael D. Eisner accepted the position of chairman and chief executive officer of Walt Disney Co. Through dedication, imagination, and intelligence, Eisner and his team of top executives have been successful in putting the magic back into Disney. Eisner's strategy has been to enable Disney to profit fully from the value of its existing assets while also creating new ones for the future. Existing Disney assets include its theme parks, hotels, movies, and world-famous characters such as Mickey Mouse and Donald Duck. With the recent acquisition of Henson Associates Inc., Disney has added the Muppets to its cute and cuddly arsenal.

Disney executives are now beginning to realize the benefits of linking the marketing efforts of separate Disney businesses. Cross-promotional deals and selective licensing of Disney characters to other high-quality companies are typical of the company's new direction. Licensed products include clothes, toys, watches, stuffed animals, and school supplies displaying Disney characters.

The volume of visitors to Disney's theme parks has increased as a result of Eisner's decision to more actively advertise them. In addition, the parks have been exported: the Tokyo Disneyland attracts millions of people a year. A $2.5 billion Euro Disneyland is soon scheduled to open in Paris. Disney officials want to channel the revived creativity into technologically and otherwise improved theme parks. They think the parks will in turn draw increased interest to Disney films.

While continuing to appeal to the family market with animated adventures, Disney has been turning out successful films for adults through its Touchstone Pictures division. This division has produced hit after hit and is now consistently among the industry leaders in box office share.

Disney's turnaround has been truly remarkable. Eisner and his associates have transformed Disney from a lifeless giant into a strong and growing company with studio operating profits alone totaling over $250 million a year. The rejuvenation of Disney is indeed a real-life story with a happy ending.[1]

free enterprise   *the system of business in which individuals are free to decide what to produce, how to produce it, and at what price to sell it*

*P*erhaps the most important characteristic of American business is the freedom of individuals to start a business, to work for a business, to buy or sell ownership shares in a business, and to sell a business outright. Within certain limits imposed mainly to ensure public safety, the owners of a business can produce any legal product or service they choose and sell it at any price they set. This system of business, in which individuals decide what to produce, how to produce it, and at what price to sell it, is called **free enterprise.** It is rooted in our traditional and constitutional right to own property.

The American system of free enterprise ensures, for example, the right of Walt Disney to start an entertainment company, to hire an assortment of artists, and to experiment in developing theme parks. Our system gives the current executives at Disney and its shareholders the right to make a profit from the company's success, it gives Disney's management the right to compete with 20th Century Fox, and it gives movie-goers the right to choose between films produced by the two companies and many others.

competition   *a rivalry among businesses for sales to potential customers*

Competition like that between Disney and 20th Century Fox is a necessary and extremely important by-product of free enterprise. Because many individuals and groups can open businesses, there are sure to be a number of firms offering similar products. But a potential customer may want only one such product—say, a Jeep Cherokee or a Chevrolet S-10 Blazer—and not be interested in purchasing both. Each of the firms offering similar products must therefore try to convince the potential customer to buy its product rather than a similar item made by someone else. In other words, these firms must compete with each other for sales. Business **competition,** then, is essentially a rivalry among businesses for sales to potential customers. In free enterprise, competition works to ensure the efficient and effective operation of American business. Competition also ensures that a firm will survive only if it serves its customers well. Several airlines, for example, have failed because they were unable to serve customers as efficiently and effectively as their competitors did.

Business: A Definition

business   *the organized effort of individuals to produce and sell, for a profit, the goods and services that satisfy society's needs*

Business is the organized effort of individuals to produce and sell, for a profit, the goods and services that satisfy society's needs. The general term *business* refers to all such efforts within a society (as in "American business") or within an industry (as in "the steel business"). However, a *business* is a particular organization, such as American Airlines, Inc., or Sunnyside Country Store & Gas Pumps, Inc.

The Organized Effort of Individuals

Learning Objective 1
Understand the definition of business and its risks and rewards

No person or group of persons actually organized American business as we know it today. Rather, over the years individuals have organized their own particular businesses for their own particular reasons. All these

5

individual businesses, and all the interactions between these businesses and their customers, have given rise to what we call American business.

A person who risks his or her time, effort, and money to start and operate a business is called an **entrepreneur.** To organize a business, an entrepreneur must combine four kinds of resources: material, human, financial, and informational. *Material* resources include the raw materials used in manufacturing processes, as well as buildings and machinery. *Human* resources are the people who furnish their labor to the business in return for wages. The *financial* resource is the money required to pay employees, purchase materials, and generally keep the business operating. And *information* is the resource that tells the managers of the business how effectively the other resources are being combined and utilized (see Figure 1.1).

entrepreneur *a person who risks time, effort, and money to start and operate a business*

Businesses are generally of three types. Manufacturing businesses (or *manufacturers*) are organized to process various materials into tangible goods, such as delivery trucks or towels. *Service businesses* produce services, such as haircuts or legal advice. And some firms—called *middlemen*—are organized to buy the goods produced by manufacturers and then resell them. For example, the General Electric Company is a manufacturer that produces clock radios and stereo "boxes," among other things. These products may be sold to a retailing middleman such as K mart, which then resells them to consumers in its retail stores. **Consumers** are individuals who purchase goods or services for their own personal use rather than to resell them.

consumers *individuals who purchase goods or services for their own personal use rather than to resell them*

Satisfying Needs

All three types of businesses may sell either to other firms or to consumers. In both cases, the ultimate objective of every firm must be to satisfy the needs of its customers. People generally don't buy goods and services simply to own them; they buy products to satisfy particular needs. People rarely buy an automobile solely to store it in a garage; they do, however, buy automobiles to satisfy their need for transportation. Some of us may feel that this need is best satisfied by an air-conditioned BMW with stereo cassette player, automatic transmission, power seats and windows, and remote-control side mirrors. Others may believe that a Ford Taurus with a stick shift and an AM radio will do just fine. Both products are available

FIGURE 1.1
Combining Resources
All four resources must be combined effectively for a business to be successful.

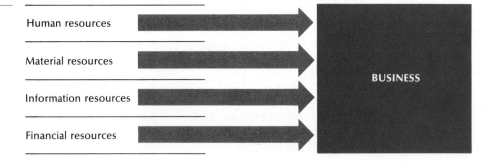

To compete with the $175 Nike Air Pressure shoe, Reebok introduced the $170 Reebok Pump, which is intended to provide customer satisfaction and to make a profit. In fact, customers do seem to be satisfied; the Reebok Pump outsold competitive brands shortly after it was introduced.

to those who want them, along with a wide variety of other products that satisfy the need for transportation.

When firms lose sight of their customers' needs, they are likely to find the going rough. But when the businesses that produce and sell goods and services understand their customers' needs and work to satisfy those needs, they are usually successful. California-based Nordstrom department stores provide the products that their customers want and offer excellent customer service. This highly successful family-owned retail organization is expanding into Virginia and New York.

profit *what remains after all business expenses have been deducted from sales revenue*

Business Profit

In the course of normal operations, a business receives money (sales revenue) from its customers in exchange for goods or services. It must also pay out money to cover the various expenses involved in doing business. If the firm's sales revenue is greater than its expenses, it has earned a profit. More specifically, as shown in Figure 1.2, **profit** is what remains after all business expenses have been deducted from sales revenue. (A negative profit, which results when a firm's expenses are greater than its sales revenue, is called a *loss*.)

The profit earned by a business becomes the property of its owners. So in one sense profit is the return, or reward, that business owners receive for producing goods and services that consumers want.

Profit is also the payment that business owners receive for assuming the considerable risks of ownership. One of these is the risk of not being paid. Everyone else—employees, suppliers, and lenders—must be paid before the owners. And if there is nothing left over (if there is no profit), there can be *no* payments to owners. A second risk that owners run is the risk of losing whatever they have put into the business. A business that cannot earn a profit is very likely to fail, in which case the owners lose whatever money, effort, and time they have invested. For business owners, the challenge of business is to earn a profit in spite of these risks.

FIGURE 1.2
The Relationship Between Sales Revenue and Profit
Profit is what remains after all business expenses have been deducted from sales revenue.

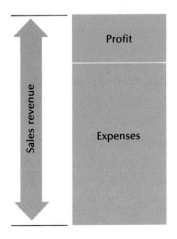

The Economics of Business

economics *the study of how wealth is created and distributed*

economy *the system through which a society answers the three economic questions— what, how, and for whom*

laissez-faire capitalism *an economic system characterized by private ownership of property, free entry into markets, and the absence of government intervention*

Adam Smith, the father of laissez-faire competition and advocate of "invisible hand" economics.

Economics is the study of how wealth is created and distributed. By *wealth* we mean anything of value, including the products produced and sold by business. "How wealth is distributed" simply means "who gets what."

According to economic theory, every society must decide on the answers to three questions:

1. What goods and services—and how much of each—will be produced?
2. How will these goods and services be produced? (That is, who will produce them and which resources will be used to do so?)
3. For whom will these goods and services be produced? (This is the question "Who gets what?")

The way in which a society answers these questions determines the kind of economic system, or **economy,** that society has chosen. In the United States, our particular answers have provided us with a *mixed* economy, which is based on laissez-faire capitalism, or private enterprise. Our free-enterprise business system is the practical application—the everyday workings—of this economic system.

Laissez-Faire Capitalism

Laissez-faire capitalism stems from the theories of Adam Smith, a Scot. In 1776, in his book *The Wealth of Nations,* Smith argued that a society's interests are best served when the individuals within that society are allowed to pursue their own self-interest.

> Every individual endeavors to employ his capital so that its produce may be of greatest value. . . . And he is in this led by an INVISIBLE HAND to promote an end which was no part of his intention. By pursuing his own interest he frequently promotes that of Society more effectually than when he really intends to promote it.

In other words, Smith believed that each person should be allowed to work toward his or her *own* economic gain, without interference from government. In doing so, each person would unintentionally be working for the good of society as a whole. And society would benefit most when there was the least interference with this pursuit of economic self-interest. Government should therefore leave the economy to its citizens. The French term *laissez faire* implies that there shall be no interference in the economy; loosely translated, it means "let them do" (as they see fit). The features of laissez-faire capitalism are summarized in Figure 1.3.

Private Ownership of Property   Smith argued that the creation of wealth (including products) is properly the concern of private individuals, not of government. Hence the resources that are used to create wealth must be owned by private individuals. Economists recognize three categories of

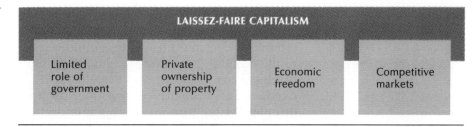

FIGURE 1.3
The Features of Laissez-Faire Capitalism
Laissez faire ("let them do") implies that there shall be no interference in the economy.

factors of production   *three categories of resources: land, labor, capital*

capital   *all the financial resources, buildings, machinery, tools, and equipment that are used in an organization's operations*

resources: land, labor, and capital, also known as the **factors of production.** Land includes the land and the natural resources on and in the land. Labor is the work performed by people. **Capital** includes financial resources, buildings, machinery, tools, and equipment that are used in an organization's operations. We have referred to these resources as material, human, and financial resources, and we shall continue to do so. Today, business people use the term *capital* to mean both capital goods and the money needed to purchase them. The private ownership and use of both kinds of capital give us the names *capitalism* and *private enterprise* for our economic system.

Smith argued further that the owners of the factors of production should be free to determine how these resources are used. They should also be free to enjoy the income and other benefits that they might derive from the ownership of these resources.

Learning Objective 2
Recognize the four main ingredients of laissez-faire capitalism

Economic Freedom   Smith's economic freedom extends to all those involved in the economy. For the owners of land and capital, this freedom includes the right to rent, sell, or invest their resources and the right to use their resources to produce any product and offer it for sale at the price they choose. For workers, this economic freedom means the right to accept or reject any job they are offered. For all individuals, economic freedom includes the right to purchase any good or service that is offered for sale by producers. These rights, however, do not include a guarantee of economic success. Nor do they include the right to harm others during the pursuit of one's own self-interest.

Competitive Markets   A crucial part of Smith's theory is the competitive market composed of large numbers of buyers and sellers. (For now, think of a market as the interaction of the buyers and sellers of a particular type of product or resource, such as shoes or secretarial skills. We discuss a more limited concept of market in Chapter 11.) Economic freedom ensures the existence of competitive markets, because sellers and buyers can enter markets as they choose. Sellers enter a market to earn profit, rent, or wages; buyers enter a market to purchase resources and want-satisfying products. Then, in a free market, sellers compete for sales and buyers compete for available goods, services, and resources.

free-market economy   *an economic system in which individuals and firms are free to enter and leave markets at will*

This freedom to enter or leave a market at will has given rise to the name **free-market economy** for the capitalism that Smith described.

Limited Role of Government   In Smith's view, the role of government should be limited to providing defense against foreign enemies, ensuring internal order, and furnishing public works and education. With regard to the economy, government should act only as rule maker and umpire. As rule maker, government should provide laws that ensure economic freedom and promote competition. As umpire, it should act to settle disputes arising from conflicting interpretations of its laws. Government, according to Adam Smith, should have no major economic responsibilities beyond these.

What, How, and for Whom in the Free-Market Economy

Learning Objective 3
Know how the three basic economic questions—what, how, and for whom—are answered in free-market and planned economies

Smith's laissez-faire capitalism sounds as though it should lead to chaos, not to answers to the three basic economic questions. How can millions of individuals and firms, all intent only on their own self-interest, produce an orderly economic system? One response might be simply, "They can and they do." Most of the industrialized nations of the world exhibit some form of modified capitalist economy, and these economies do work. A better response, however, is that these millions of individuals and firms actually provide very concrete and detailed answers to the three basic questions.

What to Produce?   This question is answered continually by consumers as they spend their dollars in the various markets for goods and services. When consumers buy Nintendo games, they are casting "dollar votes" for these products. These actions tell resource owners to produce more of this product and more of the capital goods with which the product is manufactured. Conversely, when consumers refuse to buy a product at its going price, they are voting against the product, telling producers to either reduce the price or ease off on production. In each case, consumers are giving a very specific answer concerning a very specific product.

How to Produce?   The two parts of this question are answered by producers as they enter various markets and compete for sales and profits. Those who produce for a particular market answer the question "Who will produce?" simply by being in that market. Their answer, of course, is "We will."

Competition within various markets determines which resources will be used. To compete as effectively as possible in the product markets, producers try to use the most efficient (least-cost) combination of resources. When a particular resource can be used to produce two or more different products, then producers must also compete with each other in the market for that resource. And, if the price of one needed resource becomes too high, producers will look for substitute resources—say, plastics in place of metals. The resources that will be used to produce are those that best perform their function at the least cost.

For Whom to Produce? In a market economy, goods are distributed to those who have the money to purchase them. This money is earned by individuals as wages, rents, profit, and interest—that is, as payment for the use of economic resources. Money is therefore a medium of exchange, an artificial device that aids in the exchange of resources for goods and services (see Figure 1.4). The distribution of goods and services ("who gets what") therefore depends on the *current prices* of economic resources and of the various goods and services. And prices, in turn, are determined by the balance of supply and demand.

Planned Economies

Before we discuss the workings of supply and demand in a market economy, we look quickly at two other economic systems that contrast sharply with the capitalism of Adam Smith. These systems are sometimes called **planned economies,** because the answers to the three basic economic questions are determined, at least to some degree, through centralized government planning.

planned economy *an economy in which the answers to the three basic economic questions (what, how, and for whom) are determined, to some degree, through centralized government planning*

Socialism In a *socialist* economy, the key industries are owned and controlled by the government. Such industries usually include transportation, utilities, communications, and those producing important materials such as steel. (In France, the major banks are *nationalized*, or transferred to government control. Banking, too, is considered extremely important to a nation's economy.) Land and raw materials may also be the property of the state in a socialist economy. Depending on the country, private ownership of real property (such as land and buildings) and smaller or less vital businesses is permitted to varying degrees. People

FIGURE 1.4
The Circular Flow in Smith's Laissez-Faire Economy
The use of money enhances the exchange of goods and services for resources, gives rise to the resource and product markets, and helps answer the question "For whom to produce?"

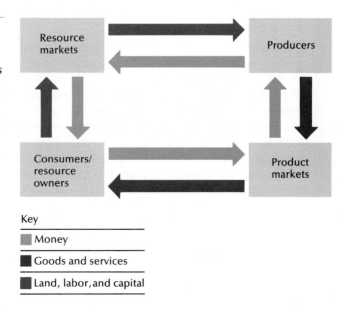

Key

⬜ Money

⬛ Goods and services

⬛ Land, labor, and capital

usually may choose their own occupations, but many work in state-owned industries.

What to produce and how to produce it are determined in accordance with national goals, which are based on projected needs, and the availability of resources—at least for government-owned industries. The distribution of goods and services is also controlled by the state to the extent that it controls rents and wages. Among the professed aims of socialist countries are the equitable distribution of income, the elimination of poverty and the distribution of social services such as medical care to all who need them, smooth economic growth, and elimination of the waste that supposedly accompanies capitalist competition.

Britain, France, Sweden, and India are democratic countries whose mixed economies include a very visible degree of socialism. Other, more authoritarian countries may actually have socialist economies; however, we tend to think of them as communist because of their almost total lack of freedom.

Communism   If Adam Smith was the father of capitalism, Karl Marx was the father of communism. In his writings (during the mid-nineteenth century), Marx advocated a classless society whose citizens together owned all economic resources. He believed that such a society would come about as the result of a class struggle between the owners of capital and the workers they had exploited. All workers would then contribute to this *communist* society according to their ability and would receive benefits according to their need.

Karl Marx, the father of communism.

The People's Republic of China, Cuba, and North Vietnam are generally considered to have communist economies. Almost all economic resources are owned by the government in these countries. The basic economic questions are answered through centralized state planning, which sets prices and wages as well. In this planning, the needs of the state generally outweigh the needs of its citizens. Emphasis is placed on the production of capital goods (such as heavy machinery) rather than on the products that consumers might want, so there are frequent shortages of consumer goods. Workers have little choice of jobs, but special skills or talents seem to be rewarded with special privileges. Various groups of professionals (bureaucrats, university professors, and athletes, for example) fare much better than, say, factory workers.

The so-called communist economies thus seem to be far from Marx's vision of communism, but rather to practice a strictly controlled kind of socialism. There is also a bit of free enterprise here and there. For example, in the Soviet Union, the farmers' markets (*rinki* in Russian) not only are allowed but are also essential to the nation's food supply. However, like all real economies, these economies are neither pure nor static. Every operating economy is a constantly changing mixture of various idealized economic systems. Some, like ours, evolve slowly. Others change more quickly, through either evolution or revolution. And, over many years, a nation, such as Great Britain, may move first in one direction—say, toward capitalism—and then in the opposite direction. It is impossible to say whether any real economy will ever closely resemble Marx's communism.

Even in a planned economy, such as the People's Republic of China, free enterprise is gaining acceptance— including government acceptance and even encouragement. China is experimenting with market incentives, and although this concept is very unfamiliar in that country, some success has been achieved and the level of entrepreneurial energy is high.

Measuring Economic Performance

productivity *the average level of output per worker per hour*

One way to measure a nation's economic performance is to assess its productivity. **Productivity** is the average level of output per worker per hour. It is a measure of the efficiency of production for an economic system. An increase in productivity results in economic growth because a larger number of goods and services are produced by a given labor force. Although U.S. workers produce more than many workers in other countries, the rate of growth in productivity has declined in the United States and has been exceeded in recent years by workers in Japan, Germany, and France. Productivity is discussed in detail in Chapter 7.

gross national product (GNP) *the total dollar value of all goods and services produced in a country for a given time period*

A general measure of a country's national economic output is called its gross national product. **Gross national product (GNP)** is the total dollar value of all goods and services produced in a country for a given time period. In 1988 the U.S. gross national product was $4.8 trillion. Comparing the GNP for several different time periods allows one to determine the extent to which a country is experiencing economic growth. Knowledge of a single year's gross national product does not provide an analyst with much information.

real gross national product *the total dollar value, adjusted for price increases, of all goods and services produced in a country during a given time period*

To make accurate comparisons of GNP figures for two different years one must adjust the figures for inflation, that is, higher price levels. By using inflation-adjusted figures, one is able to measure real gross national product. **Real gross national product** is the total dollar value, adjusted for price increases, of all goods and services produced in a country during a given time period. Comparisons of real gross national product information allows one to accurately measure differences in output from one time period to another. Figure 1.5 depicts the gross national product of the United States in current dollars and in constant 1982 dollars. The real

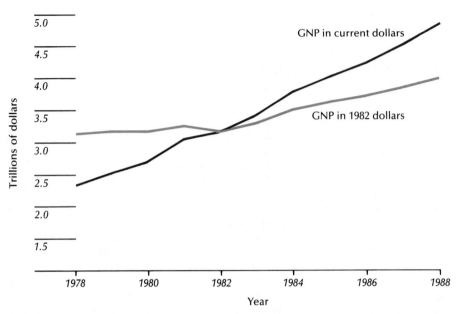

FIGURE 1.5
Gross National Product in Current Dollars and in Inflation-Adjusted Dollars
*The changes in real gross national product from one time period to another can be used to measure economic performance. (*Sources*: Survey of Current Business, Vol. 68; The National Income and Product Accounts of the U.S. 1929–1982; Statistical Abstract of the United States, 1989.)*

gross national product figures are represented in the adjusted figures. Note that between 1978 and 1988 our real gross national product grew from $3.1 trillion to $3.9 trillion.

Supply, Demand, Price, and Competition

As we have noted, a free-market system implies competition among sellers of products and resources. Economists recognize four different degrees of competition, ranging from ideal complete competition to no competition at all. These are pure competition, monopolistic competition, oligopoly, and monopoly.

Pure Competition

pure competition   the market situation in which there are many buyers and sellers of a product, and no single buyer or seller is powerful enough to affect the price of that product

Pure (or perfect) competition is the complete form of competition. **Pure competition** is the market situation in which there are many buyers and sellers of a product, and no single buyer or seller is powerful enough to affect the price of that product. Note that this definition includes several important ideas. First, we are discussing the market for a single product— say, bushels of wheat. (The definition also applies to markets for resources,

BUSINESS JOURNAL

Strengthening Competitiveness through Quality Improvement

Years ago, "Made in the U.S.A." meant high quality, unsurpassed technology, and the world's most efficient productivity. Now, in this country and overseas, foreign companies are vigorously challenging American firms. Over 70 percent of U.S. products compete with foreign goods, and this percentage will likely grow. Americans eagerly purchase German cars, Japanese electronic equipment, Russian vodka, and Italian fashion accessories. Honda has built and will build additional factories to manufacture cars in the United States.

In their struggle to be more competitive, U.S. companies have cut costs, improved efficiency, and have begun to market products and services more aggressively. Technological improvements, restructuring, and salary freezing have turned many U.S. firms into leaner, meaner machines.

Many business analysts rank poor product quality as the greatest enemy of U.S. productivity and competitiveness. Improved quality, more than anything else, enables a corporation to reduce costs and enhance profits. A typical American factory invests 20 to 25 percent of its entire operating costs on discovering and then fixing mistakes. Almost one-quarter of all factory workers must rework products that were not made correctly the first time. The cost of warranties and replacing defective merchandise is enormous. It has become a matter of survival for some U.S. companies: They must improve product quality or close the company doors.

Improving product quality often coincides with more efficient productivity. Increasing efficiency usually starts with a healthy research and development program. Funds spent on new processes and new methods have been found to be good investments. More and more American companies

are cooperating with each other on joint research and development projects and are linking up with the services and expertise of universities. This has had a positive effect on U.S. competitiveness. The combination of the best minds in industry and the sharpness and eagerness found on American college campuses will undoubtedly lead to better productivity.

Efficient productivity is also tied to employee involvement. Motivated workers produce better products and services than apathetic ones. Company officials in the United States have discovered that if front-line workers are asked for their opinions, efficiency improves and so does worker morale. If enthusiasm, pride, and craftsmanship are at the core of a company's philosophy, employees will respond and increase their value as a company asset.

U.S. companies that compete with foreign firms are fighting for their survival. For just as U.S. businesses are trying to improve their products and their productivity and lower costs, so are all of their foreign competitors. Building better, stronger companies is a continual process. Companies in the United States cannot contentedly rest on past achievements. They will need to continue to fight for their position in the international marketplace.

Based on information from A. Gary Shilling, "Hold That Body Count," *Forbes*, January 22, 1990, p. 150; Edward L. Hennessy, "Technology, Capital and People; The ABC's of U.S. Competitiveness," *CPA Journal*, August 1987, pp. 4, 6, 8; Sylvia Nasar, "America's Competitive Revival," *Fortune*, January 4, 1988, pp. 44–50, 52; Sylvia Nasar, "Competitiveness: Getting It Back," *Fortune*, April 27, 1987, pp. 217–218, 220–221, 223; and Otis Port, "The Push for Quality," *Business Week*, June 8, 1987, pp. 131–135.

but we'll limit our discussion here to products.) Second, all sellers offer essentially the same product for sale; a buyer would be just as satisfied with seller A's wheat as with that offered by seller B or seller Z. Third, all buyers and sellers know everything there is to know about the market (including, in our example, the prices that all sellers are asking for their wheat). And fourth, the market is not affected by the actions of any one buyer or seller.

In such a situation, every seller would do best by asking the same price that every other seller is asking. Why is this so? Suppose one seller wanted 50 cents more than all the others per bushel of wheat. That seller would not be able to sell a single bushel, because buyers could—and would—do better by purchasing wheat from the competition. On the other hand, a firm that was willing to sell below the going price would sell all its wheat quickly. But that seller would lose sales revenue (and profit), because buyers are actually willing to pay more.

In pure competition, then, sellers—and buyers as well—must accept the going price. But who or what determines this price? Actually, everyone does. The price of each product is determined by the actions of *all buyers and all sellers together,* through the forces of supply and demand. It is this interaction of buyers and sellers, working for their best interest, that Adam Smith referred to as the "invisible hand" of competition. Let us see how it operates.

supply *the quantity of a product that producers are willing to sell at each of various prices*

The **supply** of a particular product is the quantity of the product that producers are willing to sell at each of various prices. Supply is thus a relationship between prices and the quantities offered by producers and is represented by a supply curve as shown in Figure 1.6. Producers are rational people, so we would expect them to offer more of a product for sale at higher prices and to offer less of the product at lower prices.

demand *the quantity of a product that buyers are willing to purchase at each of various prices*

The **demand** for a particular product is the quantity that buyers are willing to purchase at each of various prices. Demand is thus a relationship between prices and the quantities purchased by buyers. This relationship is represented by a demand curve as depicted in Figure 1.6. Buyers, too, are usually rational, so we would expect them—as a group—to buy more of a product when its price is low and to buy less of the product when its price is high. This is exactly what happens when the price of fresh strawberries rises dramatically. People buy other fruit or do without and reduce their purchases of strawberries. They begin to buy more fresh strawberries only when prices drop.

FIGURE 1.6
Demand Curve and Supply Curve
The intersection of a demand curve and a supply curve indicates a single price and quantity at which buyers will purchase products and suppliers will sell them.

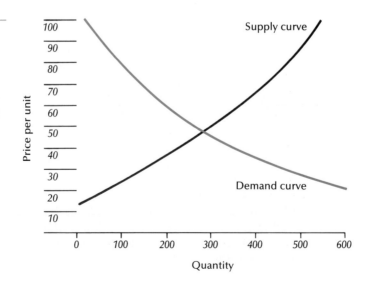

Learning Objective 4
Comprehend how supply and demand determine price in competitive markets

Of course, neither sellers nor buyers exist in a vacuum. What they do is interact within a market. (Recall our working definition of *market*.) And there is always one certain price at which the quantity of a product that is demanded is exactly equal to the quantity of that product that is produced. Suppose producers are willing to *supply* 2 million bushels of wheat at a price of $5 per bushel and that buyers are willing to *purchase* 2 million bushels at a price of $5 per bushel. In other words, supply and demand are in balance, or *in equilibrium*, at the price of $5. Therefore, if suppliers produce 2 million bushels then no one who is willing to pay $5 per bushel will have to go without wheat, and no producer who is willing to sell at $5 per bushel will be stuck with unsold wheat.

Obviously, $5 per bushel is the "going price" at which producers should sell their 2 million bushels of wheat. Economists call this price the *equilibrium price* or *market price*. Under pure competition, the **market price** of any product is the price at which the quantity demanded is exactly equal to the quantity supplied.

market price   *in pure competition, the price at which the quantity demanded is exactly equal to the quantity supplied*

In theory and in the real world, market prices are affected by anything that affects supply and demand. The *demand* for wheat, for example, might change if researchers suddenly discovered that it had very beneficial effects on users' health. Then more wheat would be demanded at every price. The *supply* of wheat might change if new technology permitted the production of greater quantities of wheat from the same amount of acreage. In that case, producers would be willing to supply more wheat at each price. Either of these changes would result in a new market price. Other changes that can affect competitive prices are shifts in buyer tastes, the development of new products that satisfy old needs, and fluctuations in income due to inflation or recession. For example, generic or "no-name" products are now available in supermarkets. Consumers can satisfy their needs for products ranging from food to drugs to paper products at a lower cost, with quality comparable to brand name items. Bayer was recently forced to lower the price of its very popular aspirin because of competition from generic products.

Monopolistic Competition

monopolistic competition   *a market situation in which there are many buyers along with relatively many sellers who differentiate their products from the products of competitors*

Pure competition is only a theoretical concept. Some specific markets (such as auctions of farm products) may come close, but no real market totally exhibits perfect competition. Many real markets, however, are examples of monopolistic competition. **Monopolistic competition** is a market situation in which there are many buyers along with relatively many sellers who differentiate their products from the products of competitors. The various products available in a monopolistically competitive market are very similar in nature, and they are all intended to satisfy the same need. However, each seller attempts to make its product somewhat different from the others by providing unique product features—an attention-getting brand name, unique packaging, or services such as free delivery or a "lifetime" warranty. For example, Hanes has differentiated L'eggs pantyhose from numerous competing brands through unique branding and packaging.

THE PEPSI GENERATION IS IN EFFECT.

An oligopoly is a market situation (or industry) in which there are few sellers. The soft-drink cola market is one such situation. The leading cola producers commit large amounts of money to competitive advertising. A recent Pepsi campaign includes slogans such as "The most refreshing pop in rock," and "The Pepsi generation is in effect."

Product differentiation is a fact of life for the producers of many consumer goods, from soaps to clothing to personal computers. The individual producer sees what looks like a mob of competitors, all trying to chip away at its market. (Actually, monopolistic competition is characterized by fewer sellers than pure competition, but there are enough sellers to ensure a highly competitive market.) By differentiating its product from all similar products, the producer obtains some limited control over the market price of its product. For example, the prices of various brands of pantyhose vary. Under pure competition, the price of all pantyhose brands would simply be the equilibrium price of pantyhose products.

Oligopoly

oligopoly   a market situation (or industry) in which there are few sellers

An **oligopoly** is a market situation (or industry) in which there are few sellers. Generally these sellers are quite large, and sizable investments are required to enter into their market. For this reason, oligopolistic industries tend to remain oligopolistic. Examples of oligopolies are the American automobile, industrial chemicals, and oil refining industries.

Because there are few sellers in an oligopoly, each seller has considerable control over price. At the same time, the market actions of each seller can have a strong effect on competitors' sales. If one firm reduces its price, the other firms in the industry usually do the same to retain their market shares. If one firm raises its price, the others may wait and watch the market for a while, to see whether their lower price tag gives them a competitive advantage, and then eventually follow suit. All this wariness usually results in similar prices for similar products. In the absence of much price competition, product differentiation becomes the major competitive weapon; this is very evident in the advertising of the

BUSINESS JOURNAL

The Best Competitors

There are many successful companies in business. However, a few of these have a reputation for completely dominating their markets. These "best" competitors often share some basic common characteristics. For example, the executives of the leading competitors are likely to be obsessed with market share: They scratch and claw viciously to not only maintain but increase the market share of their products. Also, these managers consistently work to improve their products or services, their management techniques, their marketing strategies, and every other possible aspect of their business. The best competitors are innovators totally committed to quality, who believe that good is simply not good enough. Also, strong competitors seem to favor the acquisition of other companies that either are in a related industry or possess a desired technology. The officials of these organizations are usually very cost conscious, though, and very conservative when it comes to their respective companies' capital structure. They can afford to be conservative since cash flow is rarely a problem.

Eastman Kodak Co. is one of the best competitors. Kodak currently controls 80 percent of the U.S. consumer film market and 50 percent of the global consumer film market. When you consider that one market share point of the global market is equal to about $40 million in revenues, then you begin to realize how successful a competitor Kodak really is. Since Fuji Photo Film Co. surprisingly outbid Kodak to become the official supplier of film to the 1984 Los Angeles Olympic Games, Kodak has been on a rampage, introducing one new film after another, with each new product being the result of improved technology and being vastly superior to the preceding one. Kodak is producing the best film ever made. Recently, Kodak has purchased several independent film processors, such as American Photographic Group, Fox Photo, and CX to further enhance its number-one position.

Riddell Inc., a sporting goods company, controls 65 percent of the market for football helmets. One reason for the size of its market share is that Riddell executives convinced officials of the National Football League to adopt the use of their company's helmets for NFL players. The NFL granted Riddell the exclusive right to feature its name on each helmet in exchange for product discounts. Riddell purchased a firm that makes shoulder pads, and now Riddell officials are trying to persuade the NFL to use Riddell shoulder pads exclusively. Riddell executives want to enter the consumer athletic-wear industry soon and are shopping around for a sportswear company.

Another successful competitor is Minneapolis-based Josten's, Inc., a company that specializes in class rings, graduation caps and gowns, diplomas, yearbooks, and video yearbooks. Josten's supplied medals to the 1988 Winter Olympic Games and rings to the winners of the Super Bowl and the American Football Conference championship. Its primary market, and the market it knows better than any other firm, is the students who attend the approximately 12,000 high schools and colleges in the United States. Sales at Josten's have grown at an average annual rate of about 13 percent since 1958. Josten's officials are enthusiastically entering the audio-visual educational aids industry and computer software market. The company's fastest-growing division is Artex (sportswear), and its newest division specializes in school pictures.

Based on information from "Josten's," Moody's Handbook of Common Stocks, Spring 1990 ed., Moody's Investor's Service, 99 Church Street, New York, NY 10007; Jerry Jakubovics, "Sports Mania and School Spirit: A Lucrative Combination," *Management Review*, October 1988, pp. 14–15; Carol J. Loomis, "Secrets of the Superstars," *Fortune*, April 24, 1989, pp. 50–51; and Bill Saporito, "Companies that Compete Best," *Fortune*, May 22, 1989, pp. 36–40, 42, 44.

major American auto manufacturers. For example, General Motors recently began offering 2.9 percent financing on three-year loans for all of its cars—its biggest financing inducement. The day after GM's announcement, Ford and Chrysler launched competitive financing offers. American Motors undercut them all by bringing out the ultimate in low rates: financing at 0.0 percent.[2]

Monopoly

monopoly *a market (or industry) with only one seller*

A **monopoly** is a market (or industry) with only one seller. Because only one firm is the supplier of a product, it has complete control over price. However, no firm can set its price at some astronomical figure just because there is no competition; the firm would soon find that it had no sales revenue, either. Instead, the firm in a monopoly position must consider the demand for its product and set the price at the most profitable level.

natural monopoly *an industry requiring huge investments in capital and within which duplication of facilities would be wasteful and, thus, not in the public interest*

The few monopolies in American business don't have even that much leeway in setting prices because they are all carefully regulated by government. Each of them operates in a **natural monopoly,** an industry that requires a huge investment in capital and within which any duplication of facilities would be wasteful. Most monopolies in America are public utilities, such as we find in electric power distribution. They are permitted to exist because the public interest is best served by their existence, but they operate under the scrutiny and control of various state and federal agencies. Our Constitution permits the federal government to issue copyrights, patents, and trademarks—all legal monopolies or legal limited monopolies.

Except for such regulated monopolies, federal laws prohibit not only monopolies but also attempts to form them. The Sherman Antitrust Act of 1890 made any such attempt a criminal offense, and the Clayton Antitrust Act of 1914 prohibited a number of specific actions that could lead to monopoly. The goal of these and other antitrust laws is to ensure the competitive environment of American business.

The Development of American Business

American business and the American economy developed together with the nation itself. All three have their roots in the knowledge, skills, and values that were brought to this country by the earliest settlers. Refer to Figure 1.7 for an overall view of the relationship between our history and economy and some of the major inventions that had an influence on them.

The Colonial Period

Learning Objective 5
Become aware of the origins and development of our modified capitalist business system

The first settlers in the New World were concerned mainly with providing themselves with the necessities—food, clothing, and shelter. Almost all families lived on farms, and the entire family worked at the business of surviving.

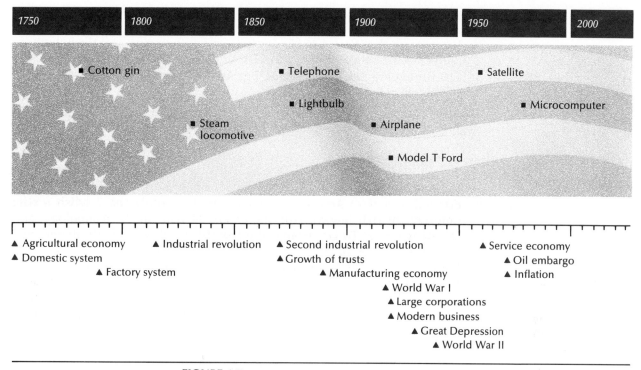

| 1750 | 1800 | 1850 | 1900 | 1950 | 2000 |

■ Cotton gin

■ Telephone

■ Satellite

■ Lightbulb

■ Microcomputer

■ Steam locomotive

■ Airplane

■ Model T Ford

▲ Agricultural economy ▲ Industrial revolution ▲ Second industrial revolution ▲ Service economy
▲ Domestic system ▲ Growth of trusts ▲ Oil embargo
▲ Factory system ▲ Manufacturing economy ▲ Inflation
▲ World War I
▲ Large corporations
▲ Modern business
▲ Great Depression
▲ World War II

FIGURE 1.7
Time Line of American Business
Notice how invention and innovation naturally led to changes in transportation.
This in turn caused a shift to more of a manufacturing economy.

The colonists did indeed survive, and eventually they were able to produce more than they consumed. They used their surplus for trading, mainly by barter, among themselves and with the English trading ships that called at the colonies. **Barter** is a system of exchange in which goods or services are traded directly for other goods and/or services—without using money. As this trade increased and capital was accumulated, small-scale business enterprises began to appear. The predominant form of ownership was the *sole proprietorship*, a business owned by only one individual. Most of these businesses produced farm products, primarily rice and tobacco for export. Other industries that had been founded by 1700 were shipbuilding, lumbering, fur trading, rum manufacturing, and fishing. These industries also produced mainly for export. Trade with England grew, but British trade policies heavily favored British merchants.

About 90 percent of the population was still engaged in farming. As late as the Revolutionary War period, farm families were engaged primarily in meeting their own needs. Some were able to use their skills and whatever time they had left over to work under the domestic system of production. The **domestic system** was a method of manufacturing in which an entrepreneur distributed raw materials to various homes, where families would process them into finished goods. The goods were then offered for sale by the merchant entrepreneur.

barter *a system of exchange in which goods or services are traded directly for other goods and/or services—without using money*

domestic system *a method of manufacturing in which an entrepreneur distributed raw materials to various homes, where families would process them into finished goods to be offered for sale by the merchant entrepreneur*

During and after the Revolutionary War, Americans began to produce a wider variety of goods, including gunpowder, tools, hats, and cutlery. Later, after the War of 1812, domestic manufacturing and trade became much more important as trade with England and other nations declined. The timing may be coincidental, but American industry began to grow in earnest just when Adam Smith's economic theory was becoming widespread. In any case, private ownership of resources and free enterprise were already a part of American political and business life.

The Industrial Revolution

In 1790 a young English apprentice mechanic named Samuel Slater decided to sail to America. At this time, to protect the English textile industry, British law forbade the export of machinery, technology, and skilled workers. To get around the law, Slater painstakingly memorized the plans for Arkwright's water-powered spinning machine and left England disguised as a farmer. A year later he set up a textile factory in Pawtucket, Rhode Island, to spin raw cotton into thread. Slater's ingenuity resulted in America's first use of the **factory system** of manufacturing, in which all the materials, machinery, and workers required to manufacture a product are assembled in one place.

By 1814 Francis Cabot Lowell had established a factory in Waltham, Massachusetts, to spin, weave, and bleach cotton all under one roof. He organized the various manufacturing steps into one uninterrupted sequence, hired professional managers, and was able to produce 30 miles of cloth each day! In doing so, Lowell seems to have made use of another concept put forth by Adam Smith: specialization. **Specialization** is the separation of a manufacturing process into distinct tasks and the assignment of different tasks to different individuals. Its purpose is to increase the efficiency of industrial workers.

With Lowell's factory the Industrial Revolution, which had already started in England, arrived in America. The three decades from 1820 to 1850 were the golden age of invention and innovation in machinery. The cotton gin of Eli Whitney greatly increased the supply of cotton for the textile industry. Elias Howe's sewing machine became available to convert materials into clothing. The agricultural machinery of John Deere and Cyrus McCormick revolutionized farm production.

At the same time, new means of transportation greatly expanded the domestic markets for American products. The Erie Canal was opened in the 1820s. Soon, thanks to Robert Fulton's engine, steamboats appeared that could move upstream against the current; they were able to use the rivers as highways for hauling bulk goods. During the 1830s and 1840s, the railroads began to extend the existing transportation system to the west, carrying goods and people much farther than was possible by waterways alone. Between 1860 and 1880 the number of miles of railroad track tripled; by 1900 it had doubled again. The phenomenal growth of the railroads in these four decades paralleled the industrial growth that the railroads had fostered.[3]

factory system   *a system of manufacturing in which all of the materials, machinery, and workers required to manufacture a product are assembled in one place*

specialization   *the separation of a manufacturing process into distinct tasks and the assignment of different tasks to different individuals*

A Second Revolution

Many business historians view the period from 1870 to 1900 as the second industrial revolution; certainly, many of the characteristics of our modern business system took form during these three decades. In this period, for example, the nation shifted from a farm economy to a manufacturing economy. The developing oil industry provided fuel for light, heat, and energy. Greatly increased immigration furnished the labor for expanded production. New means of communication brought sophistication to banking and finance. All the tools of industrialization were at hand and Smith's private enterprise was put to work. The United States became not only an industrial giant but a leading world power as well.

Industrial growth and prosperity continued well into the twentieth century. Henry Ford's moving assembly line, which brought the work to the worker, refined the concept of specialization and spawned the mass production of consumer goods. By the 1920s the automobile industry had begun to influence the entire economy. The steel industry, which supplies materials to the auto industry, grew along with it. The oil and chemical industries grew just as fast and provided countless new synthetic products—new ways to satisfy society's wants. And the emerging airplane and airline industries promised better and faster transportation.

Fundamental changes occurred in business ownership and management as well. The largest businesses were no longer each owned by one individual; instead, ownership was in the hands of thousands of corporate shareholders who were willing to invest in—but not to operate—a business. A new breed of business professional emerged to manage the huge and growing corporations. To prepare these business managers, colleges and universities began to offer degree programs in accounting, production,

No industrial innovation captured the essence of the "second revolution" more clearly than the Ford Motor Company moving assembly line. It represented the movement of the American economy away from farming and toward industrial production. Shown here is the final line in the assembly process, in which the car bodies were lowered and bolted into chassis.

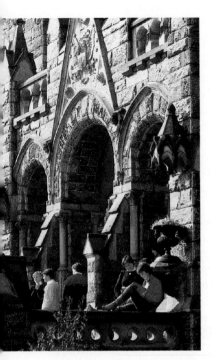

A service economy is one in which more effort is devoted to the production of services than to the production of goods. Today 80 percent of American workers are employed in service organizations, such as the college pictured here.

industrial engineering, and marketing. New philosophies of business management and personnel relations focused attention on human problems and employee morale.

Certain modern marketing techniques are products of this era, too. Large corporations developed new methods of advertising and selling. Time payment plans made it possible for the average consumer to purchase costly durable goods, such as automobiles, appliances, and furnishings. Advertisements counseled the public to "buy now and pay later." A higher standard of living was indeed created for most people—but it was not to last.

The Great Depression

The "roaring twenties" ended with the sudden crash of the stock market in 1929 and the near collapse of the economy. The Great Depression that followed in the 1930s was a time of misery and human suffering. The unemployment rate varied between 16 and 25 percent in the years 1931 through 1939, and the value of goods and services produced in America fell by almost half. Business investment came to a complete halt. People lost their faith in business and its ability to satisfy the needs of society without government interference.

After the election of President Franklin D. Roosevelt, the federal government devised a number of programs to get the economy moving again. In implementing these programs, the government got deeply involved in business for the first time—as both a regulator of business activity and a provider of social services to individuals. Many business people opposed this government intervention, but they reluctantly accepted the fact that they were no longer operating within a purely capitalist economy.

Recovery and Beyond

The economy was on the road to recovery when World War II broke out in Europe in 1939. The need for vast quantities of war materials—first for our allies and then for the American military as well—spurred business activity and technological development. This rapid economic pace continued after the war, and the 1950s and 1960s witnessed both increasing production and a rising standard of living. **Standard of living** is a loose, subjective measure of how well off an individual or a society is, mainly in terms of want satisfaction through goods and services.

standard of living *a loose, subjective measure of how well off an individual or a society is, mainly in terms of want satisfaction through goods and services*

In the mid-1970s, however, a shortage of crude oil, along with constantly rising prices for petroleum products, led to a new set of problems for business. Petroleum products supply most of the energy required to produce goods and services and to transport goods around the world. As the cost of petroleum products increased, the cost of energy increased along with it, and the cost of goods and services increased as well. The result was **inflation,** a general rise in the level of prices, at a rate well over 10 percent per year. Interest rates also increased dramatically, so borrowing by both businesses and consumers was reduced.

inflation *a general rise in the level of prices*

Business profits fell as the consumer's purchasing power was eroded by inflation and high interest rates, and unemployment reached alarming levels.

These problems seem now to have been solved—at least partially. The inflation rate, interest rates, and unemployment have all declined. Consumers have become more willing to spend money, and business people are cautiously optimistic. Production is again increasing. Recently, for example, the gross national product of the U.S. economy rose to over $4.8 trillion. Services have become a dominant part of our economy. Since well over half of the American work force is involved in service industries, ours is often called a **service economy.** (Service economy is discussed more fully in Chapter 7.) If GNP is any indication at all of a country's standard of living, then ours is high and moving higher.

service economy *an economy in which the majority of the work force is involved in service industries; one in which more effort is devoted to the production of services than to the production of goods*

Our Business System Today

So far we have looked at several different aspects of our business system. Its theoretical basis is the laissez-faire economic system of Adam Smith. However, our real-world economy is not as "laissez faire" as Smith would have liked, because government participates as more than umpire and rule maker. Ours is, in fact, a **mixed economy,** one that exhibits elements of both capitalism and socialism.

mixed economy *an economy that exhibits elements of both capitalism and socialism*

We also looked at the development of our business system. Again we saw government participation, which began in earnest during the Great Depression of the 1930s and has generally increased since those years, for a variety of economic and social reasons. Our business system is still guided by the interplay of buyers and sellers, but obviously the role of government must also be taken into account.

In today's economy, then, the three basic economic questions (what, how, and for whom) are answered by three groups:

Learning Objective 6
Identify the roles that households, businesses, and governments play in our business system

1. *Households*, made up of consumers who seek the best value for their money and the best prices for the economic resources they own
2. *Businesses*, which seek to maximize their long-term profits
3. *Federal, state, and local governments*, which seek to promote public safety and welfare and to serve the public interest

The interactions among these three groups are shown in Figure 1.8, which is similar to Figure 1.4 with government included.

Households

Households are both consumers of goods and owners of the productive resources of land, labor, and capital. As *resource owners*, the members of households provide businesses with the means of production. In return, businesses pay rent, wages, and interest, which households receive as income.

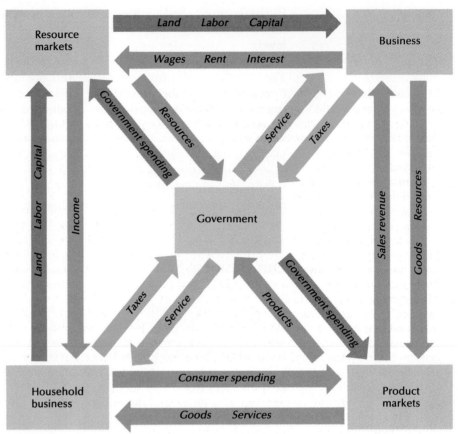

FIGURE 1.8
The Circular Flow in Our Modified Capitalist System Today
Our business system is guided by the interplay of buyers and sellers, but the role
of government is taken into account.

As *consumers*, household members use this income to purchase the
goods and services produced by business. Today almost two-thirds of our
nation's GNP consists of **consumer goods:** products purchased by individuals for personal consumption. (The remaining one-third is purchased by
business and government.) This means that consumers, as a group, are
the biggest customer of American business. So it should come as no
surprise that business does as consumers wish. And, as we saw earlier,
consumers make their wishes known through their "dollar votes."

consumer goods *products purchased by individuals for personal consumption*

Businesses

Like households, businesses are engaged in two exchanges. They exchange
money for the factors of production, and they use these resources to
produce goods and services. Then they exchange their products for sales
revenue. This sales revenue, in turn, is exchanged for additional resources,

BUSINESS JOURNAL

How to Become a Millionaire

$1,000,000. That's a large and magical number. But besides winning a lottery, being a superstar athlete, or being born into an extremely wealthy family, how does one become a millionaire? When you examine the lives and lifestyles of millionaires, you might be surprised to find out how they do it.

Contrary to popular belief, most current millionaires didn't inherit their wealth. About 80 percent of American millionaires come from middle- or working-class families.

Doctors, lawyers, and business executives have highly prestigious jobs, but they don't necessarily make the most money. Owners of small, often mundane, businesses have a much greater chance of becoming millionaires. Close to 85 percent of America's millionaires own their own companies or own sizable portions of private firms. Athletes, entertainers, and artists do not represent a large proportion of American millionaires—in fact, less than 1 percent!

Thomas J. Stanley, a marketing professor at Georgia State University and an expert on the American rich, has come up with a list of businesses that he thinks might bring the industrious, hard-working, ambitious individual his or her first million. The list includes: operation of a dry-cleaning chain; computer program design; commercial printing; jewelry retailing; specialized tool-and-die manufacturing; real estate–related businesses; plumbing, heating, and air-conditioning contracting; money managing; and independent insurance brokerage services.

Millionaires are typically workaholics: Sixty-eight percent claim that they don't ever plan on retiring. Rich people work even though they don't have to. And not only do millionaires work hard, they do not spend their money carelessly or extravagantly. Fewer than half of the millionaires in this country send their children to private elementary or high schools. And most millionaires don't own expensive watches or yachts. Intense saving, not spending, might be the key to making your first million.

So if you have ideas about reaching that million-dollar plateau, it might be a wise idea to forget about the fancy cars and cancel that plane reservation to Las Vegas. Or at least if you go to Vegas, spend less time inside the casinos and more time checking out the acts.

———————

Based on information from Charles Whitaker, "How to Make a Million Dollars," *Ebony*, September 1989, p. 134 + ; "Affluent and Active," *Wall Street Journal*, July 9, 1987, p. 31(E); Beth Brophy, "Ordinary Millionaires," *U.S. News & World Report*, January 13, 1986, pp. 43–49; and Martha T. Moore, "They're Like Us, Except They're Rich," *USA Today*, May 22, 1987, pp. 1B–2B.

which are used to produce and sell more products. So the circular flow of Figure 1.8 is continuous: Business pays *wages, rent, and interest* which become *household income* which becomes *consumer spending* which becomes *sales revenue* which again becomes *wages, rent, and interest*. And so on.

Along the way, of course, business owners would like to remove something from the circular flow in the form of profits. And households try to retain some income as savings. But are profits and savings really removed from the flow? Usually not! When the economy is running smoothly, households are willing to invest their savings in business. They can do so directly, by buying ownership shares in business or lending money to business. They can also invest indirectly, by placing their savings in bank accounts; banks then invest these savings as part of their normal business operations. In either case, savings usually find their way back into the circular flow.

It is the responsibility of government to protect and promote the public welfare. Safety on our highways depends on police patrolling and periodic inspections of transportation vehicles.

When business profits are distributed to business owners, these profits become household income. (Business owners are, after all, members of households.) And, as we saw, household income is retained in the circular flow as either consumer spending or invested savings. So business profits, too, are retained in the business system, and the circular flow is complete. How, then, does government fit in?

Governments

The framers of our Constitution desired as little government interference with business as possible. At the same time, the Preamble to the Constitution set forth the responsibility of government to protect and promote the public welfare. Local, state, and federal governments discharge this responsibility through regulation and the provision of services. Government regulation of business has already been mentioned; specific regulations are discussed in detail in various chapters of this book. In addition, government provides a variety of services that are considered important but either (1) would not be produced by private firms in a free-enterprise system or (2) would be produced only for those who could afford them. Among these services are

▶ National defense

▶ Police and fire protection

▶ Welfare payments and retirement income

▶ Education

▶ National and state parks, forests, and wilderness areas

▶ Roads and highways

▶ Disaster relief

▶ Unemployment insurance programs

▶ Medical research

▶ Development of purity standards for foods and drugs

This list could go on and on, but the point is clear: Governments are deeply involved in business life. To pay for all these services, governments collect a variety of taxes from households (such as personal income taxes and sales taxes) and from businesses (corporate income taxes).

Figure 1.8 shows this exchange of taxes for government services. It also shows government spending of tax dollars for resources and products required to provide these services. In other words, governments, too, return their incomes to the business system through the resource and product markets. The circular flow of business activity, including government, is thus complete and self-contained. That is, the system works.

Actually, with government included, our so-called circular flow looks more like a combination of several flows. And in reality it is. The important point is that, together, the various flows make up a single unit—a complete system that effectively provides answers to the basic economic questions.

The Challenges Ahead

There it is—the American business system in brief. When it works well, it provides jobs for those who are willing to work, a standard of living that few countries can match, and almost unlimited opportunity for personal advancement. But, like every other system devised by humans, it is far from perfect. Our business system may give us prosperity, but it also gave us the Great Depression of the 1930s and the economic problems of the 1970s and early 1980s.

The system obviously can be improved. It may need no more than a bit of fine tuning, or it may require something more extensive. Certainly there are plenty of people who are willing to tell us exactly what *they* think it needs. But these people provide us only with conflicting opinions. Who is right and who is wrong? Even the experts can't agree.

The experts do agree, however, that several key issues will challenge our business system over the next decade or two. Some of the questions to be resolved are:

▶ How much government involvement in our economy is necessary for its continued well-being? In what areas should there be less involvement? In what areas, more?

▶ How can we balance national growth with the conservation of natural resources and the protection of our environment?

▶ How can we evaluate the long-term economic costs and benefits of various existing and proposed government programs?

▶ How can we hold down inflation and yet stimulate the economy to provide jobs for all who want to work?

▶ How can we preserve the benefits of competition in our American economic system and still meet the needs of the less fortunate?

The answers to such questions are anything but simple. Yet they will directly affect our own future, our children's future, and that of our nation. Within the American economic and political system, the answers are ours to provide.

CHAPTER REVIEW

Summary

Business is the organized effort of individuals to produce and sell, for a profit, the goods and services that satisfy society's needs. Four kinds of resources—material, human, financial, and informational—must be combined to start and operate a business. The three general types of businesses are manufacturers, service businesses, and middlemen.

Profit is what remains after all business expenses are deducted from sales revenue. It is thus the payment that business owners receive for assuming the risks of business: primarily the risk of not receiving payment and the risk of losing whatever has been invested in the firm. Most often, a business that is operated to satisfy its customers earns a reasonable profit.

An economic system is a means of deciding what goods and services will be produced, how they will be produced, and for whom they will be produced. The pure laissez-faire capitalism of Adam Smith is an economic system in which these decisions are made by individuals and businesses as they pursue their own self-interest. In a laissez-faire capitalist system, the factors of production are owned by private individuals, and all individuals are free to use (or not to use) their resources as they see fit; prices are determined by the workings of supply and demand in competitive markets; and the economic role of government is limited to protecting competition.

In planned economies, government, rather than individuals, owns the factors of production and provides the answers to the three basic economic questions. Socialist and communist economies are—at least in theory—planned economies. In the real world, however, no economy attains "theoretical perfection."

One criterion for evaluating the performance of an economic system is to assess changes in productivity, which is the average level of output per worker per hour. A general economic performance measure is gross national product (GNP), which is the total dollar value of all goods and services produced in a country for a given time period.

Economists recognize four degrees of competition among sellers. Ranging from most competitive to least, the four degrees are: pure competition, monopolistic competition, oligopoly, and monopoly.

Since its beginnings in the seventeenth century, American business has been based on private ownership of property and freedom of enterprise. And from this beginning, through the Industrial Revolution of the early nineteenth century, to the phenomenal expansion of American industry in the nineteenth and early twentieth centuries, our government maintained an essentially laissez-faire attitude toward business. However, during the Great Depression of the 1930s, the federal government began to provide a number of social services to its citizens. Government's role in business has expanded continually since that time.

Our economic system is thus a mixed economy—capitalism cut with some socialism. Our present business system is called modified capitalism; it is essentially capitalist in nature, but government takes part in it along with households and businesses. In the circular flow that characterizes our business system, households and businesses exchange resources for goods and services, using money as the medium of exchange. Government collects taxes from businesses and households and uses tax revenues to purchase the resources and products with which to provide its services.

The American business system is not perfect by any means, but it does work reasonably well. We shall discuss some of its problems in the next chapter, wherein we examine the role of business as part of American society.

Key Terms

You should now be able to define and give an example relevant to each of the following terms:

free enterprise	monopolistic
competition	competition
business	oligopoly
entrepreneur	monopoly
consumers	natural monopoly
profit	barter
economics	domestic system
economy	factory system
laissez-faire capitalism	specialization
factors of production	standard of living
capital	inflation
free-market economy	service economy
planned economy	mixed economy
productivity	consumer goods
gross national product (GNP)	
real gross national product	
pure competition	
supply	
demand	
market price	

Questions and Exercises

Review Questions

1. What basic rights are accorded to individuals and businesses in our modified capitalist business system?
2. What is meant by free enterprise? Why does free enterprise naturally lead to competition among sellers of products?
3. Describe the four resources that one must combine to organize and operate a business. How do they differ from the economist's factors of production?

4. What distinguishes consumers from other buyers of goods and services?
5. Describe the relationship among profit, business risk, and the satisfaction of customers' needs.
6. Describe the four main ingredients of a laissez-faire capitalist economy.
7. What are the three basic economic questions? How are they answered in a capitalist economy? In a planned economy?
8. Identify and compare the four forms of competition that are recognized by economists.
9. Explain how the market price of a product is determined under pure competition.
10. Trace the steps that led from farming for survival in the American colonial period to today's mass production.
11. Why is the American economy called a mixed economy?
12. Outline the economic interactions between government and business in our business system. Outline those between government and households.

Discussion Questions

1. Who are the major competitors of the products produced by the Disney Company?
2. Why has the Disney Company become successful after having been in a slump?
3. Does one individual consumer really have a voice in answering the three basic economic questions?
4. Discuss this statement: Business competition encourages efficiency of production and leads to improved product quality.
5. What factors caused American business to develop into a modified capitalist system rather than some other type of system?
6. Is gross national product really a reliable indicator of a nation's standard of living? What might be a better indicator?
7. In our business system, how is government involved in answering the three basic economic questions? Does government participate in the system or interfere with it?

Exercises

1. Choose a type of business that you are familiar with or interested in. Then list the *specific* material, human, financial, and informational resources that you would have to combine to start such a business.
2. Cite four methods (other than pricing) that American auto manufacturers use to differentiate their

products. (The best way to do this is to scan their magazine and newspaper ads.) Rate these methods from least effective to most effective, using your own judgment and experience.
3. A retailing middleman like K mart does not process goods in any way, yet it helps satisfy consumer wants. List and explain several ways in which it does so.

Case 1.1

Hasbro, Inc., The World's Largest Toy Company

Over a decade ago, Hasbro, Inc., the largest U.S. toy company, faced a major decision about what to produce. Everyone, it seemed, was convinced that future playthings would be electronic, and most toy companies were rushing to come out with their own video games. Hasbro hesitated. It had lost money in 1978 for only the third time in its fifty-five years by spending too much to advertise toys that didn't sell. It had a huge inventory and wasn't collecting on its bills efficiently. Its day-care centers had flopped, and termites had eaten their way through a warehouse full of wooden salad bowls that were part of the company's new gourmet cookware line. The wrong move could have meant disaster for the company.

Two brothers, Alan and Stephen Hassenfeld, shouldered the burden of the decision. In fact, Hassenfeld brothers have always made the decisions at Hasbro. The grandfather and uncles of the current brothers started the company in 1923, and then passed it down to Harold and his brother Merril, Alan and Stephen's father.

The Hassenfeld family, Polish immigrants, first produced cloth-covered pencil boxes and hat liners made out of cloth scraps from textile mills. When pencil companies began making their own pencil boxes, the brothers responded by making their own pencils. When plastics were in short supply during World War II, the brothers moved into toys, transforming their pencil boxes into doctors' kits and junior-air-raid-warden sets. As a toy company, Hasbro has always had to predict the future tastes and demands of a notoriously fickle group of customers—children.

Alan and Stephen planned to put out a line of electronic toys in 1979, but they saw the market becoming flooded. All the products seemed about the same. The brothers didn't want to be imitators, even if electronic toys were the current rage. So, they stayed away from high tech. Many on Wall Street thought the decision would ruin the company, which some market analysts began to call "Hasbeen."

The video and electronics toy business turned out to be a roller coaster that tossed many companies out along the way and left others with huge inventories. However, Hasbro's nonelectronic toy sales have grown rapidly over the last decade. "I think we've become the best 'niche marketing' people in the world," Alan boasts. "We see an opening, we go after it, and we cover the sides so nobody else gets in." Those openings have included a new wave of war toys, led by the reintroduction of G.I. Joe and the creation of the tremendously successful Transformers. My Little Pony and the rejuvenated Mr. Potato Head have also been wildly successful.

The success of G.I. Joe allowed Hasbro to acquire Milton Bradley, the number-one producer of board games. But the Hassenfeld brothers know they can't just rest on their successes; that could be a fatal mistake in a business that changes as quickly as theirs does. Instead, they continue to search for new niches to fill and new products to fill them.*

Questions

1. Why would toy manufacturers be especially likely to face the problems that hurt Hasbro in the 1970s?
2. What changes in supply and demand take place during the life of a popular toy fad?
3. Can you justify Alan and Stephen Hassenfeld's decision not to go into electronic video toys?

Case 1.2

Business Philosophy at the J. M. Smucker Company

"With a name like Smucker's, it has to be good." Based on Smucker's recent success and growth in the jam, jelly, preserves, and marmalade industry, it would be hard for anyone to doubt that statement. The total jam and jelly sales for Smucker's is over $1 billion a year. By first chasing and then surpassing jelly giants Kraft, Inc. and Welch's, Smucker's now has a 37 percent share of the total jam and jelly market and is the leading manufacturer in the industry. In a

nongrowth market, Smucker's is steadily growing, increasing its market share about 1 percent a year.

The J. M. Smucker Company, based in Orrville, Ohio, is a family-run, sometimes secretive, operation. In 1897 Jerome Monroe Smucker decided to bring in extra income by making apple cider and apple butter from old family recipes. On the same property where today's modern factory now stands, Jerome carefully monitored the quality of his products, personally signing the paper tied over each container of apple butter. Now, at all of Smucker's ten plants around the country, a devotion to quality remains a key element of Smucker's business.

Soon after he began his business, Jerome was selling apple butter all over northeastern Ohio. Other members of the Smucker family became involved, and they took most of their earnings and poured them back into the company. In 1969 the Smucker family decided to take their company public. They retained 30 percent of the stock, selling 25 percent to institutions and pension funds and the rest to individual investors.

Paul Smucker (the chief executive and grandson of the founder) and his sons Tim (the chairman) and Richard (the president) are not taking their number-one position in the jam and jelly market for granted. The Smuckers know they must fend off foreign jam companies, as well as a variety of domestic competitors. Smucker's must also respond to the new waves of health awareness and calorie consciousness in the United States, as well as changes in consumers' tastes.

Part of the Smuckers' strategy for keeping on top is the introduction of new products. Recently, Smucker's has had a number of successful new entries into the market. "Simply Fruit," a spreadable fruit with no preservatives or artificial flavors and no extra sugar added, has been well received. Smucker's is also happy with the sales of its Fresh Pack Strawberry Preserves, available for only a few weeks each year. Smucker's makes peanut butter (regular and a no-salt variety) and has done well with it and a related product named "Goober," peanut butter already mixed with either grape or strawberry jelly. Smucker's has its own line of ice-cream toppings (available in microwaveable containers) and also has a line of upscale jams and jellies sold under the Dickinson brand name.

The Smuckers pride themselves on innovations of all kinds. Smucker's, sensing the coming of a trend, was the first company in the jam and jelly industry to print nutritional information on individual product labels. It was the first company to use re-sealable lids on its jars. Smucker's was also the first to offer single-portion jam and syrup packets to fast-food restaurants

---

* Based on information from David S. Leibowitz, "Toys in the Cellar," *Financial World*, June 14, 1988, p. 89; Alan Richman, "The Toys That Bind," *Esquire*, December 1986, p. 132; Howard Rudnitsky, "Bang, Mom, You're Dead," *Forbes*, June 16, 1986, p. 86; and Lois Therrien, "How Hasbro Became King of the Toymakers," *Business Week*, September 22, 1986, p. 90.

and airlines. Smucker's even has a special "invention group" that gets together to discuss ideas. All ideas, no matter how outrageous, are encouraged: All negative comments in these meetings are prohibited.

Quality, integrity, and customer relations make up the foundation of Smucker's company philosophy. When visiting the Orrville plant, a visitor receives a card on which is printed: "Quality is the key word and shall apply to our people, our products, our manufacturing methods, and our marketing efforts. . . . Quality comes first; earnings and sales growth will follow." Paul Smucker personally writes thank-you notes to all new shareholders. He also suggests that they tell a friend to try Smucker's products.

Smucker's refuses to purchase advertising time during any television show that contains violence or sex scenes. It wants to maintain its wholesome, old-fashioned image. Smucker's also pays for full-time federal government inspectors to monitor the entire jam and jelly manufacturing process. Because of this,

Smucker's is the only company to carry the Agricultural Department's top U.S. Grade A designation on all its products.†

Questions

1. What are the major components of Smucker's business philosophy that have helped this organization survive for over ninety years?
2. Economists recognize four different degrees of competition. In which type of competitive situation does Smucker's participate?
3. Why has Smucker's been able to compete against jelly giants such as Kraft and Welch's?

---

† Based on information from "The Corporate Elite," *Business Week*, October 21, 1988, p. 276; Robert McMath, "Jelly Companies Unveil Preserves at Jam Session," *Adweek's Marketing Week*, July 25, 1988, p. 8; Andrew N. Malcolm, "Of Jams and a Family," *New York Times Magazine*, November 15, 1987, pp. 83, 88, 108-109; and Julianne Slovak, "J. M. Smucker Co.," *Fortune*, January 16, 1989, p. 80.

ETHICS AND SOCIAL RESPONSIBILITY

1 Understand the types of ethical concerns that arise in the business world

2 Recognize the ethical pressures placed on decision makers

3 Understand how ethical decision making can be encouraged

4 Be aware of how our current views on the social responsibility of business have evolved

5 Understand the factors that led to the consumer movement and list some of its results

6 Recognize how present employment practices are being used to counteract past abuses

7 Be aware of the major types of pollution, their causes, and their cures

8 Become familiar with the steps a business must take to implement a program of social responsibility

CHAPTER PREVIEW

We begin by defining business ethics and examining ethical issues confronting business people. Next, we look at the pressures that influence ethical decision making and how it can be encouraged. Then we initiate our discussion of social responsibility by reviewing questionable business practices common before the 1930s and describe how public pressure brought about changes in the business environment after the Great Depression. We define and contrast two present-day models of social responsibility, the economic model and the socioeconomic model. Next, we present the major tenets of the consumer movement, which include consumers' rights to safety, to information, to choice, and to a full hearing of complaints. We discuss how ideas of social responsibility in business have affected employment practices and environmental concerns. We consider the commitment, planning, and funding that go into a firm's program of social responsibility.

INSIDE BUSINESS

Exxon Oil Spill

When the 987-foot *Exxon Valdez* ran aground on Bligh Reef in the beautiful waters of Alaska's Prince William Sound, 240,000 barrels, 11 million gallons, of oil gushed out of its tanks. An investigation conducted immediately after the accident determined that the ship's captain had a high blood-alcohol level and that the ship's third mate was steering the huge ship. The oil spill did massive damage to the wildlife and the environment. The waters and shorelines were coated with crude oil, and thousands of birds, sea otters, and fish perished when they ingested the poisonous oil or when it came into contact with their bodies.

Since the spill, Exxon Corporation has faced an intense amount of criticism for its response to the accident. Many observers found Exxon to be completely unprepared for an accident of this magnitude and slow to respond, causing the serious spill to turn into a catastrophic one. So far, 800 miles of shoreline are spotted with oil; oil covers over 1,000 square miles of water.

The oil spill shut down the area's herring season—Alaskan officials thought that the herring might be contaminated and that fishermen's boats might interfere with cleanup crews. The $75-million salmon industry is also in danger because adult fish might already be poisoned and young fish might become crippled and then die. The shrimp, black cod, rockfish, and halibut businesses will also suffer tremendously. In addition, businesses related to the fishing industry, such as restaurants and fishing guides, are in for rough economic times.

Exxon's company image has been badly tarnished by the spill. Oil and environmental experts are not sure that the oil can ever be removed entirely. They do agree, though, that the cost will be high and the task extremely difficult.

A high-ranking Exxon official has vowed: "One way or another, we are going to pick up all the oil that's out there." Another Exxon executive has stated that consumers will pay for the oil cleanup costs through increased gas prices. Because of a legal limitation, an industrywide disaster fund, and insurance, Exxon may be financially liable for only $14 million worth of damages—a relatively small amount for a company that produces profits of $5 billion annually. Exxon may be ethically liable for much more than millions of dollars. The waters and beaches, the birds and mammals, the fish and fishermen, the natives and native business people may never be the same.[1]

*O*bviously, organizations such as Exxon try to avoid accidents, especially catastrophic ones such as a major oil spill. When these events occur, people expect the company to respond not just within the limits of the law, but also in an ethical and socially responsible way.

Today, some managers still regard the costs of ethical and socially responsible business practices as not worth the return. Most managers, however, view the costs as a business expense, just like wages or rent. And an increasing number of firms are making ethics and social responsibility an essential part of business operations.

Business Ethics Defined

ethics the study of right and wrong and of the morality of choices made by individuals

business ethics the application of moral standards to business situations

Ethics is the study of right and wrong and of the morality of choices made by individuals. An ethical decision or action is one that is "right" according to some standard of behavior. **Business ethics** is the application of moral standards to business situations. Business ethics has become a public concern because of recent cases of unethical behavior. The Wall Street insider trading scandals and the questionable pricing tactics of federal defense contractors such as General Dynamics Corp. are just two examples of unethical behavior.

Ethical Issues

Business people face ethical issues daily. These issues stem from a variety of sources. While some issues arise infrequently, others occur regularly. Let's take a closer look at several ethical issues.

Fairness and Honesty

Learning Objective 1
Understand the types of ethical concerns that arise in the business world

Fairness and honesty in business are important ethical concerns. Besides obeying all laws and regulations, business persons are expected to refrain from knowingly deceiving, misrepresenting, or intimidating others. Lying is also a business problem. According to a Roper Public Opinion Research Center poll, 72 percent of Americans surveyed sometimes lie. Also, 54 percent of the respondents believe that people are less honest than they were ten years ago.[2]

Organizational Relationships

It is sometimes tempting to place personal welfare above the welfare of others or the welfare of an organization. Relationships with customers and coworkers often create ethical problems since confidential information is expected to be kept secret and all obligations are expected to be honored. Specific issues that arise include taking credit for others' ideas or work, not meeting one's obligations in a mutual agreement, and pressuring people to behave unethically.

Conflict of Interest

Conflict of interest results when a business person takes advantage of a situation for his or her own personal interest rather than for the interest of his or her employer. Sometimes payments and gifts make their way into business deals. A bribe is anything given to a person that might unfairly influence that person's business decision. All bribes are unethical.

Communications

Business communications, especially advertising, can present ethical questions. False and misleading advertising is unethical and can infuriate customers. Sponsors of advertisements aimed at children must be especially careful to avoid messages that are misleading. Advertisers of health-related products must also take precautions to guard against deception.

Pressures Influencing Ethical Decision Making

Learning Objective 2
Recognize the ethical pressures placed on decision makers

Customers expect products to be safe. Johnson and Johnson recalled 31 million bottles of Tylenol pain reliever and offered a $100,000 reward for the person or persons responsible for the deaths caused by the poisoned Tylenol.

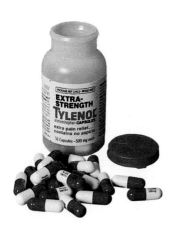

Business ethics involves relationships between a firm and its investors, customers, employees, creditors, and competitors. Each group has specific concerns, and each exerts some type of pressure on management.

Investors want management to make sensible financial decisions that will boost sales, profits, and returns on their investments.

Customers expect that a firm's products will be safe, reliable, and reasonably priced.

Employees want to be treated fairly in hiring, promotion, and compensation.

Creditors require that bills be paid on time and that the accounting information furnished by the firm be accurate.

Competitors expect that the firm's marketing activities will truthfully portray its products.

Although there are exceptions, when business is good and profit is high, it is relatively easy for management to respond to these expectations in an ethical manner. However, concern for ethics can dwindle under the pressure of low or declining profit. In such circumstances, ethical behavior is most likely to be compromised.

Expanding international trade has also led to an ethical dilemma for many American firms. In some countries, bribes and payoffs are an accepted part of business. In 1977, the U.S. government passed the Foreign Corrupt Practices Act, which prohibits these types of payments, but it is hard to enforce this act. By 1978, in response to the government's promise of leniency for firms disclosing information voluntarily, more than 400 U.S. companies admitted to making $800 million in questionable foreign payments. Government agencies have prosecuted several companies for "illegal payoffs," in spite of the fact that there is as yet no international code of business ethics. Some U.S. firms that refuse to make direct payoffs are forced to hire local consultants, public relations firms, or advertising agencies. Without stronger international laws or ethics codes, such cases are difficult to investigate. Much of the evidence and many of the people are overseas and cannot be prosecuted effectively.

Encouraging Ethical Behavior

A quick test to check if a behavior is ethical, if there is not a company policy regarding it, is to see if others approve of it. Ethical decisions will always withstand scrutiny. Openness will often create trust and help build solid business relationships.

What affects a person's inclination to make either ethical or unethical decisions is not entirely clear. Three general sets of factors are believed to influence the ethics of decision making.[3] First, an individual's values, attitudes, experiences, and knowledge influence decision making. Second, the absence of an employer's official code of ethics may indirectly encourage unethical decisions. Third, the behaviors and values of others, such as coworkers, supervisors, and company officials, affect the ethics of a person's decisions.

McDonald's, which produces hundreds of millions of pounds of paper and plastic waste annually, has become a proponent of recycling. The company urges its New England customers to dispose separately of polystyrene packaging and then collects and recycles it. McDonald's has taken other steps as well, including making its napkins from recycled paper.

BUSINESS JOURNAL

Codes of Ethics

Has the golden rule of business become "Make more gold—at any cost!"? According to Big Eight accounting firm Arthur Andersen & Co., 39 percent of the small-business executives surveyed think that their companies have been hurt by unethical business practices like bribes, kickbacks, price collusion, and conflicts of interest. Unethical behavior in a company can lower employee morale and productivity. Employees who know their firm indulges in unethical pursuits may be more apt to steal office supplies, set lax inspection standards, and spend too much time in the company lounge. Many organizations are trying to change their corporate culture by instilling a more ethical image in employees' minds.

More than 200 of the *Fortune* 500 companies now have codes of ethics. By becoming more ethical, company executives think that they will be able to attract talented employees, gain loyal customers and suppliers, and earn the public's trust and goodwill. Severe and well-publicized problems at General Electric, E. F. Hutton, Manville, General Dynamics, Union Carbide, and Morton-Thiokol have caused these and other firms to devote themselves to ethical business practices.

Several major U.S. firms are taking a strong ethical stance by trying to bring ethics to the forefront of company policy. Johnson & Johnson holds companywide meetings to discuss the company's credo of business values; the firm conducts company surveys to determine the amount of compliance to this credo. Xerox Corporation offers employees handbooks and policy statements that emphasize integrity. A Xerox ombudsman, open to all employees who have questions or reports on ethical practices, meets face-to-face with the chief executive officer. At Boeing Co., line managers lead ethics training sessions, and there is a toll-free phone number for employees who wish to confidentially communicate ethical violations. A Boeing ethics committee reports directly to the board of directors. At General Mills, there are specific guidelines for dealing with customers, vendors, and competitors. Executives actively promote open decision making. General Mills recruits employees who share company values.

There have always been, and will always be, conflicts between ethical and commercial considerations. Business managers often face many difficult decisions. Managers must consider their own personal ethics, their company's ethics, the interests of employees, and the interests of stockholders in resolving business dilemmas. Often, only time tells the appropriateness of a manager's decisions.

With government deregulation, widespread mergers, growing international trade, computerization, and the electronic transfer of funds, the potential for unethical behavior in business is great. The companies that do not have codes of ethics should create them; the companies with codes of ethics should abide by them. Ethical behavior should start with owners and CEOs so that ethics can have a sound and stable base in an organization.

Based on information from William A. Dimma, "Corporate Ethics Revisited," *Vital Speeches,* February 15, 1990, pp. 283–286; Michael Allen, "Small-Business Jungle," *Wall Street Journal,* June 10, 1988, p. 22R; John A. Byrne, "Businesses Are Signing Up for Ethics 101," *Business Week,* February 15, 1988; pp. 56–57; Sir Adrian Cadbury, "Ethical Managers Make Their Own Rules," *Harvard Business Review,* September–October 1987, pp. 69–73; Michael Davis, "Working with Your Company's Code of Ethics," *Management Solutions,* June 1988, pp. 5–10.

Learning Objective 3
Understand how ethical decision making can be encouraged

Most authorities agree that there is room for improvement in business ethics. A more problematic issue is whether business can be made more ethical in the real world. The majority of viewpoints on this issue suggest that government, trade associations, and individual firms can establish acceptable levels of behavior.

The government can do so by passing more stringent regulations. But regulations require enforcement, and the unethical business person always seems to "slip something by" without getting caught. Increased regulation may help, but it surely cannot solve the entire ethics problem.

Trade associations can provide (and some have provided) ethical guidelines for their members to follow. These organizations of firms within a particular industry are also in a position to exert pressure on members that stoop to questionable business practices. However, enforcement varies from association to association, and because trade associations exist for the benefit of their members, very strong measures may be self-defeating.

corporate code of ethics   *a guide to acceptable and ethical behavior as defined by an organization*

Employees have an easier time determining what is acceptable behavior if a company provides them with a code of ethics. This is perhaps the most effective way to encourage ethical behavior. A **corporate code of ethics** is simply a guide to acceptable and ethical behavior as defined by an organization. Uniform policies, standards, and punishments for violations encourage employees to behave ethically. Of course, such a code cannot possibly cover every situation, but general guidelines should be sufficient for most employees. Specific details could deal with prohibited practices such as bribery.

whistle blowing   *informing the press or government officials about unethical practices within one's organization*

Even if employees want to act ethically, it may be difficult to do so. Unethical practices often become ingrained in an organization. Employees with high personal ethics may then take a controversial step called whistle blowing. **Whistle blowing** is informing the press or government officials about unethical practices within one's organization. Whistle blowing could have averted disasters and prevented needless deaths and injuries in the *Challenger* space shuttle disaster and the toxic gas leak at Union Carbide Corp. in Bhopal, India. Engineers in both cases voiced their concerns to upper-level management but were reluctant to present their apprehensions to the press or news media. How can it be that employees know about life-threatening problems and let them pass? In the words of one Union Carbide employee, "Most of the engineers at Union Carbide think of themselves as part of the company. Besides, if you were identified, that would be the end of your career."[4] Naturally, whistle blowing can have serious repercussions for an employee, yet those who take this step feel that the benefit to society outweighs any personal consequences they may suffer.

Social Responsibility

social responsibility   *the recognition that business activities have an impact on society, and the consideration of that impact in business decision making*

Social responsibility is the recognition that business activities have an impact on society, and the consideration of that impact in business decision making. Obviously, social responsibility costs money. It is perhaps not so obvious—except in isolated cases—that social responsibility is good business. Consumers eventually find out which firms are acting responsibly and which are not. And, just as easily as they cast their dollar votes for a product produced by a company that is socially responsible, they can vote against the firm that is polluting the air or waterways, against the food product that contains the insecticide EDB, and against the company that survives mainly through bribery.

Meet the information managers of 1997.

Street kids or streetwise business professionals? You already know what the statistics say. It's going to take some pretty fancy footwork to turn it around.

NYNEX Foundation is doing more than just talking about it. We've joined with business, education and community leaders to support educational programs at all levels.

Now the ball's in your court.

Your first question, naturally, is does it work? So just look at the results we've seen so far.

For example, consider the MITES Program (Minority Introduction to Engineering and Science) for gifted disadvantaged high school students at M.I.T., which we support. A recent study shows that 95 percent have gone on to college.

And there's BIPED Corporation's Office Technologies program, which we also assist. It's helping disabled persons gain employment in information processing.

Educational programs like these will soon be looking for your support, and their graduates will be coming to you for a job.

We hope that you will join us in making a streetwise decision.

FOUNDATION

The NYNEX Foundation has joined with business, education, and community leaders to support educational programs at all levels.

The Evolution of Social Responsibility

Business is far from perfect in many respects, but its social responsibility record today is much better than in past decades. In fact, present demands for social responsibility have their roots in outraged reactions to the abusive business practices of the early 1900s.

Social Responsibility Before the 1930s

Learning Objective 4
Be aware of how our current views on the social responsibility of business have evolved

During the first quarter of the twentieth century, businesses were free to operate pretty much as they chose. Government protection of workers and consumers was minimal. This was indeed a period of laissez-faire business conditions. (Remember, *laissez-faire* is a French term that implies there shall be no government interference in the economy.) As a result, people either accepted what business had to offer or they did without.

Working Conditions   Before 1930, working conditions were often deplorable by today's standards. The average workweek was in excess of sixty hours for most industries, and there was no minimum-wage law. Employee benefits such as paid vacations, medical insurance, and paid overtime were almost nonexistent. Work areas were crowded and unsafe, and industrial accidents were the rule rather than the exception.

In an effort to improve working conditions, employees organized and joined labor unions. But during the early 1900s, businesses—with the help of government—were able to use such weapons as court orders, force, and even the few existing antitrust laws to defeat the attempts of unions to improve working conditions.

Consumer Rights Then as now, most people in business were honest people who produced and sold acceptable products. However, some business owners, eager for even greater profits, engaged in misleading advertising and sold shoddy and unsafe merchandise.

caveat emptor *a Latin phrase meaning "let the buyer beware"*

During this period, consumers were generally subject to the doctrine of **caveat emptor,** a Latin phrase meaning "let the buyer beware." In other words, "what you see is what you get," and too bad if it's not what you expected. Victims of unscrupulous business practices could take legal action, but going to court was very expensive and consumers rarely won their cases. Moreover, there were no consumer groups or government agencies to publicize their discoveries and hold sellers accountable for their actions.

In such an atmosphere, government intervention to curb abuses by business would seem almost inevitable. But there was as yet no great public outcry for such intervention.

In the early 1900s it was not unusual for children to work twelve-hour days under highly dangerous conditions. The "breaker boys," some of the most exploited children during this period, worked in mines separating rocks from chunks of coal.

Government Regulation   Prior to the 1930s, most people believed that competition and the action of the marketplace would correct abuses in time. Government became involved in day-to-day business activities only when there was an obvious abuse of the free-market system.

Six of the more important federal laws passed between 1887 and 1914 are described in Table 2.1. As you can see, these laws were aimed more at encouraging competition than at correcting business abuses, although two of them did deal with the purity of food and drug products. Such laws did little to curb abuses that occurred on a regular basis.

Social Responsibility After the 1930s

The collapse of the stock market on October 29, 1929, triggered the Great Depression and years of economic problems for the United States. As we noted in Chapter 1, U.S. production fell by almost one-half, and up to 25 percent of the nation's work force was unemployed. At last public pressure mounted for government to "do something" about the economy and about worsening social conditions.

When Franklin Roosevelt was inaugurated president in 1933, he instituted programs to restore the economy and to improve social conditions. Laws were passed to correct what many viewed as the monopolistic abuses of big business, and various social services were provided for individuals. These massive federal programs became the foundation for increased government involvement in the dealings between business and American society.

As government involvement has increased, so has everyone's awareness of the social responsibility of business. Today business owners are concerned about the return on their investment, but at the same time most of them demand ethical behavior from professional business managers. In addition, employees demand better working conditions, and

TABLE 2.1   Early Government Regulations that Affected American Business

Government Regulation	Major Provisions
Interstate Commerce Act (1887)	First federal act to regulate business practices; provided regulation of railroads and shipping rates
Sherman Antitrust Act (1890)	Prevented monopolies or mergers where competition was endangered
Pure Food and Drug Act (1906)	Established limited supervision of interstate sale of food and drugs
Meat Inspection Act (1906)	Provided for limited supervision of interstate sale of meat and meat products
Federal Trade Commission Act (1914)	Created the Federal Trade Commission to investigate illegal trade practices
Clayton Act (1914)	Eliminated many forms of price discrimination that gave large businesses a competitive advantage over smaller firms

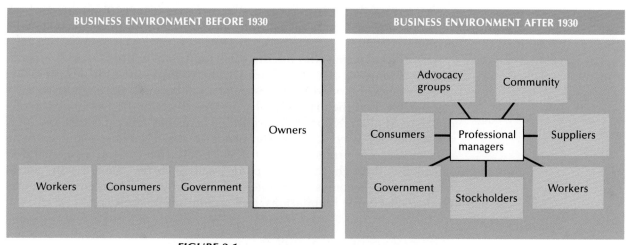

FIGURE 2.1
The Business Environment Before and After 1930
The owners of businesses were very powerful prior to 1930, and government, consumers, and workers had little or no influence. After 1930, several different groups were able to affect the way businesses were managed.

consumers want safe, reliable products. Various advocacy groups echo these concerns and also call for careful consideration of our delicate ecological balance. Managers must therefore operate in a complex business environment—one in which they are just as responsible for their managerial actions as for their actions as individual citizens. Figure 2.1 illustrates the change in emphasis in the business environment before and after the 1930s.

Two Views of Social Responsibility

Government regulation and public awareness are *external* forces that have increased the social responsibility of business. But business decisions are made *within* the firm—and there, social responsibility begins with the attitude of management. Two contrasting philosophies, or models, define the range of management attitudes toward social responsibility.

The Economic Model

economic model of social responsibility *the view that society will benefit most when business is left alone to produce and market profitable products that are needed by society*

According to the traditional concept of business, a firm exists to produce quality goods and services, earn a reasonable profit, and provide jobs. In line with this concept, the **economic model of social responsibility** holds that society will benefit most when business is left alone to produce and market profitable products that are needed by society. The economic model can be traced back to the eighteenth century when businesses were owned primarily by entrepreneurs or owner-managers. Competition was vigorous among small firms, and short-run profits and survival were primary concerns.

To the manager who adopts this traditional attitude, social responsibility is someone else's job. After all, stockholders invest in a corporation to earn a return on their investment, not because the firm is socially responsible, and the firm is legally obliged to act in the economic interest of its stockholders. Moreover, profitable firms pay federal, state, and local taxes that are used to meet the needs of society. Thus, managers who concentrate on profit feel that they fulfill their social responsibility indirectly, through the taxes paid by their firms. As a result, social responsibility becomes the problem of government, various environmental groups, charitable foundations, and similar organizations.

The Socioeconomic Model

socioeconomic model of social responsibility *the concept that business should emphasize not only profits, but the impact of its decisions on society*

In contrast, some managers believe they have a responsibility not only to stockholders but also to customers, employees, suppliers, and the general public. This broader view is referred to as the **socioeconomic model of social responsibility.** It places emphasis not only on profits, but also on the impact of business decisions on society.

Recently, increasing numbers of managers and firms have adopted the socioeconomic model, and they have done so for at least three reasons: First, business is dominated by the corporate form of ownership, and the corporation is a creation of society. If a corporation doesn't perform as a good citizen, society can and will demand changes. Second, many firms are beginning to take pride in their social responsibility records. IBM, Arco, John Hancock, and Johnson & Johnson are very proud of their commitment to social responsibility. And, of course, there are many other corporations that are more socially responsible today than they were ten years ago. Third, many business people feel it is best to take the initiative in this area. The alternative may be legal action brought against the firm by some special-interest group; in such a situation, the firm may lose control of its activities.

The Pros and Cons of Social Responsibility

The merits of the economic and socioeconomic models have been debated for years by business owners, managers, consumers, and government officials. Each side seems to have four major arguments to reinforce its viewpoint.

Arguments for Increased Social Responsibility Proponents of the socioeconomic model maintain that a business must do more than simply seek profits. To support their position, they offer the following arguments:

1. Business cannot ignore social issues because it is a part of our society.
2. Business has the technical, financial, and managerial resources that are needed to tackle today's complex social issues.

3. By helping resolve social issues, business can create a more stable environment for long-term profitability.

4. Socially responsible decision making by business firms can prevent increased government intervention, which would force businesses to do what they fail to do voluntarily.

These arguments are based on the assumption that a business has a responsibility not only to stockholders but also to customers, employees, suppliers, and the general public.

Arguments Against Increased Social Responsibility   Opponents of the socio-economic model argue that business should do what it does best: earn a profit by manufacturing and marketing products that people want. To support their position, they argue as follows:

1. Business managers are primarily responsible to stockholders, so management must be concerned with providing a return on owners' investments.

2. Corporate time, money, and talent should be used to maximize profits, not to solve society's problems.

3. Social problems affect society in general, so individual businesses should not be expected to solve these problems.

4. Social issues are the responsibility of government officials who are elected for that purpose and who are accountable to the voters for their decisions.

These arguments are obviously based on the assumption that the primary objective of business is to earn profits, whereas government and social institutions should deal with social problems.

Table 2.2 compares the economic and socioeconomic viewpoints in terms of business emphasis. Today, few firms are either purely economic or purely socioeconomic in outlook; most have chosen some middle ground between the two. However, our society generally seems to want—and even

TABLE 2.2   *A Comparison of the Economic and Socioeconomic Models as Implemented in Business*

Economic Model			Socioeconomic Model
Primary emphasis is on			**Primary emphasis is on**
1. Production	M	G	1. Quality of life
2. Exploitation of natural resources	I	R	2. Conservation of natural resources
3. Internal, market-based decisions	D	O	3. Market-based decisions, with some community controls
4. Economic return (profit)	D	U	4. Balance of economic return and social return
5. Firm's or manager's interest	L	N	5. Firm's and community's interest
6. Minor role for government	E	D	6. Active government involvement

Source: Adapted from Keith Davis, William C. Frederick, and Robert L. Blomstrom, *Business and Society: Concepts and Policy Issues* (New York: McGraw-Hill, 1980), p. 9. Used by permission of McGraw-Hill Book Company.

to expect—some degree of social responsibility from business. Thus, within this middle ground between the two extremes, businesses are leaning toward the socioeconomic view. In the next several sections, we shall look at some results of this movement in four specific areas: consumers' rights, employment practices, environmental quality, and business ethics.

Consumerism

consumerism *all those activities intended to protect the rights of consumers in their dealings with business*

Consumerism consists of all those activities that are undertaken to protect the rights of consumers in their dealings with business. Consumerism has been with us to some extent since the early nineteenth century, but the movement came to life only in the 1960s. It was then that President John F. Kennedy declared that the consumer was entitled to a new "bill of rights."

The Four Basic Rights of Consumers

Learning Objective 5
Understand the factors that led to the consumer movement and list some of its results

Kennedy's consumer bill of rights asserted that consumers have a right to safety, to be informed, to choose, and to be heard. These four rights are the basis of much of the consumer-oriented legislation that has been passed during the last twenty-five years. These rights also provide an effective outline of the objectives and accomplishments of the consumer movement.

The Right to Safety   The right to safety means that products purchased by consumers must

- Be safe for their intended use
- Include thorough and explicit directions for proper use
- Have been tested by the manufacturer to ensure product quality and reliability

There are several reasons why American business firms must be concerned about product safety. Federal agencies such as the Food and Drug Administration and the Consumer Product Safety Commission have the power to force businesses that make or sell defective products to take corrective actions. Such actions include offering refunds, recalling defective products, issuing public warnings, and reimbursing consumers—all of which can be expensive. Second, consumers and the government have been winning an increasing number of product-liability lawsuits against sellers of defective products. Moreover, the awards in these suits have been getting bigger and bigger. Producers of all-terrain vehicles, for example, have faced a number of personal injury lawsuits. Another major reason for improving product safety is the consumer's demand for safe products. People will simply stop buying a product that they believe is unsafe or unreliable.

A consumer's right to safety includes the assurance of a safe food supply. The recent detection of cyanide in grapes, alar in apples, and other contaminants in food has heightened concern about this among consumer advocates and environmentalists. Governmental responsibility for maintaining the safety of foods resides with the Food & Drug Administration and the Agriculture Department.

The Right to Be Informed   The right to be informed means that consumers must have access to complete information about a product before they buy it. Detailed information about ingredients must be provided on food containers, information about fabrics and laundering methods must be attached to clothing, and lenders must disclose the true cost of borrowing the money that they make available for customers to purchase merchandise on credit.

In addition, manufacturers must inform customers about the potential dangers of using their products. When they do not, they can be held responsible for personal injuries suffered because of their products. For example, General Electric provides customers with a twenty-page booklet that describes how they should use an automatic clothes washer. Sometimes such warnings seem excessive, but they are necessary if user injuries (and resulting lawsuits) are to be avoided.

The Right to Choose   The right to choose means that consumers have a choice of products, offered by different manufacturers and sellers, to satisfy a particular need. The government has done its part by encouraging competition through antitrust legislation. The more competition there is, the greater the choice available to consumers.

Competition and the resulting freedom of choice provide an additional benefit for consumers: They work to reduce the price of goods and services. Consider the electronic calculators that are so popular today. The Bowmar Brain, one of the first calculators introduced, carried a retail price tag in excess of $150. The product was so profitable that Texas Instruments, Rockwell International Corp., and many other firms began to compete with Bowmar Instrument Corp. As a result, calculators can now be purchased for under $10.

The Right to Be Heard   This fourth right means that someone will listen and take appropriate action when consumers complain. Actually, management began to listen to consumers after World War II, when competition between businesses that manufactured and sold consumer goods increased. One way firms got a competitive edge was to listen to consumers and provide the products they said they wanted and needed. Today, businesses are listening even more attentively, and many larger firms have consumer relations departments that the buying public can easily contact via toll-free phone numbers. Other groups listen too. Most large cities and some states have consumer affairs offices to act on the complaints of citizens.

Recent Developments in Consumerism

The greatest advances in consumerism have come through federal legislation. Some laws that have been passed in the last thirty years to protect your rights as a consumer are listed and described in Table 2.3. In addition, most business people have come to realize that they ignore consumer issues only at their own peril. Managers know that improper handling of complaints can mean lost sales, bad publicity, and lawsuits.

Employment Practices

Learning Objective 6
Recognize how present employment practices are being used to counteract past abuses

We have seen that a combination of managers who subscribe to the socioeconomic view of business's social responsibility and significant government legislation enacted to protect the buying public has considerably broadened the rights of consumers. The last two decades have seen similar progress in affirming the rights of employees to equal treatment in the workplace.

Everyone who works for a living should have the opportunity to land a job for which he or she is qualified and to be rewarded on the basis of ability and performance. This is an important issue for society, and it also makes good business sense. Yet, over the years, this opportunity has been denied to members of various minority groups. **A minority** is a racial, religious, political, national, or other group regarded as different from the larger group of which it is a part, often singled out for unfavorable treatment.

minority *a racial, religious, political, national, or other group regarded as different from the larger group of which it is a part, often singled out for unfavorable treatment*

TABLE 2.3   Major Federal Legislation Protecting Consumers Since 1960

Legislation	Main Provisions
Federal Hazardous Substances Labeling Act (1960)	Requires warning labels on household chemicals if they are highly toxic
Color Additives Amendment (1960)	Requires manufacturers to disclose when colorings are added to foods
Kefauver-Harris Drug Amendments (1962)	Established testing practices for drugs and requires manufacturers to label drugs with generic names in addition to trade names
Cigarette Labeling Act (1965)	Requires manufacturers to place standard warning labels on all cigarette packages and advertising
Fair Packaging and Labeling Act (1966)	Calls for all products sold across state lines to be labeled with net weight, ingredients, and manufacturer's name and address
Motor Vehicle Safety Act (1966)	Established standards for safer cars
Wholesome Meat Act (1967)	Requires states to inspect meat (but not poultry) sold within the state
Flammable Fabrics Act (1967)	Strengthened flammability standards for clothing, to include children's sleepwear in sizes 0 to 6X
Truth in Lending Act (1968)	Requires lenders and credit merchants to disclose the full cost of finance charges in both dollars and annual percentage rates
Land Sales Disclosure Act (1968)	Provides protection for consumers from unscrupulous practices in interstate land sales
Child Protection and Toy Act (1969)	Bans from interstate commerce toys with mechanical or electrical defects
Credit Card Liability Act (1970)	Limits credit-card holder's liability to $50 per card and stops credit-card companies from issuing unsolicited cards
Fair Credit Reporting Act (1971)	Requires credit bureaus to provide credit reports to consumers regarding their own credit files; also provides for correction of incorrect information
Consumer Product Safety Commission Act (1972)	Established the Consumer Product Safety Commission
Trade Regulation Rule (1972)	Established a "cooling-off" period of 72 hours for door-to-door sales
Fair Credit Billing Act (1974)	Amended the Truth in Lending Act to enable consumers to challenge billing errors
Equal Credit Opportunity Act (1974)	Provides equal credit opportunities for males and females and for married and single individuals
Magnuson-Moss Warranty-Federal Trade Commission Act (1975)	Provides for minimum disclosure standards for written consumer product warranties for products that cost more than $15
Amendment to Equal Credit Opportunity Act (1976)	Prevents discrimination based on race, creed, color, religion, age, and income when granting credit
Fair Debt Collection Practices Act (1977)	Outlaws abusive collection practices by third parties
Drug Price Competition and Patent Restoration Act (1984)	Established an abbreviated procedure for registering certain generic drugs
Orphan Drug Act (1985)	Amended the original 1983 Orphan Drug Act and extends tax incentives to encourage the development of drugs for rare diseases

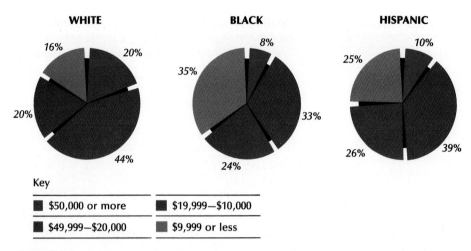

WHITE

16%
20%
20%
44%

BLACK

8%
35%
33%
24%

HISPANIC

10%
25%
26%
39%

Key

| ■ $50,000 or more | ■ $19,999–$10,000 |
| ■ $49,999–$20,000 | ■ $9,999 or less |

FIGURE 2.2
Comparative Income Levels
Charts represent total money earnings of white, black, and Hispanic workers in 1987. (Source: Statistical Abstract of the United States, 1989, U.S. Bureau of the Census, p. 449.)

The federal government responded to the outcry of minority groups during the 1960s and 1970s by passing a number of laws forbidding job discrimination. (These laws are discussed in Chapter 9 in the context of human resources management.) Now, more than twenty-five years since passage of the first of these (the Civil Rights Act of 1964), abuses still exist. An example is the disparity in income levels for whites, blacks, and Hispanics, as illustrated in Figure 2.2. Lower incomes and higher unemployment rates also affect Native Americans, handicapped persons, and women. Responsible managers have instituted a number of programs to counteract the results of discrimination.

Affirmative Action Programs

affirmative action program
a plan designed to increase the number of minority employees at all levels within an organization

An **affirmative action program** is a plan designed to increase the number of minority employees at all levels within an organization. Employers with federal contracts of more than $50,000 per year must have written affirmative action plans. The objective of such programs is to ensure that minorities are represented within the organization in approximately the same proportion as in the surrounding community. If 25 percent of the electricians in a geographic area where a company is located are black, then approximately 25 percent of the electricians it employs should also be black. Affirmative action plans encompass all areas of human resources management: recruiting, hiring, training, promotion, and pay.

Unfortunately, affirmative action programs have been plagued by two problems. The first involves quotas. In the beginning, many firms pledged to recruit and hire a certain number of minority members by a specific date. To achieve this goal, they were forced to consider only minority applicants for job openings; if they hired nonminority workers, they would be defeating their own purpose. But the courts have ruled that such quotas are unconstitutional even though their purpose is commendable. They are, in fact, a form of discrimination called reverse discrimination.

The second problem is that not all business people are in favor of affirmative action programs, although most such programs have been reasonably successful. Managers not committed to these programs can "play the game" and still discriminate against workers. To help solve this problem, Congress created (and later strengthened) the **Equal Employment Opportunity Commission (EEOC),** a government agency with the power to investigate complaints of employment discrimination and the power to sue firms that practice it.

The threat of legal action has persuaded some corporations to amend their hiring and promotional policies, but the discrepancy between men's and women's salaries has not really been affected, as illustrated in Figure 2.3. For more than thirty years, women have consistently earned only about 60 cents for each dollar earned by men.

Equal Employment Opportunity Commission (EEOC) *a government agency with the power to investigate complaints of employment discrimination and the power to sue firms that practice it*

FIGURE 2.3
The Relative Earnings of Male and Female Workers
For more than thirty years, women have consistently earned only about 60 cents for each dollar earned by men. (Source: Statistical Abstract of the United States, 1989, U.S. Bureau of the Census, p. 447.)

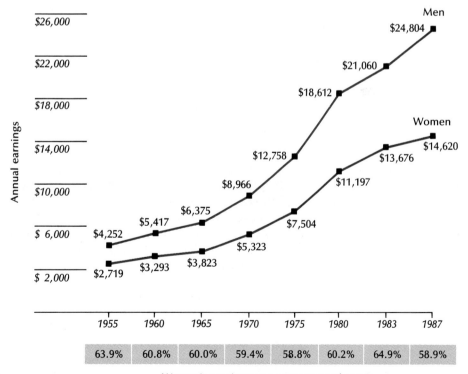

Year	1955	1960	1965	1970	1975	1980	1983	1987
	63.9%	60.8%	60.0%	59.4%	58.8%	60.2%	64.9%	58.9%

Women's earnings as a percentage of men's

Training Programs for the Hard-Core Unemployed

For some firms, social responsibility extends far beyond placing a help-wanted ad in the local newspaper. These firms have assumed the task of helping the **hard-core unemployed:** workers with little education or vocational training and a long history of unemployment. In the past, such workers were often routinely turned down by personnel managers, even for the most menial jobs.

Obviously such workers require training; just as obviously this training can be expensive and time-consuming. To share the costs, business and government have joined together in a number of cooperative programs. One particularly successful partnership is the **National Alliance of Businessmen (NAB),** a joint business-government program to train the hard-core unemployed. The NAB is sponsored by participating corporations, whose executives contribute their talents to do the actual training. The government's responsibilities include setting objectives, establishing priorities, offering the right incentives, and providing limited financing.

Concern for the Environment

The social consciousness of responsible managers and the encouragement of a concerned government have also made the public and the business community partners in a major effort to reduce environmental pollution, conserve natural resources, and reverse some of the worst effects of past negligence in this area.

Pollution is the contamination of water, air, or land through the actions of people in an industrialized society. For several decades, environmentalists have been warning us about the dangers of industrial pollution. Unfortunately, business and government leaders either ignored the problem or weren't concerned about it until pollution became a threat to life and health in America. Consider the following list.

Learning Objective 7
Be aware of the major types of pollution, their causes, and their cures

▶ According to the Environmental Protection Agency, sixty-eight areas are known to exceed the national air-quality standards for ozone, with an additional twenty-eight areas expected to be added to the list. Approximately 140 million Americans populate these polluted regions.[5]

▶ Approximately 2.7 billion pounds of toxics, some carcinogens, were released into the air by American industry in 1987.[6]

▶ Only 38 of the 1,175 hazardous waste sites included on the Superfund national cleanup priority list have been cleaned up. The General Accounting Office predicts that more than 425,000 sites may actually need cleanup.[7]

These are not isolated cases. Such situations, occurring throughout the United States, have made pollution a matter of national concern. Today Americans expect business and government leaders to take swift action to clean up our environment—and to keep it clean.

BUSINESS JOURNAL

Businesses Assist Public Schools

Eric can't read, add, use a map, and doesn't know the capital of Ecuador. Twenty-three million Americans are functionally illiterate: They can't read at the fourth-grade level. Thirty million more Americans can't read at the ninth-grade level. Thirty percent of the students who enter high school don't graduate. Half of the young adults in their twenties can't use a bus schedule, follow the directions on a pay phone, or calculate the tip on a restaurant bill. There is an educational crisis in America today.

The common cycle of ignorance, poverty, and crime is well known. Violence, narcotics, and apathy are everyday factors in public schools. Test scores are falling, and the academic skills of American youngsters seem to be consistently lower than the skills of students in other countries. The modern American educational system is in a state of decay.

All this is happening at a time when employers need highly skilled workers. Businesses need workers skilled not only in trades but also in cognitive processes. Problem-solving capabilities, creativity, the ability to assimilate material and communicate findings—these are the traits that American firms now look for in personnel and will continue to look for as skill requirements rise.

While educators and administrators strive to find the answers to education problems, businesses are not standing still. Many firms, large and small, are trying to improve schooling. In New York City, fifty companies, including Oppenheimer, Salomon Brothers, and Standard & Poor's, offer high schools financial support, curriculum advice, and other aid. American Express Company and Shearson Lehman Hutton started the Academy of Finance. High school juniors and seniors enter a two-year program that combines classroom instruction with on-the-job experience. Both Procter & Gamble and General Electric have school-aid programs.

American businesses contribute about $2 billion to educational programs every year, and this amount will probably grow substantially. Honeywell Inc. gives about 2 percent of its pretax profit to the Honeywell Foundation, which distributes funds to elementary and secondary schools, colleges, and universities. Shell Oil Company donates more than $11 million annually to educational programs.

Businesses are also trying to help teachers. The Exxon Education Foundation supports the Coalition of Essential Schools, fifty-six high schools across the United States that experiment with new teaching methods. Polaroid Corp., concerned with the shortage of science and math teachers, has started "Project Bridge." Each year this program enables up to ten Polaroid employees to become science or math teachers. Polaroid pays their salaries while the participants complete a one-year certification program.

Businesses offer schools and universities cash contributions, services, and political and economic coalitions. A partnership between business and education seems logical since both can stand to benefit greatly. But for any partnership to be successful, coordination, leadership, and sustained commitment are needed. The resources are there; the motivation should be there. If businesses and educational institutions continue to join forces, Americans can look forward to a bright future.

Based on information from Patricia A. Galagan, "Joining Forces: Business and Education Take on Competitiveness," *Training and Development Journal,* July 1988, pp. 26–29; Dale Mann, "Business Involvement and Public School Improvement, Part 2," *Phi Delta Kappan,* November 1987, pp. 228–232; George Melloan, "Public Education's Failures Plague Employers," *The Wall Street Journal,* June 21, 1988, p. 39E; and Nancy J. Perry, "Saving the Schools," *Fortune,* November 7, 1988, pp. 42–46, 50, 52, 54, 56.

Effects of Environmental Legislation

As in other areas of concern to our society, legislation and regulations play a crucial role in pollution control. The laws outlined in Table 2.4 reflect the scope of current environmental legislation. Of major importance was creation of the **Environmental Protection Agency (EPA),** the federal agency charged with enforcing laws designed to protect the environment.

TABLE 2.4   Summary of Major Environmental Laws

Legislation	Major Provisions
National Environmental Policy Act of 1970	Established the Environmental Protection Agency (EPA) to enforce federal laws that involve the environment
Clean Air Amendment of 1970	Provides stringent automotive, aircraft, and factory emission standards
Water Quality Improvement Act of 1970	Strengthened existing water pollution regulations and provides for large monetary fines against violators
Resource Recovery Act of 1970	Enlarged the solid-waste disposal program and provides for enforcement by the EPA
Water Pollution Control Act Amendment of 1972	Established standards for cleaning navigable streams and lakes and eliminating all harmful waste disposal by 1985
Noise Control Act of 1972	Established standards for major sources of noise and required the EPA to advise the Federal Aviation Administration on standards for airplanes
Clean Air Act Amendment of 1977	Established new deadlines for cleaning up polluted areas; also required review of existing air-quality standards
Resource Conservation and Recovery Act of 1984	Amended the original 1976 act and required federal regulation of potentially dangerous solid-waste disposal
Clean Act Amendment of 1987	Established a national air-quality standard for ozone

Once they are aware of a problem of pollution, most firms respond to it rather than wait to be cited by the EPA. But other owners and managers take the position that environmental standards are too strict. (Loosely translated, this means that compliance with present standards is too expensive.) Consequently, it has often been necessary for the EPA to take legal action to force firms to install antipollution equipment and clean up waste storage areas.

Experience has shown that the combination of environmental legislation, voluntary compliance, and EPA action can succeed in cleaning up the environment and keeping it clean. However, much still remains to be done.

Water Pollution   The task of water cleanup has proved to be extremely complicated and costly because of pollution run-off and toxic contamination. And yet, improved water quality is not only necessary; it is also achievable. Consider Cleveland's Cuyahoga River. A few years ago the river was so contaminated by industrial wastes that it burst into flames one hot summer day! Now, after a sustained community cleanup effort, the river is pure enough for fish to live in.

Today acid rain, which results from sulfur emitted by smokestacks in industrialized areas, is destroying many lakes and reservoirs. It is

BUSINESS JOURNAL

Renewed Environmental Awareness

There is good news and bad news about the environment. First, the bad news: Chlorofluorocarbons are eating away at the ozone layer that shields us from cancer-causing ultraviolet rays; carbon dioxide in the atmosphere is threatening to raise the earth's temperature; and acid rain, radon gas, polluted ground water, and toxic wastes are all around us. Now for the good news: Today there is a renewed environmental movement, and it is gaining strength.

Even better news is that businesses are taking the initiative to keep the earth healthy. Although the stiff regulations of the early 1970s have curbed pollution a great deal, we still face many critical environmental problems. Now, businesses—with ingenious executives and a stockpile of funds—have declared war on pollution. These companies have found that they have economic incentives to clean up the environment. Through improved public images and more efficient technological processes, companies realize that considering the ecology makes sense—dollars and sense.

Dow Chemical Co. has a pollution control program called "WRAP" (Waste Reduction Always Pays). WRAP has saved Dow money and boosted product yields. Through WRAP's activities, the resulting air pollution involved in several chemical processes has been significantly reduced. 3M Company's "Pollution Prevention Pays" program has saved 3M over $400 million. Since disposing of hazardous wastes is extremely expensive, companies are now trying to figure out how not to produce these dangerous wastes in the first place. Businesses, consumers, and the environment all benefit.

Plastics pose an especially threatening problem to the environment because they are not readily degradable. Microorganisms that naturally decay other substances do not break down traditional plastics. It takes literally hundreds of years for plastics to decompose. Due to the widespread use of plastics by society and the growing shortage of acceptable disposal sites, some pioneers in the plastics industry set out to make degradable plastics. They were successful. These new kinds of plastics—some biodegradable, others photodegradable (capable of being broken down by the sun)—have revolutionized the plastics industry. Companies like Agri-Tech, ICI Chemicals, and Webster Industries, have found that there is a fast-growing, profitable market for these new plastics, which don't contribute to the plastic pollution problem and can have special agricultural uses.

Very often, there seem to be conflicts between acting socially responsible and making profits. Businesses, though, can do both. "Free-market environmentalism" can help the environment and the business climate of the whole world. If necessity is the mother of invention, then profit is the father. If company executives must face environmental goals, chances are that in time they'll figure out how to meet those challenges economically and efficiently.

Based on information from Eric Jay Dolin, "Industry Is Going on a Waste-Watcher's Diet," *Business Week,* August 22, 1988, pp. 94–95; T.A. Heppenheimer, "Plastics Makers Clean Up from Litter," *High Technology Business,* August 1988, pp. 30–32; Jo Ann Kwong, "Corporate Donors Embrace Free-Market Environmentalism," *The Wall Street Journal,* June 23, 1988, p. 32; and Jeremy Main, "Here Comes the Big New Cleanup," *Fortune,* November 21, 1988, pp. 102, 104, 106, 110, 112, 114, 118.

contributing significantly to the deterioration of coastal waters and marine life in the eastern United States.[8] The sulfur combines with moisture in the atmosphere to form acids that are spread by winds. The acids fall to the earth in rain, which finds its way into streams, rivers, and lakes. The acid-rain problem has spread rapidly in recent years, and experts fear that the situation will worsen if the nation begins to burn more coal to generate electricity. To solve the problem, investigators must first determine where the sulfur is being emitted. The expenses that this vital

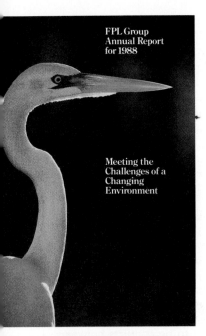

FPL Group
Annual Report
for 1988

Meeting the
Challenges of a
Changing
Environment

The FPL group is one of many organizations that are responding to concerns about the quality of the environment. Its annual report features several photographs of endangered and protected species of wildlife that safely inhabit Florida Power & Light Company's electric generating plant sites.

investigation and cleanup entail are going to be high. The human costs of having ignored the problem so long may be higher still.

Air Pollution   Usually two or three factors combine to form air pollution in any given location. The first factor is large amounts of carbon monoxide and hydrocarbons emitted by motor vehicles concentrated in a relatively small area. The second is the smoke and other pollutants emitted by manufacturing facilities. These two factors can be partially eliminated through pollution-control devices on cars, trucks, and smokestacks.

The third factor that contributes to air pollution—one that cannot be changed—is the combination of weather and geography. The Los Angeles basin, for example, combines just the right weather and geographic conditions for creating dense smog. Los Angeles has strict regulations regarding air pollution. If other U.S. cities adopted such strict regulations, they would be able to meet the national air-quality standards.[9] Even with these strict regulations, however, Los Angeles still struggles with air pollution problems because of uncontrollable conditions.

How effective is air pollution control? Most authorities agree that there has been progress since the mid-1970s. A number of cities have cleaner air today than they did fifteen years ago. Numerous chemical companies have recognized that they must take responsibility for operating their plants in an environmentally safe manner. Some of them now devote as much as 20 percent of their capital expenditures to purchasing anti-pollution devices.[10] However, air levels of sulfur dioxide and nitrogen dioxide—the main elements that cause acid rain—as well as of soot continue to increase.

Land Pollution   Air and water quality may be improving, but land pollution is still a serious problem in many areas. The fundamental issues are (1) how to restore damaged or contaminated land at a reasonable cost and (2) how to protect unpolluted land from future damage.

The land pollution problem has been worsening over the past few years, as modern technology has continued to produce more and more chemical and radioactive waste. U.S. manufacturers produce an estimated 40 to 60 million tons of contaminated oil, solvents, acids, and sludges each year. Service businesses, utility companies, hospitals, and other industries dump vast amounts of wastes into the environment.

Individuals in the United States also contribute to the waste disposal problem. On the average, each person accounts for approximately 1,547 pounds of garbage per year.[11] A nationwide shortage of landfills makes garbage disposal an especially serious predicament. Incinerators are a possible solution to the problem of a landfill shortage. They reduce the amounts of garbage but also leave tons of ash to be buried. This ash often has a higher concentration of toxicity than the original garbage.[12] Other causes of land pollution include strip-mining of coal, nonselective cutting of forests, and the development of agricultural land for housing and industry.

To help pay the enormous costs of cleaning up land polluted with chemicals and industrial wastes, Congress created a $1.6 billion Superfund in 1980. Originally, money was to flow into the Superfund from a tax paid by 800 oil and chemical companies that produce toxic waste. Then the EPA was to use the money in the Superfund to finance the cleanup of hazardous waste sites across the nation. To replenish the Superfund, the EPA had two options: It could sue the companies that were guilty of dumping chemicals at specific waste sites, or it could negotiate with guilty companies and thus completely avoid the legal system. During the 1980s, officials at the EPA came under fire because they preferred negotiated settlements. Critics referred to these settlements as "sweetheart deals" with industry. They felt the EPA should be much more aggressive in reducing land pollution in the United States. Of course, most corporate executives believe that cleanup efficiency and quality might be improved if companies were more involved. A 1986 amendment to the Superfund Act established strict guidelines for cleanups and gives residents the right to know what substances local chemical plants are producing.[13]

Noise Pollution   Excessive noise caused by traffic, aircraft, and machinery can do physical harm to human beings. Research has shown that people who are exposed to loud noises for long periods of time can suffer permanent hearing loss. The Noise Control Act of 1972 established noise emission standards for aircraft and airports, railroads, and interstate motor carriers. The act also provides funding for noise research at state and local levels.

Noise levels can be reduced by two methods. The source of noise pollution can be isolated as much as possible. (Thus, many metropolitan airports are located outside the cities.) And engineers can modify machinery and equipment to reduce noise levels. If it is impossible to reduce industrial noise to acceptable levels, workers should be required to wear earplugs to guard against permanent hearing damage.

Who Should Pay for a Clean Environment?

Governments and businesses are spending billions of dollars annually to reduce pollution—approximately $35 billion to control air pollution, $25 billion to control water pollution, and $12 billion to treat hazardous wastes. Proposed amendments to the 1970 Clean Air Act could add as much as $35 billion yearly to cleanup costs.[14]

To make matters worse, much of the money required to purify the environment is supposed to come from already depressed industries, such as the chemical industry. And a few firms have discovered that it is cheaper to pay a fine than to install expensive pollution control equipment.

Who, then, will pay for the environmental cleanup? Many business leaders believe that tax money should be used to clean up the environment and keep it clean. They reason that business is not the only source of pollution, so business should not be forced to absorb the entire cost of the cleanup. On the other hand, environmentalists believe that the cost of proper treatment and disposal of industrial wastes is an expense of doing business. In either case, consumers are likely to pay a large part of the cost—either as taxes or in the form of higher prices for goods and services.

Implementing a Social Responsibility Program

A firm's decision to be socially responsible is a step in the right direction—but only a first step. The firm must then develop and implement a tangible program to reach this goal. The factors that affect a particular firm's social responsibility program include its size, financial resources, past record in the area of social responsibility, and competition. But above all, the program must have total commitment or it will fail.

Developing a Social Responsibility Program

Learning Objective 8
Become familiar with the steps a business must take to implement a program of social responsibility

An effective program for social responsibility takes time, money, and organization. In most cases, four steps are involved in developing and implementing such a program.

Commitment of Top Executives   Without the support of top executives, any program will soon falter and become ineffective. As evidence of their commitment to social responsibility, top managers should develop a policy statement that outlines key areas of concern. This statement "sets the tone" (one of positive enthusiasm) and will later serve as a guide for other employees as they become involved in the program.

Effective social responsibility programs require the commitment of top-level executives who are directly involved in the planning and implementation of the program. This commitment is evident in the fire prevention program developed by Walgreen Company.

Planning   Next, a committee of managers should be appointed to plan the program. Whatever the form of their plan, it should deal with each of the issues described in the policy statement. If necessary, outside consultants can be hired to help develop the plan.

Appointment of a Director   After the social responsibility plan is established, a top-level executive should be appointed to direct the organization's activities in implementing it. This individual should be charged with recommending specific policies and helping individual departments understand and live up to the social responsibilities that the firm has assumed. Depending on the size of the firm, the director may require a staff to handle the program on a day-to-day basis.

The Social Audit   The director of the program should prepare a social audit for the firm at specified intervals. A **social audit** is a comprehensive report of what an organization has done, and is doing, with regard to social issues that affect it. This document provides the information that is needed for evaluation and revision of the social responsibility program. Typical subject areas include human resources, community involvement, the quality and safety of products, business practices, and efforts to reduce pollution and improve the environment. The information included in a social audit should be as accurate and as quantitative as possible, and it should reveal both positive and negative aspects of the program.

social audit *a comprehensive report of what an organization has done, and is doing, with regard to social issues that affect it*

Funding the Program

We have noted several times that social responsibility costs money. Thus, a program to improve social responsibility must be funded just like any other program. Funding can come from three sources: (1) Management can pass the cost on to consumers in the form of higher prices. (2) The corporation may be forced to absorb the cost of the program if, for example, the competitive situation does not permit a price increase. In this case, the cost is treated as a business expense, and profit is reduced. (3) The federal government may pay for all or part of the cost through special tax reductions or other incentives.

CHAPTER REVIEW

Summary

Ethics is the study of right and wrong and of the morality of choices. Business ethics is the application of moral standards to business situations. Because ethical issues arise in business situations every day, the business person should make an effort to be fair, to consider the welfare of customers and others within a firm, to avoid conflicts of interest, and to communicate honestly.

Investors, customers, employees, creditors, and competitors each exert specific pressures on a firm. Business people should not compromise their ethics to either satisfy or mislead any group. Because no international business code of ethics exists and since payoffs are sometimes part of international business practices, U.S. firms are sometimes directly or indirectly faced with ethical dilemmas when engaged in foreign business operations.

Any ethical action should be able to withstand open scrutiny. A person's individual values, the absence of an employer's code of ethics, and coworkers' attitudes and behaviors all influence a person's ethical decision making. The government, trade associations, and individual firms can help establish a more ethical business environment. An ethical employee working in an unethical environment sometimes resorts to whistle blowing to bring a particular situation to light.

In a socially responsible business, management realizes that its activities have an impact on society, and that impact is considered in the decision-making process. Before the 1930s neither workers, consumers, nor government had much influence on business activities; as a result, business gave little thought to its social responsibility. All this changed with the Great Depression. Government regulation and a new public awareness combined to create a demand that businesses act in a socially responsible manner.

According to the economic model of social responsibility, society benefits most when business is left alone to produce profitable goods and services. According to the socioeconomic model, business has as much responsibility to society as it has to its owners. Most managers adopt a viewpoint somewhere between these two extremes.

Three major areas of social concern to business and society are consumerism, employment practices, and the environment. The consumer movement has generally demanded—and received—attention from business in the areas of product safety, product information, product choices through competition, and the resolution of complaints about products and business practices.

Legislation and public demand have prompted some businesses to correct past abuses in employment practices—mainly with regard to minority groups. Affirmative action and training of the hard-core unemployed are two types of programs that have been used successfully.

Industry has contributed to the pollution of our land and water through the dumping of wastes, and to air pollution through vehicle and smokestack emissions. This contamination can be cleaned up and controlled, but the big question is who will pay for it. Present cleanup efforts are funded partly by government tax revenues, partly by business, and, in the long run, by consumers.

A program to implement social responsibility in a business begins with total commitment by top management. The program should be carefully planned, and a capable director should be appointed to implement it. Social audits should be prepared periodically as a means of evaluating and revising the program. Programs may be funded through federal incentives or through price increases.

In this chapter and in Chapter 1, we have used the general term *business owners* and the more specific term *stockholders*. In the next chapter, wherein we discuss the various forms of business and business ownership, you will see who these people are.

Key Terms

You should now be able to define and give an example relevant to each of the following terms:

ethics
business ethics
corporate code of ethics
whistle blowing
social responsibility
caveat emptor
economic model of
   social responsibility
socioeconomic model of
   social responsibility
consumerism
minority
affirmative action
   program
Equal Employment
   Opportunity
   Commission (EEOC)
hard-core unemployed
National Alliance of
   Businessmen (NAB)

pollution
Environmental
   Protection Agency
   (EPA)
social audit

Questions and Exercises

Review Questions

1. Why might an individual with high ethical standards act less ethically in business than in his or her personal life?

2. How would an organizational code of ethics help ensure ethical business behavior?

3. How and why did the American business environment change after the Great Depression?

4. What are the major differences between the economic model of social responsibility and the socioeconomic model?

5. What are the arguments for and against increased social responsibility for business?

6. Describe and give an example of each of the four basic rights of consumers.

7. There are more women than men in the United States. Why, then, are women considered a minority with regard to employment?

8. What is the goal of affirmative action programs? How is this goal achieved?

9. What is the primary function of the Equal Employment Opportunity Commission?

10. How do businesses contribute to each of the four forms of pollution? How can they avoid polluting the environment?

11. Our environment *can* be cleaned up and kept clean. Why haven't we simply done so?

12. Describe the steps involved in developing a social responsibility program within a large corporation.

Discussion Questions

1. Besides the catastrophic effects of the oil spill on the environment, what has been the effect on Exxon?

2. To what extent can and should an oil company prepare for a major oil spill?

3. How can an employee take an ethical stand regarding a business decision when his or her superior has already taken a different position?

4. Overall, would it be more profitable for a business to follow the economic model or the socioeconomic model of social responsibility?

5. Why should business take on the task of training the hard-core unemployed?

6. To what extent should the blame for vehicular air pollution be shared by manufacturers, consumers, and government?

7. Why is there so much government regulation involving social responsibility issues? Should there be less?

Exercises

1. Write out four "guidelines" that can be included as part of the code of ethics that prevails at your school or at a firm where you have worked.

2. Research and report on one case in which the EEOC or the EPA successfully brought suit against one or more firms. Give your own evaluation of the merits of the case.

3. List some items that should be included in a social audit for a small business other than a retail store.

Case 2.1

Legal Problems at Union Carbide

In December 1984, Union Carbide's chemical plant in Bhopal, India, sprang a deadly leak. Methyl isocyanate gas streamed into the air, causing the deaths of 3,500 persons. People are still dying at the rate of one a day. More than 200,000 persons were hospitalized, and nearly 25 percent of the women in the first trimester of pregnancy at the time of the accident miscarried, gave birth prematurely, or gave birth to handicapped children. More than 60,000 Bhopalis cannot do a full day's work. Clearly this is one of the worst industrial accidents in history.

Initially, Warren M. Anderson, then chairman of Union Carbide, said he would devote the rest of his career to resolving the problems caused by the accident. The company immediately donated $1 million to the Bhopal relief effort, while Union Carbide's employees donated an additional $150,000. A year later Anderson told reporters that he had overreacted. His admitting that he felt sorry about the accident increased Union Carbide's liability, thus jeopardizing the stockholders' investment and weakening the insurance carrier's position. Eventually, the Indian government charged Anderson with culpable homicide.

In April 1986, Union Carbide announced that it had reached a tentative settlement with U.S. lawyers representing victims of the Bhopal accident. The company agreed to pay $350 million in damages. But after Union Carbide's announcement, the Indian government rejected the offer. Rajiv Gandhi, the prime minister of India, called the settlement "inadequate." The Indian government insisted that it would agree only to a settlement that fully and fairly compensated all of the Bhopal victims. Privately, Indian officials suggested that a settlement in the range of $700 million to $1 billion would be more acceptable.

Although much suffering and many questions still surround the Bhopal incident, Union Carbide's legal battles have finally ended in a settlement. India's highest court ruled that Union Carbide should pay the Bhopal survivors (500,000 claimants in all) $470 million in damages. The Indian government charged that flaws in the chemical plant's design and poor maintenance caused the disaster. Union Carbide insists that an unhappy and vengeful employee (whom they refuse to name) sabotaged the plant. India's Supreme Court, however, did not address the issue of blame and, as part of the settlement, dismissed all criminal charges and civil suits against Union Carbide and its officials.

The Bhopal incident cost Union Carbide more than $24 million for its own investigation and legal fees. The price Union Carbide paid in terms of damage to its reputation was also very high. Now that a settlement has been reached, the management at Union Carbide can fully concentrate on business. Considering the turmoil, Union Carbide has done surprisingly well: The profits from its chemicals and plastics businesses have doubled since the disaster. After the accident, when the firm's stock prices dropped, Union Carbide reduced its work force from 98,000 to 43,000 workers. This streamlining must have helped the company substantially because today many analysts agree that Union Carbide is making a strong comeback.*

Questions

1. Warren M. Anderson initially said he would devote the rest of his career to resolving the problems caused by the Bhopal accident. A year later he said that he had overreacted. Why do you think he changed his position?

2. Do you think that the settlement was fair to the claimants? Why or why not?

---

* Based on information from Steve Dodson, "470 Million Accord in Bhopal Tragedy," *New York Times*, February 19, 1989, p. 14F; William B. Glaberson, Marilyn A. Harris, Patrick Houston, and Paula Dwyer, "How a Deal on Bhopal Eluded Carbide," *Business Week*, April 7, 1986, p. 39; William B. Glaberson, Marilyn A. Harris, and James R. Norman, "Why All Eyes Will Be on a Carbide Ruling," *Business Week*, January 13, 1986, p. 37; Sanjoy Hazarika, "Bhopal Payments Set at $470 Million for Union Carbide," *New York Times*, February 15, 1989, pp. 1, 27; Sanjoy Hazarika, "Many Details Unsettled on Bhopal Distributions," *New York Times*, February 16, 1989, p. 29; Jonathan P. Hicks, "After the Disaster, Carbide Is Rebuilt," *New York Times*, February 15, 1989, p. 27; Richard Koenig, Beatrice E. Garcia, and Anthony Spaeth, "Union Carbide Agrees to Settle All Bhopal Litigation for $470 Million in Pact with India's Supreme Court," *Wall Street Journal*, February 15, 1989, p. A3; "The Talk of the Town," *The New Yorker*, January 13, 1986, p. 17; and "Thumbs Down," *Time*, April 7, 1986, p. 48.

3. Based on feasibility studies, management at Union Carbide was concerned about whether this type of plant could be maintained in India. What could have been done to minimize this concern and to ensure the safety of the Bhopal workers?

Case 2.2

Absolut and Social Responsibility

Michel Roux is president of Carillon Importers Ltd., a subsidiary of Grand Metropolitan PLC. As such, Roux personally manages such brands as Bombay Gin, Grand Marnier, La Grande Passion liqueurs, Bertani wines, Laurent Perrier champagne, and Absolut vodka. Nevertheless, Roux still finds the time to take on more than his share of social responsibility efforts.

Roux built Absolut into the hottest brand in the liquor business. Since its introduction in the United States, Absolut has blossomed from an unknown into the nation's best-selling imported vodka, overtaking Stolichnaya. The American success of this 140-year-old Swedish vodka is mostly the result of Roux's business techniques, a blending of art and marketing. Roux once remarked, "Too many people take their business too seriously. Business is not such a serious thing." Based on the results of Absolut, maybe more business people should adopt this same viewpoint.

What is serious business to Roux is a variety of causes. After a successful advertising campaign that featured Absolut vodka bottles painted by artists such as Andy Warhol, Ed Ruscha, and Keith Haring, Roux began to commission lesser-known painters for his ads, greatly helping the careers of these struggling artists. He is now known among artists as "Le Patron."

Roux clearly enjoys doing good deeds. One day he read about a Swedish flautist, studying music at the Juilliard School in New York City, whose silver flute had been stolen. Roux promptly bought her another flute. Under Roux's direction, Carillon financed the restoration of a statue of Joan of Arc in New York's Riverside Park. At the restored Joan of Arc–statue festivities, Roux found out that a World War I veterans' memorial in the Bronx was also in need of repair. Carillon paid to restore that too.

Roux and Carillon believe they must help society at all levels. "You have to take care of the basement, or the house falls down," Roux once said. Carillon has one program that specializes in working with juvenile delinquents, and another one that works with Native Americans now on reservations.

Though his business is spirits, Roux has stated, "Liquor is also a drug, and moderation must be a part of our message." Roux would not consider a special Absolut St. Patrick's Day advertisement because he thought it would promote irresponsible drinking.†

† Based on information from Andrea Adelson, "Unusual Ads Help a Foreign Vodka to the Top," *New York Times*, November 28, 1988, p. D14; David Kalish, "Absolut-ly," *Marketing & Media Decisions*, April 1988, pp. 34–35; and Nancy Youman, "Michel Roux's Absolut Power," *Adweek's Marketing Week*, December 19, 1988, pp. 20–23.

Questions

1. In what ways is Michel Roux being socially responsible?
2. When a company sells products, such as tobacco or alcohol, that can be hazardous to users' health, to what extent is the firm obligated to tell customers about the risks of using such products?
3. Evaluate Roux's decision not to run a St. Patrick's Day advertisement for Absolut Vodka.

THE FORMS OF BUSINESS OWNERSHIP

3

1 Understand the basic differences among the three most common forms of business ownership: sole proprietorships, partnerships, and corporations

2 Be aware of the advantages and disadvantages of proprietorships, partnerships, and corporations

3 Know how a corporation is formed, who owns it, and who is responsible for its operation

4 Recognize the basic structure of a corporation

5 Name three types of corporations organized for special purposes, and explain how they differ from the more typical open or close corporation

6 Identify how corporations grow

7 Recognize three additional forms of ownership: cooperatives, joint ventures, and syndicates

CHAPTER PREVIEW

Our initial focus in this chapter is on three common forms of business ownership: sole proprietorships, partnerships, and corporations. We discuss how these types of businesses are formed and note the advantages and disadvantages of each. Next, we consider several types of corporations organized for special purposes, including government-owned corporations, not-for-profit corporations, and S-corporations. We also describe corporate patterns of growth, which may result from internal expansion or from mergers with other corporations. We conclude the chapter with a discussion of cooperatives, joint ventures, and syndicates—less common forms of business ownership that are useful in special situations.

Lettuce Entertain You Enterprises: Two Heads Are Better Than One

Richard Melman, the founder of Chicago-based Lettuce Entertain You Enterprises, is always eager to listen to a new concept for a restaurant. Melman's expertise is dining establishments, but his eateries provide much more than just good food and a place to eat it. With a knack for intriguing the public and obsessive attention to decor, Melman creates total dining experiences. Revenues at Melman's thirty restaurants are around $95 million a year.

An enormous number of restaurants fail every year, but Melman, using partnerships primarily, seems to build successful restaurants wherever he desires. By entering into business with different partners in different parts of the country, Melman has achieved a comfortable and successful balance between strict control of his interests and freedom to pursue new ventures.

When Melman was a youngster, he worked in his father's delicatessens. In 1967, he asked his father and his father's partner if he could become a third partner. When they turned him down, he became very dejected, quit, and decided to start his own restaurant. He has subsequently built a chain of lucrative restaurants that relies heavily on partnerships.

About twenty-one of his thirty establishments are run as partnerships. The partnership for a given restaurant consists of Melman, his three most senior partners, other investors, and a managing partner who operates the restaurant. The managing partner is totally responsible for the day-to-day activities of the business unless something goes wrong. In that situation, Melman is called in to rectify any problems. Melman makes frequent visits to all his restaurants to make sure the food is up to his standards and the service is impeccable.

The managing partner, when he or she enters into an agreement with Melman, is locked into a set salary. The only way for the managing partner to increase his or her base pay is to open a new restaurant. However, the managing partner can embark on another venture only when Melman is convinced that a replacement is ready to manage the existing restaurant.

Melman's partners include several celebrities. He opened The Eccentric, a restaurant in Chicago, with actress and talk-show host Oprah Winfrey and opened another one with quarterback Jim McMahon. Melman's successes should continue to attract partners of all kinds, which in turn should free up Melman's time to continue creating additional unique dining experiences.[1]

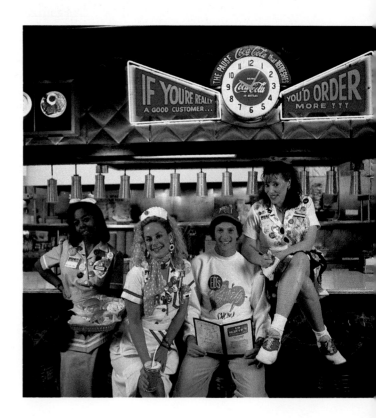

*P*eople like Richard Melman who start businesses must decide how their "something of value" will be owned. Should it be made part of their own personal assets, like a car or a house, for which they are responsible? Or should it be entirely separate from their personal finances? And should they retain ownership of the whole business or exchange part of that ownership for such assets as capital resources or management skills?

Obviously, the answers to these questions depend on the particular situation. And the answers change as the situation changes. Toward the end of the nineteenth century, Richard Sears was the sole owner of a small business in the Midwest. Later this business became a partnership known as Sears, Roebuck. And eventually Sears, Roebuck became a corporation owned by thousands of stockholders.

The three most common forms of business ownership in the United States are the sole proprietorship, partnership, and corporation (see Figure 3.1). In terms of ownership, corporations are generally the most complex, and sole proprietorships are the simplest. In terms of organization, however, all three usually start small and simple. Some, like IBM, grow and grow.

Sole Proprietorships

sole proprietorship *a business that is owned (and usually operated) by one person*

Learning Objective 1
Understand the basic differences among the three most common forms of business ownership: sole proprietorships, partnerships, and corporations

A **sole proprietorship** is a business that is owned (and usually operated) by one person. Sole proprietorship is the oldest and simplest form of business ownership, and it is the easiest to start. In most instances, the owner (the *sole* proprietor) simply decides that he or she is in business and begins operations. Some of the largest of today's corporations, including Ford Motor Company, H.J. Heinz Company, and J.C. Penney Company, started out as tiny—and, in many cases, struggling—sole proprietorships.

As you can see in Figure 3.1, there are more than 11.9 million sole proprietorships in the United States. They account for more than two-thirds of the country's business firms. Sole proprietorships are most

FIGURE 3.1
The Relative Percentages of Sole Proprietorships, Partnerships, and Corporations in the United States
Sole proprietorships, the most common form of business ownership, are most common in retailing, agriculture, and the service industries. (Source: U.S. Department of Commerce, Bureau of the Census, Statistical Abstract of the United States, 1989, p. 516.)

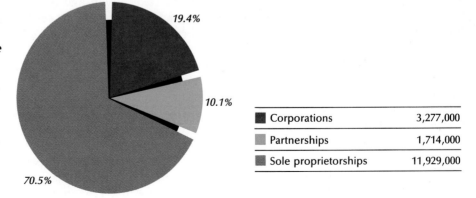

■ Corporations	3,277,000
■ Partnerships	1,714,000
■ Sole proprietorships	11,929,000

common in the retailing, agriculture, and service industries. Thus the specialty clothing shop, corner grocery, and television repair shop down the street are likely to be sole proprietorships.

Most of the advantages and disadvantages of sole proprietorships arise from the two main characteristics of this form of ownership: simplicity and individual control.

Advantages of Sole Proprietorships

Learning Objective 2
Be aware of the advantages and disadvantages of proprietorships, partnerships, and corporations

Ease and Low Cost of Formation and Dissolution   No contracts, agreements, or other legal documents are required to start a sole proprietorship. Most are established without even an attorney. A state or city license may be required for certain types of businesses, such as restaurants or catering services, that are regulated in the interest of public safety. But beyond that, a sole proprietor does not pay any special start-up fees or taxes. Nor are there any minimum capital requirements.

If the enterprise does not succeed, or the owner decides to enter another line of business, the firm can be closed as easily as it was opened. Creditors must be paid, of course. But the owner does not have to go through any legal procedure before hanging up an "Out of Business" sign.

Retention of All Profits   All profits earned by a sole proprietorship become the personal earnings of its owner. This provides the owner with a strong incentive to succeed—perhaps the strongest incentive—and a great deal of satisfaction when the business does succeed. It is this direct financial reward that attracts many entrepreneurs to the sole proprietorship form of business.

Sole proprietor Rachel London produces dresses with brilliant polyester flowers that carry the label Petal Pusher. Her boutique is in Los Angeles, but her creations have also been displayed at the Louvre in Paris.

Flexibility   The sole owner of a business is completely free to make decisions about the firm's operations. Without asking or waiting for anyone's approval, a sole proprietor can switch from retailing to wholesaling, move a shop's location, or open a new store and close an old one.

A sole owner can also respond to changes in market conditions much more quickly than the operators of other forms of business. Suppose the sole owner of an appliance store finds that many customers now prefer to shop on Sunday afternoons. He or she can make an immediate change in business hours to take advantage of that information (provided that state laws allow such stores to open on Sunday). The manager of one store in a large corporate chain may have to seek the approval of numerous managers before making such a change. Furthermore, a sole proprietor can quickly switch suppliers to take advantage of a lower price, whereas such a switch could take weeks in a more complex business.

Possible Tax Advantages   The sole proprietorship's profits are taxed as personal income of the owner. Thus a sole proprietorship does not pay the special state and federal income taxes that corporations pay. (As you will see later, the result of these special taxes is that a corporation's profits are taxed twice. A sole proprietorship's profits are taxed only once.) Also, recent changes in federal tax laws have resulted in higher tax rates for corporations than for individuals at certain income levels.

Secrecy Sole proprietors are not required by federal or state governments to publicly reveal their business plans, profits, or other vital facts. Therefore, competitors cannot get their hands on this information. Of course, sole proprietorships must report certain financial information on their personal tax forms, but that information is kept secret by taxing authorities.

Disadvantages of Sole Proprietorships

unlimited liability *a legal concept that holds a sole proprietor personally responsible for all the debts of his or her business*

Unlimited Liability **Unlimited liability** is a legal concept that holds a sole proprietor personally responsible for all the debts of his or her business. This means there is no legal difference between the debts of the business and the debts of the proprietor. If the business fails, the owner's personal property—including house, savings, and other assets—can be seized (and sold if necessary) to pay creditors.

Unlimited liability is thus the other side of the owner-keeps-the-profits coin. It is perhaps the major factor that tends to discourage would-be entrepreneurs from using this form of business organization.

Lack of Continuity Legally, the sole proprietor *is* the business. If the owner dies or is declared legally incompetent, the business essentially ceases to exist. In many cases, however, the owner's heirs take over the business and continue to operate it, especially if it is a profitable enterprise.

Limited Ability to Borrow Banks and other lenders are usually unwilling to lend large sums to sole proprietorships. Only one person—the sole proprietor—can be held responsible for repaying such loans, and the assets of most sole proprietors are fairly limited. Moreover, these assets may already have been used as the basis for personal borrowing (a mortgage loan or car loan) or for short-term credit from suppliers. Lenders also worry about the lack of continuity of sole proprietorships: Who will repay a loan if the sole proprietor is incapacitated?

The limited ability to borrow can keep a sole proprietorship from growing. It is the main reason why many business owners change from the sole proprietorship to some other ownership form when they need relatively large amounts of capital.

Limited Business Skills and Knowledge In Parts 2, 3, 4, and 5, we see managers perform a variety of functions (including planning, organizing, and controlling) in such areas as finance, marketing, human resources management, and operations. Often the sole proprietor is also the sole manager—in addition to being a salesperson, buyer, accountant, and, on occasion, janitor.

Even the most experienced business owner is unlikely to have expertise in all these areas. Consequently, the business can suffer in the areas in which the owner is less knowledgeable, unless he or she obtains the necessary expertise by hiring assistants or consultants.

Lack of Opportunity for Employees The sole proprietor may find it hard to attract and keep competent help. Potential employees may feel that there is no room for advancement in a firm whose owner assumes all managerial responsibilities. And when those who *are* hired are ready to take on added responsibility, they may find that the only way to do so is to quit the sole proprietorship and either work for a larger firm or start up their own business.

Beyond the Sole Proprietorship

The major disadvantages of a sole proprietorship stem from its one-person control—and the limited amount that one person can do in a workday. One way to reduce the effect of these disadvantages (while retaining many of the advantages) is to have more than one owner. Multiple ownership translates into more time devoted to managing, more management expertise, and more capital and borrowing ability.

Partnerships

partnership *an association of two or more persons to act as co-owners of a business for profit*

The Uniform Partnership Act, which has been adopted by many states, defines a **partnership** as an association of two or more persons to act as co-owners of a business for profit. For example, about fifteen years ago, two young black pharmacists named Cornell McBride and Therman McKenzie each put up $250 and, together, went into business making a hair spray for black men. They worked from the tiny basement of McBride's three-room house, mixing their first batch in a 55-gallon drum and stirring it with a pool cue. Today their M & M Products Company is an extremely successful firm. It is the tenth largest black-owned business in the United States, employs 165 people, and has sales of more than $50 million.[2]

There are approximately 1.7 million partnerships in the United States. As shown in Figure 3.2, partnerships account for about $368 billion in receipts. Note, however, that this form of ownership is much less common than the sole proprietorship or the corporation. In fact, partnerships represent only about 10 percent of all American businesses.

FIGURE 3.2
Total Sales Receipts of American Businesses
Although corporations account for only 19.4 percent of U.S. businesses, they bring in 90.2 percent of sales receipts. (Source: U.S. Department of Commerce, Bureau of the Census, Statistical Abstract of the United States, *1989, p. 516.)*

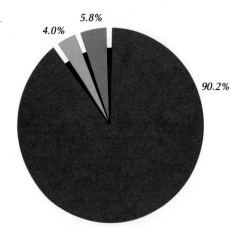

■ Corporations	$8,398 billion
■ Partnerships	$368 billion
■ Sole proprietorships	$540 billion

These partners, Richard Nicoltra (left) and Steve Beninati, operate a franchise chain of over two hundred Everything Yogurt shops, which are located primarily in the food courts of shopping malls.

Although there is no legal maximum, most partnerships have only two partners. (However, most of the largest partnerships in accounting, law, and advertising have many more than two partners.) Often a partnership represents a pooling of special talents, particularly in such fields as law, accounting, advertising, real estate, and retailing. Also, a partnership may result from a sole proprietor taking on a partner for the purpose of obtaining more capital.

Types of Partners

All partners need not be equal. Some may be fully active in running the business, whereas others may have a much more limited role.

general partner *a person who assumes full or shared operational responsibility of a business*

General Partners   A **general partner** is one who assumes full or shared operational responsibility of a business. Like sole proprietors, general partners are responsible for operating the business. They also assume unlimited liability for its debts, including debts that have been incurred by any other general partner without their knowledge or consent. The Uniform Partnership Act requires that every partnership have at least one general partner. This is to ensure that the liabilities of the business are legally assumed by at least one person.

General partners are active in day-to-day business operations, and each partner can enter into contracts on behalf of all the others. Each partner is taxed on his or her share of the profit—in the same way a sole

BUSINESS JOURNAL

Forming a Good Partnership

The Lone Ranger and Tonto, Abbott and Costello, Bonnie and Clyde—examples of partnerships are numerous in our culture. Throughout our lives, we form partnerships with family members, friends, and spouses. Usually there is not as much affection in business partnerships, but to some people, they are equally as natural. A person who might not think of starting and running a business alone might enthusiastically seize the opportunity to enter into a business partnership.

Not all partnerships work, and very few work smoothly all the time. Business partners—with egos, ambitions, and money on the line—are especially susceptible to friction. The excitement and energy surrounding the start of a new business might mask partnership problems just waiting to happen. Compatibility between persons is important, but a successful business partnership entails much more.

A good business partnership starts with a basic rule: Put everything in writing. Just as some couples opt for premarital agreements to protect themselves and their property in the event of a nasty breakup, prospective business partners should make sure they cover their assets. Items to include in a partnership agreement are who is going to make the final decisions, who is going to be responsible for what, who is going to contribute what, and what happens if a partner wants to dissolve the partnership or dies. The breakup of a partnership can be as complicated and traumatic as a divorce. Thus it is never too early, or unreasonably pessimistic, to consider what could happen in the future.

Individual co-owners should have talents that complement each other. Maybe one partner is a natural salesperson, who easily mingles with and wins over clients. The other partner can't stand working with the public and prefers to come up with brilliant ideas alone behind a computer terminal. Probably, the business will benefit from these two different areas of talent.

Partners must also trust and respect each other. To establish trust, honest and open communication is needed. Each partner should, at all times, know what the other partner or partners are doing. Partners should share both problems and triumphs equally.

Business partners must consider both the short- and long-term prospects for a new venture. Partners should have enough resources to allow for company expansion. The problems of a small business and a large business are very different. Consequently, partners should anticipate growth and understand that they may have to adapt their business relationships to fit new circumstances. A partner in a company must be flexible.

When entering into a partnership agreement, it might be wise for the partners to agree to let a neutral third party assist with any disputes that might arise. The third party may be a consultant, an accountant, a lawyer, or a mutual acquaintance. Without such an intense personal stake in the matter, a third party can look beyond personal opinion and emotions to seek a solution that is best for the company. Each partner should agree to abide by the decisions of this outsider.

Based on information from Jordan E. Cohn, "Starting a Business: Two Heads Are Better Than One," *Changing Times,* February 1987, pp. 78–80, 82–85; J. Michael Geringer, "Partner Selection Criteria for Developed Country Joint Ventures," *Business Quarterly,* Summer 1988, pp. 55–62; and Peter Wylie and Mardy Grothe, "Breaking Up Is Hard to Do," *Nation's Business,* July 1988, pp. 24–25.

proprietor is taxed. (The partnership itself pays no income tax.) If one general partner withdraws from the partnership, he or she must give notice to creditors, customers, and suppliers to avoid future liability.

limited partner   *a person who contributes capital to a business but is not active in managing it; this partner's liability is limited to the amount that he or she has invested*

Limited Partners   A **limited partner** is a person who contributes capital to a business but is not active in managing it; his or her liability is *limited* to the amount that he or she has invested. In return for their investment, limited partners share in the profits of the firm.

Not all states allow limited partnerships. In those that do, the prospective partners must file formal articles of partnership. They must publish a notice regarding the limitation in at least one newspaper. And they must ensure that at least one partner is a general partner. The goal of these requirements is to protect the customers and creditors of the limited partnership.

Partners can also be nominal, ostensible, active, secret, dormant, or silent. What type of partner individuals choose to be depends a great deal on how much involvement they want in a particular business or what special abilities they bring to a firm. The six different types of partners have the following characteristics:

1. *Nominal partner:* not a party to the partnership agreement or a true partner in any sense; by adding his or her name to the partnership, becomes liable as if he or she were a partner if persons have given credit to the firm because of such representation
2. *Ostensible partner:* active and known to the public as a partner
3. *Active partner:* active in management but may or may not be known to the public
4. *Secret partner:* active, but not known to the public or held out as a partner
5. *Dormant partner:* inactive and not known or held out as a partner
6. *Silent partner:* inactive, but may be known to the public as a partner

The Partnership Agreement

Some states require that partners draw up *articles of partnership* and file them with the secretary of state. Articles of partnership are a written agreement listing and explaining the terms of the partnership. Even when it is not required, an oral or written agreement among partners is legal and can be enforced in the courts. A written agreement is obviously preferred because it is not subject to lapses of memory.

Figure 3.3 shows a typical partnership agreement. The articles generally describe each partner's contribution to, share of, and duties in the business. They may outline each partner's responsibility—who will maintain the accounts, who will manage sales, and so forth. They may also spell out how disputes will be settled and how one partner can buy the interests of another.

Advantages of Partnerships

Ease and Low Cost of Formation   Like sole proprietorships, partnerships are relatively easy to form. The legal requirements are often limited to registering the name of the business and purchasing whatever licenses are needed. It may not even be necessary to consult an attorney, except in states that require written articles of partnership. However, it is generally a good idea to get the advice and assistance of an attorney when forming a partnership.

(1) Names of partners

(2) Nature of business

(3) Name of partnership

(4) Place of business

(5) Duration of partnership

(6) Duties of partners

(7) Contribution of capital

(8) Interest of partners

(9) Accounting

(10) Salaries of partners

(11) Drawing account

(12) Termination

ARTICLES OF PARTNERSHIP

ARTICLES OF PARTNERSHIP, made this 1st day of October, 19--, between ELIZABETH A. BORSOS, residing at 1129 Woodall Way, in the City of Boise, Idaho, and MICHAEL L. MAYO, residing at 529 Lightfoot Drive, in the City of Boise, Idaho, as follows:

THE ABOVE-NAMED PARTIES AGREE to become partners in the business of manufacturing and selling baked goods, and by these presents do agree to become partners under the firm name of Bread 'n' Bagels, at 301 North Second Street, City of Boise, Idaho, and that said partnership is to begin on the first above-mentioned date and to continue for two (2) years thereafter.

AND IT IS AGREED by and between the parties that at all times during the continuance of this partnership, they and each of them will give their entire time and attention to the business, and to the best of their endeavors and of their skill and power exert themselves for their joint interest, profit, benefit, and advantage in the aforesaid business.

AND IT IS AGREED by and between the parties that each shall contribute to the capital of the partnership the sum of Five Thousand Dollars ($5,000), the receipt of which is mutually acknowledged.

AND IT IS AGREED by and between the parties that they shall and will at all times during the continuance of said partnership bear, pay, and discharge equally between them all necessary expenses that may be required for the maintenance and management of said business, and that all profit and increase that shall arise by means of their said business shall be divided equally between them, and all loss that shall happen to their said business shall be equally borne between them.

AND IT IS AGREED by and between the parties that they shall have and keep at all times during the said partnership true books of account, and that the said partners shall render each to the other a true and perfect inventory and account of all profit and increase every six (6) months, or more often if necessary.

AND IT IS AGREED by and between the parties that each partner shall draw a salary of Nine Hundred Dollars ($900) a month, and shall be entitled to draw from the profits, beginning on the 15th day of April, 19--, and on the 15th of the month at each succeeding half-year, one quarter of the profits for the preceding period of six (6) months, or a greater equal proportion thereof, as may from time to time be agreed upon.

AND IT IS AGREED by and between the parties that at the end of the partnership they shall render complete accounts of all their dealings with the business, and all property of whatever kind of character shall be divided equally between them.

IN WITNESS WHEREOF, we have hereunto set our hands and seals this 1st day of October, 19--.

Elizabeth A. Borsos (L.S.)
Elizabeth A. Borsos

Michael L. Mayo (L.S.)
Michael L. Mayo

In the presence of:
Pierre L. Kramer

FIGURE 3.3
Articles of Partnership
Articles of partnership list and explain the terms of the partnership in a written agreement. [Source: R. Robert Rosenberg et al., College Business Law (New York: McGraw-Hill, 1978), p. 408. Copyright 1978 McGraw-Hill Book Company. Reproduced with permission.]

Availability of Capital and Credit   Partners can pool their funds so that their business has more capital than would be available to a sole proprietorship. This additional capital, coupled with the general partners' unlimited liability, can form the basis for a good credit rating. Banks and suppliers may be more willing to extend credit or grant sizable loans to such a partnership than to an individual owner.

This does not mean that partnerships can easily borrow all the money they need. Many partnerships have found it hard to get long-term financing simply because lenders worry about enterprises that take years to earn a profit. But, in general, partnerships have greater assets and so stand a better chance of obtaining the loans they need.

Retention of Profits   As in a sole proprietorship, all profits belong to the owners of the partnership. The partners share directly in the financial rewards. Thus they are highly motivated to do their best to make the firm succeed.

Personal Interest   General partners are very much concerned with the operation of the firm—perhaps even more so than sole proprietors. After all, they are responsible for the actions of all other general partners, as well as for their own.

Combined Business Skills and Knowledge   Partners often have complementary skills. If one partner is weak in, say, finances, another may be stronger in that area. Moreover, the ability to discuss important decisions with another concerned individual often takes some of the pressure off everyone and leads to more effective decision making.

Possible Tax Advantages   Like sole proprietors, partners are taxed only on their individual income from the business. The special taxes such as the state franchise tax that corporations must pay are not imposed on partnerships. Also, at certain levels of income, the new federal tax rates are lower for individuals than for corporations.

Disadvantages of Partnerships

Unlimited Liability   As we have noted, each general partner is personally responsible for all debts of the business, whether or not that particular partner incurred those debts. General partners thus run the risk of having to use their personal assets to pay creditors. Limited partners, however, risk only their original investment.

Lack of Continuity   Partnerships are terminated in the event of the death, withdrawal, or legally declared incompetence of any one of the general partners. However, that partner's ownership share can be purchased by the remaining partners. In other words, the law does not automatically provide that the business shall continue, but the articles of partnership may do so. For example, the partnership agreement may permit surviving partners to continue the business after buying a deceased partner's interest from his or her estate. However, if the partnership loses an owner whose specific skills cannot be replaced, it is not likely to survive.

Effects of Management Disagreements   The division of responsibilities among several partners means the partners must work together as a team. They must have great trust in each other. If partners begin to disagree about decisions, policies, or ethics, distrust may cloud the horizon. Such a mood tends to get worse as time passes—often to the point where it is impossible

TABLE 3.1   Questions to Ask When Forming a Partnership

Money
- ▶ Where will the start-up money come from?
- ▶ How and when will it be repaid?
- ▶ How will the partners be compensated?
- ▶ When and how will this remuneration change?
- ▶ How are employees hired, and how much will they be paid?
- ▶ How are spending priorities set?
- ▶ Who approves payments and signs the checks?
- ▶ What are the profit goals?
- ▶ How are they set and when will they be revised?
- ▶ Are profits plowed back into the business or distributed to the partners?
- ▶ If profits are taken out, at what rate are they distributed?

Goals
- ▶ What are the short-term and long-term goals of the partnership?
- ▶ Are the partners totally committed to these goals?

Separation of Responsibilities
- ▶ Who will handle personnel matters?
- ▶ Which employees report to which partners?
- ▶ How are the responsibilities divided for accounting, acquisition of new equipment and office space, new business, marketing, and other functions?
- ▶ What happens if one partner is dissatisfied with the way another partner handles a particular responsibility?

Decision-Making
- ▶ Which matters require joint decisions?
- ▶ In which areas can partners act independently?
- ▶ What criteria are used to evaluate decisions?

Individual Contributions
- ▶ How much time will each partner be required to devote to the business?
- ▶ Do all the partners value each other's contributions as much as their own?

Growth
- ▶ How will areas for growth be chosen?
- ▶ How will growth be financed?
- ▶ Who will manage the additional work created by the growth?
- ▶ If a new venture loses money, how will the partners decide whether to give up or to keep trying?

Disagreement
- ▶ What are the ground rules for resolving disagreements?
- ▶ Will conflicts be ended by deferring to the partner with the most expertise in the matter, by using facts and figures, or by an expert third party?
- ▶ Which matters require complete agreement before any action can be taken?

Communication
- ▶ How and when will information be shared?
- ▶ Will communication with employees be through the chain of command?

Source: Adapted from Patricia O'Toole, *Savvy*, January 1982, p. 63. Reprinted with permission from *Savvy* magazine. Copyright by Family Media, Inc.

to operate the business successfully. To reduce disagreements, a number of issues can be settled when forming the partnership (see Table 3.1).

Frozen Investment   It is easy to invest money in a partnership, but it is sometimes quite difficult to get it out. This is the case, for example, when remaining partners are unwilling to buy the share of the business that belongs to the partner who is leaving. To prevent such difficulties, the procedure for buying out a partner should be included in the articles of partnership.

In some cases, a partner must find someone outside the firm to buy his or her share. How easy or difficult it is to find an outsider depends on how successful the business is.

Beyond the Partnership

The advantages of a partnership over a sole proprietorship derive mainly from the added capital and expertise of the partners. However, some of the basic disadvantages of the sole proprietorship also plague the general partnership. Unlimited liability and restraints on capital resources and borrowing, for example, can hinder a partnership's growth. A third form of business ownership, the corporation, succeeds in overcoming some of these disadvantages.

Corporations

Learning Objective 3
Know how a corporation is formed, who owns it, and who is responsible for its operation

corporation *an artificial person created by law, with most of the legal rights of a real person, including the right to start and operate a business, to own or dispose of property, to borrow money, to sue or be sued, and to enter into binding contracts*

Perhaps the best definition of a corporation was given by Chief Justice John Marshall in a famous decision in 1819. A corporation, he said, "is an artificial being, invisible, intangible, and existing only in contemplation of the law." In other words, a **corporation** is an artificial person created by law, with most of the legal rights of a real person. These include the right to start and operate a business, to own or dispose of property, to borrow money, to sue or be sued, and to enter into binding contracts. Unlike a real person, however, a corporation exists only on paper.

There are more than 3.2 million corporations in the United States. They comprise only about one-fifth of all businesses, but they account for more than nine-tenths of all sales revenues and more than three-quarters of all business profits. Table 3.2 ranks the twenty-five largest industrial corporations in the United States according to sales.

Corporate Ownership

stock *the shares of ownership of a corporation*

stockholder *a person who owns a corporation's stock*

The shares of ownership of a corporation are called its **stock.** The people who own a corporation's stock—and thus own part of the corporation—are called its **stockholders,** or sometimes its *shareholders.* Once a corporation has been formed, it may sell its stock to individuals. It may also issue stock as a reward to key employees in return for certain services, or as a return to investors (in place of cash payments).

BUSINESS JOURNAL

Executive Compensation: U.S. Corporate Big Shots Get Big Bucks

Rent, food, utilities, car payments, expenses. Having trouble making ends meet? Lee Iacocca doesn't. If you break down his entire compensation package at Chrysler Corp. for a recent year, Iacocca made $38,775 an hour. Three hundred U.S. CEOs earn at least $1 million dollars annually. Probably, no more than thirty European CEOs earn that much, and the number in Asia is even smaller.

Consider the salaries of other CEOs in the automotive industry. Recently, Lee Iacocca received $77,656,000 in salary and stock options. West Germany's Edzard Reuter, CEO of Daimler-Benz A.G., made $1,200,000; France's Jacques Calvet, CEO of Peugot, made $250,000; and Japan's Tadashi Kume, CEO of Honda Motor Co., Ltd., made $450,000.

Compensation levels of CEOs in other industries are equally as disparate. Jack Welch of General Electric made $12,631,000 one year. During the same year, Karlheinz Kaske of West Germany's Siemens A.G. made $930,000; Anders Scharp of Sweden's Electrolux made $437,000; and Ichiro Shinji of Japan's JVC made $290,000. Since U.S. CEOs are unlikely to cut their own pay, look for the salaries of European and Asian executives to rise substantially in the near future.

Within the United States, executive salaries vary greatly. Studies indicate that there is a high correlation between a firm's size and its management's compensation. The larger the company, the more its CEO tends to take home. Management compensation includes salary, annual bonuses, and various long-term incentives including stock options, stock appreciation rights, and deferred compensation. Some executives have "golden parachutes," a bonus they receive when they leave a company, are fired, or are required to relocate.

Compensation packages have become so complex that it is difficult to relate compensation to performance. In fact, many compensation packages seem to be based more on tax considerations than on performance criteria. Management often gets valuable benefits no matter how the company does.

Some experts think that such generous compensation plans are hurting companies and American business in general. Since compensation is often tied to stock market–based performance, management and CEOs tend to focus on short-run profits. As a result, companies' executives have a tendency to unwisely use current assets, ignore plant updating, and prefer investments with shorter payback periods. Because there is often no clear link between performance and management compensation, there may also be a loss of innovation, research and development, and long-term investments at these companies. Executives, receiving a comfortable salary plan, tend not to take risks unless payoffs are quick and relatively certain. In view of these factors, some experts suggest that product cycle and product innovation rates—rather than new products acquired through acquisitions—be used as the criteria for evaluating management performance.

Based on information from Michael J. Mandel, "Those Fat Bonuses Don't Seem to Boost Performance," *Business Week,* January 8, 1990, p. 26; John A. Byrne, "Executive Pay: Who Gets What in '86," *Business Week,* May 4, 1987, pp. 50–54, 58; "Committee Sets Executive Pay and Incentives," *Employee Benefit Plan Review,* December 1987, p. 72; Joani Nelson-Horchler, "The Top Man Gets Richer," *Industry Week,* June 6, 1986, pp. 51–54; S. Prakash Sethi and Nobuaki Namiki, "Top Management Compensation and Corporate Performance," *Journal of Business Strategy,* Spring 1987, pp. 37–43; and Shawn Tully, "American Bosses Are Overpaid," *Fortune,* November 7, 1988, pp. 121–136.

close corporation   *a corporation whose stock is owned by relatively few people and is not traded in stock markets*

A **close corporation** is a corporation whose stock is owned by relatively few people and is not traded openly (that is, in stock markets). A person who wishes to sell the stock of such a corporation generally arranges to sell it *privately*, to another stockholder or a close acquaintance. As an example, Mr. and Mrs. DeWitt Wallace owned virtually all the stock of Reader's Digest Association, making it one of the largest corporations of this kind.

An **open corporation** is one whose stock is traded openly in stock markets and can be purchased by any individual. General Motors, the largest industrial company in the United States, is an example. Most large firms are open corporations, and their stockholders may number in the millions. For example, AT&T is owned by more than 3 million shareholders.

TABLE 3.2 **The Twenty-five Largest U.S. Industrial Corporations, Ranked by Sales**

Rank 1989	1988	Company	Sales ($ millions)	Assets ($ millions)
1	1	General Motors, Detroit	126,974.3	173,297.1
2	2	Ford Motor, Dearborn, MI	96,932.4	160,893.3
3	3	Exxon, New York	86,656.0*	83,219.0
4	4	IBM, Armonk, NY	63,438.0	77,734.0
5	5	General Electric, Fairfield, CT	55,264.0	128,344.0
6	6	Mobil, New York	50,976.0*	39,080.0
7	10	Philip Morris, New York	39,069.0*	38,528.0
8	7	Chrysler, Highland Park, MI	36,156.0	51,038.0
9	9	E. I. du Pont de Nemours, Wilmington, DE	35,209.0	34,715.0
10	8	Texaco, White Plains, NY	32,416.0	25,636.0
11	11	Chevron, San Francisco	29,443.0*	33,884.0
12	12	Amoco, Chicago	24,214.0*	30,430.0
13	13	Shell Oil, Houston[1]	21,703.0	27,599.0
14	15	Procter & Gamble, Cincinnati[2]	21,689.0	16,351.0
15	19	Boeing, Seattle	20,276.0	13,278.0
16	14	Occidental Petroleum, Los Angeles	20,068.0	20,741.0
17	16	United Technologies, Hartford[3]	19,765.5	14,598.2
18	18	Eastman Kodak, Rochester, NY	18,398.0	23,652.0
19	23	USX, Pittsburgh	17,755.0*	17,500.0
20	21	Dow Chemical, Midland, MI	17,730.0	22,166.0
21	22	Xerox, Stamford, CT	17,635.0	30,088.0
22	17	Atlantic Richfield, Los Angeles	15,905.0	22,261.0
23	26	PepsiCo, Purchase, NY	15,419.6	15,126.7
24	20	RJR Nabisco Holdings, New York[4]	15,224.0†	36,412.0
25	25	McDonnell Douglas, St. Louis	14,995.0	13,397.0

Source: *Fortune*, The Fortune 500, April 23, 1990, p. 346. © 1990 Time Inc. All rights reserved.
[1] Owned by Royal Dutch/Shell Group (1988 International 500: rank 1).
[2] Figures are for fiscal year ended June 30, 1989.
[3] Figures include Sheller-Globe (1988 rank: 368), acquired November 9, 1989.
[4] Name changed from RJR Nabisco.
* Does not include excise taxes.
† Includes sales from discontinued operations of at least 10%.

Forming a Corporation

incorporation   *the process of forming a corporation*

The process of forming a corporation is called **incorporation.** The people who actually start the corporation are its *incorporators.* They must make several decisions about the corporation before and during the incorporation process.

Where to Incorporate   A business is allowed to incorporate in any state it chooses. Most small and medium-sized businesses are incorporated in the state where they do the most business. However, the founders of larger corporations, or of those that will do business nationwide, may compare the benefits provided to corporations by various states. Some states are more hospitable than others, and some offer low taxes and other benefits to attract new firms. Delaware is acknowledged as offering the most lenient tax structure. A huge number of firms (more than 75,000) have incorporated in that state, even though their corporate headquarters may be located in another state. Figure 3.4 shows the best and worst "business climates" among the states, according to one group of experts. Best or worst business climate includes such factors as fiscal policies of state and local governments, state-regulated employment costs, labor costs, availability and productivity of labor, and other manufacturing criteria such as energy and environmental costs.

domestic corporation   *a corporation in the state in which it is incorporated*

foreign corporation   *a corporation in any state in which it does business except the one in which it is incorporated*

alien corporation   *a corporation chartered by a foreign government and conducting business in the United States*

An incorporated business is called a **domestic corporation** in the state in which it is incorporated. In all other states where it does business, it is called a **foreign corporation.** Sears, Roebuck, for example, is incorporated in New York, where it is a domestic corporation. In the remaining forty-nine states, it is a foreign corporation. A corporation chartered by a foreign government and conducting business in the United States is an **alien corporation.** Volkswagen, Sony, Lever Brothers, and Toyota are examples of alien corporations.

corporate charter   *a contract between the corporation and the state, in which the state recognizes the formation of the artificial person that is the corporation*

The Corporate Charter   Once a "home state" has been chosen, the incorporators submit *articles of incorporation* to the secretary of state. If the articles of incorporation are approved, they become the firm's corporate charter. A **corporate charter** is a contract between the corporation and the state, in which the state recognizes the formation of the artificial person that is the corporation. Usually the charter (and thus the articles of incorporation) includes the following information:

▶ Firm's name and address

▶ The incorporators' names and addresses

▶ The purpose of the corporation

▶ The maximum amount of stock and the types of stock to be issued

▶ The rights and privileges of shareholders

▶ How long the corporation is to exist (usually without limit)

Each of these key details is the result of decisions that the incorporators must make as they organize the firm—before the articles of incorporation are submitted. Let us look at one area in particular: stockholders' rights.

MANUFACTURING CLIMATE

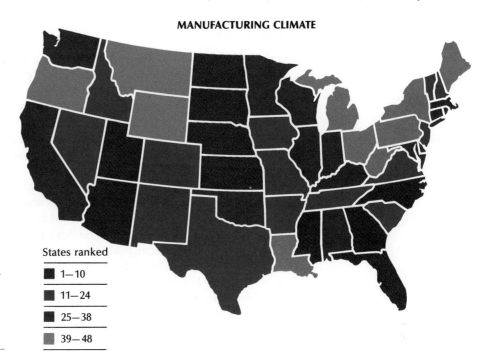

FIGURE 3.4
The Best and Worst States in Which to Incorporate a Manufacturing Firm
Data are not available for Alaska and Hawaii. (Source: Adapted with permission from Grant Thornton.)

States ranked

■ 1—10

■ 11—24

■ 25—38

■ 39—48

common stock *stock owned by individuals or firms who may vote on corporate matters, but whose claims on profit and assets are subordinate to the claims of others*

preferred stock *stock owned by individuals or firms who usually do not have voting rights, but whose claims on profit and assets take precedence over those of common-stock owners*

proxy *a legal form that lists issues to be decided at a stockholders' meeting and requests that stockholders transfer their voting rights to some other individual or individuals*

Stockholders' Rights   There are two basic kinds of stock (and some variations that are discussed in Chapters 18 and 19). Each type entitles the owner to a different set of rights and privileges. The owners of **common stock** may vote on corporate matters, but their claims on profit and assets are subordinate to the claims of others. Generally, an owner of common stock has one vote for each share owned. The owners of **preferred stock** usually do not have voting rights, but their claims on profit and assets take precedence over those of common-stock owners.

Perhaps the most important right of owners of both common and preferred stock is to share in the profit earned by the corporation. Other rights include being offered additional stock in advance of a public offering (*pre-emptive rights*); examining corporate records; voting on the corporate charter; and attending the corporation's annual stockholders' meeting, where they may exercise their right to vote.

Because common stockholders usually live all over the nation, very few actually attend the annual meeting. Instead, they vote by proxy. A **proxy** is a legal form that lists issues to be decided and requests that stockholders transfer their voting rights to some other individual or individuals. The stockholder registers his or her vote and transfers his or her voting rights simply by signing and returning the form.

Organizational Meeting   As the last step in forming a corporation, the original stockholders meet to elect their first board of directors. (Later, directors will be elected or re-elected at the corporation's annual meetings.) The board members are directly responsible to the stockholders for the way they operate the firm.

Corporate Structure

board of directors *the top governing body of a corporation, the members of which are elected by the stockholders*

Learning Objective 4
Recognize the basic structure of a corporation

Board of Directors   The **board of directors** is the top governing body of a corporation, and, as we noted, directors are elected by the shareholders. A corporation is an artificial person. Thus it can act only through its directors, who represent the corporation's owners. Board members can be chosen from within the corporation or from outside it.

Directors who are elected from within the corporation are usually its top managers—the president and executive vice presidents, for example. Those who are elected from outside the corporation are generally experienced managers with proven leadership ability and/or specific talents that the organization seems to need. In smaller corporations, majority stockholders may also serve as board members.

The major responsibilities of the board of directors are to set company goals and develop general plans (or strategies) for meeting those goals. They are also responsible for the overall operation of the firm.

corporate officer *the chairman of the board, president, executive vice president, corporate secretary and treasurer, or any other top executive appointed by the board of directors*

Corporate Officers   A **corporate officer** is appointed by the board of directors. The chairman of the board, president, executive vice presidents, and corporate secretary and treasurer are all corporate officers. They help the board make plans, carry out the strategies established by the board, and manage day-to-day business activities. Periodically (usually each month), they report to the board of directors. And once each year, at an

The advantages of a corporation, such as ease of raising capital and specialized management, facilitate the development and management of large capital-intensive projects. Shown here is the San Antonio Marriott Rivercenter, a convention hotel. The Marriott Corporation operates in fifty states and twenty-six countries.

annual meeting, the directors report to the stockholders. In theory, then, the stockholders are able to control the activities of the entire corporation through its directors (see Figure 3.5).

Advantages of Corporations

limited liability *a feature of corporate ownership that limits each owner's financial liability to the amount of money she or he has paid for the corporation's stock*

Limited Liability   One of the most attractive features of corporate ownership is **limited liability.** Each owner's financial liability is limited to the amount of money she or he has paid for the corporation's stock. This feature arises from the fact that the corporation is itself a legal being, separate from its owners. If a corporation should fail, creditors have a claim only on the assets of the corporation, not on the personal assets of its owners.

Ease of Transfer of Ownership   Let us say that a shareholder of a public corporation wishes to sell his or her stock. A telephone call to a stockbroker is all that is required to put the stock up for sale. There are usually willing buyers available for most stocks, at the market price. Ownership is transferred automatically when the sale is made, and practically no restrictions apply to the sale and purchase of stock.

Ease of Raising Capital   The corporation is by far the most effective form of business ownership for raising capital. Like sole proprietorships and partnerships, corporations can borrow from lending institutions. However, they can also sell stock to raise additional sums of money. Individuals are more willing to invest in corporations than in other forms of business because of the limited liability that investors enjoy and because of the ease with which they can sell their stock.

Perpetual Life   Because a corporation is essentially a legal "person," it exists independently of its owners and survives them. Unless its charter specifies otherwise, a corporation has perpetual life. The withdrawal, death, or incompetence of a key executive or owner is not cause for the corporation to be terminated. Sears, Roebuck, incorporated almost a century ago, is one of the nation's largest retailing corporations, even though its original owners, Richard Sears and Alvah Roebuck, have been dead for decades.

Specialized Management   Typically, corporations are able to recruit more skilled and knowledgeable managers than proprietorships and partnerships. This is because they have more available capital and are large enough to offer considerable opportunity for advancement. Within the corporate structure, administration, human resources, finance, sales, and operations are placed in the charge of experts in these fields. For instance, the Bechtel Group hired Caspar Weinberger, former Secretary of Defense.

Disadvantages of Corporations

Difficulty and Expense of Formation   Forming a corporation can be a relatively complex and costly process. The use of an attorney may be necessary to complete the legal forms and apply to the state for a charter. Charter

FIGURE 3.5
The Hierarchy of Corporate Structure
Stockholders exercise a great deal of influence by their right to vote and elect directors.

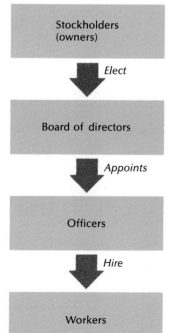

fees, attorney's fees, the costs of stock certificates and required record keeping, and other organizational costs all add up. These payments can amount to thousands of dollars for even a medium-sized corporation. The costs of incorporating, in both time and money, discourage many owners of smaller businesses from forming corporations.

Government Regulation   Most government regulation of business is directed at corporations. A corporation must meet various government standards before it can sell its stock to the public. Then it must file many reports on its business operations and finances with local, state, and federal governments. In addition, the corporation must make periodic reports to its stockholders about various aspects of the business. Also, its activities are restricted by law to those spelled out in its charter.

Double Taxation   Unlike sole proprietorships and partnerships, corporations must pay a tax on their profits. Then stockholders must pay a personal income tax on profits received as dividends. As a result, corporate profits are taxed twice—once as corporate income and again as the personal income of stockholders.

Lack of Secrecy   Because open corporations are required to submit detailed reports to government agencies and to stockholders, they cannot keep their operations confidential. Competitors can study these required corporate reports and then use the information to compete more effectively. In effect, every public corporation has to share some of its secrets with its competitors.

The characteristics of sole proprietorships, partnerships, and corporations (for example, tax rates, organizational documents needed) are summarized and compared in Table 3.3.

TABLE 3.3   Forms of Doing Business

Characteristics	Sole Proprietorship	Partnership	Corporation
Instrument of creation	None (Assumed name statement may be required.)	Agreement—oral or written	Articles of incorporation
Tax rates	Individual	Individual	Corporate
Organizational documents	None	Partnership agreement	Articles of incorporation, bylaws, minutes
Limited liability	No	No	Yes
Recognition of losses	Owner	Partners	Corporation

Source: John A. Andersen, "The Business Entity That's Best For You," *Panorama*, Number 13, Second Quarter, 1982. Reprinted by permission of Pannell Kerr Forster and the author.

Special Types of Corporations

Learning Objective 5
Name three types of
corporations organized for
special purposes, and explain
how they differ from the more
typical open or close
corporation

Most corporations are organized for the purpose of earning business profits. There are also various types of corporations that are organized for special purposes. Among these are government-owned, not-for-profit, and S-corporations.

Government-Owned Corporations

government-owned corporation   *a corporation owned and operated by a local, state, or federal government*

A **government-owned corporation** is owned and operated by a local, state, or federal government. It usually provides a service that the business sector is reluctant or unable to offer. (It is doubtful, for instance, whether private enterprise could have marshaled the financial resources needed to put astronauts on the moon.) Profit is secondary in government-owned corporations. In fact, they may continually operate at a loss, particularly in the area of public transportation. Their main objective is to ensure that a particular service is available to citizens.

The U.S. Postal Service, the Tennessee Valley Authority (TVA), the National Aeronautics and Space Administration (NASA), and the Federal Deposit Insurance Corporation (FDIC) are all government-owned corporations. They are operated by the U.S. government. Most municipal bus lines and subways are run by city-owned corporations.

quasi-government corporation   *a business owned partly by the government and partly by private citizens or firms*

In certain cases, a government will invite citizens or firms to invest in such a corporation as part owners. A business owned partly by the government and partly by private citizens or firms is called a **quasi-government corporation.**

Not-for-Profit Corporations

not-for-profit corporation
a corporation that is organized to provide a social, educational, religious, or other nonbusiness service rather than to earn a profit

A **not-for-profit corporation** is a corporation that is organized to provide a social, educational, religious, or other nonbusiness service rather than to earn a profit. Various charities, museums, and private schools (including colleges) are organized in this way, primarily to ensure limited liability. The statutes of most states contain separate provisions dealing with the organization and operation of not-for-profit corporations. These organizations do not issue stock certificates because no dividends are paid and no one is interested in buying or selling their stock. They are also exempted from income taxes.

Occasionally, some not-for-profit organizations are inspired with entrepreneurial zeal. For example, the Children's Television Workshop netted $7.7 million a few years ago by licensing Sesame Street products. In the same year, the New York Museum of Modern Art sold air rights in Manhattan for $17 million to allow the construction of a private forty-four-story residential tower. The tax-free income from the sale helped finance a new wing, doubling the size of the museum.[3]

Museums are one of the most familiar types of not-for-profit corporations. The cultural significance of museums can be international, especially when major exhibitions are assembled, such as the Monet Exhibit, which showed in Boston, Chicago, and London.

S-Corporations

If a corporation meets certain requirements, its directors may apply to the Internal Revenue Service for status as an S-corporation (formerly known as a subchapter-S corporation). An **S-corporation** is a corporation that is taxed as though it were a partnership. In other words, the corporation's income is taxed only as the personal income of shareholders.

S-corporation *a corporation that is taxed as though it were a partnership*

Becoming an S-corporation can be an effective way to avoid double taxation while retaining the legal benefits of incorporation. Moreover, shareholders can personally claim their share of losses incurred by the corporation to offset their own personal income.

To qualify for the special status of an S-corporation, a firm must meet the following criteria:

1. The firm must have no more than thirty-five shareholders.
2. The shareholders must be individuals or estates, and they must be citizens or permanent residents of the United States.
3. There can be only one class of outstanding stock.
4. The firm must not own 80 percent or more of the stock of any other corporation.
5. Income from passive sources—such as interest, rent, and royalties—cannot exceed 25 percent of the firm's gross income. (However, there is no limit on passive income for S-corporations formed after December 31, 1983.)

Corporate Growth and Mergers

Learning Objective 6
Identify how corporations grow

Growth seems to be a basic characteristic of business. At least it is for those firms that can obtain the capital needed to finance growth. One reason for seeking growth has to do with profit: A larger firm generally has greater sales revenue and thus greater profit. Moreover, in a growing economy, a business that does not grow is actually shrinking relative to the economy. And, for some executives, business growth is a means by which to boost their power, prestige, and reputation.

Should all firms grow? Certainly not until they are ready to grow. Growth poses new problems and requires additional resources that must first be available and must then be used effectively. The main ingredient in growth is capital—and, as we have noted, capital is most readily available to corporations. Thus, to a great extent, business growth means corporate growth.

Growth from Within

Most corporations grow by expanding their present operations. They may introduce and sell new but related products, such as Chrysler Corporation's van/station wagon or IBM's personal computers. They may also expand the sale of present products to new geographic markets or new groups of consumers in geographic markets already served. Currently, Wal-Mart Stores, Inc. serves customers in twenty-five states and has long-range plans for expanding into other states.

Growth from within can have relatively little adverse effect on a firm, especially if it is carefully planned and controlled. For the most part, the firm continues to do what it has been doing (and has been doing successfully), but on a larger scale. Because this type of growth is anticipated, it can be gradual and the firm can usually adapt to it easily.

Growth Through Mergers

merger *the purchase of one corporation by another*

Another way for a firm to grow is by purchasing some other corporation. The purchase of one corporation by another is called a **merger.** (The term *acquisition* means essentially the same thing, but it is usually reserved for conglomerates buying other corporations.) The firm that is expanding simply buys the stock of the purchased corporation. (This is not always as simple as it sounds. In some cases, the management and stockholders of the firm targeted for acquisition are unwilling to let their company become a subsidiary of the purchasing firm. The results may be greatly inflated stock prices, legal battles, and—at the least—general ill will between the two firms.) The underlying reason for growth by merger is the supposition that the merged companies can produce benefits for the shareholders that the individual companies cannot offer on their own.

Horizontal Mergers   A *horizontal merger* is a merger between firms that make and sell similar products in similar markets (see Figure 3.6). The

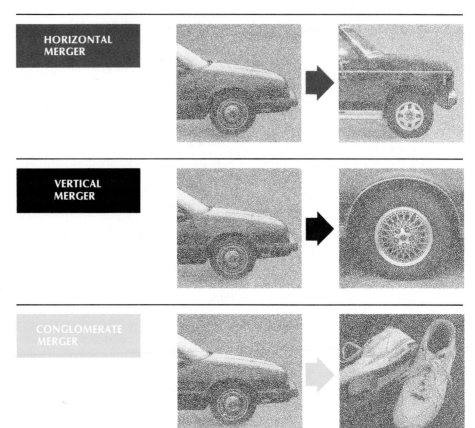

FIGURE 3.6
The Three Different Types of Growth by Merger
An automobile manufacturer acquiring another automobile manufacturer is a horizontal merger. If the same auto manufacturer buys out the company that makes its tires, a vertical merger results. A conglomerate merger results when the auto manufacturer buys a sports equipment firm.

purchase of Eastern Air Lines by Texas Air Corporation is an example of a horizontal merger. The rash of mergers between large American oil companies in the 1980s is another. Horizontal mergers tend to reduce the number of firms in an industry—and thus may reduce competition. For this reason, mergers may be reviewed carefully by federal agencies before they are permitted.

Firms may use horizontal mergers to accomplish goals other than growth. For example, the major goal of the oil-company mergers was to acquire large petroleum reserves. It was actually less costly to obtain petroleum by buying a firm that owned oil than by exploring, drilling, and pumping oil from the ground.

Vertical Mergers   A *vertical merger* is a merger between firms that operate at different but related levels in the production and marketing of a product. Generally, one of the merging firms is either a supplier or a customer of the other. For example, a vertical merger would occur if Tyson Foods, a large producer of fresh chicken, were to buy the Kentucky Fried Chicken chain.

Conglomerate Mergers   A *conglomerate merger* is a merger between firms in completely unrelated industries. Several years ago Xerox Corporation purchased Crum and Forster (an insurance firm), and Brown-Forman Distillers Corporation purchased Lenox, a producer of china. Both acquisitions were conglomerate mergers, and both enlarged the product base from which the purchasing firm receives its sales revenue.

Current Merger Trends

Future historians may focus on the explosion in mergers and company acquisitions as the most important economic trend of the 1980s and 1990s. Companies have been gobbling each other up and selling off subsidiaries at an unprecedented rate. While some results of this merger-and-acquisition mania are already evident, business experts can only guess at the long-term consequences of this major reshuffling of corporate America.

Many firms have been forced to merge to become better competitors, while others have been taken over, often against the will of top management. The recent $25-billion buy-out of RJR Nabisco by the investment firm of Kohlberg, Kravis, Roberts proved that no company is "big" enough to be safe from a takeover attempt. Relatively low stock prices and low interest rates have made company takeovers easier and cheaper to finance.[4] In some cases, companies wishing to diversify find it less expensive to buy other firms than to build them from the ground up.

The trend of mergers and acquisitions has involved some of America's most well-known companies. A short time ago, Philip Morris acquired Kraft, while Time Inc. bought Warner Communications.

Some critics of hostile takeovers claim that this wave of mergers and buy-outs hurts the U.S. economy and capitalism in general. Since top management may become overly concerned with a takeover, they may end up sacrificing solid long-term goals for profitable short-term ones.[5] Moreover, mergers and acquisitions can have a severe detrimental effect on employee morale, company productivity, and quality control. Other

The recent merger of SmithKline Beckman Corporation and Beecham Group, two pharmaceutical firms, to form SmithKline Beecham is an example of a horizontal merger. From the strengths and traditions of both companies, SmithKline Beecham seeks to grow as a major global enterprise and to build itself as a company that sets the standards for the industry.

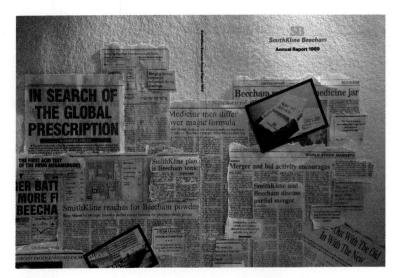

business experts disagree with this assessment, stating that morale, productivity, and quality improve because of leaner, more efficient management forces.[6]

Other Forms of Business Ownership

Learning Objective 7
Recognize three additional forms of ownership: cooperatives, joint ventures, and syndicates

Sole proprietorships, partnerships, and corporations are by far the most common forms of business ownership in the United States. Other forms of ownership do exist, however. And, like the nonstandard corporate forms, they are used primarily to serve the special needs of owners.

Cooperatives

cooperative *an association of individuals or firms whose purpose is to perform some business function for all its members*

A **cooperative** is an association of individuals or firms whose purpose is to perform some business function for all its members. Members benefit from the activities of the cooperative because it can perform its function more effectively than any member could by acting alone. For example, *buying cooperatives* are organized to purchase goods in bulk and then distribute them to members. The unit cost of the goods is lower than it would be if each member bought in a much smaller quantity.

Cooperatives such as credit unions are owned by their members, and they may or may not be incorporated. When they are, it is usually as nonprofit corporations. In either case, they generally have unlimited life; that is, a cooperative need not be dissolved when a member leaves the organization. Cooperatives that are incorporated also obtain such advantages as limited liability.

Ocean Spray Cranberries, Inc. is one of the best-known cooperatives. Growers belonging to this cooperative benefit from its resources, which no individual grower could assemble or afford. Other cooperatives include Blue Diamond, Sunkist, and Land O'Lakes.

BUSINESS JOURNAL

If You Can't Beat Them, Then Join Them in a Strategic Alliance

Your firm sells raincoats, and you know you could increase profits by entering the Korean raincoat market. What's stopping you? Nothing except hostile Korean raincoat makers and a government that wants to protect them from outside competition. You make a few phone calls, have a few conferences, hire a competent translator, and forge a major deal with a Korean rubber-boot manufacturer. Korea now has a new raincoat manufacturer.

With the costs of production, marketing, and research and development steadily climbing, many companies find it difficult to develop technology, enter new markets, and improve current market position. One solution seems to be strategic business alliances, wherein two or more companies agree in part or whole to share ideas, technology, production, and profits for the mutual benefit of all involved parties.

General Electric has a growing interest in advanced technology. So GE formed an alliance with Japan's Fanuc to acquire factory automation, with France's SNECMA to gain expertise in jet aircraft engines, and with West Germany's BMW Credit Corporation to update its financial services. GE's Medical Systems Division has joined forces with Yokogawa Electric Works of Japan in the manufacturing of sophisticated medical equipment.

Now more than ever, companies are looking to cooperation rather than confrontation to get what they want. Strategic alliances have become common in the business world. Over 2,100 alliances were created in the United States in the 1980s.

Strategic alliances are not mergers. Both companies—usually two are involved—voluntarily enter into an agreement that will theoretically benefit them both. These alliances can take the form of joint business ventures, technology-transfer agreements,

equity investments, sale and distribution ties, cooperative research and development projects, or even partnerships between competitors. A few years ago, Chrysler Corp. and Mitsubishi Motors formed a 50-50 joint venture under the name Diamond Star Corporation. Mitsubishi was in charge of the design and construction of the 2-million-square-foot plant, while Chrysler personnel supervised (and still supervise) organizational, manufacturing, legal, and financial concerns. Both companies contributed product engineers.

A strategic alliance can definitely help the companies involved, but it is not a guarantee of success or miracle cure-all. One disadvantage of a business alliance is that it often requires stringent accounting and reporting practices. Each company in an alliance must carefully monitor the other or others to ensure that there is no cheating or deception. A second disadvantage is that management may have to make a costly time commitment to start up the alliance. Third, an alliance may distract management from other important issues. The American Business Conference, an association of high-growth U.S. companies, is against sharing risks and rewards with allies. The vast majority of American Business Conference members think that strategic alliances place too much strain on management and are too limiting.

Based on information from John S. McClenahan, "Alliances for Competitive Advantage," *Industry Week,* August 24, 1987, pp. 33–36; Vladimir Pucik, "Strategic Alliances, Organizational Learning, and Competitive Advantage," *Human Resources Management,* Spring 1988, pp. 77–93; Robert Stein, "Why Fly Solo?" *Best's Review,* October 1987, pp. 30–32; and Clemens P. Work, "Business Without Borders," *U.S. News & World Report,* June 20, 1988, pp. 48–53.

The members of a cooperative are charged membership fees, which cover its operating costs. In addition, members pay for the services of the cooperative as they use those services. In a buying cooperative, for example, members pay for the goods that they have ordered through the cooperative. Perhaps a small service charge is added to that cost. Cooperatives are not profit-making organizations. Therefore, surplus funds are either returned to the members or set aside to finance future needs.

Cooperatives may be found in all segments of our economy, but they are most prevalent in agriculture. Farmers make use of cooperatives to purchase supplies, to buy services such as trucking and storage, and to market their products. The trademark *Ocean Spray*, for example, is owned by Ocean Spray Cranberries, Inc., a cooperative of some 700 cranberry growers and more than 100 citrus growers throughout the country.

Joint Ventures

joint venture   *a partnership that is formed to achieve a specific goal or to operate for a specific period of time*

A **joint venture** is a partnership that is formed to achieve a specific goal or to operate for a specific period of time. Both the scope of the firm and the liabilities of the partners are limited. Once the goal is reached or the period of time elapses, the partnership is dissolved.

Corporations, as well as individuals, may enter into joint ventures. A number of these joint ventures were formed by major oil producers in the 1970s, to share the extremely high cost of exploring for offshore petroleum deposits.

Syndicates

syndicate   *a temporary association of individuals or firms, organized to perform a specific task that requires a large amount of capital*

A **syndicate** is a temporary association of individuals or firms, organized to perform a specific task that requires a large amount of capital. The syndicate is formed because no one person or firm is willing to put up the entire amount required for the undertaking. Like a joint venture, a syndicate is dissolved as soon as its purpose has been accomplished. However, the participants in a syndicate do not form a separate firm, as do the members of a joint venture.

Syndicates are most commonly used to underwrite large insurance policies, loans, and investments. Banks have formed syndicates to provide loans to developing countries, to share the risk of default. Stock brokerage firms usually join together, in the same way, to market a new issue of stock.

CHAPTER REVIEW

Summary

The three major forms of business are the sole proprietorship, the partnership, and the corporation. A sole proprietorship is a business that is owned by one person. In essence, the owner and the business are one. All business profits become the property of the owner, and all business debts are the responsibility of the owner. Sole proprietorship is the simplest form of business to enter, control, and leave. Perhaps for these reasons, more than two-thirds of all American business firms are sole proprietorships.

A partnership is an association of two or more individuals who act as co-owners of a business for profit. Although partnership eliminates some of the disadvantages of sole proprietorship, it is the least popular of the major forms of business. Like sole proprietors, general partners are responsible for running the business and for all business debts. Limited partners receive a share of the profit in return for investing in the business. However, they are not responsible for business debts beyond the amount they have invested. A partnership agreement (or articles of partnership) is a written document setting forth the terms of a partnership.

Corporations are artificial beings created by law. These beings have the right to start and operate a business, own property, and enter into contracts.

Although corporations comprise only one-fifth of all American businesses, they account for more than nine-tenths of all business receipts. The largest businesses in the United States are organized as corporations.

Shares of ownership of a corporation are called stock, and owners are called stockholders. A corporation must be chartered, or formally recognized, by a particular state. Once the corporation has received a charter, its original stockholders elect a board of directors. The board of directors then elects or appoints corporate officers. Once each year, all stockholders have the right to vote for the firm's directors—either in person at the firm's annual meeting or by proxy.

Perhaps the major advantage of the corporate form is limited liability: Stockholders are not liable for the corporation's debts beyond the amount they have paid for its stock. Another important advantage is the perpetual life of the corporation. A major disadvantage is double taxation. The corporation's earnings are taxed once as corporate income and again as personal income (when earnings are distributed to stockholders). A corporation may grow by expanding its present operations or through merger—the purchase of another corporation.

The stock of open corporations is available to anyone who wants to buy it; the stock of close corporations is not. Government-owned corporations provide particular services, such as public transportation, to citizens. Not-for-profit corporations are formed to provide social services rather than to earn profits, but they are not owned by governments. S-corporations are corporations that are taxed as though they were partnerships. Various criteria must be met to qualify for this status.

Three additional forms of business ownership are the cooperative, joint venture, and syndicate. All are used by their owners to meet special needs, and each may be owned by either individuals or firms.

Whether they are sole proprietorships, partnerships, or corporations, most U.S. businesses are small. In the next chapter, we shall focus on these small businesses. Among other things, we shall examine the meaning of "small" as it applies to business and the place of small business in the American economy.

Key Terms

You should now be able to define and give an example relevant to each of the following terms:

sole proprietorship	general partner
unlimited liability	limited partner
partnership	corporation
stock	corporate officer
stockholder	limited liability
close corporation	government-owned corporation
open corporation	quasi-government corporation
incorporation	not-for-profit corporation
domestic corporation	
foreign corporation	
alien corporation	S-corporation
corporate charter	merger
common stock	cooperative
preferred stock	joint venture
proxy	syndicate
board of directors	

Questions and Exercises

Review Questions

1. What is a sole proprietorship? What are the major advantages and disadvantages of this form of business ownership?
2. How does a partnership differ from a sole proprietorship? Which disadvantages of sole proprietorship does the partnership tend to eliminate or reduce in effect?
3. Why is sole proprietorship the most popular form of business ownership? Why is partnership the least popular?
4. What is the difference between general partners and limited partners?
5. Explain the difference between:
   a. An open corporation and a close corporation.
   b. A domestic corporation, a foreign corporation, and an alien corporation.
   c. A government-owned corporation, a quasi-government corporation, and a not-for-profit corporation.
6. Outline the incorporation process and describe the basic corporate structure.
7. What rights do stockholders have?
8. What are the primary duties of a corporation's board of directors? How are directors elected?
9. What are the major advantages and disadvantages associated with the corporate form of business ownership?
10. How is an S-corporation different from the usual open or close corporation?
11. Describe the three types of mergers.
12. Why are cooperatives formed? Explain how they operate.
13. In what ways are joint ventures and syndicates alike? In what ways are they different?

Discussion Questions

1. What are the advantages for Richard Melman in using partnerships rather than other forms of business ownership? What are the disadvantages?
2. If you were a managing partner in one of Richard Melman's partnerships, would you prefer a different form of ownership? Explain.
3. If you were to start a business, which ownership form would you use? What factors might affect your choice of ownership form?
4. Why might an investor choose to become a limited partner instead of purchasing the stock of an open corporation?
5. Discuss the following statement: "Corporations are not really run by their owners."
6. Is growth a good thing for all firms? How can management tell when the firm is ready to grow?
7. What kinds of services do government-owned corporations provide? How might such services be provided without government involvement?

Exercises

1. Suppose you are a part-time employee working for the sole proprietor of a car wash. The owner has offered you a 29 percent partnership, and you are going to accept. Write out at least six articles of a partnership agreement that would cover your partnership.
2. You and your partner in the car wash of Exercise 1 have decided to incorporate. List the steps you would follow to form the corporation, and include specific decisions you must make at each step. Include at least six articles of incorporation (or, if you prefer, obtain and fill out a standard articles-of-incorporation form for your state).
3. Research a recent merger and determine the specific reasons why each of the two firms sought, or was agreeable to, the merger.

Case 3.1

Ownership Feud at U-Haul

Leonard Shoen started U-Haul International Inc., the do-it-yourself moving company, in 1945. Shoen built the enterprise into an American landmark, making orange moving vehicles a ubiquitous sight. However, following some questionable business decisions—namely, the building of independent rental centers and renting of such items as videocassette recorders and recreational vehicles (in addition to moving equipment)—U-Haul rapidly began losing market share to arch-rival Ryder.

Then Shoen began to dole out 95 percent of the company's stock to his children—he has twelve from three of his four marriages. In a subsequent takeover considered heartless by some, Edward "Joe" Shoen and Samuel W. Shoen forced their father out of U-Haul and took the helm of the company. But the two brothers disagreed about strategy. Joe, stressing U-Haul's original dedication to do-it-yourself moving equipment, wanted to upgrade U-Haul's battered fleet of 60,000 trucks. Sam did not and resigned as chief executive officer of U-Haul. Joe stepped into that position. The new top management includes Joe's younger brothers Mark, Paul, and Jim.

The Schoens have split into two factions—those who are involved in U-Haul business decisions and those who aren't. The "dissidents," headed by Sam Shoen and his father, want to gain control from the current managers. Needless to say, an intense sibling rivalry has erupted into a business power play. One unidentified Shoen has said, "It was inevitable. We're concerned about love among us, and what this will do. But I chalk it up to an inevitable power struggle."

Twenty-five percent of the 17 million households that move each year move themselves and lease moving trucks. With stakes this high, it is no surprise that the Shoens are battling for U-Haul. Joe Shoen and his board have taken steps to ensure their control of U-Haul's trucks, 90,000 trailers, car-top carriers, tow bars, dollies, hitches, and other equipment. First, Joe and his board issued more common and preferred stocks. Second, they required that two-thirds (a "supermajority") of the shareholders must agree on any pending issue to reach a decision. Third, Joe and his brothers in management are trying to reduce the number of shareholders of Amerco, U-Haul's parent company, to under 300 so that the board is no longer required to publicly announce certain important financial data. Joe also set up an employee stock ownership plan (ESOP). He thinks that this is the best way to acquire stock from shareholders who want cash.

Thinking they controlled more than 50 percent of U-Haul stock, the Shoens not in power were shocked when they found out they owned less than this. They then sued the Shoens in power. When all the dust clears, there is no telling which Shoens will be in power and which will not.*

---

* Based on information from Donald M. Smith, "What Marketers Should Know About Truck Rentals," *National Petroleum News*, September 1988, pp. 48–50; Stewart Toy, "A New Generation Takes the Wheel at U-Haul," *Business Week*, March 28, 1988, p. 57; and Stewart Toy and Judith Dobrzynski, "The Family That Hauls Together Brawls Together," *Business Week*, August 29, 1988, pp. 64–66.

Questions

1. What form of ownership is used by U-Haul?
2. If the founder had used a different form of ownership, would the level of family feuding have been reduced? Explain.
3. What are the negative effects of an ownership feud on the operations of U-Haul?

Case 3.2

Reebok, Rockport, and Avia

Reebok International Ltd.'s famous supple leather athletic shoes came from nowhere to take over the American aerobic-shoe market in the 1980s. They brought fashion to athletic shoes. With plenty of cash from its sudden growth, Reebok began to diversify, acquiring other companies, including two shoemakers, Rockport and Avia. Many analysts viewed the acquisitions as a defensive strategy to buy out the competition. Others saw them as an offensive, aggressive way to ensure continued growth.

Reebok makes athletic shoes for walking, running, tennis, fitness activities, and leisure—350 different models of sneakers in all. With their extra-soft leather, distinctive bright colors, and fashionable styles, Reeboks may just be the articles of clothing that best represent American life. Recognizing that it is riding a wave that might slow down, if not crash, the company has moved into new product lines. It has expanded its manufacturing to include children's shoes ("Weeboks") and sports clothing, and has purchased Elesse North America, a sportswear maker.

Few expected Reebok to buy two fast-growing competitors in the shoe business. First, it acquired Rockport, a maker of walking shoes. That kind of horizontal merger made sense to most people because Rockport's products don't overlap significantly with Reebok's, and Rockport had been growing rapidly on its own. But the takeover of Avia—the number-two aerobic shoemaker with a 15 percent market share—struck many as a defensive move, designed to make sure that Avia didn't become Reebok's serious competitor. Reebok bought the Oregon-based shoe company just before Avia was to go public with its first stock offering.

Was this a move to avoid dangerous competition or an aggressive way to keep increasing the company's profits? Although Avia and Reebok make shoes for many of the same purposes, their markets do not necessarily overlap. Avia is known for high-tech, high-performance shoes, designed for serious sportspeople who also buy from Nike, Reebok's principal competitor. Reebok may be able to maintain the sales of its good-looking, comfortable shoes, while Avia, with its fancy soles and high-tech designs, may lure customers away from Nike. So it looks as though Reebok, rather than running from competition, may be merging with its rivals to snatch even bigger percentages of market share in the shoe business. With the athletic-shoe market declining, leather prices rising, and fast-growing L.A. Gear making a play for more market share, Reebok may have to make more major moves or mergers in the future.†

Questions

1. Why would Reebok choose to buy other shoemakers instead of a fast-growing company in another industry?
2. Does anyone suffer from this kind of consolidation in an industry?
3. For Rockport and Avia, what are the advantages and the disadvantages of being taken over by a competitor?

† Based on information from Ellen Benoit, "Lost Youth," *Financial World*, September 20, 1988, pp. 28–31; Thomas Jaffe, "Reebok Redux," *Forbes*, August 22, 1988, p. 126; Linda M. Watkins, "Reebok Agrees to Acquire Rival Maker of Aerobic Shoes for About $180 Million," *Wall Street Journal*, March 11, 1987, p. 8; Lawrence M. Fisher, "Reebok to Buy Avia for $180 Million," *New York Times*, March 11, 1987, p. 32; and Lois Therrien, "Can Reebok Sprint Even Faster?" *Business Week*, October 6, 1986, p. 74.

SMALL BUSINESS, ENTREPRENEURSHIP, AND FRANCHISES

4

1 Know what a small business is and name the fields in which small businesses are concentrated

2 Describe the people who start small businesses, how some succeed, and why many fail

3 Understand the contributions of small business to our economy

4 Grasp the advantages and disadvantages of operating a small business

5 Know how the Small Business Administration helps small businesses

6 Comprehend the concept and types of franchising

7 Become aware of the growth of franchising and of its advantages and disadvantages

CHAPTER PREVIEW

In this chapter we do not take small businesses for granted. Instead we look closely at this important business sector—beginning with a definition of small business, a description of industries that often attract small businesses, and a profile of some of the people who start small businesses. Next, we consider the importance of small businesses in our economy. We also present the advantages and disadvantages of smallness in business. Then, we describe services provided by the Small Business Administration, a government agency formed to assist owners and managers of small businesses. We conclude the chapter with a discussion of the pros and cons of franchising, an approach to small business ownership that has become very popular in the last two decades.

INSIDE BUSINESS

Joanne Marlowe's Weighty Beach Towel Business

Sunning herself on a Lake Michigan beach one warm day, Joanne Marlowe's peaceful mood was disturbed by a gusting wind that raised her beach towel, spraying her with sand. A friend suggested that she figure out a way to fix the aggravating problem of flapping beach towels. So she did.

Currently in her mid-twenties, Marlowe started her first business at the age of fourteen. Her first enterprise, Furfun, capitalized on her love of stuffed animals. She sold patterns for stuffed animals in craft magazines. When her interest in stuffed toys waned, Marlowe began designing clothes for herself and her friends. Marlowe's designs, patterned after classic styles of the 1940s and 50s, soon gained her a steady clientele and a reputation as a first-rate designer.

Her clothing company eventually opened a boutique, Joanne Marlowe Designs, in an exclusive shopping district of Evanston, Illinois. The firm continued to grow until an employee embezzled $40,000 from that enterprise, forcing Marlowe to start her business career over. The theft was just the first disturbing event in a series of setbacks. According to Marlowe, in her clothing business she had inadvertently intimidated some major figures in the Evanston fashion industry, and these individuals were intent on seeing her become bankrupt. A person with less drive than Marlowe would have probably abandoned the business world altogether. She decided to leave the world of high fashion and embark on a new project.

Pursuing the beach towel idea, she took a job as a Chicago carriage driver to pay her bills until the new enterprise could get under way. For three months, she slept only about three hours a night—working on the towels during the day, caring for her horse and the carriage equipment in the afternoon, and driving people around during the evening.

It took Marlowe only five weeks to develop the product—Big Tyme towels—and eight weeks to bring it to market. With only two assistants, Marlowe guided the towels from manufacturing through sales. Through the spring of 1990, Marlowe had towel sales of near $4.5 million. The colorful weighted towels, costing between $25 and $37 each, have been a very popular item. Remembering past incidents and wanting to maintain tight control over her company's affairs, Marlowe prefers to keep her staff small, limiting it to only about ten people. Now primarily handling only the telemarketing and distribution of the towels, Marlowe hopes the sales will continue to thrive.[1]

*J*oanne Marlowe's beach towel business is experiencing considerable growth. This kind of growth is unusual. Most businesses start small, and those that survive usually stay small. They provide a solid foundation for our economy—as employers, as suppliers and purchasers of goods and services, and as taxpayers.

Small Business: A Profile

The Small Business Administration (SBA), a federal government agency created to assist, counsel, and protect the interests of small businesses, defines a **small business** as "one which is independently owned and operated for profit and is not dominant in its field." How small must a firm be not to dominate its field? That depends on the particular industry it is in. The SBA has developed specific "smallness" guidelines for the various industries:[2]

▶ *Manufacturing:* a maximum number of employees ranging from 500 to 1,500, depending on the products manufactured

▶ *Wholesaling:* a maximum number of employees not to exceed 100

▶ *Retailing:* maximum yearly sales or receipts ranging from $3.5 million to $13.5 million, depending on the industry

▶ *General construction:* average annual receipts ranging from $9.5 million to $17 million, depending on the industry

▶ *Special trade construction:* annual sales ranging up to $7 million

▶ *Agriculture:* maximum annual receipts of $0.5 million to $3.5 million

▶ *Services:* maximum annual receipts ranging from $3.5 million to $14.5 million, depending on the type of service

A new standard, based only on the number of employees, has been proposed but not yet adopted by the SBA.

Annual sales in the millions of dollars may not seem very small. However, for many firms, profit is only a small percent of total sales. Thus a firm may earn only $30,000 or $40,000 on yearly sales of $1 million—and that *is* small in comparison to the profits earned by most medium-sized and large firms. Moreover, most small firms have annual sales that are well below the limits the SBA has used in its definitions.

The Small-Business Sector

A surprising number of Americans take advantage of their freedom to start a business. There are, in fact, about 16.5 million businesses in this country. Around 90 percent are small, and many are new. Up to 4,480 new businesses are incorporated in a typical week![3]

At the same time that new firms are being created, others are going out of business. Statistically, over 70 percent of new businesses can be expected to fail within their first five years.[4] The primary reason for these failures is mismanagement resulting from a lack of business know-how.

Most businesses in the United States are classified as small businesses, such as Andrea Crawford's Kenter Canyon Farms, which grows top-quality produce for exclusive restaurants in the Los Angeles area. Crawford produces gourmet vegetables, including fifty types of lettuce, on her seven-acre farm.

The makeup of the small-business sector is thus constantly changing. While some businesses are starting up, others are closing shop. Still others are being acquired by larger firms. In spite of the high failure rate, many small businesses succeed modestly. Some, like Apple Computer, Inc., turn out to be extremely successful—to the point where they may no longer be considered small. Taken together, small businesses are also responsible for providing a high percentage of the jobs in the United States. According to some estimates, this figure is well over 60 percent.

Industries That Attract Small Businesses

Some industries, such as auto manufacturing, require huge investments in machinery and equipment. Businesses in such industries are big from the day they are started—if an entrepreneur or group of entrepreneurs can gather the capital required to start one.

By contrast, a number of industries require a low initial investment along with some special skills or knowledge. It is these industries that tend to attract new businesses. Growing industries, such as computer software, are attractive because of their sales and profit potential. However, knowledgeable entrepreneurs choose areas with which they are familiar, and these are most often the more established industries.

Small enterprise spans the gamut from corner newspaper vending to the development of optical fibers. The owners of small businesses sell gasoline, flowers, and coffee to go. They publish magazines, haul freight, teach languages, and program computers. They make wines, movies, and high-fashion clothes. They build new homes and restore old ones. They fix appliances, recycle metals, and sell used cars. They drive cabs and fly planes. They make us well when we are ill, and they sell us the products of corporate giants.

As Figure 4.1 shows, the various kinds of businesses generally fall into three broad categories of industries: service, distribution, and production. Within these categories, small businesses tend to cluster in the service industries and in retailing.

Service Industries   This category accounts for about 34 percent of all small businesses. Of these, about three-quarters provide such nonfinancial services as medical and dental care; watch, shoe, and TV repairs; haircutting and styling; restaurant meals; and dry cleaning. About 9 percent of the small service firms offer financial services such as accounting, insurance, and investment counseling.

Distribution Industries   This category includes retailing, wholesaling, transportation, and communications—industries that are concerned with the movement of goods from producers to consumers. Distribution industries account for approximately 42 percent of all small businesses. Of these, almost three-quarters are involved in retailing, the sale of goods directly to consumers. Clothing and jewelry stores, pet shops, bookstores, and grocery stores, for example, are all retailing firms. Slightly less than one-quarter of the small distribution firms are wholesalers. Wholesalers

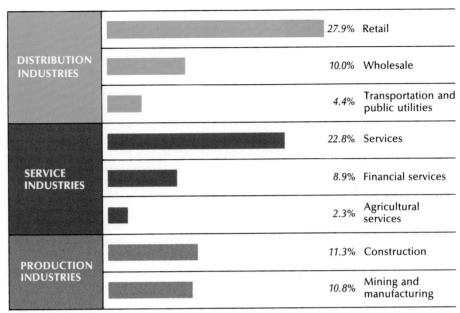

FIGURE 4.1
The Relative Proportion of Small Businesses by Industry
Small businesses are found in three major industries; most are in service and distribution. [Source: Adapted from The State of Small Business: A Report of the President *(Washington, D.C.: GPO, 1989), p. 18.]*

purchase products in quantity from manufacturers and then resell them to retailers.

Production Industries This last category includes the construction, mining, and manufacturing industries. Only about 22 percent of all small businesses are in this group, mainly because these industries require relatively large initial investments. Small firms that do venture into production generally make parts and subassemblies for larger manufacturing firms or supply special skills to larger construction firms.

The People in Small Businesses: The Entrepreneurs

Learning Objective 2
Describe the people who start small businesses, how some succeed, and why many fail

Small businesses are typically managed by the people who started and own them. Most of these people have held jobs with other firms and could still have such jobs if they wanted them. Yet owners of small businesses would rather take the risk of starting and then operating their own firms, even if the money they make is less than the salaries they might otherwise earn.

Researchers have suggested a variety of personal factors as reasons why individuals go into business. One that is often cited is the "entrepreneurial spirit"—the desire to create a new business. Other factors, such as independence, the desire to determine one's own destiny, and the

BUSINESS JOURNAL

Entrepreneurship: No Guts, No Glory

Sometimes an idea won't let you sleep. You think about it at night when you're in bed and often during the day. You know that you can make this idea work. Finally, you can't take it anymore. You want to pursue this idea. You want to be your own boss; you want to be in control; you want to achieve something worthwhile; you want to make a fortune. Welcome to the world of the entrepreneur.

So you curtail your social life and give up sleep to plan each step of your business venture. After quitting your job, you live on saved money and dreams. You divide your time between the library, telephone, and garage. At the end of seven months, it's ready: the world's first flexible dentures! You now go out in search of a personable investment banker and a graduate business student. The following spring you're living it up in the Caribbean—you're rich. But you don't sleep well at nights because you've got this idea. . . .

This is the world of individuals like Sam Walton, builder of Wal-Mart Stores, Inc., the discount-shopping empire. In 1950, Sam lost the lease on his first retail store. Having the true entrepreneurial spirit, he continued to build Ben Franklin five-and-dime stores. In 1962 Sam and his brother Bud opened the first Wal-Mart store in Arkansas. Today there are over 1,400 Wal-Mart stores scattered throughout twenty-five midwestern, southwestern, and southeastern states. Sam Walton's net worth has most recently been estimated at $6.5 to $9 billion. That's enough to rank him as the wealthiest American business person.

Entrepreneurs have the chance to become as remarkably successful as Sam Walton and other self-made business moguls. But not just anyone with a good idea can pull it off. It takes a very special person to be a successful entrepreneur. Entrepreneurs need tremendous drive and total commitment to a single goal to make an idea profitable. They also need almost boundless energy to keep their drive in high gear. If you have a hard time getting motivated, don't try to be an entrepreneur.

Patience and above-average communication skills are both crucial to the entrepreneur. Since an entrepreneur often controls a project, he or she might have a tendency to rush things like marketing research. But the successful entrepreneur learns to wait—to be patient and optimistic. No business venture can get off the ground without the cooperation of others. Through effective communication, an entrepreneur can muster the support and cooperation of financial backers, employees, and customers. The good communicator can frequently convince others to do things they might not ordinarily do.

Courage is important to the person attempting to start a business. He or she must take risks and face the possibility of failure. The entrepreneur must be willing to spend an excessive amount of time and money on something that doesn't exist and might eventually fail.

Based on information from Marc Leepson, "Building a Business: A Matter of Course," *Nation's Business,* April 1988, pp. 42–43; A. David Silver, "A Portrait of the Entrepreneur," *Accountancy,* February 1988, pp. 77, 79–80; and George Waldon, "Bargains and Billionaires," *Spirit,* November 1988, pp. 34, 36–37, 48.

---

willingness to find and accept a challenge certainly play a part. Background may come into play as well. In particular, researchers think that people whose families have been in business (successfully or not) are most apt to start and run their own businesses. The age factor is important, too. Over 70 percent of those people who start their own businesses are between 25 and 44 years old (see Figure 4.2). Women own 4.6 million businesses and are starting new businesses at twice the rate of men.[5]

Also, there must be some motivation to start a business. One person may finally decide she has simply "had enough" of working and earning a profit for someone else. Another may lose his job for some reason and

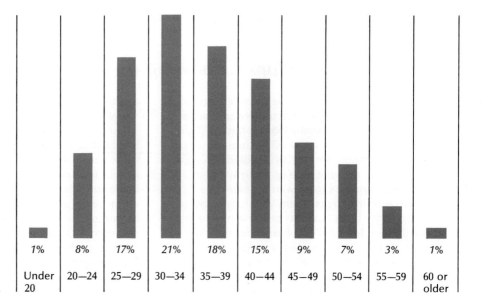

FIGURE 4.2
How Old Is the Average Entrepreneur?
People in all age groups become entrepreneurs, but almost 70 percent are between 25 and 44. (Source: Data developed and provided by The NFIB Foundation and sponsored by the American Express Travel Related Services Company, Inc.

| 1% | 8% | 17% | 21% | 18% | 15% | 9% | 7% | 3% | 1% |
| Under 20 | 20—24 | 25—29 | 30—34 | 35—39 | 40—44 | 45—49 | 50—54 | 55—59 | 60 or older |

decide to start the business he has always wanted rather than seek another job. Still another person may have an idea for a new product or a new way to sell an existing product. Or the opportunity to go into business may arise suddenly, perhaps as a result of a hobby.

When Brett Gibson was 15, he was already known around his hometown as a first-rate telephone installer. Carefully concealing his age when possible, he took over customer contracts of the local telephone company when it closed its offices. Though his grandmother drove him to business appointments and his parents had to lend him money because banks refused to take him seriously, Gibson managed to build his company, Mid American Telephone Supply, into a $700,000-a-year business. Gibson is now in his early twenties, and his firm continues to grow. However, he still runs into occasional credibility problems because of his age.[6]

In some people the motivation develops more slowly, as they gain the knowledge and ability required for success as a business owner. Knowledge and ability—especially management ability—are probably the most important factors involved. A new firm is very much built around the entrepreneur. The owner must be able to manage the firm's finances, its personnel (if there are any employees), and its day-to-day operations. He or she must handle sales, advertising, purchasing, pricing, and a variety of other business functions. The knowledge and ability to do so are most often acquired through experience working for other firms in the same area of business.

Why Small Businesses Fail

Small businesses are prone to failure. Capital, management, and planning are the key ingredients in the survival of a small business. The most common reasons for small-business failures center around these elements.

BUSINESS JOURNAL

Small-Business Failures: Knowing the Warning Signs

According to some analysts, the warning signs of a small business in deep trouble usually appear long before a firm's doors actually close for good. Those who plan to start their own small businesses should be aware of the symptoms of a company going downhill. Unfortunately, one of these symptoms is the owner's blindness to all warning signs.

Other warning signs seem painfully obvious; however, many small-business owners continuously ignore them, finding it difficult to admit that they've been wrong about a business idea. A definite warning sign of an unhealthy small business is cash-flow problems. Many persons try to open a business based on a good idea, faith, and enthusiasm. Sometimes this approach proves to be enough. At other times, it leads to complete disaster. Business owners must have the funds to cover all their expenses and also late payments by customers who may not pay promptly.

Another symptom of trouble is declining return on sales. When a small-business owner notices this trend, he or she should immediately start searching for the reason.

Wildly expanding inventories, consistently missed deadlines, and a management team that's about to have a collective nervous breakdown all point to problems. An owner who observes that there is an exceptionally high employee turnover should re-evaluate the company's structure and employee relations.

Though creditors may seem to be circling uncontrollably overhead, a small-business owner should resist filing Chapter 11 of the federal Bankruptcy Reform Act, which outlines the procedure for reorganizing a bankrupt business. By seeking protection under Chapter 11 (and attempting to work out a reorganization plan), the owner might think he or she is saving the business. However, though Chapter 11 has proved to be an effective tool for large troubled companies, it can be the final death blow for a small one. According to experts, fewer than one in ten small firms that file Chapter 11 survive. Bankruptcy lawyers, accountants, consultants, and court costs are too expensive for many a small-business owner. There is also a tendency for the owner to focus all energy on the bankruptcy, ignoring the problems that led to the bankruptcy and thus allowing them to worsen.

To avoid the pitfalls of small business, the owner should always consider long-term prospects. He or she should personally monitor and analyze all accounting information as well as maximize use of the company's computer system. Often such systems are underused. The owner should also try to learn as much as possible about marketing and planning. Many new business owners have limited expertise in marketing, accounting, and management, and either expense or pride prevents them from hiring outside help. New business owners can gain valuable insights from listening to former small-business owners and learning from their mistakes.

Based on information from C. Charles Bahr, "Sick Companies Don't Have to Die," *Vital Speeches of the Day*, September 1, 1988, pp. 685–688; Buck Brown, "For Small Firms, Perils Lie in Chapter 11," *Wall Street Journal*, July 14, 1988, p. 29; Tom McLean, "Small Companies: Failure and Success," *Accountant's Magazine*, October 1987, pp. 58–59; and William P. Sommers and Aydin Koc, "Why Most New Ventures Fail (and How Others Don't)," *Management Review*, September 1987, pp. 35–39.

Businesses can experience a number of money-related problems. It may take several years before a business begins to show a profit. Entrepreneurs need to have not only the capital to open a business but also the money to operate it in its possibly lengthy start-up phase. One cash-flow obstacle often leads to others. And a series of cash-flow predicaments usually leads to a business failure. An entrepreneur can have two separate sets of credit difficulties: He or she might be pressured into selling on credit, causing cash-flow troubles, or might rely too heavily on credit, thus becoming overwhelmed by bill collectors.[7]

Many entrepreneurs lack the management skills required to run a business. Money, time, personnel, and inventory all need to be effectively managed if a small business is to succeed. Starting a small business requires much more than optimism and a good idea.

Success and expansion sometimes lead to problems. Frequently entrepreneurs with initially successful small businesses make the mistake of overexpansion. But fast growth often results in dramatic changes in a business. Thus the entrepreneur must plan carefully and adjust competently to potentially new and disruptive situations.[8]

Every day, and in every part of the country, people plan to or actually open new businesses. Many of these businesses may not succeed. Others represent well-conceived ideas that are developed by entrepreneurs who have the expertise, resources, and determination to make their businesses succeed. As these well-prepared entrepreneurs pursue their individual goals, our society benefits in many ways from their work and creativity. Billion-dollar companies such as Apple Computer, Digital Equipment, and Tandem Computers are all examples of small businesses that expanded into industry giants.[9]

The Importance of Small Businesses in Our Economy

Learning Objective 3
Understand the contributions of small business to our economy

This country's economic history is chock full of stories of ambitious men and women who turned their ideas into business dynasties. The Ford Motor Company started as a one-man operation with a new method for industrial production. R. H. Macy & Co. can trace its beginnings to a pushcart in the streets of New York. Both Xerox Corp. and Polaroid Corp. began as small firms with a better way to do a job.

Providing Technical Innovation

Invention and innovation are among the foundations of our economy. The increases in productivity that have characterized the two hundred years of our history are all rooted in one principal source: new ways to do a job with less effort, at a lower cost. Studies show that the incidence of innovation among small-business workers is significantly higher than among workers in large businesses. Small firms produce two and a half times as many innovations as large firms, relative to the number of persons employed.[10]

According to the U.S. Office of Management and Budget, more than half the major technological advances of this century originated with individual inventors and small companies. A sampling of those innovations is remarkable:

▶ Air conditioning   ▶ Helicopter

▶ Automatic transmission   ▶ Instant camera

▶ Ball-point pen   ▶ Insulin

▶ FM radio   ▶ Jet engine

- ▶ Penicillin
- ▶ Power steering

- ▶ Xerography
- ▶ Zipper

Perhaps even more remarkable is the fact that many of these inventions sparked major new U.S. industries.

Providing Employment

Small businesses employ approximately one-half of the nation's private work force. Small businesses have thus contributed significantly to solving unemployment problems. Historically, small businesses have created the bulk of new jobs. Table 4.1 shows the small-business industries that are generating the most new jobs.

Providing Competition

Small businesses challenge larger, established firms in many ways, causing them to become more efficient and more responsive to consumer needs. A small business cannot, of course, compete with a large firm across the board. But a number of small firms, each competing in its own particular area and its own particular way, together have the desired competitive effect. Thus a small producer of portable computers, a small producer of less expensive personal computers, and a small producer of computer software together add up to reasonable competition for the no-longer-small Apple Computer.

Filling Needs of Society and Other Businesses

Large firms must, by their nature, operate on a large scale. Many may be unwilling or unable to meet the special needs of smaller groups of

TABLE 4.1 *Small-Business Industries Generating the Most New Jobs*

	Employment Increase (in thousands)	Percent Change 1987–1988
Eating and drinking places	249.9	4.0
Machinery, equipment, and supplies	99.7	6.8
Offices of physicians	91.4	8.7
Miscellaneous business services	90.9	4.3
Trucking and truck terminals	83.4	6.2
Computer and data processing services	80.4	12.5
Residential building construction	69.7	9.7
Electrical work	49.8	9.4
Miscellaneous plastic products	46.5	7.8
Masonry, stonework, and plastering	42.0	8.5

Source: *The State of Small Business: A Report of the President* (Washington, D.C.: GPO, 1989), p. 18.

Using money from outside investors, entrepreneur Jeffrey Montgomery purchased Harvey Publications, the comic book publisher that owns the rights to Richie Rich, Casper the Friendly Ghost, and other characters. Besides boosting comic book sales, Montgomery plans to re-release 248 motion picture cartoons on video cassettes.

consumers. Such groups create almost perfect markets for small companies, which can tailor their products to these groups and fill their needs profitably. A prime example is a firm that modifies automobile controls to accommodate handicapped drivers.

Small firms also provide a variety of goods and services to each other and to much larger firms. Sears, Roebuck purchases merchandise from approximately 12,000 suppliers—and most of them are small businesses. General Motors relies on more than 32,000 companies for parts and supplies. And it depends on more than 11,000 independent dealers to sell its automobiles and trucks. Large firms generally buy parts and assemblies from smaller firms for one very good reason: It is less expensive than manufacturing the parts in their own factories. This lower cost is eventually reflected in the price that consumers pay for their products.

It is clear that small businesses are a vital part of our economy and that, as consumers and as members of the labor force, we all benefit enormously from their existence. Now let us look at the situation from the viewpoint of the owners of small businesses.

The Pros and Cons of Smallness

Learning Objective 4
Grasp the advantages and disadvantages of operating a small business

Do most owners of small businesses dream of their firms growing into giant corporations—managed by professionals—while they serve only on the board of directors? Or would they rather stay small, in a firm where they have the opportunity (and the responsibility) to do everything that needs to be done? The answers depend on the personal characteristics and motivations of the individual owners. For many, the advantages of remaining small far outweigh the disadvantages.

Advantages of Small Business

Personal Relationships with Customers and Employees   For those who like dealing with people, small business is the place to be. The owners of retail shops get to know many of their customers by name and deal with them on a personal basis. Through such relationships, small-business owners often become involved in social, cultural, and political affairs within the community.

Relationships between owner-managers and employees also tend to be closer in smaller businesses. To many an employee, the owner is a friend and counselor as well as the boss.

These personal relationships provide an important business advantage. The personal service offered to customers is a major competitive weapon of small business—one that larger firms try to match but often cannot. In addition, close relationships with employees often help the small-business owner keep effective workers who might earn more with a larger firm.

Ability to Adapt to Change   Being his or her own boss, the owner-manager of a small business does not need anyone's permission to adapt to change. An owner may add or discontinue merchandise or services, change store hours, and experiment with various price strategies in response to changes in market conditions. Moreover, through personal relationships with

Yla Eason quit a $65,000-a-year job to start Olmec Corp., a small company that produces toys for children of many races. The major impetus for starting the company was that she could not find a superhero toy that her son could personally relate to. The firm began business with a single product: Sun-Man, the first black superhero toy.

customers, the owners of small businesses quickly become aware of changes in people's needs and interests—as well as the activities of competing firms.

Simplified Record Keeping Many small firms need only a simple set of records. Their record keeping might consist of a checkbook, a cash-receipts journal in which to record all sales, and a cash-disbursements journal in which to record all amounts that are paid out. Obviously, enough records must be kept to allow for producing and filing accurate tax returns.

Independence Small-business owners don't have to punch in and out, bid for vacation times, take orders from superiors, or worry about being fired or laid off. They are the masters of their own destinies—at least with regard to employment. For many people, this is the one prime advantage of owning a small business.

Other Advantages Small-business owners also enjoy a number of the advantages of sole proprietorship, which are discussed in Chapter 3. These include being able to keep all profits, the ease and low cost of going into business and (if necessary) going out of business, and being able to keep information about one's business secret.

Disadvantages of Small Business

Risk of Failure As we have noted, small firms (especially newer ones) run a heavy risk of going out of business. About two out of three firms close their doors within the first five years. Older, well-established but small firms can be hit hard by a business recession, mainly because they do not have the financial resources they need to weather a really difficult period.

Limited Potential The small businesses that survive do so with varying degrees of success. Many small firms are simply the means of making a living for the owner and his or her family. The owner may have some technical skill—as a hair stylist or an electrician does—and may have started a business to practice his or her trade. Such a business is unlikely to grow into a big business. Also, employees' potential for advancement is limited.

Limited Ability to Raise Capital Small businesses typically have a limited ability to obtain capital. Figure 4.3 shows that most small-business financing comes out of the owner's pocket. Personal loans from lending institutions provide only about one-fourth of the capital required by small businesses.

Although every person who considers starting a small business should be aware of the hazards and pitfalls we have noted, a well-conceived business plan may help avoid the risk of failure. Also, the U.S. government is dedicated to helping small businesses make it. It expresses this aim most actively through the Small Business Administration.

Own resources (cash)	75%	
Mortgage of own assets	35%	
Corporate loan from bank	33%	
Partner's assets	29%	
Personal loan from bank	23%	
Parents or other relative	20%	

FIGURE 4.3
Sources of Capital for Entrepreneurs
Small businesses get financing from various sources, but the most important is personal resources. (Source: Reprinted with permission, Inc. *magazine, June 1989. Copyright © 1989 by Goldhirsh Group, Inc., 38 Commercial Wharf, Boston, MA 02110.)*

Developing a Business Plan

business plan *a carefully constructed guide for the person starting one's own business*

When starting a small business, a lack of planning can be as deadly as a lack of money to the new enterprise. Planning is important to any business, large or small, and should never be overlooked or taken lightly. A **business plan** is a carefully constructed guide for the person starting one's own business. It also serves as a concise document that potential investors can examine to see if they would like to invest in or assist in financing a new venture.

There is a considerable amount of information available from both government and nongovernment sources that can help individuals develop a business plan. Inc. *magazine invites readers to "Be Your Own Boss" by buying and viewing their videos, which include advice from leading experts.*

Table 4.2 shows the ten sections that the business plan should include. The business person, when constructing a business plan, should strive to keep it easy to read, uncluttered, and complete. Officials of financial institutions just don't have the time to flip through pages of facts and figures. In the business plan, the business person should be sure to answer the four questions that banking officials and investors are most interested in: (1) What exactly is the nature and mission of the new venture? (2) Why is this new enterprise a good idea? (3) What are the business person's goals? (4) How much will the new venture cost?[11]

A great amount of time and consideration should go into creating a business plan. The plan will probably end up saving time later. Sharon Burch, who was running a computer software business while earning a degree in business administration, had to write a business plan as part of one course. Burch has said, "I wish I'd taken the class before I started my business. I see a lot of things I could have done differently. But it has helped me since I've been using the business plan as a guide for my business."[12]

TABLE 4.2 *Components of a Business Plan*

1. **Introduction** Basic information such as name and address of the business, nature of the business, statement of the business's financial needs (if any), and statement of confidentiality (to keep important information away from potential competitors)

2. **Executive summary** Summary of the entire business plan (a convenience for busy investors), including a justification stating why the business will succeed

3. **Industry analysis** Examination of the potential "customer," current competitors, and business's future

4. **Detailed description of the business** Information on the products or services to be offered; size and location of the business; personnel and office equipment needed; and brief history of the business

5. **Production plan** Description and cost analysis of the manufacturing process, plus an outline of the raw materials, physical plant, and heavy machinery needed

6. **Marketing plan** Discussion of pricing, promotion, distribution, and product forecasts

7. **Organizational plan** Description of the form of ownership of the venture and responsibilities of all members of the organization

8. **Assessment of risk** Evaluation of the weaknesses of the business and how the company plans to deal with these and other business problems

9. **Financial plan** Summary of the investment needed, forecasts of sales, cash-flow forecasts, breakeven analysis, estimated balance sheet, and sources of funding

10. **Appendix** Supplementary information such as market research results, copies of leases, and supplier price lists

Source: Adapted from Robert D. Hisrich and Michael P. Peters, *Entrepreneurship* (Homewood, Ill.: BPI/Irwin, 1989), pp. 126–140. Reprinted by permission.

Accuracy and realistic expectations are crucial to an effective business plan. It is unethical to deceive investors and loan officers, and it is unwise to deceive oneself.

The Small Business Administration

Small Business Administration (SBA)   *a governmental agency that assists, counsels, and protects the interests of small businesses in the United States*

Learning Objective 5
Know how the Small Business Administration helps small businesses

The **Small Business Administration (SBA),** created by Congress in 1953, is a governmental agency that assists, counsels, and protects the interests of small businesses in the United States. It helps people get into business and stay in business. The agency provides assistance to owners and managers of prospective, new, and established small businesses. Through more than one hundred offices throughout the nation, the SBA provides both financial assistance and management counseling. It helps small firms bid for and obtain government contracts, and it helps them prepare to enter foreign markets.

SBA Management Assistance

Statistics show that most failures in small business are due to poor management. For this reason, the SBA places special emphasis on improving the management ability of the owners and managers of small businesses. The SBA's Management Assistance Program is extensive and diversified. It includes free individual counseling, courses, conferences, workshops, and a wide range of publications. During a recent year the SBA indicated that it counseled or trained over 500,000 people and distributed over 3 million publications.[13]

Management Courses and Workshops   The management courses offered by the SBA cover all the functions, duties, and roles of managers. The most popular of these courses is a general survey of eight to ten different areas of business management. In follow-up studies, business people may concentrate in depth on one or more of these areas, depending on their own particular strengths and weaknesses. The SBA occasionally offers one-day conferences. These conferences are aimed at keeping owner-managers up to date on new management developments, tax laws, and the like.

Instructors may be teachers from local colleges and universities or professionals such as management consultants, bankers, lawyers, and accountants. Fees for these courses are quite low.

The SBA also invites prospective owners of small businesses to workshops, where management problems and good management practices are discussed. A major goal of these sessions is to emphasize the need for sufficient preparation before starting a new venture. Sometimes the sessions serve to convince eager but poorly prepared entrepreneurs to wait until they are ready for the difficulties that lie ahead.

Service Corps of Retired Executives (SCORE) *a group of retired business people who volunteer their services to small businesses through the SBA*

SCORE and ACE   The **Service Corps of Retired Executives (SCORE)** is a group of retired business people who volunteer their services to small businesses through the SBA. The collective experience of SCORE volunteers spans the full range of American enterprise.

A small-business owner who has a particular problem can request free counseling from SCORE. An assigned counselor visits the owner in his or her establishment and, through careful observation, analyzes the business situation and the problem. If the problem is complex, the counselor may call on other volunteer experts to assist. Finally, the counselor offers a plan for solving the problem and helping the owner through the critical period.

Active Corps of Executives (ACE) *a group of active managers who counsel small-business owners on a volunteer basis*

The **Active Corps of Executives (ACE)** is a group of active managers who counsel small-business owners on a volunteer basis. ACE was established to supplement the services available through SCORE and to keep the SBA's management counseling as current as possible. ACE volunteers come from major corporations, trade associations, educational institutions, and professions.

Help for Minority-Owned Small Businesses   Americans who are members of minority groups have had difficulty entering the nation's economic mainstream. Raising money is a nagging problem for minority business owners, who may also lack adequate training. Members of minority groups are, of course, eligible for all SBA programs, but the SBA makes a special effort to assist those who want to start small businesses or expand existing ones.

Helping women become entrepreneurs is also a special goal of the SBA. Women make up more than half of America's population, but they own less than one-fourth of its businesses. In 1980 an SBA Assistant Administrator for Women's Business Enterprise was appointed, and programs directed specifically toward this group were expanded.

Small Business Institute (SBI) *a group of senior and graduate students in business administration who provide management counseling to small businesses*

Small Business Institutes   A **Small Business Institute (SBI)** is a group of senior and graduate students in business administration who provide management counseling to small businesses. SBIs have been organized on almost 500 college campuses as another way to help business owners. The students, who work in small groups, are guided by faculty advisors and SBA management-assistance experts. Like SCORE volunteers, they analyze and help solve the problems of small-business owners at their business establishments.

Small Business Development Center (SBDC) *university-based group that provides individual counseling and practical training to owners of small businesses*

Small Business Development Centers   A **Small Business Development Center (SBDC)** is one of forty-five university-based groups that provide individual counseling and practical training to owners of small businesses. SBDCs draw from the resources of local, state, and federal governments; private business; and universities. These groups can provide managerial and technical help, data from research studies, and other types of specialized assistance that are of value to small businesses.

SBA Publications   The SBA issues management, marketing, and technical publications dealing with hundreds of topics that are of interest to present and prospective managers of small firms. Most of these publications are available from the SBA free of charge. Others can be obtained for a small fee from the U.S. Government Printing Office.

SBA Financial Assistance

Small businesses seem to be constantly in need of money, for one reason or another. An owner may have enough capital to start and operate the business. But then he or she may require more money to finance increased operations during peak selling seasons, to pay for required pollution-control equipment, to mop up after a natural disaster such as a flood, or to finance an expansion. The SBA offers special financial-assistance programs that cover all these situations. However, its primary financial function is to guarantee loans to eligible businesses.

Regular Business Loans   Most of the SBA's business loans are actually made by private lenders such as banks, but repayment is partially guaranteed by the agency. That is, the SBA may guarantee that it will repay the lender up to 90 percent of the loan if the borrowing firm cannot repay it. Guaranteed loans may be as large as $750,000. The average size of an SBA-guaranteed business loan is $165,000 and its average duration is about eight years.

Until recently, few loans were made directly to businesses by the SBA. (According to the law, the SBA could not consider making a direct loan unless a private lender had already refused to lend the business money, even with an SBA guarantee.) In a recent year, the SBA provided loan guarantees covering $3.2 billion in loans made through banks or other private-sector institutions. Included in this amount was $300 million in direct loans from the SBA to minority-owned businesses.[14]

venture capital *money that is invested in small (and sometimes struggling) firms that have the potential to become very successful*

Small Business Investment Companies   **Venture capital** is money that is invested in small (and sometimes struggling) firms that have the potential to become very successful. In many cases, only a lack of capital keeps these firms from rapid and solid growth. The people who invest in such firms expect that their investments will grow with the firms and become quite profitable.

The popularity of these investments has increased over the past ten years, but most new, small firms still have difficulty in obtaining venture capital. To help such firms, the SBA licenses, regulates, and provides financial assistance to Small Business Investment Companies. A **Small Business Investment Company (SBIC)** is a privately owned firm that provides venture capital to small enterprises that meet its investment standards. SBICs are intended to be profit-making organizations. However, SBA aid allows them to invest in small businesses that would not otherwise attract venture capital.

Small Business Investment Company (SBIC) *privately owned firm that provides venture capital to small enterprises that meet its investment standards*

We have discussed the importance of the small-business segment of our economy. We have weighed the advantages and drawbacks of operating a small business as compared to a large one. But is there a way to achieve the best of both worlds? Can one preserve one's independence as a business owner and still enjoy some of the benefits of "bigness"? Let's take a close look at franchising.

Franchising

franchise   *a license to operate an individually owned business as though it were part of a chain of outlets or stores*

A **franchise** is a license to operate an individually owned business as though it were part of a chain of outlets or stores. Often the business itself is also called a *franchise.* Among the most familiar franchises are McDonald's, KFC (Kentucky Fried Chicken), AAMCO Transmissions, Baskin-Robbins, and Pier 1 Imports. There are many other franchises with familiar names; this method of doing business has become very popular in the last two decades or so. It is an attractive means of starting and operating a small business.

What Is Franchising?

franchising   *the actual granting of a franchise*

franchisor   *an individual or organization granting a franchise*

franchisee   *a person or organization purchasing a franchise*

Franchising is the actual granting of a franchise. A **franchisor** is an individual or organization granting a franchise. A **franchisee** is a person or organization purchasing a franchise. The franchisor supplies a known and advertised business name, management skills, the required training and materials, and a method of doing business. The franchisee supplies labor and capital, operates the franchised business, and agrees to abide

A person who is seriously considering purchasing a franchise should read the Uniform Franchise Offering Circular (UFOC). This document, sometimes referred to as the "bible" of franchising, reports on where the franchisor came from, where the franchisor is today, and what the franchisor's prospects for the future are.

by the provisions of the franchise agreement. Table 4.3 lists some items that would be covered in a typical franchise agreement.

Types of Franchising Arrangements

Learning Objective 6
Comprehend the concept and types of franchising

Franchising arrangements fall into three general categories. In the first approach, a manufacturer may authorize a number of retail stores to sell a certain brand-name item. This franchising arrangement, one of the oldest, is prevalent in sales of passenger cars and trucks, farm equipment, shoes, paint, earth-moving equipment, and petroleum. About 90 percent of all gasoline is sold through franchised independent retail service stations, and franchised dealers handle virtually all sales of new cars and trucks. In the second type of franchising arrangement, a producer may

TABLE 4.3 *McDonald's Conventional Franchise as of June 1990*

McDonald's (Franchisor) Provides	*Individual (Franchisee) Supplies*
1. Nationally recognized trademarks and established reputation for quality	1. Total investment of approximately $575,000; includes initial franchise fee of $22,500 and refundable security deposit of $15,000
2. Designs and color schemes for restaurants, signs, and equipment	2. Approximate cash requirement of 40 percent of total investment
3. Formulas and specifications for certain food products	3. A minimum of 3.5 percent of gross sales annually for marketing and advertising
4. Proven methods of inventory and operations control	4. Payment of 12 percent of gross sales monthly to McDonald's Corp.
5. Bookkeeping, accounting, and policies manuals specially geared toward a franchised restaurant	5. Kitchen equipment, seating, decor, lighting, and signs in conformity with McDonald's standards (included in total investment figure)
6. A franchise term of up to 20 years	6. Willingness to relocate
7. Formal training program completed on a part-time basis in approximately 24 months in a McDonald's restaurant	7. Taxes, insurance, and maintenance costs
8. Five weeks of classroom training, including two weeks at Hamburger University	8. Commitment to assuring high-quality standards and upholding McDonald's reputation
9. Ongoing regional support services and field service staff	
10. Research and development into labor-saving equipment and methods	
11. Monthly bulletins, periodicals, and meetings to inform franchisees about management and marketing techniques	
12. The average McDonald's achieves $1.62 million a year.	

Source: McDonald's Franchising, McDonald's Corporation, Oak Brook, Ill., June 1, 1987. Used by permission.

BUSINESS JOURNAL

Sports Medicine Systems: Franchising Medical Services

With today's physical fitness craze, more people are participating in sports and physical activities—and more people are getting hurt. The nation's 5.6 million high school athletes suffer over 900,000 injuries annually; and, according to a National Institutes of Health estimation, as many as 17 million Americans suffer sports-related injuries each year. With treatment for these injuries costing as much as $4 billion, the field of sports medicine is definitely a growth industry.

One entrepreneur, realizing that there could be large profits in treating the sprained ankles, tennis elbows, and injured knees of high school athletes and "weekend warriors," has begun franchising sports medicine clinics. Dr. William Southmayd, an orthopedist and the 1963 captain of the Harvard University football team, opened a sports medicine clinic in a Boston suburb in the summer of 1976. Besides his competence as a doctor and business person, his reputation as the Boston Red Sox team physician (1978–1981) and as the author of the popular sports medicine book *Sports Health* helped him to become very successful. In 1983, Southmayd and some of his associates decided to open a second facility in Boston.

Southmayd's company, Sports Medicine Systems, Inc. (SMS), now owns five sports medicine clinics and plans to expand even more rapidly in the near future. Today the clinics receive over 61,000 annual visits from patients for a total of $6 million in gross revenues.

Southmayd is the first independent business person to start a nationwide chain of sports medicine clinics that are owned and operated by physicians. An orthopedic surgeon heads each center. The supporting staff include podiatrists, sports psychologists, physical therapists, and nutritionists.

In addition to the original five centers—in Boston and Brookline, Massachusetts; Columbus, Ohio; Portsmouth, New Hampshire; and Chicago, Illinois—two other centers (in Haverhill, Massachusetts, and Princeton, New Jersey) are wholly owned by local doctors who pay SMS $12,000 in return for use of the SMS name. Each new clinic costs about $750,000 to open, with physicians putting up 49 percent of the costs. Southmayd plans to expand into small- or medium-sized markets so that his clinics will not have to compete with well-known, highly respected sports medicine facilities in major metropolitan areas. His target markets are areas with large populations of *yuppies*—young, urban professionals known for their indulgence in sports and fitness activities—and high school students.

Southmayd offers his insights on the success and rapid growth of his full-service sports medicine centers: "We're not successful because we're smarter. It's because we have a *team* that is interested in the athlete's problem. It's as simple as the public being treated in the same way that the professional or intercollegiate athletes have been treated for years." Hospitals have been slow in responding to the sports medicine boom. It seems that unless hospitals take their sports medicine clinics out of the hospital setting, Southmayd and other sports medicine entrepreneurs will continue to make profits and expand their businesses.

Based on information from Steven Findlay, "When to See a Sports Doc," U.S. News & World Report, July 31, 1989, pp. 56–58; Richard Behar, "Medicine's $10 Billion Bonanza," Forbes, June 13, 1988, pp. 101, 104, 106; Glenn Deutsch, "The Fast Fooding of Sports Medicine," Sports Inc., March 7, 1988, pp. 16–21; and Steven Greenhouse, "The Big Bucks in Knees and Elbows," New York Times, February 1, 1987, pp. F1, F29.

license distributors to sell a given product to retailers. This arrangement is common in the soft-drink industry. Most national manufacturers of soft-drink syrups—The Coca-Cola Company, Dr Pepper Co., Pepsi-Cola, The Seven-Up Company, Royal Crown Companies Inc.—franchise independent bottlers who then serve retailers. Finally, a franchisor may supply brand names, techniques, or other services, instead of a complete product. The franchisor may provide certain production and distribution services, but its primary role in the arrangement is the careful development and control of marketing strategies. This approach to franchising, which is the most typical today, is used by Holiday Inns Inc., Howard Johnson Co., AAMCO Transmissions, McDonald's, Dairy Queen, Avis, Inc., The Hertz Corporation, KFC Corporation, and H & R Block, to name a few.

The Growth of Franchising

Learning Objective 7
Become aware of the growth of franchising and of its advantages and disadvantages

Franchising has been used since the early 1900s, primarily for filling stations and car dealerships. However, it has experienced enormous growth since the mid-1960s. This growth has generally paralleled the expansion of the fast-food industry—the industry in which franchising is used to the greatest extent. As Table 4.4 shows, *Entrepreneur* magazine's top-ranked franchises were nearly all in this industry.

Of course, franchising is not limited to fast foods. Hair salons, tanning salons, and professionals such as dentists and lawyers are expected to participate in franchising arrangements in growing numbers. Franchised health clubs, exterminators, and campgrounds are already widespread, as are franchised tax preparers and travel agencies. The real estate industry has also experienced a rapid increase in franchising. In 1988, approximately $640 billion in sales at over 509,000 franchised outlets accounted for about one-third of all retail sales in the United States.[15] The largest

TABLE 4.4 Top Ten Franchises (ranked by Entrepreneur magazine)

Rank	Name of Franchise	Minimum Start-up Costs
1	Subway	$30,400
2	Domino's Pizza	$75,000–$150,000
3	McDonald's	Varies ($575,000)
4	Little Caesars	$117,000–$120,000
5	Burger King	$311,350
6	Dairy Queen	$385,000–$595,000.
7	Arby's	$525,000–$850,000
8	Chem-Dry	$3,300–$7,000
9	Hardee's	$694,280–$1,540,000
10	Century 21	$15,000–$25,000

Source: Reprinted with permission from ENTREPRENEUR Magazine, January 1990.

franchising sectors, ranked by sales, are as follows: automobile and truck dealers (52.4 percent), gasoline service stations (14.4 percent), restaurants (9.9 percent), and retailing (nonfood; 4.5 percent).[16]

Are Franchises Successful?

Franchising is designed to provide a tested formula for success, along with ongoing advice and training. The success rate for businesses owned and operated by franchisees is significantly higher than the success rate for other independently owned small businesses. Only 5 to 8 percent of franchised businesses fail during the first two years of operation, while approximately 54 percent of independent businesses fail during that time period.[17]

Nevertheless, franchising is not a guarantee of success for either franchisees or franchisors. Too rapid expansion, inadequate capital or management skills, and a host of other problems can cause failure for both. Thus, for example, the Dizzy Dean's Beef and Burger franchise is no longer in business.

Advantages of Franchising

To the Franchisor The franchisor gains fast and selective distribution of its products without incurring the high cost of constructing and operating its own outlets. The franchisor thus has more capital available to expand production and to use for advertising. At the same time, it can ensure, through the franchise agreement, that outlets are maintained and operated according to its own standards.

The franchisor also benefits from the fact that the franchisee, being a sole proprietor in most cases, is likely to be very highly motivated to succeed. The success of the franchise means more sales, which translate into higher royalties for the franchisor.

To the Franchisee The franchisee gets the opportunity to start a business with limited capital and to make use of the business experience of others. Moreover, an outlet with a nationally advertised name, such as McDonald's, Dunkin' Donuts, or Video Biz, Inc., has guaranteed customers as soon as it opens.

If business problems arise, the franchisor gives the franchisee guidance and advice. This counseling is primarily responsible for the very high degree of success enjoyed by franchises. In most cases, the franchisee does not pay for such help.

The franchisee also receives materials to use in local advertising and can take part in national promotional campaigns sponsored by the franchisor. McDonald's and its franchisees, for example, constitute one of the nation's top twenty purchasers of advertising. Finally, the franchisee may be able to minimize the cost of advertising, of supplies, and of various business necessities by purchasing them in cooperation with other franchisees.

Disadvantages of Franchising

The disadvantages of franchising mainly affect the franchisee because the franchisor retains a great deal of control. The franchisor can dictate every aspect of the business: decor, design of employees' uniforms, types of signs, and all the details of business operations. All Burger King French fries taste the same because all Burger King franchisees have to make them the same way.

Franchise holders pay for their security, usually with a one-time franchise fee and continuing royalty and advertising fees, collected as a percentage of sales. As shown in Table 4.3, a McDonald's franchisee pays an initial franchise fee of about $22,500, an annual fee of 3.5 percent of gross sales (for advertising), and a monthly fee of 12 percent of gross sales. Table 4.4 shows how much money a franchisee needs to start a new franchise for selected organizations.

Franchise operators work hard. They often put in ten- and twelve-hour days, six days a week. And in some fields, franchise agreements are not uniform: One franchisee may pay more than another for the same services.

Even success can cause problems. Sometimes a franchise is so successful that the franchisor opens its own outlet nearby, in direct competition. A spokesperson for one franchisor says that the company "gives no geographical protection" to its franchise holders and thus is free to move in on them.

The International Franchise Association advises prospective franchise purchasers to investigate before investing and to approach buying a franchise cautiously. Franchises vary widely in approach as well as in products. Some, like Dunkin' Donuts and Baskin-Robbins ice cream stores, demand long hours. Others, like Command Performance hair salons and Uncle John's Family Restaurants, are more appropriate for those who don't want to spend many hours at their stores.

CHAPTER REVIEW

Summary

A small business is one that is independently owned and operated for profit and is not dominant in its field. The Small Business Administration (SBA) has developed guidelines that make this definition more specific and that determine whether a particular business is eligible for SBA aid.

There are about 16.5 million businesses in this country, and about 90 percent of them are small businesses. Small businesses employ about one-half of the nation's private work force, in spite of the fact that about 70 percent of new businesses can be expected to fail within five years. More than half of all small businesses are retailing and service businesses.

Such personal characteristics as independence, desire to create a new enterprise, and willingness to accept a challenge may impel individuals to start small businesses. Various external circumstances, such as special expertise or even the loss of a job, can also supply the motivation to strike out on one's own. Lack of management experience and poor planning are the major causes of failure.

Small businesses have been responsible for a wide variety of inventions and innovations, some of which have given rise to new industries. Historically, small businesses have created the bulk of the new jobs and have mounted effective competition to larger firms. They have provided things that society needs, acted as suppliers to larger firms, and served as customers of other businesses both large and small.

The advantages of smallness in business include independence, the opportunity to establish personal relationships with customers and employees, and the ability to adapt to changes quickly. The major disadvantages are the high risk of failure and the limited potential for growth.

The U.S. Small Business Administration was created in 1953 to assist and counsel the millions of small-business owners. The SBA offers management courses and workshops; managerial help, including one-to-one counseling through SCORE and ACE; various publications; and financial assistance through guaranteed loans and SBICs. It places special emphasis on aid to minority-owned businesses, including those owned by women.

A franchise is a license to operate an individually owned business as though it were part of a chain. The franchisor provides a known business name, management skills, a method of doing business, training, and required materials. The franchisee contributes labor and capital, operates the franchised business, and agrees to abide by the provisions of the franchise agreement. There are three major categories of franchise arrangements. Franchising has grown tremendously since the mid-1960s.

A major advantage of franchising is fast and well-controlled distribution of the franchisor's products, with minimal capital outlay. In return, the franchisee has the opportunity to open a business with limited capital, to make use of the business experience of others, and to sell to an existing clientele. For this, the franchisee must usually pay both an initial franchise fee and a continuing royalty based on sales. He or she must also follow the dictates of the franchise with regard to operation of the business.

This chapter ends our discussion of the foundations of American business. From here on, we shall be looking closely at various aspects of business operations. We begin, in the next chapter, with a discussion of management—what it is, what managers do, and how they work to coordinate the basic economic resources within a business organization.

Key Terms

You should now be able to define and give an example relevant to each of the following terms:

small business
business plan
Small Business
  Administration (SBA)
Service Corps of Retired
  Executives (SCORE)
Active Corps of
  Executives (ACE)
Small Business Institute
  (SBI)

Small Business
  Development Center
  (SBDC)
Small Business
  Investment Company
  (SBIC)
franchise
franchising
franchisor
franchisee

Questions and Exercises

Review Questions

1. What information would you need to determine whether a particular business is small according to SBA guidelines?
2. Which two areas of business generally attract the most small businesses? Why are these areas attractive to small business?
3. Distinguish among service industries, distribution industries, and production industries.
4. What kinds of factors impel certain people to start new businesses?
5. What are the major causes of small-business failure? Do these causes also apply to larger businesses?
6. Briefly describe four contributions of small business to the American economy.
7. What are the major advantages and disadvantages of smallness in business?
8. What are the major components of a business plan? Why should an individual develop a business plan?
9. Describe five ways in which the SBA provides management assistance to small businesses.
10. Describe two ways in which the SBA provides financial assistance to small businesses.
11. Why does the SBA concentrate on providing management and financial assistance to small businesses?
12. Explain the relationships among a franchise, the franchisor, and the franchisee.
13. What does the franchisor receive in a franchising agreement? What does the franchisee receive? What does each provide?

14. Cite one major benefit of franchising for the franchisor. Cite one major benefit for the franchisee.

Discussion Questions

1. In what ways is Joanne Marlowe similar to other entrepreneurs?
2. Why is Marlowe's towel business successful?
3. Most people who start small businesses know of the high failure rate and the reasons for it. Why, then, do they not take steps to protect their firms from failure? What steps should they take?
4. Are the so-called advantages of small business really advantages? Wouldn't every small-business owner like his or her business to grow into a large firm?
5. Do average citizens benefit from the activities of the SBA, or is the SBA just another way to spend our tax money?
6. Would you rather own your own business independently or become a franchisee? Why?

Exercises

1. From a sampling of twenty-five small businesses in your community, calculate the percentage in service industries, distribution industries, and production industries. Explain any major differences between your results and Figure 4.1.
2. Devise a plan for opening a new bicycle sales and repair shop in your community. Consider each of the components described in the business plan. Also give some thought to how you will avoid the major causes of small-business failure.

Case 4.1

No End to His Dream

The dream of many American business people is to create a company that combines both their professional skills and some personal interest or hobby. Gary Comer, founder of Lands' End, Inc., did just that. Using his expertise as a writer of advertisements, Comer created a company that sold equipment for his passion—sailing. For almost twenty-five years, Comer kept the company pretty much to himself, modifying its product line, running it as an S-corporation, paying taxes as though it were a sole proprietorship, but getting other benefits of being a corporation. Finally, in 1986, Comer offered shares to the public.

In the early 1960s, Comer was working as a copywriter for the advertising firm of Young & Rubicam, Inc. Although his writing won awards, he seemed to live for the peace and freedom provided by the weekends he spent on his sailboat. It was therefore no surprise to Comer's friends that when he quit advertising in 1962, he went to work for a sailmaker. A year later he set out on his own with Lands' End, selling sailboat hardware and equipment by mail.

From the beginning, Comer used his writing talents to make his catalogs special and to interest people in his merchandise. Customers who liked the hardware he sold would write to ask about raingear or duffel bags of the same quality, encouraging Comer to include a small clothing section in the catalogs. Gradually the clothing took over, and by 1977 he had dropped sailboat equipment entirely.

Today Comer no longer writes much for the catalogs, but they continue to be among the finest in the business. Besides describing the merchandise, they often profile a Lands' End employee or highlight some aspect of the company's product line. Of course, the company's rugged but tasteful merchandise also has much to do with its recent successes and a profit margin that, at almost 10 percent, is nearly twice the average in the apparel industry.

Until recently, Lands' End avoided paying corporate taxes by being organized as an S-corporation. Profits were divided among the shareholders, who paid taxes on their share as though it were ordinary income. When Comer finally took his company public, some Wall Street analysts said that he'd held on to his beloved company too long. They thought he would have done better to sell shares publicly five or six years earlier, when the company's huge yearly sales increases would have excited prospective stockholders. That early momentum would have given the company more money to grow with, but it would have deprived Comer of some of the joys of being an entrepreneur. And if nothing else, Comer and Lands' End have proved that joy in your work can be very rewarding.*

Questions

1. After succeeding so well as an S-corporation, why would Lands' End want to go public?

* Based on information from Barry B. Burr, "Midwest Retailer Hires N.Y. Firm for IPO," *Pensions & Investment Age,* September 29, 1986, p. 39; Susan Caminiti, "Steering His Own Course to Success," *Fortune,* January 5, 1987, p. 95; Laurie Freeman, "Lands' End a Beacon for Mail-Order Markets," *Advertising Age,* December 8, 1986, p. 4; and David Russell, "At Lands' End," *American Demographics,* September 1987, pp. 52, 55.

2. Some Wall Street analysts say that "not many entrepreneurial companies can reach sales of greater than $50 million." Why should there be such limits on what an entrepreneur can do?

Case 4.2

Big "Makudonarudo"

If you've always thought of McDonald's as an all-American company, it may surprise you to learn that the king of McDonald's franchises is named Fujita and that he doesn't eat hamburgers. In fact, Den Fujita is unusual in many respects, and his uniqueness has made him very rich. By ignoring many of the customs of both his native land and his parent company, Fujita has made McDonald's the top fast-food business in Japan and has changed the face of franchising.

Fujita was always a little different. As head cheerleader for his high school's sports teams, he wasn't content to encourage his school's racing boats from the banks of the river—instead, he dangled a member of his squad from a rope atop a bridge. When most of his classmates at the University of Tokyo were becoming bureaucrats, Fujita became an entrepreneur, establishing a trading company that imported women's accessories.

McDonald's came to Japan in 1970 searching for a Japanese partner with whom to create a Japanese McDonald's. Fujita was far from the richest potential candidate interviewed, but he was an eager entrepreneur who seemed willing to devote his energies to the new venture. McDonald's took a chance and chose him.

Almost immediately, however, Fujita began going his own way. The parent company recommended opening the first Japanese McDonald's in the suburbs, where most American fast-food stores are located. Fujita had his own ideas. He thought the young pedestrians of Japan's cities were more likely to give up Japan's fish-and-rice diet for a hamburger than were the more traditional suburban dwellers. He got

his way, opened the first Japanese McDonald's in a department store in Tokyo, didn't spend anything on advertising, and within a year had broken McDonald's world record for one-day sales: $14,000.

McDonald's learned its lesson from Fujita and has since opened inner-city restaurants around the world. Other companies might learn from the way Fujita marketed McDonald's in Japan. While the Japanese seem fascinated with Western styles and tastes, they often don't think of themselves as consumers of American products. So Fujita's McDonald's franchises play down their American origins, to the point where, according to Fujita, some Japanese who visit the United States are surprised to find that we have "Makudonarudo," as the Japanese say it, in America too.

Fujita and McDonald's continue to benefit from each other. One-third of the new McDonald's restaurants opened each year are now outside the United States. And the Tokyo McDonald's that once caused an argument is now one of 500 that Fujita owns in Japan. Fujita likes to take credit for a rise in the average weight of his people; per capita meat consumption in Japan has more than doubled in the last two decades. But Fujita himself still prefers noodles to Big Macs.†

Questions

1. Why would McDonald's have chosen an unusual entrepreneur like Den Fujita to run McDonald's in Japan?
2. What could franchises in the United States learn from Fujita?

† Based on information from "Japanese McDonald's," *Forbes*, May 19, 1986, p. 204; Frederick Hiroshi Katayama, "Japan's Big Mac," *Fortune*, September 15, 1986, p. 114; Charlene Price and Hal Linstrom, "Foodservice Franchising in International Markets," *National Food Review*, January–March 1988, pp. 15–17; and Michael Rogers, "Fast-Food Quiz: Will Takeout Sell in China?" *Fortune*, September 15, 1986, p. 116.

CAREER PROFILE

SAM WALTON   Sam Walton, or "Mr. Sam," is probably the epitome of the self-made man. Many business analysts agree that Wal-Mart Stores Inc., Sam's creation, will soon become the biggest retailer in the United States. That's quite an accomplishment for a man who started his retail career as a J.C. Penney trainee.

Sam's father was a farm-mortgage banker during the Depression. Growing up in Bentonville, Arkansas, Sam acquired a strong work ethic and an intimate knowledge of the people of rural communities. Sam became a student at the University of Missouri and eventually graduated with a degree in economics. He served in the Army during World War II and returned to Arkansas with a few retailing ideas and plenty of ambition.

He opened a Ben Franklin franchise (a five-and-dime outlet) near his home and quickly turned it into the company's largest store. Sam realized that national discount stores ignored small southern towns for the most part. Sam decided that there might be a lucrative future in pursuing small-town markets. He talked to Ben Franklin officials about his ideas, but they vehemently disagreed with him: There was no potential for real retail success in rural regions, according to them. One of Sam's slogans, though, is "If people believe in themselves, it's truly amazing what they can accomplish."

Believing in his convictions, Sam opened the first Wal-Mart store in Rogers, Arkansas in 1962. There were watermelons and donkey rides on grand opening day, and at least one observer characterized the situation as resembling a disaster area as watermelons, exploding into pieces from the intense heat of the day, mixed with donkey excrement. Sam's promotional efforts have improved significantly since then.

Sam's "Bring It Home to the USA" program has been a wide-ranging success. Sam decided to replace many foreign-made goods sold in Wal-Marts with domestic goods. This was a move designed to strengthen the U.S. economy by creating jobs and to advance Wal-Mart's public relations by attracting favorable attention. Another of Sam's programs, the ardent promotion of environmentally safe products, is boosting Wal-Mart's sales as consumers become more concerned about environmental issues.

There are no "employees" at Wal-Mart; workers are called "associates." Associates at Wal-Mart share in Sam's success through the company's profit-sharing trust, stock options, and stock-purchase plan. Sam's belief is that if you give more to your workers, they will give more to the company. He also believes in cultivating his managers. At 7:30 on Saturday mornings, 300 Wal-Mart managers get together for a pep rally. There are special Wal-Mart cheers, and prizes are awarded to managers whose stores have done especially well.

A recent *Fortune* magazine annual poll of America's most admired corporations, ranks Wal-Mart number five. Wal-Mart shareholders have also been pleased with the company's performance: A $1,000 investment in Wal-Mart in 1970 is worth half a million dollars today. Though Wal-Mart sells about $20 billion worth of goods a year and stocks around 50,000 items per store, Wal-Mart is really just getting started. Sam plans to build Wal-Marts in all fifty states; currently, there are Wal-Marts in only twenty-five. Today, Wal-Mart Stores is composed of approximately 1,400 Wal-Marts, 125 Sam's Wholesale Clubs, four Hypermarts, and a few Supercenters. Sam intends to construct more of each. Sam also aims to keep Wal-Mart headquarters in Bentonville, Arkansas.

Sam Walton is now a multibillionaire and considered by many to be a business genius. He made a fortune by combining the best characteristics of a die-hard entrepreneur with the talents of an effective small business person. Though some regard him as a bit eccentric—he insists on driving a 1978 Ford pickup truck and immortalized his late favorite hunting dog, Ol' Roy, on the label of Wal-Mart dog food—no one can deny his expertise in providing the public what it wants.

Though Sam retains the title of Chairman of the Board and remains Wal-Mart's clear inspirational leader, recently he named David Glass as CEO. At over 70 years of age and fighting leukemia, Sam has opted to relinquish the day-to-day control of his operation. Sam is still involved with Wal-Mart however. As Glass once stated, "Sam's only hobby besides bird hunting is working."

Based on information from John Huey, "Wal-Mart," *Fortune*, January 30, 1989, pp. 52–56, 58, 61; Kevin Kelly, "Sam Walton Chooses a Chip off the old CEO," *Business Week*, February 15, 1988, p. 29; and Jack Shewmaker, "The Master Sellers," *Nation's Business*, November 1988, pp. 20–21, 24, 26.

"Mr. Sam" stands as a monument to confidence, drive, ambition, foresight, and dedication to the goal of making Wal-Mart Stores the number one American retailer. His success with Wal-Mart inspires entrepreneurs and small business people everywhere to pursue their dreams and realize their potential.

CAREER PLANNING The future looks bright for individuals who possess the training and skills needed to meet the technological challenges of the future. The courses that you take in college, your early employment experience, and early career exploration become increasingly important. To help you explore different employment opportunities and plan for your future, we have included profiles of successful business people, together with specific career information, at the end of each major part in *Business*. Most of this career information is from the U.S. Department of Labor's *Occupational Outlook Handbook*. It is presented in an easy-to-use grid format like the example shown below.

We have emphasized in each career section that the business environment is undergoing rapid changes. Your success in career planning will be based to some extent on your ability to adapt to these changes.

SAMPLE CAREER PROFILE TABLE

The number in the salary column approximates the expected annual income after two or three years of service. 1 = $14,000–$16,000   2 = $18,000–$22,000   3 = $23,000–$28,000   4 = $28,000–$35,000 5 = $36,000 and up

Job Title	Educational Requirements	Salary Range	Prospects
Administrative management assistant	Two years of college; on-the-job experience	2	Gradual growth
Clerical supervisor	High school diploma; some college preferred	2	Greatest growth
Purchasing agent	Bachelor's degree in business; on-the-job experience helpful	3	Gradual growth
Secretarial supervisor	High school diploma; on-the-job experience; some college preferred	2	Gradual growth

Column	Explanation
Job Title	This column lists common job titles that correspond to job opportunities in the employment world today. Entries are alphabetized for easy reference.
Educational Requirements	Here, the general educational levels and degree requirements for each job title in column 1 are shown. In some cases, on-the-job experience is also necessary.
Salary Range	Salary ranges for each job title are included in this column. Of course, actual salary will be determined by employee qualifications, geographical difference in salary levels, and other factors.
Prospects	Employment prospects for each job title are indicated by a relative scale. In descending order, the scale ranges from greatest growth and gradual growth to limited growth and no growth.

Part 2

MANAGEMENT AND ORGANIZATION

This part of the book deals with the organization—the "thing" that is a business. We begin with a discussion of the functions involved in developing and operating an organization. Then we analyze the organization itself, to see what makes it tick. Next we put the two together, to examine the part of a business that is concerned with the conversion of material resources into products. Included in this part are:

THE MANAGEMENT PROCESS

1 Become aware of what management is
2 Understand the four basic management functions: goal setting and planning, organizing, leading and motivating, and controlling
3 Distinguish among the various kinds of managers, in terms of both level and area of management
4 Know the key management skills and the management roles in which these skills are used
5 Become aware of the different types of leadership
6 Learn the various stages of the managerial decision-making process
7 Recognize the sources companies turn to for managers
8 Understand three important contemporary approaches to management: Theory Z, corporate culture, and management excellence

CHAPTER PREVIEW

In this chapter we define the process of management and describe the four basic management functions of goal setting and planning, organizing, leading and motivating, and controlling. Then we focus on the types of managers with respect to levels of responsibility and areas of expertise. Next, we focus on the skills of effective managers and the different roles managers must play. We examine several styles of leadership and explore the process by which managers make decisions. We look at various sources of managers, both inside and outside an organization. We conclude this chapter by analyzing three innovative theories of management—Theory Z, corporate culture, and management excellence.

INSIDE BUSINESS

Management Hits Home Runs at Easton Aluminum

James L. Easton inherited the presidency of Easton Aluminum, Inc. from his father who started the firm in 1922. The younger Easton managed to transform his father's business from a moderately successful sporting goods company into an aluminum-baseball-bat institution and an $100-plus-million-a-year sporting goods operation. Located in Van Nuys, California, Easton Aluminum dominates a large majority of the $55-million-a-year aluminum-bat market. Ninety-eight percent of all NCAA baseball batters swing Easton bats when facing opposing pitchers, and many weekend athletes delight when they hear the familiar "ping" of a softball striking brightly colored aluminum.

Many professional Nordic and alpine skiers use Easton's aluminum ski poles. The firm also makes bows for archers, and its arrows have dominated archery competition for well over fifty years. A great number of National Hockey League players now use Easton hockey sticks.

Easton's engineers are athletes who design from their personal experience in the sport. They also explore advanced materials and routinely custom-design machines and production techniques. Easton's development of a new carbon (graphite) technology has revolutionized the manufacture of arrow shafts, bicycle tubing, and golf shafts.

Much of the manufacturer's success is due to the effective management practices of James Easton. Easton believes that managers should be intimately involved in every aspect of his privately owned company. For example, for over a year, company managers attended planning meetings for the firm's new distribution center. The managers met regularly to decide what they wanted and needed from the new center; they made five-year projections of distribution requirements. Using computer simulations for distribution planning, the managers were able to build an efficient system without hiring outside consultants. They stayed within their $5-million budget, too. After the distribution center began operation, Kenneth DuVall, vice president of Easton Aluminum, happily stated, "By and large, we have succeeded in building the distribution center of our dreams." On the role of managers, DuVall commented, "We developed a clear understanding of what we're about and what we need to do to stay competitive...." The exceptionally high level of inventory accuracy at the Salt Lake City distribution center has improved customer service tremendously.

Easton Aluminum is clearly a successful sporting goods company that is getting bigger and better every day. Through effective management, this looks like one company that may continue to hit home runs for a long time.[1]

itout a doubt, management is one of the most exciting, challenging, and rewarding of professions. The men and women who manage business firms play an important part in shaping the world we live in. Easton Aluminum is successful largely because of its effective management. Through the application of appropriate management skills and techniques, Easton Aluminum is experiencing significant growth in a low-growth industry.

Depending on its size, an organization may employ a number of specialized managers who are responsible for particular areas of management. An organization also includes managers at its several operational levels to coordinate resources and activities at those levels. Must every organization employ all these managers in area after area and level upon level? Well, yes and no. A very large organization may actually field a battalion of managers, each responsible for activities on one particular level of one management area. On the other hand, the owner of a sole proprietorship may be the only manager in the organization. He or she is responsible for all levels and areas of management (and probably for getting the mail out on time, as well).

What is important to an organization is not the number of managers it employs but the ability of these managers to achieve the organization's goals, such as those established by the management at Easton Aluminum. As you will see, this task requires the application of a variety of skills to a wide range of functions and roles.

What Is Management?

Learning Objective 1
Become aware of what management is

Management is the process of coordinating the resources of an organization to achieve the primary goals of the organization. As we saw in Chapter 1, most organizations make use of four kinds of resources: material, human, financial, and informational (see Figure 5.1).

Material resources are the tangible, physical resources that an organization uses. For example, General Motors uses steel, glass, and fiber-glass to produce cars and trucks on complex machine-driven assembly lines. Both the assembly lines and the buildings that house them are material resources, as are the actual materials from which vehicles are built. A college or university uses books, classroom buildings, desks, and computers to educate students. And the Mayo Clinic uses beds, operating room equipment, and diagnostic machines to provide health care.

FIGURE 5.1
The Four Main Resources of Management
Managers coordinate an organization's resources to achieve the primary goals of the organization.

MANAGEMENT				
Material resources	Human resources	Financial resources	Informational resources	→ Organizational goals

These three managers represent the sales, marketing, and service areas of the Cargo Division of America West Airlines. Although America West's primary business is passenger transportation, this successful division has made important contributions to the company's bottom line.

Perhaps the most important resources of any organization are its *human resources*—people. In fact, some firms live by the philosophy that their employees are their most important assets. To keep people happy, a variety of incentives or perks are used, including higher-than-average pay, flexible working hours, recreational facilities, day-care centers, lengthy paid vacations, cafeterias offering inexpensive meals, and generous benefit programs. At Southwest Airlines, employees are encouraged to have fun. A list of notable employee-oriented firms can be found in a book entitled *The 100 Best Companies to Work for in America*, by Levering, Moskowitz, and Katz.

Financial resources are the funds that the organization uses to meet its obligations to various creditors. A Safeway store obtains money from customers at the check-out counters and uses a portion of that money to pay the wholesalers from which it buys food. Citicorp, a large New York bank, borrows and lends money. A college obtains money in the form of tuition, income from its endowment, and state and federal grants. It uses the money to pay utility bills, insurance premiums, and professors' salaries. Each of these transactions involves financial resources.

Finally, many organizations are increasingly finding that they cannot afford to ignore *information*. External environmental conditions—including the economy, consumer markets, technology, politics, and cultural forces—are all changing so rapidly that an organization that does not adapt will probably not survive. And, to adapt to change, the organization must know what is changing and how it is changing. Companies are finding it increasingly important to gather information about their competitors in today's business environment. Companies such as Ford Motor

Company and General Electric are known to collect information about their competitors. McDonnell Douglas used competitive intelligence to beat Boeing in the development of a new prop-fan airliner.[2] These companies are technology based, but other types of companies, such as Kraft and J.C. Penney, collect this information as well. As we discuss in Part 5, information that is generated within the organization is just as important as external information.

It is important to realize that these are only general categories of resources. Within each category are hundreds or thousands of more specific types, from which management must choose the set of resources that can best accomplish its goals. Consider, for example, the wide variety of skills and talents that people have to offer. Of these, Metro-Goldwin-Mayer Film Co. would certainly choose a different set of skills from, say, the American Red Cross. A Burger King outlet would require still a different set. When we consider choices from all four categories, we end up with an extremely complex group of specific resources. It is this complex group of specific resources—and not simply "some of each" of the four general categories—that managers must coordinate to produce goods and services.

Another interesting way to look at management is in terms of the functions that managers perform. These functions have been identified as goal setting and planning, organizing, leading and motivating employees, and controlling ongoing activities. We shall explore them in some detail in the next section.

Basic Management Functions

Learning Objective 2
Understand the four basic management functions: goal setting and planning, organizing, leading and motivating, and controlling

A number of management functions must be performed if any organization is to succeed. Some seem to be most important when a new enterprise is first formed or when something is obviously wrong. Others seem to be essentially day-to-day activities. In truth, however, all are part of the ongoing process of management.

First, goals must be established for the organization, and plans must be developed to achieve those goals. Next, managers must organize people and other resources into a logical and efficient "well-oiled machine" that is capable of accomplishing the goals that have been chosen. Then, managers must lead employees in such a way that they are motivated to work effectively to help achieve the goals of the organization. Finally, managers need to maintain adequate control to ensure that the organization is working steadily toward its goals.

For example, when Lee Iacocca took the reins at Chrysler Corp., that firm was on the brink of bankruptcy. One of the first things Iacocca did was to establish a series of specific goals for sales growth and a strategy for achieving them. He changed the basic structure of the organization. Then he provided effective leadership by working for $1 a year until he had turned the company around. He also developed an elaborate control system to keep Chrysler on track.

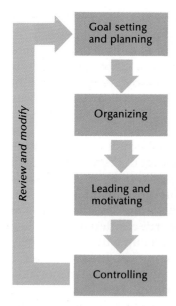

FIGURE 5.2
The Management Process
Note that management is not a step-by-step procedure, but a process with a feedback loop that represents a flow.

These functions do not occur according to some rigid, preset timetable. Managers don't plan in January, organize in February, lead and motivate in March, and control in April. At any given time, managers are likely to be engaged in a number of functions simultaneously. However, each of the functions tends to lead naturally to others. Figure 5.2 provides a visual framework for discussion of these management functions.

Goal Setting and Planning

As we have noted, management must set goals for the organization. Then the managers must develop plans by which to achieve those goals.

Goal Setting   A **goal** is an end state that the organization is expected to achieve. **Goal setting,** then, is the process of developing—and committing an organization to—a set of goals. Every organization has goals of several types.

The most fundamental type of goal is the organization's **purpose,** which is the reason for the organization's existence. Texaco Inc.'s purpose is to earn a profit for its owners. Houston Community College System's purpose is to provide an education for local citizens. The purpose of the Secret Service is to protect the life of the president. The organization's **mission** is the means by which it is to fulfill its purpose. Apple Computer attempts to fulfill its purpose by manufacturing computers, whereas Ford Motor Company fulfills the same purpose (making a profit) by manufacturing cars. Finally, an **objective** is a specific statement detailing what the organization intends to accomplish as it goes about its mission. For McDonald's, one objective might be that all customers will be served within two minutes of their arrival. Sears, Roebuck might adopt the objective that sales will be increased by 7 percent this year. For IBM, one objective might be that the average delivery time for personal computers to reach retailers will be reduced by four days next year.

Goals can deal with a variety of factors, such as sales, company growth, costs, customer satisfaction, and employee morale. They can also span various periods of time. A small manufacturer may focus primarily on sales objectives for the next six months, whereas Exxon Corporation may be more interested in objectives for the year 2000. Finally, goals are set at every level of the organization. Every member of the organization—the president of the company, the head of a department, and an operating employee at the lowest level—has a set of goals that he or she hopes to achieve.

The goals developed for these different levels must be consistent with one another. However, it is likely that some conflict will arise. A production department, for example, may have a goal of minimizing costs. One way to do this is to produce only one type of product and offer no "frills." Marketing, on the other hand, may have a goal of maximizing sales. And one way to implement this goal is to offer prospective customers a wide range of products with many options available. As part of his or her own goal setting, the manager who is ultimately responsible for *both* depart-

goal   *an end state that the organization is expected to achieve*

goal setting   *the process of developing and committing an organization to a set of goals*

purpose   *the reason for an organization's existence*

mission   *the means by which an organization is to fulfill its purpose*

objective   *a specific statement detailing what an organization intends to accomplish as it goes about its mission*

ments must achieve some sort of balance between such competing or conflicting goals. This balancing process is called *optimization.*

The optimization of conflicting goals requires insight and ability. When faced with the marketing-versus-production conflict we have just described, most managers would probably not adopt either viewpoint completely. Instead, they might decide on a reasonably diverse product line offering only the most widely sought-after options. Such a compromise would seem to be best for the organization as a whole.

plan   *an outline of the actions by which an organization intends to accomplish its goals*

planning   *the processes involved in developing plans*

strategy   *an organization's broadest set of plans, developed as a guide for major policy setting and decision making; it defines what business the company is in or wants to be in and the kind of company it is or wants to be*

Planning   Once goals have been set for the organization, managers must develop plans for achieving them. A **plan** is an outline of the actions by which the organization intends to accomplish its goals. The processes involved in developing plans are referred to as **planning.** Just as it has several goals, the organization should develop several types of plans.

An organization's **strategy** is its broadest set of plans and is developed as a guide for major policy setting and decision making. A firm's strategy defines what business the company is in or wants to be in and the kind of company it is or wants to be. When the Surgeon General issued a report linking smoking and cancer in the 1950s, top management at Philip Morris Companies recognized that the company's very survival was threatened. Action was needed to broaden the company's operations. Major elements in the overall Philip Morris strategy were first to purchase several non-tobacco-related companies (such as Miller Brewing) and then the Seven-Up Company and to aggressively promote the companies' products. As a

Fred Lager, as former CEO, was responsible for all basic management functions at Ben & Jerry's Homemade. Almost ten years ago Lager invested $50,000 in the original Ben & Jerry's and became the general manager. Today, this $60-million-a-year company has become well known for its high-fat ice cream and its no-fat management.

result of its strategy, Philip Morris seems to have attained the goal of being less dependent on tobacco sales.

Most organizations also employ several narrower kinds of plans. A **tactical plan** is a smaller-scale (and usually shorter-range) plan developed to implement a strategy. If a strategic plan will take five years to complete, the firm may develop five tactical plans, one covering each year. Tactical plans may need to be updated periodically as conditions and experience dictate. Their narrower scope permits them to be changed more easily than strategies.

Another category of plans is referred to as *standing plans*. These result from—and implement—decisions that have previously been made by management. A **policy** is a general guide for action in a situation that occurs repeatedly. A **standard operating procedure (SOP)** is a plan that outlines the steps to be taken in a situation that arises again and again. An SOP is thus more specific than a policy. For example, a Sears, Roebuck department store may have a policy of accepting deliveries only between 9 A.M. and 4 P.M. Standard operating procedure might then require that each accepted delivery be checked, sorted, and stored before closing time on the day of the delivery.

Organizing the Enterprise

After goal setting and planning, the second major function of the manager is organization. **Organizing** is the grouping of resources and activities to accomplish some end result in an efficient and effective manner. Consider the case of an inventor who creates a new product and goes into business to sell it. At first, he will probably do everything himself—purchase raw materials, make the product, advertise it, sell it, and keep his business records up to date. Eventually, as his business grows, he will find that he needs help. To begin with, he might hire a professional sales representative and a part-time bookkeeper. Later he might need to hire full-time sales personnel, other people to assist with production, and an accountant. As he hires each new person, he must decide what that person will do, to whom that person will report, and generally how that person can best take part in the organization's activities. We shall discuss these and other facets of the organizing function in much more detail in the next chapter.

Leading and Motivating

The leading and motivating functions are concerned with the human resources within the organization. **Leading** is the process of influencing people to work toward a common goal. **Motivating** is the process of providing reasons for people to work in the best interests of the organization. Together, leading and motivating are often referred to as **directing.**

We have already noted the importance of an organization's human resources. Because of this importance, leading and motivating are critical activities. Obviously, different people do things for different reasons— that is, they have different *motivations*. Some are primarily interested in earning as much money as they can. Others may be spurred on by

---

tactical plan   *a small-scale, short-range plan developed to implement a strategy*

policy   *a general guide for action in a situation that occurs repeatedly*

standard operating procedure (SOP)   *a plan that outlines the steps to be taken in a situation that arises again and again*

organizing   *the grouping of resources and activities to accomplish some end result in an efficient and effective manner*

leading   *the process of influencing people to work toward a common goal*

motivating   *the process of providing reasons for people to work in the best interests of the organization*

directing   *the combined processes of leading and motivating*

opportunities to get ahead in an organization. Part of the manager's job, then, is to determine what things motivate subordinates and to try to provide those things in a way that encourages effective performance.

Quite a bit of research has been done on both motivation and leadership. As you will see in Chapter 8, research on motivation has yielded very useful information. Research on leadership has been less successful. In spite of decades of study, no one has discovered a general set of personal traits or characteristics that makes a good leader. Later in this chapter, leadership is discussed in more detail.

Controlling Ongoing Activities

controlling *the process of evaluating and regulating ongoing activities to ensure that goals are achieved*

Controlling is the process of evaluating and regulating ongoing activities to ensure that goals are achieved. To see how controlling works, consider a rocket launched by NASA to place a satellite in orbit. Do NASA personnel simply fire the rocket and then check back in a few days to find out whether the satellite is in place? Of course not. The rocket is constantly monitored, and its course is regulated and adjusted as needed to get the satellite to its destination. Similarly, managerial control involves both close monitoring of the progress of the organization as it works toward its goals, and the regulating and adjusting required to keep it on course.

For example, suppose that United Air Lines, Inc. establishes a goal of increasing its profit by 12 percent next year. To ensure that this goal is reached, United's management might monitor its profit on a monthly basis. After three months, if profit has increased by 3 percent, management might be able to assume that everything is going according to schedule. Probably no action will be taken. However, if profit has increased by only 1 percent after three months, some corrective action would be needed to get the firm on track. The particular action that is required depends on the reason for the low increase in profit.

The control function includes three steps (see Figure 5.3). The first is *setting standards*, or specific goals to which performance can be compared.

FIGURE 5.3
The Control Function
The control function includes the three steps of setting standards, measuring actual performance, and taking corrective action.

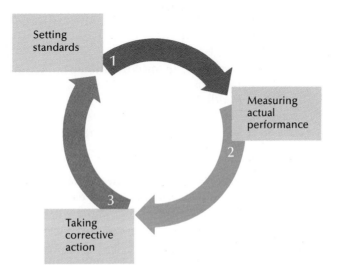

(Quantitative goals, such as United's 3 percent profit increase in three months, are perhaps the most useful.) The second step is *measuring actual performance* and comparing it with the standard. And the third step is *taking corrective action* as necessary. The results of this third step may affect the setting of standards. Notice that the control function is circular in nature. The steps in the control function must be repeated periodically until the primary goal is achieved.

Kinds of Managers

Learning Objective 3
Distinguish among the various kinds of managers, in terms of both level and area of management

Managers can be classified along two dimensions: level within the organization and area of management. We will use these two perspectives to explore the various types of managers.

top manager   *an upper-level executive who guides and controls the overall fortunes of the organization*

Levels of Management

For the moment, think of an organization as a three-story structure (as illustrated in Figure 5.4). Each story corresponds to one of the three general levels of management: top managers, middle managers, and lower-level managers.

Top Managers   A **top manager** is an upper-level executive who guides and controls the overall fortunes of the organization. Top managers constitute a small group. In terms of planning, they are generally responsible for interpreting the organization's purpose and developing its mission. They also determine the firm's strategy and define its major policies. It takes years of hard work and determination, as well as talent and no small share of good luck, to reach the ranks of top management in large companies. Common titles associated with top managers are president, vice president, chief executive officer (CEO), and chief operating officer (COO).

Middle Managers   A **middle manager** is a manager who implements the strategy and major policies handed down from the top level of the organization. Middle managers develop tactical plans and standard operating procedures, and they coordinate and supervise the activities of lower-level managers. Titles at the middle-management level include division manager, department head, plant manager, and operations manager.

Lower-Level Managers   A **lower-level manager** is a manager who coordinates and supervises the activities of operating employees. Lower-level managers spend most of their time working with and motivating employees, answering questions, and solving day-to-day problems. Most lower-level managers are former operating employees who, owing to their hard work and potential, were promoted into management. Many of today's

FIGURE 5.4
Management Levels Found in Most Companies
The coordinated effort of all three levels of managers is required to implement the goals of any company.

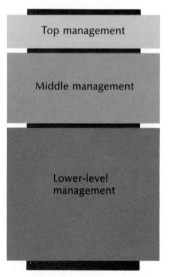

Top management

Middle management

Lower-level management

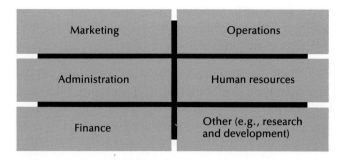

FIGURE 5.5
Areas of Management Specialization
Other areas may have to be added, depending on the nature of the firm and the industry.

middle and top managers began their careers on this lowest management level. Common titles for lower-level managers include office manager, supervisor, and foreman.

Areas of Management

Our organizational structure can also be divided more or less vertically into areas of management specialization (see Figure 5.5). The most common areas are finance, operations, marketing, human resources, and administration. Depending on its purpose and mission, an organization may include other areas as well—research and development, for example.

middle manager *a manager who implements the strategy and major policies developed by top management*

lower-level manager *a manager who coordinates and supervises the activities of operating employees*

financial manager *a manager who is primarily responsible for the organization's financial resources*

Financial Managers   A **financial manager** is a manager whose primary responsibility is the organization's financial resources. Accounting and investment are specialized areas within financial management. Because financing affects the operation of the entire firm, many of the presidents of this country's largest companies are people who got their "basic training" as financial managers.

operations manager *a manager who creates and manages the systems that convert resources into goods and services*

Operations Managers   An **operations manager** is a manager who creates and manages the systems that convert resources into goods and services. Traditionally, operations management has been equated with manufacturing—the production of goods. However, in recent years many of the techniques and procedures of operations management have been applied to the production of services and to a variety of nonbusiness activities. Like financial management, operations management has produced a good percentage of today's company presidents.

marketing manager *a manager who is responsible for facilitating the exchange of products between the organization and its customers or clients*

Marketing Managers   A **marketing manager** is a manager responsible for facilitating the exchange of products between the organization and its customers or clients. Specific areas within marketing are marketing research, advertising, promotion, sales, and distribution. A sizable number of today's company presidents have risen from the ranks of marketing management.

human resources manager *a person charged with managing the organization's formal human resources programs*

Human Resources Managers   A **human resources manager** is a person charged with managing the organization's formal human resources programs. He or she engages in human resources planning; designs systems for hiring, training, and appraising the performance of employees; and ensures that the organization follows government regulations concerning employment practices. Because human resources management is a relatively new area of specialization in many organizations, there are not many top managers with this kind of background. However, this situation should change with the passage of time.

administrative manager *a manager who is not associated with any specific functional area but who provides overall administrative guidance and leadership*

Administrative Managers   An **administrative manager** (also called a *general manager*) is a manager who is not associated with any specific functional area but who provides overall administrative guidance and leadership. A hospital administrator is a good example of an administrative manager. He or she does not specialize in operations, finance, marketing, or personnel management but instead coordinates the activities of specialized managers in all these areas. In many respects, most top managers are really administrative managers.

Whatever their level in the organization and whatever area of management they specialize in, successful managers generally exhibit certain key skills and are able to play certain managerial roles. But, as we shall see, some skills may be more critical at one level of management than at another.

What Makes Effective Managers?

Learning Objective 4
Know the key management skills and the management roles in which these skills are used

In general, effective managers are those who (1) possess certain important skills and (2) are able to use these skills in a number of managerial roles. Probably no manager is called on to use any particular skill *constantly* or to play a particular role all the time. However, these skills and abilities must be available when they are needed.

Key Management Skills

The skills that typify effective managers tend to fall into five general categories: technical, conceptual, interpersonal, diagnostic, and analytic.

technical skill *a specific skill needed to accomplish a specialized activity*

Technical Skills   A **technical skill** is a specific skill needed to accomplish a specialized activity. For example, the skills that engineers, lawyers, and machinists need to do their jobs are technical skills. Lower-level managers (and, to a lesser extent, middle managers) need the technical skills that are relevant to the activities they manage. Although these managers may not have to perform the technical tasks themselves, they must be able to

BUSINESS JOURNAL

Executive Celebrities: There's No Business Like Show Business

Executive celebrities are highly visible. They're in commercials, on television shows, at fashionable Manhattan parties. T. Boone Pickens, Jr., Lee Iacocca, Ted Turner, Steven Jobs, Donald Trump, Victor Kiam—these individuals are all as familiar to us as a movie star or a famous athlete. Why are some of our most prominent national figures and cultural heroes business executives?

Lee Iacocca seems to thrive on his celebrity status. The brash, outspoken head of Chrysler Corp., fired from his position at Ford, personally took the lead in saving his new company. He made the right decisions, collected a competent staff, and even starred in Chrysler commercials. Iacocca has appeared on "Miami Vice" and was instrumental in the restoration effort of the Statue of Liberty. Iacocca has an opinion on everything from taxes to foreign policy, and is more than happy to express these ideas. Iacocca's appearances, candor, and best-selling biography have all made him a business star.

Victor Kiam is the chief executive officer (CEO) and sole shareholder of Remington. He came to struggling Remington and quickly made some major changes. He drastically reduced the number of executives, brought all production plants back to the United States, and aggressively promoted Remington's electric shavers himself. He became Remington's primary salesperson and sales figures soared. Kiam, like Iacocca, has also published a book, and he is marketing it as vigorously as he does his shavers.

Donald Trump, the real estate magnate, is also a celebrity. He can be seen anywhere from his luxury ocean cruiser to his Atlantic City hotel to a major sporting event. Recognized wherever he goes, Trump greatly enjoys the limelight.

These—and others like T. Boone Pickens of Mesa Limited Partnership and Steven Jobs of NeXT Computers—are just some examples of celebrity executives. Celebrity CEOs have naturally drawn public attention to the businesses they control. Chrysler, Remington, and Trump's real estate holdings have all benefited substantially by the attention paid to their CEOs.

Other CEOs dread the spotlight. They think that being a celebrity is dangerous and that persons like Iacocca spend entirely too much time away from their desks. Iacocca especially has been criticized for neglecting new car development at Chrysler. Executives also avoid stardom because they think that executive celebrities become overconfident. With constant media exposure, talk-show appearances, and devoted fans, a celebrity executive might have a tendency to feel invincible and infallible. One major bad decision by a CEO could lead to problems or even disaster for an organization. Furthermore, training the successor to a celebrity executive is difficult. The new CEO will probably not be able to fill the shoes of a celebrity predecessor. Celebrity executives also face a security risk. Ambitious kidnappers or fanatical followers pose a potential threat to celebrity executives and their families.

Based on information from S. C. Gwynne, "Can Iacocca Do It Again?" *Time,* March 5, 1990, p. 40; Judith H. Dobrzynski, "Business Celebrities," *Business Week,* June 23, 1986, pp. 100–107; "Federal Express Spreads Its Wings," *Journal of Business Strategy,* July/August 1988, pp. 15–20; Marilyn Much, "Would You Buy a Shaver from This Man?" *Industry Week,* August 24, 1987, pp. 37–38; and Bob Spitz, "Mr. America," *Life,* June 1986, pp. 35–42.

train subordinates, answer questions, and otherwise provide guidance and direction. In general, top managers do not rely on technical skills as much as managers at other levels. Still, understanding the technical side of things is an aid to effective management at every level.

conceptual skill *the ability to conceptualize and think in abstract terms*

Conceptual Skills **Conceptual skill** is the ability to think in abstract terms. Conceptual skill allows the manager to see the "big picture" and to understand how the various parts of an organization or an idea can fit together. In 1951 a man named Charles Wilson decided to take his family on a cross-country vacation. All along the way, the family was forced to put up with high-priced but shabby hotel accommodations. Wilson reasoned that most travelers would welcome a chain of moderately priced, good-quality roadside hotels. You are no doubt familiar with what he conceived: Holiday Inns. Wilson was able to identify a number of isolated factors (existing accommodation patterns, the need for a different kind of hotel, and his own investment interests) to "dream up" the new business opportunity and to carry it through to completion.

Conceptual skills are useful in a wide range of situations, including the optimization of goals described earlier. They appear, however, to be more crucial for top managers than for middle or lower-level managers.

interpersonal skill *the ability to deal effectively with other people*

Interpersonal Skills An **interpersonal skill** is the ability to deal effectively with other people, both inside and outside the organization. Examples of interpersonal skills are the ability to relate to people, understand their needs and motives, and show genuine compassion. When all other things are equal, the manager who is able to exhibit these skills will be more successful than the manager who is arrogant and brash and who doesn't care about others.

diagnostic skill *the ability to assess a particular situation and identify its causes*

Diagnostic Skills **Diagnostic skill** is the ability to assess a particular situation and identify its causes. The diagnostic skills of the successful manager parallel those of the physician, who assesses the patient's symptoms to pinpoint the underlying medical problem. We can take this parallel one step further, too. In management as in medicine, correct diagnosis is often critical in determining the appropriate action to take. All managers need to make use of diagnostic skills, but these skills are probably used most by top managers.

analytic skill *the ability to identify the relevant issues or variables in a situation, to determine how they are related, and to assess their relative importance*

Analytic Skills **Analytic skill** is used to identify the relevant issues (or variables) in a situation, to determine how they are related, and to assess their relative importance. All managers, regardless of level or area, need analytic skills. Analytic skills often come into play along with diagnostic skills. For example, a manager assigned to a new position may be confronted with a wide variety of problems that all need attention. Diagnostic skills will be needed to identify the causes of each problem. But first the manager must analyze the problem of "too many problems" to determine which problems need immediate attention and which ones can wait.

Managerial Roles

Research suggests that managers must, from time to time, act in ten different roles if they are to be successful.[3] (By *role* we mean a part that someone plays.) These ten roles can be grouped into three categories: decisional, interpersonal, and informational.

decisional role *a role that involves various aspects of management decision making*

Decisional Roles   As you might suspect, a **decisional role** is one that involves various aspects of management decision making. In the role of *entrepreneur*, the manager is the voluntary initiator of change. For example, the manager who develops a new strategy or expands the sales force into a new market is playing the entrepreneur's role. A second decisional role is that of *disturbance handler*. A manager who settles a strike, or finds a new supplier of raw materials because there have been inventory shortages, is handling a disturbance. Third, the manager also occasionally plays the role of *resource allocator*. In this role, the manager might have to decide which departmental budgets to cut and which expenditure requests to approve. The fourth and last decisional role is that of *negotiator*. Being a negotiator might involve settling a dispute between a manager and the manager's subordinate or negotiating a new labor contract.

interpersonal role *a role in which the manager deals with people*

Interpersonal Roles   By now you should realize that dealing with people is an integral part of the manager's job. An **interpersonal role** is a role in which the manager deals with people. The manager may be called on to serve as a *figurehead*, perhaps by attending a ribbon-cutting ceremony or taking an important client to dinner. The manager may also have to play

The Gerber Products Company prides itself on being a leader in infant nutrition research. Pictured here is the team of managers who combined their skills to produce "Dietary Guidelines for Infants," a pamphlet that was distributed to pediatricians, government agencies, and individuals who call Gerber's consumer response line.

BUSINESS JOURNAL

Would You Be a Good Business Leader?

A football team needs a good quarterback, an army needs a good general, and a business needs a good leader. With global competition, deregulation, and continually developing technology, both large and small businesses must face constant change. To overcome any crisis and to succeed in an ever-changing environment, a business needs a chief executive officer (CEO) who is more than an effective manager. The CEO who is ready to bring a business into the twenty-first century must be able to understand where the company is, where it wants to be, and where it will be in the future. This person must be like CEOs Lee Iacocca of Chrysler, John Reed of Citicorp, or John F. Welch, Jr., of General Electric.

A good leader has the ability to create a business strategy, communicate this strategy, and inspire employees to carry it out effectively. Currently, business leadership is a hot topic. Many books have recently been published on business leadership, on organizational leaders themselves, and on how to become a better leader. Leadership seminars and workshops are becoming very popular.

Can leadership abilities be taught? Among professors and business people alike, this is a controversial question. Johnson & Johnson management seems to think so. Johnson & Johnson attempts to spot potential leaders early in their careers so that they can be given extra freedom and responsibility. Officials at General Foods Corp. see leadership as the foundation for all business growth and expansion. As a result, General Foods puts a massive effort into developing leaders. Other companies do not believe that leadership can be taught, and they prefer to hire experienced, proven leaders from other firms.

A good leader motivates employees, monitors their performance, helps, coaches, and makes de-

cisions. Flexibility, intelligence, and integrity are all key characteristics of an effective leader. In addition to having these personality traits, a good leader should follow seven guidelines:

1. Develop a vision.
2. Be an expert (this builds employee confidence).
3. Trust subordinates. (A good leader delegates authority.)
4. Encourage openness and discussion, and be able to integrate different ideas.
5. Encourage risks and accept errors.
6. Simplify—to focus on important matters.
7. Maintain composure under any circumstances.

Top leaders must be supported by other good leaders throughout their companies' ranks. Chief executives need operational leaders that can complement their efforts. Good operational leaders are involved with structure, rewards, and punishments, to allow their superiors to concentrate on inspiring dedication and productivity. Good leadership throughout an organization lets the CEO be the organization's catalyst and attractive public figure.

Based on information from Edward A. Kazemek, "Leadership: Style Makes the Difference," *Healthcare Financial Management*, March 1988, p. 98; Sharon R. King, "The Leading Edge," *Black Enterprise*, May 1988, pp. 87, 89–93; Ray Kulwiec, "What Does a Leader Do?" *Modern Materials Handling*, May 1988, p. 63; Kenneth Labich, "The Seven Keys to Business Leadership," *Fortune*, October 24, 1988, pp. 58–66; Jeremy Main, "Wanted: Leaders Who Can Make a Difference," *Fortune*, September 28, 1987, pp. 92–94, 99–100, 102; and David A. Nadler and Michael L. Tushman, "What Makes for Magic Leadership," *Fortune*, June 6, 1988, pp. 261–262.

---

the role of *liaison* by serving as a go-between for two different groups. In this case, one of the two groups is the manager's own company. As a liaison, a manager might represent his or her firm at meetings of an industrywide trade organization. Finally, the manager often has to serve as a *leader*. Playing the role of leader includes being an example for others in the organization as well as developing the skills, abilities, and motivation of subordinates.

Informational Roles   An **informational role** is one in which the manager either gathers or provides information. In the role of *monitor*, the manager actively seeks information that may be of value to the organization. For example, a manager who hears about a good business opportunity, or is told by subordinates that employees are contemplating a strike, is engaging in the role of monitor. The second informational role is that of *disseminator*. In this role, the manager transmits key information to those who can make use of it. As a disseminator, the above-mentioned manager would tip off the appropriate marketing manager about the business opportunity and warn the human resources manager about the possible strike. The third informational role is that of *spokesperson*. In this role, the manager provides information to people outside the organization, such as the press and the public.

Leadership

leadership   *the ability to influence others*

Leadership has been broadly defined as the ability to influence others. A leader has power and can use it to affect the behavior of others.[4] If the power is granted by an organization, the leader is said to have *authority* as well. Leadership is different from management in that a leader strives for voluntary cooperation, whereas a manager may depend on coercion to change behavior. A leader can be a manager, however, and an effective manager will probably display leadership skills.[5]

Formal and Informal Leadership

Learning Objective 5
Become aware of the different types of leadership

Some experts make a distinction between formal leadership and informal leadership. Formal leaders have power of position; that is, they hold authority from an organization and influence others to work for the organization's objectives. Informal leaders usually have no authority and may or may not exert their influence in support of the organization. Both formal and informal leaders make use of several kinds of power, including the ability to grant rewards or impose punishments, the possession of expert knowledge, and personal attraction or charisma.

Styles of Leadership

For many years leadership was viewed as a combination of personality traits, such as self-confidence, intelligence, and dependability. A consensus on which traits were most important was difficult to achieve, however, and attention turned to styles of leadership behavior. In the last few decades several styles of leadership have been identified: authoritarian, laissez-faire, and democratic.[6] The **authoritarian leader** holds all authority and responsibility, with communication usually moving from top to bottom. This leader assigns workers to specific tasks and expects orderly,

authoritarian leader   *one who holds all authority and responsibility, with communication usually moving from top to bottom*

laissez-faire leader *one who waives responsibility and allows subordinates to work as they choose with a minimum of interference; communication flows horizontally among group members*

democratic leader *one who holds final responsibility but also delegates authority to others, who help determine work assignments; communication is active upward and downward*

precise results. At the other extreme is the **laissez-faire leader,** who waives responsibility and allows subordinates to work as they choose with a minimum of interference. Communication flows horizontally among group members. The **democratic leader** holds final responsibility but also delegates authority to others, who participate in determining work assignments. In this leadership style, communication is active both upward and downward.

Each of these styles has its advantages and disadvantages. For example, democratic leadership can motivate employees to work effectively because it is *their* decisions that they are implementing. On the other hand, the decision-making process takes time that subordinates could otherwise be devoting to their tasks. Actually, each of the three leadership styles can be effective. The style that is *most* effective depends on the interaction among the subordinates, the characteristics of the work situation, and the manager's personality.

Managerial Decision Making

decision making *the process of developing a set of possible alternative solutions and choosing one alternative from among that set*

Learning Objective 6
Learn the various stages of the managerial decision-making process

Decision making is the process of developing a set of possible alternative solutions and choosing one alternative from among that set.[7] In ordinary, everyday situations our decisions are made casually and informally. We encounter a problem, mull it over for a way out, settle on a likely solution, and go on. Managers, however, require a more systematic method for solving complex problems in a variety of situations. As shown in Figure 5.6, managerial decision making involves four steps: (1) identifying the problem or opportunity, (2) generating alternatives, (3) selecting an alternative, and (4) implementing the solution.[8]

Identifying the Problem or Opportunity

A problem is the discrepancy between an actual condition and a desired condition—the difference between what is occurring and what one wishes to occur. A "problem" may be negative or positive. A positive problem may be viewed as an "opportunity."

Although accurate identification of a problem is essential for the solving of that problem, this stage of decision making creates many difficulties for managers. Sometimes managers' preconceptions of the problem prevent them from seeing the situation as it actually is. They produce an answer before the proper question has ever been asked. In other cases, managers overlook truly significant issues by focusing on unimportant matters. Also, managers may analyze problems in terms of symptoms rather than underlying causes.

Effective managers learn to look ahead so that they are prepared when decisions must be made. They clarify situations and examine the causes of problems, asking whether the presence or absence of certain

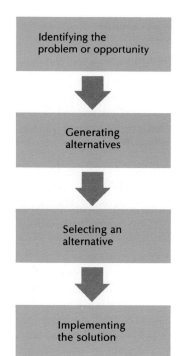

FIGURE 5.6
Major Steps in the Managerial Decision-Making Process
Managers require a systematic method for solving problems in a variety of ways. (Source: Robert Kreitner, Management, 4/e. Copyright © 1989 by Houghton Mifflin Company. Used by permission.)

variables alters a given situation. Finally, they consider how individual behaviors and values affect the way problems or opportunities are defined.

Generating Alternatives

After a problem has been suitably defined, the next task is to generate alternatives. Generally, the more important the decision, the more attention is devoted to this stage. Managers should be open to fresh, innovative ideas as well as to more obvious answers.

Certain techniques can aid in the generation of creative alternatives. Brainstorming, commonly used in group discussions, encourages participants to come up with as many new ideas as possible, no matter how outrageous. Other group members are not permitted to criticize or ridicule. Another approach to generating alternatives, developed by the U.S. Navy, is called "Blast! Then Refine." Group members tackle a recurring problem afresh, erasing from their minds all solutions and procedures tried in the past. The group then re-evaluates its original objectives, modifies them if necessary, and devises new solutions to the problem. Other techniques for stimulating new ideas are also useful in this stage of decision making.

Selecting an Alternative

A final decision is influenced by a number of considerations, including financial constraints, finite human and information resources, time limits, legal obstacles, and political factors. Managers must select the alternative that will be most effective and practical under the circumstances. At times two or more alternatives, or some combination of alternatives, will be equally appropriate.

Managers may choose solutions to problems on several levels. The word *satisfice* has been coined to describe solutions that are only adequate, not the best possible. Although managers often make decisions that satisfice if they lack time or information, this is not the most productive approach in the long run. Managers should try to optimize—that is, to carefully investigate alternatives and select the one that best solves the problem. In a few cases managers may be able to maximize, or achieve all of their goals. Finally, managers may change the basic situation so that the problem no longer exists.

Implementing the Solution

Implementation of a decision requires time, planning, and preparation of personnel. Managers must usually deal with unforeseen consequences as well, even when alternatives have been carefully considered.

If the chosen course of action removes the difference between the actual conditions and the desired conditions, then it is judged effective. If the problem persists, however, managers may decide to give the alternative more time to work, adopt a different alternative, or start the problem identification process all over again.

Sources of Managers

We have discussed a number of functions that managers must perform, skills they must use, and roles they must play. But where do they acquire the ability to do all this? We can best answer this question by turning it around and asking where organizations get management personnel. There are three primary sources of managers: lower levels in the organization, other organizations, and schools and universities (see Figure 5.7).

Inside the Organization

You have probably heard about firms whose policy is to "promote from within." This simply means that, whenever a position needs to be filled, the firm makes a genuine effort to promote someone from a lower level in the firm to that position. This approach has two advantages. First, the person promoted from within is already familiar with how the organization operates, its strategy, its people, and most other facets of the organization. Second, promotion from within may increase job motivation for all employees. That is, if employees recognize that good work can lead to a promotion, they are more likely to work harder and better and to stay with the company rather than seek advancement elsewhere.

On the other hand, promoting from within may limit innovation. The new manager may simply continue to do things the way the previous manager did them—the way they have always been done in the organization. Furthermore, at the time a particular position needs to be filled, there might not be anyone in the organization who is truly qualified for that position. Hence, even firms that seek to promote from within may have to hire someone from another organization occasionally.

FIGURE 5.7
Sources of Managers
Potential managers may be promoted from within, hired away from other companies, or hired directly from college.

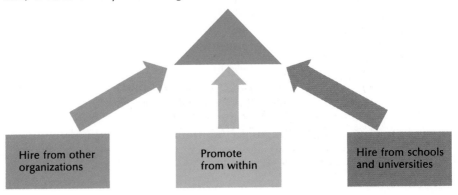

Hire from other
organizations

Promote
from within

Hire from schools
and universities

Other Organizations

The practice of hiring managers from other organizations seems to be used particularly to fill top management positions. Specialized executive employment agencies (sometimes unflatteringly called "head-hunters") search out qualified personnel who may be interested in leaving their organizations for better jobs. The agencies then match these people with firms seeking top managers. For example, recently head-hunters were responsible for replacing CEOs at Gerber Products, United Air Lines, Firestone Tire & Rubber Co., Mellon Bank, Datapoint, and Reebok.[9] Of course, many managers are hired by the more direct process of simply applying to the firm that has advertised an opening.

The primary advantages of hiring from the outside are that applicants may be judged objectively, based on their work record in the previous organization, and may bring new ideas and fresh perspectives to the firm. On the other hand, the hiring firm may not be able to learn as much about the applicant as it might like. Also, hiring from outside may cause resentment among present employees.

Schools and Universities

The third important source of managers is school and university campuses. Most large companies—and many smaller ones as well—routinely interview prospective graduates who might be interested in working for them. A number of recruiters look for people who are well trained and who have participated in internship programs and campus organizations. Those who are hired usually go through a management training program before being assigned a position. The program acquaints them with the firm and its products and prepares them for higher-level positions in the firm. Hence, educational institutions provide a pool of management talent that the organization then develops further, with the eventual goal of promotion to higher management levels.

Even after potential managers leave school and begin their working careers, their education is often not finished. Many return to school for an advanced degree, such as an M.B.A. (Master of Business Administration), or to receive specialized training in management development programs and seminars.

Contemporary Management Issues

Learning Objective 8
Understand three important contemporary approaches to management: Theory Z, corporate culture, and management excellence

In recent years, there has been much interest in the development and application of new and innovative management approaches. Three of the best-known and most influential approaches to management are Theory Z, corporate culture, and management excellence.

Theory Z

Japanese management practices and techniques have received much attention lately from managers and management theorists. One cause of this interest has been the difference in productivity trends in the United States and Japan. Simply defined, **productivity** is the average output per hour for all workers in the private business sector. In the United States, manufacturing productivity increased at the rate of 3.2 percent per year from 1960 to 1973. The annual growth rate dropped to less than half that figure between 1973 and 1979, though the rate rose again to 3.1 percent per year from 1979 to 1986. By contrast, Japanese manufacturing productivity increased by 10.3 percent per year until 1973 and is still increasing at a rate of more than 5 percent per year. This productivity is particularly visible in the Japanese automotive and electronics industries.

productivity   the average output per hour for all workers in the private business sector

In the 1970s William Ouchi, a management professor at UCLA, began to study business practices in United States and Japanese firms. He concluded that different types of management systems dominate in these two countries.[10]

In Japan, Ouchi found what he calls *Type J* firms. They are characterized by lifetime employment for employees, collective (or group) decision making, collective responsibility for the outcomes of decisions, slow evaluation and promotion, implied control mechanisms, nonspecialized career paths, and a holistic concern for employees as people.

American industry is dominated by what Ouchi calls *Type A* firms, which follow a different pattern. They emphasize short-term employment, individual decision making, individual responsibility for the outcomes of decisions, rapid evaluation and promotion, explicit control mechanisms, specialized career paths, and a segmented concern for employees only as employees.

A few very successful American firms represent a blend of the Type J and Type A patterns. These *Type Z* organizations emphasize long-term employment, collective decision making, individual responsibility for the outcomes of decisions, slow evaluation and promotion, informal control along with some formalized measures, moderately specialized career paths, and a holistic concern for employees. Examples of Type Z firms are IBM, Eastman Kodak, and Hewlett-Packard.

Theory Z   the belief that some middle ground between Ouchi's type A and Type J practices is best for American business

Theory Z is the belief that some middle ground between Ouchi's Type A and Type J practices is best for American business (see Figure 5.8). A major part of Theory Z is the emphasis on participative decision making. The focus is on "we" rather than on "us versus them." Theory Z employees and managers view the organization as a family. This participative spirit fosters cooperation and the dissemination of information and organizational values.

Corporate Culture

corporate culture   the inner rites, rituals, heroes, and values of a firm

Another idea that has attracted a great deal of interest among managers is the concept of corporate culture. A **corporate culture** is generally defined

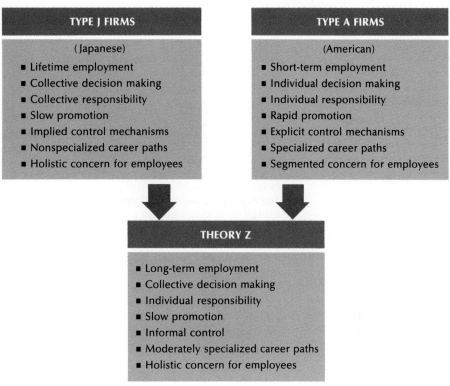

FIGURE 5.8
The Features of Theory Z
The best aspects of Japanese and American management theories combine to form the nucleus of Theory Z.

as the inner rites, rituals, heroes, and values of a firm (see Figure 5.9). Rituals that might seem silly to an outsider can have a powerful influence on how the employees of a particular organization think and act. For example, new employees at Honda Motor Co.'s Marysville, Ohio, manufacturing facility are encouraged to plant a small pine tree on the company's property. Symbolically, the growth of each employee's tree represents his or her personal growth and development at Honda.[11]

Terrence Deal (a Harvard University professor) and Allan Kennedy (a management consultant) have identified several key types of cultures.[12] One is the *tough-guy, macho culture,* in which people act as rugged individuals who like to take chances. Another is referred to as the *work hard/play hard culture.* Here the emphasis is on fun and action with few risks. A third major form of corporate culture is the *bet-your-company culture.* In this corporate situation, the emphasis is on big-stakes decisions and gambles that may pay off far in the future. Finally, there is the *process culture,* in which the organization functions mechanically, with much "red tape" and little actual exchange of information.

CORPORATE CULTURE	MANAGEMENT EXCELLENCE
▪ Inner rites, rituals, heroes, and values have a strong influence on a firm's performance ▪ Several key types of culture: tough guy, work hard/play hard, bet-your-company, and process ▪ Culture must change when firm or its environment is changing	▪ Creates an environment in which employees feel like winners ▪ Gives employees a voice in how they do their work ▪ Allows employees to control the quality of their output

FIGURE 5.9
The Principal Features of Corporate Culture and Management Excellence
Compare aspects of these two theories with those of Theory Z.

Corporate culture is generally thought to have a very strong influence on a firm's performance over time. Hence it is useful to be able to assess a firm's corporate culture. Common indicators include the physical setting (building, office layouts, and so on); what the company itself says about its corporate culture (in its advertising and public-relations news releases, for example); how the company greets its guests (does it have formal or informal reception areas?); and how employees spend their time (working alone in an office most of the time or spending much of the day working with others).

Deal and Kennedy believe that cultural change is needed when the company's environment is changing, when the industry is becoming more competitive, when the company's performance is mediocre, when the company is growing rapidly, or when the company is about to become a truly large corporation. Moreover, they believe that organizations of the future will look quite different from those of today. In particular, they predict that tomorrow's business firms will be made up of small task-oriented work groups, each with control over its own activities. These small groups will be coordinated through an elaborate computer network and held together by a strong corporate culture.

Management Excellence

The most recent perspective on management theory focuses on excellence. This focus results in such management practices as making average employees feel like heroes and winners, giving employees a voice in how they do their work, and letting people control the quality of their own output.[13] **Management excellence,** then, is a point of view that promotes feelings of excellence in employees.

Companies that stress management excellence include IBM and Procter & Gamble. At IBM, for example, sales quotas are purposely set so

management excellence *an approach to management that promotes feelings of excellence in employees*

BUSINESS JOURNAL

Growing a Healthy Corporate Culture

Corporate culture is the shared values and beliefs of a company's employees. It involves the long-term goals of the company and the day-to-day routines. Though corporate culture is often a tacit set of values and beliefs, it is crucial to a company's strategy and success.

IBM is known for a corporate culture that is based on promotion of products and quick responsiveness. 3M Company's culture is founded on innovation and experimentation. Two very profitable firms with two different visions for achieving success. Where would you best fit in? Do you see yourself as a team player unselfishly devoted to maintaining the high status of your organization? Or would you be more comfortable taking risks by experimenting with ideas? When looking for a job, it is a good idea to examine the corporate cultures of prospective employers. Being happy and productive in your work could depend on it.

Different ingredients can make up a successful corporate culture. It depends on many factors, including company size, industry characteristics, technology, and company history. A large commercial airline like Delta Air Lines, Inc., has a culture that stresses efficiency and customer service, while a small advertising firm has a culture that emphasizes creativity and independence. RJR Nabisco's long-term outlook focuses on diversification, while Hershey Foods Corp. is satisfied with remaining primarily in the candy and snack-food business.

Recently Capital Cities Communications acquired ABC. ABC's corporate culture revolved around ex-panding its viewer base. It eagerly sought large, expensive contracts and was committed to programs with high budgets. Capital Cities officials have a corporate culture that stresses profits and careful spending. As a result, there was severe conflict between Capital Cities' and ABC's executives. There was corporate-culture shock, not to mention many unhappy employees.

It is up to a company's chief executive officer and high-ranking officials to create a corporate culture. These officials must understand what makes their organization different and effectively communicate these differences to employees. The employees must recognize what the organization stands for and why it is valuable to them.

Based on information from Brian Dumaine, "Creating a New Company Culture," *Fortune*, January 15, 1990, pp. 127, 128+; Bernard Arogyaswamy and Charles M. Byles, "Organizational Culture: Internal and External Fits," *Journal of Management*, Winter 1987, pp. 647–658; John K. Clemens, "A Lesson from 431 B.C.," *Fortune*, October 13, 1986; and Bill Nixon, "You Can't Ignore Corporate Culture," *Accountancy*, May 1987, pp. 99–101.

that 70 to 80 percent of all sales representatives can meet them. As a result, sales reps tend to feel like winners and to work even harder and more effectively. Contrast this with a firm that sets sales goals that only 30 percent of its representatives can meet. As a result, 70 percent of its sales reps cannot help but feel like failures and losers.

In many ways, the concept of management excellence builds on the ideas of Theory Z and corporate culture. All three approaches emphasize the important role that people play in determining the success or failure of an organization.

CHAPTER REVIEW

Summary

Management is the process of coordinating the resources of an organization to achieve the primary goals of the organization. Managers are concerned with four types of resources—material, financial, human, and informational.

Managers perform four basic functions. The amount of time they devote to each depends on the situation of the firm and of the manager within the firm. First, managers engage in goal setting and planning (determining where the firm should be going and how to get there). Three types of plans, from the broadest to the most specific, are strategies, tactical plans, and standing plans. Next, managers organize resources and activities to accomplish results in an efficient and effective manner. Then, managers must lead and motivate others to inspire them to work in the best interest of the organization. Finally, managers must control ongoing activities, through continual evaluation and regulation, to keep the organization on course as it pursues its goals.

Managers—or management positions—may be classified from two different perspectives. From the perspective of level, there are top managers, who control the fortunes of the organization; middle managers, who implement strategies and major policies; and lower-level managers, who supervise the activities of operating employees. From the viewpoint of area of management, managers most often deal with the functions of finance, operations, marketing, human resources, and administration.

Effective managers tend to possess a specific set of skills and to fill ten basic managerial roles. Technical, conceptual, interpersonal, diagnostic, and analytic skills are all important, though the relative importance of each varies with the level of management. All the key managerial roles can be classified as decisional, interpersonal, or informational.

Managers' own effectiveness often depends on their styles of leadership—that is, their ability to influence others, either formally or informally. Leadership styles include the authoritarian "do it my way" style, the laissez-faire "do it your way" style, and the democratic "let's do it together" style.

Decision making, an integral part of a manager's work, is the process of developing a set of possible alternative solutions and choosing one alternative from among that set. Managerial decision making involves four steps. Managers must accurately identify problems, come up with several possible solutions, choose the solution that will be most effective under the circumstances, and finally implement the chosen course of action.

Candidates for management positions learn their skills and roles in lower levels within the organization, in other organizations, and in schools and universities.

Contemporary management theory features three interrelated concepts. Theory Z attempts to combine Japanese and American management practices. Corporate culture focuses on the rites, rituals, heroes, and values of the firm. Management excellence focuses on instilling a feeling of excellence in employees. All three approaches to management stress the prime importance of people in the organization.

In the next chapter we shall examine the organizing function in some detail. We shall look specifically at various forms that organizations take and the management concepts that result in these forms. Like most things in management, the form of an organization depends on the organization's goals, strategies, and personnel.

Key Terms

You should now be able to define and give an example relevant to each of the following terms:

management	top manager
goal	middle manager
goal setting	lower-level manager
purpose	financial manager
mission	operations manager
objective	marketing manager
plan	human resources
planning	manager
strategy	administrative manager
tactical plan	technical skill
policy	conceptual skill
standard operating	interpersonal skill
procedure (SOP)	diagnostic skill
organizing	analytic skill
leading	decisional role
motivating	interpersonal role
directing	informational role
controlling	leadership

authoritarian leader

laissez-faire leader

democratic leader

decision making

productivity

Theory Z

corporate culture

management excellence

Questions and Exercises

Review Questions

1. Define the term *manager* without using the word *management* in your definition.
2. What are the purpose and the mission of a neighborhood restaurant? of the Salvation Army? What might be reasonable objectives for these organizations?
3. How do a strategy, a tactical plan, and a policy differ? What do they all have in common?
4. What exactly does a manager organize, and for what reason?
5. Why are leadership and motivation necessary in a business where people are paid for their work?
6. Explain the steps involved in the control function.
7. How are the two perspectives on kinds of managers—that is, level and area—different from each other?
8. In what way are management skills related to the roles managers play? Provide a specific example to support your answer.
9. Compare and contrast the major styles of leadership.
10. Discuss what happens during each stage of the managerial decision-making process.
11. What are the advantages and disadvantages of promoting from within, compared to hiring new managers from outside the organization?
12. In what ways are Theory Z and the concept of management excellence alike?
13. What is meant by corporate culture?

Discussion Questions

1. Why is Easton Aluminum successful?
2. What types of management skills are demonstrated by James Easton?
3. Does a healthy firm (one that is doing well) have to worry about effective management? Explain.
4. Which of the management functions, skills, and roles don't really apply to the owner-operator of a sole proprietorship?
5. Which leadership style might be best suited to each of the three general levels of management?
6. Do you think people are really as important to an organization as this chapter seems to indicate?

Exercises

1. You are the owner and only employee of a firm that you started this morning. Your firm is to produce and sell hand-sewn canvas work pants to clothing stores. (You, of course, are an expert tailor.)
   a. Write out your firm's purpose, its mission, and at least two of its objectives.
   b. Write out your firm's sales strategy and a tactical plan that follows from the sales strategy. Make sure the strategy is in keeping with your goals.
   c. Write out one sales policy to be followed by your firm, and one SOP that implements the policy.
2. Rate yourself on each of the five key management skills and on your proven ability to perform each of the four management functions. (Use a scale of 1 to 5, with 5 being the highest.) Based on your ratings, explain why you would or wouldn't hire yourself for a lower-level management position.

Case 5.1

The NeXT Computer

Determined to regain his position at the top of the computer industry, Steven Jobs is betting his tarnished reputation and a substantial amount of cash on his new brainchild—the NeXT computer. Jobs is trying to prove that he really can build and manage a successful computer company, although some business analysts maintain that his triumphs as cofounder of Apple Computer, Inc. were mostly a fluke. After losing a power struggle at Apple to his one-time friend John Sculley, Jobs started a company called NeXT, Inc., and, with five former Apple employees, attempted to build a revolutionary computer. Because of Jobs' abilities and personality, and some impressive engineering feats, he achieved his objectives.

During the three years it took to develop the NeXT computer, Jobs followed a simple managerial strategy: He demanded devotion, sacrifice, and, most importantly, perfection from his employees. Leaving Apple with a damaged ego and a reputation for throwing tantrums, Jobs used his charm and infectious enthusiasm to recruit the best personnel he could. Despite being extremely demanding at times, Jobs is able to keep employee morale high at NeXT by providing a work atmosphere teeming with competency and style. One of the first people Jobs hired after he set up headquarters in California was an interior designer. NeXT's corporate headquarters and high-tech, automated computer-manufacturing plant are as slick as the NeXT computer itself. From the headquarters' polished wood floors, white furniture, and exotic juice–stocked refrigerator to the stylish gray and black robots, NeXT employees are surrounded by testimonials to their elite (at least in the eyes of Jobs) standing.

Jobs, a college dropout at 19 and a multimillionaire by 26, claims he is a better manager now than when he was at Apple. Today, in his thirties, he is proud of his new management style. "I think of myself as a pretty good operations person," says Jobs. "I'm concerned about how things are going to work at NeXT and how to avoid too many layers of management. We don't sit around in a dark room with a crystal ball. A lot of macro insights come after you've spent time on microscopic detail."

Jobs designed the NeXT computer especially for the academic community. Before product development began, he surveyed faculty members of thirty universities to determine what professors and students wanted in a personal computer. Some computer experts have expressed surprise and skepticism about Jobs' pursuit of the academic market. The competition from other firms to supply colleges and universities with computers is fierce, and college students might have a difficult time paying the $6,500 price (a NeXT laser printer costs an additional $2,000). Nevertheless, Jobs is as confident as he ever was. He firmly believes in a slogan he often quotes to his employees: "Trust the technology."*

Questions

1. How would you characterize Steven Jobs' leadership style?
2. Would you like to work for Jobs? Why or why not?

Case 5.2

Management Practices at CBS

In the past, Laurence Tisch, CEO at Columbia Broadcasting System (CBS), proved himself to be a first-rate accountant and financial wizard. So it is no

---

* Based on Katherine M. Hafner and Richard Brandt, "Steve Jobs: Can He Do It Again?" *Business Week*, October 24, 1988, pp. 74–78, 80; Brian O'Reilly, "Steve Jobs: What's Next?" *Fortune*, November 7, 1988, pp. 12, 16; Brenton R. Schlender, "Next Project," *Wall Street Journal*, October 13, 1988, pp. A1, A16; and John Schwartz, "Steve Jobs Comes Back," *Newsweek*, October 24, 1988, pp. 46–49, 51.

surprise that this confident and articulate man has been hurt because many observers have openly questioned his ability to run CBS. CBS's current board of directors, network affiliates, and investors have harshly criticized Tisch's strategy at CBS or, more precisely, his *lack* of a concrete company strategy. However, others claim that Tisch's decisions at CBS have been excellent and have brought financial stability to the firm.

Before Tisch came along, CBS was a diverse entertainment giant. CBS/Records Group was the world's largest record company. Tisch sold CBS Records to Sony Corp. (for $2 billion), just when the compact-disc revolution began to breathe a strong rush of air into the music industry. Tisch sold CBS's publishing holdings to Harcourt Brace Jovanovich, Inc., and its magazine division to Diamandis Communications, Inc. And, while ABC is expanding its commitment to cable programming—by investing in such networks as ESPN, Lifetime, and Arts & Entertainment Network—and NBC (which has been trying to increase its involvement in cable for years) is now leasing the Tempo Television Network, Tisch sold off CBS's interests in Rainbow Services (a cable programming venture) and several regional SportsChannel networks.

Tisch argues that he wants to concentrate on broadcasting, even though the evening viewing audience for CBS programs has diminished by two million households since Tisch took command. Tisch says that CBS will regain its lead in the broadcast industry with improved programming, aggressive promotion to attract new viewers, and marketing innovations that appeal to advertisers. Some television analysts expect Tisch's plans to fail; they think that CBS must diversify to grow at a time when network television is shrinking so dramatically.

Tisch's management style irritates many people. He hates memos, meetings, and traditional channels of communication. Though decisions at CBS are now made more rapidly, the bureaucratic culture of the company has been upset. Over a two-year period after Tisch became CEO, CBS reduced its work force from 16,000 to 6,800 employees. Its revenues also shrank, from about $5 billion to $2.8 billion a year, and it slipped to last place in the crucial A. C. Nielsen Co. television ratings. In contrast, when Capital Cities took over ABC and made cuts as deep as CBS's in the work force, ABC ratings improved.

One of CBS's directors said in a recent *Business Week* interview: "We're not happy. Tisch has dismantled the company in a piecemeal fashion, and it's too late to stop him. We've asked for a plan or a strategy. But it's not in his nature to lay out a strategy." To

Tisch's credit, CBS did land the 1992 Winter Olympic Games, and the company has more than $3 billion in the bank. Stock analysts, however, are still predicting a dull future for CBS. But, since Tisch controls nearly 25 percent of CBS's stock, Tisch's critics and dissatisfied colleagues will probably have to accept his way of doing business for a long time.†

† Based on information from Laurie Baum and David Lieberman, "Has Larry Tisch Sold Too Much of CBS's Future?" _Business Week_, July 25, 1988, pp. 52–54; Subrata N. Chakravarty, "Behind All That Shuffling and Reshuffling at CBS," _Forbes_, August 8, 1988, pp. 77–79; David Lieberman, "Laurence Tisch," _Business Week_, April 15, 1988, p. 146; and "Tisch Talks Programming," _Broadcasting_, October 24, 1988, p. 57.

Questions

1. Does the fact that Tisch does not like memos, meetings, and traditional channels of communication indicate that he is not an effective manager?
2. Given that several groups, such as the board of directors, network affiliates, and investors, have been critical of Tisch's actions, should he take corrective measures? Explain.

CREATING THE ORGANIZATION

1 Understand what organizations are and what their organization charts show

2 Be aware of the overall dimensions of organizational structure

3 Know why job specialization is important and why some firms are using less of it

4 Be aware of the various bases for departmentalization

5 Perceive how decentralization follows from delegation

6 Understand the span of management and how it describes an organization

7 Comprehend the distinction between line and staff management

8 Grasp the three basic forms of organizational structure: bureaucratic, organic, and matrix

9 Define what an informal organization is and how it operates through informal groups and the grapevine

CHAPTER PREVIEW

We begin this chapter by examining the business organization—what it is and how its various positions are structured. Next, we focus one by one on five dimensions of organizational structure. We discuss job specialization within a company; the grouping of jobs into manageable units or departments; the delegation of power from management to subordinates; the span of management; and the differences between line and staff management. Then, we step back for an overall view of three approaches to organizational structure—the bureaucratic structure, the organic structure, and the matrix structure. Finally, we look at the network of social interactions—the informal organization—that operates within the formal business structure.

INSIDE BUSINESS

Burger King: Reorganizing to Fix a Whopper of a Problem

Pillsbury Company's long succession of problems with its largest and most profitable division, number-two hamburger chain Burger King, has been well documented in business publications. When Pillsbury owned Burger King, its marketing efforts were in disarray, many of its restaurants needed to be refurbished, there was a great deal of management turnover, and its sales lagged behind those of arch-rival McDonald's. In a hostile takeover, the British firm Grand Metropolitan PLC purchased Pillsbury to add the food-and-restaurant business to its already hefty portfolio of real estate, distilling, and gambling enterprises. High on the priority list of Grand Metropolitan is the revitalization of Burger King, which its new owner thinks has a substantial store of untapped potential.

A large number of Burger King franchisees had been very dissatisfied with Pillsbury. To smooth out relations, the Grand Metropolitan management team is listening to the franchisees' suggestions and putting more funds into renovation of shabby outlets. The executive in charge of turning Burger King around says he doesn't have a bag of magical solutions but believes that the crucial ingredient is what Burger King delivers to the customer at the point of sale. To that end, Grand Metropolitan's management is trying to ensure that there is a higher level of quality control and consistency among all outlets. When Burger King was under Pillsbury's control, many customers complained that they never knew what the food would taste like.

Months before Grand Metropolitan actually finalized the Pillsbury deal, retailing experts had started evaluating the problems at Burger King. The new Burger King team is now concentrating heavily on marketing. Hoping to erase a notoriously bad reputation, they are increasing Burger King's marketing budget. Grand Met's commercial affairs director remarked, "Our belief is that Burger King needs a very superb advertising campaign, and we'd go to a lot of trouble to get the best creative product. We've already pinpointed advertising that has not been consistent over time. A big idea is needed that can be built over time."

Grand Metropolitan executives, the majority of whom have absolutely no background in the fast-food business, face a major challenge in taking market share away from McDonald's. But they think that the battle will be fought—and eventually won—at each of Burger King's 5,500 outlets.[1]

*B*urger King, like many other companies, is changing its organization to be more competitive. When firms are reorganized, the focus is sometimes on cost cutting. In other cases, the emphasis is on improving product or service quality to increase customer satisfaction. The way that a firm is organized influences its performance. Thus, the issue of organization is important.

What Is an Organization?

We used the term *organization* throughout Chapter 5 without really defining it, mainly because its everyday meaning is close to its business meaning. Here, however, let us agree that an **organization** is a group of two or more people working together in a predetermined fashion to achieve a common set of goals. A neighborhood grocery store owned and operated by a husband-and-wife team is an organization. Exxon Corporation, employing hundreds of thousands of workers worldwide, is also an organization in the very same sense. Both need to be organized, although Exxon's organizational structure is vastly more complex than that of the grocery store.

organization *a group of two or more people working together in a predetermined fashion to achieve a common set of goals*

Learning Objective 1
Understand what organizations are and what their organization charts show

Organizing

An inventor who goes into business to produce and market a new invention adds people to the organization and then decides what each will do, who will report to whom, and so on. These activities are the essence of organizing, or creating, the organization. *Organizing,* as we saw in Chapter 5, is the process of grouping resources and activities to accomplish some end result in an efficient and effective manner. Out of the organizing process comes an **organizational structure,** which is a fixed pattern of (1) positions within the organization and (2) relationships among those positions.

organizational structure
a fixed pattern of (1) positions within an organization and (2) relationships among those positions

Developing Organization Charts

organization chart *a diagram that represents the positions and relationships within an organization*

An **organization chart** is a diagram that represents the positions and relationships within an organization—that is, it reveals the company's organizational structure. An example of an organization chart is shown in Figure 6.1. What does it tell us?

Each rectangle in the chart represents a particular position or person in the organization. At the top of the chart is the president; at the next level are the vice presidents. The solid vertical lines connecting the vice presidents to the president indicate that the vice presidents are in the chain of command. The **chain of command** is the line of authority that extends from the highest to the lowest levels of the organization. Moreover, each vice president reports directly to the president. Similarly, the plant managers, regional sales managers, and accounting department managers report directly to the vice presidents.

chain of command *the line of authority that extends from the highest to the lowest levels of an organization*

163

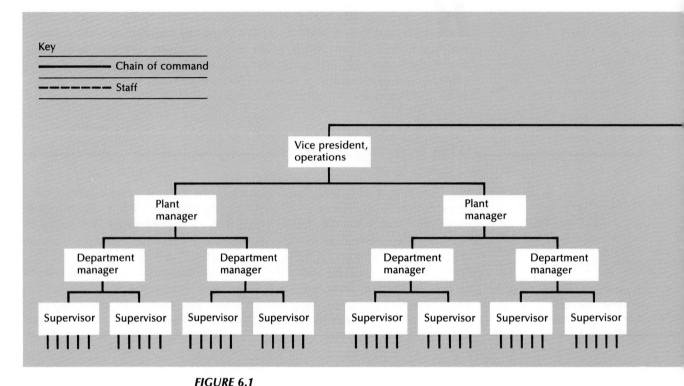

FIGURE 6.1
A Typical Corporate Organization Chart
A company's organization chart represents the positions and relationships within an organization and shows the managerial chains of command.

The fact that the directors of legal services, public affairs, and human resources are shown with a broken line means that these people are not part of the direct chain of command. Instead, they hold *advisory,* or *staff,* positions. This difference will be made clear later in the chapter, when we discuss line and staff positions.

Most smaller organizations find organization charts useful. They clarify positions and reporting relationships for everyone in the organization, and they help managers track growth and change in the organizational structure. For two reasons, however, many large organizations do not maintain complete, detailed charts. It is difficult to chart accurately even a few dozen positions, much less the thousands that characterize larger firms. And larger organizations are almost always changing one part of their structure or another. An organization chart would probably be outdated before it was completed.

In the next several sections we shall consider five major dimensions of organizational structure, most of which are not immediately apparent on the company's organization chart.

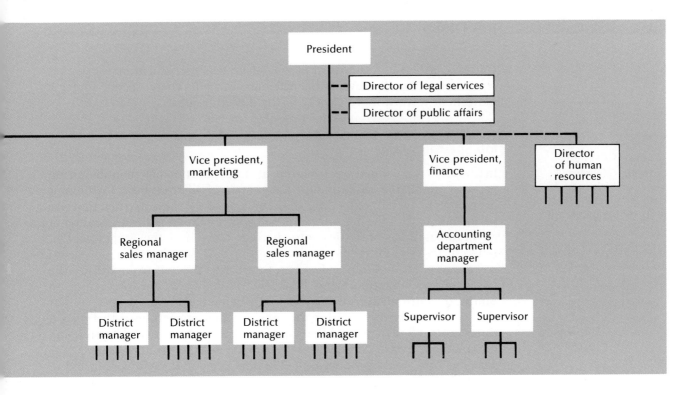

The Dimensions
of Organizational Structure

An inventor who goes into business has to make decisions about how to organize the firm. These decisions are all part of five major steps that sum up the organizing process. The results of these steps are often called the *dimensions of organizational structure* because they are reflected in the organization and its organization chart. The five steps are as follows:

Learning Objective 2
Be aware of the overall dimensions of organizational structure

1. Divide the work that is to be done by the entire organization into separate parts, and assign those parts to positions within the organization. This step is sometimes called job design. The resulting dimension is the *degree of specialization* within the organization.

2. Group the various positions into manageable units. This step determines the *nature and degree of departmentalization* of the organization.

3. Distribute responsibility and authority within the organization. This step results in a particular *degree of centralization* for the organization.

4. Determine the number of subordinates who will report to each manager. The resulting dimension is called the *span of management*.

5. Distinguish between those positions with direct authority and those that are support positions. This establishes the organization's *chain of command*.

Job Design

Until recently, the watchword in job design was specialization for worker efficiency. Now, however, the tide has turned. There seems to be a movement toward more variety in the design of jobs.

Job Specialization

Learning Objective 3
Know why job specialization is important and why some firms are using less of it

job specialization *the separation of all organizational activities into distinct tasks and the assignment of different tasks to different people*

In Chapter 1 we defined *specialization* as the separation of a manufacturing process into distinct tasks and the assignment of different tasks to different people. Here we are extending that concept to *all* the activities that are performed within the organization. **Job specialization** is the separation of all organizational activities into distinct tasks and the assignment of different tasks to different people.

As we noted in Chapter 1, Adam Smith was the first to emphasize the power of specialization in his book *The Wealth of Nations*. According to Smith, the various tasks in a particular pin factory were arranged so that one worker drew the wire for the pins, another straightened the wire, a third cut it, a fourth ground the point, and a fifth attached the head. Using this method, Smith claimed, ten men were able to produce 48,000 pins per day. They could produce only 200 pins per day if each worker had to perform all five tasks!

The tasks in producing Saturday Night Live are varied and specific. The actors are just one element in the job specialization involved. Shown here are the actors, who have been members of the Saturday Night Live cast since 1986.

The Rationale for Specialization

There are a number of reasons that at least some specialization is needed. First and foremost is the simple fact that the "job" of most organizations is simply too large for one person to handle. In a firm that produces goods, several production people may be needed. Others will be needed to sell the product, to control the firm's finances, and so on.

Second, when a worker has to learn only a specific, highly specialized task, that individual should be able to learn to do it very efficiently. Third, the worker who is doing the same job over and over does not lose time changing from one operation to another, as the pin workers probably did when each was producing a complete pin. Fourth, the more specialized the job, the easier it may be to design specialized equipment for those who do it. And finally, the more specialized the job, the easier it is to train new employees when an employee quits or is absent from work.

Unfortunately, specialization can lead to some negative consequences as well. The most significant of these is the boredom and dissatisfaction that many employees feel when they do the same job over and over. Monotony can be deadening. Bored employees may be absent from work frequently, may not put much effort into their work, and may even sabotage the company. Because of these negative side effects, in recent years managers have begun to search for alternatives to specialization in the design of jobs.

Alternatives to Job Specialization

The three most common antidotes to the problems that job specialization can breed are job rotation, job enlargement, and job enrichment.

job rotation *the systematic shifting of employees from one job to another*

Job Rotation   **Job rotation** is the systematic shifting of employees from one job to another. For example, a worker may be assigned to a different job every week for four weeks and then return to the first job in the fifth week. The idea behind job rotation is to provide a variety of jobs so that workers are less likely to get bored and dissatisfied. Companies that use job rotation include Ford, Bethlehem Steel Corp., and The Prudential Insurance Co. of America.

Unfortunately, many firms have had less than total success with job rotation. Often each of the jobs to which a worker is shifted is itself narrow and boring. Therefore, although there may be a short period of revived interest after each new assignment, this interest wears off quickly. Still, job rotation is widely used, and it offers the added advantage of being an excellent tool for teaching employees new skills.

job enlargement *giving a worker more things to do within the same job*

Job Enlargement   In job rotation, the employee is shifted from job to job, but the jobs are not changed. In **job enlargement**, on the other hand, the worker is given more things to do within the same job. For example, under job specialization, each worker on an assembly line might connect three wires to the product as it moves down the line. After job enlargement, each worker might connect five wires. Unfortunately, the added tasks are often just as routine as those that the workers performed before the change. In such cases, enlargement may not be effective. American Telephone & Telegraph, IBM, and the Maytag Co. have all experimented with job enlargement.

Job Enrichment   Job enrichment is perhaps the most advanced alternative to job specialization. Whereas job rotation and job enlargement do not really change the routine and monotonous nature of jobs, job enrichment does. **Job enrichment** is, in essence, providing workers with both more tasks to do and more control over how they do their work. In particular, under job enrichment many controls are removed from jobs, workers are given more authority, and work is assigned in complete, natural units. Moreover, employees are frequently given new and challenging job assignments. By blending more planning and decision making into jobs, job enrichment builds more depth and complexity into jobs. These changes tend to increase the employee's sense of responsibility and provide motivating opportunities for growth and advancement.

job enrichment   *providing workers with both more tasks to do and more control over how they do their work*

Job enrichment works best when employees seek more challenging work. Not all workers, however, respond positively to job enrichment programs. Employees must desire personal growth and have the skills and knowledge to perform enriched jobs. Lack of self-confidence, fear of failure, or distrust of management's intentions is likely to lead to ineffective performance of enriched jobs. The company that uses job enrichment as an alternative to specialization faces extra expenses such as the costs of retraining. Among the companies that have used job enrichment are General Foods and Texas Instruments.

Departmentalization

After jobs are designed, they must be grouped together into "working units" in keeping with the organization's goals. This process is called departmentalization. More specifically, **departmentalization** is the process of grouping jobs into manageable units according to some reasonable scheme. Several departmentalization schemes, or bases, are commonly used. And most firms use more than one of them. The groups of positions that result from the departmentalization process are usually called *departments*, although they are sometimes known as units, groups, or divisions.

departmentalization   *the process of grouping jobs into manageable units according to some reasonable scheme*

Departmentalization Bases

A **departmentalization basis** is the scheme or criterion by which jobs are grouped into units. The most common bases are function, product, location, and customer.

departmentalization basis   *the scheme or criterion by which jobs are grouped into units*

The Dixie Ti-Caro Yarns Group is the nation's biggest supplier of ring-spun, fine-count, singles, and plied yarns made from cotton, synthetic materials, or synthetic blends. This division of Dixie Yarns, Inc. is departmentalized based on both product and customer type.

departmentalization by function *the grouping together of all jobs that relate to the same organizational activity*

Learning Objective 4
Be aware of the various bases for departmentalization

departmentalization by product *the grouping together of all activities related to a particular product or product group*

By Function   **Departmentalization by function** is the grouping together of all jobs that relate to the same organizational activity. Under this scheme, all marketing personnel are grouped together in the marketing department, all production personnel are grouped into the production department, and so on.

Most smaller and newer organizations base their departmentalization on function. Such grouping permits each department to be efficiently staffed by experts. Supervision is simplified because everyone is involved in the same kinds of activities, and coordination is fairly easy. On the other hand, this method of grouping jobs can lead to slow decision making, and it tends to emphasize the department rather than the organization as a whole.

By Product   **Departmentalization by product** is the grouping together of all activities related to a particular product or product group. This scheme is often used by older and larger firms that produce and sell a variety of products. Each product department handles its own marketing, production, financial management, and human resources activities.

Departmentalization by product makes decision making easier and provides for the integration of all activities associated with each product or product group. However, it causes some duplication of specialized activities, such as finance, from department to department. And the emphasis is placed on the product rather than on the whole organization.

Digital Equipment Corporation, one of the largest computer manu-facturers in the world, was originally organized around eighteen separate product groups. Each product group competed with the others and became protective rather than cooperative. Instead of working for the common goals of the company, members of the product group were working for the good of the product group. As a result, the company's efficiency and profits suffered.

departmentalization by location *the grouping together of all activities according to the geographic area in which they are performed*

By Location   **Departmentalization by location** is the grouping together of all activities according to the geographic area in which they are performed. Departmental areas may range from whole countries (for multinational firms) to regions within countries (for national firms) to areas of several city blocks (for police departments organized into precincts). Departmen-talization by location allows the organization to respond readily to the unique demands or requirements of different locations. On the other hand, a large administrative staff and an elaborate control system may be needed to coordinate operations in many locations.

One of the ways that the president of Digital Equipment solved the problem of counterproductive product groups was to combine the twelve U.S. product groups into three regional management centers. This helped to clear up communication among different departments and consolidated much of the administrative paperwork, which had been slowing down important decisions.

departmentalization by customer *the grouping together of all activities according to the needs of various customer groups*

By Customer   **Departmentalization by customer** is the grouping together of all activities according to the needs of various customer groups. A car dealership, for example, may have one sales staff to deal with individual consumers and a different sales staff to work with corporate fleet buyers. The obvious advantage of this approach is that it allows the firm to deal efficiently with unique customers or customer groups. The biggest draw-back is that a larger-than-usual administrative staff is needed.

Another part of Digital Equipment's reorganization was the assigning of the sales force to specific customers rather than to specific markets. Before the reorganization, as many as six salespeople, each from a different product group, could call on one large customer. The situation was confusing and frustrating for customers, and not very profitable for Digital Equipment.

Using Combinations of Bases

Few organizations exhibit only one departmentalization base. In fact, many firms make use of several different bases within a single organization (see Figure 6.2). An example is General Motors Corp. GM has realigned its divisions into small-vehicle and large-vehicle groups. Each GM division, in turn, is departmentalized by function; each has its own marketing, finance, and personnel groups. Production groups might be further de-partmentalized by plant location, with each plant comprising an individual unit. Similarly, a divisional marketing group might be divided in such a

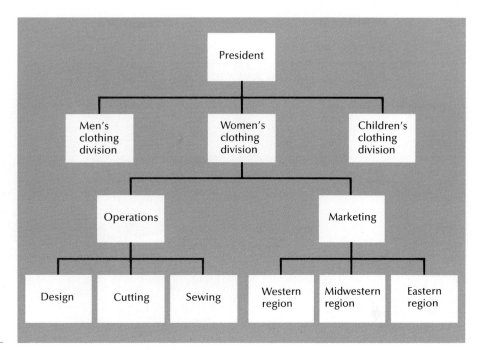

FIGURE 6.2
Multibase
Departmentalization
Most firms use more than one basis for departmentalization to improve efficiency and to avoid overlapping positions.

way that one unit handles consumer sales and another handles fleet and corporate sales.

All this adds up to the fact that multibase departmentalization is the rule rather than the exception for larger firms. Like every management tool, departmentalization is used however and wherever it will benefit the organization most.

Delegation, Decentralization, and Centralization

Learning Objective 5
Perceive how decentralization follows from delegation

The third major step in the organizing process is to distribute power in the organization. Delegation is the act of distributing power from management to subordinates. The degree of centralization or decentralization of authority is determined by the overall pattern of delegation within the organization.

Delegation of Authority

delegation the assigning of part of a manager's work and power to a subordinate

Delegation is the assigning of part of a manager's work and power to a subordinate. Because no manager can do everything alone, delegation is vital to the completion of a manager's work. Delegation is also important in developing the skills and abilities of subordinates. It allows those who are being groomed for higher-level positions to play increasingly important roles in decision making.

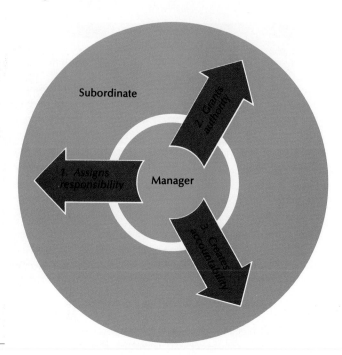

FIGURE 6.3
Steps in the Delegation Process
To be successful, a good manager must learn how to delegate. No one can do everything alone.

responsibility *the duty to do a job or perform a task*

authority *the power, within the organization, to accomplish an assigned job or task*

accountability *the obligation of a subordinate to accomplish an assigned job or task*

Steps in Delegation   Three steps are generally involved in the delegation process (see Figure 6.3). First, the manager must *assign responsibility*. **Responsibility** is the duty to do a job or perform a task. Along with assigning responsibility, the manager must *grant authority*. **Authority** is the power, within the organization, to accomplish an assigned job or task. This might include the power to obtain specific information, order supplies, authorize relevant expenditures, and make certain decisions. Finally, the manager must *create accountability*. **Accountability** is the obligation of a subordinate to accomplish an assigned job or task.

Note that accountability is created but that it cannot be delegated away. Suppose we are responsible for performing some job. We, in turn, delegate part of the work to a subordinate. We nonetheless remain accountable to our immediate superior for getting the job done properly. If our subordinate fails to complete the assignment, we—not the subordinate—will be called on to account for what has become *our* failure.

Barriers to Delegation   For several reasons, managers may be unwilling to delegate work. One reason is that the person who delegates remains accountable for the work. Many managers are reluctant to delegate simply because they want to be sure that the work gets done properly. In other words, they just don't trust their subordinates. Another reason for reluctance to delegate stems from the opposite situation: A manager may fear that a subordinate will do the work so well that he or she will attract the approving notice of top management and will become a threat to the manager. Finally, some managers don't delegate because they are so disorganized that they simply are not able to plan and assign work in an effective way.

Decentralization of Authority

The general pattern of delegation throughout an organization determines the extent to which that organization is decentralized or centralized. An organization in which management consciously attempts to spread authority widely in the lower organization levels is said to be a **decentralized organization.** An organization that systematically works to concentrate authority at the upper levels is said to be a **centralized organization.**

decentralized organization *an organization in which management consciously attempts to spread authority widely in the lower levels of the organization*

centralized organization *an organization that systematically works to concentrate authority at the upper levels of the organization*

A variety of factors can influence the extent to which a firm is decentralized. One is the external environment in which the firm operates. The more complex and unpredictable this environment is, the more likely it is that top management will let lower-level managers make important decisions. Another factor is the nature of the decision itself. The riskier the decision, the greater the tendency to centralize decision making. A third factor is the abilities of lower-level managers. If these managers do not have strong decision-making skills, top managers will be reluctant to decentralize. On the other hand, strong lower-level decision-making skills encourage decentralization. Finally, a firm that has traditionally practiced centralization is likely to maintain that centralization in the future, and vice versa.

Neither decentralization nor centralization is, in principle, either right or wrong. What works for one organization may or may not work for another. K mart Corporation, Toys "Я" Us, Inc., and McDonald's have all been very successful—and they all practice centralization. By the same token, decentralization has worked very well for General Electric, Du Pont, and Sears, Roebuck. Every organization must assess its own situation and then choose the level of centralization or decentralization that it feels will work best in that situation.

The Span of Management

span of management (or **span of control**) *the number of subordinates who report directly to one manager*

The fourth major dimension of organizational structure, the **span of management** (or **span of control**) is the number of subordinates who report directly to one manager. For hundreds of years, theorists have searched for an optimal span of management. When it became apparent that there is no perfect number of subordinates for a manager to supervise, they turned their attention to the more general issue of whether the span should be wide or narrow.

Wide and Narrow Spans of Control

Learning Objective 6
Understand the span of management and how it describes an organization

A *wide* span of management exists when a manager has a large number of subordinates. A *narrow* span exists when the manager has only a few subordinates. Several factors determine the span that is better for a particular manager (see Figure 6.4). Generally, the span should be narrow (1) when subordinates are physically located far from each other, (2) when the manager has much work to do in addition to supervising subordinates, (3) when a great deal of interaction is required between supervisor and

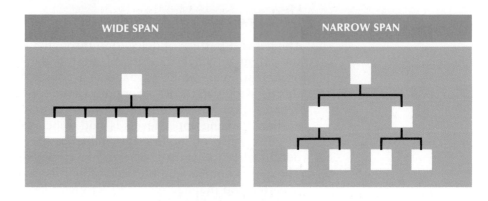

FIGURE 6.4
The Span of Management
Several criteria determine whether a firm uses a wide span of management, in which several subordinates report to one manager, or a narrow span, in which a manager has few subordinates.

Deciding factors

Physical dispersion
Managerial tasks
Interaction required
Frequency of new problems
Competence level
Existence of standard operating procedures

subordinates, and (4) when new problems arise frequently. The span of control may be wide (1) when the manager and the subordinates are very competent, (2) when the organization has a well-established set of standard operating procedures, and (3) when few new problems are expected to arise.

Organizational Height

organizational height *the number of layers, or levels, of management in a firm*

The span of management has an obvious impact on relations between superiors and subordinates. It has a more subtle but equally important impact on the height of the organization. **Organizational height** is the number of layers, or levels, of management in a firm. An organization with many layers of management is considered *tall*, whereas one with fewer layers is *flat*.

The span of management plays a direct role in determining the height of the organization, as shown in Figure 6.4. If spans of management are generally narrow, more levels are needed and the resulting organization is tall. If spans of management are wider, fewer levels are needed and the organization is flat.

In a taller organization, administrative costs are higher because more managers are needed. And communication among levels may become distorted because information has to pass up and down through more people. On the other hand, the managers in a flat organization may all have to perform more administrative duties simply because there are fewer managers. They may have to spend considerably more of their time supervising and working with subordinates.

Line and Staff Management

line management position
a position that is part of the chain of command and that includes direct responsibility for achieving the goals of the organization

staff management position
a position created to provide support, advice, and expertise within an organization

Our last major organizational dimension is the chain of command (or line of authority) that reaches from the uppermost to the lowest levels of management. A **line management position** is part of the chain of command; it's a position in which a person makes decisions and gives orders to subordinates to achieve the goals of the organization. A **staff management position,** by contrast, is a position created to provide support, advice, and expertise to someone in the chain of command. Staff positions are not part of the chain of command but do have authority over their assistants. Staff personnel are not specifically accountable for accomplishing the goals of the firm. A marketing executive is generally a line manager because marketing is directly related to accomplishing the firm's purpose, mission, and objectives. A legal advisor, however, doesn't actively engage in profit-making activities but rather provides legal support to those who do. Hence the legal advisor occupies a staff position (see Figure 6.5).

Line and Staff Positions Compared

Learning Objective 7
Comprehend the distinction between line and staff management

Both line and staff managers are needed for effective management, but there are important differences between the two kinds of positions. The basic difference is in terms of authority. Line managers have *line authority*, which means that they can make decisions and issue directives that relate to the organization's goals. Staff managers, on the other hand, seldom have this kind of authority. Instead, they usually have either advisory authority or functional authority.

FIGURE 6.5
Line and Staff Management
A line manager has direct responsibility for achieving the company's goals and is in the direct chain of command. A staff manager supports and advises the line managers.

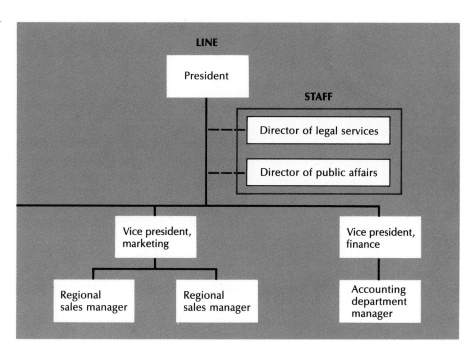

At Walgreens, employee relations attorneys (staff positions) are responsible for addressing and resolving employee complaints by working closely with district and store management (line positions). Here, Deidra Wasp, an employee relations attorney, confers with Mike Arnoult, the District Manager for Chicago.

Advisory authority is simply the expectation that line managers will consult the appropriate staff manager when making decisions. (Even so, line managers generally don't have to follow the advice they get from staff managers.) Functional authority is stronger, and in some ways it is like line authority. *Functional authority* is the authority of staff managers to make decisions and issue directives, but only about their own areas of expertise. For example, a legal advisor can decide whether to retain a particular clause in a contract, but not what price to charge for a new product. Contracts are part of the legal advisor's area of expertise; pricing is not.

Line-Staff Conflict

For a variety of reasons, conflict between line managers and staff managers is fairly common in business. Staff managers often have more formal education and are sometimes younger (and perhaps more ambitious) than line managers. Line managers may perceive staff managers as a threat to their own authority, or they may resent them. For their part, staff managers may become resentful if their expert recommendations—in public relations or human resources management, for example—are not adopted by line management.

Fortunately, there are several ways to minimize the possibility of such conflict. One way is to integrate line and staff managers into one team working together on problems. Another is to ensure that the areas of responsibility of line and staff managers are clearly defined. Finally, line and staff managers can both be held accountable for the results of their activities.

Other Elements
of Organizational Structure

We have now discussed the five major dimensions of organizational structure. In this section we shall look at three other elements of organization: work schedules, committees, and coordination techniques (see Table 6.1).

Work Schedules

To most people, *work schedule* means the standard 9 A.M.-to-5 P.M. forty-hour workweek. In reality, though, many people have work schedules that are quite different from this. Police officers, firefighters, restaurant per-

TABLE 6.1   *Eight Dimensions of Organizational Structure*

Dimension	Purpose
Job design	To divide the work performed by an organization into parts and assign each part a position within the organization. Job specialization, job rotation, job enlargement, and job enrichment are key elements in the job design process.
Departmentalization	To group various positions in an organization into manageable units. Departmentalization may be based on function, product, location, customer, or a combination of these bases.
Delegation	To distribute part of a manager's work and power to subordinates. A deliberate concentration of authority at the upper levels of the organization creates a centralized structure. A wide distribution of authority into the lower levels of the organization creates a decentralized structure.
Span of management	To set the number of subordinates who report directly to one manager. A narrow span has only a few subordinates reporting to one manager. A wide span has a large number of subordinates reporting to one manager.
Line and staff management	To distinguish between those positions that are part of the chain of command and those that provide support, advice, or expertise to those in the chain of command.
Work schedules	To assign the time in which a subordinate is to perform assigned responsibilities. A compressed workweek, a flexible workweek, and job sharing are three alternatives to the traditional 9 A.M.-to-5 P.M. forty-hour workweek.
Committees	To accomplish a specific task by assigning it to a group of individuals within the organization.
Coordination techniques	To coordinate organizational resources to minimize duplication and maximize effectiveness. Managerial hierarchy, rules and procedures, liaisons, and committees are four coordination techniques.

sonnel, airline employees, and medical personnel, for example, usually have work schedules that are far from standard. Some manufacturers also rotate personnel from shift to shift. And many professional people—such as managers, artists, and lawyers—work more than forty hours per week because they need the extra time to get their work done or simply because they want to.

In recent years, organizations have begun to experiment with alternative work schedules. One such schedule is called the compressed workweek. A **compressed workweek** is an arrangement whereby an employee works a full forty hours per week, but in less than the standard five days. The most common variation is to have people work ten hours per day for four days and then give them a three-day weekend.

A second alternative work schedule is called the flexible workweek. A **flexible workweek** is an arrangement in which each employee chooses the hours during which he or she will work, subject to certain limitations. Typically the firm establishes two bands of time: the *core time*, when all employees must be at work, and the *flexible time*, when employees may choose whether to be at work. The only condition is that every employee must work a total of eight hours per day. For example, the hours between 9 and 11 A.M. and 1 and 3 P.M. might be core time, whereas the hours between 6 and 9 A.M., between 11 A.M. and 1 P.M., and between 3 and 6 P.M. might be flexible time. This would give employees the option of coming in early and getting off early, coming in later and leaving later, or simply taking extra-long lunch hours. But it would also ensure that everyone would be present at certain times, when conferences with supervisors and department meetings could be held.

Finally, some firms are experimenting with job sharing, which is similar to permanent part-time work in some ways. **Job sharing** is an arrangement whereby two people share one full-time position. One person may work from 8 A.M. to noon and the other from 1 to 5 P.M. Job sharing provides the security of a permanent job along with the flexibility of a part-time job. It is of special interest to parents who want more time with their children and people who simply desire more leisure time. For the firm, it provides an opportunity to attract highly skilled employees who might not be available on a full-time basis.

Committees

Several types of committees can be used within an organizational structure. An **ad hoc committee** is a committee created for a specific short-term purpose, such as reviewing the firm's employee benefits plan. Once its work is finished, the ad hoc committee disbands. A **standing committee** is a relatively permanent committee charged with performing some recurring task. A firm might establish a budget review committee, for example, to review departmental budget requests on an ongoing basis. Finally, a **task force** is a committee established to investigate a major problem or pending decision. If a firm were contemplating a merger with another company, it might form a task force to assess the pros and cons of the merger.

Margin glossary:

compressed workweek *an arrangement whereby an employee works a full forty hours per week, but in less than the standard five days*

flexible workweek *an arrangement in which each employee chooses the hours during which he or she will work, subject to certain limitations*

job sharing *an arrangement whereby two people share one full-time position*

ad hoc committee *a committee created for a specific short-term purpose*

standing committee *a relatively permanent committee charged with performing some recurring task*

task force *a committee established to investigate a major problem or pending decision*

Committees offer some advantages over individual action. Their several members are, of course, able to bring more information and knowledge to the task at hand. Furthermore, committees tend to make more accurate decisions and to transmit their results through the organization more effectively. On the other hand, committee deliberations take much longer than individual actions. Unnecessary compromise may take place within the committee. Or the opposite may occur as one person dominates (and thus negates) the committee process.

Coordination Techniques

managerial hierarchy *the arrangement that provides increasing authority at higher levels of management*

Our final element of organization is the *coordination of organizational resources*, which is the integration of resources to minimize duplication and maximize effectiveness. Several coordination techniques have proved useful. One technique is simply to make use of the **managerial hierarchy,** which is the arrangement that provides increasing authority at higher levels of management. One manager is placed in charge of all the resources that are to be coordinated. That person is able to coordinate them by virtue of the authority accompanying that position.

Resources can also be coordinated through rules and procedures. For example, a rule can govern how a firm's travel budget is to be allocated. This particular resource, then, would be coordinated in terms of that rule.

In complex situations, more sophisticated coordination techniques may be called for. One approach is to establish a liaison. Recall from Chapter 5 that a liaison is a go-between—a person who coordinates the activities of two groups. Suppose Ford Motor Company is negotiating a complicated contract with a supplier of steering wheels. The supplier might appoint a liaison whose primary responsibility is to coordinate the contract negotiations. Finally, for *very* complex coordination needs, a committee (that is, a task force) could be established. Suppose Ford is in the process of purchasing the steering-wheel supplier. In this case a task force might be appointed to integrate the new firm into Ford's larger organizational structure.

Forms of Organizational Structure

Learning Objective 8
Grasp the three basic forms of organizational structure: bureaucratic, organic, and matrix

Up to this point, we have focused our attention on the major dimensions of organizational structure. In many ways, this is like discussing the important parts of a jigsaw puzzle one by one. Now it is time to put the puzzle together. In particular, we discuss three basic forms of organizational structure: bureaucratic, organic, and matrix.

The Bureaucratic Structure

The term *bureaucracy* is often used in an unfavorable context, and it tends to suggest rigidity and red tape. This image may be a negative one, but it does capture something of the bureaucratic structure.

BUSINESS JOURNAL

Demassing: Building a Lean, Mean, Competitive Machine

Besides shutting down, how can a company cut costs? Today many companies have found demassing to be effective in reducing budgets. *Demassing,* or downsizing, refers to reducing an organization's staff. This can lead to quicker decision making, more precise accountability, and harder-working employees. Why don't more companies downsize their labor forces? It is because demassing, if not planned and carried out carefully, can produce more disadvantages than advantages, and it can ruin a firm's reputation.

Du Pont, Monsanto Company, and Union Carbide have all successfully demassed their companies. Initially demassing is expensive, since most companies must make severance payments and fund retirement plans. Du Pont spent $125 million in the first quarter after demassing; Union Carbide spent $70 million. However, Du Pont saves about $230 million each year, while Union Carbide saves approximately $250 million annually.

After a business is involved in an acquisition or merger, there may be an excess of personnel. Technological innovations or automation may mean that fewer workers are needed. A sluggish economy and a dynamic business environment might cause a company to be highly cost competitive. Any one of these factors, or a combination, should make a business consider demassing.

Demassing can take a number of forms: early retirement programs, transfers to other locations, hiring freezes, pay and benefit reductions, and terminations. Whatever methods a company uses must be studied thoroughly. Many companies avoid demassing because terminations can be painful and stressful. Managers do not like firing subordinates because it reduces their own responsibility (less people will report to them), poses a potential threat to their own job security, and because it is personally difficult to deprive a colleague of a job.

Demassing is not easy to reverse. Therefore, management should consider long-term market situations and other factors like the size of the company, impact on terminated *and* retained employees, and impact on the competition. If a company does make the decision to downsize, it should follow these guidelines:

1. Form a strategy.
2. Consider alternatives.
3. Identify who will be kept, transferred, and terminated. There should be set criteria for these decisions. Management should take into account job analyses, seniority, work appraisals, and market forecasts.
4. Develop good communications with employees. Communication is vital to demassing. Employees should be well informed.
5. Allow a sufficient time for demassing to occur.
6. Assist displaced employees through résumé workshops, placement programs, and opportunities for counseling.
7. Provide early-retirement and voluntary-separation incentives.
8. Follow up demassing by building the confidence and morale of the remaining workers.

A company must deal with its present and former employees equitably and compassionately. If it does not, it runs the double risk of putting current workers in a constant state of fear and of driving away potential employees. Also, the community where a company is located can be affected by demassing. An effective information program should be used to ensure that the community, customers, shareholders, and suppliers are accurately informed.

Based on information from Ronald Henkoff, "Cost Cutting: How to Do It Right," *Fortune,* April 9, 1990, pp. 40–43+; Steven H. Appelbaum, Roger Simpson, and Barbara T. Shapiro, "Downsizing: The Ultimate Human Resource Strategy," *Business Quarterly,* Fall 1987, pp. 52–60; Thomas Moore, "Goodbye, Corporate Staff," *Fortune,* December 21, 1987, p. 65; and Lester C. Thurow, "White-Collar Overhead," *Across the Board,* November 1986, pp. 25–27, 30–32.

bureaucratic structure
a management system based on a formal framework of authority that is carefully outlined and precisely followed

A **bureaucratic structure** is a management system based on a formal framework of authority that is carefully outlined and precisely followed. In terms of the major structural dimensions, a bureaucracy is likely to have the following characteristics:

1. A high level of job specialization
2. Departmentalization by function
3. Precise and formal patterns of delegation
4. A high degree of centralization
5. Narrow spans of management, resulting in a tall organization
6. Clearly defined line and staff positions, with formal relationships between the two

Perhaps the best examples of contemporary bureaucracies are government agencies, colleges, and universities. Consider the very rigid and formal college entrance and registration procedures. The reason for such procedures is to ensure that the organization is able to deal with large numbers of people in an equitable and fair manner. We may not enjoy them, but regulations and standard operating procedures pretty much guarantee uniformity.

The biggest drawback to the bureaucratic structure is its lack of flexibility. The bureaucracy has trouble adjusting to change and coping with the unexpected. Because today's business environment is dynamic and complex, many firms have found that the bureaucratic structure is not appropriate.

The Organic Structure

organic structure   *a management system founded on cooperation and knowledge-based authority*

An **organic structure** is a management system founded on cooperation and knowledge-based authority. It is much less formal than the bureaucracy and much more flexible. An organic structure tends to have the following structural dimensions:

1. A low level of job specialization
2. Departmentalization by product, location, or customer
3. General and informal patterns of delegation
4. A high degree of decentralization
5. Wide spans of management, resulting in a flat organization
6. Less clearly defined line and staff positions, with less formal relationships between the two

The organic structure tends to be more effective when the environment of the firm is complex and dynamic. This structure allows the organization to monitor the environment and react quickly to changes. Of course, the organic structure requires more cooperation among employees than the bureaucracy does. Employees must be willing and able to work together in an informal atmosphere where lines of authority may shift according to the situation.

The Matrix Structure

The matrix structure is the newest and most complex organizational structure. Its hallmark is a multiple command system, in which individuals report to more than one superior at the same time. The **matrix structure** is an organizational structure that combines vertical and horizontal lines of authority. The matrix structure occurs when product departmentalization is superimposed on a functionally departmentalized organization. In a matrix organization, authority flows both down and across.

To see what this is like, first consider the usual functional arrangement, with people working in departments such as marketing and finance. Now suppose we assign people from these departments to a special group that is working on a new project as a team. This special group is really a product department. The manager in charge of the group is usually called a *project manager*. Any individual who is working with the group reports *both* to the project manager and to his or her superior in the functional department (see Figure 6.6).

A matrix structure usually evolves through four stages. At first the firm is organized simply as a functional structure. Then a smaller number of interdepartmental groups are created to work on especially important projects. Next, more groups are created, and they become an integral and important part of the organization. Finally, the firm becomes what is called a *mature matrix*. In the mature matrix, project managers and functional managers have equal authority. Some employees float (or shift) from group to group without ever being "tied" to a particular functional department. Eventually the activities of the project teams become the major focus of the organization.

Many firms have experimented with matrix structures. Notable examples include Texas Instruments, Monsanto, and Chase Manhattan Bank.

matrix structure   *an organizational structure that combines vertical and horizontal lines of authority by superimposing product departmentalization on a functionally departmentalized organization*

FIGURE 6.6
A Matrix Organization
A matrix is usually the result of combining product departmentalization with function departmentalization. It is a complex structure in which employees have more than one supervisor. (Source: Ricky W. Griffin, Management, *3/e. Copyright © 1990 by Houghton Mifflin Company. Used by permission.)*

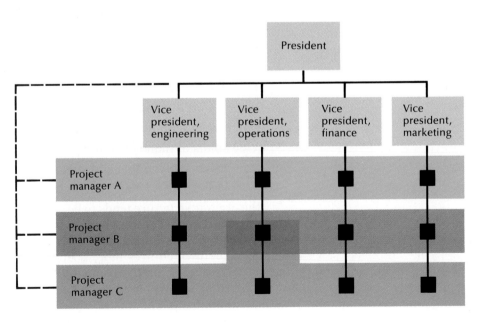

Matrix structures offer several advantages over the conventional organizational forms. Added flexibility is probably the most obvious advantage. Motivation also improves because people become more deeply committed to their special projects. In addition, employees experience personal development through doing a variety of jobs. And people communicate more as they become liaisons between their project groups and their functional departments.

The matrix structure also has some disadvantages. The multiple command system can cause confusion about who has authority in various situations. Like committees, groups may take longer to resolve problems and issues than individuals working alone. And, because more managers and support staff may be needed, a matrix structure may be more expensive to maintain than a conventional structure. All things considered, though, the matrix appears to offer a number of benefits to business. It is likely that in the future more and more firms will begin to explore and experiment with this innovative method of organization.

Intrapreneurship

Since innovations are important to companies, and entrepreneurs are among the most innovative people around, it seems almost natural that an entrepreneurial character would prominently surface in many of today's larger organizations. An **intrapreneur,** in essence an entrepreneur working in an organizational environment, develops an idea into a product and manages the product within the firm.[2] An intrapreneur possesses the confidence and drive of an entrepreneur but is allowed to use organizational resources for idea development.

Arthur Fry, inventor of the colorful Post-it Notes that are now seen in offices everywhere, is a devoted advocate of intrapreneurship. Nurturing his note-pad idea at 3M for years, Fry speaks highly of the intrapreneurial commitment at 3M. On being an intrapreneur, Fry says, "First you need a product champion to get that core vision going. Then, you need the facilities that 3M has and a willingness to pull the concept together."[3] Fry suggests that an intrapreneur is an individual who doesn't have all the skills to get the job done, and, thus, has to work within an organization, making use of its skills and attributes.

Arthur Fry, inventor at 3M, developed Post-it Notes in 1980. 3M is a leader in encouraging intrapreneurship. Today, intrapreneur Fry continues to work on extensions of this highly successful product.

intrapreneur *an entrepreneur working in an organizational environment who develops an idea into a product and manages the product within the firm*

The Informal Organization

So far we have discussed the organization as a more or less formal structure consisting of positions and relationships among those positions. This is the organization that is shown on an organization chart. There is another kind of organization, however, that does not show up on any chart. We shall define this **informal organization** as the pattern of behavior and interaction that stems from personal rather than official relationships. Firmly embedded within every informal organization are informal groups and the notorious grapevine.

informal organization *the pattern of behavior and interaction that stems from personal rather than official relationships*

Informal Groups

informal group *a group created by the members themselves to accomplish goals that may or may not be relevant to the organization*

A formal group is one that is created by the organization to help accomplish the organization's goals. Such groups as departments, task forces, and committees are thus formal groups. On the other hand, an **informal group** is one that is created by the members of the group themselves to accomplish goals that may or may not be relevant to the organization. Workers may create an informal group to go bowling, play softball, form a union, get a particular manager fired or transferred, or have lunch together every day. The group may last for several years or only a few hours.

Learning Objective 9
Define what an informal organization is and how it operates through informal groups and the grapevine

Employees choose to join informal groups for a variety of reasons. Perhaps the main reason is that people like to be with others who are similar to themselves. The activities of a particular group may also be appealing. (A person who likes to bowl may be inclined to join a group of Thursday night bowlers.) Or it may be that the goals of the group appeal to the individual. (If a group has been formed to try to get the company to install a new cafeteria, and if a particular employee happens to think a new cafeteria is needed, he or she will probably join the group.) Others may join informal groups simply because they have a need to be with their associates and be accepted by them.

Informal groups can be powerful forces in organizations. They can restrict output, or they can help managers through tight spots. They can cause disagreement and conflict, or they can help boost morale and job satisfaction. They can show new people how to contribute to the organization, or they can help people get away with substandard performance. Clearly, managers should be aware of these informal groups. Those who make the mistake of fighting the informal organization have a major obstacle to overcome.

The Grapevine

grapevine *the informal communications network within an organization*

The **grapevine** is the informal communications network within an organization. It is completely separate from—and sometimes much faster than—the organization's formal channels of communication. Formal communication usually follows a path that parallels the organizational chain of command. By contrast, information can be transmitted through the grapevine in any direction—up, down, diagonally, or horizontally across the organizational structure. Subordinates may pass information to their bosses, an executive may relay something to a maintenance worker, or there may be an exchange of information between people who work in totally unrelated departments.

Grapevine information may be concerned with topics ranging from the latest management decisions to the results of today's World Series game to pure gossip. It can be important or of little interest. And it can be highly accurate or totally distorted and inaccurate.

How should managers treat the grapevine? Certainly they would be making a big mistake if they tried to eliminate it. Wherever people work together day in and day out, they are going to communicate. And even if a manager could eliminate informal communication at work, employees

BUSINESS JOURNAL

The Intrapreneur—Going Out on a High Wire . . . with a Safety Net

There's a confident, quick-thinking hero on the American business scene. This hero mixes the creativity, daring, innovation, and spirit of an independent entrepreneur with the structure, skills, experience, and financial strength of a company team player. America's competitive edge and the productivity of individual businesses may rest on the shoulders of the intrapreneur.

Intrapreneurship is the means by which an organization identifies, supports, and promotes original ideas and new products. In a sense, an existing company transforms an employee's dream into a business venture. If intrapreneurship sounds like a variation of entrepreneurship, it is because these two have much in common. Typically, both intrapreneurs and entrepreneurs are strong-minded, independent, goal-oriented persons. Both take risks, and both stand the chance of reaping great benefits if their ideas are successful.

There are also extreme differences between the two. Intrapreneurs dwell in big companies with established corporate cultures. These large companies have consistent policies and bureaucratic procedures that, even though they may bog down the creative process, are effective safeguards against production and marketing mistakes. An intrapreneur can explore new ideas with the safety net of job security. Entrepreneurs are on their own, risking their personal finances in an inconsistent and highly pressurized environment. There are no set procedures and no support systems. Patience is a must for the intrapreneur; too much patience may destroy the drive of the entrepreneur. Entrepreneurs need no one's approval for action, and, though large businesses might frown on change, change to an entrepreneur almost always is a sign of progress. When an entrepreneur fails, there is no stable job to go back to.

Companies in a variety of fields are anxious to cultivate a successful intrapreneurial culture. To develop the right climate for intrapreneurs, management should follow six steps.

1. Management should encourage new ideas and should be willing to accept these ideas from anyone voicing them.

2. Management should become practiced at screening these new ideas so that resources—time, equipment, and money—may be allocated efficiently. Also, screening will let managers gauge the amount of support a venture can garner.

3. Management should actively support idea development by rewarding achievements and recognizing even small accomplishments.

4. Managers should encourage flexibility; they should try to find the proper combination of project control and entrepreneurial freedom. Many sound ideas have succumbed to strict company regulations.

5. Management should generously reward any and all contributors to a new idea or product. This reward can take the shape of a bonus, salary increase, or more research freedom.

6. Management must be fully committed to innovation. It should be willing to provide leadership and promote creativity.

Based on information from Ira D. Hill, "An Intrapreneur-Turned-Entrepreneur Compares Both Worlds," *Research Management,* May–June 1987, pp. 33–37; "Lessons from a Successful Intrapreneur," *Journal of Business Strategy,* March/April 1988, pp. 20–24; Joel E. Ross and Darab Unwalla, "Who Is an Intrapreneur?" *Personnel,* December 1986, pp. 45–49; and Erik G. Rule and Donald W. Irwin, "Fostering Intrapreneurship: The New Competitive Edge," *Journal of Business Strategy,* May/June 1988, pp. 44–47.

would still get together and talk outside the office. A more rational approach is to recognize the existence of the grapevine as a part—though an unofficial part—of the organization. For example, managers should respond promptly and aggressively to inaccurate grapevine information to minimize the damage that such misinformation might do. Moreover, the grapevine can come in handy when managers are on the receiving end of important communications from the informal organization.

CHAPTER REVIEW

Summary

Organizing is the process of grouping resources and activities to accomplish some end in an efficient and effective manner. The purpose of this process is to mold an organizational structure, which is a fixed pattern of positions and relationships. An organization chart is a diagram that represents the organizational structure. The five steps in the organizing process result in five basic dimensions of organizational structure. These are degree of job specialization, nature and degree of departmentalization, degree of centralization, the span of management, and the chain of command as determined by line-staff arrangements.

Job specialization is the separation of all the activities within the organization into smaller component parts and the assignment of different components to different people. Several factors combine to make specialization a useful technique for designing jobs, but high levels of specialization may cause employee dissatisfaction and boredom. Techniques for overcoming these problems include job rotation, job enlargement, and job enrichment.

Departmentalization is the grouping of jobs into manageable units according to some reasonable scheme or basis. These bases include departmentalization by function, product, location, and customer. Because each of these bases provides particular advantages, most firms use different bases in different organizational situations.

Delegation is the assigning of part of a manager's work to a subordinate. It involves the assignment of responsibility, the granting of authority, and the creation of accountability. A decentralized firm is one that delegates as much power as possible to people in the lower management levels. In a centralized firm, on the other hand, power is systematically retained at the upper levels.

The span of management is the number of subordinates who report directly to a manager. Spans are generally characterized as wide (many subordinates per manager) or narrow (few subordinates per manager). Wide spans generally result in flat organizations (few layers of management); narrow spans generally result in tall organizations (many layers of management).

A line position is one that is in the organization's chain of command (line of authority), whereas a staff position is supportive in nature. Staff positions may carry some authority, but it usually applies only within staff areas of expertise.

Additional elements that must be considered in structuring an organization are the establishment of work schedules, use of committees, and techniques for achieving coordination among various groups within the organization.

There are three basic forms of organizational structure. The bureaucratic structure is characterized by formality and rigidity. The organic structure is characterized by flexibility. And the newer matrix structure may be visualized as product departmentalization superimposed on functional departmentalization. An intrapreneur is an entrepreneur working in an organizational environment to develop an idea into a product.

The informal organization consists of social and personal interactions within the more formal organizational structure. Key aspects of the informal organization are informal groups created by the group members themselves and the grapevine, which is an informal information network. Managers must recognize the existence of the informal organization and even learn to use the grapevine to their advantage.

In the next chapter, we apply these and other management concepts to an extremely important business function: the production of goods and services.

Key Terms

You should now be able to define and give an example relevant to each of the following terms:

organization
organizational structure
organization chart
chain of command
job specialization
job rotation
job enlargement
job enrichment
departmentalization
departmentalization basis
departmentalization by function
departmentalization by product
departmentalization by location
departmentalization by customer
delegation
responsibility
authority
accountability
decentralized organization
centralized organization

span of management (or span of control)
organizational height
line management position
staff management position
compressed workweek
flexible workweek
job sharing
ad hoc committee
standing committee
task force
managerial hierarchy
bureaucratic structure
organic structure
matrix structure
intrapreneur
informal organization
informal group
grapevine

Questions and Exercises

Review Questions

1. In what way do organization charts illustrate our definition of organizational structure?
2. What determines the degree of specialization within an organization?
3. Describe and contrast the three alternatives to job specialization.
4. What are the major differences among the four departmentalization bases?
5. Why do most firms employ several departmentalization bases?
6. What three steps are involved in delegation? Explain each.
7. How does a firm's top management influence its degree of centralization?

8. How is organizational height related to the span of management?
9. What are the key differences between line and staff positions and the authority their occupants wield?
10. Describe three alternatives to the standard five-day, forty-hour workweek.
11. How may the managerial hierarchy be used to coordinate the organization's resources?
12. Contrast the bureaucratic and organic forms of organizational structure.
13. Which form of organizational structure would probably lead to the strongest informal organization? Why?

Discussion Questions

1. Why is Burger King being reorganized at the corporate level?
2. What major problems is Burger King hoping to resolve through its reorganization?
3. Explain how the five steps of the organizing process determine the dimensions of the resulting organizational structure. Which steps are most important?
4. Which kinds of firms would probably operate most effectively as centralized firms? as decentralized firms?
5. How do decisions concerning work schedules, the use of committees, and coordination techniques affect organizational structure?
6. How might a manager go about formalizing the informal organization?

Exercises

1. Draw the organizational chart for the academic institution that you are attending. State your assumptions if you must make them.
2. Chart your own workweek and determine what type it is (standard, compressed, or flexible).

Case 6.1

Western Union's Reorganization

Although Western Union Corporation is nearly 140 years old, its future may be anything but old-fashioned. A recent radical reorganization of the ailing company may halt its losses and transform it into a high-tech communications leader.

Company president and CEO Robert J. Amman's first move to bring the company back to health was the purchase of ITT World Communications Inc. for

$178 million, which brought more modern technology to Western Union.

Amman's restructuring plan divides Western Union's services into totally separate business units that operate independently. The five new units are Business Communications Services, Consumer Communications and Financial Services, Priority Mail Services, Advanced Transmission Systems, and Network Services. Business Communications, the largest group, is responsible for international and domestic telex services and the EasyLink electronic mail service. Consumer Communications handles money transfer services, Mailgrams (telegrams delivered by the postal service), and telegrams for the public through Western Union's nationwide network of 11,000 agents. Priority Mail Services provides commercial Mailgrams, computer letters to businesses, and priority letters. Advanced Transmissions is involved in building and operating fiber-optic telecommunication facilities, and Network Services is marketing Western Union's international transmission service.

To cut company costs, Amman trimmed Western Union's work force by 25 percent, laying off about 1,800 workers. The layoffs, which eliminated overlapping jobs, affected almost every job category. By working closely with union representatives, Western Union was able to avoid labor disputes and draw up new labor contracts without much trouble.

In a further attempt to cut costs, Amman also closed down Western Union's nationwide microwave network and sold the company's four-satellite network. He also unloaded its little-known but expensive-to-operate domestic long-distance service.

Once on the verge of bankruptcy, Western Union is now committed to innovation—operational as well as technological. Western Union executives plan to implement many new ideas that they hope will save money and make the company more competitive. Amman thinks the company's $300-million telegram and money-transfer businesses will grow even faster with a new money-order service and a service that allows customers to obtain cash advances with their credit cards.*

---

* Based on information from Betsy August, "Western Union Says Its Merger Spurred Cuts," *The Record* (Hackensack, N.J.), April 14, 1988; Neil Barsky, "Western Union Wire: Hit the Road, Workers," *New York Daily News*, April 14, 1988; John T. Harding, "Western Union to Cut Workforce by 25%," *Star-Ledger* (Newark, N.J.), April 13, 1988; John J. Keller, "Bob Amman Tries to Reinvent the Onion," *Business Week*, June 13, 1988, p. 33.

Questions

1. What are the major objectives of Western Union's restructuring of its organization?
2. Evaluate Amman's decision to establish separate business units within Western Union.

Case 6.2

Travelers Insurance Seeks Better Communication and Coordination Through Technology

Travelers Insurance Co. entered the personal-computer age several years ago when an insurance agent in Ohio said he'd like to compute auto insurance premiums on his Apple computer. Working weekends, a Travelers executive developed a modest program that he sent to the Ohio agent on a diskette. Soon a dozen agents were using the program to figure premiums faster and more accurately.

Now there are 35,000 computer terminals in use at Travelers, both at the company's Hartford, Connecticut, home office and in the field. Unlike the managers at many U.S. corporations who hesitate to get involved with personal computers (or "PCs"), Travelers executives have been enthusiastic. They are working to transform their employees from transaction processors into knowledge workers. They plan to take office technology beyond office automation and into office communications. Travelers officials feel that the productivity of both the clerical staff and knowledge workers will greatly improve because of technical advancements. They think that business quality depends on efficient communications within and between departments, and on competent decision making among knowledge workers.

About 5,000 of Travelers' personal computers are owned by independent Travelers agents. The PCs calculate premiums for agents and provide immediate printouts for clients, showing rates and coverages. Agents using PCs have a better bottom line than those agents who mail in paperwork.

Travelers concedes, however, that while the PCs have unquestionably improved productivity, they have also introduced a new set of problems. Some agents, for example, feel pressure to buy PCs but then experience frustration when the PCs don't provide immediate solutions to their problems. Agents also complain that sales drop when they take time out to learn to operate the PCs. In addition, the agents are realizing that their present hardware will eventually have to be replaced with newer systems that may be more expensive and more complicated.

These complaints, though, will not affect Travelers' aggressive charge into the electronic age. Voice mail, teleconferencing, and a substantial telecommunications program have already been introduced at Travelers. All of these will act as tools that knowledge workers will be able to use to process important information more rapidly.

Managers at Travelers have also experimented with interactive video stations. These stations house computer terminals that respond to a person's touch. After completing a question-and-answer session, the potential customer is provided with an appropriate insurance quote. The customer can anonymously select information on home owners', automobile, term, or universal life insurance, and estimates on home replacement costs. Officials at Travelers are currently testing these stations and, after analyzing the results, will make adjustments.

Having spent more than $100 million on agency automation, Travelers is committed to the complex process of changing the way its work is done. Because of more direct communication between agents and the home office, for example, Travelers has reduced the number of its field offices from about ninety to fifteen. Company analysts now examine total agency performance, instead of just individual policies. The company also provides technical support to employees and agents, and offers an incentive loan program to help agents buy electronic equipment. Travelers isn't pushing its employees to become computer technicians, but the company does intend to use available technology to reduce inefficiencies. Integration is the key to Travelers' future. Executives feel confident that productivity and quality will be improved if they can effectively integrate technologies, business plans, products, and services with customer needs.†

Questions

1. In your opinion, what sort of work should a computer do, and what sort of work should people do?
2. Imagine that the CEO of a large firm could look at the reports, decisions, and budgets of any manager at any level in his firm. What effect would that have on his span of control?

---

† Based on information from Barbara Tzivanis Benham, "Telecommuting: There's No Place Like Home," *Best's Review*, May 1988, pp. 46, 48; William Bowen, "The Puny Payoff from Office Computers," *Fortune*, May 26, 1986, pp. 20–24; Joseph T. Brophy, "Linking Knowledge Workers and Information Technology," *Office*, September 1987, pp. 88, 90; Joseph T. Brophy and Trav Waltrip, "Linking the Knowledge Work Force," *Best's Review*, November 1986, pp. 56–57; Lynn G. Coleman, "Interactive Video May Make Insurance Agents Obsolete," *Marketing News*, July 17, 1987, p. 2; "H-P Asks: Can We Create a Less Technical Environment?" *Management Review*, December 1986, p. 18; and Ron Winslow, "Everybody with a PC," *Wall Street Journal*, September 16, 1985, p. 28ff.

OPERATIONS MANAGEMENT

1 Understand the nature of operations management

2 Be able to outline the conversion process, which transforms input resources into products

3 Recognize the need for research and development, and know the activities it includes

4 Distinguish between the two phases of operations planning: design planning and operational planning

5 Know the four major areas of operations control: purchasing, inventory control, scheduling, and quality control

6 Understand the increasing role of automation and robotics in production processes

7 Be aware of the reasons for recent trends in productivity and identify some methods of enhancing productivity

CHAPTER PREVIEW

We begin this chapter with an overview of operations management—the activities that are involved in the conversion of resources into products. We describe the technology or conversion systems that make production possible and also note the growing role of services in our economy. Then we examine more closely three important aspects of operations management: developing ideas for new products, planning product design and production facilities, and effectively controlling operations once production has begun. Next, we discuss changes in production as a result of automation, robotics, and computer-aided manufacturing. We close the chapter with a look at productivity trends and ways productivity can be improved.

INSIDE BUSINESS

Hoover Company Achieves High Quality, Low Costs Through High-Tech Automation

The Hoover Co., a division of The Maytag Corporation that has long held the number-one position in market share for upright vacuum cleaners, has no intention of relinquishing its lead. Recently Hoover spent $38 million to modernize its manufacturing plants with state-of-the-art equipment. It has deployed this machinery so efficiently that Hoover now has not only the most sophisticated vacuum-cleaner plant but also one of the most advanced manufacturing facilities in the United States. "What we have refined and learned in regard to manufacturing and engineering interface are lessons that won't be lost on future projects," says the manager responsible for Hoover's manufacturing in the United States.

Hoover took a significant risk by investing so heavily in high tech, and the investment is providing significant returns. At Hoover's North Canton, Ohio factory, a complex assembly-line mixture of workers, robots, and conveyer belts creates a Hoover Elite cleaner in half the time it took to assemble one of the previous models. With redesigned products, simplified production methods, and improved manufacturing, Hoover workers can now make a cleaner that weighs 26 percent less than its predecessor and has much fewer parts. For instance, fifty-six fasteners used to hold an old model together, while twelve do the same job in the new Elites. A system of robotics installs the complex wiring that provides improved quality and speed in the new cleaners. The production cycle rarely slows since changes that differentiate each new cleaner model are worked into the assembly process at a later stage.

At each work station in the highly integrated plant are computers that "communicate" with each other. Hoover officials call this setup a "factory-within-a-factory" system and are very pleased with the results. Eventually, engineers will link the factory-within-a-factory system to other shop-floor systems and departments.

Hoover's own manufacturing resource planners had to rearrange about 250,000 square feet of plant space to accommodate its new assembly line. Although entire departments had to be relocated, daily plant operations were never interrupted.

Hoover managers claim that the system has improved product quality tremendously. Computers inspect each unit at every level of production. Workers also check sixteen important characteristics on each unit before they package it. A separate quality-appraisal department randomly samples cleaners and completely disassembles them to make sure that units made at similar times are defect-free.[1]

*T*he use of automation by U.S. manufacturers such as Hoover is increasing. Robots and other types of automated production devices are helping U.S. producers become more efficient. Automation is allowing manufacturers like Hoover to cut their production costs and to improve significantly the quality of their products.

Operations management encompasses numerous activities. Transforming new materials and other resources into goods and services is a part of operations management. The purpose of this transformation of resources into goods and services is to provide utility to customers. **Utility** is the ability of a product to satisfy a human need. Although there are four types of utility—form, place, time, and possession—operations management and production focus primarily on the creation of form utility. **Form utility** is created by converting production inputs into finished products. Controlling product quality is another prime responsibility of operations managers. A firm that consistently produces goods or services of poor quality will, at the very least, lose customers in droves. In more extreme cases, faulty goods or services may involve a firm in costly legal battles.

Another key part of operations management is effective use of resources—especially human resources—in the production of goods and services. Detroit automakers have found that their operating employees are a valuable resource in more ways than one. Not only are workers producing cars, but they are also helping to solve quality control problems through such techniques as quality circles.

Inventory management is still another responsibility of operations managers. Every part that is stored for future use (such as on an auto assembly line) must be financed. And these financing costs eventually find their way into the price of the product, or else they eat away at profit. Scheduling control is closely allied to inventory control. The better the scheduling of incoming parts, the smaller the required inventory. The ideal is to have every part become available just when it is needed—just in time.

Excessive inventory, poor scheduling, less than full use of resources, and even excess management all increase costs and thus raise prices for consumers. These higher prices and the lack of superior quality to make up for it—poor fuel economy in cars, for example—caused American consumers to switch to Japanese products in the 1970s. But, as we have seen, American manufacturers have begun to fight back, primarily through more effective operations management. Operations management is clearly a topic that warrants careful study.

Learning Objective 1
Understand the nature of operations management

utility *the ability of a product to satisfy a human need*

form utility *utility created by converting production inputs into finished products*

Production and Operations Management

In Chapter 5, operations managers were described as the people who create and manage systems that convert resources into goods and services. In this chapter, we shall examine the activities that are part of the operations manager's job. In fact, we shall begin by defining operations management in terms of those activities. **Operations management** consists of all the activities that managers engage in for the purpose of producing goods and services.

This set of activities was once referred to as production management. However, at that time the term *production* was applied only to the manufacture of tangible goods. Then, as managers began to realize that many production techniques are just as relevant and useful to firms that produce services, such as insurance protection, the function came to be called *production and operations management*. The idea of production was also extended to include services. Thus **production** is now considered to be the process of converting resources into goods, services, or ideas.

Finally, the phrase was shortened to *operations management*, and that's the phrase we use. When the word *production* creeps into our discussions, remember that we are using it in the enlarged sense. It includes the creation of goods, services, and ideas. To refer to goods, services, and ideas themselves, we use the word *products*.

A number of activities are involved in operations management. First, the organization may engage in product development to come up with the goods and services it will produce. Next, production must be planned. As you will see, planning takes place both *before* anything is produced and *during* production. Finally, managers must concern themselves with the control of operations, to ensure that goals are being achieved. We discuss each of these major activities in the sections that follow. But first we need to take a closer look at the nature of production itself.

The Conversion Process

Production is the conversion of resources into goods, services, and ideas. These resources are materials, finances, people, and information. The goods and services are varied and diverse. But how does the conversion take place? How does General Motors convert steel and glass, money from previous auto sales and stockholders' investments, production workers and managers, and economic and marketing forecasts into automobiles? How does Aetna Life and Casualty convert office buildings, insurance premiums, actuaries, and mortality tables into life insurance policies? They do so through the use of technology or a particular conversion system (see Figure 7.1). A **technology** is the knowledge and process required to transform input resources into outputs such as specific products. As indicated by our Aetna example, a technology need not involve heavy machinery and equipment.

The Nature of the Conversion

The conversion of inputs into outputs can be described in several ways. We shall limit our discussion to three: the focus of the conversion, its magnitude, and the number of technologies employed.

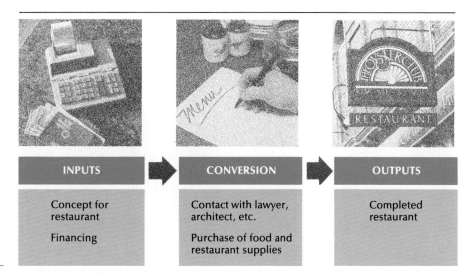

FIGURE 7.1
The Conversion Process
The conversion process converts resources such as materials, finances, and people into useful goods, services, and ideas. The conversion process is a crucial step in the economic development of any nation.

INPUTS	CONVERSION	OUTPUTS
Concept for restaurant	Contact with lawyer, architect, etc.	Completed restaurant
Financing	Purchase of food and restaurant supplies	

Focus   By the *focus* of a conversion process we mean the resource or resources that comprise the major input. For a bank like Citicorp, financial resources are of prime concern in the conversion process. A refiner such as Exxon concentrates on material resources. A college or university is primarily concerned with information. And a barbershop focuses on the use of human resources.

Learning Objective 2
Be able to outline the conversion process, which transforms input resources into products

Magnitude   The *magnitude* of a conversion is the degree to which the input resources are physically changed by the conversion. At one extreme lie such processes as the one by which Union Carbide produces Glad Wrap. Various chemicals in liquid or powder form are combined to form long, thin sheets of plastic Glad Wrap. Here the inputs are totally unrecognizable in the finished product. At the other extreme, American Airlines' technology produces *no* physical change in its inputs. The airline simply transports people from one place to another.

Number of Technologies   A single firm may employ one technology or many. In general, larger firms that make a variety of products use multiple technologies. For example, Sears, Roebuck manufactures some of its own products, buys other merchandise from wholesalers, and operates a credit division, an insurance company, and a property development division. Clearly a number of different conversion processes are involved in these activities. Smaller firms, by contrast, may operate in one fairly small and narrow market in which few conversion processes are required.

The Increasing Importance of Services

The application of operations management to the production of services has coincided with a dramatic growth in the number and diversity of service organizations. For example, only 28 percent of American workers

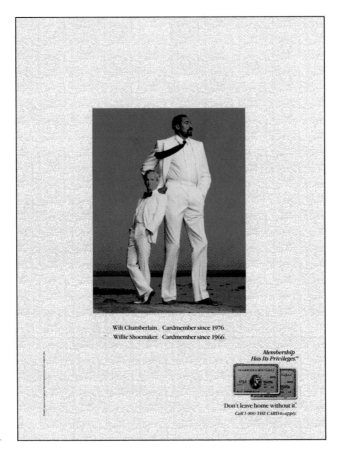

Wilt Chamberlain. Cardmember since 1976.
Willie Shoemaker. Cardmember since 1966.

*Membership
Has Its Privileges.*

Don't leave home without it.
Call 1-800-THE CARD to apply.

American Express Company is a service provider in our economy, which is now dominated by service industries. In its advertising, American Express emphasizes the long-term satisfaction its members (some of whom are quite famous!) have felt with the services the company provides.

were employed in service organizations in 1900. By 1950 this figure had grown to 40 percent, and by 1990 it had risen to 80 percent (beginning in 1984, forestry and fishery services are included in these figures). Moreover, in 1962 approximately $58 billion was spent in this country on services. By 1987 this figure had increased to $794 billion. By any yardstick, service firms have become a dominant part of our economy. In fact, the American economy is now characterized as a service economy (see Figure 7.2). A **service economy** is one in which more effort is devoted to the production of services than to the production of goods.

service economy   an economy in which more effort is devoted to the production of services than to the production of goods

This rapid growth is the primary reason for the increased emphasis on production techniques in service firms. The managers of restaurants, dry cleaners, real estate agencies, banks, movie theaters, airlines, travel agencies, and other service firms have realized that they can benefit from the experience of manufacturers, construction firms, and retailers.

Now that we understand something about the conversion process as it is carried out to transform resources into goods and services, it is time to consider three major activities that are involved in operations management. These are product development, operations planning, and operations control.

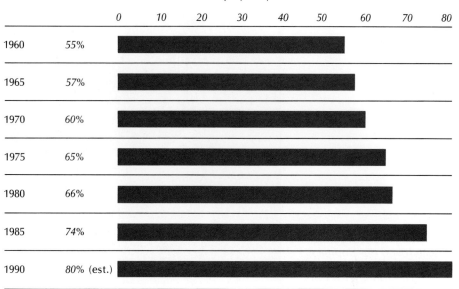

Percent of American workers
employed by service industries

		0	10	20	30	40	50	60	70	80
1960	55%									
1965	57%									
1970	60%									
1975	65%									
1980	66%									
1985	74%									
1990	80% (est.)									

FIGURE 7.2
Service Industries
The growth of service firms has increased so dramatically that we live in what is now referred to as a service economy. (Source: "Employees in Nonagricultural Establishments," Bureau of Labor Statistics, 1984; and "Employment of Workers on Nonagricultural Payrolls," Monthly Labor Review, March 1990.)

Where Do Products Come From?

No firm can produce a product until it has a product to produce. In other words, someone must first come up with a new way to satisfy a need—a new product or an improvement in an existing product. Only then will the firm be able to begin the variety of activities that make up operations management.

Research and Development

Learning Objective 3
Recognize the need for research and development, and know the activities it includes

How did we get electric pencil sharpeners and electronic word processors? We got them the same way we got light bulbs and automobile tires: from people working with new ideas and technical advances. Thomas Edison created the first light bulb and Charles Goodyear discovered the vulcanization process that led to tires. In the same way, scientists and researchers working in businesses and universities have produced many of the newer products that we may already have started to take for granted.

research and development
(R&D)   *an organized set of activities intended to identify new ideas and technical advances that have the potential to result in new goods and services*

These activities are generally referred to as research and development. For our purposes, **research and development (R&D)** is an organized set of activities intended to identify new ideas and technical advances that have the potential to result in new goods and services.

In general, there are three types of R&D activities. *Basic research* consists of activities aimed at uncovering new knowledge. The goal of basic research is scientific advancement, without regard for its potential use in the development of goods and services. *Applied research*, on the

To refine products during research and development, companies like Atari employ potential product users to test products. At Atari, games are played and tested dozens of times to assure perfect performance.

other hand, consists of activities geared to discovering new knowledge that has some potential use. And *development and implementation* are research activities undertaken to put new or existing knowledge to use in producing goods and services.

The Costs of Research   Research is costly. American businesses spend approximately $63 billion per year, and the federal government spends about $65 billion each year on research and development.[2] (Some federal research is done at colleges and universities and is funded through contracts or grants.)

R&D Organization   Most firms organize their R&D activities as a staff function, either at the corporate level or within product-based departments. When R&D activities are placed at the corporate level, they are somewhat centralized. This arrangement allows the firm to concentrate research activities within one group, so that there is no duplication of effort among departments. However, a corporate R&D staff may not be sensitive to the needs of each separate department. Placing separate R&D staffs within product departments overcomes this problem. But costs are higher because R&D facilities must be duplicated for the various departments. Some firms try to combine the two approaches by centralizing basic research and some applied research but decentralizing the remaining R&D effort.

Several years ago, a few computer manufacturers banded together to establish a research partnership called the Micro Computer Consortium (MCC). Each firm contributed a fixed amount of money to operate MCC's research laboratory in Austin, Texas. In return, the contributing firms have the right to exclusive use of any of MCC's results for three years. After that time, results may be licensed to other firms. This practice is widespread in Japan. The high cost of research and increased international business competition may encourage many more joint R&D ventures.

Product Extension and Refinement

When a brand-new product is first marketed, its sales slowly increase from no sales at all. If the product is successful, annual sales increase more and more rapidly until they reach some peak. Then, as time passes, annual sales begin to decline, and they continue to decline until it is no longer profitable to market the product. (This rise-and-decline pattern is called the *product life cycle;* it is seen in more detail in Chapter 12.)

If a firm sells only one product, when that product reaches the end of its life cycle, the firm, too, will die! To stay in business, the firm must, at the very least, find ways to extend or refine the want-satisfying capability of its product. Consider television sets. Since they were first introduced in the late 1930s, television sets have been constantly *refined*, so that they now provide clearer, sharper pictures with less dial adjusting. They are tuned electronically for better picture control and can even compensate for variations in room lighting and picture-tube wear. During the same time, television sets were also *extended*. Full-color as well as black-and-white sets can be purchased. There are television-only sets and others that include video games, digital clocks, and telephones. Both manual and remote control are available.

Each refinement or extension results in an essentially "new" product whose sales make up for the declining sales of a product that was introduced earlier. General Foods, for example, introduced Jell-O to the public over sixty years ago. One of their newer products is still based on Jell-O. This relatively new product, Jell-O Pudding Pops, has been bringing in sales of more than $100,000,000 annually. For most firms, extension and refinement are expected results of their development and implementation effort. Most often, they result from the application of new knowledge to existing products.

Operations Planning

Learning Objective 4
Distinguish between the two phases of operations planning: design planning and operational planning

Only a fraction of the many ideas for new products, refinements, and extensions ever gets to the production stage. But for those ideas that do, the next step in the process of operations management is operations planning. Operations planning involves two major phases: design planning and operational planning.

Design Planning

When the R&D staff at IBM recommended to top management that it produce and market an affordable personal computer, the company could not simply swing into production the next day. Instead, a great deal of time and energy had to be invested in determining what the new computer would look like, where and how it would be produced, what options would be included, and so on. These decisions are a part of design planning. **Design planning** is the development of a plan for converting a product idea into an actual commodity ready for marketing. This plan must, of course, be developed before a production facility is acquired or adapted. The major decisions involved in design planning deal with product line, capacity, technology, facilities, and human resources.

design planning *the development of a plan for converting a product idea into an actual commodity ready for marketing*

Product Line **A product line** is a group of similar products that differ only in relatively minor characteristics. During the design-planning stage, operations personnel must determine how many different product variations there will be. An automobile manufacturer needs to determine how many different models to produce, what major options to offer, and the like. A restaurant owner must decide how many menu items to offer. An important issue in deciding on the product line is to balance customer preferences and production requirements. It is also important to identify the most effective combination of product alternatives. For this reason, marketing managers play an important role in making product-line decisions.

product line *a group of similar products that differ only in relatively minor characteristics*

Intel designs and constructs state-of-the-art production facilities for producing computer chips in New Mexico. To ensure high quality, computer chips are produced in "clean rooms," which are much cleaner than surgical hospital areas.

BUSINESS JOURNAL

Making It Simple

According to Earl Powell, director of the Design Management Institute, "The trade deficit is actually a design deficit." Simplifying product design is a way to both improve product quality and reduce costs. And companies are finding out that simplified designs also lead to fewer problems on the factory floor.

The executives at CalComp Inc. are outspoken advocates of streamlining and simplifying product designs. Based in Anaheim, California, CalComp builds plotters that produce computer drawings for architects and engineers. This once-struggling company has become prosperous, and its executives attribute the turnaround to design simplification. At industry gatherings, CalComp representatives even offer their competitors a free videotape and brochure on the rewards of simplification. Since CalComp officials have begun their drive to simplify designs and methods, company sales revenues have risen 62 percent. CalComp's latest model, the Drawing Master plotter, contains only 95 parts; its predecessor was composed of 494 parts. The new plotter is more efficient and prints out drawings twice as fast as the previous model.

The executives at Ford Motor Company are also committed to design simplification. Ford has become the design leader among U.S. automobile manufacturers as its simplified designs and design methods have led to increased sales and profits. In former times, a cumbersome four-step process was used to produce Ford's cars. First, a group of product planners would come up with a new car design. Then, designers would take over. Next, engineers would add their expertise. Finally, the manufacturers themselves tried to construct the model. Changes in design often translated into incredibly inefficient delays. Ford's simpler design scheme now has designers, engineers, production specialists, and additional groups working together simultaneously to produce a new automobile. Mistakes or suggestions are acted on immediately. As a result of this new system, Ford workers have drastically compressed development-cycle times on new models and thus increased the pressure on competitors. In response, both Chrysler and General Motors are restructuring their manufacturing processes to incorporate simplified designs.

Based on information from Patrick E. Cole, "Simpler Designs, Simpler Factories," *Business Week*, June 1989, p. 150; Roxane Farmanfarmaian, "Does Good Design Pay Off?" *Working Woman*, July 1989, pp. 47, 49–50; and Alex Taylor III, "Why Fords Sell Like Big Macs," *Fortune*, November 21, 1988, pp. 123–125.

---

product design *the process of creating a set of specifications from which a product can be produced*

Each distinct product within the product line must be designed. **Product design** is the process of creating a set of specifications from which the product can be produced. The need for a careful and complete design of tangible goods is fairly obvious; they cannot be manufactured without it. But services should be carefully designed as well, and *for the same reason.*

capacity *the amount of input a facility can process or output it can produce in a given time*

Required Capacity   **Capacity** is the amount of input a production facility can process or the amount of output it can produce in a given time. (The capacity of an automobile assembly plant, for instance, might be 500,000 cars per year.) Operations managers—again working with the firm's marketing managers—must determine what the required capacity will be. This determines the size of the production facility. Capacity planning is vitally important. If the facility is built with too much capacity, valuable resources (plant, equipment, and money) will lie idle. If the facility offers insufficient capacity, capacity may have to be added later, which is much more expensive than building a large-enough facility to begin with.

Suppose an automobile assembly plant is constructed with the capacity to produce 500,000 cars per year. If customers then want only 400,000 cars per year, 20 percent of the capital invested in the plant will be wasted. On the other hand, if customers want as many as 600,000 units per year, the company may have to build a costly addition onto the plant to produce all the cars it can sell.

Capacity means about the same thing to service businesses. The capacity of a restaurant is the number of patrons it can serve at one time. The capacity of a hospital is the number of patients it can care for at any one time (usually given as the number of beds).

Technology   A technology, as we saw earlier, is a process used to transform input resources into a specific product. During the design-planning stage, operations personnel must specify all the details of the process that will be used.

A major decision for many contemporary operations managers is the degree to which *automation*—including industrial robots—should be enlisted in place of human labor. Here, there is a tradeoff between high initial costs and low operating costs (for automation) and low initial costs and higher operating costs (for human labor). To a great extent, however, such decisions depend on the available technologies. A **labor-intensive technology** is one in which people must do most of the work. Housecleaning services and professional baseball teams, for example, are labor intensive. A **capital-intensive technology** is one in which machines and equipment do most of the work. An automated assembly plant is highly capital intensive.

labor-intensive technology
one in which people must do most of the work

capital-intensive technology
one in which machines and equipment do most of the work

Facilities   A very complex set of design-planning decisions deals with the facilities to be used in creating the products and services that the organization offers. Major decisions include the number of facilities to be used, their locations, and their layout.

Should all the required capacity be placed in one or two large facilities? Or should it be divided among several smaller facilities? In general, firms that market a wide variety of products find it more economical to have a number of smaller facilities. Firms that produce only a few products tend to have fewer but larger facilities. There are many exceptions to this general rule, and decisions concerning facility size must often be made in light of zoning and other restrictions.

In determining where to locate production facilities, operations managers need to consider a number of variables:

▶ Geographic locations of suppliers of parts and raw materials

▶ Locations of major markets for their companies' products

▶ Transportation costs to suppliers and to various markets

▶ Availability of skilled and unskilled labor in various geographic areas

▶ Special requirements of the technologies used, such as great amounts of energy or water

plant layout *the arrangement of machinery, equipment, and personnel within a facility*

FIGURE 7.3
Facilities Planning
The product layout is used when all products undergo the same operations in the same sequence. The process layout is used when small batches of different products are created in a different operating sequence.

The choice of a particular location often involves *optimizing,* or balancing, the applicable variables.

Finally, the **plant layout,** which is the arrangement of machinery, equipment, and personnel within the facility, must be determined. Two general types of plant layout are used (see Figure 7.3).

The *process layout* is used when different sequences of operations are required for creating small batches of different products. The plant is arranged so that each operation is performed in a particular area, and the work is moved from area to area to match its own sequence of operations. An auto repair shop provides an example of a process layout. The various operations might be engine repair, body work, wheel alignment, and safety inspection. Each is performed in a different area. A

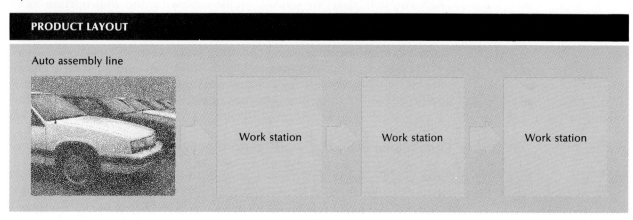

PRODUCT LAYOUT

Auto assembly line

Work station   Work station   Work station

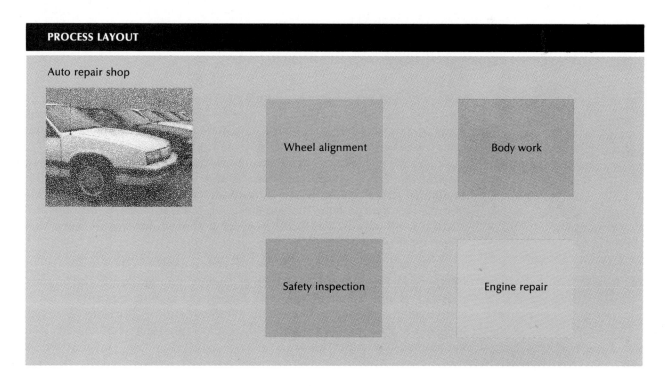

PROCESS LAYOUT

Auto repair shop

Wheel alignment   Body work

Safety inspection   Engine repair

particular car "visits" only areas where the kinds of work it needs are performed.

A *product layout* is used when all products undergo the same operations in the same sequence. The work stations are arranged to match the sequence of operations, and the work flows from station to station. An assembly line is the best example of a product layout.

Human Resources   In many ways, human resources are more the concern of human resources managers than of operations managers, but the two must work together at the design-planning stage. Several design-planning activities affect the work of human resources managers. For example, suppose a sophisticated technology requiring special skills is called for. The firm will have to recruit employees with the appropriate skills, develop training programs, or do both. And, depending on where facilities are to be located, arrangements may have to be made to transfer skilled workers to the new locations or to train local workers.

Human resources managers can also obtain and provide valuable information on availability of skilled workers in various areas, wage rates, and other factors that may influence choices of technology and location.

Operational Planning

operational planning   *the development of plans for utilizing production facilities and resources*

Once the production process and facilities have been designed, operations personnel must plan for their use. **Operational planning** is the development of plans for utilizing production facilities and resources. In contrast to one-time-only design plans, operational plans are developed periodically for each facility. The objective of operational planning is to decide on a level of output for the facility. Four steps are required: (1) select a planning horizon, (2) estimate market demand, (3) compare demand with capacity, and (4) adjust output to demand.

planning horizon   *the period during which a plan will be in effect*

Select a Planning Horizon   A **planning horizon** is simply the period during which a plan will be in effect. A common planning horizon for operational plans is one year. That is, operations personnel plan production output one year in advance. Before each year is up, they plan for the next.

A planning horizon of one year is generally long enough to average out seasonal increases and decreases in sales. At the same time, it is short enough for planners to adjust output to accommodate long-range sales trends. However, firms that operate in a rapidly changing business environment may find it best to select a shorter horizon to keep their operational planning current.

Estimate Market Demand   The *market demand* for a product is the quantity that customers will demand at the going price. This quantity must be estimated for the period covered by the planning horizon. The sales forecasts and projections developed by marketing managers are the basis for market-demand estimates.

BUSINESS JOURNAL

CAD/CAM: It's High Time for High Tech

CAD/CAM (computer-aided design/computer-aided manufacturing) has made life much easier for many designers, draftspeople, and engineers. CAD/CAM makes the journey between an idea and an actual product shorter. Firms in highly competitive industries rely on this technology for shorter product-development time spans that allow their products to get on store shelves, in warehouses, and onto display floors more quickly.

Using CAD/CAM, an engineer can have a computer do all the tedious drawing and calculating. Computer drawings are often more accurate, legible, and consistent than comparable human designs. Moreover, engineers can make design changes quickly. By-passing costly and time-consuming physical models, engineers can perform tolerance and stress tests on new products while those products are just computer-screen renderings.

Aerospace, automobile, architectural, and tool-and-die firms all use CAD/CAM systems extensively. Since the costs of these complicated systems have come down recently, smaller firms are also being swept into the CAD/CAM mainstream. Large and small companies alike are gambling that the costs involved in installing a system and training employees to use it will be offset by gains in product quality, manufacturing efficiency, and time saved.

CAD/CAM clearly has remarkable potential, but it also has serious drawbacks. CAD/CAM software is very difficult to learn; as a result, training can be extremely taxing on both employees and the company's budget. Furthermore, there is usually a substantial time lag on the learning curve between initial training and proficiency. A firm must also consider the possibility that once an employee has been trained, he or she might then leave the company to take a more lucrative position with a rival organization. Hiring CAD/CAM consultants or workers trained in CAD/CAM may be a more sensible, but very costly, move in certain cases.

Another downside to CAD/CAM is that sometimes the increased engineering efficiency and productivity it achieves cause problems in other divisions of the organization. Other departments may not be equipped to handle the increased workload. In addition, lowered employee morale or interdepartmental squabbling may result.

As more researchers continue to construct better, less expensive, and easier-to-use CAD/CAM systems, many of CAD/CAM's limitations will disappear. Though CAD/CAM will most likely reach its prime in the coming century, it is definitely thriving today.

Based on information from Andrew Csinger and Robert Rohonczy, "When Should You Use a CAD Consultant?" *Machine Design*, August 25, 1988, pp. 91–94; Suzanne Loeffelholz, "CAD/CAM Comes of Age," *Financial World*, October 18, 1988, pp. 38–40; and Robert E. Perri, "CAD/CAM Productivity," *Design News*, July 8, 1985, pp. 107–109.

Compare Demand and Capacity   The third step in operational planning is to compare the projected market demand with the facility's capacity to satisfy that demand. Again, demand and capacity must be compared for the same period—the planning horizon. One of three outcomes may result: Demand may exceed capacity, capacity may exceed demand, or capacity and demand may be equal. If they are equal, the facility should be operated at full capacity. But if market demand and capacity are not equal, an adjustment may be necessary.

Adjust Output to Demand   When market demand exceeds capacity, several options are available to the firm. Output may be increased (to match demand) by operating the facility overtime with existing personnel or by starting a second or third work shift. Another response is to subcontract a portion of the work out to other manufacturers. If the excess demand is likely to be permanent, the firm may expand the facility.

Another option that firms occasionally pursue is to ignore the excess demand and allow it to remain unmet. For several years, this strategy was used by the Adolph Coors Co. Gradually a mystique developed around Coors beer because it was not available in many parts of the country. Then, when the firm's brewing capacity was finally expanded, an eager market was waiting.

When capacity exceeds market demand, there are again several options. To reduce output temporarily, workers may be furloughed (laid off) and part of the facility shut down. Or the facility may be operated on a shorter-than-normal workweek for as long as the excess persists. To adjust to a permanently decreased demand, management may shift the excess capacity to the production of other goods or services. The most radical adjustment is to eliminate the excess capacity by selling unused facilities.

Operations Control

Learning Objective 5
Know the four major areas of operations control: purchasing, inventory control, scheduling, and quality control

So far we have discussed the development of a product idea and the planning that translates that idea into the reality of a production facility and a level of output. Now it's time to push the "start button" to get the facility into operation.

While it is operating, the facility must be monitored and regulated— that is, controlled—to ensure that plans are being implemented and goals are being achieved. In this section we examine four important areas of operations control: purchasing, inventory control, scheduling, and quality control (see Figure 7.4).

Purchasing

purchasing   *all the activities involved in obtaining required materials, supplies, and parts from other firms*

Purchasing consists of all the activities involved in obtaining required materials, supplies, and parts from other firms. The purchasing function is far from routine, and its importance should not be underestimated. For some products, purchased materials make up more than 50 percent of their wholesale cost.[3]

The objective of purchasing is to ensure that required materials are available when they are needed, in the proper amounts, and at minimum cost. In keeping with this objective, the two major functions of purchasing are supplier selection and purchase planning.

Supplier Selection   Purchasing personnel should constantly be on the lookout for new or "back-up" suppliers, even when their needs are being met by their present suppliers. It may become necessary to change suppliers for any of a variety of reasons. Or such problems as strikes and equipment breakdowns may cut off the flow of purchased materials from a primary supplier.

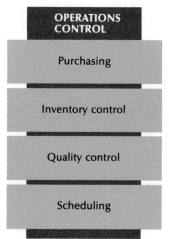

FIGURE 7.4
Four Aspects of Operations Control
To implement the operations control system in any business requires the effective use of purchasing, inventory control, scheduling, and quality control by all managerial levels.

The choice of suppliers should result from careful analysis of a number of factors:

▶ *Price:* Even tiny differences in price can add up to good-sized sums when large quantities are purchased. (A saving of 2 cents per unit on annual purchases of 100,000 units yields a yearly savings of $2,000.) Moreover, some suppliers will give discounts on large purchases, and some may assume part or all of the cost of transportation. These arrangements are essentially price reductions. Purchasers should always take them into account.

▶ *Quality:* The idea is not necessarily to find the highest quality available, but to buy materials at a level of quality that is in keeping with their intended use. The minimum acceptable quality is usually specified by product designers. Beyond that, purchasing personnel need to weigh quality against price, because higher quality usually costs more.

▶ *Reliability:* An agreement to purchase high-quality materials at a low price is the purchaser's dream. But such an agreement becomes a nightmare if the supplier doesn't deliver. Purchasing personnel should check the reliability of potential suppliers as well as their ability to meet delivery schedules.

Purchase Planning   If a production facility runs out of a part or material, it will probably have to shut down. And because costs such as rent, wages, and insurance expenses must still be paid, a shutdown can be expensive. Conversely, large stockpiles of materials are also costly because the money invested in stored materials does not contribute to the firm or its operations. The objective of purchase planning is to balance these two opposing factors to ensure that sufficient purchased materials are on hand without paying excessive storage costs.

Inventory Control

inventory   *stocks of goods and materials*

An **inventory** is a stock of goods and materials. Operations managers are concerned with three types of inventories. A *raw materials inventory* consists of materials that will become part of the product during the conversion process; these include purchased materials, parts, and subassemblies. The *work-in-process inventory* consists of products that have been partially completed but require further processing. The *finished goods inventory* consists of completed goods that are awaiting shipment to customers.

inventory control   *the process of managing inventories in such a way as to minimize inventory costs, including both holding costs and potential stock-out costs*

Associated with each type of inventory are a *holding cost*, or storage cost, and a *stock-out cost*, the cost of running out of inventory. **Inventory control** is the process of managing inventories in such a way as to minimize inventory costs, including both holding costs and potential stock-out costs. We have already discussed these costs with regard to raw materials or purchased inventories. For work in process, the stock-out cost is the cost of the resulting shutdown or partial shutdown of a production line or facility. For finished goods, the cost of running out is the resulting loss of sales.

Computerization is being utilized increasingly to make inventory control more accurate and efficient. At the Hayward, California distribution center for Baxter International, a manufacturer, marketer, and supplier of health-care products, customized software guides the sorting and inventory operations.

Various mathematical models can be used to minimize the total cost of ordering and carrying inventory. One such model—*the economic order quantity (EOQ)*—provides the least-cost order quantity via a simple arithmetic calculation.[4] Using this information, an inventory manager can determine what quantity to order when reordering merchandise.

Because large firms can incur huge inventory costs, much attention has been devoted to inventory control. The "just-in-time" system being used by some businesses is one result of all this attention. A **just-in-time inventory system** is designed to ensure that materials or supplies arrive at a facility just when they are needed so that storage is minimized. The just-in-time system reduces carrying costs and excessive inventory. It requires considerable cooperation between the supplier and the customer. The customer must specify what will be needed, when, and in what amounts. The supplier must be sure that the right supplies arrive at the agreed-upon time and location.

just-in-time inventory system *a system designed to ensure that materials or supplies arrive at a facility just when they are needed*

Computer-controlled inventory systems are also being used. For smaller firms, microcomputer-based systems can be used to keep track of inventories, provide periodic inventory reports, and alert managers to impending stock-outs. For larger firms, more complex computer-based systems maintain inventories of thousands of individual items, perform routine purchasing chores in accordance with a purchasing plan, and schedule the production of both subassemblies and finished goods.

What is most important, however, is not *how* inventories are controlled but the fact that they *are* controlled. Operations managers are responsible for making sure that sufficient inventories are on hand and that they are acquired at the lowest possible cost.

BUSINESS JOURNAL

Just-In-Time: Better to Wait Until the Last Minute?

We have always been told, "Don't put off until tomorrow what you can do today." But, in some cases, it might not be such a bad idea to wait until the very last minute to get something done. As evidence of this, an increasing number of companies have partially or completely adopted the *Just-In-Time (JIT)* supply system.

Years ago, it was almost mandatory for a company to stockpile a massive inventory of parts. After all, no one ever knew when a cruicial, big order would come in. This "massive inventory" approach proved to be very costly (though many companies still believe in it today). Warehousing inventory can be very expensive, and defective parts usually cannot be spotted until they are individually handled by workers.

JIT eliminates large storage costs. JIT works like this: A part or component arrives at an assembly plant a few hours, or even minutes, before it is actually used. For example, on an auto assembly line, managers synchronize the arrival of car seats so that workers can move them directly from the loading dock to the car shells. The car-seat manufacturer even loads the seats in the order they will be used.

Of course, to use the JIT method, a company and its suppliers must put a maximum effort into coordinating transportation methods and means. A supplier must know exactly how long it takes a truck to get from one location to another. Since one mistake could upset an assembly-line operation for several days, fast, reliable, and efficient transportation is mandatory for JIT to work. Though JIT may take some time to perfect, once all parties are coordinated

and running smoothly, it can reduce waste, save money, and allow a company to provide superior customer service.

A few years ago, Kasle Steel Corp. built its Auto Blankers plant inside a General Motors plant in Flint, Michigan. Blanks—the sheet metal that eventually becomes auto roofs, fenders, and hoods—are delivered JIT to GM's stamping presses. Through a computerized system, GM tells the Auto Blankers plant thirty days in advance how much steel will be needed on the thirty-first day. Ten days before production, GM either confirms or adjusts the order. Twenty-four hours before GM is scheduled to stamp the blanks, the Auto Blankers plant receives an electronic go-ahead notice. As a result of this system, GM gets the steel it needs for stamping already uncoiled, washed, oiled, cut, and completely inspected. Auto Blankers has set the JIT standard for steel.

Flexible, reliable overnight-delivery firms and computerized communications have turned JIT from a theory into a business practice. The ultimate aim of a producer is to reliably supply customers with superior products. Since retailers want to keep inventory and quality control costs down, manufacturers employing effective JIT networks will be more appealing than those that do not.

Based on information from Ken Ackerman, "Just-In-Time's American Practitioners," *Management Review*, June 1988, pp. 55–57; William C. Copacino, "Four Keys to Effective JIT," *Traffic Management*, June 1988, p. 37; Ernest Raia, "JIT in Detroit," *Purchasing*, September 15, 1988, pp. 68–69, 71–72, 74, 76–77; and Tom Stundza, "Metals Suppliers Take on JIT," *Purchasing*, September 15, 1988, pp. 80A2–80A3, 80A4.

Scheduling

scheduling *the process of ensuring that materials are at the right place at the right time*

Scheduling is the process of ensuring that materials are at the right place at the right time. These "materials" may be raw materials, subassemblies, work in process, or finished goods. They may be moved from the warehouse to the work stations at which they are needed; they may move from station to station along an assembly line; or they may arrive at work stations "just in time" to be made part of the work in process there. For finished goods, scheduling involves both shipment to customers to fill orders and movement into finished-goods inventory.

As our definition implies, both place and time are important to scheduling. (This is no different from, say, the scheduling of classes. You cannot attend your classes unless you know both where and when they are held.) The *routing* of materials is the sequence of work stations that the materials will follow. The *timing* specifies when the materials will arrive at each station and, perhaps, how long they will remain there. Scheduling personnel may also be responsible for specifying which operations are to be performed at each work station, especially in plants that utilize the process layout. They are also responsible for monitoring schedules (called *follow-up*) to ensure that the work flows according to schedule.

Gantt chart *a graphic scheduling device that displays the tasks to be performed on the vertical axis and the time required for each task on the horizontal axis*

Scheduling Through Gantt Charts   A **Gantt chart,** developed by Henry L. Gantt, is a graphic scheduling device that displays the tasks to be performed on the vertical axis and the time required for each task on the horizontal axis. As shown in Figure 7.5, completed tasks can also be shown on a Gantt chart, which allows for actual progress to be monitored against planned activities. Gantt charts are used for scheduling routine production activities and for larger, more complex projects. They can be used for scheduling the work of one worker or the work of a group of employees. Although Gantt charts were originally designed for production scheduling, today they are used in scheduling many types of organizational activities. Gantt charts are not particularly suitable for scheduling extremely complex situations. Nevertheless, using Gantt charts forces a manager to plan

FIGURE 7.5
A Gantt Chart
The job that this chart details is to build three dozen electric golf carts between August 1 and August 25.
(Source: Robert Kreitner, Management, 4/e. Copyright © 1989 by Houghton Mifflin Company. Used by permission.)

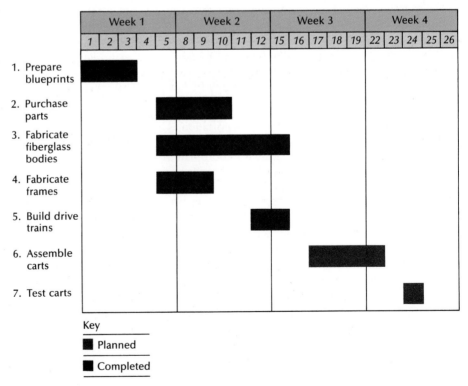

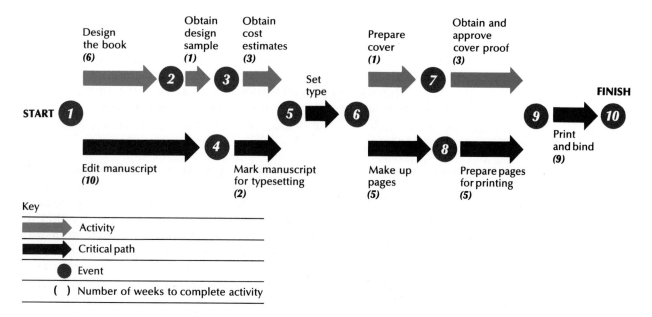

Design the book *(6)* — 2 — Obtain design sample *(1)* — 3 — Obtain cost estimates *(3)* — Set type

START 1

Prepare cover *(1)* — 7 — Obtain and approve cover proof *(3)* — FINISH

5 — 6

Edit manuscript *(10)* — 4 — Mark manuscript for typesetting *(2)*

Make up pages *(5)* — 8 — Prepare pages for printing *(5)*

9 — 10 — Print and bind *(9)*

Key

→ Activity

→ Critical path

● Event

( ) Number of weeks to complete activity

FIGURE 7.6
Simplified PERT Diagram for Producing This Book
A PERT diagram identifies the activities necessary to complete a given project and arranges the activities based on the total time required for each to become an event. The activities on the critical path determine the minimum time required.

PERT (Program Evaluation and Review Technique) *a technique for scheduling a process or project and maintaining control of the schedule*

the steps required to get a job done and to specify time requirements for each part of the job.[5]

Scheduling Control via PERT

PERT (Program Evaluation and Review Technique) is a technique for scheduling a process or project and maintaining control of the schedule. PERT was developed for use in constructing the *Polaris* submarine in the late 1950s. It has since been applied successfully in a wide range of industries.

To use PERT, we begin by identifying all the major *activities* involved in the project. The completion of each activity is called an *event*. For example, producing a textbook consists of editing the manuscript, designing the book, obtaining cost estimates, marking the manuscript for typesetting, setting type, and carrying out other activities. The completion of each of these activities is an event.

Next we arrange the events in a sequence. In doing so, we must be sure that an event that must occur before another event in the actual process also occurs before that event in the sequence. For example, the manuscript must be edited before the type is set. Therefore, in our sequence, the event "edit manuscript" must precede the event "set type."

Next we use arrows, representing activities, to connect events that must occur in sequence. We then estimate the time required for each activity and mark it near the corresponding arrow. The longest path through the sequence (the path that takes the longest time, from start to finish) is called the *critical path*. The activities on this path determine the minimum time in which the process can be completed. These activities are the ones that must be scheduled and controlled carefully. A delay in any one of them will cause a delay in completion of the project as a whole.

Figure 7.6 is a PERT diagram for the production of this book. The critical path runs from event 1 to event 4 to event 5 (which takes 12 weeks) rather than connecting events 1, 2, 3, and 5 (which takes only 10 weeks). It then runs through events 6, 8, and 9 to the finished book at event 10. Note that even a six-week delay in preparing the cover will not delay the production process. However, *any* delay in an activity on the critical path will hold up publication. Thus, if necessary, resources could be diverted from cover preparation to, say, makeup of pages.

Quality Control

quality control *the process of ensuring that goods and services are produced in accordance with design specifications*

Quality control is the process of ensuring that goods and services are produced in accordance with design specifications for the products. These specifications should reflect the organization's goals and strategies regarding quality. The major objective of quality control is to see that the organization lives up to the standards that it has set for itself on quality. Some firms, such as Volvo and Neiman-Marcus, have built their reputations on quality. Customers pay more for their products in return for assurances of high quality. Other firms adopt a strategy of emphasizing lower prices along with reasonable (but not particularly high) quality.

quality circle *a group of employees who meet on company time to solve problems of product quality*

American automakers have recently adopted a strategy that calls for better quality in their products. The use of a **quality circle**, a group of employees who meet on company time to solve problems of product quality, is one way that automakers are implementing this strategy at the operations level. Quality circles have also been used successfully in some high-technology companies, such as Digital Equipment.

inspection *the examination of output to control quality*

Increased effort is also being devoted to **inspection**, which is the examination of output to control quality. Inspections are performed at various times during production, depending on both the process and the product. Purchased materials may be inspected when they arrive at the production facility. Subassemblies and manufactured parts may be inspected before they become part of a major assembly or finished product. And finished goods may be inspected before they are shipped to customers. Items that are within design specifications continue on their way. Those that are not within specs are removed from production.

The method of inspection used depends on the item that is being examined. Visual inspection may be sufficient for products such as furniture and rug-cleaning services. Or one or two light bulbs may be tested out of every hundred produced. At the other extreme, complete x-ray inspection may be required for the vital components of airplanes and nuclear reactors.

Historically, quality control has been viewed largely as an activity that takes place somewhere near the end of the production process, an after-the-fact measurement of production success. As such, efforts to ensure quality increased the costs associated with making that good or service. For that reason, quality and productivity were viewed as conflicting; one was increased at the other's expense. Over the years, more and more managers have realized that quality is *not* something that is measured at or near the end of the production process, but rather is an essential "ingredient" of the good or service being provided. Viewed in this light, quality orientation becomes an overall approach to doing business and becomes the concern of all members of the organization. This view of quality provides several benefits. The number of defects decreases, which causes yield to increase. Making it right the first time reduces many of the rejects and much of the rework. Making the operative employees responsible for quality eliminates the need for inspection. An operator is indoctrinated to accept full responsibility for quality in his or her work.

Automation and Robotics

Learning Objective 6
Understand the increasing role of automation and robotics in production processes

Automation, a development that is revolutionizing the workplace, is the total or near-total use of machines to do work. The rapid increase in automated procedures in recent years has been made possible by the microprocessor, a silicon chip one-quarter-inch square that does the electronic switching work of 100,000 vacuum tubes. Microprocessors have led to the production of desk-top computers for offices, where clerical tasks, information retrieval and storage, and interoffice communications are being transformed. In factories, computers are being used in robots and in flexible manufacturing systems.

Robotics

robotics *the use of programmable machines to perform a variety of tasks by manipulating materials and tools*

Robotics is the use of programmable machines to perform a variety of tasks by manipulating materials and tools.[6] Robots work quickly, accurately, and steadily. They are especially effective in tedious assembly-line

Robots are used to perform tasks more efficiently than a human worker could. Jobs that involve working in high or low temperature areas or in polluted atmospheres, such as painting, are appropriate candidates for robotics.

jobs and for handling hazardous materials. To date, the automotive industry has made the most extensive use of robotics, but robots have also been used to mine coal, inspect the inner surfaces of pipes, assemble computer components, provide certain kinds of patient care in hospitals, and clean and guard buildings at night. It is estimated that more than 50,000 robots will be functioning in U.S. businesses by the mid-1990s.

Flexible Manufacturing Systems

flexible manufacturing system (FMS) *a recent development in automation that combines robotics and computer-aided manufacturing in a single system*

The **flexible manufacturing system (FMS)**, one of the most recent developments in automation, combines robotics and computer-aided manufacturing in a single system. Robots feed basic wood, metal, or plastic parts into computer-controlled machines and retrieve the parts when they emerge. Automated carts and bins keep the parts moving from one work station to another, while a complex set of electronic controls coordinates the functioning of the entire system. A related technology is computer-aided design, which allows engineers to draft and revise plans for new products by computer, rather than on paper.

FMSs have several advantages over traditional assembly lines, which are fairly rigid arrangements of machines and work stations. Assembly lines turn out large numbers of identical products economically, but they require expensive, time-consuming retooling of equipment when new products are to be manufactured. In contrast, FMSs are rearranged by reprogramming machines, so that smaller batches of a variety of products can be made without raising the cost. Although the design and installation costs of FMSs are high, the electronic equipment is used more frequently and efficiently than tools in traditional shops.

Technological Displacement

Automation is expected to increase productivity by cutting manufacturing time, reducing error, and simplifying retooling procedures. No one knows, however, what the effect will be on the work force. Some experts estimate that automation will bring changes to as many as 45 percent of all jobs by the end of the century. Total unemployment may not increase, but many workers will be faced with the choice of retraining for new jobs or seeking jobs in other sectors of the economy. Institutions of government, of business, and of education will have to cooperate to prepare workers for new roles in an automated workplace.[7]

The Management of Productivity

We should not conclude this chapter without discussing the management of productivity. Productivity concerns all managers, but it is especially important to operations managers. They are the people who must oversee the creation of the firm's goods and services. We define **productivity** as a measure of output per unit of time per worker. Hence, if each worker at

productivity *a measure of output per unit of time per worker*

plant A produces 75 units per day, and each worker at plant B produces only 70 units per day, the workers at plant A are more productive. If one bank teller serves 25 customers per hour and another serves 28 per hour, the second teller is more productive.

Productivity Trends

Learning Objective 7
Be aware of the reasons for recent trends in productivity and identify some methods of enhancing productivity

When we discussed Theory Z in Chapter 5, we noted that in recent years the productivity growth rate in the United States has fallen considerably behind those in other countries. American workers still produce more than their counterparts in some of the other industrialized countries, such as West Germany, Canada, Denmark, and Sweden. But our *rate of productivity growth* is lagging behind the productivity growth rates of some other countries, such as Japan, France, Italy, and the United Kingdom.[8]

Causes of Productivity Declines

There are several factors that have been cited as possible causes of reduced productivity. First, in recent years the United States has experienced major changes in the composition of its work force. In particular, many women and young people have entered the work force for the first time. The majority of these new entrants have relatively little work experience. Therefore, their productivity might be lower than average. As they develop new skills and experience, their downward influence on productivity trends should diminish.

Another potential cause of stagnation in productivity is recent changes in industrial composition. By *industrial composition* we mean the relative numbers of workers in various industries. Specifically, many workers moved from agricultural jobs (which are low in productivity) to nonagricultural jobs (which are more productive) during the period beginning shortly after World War II and ending in the mid-1960s. This movement alone gave a boost to productivity growth. When it ended, productivity growth slowed down again.

There has also been a shift in the ratio of capital input to labor input in American industry. During the last decade, businesses have slowed their rate of investment in new equipment and technology. As workers have had to use increasingly outdated equipment, their productivity has naturally declined.

Another factor that may contribute to the decline in productivity growth is a decrease in spending for research and development. The amount of money spent for R&D by government and industry, expressed as a percentage of gross national product, has been falling since 1964. As a result, there have been fewer innovations and new products.

Finally, increased government regulation is frequently cited as a factor that has affected productivity. Federal agencies such as the Occupational Safety and Health Administration (OSHA) and the Food and Drug Administration (FDA) are increasingly regulating and intervening in business practices. The Goodyear Tire & Rubber Company recently generated

345,000 pages of computer printout weighing 3,200 pounds to comply with one new OSHA regulation! Furthermore, the company spends over $35 million each year solely to meet the requirements of six regulatory agencies. These resources could increase productivity if they were invested elsewhere.

Improving Productivity

Several techniques and strategies have been suggested as possible cures for these downward productivity trends. Some involve the removal of major barriers to productivity growth. For example, research and development could be stimulated by tax credits or other inducements. Similarly, various government policies that may be hindering productivity could be eliminated or at least modified.

Increased cooperation between management and labor could improve productivity. When unions and management work together, quite often the result is an improved situation for both.

In a related area, many managers believe that increased employee participation can enhance productivity. Employee participation is a primary element in Theory Z. Another popular method of increasing participation is the quality circle now being used by a number of firms. As we have noted, a quality circle is a group of employees who meet periodically, on company time, to solve problems related to product quality. Quality circles are not only helpful in controlling quality; they can also increase employee morale and motivation through employee participation in decision making.

Still another potential solution to productivity problems is to change the incentives for work. Many firms simply pay employees for their time, regardless of what or how much they produce. That is, employees are paid by the hour. As long as they produce at some minimal level, everything is fine. By changing the reward system so that people are paid for what they contribute, rather than for the time they put in, it may be possible to motivate employees to produce at higher levels.

CHAPTER REVIEW

Summary

Operations management consists of all the activities that managers engage in to create products (goods, services, and ideas). Operations are as relevant to service organizations as to manufacturing firms. In fact, production is defined to include the conversion of resources into either goods or services.

A technology is the knowledge and process the firm uses to convert input resources into output goods or services. Conversion processes vary in terms of their major input (focus), the degree to which inputs are changed (magnitude), and the number of technologies employed in the conversion.

Operations management often begins with the research and product development effort. The results of R&D may be entirely new products or extensions and refinements of existing products. The limited life cycle of every product spurs companies to invest continuously in R&D.

Operations planning is planning for production. First, design planning is undertaken to address questions related to the product line, required production capacity, the technology to be used, the design of production facilities, and human resources. Next, operational planning focuses on the use of production facilities and resources. The steps in this periodic planning are (1) to select the appropriate planning horizon, (2) to estimate market demand, (3) to compare demand and capacity, and (4) to adjust output to demand.

The major areas of operations control are purchasing, inventory control, scheduling, and quality control. Purchasing involves both selecting suppliers and planning purchases. Inventory control is the management of stocks of raw materials, work in process, and finished goods to minimize the total inventory cost. Scheduling ensures that materials are at the right place at the right time—for use within the facility or for shipment to customers. Quality control ensures that products meet their design specifications.

Automation, the total or near-total use of machines to do work, is rapidly changing the way work is done in both factories and offices. A growing number of industries are using programmable machines called robots to perform tasks that are tedious or hazardous to human beings. The flexible manufacturing system combines robotics and computer-aided manufacturing to produce smaller batches of products more efficiently than the traditional assembly line.

In recent years, the productivity growth rate in this country has fallen behind the rates of productivity growth in some of the other industrialized nations. Several factors have been cited as possible causes for this trend, and managers have begun to explore techniques for overcoming it.

The next chapter treats a very important aspect of management in general and of productivity management in particular—employee motivation and morale. In Chapter 8, we discuss a number of major theories of employee motivation. And we see how managers use various reward systems to boost motivation and morale.

Key Terms

You should now be able to define and give an example relevant to each of the following terms:

utility	service economy
form utility	research and
operations management	development (R&D)
production	design planning
technology	product line
product design	scheduling
capacity	Gantt chart
labor-intensive technology	PERT (Program Evaluation and Review Technique)
capital-intensive technology	quality control
plant layout	quality circle
operational planning	inspection
planning horizon	robotics
purchasing	flexible manufacturing system (FMS)
inventory	productivity
inventory control	
just-in-time inventory system	

Questions and Exercises

Review Questions

1. List all the activities or functions that are involved in operations management.
2. In terms of focus, magnitude, and number, characterize the technologies used by a local pizza parlor, a dry-cleaning establishment, and an auto repair shop.
3. Identify and briefly describe the two major aspects of product development.
4. What are the major elements of design planning?
5. What are the four steps in operational planning? What is its objective?
6. What is the difference between capacity and output?
7. Describe the two major functions of purchasing.
8. What are the costs that must be balanced and minimized through inventory control?
9. Explain in what sense scheduling is a *control* function of operations managers.
10. How might productivity be measured in a restaurant? in a department store? in a public school system?

Discussion Questions

1. What are the major benefits of the high-tech automated production facilities of the Hoover Company?
2. What possible problems may result from the changes at Hoover?
3. Do certain kinds of firms need to stress particular areas of operations management? Explain.
4. Is it really necessary for service firms to engage in research and development? in operations planning and control?

5. How are the four areas of operations control interrelated?
6. Is operations management relevant to nonbusiness organizations such as colleges and hospitals? Why?

Exercises

1. Assume you have decided to go into the business of assembling and selling desk lamps with built-in electronic calculators. Decide whether you would use a process layout or a product layout in your production facility. Then sketch the layout of the facility.
2. For the calculator lamp of Exercise 1, explain in detail what arrangements you would make in each of the four areas of operations control.
3. Draw a PERT diagram for the development of a term paper—start with identifying the topic and end with the final typed draft.

Case 7.1

Caterpillar Streamlines Its Production Plants

Big, yellow Caterpillar earth-moving, construction, and materials-handling machinery can be seen along the highways and at construction sites across the United States. But Caterpillar Inc., known for its high-quality, rugged equipment, has not always rolled along smoothly. During the mid-1980s, Caterpillar faced strong competition from Japanese firms, namely Komatsu, Ltd., and Caterpillar's market share suffered badly. The conservative executives at Caterpillar knew it was time to act. They dramatically changed their business by streamlining the manufacturing plants.

Caterpillar executives decided to invest over $1 billion in a program called "Plant With a Future" (PWAF), which was a total modernization of all Caterpillar facilities. PWAF has led to reduced inventories, faster production times, an improvement of Caterpillar's already-high quality, and a new sense of teamwork among Caterpillar workers. Before PWAF, it took employees twenty days to assemble a single clutch housing for a vehicle. Now, the process takes only four hours. Formerly, workers produced transmissions in five different locations. Today, transmission assembly takes place in one plant under one manager's control. Caterpillar employees even visit the plants of their suppliers to make suggestions about how they might improve production.

Caterpillar officials have also begun a policy of "certifying" suppliers who meet their standards. These

certified suppliers, 800 of Caterpillar's 4,000 major suppliers, receive preferential treatment. Caterpillar receives near-perfect quality in return. The reject rate from these suppliers is very low.

In addition, Caterpillar officials are reinvesting heavily in their five remaining European plants. By installing computerized inventory systems and rearranging factory floor space, they hope to make these factories more efficient. Caterpillar knows it must cut costs and prices to compete with European manufacturers such as Fiat-Allis and Volvo AB. Streamlining factories is a key step in this direction.

At one time, Komatsu controlled 20 percent of the U.S. heavy-machinery market, which had formerly been dominated by Caterpillar. Since then, Caterpillar has regained another 5 percent from Komatsu. Officials at Caterpillar are very proud of the results of their PWAF program. An executive vice president at Caterpillar indicated that executives made the strategic decision early not to give up market share to anyone. To do this, Caterpillar must be competitive worldwide.*

Questions

1. What major factors led to Caterpillar's decision to streamline its production operations?
2. In what ways has Caterpillar benefited from the changes made in its manufacturing plants?

Case 7.2

Chrysler Gets an Overhaul

Chrysler Corp. has strongly bounced back from near bankruptcy in the early 1980s because of improved quality, greater production economy, increased assembly-line efficiency, and a new corporate strategy. Chrysler has also renewed its commitment to engineering, product development, and marketing.

Chrysler purchased American Motors Corp. (AMC) from Renault for $835 million. Even though bringing AMC into Chrysler has been a longer process than Chrysler officials expected it to be, many business analysts believe that AMC will make Chrysler more competitive in the U.S. auto market. Through the purchase of AMC, Chrysler acquired the very popular

---

* Based on information from Brian Bremner, "Cat's Fight to Stay King of the Jungle," *Business Week*, December 12, 1988, p. 58; Kathleen Deveny, "Going for the Lion's Share," *Business Week*, July 18, 1988, pp. 70–72; and Keven Kelly, "A Weakened Komatsu Tries to Come Back Swinging," *Business Week*, February 22, 1988, p. 48.

Jeep line of vehicles. Today customers are buying Jeeps as fast as Chrysler can build them.

The Liberty Project, as Chrysler calls its effort to streamline production, is designed to cut costs by 30 percent—about $2,500 per car—by 1995. About $500 of the per-car savings will be from fixed costs; the rest will come from reduced labor per car, better assembly methods, and heavier use of preassembled parts from outside suppliers.

A simplification program has cut the number of parts a plant must handle. That means more usable plant space and less money and personnel tied up in inventory control. Handling fewer parts also cuts down on errors in assembly and on warranty repair problems. This simplification, along with a Performance Feedback (PFB) quality-control system that spots assembly-line mistakes quickly, has increased the quality of Chrysler's cars.

Cost-cutting measures are affecting older Chrysler plants. New robots are automating procedures, reducing labor costs, and keeping breakeven points low. Chrysler can thus increase profits as production moves from the breakeven point to "full" capacity; the company can also make a profit at lower volumes if new car sales are down.

Chrysler is investing heavily to bring its technology into the twenty-first century. The automaker has adopted computer-aided design methods that decrease product-development time by 40 percent. Chrysler has also spent $250 million on information systems, such as an electronic mail network that allows Chrysler to communicate daily with 6,500 dealerships.

Chrysler officials believe that their company must match Japanese production costs to be competitive in U.S. markets. For this reason, Chrysler closed its Kenosha, Wisconsin, plant. In its search for cost advantages, Chrysler also looks for low-cost components, even from foreign vendors, rather than making all parts itself.

Management at Chrysler replaced a previous strategy of trimming budgets, reducing staff, and cutting overtime with a strategy that emphasizes future market-share gains. Short-term profits are of minor concern to Chrysler. Chrysler's immediate objective is to improve the quality, reliability, and durability of its cars, and to remain the number-one low-cost producer of automobiles in the United States.†

Questions

1. Does the use of robots help Chrysler produce higher-quality products? Explain.
2. One of Chrysler's goals is to operate its plants at full capacity. How does this help Chrysler to reduce its production costs by $2,500 per car?
3. Can you think of any negative effects resulting from Chrysler's actions to reduce costs?

† Based on information from "Chrysler Pours Millions into Plant Upgrade," *Production*, March 1986, p. 11+; Mary Connelly, "Iacocca Returns as Saviour," *Automotive News*, May 9, 1988, p. 1+; Paul Eisenstein, "Detroit's Counterattack Strategy," *Computer Decisions*, May 1988, pp. 52–56; Fred Frailey, "What Chrysler, AMC Get from Their Alliance," *U.S. News & World Report*, July 14, 1986, pp. 39–40; Melinda Grenier Guiles and Doron P. Levin, "Buying AMC Could Strengthen Chrysler," *Wall Street Journal*, March 11, 1987, p. 2; William J. Hampton, "The Next Act at Chrysler," *Business Week*, November 3, 1986, p. 66+; Elizabeth Horwitt, "Network Links Chrysler, Dealers," *Computerworld*, January 11, 1988, pp. 37, 40; John McElroy, "1987 Industry Report Card," *Automotive Industries*, April 1988, p. 28; Alex Taylor III, "Iacocca's Time of Trouble," *Fortune*, March 14, 1988, p. 79+; Alex Taylor III, "Lee Iacocca's Production Whiz," *Fortune*, June 22, 1987, pp. 36–39, 42, 44; and James B. Treece, "Digesting AMC: So Far, So Good," *Business Week*, February 22, 1988, pp. 130–132.

CAREER PROFILE

BILL MARRIOTT John Willard ("Bill") Marriott Jr. stands firmly behind his beliefs, and he whole-heartedly believes in hard work, clean living, his family, and a successful company. The current chairman of Marriott Corp. runs an organization operating about 550 hotels; 1,100 restaurants; and a food services division that serves airlines, airports, over 500 colleges, about 600 hospitals, and 1,200 companies including Exxon, Xerox, IBM, and Avon. Marriott Corp. is one the ten largest employers in the U.S., having over 230,000 on the payroll. Bill Marriott cares about every one of them.

Marriott Corp. started as a nine-seat root-beer stand in Washington, D.C. built by J. Willard Marriott Sr. in 1927. The industrious and ambitious senior Marriott soon turned his root-beer stand into a thriving restaurant business. When Bill was only eight years old, he began accompanying his father on business trips, sitting through company meetings and product testings. When Bill became a teenager, he took a job cooking French fries at one of his father's restaurants. He continued to work for his father while attending the University of Utah. Bill took over the reins of Marriott Corp. when he became president in 1964. His father remained chairman until he died in 1985.

Bill Marriott's rise as head of one of the most consistently successful service companies has not been easy. During much of his career, Marriott worked fourteen-hour days, traveled over 200,000 miles a year visiting Marriott operations, and gave over forty speeches a year. He has also survived one serious accident (the explosion of the gas tank of a boat he was trying to start) and a heart attack. Since his heart attack, he has worked only ten to twelve hours a day.

The heart attack took Marriott and his family and friends by surprise. Marriott is a devout Mormon and neither drinks alcohol nor smokes. Regular medical check-ups indicated that he had low cholesterol levels and good blood pressure. The stress, strain, and lack of exercise took their toll, however. Now, Marriott exercises regularly (under supervision), watches his diet more closely, and spends more time relaxing with his family. Marriott's brother, Richard, Marriott Corp.'s vice chairman, is doing more traveling, relieving Bill of some responsibilities and leaving him more time and energy for important decision making.

Besides his brother Richard, several other of Bill's relatives play important roles in Marriott Corp. Bill's mother Alice is a vice-president and director; his eldest son Steve is a marketing director of a Marriott hotel in Maryland; his son John manages food and beverages at an airport outside of Washington, D.C.; and his son-in-law works at a Marriott in California. Bill's youngest son will soon work for the company.

Bill thinks that family members are more dedicated and committed to Marriott Corp. than hired managers ever could be. A family-operated business can often move more quickly when it comes to major decisions, and the added measure of job security allows family members the opportunity to take more risks and to more seriously consider the long-term direction of the company.

Marriott devotes a considerable amount of his time to outside activities. He is the president of the Washington, D.C. Mormon church stake, a group of eight to ten congregations. He also serves on the boards of Boy Scouts of America, the National Geographic Society, and General Motors Corp., among others.

Those who know Bill Marriott claim that he is a shy, soft-spoken man. Despite his bashful nature, he has appeared in a number of print and television advertisements because he thinks it is good publicity for his company. He is hospitable and polite, and he and his wife Donna avoid the extravagant lifestyle adopted by many CEOs. Marriott plans to keep his corporation financially healthy and growing. When the time comes for him to pass the management of Marriott Corp. to a new generation, he wants to be sure that they have all the advantages he did—and more. To continue the history of Marriott's astounding success, they will also need the same intelligence, energy, dedication, and commitment.

"Bill Marriott: Still Building in an Overbuilt Market," *(Phoenix) Arizona Trend,* May 1, 1988, E4–E7; Doug Carroll, "Heart Attack Forces Exec to Downshift," *USA Today,* December 11, 1989, pp. 1B, 2B; "How Master Lodger Bill Marriott Prophesied Profit and Prospered," *Fortune,* June 5, 1989, pp. 56–57; Tom Ichniowski, "A Marriott Kid's Place Is in the Company Kitchen," *Business Week,* April 4, 1988, p. 109; and Edward C. Baig, "Rooms at the Inn," *Fortune,* January 2, 1989, p. 62.

The figure in the salary column approximates the expected annual income after two or three years of service. 1 = $12,000–$15,000 2 = $16,000–$20,000 3 = $21,000–$27,000 4 = $28,000–$35,000 5 = $36,000 and up

Job Title	Educational Requirements	Salary Range	Prospects
Accounting manager	Bachelor's degree in accounting; on-the-job experience; master's degree in business administration preferred	4	Greatest growth
Administrative management assistant	Two years of college; on-the-job experience	2	Gradual growth
Clerical supervisor	High school diploma; some college preferred	2	Greatest growth
Food services manager	Two years of college or trade school; on-the-job experience	2	Gradual growth
General clerical employee	High school diploma; on-the-job experience; some college helpful	1–2	Gradual growth
Health services manager	Bachelor's degree in business or hospital administration; master's degree preferred	4	Greatest growth
Hospital administrator	Bachelor's degree in business or hospital administration; master's degree preferred	4	Gradual growth
Hotel manager	Some college helpful; bachelor's degree preferred; on-the-job experience	4	Gradual growth
Industrial designer	Bachelor's degree; on-the-job experience	2–3	No growth
Industrial engineer	Bachelor's degree; on-the-job experience	3	Gradual growth
Management analyst	Bachelor's degree in management; on-the-job experience	4	Greatest growth
Management trainee	Two years of college; bachelor's degree preferred	2–3	Gradual growth
Operations analyst	Bachelor's degree in math, statistics, or management	2–3	Greatest growth
Operations manager	Bachelor's degree in math, engineering, or management; several years of experience	3–4	Gradual growth
Operations research analyst	Bachelor's degree in math, statistics, or computers	2–3	Gradual growth
Public relations manager	Bachelor's degree in business; on-the-job experience	4	Gradual growth
Purchasing agent	Bachelor's degree in business; on-the-job experience helpful	3	Gradual growth
Secretarial supervisor	High school diploma; on-the job experience; some college preferred	2	Gradual growth
Systems analyst	College degree in business, math, computers, or engineering	3	Greatest growth
Traffic manager	Some college; degree helpful	Varies widely	Limited growth

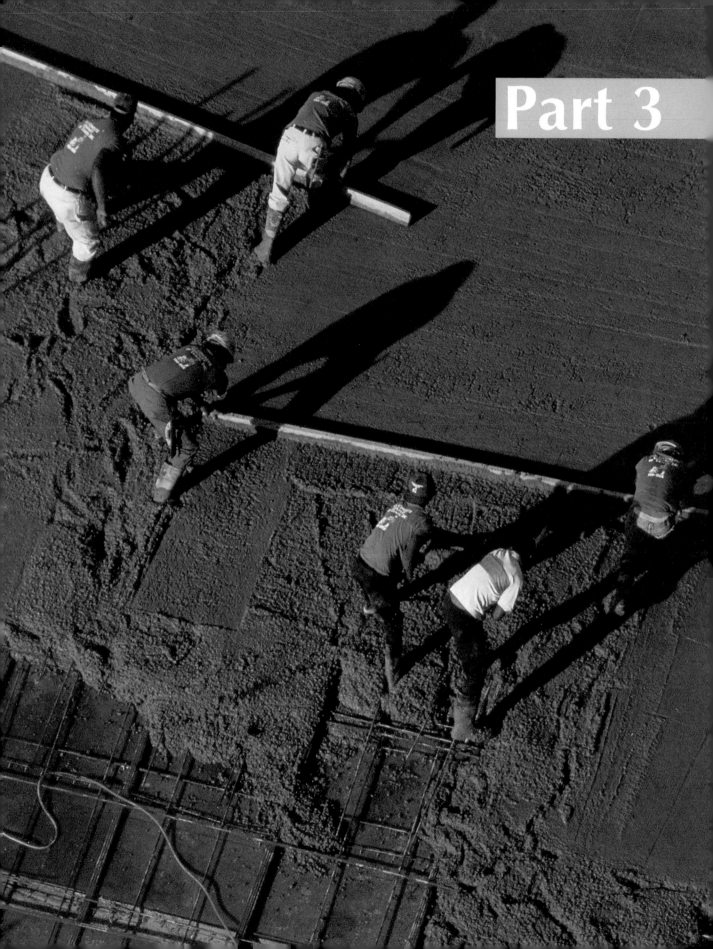

Part 3

THE HUMAN RESOURCE

This part of *Business* is concerned with the most important and least predictable of all resources—people. We begin by discussing various ideas about why people behave as they do, paying special attention to the work environment. Then we apply these ideas to the management of a firm's work force. Finally, we look at organized labor in the United States and probe the sometimes controversial relationship between business management and labor unions. Included in this part are:

PEOPLE AND MOTIVATION

CHAPTER PREVIEW

First, to provide a perspective of current motivational theories, we present several early views of motivation that influenced management practices, including Taylor's ideas of scientific management, Mayo's Hawthorne Studies, and McGregor's Theory X and Theory Y. We also describe two widely known theories of human motivation—Maslow's hierarchy of needs and Herzberg's concepts of satisfaction and dissatisfaction. Then, turning our attention to ` contemporary ideas, we examine equity, expectancy, and reinforcement theories, and explain how these motivational theories can be applied in an organization's reward system. Finally, we discuss specific techniques that managers can use to improve employee motivation.

Japanese Techniques Come to America

In a total of six states in the middle of America, 15,000 assembly-line workers are putting Japanese cars together. These autoworkers are assembling Hondas in Ohio, Toyotas in Kentucky, Mazdas in Michigan, and Nissans in Tennessee. Mitsubishi and Chrysler are jointly making cars in Illinois, and Subaru and Isuzu have set up shop in Indiana. The Japanese have brought more than their technology to their auto plants—they have also brought their own way of doing things.

Using Japanese management techniques, managers at these plants have motivated American workers to produce cars of the same high quality as those made in Japan. There is a definite Japanese philosophy of all-for-one and one-for-all running through the day-to-day operations of these plants. For example, there are no narrow job classifications: No one is a welder or a painter. Instead, a visitor finds "technicians" at Nissan, "associates" at Honda, and "team members" at Mazda and Toyota.

Employees at these manufacturing plants work in small, highly coordinated groups. Every worker on an assembly line is responsible for his or her particular job, for inspecting the overall quality of the product at hand, and for improving the production process. Management tries to make all workers feel equally important. Assembly-line workers actively participate in decisions on scheduling overtime and rotating jobs.

In the Japanese-managed plants in the United States, an air of equality appears to be present. There are no private offices for those in management—even senior executives share large, simple offices. Executives do not have reserved parking spots; they eat in the same cafeterias and even wear the same uniforms as line workers. No office workers can drink coffee at their desks because line workers are not allowed to.

The Japanese managers spend a great amount of time and energy building the morale of workers and trying to ensure company harmony. Toyota encourages its "personal touch program," an effort to promote after-hours socializing between Japanese and American workers. All the cheerleading that goes on in these plants must work very well: Nissan has the best attendance record in the U.S. auto industry, and it does not use time clocks.

For the Japanese management system to be effective, the Japanese companies need highly skilled and motivated workers. Japanese car companies spend weeks testing potential employees and training recently hired ones. The Japanese companies sometimes send workers to training sessions in Japan.

Team participation and strong interpersonal skills are definite requirements for workers in Japanese companies. Workers are rewarded for the impact they have on their "job team," and not for any personal performance. Many autoworkers love the Japanese system; others say it is too stressful.[1]

o achieve high production goals, Japanese automakers in the United States need more than the right raw materials and the latest production equipment. They must also have motivated employees. Although from time to time workers are dissatisfied, most of their employees are quite satisfied with their jobs and are motivated to meet high production standards. To some extent, this high level of worker motivation derives from the companies' management practices such as job rotation, employee participation, rewarding "job team" performance, and a philosophy of worker equality.

What Is Motivation?

We look at various levels of needs and motivation later in this chapter, but first we must ask, what exactly is motivation? Most often, the term is used to explain people's behavior. Successful athletes are said to be highly motivated. A student who avoids work is said to be unmotivated. (From another viewpoint, the student might be thought of as motivated—to avoid work.)

motivation *the individual, internal process that energizes, directs, and sustains behavior; the personal "force" that causes one to behave in a particular way*

We shall define **motivation** as the individual, internal process that energizes, directs, and sustains behavior. Motivation is the personal "force" that causes one to behave in a particular way. When we say that job rotation motivates employees, we mean that it activates this force or process within employees.

Developing and maintaining effective motivational programs raises employee morale, which results in increased satisfaction with regard to their jobs, their superiors, and the organization in general. This photo appears on the opening page of the Philadelphia Electric Company annual report. The report emphasizes the vitality and talent of the company's employees.

morale   *a person's attitude toward his or her job, superiors, and the firm itself*

Learning Objective 1
Understand the meaning of motivation

Most of the employees at Japanese auto plants in the United States are satisfied with their jobs and with their companies. Their dedication to their employers is an indicator of high morale. An employee's **morale** is his or her attitude toward the job, his or her superiors, and the firm itself.

High morale—a positive attitude—results mainly from the satisfaction of needs on the job or as a result of the job. One need that might be satisfied on the job is the need for *recognition* as an important contributor to the organization. Another need satisfied as a result of the job is the need for *financial security*. High morale, in turn, leads to the dedication and loyalty that are in evidence at the Japanese auto plants in the United States, as well as to the desire to do the job well. Low morale can lead to shoddy work, absenteeism, and high rates of turnover, as employees leave to seek more satisfying jobs with other firms.

Motivation, morale, and the satisfaction of employees' needs are thus intertwined. Along with productivity, they have been the subject of much study since the end of the nineteenth century. Let us begin our treatment of motivation by outlining some landmarks of that early research.

Historical Perspectives on Motivation

Learning Objective 2
Recognize some earlier perspectives on motivation: scientific management, Theory X, and Theory Y

Often researchers begin a study with some fairly narrow goal in mind. But after they develop an understanding of their subject, they realize that both their goal and their research should be broadened. This is exactly what happened when early research into productivity blossomed into the more modern study of employee motivation.

Scientific Management

scientific management   *the application of scientific principles to management of work and workers*

During the early part of the twentieth century, Frederick W. Taylor became interested in improving the efficiency of individual workers. This interest stemmed from his own experiences in manufacturing plants. It eventually led to **scientific management,** the application of scientific principles to management of work and workers.

One of Taylor's first jobs was with the Midvale Steel Company in Philadelphia, where he developed a strong distaste for waste and inefficiency. He also observed a practice he called soldiering. Workers "soldiered," or worked slowly, because they feared if they worked faster, they would run out of work and lose their jobs. Taylor realized managers were not aware of this practice because they had no idea what the workers' productivity level *should* be.

Taylor later left Midvale and spent several years at Bethlehem Steel. It was there that he made his most significant contribution. In particular, he suggested that each job should be broken down into separate tasks. Then management should determine (1) the best way to perform these tasks and (2) the job output to expect when the tasks were performed properly. Next, management should carefully choose the best person for

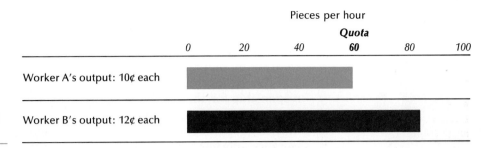

Pieces per hour

| | Quota | | | | |
| 0 | 20 | 40 | **60** | 80 | 100 |

Worker A's output: 10¢ each

Worker B's output: 12¢ each

FIGURE 8.1
The Piece-Rate System
When workers exceeded their quota, they were rewarded by being paid at a higher rate per piece for all the pieces they produced.

piece-rate system *a compensation system under which employees are paid a certain amount for each unit of output they produce*

Frederick W. Taylor (1856–1915), an American efficiency engineer, implemented scientific management—the application of scientific principles to the management of work and workers.

each job and train that person to do the job properly. Finally, management should cooperate with workers to ensure that jobs were performed as planned.

Taylor also developed the idea that most people work only to earn money. He therefore reasoned that pay should be tied directly to output. The more a person produced, the more he or she should be paid. This gave rise to the **piece-rate system,** under which employees are paid a certain amount for each unit of output they produce. Under Taylor's piece-rate system, each employee was assigned an output quota. Those exceeding the quota were paid a higher per-unit rate for *all* units they produced (see Figure 8.1).

Taylor's system was put into practice at Bethlehem Steel, and the results were dramatic. Average earnings per day for steel handlers rose from $1.15 to $1.88. (Don't let the low wages that prevailed at the time obscure the fact that this is an increase of better than 63 percent!) The average amount of steel handled per day increased from 16 to 57 tons.

Taylor's ideas were revolutionary and had a profound impact on management practice. However, his view of motivation was soon recognized as overly simplistic and narrow. It is true that most people expect to be paid for their work. But it is also true that people work for a variety of reasons other than pay. Simply increasing a person's pay may not increase his or her motivation.

The Hawthorne Studies

Between 1927 and 1932, two experiments were conducted by Elton Mayo at the Hawthorne plant of the Western Electric Company in Chicago. The original objective of these studies, now referred to as the Hawthorne Studies, was to determine the effects of the work environment on employee productivity.

In the first set of experiments, lighting in the workplace was varied for one group of workers but not a second group. Then the productivity of both groups was measured to determine the effect of the variations in light. To the amazement of the researchers, productivity increased for *both* groups. And for the group whose lighting was varied, productivity remained high until the light was reduced to the level of moonlight!

The second set of experiments focused on the effectiveness of the piece-rate system in increasing the output of *groups* of workers. Researchers

Studies by Elton Mayo revealed the importance of human factors in motivating employees.

expected that output would increase because faster workers would put pressure on slower workers to produce more. Again, the results were not as expected. Output remained constant, no matter what "standard" rates were set by management.

The researchers came to the conclusion that *human factors* were responsible for the results of the two experiments. In the lighting experiments, researchers had given both groups of workers a *sense of involvement* in their jobs merely by asking them to participate in the research. These workers—perhaps for the first time—felt as though they were an important part of the organization. In the piece-rate experiments, each group of workers informally set the acceptable rate of output for the group. To gain the *social acceptance* of the group, each worker had to produce at that rate. Slower or faster workers were pressured to maintain the group's pace.

The Hawthorne Studies showed that such human factors are at least as important to motivation as pay rates. From these and other studies, the *human relations movement* in management was born. Its premise was the assumption that employees who are happy and satisfied with their work will be motivated to perform better. Hence, management would do best to provide a work environment that maximizes employee satisfaction.

Theory X and Theory Y

The concepts of Theory X and Theory Y were advanced by Douglas McGregor in his 1960 book *The Human Side of Enterprise*.[2] They are, in reality, sets of assumptions that underlie management's attitudes and beliefs regarding worker behavior.

Theory X is a concept of employee motivation generally consistent with Taylor's scientific management. Theory X assumes that employees dislike work and will function effectively only in a highly controlled work environment:

1. People dislike work and try to avoid it.

2. Because people dislike work, managers must coerce, control, and frequently threaten employees to achieve organizational goals.

3. People generally must be led because they have little ambition and will not seek responsibility. They are concerned mainly with security.

The logical outcome of such assumptions will be a highly controlled work environment—one in which managers make all the decisions and employees just take orders.

On the other hand, **Theory Y** is a concept of employee motivation generally consistent with the ideas of the human relations movement. Theory Y assumes that employees accept responsibility and work toward organizational goals if by so doing they also achieve personal rewards:

1. People do not naturally dislike work. In fact, work is an important part of their lives.

2. People will work toward goals to which they are committed.

Theory X *a concept of employee motivation generally consistent with Taylor's scientific management; assumes that employees dislike work and will function only in a highly controlled work environment*

Theory Y *a concept of employee motivation generally consistent with the ideas of the human relations movement; assumes that employees accept responsibility and work toward organizational goals if by so doing they also achieve personal rewards*

According to Douglas McGregor, managers adopt either a negative (Theory X) or a positive (Theory Y) view of human behavior.

3. People become committed to goals when it is clear that accomplishing the goals will bring personal rewards.
4. People often seek out and willingly accept responsibility.
5. Employees have the potential to help accomplish organizational goals.
6. Organizations generally do not make full use of their human resources.

Obviously this view is quite different from—and much more positive than—that of Theory X. McGregor argued that most managers behave in accordance with Theory X. But he maintained that Theory Y is more appropriate and effective as a guide for managerial action (see Table 8.1).

The human relations movement and Theories X and Y increased managers' awareness of the importance of social factors in the workplace. However, human motivation is a complex and dynamic process to which there is no simple key—neither money alone nor social factors alone. Rather, a variety of factors must be considered in any attempt to increase motivation. We turn now from research on human productivity to research that focused directly on human needs.

Maslow's Hierarchy of Needs

Learning Objective 3
Become familiar with Maslow's hierarchy of needs

need   *a personal requirement*

hierarchy of needs   *Maslow's sequence of human needs in the order of their importance*

physiological needs   *the things human beings require for survival*

safety needs   *the things human beings require for physical and emotional security*

The concept of a hierarchy of needs was advanced by Abraham Maslow, a psychologist. A **need** is a personal requirement. Maslow assumed that humans are "wanting" beings who seek to fulfill a variety of needs. He assumed that these needs can be arranged according to their importance in a sequence known as Maslow's **hierarchy of needs** (see Figure 8.2).

At the most basic level are **physiological needs,** the things we require to survive. These needs include food and water, clothing, shelter, and sleep. In the employment context, these needs are usually satisfied through adequate wages.

At the next level are **safety needs,** the things we require for physical and emotional security. Safety needs may be satisfied through job security, health insurance, pension plans, and safe working conditions.

TABLE 8.1   *Theory X and Theory Y Contrasted*

Area	Theory X	Theory Y
Attitude toward work	Indifference	Involvement
Control systems	External	Internal
Supervision	Direct	Indirect
Level of commitment	Low	High
Employee potential	Ignored	Identified
Use of human resources	Limited	Utilized

BUSINESS JOURNAL

Inspiring Motivation

The drive for success and improvement is causing many companies to go out on a limb—literally. Dow Chemical, General Motors, Hewlett-Packard, and Sears, Roebuck have all sent company managers to the Pecos River Learning Center near Santa Fe, New Mexico. Senior company officials think that if managers can learn to cope with nature and face certain "treacherous" situations, they will become more self-confident, more self-reliant, more daring, and ultimately, more productive. Outdoor programs are just one of the unconventional methods executives are employing to increase the efforts of management and sales staffs. In their effort to become even more competitive, some companies are turning to motivational speakers or the controversial human potential movement.

Mountain climbers, baseball stars, National Football League coaches, and gymnasts are all giving advice on how to become leaders, how to be competitive, and how to win. Ford Motor Company has used former baseball player Lou Brock and former pro quarterback Pat Hayden to motivate sales managers. The Arrow Shirts division of Cluett, Peabody & Co. employs Miami Dolphin quarterback Dan Marino to give inspiring speeches. Retired football players Roger Staubach and Fran Tarkenton frequently give talks to salespeople and company managers. They stress the importance of teamwork and the worth of unselfishness in team leaders.

The price tags on these motivational speeches are high. In addition to a flat fee, many sports-business speakers require reimbursement for lodging and transportation. As a flat fee, Mike Ditka charges $15,000, Roger Staubach charges $10,000, and gymnast Cathy Rigby collects $5,000. Fees usually range between $2,000 and $10,000. If this is beyond a small company's budget, several sports figures have developed motivational videotapes. College football coach Lou Holtz, golf great Arnold Palmer, hockey legend Bobby Hull, and baseball hero Reggie Jackson each have videotapes. Some business people question the effectiveness of these motivational speakers, claiming that they might inspire salespeople for a short while but that they have no long-term effects.

The most controversial of motivational techniques is the human potential movement. Human potential organizations believe that they can improve a company's performance by appealing to employees' emotions rather than reason. Human potential groups try to drastically alter people by showing them how to unleash stored, normally unused, personal energy. Three organizations known for business programs in increasing human potential are Werner Erhard's Transformational Technologies, Inc., John-Roger's MSIA (pronounced *Messiah*), and the Church of Scientology founded by science-fiction author L. Ron Hubbard. MSIA's popularity in particular has increased because of its celebrity clientele, which includes actress-singer Barbara Streisand and Scott Paper's CEO Philip Lippincott.

Based on information from Bill Kelly, "Can Sports Stars Really Motivate Your Sales Force?" *Sales and Marketing Management*, December 1987, pp. 36–40; Jeremy Main, "Trying to Bend Manager's Minds," *Fortune*, November 23, 1987, pp. 95–96, 100, 104–106; "Tarkenton on Teambuilding," *Management Solutions*, October 1986, pp. 30–31; and Ken Wells, "The Athletic Approach," *Wall Street Journal*, February 26, 1988, pp. 9D–10D.

---

social needs *the human requirements for love and affection and a sense of belonging*

Next are the **social needs,** the human requirements for love and affection and a sense of belonging. To an extent, these needs can be satisfied through the work environment and the informal organization. But social relationships beyond the workplace—with family and friends, for example—are usually needed too.

esteem needs *the human requirements for respect, recognition, and a sense of one's own accomplishment and worth*

At the level of **esteem needs,** we require respect and recognition (the esteem of others), as well as a sense of our own accomplishment and worth (self-esteem). These needs may be satisfied through personal accom-

Abraham Maslow, developer of the concept of a hierarchy of needs.

self-realization needs *the needs to grow and develop as people and to become all that we are capable of being*

plishment, promotion to more responsible jobs, various honors and awards, and other forms of recognition.

At the uppermost level are **self-realization needs,** the needs to grow and develop as people and to become all that we are capable of being. These are the most difficult needs to satisfy, and the means of satisfying them tend to vary with the individual. For some people, learning a new skill, starting a new career after retirement, or becoming "the best there is" at some endeavor may be the way to satisfy the self-realization needs.

Maslow suggested that people work to satisfy their physiological needs first, then their safety needs, and so on up the "needs ladder." In general, they are motivated by the needs at the lowest (most important) level that remain unsatisfied. However, needs at one level do not have to be completely satisfied before needs at the next-higher level come into play. If the majority of a person's physiological and safety needs are satisfied, that person will be motivated primarily by social needs. But any physiological and safety needs that remain unsatisfied will also be important.

Maslow's hierarchy of needs provides a useful way of viewing employee motivation, as well as a guide for management. By and large, American business has been able to satisfy workers' basic needs, but the higher-order needs present more of a problem. They are not satisfied in a simple manner, and the means of satisfaction vary from one employee to another.

FIGURE 8.2
Maslow's Hierarchy of Needs
Maslow believed that people seek to fulfill five categories of needs.

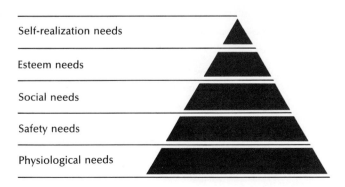

Self-realization needs

Esteem needs

Social needs

Safety needs

Physiological needs

Herzberg's Theory

In the late 1950s, Frederick Herzberg interviewed approximately two hundred accountants and engineers in Pittsburgh. During the interviews, he asked them to think of a time when they had felt especially good about their jobs and their work. Then he asked them to describe the factor or factors that had caused them to feel that way. Next, he did the same regarding a time when they had felt especially bad about their work. He was surprised to find that feeling good and feeling bad resulted from entirely different sets of factors. That is, low pay might have made a particular person feel bad, but it was not high pay that had made him or her feel good. Instead, it was some completely different factor.

Satisfaction and Dissatisfaction

motivation-hygiene theory *the idea that satisfaction and dissatisfaction are separate and distinct dimensions*

Prior to Herzberg's interviews, the general assumption was that employee satisfaction and dissatisfaction lay at opposite ends of the same scale. People felt satisfied, dissatisfied, or somewhere in between the two. Herzberg's interviews, however, convinced him that satisfaction and dissatisfaction may well be different dimensions altogether. One dimension might range from satisfaction to no satisfaction, and the other might range from dissatisfaction to no dissatisfaction. The opposite of satisfaction is not dissatisfaction. The idea that satisfaction and dissatisfaction are separate and distinct dimensions is referred to as the **motivation-hygiene theory** (see Figure 8.3).

The job factors that Herzberg found most frequently associated with satisfaction are achievement, recognition, responsibility, advancement, growth, and the work itself. These factors are generally referred to as

FIGURE 8.3
Motivation-Hygiene Theory
Herzberg's theory takes into account that there are different dimensions to job satisfaction and dissatisfaction and that these factors do not overlap.

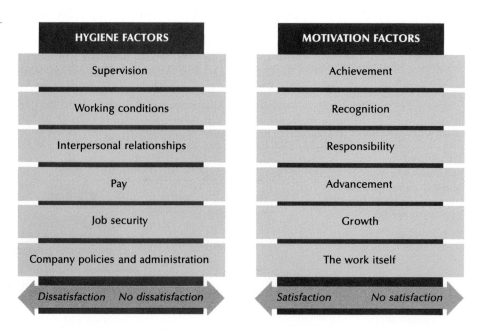

HYGIENE FACTORS	MOTIVATION FACTORS
Supervision	Achievement
Working conditions	Recognition
Interpersonal relationships	Responsibility
Pay	Advancement
Job security	Growth
Company policies and administration	The work itself
Dissatisfaction No dissatisfaction	Satisfaction No satisfaction

motivation factors   *job factors that increase motivation, but whose absence does not necessarily result in dissatisfaction according to the motivation-hygiene theory*

hygiene factors   *job factors that reduce dissatisfaction when present to an acceptable degree, but do not necessarily result in high levels of motivation, according to the motivation-hygiene theory*

motivation factors because their presence increases motivation. However, their absence does not necessarily result in feelings of dissatisfaction. When motivation factors are present, they act as *satisfiers*.

Job factors cited as causing dissatisfaction are supervision, working conditions, interpersonal relationships, pay, job security, and company policies and administration. These factors, called **hygiene factors,** reduce dissatisfaction when they are present to an acceptable degree. However, they do not necessarily result in high levels of motivation. When hygiene factors are absent, they act as *dissatisfiers*.

Using Herzberg's Theory

Herzberg provides explicit guidelines for using the motivation-hygiene theory of employee motivation. He suggests that the hygiene factors must be present to ensure that a worker can function comfortably. But he warns that a state of *no dissatisfaction* never exists. In any situation, people will always be dissatisfied with something.

Managers should make hygiene as good as possible, but should then expect only short-term, not long-term, improvement in motivation. Managers must work to provide the motivation factors, which will presumably enhance motivation and long-term effort.

One practical application of the motivation-hygiene theory is job enrichment, which was discussed in Chapter 6. Job enrichment provides or strengthens such motivation factors as achievement, recognition, and responsibility.

We should note that employee pay has more effect than is explained by Herzberg's theory. His theory suggests that pay provides only short-term change and not motivation. Yet, in many organizations, pay provides recognition and reward for achievement—and recognition and achievement are both motivation factors. The effect of pay may depend on how it is distributed. If a pay increase does not depend on performance (as in across-the-board or cost-of-living raises), it may not motivate people. However, if pay is increased as a form of recognition (as in bonuses or awards), it may play a powerful role in motivating employees to higher performance.

Contemporary Views on Motivation

Learning Objective 5
Become aware of three contemporary theories of motivation: equity, expectancy, and reinforcement

Maslow's hierarchy of needs and Herzberg's two-factor theory are popular and widely known theories of motivation. Each is also a significant step up from the relatively narrow views of scientfic management and Theories X and Y. But they do have one weakness: Each is an attempt to specify *what* motivates people, but neither explains *why* or *how* motivation is caused or how motivation is sustained over time. In recent years, managers have begun to explore three other models that take a more dynamic view of motivation. These are equity theory, expectancy theory, and reinforcement theory.

Equity Theory

The **equity theory** of motivation is based on the premise that people are motivated first to achieve and then to maintain a sense of equity. As used here, *equity* is the distribution of rewards in direct proportion to the contribution of each employee to the organization. Everyone need not receive the *same* rewards, but the rewards should be in accordance with individual contributions.

According to the theory, we tend to implement the idea of equity in the following way. First, we develop our own outcome-to-input ratio. Inputs are the things we contribute to the organization, such as time, effort, skills, education, experience, and so on. Outcomes are the things we get from the organization, such as pay, benefits, recognition, promotions, and other rewards. Next, we compare this ratio to what we perceive as the outcome-to-input ratio for some other person. It might be a coworker, a friend who works for another firm, or even an average of all the people in our organization. This person is called the "comparison other." Note that our perception of this person's outcome-to-input ratio may be absolutely correct or completely wrong. However, we believe it is correct.

If the two ratios are roughly the same, we feel that the organization is treating us equitably. In this case we are motivated to leave things as they are. However, if our ratio is the lower of the two, we feel underrewarded and are motivated to change things. We may (1) decrease our own inputs by not working so hard, (2) try to increase our total outcome by asking for a raise in pay, (3) try to get the comparison other to increase some inputs or receive decreased outcomes, (4) leave the work situation, or (5) do a new comparison with a different comparison other.

Equity theory is most relevant to pay as an outcome. Because pay is a very real measure of a person's worth to the organization, comparisons involving pay are a natural part of organizational life. Managers can avoid problems arising from inequity by doing everything possible to avoid inequity. For instance, they can make sure that rewards are distributed on the basis of performance and that everyone clearly understands the basis for his or her own pay.

Expectancy Theory

Expectancy theory, developed by Victor Vroom, is a very complex model of motivation that is based on a deceptively simple assumption. According to expectancy theory, motivation depends on how much we want something and on how likely we think we are to get it (see Figure 8.4). Consider, for example, the case of three sales representatives who are candidates for promotion to one sales manager's job. Bill has had a very good sales year and always gets good performance evaluations. However, he isn't sure he wants the job because it involves a great deal of travel, long working hours, and much stress and pressure. Paul wants the job badly but doesn't think he has much chance of getting it. He has had a terrible sales year and gets only mediocre performance evaluations from his

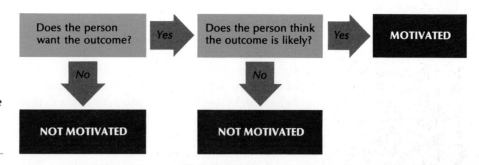

FIGURE 8.4
Expectancy Theory
Vroom's theory is based on the idea that motivation depends on how much people want something and on how likely they think they are to get it.

present boss. Susan wants the job as much as Paul, and she thinks she has a pretty good shot at it. Her sales have improved significantly this past year, and her evaluations are the best in the company.

Expectancy theory would predict that Bill and Paul are not very motivated to seek the promotion. Bill doesn't really want it, and Paul doesn't think he has much of a chance of getting it. Susan, however, is very motivated to seek the promotion because she wants it *and* thinks she can get it.

Expectancy theory is complex because each action we take is likely to lead to several different outcomes, some that we may want and others that we may not want. For example, if people work hard and put in many extra hours, several things may happen. They may get a pay raise, they may be promoted, they may have less time with their families, they may have to cut back on their social life, and they may gain valuable new job skills.

For one person, the promotion may be paramount, the pay raise and new skills fairly important, and the loss of family and social life of negligible importance. For someone else, the family and social life may be most important, the pay raise of moderate importance, the new skills unimportant, and the promotion undesirable because of the additional hours it would require. The first person would be motivated to work hard and put in extra hours, whereas the second person would not be at all motivated to do so. In other words, it is the entire bundle of outcomes—and the individual's evaluation of the importance of each outcome—that determines motivation.

Expectancy theory is difficult to apply, but it does provide several useful guidelines for managers. It suggests that managers must recognize that (1) employees work for a variety of different reasons; (2) these reasons, or expected outcomes, may change over time; and (3) it is necessary to clearly show employees how they can attain the outcomes they desire.

Reinforcement Theory

reinforcement theory a theory of motivation based on the premise that behavior that is rewarded is likely to be repeated, whereas behavior that has been punished is less likely to recur

The contemporary motivation theory with perhaps the greatest potential for business application is reinforcement theory. **Reinforcement theory** is based on the premise that behavior that is rewarded is likely to be repeated, whereas behavior that has been punished is less likely to recur.

Kinds of Reinforcement   A *reinforcement* is an action that follows directly from a particular behavior. It may be a pay raise following a particularly large sale to a new customer or a reprimand for coming to work late. Reinforcements can take a variety of forms and can be used in a number of different ways. A *positive reinforcement* is one that strengthens desired behavior by providing a reward. For example, many employees respond well to praise. Recognition from their supervisor after they have done a good job increases (strengthens) their willingness to perform well in the future.

A *negative reinforcement* strengthens desired behavior by eliminating an undesirable task or situation. Suppose that a machine shop must be cleaned every month. Because of the nature of the work, cleaning up is a dirty, miserable task. During one particular month when the workers do a less-than-satisfactory job at their normal work assignments, the boss requires the workers to clean up the factory rather than hiring a private maintenance service to clean the facility. The employees will be motivated to work harder during the next month, to avoid the unpleasant cleanup task again.

Punishment is an undesired consequence that follows from undesirable behavior. Common forms of punishment used in organizations include reprimands, docked (reduced) pay, disciplinary layoffs, and termination (firing). Punishment often does more harm than good. It tends to create an unpleasant environment, fosters hostility and resentment, and suppresses undesirable behavior only until the supervisor's back is turned.

Managers who rely on *extinction* hope to eliminate undesirable behavior by ignoring it. The idea is that the behavior will eventually become "extinct." Suppose, for example, that an employee has the habit of writing memo after memo to his or her manager about insignificant events. If the manager doesn't respond to any of these memos, the employee will probably stop writing them; and the behavior will be extinguished.

Using Reinforcement   The effectiveness of reinforcement depends on which type is used and how it is timed. Each of the four types is best in certain situations. However, many situations lend themselves to the use of more than one type. Generally, positive reinforcement is considered the most effective, and it is recommended when the manager has a choice.

Continual, repetitive reinforcement can become tedious for both manager and employees, especially when the same behavior is being reinforced over and over in the same way. At the start, it may be necessary to reinforce a desired behavior every time it occurs. However, once a desired behavior has become more or less established, occasional reinforcement seems to be most effective.

A number of firms have applied reinforcement theory in the workplace. Procter & Gamble, Warner-Lambert, Ford, and Emery Air Freight have all reported success with the systematic use of positive reinforcement to reward desired behavior. At Emery, for example, management believed that air-freight containers (used to consolidate many small shipments into fewer large ones) were not being utilized effectively. Through an innovative system based on positive reinforcement, Emery was able to increase container utilization from 45 percent of capacity to over 95 percent. As a result, Emery saved $3 million in the first three years of the program.

Motivating Through Reward Systems

Up to now, we have focused our attention on theories and models of employee motivation. Many of these may be difficult for the practicing manager to apply. Those that are used generally become part of the organization's **reward system,** which is the formal mechanism for defining, evaluating, and rewarding employee performance. A reward system should motivate employees to work effectively to receive desired outcomes from the organization. It should also have a positive impact on employee satisfaction and morale.

reward system   *the formal mechanism for defining, evaluating, and rewarding employee performance*

Effective Reward Systems

Learning Objective 6
Know the characteristics of effective reward systems and several relatively new kinds of reward systems

A reward system must accomplish four things if it is to be truly effective. First, it must enable people to satisfy their basic needs. In terms of Maslow's hierarchy of needs, for example, rewards should enable employees to satisfy the first two levels.

Second, an effective reward system should provide rewards comparable to those offered by other organizations. According to equity theory, employees at one firm will experience inequity if they think their outcome-to-input ratios are lower than those of employees at some other firm. This can result in decreased effort or increased turnover.

Third, rewards must be distributed fairly and equitably within the organization. People are more likely to compare themselves with others in their own firm than with workers elsewhere. Hence, perceptions of equity come into play here as well. Moreover, a strong relationship between performance and reward is consistent with both expectancy theory and reinforcement theory.

Fourth, an effective reward system must recognize the fact that different people have different needs and may choose different paths to the fulfillment of those needs. Some people want economic gain, while others want more leisure time. Some people may want to earn more money by simply working longer hours in their current positions. Other people may prefer to earn more money through promotions and new job opportunities.

Companies reward their top-performing employees, such as Estrella Linch, an outstanding salesperson with The Prudential Insurance Company of America.

New Kinds of Reward Systems

Money will always be an important part of the rewards employees expect. The two most commonly used monetary reward systems are fixed-rate systems and incentive systems. In *fixed-rate systems,* employees are paid a set amount for the work they do during some specified period—an hour, a day, a week, a month, or a year. In *incentive systems,* employees are paid a set amount for each unit they produce. Taylor's piece-rate system, which we described earlier, is an incentive system. The commission system, in which an employee is paid a percentage of his or her sales volume, is also an incentive system.

In their attempt to discover new and effective ways to enhance employee motivation, managers have begun to search for innovative reward systems. Among those now being explored are the all-salaried work force, the skill-based job-evaluation system, lump-sum salary increases, and the cafeteria benefits plan.

All-Salaried Work Force No member of an all-salaried work force punches a time clock or has a rigidly defined work schedule. Instead, every employee receives a guaranteed monthly salary, regardless of the time actually worked. Performance—rather than time—is the basis for this reward system, and employees are expected to get a certain amount of work done. If some employees need more time to complete their work, they are expected to put in that time without additional compensation, just as managers typically do.

Skill-Based Job Evaluation In conventional reward systems, all employees who do the same job are paid about the same amount, regardless of how well they perform. In the skill-based job-evaluation system, however, it is the person rather than the job that defines the compensation. If two people work at the same job, but one is considerably more skilled than the other, then the more skilled employee receives the higher pay. Usually a person's pay is adjusted upward for each new skill or job that she or he masters. Texas Instruments and General Foods have reported successful experiences with skill-based job-evaluation systems.

Lump-Sum Salary Increases In traditional reward systems, an employee who receives an annual pay increase is given part of the increase in each pay period. For example, suppose an employee on a monthly salary gets a 10 percent annual pay hike. He or she actually receives 10 percent of the former monthly salary added to each month's paycheck for a year. Companies that offer lump-sum salary increases give the employee the option of taking the entire pay raise in one lump sum at the beginning of the year. The employee then draws his or her "regular" pay for the rest of the year. The lump-sum payment is typically treated as an interest-free loan that must be repaid if the employee leaves the firm during the year. B. F. Goodrich, Aetna Life and Casualty, and Timex have all used variations of this plan.

Cafeteria Benefits Plan The usual reward system includes not only pay but also a set "package" of benefits. These may include health insurance, paid vacations, paid holidays, a retirement plan, life insurance, and other benefits. Some employees take advantage of all these benefits; others do not. Those who do not use certain benefits simply don't get them. For example, employees who choose not to take all their allotted vacation receive nothing in return; they just don't get all their vacation time.

Under the cafeteria benefits plan, employees are allotted a certain amount of benefits money to "spend" as they see fit in the "benefits

BUSINESS JOURNAL

Motivation Through Company-Funded Child Care

What have I done to my baby? What kind of person is taking care of my child? Besides the ordinary stress of working, working parents may also face the panic and guilt of not staying home with their young children. Though bad accidents, mistreatment, and incidents of sexual abuse in licensed day-care centers are rare, several recent horror stories have left working parents worried and skeptical about the welfare of their children.

By helping parents pay for baby sitters, providing company-sponsored child-care centers, or offering child-care referral services to employees, businesses can ease the minds of anxious parents and thus create a more stable and productive work force. Because of an impending labor shortage that will almost certainly get worse, it is very likely that more and more companies will provide employees with some form of child-care assistance.

Some companies already have child-care plans. BankAmerica Corp. organized the California Child Care Initiative to help its employees with their child-care responsibilities. The California Child Care Initiative is a partnership of thirty-three public and private organizations including the American Express Foundation, Los Angeles County, and the city of Santa Monica. Polaroid Corp. has set up a voucher program that pays up to 80 percent of an employee's costs at selected child-care facilities. Apple Computer, Inc. spent $750,000 to open a child-care center for seventy children in Cupertino, California. Parents working for Apple, selected by lottery, pay up to $575 a month (depending on their salary) to have their children cared for at this on-site company center. Other companies, like Hewlett-Packard, are allowing employees to personally design more flexible work schedules.

With day care hard to find, hard to afford, and sometimes questionable in quality, firms can assist parents tremendously by helping employees with child care. In addition, child-care programs usually benefit businesses by raising employee morale, reducing absenteeism, and relieving employers of recruiting and retraining costs. Furthermore, because of the federal deficit, employees will not be able to look to the government for child-care assistance. Any form of organized help will have to come from the private sector.

Today the number of firms offering meaningful child-care aid is still small. Of the 1.2 million businesses with ten or more employees, only 2 percent, 25,000 firms, have employer-sponsored day-care programs. Only 3 percent of U.S. employers assist employees in paying for child-care expenses. Statistics show that large companies are more likely to offer employees child-care benefits than smaller companies. Some large organizations housed in tall buildings are limited in their ability to set up day-care centers, though, because fire regulations typically mandate that children be cared for on the ground floor. Insurance premiums and liability costs also steer many wary employers away from child-care involvement.

David Bloom and Todd P. Steen, "Why Child Care Is Good for Business," *American Demographics*, August 1988, pp. 22–27, 57–59; Jaclyn Fierman, "Child Care: What Works—and Doesn't," *Fortune*, November 21, 1988, pp. 163, 166, 170, 174, 176; Jon D. Hull, Melissa Ludtke, and Elizabeth Taylor, "The Child-Care Dilemma," *Time*, June 22, 1987, pp. 54–60; and Cheryl Russell, "Who Gives and Who Gets," *American Demographics*, May 1988, pp. 17–18.

cafeteria." They may use it to purchase whatever benefits they would like most. In a two-income family, one spouse might elect not to take health insurance (because the other spouse has a better plan) and to take additional vacation time instead. Similarly, a single employee with no dependents may by-pass life insurance in favor of other options.

Many employees like this approach, but it is quite costly to manage and administer. In spite of the cost, American Can Company, PepsiCo, and Quaker Oats have set up cafeteria benefits plans for their employees.

TABLE 8.2   Types of Reward Systems

Type	Description
Fixed-rate	Employees are paid a set amount of money for the work they do during a specific time.
Incentive	Employees are paid a set amount of money for each unit produced. Taylor's piece-rate system and a commission sales system are two examples.
All-salaried work force	Employees receive a guaranteed monthly salary, regardless of the time actually worked.
Skill-based job evaluation	If two people work at the same job, but one is considerably more skilled than the other, then the more skilled employee receives the higher pay. Texas Instruments and General Foods have reported success with this system.
Lump-sum salary increases	Employees are allowed to take their entire pay raise in one lump sum at the beginning of the year and draw their "regular" pay the rest of the year. B. F. Goodrich, Aetna Life and Casualty, and Timex have all used variations of this plan.
Cafeteria benefits plan	Employees are allotted a certain amount of benefits money to "spend" as they see fit in the "benefits cafeteria." American Can Company, PepsiCo, and Quaker Oats have used this plan.

Offering rewards (see Table 8.2) is not the only way organizations can motivate employees. In the next section we will look at several other inducements to high performance.

Key Motivation Techniques

Several specific techniques have been developed to help managers boost employee motivation. Some of these have already been discussed in other contexts, but we will review them here.

Management by Objectives

management by objectives (MBO) *a motivation technique in which a manager and his or her subordinates collaborate in setting goals*

Learning Objective 7
Learn several techniques for increasing employee motivation

Management by objectives (MBO) is a motivation process in which a manager and his or her subordinates collaborate in setting goals. The primary purpose of MBO is to clarify the roles that the subordinates are expected to play in reaching the organization's goals; it allows subordinates to participate in goal setting and in performance evaluation, thus increasing their motivation. Most MBO programs consist of a series of five steps, as shown in Figure 8.5.

The first step in setting up an MBO program is to secure the acceptance of top management. It is essential that top managers endorse and participate in the program if others in the firm are to accept it. The acceptance of top management also provides a natural starting point for educating employees about the purposes and mechanics of MBO.

Next, preliminary goals must be established. Top management also plays a major role in this activity because the preliminary goals reflect the firm's mission and strategy. The intent is to have these goals filter down through the organization.

The third step, which actually consists of several smaller steps, is the essence of MBO. (1) The manager explains to the subordinate that he or she has accepted certain goals for the group (manager plus subordinates) and asks the subordinate to think about how he or she can help achieve these goals. (2) The manager later meets with each subordinate individually. Together, the two of them establish goals for the subordinate. Whenever possible, the goals should be measurable and should include a time within which they will be fulfilled (usually one year). K mart, for example, sets annual goals in terms of sales dollars per square foot of floor space. (3) The manager and the subordinate decide what resources the subordinate will need to accomplish his or her goals.

As the fourth step, the manager and each subordinate meet periodically to review the subordinate's progress. Goals may be modified during these meetings if circumstances have changed. For example, a sales representative may have accepted a goal of increasing sales by 20 percent. However, a new competitor may have entered the marketplace, making this goal unattainable. In light of this new information, the goal may be revised downward to 10 or 15 percent.

The fifth step in the MBO process is evaluation. At the end of the designated period, the manager and each subordinate meet again to determine which of the subordinate's goals were met, which goals were not met, and why. The employee's reward (in the form of a pay raise, praise, or promotion) is based on the degree of attainment.

Like many other management methods, MBO has advantages and disadvantages. MBO can motivate employees by involving them in the MBO process. By discussing goals and performance appraisal, communication is improved within an organization. Periodic goal setting and

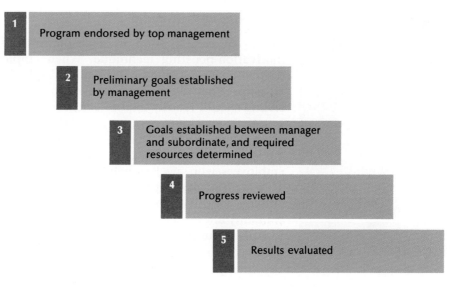

FIGURE 8.5
The Five Steps Required for an Effective MBO Program
An MBO program clarifies the roles that subordinates are expected to play in reaching the organization's goals while allowing subordinates to participate in goal setting and performance evaluation.

1   Program endorsed by top management

2   Preliminary goals established by management

3   Goals established between manager and subordinate, and required resources determined

4   Progress reviewed

5   Results evaluated

review enhances control within an organization. A major problem with MBO is that it does not work unless the process begins at the top of an organization. In some cases, MBO results in excessive paperwork. Finally, some managers have difficulty sitting down and working out goals with their subordinates and instead may actually assign goals to their subordinates. This practice undermines an MBO program and leads to resentment by subordinates.[3]

MBO has proved to be an effective motivational tool in many organizations. Tenneco, Black & Decker, Du Pont, General Foods, RCA, and General Motors have all reported success with MBO. Like any management technique, however, it must be applied with caution and in the right spirit if it is to work.

Job Enrichment

This concept was discussed in Chapter 6. There, we noted that job enrichment is an alternative to job specialization. It is an attempt to provide workers with variety in their tasks, and it accords them some responsibility for, and control over, their jobs. In this chapter we noted that Herzberg's motivation-hygiene theory is one basis for the use of job enrichment; that is, the added responsibility and control that job enrichment confers on employees increase their satisfaction and motivation.

Modified Workweeks

Modified workweeks were also discussed in Chapter 6. The compressed workweek, the flexible workweek, and job sharing were described as alternatives to traditional work schedules. Modified workweeks can also be used to enhance employee motivation. If an employee is permitted to decide when to work, he or she will develop a feeling of autonomy and professionalism. This, in turn, leads to increased motivation.

Employee Participation

Employee participation in decision making is frequently cited as a motivation-boosting technique. When employees are given a voice in determining what they will be doing and where the organization should be going, they develop a sense of involvement and commitment. This feeling should readily lead to enhanced motivation.

An increasingly popular method of soliciting employee participation is applying Ouchi's Theory Z (Chapter 5)—and, in particular, quality circles. Recall from Chapter 7 that *quality circles* are groups of volunteer employees who meet to help solve problems related to product quality. This form of participation actually provides two advantages: increased employee motivation and solutions to organizational problems. At a steel company in Cleveland, labor-and-management teams have sought out and identified solutions for several difficult production and maintenance problems.

Employee participation pays off handsomely for the organization and its employees. These employees at Lyondell Petrochemical Company, through employee participation, suggested methods by which the company could increase its production of ethylene by 70 million pounds per year.

BUSINESS JOURNAL

For Beehivers, There's No Place Like Home

The television, VCR, stereo system, and a comfortable couch are in the living room. One of the spare bedrooms houses the stationary bike, the rowing machine, a weight bench, and various weights. In the den there is a home computer, printer, small copier, facsimile machine, and an impressive desk. The person who lives here doesn't do any commuting to work—it's a short trip between the breakfast table and the den. What do you get when you cross a yuppie with a recluse? You get a *beehiver*, or *telecommuter*.

There are both advantages and disadvantages to working at home. One of the big advantages in the recent past—income tax deductions—has been curbed by new federal tax laws. Still, a person using part of his or her home for business purposes may claim portions of the rent, utilities, and structural modifications as business expenses. The purchase of a computer, telephone-answering machine, or other electronic office equipment also qualifies as an expense. But federal tax laws are complicated and specific, and if the tax auditor suddenly comes around, the beehiver better have all the receipts and physical proof necessary to justify the write-offs. Beehivers aren't exempt from penalties and interest.

Beehivers, whether they are entrepreneurs or they work for a company, spend more time with their children than their office counterparts. Studies indicate that beehivers who work for others are also more productive. Closing an important deal with a client while sitting on the couch might be just the thing for some people. Companies like IBM, J.C. Penney, American Express, and Johnson & Johnson all employ beehivers.

Working at home has it shortcomings, though. Employers, not actually seeing what their workers are doing, may pass up beehivers for promotions. The lack of social contact may cause beehivers to feel isolated and alienated. Also, beehivers might miss the intellectual and creative stimulation often provided by peers and superiors. Feeling cooped up, beehivers might also get a little stir crazy. In addition, telecommuters may face zoning restrictions. They may be legally limited in the amount of deliveries they can receive or in the size of office equipment they can bring into a residence. Finally, every beehiver must face the constant temptations of the television and a comfortable bed.

Despite any disadvantages, however, with the growing difficulties in finding adequate, affordable child-care facilities, the stress and cost involved in commuting, and the rising number of "microbusinesses" (businesses employing four or less people), the ranks of beehivers should continue to expand. For some, home is where the heart is *and* the office, too.

Based on information from Ronaleen R. Roha, "Tax-Proofing Your Home Office," *Changing Times*, June 1989, pp. 75–76; Janice Castro, "Staying Home Is Paying Off," *Time*, October 26, 1987, pp. 112–113; Walter Kiechel III, "The Microbusiness Alternative," *Fortune*, October 24, 1988, pp. 219–220; and Paul Plawin, "Your Home Business: Starting It Right," *Changing Times*, August 1987, pp. 71–75.

Behavior Modification

behavior modification   *the use of a systematic program of reinforcement to encourage desirable organizational behavior*

Behavior modification is a technique based on reinforcement theory, which we discussed earlier in this chapter. As applied to management, **behavior modification** is the use of a systematic program of reinforcement to encourage desirable organizational behavior.

Use of this technique begins with the identification of target behavior—behavior that is to be changed. (It may be low production levels or a high rate of absenteeism, for example.) Existing levels of this behavior are then measured. Next, managers provide positive reinforcement in the form of rewards when employees exhibit the desired behavior (such as increased production or less absenteeism). Finally, the levels of the target behavior are measured again, to determine whether the desired changes have been achieved. If they have, the reinforcement is maintained to avoid extinction. However, if the target behavior has not changed in the desired direction, the reinforcement (reward) system must be changed to one that is likely to be more effective.

CHAPTER REVIEW

Summary

Motivation is the individual, internal process that energizes, directs, and sustains behavior. One of the first approaches to employee motivation was Frederick Taylor's scientific management. Taylor believed that employees work only for money and that they must be closely supervised and managed. Douglas McGregor labeled this view Theory X and then described an alternative view called Theory Y. Theory Y is more in keeping with the results of the Hawthorne Studies (which showed the importance of social processes in the workplace) and with the human relations movement (which was based on the idea that employees can be motivated to behave as responsible members of the organization).

Maslow's hierarchy of needs suggests that people may be motivated by five sets of needs. In order of decreasing importance, these needs are called the physiological, safety, social, esteem, and self-realization needs. People are motivated by the lowest (most important) set of needs that remains unfulfilled. As needs at one level are satisfied, people try to satisfy needs at the next level.

Frederick Herzberg found that satisfaction and dissatisfaction are influenced by two different sets of factors. Hygiene factors, including pay and working conditions, affect an employee's degree of dissatisfaction but do not affect satisfaction. Motivation factors, including recognition and responsibility, affect an employee's degree of satisfaction but do not affect the degree of dissatisfaction.

There are three major contemporary motivation theories. Equity theory maintains that people are motivated to obtain and preserve equitable treatment for themselves. Expectancy theory suggests that our motivation depends on how much we want something and how likely we think we are to get it. And reinforcement theory is based on the idea that people will repeat behavior that is rewarded and won't repeat behavior that is punished.

Effective reward systems must satisfy basic needs, they must be both externally and internally equitable, and they must recognize that people have a variety of needs. Traditional reward systems are based on fixed rates or incentives. Several new types of reward systems seem to provide additional motivation to employees.

Managers can use a variety of techniques to enhance employee motivation. Key techniques include management by objectives, in which the manager and subordinate set goals for the subordinate together, and behavior modification, which is based on reinforcement theory. Job enrichment, modified workweeks, and employee participation can also be used to motivate employees.

The design of reward systems (and other personnel-related systems) is part of a broader set of activities called human resources management. These activities are the subject of the next chapter.

Key Terms

You should now be able to define and give an example relevant to each of the following terms:

motivation	self-realization needs
morale	motivation-hygiene theory
scientific management	motivation factors
piece-rate system	hygiene factors
Theory X	equity theory
Theory Y	expectancy theory
need	reinforcement theory
hierarchy of needs	reward system
physiological needs	management by objectives (MBO)
safety needs	behavior modification
social needs	
esteem needs	

Questions and Exercises

Review Questions

1. Compare the two earlier schools of thought on motivation: scientific management and Theory X versus the human relations movement and Theory Y.
2. How did the results of the Hawthorne Studies influence researchers' thinking about employee motivation?
3. What are the five sets of needs in Maslow's hierarchy? How are a person's needs related to motivation?
4. What are the two dimensions in Herzberg's motivation-hygiene theory? What kinds of things affect each dimension?
5. According to equity theory, how does an employee determine whether he or she is being treated equitably?
6. According to expectancy theory, what two things determine motivation?
7. What is the fundamental premise of reinforcement theory?
8. What are the four attributes of an effective reward system?
9. What is the prime motivating factor in the all-salaried reward system? in the skill-based job-evaluation system?
10. Describe the steps involved in the MBO process.
11. What are the objectives of MBO? What do you think might be its disadvantages?
12. How does employee participation—as in quality circles—increase motivation?
13. Describe the steps in the process of behavior modification.

Discussion Questions

1. What types of motivational techniques are being used by Japanese auto plants in the United States?
2. What are the potential problems associated with motivational techniques employed by Japanese managers?
3. How might managers make use of the hierarchy of needs in motivating employees? What problems would they encounter?
4. Do the various theories of motivation contradict each other or complement each other? Explain.
5. What combination of motivational techniques do you think would result in the best overall motivation and reward system?
6. Reinforcement theory and behavior modification have been called demeaning because they tend to treat people "like mice in a maze." Do you agree?

Exercises

1. Analyze the system that is used in your school to motivate and reward students. Determine (a) the theory or theories on which it is based and (b) how it could be improved.
2. Suppose you are the owner of a neighborhood hardware store and have two employees besides yourself. What motivational problems might you encounter? What techniques could you use to minimize these problems?
3. Devise a reward system for the hardware store of Exercise 2. Make sure it has all the attributes of an effective reward system *and* takes into consideration the hardware store "environment."

Case 8.1

Quad/Graphics Motivates Employees

"The average employee who joins my company looks like a misfit," says the founder and president of Quad/Graphics, Harry V. Quadracci, explaining that his Wisconsin-based printing company isn't full of college graduates or high-tech engineers. But, Quadracci adds, "we get extraordinary results from ordinary people." With its cutting-edge technology, employee education program, and creative management practices, Quad/Graphics turns novice printers into skilled technicians who are proud of their work. The bottom line for the company includes satisfied employees, high-quality products, and annual sales of more than $400 million.

The largest privately held printing company in the country, Quad/Graphics prints more than a hundred magazines and catalogs, including *Time, Newsweek, Playboy,* and *U.S. News & World Report.* Since its founding in 1971 with a single press in a 20,000-square-foot plant in Pewaukee, Wisconsin, Quad/Graphics has expanded to several printing plants, millions of square feet of floor space, and more than 3,500 employees. Through its Quad/Tech division, the company develops state-of-the-art printing technology to use in its own operations and to sell to other printers.

But a "knowledge company," as Quad/Graphics calls itself, begins with people. "Where else are the ideas going to come from?" asks Quadracci. So the company often hires high school graduates who don't have clear career goals—and teaches them that, with training, they can become more than mere printers.

At Quad/Graphics, employees learn to think of themselves as printing specialists who operate sophisticated, computer-controlled presses.

What's more, through Quad/Graphics' employee stock ownership program, workers can acquire a financial interest in the company. Quad/Graphics makes regular tax-deductible contributions to a trust fund for buying stock. Based on employees' years of membership in the plan and salaries, each year the amount of stock allocated to them increases. When they retire or leave the company, they receive the stock and can sell it back to Quad/Graphics for a liberal retirement income. At present, more than 4 percent of the company's stock belongs to employees, and Quad/Graphics predicts that some day the firm will be wholly owned by its employees.

Quad/Graphics' ownership plan motivates employees for several reasons. If the company does well, they have the opportunity to earn more money. They also view the company's contribution as an expression of respect for the work they do, especially since it's combined with other forms of participative management. Moreover, Quad/Graphics' open communication policy keeps employees informed about the stock plan and reinforces their sense of company ownership.

Quad/Graphics' approach to partnership has resulted in an extensive program of training and education. In addition to various orientation classes, employees can take extra courses. Years ago Quad/Graphics converted to a three-day workweek, which allows people to work three twelve-hour shifts and keeps the presses running around the clock. The company saved on overtime, and productivity rose 20 percent. Now the company's educational division uses Fridays to teach classes ranging from remedial math and reading to safety skills and computer programming. Students and teachers participate voluntarily, without pay. Employees aren't promoted just because they take classes, but they're often better prepared when job openings do come along.

Not surprisingly, Quadracci calls his company a "social experiment." But, from the beginning, the operation has thrived on change—on the never-ending search for a better way to do things. Experimentation doesn't always pay off, as in the case of the three employees who were given the freedom to develop a page-folding machine. After an investment of $780,000, the machine still didn't work. Quadracci is philosophical about mistakes, figuring that they are inevitable in any aggressive research and development program. The important thing at Quad/Graphics is to start early and keep trying. With the help of training, technology, and a piece of the corporate pie, Quad/Graphics wants its employee-partners to keep on looking for a better way.*

Questions

1. What types of motivational techniques are being used at Quad/Graphics?
2. Are these motivational techniques effective? Explain your answer.
3. Would you like to work at Quad/Graphics? Why or why not?

Case 8.2

United Parcel Service Runs a Tight Ship

In this era of high-tech equipment and sophisticated management techniques, United Parcel Service, Inc.'s industrial engineers are sticking to old-fashioned time and motion studies to set standards for many tasks. UPS, however, has no intention of being left behind in the electronics revolution.

UPS, the nation's largest deliverer of packages, employs more than 215,000 (about half are full-time workers) persons who are expected to provide a fair day's work for a fair day's pay. Pay for drivers averages about 6 percent more than that of the best-paid drivers at other trucking companies.

To earn that better pay, UPS employees are expected to precisely follow UPS policy in everything from stepping efficiently in and out of a delivery truck to accurately sorting the 10 million packages that are picked up and delivered daily. A sorter, for example, is expected to handle 1,124 packages an hour with no more than one mistake per 2,500 packages.

UPS employees are also closely supervised. Drivers are sometimes accompanied on their rounds by UPS industrial engineers (with digital timers) who even time trips to the bathroom. To obtain maximum output from drivers, the engineers correct deviations on the spot. Supervisors ride with "least-best drivers" until the drivers learn to finish their rounds on time. A UPS district manager comments, "We bring workers up to our level of acceptance; we don't go down to

---

* Based on information from George Gendron and Bo Burlingham, "Printer Harry Quadracci," *Inc.*, December 1986, pp. 25–26+; Daniel M. Kehrer, "The Miracle of Theory Q," *Business Month*, September 1989, pp. 45–49; Patty Murphy, "Never Too Late to Learn," *American Printer*, September 1989, pp. 87–89; and Corey Rosen, Katherine J. Klein, and Karen M. Young, "When Employees Share the Profits," *Psychology Today*, January 1986, pp. 30–36.

their level." One former UPS supervisor said he would ask, "Are you falling asleep? Do you want a sleeping bag?" in order to embarrass less-efficient drivers into working faster.

Today the UPS corporate culture stresses achievement and teamwork as well as efficiency. A company official says that the rigid UPS standards aren't intended to be "hammers"; instead they provide a measure of accountability. That accountability, along with the company's skill in managing its work force, are considered the keys to success for UPS in what is becoming an increasingly competitive market.

Some UPS drivers are very happy with their jobs, taking pride in meeting standards day after day. Up to 80 percent of the full-time work force attends voluntary workshops after hours. Other workers complain that they can't relax, are always in a hurry, and have to shorten breaks to finish on time. The company "squeezes every ounce out of you," says one driver.

Still, UPS managers indicate that the company's standards help employees work smarter, not harder. Some productivity experts call UPS one of the most efficient companies anywhere. At least one transportation executive states that UPS has taken "people engineering" as far as it can be taken.

Though UPS clearly dominates small-package delivery, it ranks second to Federal Express in the overnight-package delivery business. To gain a greater market share, UPS is trying to improve its public image and aggressively develop more modern methods. UPS now has its own airline because company officials found they needed more transportation flexibility. Training its own flight crews, UPS expects its pilots to be as efficient as its truck drivers.

UPS officials trying to match and surpass Federal Express have placed electronic scanners in the company's sorting centers and on-board computers in its vans. Growing rapidly, UPS has its priorities straight—efficiency, improvement, company loyalty, and profits.†

Questions

1. Would you like to work for UPS? Why or why not?
2. How do you think participative management techniques such as quality circles would work at UPS?
3. What motivates you? Doing a good job? Being complimented for doing a good job? Money? Recognition? Awards publicly given?

---

† Based on information from Leo Abruzzese, "Low-Key Base Profits UPS," *Journal of Commerce*, July 25, 1985, p. 1A; Leo Abruzzese, "UPS Runs Bare-Bone Operation, Works for Maximum Efficiency," *Journal of Commerce*, July 26, 1985, p. 7A; Christopher Fotos, "UPS Establishes Its Own Airline to Simplify Flight Operations," *Aviation Week & Space Technology*, October 3, 1988, pp. 108–109; Kenneth Labich, "Big Changes at Big Brown," *Fortune*, January 18, 1988, p. 56+; Daniel Machalaba, "United Parcel Service Gets Deliveries Done by Driving Its Workers," *Wall Street Journal*, April 22, 1986, p. 1; and Mark Magnier, "UPS Gives Up on Fuel Blend," *Journal of Commerce*, March 15, 1988, pp. 1A, 10A.

HUMAN RESOURCES MANAGEMENT

1 Understand the definition of human resources management

2 Be aware of the steps in human resources planning

3 Understand the objectives and uses of job analysis

4 Be able to describe the processes of recruiting, employee selection, and orientation

5 Know the primary elements of employee compensation and benefits

6 Understand the purposes and techniques of employee training, development, and performance appraisal

7 Know some of the major legislation affecting human resources management

CHAPTER PREVIEW

We begin our study of human resources management, or HRM, with an overview of how businesses acquire, maintain, and develop their human resources. After listing the steps by which firms match their human resources needs with the supply of human resources available, we examine the concept of job analysis. Then we focus on a firm's recruiting, selection, and orientation procedures as the means of acquiring employees. We also describe forms of employee compensation that motivate employees to remain with the firm and to work effectively. Next, we discuss employee training, management development, and performance appraisal methods. Finally, we consider legislation that affects HRM practices.

INSIDE BUSINESS

Motorola's Education Program

Recently Motorola was the world's largest producer of semiconductors; now it is in fourth place. Motorola's other electronic devices—two-way radios, pagers, cellular telephones, and modems—are also facing fierce competition from other domestic and foreign products. But Motorola is fighting back by improving product quality. Company executives are trying to create a new corporate culture that focuses on "total customer satisfaction." Motorola's quality goal is stated in six words: "Zero defects in everything we do."

Motorola officials believe they can reach this goal by investing in what they consider their most valuable company resource—their employees. Everyone at Motorola, from the chief executive officer to the janitors, takes classes in customer satisfaction. Motorola stands firmly behind its education program that teaches new skills to *all* of its 104,000 workers.

While other U.S. companies may opt for layoffs and plant closings, Motorola executives think that educated employees are more advantageous to their firm than are severe cost-cutting tactics. Motorola spends more than $60 million annually on employee education. This figure amounts to 3 percent of Motorola's payroll.

Motorola workers who do poorly on reading and mathematics tests enroll in remedial classes. Other plant workers attend classes in statistical process control, idea sharing, and teamwork (teamwork is reinforced by company volleyball games). Employees also take courses in design-for-assembly techniques, risk taking, and managing change. Since 1984, Motorola managers have spent more than 3.2 million classroom hours in courses lasting from four hours to eight weeks. Motorola even has its suppliers enroll in classes on quality.

At the Motorola Training and Education Center in Schaumburg, Illinois, the $14-million Galvin Center for Continuing Education provides Motorola employees all over the world with state-of-the-art technical and managerial instruction. The Motorola center is using high-tech equipment to teach high-tech procedures. A sophisticated satellite communications system, for example, is used to allow workers to participate in live training programs from their particular work locations.

By linking its employee education effort to its overall corporate strategy, 62-year-old Motorola is demonstrating its commitment to education. Thus far the company has had very positive results: Compared to three years ago, Motorola workers can build one cellular telephone ten times faster, and defects in phones have dropped dramatically. At Motorola, intensified employee education has been a key to greater productivity and higher-quality products.[1]

Motorola attributes its growth and success to its employees. Training and education are viewed as essential for long-term employee development. To increase productivity and make higher-quality products, Motorola officials recognize that well-trained personnel are required.

Human Resources Management: An Overview

The human resource is not only unique and valuable; it is an organization's most important resource. It seems logical that the organization would expend a great deal of effort to acquire and utilize such a resource, and most organizations do. That effort is now known as *human resources management,* or *HRM.* It has also been called *staffing* and *personnel management.*

human resources management *all the activities involved in acquiring, maintaining, and developing an organization's human resources*

Human resources management consists of all the activities involved in acquiring, maintaining, and developing an organization's human resources. As the definition implies, HRM begins with acquisition—getting people to work for the organization. Next, steps must be taken to keep these valuable resources. (This is important; after all, they are the only business resources that can leave the organization at will.) Finally, the human resources should be developed to their full capacity to contribute to the firm.

HRM Activities

Learning Objective 1
Understand the definition of human resources management

Each of the three phases of HRM—acquiring, maintaining, and developing human resources—consists of a number of related activities. Acquisition, for example, includes planning as well as the various activities that lead to hiring new personnel. Altogether, this phase of HRM includes five separate activities:

▶ *Human resources planning:* to determine the firm's future human resources needs

▶ *Job analysis:* to determine the exact nature of positions that are to be filled

▶ *Recruiting:* to attract people to apply for positions in the firm

▶ *Selection:* to choose and hire the most qualified applicants

▶ *Orientation:* to acquaint new employees with the firm

Maintaining human resources consists primarily of motivating employees to remain with the firm and to work effectively. Since motivation is discussed at length in Chapter 8, we concentrate here on some additional aspects of maintaining human resources:

▶ *Compensation and benefits:* to reward employee effort

The development phase of HRM is concerned with improving employees' skills and expanding their capabilities. There are two important activities within this phase:

▶ *Training and development:* to teach employees new skills, new jobs, and more effective ways of doing their present jobs

▶ *Performance appraisal:* to assess employees' current and potential performance levels

These activities are discussed in more detail shortly, when we have completed this overview of human resources management.

Responsibility for HRM

In general, human resources management is a shared responsibility of line managers and staff HRM specialists.

In very small organizations, the owner is usually both a line manager and the staff personnel specialist. He or she handles all or most HRM activities. As the firm grows in size, a personnel manager is generally hired to take over most of the staff responsibilities. As growth continues, additional staff positions are added as needed. In firms as large as, say, Bristol-Myers Co., HRM activities tend to be very highly specialized. There may be separate groups to deal with compensation, training and development programs, and the other staff activities.

Specific HRM activities are assigned to those who are in the best position to perform them. Human resources planning and job analysis are usually done by staff specialists, with input from line managers. Similarly, recruiting and selection are generally handled by staff experts, although line managers are involved in the actual hiring decisions.

Training and development activities are sometimes accomplished through unique experiences, such as those provided by Outward Bound. Outward Bound's guiding principles include undefeatable spirit, tenacity in pursuit, sensible self-denial, enterprise, curiosity, and compassion.

Orientation programs are usually devised by staff specialists, and the orientation itself is carried out by both staff specialists and line managers. Compensation systems (including benefits) are most often developed and administered by the HRM staff. However, line managers recommend pay increases and promotions. Training and development activities are usually the joint responsibility of staff and line managers. Performance appraisal is the job of the line manager, although HRM staff personnel are likely to design the firm's appraisal system.

Human Resources Planning

human resources planning
the development of strategies to meet a firm's future human resources needs

Human resources planning is the development of strategies to meet the firm's future human resources needs. The starting point for this planning is the organization's overall strategic plan. From this, human resources planners can forecast the firm's future demand for human resources. Next, the planners must determine whether the needed human resources will be available; that is, they must forecast the supply of human resources within the firm. Finally, they have to take steps to match supply with demand.

Forecasting Human Resources Demand

Learning Objective 2
Be aware of the steps in human resources planning

Forecasts of human resources demand should be based on as much relevant information as planners can gather. The firm's overall strategic plan will provide information about future business ventures, new products, and projected expansions or contractions of particular product lines. Information on past staffing levels, evolving technologies, industry staffing practices, and projected economic trends can also be very helpful.

All this information should be used to determine both the number of employees who will be required and their qualifications—including skills, experience, and knowledge. There are a variety of methods for forecasting specific personnel needs. With one simple method, personnel requirements are projected to increase or decrease in the same proportion as sales revenue. Thus, if a 30 percent increase in sales volume is projected over the next two years, a 30 percent increase in personnel requirements would be forecast for the same period. (This method can be applied to specific positions as well as to the work force in general. It is not, however, a very precise forecasting method.) At the other extreme are the elaborate computer-based personnel planning models used by some larger firms such as Exxon.

Forecasting Human Resources Supply

The human resources supply forecast must take into account both the present work force and any changes, or movements, that may occur within it. For example, suppose planners project that, in five years, the firm will need 100 more engineers than the 100 that are currently employed. The planners cannot simply assume that they will have to hire 100 engineers over the next five years. During that period, some of the firm's present engineers are likely to be promoted, leave the firm, or move to other jobs within the firm. Thus planners might project the supply of engineers in five years at 87, which means that a total of 113 (or more) would have to be hired.

Two useful techniques for forecasting human resources supply are the replacement chart and the skills inventory. A **replacement chart** is a list of key personnel, along with possible replacements within the firm. The chart is maintained to ensure that top management positions can be filled fairly quickly in the event of an unexpected resignation or retirement. Some firms also provide additional training for those employees who might eventually replace top managers.

A **skills inventory** is a computerized data bank containing information on the skills and experience of all present employees. It is used to search for candidates to fill new or newly available positions. For a special project, a manager might be seeking a current employee with an engineering degree, at least six years of experience, and fluency in French. The skills inventory can quickly identify the employees who possess such qualifications.

replacement chart   *a list of key personnel and their possible replacements within the firm*

skills inventory   *a computerized data bank containing information on the skills and experience of all present employees*

Matching Supply with Demand

Once they have forecasts of both the demand for personnel and the firm's supply of personnel, planners can devise a course of action for matching the two. When demand is forecast to be greater than supply, plans must be made to recruit and select new employees. The timing of these actions depends on the types of positions to be filled. Suppose we expect to open a new plant in five years. Along with other employees, a plant manager and twenty-five maintenance workers will be needed. We can probably wait quite a while before we begin to recruit maintenance personnel. However, because the job of plant manager is so critical, we may start searching for the right person for that position immediately.

When supply is forecast to be greater than demand, the firm must take steps to reduce the size of its work force. Several methods are available, although none of them is especially pleasant for managers or discharged employees. When the oversupply is expected to be temporary, some employees may be *laid off*—dismissed from the work force until they are needed again.

Perhaps the most humane method for making personnel cutbacks is through attrition. *Attrition* is the normal reduction in the work force that occurs when employees leave the firm. If these employees are not replaced, the work force eventually shrinks to the point where supply matches demand. Of course, attrition may be a very slow process—too slow to really help the firm.

Early retirement is another option that can sometimes be used. Under this method of reducing the size of the work force, people who are within a few years of retirement are permitted to retire early with full benefits. Depending on the age makeup of the work force, this may or may not reduce the staff enough. As a last resort, unneeded employees are sometimes

Every employer faces specific challenges in filling its need for experienced, skilled workers. Transporting workers to the work site is a specific requirement for NERCO, a subsidiary of PacifiCorp, which owns oil reserves in the Gulf of Mexico. NERCO accomplishes this by providing transportation via ship to off-shore oil rig.

simply *fired*. Because of its negative impact, this method is generally used only when absolutely necessary.

Even when human resources planners know how many new employees the firm will need, one further step intervenes before these people can actually be hired. This step is job analysis.

Job Analysis

Learning Objective 3
Understand the objectives and uses of job analysis

job analysis *a systematic procedure for studying jobs to determine their various elements and requirements*

There is no sense in trying to hire people unless we know what we are hiring them for. In other words, we need to know the exact nature of a job before we can find the right person to do it.

Job analysis is a systematic procedure for studying jobs to determine their various elements and requirements. Consider the position of secretary, for example. In a large corporation, there may be fifty different kinds of secretarial positions. They all may be called "secretary," but each may be different from the others in the activities to be performed, the level of proficiency required for each activity, and the particular set of qualifications that the position demands. These are the things that job analysis focuses on.

job description *a list of the elements that make up a particular job*

The job analysis for a particular position typically consists of two parts—a job description and a job specification. A **job description** is a list of the elements that make up a particular job. It includes the duties the jobholder must perform; the working conditions under which the job must be performed; the jobholder's responsibilities (including number and types of subordinates, if any); and the tools and equipment that must be used on the job (see Figure 9.1).

job specification *a list of the qualifications required to perform a particular job*

A **job specification** is a list of the qualifications required to perform a particular job. Included are the skills, abilities, education, and experience that the jobholder must have.

The job analysis is the basis for recruiting and selecting new employees—for either existing positions or new ones. It is also used in other areas of human resources management, including evaluation and the determination of equitable compensation levels.

Recruiting, Selection, and Orientation

Learning Objective 4
Be able to describe the processes of recruiting, employee selection, and orientation

In an organization with jobs waiting to be filled, HRM personnel need to (1) find candidates for those jobs and (2) match the right candidate with each job. Three activities are involved: recruiting, selection, and (for new employees) orientation.

Recruiting

recruiting *the process of attracting qualified job applicants*

Recruiting is the process of attracting qualified job applicants. Because it is a vital link in a costly process (for example, fees plus expenses paid to private employment agencies can total more than $30,000 for executive

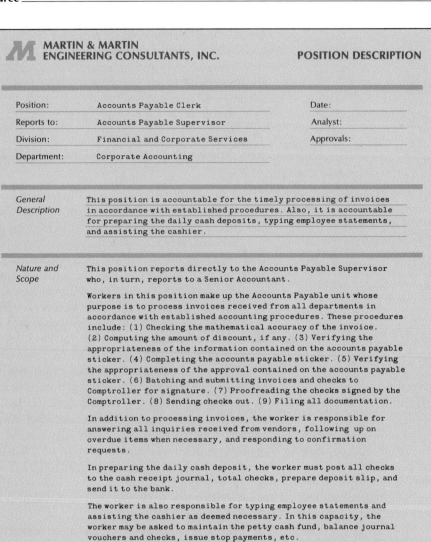

MARTIN & MARTIN
ENGINEERING CONSULTANTS, INC.   **POSITION DESCRIPTION**

Position:	Accounts Payable Clerk	Date:
Reports to:	Accounts Payable Supervisor	Analyst:
Division:	Financial and Corporate Services	Approvals:
Department:	Corporate Accounting	

General Description

This position is accountable for the timely processing of invoices in accordance with established procedures. Also, it is accountable for preparing the daily cash deposits, typing employee statements, and assisting the cashier.

Nature and Scope

This position reports directly to the Accounts Payable Supervisor who, in turn, reports to a Senior Accountant.

Workers in this position make up the Accounts Payable unit whose purpose is to process invoices received from all departments in accordance with established accounting procedures. These procedures include: (1) Checking the mathematical accuracy of the invoice. (2) Computing the amount of discount, if any. (3) Verifying the appropriateness of the information contained on the accounts payable sticker. (4) Completing the accounts payable sticker. (5) Verifying the appropriateness of the approval contained on the accounts payable sticker. (6) Batching and submitting invoices and checks to Comptroller for signature. (7) Proofreading the checks signed by the Comptroller. (8) Sending checks out. (9) Filing all documentation.

In addition to processing invoices, the worker is responsible for answering all inquiries received from vendors, following up on overdue items when necessary, and responding to confirmation requests.

In preparing the daily cash deposit, the worker must post all checks to the cash receipt journal, total checks, prepare deposit slip, and send it to the bank.

The worker is also responsible for typing employee statements and assisting the cashier as deemed necessary. In this capacity, the worker may be asked to maintain the petty cash fund, balance journal vouchers and checks, issue stop payments, etc.

During the course of work the worker may speak to personnel throughout the company as well as outside vendors.

Principal Accountabilities

(1) Timely processing of invoices in accordance with established procedures. (2) Analyzing vendor statements, following up on overdue items. (3) Answering inquiries received from outside vendors. (4) Responding to audit confirmation requests. (5) Calculating cash discounts earned. (6) Preparing the daily cash deposit. (7) Typing employee statements.

positions),[2] recruiting needs to be a systematic rather than haphazard process. One goal of recruiters is to attract the "right" number of applicants. The right number is enough to allow a good match between applicants and open positions, but not so many that matching them requires too much time and effort. For example, if there are five open positions and five applicants, the firm essentially has no choice. It must hire those five applicants (qualified or not) or the positions will remain open. At the other extreme, if several hundred people apply for the five positions, HRM personnel will have to spend weeks processing their applications.

Recruiters may seek applicants outside the firm, within the firm, or both. Which source is used generally depends on the nature of the position, the situation within the firm, and (sometimes) the firm's established or traditional recruitment policies.

External Recruiting   **External recruiting** is the attempt to attract job applicants from outside the organization. Among the means available for external recruiting are newspaper advertising, recruiting on college campuses and in union hiring halls, utilizing employment agencies, and soliciting the recommendations of present employees. In addition, many people who are looking for work simply apply at the firm's employment office.

external recruiting *the attempt to attract job applicants from outside the organization*

Clearly, it is best to match the recruiting means with the kind of applicant being sought. For example, private employment agencies most often handle professional people, whereas public employment agencies (operated by state or local governments) are usually more concerned with operations personnel. Hence we might approach a private agency if we were looking for a vice president, but we would be more inclined to contact a public agency if we wanted to hire a machinist.

The primary advantage of external recruiting is that it enables the firm to bring in people with new perspectives and varied business backgrounds. It may also be the only way to attract applicants with the required skills and knowledge. On the other hand, external recruiting is often quite expensive, especially if private employment agencies must be used. External recruiting may also provoke resentment among present employees.

Internal Recruiting   **Internal recruiting** means considering present employees as applicants for available positions. Generally, current employees are considered for *promotion* to higher-level positions. However, employees may also be considered for *transfer* from one position to another at the same level.

internal recruiting *considering present employees as applicants for available positions*

Promoting from within provides strong motivation for current employees and helps the firm to retain quality personnel. General Electric, Exxon, Bell Telephone Laboratories, and Eastman Kodak are companies dedicated to promoting from within. (In cases where there is a strong union, the practice of *job posting*, or informing current employees of upcoming new openings, may be required by the union contract.) The primary disadvantage of internal recruiting is that promoting a current

BUSINESS JOURNAL

Moving Up Through the Glass Ceiling

Women executives, and women who want to be executives, face many difficulties. The life of an executive is demanding—constant pressure, exhausting workdays, and long hours. Though some women manage to do both surprisingly well, it is very hard to lead the executive life and to nurture a family. The time, energy, and attention that growing children require is enormous. Any executive is hard-pressed to devote time to a family, but to women, traditional preservers of the home, this struggle often proves to be too much. Women are then obliged to sacrifice either their careers or the time they spend with their families. For some women, no sacrifice is involved. They decisively choose the life of the business executive and are willing to dedicate themselves fully to their careers. These women must deal with another type of problem.

Some businesses resist placing women, however dedicated, in executive positions. The "locker-room" mentality of male camaraderie still abides. Women, though respected, are still considered outsiders. Other firms see the sacrifices that a woman executive must make as too taxing. They think that hiring a female executive is too risky: If the woman suddenly decides that she would rather stay at home with her children, they lose a trained, valuable executive.

In *Breaking the Glass Ceiling*, author Ann Morrison and her colleagues at the Center for Creative Leadership, an organization that gives seminars and programs on leadership, discuss the problems many competent, ambitious women face. The term "glass ceiling" refers to an imaginary barrier that separates women from top-management positions. As women ascend the corporate ladder, they find that they are shut off from executive jobs. Some women do break through, however, to become important assets to their companies.

Women are especially successful in high-tech, high-growth industries, where they seem to be promoted faster than in other fields. The publishing industry also has a history of being receptive to women executives. Health services, social services, the retail-clothing business, and education have large numbers of women in executive positions. Other industries—like steel, railroads, and mining—have a disproportionately low number of women in top management.

Today, more than one-third of all M.B.A. graduates are women, and about 49 percent of all managers are women. In the future these women will probably rise to higher and higher levels in organizations. Thus, companies would be wise to start grooming women for top-level positions. Any company that does not will likely face a shortage of able leaders.

Based on information from Laurie Baum, "Corporate Women," *Business Week*, June 22, 1987, pp. 72–78; Anne B. Fisher, "Where Women Are Succeeding," *Fortune*, August 3, 1987, pp. 78–81, 84, 86; Monci Jo Williams, "Women Beat the Corporate Game," *Fortune*, September 12, 1988, pp. 128–129, 132, 134, 136, 138; and "A Woman's World," *American Demographics*, August 1988, pp. 18–19.

employee leaves another position to be filled. Not only does the firm still incur recruiting and selection costs, but it must also train two employees instead of one.

In many situations, it may be impossible to recruit internally. For example, a new position may be such that no current employee is qualified to fill it. Or the firm may be growing so rapidly that there is no time to go through the reassigning of positions that promotion or transfer might require.

Selection

selection *the process of gathering information about applicants for a position and then using that information to choose the most appropriate applicant*

Selection is the process of gathering information about applicants for a position and then using that information to choose the most appropriate applicant. Note the use of the word *appropriate*. In selection, the idea is not to hire the person with the "most" qualifications, but rather to choose the applicant with the qualifications that are most appropriate for the job. The actual selection of an applicant often is made by one or more line managers who have responsibility for the position being filled. However, HRM personnel usually facilitate the selection process by developing a pool of applicants and expediting the assessment of these applicants. The most common means of obtaining information about applicants' qualifications are employment applications, tests, interviews, references, and assessment centers.

Employment Applications Just about everyone who applies for anything must submit an application. You probably filled one out to apply to your school. Employment applications are useful in collecting factual information on a candidate's education, work experience, and personal history (see Figure 9.2). The data obtained from applications are usually used for two purposes: to identify candidates who are worthy of further scrutiny and to familiarize interviewers with applicants' backgrounds.

Many job candidates submit résumés to prospective employers, and some firms require them. A *résumé* is a one-or-two-page summary of the candidate's background and qualifications; it includes a description of the type of job the applicant is seeking. A résumé may be sent to a firm to request consideration for available jobs, or it may be submitted along with an employment application.

In recent years, a technique has been developed to determine the relative importance of information that is provided on applications and résumés. Current employees are asked which factors in their own backgrounds are most strongly related to their current jobs. Then these factors are given extra weight in assessing new applicants' qualifications to perform similar jobs.

Employment Tests Tests that are given to job candidates usually focus on aptitudes, skills, abilities, or knowledge relevant to the jobs that are to be performed. Such tests (typing tests, for example) indicate how well the applicant will do on the job. Occasionally companies use general intelligence or personality tests, but these are seldom useful in predicting specific job performance.

At one time, a number of companies were criticized for using tests that were biased against members of certain minority groups—in particular, blacks. This practice of testing has largely been eliminated for two reasons. The test results were, to a great extent, unrelated to job performance. And to prove that they are not discriminating, firms must be able to demonstrate that the results of any tests they use are valid predictors of on-the-job performance. Applicants who believe they have been discriminated against in a test may file a complaint with the EEOC.

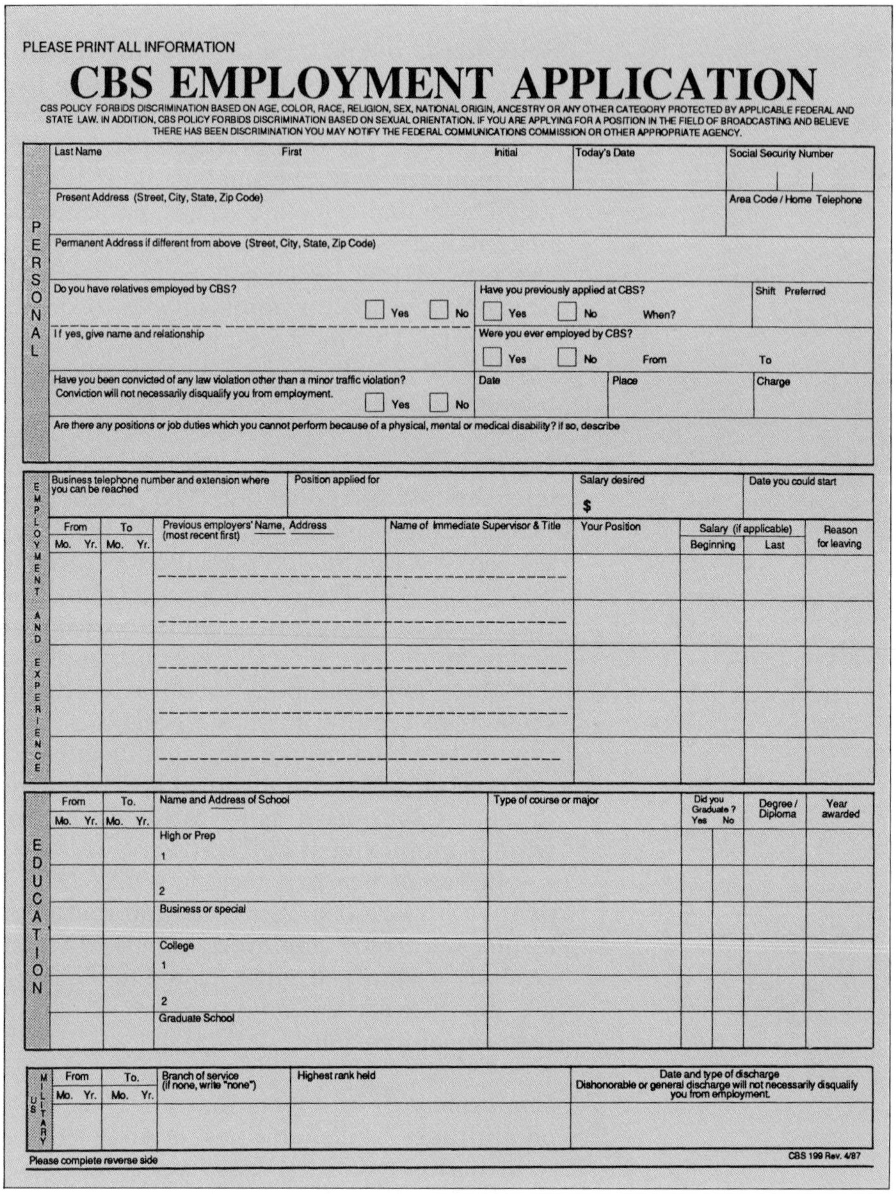
PLEASE PRINT ALL INFORMATION

CBS EMPLOYMENT APPLICATION

CBS POLICY FORBIDS DISCRIMINATION BASED ON AGE, COLOR, RACE, RELIGION, SEX, NATIONAL ORIGIN, ANCESTRY OR ANY OTHER CATEGORY PROTECTED BY APPLICABLE FEDERAL AND STATE LAW. IN ADDITION, CBS POLICY FORBIDS DISCRIMINATION BASED ON SEXUAL ORIENTATION. IF YOU ARE APPLYING FOR A POSITION IN THE FIELD OF BROADCASTING AND BELIEVE THERE HAS BEEN DISCRIMINATION YOU MAY NOTIFY THE FEDERAL COMMUNICATIONS COMMISSION OR OTHER APPROPRIATE AGENCY.

PERSONAL

Last Name | First | Initial | Today's Date | Social Security Number

Present Address (Street, City, State, Zip Code) | Area Code / Home Telephone

Permanent Address if different from above (Street, City, State, Zip Code)

Do you have relatives employed by CBS? ☐ Yes ☐ No | Have you previously applied at CBS? ☐ Yes ☐ No When? | Shift Preferred

If yes, give name and relationship | Were you ever employed by CBS? ☐ Yes ☐ No From To

Have you been convicted of any law violation other than a minor traffic violation? Conviction will not necessarily disqualify you from employment. ☐ Yes ☐ No | Date | Place | Charge

Are there any positions or job duties which you cannot perform because of a physical, mental or medical disability? If so, describe

EMPLOYMENT AND EXPERIENCE

Business telephone number and extension where you can be reached | Position applied for | Salary desired $ | Date you could start

From Mo. Yr.	To Mo. Yr.	Previous employers' Name, Address (most recent first)	Name of Immediate Supervisor & Title	Your Position	Salary (if applicable) Beginning	Salary (if applicable) Last	Reason for leaving

EDUCATION

From Mo. Yr.	To. Mo. Yr.	Name and Address of School	Type of course or major	Did you Graduate? Yes No	Degree / Diploma	Year awarded
		High or Prep 1				
		2				
		Business or special				
		College 1				
		2				
		Graduate School				

US MILITARY

From Mo. Yr.	To. Mo. Yr.	Branch of service (if none, write "none")	Highest rank held	Date and type of discharge Dishonorable or general discharge will not necessarily disqualify you from employment.

Please complete reverse side — CBS 199 Rev. 4/87

FIGURE 9.2
A Typical Employment Application
Employers use applications to collect factual information on a candidate's education, work experience, and personal history. (Source: Used by permission of CBS Inc.)

Interviews The employment interview is perhaps the most widely used selection technique. Job candidates are usually interviewed by at least one member of the HRM staff and by the person for whom they will be working. Candidates for higher-level jobs may also meet with a department head or vice president and may have several additional interviews.

Interviews provide an opportunity for the applicant and the firm to learn more about each other. Interviewers can pose problems to test the candidate's abilities. They can probe employment history more deeply and learn something about the candidate's attitudes and motivation. The candidate, meanwhile, has a chance to find out more about the job and the people with whom he or she would be working.

Unfortunately, interviewing may be the stage at which discrimination enters the selection process. For example, suppose a female applicant mentions that she is the mother of small children. Her interviewer may automatically (and mistakenly) assume that she would not be available for job-related travel. In addition, interviewers may be unduly influenced by irrelevant factors such as appearance. Or they may ask different questions of different applicants, so that it becomes impossible to compare candidates' qualifications.

Some of these problems can be solved through better interviewer training and the use of structured interviews. A *structured interview* is one in which the interviewer is given a prepared set of questions to ask. The firm may also consider using several different interviewers for each applicant, but that solution is likely to be a costly one.

References   A job candidate is generally asked to furnish the names of references—people who can verify background information and provide personal evaluations of the candidate. Naturally, applicants tend to list only references who are likely to say good things about them. Thus personal evaluations obtained from references may not be of much value. However, references are often contacted to verify such information as previous job responsibilities and the reason an applicant chose to leave a former job.

Assessment Centers   A newer selection technique is the assessment center, which is used primarily to select current employees for promotion to higher-level management positions. Typically, a group of employees is sent to the center for two or three days. While they are there, these employees participate in a variety of activities designed to simulate the management environment and predict managerial effectiveness. Trained observers (usually managers) make recommendations regarding promotion possibilities. Although this technique is gaining popularity, the expense involved limits its use to larger organizations.

Orientation

Once all the available information about job candidates has been collected and analyzed, those involved in the selection decide which candidate they would like to hire. A job offer is extended to the candidate. If it is accepted, the candidate becomes an employee and starts to work for the firm.

Soon after a candidate joins the firm, he or she goes through the firm's orientation program. **Orientation** is the process of acquainting new employees with the organization. Orientation topics range from such basic items as the location of the company cafeteria to such concerns as various career paths within the firm. The orientation itself may consist of a half-hour informal presentation by a human resources manager. Or it may be

orientation   *the process of acquainting new employees with an organization*

Rite Aid Corporation operates the largest retail drug chain in the United States. Over a two-year period, Rite Aid hired 8,000 new associates in its drugstores. In support of this dramatic growth, the company has reinforced training programs through such means as an employee orientation video.

an elaborate program involving many different people and lasting several days or weeks.

In some firms, special orientation techniques are used for both new and present employees. For example, Ford Motor Company conducts a three-month workshop for disadvantaged workers. The program acquaints these employees with efficient work habits, ways of getting to and from work, and the basic principles of money management. Atlantic Richfield Co. in Dallas holds retirement seminars in its regional and district offices to keep its employees up to date on the latest retirement benefits.

Of course, attracting and hiring new employees is of vital importance. Many prospective employees will decide whether to join the firm on the basis of our next topic, the compensation and benefits it offers.

Compensation and Benefits

Learning Objective 5
Know the primary elements of employee compensation and benefits

In Chapter 8 we note that an effective employee reward system must (1) enable employees to satisfy their basic needs, (2) provide rewards comparable to those offered by other firms, (3) be distributed fairly within the organization, and (4) recognize the fact that different people have different needs.

The firm's compensation system can be structured to fill the first three of these requirements. The fourth is more difficult; it must take into account the many differences among people. Most firms offer a number of benefits that, taken together, generally help provide for employees' varying needs.

BUSINESS JOURNAL

Pay-for-Performance: Employers Want to Get What They Pay For

"Pull your own weight or you're history!" That may seem harsh, but how else can a company reduce labor costs *and* motivate employees? Since the early 1980s, firms have tried to control "runaway" salaries by installing pay-for-performance systems. Instead of yearly across-the-board salary increases, some organizations individually reward outstanding workers through bonuses. A pay-for-performance strategy allows management to control labor costs while encouraging employees to work harder.

Recently General Motors overhauled its employee compensation system. GM stopped annual cost-of-living increases for salaried employees and temporarily eliminated all salary increases. A high-ranking GM executive explained, "To treat people fairly, you have to treat people differently." Today GM ranks its employees against each other. Managers choose the top 10 percent of employees, the next 25 percent, the next 55 percent, and the bottom 10 percent. An employee's merit pay under this system depends on individual accomplishment.

Traditionally, a good worker is rewarded with a higher base salary. This salary increase is distributed during the year until the next increase. This can be costly to a company because, since benefits and pensions are often tied to salaries, labor costs rise exponentially.

The current business trend is toward merit payments. A worker gets a bonus, but his or her base salary remains the same. This policy is good for the company because employers can control costs and compensate a worker based on performance. Also, benefit costs can be contained because a lump sum is not added to the salary. Furthermore, employees may perceive lump-sum performance bonuses as more meaningful. A $3,000 yearly bonus check may seem more substantial than a $250-a-month raise.

When using a performance-based lump-sum program, a company can be flexible. For a good year, bonuses can be higher than for a bad year. Excellent workers can receive larger bonuses than average workers, with poor workers receiving no bonuses at all. Allied-Signal is pleased with the results of linking employee ability to compensation; General Mills has a successful pay-for-performance program

in place as well. Other companies are following their lead.

But is a pay-for-performance system right for every company? If a company cannot afford to increase salaries every year, if top company performers are not motivated because weaker performers are earning the same relative salary increases, if merit guidelines are too low, or if a company provides all its employees with the same bonus at the end of a year, then management should consider a lump-sum pay-for-performance system.

If a company decides that this is a good move, it must proceed carefully when implementing the system. Salaries may have to be adjusted, and then a proper appraisal program established and thoroughly explained. A complete explanation is crucial to the success of a pay-for-performance system. Since workers will be sensitive to anything affecting their paychecks, managers should make every effort to design a communication strategy that includes easy-to-read documents about the program, employee meetings, and employee feedback sessions. Employees should be given enough time to understand and accept the change. Without this time and communication effort, employees might totally reject the program and become even less motivated.

Based on information from "Labor Letter," *Wall Street Journal*, February 9, 1988, p. 1; Suzanne L. Minken, "Does Lump-sum Pay Merit Attention?" *Personnel Journal*, June 1988, pp. 77–83; Jacob M. Schlesinger, "GM's New Compensation Plan Reflects General Trend Tying Pay to Performance," *Wall Street Journal*, January 25, 1988, p. 39E; John F. Sullivan "The Future of Merit Pay Programs," *Compensation & Benefits Review*, May–June 1988, pp. 22–30; and Michael A. Verespej, "We'll Have to Earn Our Keep," *Industry Week*, April 18, 1988, p. 57.

Compensation Decisions

compensation *the payment that employees receive in return for their labor*

compensation system *the policies and strategies that determine employee compensation*

Compensation is the payment that employees receive in return for their labor. Its importance to employees is obvious. And, because compensation can account for up to 80 percent of a firm's operating costs, it is equally important to management. The firm's **compensation system**—the policies and strategies that determine employee compensation—must therefore be carefully designed to provide for employee needs while keeping labor costs within reasonable limits. For most firms, designing an effective compensation system requires three separate management decisions (see Figure 9.3).

The Wage-Level Decision   Management must first position the firm's general pay level relative to pay levels of comparable firms. In other words, will the firm pay its employees less than, more than, or about the same as similar organizations? Most firms choose a pay level near the industry average. A firm that is not in good financial shape may pay less than the going rate. Large, prosperous organizations, by contrast, may pay a little more than average to attract and retain the most capable employees.

wage survey *a collection of data on prevailing wage rates within an industry or a geographic area*

To determine what the average is, the firm may use wage surveys. A **wage survey** is a collection of data on prevailing wage rates within an industry or a geographic area. Such surveys are compiled by industry associations, local governments, personnel associations, and (occasionally) individual firms.

The Wage-Structure Decision   Next, management must decide on relative pay levels for all the positions within the firm. Will managers be paid more than secretaries? Will secretaries be paid more than custodians? The result of this decision (actually, it is a set of decisions) is often called the firm's *wage structure*.

job evaluation *the process of determining the relative worth of the various jobs within a firm*

The wage structure is almost always developed on the basis of a job evaluation. **Job evaluation** is the process of determining the relative worth

FIGURE 9.3
Compensation Decisions
Management decides how competitive salaries will be with those of similar firms (wage level); the relative importance of different positions (wage structure); and the specific wages of each employee (individual wages).

MANAGEMENT		
Wage level	Wage structure	Individual wages

of the various jobs within a firm. Most observers would probably agree that a secretary should make more money than a custodian, but how much more? Twice as much? One and one-half times as much? Job evaluation should provide the answers to such questions.

A number of techniques may be used to evaluate jobs. The simplest is to rank all the jobs within the firm according to their value to the firm. Of course, if there are more than a few jobs, this technique loses its simplicity very quickly. A more frequently used method is based on the job analysis. "Points" are allocated to each job for each of its elements and requirements, as set forth in the job analysis. For example, "college degree required" might be worth 50 points, whereas the need for a high school education might be allocated only 25 points. The more points a job is allocated, the more important it is presumed to be (and the higher its level in the firm's wage structure).

The Individual-Wage Decision Finally, the specific payments that individual jobholders will receive must be determined. Consider the case of two secretaries working side by side. Job evaluation has been used to determine the relative level of their pay within the firm's wage structure. However, suppose one secretary has fifteen years of experience and can accurately type 80 words per minute. The other has two years of experience and can type only 55 words per minute. In most firms, these people would not receive the same pay. Instead, a wage range would be established for the secretarial position. Suppose this range were $7 to $9.50 per hour. The more experienced and proficient secretary would then be paid an amount near the top of the range (say, $8.90 per hour). The less experienced secretary would receive an amount that was lower but still within the range (say, $7.75 per hour).

Two wage decisions actually come into play here. First the employee's intitial rate must be established. It is based on experience, other qualifications, and expected performance. Later the employee may be given pay increases based on seniority and performance.

Comparable Worth

comparable worth *a concept that seeks equal compensation for jobs requiring about the same level of education, training, and skills*

There is growing concern that one reason women in the work force are paid less than men is that a certain proportion of women occupy female-dominated jobs—nurses, clerk typists, and medical records analysts, for example—that require education, skills, and training equal to higher-paid positions that are predominantly occupied by men. **Comparable worth** is a concept that seeks equal compensation for jobs requiring about the same level of education, training, and skills. Several states have enacted laws that require equal pay for comparable work in government positions. Critics of comparable worth argue that the market has determined the worth of these jobs and that laws should not be enacted to tamper with the pricing mechanism of the market. They also point out that artificially inflating salaries for these female-dominated occupations encourages women to keep these jobs rather than to seek out other higher-paying jobs.

Types of Compensation

hourly wage *a specific amount of money paid for each hour of work*

Hourly Wage An **hourly wage** is a specific amount of money paid for each hour of work. People who earn wages are paid their hourly wage for the first forty hours worked in any week. They are then paid one and one-half times their hourly wage for time worked in excess of forty hours. (That is, they are paid "time and a half" for overtime.) Workers in retailing and fast-food chains, on assembly lines, and in clerical positions are usually paid an hourly wage.

salary *a specific amount of money paid for an employee's work during a set calendar period, regardless of the actual number of hours worked*

Weekly or Monthly Salary A **salary** is a specific amount of money paid for an employee's work during a set calendar period, regardless of the actual number of hours worked. Salaried employees receive no overtime pay, but they do not lose pay when they are absent from work (within reasonable limits). Most professional and managerial positions are salaried.

commission *a payment that is some percentage of sales revenue*

Commissions A **commission** is a payment that is some percentage of sales revenue. Sales representatives and sales managers are often paid entirely through commissions or through a combination of commissions and salary.

bonus *a payment in addition to wages, salary, or commissions, usually an extra reward for outstanding job performance*

Bonuses A **bonus** is a payment in addition to wages, salary, or commissions. Bonuses are really extra rewards for outstanding job performance. They may be distributed to all employees or only to certain employees within the organization. Some firms distribute bonuses to all employees every Christmas. The size of the bonus depends on the firm's earnings and the particular employee's length of service with the firm. Other firms offer bonuses to employees who exceed specific sales or production goals. Kollmorgen Corporation of Stamford, Connecticut, is a large conglomerate that nurtures a feeling of smallness for the sake of its employees. One of the ways Kollmorgen maintains this feeling is to split any division that grows beyond a few hundred employees. Workers in that division receive a bonus for the good work that led to the growth and split; and then they return to a new division small enough to give each employee recognition.

profit sharing *the distribution of a percentage of the firm's profit among its employees*

Profit Sharing **Profit sharing** is the distribution of a percentage of the firm's profit among its employees. The idea is to motivate employees to work effectively by giving them a stake in the company's financial success. Some firms—including Sears, Roebuck—have linked their profit-sharing plans to employee retirement programs; that is, employees receive their profit-sharing distributions, with interest, when they retire. Olga Company, a maker of lingerie and underwear, places 20 to 25 percent of its annual pretax earnings in a profit-sharing plan for its employees.

Employee Benefits

employee benefit *a reward that is provided indirectly to employees—mainly a service (such as insurance) paid for by the employer or an employee expense (such as college tuition) reimbursed by the employer*

An **employee benefit** is a reward that is provided indirectly to employees. Employee benefits consist mainly of services that are paid for by employers (such as insurance) and employee expenses that are reimbursed by employers (such as college tuition). Nowadays, the average cost of these benefits is more than one-third of the total cost of wages and salaries.

Health insurance is one of the most common forms of insurance coverage offered in an employee benefit package. Many health insurance providers, including Blue Cross & Blue Shield, emphasize preventive health care measures, including fitness programs. This emphasis is backed up in a concrete way by offering discounts at fitness centers.

Thus a person who earns $15,000 a year is likely to receive, in addition, over $5,000 worth of employee benefits.

Employee benefits take a variety of forms. *Pay for time not worked* covers such things as vacation time, holidays, and sick leave. *Insurance packages* may include health, life, and dental insurance for employees and their families. Some firms pay the entire cost of the insurance package, and others share the cost with the employee. The costs of *pension and retirement programs* may also be borne entirely by the firm or shared with the employee.

Some benefits are required by law. For example, employers must maintain *workers' compensation insurance*. This insurance pays medical bills for injuries that occur on the job, and it provides income for employees who are disabled by job-related injuries. Employers must also pay for *unemployment insurance* and must contribute to each employee's federal *Social Security* account.

Other benefits provided by employers include *tuition-reimbursement plans, credit unions, child care,* company *cafeterias* selling reduced-price meals, and various *recreational facilities.* Tenneco provides an elaborate health facility for its Houston employees.

Employees generally want to improve their performance and their compensation as well. It is certainly in the firm's interest to provide opportunities for them to do so. Training and development, then, are important aspects of human resources management.

Training and Development

Training and development are both aimed at improving employees' skills and abilities. However, the two are usually differentiated as follows: **Employee training** is the process of teaching operations and technical employees how to do their present jobs more effectively and efficiently. **Management development** is the process of preparing managers and other professionals to assume increased responsibility in both present and future positions. Thus training and development differ in who is being taught and in the purpose of the teaching. Both are necessary for personal and organizational growth. Companies that hope to stay competitive typically make huge commitments to employee training and development. For example, IBM spends $900 million annually for employee education and training. Most new IBMers spend most of their first six weeks in company-run classes, and the average employee receives twelve days of training annually.[3]

employee training *the process of teaching operations and technical employees how to do their present jobs more effectively and efficiently*

management development *the process of preparing managers and other professionals to assume increased responsibility in both present and future positions*

Training and Development Methods

Learning Objective 6
Understand the purposes and techniques of employee training, development, and performance appraisal

A variety of methods are available for employee training and management development. Some of these methods may be more suitable for one or the other, but most can be applied to both. These methods are as follows:

▶ *On-the-job methods*, in which the trainee learns by doing the work under the supervision of an experienced employee

▶ *Vestibule training*, in which the work situation is simulated in a separate area so that learning takes place away from the day-to-day pressures of work

▶ *Classroom teaching* and *lectures*, methods that you probably already know quite well

▶ *Conferences* and *seminars*, in which experts and learners meet to discuss problems and exchange ideas

▶ *Role playing*, in which participants act out the roles of others in the organization, for better understanding of these roles (primarily a management development tool)

Evaluation of Training and Development

Training and development are very expensive. The training itself costs quite a bit, and employees are usually not working—or are working at a reduced pace—during training sessions. To ensure that training and development are cost effective, the managers responsible should evaluate these efforts periodically.

The starting point for this evaluation is a set of verifiable objectives that are developed *before* the training is undertaken. Suppose a training program is expected to improve the skills of machinists. The objective of the program might be stated as follows: "At the end of the training period, each machinist should be able to process 30 parts per hour with no more than 1 defective part per 90 parts completed." This objective clearly specifies what is expected and how training results may be measured or verified. Evaluation then consists of measuring machinists' output and the number of defective parts produced, after the training.

The results of training evaluations should be made known to all those involved in the program—including trainees and upper management. For trainees, the results of evaluations can enhance motivation and learning. For upper management, the results may be the basis for making decisions about the training program itself.

Another form of evaluation—performance appraisal—is an equally important part of human resources management.

Performance Appraisal

performance appraisal *the evaluation of employees' current and potential levels of performance to allow superiors to make objective human resources decisions*

Performance appraisal is the evaluation of employees' current and potential levels of performance to allow managers to make objective human resources decisions. It has three main objectives. First, performance appraisal allows a manager to let subordinates know how well they are doing and how they can do better in the future. Second, it provides an effective basis for distributing rewards such as pay raises and promotions. Third, performance appraisal helps the organization monitor its employee

Many managers find that their performance appraisals are most accurate when they have regular contact with their subordinates and are knowledgeable about the progress, content, and style of their work.

selection, training, and development activities. If large numbers of employees continually perform below expectations, the firm's selection process may need to be revised, or additional training and development may be required. Considering that experts believe that half of the three million employees who are fired each year in the United States are fired unfairly, managers are challenged to do a much better job of improving performance through performance appraisal.[4]

Common Evaluation Techniques

The various techniques and methods for appraising employee performance are either objective or judgmental in nature.

Objective Methods Objective appraisal methods make use of some measurable quantity as the basis for assessing performance. Units of output, dollar volume of sales, number of defective products, and number of insurance claims processed are all objective, measurable quantities. Thus an employee who processes an average of twenty-six claims per week is evaluated higher than one whose average is nineteen claims per week.

Such objective measures cannot always be applied without some adjustment for the work environment. Suppose the first of our insurance claims processors works in New York City, whereas the second works in rural Iowa. Both must visit each client, perhaps because they are processing home-insurance claims. In this case the two may very well be equally competent and motivated. The difference in their average weekly output may be due entirely to the long distances that the Iowan must travel to reach clients' homes. Thus, a manager must take into account circumstances that may be hidden by a purely statistical measurement.

Judgmental Methods Judgmental appraisal methods are used much more frequently than objective methods. They require that the manager judge or estimate the employee's performance level, relative to some standard (see the performance appraisal form in Figure 9.4). In one such method, the manager ranks subordinates from best to worst. This approach has a number of drawbacks, including the lack of any absolute standard.

Rating scales comprise the most popular judgmental appraisal technique. A *rating scale* consists of a number of statements. Each employee is rated on the degree to which he or she is described by each statement. For example, one statement might be, "This employee always does high-quality work." The employee would be given a rating of any number from 5 down to 1, corresponding to gradations ranging from "strongly agree" to "strongly disagree." The ratings on all the statements are added to obtain the employee's total evaluation.

Avoiding Appraisal Errors Managers must be cautious if they are to avoid making mistakes when appraising subordinates. It is common to overuse one portion of an evaluation instrument, thus overemphasizing some issues and underemphasizing others. A manager must guard against allowing an employee's poor performance on one activity to influence his

POLAROID CORPORATION

INDIVIDUAL PROGRESS REPORT

PURPOSE

This progress report is issued three times during the member's first year of employment to allow you to give extensive thought to whether the individual is going to be the kind of member we want to continue employing at Polaroid.

PROCEDURE

1. Please judge this member on the characteristics listed below. Base your evaluation on your knowledge of the member's current performance on this job.

2. Concentrate on only one characteristic at a time. Place a check (✓) in the space provided which best expresses your judgement of each characteristic.

This is (3) ___ (8) ___ (11) ___ Month Rating   NAME ___

JOB CLASSIFICATION ___   DATE HIRED ___
SUPERVISOR ___   DATE OF THIS RATING ___
TIME UNDER YOUR SUPERVISION ___   DEPARTMENT ___

QUALITY OF WORK - (Do not consider amount of work). Is work done correctly and accurately? Does work meet the required standards of quality? Is there little waste or spoilage?

| Work is carelessly done or not done correctly. Produces waste or rejected material. | Does not produce work up to standards. Has to be checked frequently to get required results. Work frequently not accurate. | Does acceptable work. Results meet normal standards. Work performed is satisfactory. | Performs work of high quality. Makes few errors. Work can be depended upon. | Work is of highest quality. Very accurate. Does job exactly as it should be done. Never spoils a job or creates waste. |

Additional comments: ___

SAFETY HABITS AND ATTITUDES - Works carefully? Follows safety instructions and rules? Points out unsafe conditions?

| Unsafe; careless. Disregards safety rules. Creates hazards. | Obeys safety rules when recommended. Takes some chances. | Works with reasonable care. Usually and normally safe. | Works carefully. Observes all safety rules. Aware of safety problem. | Very safety-conscious. Considers safety promotion part of job. Makes suggestions. |

Additional comments: ___

ABILITY TO UNDERSTAND AND FOLLOW INSTRUCTIONS - Understands instructions? Remembers what to do? Completes task?

| Dull. Requires repeated and constant instructions. Poor memory. | Needs detailed instructions on every point. Must be reminded of original instructions. | Seems to understand instructions. May require occasional follow-up. | Rarely has to have instructions repeated. Understands and follows instructions as given. | Seems to anticipate instructions. "Catches on" immediately. Understands with great ease and follows through. |

Additional comments: ___

WORK OUTPUT - (Do not consider quality of work). General work habits? Work habits compared to others in the group?

| Slow worker. Lazy. Stalls around. Low production. | Takes it easy. Requires some pushing. Below normal production. Clock watcher. | Works steadily. Does job in reasonable manner. Does normal amount of work. | Works hard. Always steady at job. Does more than others doing same job. | Fast and hard worker. Outstanding for amount of work done. High production. Keeps driving throughout the day. |

Additional comments: ___

POLAROID STOCK NO. 27-094

FIGURE 9.4
Performance Appraisal Form
Judgmental appraisal methods are used much more often than objective methods. Using judgmental methods requires the manager to estimate the employee's performance level, relative to some standard. (Source: Courtesy of Polaroid Corporation.)

or her judgment of that subordinate's work on other activities. Allowing recent performance to be overemphasized distorts an employee's performance evaluation. For example, if the employee is being rated on performance over the last year, a manager should not permit last month's performance to overshadow the quality of the work done in the first eleven months of the year. Finally, a manager must guard against discrimination on the basis of race, age, or sex.

Performance Feedback

No matter which appraisal technique is used, the results should be discussed with the employee soon after the evaluation is completed. The manager should explain the basis for present rewards and should let the employee know what he or she can do to be recognized as a better performer in the future. The information provided to an employee in such discussions is called *performance feedback.*

Performance feedback should occur in two stages, and these two stages should not take place in a single sitting. The first is the *evaluation interview.* At this interview the manager plays the role of the evaluator

BUSINESS JOURNAL

Expensive Business Lawsuits

Mr. Duncan, the founder and owner of a building construction company, decides he must streamline his struggling firm to reduce costs. After much thought, he fires an office worker who is no longer needed. Mr. Duncan is slapped with a million-dollar lawsuit by the former employee—and Mr. Duncan loses. Judges and juries across the United States have not only chipped away at but have carved huge gaps out of the employment-at-will doctrine.

Employment-at-will mandates that, as long as no laws are violated, any employment relationship may be terminated by either the employer or employee at any time for good cause, no cause, or a morally wrong cause. Traditionally, the United States has been an employment-at-will nation. Judging by the recent number of successful lawsuits challenging this tradition, however, the relationship between employers and employees is changing dramatically.

There are two basic kinds of employee lawsuits: the public policy suit and the implied contract suit. A supervisor cannot fire an employee for refusing to do something that is contrary to public policy. In addition, leaving work for a short time to vote, filing a workers' compensation claim, and refusing to take part in an illegal activity are all reasons that an employer cannot use to fire a worker. The courts in several states have agreed that an employee cannot be terminated for doing something that is protected by law.

An employee handbook, an oral agreement, or even a letter promising employment can contain implied contracts. An employee may claim that, because of either a written or oral statement, the employer has failed to live up to its "end of a deal." If an employer's handbook mentions that an employee will not be fired unless his or her work performance does not meet an objective level, and the employer discharges an employee without evidence that he or she did not meet these specific levels, then it is likely that the employee would win a lawsuit based on breach of an implied contract.

Dispute-resolution systems are an alternative means of dealing with conflicts between dismissed employees and employers. Dispute-resolution systems can perform functions similar to labor-union grievance committees. BankAmerica, NBC, and Aetna Life and Casualty all have nonunion grievance systems. The chief executive officer, chairman, and personnel director of Federal Express Corp. meet each Tuesday to discuss employee complaints.

Many lawyers think that the most effective (and safest from the employer's standpoint) dispute-resolution systems use outside arbitrators. Arbitration benefits the employee, too. Using arbitration, an employee continues to work at a firm until the arbitrator makes a decision. This decision usually takes only a few weeks. Arbitration may be preferable to a lawsuit because even if an employee wins the lawsuit, at least half of his or her settlement is spent on lawyers and taxes. Furthermore, a suing ex-employee faces the stigma of being branded a potential troublemaker.

Based on information from Jill Andresky, "Fear of Firing," *Forbes*, December 2, 1985, p. 90; Aaron Bernstein, "More Dismissed Workers Are Telling It to the Judge," *Business Week*, October 17, 1988, pp. 68–69; David L. Bacon and Angel Gomez, III, "How to Prevent Wrongful Termination Lawsuits," *Personnel*, February 1988, pp. 70–72; David A. Bradshaw and Linda Van Winkle Deacon, "Wrongful Discharge: The Tip of the Iceberg," *Personnel Administrator*, November 1985, pp. 74–76; James E. Challenger, "If You Sue Your Boss, You May Not Have Another," *Wall Street Journal*, March 16, 1988, p. 16; Laurence P. Corbett, "Avoiding Wrongful Discharge Suits," *Management Solutions*, June 1986, pp. 19–23; David S. Hames, "The Current Status of the Doctrine of Employment-at-Will," *Labor Law Journal*, January 1988, pp. 19–32; Marisa Manley, "Charges and Discharges," *Inc.*, March 1988, pp. 126–128; Mary-Margaret Wantuck, "Avoiding Employee Lawsuits," *Nation's Business*, January 1986, p. 13; Stephen Wermiel, "Justices Expand Union Workers' Right to Sue," *Wall Street Journal*, June 7, 1988, p. 4; and John Wilcox, "Business Suits," *Training and Development Journal*, April 1988, pp. 12–13.

and makes the subordinate aware of what he or she is doing right and wrong. The subordinate should understand how the manager reached these decisions and what criteria were used by the manager. In the second stage, or *feedback interview*, the manager should specify how the employee can improve individual performance. Suggestions should be made regarding methods, techniques, and perhaps training that is necessary to perform better in that position.[5]

Many managers find it difficult to discuss the negative aspects of an appraisal. Unfortunately, they may ignore performance feedback or provide it in a very weak and ineffectual manner. In truth, though, most employees have strengths that can be emphasized while their weaknesses are discussed. An employee may not even be aware of weaknesses and their consequences. If they are not pointed out through performance feedback, they cannot possibly be eliminated. Only through tactful, honest communication can the results of an appraisal be fully utilized.

The Legal Environment of HRM

Learning Objective 7
Know some of the major legislation affecting human resources management

Legislation regarding personnel practices has been passed mainly to protect the rights of employees, to promote job safety, and to eliminate discrimination in the workplace. Seven pieces of legislation (see Table 9.1) and one set of executive orders are of primary concern.

Title VII of the Civil Rights Act of 1964

This law applies directly to selection and promotion. It forbids organizations to discriminate in those areas on the basis of sex, race, color, religion, or national origin. Hence the purpose of Title VII is to ensure that employers make personnel decisions on the basis of employee qualifications only. As a result of this act, discrimination in employment (especially against blacks) has been sharply curtailed in this country.

The Equal Employment Opportunity Commission (EEOC) is charged with enforcing Title VII. If a person believes that he or she has been discriminated against, that person can file a complaint with the EEOC. The EEOC investigates the complaint. If it finds that the person has, in fact, been the victim of discrimination, it can take legal action on his or her behalf.

Age Discrimination in Employment Act

This act was passed in 1967 and amended in 1978. Its general purpose is the same as that of Title VII—to eliminate discrimination. However, as the name implies, the Age Discrimination in Employment Act is concerned only with discrimination based on age. In particular, it outlaws personnel practices that discriminate against people aged 40 to 69. (No federal law

TABLE 9.1   *Federal Legislation That Focuses on Human Resources Management*

Law	Purpose
Title VII of the Civil Rights Act of 1964	Eliminates discrimination in employment practices based on sex, race, color, religion, or national origin.
Age Discrimination in Employment Act of 1967/1978	Outlaws personnel practices that discriminate against people aged 40 to 69. The 1978 amendment outlaws company policies that require employees to retire before age 70.
Fair Labor Standards Act of 1938	Establishes a minimum wage and an overtime pay rate for employees working more than forty hours per week.
Equal Pay Act of 1963	Specifies that men and women who are doing equal jobs must be paid the same wage.
Employment Retirement Income Security Act of 1974	Regulates company retirement programs and provides a federal insurance program for retirement plans that go bankrupt.
Occupational Safety and Health Act of 1970	Regulates the degree to which employees can be exposed to hazardous substances, and specifies the safety equipment that must be provided by the employer.
National Labor Relations Act of 1935	Establishes a collective bargaining process in labor-management relations. It also establishes the National Labor Relations Board (NLRB).
Labor-Management Relations Act of 1947	Provides a balance between union power and management power. Also known as the Taft-Hartley Act.

forbids discrimination against people younger than 40, but several states have adopted age-discrimination laws that apply to a variety of age groups.) Also outlawed are company policies that require employees to retire before age 70.

Fair Labor Standards Act

This act, which was originally passed in 1938 and has been amended many times, applies primarily to wages. It establishes such things as minimum wages and overtime pay rates. Many managers and other professionals, however, are exempt from this law. Managers, for example, seldom get paid overtime when they work more than forty hours in a week.

Equal Pay Act

This law, passed in 1963, overlaps somewhat with Title VII of the Civil Rights Act. The Equal Pay Act specifies that men and women who are doing equal jobs must be paid the same wage. Equal jobs are jobs that demand equal effort, skill, and responsibility and that are performed under the same conditions. Differences in pay are legal if they can be

BUSINESS JOURNAL

Keep Your Hands, Comments, and Jokes to Yourself!

▶ Marsha, the owner of a video-rental store that had become very busy and successful, decided to hire a manager. The person she hired, Todd, seemed qualified, competent, and eager to assume the day-to-day running of the store and the supervision of the six employees working there. After a month, Tina (one of these employees) asked Todd if she could have a Saturday off. Todd, with a smile, said that he might be able to reschedule her if she were available for dinner that evening. When Tina said no, Todd angrily let her know that he was in charge of hiring and firing and that it would be a good idea for her to reconsider. According to the law, Tina has been sexually harassed.

▶ Mike had a new job with a major retailing firm. He was one of three men who worked in the eighteen-person data processing department. During one of his breaks, Mike went into the lounge to grab a snack and soft drink. Sitting down, Mike was shocked when he heard some of the comments his women coworkers were making. They were graphically discussing the anatomies of their male coworkers and laughing hysterically. Mike was very embarrassed and quickly left. He never entered the lounge again and always felt extremely uncomfortable when he heard a woman giggling at her work station. According to the law, Mike has been sexually harassed.

In 1980, the Equal Employment Opportunity Commission (EEOC) issued sexual harassment guidelines to Title VII of the 1964 Civil Rights Act. The EEOC stated: "Unwelcome sexual advances, requests for sexual favors, and other verbal or physical conduct of a sexual nature constitute sexual harassment when submission to such conduct is made either explicitly or implicitly a term or condition of an individual's employment, submission to or rejection of such conduct by an individual is used as the basis for employment decisions affecting such individual, or such conduct has the purpose or effect of substantially interfering with an individual's work performance or creating an intimidating, hostile, or offensive working environment." Currently, 70 percent of all sexual harassment claims filed with the EEOC are "hostile environment" cases.

Since the Supreme Court held that an employer is liable for employees who sexually harass, there has been a new drive to educate employees on sexual harassment. A good rule to keep in mind is: If you think it might be offensive, don't do it or say it. If you think you have been sexually harassed, there are several steps you can take.

Some think the most effective method to combat sexual harassment is to ask or tell the offender to stop. Threatening to tell or actually telling others, including supervisors and high company officials, is another option. Avoiding the harasser, making a joke of the situation, or entirely ignoring the behavior might make the offender think you are receptive to the questionable actions. If the offensive behavior persists, there is always legal action. Before contacting a lawyer, though, you should know that these lawsuits are often embarrassing, emotionally difficult, hard to win without careful documentation, and extremely lengthy.

Based on information from Marcy O'Koon, "Sexual Harassment," *Good Housekeeping*, January 1989, p. 171; Amy Saltzman, "Hands Off at the Office," *U.S. News & World Report*, August 1, 1988, pp. 56–58; Michael A. Verespej, "Hostile Environment," *Industry Week*, March 21, 1988, p. 21; and Stefanie Weiss, "Confronting Sexual Harassment," *NEA Today*, April 1988, p. 6.

attributed to differences in seniority, qualifications, or performance. But women cannot be paid less (or more) for the same work solely because they are women.

Employee Retirement Income Security Act

This act was passed in 1974 to protect the retirement benefits of employees. It does not require that firms provide a retirement plan. However, it does specify that *if* a retirement plan is provided, it must be managed in such a way that the interests of employees are protected. It also provides federal insurance for retirement plans that go bankrupt.

Occupational Safety and Health Act

This law, passed in 1970, is concerned mainly with issues of employee health and safety. For example, the act regulates the degree to which employees can be exposed to hazardous substances. It also specifies the safety equipment that must be provided.

The Occupational Safety and Health Administration (OSHA) was created to enforce this act. Inspectors from OSHA investigate employee complaints regarding unsafe working conditions. They also make spot checks on companies operating in particularly hazardous industries, such as chemicals and mining, to ensure compliance with the law. A firm that is found to be in violation of federal standards can be heavily fined or shut down.

National Labor Relations Act and Labor-Management Relations Act

These laws are concerned with dealings between business firms and labor unions. This general area is, in concept, a part of human resources management. However, because of its importance, it is often treated as a separate set of activities. We discuss both labor-management relations and these two acts in detail in Chapter 10.

Affirmative Action

A series of executive orders, issued by the president of the United States, established the requirement for affirmative action in personnel practices. This requirement applies to all employers holding contracts with the federal government. It prescribes that such employers (1) actively encourage job applications from members of minority groups and (2) hire qualified employees from minority groups that are not fully represented in their organizations. Many firms that do not hold government contracts take part voluntarily in this affirmative-action program.

It is against this background of regulations and guidelines that human resources planners must make decisions involving personnel recruiting and selection. But even before considering *whom* they need, they must forecast *how many*.

CHAPTER REVIEW

Summary

Human resources management (HRM) is the set of activities involved in acquiring, maintaining, and developing an organization's human resources. Responsibility for HRM is shared by line and staff managers.

Human resources planning consists of forecasting the human resources that the firm will need and those that it will have available and then planning a course of action to match supply with demand. Attrition, layoffs, early retirement, and (as a last resort) firing can be used to reduce the size of the work force. Supply is increased through hiring.

Job analysis provides a job description and a job specification for each position within the firm. These serve as the basis for recruiting and selecting new employees. Candidates for open positions may be recruited from within or outside the firm. In the selection process, applications, résumés, tests, interviews, references, and assessment centers may be used to obtain information about candidates. This information is then used to select the most appropriate candidate for the job. Newly hired employees should go through a formal or informal orientation program to acquaint them with the firm.

In developing a system for compensating, or paying, employees, management must decide on the firm's general wage level (relative to other firms), the wage structure within the firm, and individual wages. Wage surveys and job analysis are useful in making these decisions. Employees may be paid hourly wages, salaries, or commissions. They may also receive bonuses and profit-sharing payments. Employee benefits, which are nonmonetary rewards to employees, add about one-third to the cost of compensation.

Employee training and management development programs enhance the ability of employees to contribute to the firm. Several training techniques are available. Because training is expensive, its effectiveness should be evaluated periodically.

Performance appraisal, or evaluation, is used to provide employees with performance feedback, to serve as a basis for distributing rewards, and to monitor selection and training activities. Both objective and judgmental appraisal techniques are used. Their results must be communicated to employees if they are to help eliminate job-related weaknesses. A number of laws that affect HRM practices were passed to protect the rights and safety of employees.

In this chapter we note that although relations between firms and labor unions are an extremely important part of human resources management, they are usually treated separately from HRM. In the next chapter, we discuss this topic in detail.

Key Terms

You should now be able to define and give an example relevant to each of the following terms:

human resources management	compensation system
human resources planning	wage survey
replacement chart	job evaluation
skills inventory	comparable worth
job analysis	hourly wage
job description	salary
job specification	commission
recruiting	bonus
external recruiting	profit sharing
internal recruiting	employee benefit
selection	employee training
orientation	management development
compensation	performance appraisal

Questions and Exercises

Review Questions

1. List the three main HRM activities and their objectives.
2. In general, on what basis is responsibility for HRM divided between line and staff managers?
3. How is a human resources demand forecast related to the firm's organizational planning?
4. Describe the two techniques used in forecasting human resources supply.
5. How do human resources managers go about matching the firm's supply of workers with its demand for workers?
6. How are a job analysis, job description, and job specification related?
7. What are the advantages and disadvantages of external recruiting? of internal recruiting?
8. In your opinion, what are the two best techniques for gathering information about job candidates?

9. Why is orientation an important HRM activity?
10. Explain how the three wage-related decisions result in a compensation system.
11. How is a job analysis used in the process of job evaluation?
12. Suppose you have just opened a new Ford automobile sales showroom and repair shop. Which of your employees would be paid wages, which would receive salaries, and which would receive commissions?
13. What is the difference between the objective of employee training and the objective of management development?
14. Why is it so important to provide feedback after a performance appraisal?

Discussion Questions

1. Is Motorola's practice of spending more on employee education than do competitors a wise practice? Explain.
2. Why is Motorola concerned about providing additional education for all employees?
3. How accurately can managers plan for future human resources needs?
4. How might an organization's recruiting and selection practices be affected by the general level of employment?
5. Are employee benefits really necessary? Why?
6. What actions would you take, as a manager, if an operations employee with six years of experience on the job refused ongoing training and ignored performance feedback?
7. Why are there so many laws relating to HRM practices? Which are the most important laws, in your opinion?

Exercises

1. Construct a job analysis for the position of "entering first-year student" at your school.
2. Write a newspaper ad to attract applicants for the position of retail salesperson in your small business.
3. Describe the orientation procedure used by a firm that you have worked for or by your school. Then devise an *improved* orientation procedure for that organization.

Case 9.1

Employee Selection and Recruiting at Formula 409

Just as individuals may be broadly categorized as "extroverts" or "introverts," so organizations may be viewed as having particular personalities. Often, in-dividuals who thrive in one type of organization are ill-suited for other types of organizations.

One entrepreneur learned this lesson the hard way. As soon as Wilson Harrell bought into the company that made the spray cleaner Formula 409, he began competing for shelf space and market share with such giants as Procter & Gamble. Harrell's small company began to succeed in this venture, largely because of the innovative, hard-driving, entrepreneurial types employed by the company.

But Harrell didn't fully grasp the reason for his firm's success. He sought advice from management consultants about what to do next. The consultants recommended that Harrell bring in big-company types: a marketing vice president, for example, who'd instill a sense of professionalism in the sales force. One consultant in particular was surprised to see Harrell still in business, noting that Harrell's sales force was undisciplined and fiercely independent. Harrell could see this, but he failed to realize that this unconventional sales force was precisely what had propelled his small firm into big-time competition in the first place.

When Harrell recruited a marketing vice president with full managerial authority, the problems began. The vice president sized up the sales force and concluded that the company couldn't survive with such a crew of misfits. Harrell agreed, and he began to replace them with employees better suited to a large firm.

Next, Harrell hired professional managers, just as large corporations did. Gradually Harrell's small enterprise began to fail. The vitality and originality that had been the mark of Formula 409 were replaced by unimaginative marketing plans that resulted in a loss of market share. Only a takeover by Clorox Co. saved Harrell from complete financial disaster.

Harrell, however, didn't blame his team of managers, who were competent executives. He realized instead that the managers were in the wrong company. They were not suited to the type of ongoing, strategic efforts required in a small company. Harrell had learned that recruiting and selection decisions must be made in the context of such requirements.*

Questions

1. Why don't all organizations need personnel with the same type of personalities?

* Based on information from Wilson Harrell, "Betting on the Right Horses," *Inc.*, September 1986, pp. 103–104; and Joseph P. Kahn, "Portrait of a Compulsive Entrepreneur," *Inc.*, April 1985, pp. 79–80+. Reprinted with permission, *Inc.* magazine. Copyright © 1985, 1986 by INC. Publishing Company, 38 Commercial Wharf, Boston, MA 02110.

2. Was it faulty recruiting or faulty selection that led Formula 409 to hire the wrong type of sales and managerial employees?

Case 9.2

HRM: Top Priority at Herman Miller, Inc.

Max DePree, chairman of the office-furniture manufacturing company Herman Miller, Inc., is optimistic about his company's future. He is confident that Herman Miller can handle the aggression of expanding foreign furniture makers and eventually displace the number-one office-furniture producer in the United States, Steelcase Inc.

Back in 1923, long before employee profit sharing, incentive programs, and human resources management were popular, Max's father and company founder, D. J. DePree, stongly believed in a company ethic that stressed employee involvement and employer compassion. In the ensuing years, employer-employee relationships have been so good at Herman Miller that there has never been a serious attempt to unionize the company. Max DePree is proud of the trust that exists between management and workers, and many industry analysts attest to the comfortable and efficient work environment of Herman Miller's plants. Herman Miller (D. J. DePree named the company after his father-in-law, who gave him the start-up money) may be the only company in the United States with a vice president for people, who supervises human resources and employee relations.

When hiring new employees, Herman Miller managers focus more on a person's character and interpersonal abilities than on a résumé. Managers organize employees into work teams with team leaders. Every six months, the leader evaluates his or her workers; the workers also evaluate the leader. Company meetings that bring together line supervisors and elected team representatives attempt to resolve any grievances. Workers also have the option of meeting directly with executives. Each employee is concerned with cost cutting and product improvement, receiving bonuses that reward individual or group suggestions. Worker suggestions have saved Herman Miller more than $12 million in one year.

In the event of a hostile takeover, workers as well as executives will receive "silver parachutes" (large checks) if they lose their jobs. Other measures Herman Miller has taken to ensure that workers stay satisfied are the limitation of the CEO's salary to twenty times that of the average line worker and the establishment of an ethically sound managerial promotion plan. Max DePree, who recently stepped down as CEO (he retained his title as chairman), will be the last DePree to head the company. The next generations of DePrees are not allowed to work for the company to guard against nepotism.

Max DePree once stated, "Capitalism can only reach its potential when it capitalizes on all workers' gifts and lets them share in the results." The management of his company seems to be deeply dedicated to this idea. Herman Miller's unique management practices and incentive programs have resulted in one of the fastest growth rates of any business in the office-furniture industry.

Cost cutting—which has led to layoffs and hard feelings at many large U.S. companies—has actually strengthened the management-worker relationships at Herman Miller as workers and executives work together to achieve company objectives. In the office-furniture business, nice guys certainly don't finish last. The executives and workers at Herman Miller have their goals set much higher than that.†

Questions

1. In what ways does a company like Herman Miller benefit from highly favorable employer-employee relationships created by effective HRM activities and programs?
2. Herman Miller appears to provide more employee benefits than do many other companies. What are the advantages and disadvantages of these management practices to the company?

---

† Based on information from Kenneth Labich, "Hot Company, Warm Culture," *Fortune*, February 27, 1989, pp. 74–76, 78; "Making Open Offices a Little Less Open," *Wall Street Journal*, November 8, 1988, p. B1; and Dana Wechsler, "A Comeback in Cubicles," *Forbes*, March 21, 1988, pp. 54, 56.

UNION-MANAGEMENT RELATIONS

1 Be able to explain how and why labor unions came into being

2 Understand the sources of unions' negotiating power and trends in union membership

3 Become familiar with major labor-management legislation

4 Be aware of the steps involved in forming a union, and show how the National Labor Relations Board is involved in the process

5 Understand the major elements in the collective bargaining process

6 Know the major issues covered in a union-management contract

7 Recognize the major bargaining tools available to unions and management

We open this chapter by reviewing the history of labor unions in this country. Then we turn our attention to organized labor today, noting current membership trends and summarizing important labor-relations laws. We discuss the unionization process—why employees join unions, how a union is formed, and what the National Labor Relations Board does. Collective bargaining procedures are then explained. Next, we consider such issues as employee pay, working hours, security, management rights, and grievance procedures, all of which are issues included in a union-management contract. We close with a discussion of various labor and management negotiating techniques, including strikes, lockouts, mediation, and arbitration.

INSIDE BUSINESS

UAW and GM Working Together

In the past, General Motors Corp. had been heavily criticized for overlooking the importance of its workers while it poured billions of dollars into plant modernization and improved technology. But, in an unprecedented move, GM and union representatives from the United Auto Workers (UAW) came together to try to bring improved quality, productivity, and customer satisfaction to the automaker. GM knew that it had to restructure its entire corporate culture and human resources management to keep from sliding further behind in the very competitive auto industry.

Since the UAW and GM agreed to work together to improve quality and customer satisfaction, GM has made manufacturing improvements. Workers' suggestions have resulted in better production methods. For example, at GM's Inland Division plant in Livonia, Michigan, workers can now complete the interior of a Chevy Cavalier sedan in one-fourth the time that it formerly took. Today every plant has a quality improvement process.

Combining ideas, GM and the UAW came up with the "Quality Network," a general process that symbolizes GM's new commitment to improving its relationships with suppliers, dealers, and customers. The Quality Network stresses the importance of GM people. As GM's president has stated, "People are the ones who make technology work."

Every GM employee is given a booklet that emphasizes the importance of customer satisfaction through people, teamwork, and continuous improvement.

GM is so serious about getting workers involved in company decisions at every level that the UAW was even instrumental in selecting the advertising agency for GM's new Saturn division. The UAW also had representatives on the committee that oversaw the design of the Saturn assembly plant. Clearly, Saturn executives are making their business a totally joint effort between the union and management.

GM and the UAW have concluded that workers who feel satisfied with themselves take more interest in doing a good job and are also more willing to learn new skills. GM, working with the UAW, has thus given high priority to worker training or retraining, when necessary. GM has also instituted a self-enrichment training program for workers.[1]

The cooperation between the UAW and GM provides greater job satisfaction to the workers, makes the organization more productive, allows GM to be more competitive, and thus improves workers' job benefits and security. Not all companies and unions get along as well as the UAW and GM, however. Wages, work rules, and benefits programs are common issues that sometimes lead to disputes between management and labor.

A **labor union** is an organization of workers acting together to negotiate their wages and working conditions with employers. In the United States, nonmanagement employees have the legal right to form unions and to bargain, as a group, with management. The result of the bargaining process is a *labor contract*, a written agreement that is in force for a set period of time (usually one to three years). The dealings between labor unions and business management, both in the bargaining process and beyond it, are called **union-management relations** or, more simply, **labor relations.**

There is a dual relationship between labor and management. The two groups have different goals, which tend to place them at odds with each other. But these goals must be attained by the same means—through the production of goods and services. And, even at contract bargaining sessions, the two groups must work together to attain their goals. Perhaps mainly for this reason, antagonism now seems to be giving way to cooperation in union-management relations.

Before we examine how organized labor operates today, we should take a look at its roots in the history of the labor movement.

The Historical Development of Unions

Until the middle of the nineteenth century, there was very little organization of labor in this country. Groups of workers did occasionally form a **craft union,** which is an organization of skilled workers in a single craft or trade. These unions were usually limited to a single city, and they often did not last very long. The first known strike in the United States involved a group of Philadelphia printers who stopped working over demands for higher wages. When the printers were granted a pay increase by their employers, the group disbanded.

Early History

In the mid-1800s, improved transportation began to open new markets for manufactured goods. New manufacturing methods made it possible to supply those markets, and American industry began to grow. The Civil War and the continued growth of the railroads after the war led to further industrial expansion.

Large-scale production required more and more skilled industrial workers. As the skilled labor force grew, craft unions emerged in the more industrialized areas. From these craft unions, three significant labor organizations evolved. See Figure 10.1 for a historical overview of unions and their patterns of membership.

Knights of Labor   The first significant labor organization to emerge was the Knights of Labor. The *Knights of Labor* was formed as a secret society in 1869 by Uriah Stephens. One major goal of the Knights was to eliminate the depersonalization of the worker that resulted from mass-production technology. Another was to improve the moral standards of both employees and society. The Knights of Labor was the first truly national labor union. Membership increased steadily, and by 1886 the Knights had approximately 700,000 members.

The moralistic goals of the Knights ultimately contributed to its downfall. The group's leaders concentrated so hard on social and economic change that they did not recognize the effects of technological change. Moreover, they assumed that all employees had the same goals—those of the Knights' leaders—and wanted social and moral reform.

The major reason for the demise of the Knights, however, was the Haymarket riot of 1886. At a rally (called to demand a reduction in the length of a workday from ten to eight hours) in Chicago's Haymarket Square, a bomb exploded. Several police officers and civilians were killed

FIGURE 10.1
Historical Overview of Unions
The total number of members for all unions has risen dramatically since 1869, when the first truly national union was organized. The dates of major events in the history of labor unions are singled out along the line of membership growth.
(Sources: U.S. Bureau of Labor Statistics and Directory of U.S. Labor Organizations, 1986–87; U.S. Bureau of Labor Statistics, Current Population Survey of Households, 1988.)

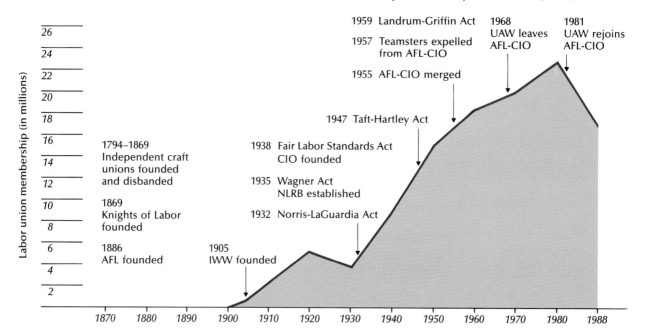

Samuel Gompers, President of the American Federation of Labor, at a meeting with its executive council in 1924.

or wounded. The Knights were not directly implicated, but they quickly lost public favor.

American Federation of Labor   In 1886 several leaders of the Knights joined with independent craft unions to form the *American Federation of Labor (AFL)*. Samuel Gompers, one of the AFL's founders, became its first president. Gompers believed that the goals of the union should be those of its members rather than those of its leaders. Moreover, the AFL did not seek to change the existing business system, as the Knights of Labor had. Instead, its goal was to improve its members' living standards within that system.

Another major difference between the Knights of Labor and the AFL was in their positions regarding strikes. A **strike** is a temporary work stoppage by employees, calculated to add force to their demands. The Knights did not favor the use of strikes, whereas the AFL strongly believed that striking was an effective labor weapon. The AFL also believed that organized labor should play a major role in politics. As we will see, the AFL is still very much a part of the American labor scene.

Industrial Workers of the World   The *Industrial Workers of the World (IWW)* was created in 1905 as a radical alternative to the AFL. Among its goals was the overthrow of capitalism. This radical stance prevented the IWW from gaining much of a foothold. Perhaps its major accomplishment was to make the AFL seem less threatening, by comparison, to the general public and to business leaders.

Nevertheless, during the first two decades of this century, both business and government attempted to keep labor unions from growing. This period

strike *a temporary work stoppage by employees, calculated to add force to their demands* is characterized by strikes and violent confrontations between management and unions. In steelworks, garment factories, and auto plants, clashes took place in which striking union members fought bitterly against nonunion workers, police, and private security guards.

Between the World Wars

The AFL continued to be the major force in organized labor. By 1920 its membership included 75 percent of all those who had joined unions. Throughout its existence, however, the AFL had been unsure of the best way to deal with unskilled and semiskilled workers. Most of its members were skilled workers in specific crafts or trades. But technological changes during World War I had brought about a significant increase in the number of unskilled and semiskilled employees in the work force. These people sought to join the AFL, but they were not well received by its established membership.

Some unions within the AFL did recognize the need to organize unskilled and semiskilled workers, and they began with the automotive and steel industries. The type of union they formed was an **industrial union,** an organization of both skilled and unskilled workers in a single industry. Soon workers in the rubber, mining, newspaper, and communications industries were also organized into unions. Eventually these unions left the AFL and formed the *Congress of Industrial Organizations (CIO)*.

During this same time (the late 1930s), there was a major upswing in membership—in the AFL, CIO, and independent unions. Strong union leadership, the development of new negotiating tactics, and favorable legislation combined to increase total union membership to 9 million in 1940. At this point the CIO began to rival the AFL in size and influence. There was other rivalry as well: The AFL and CIO often clashed over which of them had the right to organize and represent particular groups of employees.

industrial union *an organization of both skilled and unskilled workers in a single industry*

Recent History

Since World War II, the labor scene has gone through a number of changes. For one thing, during and after the war years there was a downturn in public opinion regarding unions. A few isolated but very visible strikes during the war caused public sentiment to shift against unionism.

Perhaps the most significant occurrence, however, was the merger of the AFL and the CIO. After years of bickering, the two groups recognized that they were wasting effort by fighting each other and that a merger would greatly increase the strength of both. The merger took place on December 5, 1955. The new organization, called the *AFL-CIO*, had a membership of as many as 16 million workers, which made it the largest labor organization of its kind in the world. Its first president was George Meany, who served until 1979.

Organized Labor Today

Learning Objective 2
Understand the sources of unions' negotiating power and trends in union membership

The power of unions to negotiate effectively with management is derived from two sources. The first is their membership. The more workers a union represents within an industry, the greater its clout in dealing with firms operating in that industry. The second source of union power is the laws that guarantee unions the right to negotiate and, at the same time, regulate the negotiating process.

Union Membership

At present, union members account for a relatively small portion of the American work force. (Less than one-quarter of the nation's workers belong to unions.) Union membership is concentrated in a few industries and job categories. Within these industries, unions wield considerable power.

The AFL-CIO is still the largest union organization in this country, boasting approximately 14,100,000 members. Those represented by the AFL-CIO include actors, barbers, construction workers, carpenters, retail clerks, musicians, teachers, postal workers, painters, steel and iron workers, firefighters, bricklayers, and newspaper reporters. The membership

At Preston Trucking, management and union members are developing a strong, positive relationship. This is being done primarily by increasing the level of trust by the use of bottom-up communication tools, such as surveys and an employee suggestion program.

represented by the AFL-CIO is obviously very diverse (see Figure 10.2, which shows the organization of the AFL-CIO).

One of the largest unions not associated directly with the AFL-CIO is the Teamsters' union. The *Teamsters* were originally part of the AFL-CIO, but in 1957 they were expelled for corrupt and illegal practices. The union started out as an organization of professional drivers, but it has recently begun to recruit employees in a wide variety of jobs. Current membership is slightly below 2 million workers.

The *United Auto Workers* represents employees in the auto industry. The UAW, too, was originally part of the AFL-CIO, but it left the parent union—of its own accord—in 1968. The current membership of the UAW is around 1 million. For a while, the Teamsters and the UAW formed a semistructured partnership called the Alliance for Labor Action. This partnership was eventually dissolved, and the UAW again became part of the AFL-CIO in 1981.

Membership Trends

The proportion of union members, relative to the size of the nation's work force, has declined over the last twenty years. Moreover, total union membership has dropped since 1980, despite steadily increasing membership in earlier years (see Figure 10.1). To a great extent, this decline in membership is due to changing trends in business:

▶ Heavily unionized industries have either been decreasing in size or have not been growing as fast as nonunionized industries. For example, recent cutbacks in the steel and auto industries have tended to reduce union membership. At the same time, the growth of high-tech industries has increased the ranks of nonunion workers.

▶ Many firms have moved from the heavily unionized Northeast and Great Lakes regions to the less unionized Southeast and Southwest—the "Sunbelt." At the new plants, formerly unionized firms tend to hire nonunion workers.

▶ The largest growth in employment is occurring in the service industries, and these industries are typically not unionized.

▶ Management is providing benefits that tend to reduce employees' need for unionization. Increased employee participation and better wages and working conditions are goals of unions. When these benefits are already supplied by management, workers are less likely to join unions.

Unions are increasing the pace of their organizing activities in the Sunbelt and the service industries. It remains to be seen whether they will be able to regain the prominence and power they enjoyed between the world wars and during the 1950s. There is little doubt, however, that they will remain a powerful force in particular industries. And their membership among professional and white-collar workers will probably increase.

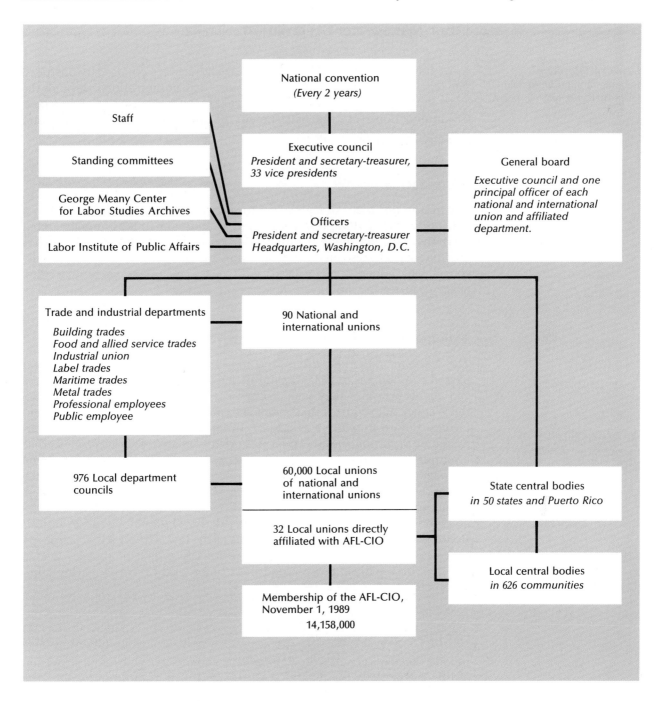

FIGURE 10.2
AFL-CIO Organization Chart
Like a big corporation, the AFL-CIO has organized its chain of command to best attain its goals as well as the goals of the various unions it represents. (Source: "Structure of the AFL-CIO," American Federation of Labor and Congress of Industrial Organizations, Washington, D.C., December 1989, p. 2.)

Labor-Management Legislation

Learning Objective 3
Become familiar with major
labor-management legislation

As we have noted, early efforts to organize labor were opposed by business. The federal government generally supported antiunion efforts through the court system, and in some cases federal troops were used to end strikes. Gradually, however, the government began to correct this imbalance through the legislative process.

Norris-LaGuardia Act

The first major piece of legislation to secure rights for unions, the *Norris-LaGuardia Act* of 1932, was considered a landmark in labor-management relations. This act made it difficult for businesses to obtain court orders that banned strikes, picketing, or union membership drives. Previously, courts had issued such orders readily as a means of curbing strikes, peaceful picketing, and even membership drives.

National Labor Relations Act

The *National Labor Relations Act*, also known as the *Wagner Act*, was passed by Congress in 1935. It established procedures by which employees can decide whether they want to be represented by a union. If they do, the Wagner Act requires that management negotiate with union representatives. Before this law was passed, union efforts were sometimes interpreted as violating the Sherman Act (1890) because they were viewed as attempts to monopolize. It also forbids certain unfair labor practices on the part of management, such as firing or punishing workers because they are prounion, spying on union meetings, and bribing employees to vote against unionization.

National Labor Relations Board (NLRB) *the federal agency that enforces the provisions of the Wagner Act*

Finally, the Wagner Act established the **National Labor Relations Board (NLRB)** to enforce the provisions of the law. The NLRB is primarily concerned with (1) overseeing the elections in which employees decide whether they will be represented by a union and (2) investigating complaints lodged by unions or employers.

Fair Labor Standards Act

In 1938 Congress enacted the *Fair Labor Standards Act*. One major provision of this act permits the federal government to set a minimum wage. The first minimum wage, which was set in the late 1930s and did not include farm workers and retail employees, was $0.25 an hour. Today the minimum wage is $4.25 an hour. Some employees, such as professional, executive, and administrative personnel, are exempt from the minimum wage provisions. The act also requires that employees be paid at overtime rates for work in excess of forty hours a week. Finally, this law prohibits the use of child labor.

Labor-Management Relations Act

The legislation of the 1930s sought to discourage unfair practices on the part of employers. As can be seen in Figure 10.1, union membership grew from approximately 3 million in 1910 to almost 14 million members by 1945. Unions represented over 35 percent of all nonagricultural employees in 1945. As union membership and power grew, however, the federal government began to examine the practices of labor. Several long and bitter strikes, mainly in the coal and trucking industries in the early 1940s, led to a demand for legislative restraint on unions. As a result, in 1947 Congress passed the *Labor-Management Relations Act,* also known as the *Taft-Hartley Act,* over President Harry Truman's veto.

The objective of the Taft-Hartley Act is to provide a balance between union power and management power. It lists unfair labor practices that *unions* are forbidden to use. These include refusal to bargain with management in good faith, charging excessive membership dues, harassing nonunion workers, and using various means of coercion against employers.

The Taft-Hartley Act also gives management more rights during union organizing campaigns. For example, management may outline for employees the advantages and disadvantages of union membership, as long as the information it presents is accurate. The act gives the president of the United States the power to obtain a temporary injunction to prevent or stop a strike that endangers the national health and safety. An **injunction** is a court order requiring a person or group either to perform some act or to refrain from performing some act. Finally, the Taft-Hartley Act authorized states to enact laws to allow employees to work in a unionized firm without joining the union. About twenty states (many in the South) have passed such legislation, called *right-to-work laws.*

injunction   *a court order requiring a person or group either to perform some act or to refrain from performing some act*

Landrum-Griffin Act

In the 1950s, Senate investigations and hearings exposed labor racketeering in unions and uncovered cases of bribery, extortion, and embezzlement among union leaders. It was discovered that a few union leaders had taken union funds for personal use and accepted payoffs from employers for union protection. Some were involved in arson, blackmail, and murder. Public pressure for reform resulted in the 1959 *Landrum-Griffin Act.*

This law was designed to regulate the internal functioning of labor unions. Provisions of the law require unions to file annual reports with the U.S. Department of Labor regarding their finances, elections, and various decisions made by union officers. The Landrum-Griffin Act also ensures each union member the right to seek, nominate, and vote for each elected position in his or her union. It provides safeguards governing union funds, and it requires management and unions to report the lending of management funds to union officers, union members, or local unions.

The various pieces of legislation that we have reviewed here effectively regulate much of the relationship between labor and management once a union has been established. The next section demonstrates that forming a union at one's firm is also a carefully regulated process.

The Unionization Process

Learning Objective 4
Be aware of the steps
involved in forming a union,
and show how the National
Labor Relations Board is
involved in the process

For a union to be formed at a particular firm, some employees of the firm must first be interested in being represented by a union. They must then take a number of steps to formally declare their desire for a union. To ensure fairness, most of the steps in this unionization process are supervised by the NLRB.

Why Some Employees Join Unions

Obviously, employees have a variety of reasons for wishing to start or join a union. One commonly cited reason is to combat alienation. Some employees—especially those whose jobs are dull and repetitive—can begin to perceive themselves as merely parts of a machine. They may feel that, at work, they lose their individual or social identity. Union membership is one way to establish contact with others in the firm.

Another common reason for joining a union is the perception that union membership increases job security. No one wants to live in fear of arbitrary or capricious dismissal from a job. Unions actually have only limited ability to guarantee a member's job, but they can help increase job security by using seniority rules.

Employees may also join a union because of dissatisfaction with one or more elements of their jobs. If they are unhappy with their pay, benefits, or working conditions, they may look to a union to correct the perceived deficiencies.

Some people join unions because of their personal background. For example, a person whose parents are strong believers in unions might be inclined to feel just as positive about union membership.

We should also note that there are situations in which employees *must* join a union to keep their jobs. Many unions try, through their labor contracts, to require that all new employees join the union after a specified probationary period. Under the Taft-Hartley Act, states may pass right-to-work laws prohibiting this practice.

Steps in Forming a Union

The first step in forming a union is the *organizing campaign* (see Figure 10.3). Its primary objective is to develop widespread employee interest in having a union. To kick off the campaign, a national union may send organizers to the firm to develop this interest. Alternatively, the employees themselves may decide that they want a union. Then they contact the appropriate national union and ask for organizing assistance.

The organizing campaign can be quite emotional, and it may lead to conflict between employees and management. On the one hand, the employees who want the union are dedicated to its creation. On the other hand, management is extremely sensitive to what it sees as a potential threat to its power and control.

At some point during the organizing campaign, employees are asked to sign *authorization cards* (see Figure 10.4) to indicate—in writing—their

FIGURE 10.3
Steps in Forming a Union
The unionization process consists of a campaign, authorization cards, a formal election, and certification of the election by the National Labor Relations Board.

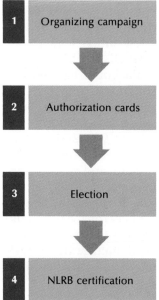

BUSINESS JOURNAL

Unions on the Rebound

Although you may see many smiling faces in television ads promoting unions, there haven't been too many smiles on the faces of union officials in the recent past. Union membership has been down and is continuing to drop steadily. With the shutdown of unionized factories, well-publicized charges of racketeering and underworld connections, and deregulation in the transportation industries, union membership has suffered severely. The unions, however, are not about to peacefully roll over and die. Using aggressive marketing practices, they may, in fact, be on the rise again.

The AFL-CIO is trying to expand its 14 million-member roster by offering a wide range of special benefits, or perks, to full and associate members. Associate members pay half the monthly union dues ($6 or $7) and are not represented in collective bargaining, but they get all the union perks. The union hopes that eventually they will become full members. The AFL-CIO now offers union employees a special low-interest credit card. In addition, members receive special deals on legal assistance, health care, automobile insurance, vacation packages, rental cars, and even funerals. So far it seems all the perks have worked in attracting new members.

The unions think that their union image needs to be upgraded. The AFL recently set aside more than $13 million for a two-year "Union Yes" campaign. The United Auto Workers (UAW) and the United Food and Commercial Workers (UFCW) have both committed large amounts of money to advertising campaigns. Unions are looking to Hollywood for spokespersons, employing well-known actors and actresses. Union slogans will likely be appearing on everything from bumper stickers to T-shirts and billboards.

The main reason unions are so concerned about changing their image is that they want to attract members from occupations that traditionally have not been unionized. Their prime target is white-collar workers, particularly in the growing ranks of service industries. But union organizers have discovered that white-collar employees do not react to unions in the same ways that blue-collar employees do. White-collar workers respond more positively to a more personal approach, which means that union organizing committees have to expand to reach more people. Also, white-collar workers pay more attention to the style and appearance of union literature—crude handbills seem to offend these workers.

Union officials are actively seeking to recruit members from the health-care, data-entry, hotel, restaurant, and clerical fields. Unions recently won a major victory in the health-care field when the National Labor Relations Board (NLRB) ruled that it would recognize eight separate categories of hospital workers at nonpublic, acute-care hospitals. And unions came out on top in another big battle when employees narrowly approved a 3,500-member clerical union at Harvard University.

Based on information from Bob Cohn, "Perks for the Rank and File," *Newsweek*, April 6, 1987, p. 42; Daniel Forbes, "With Its Image at an All-Time Low, Labor Turns to Madison Avenue," *Adweek's Marketing Week*, August 1, 1988, pp. 30, 32; Matthew Goodfellow, "Unions: Is It Time?" *Best's Review*, October 1988, pp. 19–20, 22, 24, 27; "Harvard Decides to Allow Certifying Clerical Union," *Wall Street Journal*, November 7, 1988, p. B10; and Harris Meyer, "Unionizing MDs Still Face Legal Roadblocks," *American Medical News*, September 16, 1988, p. 3.

support for the union. Because of various NLRB rules and regulations, both union organizers and company management must be very careful in their behavior during this authorization drive. For example, employees cannot be asked to sign the cards when they are supposed to be working. And management may not indicate in any way that employees' jobs or job security will be in jeopardy if they *do* sign the cards.

If at least 30 percent of the eligible employees sign authorization cards, the organizers generally request that the firm recognize the union

FIGURE 10.4
Sample Authorization Card
*Unions must have written
authorization to represent
employees. (Source: Printed
with permission of NLRB.)*

as the employees' bargaining representative. Usually the firm rejects this request, and a *formal election* is held to decide whether to have a union. This election usually involves secret ballots and is conducted by the NLRB. The outcome of the election is determined by a simple majority of eligible employees who choose to vote.

If the union obtains a majority, it becomes the official bargaining agent for its members. It may immediately begin the process of negotiating a labor contract with management. If the union is voted down, the NLRB will not allow another election for one year.

Several factors can complicate the unionization process. For example, the **bargaining unit,** which is the specific group of employees that the union is to represent, must be defined. Union organizers may want to represent all hourly employees at a particular site (such as all workers at a manufacturing plant). Or they may wish to represent only a specific group of employees (such as all electricians in a large manufacturing plant).

bargaining unit   *the specific group of employees represented by a union*

Another issue that may have to be resolved is that of **jurisdiction,** which is the right of a particular union to organize particular workers. Where jurisdictions overlap or are unclear, the employees themselves may decide who will represent them. In some cases, two or more unions may be trying to organize some or all of the employees of a firm. Then the election choices may be union A, union B, or no union at all.

jurisdiction   *the right of a particular union to organize particular workers*

The Role of the NLRB

As we have indicated, the NLRB is heavily involved in the unionization process. Generally, the NLRB is responsible for overseeing the organizing campaign, conducting the election (if one is warranted), and certifying the results.

The unionization process by the UAW failed at the Nissan plant in Smyrna, Tennessee when employees voted against unionization by a 2-to-1 margin in 1989.

During the organizing campaign, both employers and union organizers can take steps to educate employees regarding the advantages and disadvantages of having a union. However, neither is allowed to use underhanded tactics or distort the truth. If violations occur, the NLRB can stop the questionable behavior, postpone the election, or set aside the results of an election that has already taken place.

The NLRB usually conducts the election within forty-five days after the organizers submit the required number of signed authorization cards. A very high percentage of the eligible voters generally participate in the election, and it is held at the workplace during normal working hours. In certain cases, however, a mail ballot or other form of election may be called for.

Certification of the election involves counting the votes and considering challenges to the election. After the election results are announced, management and the union organizers have five days in which to challenge the election. The basis for a challenge might be improper conduct prior to the election or participation by an ineligible voter. After considering any challenges, the NLRB passes final judgment on the election results.

Once union representation is established, union and management get down to the serious business of contract negotiations.

Collective Bargaining

collective bargaining *the process of negotiating a labor contract with management*

Once a new union is certified by the NLRB, its first task is to establish its own identity and structure. It will immediately sign up as many members as possible. Then, in an internal election, members will choose officers and representatives. A negotiating committee will also be chosen to begin **collective bargaining,** the process of negotiating a labor contract with management.

Learning Objective 5
Understand the major
elements in the collective
bargaining process

The First Contract

To prepare for its first contract session with management, the negotiating committee decides what position it will take on the various contract issues. The committee is likely to determine which issues are of most importance to the union's members. To the members of a newly formed union, the two most pressing issues might be a general wage increase and an improved benefits package.

The union then informs management that it is ready to begin negotiations, and a time and location are agreed on. Both sides continue to prepare for the session up until the actual date of the negotiations.

The negotiations are occasionally held on company premises, but it is more common for the parties to meet away from the workplace—perhaps in a local hotel. The union is typically represented by the negotiating committee and by one or more officials from the regional or national union office. The firm is normally represented by managers from the industrial-relations, operations, HRM, and legal departments. Each side is required by law to negotiate in good faith and not to stall or attempt to extend the bargaining proceedings unnecessarily.

The union normally presents its contract demands first. Management then responds to the union's demands, often with a counterproposal. The bargaining may move back and forth, from proposal to counterproposal, over a number of meetings. Throughout the process, union representatives constantly keep their members informed of what is going on and how the committee feels about the various proposals and counterproposals.

Each side clearly tries to "get its own way" as much as possible, but each also recognizes the need for compromise. For example, the union may begin the negotiations by demanding a wage increase of $1 per hour but may be willing to accept 60 cents per hour. Management may initially offer 40 cents but may be willing to pay 75 cents. Eventually, the two sides will agree on a wage increase of somewhere between 60 and 75 cents per hour.

If an agreement cannot be reached, the union may go on strike. Strikes are rare during a union's first contract negotiations. In most cases, the initial contract is eventually developed by the negotiating teams.

ratification *approval of a labor contract by a vote of the union membership*

The final step in collective bargaining is **ratification,** which is approval of the contract by a vote of the union membership. If the membership accepts the terms of the contract, it is signed and becomes a legally binding agreement. If the contract is not ratified, the negotiators must go back and try to iron out a more acceptable agreement.

Later Contracts

A labor contract may cover a period of from one to three years or more, but every contract has an expiration date. As that date approaches, both management and the union begin to prepare for new contract negotiations. Now, however, the entire process is likely to be much thornier than the first negotiation.

For one thing, the union and the firm have "lived with each other" for several years. There may have been some difficulties during this time, and issues may have arisen that each side sees as being of critical importance. Such issues can result in a great deal of emotion at the bargaining table, and they are often difficult to resolve. For another thing, each side has learned from the earlier negotiations. Each may take a harder line on certain issues and be less willing to compromise.

And then there is the contract deadline. As the expiration date of the existing contract draws near, each side feels pressure—real or imagined—to reach an agreement. This pressure may nudge the negotiators toward agreement, but it can also produce even greater difficulty in reaching an accord. Moreover, at some point during the negotiations, union leaders are likely to take a *strike vote*. This vote reveals whether union members are willing to strike in the event that a new contract is not negotiated before the old one expires. In almost all cases, this vote supports a strike. So the threat of a strike may add to the pressure mounting on both sides, as they go about the business of negotiating a new contract.

Union-Management Contract Issues

Learning Objective 6
Know the major issues covered in a union-management contract

As might be expected, many diverse issues are negotiated by unions and management, and are made a part of their labor contract. Unions tend to emphasize issues related to members' income and standard of living, and the strength of the union. Management's primary goals are to retain as much control as possible over the operations of the firm and to maximize its strength relative to that of the union. The balance of power between the union and management varies from firm to firm.

Employee Pay

An area of bargaining that is central to union-management relations is employee pay. Three separate issues are usually involved: the forms of pay, magnitude of pay, and means by which the magnitude of pay will be determined.

Forms of Pay   The primary form of pay is direct compensation—the wage or salary that an employee receives in exchange for his or her contribution to the organization. Because direct compensation is a fairly straightforward issue, negotiators often spend much more of their time developing a benefits package for employees. And, as the range of benefits and their costs have escalated over the years, this element of pay has become increasingly important and complex.

We discussed the various employee benefits in Chapter 9. Of these, health, life, disability, and dental insurance are important benefits that unions try to obtain for their members. Deferred compensation, in the form of pension or retirement programs, is also a common focal point of concern.

Other benefits commonly dealt with in the bargaining process include paid vacation time and holidays. Policy on paid sick leave may also be

BUSINESS JOURNAL

ESOPs: Letting Employees Take Stock

ESOPs don't have anything to do with fairy tales, but to some business owners and employees, they seem to have happy endings. *ESOP* stands for Employee Stock-Ownership Plan, a relatively new and revolutionary way of transferring ownership of a business. Depending on who you listen to, ESOPs are either a sound idea that's here to stay or a passing trend that's doomed. The fact is, ESOPs are still in the developmental stage, and until certain business laws and ethics are addressed and revised, there is no telling how popular, successful, or widespread ESOPs will be.

ESOPs can work in one of three ways. In an ordinary ESOP plan, an employer contributes cash or stock to an employee stock trust. The trust then buys or receives the company's stock. The trust, governed by a company-appointed board, is in charge of the individual accounts of all employees who get shares in the company by means of the employer's contribution.

In a leveraged ESOP, the employer sets up a trust that borrows money from a lending institution and then uses that money to buy stock from the company. The stock, under specific guidelines, is given to employees. Leveraged ESOPs offer a company a great tax break since the money a company contributes into the stock trust is not treated as a loan repayment but as a contribution to an employee benefits plan. Contributions to such benefits plans are completely tax-deductible.

The most common ESOP is the transfer-of-ownership plan. A company makes a cash contribution into a trust to buy shares from existing shareholders. The company then transfers stock to individual employees. This plan lets employers carefully control how much and when stock is transferred.

The largest totally employee-owned company is Avis, Inc., the rental-car firm. Avis employees appear to be satisfied with their ESOP, and the company itself has been gaining market share. Wyatt Cafeterias, Amsted Industries (a diversified manufacturer), and Dan River (a textiles company) are examples of other successful businesses that are wholly owned by employees through ESOPs.

ESOPs can let employers take advantage of tax incentives and increase their cash flow. Many owners of businesses that have adopted ESOPs have found that employee morale, productivity, efficiency, and product quality all improve dramatically when employees realize that they are the actual owners. Employee turnover rates decrease. Employees that participate as well as those that are encouraged to participate in company matters—from everyday problem solving to financial planning—seem more content and willing to put forth extra effort. Also, ESOPs are a good marketing tool; studies indicate that consumers tend to look favorably on employee-owned companies.

Not all ESOPs are successful, however. Some have been major failures. Sometimes the restructuring an ESOP allows is not enough to keep a struggling firm alive. In other cases, ESOPs have served as the means by which owners of unprofitable companies have unloaded them onto employees at great profits. Some owners have used ESOPs merely as a way of preventing takeovers. Also, in some ESOPs, employees, though technically owners, have nothing to say regarding the way the company is run. All of these scenarios have aroused controversy and caused several members of Congress to call for a ban on ESOPs.

Based on information from Bartlett Naylor, "ESOP Fables: Not Just a Capitalist Tool," *The Nation*, January 22, 1990, p. 90+; Susan Dentzer, "The Foibles of ESOP's," *Newsweek*, October 19, 1987, pp. 58–59; David Kirkpatrick, "How the Workers Run Avis Better," *Fortune*, December 5, 1988, pp. 103, 106, 110, 114; and Norman M. Scarborough and Thomas W. Zimmerer, "The Entrepreneur's Guide to ESOPs," *Business*, January–March 1988, pp. 31–36.

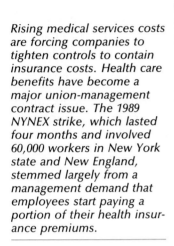

Rising medical services costs are forcing companies to tighten controls to contain insurance costs. Health care benefits have become a major union-management contract issue. The 1989 NYNEX strike, which lasted four months and involved 60,000 workers in New York state and New England, stemmed largely from a management demand that employees start paying a portion of their health insurance premiums.

negotiated. Obviously, unions argue for as much paid vacation and holiday time as possible and for liberal sick-leave policies. Management naturally takes the opposition position.

Magnitude of Pay   Of considerable importance is the *magnitude,* or amount, of pay that employees receive as both direct and indirect compensation.

The union attempts to ensure that pay is equitable with that received by other employees, both locally and nationally, in the same or similar industries. The union also attempts to include, in the contract, clauses that provide pay increases over the life of the agreement. The commonest is the *cost-of-living clause,* which ties periodic pay increases to increases in the cost of living, as defined by various economic statistics or indicators.

Of course, the magnitude of pay is also affected by the organization's ability to pay. If the firm has recently posted large profits, the union may expect large pay increases for its members. On the other hand, if the firm has not been very profitable, the union may agree to smaller pay hikes or even to a pay freeze. In an extreme situation (for example, when the firm is bordering on bankruptcy), the union may agree to pay cuts. Very stringent conditions are usually included in any agreement to a pay cut. Recently, the union at Chrysler agreed to a pay cut of $1.51 per hour and to relax work rules and raise productivity so that the labor force could be reduced by 25 percent over a five-year period. In return, management had to agree to reduce the work force only through attrition.

Bargaining with regard to magnitude also revolves around employee benefits. At one extreme, unions seek a wide range of benefits, entirely or largely paid for by the firm. At the other extreme, management may be willing to offer the benefits package but may want its employees to bear most of the cost. Again, factors such as equity (with similar firms and jobs) and ability to pay enter into the final agreement.

Pay Determinants   Negotiators also address the question of how individual pay will be determined. For management, the ideal arrangement is to tie wages to each employee's productivity. As we saw, this method of payment tends to motivate and reward effort. Unions, on the other hand, feel that this arrangement can also create unnecessary competition among employees. They generally argue that employees should be paid—at least in part—according to seniority. **Seniority** is the length of time an employee has worked for the organization.

Determinants regarding benefits are also negotiated. For example, management may want to provide retirement benefits only to employees who have worked for the firm for a specified number of years. The union may want these benefits provided to all employees.

Working Hours

Of special interest relative to working hours is the matter of overtime. Federal law defines **overtime** as time worked in excess of forty hours in one week. And it specifies that overtime pay must be at least one and one-half times the normal hourly wage. Unions may attempt to negotiate overtime rates for all hours worked beyond eight hours in a single day. Similarly, the union may attempt to obtain higher overtime rates (say, twice the normal hourly wage) for weekend or holiday work. Still another issue is an upper limit to overtime, beyond which employees can refuse to work.

In firms with two or more work shifts, workers on less desirable shifts are paid a premium for their time. Both the amount of the premium and the manner in which workers are chosen for (or choose) particular shifts are negotiable issues. Other issues related to working hours are the work starting times and the length of lunch periods and coffee breaks.

Security

Security actually covers two issues: the job security of the individual worker and the security of the union as the bargaining representative of the firm's employees.

Job security is protection against the loss of employment. It is and probably always will be a major concern of individuals. As we noted earlier, the desire for increased job security is a major reason for joining unions in the first place. In the typical labor contract, job security is based on seniority. If employees must be laid off or dismissed, those with the least seniority are the first to go. Some of the more senior employees may have to move to lower-level jobs, but they remain employed.

Union security is protection of the union's position as the employees' bargaining agent. Union security is frequently a more volatile issue then job security. Unions strive for as much security as possible, but management tends to see an increase in union security as an erosion of its control.

seniority *the length of time an employee has worked for the organization*

overtime *time worked in excess of forty hours in one week; under some union contracts, it can be time worked in excess of eight hours in a single day*

job security *protection against the loss of employment*

union security *protection of the union's position as the employees' bargaining agent*

Union security arises directly from its membership. The greater the ratio of union employees to nonunion employees, the more secure the union. In contract negotiations, unions thus attempt to establish various union-membership conditions. The most restrictive of these is the **closed shop,** in which workers must join the union before they are hired. This condition was outlawed by the Taft-Hartley Act, but several other arrangements are subject to negotiation:

closed shop *a workplace in which workers must join the union before they are hired; outlawed by the Taft-Hartley Act*

▶ The **union shop,** in which new employees must join the union after a specified probationary period.

union shop *a workplace in which new employees must join the union after a specified probationary period*

▶ The **agency shop,** in which employees can choose not to join the union but must pay dues to the union anyway. (The idea is that nonunion employees benefit from union activities and should help support them.)

agency shop *a workplace in which employees can choose not to join the union but must pay dues to the union anyway*

▶ The **maintenance shop,** in which an employee who joins the union must remain a union member as long as he or she is employed by the firm.

maintenance shop *a workplace in which an employee who joins the union must remain a union member as long as he or she is employed by the firm*

Management Rights

Of particular interest to the firm are those rights and privileges that are to be retained by management. For example, the firm wants as much control as possible over whom it hires, how work is scheduled, and how discipline is handled. The union, on the other hand, would like some control over these and all other matters affecting its members. Interestingly, unions in the United States are making surprisingly rapid progress toward their goal of playing a more direct role in corporate governance. In exchange for union concessions that helped Chrysler fend off bankruptcy, Douglas Fraser, a high-ranking union official, was given a seat on Chrysler's board of directors. He participated fully in all company business except labor-management strategy. Since that time, union employees have taken seats on a number of corporate boards.

Grievance Procedures

grievance procedure *a formally established course of action for resolving employee complaints against management*

A **grievance procedure** is a formally established course of action for resolving employee complaints against management. Virtually every labor contract contains one grievance procedure. Procedures vary in scope and detail, but most include the following four steps (see Figure 10.5).

Original Grievance   The process begins with an employee who believes that he or she has been treated unfairly, in violation of the labor contract. For example, an employee may be entitled to a formal performance review after six months on the job. If no such review is conducted, the employee may file a grievance. To do so, the employee explains the grievance to a **shop steward,** an employee who is elected by union members to serve as their representative. The employee and the steward then discuss the grievance with the employee's immediate supervisor. Both the grievance and the supervisor's response are put in writing.

shop steward *an employee who is elected by union members to serve as their representative*

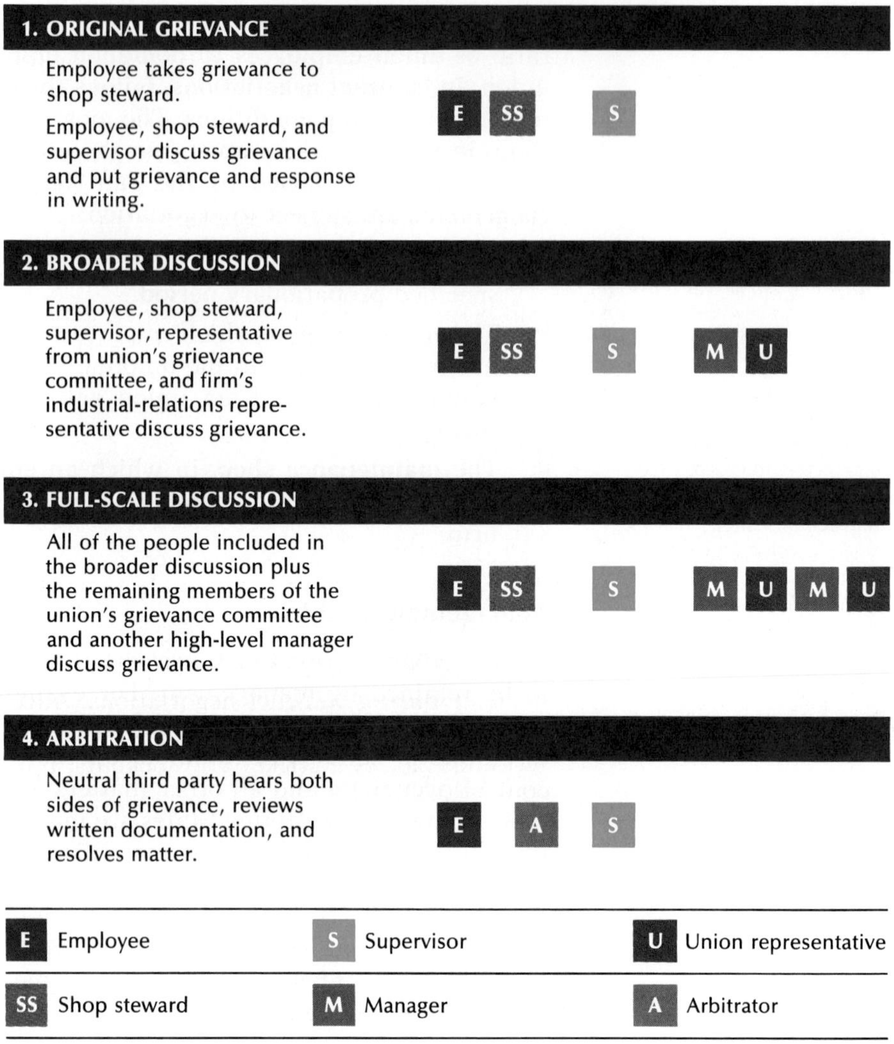

1. ORIGINAL GRIEVANCE

Employee takes grievance to shop steward.

Employee, shop steward, and supervisor discuss grievance and put grievance and response in writing.

`E` `SS` `S`

2. BROADER DISCUSSION

Employee, shop steward, supervisor, representative from union's grievance committee, and firm's industrial-relations representative discuss grievance.

`E` `SS` `S` `M` `U`

3. FULL-SCALE DISCUSSION

All of the people included in the broader discussion plus the remaining members of the union's grievance committee and another high-level manager discuss grievance.

`E` `SS` `S` `M` `U` `M` `U`

4. ARBITRATION

Neutral third party hears both sides of grievance, reviews written documentation, and resolves matter.

`E` `A` `S`

| `E` Employee | `S` Supervisor | `U` Union representative |
| `SS` Shop steward | `M` Manager | `A` Arbitrator |

FIGURE 10.5
Steps in Resolving a Grievance
The employee grievance procedure for most organizations consists of four steps. Each ensuing step involves all the personnel from the preceding step plus at least one higher-level person. The final step is to go to a neutral third party, the arbitrator.

Broader Discussion In most cases the problem is resolved during the initial discussion with the supervisor. If it is not, a second discussion is held. Now the participants include the original parties (employee, supervisor, and steward); a representative from the union's grievance committee; and the firm's industrial-relations representative. Again a record is kept of the discussion and its results.

Full-Scale Discussion If the grievance is still not resolved, a full-scale discussion is arranged. This discussion includes everyone involved in the broadened discussion, as well as all remaining members of the union's grievance committee and another high-level manager. As usual, all proceedings are put in writing. All participants are careful not to violate the labor contract during this attempt to resolve the complaint.

arbitration *the procedure by which a neutral third party hears the two sides of a dispute and renders a decision; the decision is binding when arbitration is part of the grievance procedure, but may not be binding when arbitration is used to settle labor-contract disputes*

Arbitration The final step in almost all grievance procedures is **arbitration,** in which a neutral third party hears the grievance and renders a binding decision. As in a court hearing, each side presents its case with the right to cross-examine witnesses. In addition, the arbitrator reviews the written documentation of all previous steps in the grievance procedure. Both sides may then give summary arguments and/or present briefs. The arbitrator then decides whether a provision of the labor contract has been violated and proposes a remedy. The arbitrator cannot make any decision that would add to, detract from, or modify the terms of the contract. If it can be proved that the arbitrator exceeded the scope of his or her authority, either party may appeal the decision to the courts.

What actually happens when union and management "lock horns" over all the issues we have mentioned? We can answer this question by looking at the following negotiating tools.

Union and Management Negotiating Tools

Learning Objective 7
Recognize the major bargaining tools available to unions and management

Both management and unions can draw on certain tools to influence one another during contract negotiations. Advertising and publicity may be used by both sides to gain support for their respective positions. The most extreme tools are strikes and lockouts, but there are other, milder techniques as well.

Strikes

Unions make use of strikes only in a very few instances, and it is almost always after an existing labor contract has expired. Even then, if new contract negotiations seem to be proceeding smoothly, a union does not actually start a strike. The union does take a strike vote, but the vote may be used primarily to show members' commitment to a strike if negotiations fail.

picketing *marching back and forth in front of one's place of employment with signs informing the public that a strike is in progress*

When union members do go out on strike, it is usually because negotiations seem to be stalled. A strike is simply a work stoppage: Employees do not report for work. In addition, striking workers engage in **picketing,** marching back and forth in front of their place of employment with signs informing the public that a strike is in progress. In doing so, they hope that (1) the public will be sympathetic to the strikers and will not patronize the struck firm; (2) nonstriking employees of the firm will honor the picket line and not report to work either; and (3) members of other unions will not cross the picket line (for example, to make deliveries or pickups) so as to further restrict the operations of the struck firm.

Obviously, strikes are expensive to both the firm and the strikers. The firm loses business and earnings during the strike. In fact, the main objective of a strike is to put financial pressure on the firm. At the same time, the striking workers lose the wages they would have earned if they had been at their jobs.

Picket lines during a strike, like the one at Boeing, attract public support and sympathy. This strike, which occurred in October 1987, involved 57,000 members of the International Association of Machinists and Aerospace workers. It was the first strike against Boeing in twelve years.

Unions try to support striking members as much as possible. Larger unions put a portion of their members' dues into a *strike fund*. The fund is used to provide financial support for striking union members.

wildcat strike *a strike that has not been approved by the strikers' union*

At times, workers may go out on a **wildcat strike,** which is a strike that has not been approved by the union. In this situation, union leaders typically work with management to convince the strikers to return to work.

Slowdowns and Boycotts

Almost every labor contract contains a clause that prohibits strikes during the life of the contract. (This is why strikes usually take place after a contract has expired.) However, a union may strike a firm while the contract is in force if members believe that management has violated the terms of the contract. Workers may also engage in a **slowdown,** which is a technique whereby workers report to their jobs but work at a slower pace than normal.

slowdown *a technique whereby workers report to their jobs but work at a slower pace than normal*

A **boycott** is a refusal to do business with a particular firm. Unions occasionally bring this technique to bear by urging their members (and sympathizers) not to purchase the products of a firm with which they are having a dispute. A *primary boycott*, which is aimed at the employer directly involved in the dispute, can be a powerful weapon. A *secondary boycott*, which is aimed at a firm doing business with the employer, is prohibited by the Taft-Hartley Act.

boycott *a refusal to do business with a particular firm*

Management Weapons

lockout *a firm's refusal to allow employees to enter the workplace*

Management's most potent weapon is the lockout. In a **lockout,** the firm refuses to allow employees to enter the workplace. Like strikes, lockouts are expensive for both the firm and its employees. For this reason they are rarely used, and then only in certain special circumstances. A firm that produces perishable goods, for example, may use a lockout if management believes it employees will soon go on strike. The idea is to stop production in time to ensure that there is minimal spoilage of finished goods or work in process.

strikebreaker *a nonunion employee who performs the job of a striking union member*

Management may also attempt to hire strikebreakers. A **strikebreaker** is a nonunion employee who performs the job of a striking union member. Hiring strikebreakers can result in violence when picketing employees confront the nonunion workers at the entrances to the struck facility. For the firm, there is also the problem of finding qualified replacements for the striking workers. Sometimes management personnel take over the jobs of strikers. Bell Telephone managers have done this on more than one occasion.

Mediation and Arbitration

Strikes and strikebreaking, lockouts and boycotts, all pit one side against the other. Ultimately one side "wins" and the other "loses." Unfortunately, the negative effects of such actions—including resentment, fear, and distrust—may linger for months or years after a dispute has been resolved.

More productive techniques that are being used increasingly are mediation and arbitration. These techniques may come into play before a labor contract expires or after some other strategy, such as a strike, has proved ineffective.

mediation *the use of a neutral third party to assist management and the union during their negotiations*

Mediation is the use of a neutral third party to assist management and the union during their negotiations. This third party (the mediator) listens to both sides, trying to find common ground for agreement. The mediator also tries to facilitate communication between the two sides, to promote compromise, and generally to keep the negotiations moving. At first the mediator may meet privately with each side. Eventually, however, his or her goal is to get the two to settle their differences at the bargaining table.

Unlike mediation, the *arbitration* step is a formal hearing. Just as it is used as the final step in a grievance procedure, it may also be used in contract negotiations (perhaps after mediation attempts) when the two sides cannot agree on one or more issues. Here, the arbitrator hears the formal positions of both parties on outstanding, unresolved issues. The arbitrator then analyzes these positions and makes a decision on the possible resolution of the issues. If both sides have agreed in advance that the arbitration will be binding, they must accept the arbitrator's decision.

If mediation or arbitration is unsuccessful, then, under the provisions of the Taft-Hartley Act, the president of the United States can obtain a temporary injunction to prevent or stop a strike if it would jeopardize national health or security.

CHAPTER REVIEW

Summary

A labor union is an organization of workers who act together to negotiate wages and working conditions with their employers. Labor relations are the dealings between labor unions and business management.

The first major union in the United States was the Knights of Labor, formed in 1869. The Knights were followed in 1886 by the American Federation of Labor and in 1905 by the radical Industrial Workers of the World. Of these three, only the AFL remained when the Congress of Industrial Organizations was founded as an organization of industrial unions between World War I and World War II. After years of bickering, the AFL and CIO merged in 1955. The largest union not affiliated with the AFL-CIO is the Teamsters' union.

At present, union membership accounts for less than one-quarter of the American work force, and it seems to be decreasing for various reasons. Nonetheless, unions wield considerable power in many industries—those in which their members comprise a large proportion of the work force.

Important laws that affect union power are the Norris-LaGuardia Act (which limits management's ability to obtain injunctions against unions), the Wagner Act (which forbids certain unfair labor practices by management), the Fair Labor Standards Act (which allows the federal government to set a minimum wage and to mandate overtime rates), the Taft-Hartley Act (which forbids certain unfair practices by unions), and the Landrum-Griffin Act (which regulates the internal functioning of labor unions). The National Labor Relations Board, a federal agency that oversees union-management relations, was created by the Wagner Act.

Employees start or join unions for a variety of reasons, including alienation, concern about job security, and dissatisfaction with their jobs. Attempts to form a union begin with an organizing campaign and end with a formal election in which employees decide whether they want a union. The entire process is supervised by the NLRB, which also certifies the results of the election.

Once a union is established, it may negotiate a labor contract with management through the process called collective bargaining. Contract issues include employee pay and benefits, working hours, job and union security, management rights, and grievance procedures. As the expiration date of an existing contract approaches, management and the union begin to negotiate a new contract.

When contract negotiations do not run smoothly, unions may apply pressure on management through strikes, slowdowns, or boycotts. Management may counter by imposing lockouts or hiring strikebreakers. Less drastic techniques for breaking contract deadlocks are mediation and arbitration. In both, a neutral third party is involved in the negotiations.

This chapter ends our discussion of human resources. In the next part of the book, we examine the marketing function of business. We begin, in Chapter 11, by discussing the meaning of the term *marketing* and the various markets for products and services.

Key Terms

You should now be able to define and give an example relevant to each of the following terms:

labor union

union-management (labor) relations

craft union

strike

industrial union

National Labor Relations Board (NLRB)

injunction

bargaining unit

jurisdiction

collective bargaining

ratification

seniority

overtime

job security

union security

closed shop

union shop

agency shop

maintenance shop

grievance procedure

shop steward

arbitration

picketing

wildcat strike

slowdown

boycott

lockout

strikebreaker

mediation

Questions and Exercises

Review Questions

1. Briefly describe the history of unions in the United States.
2. How has government regulation of union-management relations evolved during this century?
3. For what reasons do employees start or join unions?
4. Describe the process of forming a union and explain the role of the NLRB in that process.
5. List the major areas that are negotiated in a labor contract.
6. Explain the three issues involved in negotiations concerning employee pay.
7. What is the difference between job and union security? How do unions attempt to enhance union security?
8. What is a grievance? Describe the typical grievance procedure.
9. What steps are involved in collective bargaining?
10. For what reasons are strikes and lockouts relatively rare nowadays?
11. What are the objectives of picketing?
12. In what ways do the techniques of mediation and arbitration differ from each other?

Discussion Questions

1. In what ways are the UAW and GM working together to improve productivity and product quality?
2. Discuss the major advantages to the UAW and GM that can result from their cooperative efforts.
3. Do unions really derive their power mainly from their membership and labor legislation? What are some other sources of union power?
4. Which labor-contract issues are likely to be the easiest to resolve? Which are likely to be the most difficult?
5. Discuss the following statement: Union security means job security for union members.
6. How would you prepare for labor contract negotiations as a member of management? as head of the union negotiating committee?
7. Under what circumstances are strikes and lockouts justified in place of mediation or arbitration?

Exercises

1. Develop a labor contract to govern student-teacher relations in your school. Include at least four major issues.

2. Find two or more articles describing a recent strike.
   a. Try to determine the exact nature of the issue or issues on which negotiators could not agree.
   b. Determine the means by which these issues were finally resolved.
   c. Explain how these issues could have been resolved without a strike.
3. Find a copy of a labor contract in your library. List the issues that are covered in the contract and compare them with the issues cited in this chapter.

Case 10.1

Union Work Rules Change at Cablec

Imagine work rules so rigid that before a mechanic can repair a fork lift, a union electrician must first unhook the battery cables. That was the situation when Cablec Corporation, a New York City-based maker of high-voltage power cables, bought a Marion, Indiana, cable plant that was still using work rules dating back to the 1930s.

Moreover, when Cablec needed a skilled technician to operate a cable-insulating machine, six workers with high seniority ended up back on the payroll because of seniority rights. The first five in line didn't have the needed skills and were put to work sweeping floors. The worker sixth in seniority did have the right skills—so he ran the machine. According to Cablec's management, something had to change.

Cablec is a company that has successfully wrestled with changes in work rules and seniority rights. Many businesses feel that changes in work rules will help boost productivity, cut costs, increase profits, and even increase the chances of survival. But unions see work-rule changes as a threat to their twin goals of preserving jobs and maintaining union strength. Also, unions consider work rules powerful bargaining tools in labor negotiations with management. In some cases, management, eager for work-rule changes, has given in to union demands to reach an agreement.

Although no one has done detailed cost/benefit analyses of work-rule changes, some business experts say that a work-rule change generally increases the need for worker training because job descriptions are enlarged. Training, of course, costs time and money, and the extra cost offsets gains from the work-rule change.

Before buying the Marion cable plant, Cablec arranged with the plant's two unions to cut job classifications by two-thirds—from 217 to 69. The company also specified a reduction in worker seniority rights, so that skills would have to be considered along with seniority when workers were to be rehired. Those rule changes cut the Marion plant's work force by 6 percent and—along with other economies, such as scrap reduction—saved about $3 million a year.

Some Cablec workers still worry that the work-rule changes will subject them to the whims of management. For example, workers no longer have a choice about working overtime or not. Older workers are concerned that, with changes in seniority rights, they could be laid off while younger workers keep working. Some skilled workers have left Cablec for jobs in other companies where they feel they have more job security.

Recently, though, any union unrest at Cablec has been overshadowed by the company's growth. Since Cablec's buyout of Phelps Dodge Corporation's power cable business, Cablec owns the best power cable technology in the United States. Also, through business dealings with both Japanese and British companies, Cablec has been able to acquire the most sophisticated power cable knowledge of these two countries. Because of these business maneuvers, Cablec finds itself firmly entrenched as a world leader in the power cable industry. It seems as long as Cablec lives up to its philosophy that employees are a company's most important asset, management and labor will peacefully and successfully work together.*

Questions

1. How do you feel about Cablec's cutting costs by reducing the Marion plant's work force by 6 percent and enlarging other jobs there, especially when Cablec seems to be doing so well financially?
2. Suppose that during contract renewal talks, (a) Cablec had insisted that its new union contract contain more work-rule changes and (b) the union didn't agree. What could Cablec have done to get its way? What could the union have done to get its way?
3. If you were a worker at the Marion cable plant, how would you feel if your job had been enlarged but your pay remained the same?

---

* Based on information from "Companies to Watch," *Fortune,* September 15, 1986, p. 68; "Executive Changes," *New York Times,* August 1, 1986, p. D2; Alex Kotlowitz, "Work Rules Shape Up as Major Battleground in U.S. Labor Disputes," *Wall Street Journal,* June 4, 1986, p. 1+; and John S. McClenahen, "Team Plays at Cablec Corporation," *Industry Week,* April 4, 1988, pp. 81–82.

Case 10.2

Eastern Airlines and the IAM

It seems as if Frank A. Lorenzo, CEO of Eastern Air Lines, and labor unions have been at war for years. The unions claim that Lorenzo is a union buster, and Lorenzo insists that labor costs are the primary enemy of the airline industry. Lorenzo wants to lower salaries to improve Eastern's financial performance. Recent events at Eastern Airlines have been extremely turbulent as management and labor battle for control of an airline that may already be dead.

The International Association of Machinists and Aerospace Workers (IAM) insists that Lorenzo is trying to systematically dismantle Eastern Airlines to benefit his other enterprise, nonunion Continental Airlines Corp. Members of the IAM at Eastern—mechanics, baggage handlers, and ground-crew personnel—went on strike when Lorenzo's new proposed contract lowered salaries across the board, wiped out worker seniority rights, and reduced pension benefits. The IAM was joined by other sympathetic airline unions: Pilots and flight attendants also went on strike at Eastern.

Lorenzo reacted to the strike by declaring Eastern bankrupt and filing for company reorganization under Chapter 11 of the Bankruptcy Reform Act. (In 1983, Lorenzo had triumphantly broken union contracts at Continental when he declared the airline to be bankrupt.) In a move that union officials claim was intended to massacre the once-successful Eastern, Lorenzo then sold Eastern's profitable East Coast shuttle service to billionaire real estate developer Donald Trump.

In a surprise counterattack on Lorenzo, airline union members began to make severe safety-violation complaints against Eastern and Continental. In an unprecedented investigation, the Federal Aviation Administration (FAA) thoroughly inspected Eastern and Continental planes. The FAA concluded that the airlines were safe but that the continuing feud between the unions and Lorenzo might jeopardize passenger safety.

As the situation now stands, it appears that Lorenzo is winning the battle. Strikers are still marching at airports, and union lobbyists are still asking Congress to intervene in Eastern's bankruptcy reorganization, but Eastern is attracting many new customers with reduced fares and improved service. Eastern's schedule has expanded to 600 flights and will grow even larger in the future. And, though striking Eastern pilots have asked the Air Line Pilots Association to order a work stoppage by pilots across the nation, hundreds of union pilots have crossed picket lines.

The president of Eastern has said, "We feel better about Eastern's prospects, longevity, and future success than we've ever felt about them." The unions vow that the war over Eastern is just beginning. They may be in for a long, hard fight because, if Lorenzo's plan for a smaller airline doesn't fly, Lorenzo will probably attempt to merge Eastern and Continental—and the unions will lose anyway.†

---

† Based on information from Doug Carroll, "Eastern's Past Threatens Its Future," *USA Today*, March 6, 1989, p. 2; Doug Carroll, "It's Winning Passengers, Adding Flights," *USA Today*, August 18, 1989, pp. B1–B2; Jo Ellen Davis and Pete Engardio, "Showdown Time at Eastern," *Business Week*, February 8, 1988, pp. 20–21; David Landis, "Eastern Chops Fares Below Industry Cuts," *USA Today*, August 16, 1989, p. B1; and Barbara Sturken, "Texas Air Plan to Spin Off Shuttle May Meet Challenge from Unions," *Travel Weekly*, February 15, 1988, pp. 1, 47.

Questions

1. Are Eastern's dealings with the unions fair to Eastern employees who are union members? Are these dealings fair to stockholders of Eastern's parent company?

2. In your opinion, should a company be able to use the bankruptcy laws to reduce unions' bargaining power?

CAREER PROFILE

LIZ CLAIBORNE Elizabeth Claiborne Ortenberg, along with her husband Arthur Ortenberg, runs the largest women's apparel company in the world. When they started Liz Claiborne, Inc. in 1976, the Ortenbergs never envisioned that their sportswear company would turn into a clothing and accessory giant with sales of over $1 billion a year. As president and chief executive officer of Liz Claiborne, Liz used her sense of fashion and business skills to build the first company headed by a woman to make *Fortune* magazine's list of the top 500 U.S. firms.

Born in Brussels, Belgium, to American parents in 1929, Liz spent her early childhood touring museums with her father and learning to sew and cook from her mother. Her father, a banker with Morgan Guaranty Trust Co., decided his family should leave Belgium before the Nazis arrived. They moved to New Orleans, where her father had family ties.

Liz's interest in fashion began when she was very young, but her conservative father was strongly opposed to her entering the fashion business. He sent her back to Europe to study fine arts in Brussels and later in Nice. Liz never received a high school diploma but that—like her father's warnings about the fashion business—didn't deter her.

In 1949, Liz won a design contest sponsored by *Harper's Bazaar* magazine for her sketch of a woman's overcoat. In 1951 she moved to New York and soon landed a job as a sketcher for Tina Lesser in the heart of Manhattan's garment district. She worked at several design firms, eventually marrying one of her employers, Arthur Ortenberg.

Liz quickly earned a reputation as a talented designer, preferring to design updated versions of classic women's clothes rather than trendy or avant-garde fashions. For sixteen years, she directed the design room for the Dress Designer Youth Guild. She decided to form her own company because Youth Guild officials disagreed with her ideas for women's apparel—mix and match coordinated separates. So she, her husband, and Leonard Boxer founded their own firm funded with their savings and another $180,000 raised from family and friends.

By the end of their first year in business, their company was realizing a profit. Liz, by designing fashionable, comfortable clothes for working women, tapped into a huge and enthusiastic market. Besides women's sportswear, the Liz Claiborne name now finds itself on accessories, shoes, jeans, dresses, fragrances, and menswear. Claiborne executives have decided to enter the retail business by opening Liz Claiborne boutiques in malls and setting up Liz Claiborne areas in department stores.

Liz Claiborne has plans to expand production of its line of large-size women's clothing. With an estimated 40 million women in the United States who wear a size 14 or larger, Liz wants a part of this $10 billion market and will promote the line under the brand name Elizabeth. The company will also expand its menswear division. While venturing into new and risky territory with their business, both Liz and Arthur plan to curtail their respective responsibilities. They want to be able to spend more time at their vacation homes and they also have full confidence in the abilities of the managers they have trained. Liz has given up designing altogether and now exclusively "edits" the work of others.

Liz Claiborne has built a successful and stable company in an industry noted for chaos and failures. Her business serves as a model for human resources management, especially in issues affecting working mothers. The unassuming Claiborne shies away from the spotlight and interviews, but is no prima donna. She happily rides to her New Jersey plant in a van crowded with her employees, and everyone at the company is on a first-name basis.

Liz is a fashion artist who enjoys fostering new talent and ideas. There must be something to Liz's formula for success: She is one of the most successful individuals in American business and living proof that the American dream continues to thrive.

Based on information from Kathleen Deveny, "Can Ms. Fashion Bounce Back?" *Business Week,* January 16, 1989, pp. 64–67, 70; "Liz Claiborne," *Business Month,* December 1987, p. 46; and Michele Morris, "The Wizard of the Working Woman's Wardrobe," *Working Woman,* June 1988, pp. 74–75, 78, 80.

The figure in the salary column approximates the expected annual income after two or three years of service. 1 = $12,000–$15,000 2 = $16,000–$20,000 3 = $21,000–$27,000 4 = $28,000–$35,000 5 = $36,000 and up

Job Title	Educational Requirements	Salary Range	Prospects
Affirmative action coordinator	Some college; degree helpful	2–3	Gradual growth
Blue-collar worker supervisor	High school diploma; some college helpful	2–3	Limited growth
Employment counselor	Degree in business or human relations management	3	Limited growth
Employment development specialist	Bachelor's degree in business or management; on-the-job experience	4	Limited growth
Industrial relations analyst	Bachelor's degree in business or management; on-the-job experience	3–4	Limited growth
Labor relations specialist	Bachelor's degree; on-the-job experience	4	Limited growth
Management services trainee—personnel	Two years of college; bachelor's degree helpful	1–3	Gradual growth
Mediator	Bachelor's degree; on-the-job experience	4–5	Limited growth
Personnel administrator	Bachelor's degree in personnel; master's degree helpful	4	Gradual growth
Personnel interviewer	Some college; degree helpful	2	Greatest growth
Personnel worker	Some college; college degree preferred	2	Gradual growth
Records analyst	Bachelor's degree; on-the-job experience	2–3	Gradual growth
Regulatory inspector	High school diploma; some college preferred	2–3	Limited growth
Safety inspector	High school diploma; some college preferred	2–3	Limited growth
Salary and wage administrator	Some college; degree in personnel helpful	3	Limited growth
Social worker	College degree; graduate degree preferred	2–3	Limited growth
Training officer	Some college; degree helpful; on-the-job experience	2–3	Limited growth

Part 4

MARKETING

The business activities that make up a firm's marketing efforts are those most directly concerned with satisfying customers' needs. In this part, we discuss these activities in some detail. We begin with a general discussion of marketing and the market for consumer goods. Then, in turn, we discuss the four elements that are combined into a marketing mix: product, price, distribution, and promotion. Included in this part are:

AN OVERVIEW
OF MARKETING

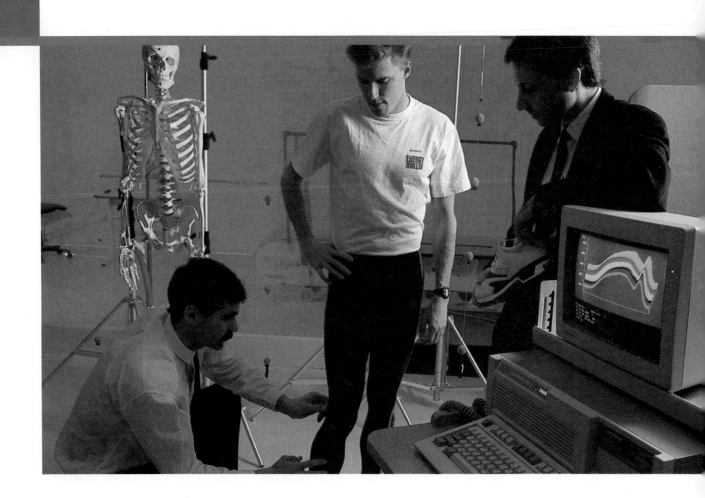

LEARNING OBJECTIVES

LEARNING OBJECTIVES

1 Understand *marketing* and explain how it creates utility for purchasers of products

2 Trace the development of the marketing concept and understand how it is implemented

3 Know what markets are and how they are classified

4 Identify the four elements of the marketing mix and become aware of their importance in developing a marketing strategy

5 Comprehend how the marketing environment affects strategic market planning

6 Describe how market measurement and sales forecasting are used

7 Know the difference between a marketing information system and marketing research

8 Understand several factors that may influence buying behavior

9 Recognize three ways of measuring consumer income

10 Understand the marketing implications of several socioeconomic changes occurring in the United States

11 Recognize the relative costs and benefits of marketing

CHAPTER PREVIEW

In this chapter we examine some of the important marketing activities that add value, or utility, to products. We trace the evolution of the marketing concept and describe how organizations put the marketing concept into practice. Next, our focus shifts to market classifications and marketing strategy. We analyze the four elements of a marketing mix—elements that a business firm can control— and also discuss factors in the marketing environment that a firm cannot control. We consider effective tools for strategic market planning, including market measurement, sales forecasts, marketing information systems, and marketing research. Then we look at some of the major forces that influence both consumer and organizational buying behavior. We examine the marketing implications of socioeconomic changes occurring in the United States. We close the chapter with an evaluation of marketing's costs and benefits.

INSIDE BUSINESS

Catering to Customers

Club Med Inc., an international chain of resorts, is broadening its marketing orientation. Until the 1980s, the Club Med villages in the Americas were for singles only; now its clients include couples, particular sports enthusiasts, people wishing upscale vacations, and families. In catering to the needs of families, the clubs have added day-care services ("baby clubs") and recreational programs for children ("mini-clubs"). Half of Club Med's one million members are married, and in a recent year 72,437 parents and children stayed at Club Med resorts.

Consequently, you will no longer see only sensual, leggy swimsuit models in Club Med's television commercials. You will also see a middle-aged couple walking on a beach or a family of four making home movies of themselves in a scenic Club Med village.

Club Med is seeking to further past successes by anticipating and responding to the needs of its clients, or "GMs" (gentle members). It is evolving beyond its old playboy-playgirl image; its vacation offerings are more varied than ever, including golfing vacations, cruises, and trips to archeological sites.

Marketing is simply catering to the wants and needs of customers. One trend that Club Med has discovered is that the younger clientele that made its resorts successful in the seventies is aging. These customers now demand once-nonexistent frills such as child-care services and rooms with locks, telephones, and televisions. Serge Trigano, vice chairman of the board and CEO, says that what worked for Club Med for twenty years does not work anymore. So the famed era of its "open-door" (rooms with no keys) policy has come to a close. By the end of 1989 all of Club Med's North American villages had room locks and keys for its guests. According to Jacques Gann, Club Med's president, "Our goal is to have keys everywhere," adding that guests did not appreciate waiting in line to get to a central safe where their valuables were kept.

Club Med wants to keep its present loyal clientele (47 percent of the guests are repeaters), while also attracting vacationers who have never stayed at a Club Med resort village. Therefore, to broaden its market and renovate its clubs, the chain is spending $208 million.

Will the expanded market orientation pay off? Doubting skeptics think not. They feel that Club Med will always be a vacation package, not a Hilton. But Club Med's management is counting on its marketing formula to enable it to be everything to everybody. Time will tell.[1]

arketing encompasses a diverse set of decisions and activities performed by individuals and by both business and nonbusiness organizations. Marketing begins and ends with the customer. As Club Med Inc. spends $208 million to renovate its resorts and change its customer focus, the firm is attempting to attract new customers and keep its old ones. Club Med discovered, among other things, that its guests prefer room locks. By listening to its customers, Club Med is in an excellent position to offer products at prices its customers can afford.

marketing *the process of planning and executing the conception, pricing, promotion, and distribution of ideas, goods, and services to create exchanges that satisfy individual and organizational objectives*

The American Marketing Association defines **marketing** as "the process of planning and executing the conception, pricing, promotion, and distribution of ideas, goods, and services to create exchanges that satisfy individual and organizational objectives." The marketing process involves eight major functions and numerous related activities (see Table 11.1). All of these functions are essential if the marketing process is to be effective.

Utility: The Value Added by Marketing

utility *the power of a good or service to satisfy a human need*

As defined in Chapter 7, **utility** is the power of a good or service to satisfy a human need. A lunch at a Pizza Hut, an overnight stay at a Holiday Inn, and a Mercedes 420 SEL all satisfy human needs. Each possesses utility. There are four kinds of utility.

form utility *utility that is created by converting production inputs into finished products*

Form utility is utility that is created by converting production inputs into finished products, as indicated in Chapter 7. Marketing efforts may indirectly influence form utility because the data gathered as part of marketing research are frequently used to determine the size, shape, and features of a product.

The three kinds of utility that are directly created by marketing are place, time, and possession utility. **Place utility** is utility that is created by making a product available at a location where customers wish to purchase it. A pair of shoes is given place utility when it is shipped from a factory to a department store.

place utility *utility that is created by making a product available at a location where customers wish to purchase it*

time utility *utility that is created by making a product available when customers wish to purchase it*

Time utility is utility that is created by making a product available when customers wish to purchase it. For example, tennis shoes might be manufactured in December but not displayed until April, when consumers in a northern city start thinking about summer sports. By storing the shoes until they are wanted, the manufacturer or retailer provides time utility.

possession utility *utility that is created by transferring title (or ownership) of a product to the buyer*

Possession utility is utility that is created by transferring title (or ownership) of a product to the buyer. For a product as simple as a pair of shoes, ownership is usually transferred by means of a sales slip or receipt. For such products as automobiles and homes, the transfer of title is a more complex process. Along with the title to its product, the seller transfers the right to use that product to satisfy a need (see Figure 11.1).

Time, place, and possession utility have real value in terms of both money and convenience. This value is created and added to goods and services through a wide variety of marketing activities—from research

Learning Objective 1
Understand *marketing* and explain how it creates utility for purchasers of products

TABLE 11.1 Major Marketing Functions

Exchange Functions: All companies such as manufacturers, wholesalers, and retailers buy and sell to market their merchandise.

1. **Buying** includes such functions as obtaining raw materials to make products, knowing how much merchandise to keep on hand, and selecting suppliers.
2. **Selling** creates possession utility by transferring the title of a product from seller to customer.

Physical Distribution Functions: These functions involve the flow of goods from producers to customers. Transportation and storage provide time utility and place utility, and require careful management of inventory.

3. **Transporting** involves selecting a mode of transport that provides an acceptable delivery schedule at an acceptable price.
4. **Storing** goods is often necessary to sell them at the best selling time.

Facilitating Functions: These functions help the other functions take place.

5. **Financing** helps at all stages of marketing. To buy raw materials, manufacturers often borrow from banks or receive credit from suppliers. Wholesalers may be financed by manufacturers, and retailers may receive financing from the wholesaler or manufacturer. Finally, retailers often provide financing to customers.
6. **Standardizing** sets uniform specifications for products or services. **Grading** classifies products by size and quality, usually through a sorting process. Together, standardization and grading facilitate production, transportation, storage, and selling.
7. **Risk taking**—even though competent management and insurance can minimize risks—is a constant reality of marketing because of such losses as bad debt expense, obsolescence of products, theft by employees, and product-liability lawsuits.
8. **Gathering market information** is necessary for making all marketing decisions.

indicating what customers want to product warranties ensuring that customers get what they pay for. Overall, these marketing activities account for about half of every dollar spent by consumers. When they are part of an integrated marketing program that delivers maximum utility to the customer, most of us would agree that they are worth the cost.

Place, time, and possession utility are only the most fundamental applications of marketing activities. In recent years, marketing activities have resulted from a broad business philosophy known as the marketing concept.

The Marketing Concept

Learning Objective 2
Trace the development of the marketing concept and understand how it is implemented

The process that leads any business to success seems simple. First, the firm must talk to its potential customers to assess their needs for its products or services. Then the firm must develop a product or service to satisfy those needs. Finally, the firm must continue to seek ways to provide customer satisfaction. This process is an application of the marketing concept, or marketing orientation. As simple as it seems, American business took about a hundred years to accept it.

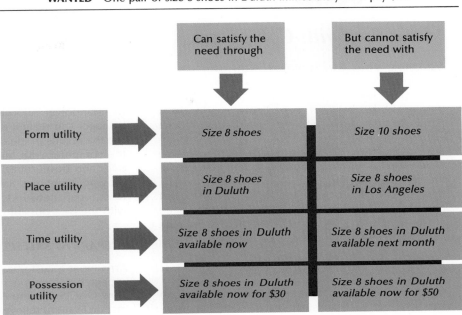

WANTED   One pair of size 8 shoes in Duluth immediately. Will pay $30.

	Can satisfy the need through	But cannot satisfy the need with
Form utility	*Size 8 shoes*	*Size 10 shoes*
Place utility	*Size 8 shoes in Duluth*	*Size 8 shoes in Los Angeles*
Time utility	*Size 8 shoes in Duluth available now*	*Size 8 shoes in Duluth available next month*
Possession utility	*Size 8 shoes in Duluth available now for $30*	*Size 8 shoes in Duluth available now for $50*

FIGURE 11.1
Types of Utility
Form utility is created by the production process, but marketing creates time, place, and possession utility.

Evolution of the Marketing Concept

From the start of the Industrial Revolution until the early twentieth century, business effort was directed mainly toward the production of goods. Consumer demand for manufactured products was so great that manufacturers could almost bank on selling everything they produced. Business had a strong *production orientation*, in which emphasis was placed on increased output and production efficiency. Marketing was limited to taking orders and distributing finished goods.

In the 1920s, production began to catch up with demand. Now producers had to direct their efforts toward selling goods to consumers whose basic wants were already satisfied. This new *sales orientation* was characterized by increased advertising, enlarged sales forces, and occasionally high-pressure selling techniques. Manufacturers produced the goods they expected consumers to want, and marketing consisted primarily of taking orders and delivering goods, along with personal selling and advertising.

During the 1950s, however, business people started to realize that even enormous advertising expenditures and the most thoroughly proven sales techniques were not enough. Something else was needed if products were to sell as well as expected. It was then that business managers recognized that they were not primarily producers or sellers but rather

BUSINESS JOURNAL

Marketing with Computers

Marketing is being transformed by the computer. A salesperson's primary equipment used to consist of good shoe leather and intuitions about products that might be best for a particular market at a particular time. Now, with the development of specialized computer programs, marketers—from high-level chain-store executives to salespeople working a "territory"—rely on computers to help them make the most efficient use of their time and money. Impressed by the computer's ability to quickly get important sales information to the people who need it, marketers are using this information to coordinate advertising and human resources in new ways.

COMPUTERIZING CASH REGISTERS

Marketers like The J. M. Smucker Co. are relying on computerized cash registers to steal customers from competitors. For example, a computerized cash register can automatically print out a free coupon for Smucker's jam when it records a customer's purchase of competitor Sorrell Ridge's all-fruit jam.

R. J. Reynolds Tobacco USA keeps 40 million customer profiles in its mainframe computers, which can thus tailor the firm's premiums to its customers' lifestyles. A golfer, for example, would receive free golf balls in a promotional mailing, while a photographer would be offered free camera accessories. Similarly, Seagram and General Foods Corp. have been compiling millions of customers' names for their promotional campaigns. Nabisco Brands, Inc. handles 235,000 consumer contacts each year, usually inquiries about product usage, nutrition, and ingredients. This consumer feedback is computerized and available on demand throughout Nabisco's operating divisions. To keep its customers flying in the friendly skies, United Air Lines' Covia subsidiary spends $120 million a year maintaining and updating software for its computerized reservation system.

REDRAWING TERRITORIES

One difficulty of assigning a salesperson to a particular geographic "territory" has been what to do when the territory changes. As certain areas grow faster than others, imbalances result in the workloads and potential sales for the salespeople in those areas.

Redrawing the territories has traditionally been such a slow and tedious process that managers were reluctant to do it. Now, with software called Maps III (Manpower Allocation and Planning System), a manager can realign a territory and within minutes see the results of the change. The manager supplies the computer with business data such as potential sales and travel times between customers, and the program combines these data with geographic features, road networks, and zip codes to come up with the best possible territory assignments.

PREPARING SALESPEOPLE

Arriving at a customer's door not knowing what to expect has long been a salesperson's nightmare. Now OACIS (Online Automated Commercial Information System) relieves salespeople of many of their daily worries by supplying them with up-to-the-minute data. Monsanto Chemical Co./Plastics Division uses such a system linked to its automated order billing network. Any of the company's salespeople can use a company terminal to access freshly updated information on accounts, products, and performance. Before calling on an account, the salesperson thus knows what a customer has bought in the past month or year, and how good the customer's payment record is. Perhaps just as important, the salesperson can see whether Monsanto has been behind on a delivery and will have an answer when the customer asks, "Where's that product I ordered last month?"

Based on information from Anthony Ramirez, "Department Stores Shape Up," *Fortune*, September 1, 1986, p. 50; Howard L. Green, "Retail Sales Forecasting Systems," *Journal of Retailing*, Fall 1986, p. 227; Joshua Levine, "Stealing the Right Shoppers," *Forbes*, July 10, 1989, p. 104; William M. Pride and O. C. Ferrell, *Marketing: Concepts and Strategies*, 6th ed. (Boston: Houghton Mifflin, 1989), p. 179; and Brenton R. Schlender, "How to Break the Software Logjam," *Fortune*, September 25, 1989, p. 100.

were in the business of satisfying customers' wants. As Phillip E. Benton, Jr., president of Ford Automotive Group, states, "What our customers define as quality is what we must deliver. We have re-learned in recent years that the successful automakers consistently provide customers with what they need and want, at a price they feel offers good value, in a product that meets their expectations of safety and quality. Our challenge is to go beyond that—to exceed customer expectations and, indeed, to generate customer enthusiasm."[2] Marketers realized that the best approach was to adopt a customer orientation—in other words, the organization had to first determine what customers need and then develop goods and services to fill those particular needs (see Figure 11.2).

marketing concept   *the business philosophy that involves the entire organization in the process of satisfying customers' needs while achieving the organization's goals*

This **marketing concept** is a business philosophy that involves the entire organization in the process of satisfying customers' needs while achieving the organization's goals. All functional areas—from product development through production to finance and, of course, marketing—are viewed as playing a role in providing customer satisfaction.

Implementing the Marketing Concept

The marketing concept has been adopted by many of the most successful business firms. Some firms, such as Ford Motor Company and Apple Computer, have gone through minor or major reorganizations in the process. Because the marketing concept is essentially a business philosophy, anyone can say, "I believe in it." But to make it work, management must fully adopt and then implement it.

To implement the marketing concept, a firm must first obtain information about its present and potential customers. The firm must determine not only what customers' needs are but also how well those needs are being satisfied by products currently on the market—both its own products and those of competitors. It must ascertain how its products might be improved and what opinions customers have of the firm and its marketing efforts.

The firm must then use this information to pinpoint the specific needs and potential customers toward which it will direct its marketing activities and resources. (Obviously, no firm can expect to satisfy all needs. And not every individual or firm can be considered a potential customer for every product manufactured or sold by a firm.) Next, the firm must mobilize its marketing resources to (1) provide a product that will satisfy its customers; (2) price the product at a level that is acceptable to buyers and that will yield a profit; (3) promote the product so that potential customers will be aware of its existence and its ability to satisfy their needs; and (4) ensure that the product is distributed so that it is available to customers where and when needed.

Finally, the firm must again obtain marketing information—this time regarding the effectiveness of its efforts. Can the product be improved? Is it being promoted properly? Is it being distributed efficiently? Is the price too high? The firm must be ready to modify any or all of its marketing activities on the basis of this feedback.

FIGURE 11.2
Evolution of the Customer Orientation
Business managers recognized that they were not primarily producers or sellers but rather were in the business of satisfying customers' wants.

PRODUCTION ORIENTATION

- Take orders
- Distribute goods

SALES ORIENTATION

- Increase advertising
- Enlarge sales force
- Develop sales techniques

CUSTOMER ORIENTATION

- Determine customer needs
- Develop goods and services to fill needs

Markets and Their Classification

market   *a group of individuals, organizations, or both who have needs for products in a given category and who have the ability, willingness, and authority to purchase such products*

Learning Objective 3
Know what markets are and how they are classified

A **market** is a group of individuals, organizations, or both who have needs for products in a given category and who have the ability, willingness, and authority to purchase such products. The people or organizations must require the product. They must be able to purchase the product with money, goods, or services that can be exchanged for the product. They must be willing to use their buying power. Finally, they must be socially and legally authorized to purchase the product.

Markets are classified as consumer, industrial, or reseller markets. These classifications are based on the characteristics of the individuals and organizations within each market. Because marketing efforts vary depending on the intended market, marketers should understand the general characteristics of these three groups.

Consumer markets consist of purchasers and/or individual household members who intend to consume or benefit from the purchased products and who do not buy products to make a profit.

Industrial markets are grouped broadly into producer, governmental, and institutional categories. These markets purchase specific kinds of products for use either in day-to-day operations or in making other products for profit. *Producer markets* consist of individuals and business organizations that intend to make a profit by buying certain products to use in the manufacture of other products. *Governmental markets* comprise federal, state, county, and local governments. They buy goods and services to maintain internal operations and to provide citizens with such products as highways, education, water, energy, and national defense. Their pur-

Software Toolworks Inc.'s marketing strategy focuses on its target market of home computer game enthusiasts. Toolworks has sold 1 million copies of its programs in the game and educational markets. Its seventy offerings include the two best-selling computerized chess games.

chases total billions of dollars each year. *Institutional markets* inc
churches, private schools and hospitals, civic clubs, fraternities an
sororities, charitable organizations, and foundations. Their goals are
different from such typical business goals as profit, market share, or return
on investment.

Reseller markets consist of intermediaries such as wholesalers and
retailers who buy finished products and sell them for a profit.

After classifying and identifying its market or markets, an organization
must develop marketing strategies to reach this audience.

Developing Marketing Strategies

marketing strategy *a plan that will enable an organization to make the best use of its resources and advantages to meet its objectives*

A **marketing strategy** is a plan that will enable an organization to make
the best use of its resources and advantages to meet its objectives. A
marketing strategy consists of (1) the selection and analysis of a target
market and (2) the creation and maintenance of an appropriate **marketing
mix,** a combination of product, price, distribution, and promotion developed to satisfy a particular target market.

marketing mix *a combination of product, price, distribution, and promotion developed to satisfy a particular target market*

Target Market Selection and Evaluation

target market *a group of persons for whom a firm develops and maintains a marketing mix suitable for the specific needs and preferences of that group*

A **target market** is a group of persons for whom a firm develops and
maintains a marketing mix suitable for the specific needs and preferences
of that group. In selecting a target market, marketing managers examine
potential markets for their possible effects on the firm's sales, costs, and
profits. The managers attempt to determine whether the organization has
the resources to produce a marketing mix that meets the needs of a
particular target market and whether satisfying those needs is consistent
with the firm's overall objectives. They also analyze the strength and
number of competitors already selling in a potential target market.
Marketing managers generally take either the total market approach or
the market segmentation approach in choosing a target market.

total market approach *a single marketing mix directed at the entire market for a particular product*

Total Market Approach   When a company designs a single marketing mix
and directs it at the entire market for a particular product, it is using a
total market approach (see Figure 11.3). This approach, also known as an
undifferentiated approach, assumes that individual customers in the target
market for a specific kind of product have similar needs and, therefore,
that the organization can satisfy most customers with a single marketing
mix. This single marketing mix consists of one type of product with little
or no variation, one price, one promotional program aimed at everyone,
and one distribution system to reach all customers in the total market.
Products that can be marketed successfully with the total market approach
include staple food items such as sugar and salt, and certain kinds of farm
produce. A total market approach is useful only in a limited number of
situations because for most product categories, buyers have different
needs. When customers' needs vary, the market segmentation approach
should be used.

TOTAL MARKET APPROACH

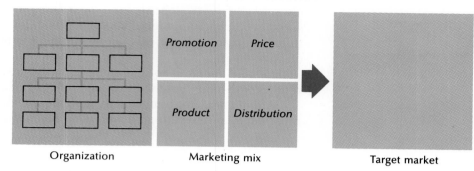

Organization · Marketing mix · Target market

FIGURE 11.3
General Approaches for Selecting Target Markets
The total market approach (top) assumes that individual customers have similar needs and that most customers can be satisfied with a single marketing mix. When customers' needs vary, the market segmentation approach (bottom) should be used. (Source: Adapted from William M. Pride and O. C. Ferrell, Marketing: Concepts and Strategies, 6/e. Copyright © 1989 by Houghton Mifflin Company. Used by permission.)

MARKET SEGMENTATION APPROACH

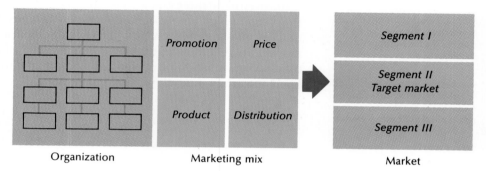

Organization · Marketing mix · Market

market segment *a group of individuals or organizations, within a market, that share one or more common characteristics*

market segmentation *the process of dividing a market into segments and directing a marketing mix at a particular segment or segments rather than at the total market*

Market Segmentation Approach A firm that is marketing 40-foot yachts would not direct its marketing effort toward every person in the total boat market. Some might want a kayak or a canoe. Others might want a speedboat or an outboard-powered fishing boat. Still others might be looking for something resembling a small ocean liner. Any marketing effort directed toward such people would be wasted.

Instead the firm would direct its attention toward a particular portion, or *segment*, of the total market for boats. A **market segment** is a group of individuals or organizations, within a market, that share one or more common characteristics. The process of dividing a market into segments is called **market segmentation.** As Figure 11.3 shows, a firm using this approach directs a marketing mix at a segment or segments rather than at the total market. In our example, one common characteristic, or *basis*, for segmentation might be "end use of a boat." The firm would be interested primarily in that market segment whose uses for a boat could lead to the purchase of a 40-foot yacht. Another basis for segmentation might be income; still another might be geographic location. Each of these variables has an effect on the type of boat an individual might purchase. When choosing a basis for segmentation, it is important to select a characteristic that relates to differences in people's needs for a product. The yacht producer, for example, would not use religion to segment the boat market because people's needs for boats do not vary based on religion.

TABLE 11.2   *Common Bases of Market Segmentation*

Product-Related	Demographic	Psychographic	Geographic
Volume usage	Age	Personality attributes	Region
End use	Sex	Motives	Urban, suburban, rural
Benefit expectations	Race	Lifestyles	Market density
Brand loyalty	Nationality		Climate
Price sensitivity	Income		Terrain
	Educational level		
	Occupation		
	Family size		
	Religion		
	Home ownership		
	Social class		

Source: Adapted from William M. Pride and O. C. Ferrell, *Marketing: Concepts and Strategies*, 6/e. Copyright © 1989 by Houghton Mifflin Company. Used by permission.

Marketers make use of a wide variety of segmentation bases. Those bases that are most commonly applied to consumer markets are shown in Table 11.2. Each of them may be used as a single basis for market segmentation or in combination with other bases.

Creating a Marketing Mix

Learning Objective 4
Identify the four elements of the marketing mix and become aware of their importance in developing a marketing strategy

A business firm controls four important elements of marketing—elements that it must combine in such a way as to reach its target market. These are the *product* itself, the *price* of the product, the means chosen for its *distribution*, and the *promotion* of the product. When they are combined, these four elements form a marketing mix (see the circular area in Figure 11.4).

The firm can vary its marketing mix by changing any one or more of these ingredients. Thus a firm may use one marketing mix to reach one target market and a second, somewhat different marketing mix to reach another target market. For example, the Neiman Marcus Group's specialty retailing businesses—Neiman Marcus, Bergdorf Goodman, and Contempo Casuals—use one marketing mix for its most affluent and discriminating customers and another mix for younger, 17- to 24-year-old women who are interested in the most fashion-forward apparel available at moderate prices. Neiman Marcus and Bergdorf Goodman offer the highest possible levels of customer service to their most affluent customers, while moderate prices are emphasized at Contempo Casuals.[3] Different products and prices immediately result in different marketing mixes.

The *product* ingredient of the marketing mix includes decisions about the design of the product, brand name, packaging, warranties, and the like. Thus, when McDonald's Corp. decides on brand names, package designs, sizes of orders, flavors of sauces, and recipes, these are all part of the product ingredient.

FIGURE 11.4
The Marketing Mix and the Marketing Environment
The marketing mix consists of elements that the firm controls—product, price, physical distribution, and promotion. The firm generally has no control over the external marketing environment. (Source: Adapted from William M. Pride and O. C. Ferrell, Marketing: Concepts and Strategies, 6/e. Copyright © 1989 by Houghton Mifflin Company. Used by permission.)

The *pricing* ingredient is concerned with both base prices and discounts of various kinds. Pricing decisions are intended to achieve particular goals, such as to maximize profit or even to make room for new models. The rebates offered by automobile manufacturers are a pricing strategy developed to boost low auto sales. Product and pricing are discussed in detail in Chapter 12.

The *distribution* ingredient involves not only transportation and storage but also the selection of intermediaries. How many levels of intermediaries should be used in the distribution of a particular product? Should the product be distributed as widely as possible? Or should distribution be restricted to a few specialized outlets in each area? These and other questions related to distribution are considered in Chapter 13.

The *promotion* ingredient focuses on providing information to target markets. The major forms of promotion include advertising, personal selling, sales promotion, and publicity. These forms are discussed in Chapter 14.

The "ingredients" of the marketing mix are controllable elements. The firm can vary each of them to suit its organizational goals, marketing goals, and target markets. As we extend our discussion to the firm's overall marketing plan, we will see that the marketing environment also includes a number of *uncontrollable* elements.

Marketing Strategy and the Marketing Environment

Learning Objective 5
Comprehend how the marketing environment affects strategic market planning

The marketing mix consists of elements that the firm controls and uses to reach its target market. In addition, the firm has control over such organizational resources as finances and information. These resources, too, may be used to accomplish marketing goals. However, the firm's marketing activities are also affected by a number of external—and generally uncontrollable—forces. As Figure 11.4 illustrates, the forces that make up the external *marketing environment* are:

▶ *Economic forces*—the effects of economic conditions on customers' ability and willingness to buy

▶ *Legal forces*—the laws enacted either to protect consumers or to preserve a competitive atmosphere in the marketplace

▶ *Societal forces*—consumers' social and cultural values, the consumer movement, and environmental concerns

▶ *Competitive forces*—the actions of competitors, who are in the process of implementing their own marketing plans

▶ *Political forces*—government regulations and policies that affect marketing, whether or not they are directed specifically at marketing

▶ *Technological forces*—in particular, technological changes that can cause a product (or an industry) to become obsolete almost overnight

These forces influence decisions about marketing-mix ingredients. Changes in the environment can have a major impact on existing marketing strategies. In addition, changes in environmental forces may lead to abrupt shifts in target-market needs.

Strategic Market Planning

The development of a marketing strategy begins with an assessment of the marketing environment. Marketers should gather and analyze all available information concerning the marketing environment, the effectiveness of previous marketing programs or strategies, the firm's present and potential markets and their needs, and the availability of resources. Obviously, marketing research and the firm's system for managing its marketing information play an important role in this first stage of the planning process.

Next, particular and detailed marketing objectives should be formulated. These objectives should be developed in accordance with organizational goals. They must also be measurable and realistic—in line with both the marketing situation and available resources.

BUSINESS JOURNAL ▰▰▰▰

Telemarketing: A Tool for the 1990s

Telemarketing is defined as selling on the telephone; it does not include customer service provided on the phone. Direct marketing by telephone was the fastest-growing sales medium of the 1980s; it now employs nine million telemarketers. Annoying as the calls are to most people, telemarketing does sell, and it is used by both large and small companies to control costs and maximize sales.

ADVANTAGES OF TELEMARKETING

A combination of telemarketing, traditional advertising, and sales promotions allows companies to almost immediately increase sales volume. Telemarketing has other advantages as well:

▶ Telemarketing can help firms reduce their overall marketing costs while allowing them to gauge results with greater precision. Companies that have successfully supplemented personal selling with telemarketing include IBM, MCI Communications, Chrysler, and General Electric.

▶ Telemarketing speeds up order taking and shipping. Integrated services digital network (ISDN) technology is already making the telemarketer's job much easier and faster. ISDN automatic number identification (ANI) helps the telemarketer process calls, increase productivity, and improve call handling.

▶ Telemarketing is flexible. Scripts can be adapted to the responses of the listener, and entire campaigns can be adjusted midway, if necessary.

▶ Telemarketing provides immediate, measurable results, unlike other sales strategies.

▶ Telemarketing boosts the effectiveness of print, radio, and television ads.

GUIDELINES FOR SETTING UP A SUCCESSFUL TELEMARKETING PROGRAM

▶ Marketing managers must clearly define objectives and communicate them to telemarketers.

▶ Management must delegate responsibility for the telemarketing program to a high-level decision maker.

▶ Telemarketing representatives should be trained to focus on the call objectives and not go off on a tangent.

▶ Management should recruit persons who have little or no experience in the field but who demonstrate sales potential and have good telephone voices.

▶ Telemarketing employees should be adequately compensated. The compensation package should motivate these employees to meet and exceed such goals as closing sales, making calls, and servicing accounts.

▶ Telemarketing should be integrated with all other marketing functions of the business.

TELEMARKETING FRAUD AND GOVERNMENT'S RESPONSE

Many executives are convinced that telemarketing works. Now that the industry is booming, however, state and federal lawmakers are eager to crack down on fraudulent operations. California became the first state to require registration of telemarketers. The Telemarketing Fraud Prevention Act of 1989 seeks to regulate telemarketing; the act gives state attorneys general the power to sue telemarketers suspected of fraud in federal court and establishes a three-day period in which consumers can back out of telemarketing purchases.

Recognizing that telemarketing's past reputation has been a bit shady, legitimate telemarketers are anxious to keep the industry clean, upgrade its image, and explore new uses for telemarketing—without unduly pestering the consumer.

Based on information from Richard Edel, "Companies Clamping Down on Telemarketing," *Advertising Age,* March 6, 1986, pp. 18–20; Kevin T. Higgins, "Telemarketing Focuses on Recruiting, Training," *Marketing News,* April 25, 1986, p. 1; Cyndee Miller, "Lawmakers Eager to Crack Down on Telemarketing Fraud," *Marketing News,* July 3, 1989, p. 1; Neal Kay and David Keeler, "High-tech High-volume Telemarketing," *Direct Marketing,* June 1989, p. 85; Richard Herzog, "Telemarketing Spurs High-Tech Sales," *Direct Marketing,* February 1988, p. 88; and Julie Johnson, "ANI Leads the Way," *Telephony,* April 10, 1989, p. 32.

Then a target market must be selected, and a marketing mix must be designed to reach that market. Here, product, pricing, distribution, and promotional strategies need to be coordinated in a unified mix. As we have noted, the marketing strategy must be designed to operate effectively within the external marketing environment.

Finally, the performance of the marketing strategy should be evaluated. Both marketing research and the marketing information system come into play as monitoring tools. The information that is obtained should be used to evaluate the strategy and modify it as necessary. This information should also be used to begin the next round of market planning.

Market Measurement and Sales Forecasting

Learning Objective 6
Describe how market measurement and sales forecasting are used

An organization must measure the sales potential for specific types of market segments to evaluate the feasibility of entering new segments. Estimates of sales potential also allow an organization to decide how best to allocate the company's marketing resources and activities among market segments in which the firm is already active. All such estimates should identify the relevant time frame. Short-range estimates are for less than one year, medium-range estimates are for one to five years, and long-range estimates are for longer than five years. The estimates should also define the geographic boundaries of the forecast. For example, sales

Automobile dealers must revise their sales forecasts when the trend is toward a decline in auto sales. When they anticipate slow sales, dealers are cautious about stocking up on new models.

potential can be estimated for a city, county, state, or group of nations. Finally, forecasters should confine their estimates to a specific product line or item.

sales forecast *an estimate of the amount of a product that an organization expects to sell during a certain period of time, based on a specified level of marketing effort*

A company **sales forecast** is the amount of a product that an organization expects to sell during a certain period of time, based on a specified level of marketing effort. Managers in different divisions of the organization rely on sales forecasts when they purchase raw materials, schedule production, secure financial resources, consider plant or equipment purchases, hire personnel, and plan inventory levels. Since the accuracy of a sales forecast is important, many organizations use several methods for forecasting sales, including executive judgments, surveys of buyers or sales personnel, time series analyses, correlation analyses, and market tests. The specific methods used depend on the cost involved, type of product, characteristics of the market, time span of the forecast, purposes for which the forecast is used, stability of historical sales data, availability of the required information, and expertise and experience of forecasters.

Marketing Information

Learning Objective 7
Know the difference between a marketing information system and marketing research

Accurate and timely information is the foundation of effective marketing—and, in particular, of the marketing concept. A wealth of marketing information is available, both within the firm and from outside sources, but this information must be gathered, analyzed, and put to use by marketing personnel.

There are two general approaches to collecting marketing information. A marketing information system provides information on a continuing basis, whereas marketing research is used to obtain information for specific marketing projects.

Marketing Information Systems

marketing information system *a system for managing marketing information that is gathered continually from internal and external sources*

A **marketing information system** is a system for managing marketing information that is gathered continually from internal and external sources. A computer is frequently used because of the amount of data that the system must accept, store, sort, and retrieve. *Continual* collection of data is essential if the system is to incorporate the most up-to-date information.

In concept, the operation of a marketing information system is not complex. Data from a variety of sources are fed into the system. Data from *internal* sources include sales figures, product and marketing costs, inventory levels, and activities of the sales force. Data from *external* sources relate to the firm's suppliers, intermediaries, and customers; competitors' marketing activities; and economic conditions. All these data are stored and processed within the marketing information system. Its output is a flow of information in the form that is most useful for marketing decision making. Included in this information might be daily sales reports by territory and product, forecasts of sales or buying trends, and reports on

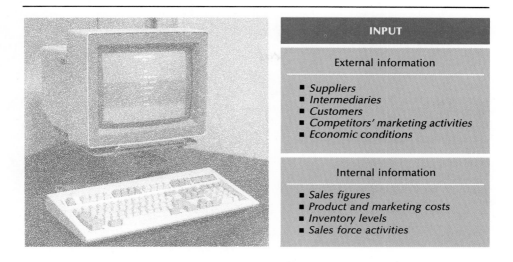

INPUT
External information
<ul><li>*Suppliers*</li><li>*Intermediaries*</li><li>*Customers*</li><li>*Competitors' marketing activities*</li><li>*Economic conditions*</li></ul>
Internal information
<ul><li>*Sales figures*</li><li>*Product and marketing costs*</li><li>*Inventory levels*</li><li>*Sales force activities*</li></ul>

OUTPUT
Information in useful form

FIGURE 11.5
Marketing Information System
Using a computer, the system compiles and converts information from inside and outside the company into a form useful for decision making.

changes in market share for the major brands in a specific industry. Both the information outputs and their form depend on the requirements of the personnel in the firm (see Figure 11.5).

Marketing Research

marketing research *the process of systematically gathering, recording, and analyzing data concerning a particular marketing problem*

Marketing research is the process of systematically gathering, recording, and analyzing data concerning a particular marketing problem. Thus marketing research is used in specific situations to obtain information that is not otherwise available to decision makers. It is an intermittent, rather than a continuous, source of marketing information.

A six-step procedure for conducting marketing research is given in Table 11.3. This procedure is particularly well suited to testing new products, determining various characteristics of consumer markets, and evaluating promotional activities. General Foods Corp. makes extensive use of marketing research—in the form of taste tests—to determine whether proposed new products will appeal to consumers.

Marketing research conducted by Borden revealed that retail sales of Eagle Brand sweetened condensed milk—"The Dessert Maker"—rise as much as 50 percent when it is merchandized side-by-side with produce and other dessert ingredients.

TABLE 11.3 **The Six Steps of Marketing Research**

1. Define the problem	In this step, the problem is clearly and accurately stated to determine what issues are involved in the research, what questions to ask, and what types of solutions are needed. This is a crucial step that should not be rushed.
2. Make a preliminary investigation	The objective of preliminary investigation is to develop both a sharper definition of the problem and a set of tentative answers. The tentative answers are developed by examining internal information and published data, and by talking with persons who have some experience with the problem. These answers will be tested by further research.
3. Plan the research	At this stage researchers know what facts are needed to resolve the identified problem and what facts are available. They make plans on how to gather needed but missing data.
4. Gather factual information	Once the basic research plan has been completed, the needed information can be collected by mail, telephone, or personal interviews; by observation; or from commercial or government data sources. The choice depends on the plan and the available sources of information.
5. Interpret the information	Facts by themselves do not always provide a sound solution to a marketing problem. They must be interpreted and analyzed to determine the choices that are available to management.
6. Reach a conclusion	Sometimes the conclusion or recommendation becomes obvious when the facts are interpreted. However, in some cases, reaching a conclusion may not be so easy because of gaps in the information or intangible factors that are difficult to evaluate. If and when the evidence is less than complete, it is important to say so.

Source: Adapted from Small Business Administration (Washington, D.C.), *Small Business Bibliography No. 9.*

Types of Buying Behavior

buying behavior   *the decisions and actions of people involved in buying and using products*

consumer buying behavior   *the purchasing of products for personal or household use, not for business purposes*

organizational buying behavior   *the purchasing of products by producers, governmental units, institutions, and resellers*

Learning Objective 8
Understand several factors that may influence buying behavior

Buying behavior may be defined as the decisions and actions of people involved in buying and using products.[4] **Consumer buying behavior** refers to the purchasing of products for personal or household use, not for business purposes. **Organizational buying behavior** is the purchasing of products by producers, governmental units, institutions, and resellers. Since a firm's success depends greatly on buyers' reactions to a particular marketing strategy, it is important to understand buying behavior. Marketing managers are better able to predict consumer responses to marketing strategies and develop a satisfying marketing mix if they are aware of the factors that affect buying behavior.

Consumer Buying Behavior

Consumers use different types of decision behaviors when buying different products. For frequently purchased, low-cost items, a consumer employs routine response behavior. Very little search or decision effort is necessary to complete these purchases. The buyer uses limited decision making for purchases made occasionally and when more information is needed about an unknown product in a well-known product category. The consumer engages in extensive decision making when buying an unfamiliar, expensive item or one that is seldom purchased.

A person deciding on a purchase goes through some or all of the steps shown in Figure 11.6. First, the consumer acknowledges that a problem exists. Then the buyer looks for information that may include brand names, product characteristics, warranties, and other features. Next, the buyer weighs the various options that have come to light and then finally

Buyer behavior is influenced by psychological and social factors, such as peer group pressure.

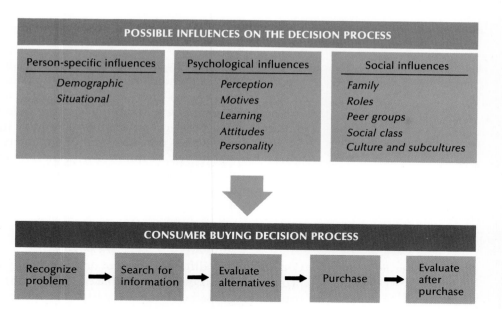

FIGURE 11.6
Consumer Buying Decision Process and Possible Influences on the Process
A buyer goes through some or all of these steps when making a purchase. (Source: Adapted from William M. Pride and O. C. Ferrell, Marketing: Concepts and Strategies, 6/e. *Copyright © 1989 by Houghton Mifflin Company. Used by permission.)*

makes a choice and acquires the item. In the after-purchase stage, the consumer evaluates the suitability of the product. This judgment will have an effect on future purchases. As Figure 11.6 shows, the buying process is influenced by person-specific factors (demographic, situational), psychological factors (perception, motives, learning, attitudes, personality), and social factors (family, roles, peer groups, social class, culture and subculture).

Organizational Buying Behavior

Organizational buyers consider a product's quality, its price, and the service provided by suppliers. Organizational buyers are usually better informed than consumers about the products they buy and generally buy in larger quantities. In an organization, a committee or group of people, rather than single individuals, often decide on purchases. Committee members must consider the organization's objectives, purchasing policies, resources, and personnel. Organizational buying occurs through description, inspection, sampling, or negotiation.

The American Consumer

In this section we examine several measures of consumer income, a major source of buying power. By looking at why, what, where, and when consumers buy, we explain how this income is spent. Our focus then shifts to socioeconomic trends that influence consumption patterns and marketing activities.

Consumer Income

Learning Objective 9
Recognize three ways of
measuring consumer income

personal income   *the income
an individual receives from all
sources less the Social Security
taxes that the individual must
pay*

disposable income   *personal
income less all additional
personal taxes*

discretionary income   *disposable income less savings and expenditures on food, clothing,
and housing*

Purchasing power is created by income. However, as every taxpayer knows, not all income is available for spending. For this reason, marketers consider income in three diffrent ways: **Personal income** is the income an individual receives from all sources *less* the Social Security taxes that the individual must pay. In 1989 total U.S. personal income was $4.4 trillion!

Disposable income is personal income *less* all additional personal taxes. These taxes include income, estate, gift, and property taxes levied by local, state, and federal governments. About 5 percent of all disposable income is saved. On the average, just over 50 percent is spent on such necessities as food, clothing, and shelter. In 1989 total U.S. disposable income was $3.7 trillion.[5]

Discretionary income is disposable income *less* savings and expenditures on food, clothing, and housing. Discretionary income is of particular interest to marketers because consumers have the most choice in spending it. Consumers use their discretionary income to purchase items ranging from automobiles and vacations to movies and pet food. In 1989 total U.S. discretionary income was $1.95 trillion.[6]

According to a study by the U.S. Census Bureau and the Conference Board, 60 percent of the households headed by a person with five or more years of college education have an average discretionary income of $18,250 per year. Forty-one percent of married couples with both spouses working have discretionary income averaging $13,300 per household.[7]

Why Do Consumers Buy?

Consumers buy with the hope of getting a large amount of current and future satisfaction relative to their buying power. Consumers buy because they would rather have a particular good or service than the money they have to spend to buy it! More specifically, consumers may choose to buy a given product for five reasons:

1. *They have a use for the product.* Many items fill an immediate "use" need. A kitchen needs pots and pans; a student needs books.

2. *They like the convenience a product offers.* Such items as electric can openers and ice crushers are not essential, but they offer convenience and thus satisfaction.

3. *They believe the purchase will enhance their wealth.* People collect antiques or gold coins as investments as well as for enjoyment. Home owners buy aluminum siding, awnings, and fences to add to the value of their property.

4. *They take pride in ownership.* Many consumers purchase items such as a compact disc player or gold Rolex watch because such products provide status and pride of ownership as well as utility.

5. *They buy for safety.* Consumers buy health, life, and fire insurance to protect themselves and their families. Smoke detectors, automatic appliance timers, traveler's checks, and similar products also provide safety and protection.

What Do Consumers Buy?

Figure 11.7 shows how consumer spending is divided among various categories of products and services. The average American household spent $24,414 in 1987, according to the latest available data from the Census Bureau. As we have noted, the greatest proportion of disposable income is spent on food, clothing, and shelter. The largest share—$7,569— went toward housing and related expenses, from taxes to furnishings. The second-largest expense was transportation, with families spending an average of $4,600 on cars and other vehicles, insurance, repairs, and public transportation. The average household spent $3,664 on food, including $2,099 to eat at home. Clothing and related services, such as dry cleaning, used up $1,446. Another $1,193 went toward entertainment, and slightly

FIGURE 11.7
Consumer Spending
What percentage of disposable income is spent on various categories of products and services?
(Sources: U.S. Department of Labor, Bureau of Statistics, Survey of Consumer Expenditures, 1989; Wall Street Journal, August 21, 1989, p. B1.)

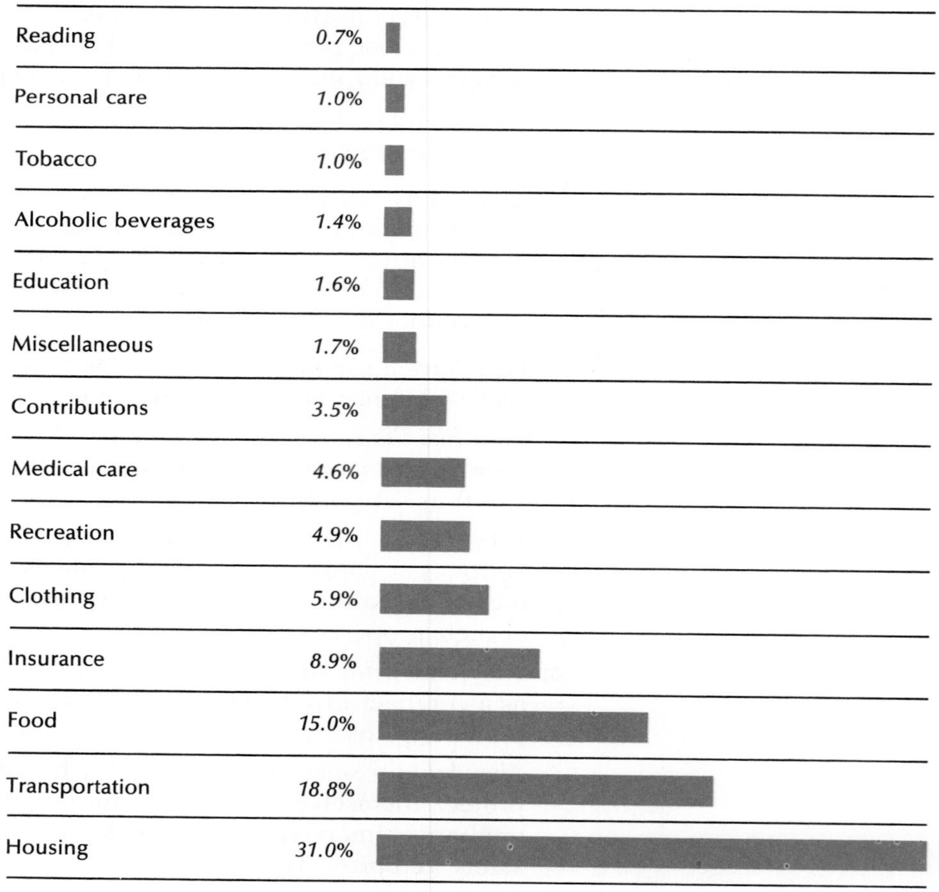

Category	Percentage
Reading	0.7%
Personal care	1.0%
Tobacco	1.0%
Alcoholic beverages	1.4%
Education	1.6%
Miscellaneous	1.7%
Contributions	3.5%
Medical care	4.6%
Recreation	4.9%
Clothing	5.9%
Insurance	8.9%
Food	15.0%
Transportation	18.8%
Housing	31.0%

more than $1,135 was spent on health care.[8] (A mere 1 percent of total disposable income amounts to around $30 billion. Thus none of the categories in Figure 11.7 is really small in terms of total dollars spent.)

Where Do Consumers Buy?

Probably the most important factor that influences a consumer's decision about where to buy a particular product is his or her perception of the store. Consumers' general impressions of an establishment's products, prices, and sales personnel can mean the difference between repeat sales and lost business. Consumers distinguish among various types of retail outlets (such as specialty shops, department stores, and discount outlets), and they choose particular types of stores for specific purchases.

Many retail outlets go to a great deal of trouble to build and maintain a particular "image." Products that do not fit the image are not carried. For example, at today's Tiffany & Co. image is everything. When Avon Products, Inc. owned Tiffany from 1979 to 1984, customers were shocked to see cheap glassware and crystal on display. Avon's mismarketing destroyed the once-renowned Tiffany's image and resulted in a $5 million loss in 1984. Today, with new ownership, Tiffany is again selling necklaces worth $7 million, and the Tiffany magic has been recaptured. For fiscal 1989, Tiffany's earnings jumped 50 percent to $24 million.[9]

Consumers also select the businesses they patronize on the basis of location, product assortment, and such services as credit terms, return privileges, and free delivery.

When Do Consumers Buy?

In general, consumers buy when buying is most convenient. Certain business hours have long been standard for establishments that sell consumer products. However, many of these establishments have stretched their hours to include evenings and Sundays (where local laws permit Sunday business). Ultimately, within each area, the consumers themselves control when they will do their buying.

Some Noteworthy Demographic Trends*

Learning Objective 10
Understand the marketing implications of several socioeconomic changes occurring in the United States

American consumers are an especially dynamic group. They change their jobs and places of residence, their attitudes, and their lifestyles at a rate that would be alarming in most other countries. Marketers, of course, must keep up with these changes. A shift in population from the cold North to the warm South and Southwest, for example, affects both the marketing environment and the makeup of the firm's marketing mix. Let's outline several trends that researchers expect to be important to marketers over the next decade or so.

---

* Data for this section came from *Population Profile of the United States*, 1989, U.S. Department of Commerce, Bureau of the Census.

Men and Women Are Delaying First Marriage   There has been a dramatic increase in the proportion of people of prime marrying age who have not yet married for the first time. Among women in their early twenties, 61 percent had not yet married in 1988, compared with 36 percent in 1970. For men in this group, the figures were 78 and 55 percent, respectively.

Even more striking are the sizable proportions of older young adults who remain unmarried. Of 25-to-29-year-olds in 1988, 30 percent of the women and 43 percent of the men had not yet married; this figure contrasts with 11 percent and 19 percent, respectively, in 1970.

Marketing implications: It is expected that a large proportion of the over-30 age group will remain single or, if they marry, will remain childless. Single people and childless couples have quite different spending patterns from young couples with families. They are less likely to be home owners; therefore, they buy less furniture and fewer appliances and home furnishings. On the other hand, they spend more heavily on luxuries and leisure activities—travel, entertainment, restaurant meals, and recreation.

Decline in Teen-Age Population   The high school group (aged 14 to 17 years) declined from 14.5 million in 1987 to 13.2 million in 1990. By 1995, it should return to the 1987 level, then remain at least that large through 2010.

Although older Americans were often overlooked in the past, the increase in the number of elderly citizens has created a growing market for products and services such as travel, retirement housing, and health foods. General Foods uses older celebrities such as Lena Horne in ads for Post Natural Bran Flakes.

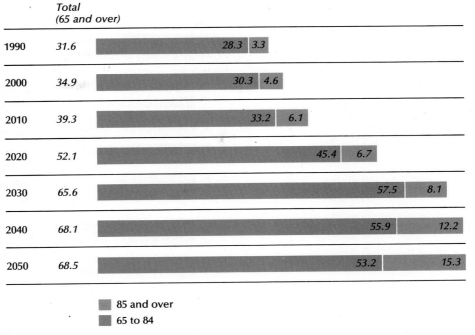

	Total (65 and over)		
1990	31.6	28.3	3.3
2000	34.9	30.3	4.6
2010	39.3	33.2	6.1
2020	52.1	45.4	6.7
2030	65.6	57.5	8.1
2040	68.1	55.9	12.2
2050	68.5	53.2	15.3

■ 85 and over
■ 65 to 84

FIGURE 11.8
Projections of the Elderly Population of the United States, by Age: 1990 to 2050 (in millions)
Projected population figures reveal a trend toward increasing proportions of older people in America. (Source: U.S. Department of Commerce, Bureau of the Census, Current Population Reports, Population Profile of the United States, *1989, p. 40.)*

Marketing implications: The market for youth-oriented products will obviously shrink. Soft drinks, snack foods, video games, music tapes and compact discs, certain cosmetics, designer clothes, and similar products are likely to be the hardest hit. John Wyek, Director of the Office of Strategic Research at Levi Strauss, recently stated, "In fact, we sell more jeans to men aged 25 and older than we do to teens and college kids. And last fall we broke a new campaign aimed at the 35-plus market."[10] Many marketers are currently redirecting their marketing efforts toward an older clientele, as noted in the case of Club Med.

Increase in the Number of Elderly Citizens   The United States will be an aging society until the middle of the next century. Between 1977 and 1987, the number of elderly people increased from 23.9 million to 29.9 million. From now until 2010, the population 65 years and older will have grown at a rate of 1.2 percent. After 2010, however, baby-boomers will enter this age group, causing it to increase at a more marked rate. As shown in Figure 11.8, the elderly will number 39.3 million in 2010, and 65.6 million by 2030.

Marketing implications: There has been a tendency to overlook this market because senior citizens have relatively small incomes and, according to

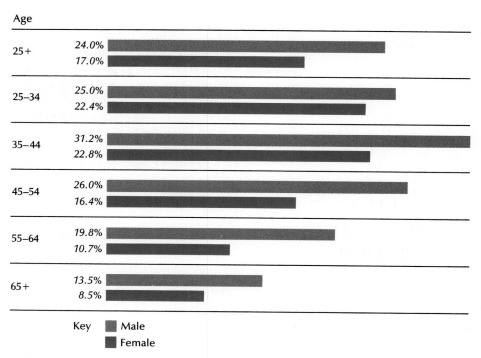

Age

FIGURE 11.9
College Graduates in the United States, by Age and Sex: 1988
In 1988, 24 percent of men and 17 percent of women aged 25 years of age or older had completed four or more years of college. (Source: U.S. Department of Commerce, Bureau of the Census, Current Population Reports, Population Profile of the United States, 1989, p. 22.)

marketing research, have passed the prime acquiring years. However, the over-65 population has become a growing market for many products and services—including travel, recreation, retirement housing, single-portion foods, special cosmetics, and health care.

A Better-Educated Population, with Greater Purchasing Power   The educational level of the population continued to rise in the 1980s. The proportion of persons aged 25 years and older who are high school graduates reached an all-time high of 76 percent in 1988, compared with 24 percent in 1940. As shown in Figure 11.9, in 1988, 24 percent of men and 17 percent of women had completed four or more years of college.

A U.S. Census Bureau study indicates that today's 18-year-old man who goes on to college and obtains a bachelor's degree can expect lifetime earnings of $1,438,000 to $3,000,000, compared with earnings of $933,000 to $1,980,000 for a man with a high school diploma. A man who does not complete high school will earn only $781,000. For women, the earnings are about one-third less than their male counterparts'.

Marketing implications: Educated parents seek even better opportunities for their children. Private-school enrollment is on the upswing. The market for children's books, educational toys, and developmental experiences should benefit from college-educated parents' eagerness to produce "super babies."[11] Children's books are the fastest-growing segment in publishing today.[12]

Increase in the Number of Working Women Women's increased participation in the labor force has also added greatly to the number of two-income families in America and will continue to do so throughout the rest of the century. Since 1950 the number of two-income families has more than tripled. These families now represent over 46 percent of all households.

Marketing implications: The working woman has been a key factor in the growth of the fast-food industry and the development of convenience appliances, such as the slow cooker and the microwave oven. The increase in female workers has also created the present day-care industry. Further growth over the next ten years is anticipated for such products as convenience foods, women's clothing, cosmetics, grooming aids, and labor-saving appliances.

Costs and Benefits of Marketing

Learning Objective 11
Recognize the relative costs and benefits of marketing

American marketing is often criticized as being costly and wasteful. Many critics feel that marketing costs are excessive when they make up as much as half the retail price of a consumer product. One of the major difficulties here is that marketing provides services, which are intangible and therefore hard to pinpoint. How much, exactly, is it worth to be able to buy Tylenol (and other over-the-counter drugs) in tamper-resistant packages? What price would you put on the convenience of being able to purchase camera film in every city and town in this country? Such questions are difficult—perhaps impossible—to answer.

Some reasons for the general increase in marketing costs over the years are:

1. Consumer demands for such services as conveniently located shopping centers, wide assortments of attractively displayed merchandise, credit, merchandise-return privileges, guarantees and warranties, after-sale service, and free delivery all add to marketing costs.

2. Skyrocketing costs of energy, labor, transportation, packaging materials, labels, and most other inputs used by suppliers of goods and services have directly increased marketing costs.

3. Government regulations on packaging, labeling, grading, and a host of other marketing activities have increased the benefits of marketing, but they have increased its costs as well.

Though critics tend to focus on the costs of marketing, they do not deny that it serves a useful purpose. Some of the benefits of marketing activities include the following:

▶ *Development of new or improved products:* Marketing research discovers consumers' changing needs and wants, and translates them into new or modified products and services. The consumer gains through increased want satisfaction, often at lower prices.

▶ *Creation of time, place, and possession utility:* Marketing provides goods and services where and when customers want them. Through financing, marketing also permits consumers to own and use products well before they have accumulated the money to purchase these products outright. Marketing also provides a great deal of information (concerning such things as product contents, use, and repair) that is valuable to purchasers.

▶ *Creation of jobs:* The jobs provided by approximately 2,000,000 retailers, 400,000 wholesalers, 22,000 transportation companies, and thousands of advertising agencies are directly related to marketing.

▶ *Improved standard of living:* Finally, by creating and delivering an immense variety of goods and services, marketing improves the standard of living.

CHAPTER REVIEW

Summary

Marketing is the process of planning and executing the conception, pricing, promotion, and distribution of ideas, goods, and services to create exchanges that satisfy individual and organizational objectives. Marketing adds value in the form of utility, or the power of a product or service to satisfy a need. It creates time utility by making products available when customers want them, place utility by making products available where customers want them, and possession utility by transferring the ownership of products to buyers.

Business people focused on the production of goods from the Industrial Revolution until the early twentieth century, and on the selling of goods from the 1920s to the 1950s. Marketing received little attention up to that point. After 1950, however, business people recognized that their enterprises involved not only production and selling but also the satisfaction of customers' needs. They began to implement the marketing concept, a business philosophy that involves the entire business organization in the dual process of satisfying customer needs and achieving the organization's goals.

Implementation of the marketing concept begins and ends with marketing information—first to determine what customers need, and later to evaluate how well the firm is meeting those needs.

A market consists of people with needs, the ability to buy, and the desire and authority to purchase. Markets are classified as consumer, industrial, and reseller markets.

A marketing strategy is a plan for the best use of an organization's resources to meet its objectives. Developing a marketing strategy involves selecting and analyzing a target market and creating and maintaining a marketing mix that will satisfy that market. A target market is chosen through the total market approach or the market segmentation approach. A market segment is a group of individuals or organizations within a market that have similar characteristics and needs. Businesses that use a total market approach design a single marketing mix and direct it at the entire market for a particular product. The market segmentation approach directs a marketing mix at a segment or segments of a market.

A firm's marketing mix is the combination of product, price, distribution, and promotion that it uses to reach a target market. To achieve a firm's marketing objectives, marketing-mix strategies must begin with an assessment of the marketing environment, which in turn will influence decisions about marketing-mix ingredients. Market measurement and sales forecasting are used to estimate sales potential and predict product sales in specific market segments. Strategies are then monitored and evaluated through marketing research and the marketing information system, which stores and processes internal and external data in a form that is conducive to marketing decision making.

Buying behavior consists of the decisions and actions of people involved in buying and using products. Consumer buying behavior refers to the purchase of products for personal use and not for business purposes. Organizational buying behavior refers to the purchasing behavior of producers, governmental units, institutions, and resellers. Understanding buying behavior helps marketers predict how buyers will respond to marketing strategies.

Personal income is the income an individual receives less the Social Security taxes he or she must pay. Disposable income is personal income minus all other taxes. Discretionary income is what remains after savings and expenditures for necessities. Consumers use discretionary income to buy goods and services that best satisfy their needs. If marketers are to serve this vast and affluent market effectively, they must be aware of both consumer spending patterns and spending trends.

In the next chapter we discuss two elements of the marketing mix: product and price. Our emphasis will be on the development of product and pricing within a marketing strategy.

Key Terms

You should now be able to define and give an example relevant to each of the following terms:

marketing	place utility
utility	time utility
form utility	possession utility

marketing concept
market
marketing strategy
marketing mix
target market
total market approach
market segment
market segmentation
sales forecast
marketing information system
marketing research
buying behavior

consumer buying behavior
organizational buying behavior
personal income
disposable income
discretionary income

Questions and Exercises

Review Questions

1. How, specifically, does marketing create place, time, and possession utility?
2. How is a marketing-oriented firm different from a production-oriented firm or a sales-oriented firm?
3. What are the major requirements for a group of individuals and organizations to be a market? How does a consumer market differ from an industrial market?
4. What are the major components of a marketing strategy?
5. What is the purpose of market segmentation? What is the relationship between market segmentation and the selection of target markets?
6. What are the four elements of the marketing mix? In what sense are they "controllable"?
7. Describe the forces in the environment that affect an organization's marketing decision.
8. What major issues should be specified prior to conducting a sales forecast?
9. What is the difference between a marketing information system and a marketing research project? How might the two be related?
10. Why should marketers try to understand buying behavior?
11. How are personal income, disposable income, and discretionary income related? Which is the best indicator of consumer purchasing power?
12. List five reasons why consumers make purchases. What need is satisfied in each case?
13. How might a marketing manager make use of information about consumer trends?

Discussion Questions

1. Why is Club Med broadening its marketing orientation to include families? After all, Club Med's marketing efforts were quite successful in the 1970s and 1980s. Evaluate Club Med's decision not to exclusively focus its marketing efforts on the singles market.
2. Why is each of the following a marketing activity?
   a. The provision of sufficient parking space for customers at a suburban shopping mall
   b. The purchase (by a clothing store) of seven dozen sweaters in assorted sizes and colors
   c. The inclusion of nutrition information on the labels of food packages
3. How might adoption of the marketing concept benefit a firm? How might it benefit the firm's customers?
4. Is marketing information as important to small firms as it is to larger firms? Explain.
5. How does the marketing environment affect a firm's marketing strategy?

Exercises

1. Describe how a producer of computer hardware could apply the marketing concept.
2. Through library research, determine the distribution of income among American households in as much detail as possible. Then explain how you would use this information if you were marketing 40-foot yachts.
3. Explain how you would develop a marketing strategy for an in-home rug and upholstery cleaning service. Describe the marketing information you would need.

Case 11.1

Targeting New Markets

No one has been able to develop a list of superbly managed companies that withstands the test of time. Levi Strauss, one of the models of excellence in the early 1970s, faced hard times in the late 1970s and early 1980s. The company struggled in its attempts to appeal to both the youth and adult markets. The company's efforts to appeal to both markets through a single advertising strategy proved unsuccessful. New product lines of jeans came and went.

The company became determined to shine up its tarnished image. Image, sales, and profits are being improved through product diversification, acceptance of the fact that the preferences of students of the 1960s

and 1970s have evolved, and by the targeting of ethnic groups throughout the United States.

Today, Levis are again a staple for baby boomers. Different sizes, silhouettes, and fabrics have helped retain Levi's appeal. And for the younger market, Levi continues to stress hip, fit, and image. The company also uses varied commercials to appeal to specific groups and is planning to target different age and racial groups as demographics continue to change.

Demographics, especially in California, are changing rapidly, and the company is responding with new lines of casual pants. Economic and population trends in California reveal that Hispanics, blacks, and Asians will exert increasing economic influence as their numbers continue to expand. Research by the Center for the Continuing Study of the California economy predicts that California's population will expand by 500,000 people a year through 1995; due to immigration trends, around two-thirds of this increase will be Hispanics and Asians. California will represent one-fifth of the entire U.S. economic expansion during the same time period. Levi Strauss is successfully using this demographic information to develop clothing to appeal to new target markets. However, Levi Strauss's Office of Strategic Research director John Wyek, who has helped the company utilize demographic information, realizes that change will be a constant factor: "From now until the year 2,000, there's going to be a steady decline in the total number of 18-to-24-year-olds. . . . Hispanic 18-to-24-year-olds will increase by 40 percent. It changes the feel of our audience."*

By creating new products with a well-known trademark, new designs and fabrics, and by improving its advertising and image, Levi Strauss intends to capture emerging markets as well as better respond to its traditional clientele.†

Questions

1. How is Levi Strauss shining up its tarnished image?
2. In what ways is Levi Strauss implementing the marketing concept? Explain.
3. How have demographic factors influenced Levi Strauss's marketing strategies?

---

* Bickley Townsend, "Beyond the Boom," *American Demographics*, June 1989, p. 40.

† Based on information from Bickley Townsend, "Beyond the Boom," *American Demographics*, June 1989, p. 40; Marcy Magiera, "Levi Gives Women a Taste of the Blues," *Advertising Age*, July 18, 1988, p. 23; Martha Farnsworth Riche, "California Here It Comes," *American Demographics*, March 1989, p. 8; and Andrew Pollack, "Jeans Fade but Levi Strauss Glows," *The New York Times*, June 26, 1989, p. C1.

Case 11.2

Cindy's Corner: Marketing a Family Restaurant

Cindy's Corner, a family-oriented restaurant, opened for business fifteen months ago. Things weren't going well, even though Cindy Adams, the owner, felt the food was as good as that offered by most other restaurants in town.

Adams decided to get some help from a marketing consultant. During a discussion with her, the consultant asked Adams what her target market was. She responded, "Anyone who stops by." He then asked her what types of menu items her customers wanted. She said that she really wasn't sure. To focus on some of the marketing problems that Adams was experiencing, the marketing consultant shared the following story.

During World War II, the U.S. Air Force established a supply depot on an island in the South Pacific. The base and its runway, landing lights, control tower, and storage buildings were of great interest to the natives. They liked to watch planes take off and land. In time they especially looked forward to cargo shipments because they had devised ways of pilfering food and other supplies from the base.

After the war, U.S. military personnel razed the base's buildings and dismantled the runway before leaving the island for good. The natives, who had come to depend on the cargo supplies, decided that the large silver birds might return if the base were rebuilt. So they cleared off the landing strip, put up crude storage huts, and constructed a "tower" near the runway. At night they placed a line of torches on either side of the runway. The natives waited patiently for many days, but the silver birds never returned.

Questions

1. What was the consultant's purpose in sharing this story with Ms. Adams?
2. How should Ms. Adams go about developing a marketing strategy for Cindy's Corner?

PRODUCT
AND PRICE

1 Know what a product is and how products are classified

2 Understand the product life cycle and how it leads to new-product development

3 Understand the definitions of *product line* and *product mix* and be able to distinguish between the two

4 Know the methods available for changing a product mix

5 Understand the uses and importance of branding, packaging, and labeling

6 Comprehend the economic basis of pricing and the means by which sellers can control prices and buyers' perceptions of prices

7 Identify the major pricing objectives and the methods that businesses use to implement them

8 Recognize the different strategies available to companies as they set basic prices

CHAPTER PREVIEW

We look first in this chapter at products. We examine product classifications and describe the four stages, or life cycle, through which every product moves. Next, we illustrate how firms manage products effectively by modifying or deleting existing products and by developing new products. Branding, packaging, and labeling of products are also discussed. Then our focus shifts to pricing. We explain competitive factors that influence sellers' pricing decisions and also explore buyers' perceptions of prices. After considering organizational objectives that can be accomplished through pricing, we outline several methods for setting prices. Finally, we describe pricing strategies by which sellers can reach target markets successfully.

A Well-Conceived, Super-Successful Product: The Mazda Miata

Move over, Corvette, the Mazda Miata is here. Though the peppy, two-seat sports cars have just begun trickling into dealer showrooms, young professionals and sports-car enthusiasts are eager to snap them up. Harrelson Mazda, a dealership in Charlotte, North Carolina, sold its total Miata inventory of eight cars in one day—at considerably more than the manufacturer's suggested list price. At least 280 people are on Harrelson's waiting list, but the dealer will get only eight or nine Miatas a month, out of 40,000 Miatas that Mazda Motor Corp. will bring into the United States annually. Excess demand and limited supply mean high profits for Miata dealers.

National race-car champion Bobby Rahal says, "This has got to be the hottest thing going this year [1989]. . . . It should appeal to both young and middle-aged guys who are into their second childhood. This is a classic car to just go out and cruise in."

But for Mazda Motor Corp., the Miata is more than just a hot little car. It's the vehicle that may just change the automaker's image in the U.S. market. Today, Mazdas are viewed as low-priced alternatives to Hondas and Toyotas; they rank a distant fourth among Japanese cars here, after Honda, Toyota, and Nissan.

The masterminds of Miata are Toshihiko Hirai and Bob Hall. Toshihiko Hirai directed his Miata development team to aim for the ideal of "oneness between rider and horse." They came up with a product that looks British, feels Italian, and has roots that are truly American and Japanese.

In the early 1980s, Mazda's chairman, Kenichi Yamamoto had met Bob Hall, a West Coast editor for *Autoweek*, and told him to research the market for a light, entry-level roadster. Hall told Yamamoto what Mazda needed was a sports car. Later, in 1981, Hall joined Mazda and convinced top management that demand existed for an affordable sports car.

The new-product idea moved from Hall's broadly defined concept to production in early 1986 in Hiroshima. The outcome is a comfortable sports car wider than a Porsche Carrera 4, with a minimal top-down wind buffeting, an air bag, a heater, and an air conditioner.

The projected low price was a prime consideration in producing the Miata. The development team persuaded the marketing team that the car should be available in just three colors—red, white, and blue; and there are no gadgets and very few options. The project management team worked as enthusiastically as if the Miata were their own conception.

The biggest complaint about the Miata is not its styling, quality, color, or performance, but its lack of availability and the cold reality of showroom pricing. An annual supply of about 40,000 cars and high demand translate into a four-month-long waiting list for eager buyers, and a dealer profit of up to $4,000 for each car.[1]

A **product** is everything that one receives in an exchange, including all tangible and intangible attributes and expected benefits. A car, for example, includes a warranty, owner's manual, and perhaps free 3,000-mile service and free emergency road service for ten years. Some of the intangibles that may go with an automobile include the status associated with ownership and the memories generated from past rides. Developing and managing products effectively is crucial to an organization's ability to maintain successful marketing mixes.

As we noted in Chapter 1, a product may be a good, service, or idea. A *good* is a real, physical thing that we can touch. A *service* is the result of applying human or mechanical effort to a person or thing. Basically, a service is a change we pay others to make for us. A real estate agent's services result in a change in the ownership of real property. A barber's services result in a change in one's appearance. An idea may take the form of philosophies, lessons, concepts, or advice. Often, ideas are included with a good or service. Thus we might buy a book (a good) that provides ideas on how to lose weight. Or we might join Weight Watchers, for both ideas on how to lose weight and help (services) in doing so.

Our definition of the term *product* is based on the concept of an exchange. In a purchase, the thing that is exchanged for the product is money—an amount of money equal to the *price* of the product. When the product is a good, the price may include such services as delivery, installation, warranties, and training. A good *with* such services is not the same product as the good *without* such services. In other words, sellers set a price for a particular "package" of goods, services, and ideas. When the makeup of that package changes, the price should change as well.

Classification of Products

Different classes of products are directed at particular target markets. A product's classification largely determines what kinds of distribution, promotion, and pricing are appropriate in marketing the product.

Products can be grouped into two general categories—consumer and industrial. A product purchased to satisfy personal and family needs is a **consumer product.** A product bought for use in a firm's operations or to make other products is an **industrial product.** The buyer's intent—or the ultimate use of the product—determines the classification of an item. Note that a single item can be both a consumer and an industrial product. For example, a broom is a consumer product if it is used in someone's home. However, the same broom is an industrial product if it is used in the maintenance of a business. After a product is classified as a consumer or industrial product, it can be further categorized as a particular type of consumer or industrial product.

Consumer Product Classifications

The traditional and most widely accepted system of classifying consumer products consists of three categories: convenience, shopping, and specialty products. These groupings are based primarily on characteristics of buyers' purchasing behavior.

convenience product *a relatively inexpensive, frequently purchased item for which buyers want to exert only minimal effort*

A **convenience product** is a relatively inexpensive, frequently purchased item for which buyers want to exert only minimal effort. Examples include bread, gasoline, newspapers, soft drinks, and chewing gum. The buyer spends little time in either planning the purchase of a convenience item or comparing available brands or sellers.

shopping product *an item for which buyers are willing to expend considerable effort on planning and making the purchase*

A **shopping product** is an item for which buyers are willing to expend considerable effort on planning and making the purchase. Buyers allocate ample time for comparing stores and brands with respect to prices, product features, qualities, services, and perhaps warranties. Appliances, upholstered furniture, men's suits, bicycles, and stereos are examples of shopping products. These products are expected to last for a fairly long time and thus are purchased less frequently than convenience items.

specialty product *an item that possesses one or more unique characteristics for which a significant group of buyers is willing to expend considerable purchasing effort*

A **specialty product** possesses one or more unique characteristics, and a significant group of buyers is willing to expend considerable purchasing effort to obtain it. Buyers actually plan the purchase of a specialty product; they know exactly what they want and will not accept a substitute. In searching for specialty products, purchasers do not compare alternatives.

One problem with this approach to classification is that buyers may behave differently when purchasing a specific type of product. Thus, a single product can fit into all three categories. To minimize this problem, marketers think in terms of how buyers are most likely to behave when purchasing a specific item.

Industrial Product Classifications

Based on their characteristics and intended uses, industrial products can be classified into the following categories: raw materials, major equipment, accessory equipment, component parts, process materials, supplies, and services.

raw material *a basic material that actually becomes part of a physical product; usually comes from mines, forests, oceans, or recycled solid wastes*

A **raw material** is a basic material that actually becomes part of a physical product and usually comes from mines, forests, oceans, or recycled solid wastes. Raw materials are usually bought and sold according to grades and specifications.

major equipment *large tools and machines used for production purposes*

Major equipment includes large tools and machines used for production purposes. Examples of major equipment are lathes, cranes, and stamping machines. Some major equipment is custom-made for a particular organization, but other items are standardized products that perform one or several tasks for many types of organizations.

accessory equipment *standardized equipment used in a variety of ways in a firm's production or office activities*

Accessory equipment is standardized items that generally can be used in several ways within a firm's production or office activities. Examples include hand tools, typewriters, fractional-horsepower motors, and calculators. Compared with major equipment, accessory items are usually much less expensive and are purchased routinely with less negotiation.

component part *an item that becomes part of a physical product and is either a finished item ready for assembly or a product that needs little processing before assembly*

A **component part** becomes part of a physical product and is either a finished item ready for assembly or a product that needs little processing before assembly. Although it becomes part of a larger product, a component part can often be identified easily. Clocks, tires, and switches are examples of component parts.

process material *a material that is used directly in the production of another product and is not readily identifiable in the finished product*

A **process material** is used directly in the production of another product; unlike a component part, however, a process material is not readily identifiable. Like component parts, process materials are purchased according to industry standards or to the specifications of the individual purchaser. Examples include industrial glue and food preservatives.

supply *an item that facilitates production and operations but does not become part of the finished product*

A **supply** facilitates production and operations, but it does not become part of the finished product. Paper, pencils, oils, cleaning agents, and paints are examples.

industrial service *an intangible product that an organization uses in its operations*

An **industrial service** is an intangible product that an organization uses in its operations. Examples include financial, legal, marketing research, and janitorial services. Purchasers must decide whether to provide their own services internally or to hire them from outside the organization.

The Product Life Cycle

product life cycle *a series of stages in which a product's sales revenue and profit increase, reach a peak, and then decline*

In a way, products are like people: They are born, they live, and they die. Every product progresses through a **product life cycle,** which is a series of stages in which its sales revenue and profit increase, reach a peak, and then decline. A firm must be able to launch, modify, and delete products from its offering of products in response to changes in product life cycles. Otherwise, the firm's profit will disappear and the firm will fail. In this section, we discuss the stages of the life cycle and how marketers can use this information.

Learning Objective 2
Understand the product life cycle and how it leads to new-product development

Stages of the Product Life Cycle

Generally the product life cycle is assumed to be composed of four stages—introduction, growth, maturity, and decline—as shown in Figure 12.1. Some products plunge through these stages rapidly, in a few weeks or months. Others may take years to go through each stage. Pet Rocks were

FIGURE 12.1
Product Life Cycle
The graph shows sales volume and profits during the life cycle of a product.
(Source: Adapted from William M. Pride and O. C. Ferrell, Marketing: Concepts and Strategies, 6/e. Copyright © 1989 by Houghton Mifflin Company. Used by permission.)

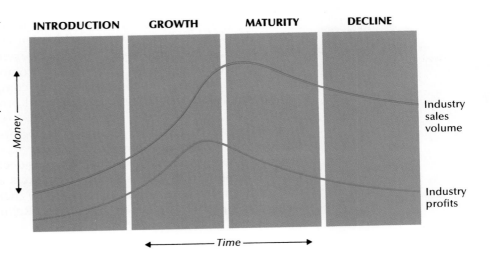

a profitable but short-lived fad. Parker Brothers' *Monopoly* game, which was introduced over fifty years ago, is still going strong.

Introduction   In the *introduction stage*, consumer awareness and acceptance of the product are low. Sales rise gradually as a result of promotion and distribution activities, but initially high development and marketing costs result in low profit, or even in a loss. There are relatively few competitors. The price is sometimes high, and purchasers are primarily people who want to be "the first on their block" to own the new product. The marketing challenge at this stage is to make potential customers aware of the product's existence and its features, benefits, and uses.

A new product is seldom an immediate success. Marketers must watch early buying patterns carefully and must be prepared to modify the new product promptly if necessary. The product should be priced to attract the particular market segment that has the greatest desire and ability to buy the product. Plans for distribution and promotion should suit the targeted market segment. As with the product itself, the initial price, distribution channels, and promotional efforts may need to be adjusted quickly to maintain sales growth during the introduction stage.

Growth   In the *growth stage*, sales increase rapidly as the product becomes well known. Other firms have probably begun to market competing products. The competition and lower unit costs (due to mass production) result in a lower price, which reduces the profit per unit. Note that industry profits reach a peak and begin to decline during this stage. To meet the needs of the growing market, the originating firm offers modified versions of its product and expands its distribution. The 3M Company, the maker of Scotch Tape, developed a variety of tape dispensers, which made its product easier to use. General Foods Corp., the maker of Jell-O, increased the number of Jell-O flavors from six to more than a dozen.

Management's goal in the growth stage is to stabilize and strengthen the product's position by encouraging brand loyalty. To beat the competition, the company may further improve the product or expand the product line to appeal to specialized market segments. Management may also compete by lowering prices if increased production efficiency has resulted in savings for the company. As the product becomes more widely accepted, marketers may be able to broaden the network of distributors. Marketers can also emphasize customer service and prompt credit for defective products. During this period promotional efforts attempt to build brand loyalty in consumers. The company's relative costs for promotion usually drop as the level of total product sales increases.

Maturity   Sales are still increasing at the beginning of the *maturity stage*, but the rate of increase has slowed. Later in this stage the sales curve peaks and begins to decline. Industry profits decline throughout this stage. Dealers' product lines are simplified, markets are segmented more carefully, and price competition increases. The increased competition forces weaker competitors to leave the industry. Refinements and extensions of the original product appear on the market.

During a product's maturity stage, market share may be strengthened by redesigned packaging or changes in promotional emphasis. In this ad, Gerber is emphasizing the natural ingredients in its baby food.

The Complete Recipe for Gerber Peas:

Fresh, tender peas.
Water.

All Gerber baby foods are perfectly prepared for your baby's nutritional needs. without added salt, artificial colors, flavors, or preservatives. Those are the facts. **Gerber** Pure and Simple.

During a product's maturity stage, its market share may be strengthened by redesigned packaging or style changes. Also, consumers may be encouraged to use the product more often or in new ways. Pricing strategies are flexible during this stage. Markdowns and price incentives are not uncommon, although price increases to offset production and distribution costs may be used as well. Marketers may offer incentives and assistance of various kinds to dealers to encourage them to support mature products, especially in the face of competition from private-label brands. New promotional efforts and aggressive personal selling may be necessary during this period of intense competition.

Decline   During the *decline stage*, sales volume decreases sharply. Profits continue to fall. The number of competing firms declines, and the only survivors in the marketplace are those firms that specialize in marketing the product. Production and marketing costs become the most important determinant of profit.

When a product adds to the success of the overall product line, the company may retain it; otherwise, management must determine when to eliminate the product. A product usually declines because of technological advances or environmental factors, or because consumers have switched to competing brands. Therefore, few changes are made in the product itself during this stage. Instead, management may raise the price to cover costs, re-price to maintain market share, or lower the price to reduce inventory. Similarly, management will narrow distribution of the declining product to the most profitable existing markets. During this period the company will not give the product a lot of promotion, although the firm may use advertising and sales incentives to slow the product's decline. The company may choose to eliminate less profitable versions of the product from the product line and, eventually, may decide to drop the product entirely.

Using the Product Life Cycle

Marketers should be aware of the life-cycle stage of each product they are responsible for. And they should know how long the product is expected to remain in that stage. Both must be taken into account in making decisions about the marketing strategy for a product. If a product is expected to remain in the maturity stage for a long time, a replacement product might be introduced later in the maturity stage. If the maturity stage is expected to be short, however, a new product should be introduced much earlier. In some cases, a firm may be willing to take the chance of speeding up the decline of existing products. According to Robert A. Fox, former president and chief operating officer of Del Monte Corp.,

> This is a fact Procter & Gamble learned long ago. Only by introducing many detergents, each differently branded and competing with one another, has it built and maintained its dominance in that business. P&G knows that if an improvement is possible and they don't exploit it, it's only a matter of time until someone else will.[2]

In other situations, a company will attempt to extend a product's life cycle. For example, General Mills has extended the life of Bisquick baking mix (launched in the mid-1930s) by significantly improving the product's formulation.

Product Line and Product Mix

product line *a group of similar products that differ only in relatively minor characteristics*

In Chapter 7, a **product line** was defined as a group of similar products that differ only in relatively minor characteristics. Generally, the products within a product line are related to each other in the way they are produced, marketed, or used. Parker Brothers, for example, manufactures and sells board games such as *Monopoly* and *Risk,* children's games such as *Winnie the Pooh,* electronic toys for children, and strategy games for adults.

Many firms tend to introduce new products within existing product lines. This permits them to apply the experience and knowledge that they have acquired to the production and marketing of new products. However, some firms develop entirely new product lines.

product mix *all the products that a firm offers for sale*

A firm's **product mix** consists of all the products that the firm offers for sale. Two "dimensions" are often applied to a firm's product mix. The *width* of the mix is a measure of the number of product lines it contains. The *depth* of the mix is a measure of the average number of individual products within each line. These are somewhat vague measures; we speak of a *broad* or a *narrow* mix, rather than a mix of exactly three or five product lines.

Learning Objective 3
Understand the definitions of *product line* and *product mix* and be able to distinguish between the two

Many firms seek new products that will broaden their product mix, just as Mazda Motor Corp. has done with the Miata. By developing new product lines, firms gain additional experience and expertise. Moreover, firms achieve stability by operating within several different markets. Problems in one particular market do not affect a multiline firm nearly as much as they would affect a firm that depended entirely on a single product line.

Managing the Product Mix

Learning Objective 4
Know the methods available for changing a product mix

To provide products that both satisfy people in a firm's target market or markets and achieve the organization's objectives, a marketer must develop, adjust, and maintain an effective product mix. Seldom can the same product mix be effective for long. Because customers' product preferences and attitudes change, their desire for a product may dwindle or grow. In some cases, a firm needs to alter its product mix to adapt to competition. A marketer may have to eliminate a product from the mix because one or more competitors dominate that product's specific market segment. Similarly, an organization may have to introduce a new product or modify an existing one to compete more effectively. A marketer may expand the firm's product mix to take advantage of excess marketing and production capacity. For whatever reason a product mix is altered, the product mix must be managed to bring about improvements in the mix. There are three major ways to improve a product mix: change an existing product, delete a product, or develop a new product.

Changing Existing Products

product modification *the process of changing one or more of a product's characteristics*

Product modification refers to changing one or more of a product's characteristics. For this approach to be effective, several conditions must be met. First, the product must be modifiable. Second, existing customers must be able to perceive that a modification has been made, assuming that the modified item is still directed at them. Third, the modification should make the product more consistent with customers' desires so that it provides greater satisfaction.

Existing products can be altered in three primary ways: quality, function, and style. *Quality modifications* are changes that relate to a product's dependability and durability and usually are achieved by alterations in the materials or production process. *Functional modifications* affect a product's versatility, effectiveness, convenience, or safety; they usually require redesign of the product. Typical product categories that have undergone extensive functional modifications include kitchen appliances, office and farm equipment, and vacuum cleaners. *Style modifications* are directed at changing the sensory appeal of a product by altering its taste, texture, sound, smell, or visual characteristics. Since a buyer's purchase decision is affected by how a product looks, smells, tastes, feels, or sounds, a style modification may have a definite impact on purchases. Through style modifications, a firm can differentiate its product from competing brands and perhaps gain a sizable market share if customers find the modified product to be more appealing.

Deleting Products

product deletion *the elimination of one or more products from a product line*

To maintain an effective product mix, a firm often has to eliminate some products. This is called **product deletion**. A weak product costs the firm too much time, money, and resources that could be available for modifying other products or developing new ones. Also, when a weak product generates an unfavorable image among customers, the negative ideas may rub off on some of the firm's other products.

Most organizations find it difficult to delete a product. Some firms drop weak products only after they have become severe financial burdens. A better approach is some form of systematic review of the product's impact on the overall effectiveness of the firm's product mix. Such a review should analyze a product's contribution to the firm's sales for a given period. It should include estimates of future sales, costs, and profits associated with the product and a consideration of whether changes in the marketing strategy could improve the product's performance.

A product deletion program can definitely improve a firm's performance. For example, Del Monte once claimed that it had the largest assortment of canned fruits and vegetables nationally. The company recently deleted a number of items that were not achieving adequate sales and profits.

Developing New Products

Developing and introducing new products is frequently time-consuming, expensive, and risky. Thousands of new products are introduced annually. Depending on how one defines it, the failure rate for new products ranges between 60 and 75 percent. Although developing new products is risky, failing to introduce new products can also present hazards. New products are generally grouped into three categories on the basis of their degree of similarity to existing products. *Imitations* are products that are designed to be similar to—and to compete with—existing products of other firms. Examples are the various brands of fluoride toothpaste that were developed to compete with Crest. *Adaptations* are variations of existing products that are intended for an established market. Freeze-dried coffee is a product adaptation. The product refinements and extensions discussed in Chapter 7 are most often considered adaptations, although imitative products may also include some refinement and extension. *Innovations* are entirely new products. They may give rise to a new industry (such as xerography or television) or revolutionize an existing one. The introduction of sound tracks, for example, permanently changed the motion picture industry. Similarly, compact discs have brought major changes to the recording industry. Innovative products take considerable time, effort, and money to develop. They are therefore less common than adaptations and imitations.

Before a new product is introduced, it goes through six phases. Figure 12.2 depicts the evolutionary nature of new-product development.

Idea Generation   Idea generation involves looking for product ideas that will help a firm achieve its objectives. Although some organizations get their ideas almost by chance, firms trying to maximize product-mix effectiveness usually develop systematic approaches for generating new-product ideas. Ideas may come from marketing managers, researchers, engineers, competitors, advertising agencies, management consultants, private research organizations, or customers.

Screening   During screening, ideas that do not match organizational resources and objectives are rejected. At this stage, firms must ask whether they have the expertise to develop and market a product. Management may reject a good idea because the company lacks needed skills and abilities. The largest number of product ideas are rejected during the screening phase.

Business Analysis   Business analysis provides a tentative outline of a product's position in the marketplace, including its probable profitability.

FIGURE 12.2
Phases of New-Product Development
Generally, marketers use six steps to develop a new product. (Source: Reprinted from William M. Pride and O. C. Ferrell, Marketing: Concepts and Strategies, 6/e. Copyright © 1989 by Houghton Mifflin Company. Used by permission.)

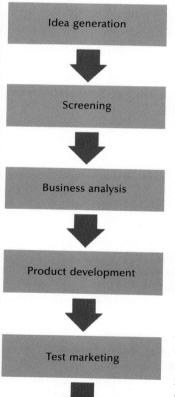

Idea generation

Screening

Business analysis

Product development

Test marketing

Commercialization

Developing new products to respond to constantly changing consumer wants and needs—although time consuming and expensive— is imperative to a firm's success. These members of Friendly's Research and Development group are testing new menu items at the company's test kitchens.

During this stage, the firm considers how the new product, if it were introduced, would affect the firm's sales, costs, and profits. Marketing personnel usually work up preliminary sales and cost projections at this point, with the help of R&D and production managers.

Product Development   In the product development phase, the company must find out first if it is technically feasible to produce the product and then if the product can be made at costs low enough to justify a reasonable price. If a product idea makes it to this point, it is transformed into a working model, or *prototype*.

Test Marketing   *Test marketing* is the limited introduction of a product in areas chosen to represent the intended market. Its aim is to determine buyers' probable reactions. Marketers can experiment with advertising, pricing, and packaging in different test areas and can measure the extent of brand awareness, brand switching, and repeat purchases that results from alterations in the marketing mix.

Commercialization   During commercialization, plans for full-scale manufacturing and marketing must be refined and completed, and budgets for the project must be prepared. In the early part of the commercialization phase, marketing management analyzes the results of test marketing to find out what changes in the marketing mix are needed before the product is introduced. The results of test marketing may tell the marketers, for example, to change one or more of the product's physical attributes, to modify the distribution plans to include more retail outlets, to alter promotional efforts, or to change the product's price. Products are not usually introduced nationwide overnight. Most new products are marketed in stages, beginning in selected geographic areas and expanding into adjacent areas over a period of time.

Why Do Products Fail? In spite of this rigorous process for developing product ideas, the majority of new products end up as failures. In fact, many well-known corporations have produced market failures (see Table 12.1).

Why does a new product fail? Mainly because the product and its marketing program are not planned and tested as completely as they should be. For example, to save on development costs, a firm may market-test its product but not its entire marketing mix. Or a firm may market a new product before all the "bugs" have been worked out. Or, when problems show up in the testing stage, a firm may try to recover its product development costs by pushing ahead with full-scale marketing anyway. Finally, some firms try to market new products with inadequate financing.

Branding, Packaging, and Labeling

Learning Objective 5
Understand the uses and importance of branding, packaging, and labeling

Three important features of a product (particularly a consumer product) are its brand, package, and label. These features may be used to associate a product with a successful product line or to distinguish it from existing products. They may be designed to attract customers at the point of sale

The girl with the umbrella has appeared on Morton Salt packaging for over seventy-five years. She never grows older, but remains ever fashionable, getting new hairstyles and dresses in 1921, 1933, 1941, 1956, and 1968.

TABLE 12.1   *Examples of Product Failures*

Food Items	Health and Beauty Aids	Other Products
Campbell's Red Kettle Soups	Colgate's Cue Toothpaste	Real (cigarettes)
Post Cereals with Freeze-Dried Fruit	Bristol-Myers Resolve Analgesic	Stanley Works' Garden Tool Line
Heinz's Great American Soup	Scott Paper's Babyscott Diapers	Golden Esso Extra
Rheingold's California Gold Label Beer	Nine Flags Men's Cologne	Prestone Long-Life Coolant
Seagram's Four Roses Premium Light Whiskey	Warner-Lambert's Reef Mouthwash	Texas Instruments' wrist watches
McDonald's McRib Sandwich	Colgate's 007 Men's Cologne	Cadillac Cimarron
Rise 'n' Shine Breakfast Drink	Revlon's Super Natural Hairspray	Federal Express Zap Mail
Nestle's New Cookery	Procter & Gamble's Hidden Magic Hairspray	
	Crazy Legs (shaving cream for women)	
	Us (unisex deodorant)	
	Rely tampons	
	Designer Diapers	

Source: Joel R. Evans and Barry Berman, *Essentials of Marketing* (New York: Macmillan, 1984); and Arthur Bragg, "Back to the Future," *Sales and Marketing Management*, November 1986, pp. 61–62.

or to provide information to potential purchasers. Because the brand, package, and label are very real parts of the product, they deserve careful attention during product planning.

What Is a Brand?

brand   *a name, term, symbol, design, or any combination of these that identifies a seller's products and distinguishes them from competitors' products*

A **brand** is a name, term, symbol, design, or any combination of these that identifies a seller's products and distinguishes them from competitors' products.[3] A **brand name** is the part of a brand that can be spoken. It may include letters, words, numbers, or pronounceable symbols, like the ampersand in *Procter & Gamble*. A **brand mark,** on the other hand, is the part of a brand that is a symbol or distinctive design, like Planters' "Mr. Peanut."

brand name   *the part of a brand that can be spoken*

brand mark   *the part of a brand that is a symbol or distinctive design*

trademark   *a brand that is registered with the U.S. Patent and Trademark Office and is thus legally protected from use by anyone except its owner*

A **trademark** is a brand that is registered with the U.S. Patent and Trademark Office and is thus legally protected from use by anyone except its owner. Among the many registered trademarks are the shape of the Coca-Cola bottle and the CBS eye.

Brands are often classified according to who owns them: manufacturers or stores. A **manufacturer** (or **producer**) **brand,** as the name implies, is a brand that is owned by a manufacturer. The majority of foods, major appliances, and gasolines, as well as all automobiles, are sold with producer branding. So is much of today's clothing. Names such as Jonathan Logan,

manufacturer (or **producer**) **brand**   *a brand that is owned by a manufacturer*

Calvin Klein, Bill Blass, and Gloria Vanderbilt are examples of producer brands that appeal to both department stores and consumers. Many consumers prefer producer brands because they are nationally known, offer consistent quality, and are widely available.

store (or **private**) **brand**
a brand that is owned by an individual wholesaler or retailer

A **store** (or **private**) **brand** is one that is owned by an individual wholesaler or retailer. Among the better-known store brands are Kenmore and Craftsman (owned by Sears, Roebuck) and KMC (owned by K mart). Owners of store brands claim that they can offer lower prices, earn greater profits, and improve customer loyalty with their own brands. Companies that manufacture a private brand often find such operations profitable because they can use excess capacity and at the same time avoid most marketing costs. About one-third of all tire, food, and appliance sales are of store-branded items. Sears generates more than one-half of its sales from its own brands.

Consumer confidence is the most important element in the success of a branded product, whether the brand is owned by a producer or a store. Because branding identifies each product completely, consumers can easily repurchase products that provide satisfaction, performance, and quality. And they can just as easily avoid or ignore products that do not. In supermarkets, among the products most likely to keep their shelf space are the brand leaders having the greatest share of sales and deepest consumer commitment.

generic product (or **brand**)
a product with no brand at all

A **generic product** (sometimes called a **generic brand**) is a product with no brand at all. Its plain package carries only the name of the product—applesauce, peanut butter, potato chips, or whatever—in black type. Usually, generic products are made by the major producers that manufacture name brands. Generic products have been available in supermarkets since 1977. They appeal mainly to consumers who are willing to sacrifice consistency in size or quality for a lower price. However, generic products are not necessarily lower in quality.

Branding Strategies

The basic branding decision for any firm—producer or seller—is whether to brand its products. A producer may market its products under its own brands, private brands, or both. A seller (store) may carry only producer brands, its own brands, or both. Once either type of firm decides to brand, it chooses one of two branding strategies: individual branding or family branding.

individual branding   *the strategy in which a firm uses a different brand for each of its products*

Individual branding is the strategy in which a firm uses a different brand for each of its products. For example, Procter & Gamble uses individual branding for its line of bar soaps, which includes Ivory, Camay, Lava, Zest, Safeguard, and Coast. Individual branding offers two major advantages. A problem with one product will not affect the good name of the firm's other products. And the different brands can be directed toward different segments of the market. For example, Holiday Inns' Hampton Inns are directed toward budget-minded travelers, Residence Inns toward apartment dwellers, and Crown Plazas toward upscale customers.

family branding   *the strategy in which a firm uses the same brand for all or most of its products*

Family branding is the strategy in which a firm uses the same brand for all or most of its products. Sunbeam, General Electric, IBM, and Xerox

BUSINESS JOURNAL ◢◢◢◢◢◢◢◢◢◢◢◢

The Name of the Game Is the Brand Name

Do you wonder how Mazda chose the name *Miata* for its hot new sports car? *Miata* is derived from an Old German word meaning "reward." Fortunately, Mazda did not have to wait for a court decision to use the name Miata. But Toyota was not so lucky. Toyota's new luxury car had to await a court decision on the name *Lexus*. Mead Data Central, Inc. had claimed that *Lexus* was too close to *Lexis*, the brand name of its computerized data base for the law profession. Finally, Toyota won the right to use the name *Lexus*.

SELECTING AND DEVELOPING BRAND NAMES

There are several different sources and methods for selecting and developing brand names. In the past, some of the most successful names have come from such sources as surnames and nicknames, names relating to product ingredients, tribal and company names, and social structures. Other traditional name sources include animal names, song titles, historical events, and language elements. New and unique brand names can be developed from association analysis, which attempts to create an association between the product and something culturally recognizable; linguistic analysis, which uses graphemics, morphemics, and semantics to create new names; and from random symbol combinations.

Products are given a brand name and often a trademark. A *brand name* identifies the product and/or its manufacturer. A *trademark* is a name, symbol, or any other device that identifies a product; it is officially registered and legally restricted for the exclusive use of the owner or manufacturer. Among trademarks that cannot be imitated are the Playboy bunny costume and the NBC chimes.

PROTECTING BRAND NAMES

Companies spend considerable time and effort selecting a brand name. But that is only half the battle. Company attorneys must be ever vigilant to ensure that the communications media do not use the brand name inappropriately. For example, multibillion-dollar Xerox Corporation of Stamford, Connecticut, spends $100,000 a year on "educational trademark ads" directed at publishers, editors, and others who may misuse its product name "Xerox" as a generic term for photocopy. Advertising people and trademark attorneys are sometimes at odds—the common use of a product name is an advertiser's dream, but a trademark attorney's nightmare. Xerox Corporation's trademark attorney protects the company's product name by actively seeking any infringements of trademark laws by competitors.

Recently, Owen Ryan & Associates (OR&A) won a summary judgment from the Trademark Trial and Appeals Board against Anheuser-Busch's claims of trademark infringement. OR&A had registered the name *Party Animals* for a snack-cracker product with the U.S. Patent and Trademark Office. Anheuser-Busch, Inc., claimed that this would cause consumer confusion with its Bud Light Spuds MacKenzie "Original Party Animal" and Eagle Snacks promotions.

Precedent and law agree that a brand name constitutes a protectable trademark if the name meets three requirements:

► It must be adopted and used by a company.

► It must be distinct from other brand names. Distinctiveness is determined through searches of federal registration lists, telephone books, trade journals, and other publications.

► It must meet the standards for valid trademarks established by the courts or the U.S. Patent and Trademark Office.

Based on information from Kevin A. Wilson, "Horse Play with Mazda," *Autoweek*, March 20, 1989, p. 18; Ken Gross, "Back to the Future," *Automotive Industries*, April 1989, p. 92; Dorothy Cohen, "Trademark Strategy," *Journal of Marketing*, January 1986, pp. 61–74; Paul A. Eisanstein, "Toyota's New Luxury Line Awaits Decision on Name," *Journal of Commerce and Commercial*, February 15, 1989, p. 1A; Clemens P. Work and Kenneth R. Sheets, "Vowels Cost More," *U.S. News & World Report*, January 16, 1989; Jim Henry, "Toyota Wins Lexus Name," *Automotive News*, January 9, 1989, p. 1; Maile A. Carlton and Donna M. Bialik, "Rhyme, Rhythm, and Reason: The Three Rs of Brand Name Selection," *Business*, April–June 1989, p. 53; Mark McLaughlin, "Trademark Attorneys Fight the Good Fight Against Idiom Blight," *New England Business*, March 17, 1986, p. 36; and Lynn G. Coleman, "David KOs Goliath, but Giant Won't Stay Down," *Marketing News*, August 14, 1989, p. 10.

use family branding for their entire product mix. A major advantage of family branding is that the promotion of any one item that carries the family brand tends to help all other products with the same brand name. In addition, new products have a head start when their brand name is already known and accepted by consumers.

Brand names should be distinctive and easy to remember, say, and spell. However, they must also be carefully protected—both from competitors and, surprisingly, from excessive popularity. Many brand names have become the names of general classes of products because they were not adequately protected by their owners. Among these are cellophane, escalator, linoleum, nylon, thermos, harmonica, aspirin, and yo-yo.

Packaging

packaging all those activities involved in developing and providing a container for a product

Packaging consists of all those activities involved in developing and providing a container for a product. The package is a vital part of the product. It can make the product more versatile, safer, or easier to use. Through its shape and what is printed on it, a package can influence purchasing decisions. It can be used to facilitate branding strategies. The L'eggs package, for example, effectively links the product to the brand name.

Packages thus have both functional and marketing value. Their primary function is to protect the product, and they should be strong enough to do so. They should be easy to open and close, to store and reuse, and to dispose of or recycle.

With regard to marketing, packages should be attention-getters if they are to be displayed at the point of sale—as in supermarkets. Various sizes of packages may be used to reach particular target markets. Single-portion food packages for single-person households and the "giant economy size" for large families are examples. Such packages as reusable containers and no-drip bottles may also attract customers to particular products. See-through plastic packaging allows the customer to see the product before it is purchased and reduces theft. Both Lipton and Ocean Spray sell fruit juices aseptically packaged in boxes that do not need refrigeration.

Finally, the package can be used to inform customers about the product's contents, uses, advantages, features, and hazards.

Labeling

labeling the presentation of information on a product or its package

Labeling is the presentation of information on a product or its package. The *label* is the part that contains the information. This information may include the brand name and mark, the registered-trademark symbol ®, the package size and contents, product claims, directions for use and safety precautions, a list of ingredients, the name and address of the manufacturer, and the Universal Product Code symbol, which is used for automated check-out and inventory control.

A number of federal regulations specify information that *must* be included in the labeling for certain products:

▶   Garments must be labeled with the name of the manufacturer, country of manufacture, fabric content, and cleaning instructions.

▶ Any food product for which a nutritional claim is made must have nutrition labeling that follows a standard format.

▶ Nonedible items such as shampoos and detergents must carry safety precautions as well as instructions for their use.

▶ The ingredients of food products must be listed in order, beginning with the ingredient that constitutes the largest percentage of the product.

Such regulations are aimed at protecting the consumer from both misleading product claims and the improper (and thus unsafe) use of products.

Labels may also carry the details of written or express warranties. An **express warranty** is a written explanation of the responsibilities of the producer in the event that the product is found to be defective or otherwise unsatisfactory. Recently, as a result of consumer discontent (along with some federal legislation), firms have begun to simplify the wording of warranties and to extend their duration. Chrysler's 70,000-mile/7-year warranty is featured heavily in that firm's advertising.

Many of the decisions and activities associated with a product have a definite impact on its price. The rest of this chapter is devoted to considerations affecting pricing goals, methods, and strategies.

express warranty   a written explanation of the responsibilities of the producer in the event that the product is found to be defective or otherwise unsatisfactory

The Product and Its Price

You should now realize that a product is more than a thing that we can touch or a change that we can see. It is, rather, a set of attributes and benefits that has been carefully designed to satisfy its market while earning a profit for the seller. But no matter how well a product is designed, it cannot perform its function if it is priced incorrectly. Few people will purchase a product with too high a price, and a product with too low a price will earn little or no profit. Somewhere between too high and too low, there is a "proper," effective price for each product. In the remainder of this chapter, we shall see how businesses go about determining what the right price is.

The Meaning and Use of Price

price   the amount of money that a seller is willing to accept in exchange for a product, at a given time and under given circumstances

The **price** of a product is the amount of money that the seller is willing to accept in exchange for the product, at a given time and under given circumstances. At times, the price results from negotiations between buyer and seller. But in many business situations, the price is fixed by the seller. Suppose a seller sets a price of $10 for a particular product. In essence, the seller is saying "Anyone who wants this product can have it here and now, in exchange for $10."

Each interested buyer then makes a very personal judgment regarding the utility of the product, often in terms of some dollar value. If a particular person feels that he or she will get at least $10 worth of want satisfaction (or value) from the product, he or she is likely to buy it. But if that person

Learning Objective 6
Comprehend the economic basis of pricing and the means by which sellers can control prices and buyers' perceptions of prices

Low prices and aggressive marketing are the two major elements in the success of Carnival Cruise Lines. This company's vacation packages are priced at least 20 percent below competing cruises. Carnival's revenues have grown 30% annually since 1980 (three times the average for the cruise business). Its customers seem elated to have found the right product at the right price.

can get more want satisfaction by spending $10 in some other way, he or she will not buy it.

Price thus serves the function of *allocator*. First, it allocates goods and services among those who are willing and able to buy them. (As we noted in Chapter 1, the answer to the economic question "For whom to produce?" depends primarily on prices.) Second, price allocates financial resources (sales revenue) among producers according to how well they satisfy customers' needs. And third, price helps customers to allocate their own financial resources among various want-satisfying products.

Can Firms Control Their Prices?

supply *the quantity of a product that producers are willing to sell at each of various prices*

Supply and Demand—Once Again In Chapter 1, we defined the **supply** of a product as the quantity of the product that producers are willing to sell at each of various prices. We can draw a graph of the supply relationship for a particular product, say, jeans (see the left graph of Figure 12.3). Note that the quantity supplied by producers *increases* as the price increases along this *supply curve*.

demand *the quantity of a product that buyers are willing to purchase at each of various prices*

As defined in Chapter 1, the **demand** for a product is the quantity that buyers are willing to purchase at each of various prices. We can also draw a graph of the demand relationship (see the middle graph of Figure 12.3). Note that the quantity demanded by purchasers *increases* as the price decreases along the *demand curve*.

As noted in Chapter 1, the sellers and buyers of a product interact in the marketplace. We can show this interaction by superimposing the supply curve on the demand curve for our product, as shown in the right graph of Figure 12.3.

The two curves intersect at point [obscured]
15 million pairs of jeans and a price of [obscured]
supply curve; thus producers are willing to [obscured]
each. Point E is also on the demand curve [obscured]
purchase 15 million pairs at $15 each. Point [obscured]
15 million pairs are produced and priced at $15, [obscured]
everyone who is willing to pay $15 will be able to [obscured]

Prices in the Real Economy In a (largely theoretic[obscured]
competition, no producer has control over the price [obscured]
producers must accept the equilibrium price. If they charg[obscured]
they will not sell their products. If they charge a lower p[obscured]
lose sales revenue and profits. In addition, the products o[obscured]
producers are indistinguishable from each other when a syst[obscured]
competition exists. Every bushel of wheat, for example, is ex[obscured]
every other bushel of wheat.

In the real economy, producers try to gain some control over [obscured]
by differentiating their products from similar products. **Product di**[obscured]
entiation is the process of developing and promoting differences betwe[obscured]
one's product and all similar products. The idea behind product differ[obscured]
entiation is to create a specific demand for the firm's product—to take
the product out of competition with all similar products. Then, in its own
little "submarket," the firm can control price to some degree. Jeans with
various designer labels are a result of product differentiation.

Firms also attempt to gain some control over price through advertising.
If the advertising is effective, it will increase the quantity demanded. This
may permit a firm to increase the price at which it sells its particular
output.

product differentiation *the process of developing and promoting differences between one's product and all similar products*

FIGURE 12.3
Supply and Demand Curves
Supply curve (left): *The upward slope (to the right)* means that producers will
supply more jeans at higher prices. **Demand curve (middle):** *The downward slope
(to the right)* means that buyers will purchase fewer jeans at higher prices. **Supply
and demand curves together (right):** *Point E indicates equilibrium in quantity and
price for both sellers and buyers.*

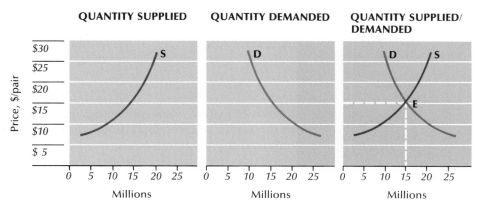

et, firms may reduce prices to obtain a competitive
hope to sell more units at a lower price, thereby
ales revenue. Although each unit earns less profit,

rge sellers in an oligopoly (an industry in which
e considerable control over price, mainly because
ortion of the total supply of its product. However,
oter 1, this control of price is diluted by each
etitors.

he real economy do exert some control over
trol depends on their pricing goals and their
ts, as well as on the workings of supply and
s.

Competition

price of a product can be set, an organization must decide on
basis it will compete—on the basis of price or some other combination
of factors. The choice influences pricing decisions as well as other marketing-mix variables.

Price competition occurs when a seller emphasizes the low price of a
product and sets a price that equals or beats competitors' prices. To use
this approach most effectively, a seller must have the flexibility to change
prices often and must do so rapidly and aggressively whenever competitors
change their prices. Price competition allows a marketer to set prices
based on demand for the product or in response to changes in the firm's
finances. Competitors can do likewise, however, which is a major drawback
of price competition. They, too, can quickly match or outdo an organization's price cuts. In addition, if circumstances force a seller to raise
prices, competing firms may be able to maintain their lower prices.

Nonprice competition is based on factors other than price. It is used
most effectively when a seller can make its product stand out from the
competition by distinctive product quality, customer service, promotion,
packaging, or other features. Buyers must be able to perceive these
distinguishing characteristics and consider them desirable. Once customers have chosen a brand for nonprice reasons, they may not be as
easily attracted to competing firms and brands. In this way a seller can
build customers' loyalty to its brand. Price is still an important part of a
marketing mix in nonprice competition, but it is possible for a firm to
increase a brand's unit sales without lowering its price.

Buyers' Perceptions of Price

In setting prices, managers should consider the price sensitivity of people
in the target market. How important is price to them? Is it always "very
important"? Members of one market segment may be more influenced by
price than members of another. For a particular product, the price may
be a bigger factor to some buyers than to others. For example, buyers

nonprice competition competition that is based on factors
other than price

on an empha-
ing a price equal to or
er than competitors' to gain
sales or market share

may be more price sensitive when purchasing gasoline than they are when purchasing jeans.

Buyers will accept different ranges of prices for different products; that is, they will tolerate a narrow range for certain items and a wider range for others. Management should be aware of these limits of acceptability and the products to which they apply. The firm should also take note of buyers' perceptions of a given product in relation to competing products. A premium price may be appropriate if a product is considered superior to others in that category or if the product has inspired strong brand loyalty. On the other hand, if buyers have a fairly negative view of a product, a lower price may be necessary.

Sometimes buyers relate price to quality. They may consider a higher price to be an indicator of higher quality. Managers involved in pricing decisions should determine whether this outlook is widespread in the target market. If it is, a higher price may improve the image of a product and, in turn, make the product more desirable.

Pricing Objectives

Learning Objective 7
Identify the major pricing objectives and the methods that businesses use to implement them

Before management can set prices for a firm's products, it must decide what it expects to accomplish through pricing. That is, management must set pricing objectives that are in line with both organizational and marketing objectives.

Of course, one objective of pricing is to make a profit, but this may not be a firm's primary objective. One or more of the following factors may be just as important (see Figure 12.4).

Survival

A firm may have to price its products to survive—either as an organization or as a factor in a particular market. This usually means that the firm will cut its price to attract customers, even if it then must operate at a loss. Of course, such a goal can't be pursued on a long-term basis. Consistent losses would cause the business to fail.

FIGURE 12.4
Pricing Objectives
One objective of pricing is to make a profit, but this may not be a company's primary pricing objective.

PRICING OBJECTIVES

- Survival
- Profit/maximization
- Return on investment
- Market share
- Status quo

Just to remain in the air transportation market, Continental Airlines Corp. offered a fare of $49 on all its nonstop flights. Although this low price was extremely attractive to the public, it was not, however, greeted with delight by competing airlines. Nevertheless, Continental's management felt it was necessary for survival.

Profit Maximization

Many firms may state that their goal is to maximize profit, but this goal is impossible to define (and thus impossible to achieve). What, exactly, is the "maximum" profit? How does a firm know when it has been reached? Firms that wish to set profit goals should express them as either specific dollar amounts or percentage increases over previous profits. For example, Campbell Soup Company's pricing goal is to post a 15 percent annual increase in earnings.[4]

Target Return on Investment

The *return on investment (ROI)* is the amount that is earned as a result of that investment. Some firms set an annual-percentage ROI as their pricing goal. ConAgra, Inc., the parent company for Banquet Foods and other subsidiaries, considers rate of return the single most significant measure

Courtyard by Marriott, a business traveler's hotel, offers low weekend rates to boost occupancies among leisure travelers. Its ad also emphasizes how much you get for your money, including king-size beds, cable TV, a whirlpool, and an exercise room.

of operating performance. The company's objective is to earn an average after-tax ROI in excess of 20 percent.[5]

Market Share Goals

A firm's *market share* is its proportion of total industry sales. Some firms attempt, through pricing, to maintain or increase their share of the market. Several years ago, Ford Motor Company used pricing to increase its share of the European car market to a record 12.4 percent.[6] And, to protect its market share against the Trump Shuttle, Pan American World Airways cut its own fares to match Trump's nonstop fare between New York and Washington, D.C.

Status Quo Pricing

In pricing their products, some firms are guided by a desire to not "make waves," or to maintain the status quo. This is especially true in industries where price stability is important. If such a firm can maintain its profit or market share simply by meeting the competition—charging about the same price as competitors for similar products—then it will do so.

Sometimes, the strongest competitor, called the *price leader*, sets its price first; other firms in the industry then follow suit. In the automobile industry, General Motors is usually the price leader. When GM announces a 2 percent increase in price, its American competitors follow with price increases.

Pricing Methods

Once a firm has developed its pricing objectives, it must select a pricing method and strategy to reach that goal. The *pricing method* provides a "basic" price for each product. *Pricing strategies* are then used to modify the basic price, depending on pricing objectives and the market situation.

Two factors are important to every firm engaged in setting prices. The first is recognition that the market, and not the firm's costs, ultimately determines the price at which a product will sell. The second is awareness that costs and expected sales can be used only to establish some sort of *price floor*, the minimum price at which the firm can sell its product without incurring a loss.

We shall look at three kinds of pricing methods: cost-based, demand-based, and competition-based pricing.

Cost-Based Pricing

Using the simplest method of pricing, cost-based pricing, the seller first determines the total cost of producing (or purchasing) one unit of the product. The seller then adds an amount to cover additional costs (such as insurance or interest) and profit. The amount that is added is called the **markup.** The total of the cost plus the markup is the selling price of the product.

markup *the amount that a seller adds to the cost of a product to determine its basic price*

Many smaller firms calculate the markup as a percentage of their total cost. Suppose, for example, that the total cost of manufacturing and marketing 1,000 portable stereos is $100,000, or $100 per unit. If the manufacturer wants a markup that is 20 percent above its costs, the selling price will be $100 plus 20 percent of $100, or $120 per unit.

Markup pricing is easy to apply, and it is used by many businesses (mostly retailers and wholesalers). However, it has two major flaws. The first is the difficulty of determining an effective markup percentage. If this percentage is too high, the product may be overpriced for its market; then too few units may be sold to return the total cost of producing and marketing the product. On the other hand, if the markup percentage is too low, the seller is "giving away" profit that it could have earned simply by assigning a higher price. In other words, the markup percentage needs to be set to account for the workings of the market, and that is very difficult to do.

The second problem with markup pricing is that it separates pricing from other business functions. The product is priced *after* production quantities are decided on, *after* costs are incurred, and almost without regard for the market or the marketing mix. To be most effective, the various business functions should be integrated. *Each* should have an impact on *all* marketing decisions.

Demand-Based Pricing

There are several ways to include product demand in the pricing process. They range from the simple but dangerous method of experimenting with several prices to complex methods involving intricate and detailed calculations. Somewhere between these two extremes is a pricing method based on *breakeven analysis.*

breakeven quantity *the number of units that must be sold for the total revenue (from all units sold) to equal the total cost (of all units sold)*

For any product, the **breakeven quantity** is the number of units that must be sold for the total revenue (from all units sold) to equal the total cost (of all units sold). **Total revenue** is the total amount received from sales of the product. We can estimate projected total revenue as the selling price multiplied by the number of units sold.

total revenue *the total amount received from sales of a product*

The costs involved in operating a business can be broadly classified as either fixed costs or variable costs. A **fixed cost** is a cost that is incurred no matter how many units of a product are produced or sold. Rent, for example, is a fixed cost; it remains the same whether 1 unit or 1,000 are produced. A **variable cost** is a cost that depends on the number of units produced. The cost of fabricating parts for a stereo receiver is a variable cost. The more units produced, the higher this cost is. The **total cost** of producing a certain number of units is the sum of the fixed costs and the variable costs attributed to those units.

fixed cost *a cost that is incurred no matter how many units of a product are produced or sold*

variable cost *a cost that depends on the number of units produced*

total cost *the sum of the fixed costs and the variable costs attributed to a product*

If we assume a particular selling price, we can find the breakeven quantity either graphically or by using a formula. Figure 12.5 graphs the

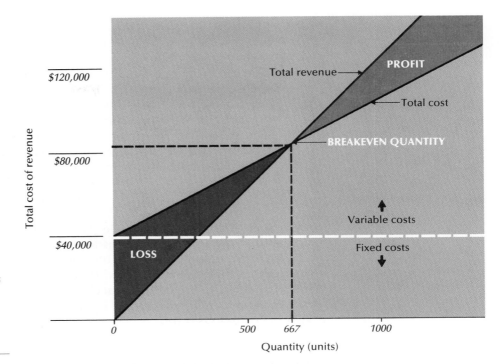

FIGURE 12.5
Breakeven Analysis
Breakeven analysis answers
the question, What is the
lowest level of production
and sales at which a com-
pany can break even on a
particular product?

total revenue earned and the total cost incurred by the sale of various
quantities of some hypothetical product. With fixed costs of $40,000,
variable costs of $60 per unit, and a selling price of $120, the breakeven
quantity is 667 units. To find the breakeven quantity, one must first deduct
the variable cost from the selling price to determine how much money
the sale of one unit contributes to offsetting fixed costs. One then divides
that contribution into the total fixed costs to arrive at the breakeven
quantity. (The breakeven quantity in Figure 12.5 is the quantity represented by the intersection of the total-revenue and total-cost axes.) If the
firm sells more than 667 units, it will earn a profit. If it sells fewer units,
it will suffer a loss.

To use this breakeven analysis for pricing, we select several reasonable
selling prices and find the breakeven quantity that is associated with each
price. For a portable-stereo manufacturer, we might come up with the
following results:

Possible price	Breakeven quantity
$100	1,000
$110	800
$120	667
$140	500

Next, on the basis of our experience in marketing stereos, along with
any additional market data that might be available, we estimate the

demand for these stereos. Our goal is to determine, as best we can, how many units we can sell at each possible price. We then combine this demand analysis with our breakeven analysis to set both the price of the stereo and the production quantity.

Suppose we determine that sales will be very weak at the high $140 price but that we could sell 1,000 stereos at a price of $100 or 900 stereos at a price of $110. We also estimate that we could sell 800 to 850 units at $120 each. Based on this information, we would set our basic price at $120 per unit, and we would produce no more than 850 units—not the 1,000 units that might be our production capacity.

Competition-Based Pricing

In competition-based pricing, the firm essentially ignores costs and market demand. Instead, it uses competitors' prices as guides in setting its own prices. This method is probably most important when competing products are very similar in nature or when the market is such that price is the key element of the marketing mix.

Competition-based pricing is popular, especially with retailers, for two main reasons. First, it is simple. There is no need to study demand, to do a breakeven analysis, or even to calculate markups. The firm simply charges the same prices that its competitors charge for similar goods and services. Second, this pricing method is considered fair to both buyer and seller, and it rarely sparks a price war.

Pricing Strategies

Learning Objective 8
Recognize the different strategies available to companies as they set basic prices

A seller may temporarily or permanently apply various pricing strategies to the basic prices of its individual products or complete product lines (see Figure 12.6). The extent to which a particular seller uses any of the following strategies depends on its pricing and marketing goals, the markets for its products, the degree of product differentiation, the life-cycle stage of the product, and other factors.

New-Product Strategies

Price Skimming   Some consumers are willing to pay a high price for an innovative product, either because of its novelty or because of the prestige or status that ownership confers. **Price skimming** is the strategy of charging the highest-possible price for a product during the introduction stage of its life cycle. The seller essentially "skims the cream" off the market, which helps to recover more quickly the high costs of research and development. Also, a skimming policy may hold down demand for the product, which is helpful if the firm's production capacity is limited during the introduction stage. The greatest disadvantage is that a skim-

price skimming *the strategy of charging the highest-possible price for a product during the introduction stage of its life cycle*

CHOOSE PRICING METHOD TO SET BASIC PRICE	IMPLEMENT PRICING STRATEGIES

■ Cost-based pricing
■ Demand-based pricing
■ Competition-based pricing
	■ New-product strategies
	  Price skimming
	  Penetration pricing
	■ Discounting
	  Trade discounts
	  Quantity discounts
	  Cash discounts
		■ Psychological pricing strategies
		  Odd pricing
		  Multiple unit pricing
		  Prestige pricing
		  Price lining
		■ Geographic pricing strategies

FIGURE 12.6
Pricing Strategies
After using a pricing method to set the basic price for a product, the seller adjusts the price according to a pricing strategy.

ming price may make the product appear lucrative to potential competitors, who may attempt to enter that market.

penetration pricing *the strategy of setting a low price for a new product*

Penetration Pricing   At the opposite extreme, **penetration pricing** is the strategy of setting a low price for a new product. The idea is to develop a large market share for the product quickly. The seller hopes that this approach will sell more units during the early life-cycle stages and thus discourage competitors from entering the market. If the low price stimulates sales, the firm may experience longer production runs that result in lower production costs per unit. A disadvantage of penetration pricing is that it places a firm in a less flexible position. It is more difficult to raise prices significantly than it is to lower them.

Psychological Pricing Strategies

odd pricing *the strategy of setting prices at odd amounts that are slightly below an even or whole number of dollars*

Odd Pricing   Many retailers believe that consumers respond more positively to odd-number prices like $4.99 than to whole-dollar prices like $5. **Odd pricing** is the strategy of setting prices at odd amounts that are slightly below an even or whole number of dollars.

Nine and five are the most popular ending figures for prices, accounting for nearly 80 percent of the marketplace. These odd prices were started by retailers in the 1890s as clerks had to make change and customers were encouraged to make impulse purchases.

Sellers who use this strategy believe that odd prices will increase sales and hence total revenue and profit. The strategy is not limited to low-priced items. Auto manufacturers may set the price of a car at $9,995 rather than $10,000. Odd pricing has been the subject of various psychological studies, but the results have not been conclusive.

multiple-unit pricing *the strategy of setting a single price for two or more units*

Multiple-Unit Pricing   Many retailers (and especially supermarkets) practice **multiple-unit pricing,** setting a single price for two or more units, such as two cans for 99 cents rather than 50 cents per can. Especially for products with a rapid turnover, this strategy can increase sales. Customers who see the single price, and who expect eventually to use more than one

BUSINESS JOURNAL

A New Price Policy for America's Largest Retailer

Crowds began forming early to eagerly await the opening of most Sears stores. When the stores opened, there were balloons, streamers, free gifts, and jazz bands to celebrate a major change for America's largest retailer. Faced with stiff competition from both specialty stores like The Gap (clothing) and Circuit City (electronics) and from discount stores like K mart and Wal-Mart, Sears, Roebuck closed 824 stores for forty-two hours and permanently lowered prices by as much as 50 percent on 50,000 items. And, to prove that it means business, Sears has promised to match any competitor's advertised price.

The new price policy is designed to recapture customers who have been shopping at cheaper discount stores or trendier specialty stores. According to management, the everyday low-price policy also eliminates the need for regularly scheduling special promotional sales because prices have already been reduced. Fewer sales promotions will save the company as much as $200 million each year—by reducing the labor (now used to change price tags), advertising, and inventory-handling costs associated with special sales.

Sears also hopes to attract more customers by placing famous-label products alongside its own store brands, such as Kenmore appliances and Craftsman tools. This tactic has already proved successful in test marketing. In fact, part of a recent Sears media blitz focuses on 1,000 brand-name items already sold at Sears, and the company is adding new brands each week. In addition, Sears is moving to convert its stores into a collection of superstore departments that can compete head-on with specialty stores. (*Superstores* are large retail stores with departments featuring housewares, clothing, automotive products, and so on.) By the end of the year, the chain will introduce a new superstore department called Brand Central to sell appliances and electronics.

Sears' new everyday low pricing is aimed at lifting the firm's sagging sales and profits. Analysts concede that price cuts will initially spur sales and profits but could later (in the long run) hurt the firm's profits unless management reduces administrative, distribution, and sales costs. Last year, Sears' overhead expense accounted for 30 cents of every sales dollar—compared with 23 cents at K mart and a mere 15 cents at Wal-Mart. For Sears, lowering costs is every bit as important as lowering prices. To be successful with everyday low pricing, a company must also have everyday low costs.

For now, management hopes that the new low-price policy and resulting increase in profits will placate the firm's stockholders. It's no secret that large numbers of stockholders have been disappointed with the firm's financial performance over the past few years. Increased profits could also help protect the company from a threatened takeover. For years, Sears—valued at just over $15 billion—believed it was too big to be taken over, but the recent $25-billion takeover of RJR Nabisco Inc. has shown that no takeover target is too large for a hostile buy-out. In addition to restructuring its retail operations, Sears has bought back 10 percent of its stock, sold the company's 110-story Sears Tower in Chicago, and tried to sell parts of its Coldwell-Banker (real estate) and Allstate Insurance divisions to improve its cash position and thus protect itself from a takeover.

Based on information from Francine Schwadel, "Sears, Hit by Disappointing Sales, Maps Ways to Stir Business, Keep Pricing Goals," *Wall Street Journal*, October 5, 1989, p. A3; Dean Foust, "Will the Big Markdown Get the Big Store Moving Again?" *Business Week*, March 13, 1989, p. 110+; "Sale Days at Sears," *Newsweek*, March 6, 1989, p. 43; Pamela Sherrid, "Attention Discount Shoppers!" *U.S. News & World Report*, March 13, 1989, p. 54; and "Sears' New Discount Policy Is Drawing Crowds, So Far," *Time*, March 13, 1989, p. 47.

unit of the product, regularly purchase it in multiple units to save the odd cents.

prestige pricing *the strategy of setting a high price to project an aura of quality and status*

Prestige Pricing   **Prestige pricing** is the strategy of setting a high price to project an aura of quality and status. Because high-quality items are generally more expensive than those of average quality, many buyers believe that high price *means* high quality for certain types of products such as cosmetics, perfumes, and jewelry. High-priced products such as Rolex watches and stores such as Neiman-Marcus Co. tend to attract quality- and prestige-conscious customers.

price lining *the strategy of selling goods only at certain predetermined prices that reflect definite price breaks*

Price Lining   **Price lining** is selling goods only at certain predetermined prices that reflect definite price breaks. For example, a store may sell men's ties only at $9 and $16. This strategy is widely used in clothing stores and boutiques. It eliminates minor price differences from the buying decision—both for customers and for purchasing managers who buy merchandise to sell in the store.

Geographic Pricing

Geographic pricing strategies deal with delivery costs. The seller may assume all delivery costs, no matter where the buyer is located. This practice is sometimes called *postage-stamp pricing.* Or the seller may share transportation costs with the buyer according to some predetermined policy. The pricing strategy that requires the buyer to pay the greatest part of the delivery costs is called *F.O.B. point of origin pricing.* It stands for "free on board at the point of origin," which means that the buyer will pay the transportation costs from the warehouse to the buyer's place of business.

Discounting

discount *a deduction from the price of an item*

A **discount** is a deduction from the price of an item. Producers and sellers offer a wide variety of discounts to their customers:

▶ *Trade discounts* are discounts from the list price that are offered to marketing intermediaries, or middlemen. A furniture retailer, for example, may receive a 40 percent discount from the manufacturer. The retailer would then pay $60 for a lamp carrying a list price of $100. Intermediaries, discussed in Chapter 13, perform various marketing activities in return for trade discounts.

▶ *Quantity discounts* are discounts given to customers who buy in large quantities. The seller's per-unit selling cost is lower for larger purchases. The quantity discount is a way of passing part of this saving on to the buyer.

▶ *Cash discounts* are discounts offered for prompt payment. A seller may offer a discount of "2/10, net 30," meaning that the buyer may take a 2 percent discount if the bill is paid within 10 days and that the bill must be paid in full within 30 days.

CHAPTER REVIEW

Summary

A product is everything that one receives in an exchange, including all attributes and expected benefits. The basic product may be a manufactured item, a service, an idea, or some combination of these.

Products are classified according to their ultimate use. Classification affects a product's distribution, promotion, and pricing. Consumer products, which include convenience, shopping, and specialty products, are purchased to satisfy personal and family needs. Industrial products are purchased for use in a firm's operations or to make other products.

Every product moves through a series of four stages—introduction, growth, maturity, and decline—which together form the product life cycle. As the product progresses through these stages, its sales and profitability increase, peak, and then decline. If a firm does not introduce new products to replace declining products, it will eventually fail.

A product line is a group of similar products marketed by a firm. The firm's product mix includes all the products that it offers for sale. Customer satisfaction and organizational objectives require marketers to develop, adjust, and maintain an effective product mix. Marketers may improve a product mix by changing existing products, deleting products, and developing new products.

New products should be developed in a series of six steps. The first two steps, idea generation and screening, remove from consideration those product ideas that do not mesh with organizational goals or are not feasible. The third step, business analysis, generates information on the marketability and profitability of the proposed product. The last three steps—product development, testing, and commercialization—provide an actual product and launch it into the marketplace. Most product failures result from inadequate product planning and development.

Branding strategies are used to associate (or not associate) particular products with existing products, with producers, or with intermediaries. Packaging protects goods and enhances marketing efforts. Labeling provides customers with product information, some of which is required by law.

Under the ideal conditions of pure competition, an individual seller has no control over the price of its products. Prices are determined by the workings of supply and demand. In our real economy, however, sellers do exert some control, primarily through product differentiation.

Before the price of a product can be set, a firm must decide whether its basis for competition will be its low price or some nonprice consideration. Also, managers must consider the relative importance of price to buyers in the target market before setting prices. Prices may be established based on costs, demands, the competition's prices, or some combination of these. Cost- and competition-based pricing are simpler than demand-based pricing, which considers additional marketing factors in the pricing process. Once basic prices are set, the seller may apply various pricing strategies to reach its target markets more effectively.

In this chapter, we discussed two ingredients of the marketing mix—product and pricing. The next chapter is devoted to a third element—distribution. As that chapter shows, distribution includes not only the physical movement of products but also the organizations that facilitate exchanges among the producers and users of products.

Key Terms

You should now be able to define and give an example relevant to each of the following terms:

product	brand mark
consumer product	trademark
industrial product	manufacturer (or
convenience product	producer) brand
shopping product	store (or private) brand
specialty product	generic product (or
raw material	brand)
major equipment	individual branding
accessory equipment	family branding
component part	packaging
process material	labeling
supply	express warranty
industrial service	price
product life cycle	supply
product line	demand
product mix	product differentiation
product modification	price competition
product deletion	nonprice competition
brand	markup
brand name	breakeven quantity

total revenue

fixed cost

variable cost

total cost

price skimming

penetration pricing

odd pricing

multiple-unit pricing

prestige pricing

price lining

discount

Questions and Exercises

Review Questions

1. What does the purchaser of a product obtain, besides the good, service, or idea itself?
2. What are the products of (a) a bank, (b) an insurance company, and (c) a university?
3. What major factor determines whether a product is a consumer or industrial product?
4. Describe each of the classifications of industrial products.
5. What are the four stages of the product life cycle? How can a firm determine which stage a particular product is in?
6. What is the difference between a product line and a product mix? Give an example of each.
7. Under what conditions does product modification work best?
8. Why do products have to be deleted from a product mix?
9. Why must firms introduce new products?
10. Briefly describe the six new-product development stages.
11. What is the difference between (a) manufacturer and store brands, and (b) family and individual branding?
12. How can packaging be used to enhance marketing activities?
13. For what purposes is labeling used?
14. What is the primary function of prices in our economy?
15. Compare and contrast the characteristics of price and nonprice competition.
16. How might buyers' perceptions of price influence pricing decisions?
17. List and briefly describe the five major pricing objectives.
18. What are the differences among markup pricing, pricing by breakeven analysis, and competition-based pricing?
19. In what way is demand-based pricing more realistic than markup pricing?
20. Why would a firm use competition-based pricing?

21. Which pricing strategies are used mainly (a) for new products, (b) by retailers, and (c) in sales to intermediaries?

Discussion Questions

1. Why is the Miata more than just a hot little car for Mazda? Can Mazda change the image of its cars as low-priced Japanese alternatives to Hondas and Toyotas?
2. Why was low price a prime consideration in producing the Miata sports car?
3. Is it a good marketing strategy to produce just three colors—red, white, and blue?
4. Why is it important to understand how products are classified?
5. What factors might determine how long a product remains in each stage of the product life cycle? What can a firm do to prolong each stage?
6. Some firms do not delete products until they become financially threatening. What problems may arise if this practice is used?
7. Which steps in the evolution of new products are most important? Which are least important?
8. Do branding, packaging, and labeling really benefit consumers? Explain.
9. To what extent can a firm control its prices in our market economy? What factors limit such control?
10. Under what conditions would a firm be most likely to use nonprice competition?
11. Can a firm have more than one pricing objective? Can it use more than one of the pricing methods discussed in this chapter? Explain.
12. What are the major problems with using price skimming?
13. What is an "effective" price?

Exercises

1. Suppose you have an idea for a new game called "Oligopoly." Explain how you would shepherd your idea through the product-development steps between idea generation and commercialization.
2. Develop a package for the game described in Exercise 1. Consider the package material, the package design, and the information you would include on the package.
3. As the manager of a clothing store, you have just received a shipment of new cheesecloth T-shirts. The T-shirts cost you $48 per dozen, and your usual markup is 40 percent. However, yours is the only store in town that will be carrying this fashionable product. What price will you set for the T-shirts? Why?

Case 12.1

Developing and Introducing New Products at American Express

Founded in 1850, American Express Company is today one of the world's leaders in travel and financial services. The company had 1988 revenues of $23 billion, and net income exceeded $1 billion.

One of the key reasons for its success is that the company is always developing new products and further improving the quality of service it provides. According to James D. Robinson III, chairman and chief executive officer, "We never lose sight of the fact that our success depends on listening and responding to the needs of the marketplace. We constantly remind ourselves that our goal is to deliver premium, high-quality products and services to carefully targeted segments of the market."

In 1988, the American Marketing Association named the Optima Card, a revolving credit card from American Express Company, one of the ten best new products for 1987.* Company president Louis Gerstner has been responsible for much of the firm's successful strategy and many of its products. For example, he launched the corporate and gold cards in the People's Republic of China and introduced new products and services in Canada, the United Kingdom, Europe, and the Soviet Union. He expanded the traditional green card's position beyond the travel market to include many other types of purchases. To exploit the appeal of the elitist charge card, Gerstner introduced the gold and platinum cards. Now he plans to sell merchandise to American Express cardholders.

Examination of the development and marketing of the Optima Card and other successful new products suggests some common characteristics. Innovativeness is emphasized over gimmickry; basically, the firm remains within the business it knows and new products are given almost entire devotion of time for months at a time.†

---

* The other nine winners were Certified Stainmaster Carpet by E. I. Du Pont de Nemours; Bull's-Eye Barbecue Sauce by Kraft, Inc.; O.N.E. Dry Dog Food by Ralston Purina Company; Sundance Natural Juice Sparkler by The Stroh Brewery Co.; the Acura Legend by American Honda Motor Co.; Lunch Buckets by The Dial Corp.; American Collection Cookies by Pepperidge Farms Inc.; Cherry 7Up by The Seven-Up Company; and Fab 1 Shot by Colgate-Palmolive Co.

† Based on the information from American Express Company, Annual Report, 1988, pp. 4, 6; "AMA Names 10 Best New Products of 1987," *Marketing News*, March 28, 1988, p. 1; Craig Mellow, "Successful Products of the Eighties," *Across the Board*, November 1988, p. 40; and Saul Hansell, "What's in the Card for Lou Gerstner?" *Institutional Investor*, December 1988, p. 48.

Questions

1. How does American Express Company come up with ideas for new products and services?
2. Why does American Express Company continue to develop new products and services when introducing new products is time-consuming, expensive, and risky?

Case 12.2

Airline Pricing: Boon or Bust?

The Airline Deregulation Act of 1978 has had a significant impact on the airline industry and its pricing policies. Until 1978, the Civil Aeronautics Board (CAB), a federal agency, dictated what fares airlines could charge and what routes airlines could fly. But the 1978 law changed all that. Now airlines' marketing executives make these decisions.

To compete for business, airlines developed new strategies such as frequent flier programs and discount pricing. Since 1978, discount fares have been more widely used, but the variety of restrictions on these fares has increased. As a result, customers often become disappointed and irritated when the fine print of an advertisement reveals that the "deal" is not what it appeared to be. For instance, the discount price that originally caught the customer's eye might be half the price of a ticket available only on a round-trip basis.

Although some fares increased in 1988 and 1989, average revenue per passenger for the airlines declined in real terms between 1976 and 1987. Some discount pricing came at the expense of more restrictions on tickets (not fully refundable, requiring advance purchase, or requiring a stay over a Saturday night). According to the Air Transport Association of America, about 90 percent of passengers now fly on discounted tickets at an average discount of 60 percent off the "regular" coach fare.

Critics allege, however, that the benefits of lower fares are not evenly distributed among classes of passengers. For example, fares tend to be higher on routes served by fewer carriers. In addition, business travelers often cannot meet the vigorous restrictions (such as time of day, particular weekdays, advance notice) for discount fares. Moreover, passengers who could afford to fly *before* the discount fares of deregulation must now endure more closely packed seats, a higher percentage of seats being filled, and the general increase in airport congestion. All in all, though, there is little doubt that the average passenger is better off.

Under deregulation, airlines can differentiate their products vis-à-vis fares *and* quality of service. The result has been cutbacks in meal service and other amenities, since most passengers have revealed a preference for lower fares even at the expense of lower-quality service.‡

---

‡ Based on information from Paul W. Bauer, "Airline Deregulation: Boon or Bust?" *Economic Commentary*, Federal Reserve Bank of Cleveland, May 1, 1989; Paul W. Bauer, and Thomas J. Zlatoper, "Determinants of Direct Air Fares to Cleveland: How Competitive?" *Economic Review*, Federal Reserve Bank of Cleveland, First Quarter 1989; "Airline Competition: DOT's Implementation of Airline Regulatory Authority," General Accounting Office *Report RCED-89-93*, June 28, 1989; "Airline Advertisers Take Consumers for a Ride," *NCL Bulletin*, National Consumer League, Fall 1989, p. 6; Alfred E. Kahn, "I Would Do It Again," *Regulation*, 1988, p. 2; Kenneth W. Thornicroft, "Airline Deregulation and the Airline Labor Market," *Journal of Labor Research*, Spring 1989, p. 163; and Lee J. Van Scyoc, "Effects of Airline Deregulation on Profitability," *Logistics and Transportation Review*, March 1989, p. 39.

Questions

1. Few people will purchase an airline ticket with too high a price, and a ticket with a deeply discounted fare will earn little or no profit for an airline. What is a "proper" or effective price for an airline ticket?

2. In the airline industry, marketing executives try to gain some control over price by differentiating their products. Give examples of product differentiation in the airline industry.

3. Why did the average revenue per passenger decline in real terms between 1976 and 1987?

4. Is the practice of discount pricing fair to business travelers? Why or why not?

WHOLESALING, RETAILING, AND PHYSICAL DISTRIBUTION

1 Know the various channels of distribution that are used for consumer and industrial products

2 Understand the concept of market coverage

3 Know what a vertical marketing system is and identify the types of vertical marketing systems

4 Recognize the need for wholesalers

5 Become aware of the major types of wholesalers and describe the services they perform for retailers and manufacturers

6 Understand the differences among the major types of retail outlets

7 Comprehend the wheel of retailing hypothesis

8 Know the categories of shopping centers and identify the factors that determine how shopping centers are classified

9 Recognize the five most important physical distribution activities

CHAPTER PREVIEW

First in this chapter we examine various channels of distribution—the company-to-company paths that products follow as they move from producer to ultimate user. Then we discuss wholesalers and retailers, two important groups of intermediaries operating within these channels. Next, we examine the types of shopping centers. Finally, we explore the physical distribution function and the major modes of transportation that are used to move goods.

Wal-Mart: Simply a Phenomenon

A $1,000 investment in Wal-Mart stock in 1970 is worth half a million dollars today. What's more, the company's annual return to investors from 1977 to 1987 was 46 percent. Net profit increased almost 35 percent to $761 million in 1988, and net sales were a record $25.8 billion in 1989. It's no wonder that Wal-Mart Stores, Inc. is the darling of Wall Street. According to financial analyst Margaret Gilliam, Wal-Mart is quite likely the finest-managed company in America.[1]

Today, Wal-Mart operates 1,300 stores. Yet, it wasn't always the successful discount-store chain that you now see in twenty-five states. Back in 1962, Sam Walton—the founder of Wal-Mart—opened his first store in the small town of Rogers, Arkansas, and then a second store in nearby Harrison, Arkansas. According to one of Sam's friends, it was the worst retail store he had ever seen. So how did Wal-Mart get to be the giant discount-store operation that it is today?

Most people will tell you the secret of Wal-Mart's success can be traced to Sam Walton. He has motivated more than 183,000 people to work as partners in the Wal-Mart organization. Employees are called "associates," a term coined by Walton to reflect the value he places on workers. Words like *we* and *our* are used constantly by both managers and associates to describe their goals and objectives. Even top management works hard at Wal-Mart. Most executives spend Monday through Thursday visiting individual stores. Then they return to the home office in Bentonville, Arkansas. On Friday and Saturday, these same managers meet to develop marketing strategies to improve the firm's overall performance.

Another reason for Wal-Mart's success can be traced to its buying policies. The company buys most inventory items directly from the manufacturers. This policy enables Wal-Mart to *sell* each item below the wholesale price that local merchants *pay* for the merchandise. Simply put, Wal-mart uses its buying power more forcefully than any other firm in America.

New distribution technology developed by Wal-Mart has made the firm even more profitable. The company has fourteen warehouses, most within a day's drive of the stores they serve. These huge "distribution centers" are automated and stock over 9,000 different items. In many cases, the warehouses receive merchandise that has been electronically ordered from vendors via direct computer/telephone hookups between Wal-Mart's and the vendors' computers. The warehouses use optical scanning devices and bar code labels to sort and store merchandise.

Because of its well-managed physical distribution system, motivated employees, and shrewd buying practices, the small company that started in the foothills of the Ozarks is now the third-largest retailer in the United States, behind Sears and K mart. And marketing experts are predicting that it will surpass both of these competitors to become the largest American retailer.[2]

More than two million firms in the United States help move products from producers to consumers. Of all marketers, retail firms that sell directly to consumers are the most visible. Store chains like Sears, K mart, and Wal-Mart operate retail outlets where consumers make purchases. Other retailers, like Avon Products and Electrolux, send their salespeople to the homes of customers. Still others, like Lands' End and L. L. Bean, sell through catalogs or through both catalogs and stores.

In addition, there are more than half a million wholesaling intermediaries, or firms that sell merchandise to other firms. Most consumers know little about these firms, which work "behind the scenes" and rarely sell directly to consumers.

These and other intermediaries are concerned with the transfer of both products and ownership. They thus help create the time, place, and possession utility that are so important in marketing. As we will see, they also perform a number of services for their suppliers and their customers.

Before we look closely at some of these important intermediaries, we should get an idea of the various channels—some simple, some complex—by which products are distributed to consumers.

Channels of Distribution

channel of distribution (or **marketing channel**) *a sequence of marketing organizations that directs a product from the producer to the ultimate user*

A **channel of distribution,** or **marketing channel,** is a sequence of marketing organizations that directs a product from the producer to the ultimate user. Every marketing channel begins with the producer and ends with either the consumer or the industrial user.

middleman (or **marketing intermediary**) *a marketing organization that links a producer and user within a marketing channel*

A marketing organization that links a producer and user within a marketing channel is called a **middleman,** or **marketing intermediary.** For the most part, middlemen are concerned with the transfer of *ownership* of products. A **merchant middleman** (or, more simply, a *merchant*) is a middleman that actually takes title to products by buying them. A **functional middleman,** on the other hand, helps in the transfer of ownership of products but does not take title to the products.

merchant middleman *a middleman that actually takes title to products by buying them*

functional middleman *a middleman that helps in the transfer of ownership of products but does not take title to the products*

Major Marketing Channels

Different channels of distribution are generally used to move industrial and consumer products. The six most commonly used channels are illustrated in Figure 13.1

Channels for Consumer Products

Learning Objective 1
Know the various channels of distribution that are used for consumer and industrial products

Producer to Consumer This channel, which is often called the *direct channel,* includes no marketing intermediaries. Practically all services, but very few consumer goods, are distributed through the direct channel. However, the sellers of some consumer goods, such as Avon Products, Mary Kay Cosmetics, and Fuller Brush, prefer to sell directly to consumers.

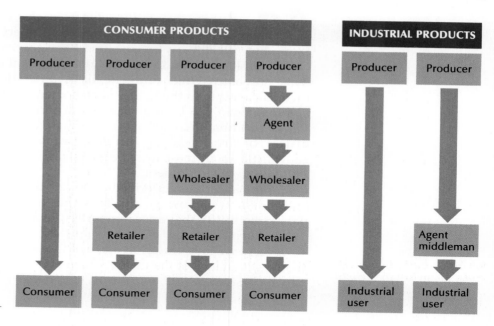

FIGURE 13.1
Distribution Channels
Producers use various channels to distribute their products.

Producers sell directly to consumers for several reasons. They can control the price of their products. They don't have to pay (through discounts) for the services of intermediaries. And they can maintain closer ties with consumers.

retailer *a middleman that buys from producers or other middlemen and sells to consumers*

Producer to Retailer to Consumer A **retailer** is a middleman that buys from producers or other middlemen and sells to consumers. Producers sell directly to retailers when retailers can buy in large quantities. This channel is most often used for products that are bulky, such as furniture and automobiles, for which additional handling would increase selling costs. It is also the usual channel for perishable products, such as fruits and vegetables, and for high-fashion products that must reach the consumer in the shortest possible time.

Producer to Wholesaler to Retailer to Consumer This indirect channel is known as the *traditional channel*, because most consumer goods (especially convenience goods) are routed through wholesalers to retailers. A **wholesaler** is a middleman that sells products to other firms. These firms may be retailers, industrial users, or other wholesalers. A producer uses wholesalers when its products are carried by so many retailers that the producer cannot deal with all of them.

wholesaler *a middleman that sells products to other firms*

Producer to Agent to Wholesaler to Retailer to Consumer This channel is used for products that are sold through thousands of outlets to millions of consumers. Often, these products are inexpensive, frequently purchased items. For example, millions of consumers buy candy bars, which are sold through numerous outlets. Some candy bars are sold through agents to

Jon Hagenbush, a wholesale route supervisor for Reiter Dairy, headquartered in Akron, Ohio, delivers milk and other dairy products to retailers who then sell Reiter's products to individual consumers.

wholesalers who, in turn, supply them to retail stores and vending machines. Agents—marketing intermediaries that facilitate exchanges—are discussed later in the chapter.

Multiple Channels for Consumer Goods   Often a manufacturer uses different distribution channels to reach different market segments. A manufacturer uses multiple channels, for example, when the same product is sold to consumers and industrial users. Multiple channels are also used to increase sales or to capture a larger share of the market. With the goal of selling as much merchandise as possible, both Firestone Tire & Rubber Co. and The Goodyear Tire & Rubber Company market their tires through their own retail outlets as well as through independent service stations and department stores.

Channels for Industrial Products

Producers of industrial products generally tend to use short channels. We will outline the two that are most commonly used.

Producer to Industrial User   In this direct channel, the manufacturer's own sales force sells directly to industrial users. Heavy machinery, large computers, and major equipment are usually distributed in this way. The very short channel allows the producer to provide customers with expert and timely services, such as delivery, machinery installation, and repairs.

Manufacturer to Agent Middleman to Industrial User   This channel is employed by manufacturers to distribute such items as operating supplies, accessory equipment, small tools, and standardized parts. The agent is an independent intermediary between the producer and the user. Generally, agents represent sellers. They receive compensation in the form of a *commission*, which is a percentage of sales revenue.

Market Coverage

How does a producer decide which distribution channels (and which particular intermediaries) to use? Like every other marketing decision, this one should be based on all relevant factors. These include the firm's production capability and marketing resources, the target market and buying patterns of potential customers, and the product itself. After evaluating these factors, the producer can choose a particular *intensity of market coverage*. Then the producer selects channels and intermediaries to implement that coverage (see Figure 13.2).

intensive distribution *the use of all available outlets for a product*

Intensive distribution is the use of all available outlets for a product. The producer that wants to give its product the widest possible exposure in the marketplace chooses intensive distribution. The manufacturer saturates the market by selling to any intermediary of good financial standing that is willing to stock and sell the product. For the consumer, intensive distribution means being able to shop at a nearby store and spending minimum time to find the product in the store. Many convenience goods, including candy, gum, and cigarettes, are distributed intensively.

selective distribution *the use of only a portion or percentage of the available outlets for a product in each geographic area*

Selective distribution is the use of only a portion or percentage of the available outlets for a product in each geographic area. Manufacturers of goods such as furniture, major electrical appliances, and clothing typically prefer selective distribution. Franchisers also use selective distribution in

FIGURE 13.2
Market Coverage
The number of outlets a producer chooses for a product depends on the type of product. Batteries, for example, are distributed intensively.

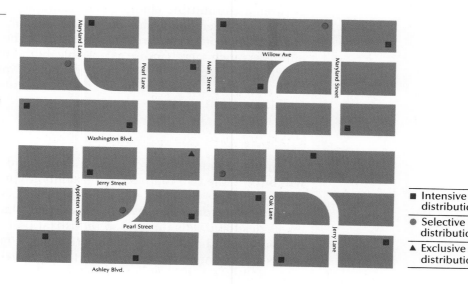

granting franchises for the sale of their goods and services in a specific geographic area.

Exclusive distribution is the use of only a single retail outlet for a product in each geographic area. Exclusive distribution is usually limited to very prestigious products. It is appropriate, for instance, for specialty goods such as expensive pianos, fine china, and automobiles.

exclusive distribution *the use of only a single retail outlet for a product in each geographic area*

Vertical Marketing Systems

Vertical channel integration occurs when two or more stages of a distribution channel are combined and managed by one firm. A **vertical marketing system (VMS)** is a centrally managed distribution channel resulting from vertical channel integration. This merging eliminates the need for certain intermediaries. One member of a marketing channel may assume the responsibilities of another member, or it may actually purchase the operations of that member. For example, a large-volume discount retailer that ships and warehouses its own stock directly from manufacturers does not need a wholesaler. Total vertical integration occurs when a single management controls all operations from production to final sale. Oil companies that own wells, transportation facilities, refineries, terminals, and service stations exemplify total vertical integration.

vertical channel integration *the combining of two or more stages of a distribution channel under a single firm's management*

vertical marketing system (VMS) *a centrally managed distribution channel resulting from vertical channel integration*

There are three types of VMSs: administered, contractual, and corporate. In an *administered VMS*, one of the channel members dominates the other members, perhaps because of its large size. Under its influence, the channel members collaborate on production and distribution. A powerful manufacturer, such as Procter & Gamble, receives a great deal of cooperation from intermediaries that carry its brands. Although the goals of the entire system are considered when decisions are made, control rests with individual channel members, as in conventional marketing channels. Under a *contractual VMS*, cooperative arrangements and the rights and obligations of channel members are defined by contracts or other legal measures. In a *corporate VMS*, actual ownership is the vehicle by which production and distribution are joined. A grocery-store chain, for example, may obtain its bread products from several of its own bakeries. Most vertical marketing systems are organized to improve distribution by combining individual operations.

Learning Objective 3
Know what a vertical marketing system is and identify the types of vertical marketing systems

Marketing Intermediaries: Wholesalers

Wholesalers may be the most misunderstood of marketing intermediaries. Producers sometimes try to eliminate them from distribution channels by dealing directly with retailers or consumers. Yet wholesalers provide a variety of essential marketing services. It may be true that wholesalers themselves can be eliminated, but their functions cannot. These functions *must* be performed by some organization within the distribution channel.

Justifications for Marketing Intermediaries

Learning Objective 4
Recognize the need for
wholesalers

The press, consumers, public officials, and other marketers often charge wholesalers, at least in principle, with inefficiency and parasitism. Consumers in particular feel strongly that the distribution channel should be made as short as possible. They assume that the fewer the intermediaries in a distribution channel, the lower the price.

Those who believe that the elimination of wholesalers would bring about lower prices, however, do not recognize that the services wholesalers perform would still be needed. Those services would simply be provided by other means, and consumers would still bear the costs. Moreover, all manufacturers would have to keep extensive records and employ enough personnel to deal with a multitude of retailers individually. Even with direct distribution, products might be considerably more expensive because prices would reflect the costs of producers' inefficiency. Figure 13.3 shows that sixteen contacts could result from the efforts of four buyers purchasing the products of four producers. With the assistance of an intermediary, only eight contacts would be necessary.

To illustrate further the useful role of wholesalers in the marketing system, assume that all wholesalers in the candy industry were abolished. With more than 1.3 million retail businesses to contact, candy manufacturers could be making as many as a million sales calls or more just to maintain the present level of product visibility. Hershey Foods Corp., for example, would have to set up warehouses all over the country, organize a fleet of trucks, purchase and maintain thousands of vending machines, and deliver all of its own candy. Sales and distribution costs for candy would soar. Candy producers would be contacting and shipping products to thousands of small businesses, instead of to a few food brokers, large retailers, and merchant wholesalers. The high costs of this inefficiency

FIGURE 13.3
Efficiency Provided by an Intermediary
The services of an intermediary reduce the number of contacts, or exchanges, between producers and buyers, thereby increasing efficiency. (Source: Adapted from William M. Pride and O. C. Ferrell, Marketing: Concepts and Strategies, 6/e. Copyright © 1989 by Houghton Mifflin Company. Used by permission.)

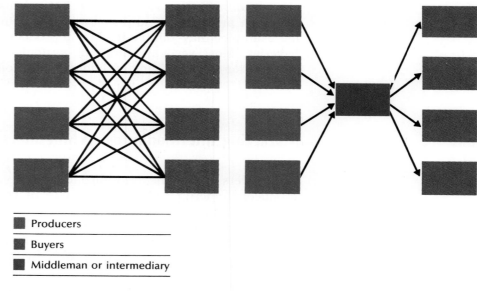

■ Producers

■ Buyers

■ Middleman or intermediary

would be passed on to consumers. Candy bars would be more expensive and perhaps in short supply.

Wholesalers are more efficient and economical not only for manufacturers but also for consumers. Because their elimination is proposed from both ends of the marketing channel, however, wholesalers should perform only those functions that are genuinely in demand. To stay in business, wholesalers should also take care to be more productive and provide better services than other channel members.

Wholesalers' Services to Retailers

Wholesalers help retailers by buying in large quantities and then selling to retailers in smaller quantities and by delivering goods to retailers. They also stock—in one place—the variety of goods that retailers would otherwise have to buy from many producers. And wholesalers provide assistance in three other vital areas: promotion, market information, and financial help.

Promotion   Most wholesalers help promote the products they sell to retailers. These services are usually either free or performed at cost. Some wholesalers are major sources of display materials designed to stimulate "impulse buying." They may also help retailers build effective window, counter, and bin displays; and they may even donate their own employees to work on the retail sales floor during special promotions.

Market Information   Wholesalers are a constant source of market information. Wholesalers have numerous contacts with local businesses and distant suppliers. In the course of these dealings, they accumulate information about consumer demand, prices, supply conditions, new developments within the trade, and even industry personnel. Most of this information is relayed to retailers informally, through the wholesaler's sales force. However, some wholesalers distribute bulletins or newsletters to their customers as well.

Information regarding industry sales and competitive prices is especially important to all firms. Dealing with a number of suppliers and many retailers, a wholesaler is a natural "clearinghouse" for such information. And most wholesalers are willing to pass it on to their customers.

Financial Aid   Most wholesalers provide a type of financial aid that retailers often take for granted. By making prompt and frequent deliveries, wholesalers enable retailers to keep their own inventory investments small in relation to sales. Such indirect financial aid reduces the amount of operating capital that retailers need.

In some trades, wholesalers extend direct financial assistance through long-term loans. Most wholesalers also provide help through delayed billing, giving customers thirty to sixty days *after delivery* to pay for merchandise. Wholesalers of seasonal merchandise may offer even longer delays. For example, a wholesaler of lawn and garden supplies may deliver seed to retailers in January but not bill them for it until May.

BUSINESS JOURNAL

The Top Three Food Wholesalers

Beginning marketing students often think that wholesalers are small and relatively unimportant. Before adopting those two attitudes, take a look at the following financial data for the top three food wholesalers in the United States.

Company	Sales (in billions)	Earnings (in millions)
Fleming Companies, Inc.	$10.5	$ 65.4
Super Valu Stores, Inc.	10.1	134.1
Wetterau Incorporated	5.0	44.0

Financial data are for the 1988 fiscal year, as reported in *Super Market News*, March 13, 1989, p. 13. Reprinted by permission.

Each of the companies listed had sales in excess of $5 billion. Also, profits ranged from $44 million to more than $134 million. Though the financial data for each firm are impressive, the numbers illustrate a basic principle: Wholesalers, large or small, cannot succeed unless they meet the needs of their customers; they must provide a service that justifies their existence.

For example, Fleming Companies, based in Oklahoma City, provides a complete line of merchandise, including both national and private-label brands, to more than 5,200 grocery retailers in thirty-six states. The company also serves as a major food-service supplier to more than 20,000 restaurants. If it were not for Fleming's distribution network, the manufacturers of the products would have to contact each of the 5,200 retailers and 20,000 restaurants.

As further evidence of Fleming's commitment to service, the company provides more than 100 services to its customers. According to company chairman Richard Harrison, all of the firm's services are designed to make the retailer more competitive and more capable of competing in the decade ahead.

Fleming has long assisted its retail buyers with store planning and merchandising. Today, such retailer support services are being expanded to include computerized shelf tags and an automated reordering system. The new shelf-tag system is completely computerized, including the shelf tag itself, which has an LED display. The shelf tag not only provides consumers with product information (price, size, and so on), but it also enables the retailer to make price changes from a single control point. This new system eliminates the need for a stock clerk to physically change the price of each item by hand. In short, the clerk goes to the shelf only to stock it.

In the near future, it will also be possible to initiate Fleming's automated reordering system. Here's how the system works: First, all merchandise is rung up at the check-out counter. Next, the computerized cash register reduces inventory in the main computer file. Finally, when inventory levels reach a predetermined level, the computer reorders the needed merchandise, and it is shipped from one of Fleming's thirty-six distribution centers without the involvement of an order clerk.

Based on information from "Unsung Giant," *Forbes*, January 9, 1989, p. 142; "Fleming Profit Declines 32%," *Supermarket News*, February 13, 1989, p. 40; "Fleming Companies," *Wall Street Transcript*, April 17, 1989, pp. 93, 352; Joel Elson, "Fleming Philadelphia Division Sets Three-Year Growth Plan," *Supermarket News*, March 27, 1989, p. 2; and "Fleming Companies, Inc.," *Moody's Handbook of Common Stocks*, Summer 1989.

Wholesalers' Services to Manufacturers

Some of the services that wholesalers perform for producers are similar to those provided to retailers. Others are quite different.

Providing an Instant Sales Force   A wholesaler provides its producers with an instant sales force so that producers' sales representatives need not call on retailers. This can result in large savings for producers. For example, Procter & Gamble and General Foods Corp. would have to spend millions of dollars each year to field a sales force that could call on all the retailers that sell their numerous products. Instead, these producers rely on wholesalers to sell and distribute their products to retailers.

Reducing Inventory Costs   Wholesalers purchase goods in sizable quantities from manufacturers and store these goods for resale. By doing so, they reduce the amount of finished goods inventory that producers must hold and, thereby, the cost of carrying inventories.

Assuming Credit Risks   When producers sell through wholesalers, it is the wholesalers who extend credit to retailers, make collections from retailers, and assume the risks of nonpayment. These services reduce the producers' cost of extending credit to customers and the resulting bad debt expense.

Furnishing Market Information   Just as they do for retailers, wholesalers supply market information to the producers they service. Valuable information accumulated by wholesalers may concern consumer demand, the producers' competition, and buying trends.

Types of Wholesalers

Learning Objective 5
Become aware of the major
types of wholesalers and
describe the services they
perform for retailers and
manufacturers

Wholesalers generally fall into three categories: merchant wholesalers; commission merchants, agents, and brokers; and manufacturers, sales branches and offices. Of these, merchant wholesalers constitute the largest portion. They account for about 58 percent of sales, three out of every four employees, and four out of every five establishments.[3]

merchant wholesaler   *a middleman that purchases goods in large quantities and then sells them to other wholesalers or retailers and to institutional, farm, government, professional, or industrial users*

Merchant Wholesalers   A **merchant wholesaler** is a middleman that purchases goods in large quantities and then sells them to other wholesalers or retailers and to institutional, farm, government, professional, or industrial users. Merchant wholesalers usually operate one or more warehouses where they receive, take title to, and store goods. These wholesalers are sometimes called *distributors* or *jobbers*.

Most merchant wholesalers are businesses composed of salespeople, order takers, receiving and shipping clerks, inventory managers, and office personnel. The successful merchant wholesaler must analyze available products and market needs. It must be able to adapt the type, variety, and quality of the products it stocks to changing market conditions.

full-service wholesaler   *a middleman that performs the entire range of wholesaler functions*

Merchant wholesalers may be classified as full-service or limited-service wholesalers, depending on the number of services they provide. A **full-service wholesaler** performs the entire range of wholesaler functions described earlier in this section. These functions include delivering goods, supplying warehousing, arranging for credit, supporting promotional activities, and providing general customer assistance.

general merchandise wholesaler   *a middleman that deals in a wide variety of products*

Under this broad heading are the general merchandise wholesaler, limited-line wholesaler, and specialty-line wholesaler. A **general merchandise wholesaler** deals in a wide variety of products, such as drugs, hardware, nonperishable foods, cosmetics, detergents, and tobacco. A

limited-line wholesaler
a middleman that stocks only a few product lines

specialty-line wholesaler
a middleman that carries a select group of products within a single line

limited-service wholesaler
a middleman that assumes responsibility for a few wholesale services only

commission merchant   *a middleman that carries merchandise and negotiates sales for manufacturers but does not take title to the goods it sells*

agent   *a middleman that facilitates exchanges, represents a buyer or a seller, and often is hired permanently on a commission basis*

broker   *a middleman that specializes in a particular commodity, represents either a buyer or a seller, and is likely to be hired on a temporary basis*

manufacturer's sales branch
essentially a merchant wholesaler that is owned by a manufacturer

manufacturer's sales office
essentially a sales agent that is owned by a manufacturer

limited-line wholesaler stocks only a few product lines, in groceries, lighting fixtures, or drilling equipment, for example. A **specialty-line wholesaler** carries a select group of products within a single line. Food delicacies such as shellfish represent the kind of product handled by this wholesaler.

In contrast to a full-service wholesaler, a **limited-service wholesaler** assumes responsibility for a few wholesale services only. Other marketing tasks are left to the manufacturer or the customer. This category includes cash-and-carry wholesalers, truck wholesalers, rack jobbers, drop shippers, and mail-order wholesalers.

Commission Merchants, Agents, and Brokers   A **commission merchant** usually carries merchandise and negotiates sales for manufacturers, but it does not take title to the goods it sells. In most cases, commission merchants have the power to set the prices and terms of sales. After a sale is made, they either arrange for delivery or provide transportation services. They are generally paid commissions by the manufacturers or producers they represent.

An **agent** is a middleman that facilitates exchanges, represents a buyer or a seller, and often is hired permanently on a commission basis. When agents represent producers, they are known as *sales agents* or *manufacturer's agents*. As long as the products represented do not compete, a sales agent may represent one or several manufacturers on a commission basis. The agent solicits orders for the manufacturers within a specific territory. As a rule, the manufacturers ship the merchandise and bill the customers directly. The manufacturers also set the prices and other conditions of the sales. What do the manufacturers gain by using a sales agent? The sales agent provides immediate entry into a territory, regular calls on customers, selling experience, and a known, predetermined selling expense (a commission that is a percentage of sales revenue).

A **broker** is a middleman that specializes in a particular commodity, represents either a buyer *or* a seller, and is likely to be hired on a temporary basis. However, food brokers, which sell grocery products to resellers, generally have long-term relationships with their clients. Brokers may perform only the selling function or both buying and selling, using established contacts or special knowledge of their field. They are generally paid commissions by the sellers.

Manufacturers' Sales Branches and Offices   A **manufacturer's sales branch** is, in essence, a merchant wholesaler that is owned by a manufacturer. Sales branches carry stock, extend credit, deliver goods, and offer help in promoting products. Their customers are retailers, other wholesalers, and industrial purchasers.

Because sales branches are owned by producers, they stock primarily the goods manufactured by their own firms. Selling policies and terms are usually established centrally and then transmitted to branch managers for implementation.

A **manufacturer's sales office** is essentially a sales agent that is owned by a manufacturer. Sales offices may sell goods manufactured by their own firms and also certain products of other manufacturers that complement their own product lines. For example, Hiram Walker & Sons imports wine from Spain to increase the number of products that its sales offices can offer to wholesalers.

Marketing Intermediaries: Retailers

Retailers are the final link between producers and consumers. Retailers may buy from either wholesalers or producers. They sell not only goods but also such services as repairs, haircuts, and tailoring. Some retailers sell both. Sears, Roebuck sells consumer goods and financial services, and many retail outlets that sell television sets also provide repair services.

Learning Objective 6
Understand the differences among the major types of retail outlets

Of the approximately more than 1.3 million retail firms in the United States, about 18 percent have annual sales of less than $25,000. On the other hand, there are giants that realize well over $1 million per day in sales revenue. Table 13.1 lists the twenty largest retail firms, the cities

TABLE 13.1   *The Twenty Largest Retail Firms in the United States*

Rank		Company	Sales	Profits
1989	1988		($ millions)	($ millions)
1	1	Sears Roebuck (Chicago)	$53,912.9	$1,508.5
2	2	K mart (Troy, Mich.)	29,557.0	323.0
3	3	Wal-Mart Stores (Bentonville, Ark.)	25,921.8	1,075.9
4	5	American Stores (Irvine, Cal.)	22,004.2	118.1
5	4	Kroger (Cincinnati)	19,087.8	(72.7)
6	6	J.C. Penney (Dallas)	16,405.0	802.0
7	7	Safeway Stores (Oakland)	14,324.6	2.5
8	8	Dayton Hudson (Minneapolis)	13,644.7	410.5
9	9	May Department Stores (St. Louis)	12,043.0	498.0
10	10	Great Atlantic & Pacific Tea (Montvale, N.J.)	10,072.7	127.6
11	11	Winn-Dixie Stores (Jacksonville, Fla.)	9,151.1	134.5
12	12	Woolworth (New York)	8,820.0	329.0
13	13	Southland (Dallas)	8,421.3	(1,306.9)
14	15	Melville (Harrison, N.Y.)	7,554.0	398.1
15	16	Albertson's (Boise, Idaho)	7,422.7	196.6
16	17	R. H. Macy (New York)	6,974.1	(53.7)
17	—	Supermarkets General Hold. (Woodbridge, N.J.)	6,298.7	(76.5)
18	18	McDonald's (Oak Brook, Ill.)	6,142.0	727.0
19	20	Walgreen (Deerfield, Ill.)	5,395.5	154.2
20	21	Publix Super Markets (Lakeland, Fla.)	5,386.2	128.5

Source: Fortune 500: © 1990 The Time Magazine Company. All rights reserved.

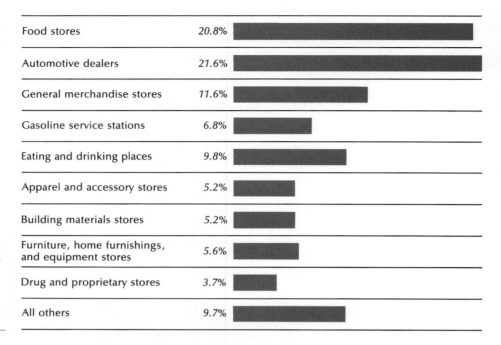

Food stores	20.8%	
Automotive dealers	21.6%	
General merchandise stores	11.6%	
Gasoline service stations	6.8%	
Eating and drinking places	9.8%	
Apparel and accessory stores	5.2%	
Building materials stores	5.2%	
Furniture, home furnishings, and equipment stores	5.6%	
Drug and proprietary stores	3.7%	
All others	9.7%	

FIGURE 13.4
Retail Sales Categorized by Merchandise Type
The numbers in this graph represent the percent of total sales for each merchandise type. [Source: Statistical Abstract of the United States, 1989, U.S. Bureau of the Census, p. 754.]

where their headquarters are located, and their approximate sales revenues, and yearly profits. Figure 13.4 shows retail sales categorized by major merchandise type and the percent of total sales for each type.

Classes of In-Store Retailers

One way to classify retailers is by ownership—in particular, by the number of stores owned and operated by the firm. An **independent retailer** is a firm that operates only one retail outlet. Approximately 79 percent of retailers are independent, and they account for about 48 percent of all retail sales.[4] One-store operators, like all small businesses, generally provide personal service and convenient locations.

A **chain retailer** is a firm that operates more than one retail outlet. By adding outlets, chain retailers attempt to reach new geographic markets. As sales increase, chains may buy in larger quantities and thus take advantage of quantity discounts. They also wield more power in their dealings with suppliers. About 21 percent of retailers operate chains, and they account for about 52 percent of all retail sales revenue.[5]

A better way to classify in-store retailers is by type of store. Each of the following types of stores may be owned independently or by a chain.

Department Stores These are large retail establishments consisting of several parts, or departments, that sell a wide assortment of products. According to the U.S. Bureau of the Census, a **department store** is a retail store that (1) employs twenty-five or more persons and (2) sells at least home furnishings, appliances, family apparel, and household linens and dry goods, each in a different part of the store. Macy's in New York,

independent retailer *a firm that operates only one retail outlet*

chain retailer *a firm that operates more than one retail outlet*

department store *a retail store that (1) employs twenty-five or more persons and (2) sells at least home furnishings, appliances, family apparel, and household linens and dry goods, each in a different part of the store*

Harrods in London, and Au Printemps in Paris are outstanding examples of large, inner-city department stores. Sears and J.C. Penney are two other department stores.

Department stores are distinctly service-oriented. Along with the goods they sell, they provide credit, delivery, personal assistance, liberal return policies, and a pleasant atmosphere. They are, for the most part, shopping stores. That is, consumers compare merchandise, price, quality, and service in competing department stores before they buy.

discount store   *a self-service, general-merchandise outlet that sells goods at lower than usual prices*

Discount Stores   A **discount store** is a self-service, general-merchandise outlet that sells goods at prices that are lower than usual. These stores can offer lower prices by operating on lower markups; locating their retail showrooms in large, low-rent areas; and offering minimal customer services. To keep prices low, discount stores operate on the basic principle of high turnover of such items as appliances, toys, clothing, automotive products, and sports equipment. To attract customers, many discount stores also offer some food items at low prices. Popular discount stores include K mart, Wal-Mart, Dollar General, and Target.

As competition among discount stores has increased, some discounters have improved their services, store environments, and locations. As a consequence, many of the better-known discount stores have assumed the characteristics of department stores. This has boosted their prices and blurred the distinction between some discount stores and department stores.[6]

catalog discount showroom   *a retail outlet that displays well-known brands and sells them at discount prices through catalog sales within the store*

Catalog Discount Showrooms   A **catalog discount showroom** is a retail outlet that displays well-known brands and sells them at discount prices through catalog sales within the store. Colorful catalogs are available in

When the new cologne Uninhibited by Cher was introduced, department stores like Macy's in New York, Marshall Field's in Chicago, and Foley's in Houston reported huge crowds, excitement, and enormous sales of the new fragrance.

BUSINESS JOURNAL ▰

Attention, K mart Shoppers

The next time you walk into K mart, take a look at the type of merchandise that the store is selling. The nation's second largest retailer—with over 2,000 discount stores in the United States and Canada—is now offering upscale merchandise. It's all part of a master plan developed by K mart's chairman, Joseph Antonini, to change the discounter's image.

AN UPSCALE IMAGE FOR K MART

Antonini believes K mart stores must upgrade their image for the 1990s in order to attract more customers. The objective is simple: Go upscale and carry better merchandise, but maintain the firm's base of loyal customers. To accomplish this objective, K mart has recruited a number of celebrities to either design or promote the firm's products. So far, big name celebrities include actress Jaclyn Smith, home decorator Martha Stewart, golfer Fuzzy Zoeller, and race car driver Mario Andretti.

According to K mart officials, their strategy is working and is one reason why the company's sales have increased in the last few years. In fact, sales growth in some divisions has exceeded the company's expectations. For example, Jaclyn Smith's line of women's clothing and her involvement in the company's advertising campaign have made K mart's apparel division the firm's fastest growing segment. Sales of household goods (linens, dishes, glasses, and flatware) have also increased since Martha Stewart began designing merchandise for K mart stores.

In addition to increased advertising and big-name endorsements by celebrities, K mart is planning to spend $1.3 billion to enlarge and remodel 700 of the firm's oldest retail outlets. Based on the firm's success in a prototype store located in suburban Detroit, remodeled stores will have wider aisles, bolder displays, and taller, deeper shelves. Again, the objective is simple: Make K mart a convenient and attractive place to shop.

IMPROVED DISTRIBUTION OF PRODUCTS

In order to keep their core customers and compete against archrival Wal-Mart, K mart lowered prices for 8,000 items in late 1989. While the price reductions increased the firm's sales, they also created a major problem. K mart's distribution system could not keep up with demand for high-volume products. To solve this problem, K mart spent over $1 billion to install a state-of-the-art computer system to monitor sales and inventory levels at individual stores. The system automatically reorders merchandise when inventory levels drop to predetermined points. According to K mart officials, it made no sense to change the company's image and carry more upscale merchandise if individual stores didn't have merchandise to sell.

Based on information from David Woodruff, "Will K mart Ever Be a Silk Purse?," *Business Week*, January 22, 1990, p. 46; Faye Rice, "Why K mart Has Stalled," *Fortune*, October 9, 1989, p. 79; Gene G. Marcial, "Attention K mart Shoppers," *Business Week*, July 10, 1989, p. 80; Patricia Sellers, "Attention K mart Shoppers," *Fortune*, January 2, 1989, p. 41; Judith H. Dobrzynski, "The CEO on the Move," *Business Week*, October 21, 1988, p. 49+; and "K mart vs. the Schlock Factor," *Fortune*, March 14, 1988, p. 9.

---

the showroom (and sometimes by mail). The customer selects the merchandise, either from the catalog or from the showroom display. Then the customer fills out an order form provided by the store and hands the form to a clerk. The clerk retrieves the merchandise from a room that is located away from the selling area and serves as a warehouse. Well-known national and regional catalog showrooms include Service Merchandise, Consumers Distributing, W. Bell, and Best Products.

specialty store *a retail outlet that sells a single category of merchandise*

Specialty Stores   A specialty store is a retail outlet that sells a single category of merchandise. Specialty stores may sell shoes, men's or women's clothing, baked goods, children's wear, photo equipment, flowers, or books. Most specialty stores cater to local markets, remain small, and are individually owned. However, there are a few large specialty chains, such as Radio Shack, Toys "Я" Us, and Hickory Farms of Ohio. Regardless of their size, all specialty stores offer specialized knowledge and service to their customers.

supermarket *a large self-service store that sells primarily food and household products*

Supermarkets   A **supermarket** is a large self-service store that sells primarily food and household products. It stocks canned, fresh, frozen, and processed foods, paper products, and cleaning products. Supermarkets may also sell such items as housewares, toiletries, toys and games, drugs, stationery, books and magazines, plants and flowers, and small items of clothing.

Supermarkets are large-scale operations that emphasize low prices and one-stop shopping for household needs. The first self-service food market opened fifty years ago. It grossed only $5,000 per week, with an average sale of just $1.31.[7] Today, a supermarket has minimum annual sales of at least $2 million. Current top-ranking supermarkets include Safeway, Kroger, Winn-Dixie, Jewel, Lucky, and A&P.

superstore *a large retail store that carries not only food and nonfood products ordinarily found in supermarkets but also additional product lines*

Superstores   A **superstore** is a large retail store that carries not only food and nonfood products ordinarily found in traditional supermarkets but also additional product lines that include housewares, hardware, small appliances, clothing, personal-care products, garden products, and automotive merchandise. Superstores also provide a number of services to entice customers. Typical services include automotive repair, snack bars/restaurants, film developing, and limited banking. Although the superstore concept originated in Europe, it is relatively new to the United States. For example, Sam Walton established Dallas-based Hypermart USA in 1987 to concentrate on high volume, low prices, and one-stop shopping for most consumer merchandise. Traditional supermarkets are finding it difficult to compete with these larger, more profitable superstores.

convenience store *a small food store that sells a limited variety of products but remains open well beyond the normal business hours*

Convenience Stores   A **convenience store** is a small food store that sells a limited variety of products but remains open well beyond the normal business hours. Almost 70 percent of the people who use convenience stores live within a mile of the store. Convenience stores are popular and are growing in number. White Hen Pantry, 7-Eleven, and Open Pantry stores, for example, are found in most areas, as are independent convenience stores. The limited stock that these stores offer and the high prices they must charge to stay open for long hours, seven days a week, keep them from becoming a threat to supermarkets.

warehouse store *a minimal-service retail food outlet*

Warehouse Stores   A **warehouse store** is a minimal-service retail food outlet. These stores appeared in the early 1970s to test discount pricing as a marketing strategy in food retailing. Escalating grocery prices in the 1970s and early 1980s made these low-price outlets extremely appealing. Many were successful.

In warehouse stores, such as Mrs. Clark's Foods and Pick 'N Save, the merchandise is left in packing cases on pallets on the floor. Prices are displayed on the cases but are not individually marked on the items. Customers may be expected to provide the paper bags or cartons in which to take their purchases home. The stores themselves are located in low-rent buildings and have large inventories on the premises.

Kinds of Nonstore Retailers

Nonstore retailers are retailers that do not sell in conventional store facilities. Instead they sell door to door, through the mail, or in vending machines.

Door-to-Door Retailers   A **door-to-door retailer** is one that sells directly to consumers in their homes. The seller's representative calls on the potential customer at home and demonstrates the product. If a sale is made, she or he writes up the order and often delivers the product to the purchaser. Encyclopedias (Encyclopaedia Britannica, Encyclopedia Americana); cosmetics and toiletries (Avon, Mary Kay); kitchenware (Tupperware); and vacuum cleaners (Electrolux) have been successfully sold door to door.

Avon Products, Inc. is the world's largest direct-selling retailer. Avon representatives sell cosmetics, fragrances and toiletries, jewelry, and accessories in consumers' homes. Avon doesn't tamper with its winning combination: The selling method it uses today was first developed when the firm was founded in 1886.

Mail-Order Retailers   A **mail-order retailer** is one that solicits orders by mailing catalogs to potential customers. To make a purchase, the customer fills out an enclosed order form and mails it to the firm. Lately, more and more mail-order firms are taking orders via toll-free telephone calls and charging the orders to customers' credit cards.

As a selling technique, catalogs work. According to the Direct Marketing Association, an industry trade group, Americans buy approximately $40 billion worth of merchandise through the mail per year. And most of this merchandise is selected from catalogs. In the last five years, mail-order sales have been increasing by about 10 percent a year; in the last ten years, sales have increased by approximately $25 billion. The annual increase in traditional retail sales is only 5 percent. The Sharper Image, Lands' End, L. L. Bean, and Spiegel are all organizations that compete with traditional retailers for customers.

Vending Machines   Vending machines dispense convenience goods automatically when customers deposit the appropriate amount of money. Vending machines do not require sales personnel, and they permit twenty-four-hour service. They can be placed in convenient locations in office buildings, educational institutions, motels and hotels, shopping malls, and service stations.

The machines make available a wide assortment of goods. They can supply candy, cigarettes, soups, sandwiches, fresh fruits, yogurt, chewing gum, postage stamps, hot and cold beverages, perfume and cosmetics, and golf balls. They are even used to sell travel insurance at airports and

Today, more and more customers are purchasing clothes, furniture, appliances, and just about every other product imaginable from mail-order firms. According to the Direct Marketing Association, the number of mail order catalogues mailed per year more than doubled during the 1980s—to 12.4 billion copies.

around-the-clock banking services at convenient urban and suburban locations.

What drawbacks plague the vending-machine business? For one thing, malfunctioning is a costly and frustrating problem, as is vandalism. The machines must also be serviced frequently to operate properly. Together, repairs and servicing result in a very high cost for vending-machine selling—often more than one-third of sales revenue.

The Wheel of Retailing

wheel of retailing   *a hypothesis that suggests that new retail operations usually begin at the bottom—in price, profits, and prestige—and gradually evolve up the cost/price scale, competing with newer businesses that are evolving in the same way*

Learning Objective 7
Comprehend the wheel of retailing hypothesis

Newly developing retail businesses strive for a secure position in the ever-changing retailing environment. One theory attempts to explain how types of retail stores originate and develop. The **wheel of retailing** hypothesis suggests that new retail operations usually begin at the bottom—in price, profits, and prestige. In time, their facilities become more elaborate, their investments increase, and their operating costs go up. Finally, the retailers emerge at the top of the cost/price scale, competing with newer businesses that are evolving in the same way.[8]

In Figure 13.5, the wheel of retailing describes the development of department and discount stores. Department stores such as Sears were originally high-volume, low-cost retailers competing with general stores and other small businesses. As the costs of services rose in department stores, discount stores began to fill the low-price retailing niche. Now many discount stores, in turn, are following the pattern by expanding services, improving locations, upgrading inventories, and raising prices. Today, some department and discount stores are not readily distinguishable from each other.

FIGURE 13.5
The Wheel of Retailing
If the "wheel" is considered to be turning slowly in the direction of the arrow, then the department stores around 1900 and the discounters later can be viewed as coming on the scene at the low end of the wheel. As it turns slowly, they move with it, becoming higher-priced operations and, at the same time, leaving room for lower-price types of firms to gain entry at the low end of the wheel. (Source: Adapted from Robert F. Harley, Retailing: Challenge and Opportunity, 3/e. Copyright © 1984 by Houghton Mifflin Company. Used by permission.)

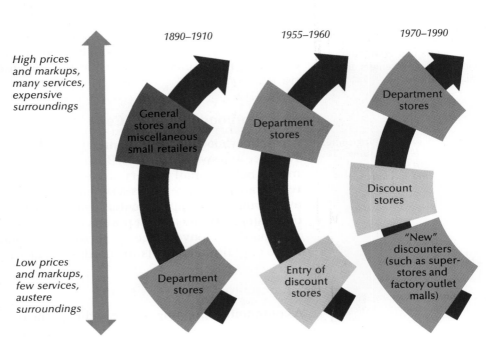

Developments in the grocery industry provide other examples of the wheel of retailing. When supermarkets were introduced in 1921, they offered lower food prices in exchange for a limited number of customer conveniences. Over the years, their services expanded to include in-store delicatessens, free coffee, gourmet food items, and children's play areas. Recently, superstores and warehouse stores have entered the field of food retailing. Superstores carry huge inventories of groceries and many commonly purchased nonfood items as well. They operate on a self-service basis and offer lower prices and a wider selection than ordinary supermarkets. Warehouse stores provide even fewer conveniences to customers but can usually offer prices as much as 20 percent lower than typical supermarkets.

Like most hypotheses, the wheel of retailing may not be universally applicable. The theory cannot predict what new retailing developments will occur, or when, for example. In industrialized, expanding economies, however, the hypothesis does help explain retailing innovations.

The Planned Shopping Center

The planned shopping center is a self-contained retail facility, constructed by private owners and comprised of various stores. Shopping centers are designed and promoted to serve diverse groups of consumers with widely differing needs. The management of a shopping center strives for a coordinated mix of stores, a comfortable atmosphere, adequate parking, landscaping, and special events to attract consumers. The convenience of shopping for most family and household needs in a single location is an important part of shopping-center appeal.

Learning Objective 8
Know the categories of shopping centers and identify the factors that determine how shopping centers are classified

A planned shopping center is one of three types: neighborhood, community, or regional. Although shopping centers vary, each offers a complementary mix of stores for the purpose of generating consumer traffic.

Neighborhood Shopping Centers

neighborhood shopping center
a planned shopping center consisting of several small convenience and specialty stores

A **neighborhood shopping center** typically consists of several small convenience and specialty stores. Businesses in neighborhood shopping centers might include small grocery stores, drugstores, gas stations, and fast-food restaurants. These retailers serve consumers who live less than ten minutes away from the shopping center, usually within a two- to three-mile radius of the stores. Because most purchases in the neighborhood shopping center are based on convenience or personal contact, these retailers generally make only limited efforts to coordinate sales activities.

Community Shopping Centers

community shopping center
a planned shopping center that includes one or two department stores and some specialty stores, along with convenience stores

A **community shopping center** includes one or two department stores and some specialty stores, along with convenience stores. It attracts consumers from a wider geographic area who will drive longer distances to find products and specialty items unavailable in neighborhood shopping centers. Community shopping centers, which are carefully planned and coordinated, generate traffic with special events such as art exhibits, automobile shows, and sidewalk sales. The management of a community shopping center maintains a balance of tenants so that the center can offer wide product mixes and deep product lines.

Regional Shopping Centers

regional shopping center
a planned shopping center containing large department stores, numerous specialty stores, restaurants, movie theaters, and sometimes hotels

A **regional shopping center** usually has large department stores, numerous specialty stores, restaurants, movie theaters, and sometimes hotels. It carries most of the merchandise offered by a downtown shopping district. Downtown merchants, in fact, have often renovated their stores and enlarged their parking facilities to meet the competition of successful regional shopping centers. Urban expressways and improved public transportation have also helped many downtown shopping areas to remain vigorous.

Regional shopping centers carefully coordinate management and marketing activities to reach the 150,000 or more consumers in their target market. These large centers usually advertise, hold special events, and provide transportation to certain groups of customers. They also maintain a suitable mix of stores. National chain stores can gain leases in regional shopping centers more easily than small independent stores because they are better able to meet the centers' financial requirements.

Physical Distribution

physical distribution   *all those activities concerned with the efficient movement of products from the producer to the ultimate user*

Learning Objective 9
Recognize the five most important physical distribution activities

Physical distribution is all those activities concerned with the efficient movement of products from the producer to the ultimate user. Physical distribution is thus the movement of the products themselves—both goods and services—through their channels of distribution. It is a combination of several interrelated business functions. The most important of these are inventory control, order processing, warehousing, materials handling, and transportation.

Not too long ago, each of these functions was considered distinct from all the others. In a fairly large firm, one group or department would handle each function. Each of these groups would work to minimize its own costs and to maximize its own effectiveness, but the end result was usually high physical distribution costs.

Various studies of the problem emphasized both the interrelationships among the physical distribution functions *and* the relationships between physical distribution and other marketing functions. Long production runs may reduce per-unit product costs, but they can cause inventory-control and warehousing costs to skyrocket. A new automated warehouse may reduce materials-handling costs to a minimum; but if it is not located properly, transportation time and costs may increase substantially.

There are many more instances of these interrelationships, and they have been duly noted. Marketers now view physical distribution as an integrated effort that provides an important marketing service: getting the right product to the right place at the right time and at minimal *overall* cost.

Inventory Management

inventory control *the process of managing inventories in such a way as to minimize inventory costs, including both holding costs and potential stock-out costs*

In Chapter 7 we discussed inventory management from the standpoint of operations. We defined **inventory control** as the process of managing inventories in such a way as to minimize inventory costs, including both holding costs and potential stock-out costs. Both the definition and the objective of inventory control apply here as well.

Holding costs are the costs of storing products until they are purchased or shipped to customers. *Stock-out costs* are the costs of sales that are lost when items are not in inventory. Of course, holding costs can be minimized by minimizing inventories, but then stock-out costs would ruin the firm. And stock-out costs can be minimized by carrying very large inventories, but then holding costs would be enormous.

Inventory management is thus a sort of "balancing act" between stock-out costs and holding costs. The latter include the cost of money invested in inventory, the cost of storage space, insurance costs, and inventory taxes. Often, even a relatively small reduction in inventory investment can provide a relatively large increase in working capital. And sometimes this reduction can best be accomplished through a willingness to incur a reasonable level of stock-out costs.

Order Processing

order processing *those activities that are involved in receiving and filling customers' purchase orders*

Order processing consists of those activities that are involved in receiving and filling customers' purchase orders. It may include the means by which customers order products as well as procedures for billing and for granting credit.

Fast, efficient order processing is an important marketing service— one that can provide a dramatic competitive edge. The people who purchase goods for intermediaries are especially concerned with their suppliers' promptness and reliability in order processing. To them it means minimal inventory costs as well as the ability to order goods when they are needed rather than weeks in advance.

Warehousing

warehousing *the set of activities that are involved in receiving and storing goods and preparing them for reshipment*

Warehousing is the set of activities that are involved in receiving and storing goods and preparing them for reshipment. Goods are stored to create time utility; that is, they are held until they are needed for use or sale. But along with storage, warehousing includes a number of other activities:[9]

▶ *Receiving goods:* The warehouse accepts delivered goods and assumes responsibility for them.

▶ *Identifying goods:* Records are made of the quantity of each item received. Items may be marked, coded, or tagged for identification.

▶ *Sorting goods:* Delivered goods may have to be sorted before being stored.

▶ *Dispatching goods to storage:* Items must be moved to their own specific storage areas, where they can be found later.

▶ *Holding goods:* The goods are kept in storage under proper protection until needed.

▶ *Recalling, selecting, or picking goods:* Items that are to leave the warehouse must be efficiently selected from storage.

▶ *Marshaling shipments:* The items making up each shipment are brought together, and the shipment is checked for completeness. Records are prepared or modified as necessary.

▶ *Dispatching shipments:* Each shipment is packaged suitably and directed to the proper transport vehicle. Shipping and accounting documents are prepared.

A firm may either use its own warehouses or rent space in public warehouses. A *private warehouse,* owned and operated by a particular firm, can be designed to serve the firm's specific needs. However, the firm must take on the task of financing the facility, determining the best location for it, and ensuring that it is fully utilized. Generally, only firms that deal in large quantities of goods can justify private warehouses.

Public warehouses offer their services to all individuals and firms. Most are huge, one-story structures on the outskirts of major cities, where rail and truck transportation are easily available. They provide storage facilities, areas for sorting and marshaling shipments, and office and display spaces for wholesalers and retailers. Public warehouses will also hold—and issue receipts for—goods that are used as collateral for borrowed funds.

Materials Handling

materials handling *the actual physical handling of goods, in warehousing as well as during transportation*

Materials handling is the actual physical handling of goods, in warehousing as well as during transportation. Proper materials-handling procedures and techniques can increase the usable capacity of a warehouse or that of any means of transportation. And proper handling can reduce breakage and spoilage as well.

Modern materials-handling efforts are aimed at reducing the number of times a product is handled. One method is called *unit loading.* Several smaller cartons, barrels, or boxes are combined into a single standard-sized load that can be handled efficiently by fork lift, conveyer, or truck.

Transportation

transportation *the shipment of products to customers*

As a part of physical distribution, **transportation** is simply the shipment of products to customers. The greater the distance between seller and purchaser, the more important is the choice of the means of transportation and the particular carrier.

carrier *a firm that offers transportation services*

A firm that offers transportation services is called a **carrier.** A *common carrier* is a transportation firm whose services are available to all shippers.

A Union Pacific trailer is loaded onto a flatcar. This type of piggyback service combines the services offered by both railroads and truck carriers to provide customers with an efficient and economical method of transporting freight. From Union Pacific's point of view as well, "intermodal traffic" is a very effective and profitable part of its business, accounting for more than $400 million in revenues during a recent year.

Railroads, airlines, and most long-distance trucking firms are common carriers. A *contract carrier* is a firm that is available for hire by one or several shippers. Contract carriers do not serve the general public. Moreover, the number of firms they can handle at any one time is limited by law. A *private carrier* is one that is owned and operated by the shipper.

In addition, a shipper can hire agents called *freight forwarders* to handle its transportation. Freight forwarders pick up shipments from the shipper, ensure that the goods are loaded onto selected carriers, and

FIGURE 13.6
Ranking of Transportation Modes
Each mode of transportation is ranked by five important criteria, from the highest to lowest. [Source: Some of this information has been adapted from J. L. Heskett, Robert Ivie, and J. Nicholas Glaskowsky, Business Logistics (New York: Ronald Press, 1973). Copyright © 1973 by Ronald Press. Used by permission.]

COST	TRANSIT TIME	RELIABILITY	ACCESSIBILITY	SECURITY
Air	Water	Pipeline	Truck	Pipeline
Truck	Rail	Truck	Rail	Water
Rail	Pipeline	Rail	Air	Rail
Pipeline	Truck	Air	Water	Air
Water	Air	Water	Pipeline	Truck

assume responsibility for the safe delivery of the shipments to their destinations. Freight forwarders are often able to group a number of small shipments into one large load (which is carried at a lower rate). This, of course, saves money for shippers.

The two prime elements in choosing a particular mode of transportation—railroad, truck, pipeline, or other—are the product itself and the firm's overall distribution system. For some combinations of these two elements, the cost of transportation may be more important. For other combinations, speed may be more crucial. Other factors that enter into this decision are the reliability of the various modes of transportation, their availability at points of shipment and delivery, and their ability to handle particular kinds of shipments. See Figure 13.6 for a ranking of transportation modes relative to several important criteria, and Figure 13.7 for a breakdown by use of different modes of transportation.

FIGURE 13.7
Changes in Ton Miles for Various Transportation Modes
The primary elements in choosing a particular mode of transportation are the product itself and the firm's distribution system. (Source: "Transportation in America," May 1989. Eno Foundation for Transportation. Reprinted with permission.)

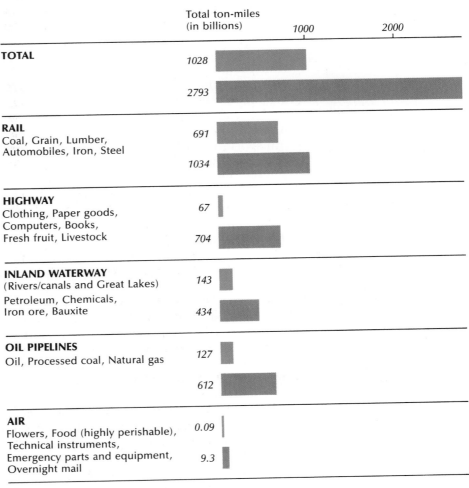

Railroads   In terms of total freight carried, railroads are the most important mode of transportation. They are also the least expensive for many products. Almost all railroads are common carriers, although a few coal-mining companies operate their own lines.

Many of the commodities carried by railroads could not be transported easily by any other means. They include a wide range of foodstuffs, raw materials, and manufactured goods. Coal ranks first by a considerable margin. Other major commodities carried by railroads include paper and pulp products, liquids in tank-car loads, heavy equipment, lumber, and cut stone.

Trucks   The trucking industry consists of common, contract, and private carriers. It has undergone tremendous expansion since the creation of a national highway system in the 1920s. Trucks can move goods to suburban and rural areas not served by railroads. They can handle freight quickly and economically, and they carry a wide range of shipments. Many shippers favor this mode of transportation because it offers door-to-door service, less stringent packaging requirements than ships and airplanes, and flexible delivery schedules.

Railroad and truck carriers have teamed up to provide a form of transportation called *piggyback*. Truck trailers are carried from city to city on specially equipped railroad flatcars. Within each city, the trailers are then pulled in the usual way by truck tractors.

Airplanes   Air transport is the fastest but most expensive means of transportation. All certified airlines are common carriers. Supplemental or charter lines are contract carriers.

Because of the high cost, lack of airport facilities in many areas, and reliance on weather conditions, airlines carry less than 1 percent of all intercity freight. Only high-value or perishable items, such as aircraft parts, pharmaceuticals, or goods that are needed immediately are usually shipped by air.

Ships   Cargo ships and barges offer the least expensive but slowest form of transportation. They are used mainly for bulky, nonperishable goods such as iron ore, bulk wheat, motor vehicles, and agricultural implements. Of course, shipment by water is limited to cities located on navigable waterways. But ships and barges account for a steady 16 percent of all intercity freight hauling.

Pipelines   Pipelines are a highly specialized mode of transportation. They are used primarily to carry petroleum and natural gas. Pipelines have become more and more important as the nation's need for petroleum products has increased. Such products as semiliquid coal and wood chips can also be shipped through pipelines continuously, reliably, and with minimal handling.

Package Carriers   The U.S. Postal Service offers *parcel post* delivery, which is widely used by mail-order houses. The Postal Service provides complete

With the use of computers, companies like Skyway Freight Systems can document and keep track of every shipment and provide customers with reliable, on-time delivery.

geographic coverage at the lowest rates, but it limits the size and weight of the shipments it will accept.

United Parcel Service, Inc. (UPS), a privately owned firm, also provides small-parcel services for shippers. Other privately owned carriers, such as Federal Express and Purolator Courier, offer fast—often overnight—parcel delivery both within and outside the United States. There are also many local parcel carriers, including specialized delivery services for various time-sensitive industries, such as publishing.

CHAPTER REVIEW

Summary

A marketing channel is a sequence of marketing organizations that directs a product from producer to ultimate user. The marketing channel for a particular product is concerned with the transfer of ownership of that product. Merchant middlemen (merchants) actually take title to products, whereas functional middlemen simply aid in the transfer of title.

The channels used for consumer products include the direct channel from producer to consumer; the channel from producer to retailer to consumer; the channel from producer to wholesaler to retailer to consumer; and that from producer to agent to wholesaler to retailer to consumer. The major channels for industrial products are producer to user, and producer to agent middleman to user. Channels and intermediaries are chosen to implement a given intensity of distribution from intensive (widest) to exclusive. A vertical marketing system (VMS) results from combining two or more channel members from different levels under one management. Administered, contractual, and corporate represent the three major types of VMSs.

Wholesalers are intermediaries that purchase from producers or other intermediaries and sell to industrial users, retailers, or other wholesalers. Wholesalers perform many functions in a channel. If they are eliminated, other channel members—such as the producer or retailers—must perform these functions. Wholesalers provide retailers with help in promoting products, collecting information, and financing. They provide manufacturers with sales help, reduce their inventory costs, furnish market information, and extend credit to retailers. Merchant wholesalers buy and then sell products. Commission merchants and brokers are essentially agents and do not take title to the goods. Sales branches and offices are owned by the manufacturers they represent and are like merchant wholesalers and agents, respectively.

Retailers are intermediaries that buy from producers or wholesalers and sell to consumers. In-store retailers include department stores, discount stores, catalog discount showrooms, specialty stores, supermarkets, superstores, convenience stores, and warehouse stores. Nonstore retailers sell door to door, by mail, or through vending machines.

The wheel of retailing hypothesis states that retailers begin as low-status, low-margin, low-priced stores and over time evolve into high-cost, high-priced operations.

There are three major types of shopping centers: neighborhood, community, and regional. A center can be classified into one of these categories based on number and types of stores and the size of the geographic area served by the center.

Physical distribution consists of activities designed to move products to ultimate users. Its five major functions are inventory management, order processing, warehousing, materials handling, and transportation. These interrelated functions are integrated into the marketing effort.

In the next chapter we discuss the fourth element of the marketing mix—promotion.

Key Terms

You should now be able to define and give an example relevant to each of the following terms:

channel of distribution (or marketing channel)
middleman (or marketing intermediary)
merchant middleman
functional middleman
retailer
wholesaler
intensive distribution
selective distribution
exclusive distribution
vertical channel integration
vertical marketing system (VMS)
merchant wholesaler
full-service wholesaler
general merchandise wholesaler
limited-line wholesaler
specialty-line wholesaler
limited-service wholesaler
commission merchant
agent
broker
manufacturer's sales branch
manufacturer's sales office
independent retailer
chain retailer
department store
discount store
catalog discount showroom
specialty store
supermarket
superstore
convenience store
warehouse store
door-to-door retailer
mail-order retailer
wheel of retailing
neighborhood shopping center
community shopping center
regional shopping center
physical distribution
inventory control
order processing
warehousing
materials handling
transportation
carrier

Questions and Exercises

Review Questions

1. In what ways is a channel of distribution different from the path taken by a product during physical distribution?
2. What are the most common marketing channels for consumer products? for industrial products?
3. What are the three general approaches to market coverage? What types of products is each used for?
4. What is a vertical marketing system? Identify examples of the three types of VMSs.
5. List the services performed by wholesalers. For whom is each service performed?
6. What is the basic difference between a merchant wholesaler and an agent?
7. Identify three kinds of full-service wholesalers. What factors are used to classify wholesalers into one of these categories?
8. Distinguish between (a) commission merchants and agents and (b) manufacturers' sales branches and manufacturers' sales offices.
9. What is the basic difference between wholesalers and retailers?
10. What is the difference between a department store and a discount store, with regard to selling orientation or philosophy?
11. How do (a) convenience stores and (b) specialty stores compete with other retail outlets?
12. What can nonstore retailers offer their customers that in-store retailers cannot?

13. What does the wheel of retailing hypothesis suggest about new retail operations?
14. Compare and contrast community shopping centers and regional shopping centers.
15. What is physical distribution? Which major functions does it include?
16. What activities besides storage are included in warehousing?
17. List the primary modes of transportation, and cite at least one advantage of each.

Discussion Questions

1. According to Sam Walton, if people believe in themselves, they can do amazing things. How has Wal-Mart used this basic philosophy to become the third-largest retailer in the United States?
2. Few traditional, old-line retailers can compete against Wal-Mart stores. They can't match the selection of merchandise or the prices that Wal-Mart offers. Why?
3. Which distribution channels would producers of services be most likely to use? Why?
4. Many producers sell to consumers both directly and through middlemen. How can such a producer justify competing with its own middlemen?
5. In what situations might a producer use agents or commission merchants rather than its own sales offices or branches?
6. If a middleman is eliminated from a marketing channel, under what conditions will costs be reduced, and under what conditions will costs increase? Will the middleman's functions be eliminated?
7. Which types of retail outlets are best suited to intensive distribution? to selective distribution? to exclusive distribution? (Explain your answer in each case.)
8. How are the various physical distribution functions related to each other? to the other elements of the marketing mix? to the other parts of the firm's marketing system?

Exercises

1. On the basis of your experience as a consumer, list the services that retailers perform for their customers. Then circle those that could be eliminated easily. Next place a check mark beside those that are most important to you. Finally, summarize your results in a sentence or two.
2. Suppose you have developed and will produce a new golf tee that increases golfers' accuracy and driving distance. Design a marketing channel (or channels) for your product. Explain why your choice of channels would be most effective for this product.
3. For the golf tees described in Exercise 2, answer the following questions:
   a. How would you package your product for sale and for ease in inventory control and handling?
   b. Where would you locate your storage facilities? (Assume nationwide distribution of your product.)
   c. What means of transportation would you use to distribute your product across the nation? Why?

Case 13.1

The Swedish Idea: IKEA

When Swedish furniture retailer IKEA opened the doors of its first U.S. store in 1985, Americans were ready and waiting. A six-month media blitz prior to opening day helped draw 150,000 shoppers to the suburban Philadelphia store in its first week. Traffic backed up on the Pennsylvania Turnpike for six miles, and at one point store officials locked the doors to slow the flood of customers. One reason for IKEA's success is that customers are attracted by the clean lines and bright colors of its sophisticated Scandinavian furniture. Another reason is its low prices, which are sometimes 50 percent less than competitors'.

IKEA, the brain child of Swedish entrepreneur Ingvar Kamprad, relies on a simple but highly successful formula: Sell quality, unassembled furniture at low prices to as many people as possible. To do this, IKEA farms out its product designs worldwide to the most efficient suppliers it can find. Because IKEA makes none of its own products, the company's suppliers work directly with IKEA designers to meet strict specifications. Items must be machine-made, attractive, economical, and, of course, packable. They must also withstand the company's rigid durability tests. Currently IKEA carries 12,000 items that are produced by 1,500 suppliers.

Kamprad also originated IKEA's knockdown packaging in the early 1950s, after observing the cumbersome distribution system of the Swedish furniture industry. Today flat-pack technology has reduced IKEA's handling and warehousing costs by more than 50 percent. IKEA's giant central warehouse in Almhult, Sweden, is staffed with three people, thirteen robots, and a line of computerized fork lifts. A keyboard operator electronically directs the fork lifts and robots to load movable pallets with the appropriate merchandise and to transport them to the trucking area.

Skillful site selection is another factor in the company's worldwide success. IKEA looks just outside big cities for inexpensive land near major highways. This tactic allows the company to target customers who live up to ninety minutes away from a store. Because IKEA customers often spend half a day at the stores anyway, they don't seem to mind the driving distance.

An IKEA store is something like a grocery warehouse, complete with special shopping carts. The U.S. stores display furniture and large items upstairs in smart room settings. Downstairs are a Swedish restaurant, a children's playroom, and the IKEA Marketplace—a showroom of lamps, fabrics, housewares, and accessories. Each of the 12,000 store items bears a tag listing its price, materials, and assembly. In the adjoining self-service area, the customer locates the appropriate flat boxes in warehouse stacks, carts purchases to the check-out counter, and then loads them in the car. Shipping is available for a fee.

The company operates seventy-seven stores in eighteen countries with total sales of $2 billion a year. In addition to the Philadelphia store, there are IKEA stores in Baltimore, Pittsburgh, and Washington, D.C. An IKEA spokesperson says the company plans to open as many as ten U.S. outlets over the next two to three years. In the meantime, the next IKEA showroom will probably be drawing its crowds of shoppers from Boston or central New Jersey.*

Questions

1. Although the median after-tax profit for the U.S. retailing industry is 2.7 percent, IKEA's after-tax profit is 7 percent. How can IKEA price its merchandise up to 50 percent less than competitors and still earn more money than they do?
2. What are the major advantages and disadvantages of using flat-pack technology—for IKEA and for its customers?

* Based on information from Peter Fuhrman, "The Workers' Friend," *Forbes*, March 21, 1988, p. 124+; Kimberley Carpenter, "Help Yourself," *Working Woman*, August 1986, p. 56; Lindsay Gruson, "IKEA Venture in USA a Hit," *New York Times*, March 22, 1986, Sec. L37; Mary Krienke, "IKEA = Simple Good Taste," *Stores*, April 1986, pp. 56–59; Jennifer Lin, "IKEA's U.S. Translation," *Stores*, April 1986, p. 60+; Kevin Maney, "Customers Flood USA IKEA Outlets," *USA Today*, November 4, 1986, p. B1; and Eleanor Johnson Tracy, "Shopping Swedish-Style Comes to the U.S.," *Fortune*, January 20, 1986, p. 63.

Case 13.2

Mrs. Fields: The Cookie Crumbles?

For Debbie Fields—the founder of Mrs. Fields Cookies—the first day of business was terrible. By noon, when she had not sold a single cookie, she decided it was time to do something. So she loaded a tray with freshly baked cookies, walked up and down the street outside her Palo Alto, California, store, and gave away her cookies to potential customers. Her strategy worked; at the end of her first day she had made $75. Today, twelve years later, Mrs. Fields Cookies operates more than 600 retail outlets, employs approximately 8,000 workers, and generates almost $90 million in annual sales revenues. Unlike many cookie retailers, the company has not franchised any of its stores; instead, all its stores are company-owned. This policy enables management to ensure that the quality standards Mrs. Fields is famous for are maintained in all its retail outlets.

Yet, for the first time, Mrs. Fields suffered operating losses in 1988. The cookie chain lost more than $15 million. Lower cookie sales (because of increased competition) and soaring rents cut into company profits. According to financial analysts, Mrs. Fields illustrates the problems that can develop with a single-product company that experiences rapid expansion.

To combat these problems, the company is now struggling to become a specialty-foods retailer that sells more than just cookies. To do this, Mrs. Fields is merging its cookie stores with those of La Petite Boulangerie. La Petite Boulangerie is a chain of 105 bakery stores that Mrs. Fields acquired from PepsiCo in 1987. The new combination stores sell not only cookies but also such items as soup, bagels, and sandwiches. Mrs. Fields has already opened more than thirty of the new combination stores.

The new strategy is a risky one, say financial analysts, because Mrs. Fields is getting away from the company's "core" business—selling gourmet cookies. Also, the new combination stores are three times as large as the old cookie stores and thus cost more to operate because of higher rents and related expenses. Finally, the company has had to absorb the costs of opening the new combination stores and retraining employees.

Randy Fields, chairman of the board and husband of Debbie Fields, believes the company will be profitable in the 1990s. The experimental test locations are already doing better than expected. In addition, the company has closed ninety-five, or about 16 percent, of the cookie stores that were either operating at a loss or overlapping the customer base of the new combination stores. Also, the company has entered a joint-venture agreement with Paris-based Midial S.A. to market products with the Mrs. Fields and La Petite Boulangerie names in the twelve-nation European Community. (The European Community is scheduled to eliminate most national trade barriers among its members by 1992.) In return for the European marketing rights, Mrs. Fields received $10 million.†

---

† Based on information from "Tough Cookies?" *Fortune*, February 13, 1989, p. 112; Tom Richman, "Their System. . .," *Inc.*, April 1989, p. 100; Buck Brown, "How the Cookie Crumbled at Mrs. Fields," *Wall Street Journal*, January 26, 1989, p. B1; "Mrs. Fields Automates the Way the Cookie Sells," *Chain Store Age Executive*, April 1988, pp. 73–74+; Mark Lewyn, "Executive Tales, Told by the Book," *USA Today*, October 12, 1987, p. 1; and Nancy Rivera Brooks, "To Entrepreneur, Success Tastes Sweet," *Los Angeles Times*, September 4, 1986, Section IV, p. 1.

Questions

1. Most companies like Mrs. Fields would have franchised their retail outlets to expand. What are the advantages of company-owned stores? What are the disadvantages?
2. Originally, Mrs. Fields Cookies was a single-product company. Should Mrs. Fields continue this single-product strategy? Why?
3. Why would Mrs. Fields enter a joint venture with Paris-based Midial S.A. to market the Mrs. Fields and La Petite Boulangerie names in Europe?

PROMOTION

1 Recognize the role of promotion

2 Know the purposes of the three types of advertising

3 Become aware of the advantages and disadvantages of the major advertising media

4 Identify the major steps in developing an advertising campaign

5 Know the various kinds of salespersons, the personal-selling process, and the major sales management tasks

6 Understand the sales promotion objectives and methods

7 Recognize the types and uses of publicity and the requirements for effective use of publicity

8 Know what factors influence the selection of promotion-mix ingredients

CHAPTER PREVIEW

In this chapter we introduce four promotion methods and describe how they are used in an organization's marketing plans. First, we examine the role of advertising in the promotion mix. We discuss different types of advertising, the process of developing an advertising campaign, and social and legal concerns in advertising. Next, we consider several categories of personal selling, noting the importance of effective sales management. We also look at sales promotion—why firms use it and which sales promotion techniques are most effective. Then, we explain how both publicity and public relations can be used to build sales. Finally, we illustrate how these four promotion methods are combined in an effective promotion mix.

Promotions Designed for Hispanics

Marketers spend billions of dollars every year to promote their goods and services. However, most of these dollars are spent on mainstream American consumers. Some critics charge that advertisers are overlooking or ignoring ethnic consumers. But this is in the process of change.

According to the U.S. Census Bureau, Hispanics will account for 42 percent of new population growth in the United States between 1990 and 2010. In 2010, there will be nearly 40 million Hispanics in the United States, more than double today's number. Already, U.S. Hispanics have $171 billion in purchasing power—a 27 percent increase from the 1987 figure.

The numbers are impressive but many firms find it difficult to tap this growing market. The problem is that U.S. Hispanics are a heterogeneous and geographically widespread group. For example, most Mexican-Americans live in California and the Southwest, Dominicans and Puerto Ricans in New York, and Cubans in Florida.

Companies are using various marketing strategies to reach different segments of the U.S. Hispanic population. Adelante Advertising Inc. specializes in working with the Hispanic market and believes that Hispanics have traits that advertisers and marketers should be aware of. For example, advertisers have found that Hispanic consumers have strong brand loyalties and will pay more for name brands. In Miami, Hispanics wear Rolex watches and drive top-of-the-line automobiles. Consequently, local jewelers and car dealers advertise on Spanish-language radio and television stations.

Marketing to the Hispanic community requires a thorough understanding of and respect for its culture. Companies such as Frito-Lay Inc. and Quaker Foods have stopped using negative stereotypes (such as the Frito Bandito), which offend Hispanic consumer groups.

Despite the inherent difficulties in reaching the Hispanic market, many companies have recognized the value of doing so, and have organized conscious and culturally sensitive promotional campaigns. Recently, in an annual Hispanic State Fair in San Antonio, Texas, exhibitors included PepsiCo, Miller Brewing Co., Colgate-Palmolive, Del Monte Foods, Avon Products, KMOL-TV San Antonio, area Lincoln-Mercury dealers, McDonald's, Quaker Oats, Old El Paso sauces, and Uncle Ben's rice.

American Express Company promotes its Money Gram consumer money transfer service through TV and radio spots in Spanish. Polaroid makes pitches for its camera in Spanish through well-known television personalities who appear on the Univision network (a Spanish-language channel that reaches 85 percent of the U.S. Hispanic population from coast to coast.) Competitor Kodak also makes appeals to Hispanics in Spanish, using the UniWorld ad agency. Kodak's promotions include point-of-purchase materials in Spanish and Spanish-language TV, radio, and print advertising.

The amount of attention paid to Hispanic consumers is bound to increase in the future as firms continue to respond to demographic trends and the potential for profit they imply.[1]

Polaroid and American Express Company use television and radio to promote their products. In addition, the firms employ direct-mail advertising, sending customers catalogs and money-saving coupons as a means of promotion.

promotion *communication that is intended to inform, persuade, or remind an organization's target markets of the organization or its products*

Promotion is communication that is intended to inform, persuade, or remind an organization's target markets of the organization or its products. The promotion with which we are most familiar—advertising—is intended to inform, persuade, or remind us to buy particular products. But there is more to promotion than advertising, and it is used for other purposes as well. For example, charities use promotion to inform us of their need for donations, to persuade us to give, and to remind us to do so in case we have forgotten. Even the Internal Revenue Service makes use of promotion (in the form of publicity) to remind us of its April 15 deadline for filing tax returns.

promotion mix *the particular combination of promotion methods that a firm uses in its promotional campaign to reach a target market*

A **promotion mix** is the particular combination of promotion methods that a firm such as PepsiCo uses in its promotional campaign to reach a target market. The makeup of a mix depends on many factors, including the characteristics of the target market. We shall discuss these factors toward the end of this chapter, after we have examined the promotion methods of advertising, personal selling, sales promotion, and publicity (which is closely related to public relations).

The Role of Promotion

Promotion is commonly the object of two misconceptions. On the one hand, people take note of highly visible promotional activities, such as advertising and personal selling, and conclude that these make up the entire field of marketing. On the other hand, people sometimes consider promotional activities to be unnecessary, expensive, and the cause of higher prices. Neither view is accurate.

Learning Objective 1
Recognize the role of promotion

The role of promotion is to facilitate exchanges directly or indirectly by informing individuals, groups, or organizations and influencing them to accept a firm's products. To expedite exchanges directly, marketers convey information about a firm's goods, services, and ideas to particular market segments. To bring about exchanges indirectly, marketers address interest groups (such as environmental and consumer groups), regulatory agencies, investors, and the general public concerning a company and its products. The broader role of promotion, therefore, is to maintain positive relationships between a company and various groups in the marketing environment.

Marketers frequently design promotional communications, such as advertisements, for specific groups, although some may be directed at wider audiences. Several different messages may be communicated simultaneously to different market segments. For example, Exxon Corporation may address customers about a new motor oil, inform investors about the firm's financial performance, and update the general public on the firm's environmental efforts to clean up the Alaskan shoreline.

FIGURE 14.1
Information Flows Into and Out of an Organization
A promotional activity's effectiveness depends on the information available to marketers. (Source: Adapted from William M. Pride and O. C. Ferrell, Marketing: Concepts and Strategies, 6/e. Copyright © 1989 by Houghton Mifflin Company. Used by permission.)

Marketers must carefully plan, implement, and coordinate promotional communications to make the best use of them. The effectiveness of promotional activities depends greatly on the quality and quantity of information available to marketers about the organization's marketing environment (see Figure 14.1). If marketers want to influence customers to buy a certain product, for example, they must know who these customers are likely to be and how they make purchase decisions for that type of product. Marketers must gather and use information about particular audiences to communicate successfully with them.

The Promotion Mix: An Overview

advertising   *a paid, nonpersonal message communicated to a select audience through a mass medium*

personal selling   *personal communication aimed at informing customers and persuading them to buy a firm's products*

sales promotion   *the use of activities or materials as direct inducements to customers or salespersons*

publicity   *a nonpersonal message delivered in news-story form through a mass medium, free of charge*

Marketers can use several promotional methods to communicate with individuals, groups, and organizations. The methods that are combined to promote a particular product make up the promotion mix for that item.

Advertising, personal selling, publicity, and sales promotion are the four major elements in an organization's promotion mix (see Figure 14.2). Two, three, or four of these ingredients are used in a promotion mix, depending on the type of product and target market involved.

Advertising is a paid, nonpersonal message communicated to a select audience through a mass medium. The key words in the definition are *nonpersonal*, which excludes personal selling by a sales force, and *paid*, which excludes publicity. Advertising is so flexible that it can reach a very large target group or a small, carefully chosen market segment. **Personal selling** is personal communication aimed at informing customers and persuading them to buy a firm's products. It is more expensive to reach one person through personal selling than through advertising, but this method provides immediate feedback and is often more persuasive than advertising. **Sales promotion** is the use of activities or materials as direct inducements to customers or salespersons. It adds extra value to the product or increases the customer's incentive to buy the product. Sales promotion is only one part of promotion, along with advertising, personal selling, and publicity. **Publicity** is a nonpersonal message delivered in news-story form through a mass medium, free of charge. Magazine, newspaper, radio, and television stories about a company's new stores, products, or personnel changes are examples of publicity. Although marketers do not pay outright for such media coverage, there are nonetheless definite costs associated with the preparation and distribution of news releases.

Advertising

Learning Objective 2
Know the purposes of the three types of advertising

selective (or **brand**) **advertising** *advertising that is used to sell a particular brand of product*

The largest share of advertising dollars goes to newspapers. Other media that are used to deliver the message are television, radio, magazines, outdoor advertising, and direct mail. Figure 14.3 shows how advertising expenditures and employment in advertising have increased since 1972. Total advertising expenditures for 1988 were 118.1 billion.[2]

Types of Advertising by Purpose

Depending on its purpose and message, advertising may be classified into three groups. Selective advertising promotes specific brands of products and services. Institutional advertising is image-building advertising for a firm. And primary-demand advertising is industry (rather than brand) advertising.

Selective Advertising   **Selective** (or **brand**) **advertising** is advertising that is used to sell a particular brand of product. It is by far the most common type of advertising, and it accounts for the lion's share of advertising expenditures. Producers use brand-oriented advertising to convince us to buy their products, from Bubble Yum to Buicks.

Selective advertising that aims at persuading consumers to make purchases within a short time is called *immediate-response advertising*. Most local advertising is of this type. It generally promotes merchandise with immediate appeal, such as fans or air conditioners during an unusually hot summer. Selective advertising aimed at keeping a firm's name or product before the public is called *reminder advertising*. Most automakers, for example, show commercials on television week after week, as a reminder of their product lines.

Comparative advertising, which has become more popular over the last decade, compares specific characteristics of two or more identified brands. Of course, the comparison always shows the advertiser's brand to be best. Comparative advertising is now fairly common among manufacturers of deodorants, toothpaste, butter, tires, and automobiles. Comparisons are often based on the outcome of surveys or research studies. Though competing firms act as effective watchdogs against each other's advertising claims, and regulations on comparative advertising are stringent, a certain sophistication on the consumer's part concerning claims based on "scientific studies" and various statistical manipulations is worth cultivating.

FIGURE 14.2
Possible Ingredients for an Organization's Promotion Mix
Depending on the type of product and target market involved, two or more of these ingredients are used in a promotion mix. (Source: Adapted from William M. Pride and O. C. Ferrell, Marketing: Concepts and Strategies, 6/e. Copyright © 1989 by Houghton Mifflin Company. Used by permission.)

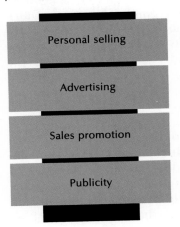

Personal selling

Advertising

Sales promotion

Publicity

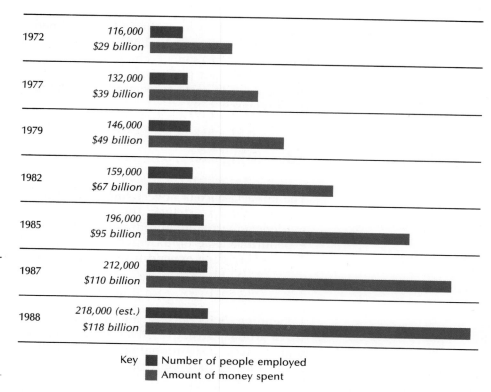

FIGURE 14.3
Growth of Advertising
Expenditures and of Employ-
ment in Advertising
Total advertising expenditures and employment in
advertising have been steadily increasing since 1972.
Both are expected to con-
tinue to rise in the 1990s.
[Sources: Bureau of Labor Statistics (Employment); Advertising Age, May 15, 1989, p. 24;
and Statistical Abstract of the
United States, 1989, U.S. Bureau of the Census, p. 401.]

Year		
1972	116,000	
	$29 billion	
1977	132,000	
	$39 billion	
1979	146,000	
	$49 billion	
1982	159,000	
	$67 billion	
1985	196,000	
	$95 billion	
1987	212,000	
	$110 billion	
1988	218,000 (est.)	
	$118 billion	

Key ▪ Number of people employed
▪ Amount of money spent

institutional advertising
advertising designed to enhance
a firm's image or reputation

primary-demand advertising
advertising whose purpose is to
increase the demand for all
brands of a good or service

advertising media   *the various*
forms of communication
through which advertising
reaches its audience

Institutional Advertising   **Institutional advertising** is advertising designed
to enhance a firm's image or reputation. Many public utilities and larger
firms, such as **AT&T** and the major oil companies, advertise to build
goodwill rather than to stimulate sales. Perhaps they feel they need to
combat what they perceive as a negative public image.

Primary-Demand Advertising   **Primary-demand advertising** is advertising
whose purpose is to increase the demand for *all* brands of a good or
service. Trade and industry associations, such as the American Dairy
Association ("Drink More Milk.") and the Association of American Railroads ("Who Needs America's Railroads? We All Do."), are the major
users of primary-demand advertising. Their advertisements promote the
product without mentioning specific brands.

Advertising Media

The **advertising media** are the various forms of communication through
which advertising reaches its audience. They include newspapers, magazines, television, radio, direct mail, and outdoor displays. Figure 14.4
shows how businesses allocate their advertising expenditures among the
various media. The *print media*—which include newspapers, magazines,
direct mail, and billboards—account for more than 50 percent of all

Learning Objective 3
Become aware of the advantages and disadvantages of the major advertising media

advertising expenditures. The *electronic media*—television and radio—account for about 28 percent.

Newspapers   Newspaper advertising accounts for about 26 percent of all advertising expenditures. More than half is purchased by retailers.

Newspaper advertising is used so extensively by retailers because it is reasonable in cost. Furthermore, because it provides only local coverage, advertising dollars are not wasted in reaching people who are outside the store's market area. It is also timely. Ads can usually be placed the day before they are to appear, and their effectiveness can be measured easily.

There are some drawbacks, however, to newspaper advertising. It has a short life span; newspapers are generally read through once and then discarded. Color reproduction in newspapers is usually poor; thus most ads must be run in black and white. Finally, marketers cannot target specific markets through newspaper ads, except with regard to geographic area.

Newspapers carry more cooperative advertising than other print media. **Cooperative advertising** is advertising whose cost is shared by a producer and one or more local retailers. The costs are shared because the advertising benefits both the producer, whose products are promoted, and the retailer, which reaches it customers through the advertising.

cooperative advertising *advertising whose cost is shared by a producer and one or more local retailers*

Magazines   The advertising revenues of magazines have been climbing dramatically since 1976. In 1988 they reached $6.1 billion, or about 5.1 percent of all advertising expenditures.

Benetton uses selective advertising to enhance sales of its line of clothing. It was one of the first advertisers to employ a trend currently sweeping the industry: ads including people of diverse nationalities. Believing that consumers want to see real people rather than idols, Benetton introduced its "United Colors of Benetton" campaign in 1984.

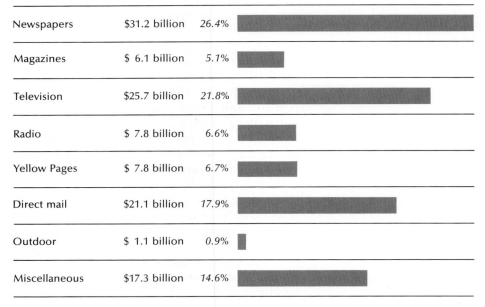

Newspapers	$31.2 billion	26.4%	
Magazines	$ 6.1 billion	5.1%	
Television	$25.7 billion	21.8%	
Radio	$ 7.8 billion	6.6%	
Yellow Pages	$ 7.8 billion	6.7%	
Direct mail	$21.1 billion	17.9%	
Outdoor	$ 1.1 billion	0.9%	
Miscellaneous	$17.3 billion	14.6%	

FIGURE 14.4
Comparison of Advertising Media in Terms of Advertising Expenditures
About 48 cents of every dollar spent on advertising are consumed in newspaper and television advertising. (Source: Reprinted with permission from AD AGE, 5/16/89. Copyright Crain Communications, Inc. All rights reserved.)

Advertisers can reach very specific market segments through ads in special-interest magazines. A boat manufacturer has a ready-made consumer audience in subscribers to *Yachting* or *Sail*. Producers of cameras and photographic equipment advertise primarily in *Travel & Leisure* or *Popular Photography*. A number of more general magazines like *Time* and *Cosmopolitan* publish regional editions, which provide advertisers with geographic segmentation as well.

Magazine advertising is more prestigious than newspaper advertising, and it provides high-quality color reproduction. In addition, magazine advertisements have a longer life span than those in other media. Issues of *National Geographic*, for example, may be retained for months or years by subscribers, and the ads they contain are viewed over and over again.

The major disadvantages of magazine advertising are high cost and lack of timeliness. Magazine ads—especially full-color ads—are expensive, although the cost per reader may compare favorably with that of other media. And, because magazine ads must normally be prepared more than a month in advance, they cannot be adjusted to reflect the latest market conditions.

direct-mail advertising
promotional material that is mailed directly to individuals

Direct Mail **Direct-mail advertising** is promotional material that is mailed directly to individuals. Direct mail is the most selective medium: Mailing lists are available (or can be compiled) to reach almost any target market, from airplane enthusiasts to zoologists. The effectiveness of direct-mail advertising can be measured easily because recipients either buy or don't buy the product that is advertised.

The success of direct-mail advertising depends on appropriate and current mailing lists. A direct-mail campaign may fail if the mailing list is outdated and the mailing does not reach the right people. In addition, this medium is relatively costly. Nevertheless, direct-mail advertising expenditures in 1988 amounted to more than $21 billion, or about 18 percent of the total.

outdoor advertising *short promotional messages on billboards, posters, and signs, and in skywriting*

Outdoor Advertising **Outdoor advertising** consists of short promotional messages on billboards, posters, and signs, and in skywriting. In 1988 outdoor advertisers spent $1.1 billion, or approximately 1 percent of total advertising expenditures, on outdoor advertising.

Sign and billboard advertising allows the marketer to focus on a particular geographic area; it is fairly inexpensive. However, because most of it is directed toward a mobile audience (the advertising on buses and taxis is itself mobile), the message must be limited to a few words. The medium is especially suitable for products that lend themselves to pictorial display.

Television Television is the newest advertising medium, and it ranks second only to newspapers in total revenue. In 1988, 21.8 percent of advertising expenditures, or $25 billion, went to television. Approximately 98 percent of American homes have at least one television set, which is used an average of seven hours each day.[3] The average U.S. household can receive nearly twenty-eight TV channels, including cable and pay stations, according to Nielson Media Research. Fifty-four percent of households receive twenty or more channels, and 39 percent can get between seven and nineteen channels.[4] Television obviously provides a massive market for advertisers.

Television advertising is the primary medium for larger firms whose objective is to reach national or regional markets. A national advertiser

Television is one of the leading media for carrying advertising messages to consumers. Here, marketing strategists plan the advertising message for an Anacin commercial, considering such factors as the product's most appealing features and its probable consumer groups.

may buy *network time,* which guarantees that its message will be broadcast by hundreds of local stations that are affiliated with the network. And both national and local firms may buy *local time* on a single station that covers a particular geographic selling area.

Advertisers may *sponsor* an entire show, alone or with other sponsors. Or they may buy *spot time* for a single 10-, 20-, 30-, or 60-second commercial during or between programs. To an extent, they may select their audience by choosing the day of the week and the time of day when their ads will be shown. Anheuser-Busch advertises Budweiser Beer and Noxell Corporation advertises Noxema shaving cream during the TV football season because the majority of viewers are men, who are likely to use these products.

Television advertising rates are based on the number of people who are expected to be watching when the commercial is aired. In 1989, a 30-second network commercial aired during the National Basketball Association Championships cost over $150,000, and a commercial of the same length ran $675,000 for Superbowl XXIII.

Unlike magazine advertising, and perhaps like newspaper ads, television advertising has a short life. If a viewer misses a commercial, it is missed forever. Viewers may also become indifferent to commercial messages. Or they may use the commercial time as a break from viewing, thus missing the message altogether. (Remote-control devices make it especially easy to banish at least the sound of commercials from the living room.)

Radio Advertisers spent about $7.8 billion, or 6.6 percent of total expenditures, on radio advertising in 1988, up from $7.2 billion in 1987. Like magazine advertising, radio advertising offers selectivity. Radio stations develop programming for—and are tuned in by—specific groups of listeners. There are almost half a billion radios in the United States (about six per household), which makes radio the most accessible medium.

Radio can be less expensive than other media. Actual rates depend on geographic coverage, the number of commercials contracted for, the time period specified, and whether the station broadcasts on AM, FM, or both. Even small retailers are able to afford radio advertisements.

Major Steps in Developing an Advertising Campaign

Learning Objective 4
Identify the major steps in developing an advertising campaign

An advertising campaign is developed in several stages. These stages may vary in number and the order in which they are implemented, depending on the company's resources, its product, and its audiences. A campaign in any organization, however, will include the following steps in some form.

1. Identify and Analyze the Advertising Target The advertising target is the group of people toward which advertisements are directed. To pinpoint the advertising target and develop an effective campaign, marketers must analyze such information as the geographic distribution of consumers;

their age, sex, race, income, and education; and their attitudes toward both the advertiser's product and competing products. How marketers use this information will be influenced by the features of the product to be advertised and the nature of the competition. Precise identification of the advertising target is crucial to the proper development of subsequent stages and, ultimately, to the success of the campaign itself.

2. Define the Advertising Objectives   The goals of an advertising campaign should be stated precisely and in measurable terms. The objectives should include the current position of the firm, indicate how far and in what direction from that original reference point the company wishes to move, and specify a definite period of time for the achievement of the goals. Advertising objectives that focus on sales will stress increasing sales by a certain percentage or dollar amount, or expanding the firm's market share. Communication objectives will emphasize increasing product or brand awareness, improving consumer attitudes, or conveying product information.

3. Create the Advertising Platform   An advertising platform includes the important selling points or features that an advertiser wishes to incorporate into the advertising campaign. These features should be those that are important to consumers in their selection and use of a product and, if possible, those features that competing products lack. Although research into consumer opinions is expensive, it is the most productive way to determine the issues of an advertising platform.

4. Determine the Advertising Appropriation   The advertising appropriation is the total amount of money designated for advertising in a given period. This stage is critical to the success of the campaign because advertising efforts based on an inadequate budget will understimulate consumer demand, and a budget too large will waste a company's resources. Advertising appropriations may be based on last year's sales or forecasted plan, on what competitors spend on advertising, or on executive judgment.

5. Develop the Media Plan   A media plan specifies exactly which media will be used in the campaign and when advertisements will appear. The primary concern of the media planner is to reach the largest possible number of persons in the advertising target for each dollar that is spent, though cost effectiveness is not easy to measure. In addition to cost, media planners must consider the location and demographics of people in the advertising target, the content of the message, and the characteristics of the audiences reached by various media. The media planner begins with general media decisions, selects subclasses within each medium, and finally chooses particular media vehicles for the campaign.

6. Create the Advertising Message   The content and form of a message are influenced by the product's features, the characteristics of people in the advertising target, the objectives of the campaign, and the choice of media. An advertiser must consider these factors to choose words and illustrations that will be meaningful and appealing to persons in the advertising target. The copy, or words, of an advertisement will vary depending on the media choice but should attempt to move the audience through attention, interest, desire, and action. Artwork and visuals should complement copy by attracting the audience's attention and communicating an idea quickly.

7. Evaluate the Effectiveness of the Advertising A campaign's success should be measured before, during, and/or after the campaign ends in terms of its original objectives. An advertiser should at least be able to estimate whether sales or market share went up because of the campaign or whether any change occurred in consumer attitudes or brand awareness. Data from past and current sales, responses to coupon offers, and consumer surveys administered by research organizations are some of the ways in which advertising effectiveness can be evaluated.

Advertising Agencies

advertising agency *an independent firm that plans, produces, and places advertising for its clients*

Advertisers can plan and produce their own advertising with help from media personnel, or they can hire advertising agencies. An **advertising agency** is an independent firm that plans, produces, and places advertising for its clients. Many larger ad agencies offer help with sales promotion and publicity as well. The media usually pay a commission of 15 percent to advertising agencies. Thus the cost to the agency's client can be quite moderate. The client, of course, pays for production and other services the agency performs. Other methods for compensating agencies are also used.

Developing an effective advertising campaign requires abundant imagination. Hal Riney of San Francisco's Hal Riney & Partners agency has been very successful with his soft-sell Calistoga ad. In fact, sales of Calistoga, a bottled-water brand owned by Perrier, rose 100% in three years.

TABLE 14.1 *The Twenty Leading National Advertisers*

Rank	Advertiser	Ad Spending ($ millions)
1	Philip Morris Cos.	$2,058.2
2	Procter & Gamble Co.	1,506.9
3	General Motors Corp.	1,294.0
4	Sears, Roebuck & Co.	1,045.2
5	RJR Nabisco	814.5
6	Grand Metropolitan PLC	773.9
7	Eastman Kodak Co.	735.9
8	McDonald's Corp.	728.3
9	PepsiCo Inc.	712.3
10	Kellogg Co.	683.1
11	Anheuser-Busch Cos.	634.5
12	K mart Corp.	632.0
13	Warner-Lambert Co.	609.2
14	Unilever NV	607.5
15	Nestle SA	573.8
16	Ford Motor Co.	569.8
17	American Telephone & Telegraph	547.5
18	Chrysler Corp.	474.0
19	General Mills	470.1
20	Johnson & Johnson	468.8

Source: Reprinted with permission from AD AGE, 9/27/89. Copyright Crain Communications, Inc. All rights reserved.

Firms that do a lot of advertising may use both an in-house advertising department and an independent agency. This approach gives the firm the advantage of being able to call on the agency's expertise in particular areas of advertising. The agency also brings a fresh viewpoint to the firm's products and advertising plans.

Table 14.1 lists the nation's twenty leading advertisers, in all media. After twenty-four years, Procter & Gamble was dethroned as the nation's number-one advertiser. In 1989 the number-one honor went to tobacco-beer-and-food giant Philip Morris Cos.

Social and Legal Considerations in Advertising

There are two main arguments against advertising—that it is wasteful and that it can be deceptive. Although advertising (like any other activity) can be performed inefficiently, it is far from wasteful. Let's look at the evidence:

▶ Advertising is the most effective and the least expensive means of communicating product information to millions of individuals and firms.

▶ Advertising encourages competition and is, in fact, a means of competition. It thus leads to the development of new and improved products, wider product choices, and lower prices.

▶ Advertising revenues support our mass communications media—newspapers, magazines, radio, and television. This means that advertising pays for much of our news coverage and entertainment programming.

▶ Advertising provides job opportunities in fields ranging from sales to film production. Total employment within the advertising industry stood at 212,000 in 1987.[5]

Along with pure fact, advertising tends to include some exaggeration, stretching of the truth, and occasional deception. Usually, consumers spot such distortion in short order. But various government and private agencies also scrutinize advertising for false or deceptive claims or offers.

At the national level, the Federal Trade Commission, the Food and Drug Administration, and the Federal Communications Commission oversee advertising practices. Advertising may also be monitored by state and local agencies, Better Business Bureaus, and industry associations. These organizations have varying degrees of control over advertising, but their overall effect has been a positive one.

Personal Selling

Personal selling is the most adaptable of all promotion methods because the person who is presenting the message can modify it to suit the individual buyer. However, personal selling is also the most expensive promotion method.

Most successful salespeople are able to communicate with people on a one-to-one basis and are strongly motivated. They have a thorough knowledge of the products they offer for sale. And they are willing and able to deal with the details involved in handling and processing orders. Sales managers tend to emphasize these qualities in recruiting and hiring, as well as in the other human resources management activities discussed in Chapter 9.

Many selling situations demand the personal contact and adaptability of personal selling. This is especially true of industrial sales, where single purchases may amount to millions of dollars. Obviously, sales of that size must be based on carefully planned sales presentations, personal contact between buyers and sellers, and thorough negotiations.

Kinds of Salespersons

Learning Objective 5
Know the various kinds of salespersons, the personal-selling process, and the major sales management tasks

Because most businesses employ different salespersons to perform different functions, marketing managers must select the kinds of sales personnel that will be most effective in selling the firm's products. Salespersons may be identified as order getters, order takers, and support personnel. A single individual can perform all three functions and frequently does so.

order getter *a salesperson who is responsible for selling the firm's products to new customers and increasing sales to present customers*

creative selling *selling products to new customers and increasing sales to present customers*

order taker *a salesperson who handles repeat sales in ways that maintain positive relationships with customers*

sales support personnel *employees who aid in selling but are more involved in locating prospects, educating customers, building goodwill for the firm, and providing follow-up service*

missionary salesperson *a salesperson—generally employed by a manufacturer—who visits retailers to persuade them to buy the manufacturer's products*

trade salesperson *a salesperson—generally employed by a food producer or processor—who assists customers in promoting products, especially in retail stores*

technical salesperson *a salesperson who assists the company's current customers in technical matters*

Order Getters   An **order getter** is responsible for what is sometimes called **creative selling:** selling the firm's products to new customers and increasing sales to present customers. An order getter must perceive buyers' needs, supply them with information about the firm's product, and persuade them to buy the product. Order-getting activities may be separated into two groups. In current-customer sales, salespeople concentrate on obtaining additional sales, or leads for prospective sales, from customers who have purchased the firm's products at least once. In new-business sales, sales personnel seek out new prospects and convince them to make an initial purchase of the firm's product. The real estate, insurance, appliance, heavy industrial machinery, and automobile industries in particular depend on new-business sales.

Order Takers   An **order taker** handles repeat sales in ways that maintain positive relationships with customers. An order taker sees that customers have products when and where they are needed and in the proper amounts. *Inside order takers* receive incoming mail and telephone orders in some businesses; they also include salespersons in retail stores. *Outside* (or *field*) *order takers* travel to customers. Often the buyer and the field salesperson develop a mutually beneficial relationship of placing, receiving, and delivering orders. Both inside and outside order takers are active salespersons and often produce most of their companies' sales.

Support Personnel   **Sales support personnel** aid in selling but are more involved in locating *prospects* (likely first-time customers), educating customers, building goodwill for the firm, and providing follow-up service. The most common categories of support personnel are missionary, trade, and technical salespersons.

A **missionary salesperson,** who usually works for a manufacturer, visits retailers to persuade them to buy the manufacturer's products. If the retailers agree, they buy the products from wholesalers, who are the manufacturer's actual customers. Missionary salespersons are often employed by producers of medical supplies and pharmaceuticals to promote these products to retail druggists, physicians, and hospitals.

A **trade salesperson,** who generally works for a food producer or processor, assists customers in promoting products, especially in retail stores. A trade salesperson may obtain additional shelf space for the products, restock shelves, set up displays, and distribute samples. Because trade salespersons are usually order takers as well, they are not strictly support personnel.

A **technical salesperson** assists the company's current customers in technical matters. He or she may explain how to use a product, how it is made, how to install it, or how a system is designed. A technical salesperson should be formally educated in science or engineering. Computers, steel, and chemicals are some of the products handled by technical salespeople.

Marketers usually require sales personnel from several of these categories. Factors that affect hiring and other personnel decisions include the number of customers and their characteristics; the product's attributes, complexity, and price; distribution channels used by the company; and the company's approach to advertising.

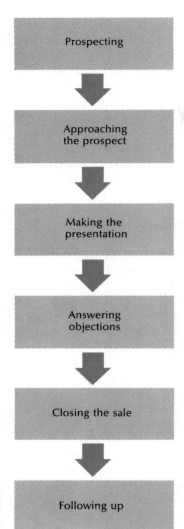

FIGURE 14.5
The Six Steps of the Personal Selling Process
Personal selling is not only the most adaptable of all promotion methods, it is also the most expensive.

The Personal-Selling Process

No two selling situations are exactly alike, and no two salespeople perform their jobs in exactly the same way. Most salespeople, however, follow the six-step procedure illustrated in Figure 14.5.

Prospecting   The first step in personal selling is to research potential buyers and choose the most likely customers, or prospects. Prospects may be suggested by business associates and customers, public records, telephone and trade-association directories, and company files. The salesperson concentrates on those prospects who have the financial resources, willingness, and authority to buy the product.

Approaching the Prospect   First impressions are often lasting impressions. Thus the salesperson's first contact with the prospect is crucial to successful selling. The best approach is one that is based on knowledge—of the prospect, of the prospect's needs, and of how the product can meet those needs. Salespeople who understand each customer's particular situation are likely to make a good first impression—and to make a sale.

Making the Presentation   The next step is the actual delivery of the sales presentation. In many cases, this includes demonstrating the product. The salesperson points out the product's features, its benefits, and how it is superior to competitors' merchandise. If the product has been used successfully by other firms, the salesperson may mention this as part of the presentation.

During a demonstration, the salesperson may suggest that the prospect try out the product personally. The demonstration and product trial should underscore specific points made during the presentation.

Answering Objections   The prospect is then given the opportunity to raise objections or ask questions. This gives the salesperson a chance to eliminate objections that might prevent a sale, to point out additional features, or to mention special services that the company offers.

Closing the Sale   To close the sale, the salesperson asks the prospect to buy the product. This is considered the critical point in the selling process. Many experienced salespeople make use of a *trial closing*, in which they ask questions that assume the customer is going to buy the product. The questions "When would you want delivery?" and "Do you want the standard or the deluxe model?" are typical of trial closings. They allow the reluctant prospect to make a purchase without having to say, "I'll take it."

Following Up   The salesperson must follow up on the order to ensure that the product is delivered on time, in the right quantity, and in good condition. During follow-up, the salesperson also makes it clear that he or she is available in case problems develop before or after delivery. Follow-up leaves a good impression and eases the way toward future sales. Hence it is essential to the selling process. The salesperson's job

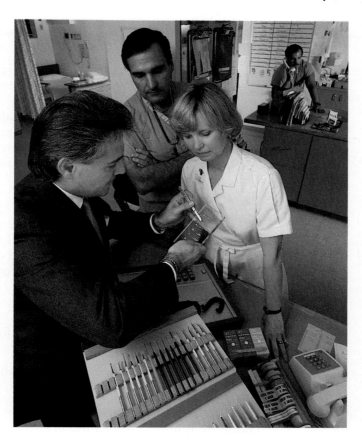

Making the sales presentation is a crucial step in the personal-selling process. The step includes demonstrating the product and pointing out the product's features. Here, a salesman from the AcuteCare Division of Becton Dickinson explains the benefits of two of the company's products, blades and scalpels for use in operating rooms.

does not end with a sale. It continues as long as the seller and the customer maintain a working relationship.

Managing Personal Selling

A firm's success often hinges on the competent management of its sales force. Without a strong sales force—and the sales revenue it brings in—a business will soon fail.

Sales managers have responsibilities in a number of areas. They must set sales objectives in concrete, quantifiable terms, specifying a certain period of time and a certain geographic area. They must adjust the size of the sales force in accord with changes in the firm's marketing plan and changes in the marketing environment. Sales managers must attract and hire effective salespersons. They must develop a training program and decide where, when, how, and for whom the training will be conducted. They must formulate a fair and adequate compensation plan to keep qualified employees. They must motivate salespersons to boost their productivity. They must define sales territories and determine scheduling and routing of the sales force. Finally, sales managers must evaluate the operation as a whole through sales reports, communications with customers, and invoices.

Sales Promotion

Sales promotion consists of activities or materials that are direct inducements to customers or salespersons. Sales promotion techniques are used primarily to enhance and supplement other promotion methods. In this role they can have a significant impact on sales of consumer products. The dramatic increase in recent spending for sales promotion shows that marketers have recognized the potential of this promotion method. Most firms now include year-round sales promotions as part of their overall promotion mix.

Sales Promotion Objectives

consumer sales promotion method   *a sales promotion method designed to attract consumers to particular retail stores and motivate them to purchase certain new or established products*

trade sales promotion method *a sales promotion method designed to encourage wholesalers and retailers to stock and actively promote a manufacturer's product*

Sales promotion activities may be used singly or in combination, both offensively and defensively, to achieve one goal or a set of goals. Marketers use sales promotion activities and materials for a number of purposes:

1. To draw new customers
2. To present a new product
3. To add to the total number of customers for an established brand
4. To boost sales to current customers
5. To convey information about product changes
6. To increase traffic in retail stores
7. To steady irregular sales patterns
8. To build up reseller inventories
9. To counter the activities of competitors
10. To improve shelf space and displays[6]

General Cinema Corporation uses promotions such as the Presidential Straw Poll to boost sales of refreshments in its theaters.

Some of these objectives focus on reseller demand; some, on consumer demand; and some, on both resellers and consumers. Any sales promotion objective should be in keeping with the organization's general goals and with its marketing and promotion objectives.

Sales Promotion Methods

Most sales promotion methods can be classified as promotion techniques either for consumer sales or for trade sales. A **consumer sales promotion method** attracts consumers to particular retail stores and motivates them to purchase certain new or established products. A **trade sales promotion method** encourages wholesalers and retailers to stock and actively promote a manufacturer's products. Incentives such as money, merchandise, marketing assistance, or gifts are commonly awarded to resellers who buy products or respond positively in other ways.

A number of factors enter into marketing decisions about which, and how many, sales promotion methods to use. Of greatest importance are the objectives of the promotional effort. Product characteristics—size, weight, cost, durability, uses, features, and hazards—and target-market

BUSINESS JOURNAL

Promoting Sales Promotions

Consumer populations and marketing environments are rapidly changing, and new markets are constantly developing. These variations force companies to develop and implement effective sales promotions.

Sales promotion materials and programs cost U.S. marketers more than advertising. Nevertheless, the impact of sales promotions may be lessening because they tend to look alike, less money is being spent on each item, and competition is intensifying.

WHY SOME SALES PROMOTIONS FAIL

Sales promotions generally focus on the consumer, who is better informed than ever before. The promotions require time to plan, execute, and evaluate. Sales promotions are likely to fail, however, if the needs of sales staff, distributors, or retailers are not properly considered. Lack of support from top management and ineffective communications also result in failures.

CHARACTERISTICS OF SUCCESSFUL SALES PROMOTIONS

Marketing research is a critical part of a promotional campaign. Once marketers have researched the target market, the firm can develop a sales promotion that explains the benefits of the product in the least amount of time possible, gives customers an incentive to purchase the product or service, and makes them feel good about themselves.

In undertaking a sales promotion, a firm should understand what its goals and objectives are and should set guidelines outlining its expectations. If the company decides to offer a premium, it should be creative and original.

Sales promotions are successful only when they are accompanied by effective advertising. An effective advertisement is one whose message stimulates consumers to purchase the product. Companies often spend considerable amounts of money on the form and content of their advertisements' message. Salespersons should use their company's advertising campaign when calling on customers. Linking sales presentations with the company's promotional campaign can increase sales.

DO CONTINUOUS SALES PROMOTIONS DESTROY BRANDS?

No and yes. Some marketing experts insist that continuous promotion does not destroy brands. Products ranging from soft drinks to breakfast cereals take advantage of promotions and contests all year long. Selling brands at cost is a common practice in supermarkets, and it does not destroy brands.

Critics of continuous promotions feel differently, however. They say that advertising builds loyalty over time, while discount promotions lead only to short-term gains. According to their outlook, excessive price promotions can ruin brands because consumers learn to buy a product by price instead of by brand loyalty.

There are no simple rules for what works, but price, competition, audience, distribution, trade support, and product features are all important ingredients to consider when developing continuous promotions.

Based on information from Bill Robinson, "No: Continuous Sales (Price) Promotion Destroys Brands," *Marketing News*, January 16, 1989, p. 4; W. E. Phillips, "Yes: Continuous Sales (Price) Promotion Destroys Brands," *Marketing News*, January 16, 1989, p. 4; William S. Pierson, "I Am Particular," *American Salesman*, June 1989, p. 6; William G. Weller, "Simple Sales Promotion Cuts Through Market Clutter," *Marketing News*, November 7, 1986, p. 16; Matthew J. Hayes, "Marketing Research: The Industry's Most Effective Tool in All Promotional Campaigns," *American Salesman*, December 1988, p. 3; Grace Conlon, "Promotional Offers Sweeten the Pot, but Ads Provide Yardstick," *Marketing News*, May 22, 1987, p. 15; and Bud Frankel, "First Fine-tune the 'Inner Game' of Sales Promotion," *Marketing News*, September 12, 1988, p. 18.

profiles—age, sex, income, location, density, usage rate, and buying patterns—must likewise be considered. Distribution channels and availability of appropriate resellers also influence the choice of sales promotion methods, as do the competitive and regulatory environments. Let's now discuss a few important sales promotion methods.

refund *a return of part of the purchase price of a product*

Refunding   A **refund** is a return of part of the purchase price of a product. Usually the refund is offered by the producer to those consumers who send in a coupon along with a specific proof of purchase. (A refund is sometimes called a *manufacturer's rebate*.) Refunding is a relatively low-cost promotion method. It was formerly used mainly for new product items, but now it is applied to a wide variety of products.

cents-off coupon *a coupon that reduces the retail price of a particular item by a stated amount at the time of purchase*

Couponing   A **cents-off coupon** is a coupon that reduces the retail price of a particular item by a stated amount at the time of purchase. These coupons may be worth anywhere from a few cents to more than $1. They are reproduced in newspapers and magazines and/or sent to consumers by direct mail. More and more firms now use coupons. About 252.7 billion coupons were distributed in 1988; of these, less than 4 percent were redeemed by consumers.[7] At an average coupon value of 44 cents, consumers redeemed coupons worth $4.66 billion in 1988.[8] Coupons seem to work best for new or improved product items. The largest single category of coupons is health and beauty aids, followed by prepared foods, frozen and refrigerated foods, cereals, and household products. Stores in some areas even deduct double the value of manufacturers' coupons from the purchase price, as a sales promotion technique of their own. Coupons may also offer free merchandise, either with or without an additional purchase of the product.

sample *a free package or container of a product*

Sampling   A **sample** is a free package or container of a product. Samples may be offered through coupons, by direct mailing, or at *in-store demonstrations*. Although sampling ensures that consumers will try the product, it is the most expensive sales promotion technique. It gives best results when it is used with new products.

premium *a gift that a producer offers the customer in return for using its product*

Premiums and Trading Stamps   A **premium** is a gift that a producer offers the customer in return for using its product. A producer of packaged foods may, for instance, offer consumers a cookbook as a premium. Most airlines offer free travel to business customers after a certain number of paid trips or air miles.

trading stamp *a stamp given out by retailers in proportion to the amount spent; redeemable for a gift*

A **trading stamp** is a stamp that is given out by retailers in proportion to the amount spent. It is redeemable for a gift. Trading stamps were very popular with supermarkets and service stations in the 1970s, but they seem to be less in vogue at present.

point-of-purchase display *promotional material that is placed within a retail store*

Point-of-Purchase Displays   A **point-of-purchase display** is promotional material that is placed within a retail store. The display is usually located near the product that is being promoted. It may actually hold merchandise (as do L'eggs hosiery displays) or inform customers of what the product offers and encourage them to buy it. Most point-of-purchase displays are prepared and set up by manufacturers and wholesalers.

trade show *an industrywide exhibit at which many sellers display their products*

Trade Shows A **trade show** is an industrywide exhibit at which many sellers display their products. Some trade shows are organized exclusively for dealers—to permit manufacturers and wholesalers to show their latest lines to retailers. Others are consumer promotions designed to stimulate buying interest in the general public. Among the latter are boat shows, home shows, and flower shows that are put on each year in large cities.

Publicity and Public Relations

Learning Objective 7
Recognize the types and uses of publicity and the requirements for effective use of publicity

public relations *all activities whose objective is to create and maintain a favorable public image*

Publicity, as mentioned earlier, is a nonpersonal message in news story form delivered through a mass medium, free of charge. Publicity differs from advertising in two ways: It is free (the media do not get paid for it), and it is not controlled by the firm. However, when it enhances the image of the firm or its products, publicity can be an effective form of promotion.

Public relations consists of all activities whose objective is to create and maintain a favorable public image. In one sense, publicity is a part of public relations—the "information" part. Actually, good public relations generally results in good publicity and thus a favorable image.

Public-relations activities are many and varied, including the sponsorship of programs on public television and radio, the sponsorship of sporting events (including the Olympics), and various informational (rather than product-oriented) advertising. For example, Philip Morris sponsors the Next Wave Festival to show its support of innovation and the arts, and General Foods Corp. sponsored the Tang March Across

Turbo Cup races, sponsored by Porsche Cars North America, Inc., make use of public relations to promote a favorable image to its potential customers. They also provide an opportunity for the promotion of automotive products by many other companies!

America for Mothers Against Drunk Driving (MADD).[9] These and other public-relations efforts tend to build sales indirectly by showing that the sponsor is a "good citizen."

Types of Publicity

news release *a typed page of generally fewer than 300 words provided by an organization to the media as a form of publicity*

feature article *a piece (of up to 3,000 words) prepared by an organization for inclusion in a particular publication*

captioned photograph *a picture accompanied by a brief explanation*

press conference *a meeting at which invited media personnel hear important news announcements and receive supplementary textual materials and photographs*

Several approaches to publicity are available to marketers. The **news release,** one of the most widely used types of publicity, is generally one typed page of fewer than 300 words provided by an organization to the media. The release includes the firm's name, address, phone number, and contact person. The **feature article,** which may run as long as 3,000 words, is usually written for inclusion in a particular publication. The **captioned photograph,** a picture accompanied by a brief explanation, is an effective way to illustrate a new or improved product. The **press conference** allows invited media personnel to hear important news announcements and to receive supplementary textual materials and photographs. Finally, letters to the editor, special newspaper or magazine editorials, films, and tapes may be prepared and distributed to appropriate media for possible use.

At times a single type of publicity will be adequate for a promotion mix. At other times, publicity will predominate in a mix, and the marketer will capitalize on several avenues of publicity. The specific kinds of publicity chosen depend on the composition of the target audience, the response of media personnel, the significance of the news item, and the nature and quantity of information to be communicated.

The Uses of Publicity

Businesses may use publicity for one purpose only or for several purposes. Publicity can raise public awareness of a company's products or activities. It can maintain a desired level of visibility for an organization. It can show a forward-looking company to its best advantage and help to downplay a negative image as well. Table 14.2 lists some of the issues that can be addressed by publicity releases.

Using Publicity Effectively

A company's publicity efforts should be thorough, well-organized, and regular. The program should be led by a designated individual or department within the business or by an advertising or public relations firm.

Because publicity functions often require personal communications with editors, reporters, and other media personnel, good professional relationships with these individuals are essential. Their advice can help ensure that a business's publicity program meshes well with the workings of the media.

A firm that is striving for effective publicity should review its news items carefully to avoid releasing those that are insignificant or poorly written. News items that do not meet media standards are usually rejected by media personnel.

TABLE 14.2   Possible Issues for Publicity Releases

Marketing Developments
New products
New uses for old products
Research developments
Changes of marketing personnel
Large orders received
Successful bids
Awards of contracts
Special events

Company Policies
New guarantees
Changes in credit terms
Changes in distribution policies
Changes in service policies
Changes in prices

News of General Interest
Annual election of officers
Meetings of the board of directors
Anniversaries of the organization
Anniversaries of an invention
Anniversaries of the senior officers
Holidays that can be tied to the organization's activities
Annual banquets and picnics
Special weeks, such as Clean-up Week
Founders' Day
Conferences and special meetings
Open house to the community
Athletic events
Awards of merit to employees
Laying of cornerstone
Opening of an exhibition

Reports on Current Developments
Reports of experiments
Reports on industry conditions
Company progress reports
Employment, production, and sales statistics
Reports on new discoveries
Tax reports
Speeches by principals
Analyses of economic conditions
Employment gains
Financial statements
Organization appointments
Opening of new markets

Personalities—Names Are News
Visits by famous persons
Accomplishments of individuals
Winners of company contests
Employees' and officers' advancements
Interviews with company officials
Company employees serving as judges for contests
Interviews with employees

Slogans, Symbols, Endorsements
Company's slogan—its history and development
A tie-in of company activities with slogans
Creation of a slogan
The company's trademark
The company's name plate
Product endorsements

Source: Albert Wesley Frey, ed., *Marketing Handbook*, 2nd ed. (New York: Ronald Press), pp. 19–35. Copyright © 1965. Reprinted by permission of John Wiley & Sons, Inc.

The number of news releases actually published or broadcast can give a company a good indication of the effectiveness of its publicity program. As one check on the print media, an organization can pay clipping services to cut out and relay published news stories to the publicity department. No similar service is available, however, for monitoring broadcast news releases. A firm can request that a notification card be returned when a station has broadcast a certain news release, but stations do not always follow through on these requests.

Promotion Planning

A **promotional campaign** is a plan for combining and using the four promotion methods—advertising, personal selling, sales promotion, and publicity—in a particular promotion mix to reach one or more marketing goals. Often the campaign is built around a *theme*, such as AT&T's "The right choice" or the American Express "Don't leave home without it."

In planning a promotion, marketers must answer two questions:

▶ What will be the role of promotion in the overall marketing mix?

▶ To what extent will each promotion method be used in the promotion mix?

The answer to the first question depends on the firm's marketing objectives, since the role of each element of the marketing mix—product, price, physical distribution, and promotion—depends on these detailed versions of the firm's marketing goals. The answer to the second question depends on the answer to the first as well as on the target market.

Promotion and Marketing Objectives

Promotion is naturally better suited to certain marketing objectives than it is to others. For example, promotion can do little to further a marketing objective such as "reduce delivery time by one-third." (It can, however, be used to inform customers that delivery time has been reduced.) Let's consider some objectives that *would* require the use of promotion as a primary ingredient of the marketing mix.

Providing Information   This is, of course, the main function of promotion. It may be used to communicate to target markets the availability of new products or product features. It may alert them to special sales or offers or give the locations of retailers that carry the firm's products. In other words, promotion can be used to enhance the effectiveness of each of the other ingredients of the marketing mix.

Increasing Market Share   Promotion can be used to convince new customers to try a product, while maintaining the product loyalty of established customers. Comparative advertising, for example, is directed mainly at those who might—but presently do not—use a particular product. Advertising that emphasizes the product's features also assures those who *do* use the product that they are doing the right thing.

Positioning the Product   The sales of a product depend, to a great extent, on its competition. The stronger the competition, the more difficult it is to maintain or increase sales. For this reason, many firms go to great lengths to position their products in the marketplace. **Positioning** is the development of a product image in buyers' minds relative to the images they have of competing products.

BUSINESS JOURNAL

Specialty Advertising: The Medium Is the Message

Specialty advertising is the use of various items to carry the advertiser's name, address, and message to the target audience. These articles (called *advertising specialties*) include credit-card-size calculators, digital compasses and alarm clocks, portable AM-FM stereo systems, push-button phones, digital watches, and 35-mm cameras. The latest specialty trend emphasizes print premiums: picture albums, collectors' editions, and health and science reference books.

Sophisticated marketing campaigns increasingly use such specialty items as product-emblazoned sweatshirts, coffee mugs, note pads, or other unique and utilitarian devices. These specialties are distributed to current customers, prospective customers, employees, or other groups that advertisers want to reach.

BANKS AND SPECIALTY ADVERTISING

Banks and other financial institutions have been using specialty advertising for decades to promote goodwill, but today they are also using it to achieve specific goals such as opening new accounts or attracting customers to new services. The budgets for specialty advertising are expanding as banks discover new applications for it. Promotional items, if picked correctly, can have a long life and can even be targeted to specific demographic groups. Specialty advertising is also being used internally to build company images and motivate employees. It is predicted that banks' use of specialty advertising to specific market segments will continue to expand over the next few years.

SPECIALTY ADVERTISING IN DIRECT-MAIL CAMPAIGNS

Recent studies indicate that dollar purchases per sale in a direct-mail campaign can be increased through specialty advertising. For example, one study found dollar purchases per sale were 321 percent higher for direct-mail advertising that included an advertising specialty as opposed to direct-mail advertising alone. Moreover, active use of specialties has been shown to increase the response rate of prospective customers unwilling to take time for interviews.

OTHER USES

Specialty advertising is a particularly versatile medium because it can be effectively used alone, in concert with another medium, or in a multimedia campaign. Because specialty advertising can be precisely focused by the advertiser, the message gets prime exposure. And because the message carrier is a useful item, potential customers are continually reminded of the company's identity.

Based on information from Joe Stratton, "Differentiation Through Specialty Advertising," *Bank Marketing*, November 1988, p. 33; G. A. Marken, "With Specialty Ads, the Medium Is the Message," *Marketing News*, June 6, 1988, p. 10; H. Ted Olson, "That Specialty Pull: Specialty Advertising Used in a Direct-Mail Campaign Can Boost Response and Dollar Purchase Per Sale," *Target Marketing*, May 1987, p. 6; and Gordon Grossman, "The Many Faces of Subscription Premiums," *Direct Marketing*, April 1989, p. 42.

Promotion is the prime positioning tool. For example, 7Up was heavily promoted as the "Uncola," to position it away from the very strong Coca-Cola and Pepsi-Cola. As an uncola, 7Up avoided competing with those two products. Instead, it was positioned against somewhat weaker, noncola soft drinks. Promotion may also be used to position one product directly against another product. For example, Miller Brewing Company's Low-enbrau beer is positioned as a German beer and is designed to compete with beers imported from Germany.

Stabilizing Sales Special promotional efforts can be used to increase sales during slack periods, such as the "off season" for certain sports equipment. By stabilizing sales in this way, a firm can use its production facilities more effectively and reduce both capital costs and inventory costs.

Promotion is also often used to increase the sales of products that are in the declining stage of their life cycle. The object is to keep them going for a little while longer.

Developing the Promotion Mix

Learning Objective 8
Know what factors influence the selection of promotion-mix ingredients

Once the role of promotion is established, the various promotion methods may be combined in a promotional campaign. As in so many other areas of business, promotion planning begins with a set of specific objectives. The promotion mix is then designed to accomplish these objectives.

Marketers often use several promotion mixes simultaneously if a firm sells multiple products. The selection of promotion-mix ingredients and the degree to which they are used depend on the organization's resources and objectives, the nature of the target market, the characteristics of the product, and the feasibility of various promotion methods.

The amount of promotional resources available in an organization influences the number and intensity of promotion methods that marketers can use. A firm with a limited budget for promotion will probably rely on personal selling, because the effectiveness of personal selling can be measured more easily than that of advertising. An organization's objectives also have an effect on its promotional activities. A company wishing to make a wide audience familiar with a new convenience item will probably depend heavily on advertising and sales promotion. If a company's objective is to communicate information to consumers—on the features of home appliances, for example—then the company may develop a promotion mix that includes some advertising, some sales promotion to attract consumers to stores, and much personal selling.

The demographics—size, geographic distribution, and socioeconomic characteristics—of the target market play a part in the composition of a product's promotion mix. If the market is small, personal selling will probably be the most important element in the promotion mix. This is true of organizations that sell to small industrial markets and businesses that use only a few wholesalers to market their goods. Companies that need to contact millions of potential customers, however, will emphasize sales promotion and advertising because these methods are relatively

Sales promotion is one of the major ingredients of a promotional campaign. Often the campaign is built around a theme, such as "You oughta be in pictures" by OshKosh B'Gosh.

inexpensive. The age, income, and education of the target market will also influence the choice of promotion techniques. For example, personal selling may be more effective with less educated consumers than ads in newspapers or magazines.

In general, industrial products require personal selling, while consumer goods depend on advertising. This is not true in every case, however. The price of the product also influences the composition of the promotion mix. Since consumers often want the advice of a salesperson on an expensive product, high-priced consumer goods may call for more personal selling. Similarly, advertising and sales promotion may be more crucial to marketers of seasonal items because having a year-round sales force is not always appropriate.

The cost and availability of promotion methods are important factors in the development of a promotion mix. Although national advertising and sales promotion activities are expensive, the cost per customer may be quite small if the campaign succeeds in reaching large numbers of people. In addition, local advertising outlets—newspapers, magazines, radio and television stations, and outdoor displays—may not be that costly for a small, local business. In some situations a firm may find that no available advertising medium reaches the target market effectively.

CHAPTER REVIEW ▰▰▰▰▰

Summary

Promotion is communication that is intended to inform, persuade, or remind an organization's target markets of the organization or its products. The major promotion-mix ingredients are advertising, personal selling, sales promotion, and publicity. The role of promotion is to facilitate exchanges directly or indirectly and to help an organization maintain favorable relationships between itself and groups in the marketing environment.

Advertising is a paid, nonpersonal message communicated to a select audience through a mass medium. Selective advertising promotes a particular brand of product. Institutional advertising is image-building advertising for a firm. Primary-demand advertising promotes the products of an entire industry rather than a single brand.

The major advertising media are newspapers, magazines, direct mail, outdoor advertising, television, and radio. Newspapers account for the greatest part of advertising expenditures, with television running a fairly close second. Magazine advertising is perhaps the most prestigious, and direct mail is certainly the most selective medium. Radio and magazine advertising can also be quite selective, and radio is relatively inexpensive.

An advertising campaign is developed in several stages. A firm's first task is to identify and analyze its advertising target. The goals of the campaign must also be clearly defined. Then the firm must develop the advertising platform, or statement of important selling points, and determine the size of the advertising budget. The next steps are to develop a media plan and create the advertising message itself. Finally, the effectiveness of the advertising campaign should be evaluated before, during, and/or after the campaign ends.

A firm may develop its own advertising, hire an advertising agency to plan and produce its ads, or both. Advertising is monitored by federal, state, and local agencies and industry organizations.

Personal selling is a personal communications process aimed at informing customers and persuading them to buy a firm's products. It is the most adaptable promotion method: The message can be modified by the salesperson to fit each buyer. Three major kinds of salespersons are order getters, order takers, and support personnel. The six steps in the personal-selling process are prospecting, approaching the prospect, making the presentation, answering objections, closing the sale, and following up. Sales managers get directly involved in setting sales force objectives; recruiting, selecting, and training salespersons; compensating and motivating sales personnel; creating sales territories; and evaluating sales performance.

Sales promotion is the use of activities and materials as direct inducements to customers and salespersons. Examples include refunding, couponing, sampling, offering premiums and trading stamps, setting up point-of-purchase displays, and taking part in trade shows.

Public-relations, or image-building, activities include the sponsorship of programs and events that are of interest to the general public. Publicity is a nonpersonal message in news story form delivered through a mass medium at no charge. It is transmitted to the media via news releases, feature articles, captioned photographs, and press conferences.

A promotional campaign is a plan for combining and using advertising, personal selling, sales promotion, and publicity to achieve one or more marketing goals. Campaign objectives are developed from marketing objectives. Then the promotion mix is developed on the basis of the organization and its marketing objectives, the nature of the target market, the product characteristics, and the feasibility of various promotional methods.

This chapter concludes our discussion of marketing. In the next chapter we begin our examination of information for business by discussing management information and computers.

Key Terms

You should now be able to define and give an example relevant to each of the following terms:

promotion	institutional advertising
promotion mix	primary-demand
advertising	advertising
personal selling	advertising media
sales promotion	cooperative advertising
publicity	direct-mail advertising
selective (or brand)	outdoor advertising
advertising	advertising agency

order getter

creative selling

order taker

sales support personnel

missionary salesperson

trade salesperson

technical salesperson

consumer sales
   promotion method

trade sales promotion
   method

refund

cents-off coupon

sample

premium

trading stamp

point-of-purchase
   display

trade show

public relations

news release

feature article

captioned photograph

press conference

promotional campaign

positioning

Questions and Exercises

Review Questions

1. What is the difference between a marketing mix and a promotion mix? How are they related?
2. What is the major role of promotion?
3. How are selective, institutional, and primary-demand advertising different from each other? Give an example of each.
4. What is cooperative advertising? What sorts of firms use it?
5. List the four major print media, and give an advantage and a disadvantage of each.
6. What types of firms use each of the two electronic media?
7. Outline the main steps required to develop an advertising campaign.
8. Why would a firm use an ad agency if it had its own advertising department?
9. Identify and give examples of the three major types of salespersons.
10. Explain how each step in the personal-selling process leads to the next step.
11. What are the major tasks involved in managing a sales force?
12. In your opinion, what are the three most effective techniques for sales promotion? How does each of these techniques supplement advertising?
13. What is the difference between publicity and public relations? What is the purpose of each?
14. Why is promotion particularly effective in positioning a product? in stabilizing or increasing sales?
15. What factors determine the specific promotion mix that should be used?

Discussion Questions

1. Why do some advertisers overlook or ignore Hispanic consumers in their advertising?
2. What advertising techniques should be used by firms attempting to reach various ethnic minority groups, especially U.S. Hispanics?
3. Discuss the pros and cons of comparative advertising from the viewpoint of (a) the advertiser, (b) the advertiser's competitors, and (c) the target market.
4. Which kinds of advertising—in which media—influence you most? Why?
5. Which kinds of retail outlets or products require mainly order taking by salespeople?
6. Why would a producer offer refunds or cents-off coupons rather than simply lowering the price of its products?
7. During the 1980s, customers were very receptive to certain types of sales promotion methods. Why?
8. How does the publicity that business firms seek help the general public?
9. What steps should a company take to avoid negative publicity?
10. What kind of promotion mix might be used to extend the life of a product that has entered the declining stage of its life cycle?

Exercises

1. Describe, sketch, or photocopy one example of each of the following types of advertisements. Explain briefly what makes it an example of its particular type.
   a. Immediate-response (selective)
   b. Reminder (selective)
   c. Institutional
   d. Primary-demand
   e. Local
   f. Cooperative
2. Briefly describe four different point-of-purchase displays that you have seen. For each, give the type of display, the product and brand displayed or promoted, and your evaluation of the effectiveness of the display.
3. Choose a particular product that was not discussed in the chapter. From your overall knowledge of the product, outline a promotion mix for it. That is, determine what percentage of your total promotion budget you would allocate to each promotion method, at whom the promotion would be directed, the media you would use. Give your reason for each decision.

Case 14.1

Multipurpose Promotion

Procter & Gamble, a consumer products promoter that practically created modern marketing, is re-creating it. The company is altering the way consumer packaged goods are marketed.

Procter & Gamble knows the importance of its retailers and retailer promotions. Among other marketing strategies, the company assigns special teams to help big customers like Wal-Mart, Kroger, and Fisher Foods of Canton, Ohio, improve their inventory, distribution, and sales promotion.

Like many marketers, Procter & Gamble offers retailers advertising allowances to promote its brands. One retailer in the P&G channel, Fisher Foods, decided to look for an alternative to newspaper advertising. A specialty advertising counselor recommended calendars as giveaways: Customers would appreciate receiving free calendars; would remember Fisher Foods; and, through the inclusion of cents-off coupons in the calendars, would take advantage of built-in savings when they redeemed the coupons at Fisher Foods.

Procter & Gamble prepared a brochure describing the calendar promotion and mailed it with a sample to fifty-three national sales coordinators. Later, the brochure was mailed to 4,000 P&G salespersons to promote the calendars to selected retail grocery chains. The stores, in turn, were to distribute the calendars to their customers.

The Procter & Gamble Calendar of Savings contained pages of coupons, recipes, and space for cooperating retailers' promotional message. The results of this promotion were excellent. A P&G spokesperson reported, "The impact . . . was outstanding. The return of calendar coupons was 619 percent over the return of newspaper store coupons."

Impressed with the results, Procter & Gamble decided to renew the calendar program for the next two years.*

Questions

1. Can you suggest other features that might make the calendar even more useful to consumers or to advertisers?

2. Fisher Foods and P&G used calendars because they created goodwill among customers and carried cents-off coupons. What other advantages might a calendar offer to advertisers?

3. Fisher Foods distributed the calendars in its stores and through the mail. What audiences for a supermarket would best be targeted by mail?

Case 14.2

Of Cigarettes and Science: MR FIT Study

R. J. Reynolds Tobacco Company, based in Winston-Salem, North Carolina, is a subsidiary of RJR Nabisco Inc. The tobacco company manufactures more than twenty brands of cigarettes and accounts for about one-third of the U.S. tobacco market.

To promote its cigarettes, R. J. Reynolds ran an advertisement entitled "Of Cigarettes and Science." The Federal Trade Commission (FTC) charged that the R. J. Reynolds advertisement made false and misleading claims about the purpose and results of the Multiple Risk Factor Intervention Trial (MR FIT) study. The MR FIT study was funded by the National Heart, Lung, and Blood Institute of the National Institutes of Health.

According to the FTC complaint, R. J. Reynolds' advertisement falsely claimed that the MR FIT study provided scientific evidence that smoking is not as hazardous as the public has been led to believe. Furthermore, charged the FTC, the advertisement falsely maintained that the MR FIT study tends to refute the theory that smoking causes heart disease. The FTC complaint also alleged that the ad was deceptive because R. J. Reynolds failed to disclose that the men in the MR FIT study who quit smoking had a significantly lower rate of heart disease than the men who continued to smoke.

The FTC's complaint was originally issued on June 16, 1986. In August 1986, the administrative law judge dismissed the case on the grounds that the ad was an editorial, fully protected by the First Amendment and not subject to regulation by the FTC. The FTC rejected the decision and remanded the matter to the administrative law judge for further proceedings.

In October 1989, the FTC announced that R. J. Reynolds Tobacco Company had agreed to settle charges that the company made false and misleading advertising claims regarding the health effects of smoking. According to one commissioner, the proposed settlement would help deter unfair or deceptive claims by

---

* Based on information from Brian Dumaine, "P&G Rewrites the Marketing Rules," *Fortune*, November 6, 1989, pp. 34–48; "Procter & Gamble Co-op Promotion Finds Another Option," Specialty Advertising Association, *1989/1990 Academic Weekly Planner*, 1989, pp. 1–2; and "Success Stories: 29 Award-Winning Specialty Advertising Promotions," *Specialty Advertising Association International*, 1989, p. 19.

other advertisers—cigarette and noncigarette companies alike—without impeding the dissemination of truthful and nondeceptive information. Another commissioner remarked that "the Commission has accorded this cigarette company treatment that is far more lenient than that ordinarily given to respondents in deceptive advertising cases."†

---

† Based on information from "R. J. Reynolds Tobacco Company Agrees to Settle FTC Charges of False Advertising," *FTC News Notes*, October 9, 1989, pp. 1–2; "Right of Rebuttal Gets New Lease, FTC Ruling on R. J. Reynolds Ad," *Advertising Age*, August 25, 1986, p. 17; Steven W. Colford, "RJR Ruling May 'Open Up' Issue Advertising," *Advertising Age*, August 18, 1986, p. 6; "The FTC vs. R. J. Reynolds," *Newsweek*, June 30, 1986, p. 48; and Steven W. Colford, "Reynolds, FTC Settle Dispute," *Advertising Age*, October 9, 1989, p. 52.

Questions

1. Do you agree with the FTC that the R. J. Reynolds Tobacco Company's advertising was false and misleading? Why or why not?

2. Do you think that the administrative law judge was correct in dismissing the case against R. J. Reynolds Tobacco Company? Why or why not?

3. Do you believe that various government and private agencies should scrutinize advertising for false or deceptive claims or offers? Explain your position.

CAREER PROFILE

FRIEDA CAPLAN For American shoppers, the Frieda of California purple heart logo found in the supermarket produce section symbolizes the best in exotic produce. Brought to the shelf by Frieda's Finest Produce Specialties, Inc., this distinctive trademark graces the labels of many unusual items such as purple potatoes, passion fruit, cherimoyas and jicama.

Frieda's Finest was founded by Frieda Caplan in 1962. At that time, there were already indications that Frieda Caplan was destined to become one of the nation's most successful female entrepreneurs. In 1962, as the owner of a tiny new produce company, she needed a sign in a hurry. The painter had only one color of paint, which proved to be a test of Caplan's marketing sense. She embraced the challenge and used the distinctive color purple to identify Frieda's Finest Produce Specialties, Inc. as the source for specialty produce across the country. In 1987, she celebrated twenty-five years in business as the first woman in the United States to successfully own and operate her own produce company.

Caplan began her career as a bookkeeper in the produce business managed by her husband's aunt and uncle. She soon worked her way "downstairs," and tried her hand at pushing California brown mushrooms—a specialty item at that time. Inspired by her success and the excitement of selling, she opened Frieda's Finest in 1962 with mushrooms as the lead item.

Today, Frieda's Finest is the nation's leading marketer and distributor of exotic fruits and vegetables, handling over 250 different items. Her marketing savvy led to the decision to add a line of complementary items, such as Fresh Crepes and Eggroll Wrappers, sold in the produce section. An ability to create consumer demand for the unusual has helped Caplan make success stories out of items like kiwifruit, spaghetti squash, jicama and shallots.

Caplan is recognized for introducing kiwifruit to North America. New Zealanders further credit her with creating the world market for the fuzzy fruit.

Strong marketing strategies, special packaging, and a sensitivity to public opinion help her create high-volume acceptance for relatively unknown items. Caplan, known as the "Queen of Kiwi," even convinced California growers to plant the fruit; today the Golden State has over 1,000 kiwifruit growers.

Communicating with consumers is the major focal point of Caplan's marketing efforts. Items are enclosed in eye-catching purple packages that describe their flavor and provide cooking and storage tips. Each label contains an invitation for the consumer to write to the company with their comments on the product. All letters of inquiry are personally answered by the Consumer Relations Department.

As a leader in the produce industry, Caplan has received numerous honors for her achievements. In 1972 she became the first woman ever to be elected a vice president of the Produce Marketing Association. She was named Produce Marketer of the Year in 1979 by *The Packer*, the major trade publication. She has also been listed in the *Cook's Magazine* "Who's Who of Cooking in America." In 1986 she received the first Harriet Alger Award from *Working Woman* magazine for being a remarkable entrepreneurial role model for women. In addition, she was selected as an outstanding California woman in business in 1987 by California's Governor Deukmejian.

Frieda's Finest is a family-run company. In 1986 Frieda promoted her eldest daughter, Karen Caplan, to president, and at that time became Chairman of the Board herself. A second daughter, Jackie Caplan Wiggins, is Vice President/National Accounts. Al Caplan, Frieda's husband of thirty-seven years, is a prominent labor relations consultant and serves as secretary/treasurer of Frieda's Finest.

"Informing the consumer as well as the produce personnel is critical when it comes to exotic produce," comments Karen Caplan. "Shoppers are reluctant to choose unfamiliar items. Our labels take the fear out of purchasing a new product." This great emphasis placed on consumer relations has helped Frieda's Finest become the leader in produce marketing.

Based on information from Frieda's Finest Produce Specialties, Inc., P.O. Box 58488, Los Angeles, CA 90058; Dave Galanti, "Stocking Up on Specialty Fruit," *Advertising Age*, September 19, 1989, p. 18; Maria LaGanga, "A Dozen Who Shaped the '80s," *Los Angeles Times*, January 1, 1990, B–1; and Erik Larson, "Strange Fruits," *Inc.*, November 1989, pp. 81–90.

The figure in the salary column approximates the expected annual income after two or three years of service. 1 = $12,000–$15,000 2 = $16,000–$20,000 3 = $21,000–$27,000 4 = $28,000–$35,000 5 = $36,000 and up

Job Title	Educational Requirements	Salary Range	Prospects
Advertising account executive	Bachelor's degree in business or liberal arts	2–3	Gradual growth
Advertising manager	Bachelor's degree in business or liberal arts	3	Limited growth
Advertising worker	Some college courses in business and marketing	2	Limited growth
Art director	College degree in art with courses in marketing and advertising	2–3	Gradual growth
Buyer (retail and wholesale trade)	High school diploma; on-the-job experience; some college preferred	2–3	Limited growth
Commercial/graphic artist	High school diploma; some college preferred	2–3	Limited growth
Manufacturer's sales-person	Some college; degree preferred; on-the-job experience	2–3	Limited growth
Market research analyst	Bachelor's degree in business, statistics, or math; graduate degree helpful	2–3	Limited growth
Marketing director	Bachelor's degree in business; on-the-job experience	3–4	Limited growth
Marketing researcher	Some college; degree helpful; on-the-job experience	2	Limited growth
Media buyer	Some college; on-the-job experience	2	Limited growth
Order clerk	High school diploma	1–2	Limited growth
Public relations specialist	College degree; on-the-job experience	2–3	Limited growth
Product marketing engineer	College degree; on-the-job experience	2–3	Limited growth
Real estate sales-person	High school diploma plus college work helpful; written state exam; varies by state	3	Gradual growth
Retail trade sales-worker	High school diploma	1–2	Limited growth
Store manager	College degree; on-the-job experience	3–4	Gradual growth
Travel agent	Some college preferred	1–2	Gradual growth
Wholesale trade sales-worker	Varies; college preferred; on-the-job experience	3	Gradual growth
Writer/editor	College degree preferred; on-the-job experience	2–3	Limited growth

Part 5

INFORMATION FOR BUSINESS

The subject of this part is information, the fourth of our business resources. First we discuss computers and the different kinds of information that are necessary for effective decision making. Then we examine the role of accounting and how financial information is collected, processed, and presented. Included in this part are:

MANAGEMENT INFORMATION AND COMPUTERS

15

LEARNING OBJECTIVES

1 Know what information is and how it differs from data
2 Understand how computers help transform data into information
3 Be able to describe the evolution of computers and explain the difference between hardware and software
4 Recognize the impact that computers have had on business
5 Be aware of management's information requirements
6 Know the four functions of a management information system
7 Be able to describe the various sources of business data
8 Understand how a management information system uses statistics to turn data into information

CHAPTER PREVIEW

In this chapter, we take a closer look at management information and computers. First, we look at the difference between data and information. Then we see how computers help managers transform data into information. We also consider the present and future impact of computers on business. Next, we analyze what types of information managers need. Finally, we examine the components of a management information system (MIS) and show how the system can be used to aid managers in the decision-making process.

Recent Developments at IBM

When discussing the future of International Business Machines (IBM), John Akers, the Chairman and CEO, tells interested parties that he has both good news and bad news.

Here's the bad news. IBM has at least three serious problems that threaten the company's future. First, the growth in corporate spending for all information technology—computers, telecommunications equipment, photocopiers, and the like—is slowing down. From the mid-1970s to the mid-1980s, the average growth in spending for high-tech information equipment was 15 percent a year. But since 1984, the growth rate has risen only 6 percent a year. And some experts predict that the growth in spending for high-tech information equipment will decrease even further in the first part of the 1990s. Reduced high-tech spending is especially damaging to IBM because of its high-priced products and high-quality image. For example, sales for IBM's mainframes—the largest and most expensive computers available today—are slowing down because customers are buying the ever-more-powerful midsized and desktop computers.

A second problem is IBM's inability to introduce new products with state-of-the-art technology. In many cases, competitors have simply beaten IBM to the marketplace. A full nine months before IBM introduced its version, for instance, Compaq Computer Corporation introduced a personal computer with the faster and more reliable Intel 80386 microchip. As a result of this and similar mistakes, IBM's share of the personal computer market decreased from almost 25 percent in the early 1980s to 13.9 percent in 1989.

A third problem is increased foreign competition. Foreign competitors like Fujitsu and NEC of Japan account for 18 percent of total domestic sales in the United States, and their market share is expected to increase well into the 1990s. To make matters worse, foreign competitors are also competing with IBM in the international marketplace. This is an especially serious problem for IBM, a company that earns almost two-thirds of its profits from overseas sales.

Now, here's the good news. IBM sells more than $160 million worth of computers and electronic equipment every day—365 days a year. With annual revenues that exceed $60 billion, the company is the fifth largest industrial corporation in the world and sells in 130 different countries. The company's annual profits are in excess of $5 billion and the return on owner's equity has averaged 17.5 percent over the last five years. The company is the largest producer of mainframes in the world and controls over 60 percent of the market. IBM also has excellent research and development facilities. And although IBM officials admit that it will be difficult to develop solutions to the problems they face, they are quick to point out that IBM is still the most successful company in the computer industry.[1]

*I*BM's current problems are common among firms that operate in the high-tech information industry. Over the past forty-five years, this industry has undergone dramatic changes. And yet, Fred Akers and IBM's top management are optimistic that they can solve the computer giant's problems and at the same time become more competitive in an ever-changing industry. Product and software engineers are already working on new products that will make the firm more competitve in the near future. And IBM is not alone. Other firms like Apple Computer Corporation, Digital Equipment, and Hewlett-Packard also know that in order to compete in the high-tech information industry, they must provide electronic equipment that can satisfy their customers' needs for accurate and up-to-date information.

As we noted in Chapter 1, information is the basic material from which plans are developed and decisions are made. To help their managers obtain and use information, most firms establish management information systems. The recent "computer revolution" has expanded the capabilities and capacities of such systems and, therefore, their usefulness.

The Need for Management Information

There is an important difference between data and information, although in many contexts the two terms are used interchangeably. Let us first look at this difference. **Data** are numerical or verbal descriptions that usually result from measurements of some sort. (The word *data* is plural; the singular form is *datum*.) An individual's current wage level, a firm's net after-tax profit last year, and the names of automobiles currently produced in the United States are all data. Most people think of data as being numerical only, but they can be nonnumerical as well. A description of an individual as a "tall, athletic woman with short, dark hair" would certainly qualify as data.

Information is data of a particular sort. Specifically, **information** is data that are presented in a form that is useful for a specific purpose. Suppose a human resources manager wants to compare the wages paid to male and female employees by the firm over the past seven years. The manager might begin with a stack of computer printouts listing every person employed by the firm, along with his or her current and past wages. But such printouts would consist of data rather than information. The manager would be hard-pressed to make any sense of the mass of names and numbers.

Now suppose the manager goes back to the computer and has it compute and graph the average wage paid to men and that paid to women in each of the seven years. The resulting graph (see Figure 15.1) is information, because the manager can use it for the purpose at hand—to compare wages paid to men and women over the seven-year period.

The wage data from the printouts became information when they were summarized in the chart shown in Figure 15.1. Often, a large set of data must be summarized if they are to be at all useful, but this is not

data *numerical or verbal descriptions that usually result from measurements of some sort*

Learning Objective 1
Know what information is and how it differs from data

information *data that are presented in a form that is useful for a specific purpose*

453

	Jan	Feb	March	April	May	June	July	Aug	Sept	Oct	Nov	Dec	Totals
Female Employees													
Employee 1	1,150	1,150	1,150	1,150	1,150	1,150	1,200	1,200	1,200	1,200	1,200	1,300	$14,200
Employee 2	1,400	1,400	1,400	1,400	1,400	1,400	1,400	1,400	1,400	1,400	1,400	1,400	$16,800
Employee 3	1,600	1,600	1,600	1,600	1,800	1,800	1,800	1,800	1,800	1,900	1,900	1,900	$21,100
Employee 4	1,200	1,200	1,200	1,200	1,200	1,200	1,250	1,250	1,250	1,250	1,250	1,250	$13,500
Male Employees													
Employee 5	1,800	1,800	1,800	1,800	1,800	1,800	1,800	1,800	1,800	1,800	1,800	1,800	$21,600
Employee 6	2,000	2,000	2,000	2,000	2,000	2,000	2,100	2,100	2,100	2,100	2,100	2,100	$24,600
Employee 7	1,900	1,900	1,900	1,900	1,900	1,900	1,950	1,950	1,950	1,950	2,000	2,000	$23,200
Employee 8	2,400	2,400	2,400	2,400	2,400	2,400	2,500	2,500	2,500	2,500	2,500	2,500	$29,400

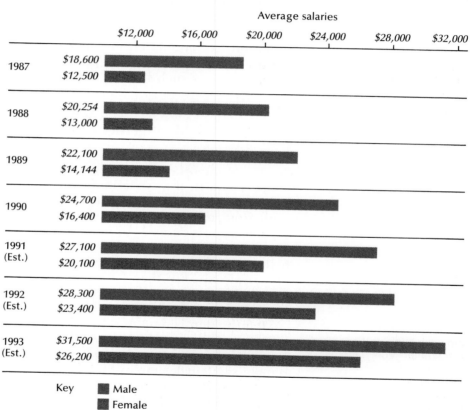

Average salaries

Year	Male	Female
1987	$18,600	$12,500
1988	$20,254	$13,000
1989	$22,100	$14,144
1990	$24,700	$16,400
1991 (Est.)	$27,100	$20,100
1992 (Est.)	$28,300	$23,400
1993 (Est.)	$31,500	$26,200

Key: ■ Male ■ Female

FIGURE 15.1
Data versus Information
Data are numerical or verbal descriptions that usually result from measurements; information is data presented in a form useful for a specific purpose.

always the case. For example, suppose the manager had wanted to know only the wage history of a specific employee. That information would be contained in the original computer printout. The manager would only have to find the employee's name in the listing to locate the required information. That is, the data would already be in the most useful form for the manager's purpose; they would need no further processing.

Most firms have access to a great deal of data that can be transformed into information. The average company maintains personnel, inventory, sales, accounting, and other types of useful data. Often, each type of data is stored in individual departments within the organization. In a large organization, this type of data is more effectively utilized when it is organized into a database. A **database** is a single collection of data that is stored in one place and can be used by people throughout the organization to make decisions. In addition to just storing data in one place, procedures for gathering, updating, and processing facts in the organization's database must be established. Computers can help ensure that the facts in a database are up to date and available when needed by employees and managers.

database *a single collection of data that is stored in one place and can be used by people throughout the organization to make decisions*

Computers and Data Processing

Learning Objective 2
Understand how computers help transform data into information

Until perhaps twenty-five years ago, most data and information were stored using manual systems. Records were kept in written form, and clerical personnel were responsible for collecting, filing, retrieving, and processing the data required by managers. Today, many clerical tasks are completed with the aid of a computer. With the advent of low-cost computers especially designed for business use, the computer came within the reach of nearly every business.

computer *an electronic machine that can accept, store, manipulate, and transmit data in accordance with a set of specific instructions*

A **computer** is an electronic machine that can accept, store, manipulate, and transmit data in accordance with a set of specific instructions. Moreover, it can store large amounts of data, process them very rapidly with perfect accuracy, and transmit (or present) results in a variety of ways. For example, Carter Hawley Hale Stores Inc. is a large corporation

Computers can be used to transform large amounts of data into information and to provide communication networks. Managers at the Virginia Department of Transportation are very enthusiastic about the benefits of Digital computing and information systems in their in-house and field-level operations. Computers have boosted the department's productivity, creativity, efficiency, and potential for growth.

that owns several retail companies, including The Broadway, Emporium-Capwell Co., and Weinstock's on the West Coast, and Thalhimer Brothers in the southeastern part of the United States. Altogether, Carter's management must keep track of more than 1,000 stores and more than eight million items of merchandise. To deal with this, Carter's management invested $75 million in a computer center near Los Angeles to keep track of all the buying, pricing, and inventory-control data and to provide management with the information it needs to run the retail network.

The Evolution of Computers

Learning Objective 3
Be able to describe the evolution of computers and explain the difference between hardware and software

Large firms such as Carter Hawley Hale are using computers on a daily basis. Even small businesses find the daily use of computers necessary. This was not always the case, however. Even after computers were developed and mass-produced, most were too large and too expensive for most businesses. Although the computer is a relatively recent invention, its development rests on centuries of research (see Figure 15.2).

FIGURE 15.2
A Chronology of Technological Developments
This chronology illustrates significant developments leading up to the invention of electronic computers that are used today.

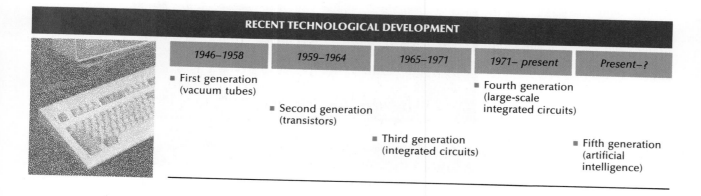

EARLY TECHNOLOGICAL DEVELOPMENTS			
Before Christ	*1600s*	*1800s*	*1900s*
▪ Abacus	▪ Slide rule developed by Napier & John William Oughtred ▪ Calculator developed by Pascal ▪ Improved calculator developed by Leibniz	▪ The difference engine and the analytical engine developed by Babbage ▪ Census punch cards developed by Hollerith	▪ Mark I computer developed by Aiken

RECENT TECHNOLOGICAL DEVELOPMENT				
1946–1958	*1959–1964*	*1965–1971*	*1971– present*	*Present–?*
▪ First generation (vacuum tubes)	▪ Second generation (transistors)	▪ Third generation (integrated circuits)	▪ Fourth generation (large-scale integrated circuits)	▪ Fifth generation (artificial intelligence)

Early Technological Developments Since the beginning of recorded history, people have had difficulty calculating answers to mathematical problems. One early mechanical calculating device, the abacus, was developed by Chinese merchants before the birth of Christ. Composed of several wires, each strung with ten beads, the abacus enabled the merchants to calculate solutions to mathematical problems and then store the results.

In the seventeenth century, the slide rule was developed through the work of John Napier and William Oughtred. And the first real mechanical "calculator" was developed in 1643 by the Frenchman Blaise Pascal. Pascal's calculator added or subtracted numbers by using a series of rotating gears, or wheels. Later in the same century, a German by the name of Gottfried von Leibniz developed a mechanical device that would not only add and subtract but also multiply, divide, and calculate square roots.

In the early 1800s, Charles Babbage, a British mathematician, designed a machine that could perform mathematical calculations and store the intermediate results in a memory unit—the forerunner of today's computer. Babbage called his device the *difference engine*. Later, Babbage designed a similar machine called the *analytical engine* that could perform addition, subtraction, multiplication, or division based on instructions coded on cards. Both the difference and analytical engines contained many features similar to those found in today's modern computers. As a result, Babbage is often called the father of modern computer technology.

In the late 1880s, Dr. Herman Hollerith was commissioned by the U.S. government to develop a system that could process the 1890 census data. His punch card system (based on Babbage's original concept) reduced the time required to process the 1890 census data to two and a half years. (It had taken seven and a half years to process the 1880 census data manually.) Based on his experience with the government project, Hollerith founded the Tabulating Machine Company to manufacture and sell punch card equipment to businesses. Later, the Tabulating Machine Company changed its name; today it is known as International Business Machines (IBM).

In 1944 Howard Aiken of Harvard University, in collaboration with IBM and the U.S. War Department, embarked on a joint project to manufacture the Mark I computer. It was not a true electronic computer because it utilized electromagnetic relays and mechanical counters to perform mathematical calculations. Nevertheless, this device did open the door for the development of the electronic computer.

Recent Technological Developments Today's electronic computers are the result of five stages (sometimes called generations) of research and development. The first generation of computers (1946 to 1958) relied on glass vacuum tubes to control the internal operations of the computer. The vacuum tubes were quite large and generated a great deal of heat. As a result, the overall computer was huge and required special air conditioning to compensate for the excessive heat build-up. For example, the ENIAC (Electronic Numerical Integrator and Calculator) was 10 feet high, 10 feet wide, and approximately 100 feet long.

The second generation (1959 to 1964) began when tiny, electronic transistors replaced vacuum tubes. Transistors greatly reduced the size of the computer. They helped solve the heat problem that plagued computers in the first generation. In addition, transistors were more reliable, required less maintenance, and processed data much faster than had the vacuum tubes. High-speed printers and card readers were introduced during the second generation. Finally, second-generation computers were programmed with high-level languages such as FORTRAN (*FOR*mula *TRAN*slation) and COBOL (*CO*mmon *B*usiness *O*riented *L*anguage).

The third generation (1965 to 1971) began when computer manufacturers started using integrated circuits (ICs), small silicon chips containing a network of transistors. Integrated circuits were quite a bit faster and more reliable than the single transistors used in the second generation. And yet, they were less expensive than second-generation transistors because of improved technology. Third-generation computers had more storage capacity and greater compatibility of computer components. The concept of remote terminals that communicate with a central computer became a reality at this time.

The fourth generation (1971 to the present) began when computer manufacturers began using large-scale integrated (LSI) circuits. LSI circuits are silicon superchips that contain thousands of small transistors. As a result of LSI circuits, fourth-generation computers are smaller than those manufactured during the third generation. Both the Apple and the IBM personal computers were developed during this generation. Also, increased storage and even greater compatibility were characteristics of computers manufactured during this period.

To date, we have experienced four generations of computer development. Now, many experts believe we are entering the *fifth generation*—computers that can simulate human decision making. This development is made possible by a refinement of LSI technology, called very large-scale integration (VLSI). All through this chapter, we stress that computers must be programmed or given step-by-step instructions to complete a specific task. Programming is necessary because the computer doesn't have common sense or the ability to think on its own. This may change in the near future. Today, researchers are studying the human brain in an attempt to learn how people reason and think. Scientists have known for years that the human brain is more efficient than any computer when comparing storage capacity, data retrieval, and information processing. The researchers' goal is to duplicate the same process with a computer and thus create a form of artificial intelligence.

artificial intelligence *a combination of computer hardware and software that exhibits the same type of intelligence as human beings*

Artificial intelligence is a combination of computer hardware and software that exhibits the same type of intelligence as human beings. Carver Mead, a noted microchip researcher, says that in five years there will be technological systems on the market—used in toys, computers, and accessories—that will see, hear, feel, and remember in ways far superior to anything that exists today.[2] The practical applications for artificial intelligence generated by a computer are unlimited. For example,

Hewlett-Packard calls its vision of future information technology the Cooperative Computing Environment. The environment will include the use of artificial intelligence, which will help people browse through databases and integrate information from many different sources.

a computer may be able to examine cells from the human body and determine which genetic factors cause cancer and other dreaded diseases. Today, artificial intelligence is so important that it is one of the fastest-growing high-tech fields. Many companies in the computer field are investing large amounts of money to either develop artificial intelligence systems or purchase existing systems developed by other companies. Later in the chapter, we examine additional technological developments and how they will affect society.

Types of Computers

The computers used in business today are generally categorized according to size as mainframes, minicomputers, or microcomputers. The *mainframe computer* is the large, powerful, and expensive (usually costing more than $1 million) computer traditionally identified with the largest businesses. IBM established its reputation by manufacturing mainframe computers and is still very active in this area. Mainframes, which may be as big as a good-sized room, can handle huge quantities of data, perform a variety of operations on these data in fractions of a second, and provide output information in several different forms. Huge organizations, like Exxon Corporation, Ford Motor Company, or the U.S. government, have the most need for mainframe computers. Today, the largest mainframe computers are sometimes referred to as *supercomputers* or *monsters*. These very large computers are used almost exclusively by universities and government agencies that are heavily involved in research activities that require large memories and high-speed processing.

Minicomputers are smaller computers (more or less desk-sized) that revolutionized the industry and made computers available to most firms. These self-contained systems can be purchased for under $10,000, and prices continue to drop steadily. With a minicomputer, most businesses can now maintain very sophisticated information systems that were previously beyond their reach. Digital Equipment Corporation's VAX series and Data General's MV series are extremely powerful minicomputers used by many businesses today.

The *microcomputer*, the latest breakthrough, is a desk-top or lap-top computer. It was made possible by the development of *microprocessor chips*, a fraction of an inch in size, that contain all the electronic circuitry required to perform large-scale data processing. Microcomputers, which are also referred to as personal computers, sell for as little as several hundred dollars or as much as a few thousand dollars. Although microcomputers are often purchased for use in the home, many smaller firms find them completely satisfactory for their limited needs. Companies like IBM, Wang Laboratories, Compaq Computer Corporation, and Apple Computer make microcomputers for the small-business market.

Computer Hardware

input unit   *the device used to enter data into a computer*

Most computers and computer systems consist of five basic components (see Figure 15.3). The **input unit** is the device used to enter data into a computer. In the past, data were fed to computers on punched cards, which were "read" by the input unit. Few modern systems use this method. Instead, data are entered manually via a keyboard (much like a typewriter keyboard) or electronically on magnetic tapes or disks that the input unit can read. Other input devices include a mouse, light pen, or touch pad. Currently, voice recognition as an input device is being developed by a number of manufacturers. When fully developed, voice recognition will make use of a computer easier for almost anyone.

FIGURE 15.3
How a Computer Works
A computer is a machine that accepts, stores, manipulates, and transmits data in accordance with a set of specific instructions. Most computers consist of five basic components.

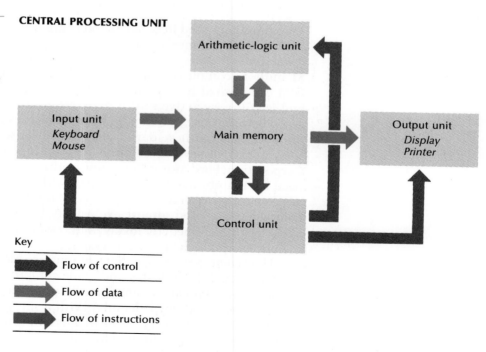

CENTRAL PROCESSING UNIT

Arithmetic-logic unit

Input unit
Keyboard
Mouse

Main memory

Output unit
Display
Printer

Control unit

Key

Flow of control

Flow of data

Flow of instructions

memory (or storage unit) *the part of a computer that stores all data entered into the computer and processed by it*

The **memory** (or **storage unit**) is the part of a computer that stores all data entered into the computer and processed by it. One measure of a computer's power is the amount of data that can be stored within it at one time. This memory capacity is given in *bytes:* One byte is the capacity to store one character, and K bytes is the capacity to store 1,024 characters. A personal computer with a 256K memory is thus capable of storing almost 60 pages of this book.

control unit *the part of a computer that guides the entire operation of the computer*

The **control unit** is the part of a computer that guides the entire operation of the computer. It transfers data and sends processing directions to the various other units, in the proper sequence to carry out the instructions of the user.

arithmetic-logic unit *the part of a computer that performs mathematical operations, comparisons of data, and other types of data transformations*

The **arithmetic-logic unit** is the part of a computer that performs mathematical operations, comparisons of data, and other types of data transformations.

output unit *the mechanism by which a computer transmits processed data to the user*

The **output unit** is the mechanism by which a computer transmits processed data to the user. Most commonly, computer output is printed on paper or displayed on a televisionlike screen called a *monitor.*

hardware *the electronic equipment or machinery used in a computer system*

All of these components make up the computer's hardware. Computer **hardware** is the electronic equipment or machinery used in a computer system. Hence, the keyboard used to enter data; the arithmetic-logic, control, and storage units; and the monitor are all hardware.

Computer Networks

computer network *a system in which several computers can either function individually or communicate with each other*

The concept of networking is perhaps the greatest boon to management decision making since the low-cost computer. A **computer network** is a system in which several computers can either function individually or communicate with each other. A typical business network revolves around a mainframe or minicomputer, which serves as the basic computer system for all areas and levels of the firm. In addition, each key manager has her or his own microcomputer. These smaller computers have sufficient capacity to store up-to-date information that the managers require on a regular basis. That is, each microcomputer maintains records that are of primary interest to a particular manager, who has immediate and personal access to that information.

In addition, each manager can communicate with the mainframe or minicomputer through his or her microcomputer. The operations manager in charge of shipping, for example, may be considering a change in the company's shipping schedule. To make the change, he or she needs to know something about sales patterns in the various sales territories. Rather than requesting the information from marketing and then waiting for it to be prepared, requesting it electronically from the mainframe can produce the needed information.

Similarly, microcomputers can communicate directly with each other. Once the new shipping schedule is drafted, the shipping manager can transmit it to other managers—computer to computer—to get their opinions.

Computer Software

software *the set of instructions that tells a computer what to do*

Software is the set of instructions that tells a computer what to do. These instructions are called the computer *program*. The program controls the manner in which a computer processes data.

The Programming Function   Writing and testing the program are probably the most critical steps in using a computer to process data. If the computer is not programmed correctly, the information it delivers is incorrect. Relying on bad information carries with it many serious risks. The old adage "garbage in, garbage out" captures this very important point.

computer programmer *a person who develops the step-by-step instructions that are contained in a computer program*

flow chart *a graphic description of the types and sequences of operations in a computer program*

Today computer programmers are in great demand as a result of the growing use of computers. But what does a computer programmer do? A **computer programmer** develops the step-by-step instructions contained in the computer program. Generally, the programmer begins the programming function by defining the problem and then designing a solution to the problem. Often, programmers use a flow chart to aid their programming efforts. A **flow chart** is a graphic description of the types and sequences of operations in a computer program. After developing the flow chart, the programmer must translate it into instructions that the computer can follow. Because the computer cannot understand English, all instructions are coded into the computer through the use of a programming language. Once the program is written, it must be debugged and tested. Only after all errors have been corrected can the program be used.

Programming is usually performed by in-house employees who create new programs, change existing programs when necessary, and maintain the computer system. Programming can also be farmed out to outside consultants who work on a fee or contract basis. In addition to developing their own software, businesses have another option. They can purchase ready-made software.

It's not always easy to find the right software to solve a firm's problems. In some cases, business firms can buy ready-made software. In other cases, the software must be developed by in-house employees. It is also possible to hire outside consultants who work on a fee or contract basis to develop software programs to meet specific needs.

Ready-Made Software   Today, ready-made software is available to handle almost any application ranging from individualized instruction to sophisticated business forecasting. Ready-made software costs range from less than $10 to more than $100,000, and total software sales exceed $40 billion a year. Using ready-made software offers the user two distinct advantages. First, ready-made software almost always costs less than programs developed in house. Second, the quality of ready-made software may be higher than programs that are developed by in-house programmers. Before deciding to purchase ready-made software, businesses must consider the following questions:

▶ Will the ready-made software enable the firm to process data and obtain the information that it needs?

▶ Can the software be adapted or changed to meet the firm's needs?

▶ Can the software be used with the computer equipment now in place?

▶ What kind of training is available with the software?

▶ Can employees contact the vendor if they have questions or encounter problems when they attempt to use the software?

▶ Do the expected benefits of using the software justify the cost?

Thanks to a software problem in inventory control, the line is temporarily on hold.

BUSINESS JOURNAL ▰▰▰▰▰▰▰▰▰▰▰

Buying a Computer

First, the good news. Competition among computer retailers has never been greater. Competition is cutthroat, and it is possible to buy a complete system for as little as $800. There are more than a hundred different brands of personal computers to choose from, with brand names ranging from ATT to Z Technology Systems.

Now, the bad news. Purchasing a computer requires careful evaluation of your needs. Anyone considering buying a computer for the first time gets bombarded by advice and opinions. Some people say they couldn't live without their Apple; others complain about their computer gathering dust in the closet. Your decisions about whether you want a computer and which one to buy should be based on your own needs and interests. Answering the following questions should help clarify those needs and make your decision a little easier.

What will you use a computer for? Many of the early computer buyers soon found they had no real need for a computer. They tired of their computer's games and discovered that they could balance their checkbooks and keep track of recipes better with pen and paper. A computer will pay off if you spend a lot of time writing (word processing), manipulating numbers (accounting), using long lists (filing), or doing extensive research.

How important is software? A computer is only as good as its software. Today, software is available to meet almost any need. Popular software packages include *WordPerfect* for word processing, *Lotus 1-2-3* for spreadsheets or accounting, and *Smart Data Manager* for filing. There are also software packages for managing your money (*Dollars and Sense*) and home budgeting (*Easy Accounting*). The manufacturer's suggested price for software packages ranges from $50 to $700, but there are substantial discounts available, especially if the software is purchased by mail.

What type of equipment should you buy? Besides the computer itself, you will need a printer, disks, and cables; and you will probably want any number of accessories. Make sure you can afford the whole package before you fall in love with one piece. When buying a computer, one of the key considerations that may affect price is the amount of memory you need. A computer's memory, known as random access memory, or RAM, is measured in kilobytes. Each kilobyte represents about a thousand characters of information. A few years ago, 64K RAM was considered adequate, but today computers come with 512K or 640K RAM. Keep in mind that many of the best software packages currently available cannot run on a machine with less than a 256K memory.

Does your machine need to be compatible with another? If your school or employer has a computer, you should consider whether you'll want to be able to take a disk from your computer and use it in another computer. You can do that only if the two computers are "compatible." Many people buy machines compatible with IBM's PC because its PC format is the closest thing to a standard that exists in the industry.

What does the future hold? Computers promise to be more powerful and smaller. In fact, you can already buy battery-operated lap-top computers that have as much power as an IBM personal computer. Most traditional lap-tops weigh only about 4 pounds and are about the size of a notebook. What's more, these electronic "gadgets" promise to be even more powerful in the future.

Based on information from David Churbuck, "Is That a Supercomputer in Your Pocket?," *Forbes*, May 15, 1989, pp. 121–122; Louis Therrien, "From Boom Boxes to Bargain-Basement PCs," *Business Week*, June 26, 1989, pp. 65–66; "How to Buy an IBM Clone," *Consumer Reports*, March 1988, pp. 179–184; "The Best-Liked Software," *Consumer Reports*, March 1988, pp. 185–187; "A Computer for the Home," *Consumers' Research*, October 1986, p. 11; and Sheldon L. Richman, "Taking the Byte Out of Buying a Computer," *Consumers' Research*, March 1985, p. 30.

While many ready-made software packages have been extremely successful, others have been dismal failures. For this reason, most computer experts suggest that you talk to someone who has used a given ready-made software package before you decide to purchase it.

Ready-made software is further discussed in the section Current Business Applications.

The Impact of Computers on Business

Learning Objective 4
Recognize the impact that computers have had on business

To solve even a simple problem, a computer must be told what to do. A computer can only manipulate data, although the speed and accuracy with which it carries out instructions is astounding. As the cost of computer memory (or storage) drops and the availability of sophisticated software packages grows, analyses, research, and record keeping that were once available only to the very largest organizations—if they were available at all—are coming within reach of all but the smallest and least sophisticated businesses.

Current Business Applications

Today, software has been developed to satisfy almost every business need. The most common types of software for business applications include packages in the following areas:

- ▶ Accounting and bookkeeping
- ▶ Computer-aided design (CAD)
- ▶ Computer-aided engineering (CAE)
- ▶ Computer-aided manufacturing (CAM)
- ▶ Computer-aided instruction (CAI)
- ▶ Database management
- ▶ Desktop publishing
- ▶ Graphics
- ▶ Spreadsheets
- ▶ Word processing

Four of the most popular packages (database management, graphics, spreadsheets, and word processing) are described in the following sections.

Database Management Programs Earlier in this chapter, we defined a database as a single collection of data that are stored in one place and can be used by people throughout the organization to make decisions. Thirty years ago, a company like Eastman Kodak would store its data in file cabinets and then retrieve data when needed. Any manipulation to transform the data contained in each file folder into useful information would be completed manually—usually by the manager who needed the information in the first place.

Today, in a large organization like Asea Brown Boveri Inc. (ABB), the use of computer-aided design (CAD) software enables the firm's engineers to design projects that meet the needs of the firm's customers. Using 3-D computer drafting, these two ABB engineers were able to create an effective solution to internal tube wall cracks in a paper mill's recovery boiler.

Today, it is possible to use database management software to electronically store and transform data into information. Data contained in a database management software package can be sorted by different criteria. For example, typical data for a firm's personnel department might include criteria such as each worker's age, sex, salary, and years of service. If management needs to know the names of workers who have at least fifteen years of experience and are at least 50 years old, an employee using database management software can print a list of employees who meet the selected criteria in a matter of minutes. While this example involves data required for personnel decisions, the same type of manipulation of data for other departments within a business is possible with database management software.

graphics program   *a software package that enables the user to display (and often print) data and conclusions in graphic form*

Graphics Programs   A **graphics program** enables the user to display (and often print) data and conclusions in graphic form. Whether you play a video game or watch a computerized scoreboard at a football stadium, you are viewing computer-generated graphics. From a business standpoint, graphics can be used for presenting financial analyses, budgets, sales projections, and the like.

Typically, graphics software allows the user to choose the type of visual aid that is desired from a menu of available graphic options. The user enters the numerical data, such as sales figures, to be illustrated into the computer. The computer program then turns the data into a graph, bar chart, or pie chart. (Graphs, bar charts, and pie charts are discussed later in this chapter.) This type of visual aid can be used to support an oral or written presentation.

BUSINESS JOURNAL

Express Packages and Instant Information

Most people would not expect a delivery company to be IBM's fifth largest customer. And yet, Federal Express Corp. has succeeded largely because of the way it uses computer power to keep track of every package in every van. A large company whose very survival depends on its reputation for reliability and speed, Federal Express maintains its competitive edge in the overnight delivery industry with 27,000 computer terminals that are connected—either directly or by satellite—to one of its twelve mainframe computers in Memphis.

The company's computerized tracking system first comes into play when a customer calls to request a package pickup. The eleven Federal Express customer service centers handle as many as 200,000 such calls a day. Once the package has been picked up, Federal Express gives it a bar code so that it can be identified by computers throughout its journey.

Then the package is flown to a regional center—the biggest one is in Memphis—between 10 P.M. and midnight. Six nights a week, the company handles an average of 650,000 packages a night, and what comes in by midnight must be back in the air by 4 A.M. The packages speed through the terminal at 500 feet per minute on conveyer belts, while computers track them and robot arms shove them into appropriate bins.

The company's DADS (digitally assisted dispatch system) continues the computerized package tracking until the moment the package is delivered. At the recipient's door, the Federal Express employee scans the bar code on the package with a computerized bar-code reader. This reader is then stuck into a slot in the delivery van's DADS, the data is radioed to a local office, and people in Memphis get the news within four seconds.

Back in Memphis, the enormous mainframe computers don't always function perfectly. Yet the company says that its system is available 99 percent of the time. Keeping everything running smoothly at the company's thousands of terminals would be impossible with the manual trouble-shooting systems of a few years ago. So Federal Express keeps its high standards through the use of diagnostic software that provides a "window" into the functioning of the computer system and automatically warns of any problems with its availability or performance. Not only does the automatic diagnostic system identify and help solve problems, it also keeps records of recurring problems and allows the company to discover the root causes of chronic errors. As a result of computerized tracking, Federal Express workers can find out almost anything about a package instantly.

Federal Express's computerized tracking system is the envy of overnight delivery firms around the world and is just one more reason why the company is so financially successful—it earns more than $165 million a year. Federal Express has used its financial success to purchase Tiger International—the world's largest heavy-cargo airline. The Federal Express–Flying Tiger acquisition is important because it enables Federal Express to fulfill a long-term goal: to provide two-day service to most cities around the globe. As a result, Federal Express's well-known reliability and top-notch service are now available worldwide.

Based on information from Stephen W. Quickel, "Wisely, Fed Ex Opted to Join 'Em," *Business Month*, March 1989, pp. 17–18; Dean Foust et al, "Mr. Smith Goes Global," *Business Week*, February 13, 1989, pp. 66–69+; Peter Middleton, "Fed Ex: Where People Matter," *Flight International*, March 28, 1987; "Network Management at Federal Express," *Business Software Review*, October 8, 1986, p. 21; and "Federal Express Backs Bold Ad Claims with DP," *Computerworld*, October 8, 1984, p. 63.

This type of visual aid has always been available, but someone had to take the time to draw it. With the aid of a graphics program, the computer can generate the drawing in seconds.

Spreadsheet Programs   In the late 1970s, Daniel Bricklin and Robert Frankston, two business students, developed VisiCalc—a software package that enabled computer users to generate electronic spreadsheets. A **spread-**

spreadsheet program *a software package that allows the user to organize data into a grid of rows and columns*

sheet program is a software package that allows the user to organize data into a grid of rows and columns. Typically, spreadsheet software such as VisiCalc and Lotus 1-2-3 allows users to build a spreadsheet by using commands such as create, format, enter, move, insert, compute, save, delete, and print.

The spreadsheet program can be used to organize numerical data, and formulas entered into the spreadsheet allow the computer to perform the mathematical calculations automatically. For example, a manager may want to project sales and expenses for the next accounting period. Numerical data for both sales and expenses are entered into the computer, and the spreadsheet software calculates the dollar amount of profit or loss based on the assumptions that the manager entered into the computer. Spreadsheet software can also be used to answer "what if" questions. By changing data to match new assumptions, the manager can see how the change will affect other data contained in the spreadsheet. This same manager might want to calculate the firm's profits based on projections that sales will increase 5, 10, and 15 percent. In this case, three additional spreadsheets could be prepared based on each set of assumptions. In fact, any variable contained in the spreadsheet could be changed and, within seconds, new information could be generated to aid the manager in the decision-making process.

word processing program *a software package that allows the user to store documents (letters, memos, reports) in the computer memory or on a magnetic disk*

Word Processing Programs   A **word processing program** allows the user to store documents (letters, memos, reports) in the computer memory or on a magnetic disk. Once entered, the material can be changed, edited, revised, deleted, or printed. In addition, materials that have been stored on a disk can be used at a later date. For example, most firms use a collection letter to urge prompt payment of past-due amounts. A word processing program can be used to send a personalized copy of the letter to all overdue accounts through the use of sort and merge features. Mail-order firms and direct-mail marketing firms make extensive use of these features to appeal to customers. Tens, hundreds, or thousands of letters—each sent to a selected individual—can be prepared from one master document.

Word processing programs can allow for quick and easy revision of documents. No longer is it necessary for secretaries to spend long hours retyping entire documents. Only the changed portions of the documents need to be retyped before they are reprinted.

Future Business Applications

In Chapter 1, information was described as the resource that tells the managers of the business how effectively the material, human, and financial resources are being utilized. The need for information will continue to increase in the future. Already, computers have transformed us into what many call an information society. An information society exists when large groups of employees generate or depend on information to perform their jobs. As discussed in the last section, most offices are already equipped with word processing equipment. Today, messages and correspondence can be prepared on a word processor and then sent electronically to their destination. This type of communication, sometimes called *electronic mail*, will increase in the future. The use of computer terminals for graphics, record keeping, data entry, and other office functions will also increase.

The ability to access information will enable more people to work at home with a personal computer that is linked to a mainframe or mini-computer at the office. Working at home will provide a type of flexibility that is needed in special situations. For example, the ability to work at home enables working mothers to raise families without sacrificing their careers. Working at home is also an attractive alternative for people with physical handicaps.

Although we have emphasized information in this section, production of manufactured goods is still necessary for our survival. In manufacturing, computers are being used to control automated equipment. In fact, some computers control entire assembly lines. Robots and robotlike equipment are already common in the automobile, steel, and other manufacturing industries. For example, General Motors, Ford Motor Company, and Chrysler Corporation are using robots to paint automobiles, weld auto-mobile bodies, and perform other jobs on assembly lines. Robots are often used when the work to be performed is dangerous. Computer-aided design and computer-aided manufacturing programs will continue to automate the way that manufactured goods are produced. The factory of the future will make increased use of automation and robotics. It will have fewer employees, and all employees will be required to work with computers. As a result, a certain amount of job displacement and unemployment will result from the increased use of computers. In many cases, the computer will simply take over the routine jobs. Although experts predict a significant number of new jobs in the computer industry and related fields, employees who don't know how to use a computer, or those who refuse to learn, will be at a definite disadvantage.

Most experts predict that in the future computers will affect every aspect of human life. As a result, computers will be as common as the toaster, the television, and the automobile. While we have tried to describe the most obvious technological trends and how computers affect business, the advances in medicine, transportation, conservation of natural re-sources, and all other areas of human life as we know it today are just as spectacular. It is safe to say that every aspect of your life will be affected by the changes that will take place in the development of computer technology.

Now that we understand how computers transform data into infor-mation, it is time to examine a management information system (MIS).

The Management Information System

management information system (MIS) *a system that provides managers with the information they need to perform their functions as effectively as possible*

Where do managers get the information they need? In many organizations, the answer lies in a **management information system (MIS),** which is a means of providing managers with the information they need to perform their functions as effectively as possible (see Figure 15.4).

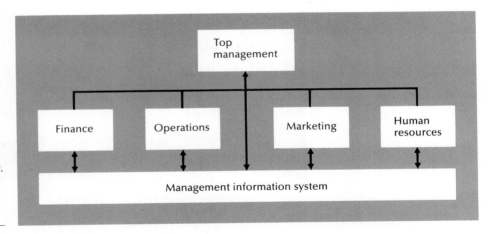

FIGURE 15.4
Management Information System (MIS)
After an MIS is installed, a user can get information directly from the MIS without having to go through other people in the organization. (Source: Adapted from David D. Van Fleet, Contemporary Management. *Copyright © 1988 by Houghton Mifflin Company. Used by permission.)*

If this sounds like the marketing information system discussed in Chapter 11, the similarity is intended. A well-designed MIS operates very much like a good marketing information system does, but it is considerably wider in scope. In many firms, the MIS is combined with a marketing information system so that it can provide information based on a wide variety of data. Accounting data should always be included in the MIS. In fact, it makes little sense to have separate information systems for the various management areas. After all, the goal is to provide needed information to all managers.

Managers' Information Requirements

Learning Objective 5
Be aware of management's information requirements

Managers have to plan for the future, implement their plans in the present, and evaluate the results against what has been accomplished in the past. Thus they need access to information that summarizes future possibilities, the present situation, and past performance. Of course, the specific types of information they need depend on their area of management and on their level within the firm.

In Chapter 5 we identified five areas of management: finance, operations, marketing, human resources, and administration. Financial managers are obviously most concerned with the firm's finances. They ponder its debts and receivables, cash flow, future capitalization needs, financial ratios, and other accounting information. Of equal importance to financial managers is information about the present state of the economy and predictions of business conditions for the near future.

Operations managers are concerned with present and future sales levels and with the availability of the resources required to meet sales forecasts. They need to know the cost of producing the firm's goods and services, including inventory costs. And they are involved with new-product planning. They must also keep abreast of any new production technology that might be useful to their firm.

Marketing managers need to have available detailed information about their firm's product mix and the products offered by competitors. Such information includes prices and pricing strategies, new and projected

Often a company must develop a computer network that allows managers in the finance, operations, marketing, human resource, and administrative areas to have access to information that summarizes the firm's future possibilities, present situation, and past performance.

promotional campaigns, and new products that are being test-marketed by competitors. Information concerning target markets and changes in those markets, market share, new and pending product legislation, and developments within channels of distribution is also important to marketing managers.

Human resources managers must be aware of anything that pertains to the firm's employees and employment in general—from plant safety to the unemployment rate. Key examples include current wage levels and benefits packages both within the firm and in firms that compete for valuable employees; current legislation and court decisions that affect employment practices; union activities; and the firm's plans for growth, expansion, or a merger.

Administrative managers are responsible for the overall management of the organization. Thus they are concerned with the coordination of information—just as they are concerned with the coordination of other business resources. First, administrators must ensure that subordinates have access to the information they need to do their jobs. Second, they are concerned that managers make use of this information. And third, they must ensure that the information is used in a consistent manner. Suppose, for example, that the operations group is designing a new plant to be opened in five years. Is the capacity of the plant consistent with marketing plans based on economic projections? Will personnel managers be able to staff the plant on the basis of their employment forecasts? And will projected sales generate enough income to cover the expected cost of financing?

Size and Complexity of the System

A management information system must be tailored to the needs of the organization it serves. In some firms there may be a tendency to save on initial costs by purchasing a system that is too small or simple. Such a system generally ends up serving only one or two management levels or a single department—the one that gets its data into the system first. Managers in other departments "give up" on the system as soon as they find that it cannot accept or process their data. They either look elsewhere for information or do without.

Almost as bad is an MIS that is too large or too complex for the organization. Unused capacity and complexity do nothing but increase the cost of owning and operating the system. In addition, a system that is difficult to use may not be used at all. Managers may find that it is easier to maintain their own records and to seek general business information from periodicals. Or, again, they may try to operate without information that could be helpful in their decision making.

Obviously, much is expected of an effective MIS. Let's examine the four functions that an MIS must perform to provide the information that managers need.

Functions of the Management Information System

Learning Objective 6
Know the four functions of a management information system

To provide information, a management information system must perform four specific functions. It must collect data; store and then update the data, as necessary; process the stored data into information; and present information to users of the system (see Figure 15.5).

Obviously, data must be collected if they are to be available for storing, processing, and presentation. The data that are entered into the system must be *relevant* to both the operation of the firm and the needs of its managers. And, perhaps most important, these data must be *accurate*. Irrelevant data are simply useless; inaccurate data can be disastrous.

The system must be capable of storing data until they are needed. And it must be able to update stored data to ensure that the information presented to managers is *timely*. An operations manager for Goodyear Tire & Rubber Company, for instance, cannot produce finished goods with last week's work-in-process inventory. She or he needs to know what is available today.

Much of the power of a management information system stems from its ability to transform data into useful information. The system must be capable of processing data in different ways to meet the particular needs of different managers.

Finally, the system must be capable of presenting the information in a *usable form*. That is, the method of presentation—tables, graphs, or charts, for example—must be in keeping with the information itself and with the uses to which it will be put.

Collecting Data

Learning Objective 7
Be able to describe the
various sources of business
data

The first step in using an MIS is to gather the information needed to establish the system—that is, the firm's *data bank*. This data bank should include all past and current data that may be useful in managing the firm. The data themselves can be obtained from within the firm and from outside sources.

Internal Sources of Data   Typically, the majority of the data gathered for an MIS come from internal sources. The most common internal sources of information include company records, reports, managers, and conferences and meetings.

Past and present accounting data can be obtained from ledgers or from financial statements. Accounting source documents can be used to obtain information about the firm's customers, creditors, and suppliers. Similarly, sales reports are a source of data on sales and sales patterns, pricing strategies, and the level and effectiveness of promotional campaigns during past years. Various management reports and the minutes of committee meetings can also yield valuable information for an MIS.

Personnel records are useful as a source of data on wage and benefits levels, hiring patterns, employee turnover, and other human resources variables. Production and inventory records can be used to reconstruct patterns of production, inventory movement, costs, and the like.

Present and past forecasts should also be included in the MIS, with data indicating how well these forecasts predicted actual events. Similarly, specific plans and management decisions—regarding capital expansion and new-product development, for example—should be made a part of the system.

The firm's managers can supply additional data concerning its economic and legal situations. For instance, financial managers can provide information about the firm's credit rating. Legal personnel can add data regarding lawsuits and the firm's compliance with pertinent government regulations.

External Sources of Data   External sources of management data include customers, suppliers, bankers, trade and financial publications, industry conferences, and firms that specialize in gathering data for organizations.

Again, these data take various forms, depending on the needs and requirements of the firm and its managers. A marketing research company may be used to acquire forecasts pertaining to product demand, consumer tastes, and other marketing variables. Suppliers are an excellent source of information about the future availability and costs of raw materials and parts used by the firm.

Bankers can often provide valuable economic insights and projections. The information furnished by trade publications and industry conferences is usually concerned as much with the future as with the present. Both are valuable sources of data on competitors and production technology.

Legal issues and court decisions that may affect the firm are occasionally discussed in local newspapers and, more often, in specialized

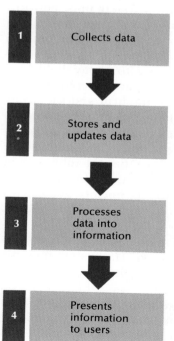

FIGURE 15.5
Four MIS Functions
*Every MIS, tailored to the
organization that it serves,
performs four functions.*

1   Collects data

2   Stores and
updates data

3   Processes
data into
information

4   Presents
information
to users

publications such as the *Wall Street Journal, Fortune,* and *Business Week.* Such publications provide a variety of other useful information as well. Government publications like the *Monthly Labor Review* and the *Federal Reserve Bulletin* are also quite useful as sources of information.

Cautions in Collecting Data   Three cautions should be observed in collecting data for an MIS. First, the cost of obtaining data from such external sources as marketing research firms can be quite high. In all cases—whether the data come from internal or external sources—the cost of obtaining data should be weighed against the potential benefits that having the data will confer on the firm.

Second, although computers do not make mistakes, the people who program them can make or cause errors. By simply pushing the wrong key on a computer keyboard, a technician can change an entire set of data, along with the information it contains. Data—from whatever source—should always be viewed in light of the manager's judgment and intuition. Where there is a disagreement between data (or information) and judgment, the data should be checked.

Third, outdated or incomplete data usually yield inaccurate information. Data collection is an ongoing process. New data must be added to the data bank as they are obtained, or they should be used to regularly update the existing store of data.

Storing and Updating Data

Data should be entered into the data bank as they are collected. Computers are especially well suited for both storing and rapidly updating MIS data.

Storing data is simply holding them for future use. A computer can store vast quantities of data in a very small space. Depending on the particular type of computer, the data may be stored on magnetic tapes or disks. Magnetic tapes and hard disks can hold the most data. Floppy (soft) disks are used with some minicomputers and with almost all microcomputers.

Large mainframes can store millions of bytes. However, that storage capacity is generally used for the particular data that are being processed at any given time (and for the processing instructions). When data are stored for an MIS, the computer is used only to transfer the data to tapes or disks: The programmer enters the data into the computer, which transfers it to a tape or disk. When the tape or disk is full, the programmer removes it from the machine, makes a note about which data it contains, stores the tape or disk on a shelf, and (if necessary) continues with another tape or disk. When the data stored on a particular disk are needed, the disk is reinserted into the computer. At this point, the data are ready to be processed by the computer.

Manual Updating   To update stored data manually, a programmer inserts the proper tape or disk into the computer, locates the data that are to be changed, and provides the new data. The computer automatically replaces the older data with the new.

BUSINESS JOURNAL

A Winning Combination: Computers and Information

A field representative for Godiva Chocolatier walks into a department store to make a sales call. She carries a complete selection of Godiva samples in one bag. In another bag, she has a lap-top computer. During her presentation, she turns on her lap-top and obtains information about the store's past sales. At the end of the presentation, she plugs the lap-top into the customer's telephone and transmits the order to the Godiva's main computer. Govida's computer acknowledges the order, transmits information about the order to the manufacturing and inventory-control departments, and also provides a shipping date for the merchandise.

If this scenario seems like it is something out of the twenty-first century, it's not. It's all part of a master plan to help the company's sixteen field representatives turn information into sales, according to Thomas Fey, president of Godiva Chocolates. Godiva Chocolates spent three years developing its lap-top computer system, which has been a primary contributor to its number-one position in the premium chocolates field.

Since the early 1980s, companies like Godiva have been trying to find ways to harness computer power to provide more information for employees' use. Today, both computer manufacturers and software vendors are doing their part to make that undertaking as easy as possible. For example, each lap-top purchased by Godiva costs approximately $3,000 and is as powerful as a microcomputer. Five years ago, a lap-top with this processing power was still on manufacturers' drawing boards.

Similarly, software vendors have increased the amount of information a computer can generate. In fact, some managers suggest that software now provides too much information. Too much information forces managers to pick and choose which information is really useful and needed. In addition, software vendors have developed personal information managers (PIMs) and executive information systems (EISs) that are easier to learn and use than *Lotus 1-2-3* and database programs like *dBase* that have been available for years.

PERSONAL INFORMATION MANAGERS (PIMs)

Personal information managers (PIMs) are designed to organize unrelated personal data, from addresses and phone numbers to project deadlines. PIMs can be used for just about anything that involves managing people, places, things, or time; and the software can be mastered in one or two days. Popular PIM software packages available today are *Info-XL* ($295); *Lotus Agenda* ($375); *Who, What, Where, When, Why* ($189.50); and *Pack Rat* ($375).

EXECUTIVE INFORMATION SYSTEMS (EISs)

Executive information systems (EISs) differ from PIMs. With a PIM, the user enters personal data, and then the PIM software organizes and presents the data in usable form. With an EIS, a manager's personal computer is linked to a mainframe computer that sorts and stores relevant data collected from internal and external sources. On the manager's command, the EIS software can examine the database, extract the facts that the manager wants, and display the data on the manager's monitor. The new EISs differ from older computer-based management information systems like *Lotus 1-2-3* and *dBase* because they can deliver information without forcing the user to become a computer expert. Companies that currently offer EIS include IBM, Comshare, Inc., and Pilot Executive Software.

Based on information from Jon Pepper, "Sweet Success in Sales Automation," *Working Woman*, April 1989, p. 59+; "Godiva Chocolate," Campbell Soup Company, Annual Report, 1988, p. 13; David Churbuck, "Next Time, Think Big," *Forbes*, June 12, 1989, pp. 155–156; Jon Pepper, "Software That Battles Chaos," *Working Woman*, April 1989, pp. 67–68; Edith Weiner and Arnold Brown, "Human Factors," *The Futurist*, May–June 1989, pp. 9–11; and Russ Lockwood, "The Searchers: On-Line Heroes of the Business World," *Personal Computing*, December 1988, pp. 128–132.

Employees at Genetic Systems, a division of Bristol Myers, are using computerized blood analysis instruments to reduce the time required to process tests of blood samples.

The frequency with which data are updated depends on how fast they change and how often they are used. When it is vital to have current data, updating may occur daily. Otherwise, new data may be collected and held for updating at a certain time each week or, perhaps, each month.

Automatic Updating   In automatic updating, the system itself updates the existing data bank as new information becomes available. The data bank, usually in the form of hard disks, is permanently connected to the MIS. The computer automatically finds the proper disk and replaces the existing data with the new data.

For example, Giant Food, a Maryland-based grocery store chain, has installed cash registers that automatically transmit, to a central computer, information regarding each item sold. The computer adjusts the store's inventory records accordingly. At any time of the day, the manager can get precise, up-to-the-minute information on the inventory of every item sold by the store. In some systems, the computer may even be programmed to reorder items whose inventories fall below some specified level.

Forms of Updating   We have been discussing the type of updating in which new data are *substituted for* old data. Although this is an efficient type of updating in terms of the use of storage, it does result in the loss of the old data. In a second form of updating, new data are *added to* the old data—much as a new file folder is placed between two folders that are already in a drawer. (In fact, on a magnetic tape or disk, existing data are actually spread apart by the computer to accommodate the new data.)

The form of updating used depends entirely on whether the existing data will be needed in the future.

Processing Data

Learning Objective 8
Understand how a management information system uses statistics to turn data into information

data processing *the transformation of data into a form that is useful for a specific purpose*

Data are collected, stored in an MIS, and updated under the assumption that they will be of use to managers. Some data are used in the form in which they are stored. This is especially true of verbal data—a legal opinion, for example. Other data require processing of some sort to extract, highlight, or summarize the information they contain. We shall define **data processing** as the transformation of data into a form that is useful for a specific purpose. For verbal data, this processing consists mainly of extracting the pertinent material from storage and combining it into a report.

Most business data, however, are in the form of numbers—large groups of numbers, such as daily sales volumes or annual earnings of workers in a particular city. Such groups of numbers are difficult to handle and to comprehend, but their contents can be summarized through the use of statistics.

statistic *a measure of a particular characteristic of a group of numbers*

Statistics as Summaries A **statistic** is a measure of a particular characteristic of a group of numbers. The statistic itself is a number that summarizes the characteristic for the entire group. In this section we discuss the most commonly used statistics (or statistical measures), using the data given in Figure 15.6. This figure contains only eleven items of data, which

FIGURE 15.6
Statistics
A statistic is a measure that summarizes a particular characteristic of an entire group of numbers.

Rondex Corporation
Employee salaries for
the month of April 199x

Employee	Monthly salary
Thomas P. Ouimet	$ 3,500
Marina Ruiz	3,500
Ronald F. Washington	3,000
Sarah H. Abrams	3,000
Kathleen L. Norton	3,000
Martin C. Hess	2,800
Jane Chang	2,500
Margaret S. Fernandez	2,400
John F. O'Malley	2,000
Robert Miller	2,000
William G. Dorfmann	1,800
Total	$29,500

simplifies our discussion. In most business situations, we would be dealing with tens or hundreds of items. Fortunately, computers can be programmed to process such large groups of numbers quickly. Managers are free to concern themselves mainly with the information that results.

The number of items in a set of data can be reduced by developing a frequency distribution. A **frequency distribution** is a listing of the number of times each value appears in the data set. For the data in Figure 15.6, the frequency distribution is as follows:

frequency distribution *a listing of the number of times each value appears in a set of data*

Monthly salary	Frequency
$3,500	2
3,000	3
2,800	1
2,500	1
2,400	1
2,000	2
1,800	1

It is also possible to obtain a grouped frequency distribution:

Salary range	No. of employees
$3,000–$3,500	5
2,500– 2,999	2
2,000– 2,499	3
1,500– 1,999	1

By summarizing the data into a grouped frequency distribution, we have reduced the number of data items by approximately 60 percent.

Measures of Size and Dispersion Perhaps the most familiar statistic is the arithmetic mean, which is commonly called the *average*. The **arithmetic mean** of a set of data is the sum of all the data values, divided by the number of items in the set. The sum of employee salaries given in Figure 15.6 is $29,500. Because there are eleven items, the average (arithmetic mean) of employee salaries is $29,500 ÷ 11 = $2,681.82.

arithmetic mean *the sum of all the values of a set of data, divided by the number of items in the set*

The arithmetic mean is a measure, or summary, of the sizes of the items in a data set. Two other summaries of size (or magnitude) are the median and the mode. The **median** of a set of data is the value that appears at the exact middle of the data when they are arranged in order. The data in Figure 15.6 are already arranged from the highest value to the lowest value. Their median is thus $2,800, which is exactly halfway between the top and bottom values.

median *the value that appears at the exact middle of a set of data when the data are arranged in order*

The **mode** of a set of data is the value that appears most frequently in the set. In Figure 15.6, the $3,000 monthly salary appears three times, which is more times than any other salary amount appears. Thus, $3,000 is the mode for this set of data.

mode *the value that appears most frequently in a set of data*

Size, of course, is an important characteristic of the items in a data set. But size alone does not describe the set. Another characteristic that

range *the difference between the highest value and the lowest value in a set of data*

is often summarized is the dispersion, or spread, of the items within the set. The simplest measure of dispersion is the **range,** which is the difference between the highest value and the lowest value in a set of data. The range of the data in Figure 15.6 is $3,500 − $1,800 = $1,700.

The smaller the range of a data set, the closer the values are to the mean—and, thus, the more effective the mean is as a measure of those values. Other measures of dispersion that are used to describe business data are the *variance* and the *standard deviation*. These are somewhat more complicated than the range, and we shall not define or calculate them here. However, you should remember that larger values of both the variance and the standard deviation indicate a greater spread among the values of the data.

With the proper software, a computer can provide these and other statistical measures almost as fast as a user can ask for them. How they are used is then up to the manager. Although statistics provide information in a much more manageable form than raw data, they can be interpreted incorrectly. Note, for example, that the average of the employee salaries given in Figure 15.6 is $2,681.82, yet not one of the employee salaries is exactly equal to that amount. This distinction between actual data and the statistics that describe them is an important one that should never be disregarded.

Presenting Information

Processed data should be presented in the form in which they have the most informational value. Verbal information may be presented in list or paragraph form. Employees are often asked to prepare formal business reports. A typical business report includes (1) an introduction, (2) the body of the report, (3) the conclusions, and (4) the recommendations. The introduction section, which sets the stage for the remainder of the report, describes the problem to be studied in the report, identifies the research techniques that were used, and serves as a preview of the material that will be presented in the report. The body of the report should objectively describe the facts that were discovered in the process of completing the report. This section of the report should provide a foundation for the conclusions and the recommendations. The conclusions section should contain statements of fact that describe the findings contained in the report. They should be specific, practical, and based on the evidence contained in the report. The recommendations section presents suggestions on how the problem under study might be solved. Like the conclusions, recommendations should be specific, practical, and based on the evidence. As part of a formal business report, visual and tabular displays may be necessary. For example, numerical information and combinations of numerical and verbal information are most easily and effectively presented in diagrams and tables.

Visual Displays A **visual display** is a diagram that represents several items of information in a manner that makes comparison easier or reflects trends among the items. The most accurate visual display is a *graph*, in

Software capable of producing visual displays is indispensable to the work of Grady C. Wright, assistant general manager of the TRW Command Support Division. As is true for many managers today, he must be able to present information in a form that other people can understand. Visual presentations of data can help fulfill this management need.

visual display   *a diagram that represents several items of information in a manner that makes comparison easier or reflects trends among the items*

which values are plotted to scale on a set of axes. Graphs are most effective for presenting information about a single variable that changes with time (such as variations in the gross national product over the last forty years). Graphs tend to emphasize trends as well as peaks and low points in the value of the variable. (See Figure 15.7 for examples of visual displays generated by a computer.)

In a *bar chart*, each value is represented as a vertical or horizontal bar. The longer a bar, the greater the value. This type of display is useful for presenting values that are to be compared. The eye can quickly pick

FIGURE 15.7
Visual Displays Used in Business Presentations

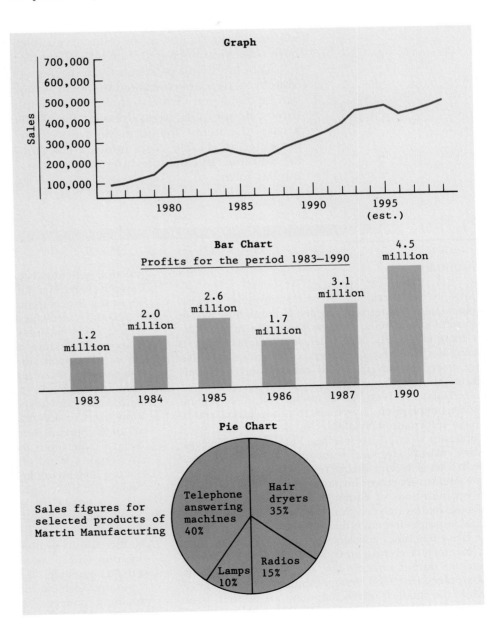

out the longest or shortest bar, or even those that seem to be of average size.

A *pie chart* is a circle ("pie") that is divided into "slices," each of which represents a different item. The circle represents the whole—for example, total sales. The size of each slice shows the contribution of that item to the whole. The larger the slice, the larger the contribution. By their nature, pie charts are most effective in displaying the relative size or importance of various items of information.

Tabular Displays   A **tabular display** is an array of verbal or numerical information in columns and rows. It is most useful in presenting information about two or more related variables (for example, variations in both sales volume and size of sales force by territory).

Tabular displays generally have less impact than visual displays. Moreover, the data contained in most two-column tables (like Figure 15.6) can be displayed visually. However, to display the information in, say, a three-column table, several bar or pie charts would be required. In such a case, the items of information are easier to compare when they are presented in a table. Also, information that is to be manipulated—used, for example, to calculate interest payments—is most often displayed in tabular form.

tabular display   *an array of verbal or numerical information in columns and rows*

CHAPTER REVIEW

Summary

Data are numerical or verbal descriptions, whereas information is data that are presented in a form that is useful for a specific purpose. Generally, information is more effectively used when it is organized into a database. A database is a single collection of data that are stored in one place and can be used by people throughout the organization to make decisions.

Today, business, government, and other organizations depend on computers to process data and to make information available for decision making. A computer is an electronic machine that can accept, store, manipulate, and transmit data in accordance with a set of specific instructions. Although computers are a relatively recent invention, we have already seen five generations of computers. Currently, firms can choose mainframe computers, minicomputers, or microcomputers to match their information needs. Each of these machines consists of at least one input unit, a memory, a control unit, an arithmetic-logic unit, and an output unit. Today, the largest mainframe computers are called supercomputers, or "monsters," while the smallest microcomputers are referred to as lap-tops. Firms can also establish a computer network—a system in which several computers can either

function individually or communicate with each other. Computers require software, or programs, which are operating instructions.

Today, software has been developed to satisfy almost every business need. Database management programs can store and transform data into information. Data contained in a database program can also be sorted by selected criteria. Graphics programs make it possible to display in graph form data and conclusions. Spreadsheets are software packages that allow users to organize data into a grid of rows and columns. Spreadsheets allow managers to answer "what if" questions by changing data to match new assumptions. Word processing programs allow users to store documents in the computer's memory or on a magnetic disk. Once entered, the material can be used at a later date. Most experts predict that in the future computers will affect every aspect of human life. Specific trends that will affect business include the increase in available information, the use of automation, and the need for employees that know how to use a computer.

A management information system is a means of providing managers with the information they need to perform their functions as effectively as possible. The data that are entered into the system must be relevant, accurate, and timely. The information provided by the system must be all of these—and it must be in usable form as well. Managers in different areas of a business generally require information pertaining to their own areas. The management information system itself should match the firm it serves in capacity and complexity.

The four functions performed by an MIS are collecting data, storing and updating data, processing data, and presenting information. Data may be collected from such internal sources as accounting documents and other financial records, conferences and meetings, and sales and production records. External sources include customers, suppliers, bankers, publications, and information-gathering organizations.

With a computer, data can be stored on magnetic tapes and disks and used whenever they are needed. Data should be updated regularly to maintain their timeliness and accuracy. Updating can be accomplished manually or via computer.

Data processing is the MIS function that transforms stored data into a form that is useful for a specific purpose. Large groups of numerical data are usually processed into summary numbers called statistics. The arithmetic mean, median, and mode are measures of the sizes of values in a set of data. The range is a measure of the dispersion, or spread, of the data values.

Finally, the processed data (which can now be called information) must be presented for use. Verbal information is generally presented in list or paragraph form. Typically, the components of a business report are the introduction, the body of the report, the conclusions, and the recommendations. Numerical information is most often displayed in graphs and charts or tables.

In the next chapter we examine the accounting process, which is a major source of information for business.

Key Terms

You should now be able to define and give an example relevant to each of the following terms:

data	control unit
information	arithmetic-logic unit
database	output unit
computer	hardware
artificial intelligence	computer network
input unit	software
memory (or storage) unit	computer programmer
flow chart	statistic
graphics program	frequency distribution
spreadsheet program	arithmetic mean
word processing program	median
	mode
management information system (MIS)	range
	visual display
data processing	tabular display

Questions and Exercises

Review Questions

1. What is the difference between data and information? Give one example of accounting data and one example of accounting information.
2. In basic terms, what is a database? How is it used in a business?
3. Briefly describe the history of computers.
4. List the five primary units within a computer, and briefly state the function of each.
5. What is meant by the term *computer network*?
6. What are the advantages of ready-made software? What are the disadvantages?
7. In your own words, define a management information system (MIS).
8. How do the information requirements of managers differ by management area?
9. Why must a management information system (MIS) be tailored to the needs of the organization it serves?
10. List the four functions of a management information system.
11. List several internal and several external sources of data.
12. What kinds of data might be updated by substituting new data for old data? by adding new data to old data?
13. What are the differences among the mean, median, and mode of a set of data? In what way are they alike?
14. Data set A has a mean of 20 and a range of 10; data set B has the same mean and a range of 4. In which data set are the values closer to each other in size? How do you know?
15. What are the components of a typical business report?

Discussion Questions

1. With annual revenues that exceed $60 billion and profits that exceed $5 billion a year, IBM is the fifth-largest industrial corporation in the world.

And yet, IBM is faced with three serious problems that threaten the company's future. In your own words, describe each problem and how it affects the future of the company.

2. According to IBM's chairman and CEO Fred Akers, one of IBM's problems was that it forgot to consider what the customer wanted. Should a large company like IBM still worry about what the customer wants? Why?

3. How can confidential data (such as the wages of individual employees) be kept confidential but be made available to managers who need them?

4. Why are computers so well suited to management information systems? What are some things that computers *cannot* do in dealing with data and information?

5. Do managers really need all the kinds of information discussed in this chapter? If not, which kinds can they do without?

6. How do you think computer technology will change in the next ten years?

Exercises

1. Leaf through a few magazines to find advertisements for three different brands of computers. For each brand, list the product attributes that are stressed in the ads. Then state whether each attribute would be important in an MIS, and why.

2. Choose a bar chart, a pie chart, or a graph, and display the data given in Figure 15.6. Why did you choose this method of presentation?

Case 15.1

A Compaq Guide to Good Business

Less than four years after it was founded in 1982, Compaq Computer Corporation made the *Fortune* 500 list of America's top industrial companies. Compaq's rise to this prestigious list—the fastest in its thirty-two-year history—provides a perfect example of how the free-market system should function. Its founders identified a need and priced their product so that it would sell. They worked hard as a team and stressed quality and efficiency.

Compaq was created by three senior managers at Texas Instruments: Bill Murto, Jim Harris, and Rod Canion. The three considered a variety of new ventures, including opening a Mexican restaurant and selling beepers to help locate misplaced keys, before deciding on a company that would build personal computers.

Their decision was based on their experience at Texas Instruments, which gave them an intimate knowledge of the computer market. Even though the growth of demand for computers slowed somewhat in the mid-1980s, Compaq's leaders correctly predicted that there would continue to be a large market for new machines. The biggest problem they faced was competition, especially from industry giants IBM and Apple Computer, Inc.

The young company took its first crucial step in product development by choosing to follow the lead of IBM, whose PCs set the standard for personal computers. Until Compaq was founded, smaller companies that survived the intense competition with IBM had done so by producing "PC clones." The makers of these clones stressed price over quality as a way to differentiate their products. But Compaq took another crucial step by deciding to differentiate itself from the clones by matching IBM's quality instead of undercutting their prices.

Compaq spent three years in the position of apprentice—learning from the master, IBM. Then the company prepared to strike out on its own. It worked hard to produce the first personal computer based on the Intel 80386, the computer chip that most experts agree has become the heart of the newest generation of personal computers. Compaq read the market well for its first big, independent step. It realized that IBM would be reluctant to bring out a machine based on the new chip because this new generation of computers would probably steal business from IBM's other, more powerful computers. Compaq's early success proved that customers would respond to its approach—building quality computers compatible with machines already in use.

The company has continued to build on its quality image and has refused to market inferior products. For example, Compaq realized that there was a large market for battery-operated lap-top computers in 1987. And yet, management refused to introduce a new product line before all the bugs could be worked out. In fact, the management team rejected the first three prototypes that were developed. Finally, Compaq's SLT lap-top was introduced in October 1988. Because of the SLT's speed and crisp screen, it became an overnight success. By the end of the year, Compaq had a 34 percent share of the lap-top market—second only to Toshiba Corporation.

According to company officials, a commitment to quality does pay off. A base of satisfied, repeat customers has made Compaq extremely profitable. Sales and profits have almost doubled each year since the company was incorporated. And financial analysts predict that Compaq's future looks bright because of its ability to incorporate the newest computer components and other technical innovations into a quality product line.*

Questions

1. Many computer companies have tried to compete with IBM by offering clones at low prices. Compaq, on the other hand, chose to compete by matching IBM's quality. What are the disadvantages and advantages of Compaq's decision?
2. Assume that you are in charge of marketing Compaq's new SLT lap-top computer. In what ways could the company's quality image be incorporated into your marketing plan?

Case 15.2

Should Computers Monitor Employee Performance?

In the past, employees have often referred to their boss as "inhuman." Today, that is not just a figure of speech. Their supervisor may, in reality, be inhuman— a computer. In thousands of U.S. offices, factories, and stores where computer systems are in use, workers can no longer goof off, take long lunch hours, make personal phone calls or enjoy extended coffee breaks. Their every move is being monitored by a computer.

About seven million Americans who work with computers are now being monitored, and that number is expected to triple in the next ten years as the use of computers increases. Monitoring requires only the installation of specially written software in a central computer that processes the work of numerous individual terminal users. In manufacturing, computers can now be linked to plant-floor machinery to alert supervisors when speed and productivity fall below an established standard of performance. In offices, computers can keep track of a typist's keystrokes or the number of payments processed by an accounting clerk.

Employees who are monitored act differently— somewhat like people having their picture taken. From the employer's viewpoint, it is hoped that having a computer monitoring an employee's performance will improve the worker's productivity. For example, Giant Food, a Maryland-based grocery store chain, uses optical scanners at check-out counters to eliminate pricing errors, improve inventory control, aid in work scheduling, and track each worker's speed. By using this technique, the grocery store chain has reportedly saved in excess of $15 million annually. Other companies using computers to monitor employees include Pacific Southwest Airlines, American Express, United Air Lines, Equitable Life Insurance, and AT&T.

There are drawbacks to monitoring employees by computers. Companies using computer monitoring systems often cite higher employee turnover, increased absenteeism, and sabotage as major problems that can offset gains in productivity. Workers argue that being watched all the time is stressful, depersonalizing, and even frightening. Some workers complain about fatigue and headaches caused by the impersonal monitoring. They emphasize that a machine cannot measure courtesy, carefulness, personal attention, and quality. Unions such as the 13,000-member Brotherhood of Railway, Airline, and Steamship Clerks are actively opposing computer monitoring. More than twenty national unions have negotiated provisions in their contracts to limit the practice of computer monitoring. Even several state legislatures have reportedly discussed laws to regulate computer monitoring.

While the majority of employees view computer monitoring as a violation of privacy, a few see it as an unbiased true appraisal of their work for which they will be paid accordingly. For these employees, computer supervision is an improvement over a supervisor's subjective judgment. Good or bad, experts believe that computer supervision is here to stay, but not without its share of employee objections and even legal battles.†

Questions

1. Explain some of the advantages and disadvantages of computer supervision from the employer's standpoint.
2. If you were an employee, would you want your work monitored by a computer?

---

* Based on information from Mark Ivey and Geoff Lewis, "How Compaq Gets There Firstest with the Mostest," *Business Week*, June 26, 1989, pp. 146–147+; Thane Peterson, "The Power Behind Compaq's European Powerhouse," *Business Week*, June 26, 1989, p. 150; Patrick Honan and Russ Lockwood, "Big Manufacturers Thinking Small," *Personal Computing*, November 1988, p. 37; Maria Shao, "PCs: The Big Three Get Bigger, and Clones Feel the Squeeze," *Business Week*, December 12, 1988, pp. 112–113; Bro Utal, "Compaq Bids for PC Leadership," *Fortune*, September 29, 1986, pp. 30–32; and Joel Kotkin, "The 'Smart Team' at Compaq Computer," *Inc.*, February 1986, p. 48.

† Based on information from Michael R. Smith, "Technologizing Office Work," *Society*, May/June 1989, pp. 65–72; Edith Weiner and Arnold Brown, "Human Factors," *Futurist*, May/June 1989, pp. 9–11. Holloway McCandless, "Computer Monitoring: Is it 'Big Brother' Watching?" *Working Woman*, November 1988, p. 38+; Stephen Koepp, "The Boss That Never Blinks," *Time*, July 28, 1986, p. 46; Carey W. English, "Is Your Friendly Computer Rating You on the Job?" *U.S. News & World Report*, February 18, 1985, p. 66; Beth Brophy, "New Technology, High Anxiety," *U.S. News & World Report*, September 29, 1986, pp. 54–55; Diana Smith, "The Electronic Supervisor," *Macleans*, June 17, 1985, p. 32.

ACCOUNTING

1 Know what accounting is and what accountants do

2 Understand the accounting equation and the concept of double-entry bookkeeping

3 Be able to list the steps of the accounting cycle

4 Know how to read and interpret a balance sheet

5 Know how to read and interpret an income statement

6 Recognize and be able to use the financial ratios that reveal how a business is doing

CHAPTER PREVIEW

We begin this chapter with an overview of the accounting process. We identify different classifications of accountants and see how their work is important both to a firm's managers and to individuals and groups outside a firm. Then we focus on the basics of an accounting system—the accounting equation, double-entry bookkeeping, and the process by which raw data are organized into financial statements. Next, we examine the two most important types of financial statements, the balance sheet and the income statement, and explain how these statements can answer a variety of questions about a firm. Finally, we show how accounting information can be expressed numerically—as financial ratios—and what these ratios say about a firm's operations.

The Arthur Andersen Worldwide Organization

For years, The Arthur Andersen Worldwide Organization, based in Chicago, was the acknowledged leader of the Big Eight accounting firms. But now the firm has dropped to number two in the rankings as a result of the merger of the accounting firms of Ernst & Whinney and Arthur Young. While Andersen's management acknowledges they are number two in the size rankings, they believe that the firm is still number one in quality and the acknowledged leader in professional services.

Arthur Andersen, with annual revenues of more than $3.4 billion, is continuing to concentrate on restructuring its global operations. Andersen realigned its services along distinct business lines reflecting the diverse client needs in the global marketplace. Two business units were established: Arthur Andersen, which provides audit, tax, and financial consulting services; and Andersen Consulting, which provides strategic services, systems integration, and information technology.

Andersen also consolidated its worldwide operations into three geographic areas: Europe, Asia/Pacific, and the Americas. Most analysts applauded this decision because it enabled Andersen to concentrate on expanding its professional services in overseas markets while expanding domestic services in the United States. Andersen derives about 60 percent of its profit from its U.S. operations, but attracting new business in North America has never been more difficult. As a result of a large number of corporate mergers, the number of companies needing auditing has diminished. In order to keep current U.S. clients or attract new ones, accounting firms have had to cut their fees. In response, Andersen is focusing on increasing the value of its services to clients and is initiating a wide range of financial consulting services, which are generating revenue growth. At the same time, Andersen is experiencing dramatic growth in new clients and revenues in

certain parts of Asia, Africa, South America, and Europe.

In addition to global reorganization, The Arthur Andersen Worldwide Organization, through its Andersen Consulting business unit, is concentrating on developing the firm's information-technology and computer-consulting activities. Andersen has been involved in the information and computer consulting field for years. As far back as 1954, Andersen installed the first commercial computer system at the General Electric Company. Today, Andersen Consulting is the most successful consulting unit of its kind with annual revenues of $1.4 billion. And it is easy to see why Andersen expanded into information and computer consulting—it's very profitable. Just one major contract—such as improving a product distribution system—may generate over $20 million in fees. In contrast, an audit contract for the same size firm typically yields less than $5 million.[1] In fact, Andersen officials predict that by 1993, information and computer consulting will produce more than half of the firm's revenues.[2]

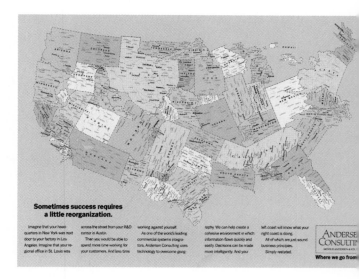

Sometimes success requires a little reorganization.

Imagine that your headquarters in New York was next door to your factory in Los Angeles. Imagine that your regional office in St. Louis was across the street from your R&D center in Austin. Then you would be able to spend more time working for your customers. And less time working against yourself.

As one of the world's leading commercial systems integrators, Andersen Consulting uses technology to overcome geography. We can help create a cohesive environment in which information flows quickly and easily. Decisions can be made more intelligently. And your left coast will know what your right coast is doing. All of which are just sound business principles. Simply restated.

ANDERSEN CONSULTING
ARTHUR ANDERSEN & CO.

Where we go from

ccording to Lawrence A. Weinbach, CEO and managing partner at The Arthur Andersen Worldwide Organization, "It isn't how big you are but how well you serve your clients' needs."[3] This philosophy has enabled his company to grow into one of the largest accounting firms in the world. And while this philosophy applies to all businesses, it is especially apt for an accounting firm. The basic product that an accounting firm sells is information—information that must meet clients' needs.

Today, it is impossible to manage a business operation without accurate and timely accounting information. For example, managers and employees, lenders, suppliers, stockholders, and government agencies rely on the information that is contained in two financial statements: the balance sheet and the income statement. Each of these reports is usually no more than one page in length. Together, they represent the results of perhaps tens of thousands of transactions that have occurred during the reporting period.

These two financial statements are thus concise summaries of a firm's activities during a specific time period. The standard unit of measurement for business operations is the dollar. The raw data are the day-to-day items of income and expense: every sale to a customer and every payment for rent, wages, raw materials, inventory, interest, and so on.

Standard accounting methods (described later) have been developed for summarizing and presenting data in financial reports. This is so that each item in each report means the same thing to everyone who reads it. Moreover, the form of the financial statements is pretty much the same for all businesses, from a neighborhood video arcade to a giant conglomerate like General Motors. This information has a variety of uses, both within the firm and outside it. However, accounting information is, first and foremost, management information. As such, it is of most use to those who are responsible for the operation of the firm.

Accounting and Accountants

Learning Objective 1
Know what accounting is and what accountants do

accounting *the process of systematically collecting, analyzing, and reporting financial information*

Accounting is the process of systematically collecting, analyzing, and reporting financial information. Because of its great value, business owners have been concerned with financial information for hundreds of years: The first book of accounting principles was written in 1494, by an Italian monk named Paciolo.

Modern accounting in the United States can be traced back to the establishment of the American Institute of Certified Public Accountants (AICPA) in 1887. By the early 1900s, accounting instruction was offered (but was optional) at many colleges and universities. Today, accounting courses are required for virtually every type of business degree.

Accounting or Bookkeeping?

Many people confuse accounting with bookkeeping, but there are important differences between the two. Accounting deals with the entire system for providing accurate and up-to-date financial information—from the design of the system through its operation to interpretation of the information that is obtained. To become an accountant, an individual must undergo years of training and chalk up a great deal of practical experience.

bookkeeping *the routine, day-to-day record keeping that is a necessary part of accounting*

Bookkeeping, on the other hand, is the routine, day-to-day record keeping that is a necessary part of accounting. Bookkeepers are responsible for obtaining the financial data that the accounting system processes. An accounting system cannot operate without good, accurate bookkeeping, but a bookkeeper can generally be trained within a year or so.

Classification of Accountants

Accountants are people who are trained and experienced in the methods and systems of accounting. They are generally classified as private accountants or public accountants.

private (or **nonpublic**) **accountant** *an accountant who is employed by a specific organization*

A **private** (or **nonpublic**) **accountant** is an accountant who is employed by a specific organization. A medium-sized or large firm may employ one or several private accountants to design its accounting system, manage its accounting department, prepare the variety of reports required by management or by law, and provide managers with advice and assistance. Private accountants provide their services only to their employers.

public accountant *an accountant whose services may be hired on a fee basis by individuals or firms*

Smaller and medium-sized firms that don't require full-time accountants can hire the services of public accountants. A **public accountant** is an accountant whose services may be hired on a fee basis by individuals or firms. Public accountants may be self-employed, or they may work for accounting firms. Accounting firms range in size from one-person operations to huge international firms with hundreds of accounting partners and thousands of employees. Table 16.1 lists the eight largest accounting firms in the United States and some of their clients.

TABLE 16.1   Accounting's "Big Eight" Certified Public Accounting Firms (in alphabetical order)

Firm	Home Office	Some Major Clients
Arthur Andersen & Co.	Chicago	ITT, Texaco, United Airlines
Coopers & Lybrand	New York	AT&T, Ford
Deloitte & Touche	New York	General Motors, Procter & Gamble
Ernst & Young	New York	Mobil, McDonald's, Coca-Cola
KPMG Peat Marwick Main	New York	General Electric, Xerox
Price Waterhouse	New York	IBM, Exxon, Du Pont
Levanthol & Horwath	Philadelphia	Lorimar, Giant Food, Reebok
Grant Thornton	Chicago	Fretter, Grainger Home Shopping Network

Source: Adapted from B. E. Needles, H. R. Anderson, and J. C. Caldwell, *Principles of Accounting*, 4th ed. Copyright © 1990 by Houghton Mifflin Company. Used by permission.

The primary users of accounting information are managers. Lenders, suppliers, stockholders, and government agencies are also interested in the information generated by a firm's accounting system.

certified public accountant (CPA) *an individual who has met state requirements for accounting education and experience and has passed a rigorous three-day accounting examination*

Most accounting firms include on their staffs at least one **certified public accountant (CPA)**, an individual who has met state requirements for accounting education and experience and has passed a rigorous three-day accounting examination. The examination is prepared by the American Institute of Certified Public Accountants and covers accounting practice, accounting theory, auditing, and business law. State requirements usually include a college accounting degree and from one to three years of on-the-job experience. Details regarding specific requirements for practice as a CPA in a particular state can be obtained by contacting the respective State Board of Accountancy. Certification as a CPA brings both status and responsibility. Only an independent CPA can officially verify the financial contents of a corporation's annual report and express an opinion—as required by law—regarding the acceptability of the corporation's accounting practices.

Users of Accounting Information

As we have noted, the primary users of accounting information are *managers*. The firm's accounting system provides a range of information dealing with revenues, costs, accounts receivable, amounts borrowed and owed, profits, return on investment, and the like. This information can be compiled for the entire firm; for each product; for each sales territory, store, or individual salesperson; for each division or department; and generally in any way that will help those who manage the organization. At a company like Kraft General Foods (a division of Philip Morris), for

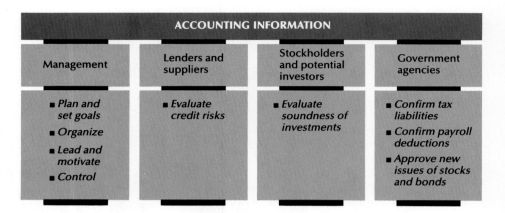

FIGURE 16.1
Accounting Information
The primary users of accounting information are managers; but certain financial information is demanded by outside individuals and organizations that the company deals with.

example, financial information is gathered for all of its hundreds of food products: Maxwell House Coffee, Birds Eye Frozen Foods, Post Cereals, Jell-O Desserts, Kool Aid, and so on. The president of the company would be interested in the combined sales for all these products. The marketing manager for desserts would be interested in sales for Birds Eye Frozen Desserts and Jell-O. The northeastern sales manager might want to look at sales figures for Kool Aid in New England. For a large, complex organization like Kraft General Foods, the accounting system must be flexible and complete because managers at different levels must be able to get the information they need.

Much of this accounting information is *proprietary;* it is not divulged to anyone outside the firm. However, certain financial information is demanded by individuals and organizations that the firm must deal with (see Figure 16.1).

▶   *Lenders* require at least the information that is contained in the firm's financial statements before they will commit themselves to either short- or long-term loans. *Suppliers* generally ask for this same information before they will extend trade credit to a firm.

▶   *Stockholders* must, by law, be provided with a summary of the firm's financial position in each annual report. In addition, *potential investors* must be provided with financial statements in the prospectus for each securities issue.

▶   *Government agencies* require a variety of information pertaining to the firm's tax liabilities, payroll deductions for employees, and new issues of stocks and bonds.

The firm's accounting system must be able to provide all this information, in the required form. An important function of accountants is to ensure that such information is accurate and thorough enough to satisfy these outside groups.

BUSINESS JOURNAL

Defensive Accounting at General Dynamics

General Dynamics Corp. is one of the top U.S. defense contractors, with annual revenues of around $9 billion. The firm is the sole supplier of the Navy's Trident submarines; and its F-16 fighter jets, M-1 tanks, and Tomahawk missiles are regarded as essential to the nation's defense. But defense contracts are just as essential to General Dynamics. They account for some 85 to 90 percent of its revenues and more than 95 percent of its operating profit.

Recently, the accounting methods used by General Dynamics have become the target of government auditors and investigators, who are checking allegedly improper cost allocations and possible overcharges. For example, General Dynamics has been accused of shifting expenses from fixed-price contracts to other contracts on which the expenses were more likely to be reimbursed. And a congressional investigating committee alleged that the firm charged the government for such expenses as country club fees (more than $18,000 worth) and the cost of boarding an executive's dog. They also found that General Dynamics had billed the government $9,609 for a single wrench.

The Defense Department expects contractors to estimate costs accurately and keep them reasonably close to original cost estimates. In fact, many contracts for the development of weapons systems are "cost-plus" contracts that involve payment by the government of all development costs, plus a fee. But whenever payment is based on costs, accurate records must be kept, and that is a function of accounting.

Officials at General Dynamics deny any wrongdoing but admit that their accounting system is less than perfect. As one official points out, accounting is probably as much an art as it is a science. True, there are generally accepted accounting practices—rules of accounting—as well as special rules that government contractors are required to follow. But many of those rules and practices are open to interpretation. The kinds of weapons systems produced by General Dynamics are not like other products—say, nuts and bolts, or even rifles and machine guns. They are extremely complex items, each one designed to perform according to a set of military specifications.

Consider, for example, that $9,609 wrench. Congressional investigators were appalled at the price, and the media made much of it. But then investigators learned that the price included the entire cost of designing and developing the wrench. Defense Department accounting rules require that all the one-time costs of developing a new tool be allocated to the first tool made (rather than spread over the entire production run of the tool).

In the wake of the accusations (and two suspensions from bidding on government contracts), General Dynamics appointed a new chief executive officer—Stanley C. Pace. Pace immediately moved to improve the company's image. One of his first acts was to tighten the firm's accounting procedures. The revamping began with the way shop workers' time is charged to specific contracts, and it included safeguards against both errors and intentional wrongdoing. The firm has also asked the government for clarification of its accounting rules.

Pace also developed ethical codes of conduct for particular jobs and initiated tough guidelines on entertainment, gratuities, and conflicts of interest. These tougher ethical guidelines helped to eliminate many of the questionable charges that plagued General Dynamics during the 1980s.

Finally, Pace directed the company's accountants to analyze all General Dynamic's defense contracts. The accountants found that questionable expenses were less than one-half of 1 percent of the total cost of defense contracts. As a result, Pace ordered that General Dynamics absorb any cost that might possibly be considered unethical or questionable. According to one accountant, the criterion for billing will be, "How would it look on the front page of the *New York Times?*"

Based on information from Harlan S. Byrne, "Aggressive Arms Merchant," *Barron's*, May 8, 1989, p. 15+; James E. Ellis, "General Dynamics: All Cleaned Up with No Place to Grow," *Business Week*, August 22, 1988, pp. 70–71; "Corporate Cleaner-Upper, *Forbes*, January 11, 1988, p. 70; and Ford S. Worthy, "Mr. Clean Charts a New Course at General Dynamics, *Fortune*, April 28, 1986, pp. 70–76.

The Accounting Process

Learning Objective 2
Understand the accounting equation and the concept of double-entry bookkeeping

Accounting can be viewed as a system for transforming raw financial *data* into useful financial *information*. In this section, we see how such a system operates. Then, in the next two sections, we describe the two most important financial statements provided by the accounting process.

The Accounting Equation

The accounting equation is a simple statement that forms the basis for the accounting process. It shows the relationship among the firm's assets, liabilities, and owners' equity.

assets   *the things of value that a firm owns*

▶ **Assets** are the things of value that a firm owns. They include cash, inventories, land, equipment, buildings, patents, and the like.

liabilities   *a firm's debts and obligations—what it owes to others*

▶ **Liabilities** are the firm's debts and obligations—what it owes to others.

owners' equity   *the difference between a firm's assets and its liabilities—what would be left over for the firm's owners if its assets were used to pay off its liabilities*

▶ **Owners' equity** is the difference between a firm's assets and its liabilities—what would be left over for the firm's owners if its assets were used to pay off its liabilities.

The relationship among these three terms is almost self-evident: Owners' equity = assets − liabilities. By moving terms algebraically, we obtain the standard form of the **accounting equation:**

accounting equation   *the basis for the accounting process: Assets = liabilities + owners' equity*

$$\textbf{Assets = liabilities + owners' equity}$$

Implementation of this equation begins with the recording of raw data— that is, the firm's day-to-day financial transactions. It is accomplished through the double-entry system of bookkeeping.

The Double-Entry Bookkeeping System

double-entry bookkeeping   *a system in which each financial transaction is recorded as two separate accounting entries to maintain the balance shown in the accounting equation*

Double-entry bookkeeping is a system in which each financial transaction is recorded as two separate accounting entries to maintain the balance shown in the accounting equation. Most often, one entry changes the left (assets) side of the equation, and the other entry changes the right (liabilities + owners' equity) side. However, for a few types of transactions, the two entries change only one side of the equation. This occurs, for example, when cash (an asset) is used to purchase equipment (another asset).

Suppose that John Thompson and Mark Martin each invest $25,000 in cash to start a new business. Before they make these investments, both sides of the accounting equation are equal to zero. The firm has no assets, no liabilities, and no owners' equity. The results of their investments are shown as transaction A in Figure 16.2. Cash (an asset) is increased by $50,000; owners' equity is also increased by a total of $50,000 to balance the increase in assets.

Note that the entries for this transaction are not lumped together as one asset increase and one owners' equity increase. Instead, the entries

	ASSETS			=	LIABILITIES		+	OWNERS' EQUITY	
	Cash	Equipment	Inventory	=	Bank Loans	Suppliers	+	Thompson	Martin
Transaction A (cash investment)	+$50,000	–0–	–0–	=	–0–	–0–	+	+$25,000	+$25,000
	$50,000 +	–0– +	–0–	=	–0– +	–0–	+	$25,000 +	$25,000
Transaction B (equipment purchase via bank loan)	–0–	+$10,000	–0–	=	+$10,000	–0–		–0–	–0–
	$50,000 +	$10,000 +	–0–	=	$10,000 +	–0–	+	$25,000 +	$25,000
Transaction C (credit purchase of inventory)	–0–	–0–	+$5,000	=	–0–	+$5,000		–0–	–0–
	$50,000 +	$10,000 +	$5,000	=	$10,000 +	$5,000	+	$25,000 +	$25,000
Transaction D (partial payoff of loan)	–$ 5,000	–0–	–0–	=	–$ 5,000	–0–		–0–	–0–
	$45,000 +	$10,000 +	$5,000	=	$ 5,000 +	$5,000	+	$25,000 +	$25,000

FIGURE 16.2
Four Business Transactions Recorded Using the Double-Entry System
Double-entry bookkeeping is used to balance the accounting equation (assets equal liabilities plus owners' equity).

are placed in separate *accounts*, which show exactly what is being increased. Here the investments are cash, so the *Cash* account is increased. Similarly, under owners' equity, there is one account for Thompson and one for Martin.

Three additional transactions are shown in Figure 16.2:

▶ In transaction B, a bank loan of $10,000 was used to purchase equipment. The loan is a liability, and the equipment is an asset.

▶ In transaction C, inventory worth $5,000 was purchased on credit. The inventory is an asset, and the amount owed is a liability.

▶ In transaction D, $5,000 in cash was used to pay off part of the bank loan. The payoff decreases cash, an asset; the reduction of the loan amount decreases a liability.

Follow through each of these transactions in Figure 16.2 to make sure you understand why each entry is recorded as shown. Also note that, after all four transactions, assets total $60,000, and liabilities and owners' equity total $60,000. Thus the books are still balanced. That is, assets are indeed equal to liabilities plus owners' equity.

The Accounting Cycle

Learning Objective 3
Be able to list the steps of the accounting cycle

In the typical accounting system, raw data are transformed into financial statements in five steps. The first three—analysis, journalizing, and posting—are performed on a continual basis throughout the accounting period. The last two—preparation of the trial balance and of the financial statements—are performed at the end of the accounting period.

Analyzing Source Documents The basic accounting data are contained in *source documents*, which are the receipts, invoices, sales slips, and other documents that show the dollar values of day-to-day business transactions. The accounting cycle begins with the analysis of each of these documents. The purpose of the analysis is to determine which accounts are affected by the documents and how they are affected.

Journalizing the Transactions Every financial transaction is next recorded in a journal—a process that is called *journalizing*. Transactions must be recorded in the firm's general journal or in specialized journals. The **general journal** is a book of original entry in which typical transactions are recorded in order of their occurrence. An accounting system may also include *specialized journals* for specific types of transactions that occur frequently. Thus a retail store might have cash receipts, cash disbursements, purchases, and sales journals in addition to its general journal.

general journal *a book of original entry in which typical transactions are recorded in order of their occurrence*

Posting Transactions Next the information recorded in the general journal or specialized journals is transferred to the general ledger. The **general**

Today, accountants often use computers to process data into information. The information is then summarized on the firm's financial statements.

general ledger *a book of accounts that contains a separate sheet or section for each account*

posting *the process of transferring journal entries to the general ledger*

trial balance *a summary of the balances of all general ledger accounts at the end of the accounting period*

ledger is a book of accounts that contains a separate sheet or section for each account. The process of transferring journal entries to the general ledger is called **posting**.

Preparing the Trial Balance A **trial balance** is a summary of the balances of all general ledger accounts at the end of the accounting period. To prepare a trial balance, the accountant determines and lists the balances for all ledger accounts. If the trial balance totals are correct, the accountant can proceed to the financial statements. If not, there is a mistake somewhere. The accountant must find and correct it before proceeding.

Preparing Financial Statements and Closing the Books The firm's financial statements are prepared from the information contained in the trial balance. This information is presented in a standardized format to make the statements as generally accessible as possible to the various parties who may be interested in the firm's financial affairs.

Once these statements have been prepared and checked, the firm's books are "closed" for the accounting period. A new accounting cycle is then begun for the next period.

Now let us consider the two most important financial statements generated by the accounting process, the balance sheet and the income statement.

The Balance Sheet

balance sheet (or **statement of financial position**) *a summary of a firm's assets, liabilities, and owners' equity accounts at a particular time, showing the various dollar amounts that enter into the accounting equation*

A **balance sheet** (or **statement of financial position**), is a summary of a firm's assets, liabilities, and owners' equity accounts at a particular time, showing the various dollar amounts that enter into the accounting equation. The balance sheet must demonstrate that the accounting equation does indeed balance. That is, it must show that the firm's assets are equal to its liabilities plus its owners' equity. As previously noted, the balance sheet is prepared at the end of the accounting period, which usually covers one year. Most firms also have balance sheets prepared semiannually, quarterly, or monthly.

Figure 16.3 shows the balance sheet for Northeast Art Supply, a small corporation that sells picture frames, paints, canvases, and other artists' supplies to retailers in New England. Note that assets are reported at the top of the statement, followed by liabilities and owners' equity. This is the standard format for these statements. Let us work through the accounts in Figure 16.3, from top to bottom.

Learning Objective 4
Know how to read and interpret a balance sheet

Assets

liquidity *the ease with which an asset can be converted into cash*

On a balance sheet, assets are listed in order, from the *most liquid* to the *least liquid*. The **liquidity** of an asset is the ease with which it can be converted into cash.

NORTHEAST ART SUPPLY, INC.

Balance Sheet
December 31, 199x

ASSETS

Current assets
Cash		$ 59,000	
Marketable securities		10,000	
Accounts receivable	$ 40,000		
Less allowance for doubtful accounts	2,000	38,000	
Notes receivable		32,000	
Merchandise inventory		41,000	
Prepaid expenses		2,000	
Total current assets			$182,000

Fixed assets
Delivery equipment	$110,000		
Less accumulated depreciation	20,000	$ 90,000	
Furniture and store equipment	62,000		
Less accumulated depreciation	15,000	47,000	
Total fixed assets			137,000

Intangible assets
Patents		$ 6,000	
Goodwill		15,000	
Total intangible assets			21,000
Total assets			$340,000

LIABILITIES AND OWNERS' EQUITY

Current liabilities
Accounts payable	$ 35,000		
Notes payable	25,000		
Salaries payable	4,000		
Taxes payable	6,000		
Total current liabilities		$ 70,000	

Long-term liabilities
Mortgage payable on store equipment	$ 40,000		
Total long-term liabilities		40,000	
Total liabilities			$110,000

Owners' equity
Common stock, 10,000 shares at $15 Par value		$150,000	
Retained earnings		80,000	
Total owners' equity			230,000
Total liabilities and owners' equity			$340,000

FIGURE 16.3
Balance Sheet
A balance sheet summarizes the firm's accounts at a particular time, showing the various dollar amounts that enter into the accounting equation and showing that the equation balances.

current assets *cash and other assets that can be quickly converted into cash or that will be used within one year*

Current Assets   **Current assets** are cash and other assets that can be quickly converted into cash or that will be used within one year. Because cash is the most liquid asset, it is listed first. Following that are *marketable securities*—stocks, bonds, and so on—that can be converted into cash in a matter of days. These are temporary investments of excess cash that Northeast Art Supply doesn't immediately need.

Next are the firm's receivables. Its *accounts receivable*, which result from the issuance of trade credit to customers, are generally due within sixty days. However, the firm expects that some of these debts will not be collected. Thus it has reduced its accounts receivable by a 5 percent *allowance for doubtful accounts.* The firm's *notes receivables* are receivables for which customers have signed promissory notes. They are generally repaid over a longer period of time.

Northeast's *merchandise inventory* represents the value of goods that are on hand for sale to customers. These goods are listed as current assets because they will be sold within the year. Since Northeast Art Supply is a wholesale operation, the inventory listed in Figure 16.3 represents finished goods that are ready for sale to retailers. For a manufacturing firm, merchandise inventory can also represent raw materials that will become part of a finished product or work in process that has been partially completed but requires further processing.

prepaid expenses   *assets that have been paid for in advance but not yet used*

Northeast's last current asset is **prepaid expenses,** which are assets that have been paid for in advance but not yet used. An example is insurance premiums. They are usually paid at the beginning of the policy year for the whole year. The unused portion (say, for the last four months of the policy year) is a prepaid expense—a current asset. For Northeast Art, all current assets total $182,000.

fixed assets   *assets that will be held or used for a period longer than one year*

Fixed Assets   **Fixed assets** are assets that will be held or used for a period longer than one year. They generally include land, buildings, and equipment. Although Northeast owns no land or buildings, it does own *delivery equipment* that originally cost $110,000. It also owns *furniture and store equipment* that originally cost $62,000.

depreciation   *the process of apportioning the cost of a fixed asset over the period during which it will be used*

Note that the values of these fixed assets are decreased by their *accumulated depreciation.* **Depreciation** is the process of apportioning the cost of a fixed asset over the period during which it will be used. The amount that is allotted to each year is an expense for that year, and the value of the asset must be reduced by that expense. In the case of Northeast's delivery equipment, $20,000 of its value has been depreciated (or used up) since it was purchased. Its value at this time is thus $110,000 less $20,000, or $90,000. In a similar fashion the value of furniture and store equipment has been reduced by accumulated depreciation of $15,000. For Northeast Art, all fixed assets total $137,000.

intangible assets   *assets that do not exist physically but have a value based on legal rights or advantages that they confer on a firm*

Intangible Assets   **Intangible assets** are assets that do not exist physically but have a value based on legal rights or advantages that they confer on a firm. They include patents, copyrights, trademarks, and goodwill. By their nature, intangible assets are long-term assets. They are of value to the firm for a number of years.

goodwill   *the value of a firm's reputation, location, earning capacity, and other intangibles that make the business a profitable concern*

Northeast Art Supply lists two intangible assets. The first is a *patent* for an oil paint that the company has developed. The firm's accountants estimate that it has a current market value of $6,000. The second intangible asset, **goodwill,** is the value of a firm's reputation, location, earning capacity, and other intangibles that make the business a profitable concern. Goodwill is not normally listed on a balance sheet unless the firm has been purchased from previous owners. In this case, the purchasers have actually paid an additional amount (over and above the value of the previous owners' equity) for this intangible asset. The firm's accountants included a $15,000 amount for goodwill. For Northeast Art, intangible assets total $21,000. Now it is possible to total all three types of assets for Northeast Art. As illustrated in Figure 16.3, total assets are $340,000.

Liabilities and Owners' Equity

The firms' liabilities are separated into two groups—current and long-term—on the balance sheet. These liability accounts and the owners' equity accounts complete the balance sheet.

current liabilities *debts that will be repaid within one year*

Current Liabilities   A firm's **current liabilities** are debts that will be repaid within one year. Northeast Art Supply purchased merchandise from its suppliers on credit. Thus its balance sheet includes an entry for accounts payable. **Accounts payable** are short-term obligations that arise as a result of making credit purchases.

accounts payable *short-term obligations that arise as a result of making credit purchases*

notes payable *obligations that have been secured with promissory notes*

Notes payable are obligations that have been secured with promissory notes. They are usually short-term obligations, but they may extend beyond one year. Only those that must be paid within the year are listed under current liabilities.

Northeast also lists *salaries payable* and *taxes payable* as current liabilities. These are both expenses that have been incurred during the current accounting period but will be paid in the next accounting period. Such expenses must be shown as debts for the accounting period in which they were incurred. For Northeast Art, current liabilities total $70,000.

long-term liabilities *debts that need not be repaid for at least one year*

Long-Term Liabilities   **Long-term liabilities** are debts that need not be repaid for at least one year. Northeast lists only a $40,000 *mortgage payable* in this group. Bonds and other long-term loans would be included here as well, if they existed. As illustrated in Figure 16.3, current and long-term liabilities total $110,000.

Owners' Equity   For a sole proprietorship or partnership, the owners' equity is shown as the difference between assets and liabilities. In a partnership, each partner's share of the ownership is reported separately by each owner's name. For a corporation, the owners' equity (sometimes referred to as *shareholders' equity*) is shown as the total value of its stock, plus retained earnings that have accumulated to date.

Northeast Art Supply has issued only common stock. Its value is shown as its par value ($15) times the number of shares outstanding (10,000). In addition, $80,000 of Northeast's earnings have been reinvested in the business since it was founded. Thus, owners' equity totals $230,000.

As the two grand totals show, Northeast's assets and the sum of its liabilities and owners' equity are equal—to $340,000.

The Income Statement

Learning Objective 5
Know how to read and interpret an income statement

An **income statement** is a summary of a firm's revenues and expenses during a specified accounting period. The income statement is sometimes called the *earnings statement* or the *statement of income and expenses*. It

income statement *a summary of a firm's revenues and expenses during a specified accounting period*

may be prepared monthly, quarterly, semiannually, or annually. An income statement covering the previous year must be included in a corporation's annual report to its stockholders.

Figure 16.4 shows the income statement for Northeast Art Supply. Note that it consists of four sections. Generally, revenues *less* cost of goods sold *less* operating expenses *equals* net income from operations.

Revenues

revenues *dollar amounts received by a firm*

gross sales *the total dollar amount of all goods and services sold during the accounting period*

Revenues are dollar amounts received by a firm. Northeast obtains its revenues solely from the sale of its products. The revenues section of its income statement begins with gross sales. **Gross sales** are the total dollar amount of all goods and services sold during the accounting period. From this are deducted the dollar amounts of

▶ *Sales returns*, or merchandise returned to the firm by its customers

▶ *Sales allowances*, or price reductions offered to customers who accept slightly damaged or soiled merchandise

▶ *Sales discounts*, or price reductions offered by manufacturers and suppliers to customers who pay their bills promptly

net sales *the actual dollar amount received by a firm for the goods and services it has sold, after adjustment for returns, allowances, and discounts*

The remainder is the firm's net sales. **Net sales** are the actual dollar amount received by the firm for the goods and services it has sold, after adjustment for returns, allowances, and discounts. For Northeast Art, net sales are $451,000.

Cost of Goods Sold

According to Figure 16.4, Northeast began its accounting period with a merchandise inventory that cost $40,000 (see *beginning inventory* under *cost of goods sold*). During the period, the firm purchased, for resale, merchandise worth $346,000. But, after taking advantage of *purchase discounts*, it paid only $335,000 for this merchandise. Thus, during the year, Northeast had *goods available for sale* valued at $40,000 + $335,000 = $375,000.

At the end of the accounting period, Northeast had an *ending inventory* of $41,000. Thus it had sold all but $41,000 worth of the available goods. The *cost of goods sold* by Northeast was therefore $375,000 *less* $41,000, or $334,000.

This is the standard method of determining the cost of the goods sold by a retailing or wholesaling firm during an accounting period. It may be summarized as follows:

cost of goods sold *the cost of the goods a firm has sold during an accounting period; equal to beginning inventory plus net purchases less ending inventory*

$$\text{Cost of goods sold} = \frac{\text{beginning}}{\text{inventory}} + \frac{\text{net}}{\text{purchases}} - \frac{\text{ending}}{\text{inventory}}$$

A manufacturer must include its raw-materials inventories, work-in-process inventories, and direct manufacturing costs in this computation.

gross profit on sales *a firm's net sales less the cost of goods sold*

A firm's **gross profit on sales** is its net sales *less* the cost of goods sold. For Northeast, this was $117,000.

NORTHEAST ART SUPPLY, INC.

Income Statement
For the Year Ended
December 31, 199x

Revenues

Gross sales		$465,000
Less sales returns and allowances	$ 9,500	
Less sales discounts	4,500	14,000
Net sales		$451,000

Cost of goods sold

Beginning inventory, January 1, 199x		$ 40,000
Purchases	$346,000	
Less purchase discounts	11,000	
Net purchases		335,000
Cost of goods available for sale		$375,000
Less ending inventory December 31, 199x		41,000
Cost of goods sold		334,000
Gross profit on sales		117,000

Operating expenses

Selling expenses

Sales salaries	$ 30,000	
Advertising	6,000	
Sales promotion	2,500	
Depreciation—store equipment	3,000	
Miscellaneous selling expenses	1,500	
Total selling expenses		$ 43,000

General expenses

Office salaries	$ 18,500	
Rent	8,500	
Depreciation—delivery equipment	4,000	
Depreciation—office furniture	1,500	
Utilities expense	2,500	
Insurance expense	1,000	
Miscellaneous expense	500	
Total general expenses		36,500
Total operating expenses		79,500

Net income from operations		$ 37,500
Less interest expense		2,000
Net income before taxes		$ 35,500
Less federal income taxes		5,325
Net income after taxes		$ 30,175

FIGURE 16.4
Income Statement
An income statement summarizes the firm's revenues and expenses during a specified accounting period—one month, three months, six months, or a year.

Operating Expenses

operating expenses *those costs that do not result directly from the purchase or manufacture of the products a firm sells*

selling expenses *costs that are related to the firm's marketing activities*

A firm's **operating expenses** are those costs that do not result directly from the purchase or manufacture of the products it sells. They are generally classed as either selling expenses or general expenses.

Selling expenses are costs that are related to the firm's marketing activities. They include salaries for members of the sales force, advertising and other promotional expenses, and the costs involved in operating stores. For Northeast Art, selling expenses total $43,000.

general expenses *costs that are incurred in managing a business*

General expenses are costs that are incurred in managing a business. They are sometimes called *administrative expenses*. Typical general expenses are the salaries of office workers and the costs of maintaining offices. A catchall account called *miscellaneous expense* is usually included in the *general expenses* section of the income statement. For Northeast Art, general expenses total $36,500. Now it is possible to total both selling and general expenses for Northeast Art. As illustrated in Figure 16.4, total operating expenses are $79,500.

Net Income

net income *the profit earned (or the loss suffered) by a firm during an accounting period, after all expenses have been deducted from revenues*

Net income is the profit earned (or the loss suffered) by a firm during an accounting period, after all expenses have been deducted from revenues. In Figure 16.4, Northeast's *net income from operations* is computed as gross profit on sales ($117,000) *less* total operating expenses ($79,500). For Northeast Art, net income from operations totals $37,500. From this, an *interest expense* of $2,000 is deducted to give a *net income before taxes* of

For a firm like Sony, advertising in newspapers and magazines to attract customers is a type of operating expense that must be reported on the firm's income statement.

BUSINESS JOURNAL

How Inventory Affects Profits

According to Thornton O'Glove, editor of the *Quality of Earnings Report*, "Companies can do wonders for their earnings by manipulating inventories."* For example, General Motors Corp. had record earnings of almost $5 billion last year. And yet, not all of that $5-billion profit was the result of operations. At least $217 million of the firm's profit came from a change in accounting procedures used to value the firm's inventories. General Motors did nothing illegal. Like many other firms, it simply used "creative accounting" to improve the profits pictured on the bottom line of its income statement.

Take the case of Saxon Industries, a large photocopy-machine manufacturer. Stanley Lurie, former chairman of the board of Saxon Industries, used fictitious accounting entries to inflate the dollar value of Saxon's merchandise inventories and sales revenues. The nonexistent inventories and sales revenues were part of a companywide scheme involving a number of high-level employees to create fraudulent profits. On paper, Saxon Industries looked good. Based on nonexistent inventories and sales revenues, Saxon was able to obtain loans that totaled more than $140 million from a consortium of more than twenty banks. Eventually, Saxon's scheme began to fall apart when high interest rates on the massive bank loans forced the company to file for bankruptcy. It then became obvious that Saxon Industries had not earned a profit in years.

METHODS USED TO EVALUATE INVENTORIES

Interested parties (investors, lenders, suppliers, and government regulatory agencies) must be on their toes to determine if profits are the result of a firm's operations, a change in accounting procedures used to value inventories, or fraud. To help eliminate the confusion surrounding inventories, accountants prepare detailed records to support the dollar amounts presented in the firm's financial statements.

Because the prices that a firm pays for the goods it sells (or the materials it uses in manufacturing) are

likely to change during an accounting period, one of four inventory methods can be used to determine the dollar value of the inventory. Under the *specific identification method,* the actual dollar cost of a particular item is assigned to the item. The *average-cost method* is based on the assumption that each inventory item carries an equal cost. To arrive at an average cost for each item, the total dollar cost of the goods available for sale is divided by the number of items. Under the *first-in, first-out (FIFO) method,* the accountant assumes that the costs of the first items purchased are assigned to the first items sold. With FIFO, the costs of the items last purchased are assigned to the items remaining in inventory. Under the *last-in, first-out (LIFO) method,* the accountant assumes that the cost of the last items purchased are assigned to the first items sold. With LIFO, the costs of the first items purchased are assigned to the items remaining in inventory.

WHICH INVENTORY METHOD IS BEST?

Each of the four methods of inventory valuation is based on a different set of assumptions. Though none is considered perfect, each method is acceptable for use in published financial statements, and each has advantages and disadvantages. Before a particular business firm chooses an inventory method, its effect on the firm's balance sheet and income statement, the amount of taxes the firm pays, and management decisions must be considered.

---

* Gary Hector, "Cute Tricks on the Bottom Line," *Fortune,* April 24, 1989, p. 194.

Based on information from Gary Hector, "Cute Tricks on the Bottom Line," *Fortune,* April 24, 1989, pp. 193–194; Philip E. Fess and Carl S. Warren, *Accounting Principles,* 16th ed. (Cincinnati: South-Western, 1990), pp. 354–361; Belverd E. Needles, Henry R. Anderson, and James C. Caldwell, *Principles of Accounting,* 4th ed. (Boston: Houghton Mifflin, 1990), pp. 431–436; Richard L. Stern, "Carl Icahn's Lucky Day," *Forbes,* February 10, 1986, p. 321; and Richard L. Stern and Paul Bornstein, "Now You See 'Em, Now You Don't, *Forbes,* July 19, 1982, p. 34.

$35,500. The interest expense is deducted in this category because it is not an operating expense. It is, rather, an expense that results from financing the business.

Northeast's *federal income taxes*, based on its pretax income, are $5,325. Although these taxes may or may not be payable immediately, they are definitely an expense that must be deducted from income. This leaves Northeast with a *net income after taxes* of $30,175. This amount may be used to pay a dividend to stockholders, retained or reinvested in the firm, used to reduce the firm's debts, or all three.

Analyzing Financial Statements

As we have seen, a firm's balance sheet provides a "picture" of the firm at a particular time. Its income statement summarizes its operations during one accounting period. Both can be used to answer a variety of questions about the firm's ability to do business and stay in business, its profitability, its value as an investment, and its ability to repay its debts.

Even more information can be obtained by comparing present financial statements with those prepared for past accounting periods. Such comparisons permit managers (and other interested people) to (1) pick out trends in growth, borrowing, income, and other business variables and (2) determine whether the firm is on the way to accomplishing its long-term goals. Most corporations include, in their annual reports, comparisons of the important elements of their financial statements for recent years. One such comparison is shown in Figure 16.5.

Many firms also compare their financial results with those of competing firms and with industry averages. Comparisons are possible as long as accountants follow the basic rules of accounting, often referred to as *generally accepted accounting principles (GAAP)*. For instance, the balance sheet and income statement for Procter & Gamble (Case 16.1) are similar to the balance sheet and income statement for Northeast Art Supply presented in Figures 16.3 and 16.4, respectively. Yet, there are minor differences in the format and terms used in each financial statement. These comparisons give managers a general idea of the firm's relative effectiveness and its standing within the industry. For example, a manager at IBM would read the financial reports for Digital Equipment Corp., Hewlett-Packard, and Data General to get a good idea of IBM's position within the office automation/computer fields. Competitors' financial statements can be obtained from their annual reports—if they are public corporations. Industry averages are published by reporting services such as Dun & Bradstreet and Standard & Poor's, as well as by some industry trade associations.

Still another type of analysis involves computation of the financial ratios discussed in the next section. Like the individual elements in the financial statements, these ratios can be compared with the firm's past ratios, with those of competitors, and with industry averages.

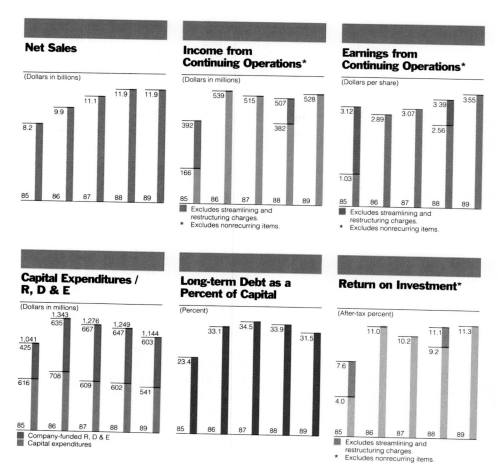

FIGURE 16.5
Comparison of Present and Past Financial Statements Most corporations include in their annual reports comparisons of the important elements of their financial statements for recent years. (Source: Allied-Signal, 1989 Annual Report, p. 20. Used by permission.)

Financial Ratios

financial ratio   *a number that shows the relationship between two elements of a firm's financial statements*

A **financial ratio** is a number that shows the relationship between two elements of a firm's financial statements. Many of these ratios can be formed, but only about a dozen or so have real meaning. Those that we discuss are generally grouped as profitability ratios, short-term financial ratios, activity ratios, and long-term debt ratios. The information required to form these ratios is found in the balance sheet and the income statement.

Profitability Ratios

A firm's net income after taxes indicates whether the firm is profitable. It does not, however, indicate how effectively the firm's resources are being used. For this latter purpose, three ratios can be computed.

net profit margin   *a financial ratio that is calculated by dividing net income after taxes by net sales*

Net Profit Margin   **Net profit margin** is a financial ratio that is calculated by dividing net income after taxes by net sales. For Northeast Art Supply,

$$\text{Net profit margin} = \frac{\text{net income after taxes}}{\text{net sales}} = \frac{\$30,175}{\$451,000}$$

$$= 0.067, \text{ or } 6.7\%$$

The net profit margin indicates how effectively the firm is transforming sales into profits. Today, the average net profit margin for all business firms is between 4 and 5 percent. With a net profit margin of 6.7 percent, Northeast Art Supply is above average. A low net profit margin can be increased by reducing expenses or by increasing the size of the average sale.

return on equity *a financial ratio that is calculated by dividing net income after taxes by owners' equity*

Return on Equity **Return on equity,** sometimes called *return on investment,* is a financial ratio that is calculated by dividing net income after taxes by owners' equity. Again, for Northeast Art Supply,

$$\text{Return on equity} = \frac{\text{net income after taxes}}{\text{owners' equity}} = \frac{\$30,175}{\$230,000}$$

$$= 0.13, \text{ or } 13\%$$

Return on equity indicates how much income is generated by each dollar of equity. Northeast is providing income of 13 cents per dollar invested in the business; the average for all businesses is between 12 and 15 cents. The only practical way to increase return on equity is to increase net income after taxes. This means reducing expenses or increasing sales, or both.

earnings per share *a financial ratio that is calculated by dividing net income after taxes by the number of shares of common stock outstanding*

Earnings per Share From the point of view of stockholders, this is one of the most widely used indicators of a corporation's success. **Earnings per share** is calculated by dividing net income after taxes by the number of shares of common stock outstanding. For Northeast Art Supply,

$$\frac{\text{Earnings}}{\text{per share}} = \frac{\text{net income after taxes}}{\text{common stock shares outstanding}} = \frac{\$30,175}{10,000}$$

$$= \$3.02 \text{ per share}$$

Learning Objective 6
Recognize and be able to use the financial ratios that reveal how a business is doing

Earnings per share is, obviously, a measure of the amount earned (after taxes) per share of common stock owned by investors. There is no meaningful average for this measure, mainly because the number of outstanding shares of a firm's stock is subject to change via stock splits and stock dividends. As a general rule, however, an increase in earnings per share is a healthy sign for any corporation. For the stockholder, such an increase may mean that common-stock dividends will also be increased.

Short-Term Financial Ratios

Two short-term financial ratios permit managers (and lenders) to evaluate the ability of a firm to cover its current liabilities. Before we discuss these ratios, we should examine one other easily determined measure: working capital. Although it is not a ratio, it is an important indicator of a firm's ability to pay its short-term debts.

working capital *the difference between current assets and current liabilities*

Working Capital

Working capital is the difference between current assets and current liabilities. It indicates how much would remain if a firm paid off all current liabilities with cash and other current assets. For Northeast Art Supply,

Current assets	$182,000
Less current liabilities	70,000
Equals working capital	$112,000

The "proper" amount of working capital depends on the type of firm, its past experience, and its particular industry. A firm with too little working capital may have to borrow money to finance its operations. A firm with too much—that is, more working capital than it needs to operate smoothly—may be able to invest its excess working capital in order to earn interest over a short period of time.

current ratio *a financial ratio that is computed by dividing current assets by current liabilities*

Current Ratio

A firm's **current ratio** is computed by dividing current assets by current liabilities. For Northeast Art Supply,

$$\text{Current ratio} = \frac{\text{current assets}}{\text{current liabilities}} = \frac{\$182,000}{\$\ 70,000} = 2.6$$

This means that Northeast Art Supply has $2.60 of current assets for every $1 of current liabilities. The average current ratio for all industries is 2.0, but it varies greatly from industry to industry. Each firm should compare its current ratio with those of its own industry to determine whether it is high or low. A low current ratio can be improved by repaying current liabilities, by converting current liabilities to long-term liabilities, or by increasing the firm's cash balance by reducing dividend payments to stockholders. An increase in owners' equity can also improve a firm's current ratio.

Acid-Test Ratio

This ratio, sometimes called the *quick ratio*, is a measure of the firm's ability to pay current liabilities quickly—with its cash, marketable securities, and receivables. The **acid-test ratio** is calculated by dividing the sum of cash, marketable securities, accounts receivable, and notes receivable by current liabilities. It is similar to the current ratio, except that the values of the firm's inventories and prepaid expenses do not enter into the calculation. Inventories are "removed" from current assets because they are not converted into cash as easily as other current assets. And prepaid expenses may not be recoverable at all. For Northeast Art Supply,

acid-test ratio *a financial ratio that is calculated by dividing the sum of cash, marketable securities, accounts receivable, and notes receivable by current liabilities*

Acid-test ratio

$$= \frac{\text{cash} + \text{marketable securities} + \text{accounts receivable} + \text{notes receivable}}{\text{current liabilities}}$$

$$= \frac{\$59,000 + \$10,000 + \$38,000 + \$32,000}{\$70,000} = \frac{\$139,000}{\$70,000} = 1.99$$

BUSINESS JOURNAL

Is Accounting Information Accurate?

How accurate is the accounting information contained in an annual report? According to financial analysts, it is not as accurate as most investors, lenders, suppliers, and government regulatory agencies think it is. While the information reported in an annual report carries the sanction of generally accepted accounting principles (GAAP), there is still room to apply questionable accounting practices that can make a firm's profits look better than they really are.

TYPICAL PROBLEM AREAS TO WATCH

Most annual reports are notorious for playing up the positive and soft-pedaling the negative. In reality, the true story behind the numbers contained in an annual report is not in the upbeat letter from the chairman of the board, but in the footnotes contained in the back. Only in the footnotes will you find the details about questionable (sometimes referred to as "creative" or "aggressive") accounting practices. According to Kenneth L. Fisher, author and money manager, that's where they bury the bodies where the fewest folks find them—in the fine print.* Watch for (1) firms that recognize income before it has actually been earned and received, (2) adjustments to inventory that inflate the firm's profits, (3) changing depreciation methods that increase a firm's profits, and (4) using one-time gains from the sale of assets to enrich the firm's bottom-line profits. All of these accounting practices are legal, but they often lead investors to make false assumptions about how financially sound a company really is.

SOME HELPFUL HINTS

While the management for most companies is honest and aboveboard, as are the auditors that audit the companies' books, there are exceptions.

First, realize that creative accounting is used mostly by those inclined to hype phony profits and hide real losses. No accountant—CPA or otherwise—can eliminate all questionable accounting practices if management is trying to conceal them.

Second, remember that the auditor's letter certifying a company's books merely signifies that the auditor found no obvious irregularities or reasons to distrust management. The letter does not guarantee that everything is aboveboard, only that the auditor didn't find anything that was not.

Third, auditors and accountants are supposed to apply generally accepted accounting procedures to paint a realistic picture of a company. Managers that are trying to inflate a firm's profits look at the same accounting standards as an obstacle to overcome.

A FINAL WORD OF CAUTION

If you still believe that all of the information contained in an annual report is beyond reproach, consider the following. A recent Securities and Exchange Commission (SEC) study examined more than 200 annual reports. Only twelve companies passed the first review. Seventy companies were ordered to amend the information contained in their annual reports. Six annual reports were so misleading that the companies were referred to the SEC's enforcement division.† As a result of their study, the SEC is now beginning to require more objective financial information.

---

† Tim Smart, "Annual Reports: The SEC Cracks the Whip," *Business Week,* April 10, 1989, p. 74.

Based on information from Gary Hector, "Cute Tricks on the Bottom Line," *Fortune,* April 24, 1989, p. 193; Kenneth L. Fisher, "If It's Too Complicated, Forget It," *Forbes,* October 3, 1988, p. 202; and Subrata N. Chakravarty, "Still Pussyfooting," *Forbes,* August 21, 1989, p. 51.

* Kenneth L. Fisher, "Thanks, Dad," *Forbes,* August 8, 1988, p. 122.

For all businesses, the desired acid-test ratio is 1.0. Northeast Art Supply is above average with a ratio of 1.99, and the firm should be well able to pay its current liabilities. To increase a low ratio, a firm would have to repay current liabilities, obtain additional cash from investors, or convert current liabilities to long-term debt.

Activity Ratios

Two activity ratios permit managers to measure how many times per year a company collects its accounts receivable or sells its inventory. Both the accounts receivable turnover ratio and the inventory turnover ratio are described below.

accounts receivable turnover *a financial ratio that is calculated by dividing net sales by accounts receivable; measures the number of times a firm collects its accounts receivable in one year*

Accounts Receivable Turnover A firm's **accounts receivable turnover** is the number of times the firm collects its accounts receivable in one year. If the data are available, this ratio should be calculated using a firm's net credit sales. Since data for Northeast Art Supply's credit sales are unavailable, this ratio can be calculated by dividing net sales by accounts receivable. Then,

$$\text{Accounts receivable turnover} = \frac{\text{net sales}}{\text{accounts receivable}} = \frac{\$451,000}{\$\ 38,000}$$

$$= 11.9 \text{ times each year}$$

Northeast Art Supply collects its accounts receivable 11.9 times each year, or about every 30 days. If the firm's credit terms call for credit customers to pay up in 25 days, then a collection period of 30 days is considered acceptable. There is no meaningful average for this measure, mainly because credit terms differ among companies. As a general rule, however, a low accounts receivable turnover ratio can be improved by pressing for payment of past-due accounts and by tightening requirements for prospective credit customers.

inventory turnover *a financial ratio that is calculated by dividing the cost of goods sold in one year by the average value of the inventory; measures the number of times the firm sells and replaces its merchandise inventory in one year*

Inventory Turnover A firm's **inventory turnover** is the number of times the firm sells and replaces its merchandise inventory in one year. It is approximated by dividing the cost of goods sold in one year by the average value of the inventory.

The average value of the inventory can be found by adding the beginning and ending inventory values (as given on the income statement) and dividing the sum by 2. For Northeast Art Supply, this comes out to $40,500. Then,

$$\text{Inventory turnover} = \frac{\text{cost of goods sold}}{\text{average inventory}} = \frac{\$334,000}{\$\ 40,500}$$

$$= 8.2 \text{ times each year}$$

Northeast Art Supply sells and replaces its merchandise inventory 8.2 times each year, or about once every month and a half.

The higher a firm's inventory turnover, the more effectively it is using the money invested in inventory. The average inventory turnover for all

W.W. Grainger, Inc. is a leading nationwide distributor of equipment, components, and supplies to the commercial, industrial, contractor, and institutional markets. Efficient inventory and distribution management techniques are crucial to this company's business. The firm's strategies include the operation of three Regional Distribution Centers and the development of a training program for district inventory specialists.

firms is about 9 times per year, but turnover rates vary widely from industry to industry. For example, supermarkets may have turnover rates of 20, whereas turnover rates for furniture stores are generally well below the national average.

Long-Term Debt Ratios

Two financial ratios are of particular interest to lenders of long-term funds. They indicate the degree to which a firm's operations are financed through borrowing.

debt-to-assets ratio *a financial ratio that is calculated by dividing total liabilities by total assets; indicates the extent to which the firm's borrowing is backed by its assets*

Debt-to-Assets Ratio   The **debt-to-assets ratio** is calculated by dividing total liabilities by total assets. It indicates the extent to which the firm's borrowing is backed by its assets. For Northeast Art Supply,

$$\text{Debt-to-assets ratio} = \frac{\text{total liabilities}}{\text{total assets}} = \frac{\$110,000}{\$340,000} = 0.32, \text{ or } 32\%$$

Northeast's debt-to-assets ratio of 32 percent means that slightly less than one-third of its assets are financed by creditors. For all businesses, the average debt-to-assets ratio is 33 percent.

The lower this ratio is, the more assets the firm has to back up its borrowing. Northeast has $3 in assets with which to repay each $1 of borrowing. A high debt-to-assets ratio can be reduced by restricting both short-term and long-term borrowing, by securing additional financing from stockholders, or by reducing dividend payments to stockholders.

TABLE 16.2 *Summary of Financial Ratios for Northeast Art Supply*

Ratio	Formula	Northeast Art Supply	Overall Business Average
Profitability Ratios			
Net profit margin	$\dfrac{\text{net income after taxes}}{\text{net sales}}$	6.7%	4%–5%
Return on equity	$\dfrac{\text{net income after taxes}}{\text{owners' equity}}$	13%	12%–15%
Earnings per share	$\dfrac{\text{net income after taxes}}{\text{common stock shares outstanding}}$	$3.02 per share	—
Short-Term Financial Ratios			
Working capital	current assets *less* current liabilities	$112,000	—
Current ratio	$\dfrac{\text{current assets}}{\text{current liabilities}}$	2.6	2.0
Acid-test ratio	$\dfrac{\text{cash + marketable securities +}}{\text{accounts receivable + notes receivable}}$ over current liabilities	1.99	1.0
Activity Ratios			
Accounts receivable turnover	$\dfrac{\text{net sales}}{\text{accounts receivable}}$	11.9	—
Inventory turnover	$\dfrac{\text{cost of goods sold}}{\text{average inventory}}$	8.2	9
Long-Term Debt Ratios			
Debt-to-assets ratio	$\dfrac{\text{total liabilities}}{\text{total assets}}$	32%	33%
Debt-to-equity ratio	$\dfrac{\text{total liabilities}}{\text{owners' equity}}$	48%	33%–50%

debt-to-equity ratio *a financial ratio that is calculated by dividing total liabilities by owners' equity; compares the amount of financing provided by creditors with the amount provided by owners*

Debt-to-Equity Ratio The **debt-to-equity ratio** is calculated by dividing total liabilities by owners' equity. It compares the amount of financing provided by creditors with the amount provided by owners. For Northeast Art Supply,

$$\text{Debt-to-equity ratio} = \frac{\text{total liabilities}}{\text{owners' equity}} = \frac{\$110,000}{\$230,000} = 0.48, \text{ or } 48\%$$

A debt-to-equity ratio of 48 percent means that creditors have provided about 48 cents of financing for every dollar provided by owners. In other words, about one-third of Northeast's total financing comes from creditors.

The debt-to-equity ratio for business in general ranges between 33 and 50 percent. The larger this ratio, the riskier the situation is for lenders. A high debt-to-equity ratio can be reduced by paying off debts or by increasing the owners' investment in the firm.

Northeast's Financial Ratios: A Summary

The formulas that we used in analyzing Northeast Art Supply's financial statements are listed in Table 16.2, along with the ratios we calculated. Northeast seems to be in good financial shape. Its net profit margin, current ratio, and acid-test ratio are all above average. Its other ratios are about average, although its inventory turnover could be improved. To do so, Northeast might consider ordering smaller quantities of merchandise at shorter intervals. Of course, the resulting decrease in inventory holding costs would have to be balanced against increased ordering costs and the possible cost of stock-outs.

CHAPTER REVIEW

Summary

Accounting is the process of systematically collecting, analyzing, and reporting financial information. Bookkeeping is essentially record keeping that is a part of the overall accounting process. A private accountant is employed by a specific organization to operate its accounting system and to interpret accounting information. A public accountant performs these functions for various individuals or firms, on a professional-fee basis. Accounting information is used primarily by management, but it is also of interest to creditors, suppliers, stockholders, and government agencies.

The accounting process is based on the accounting equation: Assets = liabilities + owners' equity. Double-entry bookkeeping ensures that the balance shown by the equation is maintained.

There are five steps in the accounting process: (1) Source documents are analyzed to determine which accounts they affect. (2) Each transaction is recorded in a journal. (3) Each journal entry is posted in the appropriate general ledger accounts. (4) At the end of each accounting period, a trial balance is prepared to make sure that the accounting equation is in balance for the period. (5) Financial statements are prepared from the trial balance. Once statements are prepared, the books are closed. A new accounting cycle is then begun for the next accounting period.

The balance sheet, or statement of financial position, is a summary of a firm's assets, liabilities, and owners' equity accounts at a particular time. This statement must demonstrate that the equation is in balance. On the balance sheet, assets are categorized as current (convertible to cash within a year), fixed (to be used or held for more than one year), or intangible (valuable solely because of the rights or

advantages that they confer). Similarly, current liabilities are those that are to be repaid within one year, and long-term liabilities are debts that will not be repaid for at least one year. For a sole proprietorship or partnership, owners' equity is reported by the owner's name in the last section of the balance sheet. For a corporation, the value of common stock, preferred stock, and retained earnings is reported in the owners' equity section.

An income statement is a summary of a firm's financial operations during a specified accounting period. On the income statement, the company's gross profit on sales is computed by subtracting the cost of goods sold from net sales. Operating expenses are then deducted to compute net income from operations. Finally, nonoperating expenses and income taxes are deducted to obtain the firm's net income after taxes.

The information contained in these two financial statements becomes more meaningful when it is compared with corresponding information for previous years, for competitors, and for the industry in which the firm operates. A number of financial ratios can also be computed from this information. These ratios provide a picture of the firm's profitability, its short-term financial position, its activity in the area of accounts receivable and inventory, and its long-term debt financing. Like the information on the firm's financial statements, the ratios can and should be compared with those of past accounting periods, those of competitors, and those representing the average of the industry as a whole.

This chapter ends our discussion of accounting information. In the next chapter, we begin our examination of business finances by discussing money, banking, and credit.

Key Terms

You should now be able to define and give an example relevant to each of the following terms:

accounting

bookkeeping

private (or nonpublic) accountant

public accountant

certified public accountant (CPA)

assets

liabilities

owners' equity

accounting equation

double-entry bookkeeping

general journal

general ledger

posting

trial balance

balance sheet (or statement of financial position)

liquidity

current assets

prepaid expenses

fixed assets

depreciation

intangible assets

goodwill

current liabilities

accounts payable

notes payable

long-term liabilities

income statement

revenues

gross sales

net sales

cost of goods sold

gross profit on sales

operating expenses

selling expenses

general expenses

net income

financial ratio

net profit margin

return on equity

earnings per share

working capital

current ratio

acid-test ratio

accounts receivable turnover

inventory turnover

debt-to-assets ratio

debt-to-equity ratio

Questions and Exercises

Review Questions

1. What is the difference between accounting and bookkeeping? How are they related?
2. What are certified public accountants? What functions do they perform?
3. List four groups that use accounting information and briefly explain why each has an interest in this information.
4. State the accounting equation and list two specific examples of each term in the equation.
5. How is double-entry bookkeeping related to the accounting equation? Briefly, how does it work?
6. Briefly describe the five steps of the accounting cycle, in order.
7. What is the principal difference between a balance sheet and an income statement?
8. How are current assets distinguished from fixed assets? Give two examples of each.
9. Why are fixed assets depreciated on a balance sheet?
10. Can a single debt (for example, a promissory note) be part current liability and part long-term liability? Explain.
11. Explain how a retailing firm would determine the cost of the goods it sold during an accounting period.
12. How does a firm determine its net income after taxes?
13. Explain the calculation procedure for and the significance of each of the following ratios:
    a. One profitability ratio
    b. One short-term financial ratio
    c. One activity ratio
    d. One long-term debt ratio

Discussion Questions

1. Since the accounting firms of Ernst & Whinney and Arthur Young merged, Arthur Andersen is no longer the largest accounting firm in the world. What is management at Arthur Andersen doing to regain the number-one ranking among accounting firms?
2. In the past ten years, most of the Big Eight accounting firms have tried to diversify their operations. Why do you think Arthur Andersen chose to diversify into the information and computer consulting field?
3. Bankers usually insist that prospective borrowers submit audited financial statements along with a loan application. Why should financial statements be audited by a CPA?
4. What can be said about a firm whose owners' equity is a negative amount? How could such a situation come about?
5. Why is it so important to compare a firm's financial statements and ratios with those of previous years, those of competitors, and the average of all firms in the industry in which the firm operates?
6. Do the balance sheet and the income statement contain all the information you might want as a potential lender or stockholder? What other information would you like to have?
7. Which do you think are the two or three most important financial ratios? Why?

Exercises

1. Table 16.3 lists the ledger account balances for the Green Thumb Garden Shop, which was started just one year ago. From that information, prepare a balance sheet and an income statement for the business.

TABLE 16.3   *Account Balances for Green Thumb Garden Shop*

Accounts	Amounts
Cash	$ 7,500
Accounts receivable	3,500
Inventory	20,000
Equipment	15,000
Accumulated depreciation	2,000
Accounts payable	11,000
Long-term debt—equipment	10,000
Owners' equity	23,000
Sales	48,000
Cost of goods sold	23,000
Sales salaries expense	8,500
Advertising expense	1,500
Depreciation expense	2,000
Rent expense	6,000
Utilities expense	1,500
Insurance expense	1,000
Miscellaneous expense	500
Income taxes	600

2. Using the financial statements you prepared in Exercise 1 and the material on ratio analysis presented in this chapter, evaluate the financial health of the Green Thumb Garden Shop. Explain how the firm's finances could be improved.

Case 16.1

Procter & Gamble

Procter & Gamble is today one of the world's leading producers of packaged consumer goods. The company produces laundry and cleaning products, personal care products, food and beverage products, and pulp and chemicals. International operations represented approximately 40 percent of the company's net sales for the fiscal year ended June 30, 1989. Net sales are more than $21 billion.

The following are Procter & Gamble's consolidated statement of earnings and consolidated balance sheet.*

Consolidated Statement of Earnings

Year Ended June 30 (millions of dollars except per-share amounts)		1989
Income	Net sales	$21,398
	Interest and other income	291
		$21,689
Costs and Expenses	Cost of products sold	13,371
	Marketing, administrative, and other expenses	5,988
	Interest expense	391
	Provision for restructuring	—
		19,750
Earnings Before Income Taxes		1,939
Income Taxes		733
Net Earnings		$ 1,206
Per Common Share	Net earnings	$7.12
	Dividends	$3.00

Consolidated Balance Sheet

June 30 (millions of dollars)		1989
Assets		
Current Assets		
	Cash and cash equivalents	$ 1,587
	Accounts receivable, less allowance for doubtful accounts of $24 in 1989	2,090
	Inventories	2,337
	Prepaid expenses and other current assets	564
		6,578
Property, Plant, and Equipment		6,793
Goodwill and Other Intangible Assets		2,305
Other Assets		675
Total		$16,351

* Procter & Gamble's consolidated statement of earnings and consolidated balance sheet are taken from the 1989 Procter & Gamble Annual Report, pp. 25–26. Used with permission.

Liabilities and Shareholders' Equity
Current Liabilities

Accounts payable—trade	$ 1,669
Accounts payable—other	466
Accrued liabilities	1,365
Taxes payable	523
Debt due within one year	633
	4,656
Long-Term Debt	3,698
Other Liabilities	447
Deferred Income Taxes	1,335

Shareholders' Equity

Convertible Class A preferred stock	1,000
Common stock—shares outstanding:	
1989—161,990,408	162
Additional paid-in capital	529
Currency translation adjustments	(63)
Reserve for employee stock ownership plan debt retirement	(1,000)
Retained earnings	5,587
	6,215
Total	$16,351

Questions

1. Using the financial information provided in this case, calculate the following ratios for Procter & Gamble.
   a. Current ratio
   b. Acid-test ratio
   c. Net profit margin
   d. Return on equity
2. Based on your analysis of available information, how would you describe Procter & Gamble's current financial condition? What actions, if any, would you consider taking to improve it? Explain your recommendations.

Case 16.2

A Classic Case of Accounting Fraud

In 1967, Equity Funding Life Insurance Company reported sales of $54 million and insurance in force totaling $109 million. By 1972, sales had grown to $1.32 billion and insurance in force had jumped to $6.5 billion. In the same five-year period, corporate profits increased nearly eightfold. For at least the first nine months of 1972, Equity Funding was ranked among the top ten American life insurance companies. It was the fastest-growing life insurance company in the United States.

In early March 1973, acting on a tip from a former employee, investigators began to look into the company's activities. By March 27, trading in Equity's stock was suspended by the New York Stock Exchange. The price of the stock had dropped almost ten points in a week, to less than $15 a share. Shortly after that, the stock was declared to be of "no value." Equity's 7,000 stockholders had lost at least $114 million.

The investigators found that, of the 97,000 policies listed on the books of an Equity Funding subsidiary, approximately 58 percent were nonexistent. Moreover, other insurance companies that had bought these policies as reinsurers had paid millions of dollars for nothing.

Reinsurance, or the practice of a company's issuing an insurance policy to a customer and then selling the policy to another insurance company to acquire cash, is not unusual in the insurance business. What was unusual in the Equity case was that there were no policyholders behind most of the policies. Nearly two-thirds of what the company claimed as its insurance business was based on bogus policies!

The chairman and president of Equity Funding received an annual salary of $100,000. In addition, in 1972, he was given a stock bonus then worth more than $150,000. He was a respected Los Angeles business leader, who until January 1972 had served as chairman of the business conduct committee of the Los Angeles branch of the National Association of Securities Dealers. He had a home with a gymnasium and tennis courts, a Rolls Royce, and a 35-foot yacht. On November 1, 1973, he and eighteen other executives of Equity Funding were indicted on 105 criminal counts. They were charged with committing felonies that included securities fraud, mail fraud, bank fraud, electronic eavesdropping, and filing false documents with the Securities and Exchange Commission.

At the time, Equity Funding had a highly computerized accounting system that facilitated the mixing of phony policies with genuine policies. However, the hoax could easily have been discovered if the policies on the books had been verified with their supposed owners. Unfortunately, not one auditor for an outside accounting firm ever confirmed a policy directly with a policyholder until after the rumors of fraud began to circulate.

It is not surprising that traditional auditing techniques failed to detect the phony policies. The company's policies looked valid, and auditors generally tend to believe the computer. In the wake of the Equity Funding scandal, the American Institute of Certified Public Accountants formed a committee to study the techniques used in auditing insurance companies and to determine how they should be changed. One change was to require that auditors obtain policy information directly from policyholders.†

_____

† Based on information from "Conning the Computer," *Newsweek*, April 23, 1973, p. 90; *Fortune*, August 1973, p. 132; *Newsweek*, April 16, 1973, p. 82; and *Newsweek*, April 23, 1973, p. 90.

Questions

1. Can strict accounting requirements stop fraudulent business practices? What group or groups should develop such requirements? Who should implement them?

2. How might an employee at Equity Funding have discovered the fraud? What would you have done if you were that employee?

CAREER PROFILE

ROBERT N. NOYCE   Consumer products like calculators, digital watches, videocassette recorders, compact disk players, and even automobiles require computer microchips to function properly. This same, small microchip has dramatically transformed banking, transportation, communications, and just about every other industry almost overnight. And although the invention of the integrated circuit has changed the way people live and the way businesses operate, most people don't know who invented the microchip.

Credit for inventing the microchip is given to two men: Jack Kilby and Robert Noyce. Kilby, a Texas Instruments engineer, came up with the idea of using silicon to produce microchips in 1958, but failed to develop a procedure for interconnecting the various components of the microchip. A year later, Noyce, a physicist at Fairchild Semiconductor, developed a process for interconnecting the various components of a microchip together with thin metal strips stamped into an oxide layer on the surface of the chip itself. Noyce's process is still used today.

Since both companies claimed legal rights to the microchip, a court battle between Texas Instruments and Fairchild Semiconductor ensued. After almost ten years, Fairchild Semiconductor and Robert Noyce eventually won the patent rights for the microchip. As part of the settlement, both Texas Instruments and Fairchild Semiconductor were allowed to use and sell the new microchips. Both companies could also license other companies to use microchips. Now, over thirty years later, the microchips and the connection process developed by Noyce are credited with starting a second industrial revolution in the information technology field.

Robert Noyce began his career with thorough academic preparation. He received a Bachelor of Arts degree from Grinnell College. He then earned a Ph.D. degree in physics from Massachusetts Institute of Technology (MIT). After leaving MIT, he worked briefly as a research engineer for both Philco Corporation and Shockley Semiconductor Laboratories. He then founded Fairchild Semiconductor—a subsidiary of Fairchild Camera & Instrument—in 1957. In 1968, Noyce and Gordon E. Moore co-founded Intel Corporation. Both companies have been extremely successful not only in generating sales revenues and profits, but also in applying microchip technology to products that both businesses and individuals use everyday. Within ten years of its inception, Fairchild Semiconductor had $130 million in annual revenues

and had become known as one of the giants in the microchip industry. Although created ten years later than Fairchild Semiconductor, Intel Corporation quickly became known as a technology leader when it developed the microprocessor that powers the personal computers that became so popular during the 1980s.

In 1988 Robert Noyce became the president and CEO of the Sematech Consortium in Austin, Texas. Sematech—short for Semiconductor Manufacturing Technology—is a cooperative effort between the federal government and fourteen U.S. computer companies to outperform foreign competitors (especially the Japanese) in the semiconductor industry.*

Unfortunately, Robert Noyce, the man who turned a sleepy area in Northern California into the world-renowned Silicon Valley, died of a heart attack in his Austin home on June 3, 1990. He was sixty-two. A successful entrepreneur who knew how to take an idea and turn it into a practical application, Robert Noyce was the acknowledged spokesperson for the semiconductor industry. In fact, his associates often called him the mayor of Silicon Valley.

---

* For more information on Sematech and the companies involved in the consortium, you may want to read the Inside Business opening case for Chapter 22.

Based on information from Jim Mitchell, "Computer Pioneer Noyce Dies," *Dallas Morning News*, June 4, 1990, p. 1A; Irwin Goodwin, "Kilby and Noyce Win Draper Prize for Developing Microchips," *Physics Today*, November 1989, p. 52; "How the U.S. Can Compete Globally," *Fortune*, June 5, 1989, p. 248; Charles A. Riley II, "Robert N. Noyce," *Fortune*, March 13, 1989, p. 132; Samuel C. Florman, *Technology Review*, January 1988, p. 20+; Otis Port, "Bob Noyce Created Silicon Valley. Can He Save It?," *Business Week*, August 15, 1988, p. 76+; Irwin Goodwin, "Bob Noyce Created Silicon Valley and Now He's Asked to Save It," *Physics Today*, September 1988, p. 50; and *Who's Who in America*, 44th ed. (Wilmette, Ill: Macmillan Directory Division, 1986), p. 2083.

The figure in the salary column approximates the expected annual income after two or three years of service. 1 = $12,000–$15,000 2 = $16,000–$20,000 3 = $21,000–$27,000 4 = $28,000–$35,000 5 = $36,000 and up

Job Title	Educational Requirements	Salary Range	Prospects
Accountant— corporate	Bachelor's degree in accounting; master's degree preferred	3–4	Greatest growth
Accountant—private practice	Bachelor's degree in accounting; state exam for Certified Public Accountant status	4–5	Gradual growth
Auditor	Bachelor's degree; master's degree helpful; on-the-job experience	3–4	Gradual growth
Bookkeeper	High school diploma; some college preferred	1–2	Limited growth
Computer application engineer	Bachelor's degree in business and computer science	3	Gradual growth
Computer operator	Two years of college in data processing; on-the-job experience	1–2	Greatest growth
Computer programming coordinator	Bachelor's degree; on-the-job experience	2–3	Gradual growth
Computer-repair technician	High school diploma; some technical training required; on-the-job experience	2	Greatest growth
Computer-systems analyst	College degree preferred; on-the-job experience	3–4	Gradual growth
Cost accountant	College degree; on-the-job experience	3–5	Limited growth
Engineering programmer	College degree in engineering	3–4	Gradual growth
File clerk	High school diploma	1	No growth
Financial controller	College degree; on-the-job experience	4–5	Limited growth
Information systems programmer	College degree in business and computer science	3–4	Gradual growth
Mail clerk	High school diploma	1	Limited growth
Office machine operator	High school diploma; some college helpful	1–2	Limited growth
Payroll clerk	High school diploma; some college preferred	1–2	Gradual growth
Process control programmer	College degree in computer science; on-the-job experience	3–4	Gradual growth
Salesperson— computer software or hardware	Some college; degree helpful	3–4	Gradual growth
Scientific programmer	College degree in computer science or engineering	3–4	Gradual growth

Part 6

FINANCE AND INVESTMENT

In this part, we are concerned with still another business resource—money. First we discuss the functions and forms of money and the institutions that are part of the U.S. monetary system. Then we examine the concept and methods of financial management, for both firms and individuals. Finally, we explore the means by which some types of financial losses can be minimized. Included in this part are:

MONEY, BANKING, AND CREDIT

1 Know the functions and important characteristics of money

2 Describe the differences between commercial banks and other financial institutions in the banking industry

3 Be able to identify the primary services provided by commercial banks and other financial institutions

4 Understand how the Federal Reserve System regulates the money supply

5 Be able to describe the Fed's role in clearing checks, controlling and inspecting currency, and administering selective credit controls

6 Recognize the function of the Federal Deposit Insurance Corporation (FDIC), Savings Association Insurance Fund (SAIF), and National Credit Union Association (NCUA)

7 Be aware of the importance of credit and credit management

CHAPTER PREVIEW

In this chapter we take a good look at money and the institutions that create and handle it. We begin by outlining the purposes of money in a society and the characteristics of money that make it an acceptable means of payment for products and resources. Then, we turn our attention to the banking industry—commercial banks, savings and loan associations, credit unions, and other institutions that offer financial services. Next, we consider the role of the Federal Reserve System in maintaining a healthy economy. We also describe the safeguards established by the federal government to protect depositors against bank failures. In closing, we examine credit transactions, sources of credit information, and effective collection procedures.

Lincoln Savings and Loan Association

On February 22, 1984, Charles Keating used $51 million obtained through the sale of high interest bonds to purchase Lincoln Savings and Loan Association of Irvine, California. At the time of the purchase, Lincoln Savings had twenty-eight branch offices with total deposits of about $1 billion. Keating quickly managed to double Lincoln Saving's deposits by offering depositors high interest on certificates of deposit. As reported in *Fortune, Forbes,* and *Time* magazines, he then used the money to finance "very" speculative investments in land developments, resort hotels, stocks, corporate bonds, and energy-generating windmills. Keating even used some of Lincoln Saving's money to finance real estate developments for American Continental Corporation, a Phoenix homebuilding company that he also managed.

As early as 1986, regulators from the Office of Thrift Supervision (OTS)—the federal agency responsible for supervising savings and loan associations—were concerned that Lincoln Savings was in serious financial trouble. Their main concerns centered around questionable lending activities. At that time, regulators held that Lincoln Savings had violated the Federal Home Loan Bank Board's rule which limits direct investments by a savings and loan association to 10 percent of its assets.

In early 1987, OTS regulators wanted to seize Lincoln Savings, but a series of events delayed government action. Apparently, Keating convinced five United States senators to intercede on his behalf. The "Keating Five" pressured regulators to drop the investigation of Lincoln Savings. Later, a federal investigation revealed that Keating had made campaign contributions in excess of $1.3 million to the same senators. Although the senators denied any wrongdoing, the Senate Ethics Committee investigated their actions.

The seizure of Lincoln Savings and Loan Association was again delayed when Danny Wall, the chief regulator for the OTS, transferred the investigation of Lincoln Savings from the San Francisco branch of the OTS to the main office in Washington, D.C. Wall later justified his action on the grounds that he wanted to make sure that this was not just a lynch mob after Keating.

Finally, in 1989 regulators did seize Lincoln Savings because of heavy operating losses and a large portfolio of bad loans. In addition, the government filed a $1.1 billion civil racketeering suit against Keating and various associates, charging them with fraud, illegal loans, and insider dealing. Regulators claim that Keating ran Lincoln Savings into the ground while reaping over $30 million for himself and his family. Keating claims that the government regulators' seizure action was improper and without just cause. And he countersued the United States government for $568 million.

Regardless of the outcome of the lawsuits, the Lincoln Savings and Loan Association bailout could wind up costing American taxpayers $2.5 billion—or about $20 each.[1]

People who deposited their money in Lincoln Savings and Loan Association did so because their deposits of $100,000 or less were insured by the federal government. Just the thought of depositing money in a bank and then losing it makes people nervous, but it does illustrate how important banks, savings and loan associations, credit unions, and other financial institutions are today.

Most people regard a bank or similar financial institution as a place to deposit or borrow money. In return for depositing their money, they receive interest. When they borrow money, they must pay interest. A firm (even a new one) may have a valuable asset in the form of a product idea. If the idea is a good one, and the firm (or its founder) has a good reputation, a bank will probably lend it the money to develop, produce, and market the product. The loan—with interest—will be repaid out of future sales revenue. In this way, both the firm and the bank will earn a reasonable profit.

Individuals may borrow to buy a home, a car, or some other high-cost item. In this case, labor is the resource that will be transformed into money to repay the loan.

In each of these situations, the borrower needs the money now and has the ability to repay it later. But also, in each situation, the money will be used to *purchase something*, and it will be repaid through the use of *resources*. This is in keeping with the concept of money that we developed in Chapter 1. Money is an artificial device that aids in the exchange of resources for goods and services.

What Is Money?

barter system *a system of exchange in which goods or services are traded directly for other goods or services*

The members of a primitive society may exchange goods and services through barter, without using money. A **barter system** is a system of exchange in which goods or services are traded directly for other goods or services. One family may raise vegetables and herbs on a plot of land, and another may weave cloth. To obtain food, the family of weavers trades cloth for vegetables, provided that the farming family is in need of cloth.

The trouble with barter is that the two parties in an exchange must need each other's product at the same time, and the two products must be roughly equal in value. It may work well when few products, primarily the necessities of life, are available. But even very primitive societies soon develop some sort of money to eliminate the inconvenience of trading by barter.

money *anything used by a society to purchase goods and services or resources*

Money is anything used by a society to purchase goods and services or resources. The members of the society receive money for their products or resources. Then they either hold that money or use it to purchase other products or resources, when and how they see fit. Different groups of people have used all sorts of objects as money—whale's teeth, stones, beads, copper crosses, clam shells, and gold and silver, for example. Today, the most commonly used objects are metal coins and paper bills, which together are called *currency*.

The Functions of Money

medium of exchange *anything that is accepted as payment for products and resources*

measure of value *a single standard or "yardstick" that is used to assign values to, and compare the values of, products and resources*

store of value *a means for retaining and accumulating wealth*

We have already noted that money aids in the exchange of goods and services for resources. And it does. But that's a rather general (and somewhat theoretical) way of stating money's function. Let us look at three specific functions of money in any society.

Serves as a Medium of Exchange   A **medium of exchange** is anything that is accepted as payment for products and resources. This definition looks very much like the definition of money. And it is meant to, because the primary function of money is to serve as a medium of exchange. The key word here is *accepted.* As long as the owners of products and resources accept money in an exchange, it is performing this function. Of course, these owners accept it because they know it is acceptable to the owners of other products and resources, which *they* may wish to purchase. For example, the family in our earlier example can sell their vegetables and use the money to purchase cloth from the weavers. This eliminates the problems associated with the barter system.

Serves as a Measure of Value   A **measure of value** is a single standard or "yardstick" that is used to assign values to, and compare the values of, products and resources. Money serves as a measure of value because the prices of all products and resources are stated in terms of money. It is thus the "common denominator" that we use to compare products and decide which we shall buy. Imagine the difficulty you would have in deciding whether you could afford, say, a pair of shoes if it were priced in terms of yards of cloth or pounds of vegetables—especially if your employer happened to pay you in toothbrushes.

Represents a Store of Value   Money that is received by an individual or firm need not be used immediately. It may be held and spent later. Hence money serves as a **store of value,** or a means for retaining and accumulating wealth. This function of money comes into play whenever we hold on to money—in a pocket, a cookie jar, a savings account, or whatever.

Value that is stored as money is affected by fluctuations in the economy. One of the major problems caused by inflation is a loss of stored value: As prices go up in an inflationary period, money loses value. Suppose you can buy a Sony stereo system for $1,000. Then we may say that your $1,000 now has a value equal to the value of that system. But let us suppose that you wait a while and don't buy the stereo immediately. If the price goes up to $1,100 in the meantime because of inflation, you can no longer buy the stereo with your $1,000. Your money has *lost* value because it is now worth less than the stereo (see Figure 17.1).

This store owner accepts money as a medium of exchange or payment for the goods purchased by his customers. He, in turn, can use money to purchase the goods needed to replenish the store's inventory.

Important Characteristics of Money

To be acceptable as a medium of exchange, money must be fairly easy to use, it must be trusted, and it must be capable of performing its functions. Together, these requirements give rise to five essential characteristics.

Base period is 1982–1984 = 100

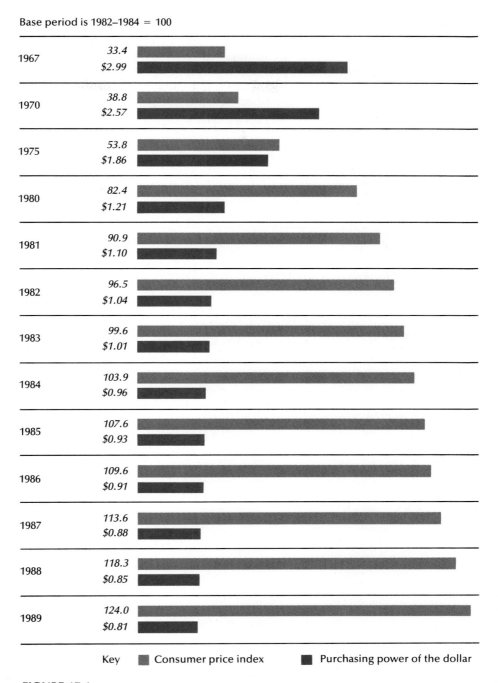

	Consumer price index	Purchasing power of the dollar
1967	33.4	$2.99
1970	38.8	$2.57
1975	53.8	$1.86
1980	82.4	$1.21
1981	90.9	$1.10
1982	96.5	$1.04
1983	99.6	$1.01
1984	103.9	$0.96
1985	107.6	$0.93
1986	109.6	$0.91
1987	113.6	$0.88
1988	118.3	$0.85
1989	124.0	$0.81

Key   ■ Consumer price index   ■ Purchasing power of the dollar

FIGURE 17.1
**The Consumer Price Index and the Purchasing Power of the Consumer Dollar
(Base period: 1982–1984 = 100)**
*Inflation causes a loss of money's stored value. As the consumer price index goes
up, the purchasing power of the consumer's dollar goes down. (Source:* Economic
Report of the President, *United States Government Printing Office, Washington, D.C., 1990,
p. 359.)*

Divisibility   The standard unit of money must be divisible into smaller units to accommodate small purchases as well as large ones. Our standard is the dollar, and it is divided into one-hundredths, one-twentieths, one-tenths, one-fourths, and one-halves through the issuance of coins (pennies, nickels, dimes, quarters, and half-dollars, respectively). These allow us to make purchases of less than a dollar and of odd amounts greater than a dollar.

Portability   Money must be small enough and light enough to be carried easily. For this reason, paper currency, is issued in larger *denominations—* multiples of the standard unit. Five-, ten-, twenty-, fifty-, and hundred-dollar bills make our money convenient for almost any purchase.

Stability   Money should retain its value over time. When it does not (during periods of high inflation), people tend to lose faith in their money. They may then turn to other means of storing value (such as gold and jewels, works of art, and real estate). In extreme cases, they may use such items as a medium of exchange as well. They may even resort to barter.

Durability   The objects that serve as money should be strong enough to last through reasonable usage. No one would appreciate (or use) dollar bills that disintegrated as they were handled or coins that melted in the sun.

Difficulty of Counterfeiting   If a nation's currency were easy to counterfeit—that is, to imitate or fake—its citizens would be uneasy about accepting it as payment. Even genuine currency would soon lose its value, because no one would want it. Thus the countries that issue currency do their best to ensure that it is very hard to reproduce.

The Supply of Money: M_1, M_2, and M_3

How much money is there in the United States? Before we can answer that question, we need to redefine a couple of familiar concepts.

demand deposit *an amount that is on deposit in a checking account*

A **demand deposit** is an amount that is on deposit in a checking account. It is called a *demand* deposit because it can be claimed immediately—on demand—by presenting a properly made-out check, withdrawing cash from an automated teller machine, or by transferring money between accounts.

time deposit *an amount that is on deposit in an interest-bearing savings account*

A **time deposit** is an amount that is on deposit in an interest-bearing savings account. Savings institutions generally permit immediate withdrawal of money from savings accounts. However, they can require written notice prior to withdrawal. The time between notice and withdrawal is what leads to the name *time* deposits.

Time deposits are not immediately available to their owners, but they can be converted to cash easily. For this reason, they are called *near-monies.* Other near-monies include short-term government securities, government bonds, and the cash surrender values of insurance policies.

The *M_1 supply of money* consists only of currency and demand deposits. (It is thus based on a narrow definition of money.) By law, currency must

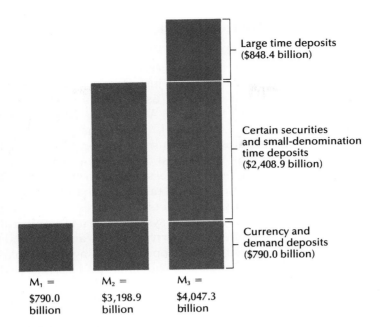

Large time deposits
($848.4 billion)

Certain securities
and small-denomination
time deposits
($2,408.9 billion)

Currency and
demand deposits
($790.0 billion)

$M_1 =$	$M_2 =$	$M_3 =$
$790.0 billion	$3,198.9 billion	$4,047.3 billion

FIGURE 17.2
The Supply of Money
Three measures of the money supply are M_1, which includes currency and demand deposits; M_2, which includes M_1 plus certain specific securities and small-denomination time deposits; and M_3, which includes M_1, M_2, plus large time deposits of $100,000 or more. (Source: Federal Reserve Bulletin, *February 1990, p. A13.*)

be accepted as payment for products and resources. Checks are accepted as payment because they are convenient, convertible to cash, and generally safe.

The *M_2 supply of money* consists of M_1 (currency and demand deposits) plus certain specific securities and small-denomination time deposits. Another common definition of money—*M_3*—consists of M_1 and M_2 plus large time deposits of $100,000 or more. The definitions of money that include the M_2 and M_3 supplies are based on the assumption that time deposits are easily converted to cash for spending. Figure 17.2 shows the elements of the M_1, M_2, and M_3 supplies. About 21 percent is coins, paper currency, and demand deposits; and the remaining 79 percent is time deposits and certain specific securities.

We have, then, at least three measures of the supply of money. (Actually, there are other measures as well, which may be broader or narrower than M_1, M_2, and M_3.) So the answer to our original question is that the amount of money in the United States depends very much on how we measure it. Generally, economy watchers tend to focus on M_1 or some variation of M_1.

We have seen that a very large part of the money that exists in this country is deposited, by those individuals and firms who possess it, in banks and other financial institutions. Let us now examine the banking industry.

The American Banking Industry

Learning Objective 2
Describe the differences between commercial banks and other financial institutions in the banking industry

commercial bank *a profit-making organization that accepts deposits, makes loans, and provides related services to its customers*

national bank *a commercial bank that is chartered by the U.S. Comptroller of the Currency*

state bank *a commercial bank that is chartered by the banking authorities in the state in which it operates*

The New Jersey Nets organization was able to construct the Meadowlands, its home court, through long-term financing from Howard Commercial Bank. Shown here are the House Officer of Howard Commercial (right) and Nets officials.

During the 1980s, a record number of banks and savings and loan associations failed. In just the past two years, more than 400 banks and 250 savings and loan associations failed. To make matters worse, the government's General Accounting Office estimates that there are still more than 1,000 "weak" banks and savings and loan associations in the United States. To help solve the problem, Congress has passed a bailout plan that is the largest federal rescue in history. The total cost for the government's plan is estimated to be $300 billion, or about $3,000 per taxpayer. And, it could take more than thirty years to correct the problem.

Certainly, these facts are distressing because they point up problems in our present banking system. Yet, it is comforting to note three important factors. First, the majority of banks and financial institutions that perform banking functions are operating at a profit. According to banking experts, roughly 10 percent of the banks and savings and loan associations in the United States are in financial trouble. Second, deposits are still insured for $100,000. Finally, the government has taken actions to help correct the situation. While the remedies will take time and are certainly not cheap, the bailout plan is solid proof that the government is committed to correcting the problems that exist in the U.S. banking system. Without a sound banking system, the nation and the economy would grind to a screeching halt.

Commercial Banks

A **commercial bank** is a profit-making organization that accepts deposits, makes loans, and provides related services to its customers. Like other businesses, the bank's primary goal—its purpose—is to earn a profit. Its inputs are money in the form of deposits, for which it pays interest. Its primary output is loans, for which it charges interest. If the bank is successful, its income is greater than the sum of its expenses, and it will show a profit.

Because banks deal with money belonging to individuals and other firms, they are carefully regulated. They must also meet certain requirements before they are chartered, or granted permission to operate, by federal or state banking authorities. A **national bank** is a commercial bank that is chartered by the U.S. Comptroller of the Currency. There are approximately 5,500 national banks, accounting for about 53 percent of all bank deposits. These banks must conform to federal banking regulations and are subject to unannounced inspections by federal auditors.

A **state bank** is a commercial bank that is chartered by the banking authorities in the state in which it operates. State banks outnumber national banks by about two to one, but they tend to be smaller than national banks. They are subject to unannounced inspections by both state and federal auditors.

Table 17.1 lists the ten largest banks in the United States. All of these are classified as national banks.

TABLE 17.1   *The Ten Largest Banks in the United States, Ranked by Total Deposits**

Rank	Commercial Bank	Deposits (in billions)
1	Citibank NA (New York)	$105.0
2	Bank of America NA & SA (San Francisco)	69.6
3	Chase Manhattan Bank NA (New York)	58.2
4	Morgan Guaranty Trust Company (New York)	45.5
5	Manufacturers Hanover Trust Company (New York)	42.9
6	Security Pacific National Bank (Los Angeles)	36.1
7	Wells Fargo Bank NA (San Francisco)	35.1
8	Chemical Bank (New York)	33.3
9	Bankers Trust Company (New York)	33.2
10	First National Bank (Chicago)	27.4

* Based on deposits as of December 31, 1988.
Source: *American Banker,* New York, 1989. Reprinted with permission.

Other Financial Institutions

savings and loan association (S&L) *a financial institution that primarily accepts savings deposits and provides home-mortgage loans*

Savings and Loan Associations   A **savings and loan association (S&L)** is a financial institution that primarily accepts savings deposits and provides home-mortgage loans. Originally, they were permitted to offer their depositors *only* savings accounts. But since Congress passed the Depository Institutions Deregulation and Monetary Control Act, which became effective on January 1, 1981, they have been able to offer interest-paying checking accounts (NOW accounts) to attract depositors. A **NOW account** is an interest-bearing checking account. (*NOW* stands for Negotiable Order of Withdrawal.)

NOW account *an interest-bearing checking account; NOW stands for Negotiable Order of Withdrawal*

During the 1980s, high interest rates, coupled with a reduced demand for homes, led to financial difficulties for many S&Ls. Much of their lending is in the form of low-interest, long-term home-mortgage loans, which were isssued to finance the purchase of homes during the 1960s and 1970s. Those older loans generate very little revenue, compared to more recent loans. In addition, because few people were taking out mortgages in the early 1980s, S&Ls were not able to lend money at the higher interest rates of that time period. As a result, the S&Ls were squeezed between the higher interest rates they paid to their depositors and the lower interest rates they received from their loans. As already mentioned earlier in this section, a large number of the troubled financial institutions are S&Ls. In fact, most experts expect that as many as 700 S&Ls will close or merge with stronger S&Ls in the next ten years.

Today, there are approximately 3,000 savings and loan associations in the United States. Federal associations are chartered under provisions of the Home Owners' Loan Act of 1933 and are supervised by the Office of Thrift Supervision—a branch of the U.S. Treasury. Approximately 40 percent of all associations have federal charters and must use the word *federal* in their names. The remaining 60 percent are chartered and supervised by state authorities.

Credit Unions

A **credit union** is a financial institution that accepts deposits from, and lends money to, only those people who are its members. Usually the membership is composed of employees of a particular firm, people in a particular profession, or those who live in a community served by a local credit union. Some credit unions require that members purchase at least one share of ownership, at a cost of about $5 to $10. Credit unions generally pay higher interest than commercial banks and S&Ls, and they may provide loans at lower cost. Credit unions are regulated by the Federal Credit Union Administration.

Mutual Savings Banks

A **mutual savings bank** is a bank that is owned by its depositors. Located primarily in the northeastern part of the United States, mutual savings banks accept deposits and lend money for home mortgages. The approximately 375 mutual savings banks in this country have no stockholders. Their profits are distributed to depositors. They operate much like S&Ls and are controlled by state banking authorities.

Organizations That Perform Banking Functions

There are three types of financial institutions that are not actually banks but that are nevertheless involved in various banking activities to a limited extent.

▶ *Insurance companies* provide long-term financing for office buildings, shopping centers, and other commercial real estate projects throughout the United States. They also invest in corporate and government bonds. The funds used for this type of financing are obtained from policyholders' insurance premiums.

▶ *Pension funds* are established by employers to guarantee their employees a regular monthly income upon retirement. Contributions to the fund may come either from the employer alone or from both the employer and the employee. Pension funds earn additional income through generally conservative investments in certain corporate stocks, corporate bonds, government securities, and real estate developments.

▶ *Brokerage firms* offer combination savings and checking accounts that pay higher-than-usual interest rates (so-called money-market rates). Many people switched to these accounts when their existence became widely recognized to get the higher rates. In the last few years, however, banks have instituted similar types of accounts, hoping to lure their depositors back.

Services Provided by Financial Institutions

If it seems to you that banks and other financial institutions are competing for your business, you're right. That is exactly what is happening. Never before have so many different financial institutions offered such a tempting array of services to attract customers. The financial services provided by the banking industry are the following:

▶ Demand deposits
▶ Time deposits

▶ Loans

▶ Electronic transfer of funds

▶ Financial advice

▶ Payroll service

▶ Certified checks

▶ Trust services

▶ Safe-deposit boxes

The three most important banking services are accepting deposits, making loans, and providing electronic funds transfers.

The Deposit Side of Banking   Firms and individuals deposit money in checking accounts (demand deposits) so that they can write checks to pay for purchases. A **check** is a written order for a bank or other financial institution to pay a stated dollar amount to the business or person indicated on the face of the check. Today, most goods and services are paid for by check. Most financial institutions charge an activity fee (or service charge) for checking accounts. It is generally somewhere between $5 and $10 per month for individuals. For businesses, monthly charges are based on the average daily balance in the checking account and on the number of checks written.

In addition to savings and loan associations, most other financial institutions offer interest-paying NOW accounts. With NOW accounts, the usual interest rate is 5.25 percent. However, individual banks may impose certain restrictions on their NOW accounts, including the following:

▶ A minimum balance before any interest is paid

▶ Fees for accounts whose balances fall below a set minimum balance

▶ Restrictions on the number of checks that may be written during each month

Some financial institutions offer Super NOW accounts. Super NOWs pay somewhat higher interest than NOW accounts and generally include unlimited check-writing privileges. But depositors may be required to maintain a minimum balance as high as $2,500 to avoid bank charges that may run between $7 and $15 per month.

Savings accounts (time deposits) provide a safe place to store money and a very conservative means of investing. The usual *passbook savings account* earns about 5.5 percent in commercial banks and S&Ls, and slightly more in credit unions. Depositors can usually withdraw money from passbook accounts whenever they wish to.

A depositor who is willing to leave money with a bank for a set period of time can earn a higher rate of interest. To do so, the depositor buys a certificate of deposit (CD). A **certificate of deposit** is a document stating that the bank will pay the depositor a guaranteed interest rate for money left on deposit for a specified period of time. The interest rates paid on CDs change weekly; they once briefly exceeded 16 percent. Rates in early 1990 ranged from 7.5 to 8.5 percent. The rate always depends on how

check   *a written order for a bank or other financial institution to pay a stated dollar amount to the business or person indicated on the face of the check*

certificate of deposit   *a document stating that the bank will pay the depositor a guaranteed interest rate for money left on deposit for a specified period of time*

BUSINESS JOURNAL

The Time Value of Money Concept

The old saying goes: "I've been rich and I've been poor, but believe me, rich is better." While being rich doesn't guarantee happiness, the accumulation of money does provide financial security and is a goal worthy of pursuit. Regardless of how much money you want or what you want to use the money for, the time value of money concept can help you obtain your financial goals.

The time value of money is a concept that recognizes that money can be invested and earn interest over a period of time. For example, assume you invest $10,000 in a certificate of deposit that pays 9 percent interest. If you let your interest accumulate, your initial $10,000 investment is worth $10,900 at the end of one year. At the end of five years, your investment is worth $15,390. At the end of ten years, your investment has increased to $23,670. In this example, you have received $13,670 in interest over a ten-year period of time as a result of letting your interest compound and grow. The money accumulated can be used for college tuition, financing a major purchase like a car or a home, retirement income, or for another investment.

THE RULE OF 72

Many people are afraid of mathematical calculations, but the *rule of 72* provides a quick, easy method to estimate how long it takes an investment to double in value. Divide the number 72 by the interest rate for any investment. Thus an investment that pays 9 percent will double in value in approximately eight years ($72 \div 9 = 8$ years).

HOW THE TIME VALUE OF MONEY CONCEPT AFFECTS INVESTMENTS

One of the first things financial planners tell clients is that there is no substitute for a long-term investment program. In simple language, this means that if you start an investment program when you are young, make conservative and safe investments, and let your investment earnings accumulate, you won't have to worry about finances when you reach retirement age.

HOW YOU CAN BECOME A MILLIONAIRE

Today, there are more than one million millionaires in the United States, and you, too, can become a millionaire. Here's a plan guaranteed to work. Let's assume you are 25 years old and invest $2,400 each year in an investment that provides a 10 percent return each year for the next forty years. When you reach 65, your investment will be worth $1,062,216. Over a forty-year period of time, you have invested a total of $96,000 ($2,400 × 40 = $96,000). The remaining $966,216 is the result of letting your investment accumulate and compound for forty years.

A WORD OF CAUTION

For this plan to work, you must be 25 years old and willing to invest $2,400 a year for over forty years. If you skip investments, use the money before you reach 65, or the interest rate should fall below 10 percent, then your investment will be worth less than $1 million. This example illustrates the time value of money concept, but it does not take into account what your money will buy when you reach retirement age. Certainly, inflation and increasing prices over the next forty years (both topics discussed in this chapter) should be taken into consideration. Yet, it is important to realize that for as little as $200 a month over a forty-year period, you, too, can become a millionaire.

Based on information from Kevin McCormally, "The Saying That a Bird in Hand Is Worth Two in the Bush Applies to Money, Too," *Changing Times*, August 1989, p. 16; Clint Willis, "Mastering the Math Behind Your Money," *Money*, May 1989, pp. 129–130 + ; and John Steele Gordon, "The Problem of Money and Time," *American Heritage*, May/ June 1989, pp. 57–58 + .

much is invested and for how long. Depositors are penalized for early withdrawal of funds invested in CDs.

The Lending Side of Banking Commercial banks, savings and loan associations, credit unions, and other financial institutions provide short- and long-term loans to both individuals and businesses. *Short-term loans* are those that are to be repaid within one year. For businesses, short-term loans are generally used to provide working capital that will be repaid with sales revenues. To ensure that short-term money will be available when it is needed, many firms establish a line of credit. A **line of credit** is a loan that is approved before the money is actually needed. Because all the necessary paperwork is already completed and the loan is preapproved, the business can later obtain the money without delay, as soon as it is required. Even with a line of credit, a firm may not be able to borrow money if the bank does not have sufficient funds available. For this reason, some firms prefer a **revolving credit agreement,** which is a guaranteed line of credit. Both types of financing are discussed in greater detail in Chapter 18.

Long-term business loans have a longer repayment period—generally three to seven years but sometimes as long as fifteen years. They are most often used to finance the growth of a firm or its product mix.

Most lenders prefer some type of collateral for both business and personal long-term loans. **Collateral** is real or personal property (stocks, bonds, land, equipment, or any other asset of value) that the firm or individual owns and that is pledged as security for a loan. For example, when an individual obtains a loan to pay for a new automobile, the automobile is the collateral for the loan. If the borrower fails to repay the loan according to the terms specified in the loan agreement, the lender can repossess the collateral pledged as security for that loan.

Repayment terms and interest rates for both short- and long-term loans are arranged between the lender and the borrower. For businesses, repayment terms may include monthly, quarterly, semiannual, or annual payments. Repayment terms (and interest rates) for personal loans vary, depending on how the money will be used and what type of collateral, if any, is pledged. Borrowers should always "shop" for a loan, comparing the repayment terms and interest rates offered by competing financial institutions.

Electronic Transfer of Funds The newest service provided by financial institutions is electronic banking. An **electronic funds transfer (EFT) system** is a means for performing financial transactions through a computer terminal or telephone hookup. Present EFT systems can be used in four ways.

1. *Automated teller machines (ATMs):* An ATM is an electronic bank teller—a machine that provides almost any service a human teller can provide. Once the customer is properly identified, the machine can dispense cash from the customer's checking or savings account or can make a cash advance charged to a credit card. Most ATMs can

---

line of credit *a loan that is approved before the money is actually needed*

revolving credit agreement *a guaranteed line of credit*

collateral *real or personal property that a firm or individual owns and that is pledged as security for a loan*

electronic funds transfer (EFT) system *a means for performing financial transactions through a computer terminal or telephone hookup*

Customers at an increasing number of supermarkets are able to purchase merchandise at point-of-sale (POS) terminals. According to company officials, customers like POS transactions because they don't have to carry a lot of cash or write checks.

also accept deposits and provide information about current account balances. ATMs are located in bank parking lots, supermarkets, drugstores, and even gas stations. Customers have access to them at all times of the day or night.

2. *Automated clearinghouses (ACHs):* Where ACHs are available, large companies can use them to transfer wages and salaries directly into their employees' bank accounts without making out individual paychecks. The ACH system saves time and effort for both employers and employees, and adds a measure of security to the transfer of these payments.

3. *Point-of-sale (POS) terminals:* A POS terminal is a computerized cash register that is located in a retail store and connected to a bank's computer. Here's how it works. You select your merchandise. At the cash register, you pull your debit card through a magnetic card reader and enter your four-to-seven-digit personal identification number. A central processing center notifies a computer at your bank that you want to make a purchase. Next, the bank's computer immediately deducts the amount of the purchase from your checking account. Then, the amount of the purchase is added to the store's account. Finally, the store is notified that the transaction is complete, and the cash register prints out your receipt. Notice the difference between a debit card and a credit card. With a debit card, money is deducted immediately from your account. A credit-card transaction, on the

other hand, involves a short-term loan made to you by the bank or credit-card company. The use of POS terminals has two advantages. First, you don't have to write a check to pay for your merchandise. Second, the retailer doesn't have to worry about nonpayment because the money is withdrawn from your account immediately.

4. *Bill payment by telephone:* Individuals can authorize their banks to make payments to various creditors by using a touch-tone telephone like a computer terminal. The customer simply punches in the required information, and the bank transfers the funds automatically.

Bankers are generally pleased with EFT systems. EFT is fast, and it eliminates some costly processing of checks. However, many bank customers are reluctant to use EFT systems. Some customers simply don't like "the machine," whereas others fear the computer will garble their accounts. Congress has responded to consumer fears by passing the Electronic Funds Transfer Act, which protects the customer in case the bank makes an error or the customer's EFT identification card is lost or stolen. No doubt the use of EFT will increase as people become more familiar with it.

A network as diverse and influential as the banking industry must be subject to uniform regulations and controls. In fact, regulation of banking in this country really amounts to regulation of our economy at large.

The Federal Reserve System

Federal Reserve System *the government agency responsible for regulating the United States banking industry*

The **Federal Reserve System** (or simply "the Fed") is the government agency responsible for regulating the United States banking industry. It was created by Congress on December 23, 1913. Its mission is to maintain an economically healthy and financially sound business environment in which banks can operate. The Federal Reserve System is controlled by the seven members of its Board of Governors, who meet in Washington, D.C. Each governor is appointed by the president and confirmed by the Senate for a fourteen-year term. The president also selects the chairman and vice chairman of the board from among the board members for four-year terms. These terms may be renewed.

The Federal Reserve System includes twelve Federal Reserve District Banks, which are located throughout the United States, as well as twenty-five branch-territory banks (see Figure 17.3). Each Federal Reserve District Bank is actually owned—but not controlled—by the commercial banks that are members of the Federal Reserve System. All national (federally chartered) banks must be members of the Fed. State banks may join if they choose to and if they meet membership requirements.

Learning Objective 4
Understand how the Federal Reserve System regulates the money supply

The primary function of the Fed is to regulate the supply of money in this country in such a way as to maintain a healthy economy. It does so by controlling bank reserve requirements and the discount rate and by running open-market operations.

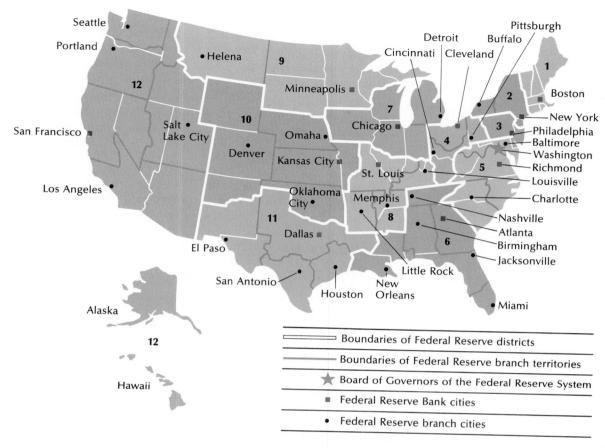

FIGURE 17.3
Federal Reserve System
The Federal Reserve System comprises twelve district banks and twenty-five branch banks. (Source: Board of Governors of the Federal Reserve System, 1990.)

Regulation of Reserve Requirements

reserve requirement   *the percentage of its deposits that a bank must retain, either in its own vault or on deposit with its Federal Reserve district bank*

When money is deposited in a bank, the bank must retain a portion of it to satisfy customers who may want to withdraw money from their accounts. The remainder is available for loans. The **reserve requirement** is the percentage of its deposits that a bank *must* retain, either in its own vault or on deposit with its Federal Reserve District Bank. For example, if a bank has deposits of $20 million and the reserve requirement is 10 percent, the bank must retain $2 million.

Through a process called *deposit expansion*, the bank can then use the remaining $18 million to actually create more money and make more loans. Here's how deposit expansion works. In this example, the bank must retain $2 million in a reserve account. The remaining $18 million can be used to fund consumer and business loans. Assume that the bank loans out all $18 million to different borrowers. Also, assume that before using any of the borrowed funds, all borrowers deposit the $18 million in their bank accounts at the lending institution. Now, the bank's deposits have increased by an additional $18 million. Since these deposits are subject to the same reserve requirement described above, the bank must maintain $1.8 million in a reserve account, and the bank can lend the additional $16.2 million to other bank customers. Of course, the bank's lending potential becomes steadily smaller and smaller as more loans are made. And it should be pointed out that, since bankers are usually very conservative by nature, they will not use deposit expansion to maximize their lending activities; they will take a more middle-of-the-road approach. Finally, the government allows banks to use the deposit-expansion process as long as the reserve requirement is maintained and the bank keeps enough cash on hand to meet the needs of customers who want to withdraw money from their accounts.

The reserve requirement is set by the Board of Governors of the Fed. When it is increased, banks have less money available for lending. Fewer loans are made, and the economy tends to slow. Thus, increasing the reserve requirement is a powerful anti-inflation weapon. On the other hand, by decreasing the reserve requirement, the Fed can make additional money available for lending to stimulate a slow economy.

The present reserve requirement for time deposits is 3 percent. For NOW accounts it can range from 3 to 12 percent, depending on such factors as the total amount on deposit, average daily deposits, and the location of the particular member bank. Because this means of controlling the money supply is so very potent and has such far-reaching effects, the Fed seldom changes the reserve requirement.

Regulation of the Discount Rate

discount rate *the interest rate that the Federal Reserve System charges for loans to member banks*

Member banks may borrow money from the Fed to satisfy the reserve requirement and to make additional loans to their customers. The interest rate that the Federal Reserve System charges for loans to member banks is called the **discount rate.** It is set by the Fed's Board of Governors.

When the Fed lowers the discount rate, money is easier to obtain. Member banks feel free to make more loans and to charge lower interest rates. This increases the money supply and generally stimulates the nation's economy. When the Fed raises the discount rate, banks begin to restrict loans. They increase the interest rates they charge and tighten their own loan requirements. The overall effect is to slow the economy— to check inflation—by making money more difficult and more expensive to obtain.

Open-Market Operations

The federal government finances its activities partly by selling U.S. government securities. These securities, which pay interest to owners, may be purchased by any individual, firm, or organization—including the

Fed. **Open-market operations** are the buying and selling of U.S. government securities by the Federal Reserve System for the purpose of controlling the supply of money. They are the most frequently used tool of the Fed.

To reduce the nation's money supply, the Fed simply *sells* government securities on the open market. The money it receives from purchasers is taken out of circulation. Thus less money is available for investment, purchases, or lending. To increase the money supply, the Fed *buys* government securities. The money that it pays for the securities goes back into circulation, making more money available to individuals and firms.

Because the major purchasers of government securities are financial institutions, open-market operations tend to have an immediate effect on lending and investment. Moreover, this effect can be controlled and adjusted by varying the amount of securities that the Fed sells or buys at any given time.

Table 17.2 summarizes the effects of open-market operations and the other tools used by the Fed to regulate the money supply.

TABLE 17.2 *Methods Used by the Federal Reserve System to Control the Money Supply and the Economy*

Method Used	Immediate Result	End Result
Open-market operations		
1. Fed **sells** government securities and bonds	Less money for banks to lend to customers—reduction in overall money supply	Economic slowdown
2. Fed **buys** government securities and bonds	More money for banks to lend to customers—increase in overall money supply	Increased economic activity
Regulating reserve requirement		
1. Fed **increases** reserve requirement	Less money for banks to lend to customers—reduction in overall money supply	Economic slowdown
2. Fed **decreases** reserve requirement	More money for banks to lend to customers—increase in overall money supply	Increased economic activity
Regulating the discount rate		
1. Fed **increases** the discount rate	Less money for banks to lend to customers—reduction in overall money supply	Economic slowdown
2. Fed **decreases** the discount rate	More money for banks to lend to customers—increase in overall money supply	Increased economic activity

Other Responsibilities

Learning Objective 5
Be able to describe the Fed's
role in clearing checks,
controlling and inspecting
currency, and administering
selective credit controls

In addition to its regulation of the money supply, the Fed is also responsible for clearing checks, controlling and inspecting currency, and applying selective credit controls.

Clearing Checks   Today people use checks to pay for nearly everything they buy. If all the checks written in one year were taped end to end, they would extend to the moon and back four times.[2] Moreover, it costs about 50 cents to *clear* the typical check—that is, to process it for payment.[3]

A check written by a customer of one bank and presented for payment to another bank in the same town may be processed through a local clearinghouse. But the procedure becomes more complicated when the banks are not in the same town. That's where the Federal Reserve System comes in. The Fed is responsible for the prompt and accurate collection and crediting of intercity checking transactions.

The steps involved in clearing a check through the Federal Reserve System are outlined in Figure 17.4. About half of all the checks written in the United States are cleared in this way. The remainder are either presented directly to the paying bank or processed through local clearinghouses. Through the use of electronic equipment, most checks can be cleared within two or three days.

Control and Inspection of Currency   As paper currency is handled, it becomes worn or dirty. The typical dollar bill has a life expectancy of less than one year (larger denominations usually last longer because they are handled less). When member banks deposit their surplus cash in a Federal Reserve Bank, the currency is automatically inspected. Bills that are unfit for further use are separated and destroyed. The destruction process is usually as follows:

► Holes are drilled in each corner of the bills by one group of employees.

► The bills are then cut in half by a second group of employees.

► Each half is pulverized by a third group.

► The end result is barely recognizable as paper. It is baled and sold for use in making such things as wrapping paper and roofing material.

Selective Credit Controls   The Federal Reserve System has the power to establish credit terms for loans involving consumer durables (automobiles, appliances, and the like) and for real estate loans. In particular, the Board of Governors can set both the amount of the down payment and the repayment period for these loans. It has not exercised this power in recent years. By exercising these powers, the Fed can increase or decrease consumer purchases of major items that typically involve credit.

In a more recent, related development, Congress gave the Fed the responsibility for implementing the Truth-in-Lending Act, which was passed by Congress in 1968. This act requires lenders to clearly state the annual percentage rate and total finance charge for a consumer loan. It also prohibits discrimination in lending based on race, color, sex, marital status, religion, or national origin.

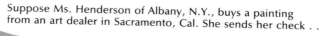

Suppose Ms. Henderson of Albany, N.Y., buys a painting from an art dealer in Sacramento, Cal. She sends her check . .

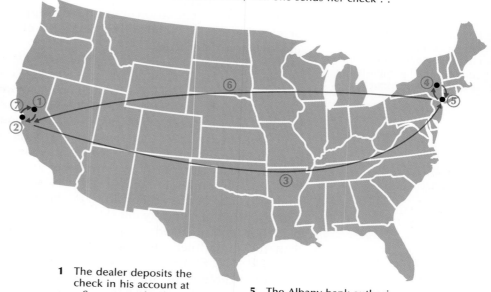

1   The dealer deposits the check in his account at a Sacramento bank.

2   The Sacramento bank deposits the check for credit in its account with the Federal Reserve Bank of San Francisco.

3   The Federal Reserve Bank of San Francisco sends the check to the Federal Reserve Bank of New York for collection.

4   The Federal Reserve Bank of New York forwards the check to the Albany bank, which deducts the amount of the check from Ms. Henderson's account.

5   The Albany bank authorizes the Federal Reserve Bank of New York to deduct the amount of the check from its deposit account with the Federal Reserve Bank.

6   The Federal Reserve Bank of New York pays the Federal Reserve Bank of San Francisco by payment from its share in the interdistrict settlement fund.

7   The Federal Reserve Bank of San Francisco credits the Sacramento bank's deposit account, and the Sacramento bank credits the art dealer's account.

FIGURE 17.4
Clearing a Check Through the Federal Reserve System
Approximately one-half of all U.S. checks are cleared this way, a process that usually takes two to three days. (Source: Federal Reserve Bank of New York, The Story of Checks, *6th ed., 1983, p. 11.)*

The Federal Reserve System is also responsible for setting the margin requirements for certain stock transactions. The *margin* is the minimum portion of the selling price that must be paid in cash. (The investor may borrow the remainder.) The current margin requirement is $2,000, or 50 percent. If an investor purchases $4,000 worth of stock, he or she must pay at least $2,000 cash. The remaining $2,000 may be borrowed from the brokerage firm or some other financial institution.

The FDIC, SAIF, and NCUA

During the Depression, a number of banks failed and their depositors lost all their savings. To make sure that this does not happen again (and to restore public confidence in the banking industry), Congress organized the *Federal Deposit Insurance Corporation (FDIC)* in 1933. The primary purpose of the FCIC is to insure deposits against bank failure. All banks that are members of the Federal Reserve System are required to belong to the FDIC. Nonmember banks are allowed to join if they qualify. Insurance premiums are paid by the banks.

Learning Objective 6
Recognize the function of the Federal Deposit Insurance Corporation (FDIC), Savings Association Insurance Fund (SAIF), and National Credit Union Association (NCUA)

The FDIC insures all accounts in each member bank for up to $100,000 per depositor. An individual depositor may obtain additional coverage by opening separate accounts in different banks. Individuals who deposit their money in savings and loan associations or credit unions receive similar protection. The newly created *Savings Association Insurance Fund (SAIF)* insures deposits in savings and loan associations. Formerly, the now defunct Federal Savings and Loan Insurance Corporation (FSLIC) was charged with this responsibility. The *National Credit Union Association (NCUA)* insures deposits in credit unions.

The FDIC, SAIF, and NCUA have improved banking in the United States. When any one of these organizations insures an institution's deposits, it reserves the right to periodically examine that institution's operations. For example, the FDIC has established regional centers in Tennessee, California, and Texas to monitor the large number of banks that are in trouble in those parts of the country. If a bank, S&L, or credit union is found to be poorly managed, it is reported to the proper banking

The Federal Deposit Insurance Corporation (FDIC) insures all accounts in each member bank for up to $100,000. One such bank is Independence Bank of Chicago, which was named 1989 Bank of the Year by Black Enterprise *magazine. The bank has also placed in the top five of the* Black Enterprise *Bank List every year for the past decade.*

authority. In extreme cases, the FDIC, SAIF, or NCUA can cancel its insurance coverage. This is a particularly unwelcome action. It causes many depositors to withdraw their money from the bank, S&L, or credit union and discourages most prospective depositors from opening an account.

Lending to individuals and firms is a vital function of banks. And deciding wisely to whom it will extend credit is one of the most important activities of any institution. The material in the next section explains the different factors that are used to evaluate credit applicants.

Effective Credit Management

credit *immediate purchasing power that is exchanged for a promise to repay it, with or without interest, at a later date*

Credit is immediate purchasing power that is exchanged for a promise to repay it, with or without interest, at a later date. A credit transaction is a two-sided business activity that involves both a borrower and a lender. The borrower is most often a person or firm that wishes to make a purchase. The lender may be a bank, some other lending institution, or an intermediary involved in the purchase.

Learning Objective 7
Be aware of the importance of credit and credit management

For example, suppose you obtain a bank loan to buy a $40,000 Porsche automobile. You, as the borrower, obtain immediate purchasing power. In return, you agree to certain terms that are imposed by the bank. As the lender, the bank requires that you make monthly payments, pay interest, and purchase insurance to protect the car until the loan is paid in full. That is, you promise to repay the purchasing power, pay interest for its use, and protect the collateral until the loan is repaid.

Banks lend money because they are in business for that purpose. The interest they charge is what provides their profit. There are at least two reasons why other businesses extend credit to their customers. First, some customers simply can't afford to pay the entire amount of their purchase immediately, but they *can* repay credit in a number of smaller payments, stretched out over some period of time. Second, some firms are forced to sell goods or services on credit to compete effectively when other firms offer credit to their customers.

Today the effective management of credit is a practical necessity for most businesses. Credit terms can be used as a competitive weapon, and firms can realize a profit from interest charges. The major pitfall in granting credit is the possibility of nonpayment and the resulting loss of income. However, if a firm follows the five C's of credit management, it can minimize this possibility.

The Five C's of Credit Management

The primary purpose of any business is to earn a profit by selling goods and services. When a business extends credit to its customers, it must face the fact that some customers will be unable or unwilling to pay for their credit purchases. With this in mind, credit managers must establish policies for determining who will receive credit and who will not. Most

BUSINESS JOURNAL

My Bank Just Failed!

After a hard day at the office, you sit down in front of the television to watch the local news. The first story is about another bank closure. But this time the story hits home because the bank in the story is your bank. Could this happen to you?

Unfortunately, there is a possibility that your bank or savings and loan association will close in the next ten years. Last year, 221 banks and 205 savings and loan associations failed in the United States. And the General Accounting Office and other federal agencies are predicting that at least 500 to 1,000 more will fail or merge with stronger institutions during the next ten years. Therefore, before you deposit money in a bank or savings and loan association, consider the following set of questions and answers.

Are my bank accounts protected? The Federal Deposit Insurance Corporation (FDIC) and a new federal fund—the Savings Association Insurance Fund (SAIF) will insure accounts for up to $100,000. It is even possible to deposit more than $100,000 in the same institution and be covered, if your money is deposited in different types of accounts. But be warned—financial analysts advise against this practice. A better approach is to move some of your money to another financial institution when your account exceeds $100,000.

Will the current crisis affect future interest rates? Yes. Interests rates on certificates of deposit (CDs) will be lower in the future because many of the most desperate or cash-hungry banks and savings and loan associations will be closed or merged with healthier financial institutions.

Are there ways to evaluate a bank or savings and loan? Yes. You can simply ask for financial data. Look at the income statement to see if a given institution is earning a profit. Also, examine any material contained in its financial statements about "nonperforming" loans. Finally, look at the ratio of equity capital to assets. Banking experts suggest that equity capital should be about 5 to 6 percent of the total assets amount. Be suspicious if a bank or savings and loan will not provide information about its financial condition.

What is the government doing? After at least six months of study, the government is now ready to take some definite steps to "fix" the problem. First, the capital standards for banks and savings and loan associations will be increased. Second, the Office of Thrift Supervision—a new branch of the Treasury Department—will replace the Federal Home Loan Bank Board and supervise the savings and loan industry. Third, a new federal agency—the Resolution Trust Corporation—will be responsible for disposing of an estimated $500 billion in assets of failed thrifts.

What will it cost? The Government Accounting Office has estimated that the total cost of the federal bailout program will exceed $150 billion. Other experts estimate that the actual cost may be as high as $300 billion. This program could end up costing the average taxpayer an extra $3,000.

What about the future? There have been at least three recommendations that may be implemented in the future. First, to increase the reserves of the FDIC and SAIF, all banks and financial institutions will pay higher premiums for insurance coverage. Second, premiums for FDIC and SAIF coverage may be increased if a financial institution makes a number of "risky" loans. Third, an individual's coverage may be limited to a total of $100,000, regardless of how many accounts or banks he or she uses.

Based on information from Jon P. Goodman, "Help! My Bank Just Failed!" *Ladies' Home Journal*, June 1989, p. 22+; Penelope Want, "All You Need to Know About the S&L Bailout," *Money*, September 1989, p. 21; M. S. Forbes, Jr., "Avoiding Another S&L Crisis," *Forbes*, May 15, 1989, p. 27; and Susan Dentzer, "The S&L Bailout Bust," *U.S. News & World Report*, June 26, 1989, pp. 20–22.

lenders build their credit policies around the five C's of credit: character, capacity, capital, collateral, and conditions. To provide this information, most lenders require borrowers to complete a credit application such as the one illustrated in Figure 17.5.

Character By *character* we mean the borrower's attitude toward his or her credit obligations. Experienced credit managers often see this as the most important factor in predicting whether a borrower will make regular payments and ultimately repay a credit obligation.

Typical questions to consider in judging a borrower's character include the following:

1. Is the borrower prompt in paying bills?
2. Have other lenders had to dun the borrower with overdue notices before receiving payment?

FIGURE 17.5
Credit Application Form
Credit managers use the information on credit application forms to help determine which customers should be granted credit.

SECTION 1

NAME First Middle Last
ADDRESS Street Apt. City State Zip
HOW LONG AT ABOVE ADDRESS ☐Own ☐Rent TELEPHONE
FORMER ADDRESS How Long
NAME OF BUSINESS TELEPHONE
BUSINESS ADDRESS Street City State Position How Long
PREVIOUS EMPLOYER (Please indicate if employed by above less than 3 years, or College/University if recent graduate.) Years with Firm or Year Graduated
NAME OF BANK ☐Reg. Check ☐Spec. Check Branch Address
NAME OF BANK ☐Savings Branch Address

CHARGE ACCOUNTS AT	ACCOUNT NUMBER IF AVAILABLE

OTHERS WHO MAY CHARGE
SPECIAL INSTRUCTIONS

SECTION 2

INFORMATION FOR JOINT APPLICANT OR AUTHORIZED SPOUSE
NAME Relationship to Applicant (if any) TELEPHONE
ADDRESS Street Apt. City State Zip ☐Own ☐Rent How Long
FORMER ADDRESS How Long
NAME OF BUSINESS TELEPHONE
BUSINESS ADDRESS Street City State Position How Long
PREVIOUS EMPLOYER (Please indicate if employed by above less than 3 years, or College/University if recent graduate.) Years with Firm or Year Graduated
NAME OF BANK ☐Reg. Check ☐Spec. Check Branch Address
NAME OF BANK ☐Savings Branch Address

3. Have lenders been forced to take the borrower to court to obtain payment?

4. Has the customer ever filed for bankruptcy? If so, did the customer make an attempt to repay debts voluntarily?

Even personal factors such as marital status and drinking or gambling habits may affect an individual's ability to repay a loan or credit obligation.

Capacity   By *capacity* we mean the borrower's financial ability to meet credit obligations—that is, to make regular loan payments as scheduled in the credit agreement. If the customer is another business, the loan officer or credit manager looks at the firm's income statement. For individuals, the loan officer or credit manager checks salary statements and other sources of income, such as dividends and interest. The borrower's outstanding financial obligations and monthly expenses are also taken into consideration before credit is approved.

Capital   The term *capital* as used here refers to the borrower's assets or net worth. In general, the greater the capital, the greater the borrower's ability to repay a loan of a specific size. The capital position of a business can be determined by examining its financial statements. (Most lenders insist that the business borrower's financial statements be prepared or audited by an independent certified public account. This helps ensure that the information contained in the statements is accurate.) For individuals, information on net worth can be obtained by requiring that the borrower complete a credit application. The borrower must also authorize employers and financial institutions to release information to confirm the claims made in the application.

Collateral   For large amounts of credit—and especially for long-term loans—the lender may require some type of collateral. *Collateral*, as defined earlier, is real or personal property (stocks, bonds, land, equipment, or any other asset of value) that the firm or individual owns and that is pledged as security for a loan. If the borrower fails to live up to the terms of the credit agreement, the collateral can be sold to satisfy the debt.

Conditions   Here we mean *general economic conditions*, which can affect a borrower's ability to repay a loan or other credit obligation. How well a business firm can withstand an economic storm may depend on the particular industry the firm is in, its relative strength within that industry, and its earnings history and earnings potential. For individuals, the basic question of conditions focuses on security—of both the applicant's job and the firm that he or she works for.

Checking Credit Information

The five C's are concerned mainly with information that is supplied by the applicant. But how can the lender determine whether this information is accurate? That depends on whether the potential borrower is a business or an individual consumer.

Credit information concerning businesses can be obtained from four sources:

▶ *National credit-reporting agencies:* Dun & Bradstreet is the most widely used credit-reporting agency in the United States. Its Dun & Bradstreet Reports present detailed credit information about specific companies. Its reference books include credit ratings for more than 9.5 million businesses.

▶ *Local credit-reporting agencies,* which may require a monthly or yearly fee for providing information on a continual basis

▶ *Industry associations,* which may charge a service fee

▶ *Other firms* that have given the applicant credit

Various credit bureaus provide credit information concerning individuals—generally for a fee of from $7 to $15 per request. The following is a list of the three major consumer credit bureaus.

▶ TRW Credentials Services (Orange, California)

▶ Trans Union Credit Information Co. (Chicago)

▶ Credit Bureau, Inc./Equifax (Atlanta)

These and other credit bureaus are subject to the provisions of the Fair Credit Reporting Act of 1970. This act safeguards consumers' rights in two ways. First, every consumer has the right to know what information is contained in his or her credit bureau file. In most states, a consumer who has been denied credit on the basis of information provided by a credit bureau can obtain a credit report without charge within thirty days of the denial. In other situations, the consumer may obtain the information for a $7 or $10 fee. The credit bureau either sends a copy of the file or specifies a local or regional office where it can be obtained.

Second, if a consumer feels that some information in the file is inaccurate, misleading, or vague, he or she has the right to request that the credit bureau verify it. If the disputed information is found to be correct, the consumer can provide an explanation of up to 100 words, giving his or her side of the dispute. This explanation must become part of the consumer's credit file. If the disputed information is found to be inaccurate, it must be deleted or changed. Furthermore, any lending institution that has been supplied the inaccurate information within the past six months must be sent a corrected update.

Sound Collection Procedures

The vast majority of borrowers follow the lender's repayment terms exactly. However, some accounts inevitably become overdue for any of a variety of reasons. Experience shows that such accounts should receive immediate attention.

Some firms handle their own delinquent accounts; others prefer to use a professional collection agency. (Charges for an agency's services are usually high—up to half of the amount collected.) Both tend to use the following standard collection techniques, generally in the order in which they are listed.

BUSINESS JOURNAL

Your Credit Rating

You graduate from college and start earning a good salary. After six months on the job, you decide that it's time to take the plunge and make your first major purchase—a new BMW. You apply for a car loan, and it is denied. What went wrong?

Many times credit applicants are turned down because they don't have a credit history or they have a "bad" credit history. Regardless of the reason, credit counselors advise that the first thing you should do is to find out why you were turned down. Then you can take some positive steps to improve your credit rating.

ESTABLISHING CREDIT FOR THE FIRST TIME

It is more difficult to establish credit for the first time than most people think. Here are seven specific actions you can take to establish a good credit history.*

1. Open both a checking and a savings account at a local bank, savings and loan association, or credit union.

2. Take out a small installment loan at the financial institution where you have your checking and savings accounts.

3. Establish credit with a local department store. Department-store accounts are often easier to establish than other types of credit accounts.

4. If a bank, department store, or oil company offers you a credit card, take it. Then be sure to make your payments on time.

5. Pay all your bills on time. If you live in a rental apartment and pay your own utilities, make sure you pay the rent and utilities promptly.

6. Don't borrow from a small-loan company (sometimes referred to as a *personal finance company*). A credit reference from this type of company may hurt you more than it can help.

7. If you are married and have a joint credit account, make sure that credit histories are reported in both names. If you are a woman, the account should be in your given name.

---

* Adapted from ''What Makes You a Good Credit Risk?'' *Consumer Reports*, May 1983, p. 256.

REBUILDING CREDIT

According to the Fair Credit Reporting Act of 1970, you should receive a written explanation of why you were denied credit. If the decision was based on information obtained from a credit bureau, your first step should be to contact the bureau and find out what information is contained in your credit report.

The Fair Credit Reporting Act requires a credit bureau to sell you a copy of your report or to provide a copy free of charge within thirty days if you have been denied credit. The average credit report contains a great deal of personal data along with information about how you pay your bills. If you spot an obvious error, phone or write the credit bureau and describe the error in detail. Federal law requires the credit bureau to investigate such complaints. But don't be surprised if you have to provide proof to substantiate your claim. Even if the bureau continues to insist that its records are correct, you can submit a 100-word explanation that must be included in your report. Unfavorable information can remain on your credit report for as long as seven years, with one exception. Information about personal bankruptcies can be retained as long as ten years.

Once you have obtained credit, make sure you protect it. If an unexpected large expense or a loss of income causes you to miss an installment payment, try to work out alternative arrangements with your creditors. Credit counseling services are available; some are free. If you need help, take action quickly before your credit rating is damaged.

Based on information from Rodolfo G. Ledesma, ''How to Check Your Credit Rating,'' *Consumer's Research*, September 1989, pp. 30–33; Don Dunn, ''When You Don't Get Credit Where Credit Is Due,'' *Business Week*, October 2, 1989, pp. 116–117; and Michele Galen, ''The Right to Privacy: There's More Loophole Than Law,'' *Business Week*, September 4, 1989, p. 77.

1. Subtle reminders and overdue notices, such as statements marked "Past Due"

2. Telephone calls to urge prompt payment

3. Personal visits to stress the necessity of paying past-due amounts immediately

4. Legal action, although the time, expense, and uncertain outcome of a lawsuit make this action a last resort

Good collection procedures should be firm, but they should also allow for compromise. Harassment is both illegal and bad business. Ideally, the customer will be convinced to make up missed payments, and the firm will retain the customer's goodwill.

CHAPTER REVIEW

Summary

Money is anything that is used by a society to purchase goods and services or resources. It must serve as a medium of exchange, a measure of value, and a store of value. To perform its functions effectively, money must be divisible into units of convenient size, light and sturdy enough to be carried and used on a daily basis, stable in value, and difficult to counterfeit.

The M_1 supply of money is made up of coins and bills (currency) and deposits in checking accounts (demand deposits). The broader M_2 supply includes M_1 plus certain specific securities and small-denomination time deposits. Another common definition—M_3—consists of M_1 and M_2 plus large time deposits of $100,000 or more.

A commercial bank is a profit-making organization that accepts deposits, makes loans, and provides related services to customers. In the United States, commercial banks may be chartered by the federal goverment or the various state governments. Savings and loan associations, credit unions, and mutual savings banks offer the same basic services that commercial banks provide. Insurance companies, pension funds, and brokerage firms provide some limited banking services.

The Federal Reserve System is responsible for regulating the banking industry and maintaining a sound economic environment. Banks with federal charters must be members of the Fed. State banks may join if they choose to and if they can meet the requirements for membership.

To control the supply of money, the Federal Reserve System regulates the reserve requirement, or the percentage of deposits that a bank must keep on hand. It also regulates the discount rate, or the interest rate the Fed charges member banks for loans. And it engages in open-market operations, in which it buys and sells government securities. The Fed is responsible for clearing checks, inspecting currency, and setting credit terms for certain consumer and stock-purchase loans.

The Federal Deposit Insurance Corporation (FDIC), Savings Association Insurance Fund (SAIF), and National Credit Union Association (NCUA) insure all accounts in member banks, S&Ls, and credit unions, up to $100,000 per depositor.

Credit is immediate purchasing power that is exchanged for a promise to repay it, with or without interest, at a later date. Businesses sell goods and services on credit because some customers can't afford to pay cash, and because they must keep pace with competitors who offer credit. Decisions on whether to grant credit to businesses and individuals are usually based on the five C's of credit: character, capacity, capital, collateral, and conditions. Credit information can be obtained from various credit-reporting agencies, credit bureaus, industry associations, and other firms. The techniques used to collect past-due accounts should be firm but flexible enough to maintain customer goodwill.

In the next chapter, we focus on money as a productive resource. You will see why firms need financing, how they obtain the money they need, and how they ensure that it is utilized efficiently, in keeping with their organizational objectives.

Key Terms

You should now be able to define and give an example relevant to each of the following terms:

barter system
money
medium of exchange
measure of value
store of value
demand deposit
time deposit
commercial bank
national bank
state bank
savings and loan association (S&L)
NOW account
credit union

mutual savings bank
check
certificate of deposit
line of credit
revolving credit agreement
collateral
electronic funds transfer (EFT) system
Federal Reserve System
reserve requirement
discount rate
open-market operations
credit

Questions and Exercises

Review Questions

1. How does the use of money solve the problems that are associated with a barter system of exchange?
2. What are the three functions that money must perform in a sound monetary system? Give an example of each.
3. Explain why money must have each of the following characteristics.
   a. divisibility
   b. portability
   c. stability
   d. durability
   e. difficulty of counterfeiting
4. What is included in the definition of the M_1 supply of money? of the M_2 supply? of the M_3 supply?
5. What is the difference between a national bank and a state bank? What other financial institutions compete with national and state banks?
6. Describe the major depositing and lending services provided by financial institutions today.
7. What is the major advantage of electronic banking? What is its major disadvantage?
8. What is the Federal Reserve System? How is it organized?

9. Explain how the Federal Reserve System uses each of the following to control the money supply.
   a. Reserve requirements
   b. The discount rate
   c. Open-market operations
10. How could the Fed use its control of consumer credit terms and the margin requirement to regulate the supply of money?
11. What is the basic function of the FDIC, SAIF, and NCUA? How do they perform this function?
12. List and explain the five C's of credit management.
13. How would you check the information provided by an applicant for credit at a department store? at a heavy-equipment manufacturer's sales office?

Discussion Questions

1. Charles Keating used money from Lincoln Savings and Loan Association to finance speculative investments in land developments, resort hotels, stocks, corporate bonds, and energy-generating windmills. Should there be a government regulation that restricts the types of loans that a bank, savings and loan association, or other financial institution can make?
2. Government regulators realized that Lincoln Savings and Loan Association was in serious financial trouble as early as 1986. Why do you think they waited three years before taking action?
3. It is said that financial institutions "create" money when they make loans to firms and individuals. Explain what this means.
4. Is competition among financial institutions good or bad for the following?
   a. these institutions
   b. their customers
   c. the economy
5. Why would banks pay higher interest on money that is left on deposit for longer periods of time (for example, on CDs)?
6. Why does the Fed use indirect means of controlling the money supply, instead of simply printing more money or removing money from circulation when necessary?
7. Lenders are generally reluctant to extend credit to individuals with no previous credit history (and no outstanding debts). Yet, they willingly extend credit to individuals who are in the process of repaying debts. Is this reasonable? Is it fair?

Exercises

1. Devise a form of money, other than coins and bills, that fulfills the functions of money and has all the required characteristics.

2. Obtain a credit application from a store or bank. Fill it out. Then answer the following questions.
   a. Does the application ask for enough information so that a credit manager could apply the five C's? What questions should be added to the application form?
   b. Would you, as a credit manager, extend credit to yourself? Explain.

Case 17.1

Bank Failures and the FDIC

Financial troubles in the Farm Belt, depressed conditions in the oil and gas industry, and unsound real estate loans throughout the United States led to major problems for U.S. banks during the 1980s. As evidence of the severity of the problems, the number of bank failures per year for the past five years averaged more than 175. Most of the failures were attributed to mismanagement—but that can mean almost anything from skullduggery and fraud to stupidity.

In the wake of these bank failures, depositors tend to worry about losing their money. In most cases, they need not worry if their deposits are insured by the federal government through the Federal Deposit Insurance Corporation (FDIC). This organization guarantees deposits for up to $100,000 per account. Currently, the FDIC has reserves of more than $15 billion. And if it should need more money to make good on deposit insurance, the FDIC is backed by the full faith and credit of the United States government. In fact, recently President Bush approved a congressional bill for more than $166 billion in federal aid to ensure that no depositor would lose money in a federally insured bank, unless his or her account contained more than $100,000.

The FDIC charges a fee of one-twelfth of 1 percent of the insured bank's total deposits. In addition, the FDIC has a stringent capital-reserve requirement, intended to help keep member banks from failing. But when they do fail—or look as though they might fail—the FDIC is there with help and, if needed, sterner measures. For example, in late 1988, the FDIC provided $4 billion in aid to Dallas-based First Republic Bank of Texas. Later, the Texas bank merged with NCNB, a large successful banking company in North Carolina. The depositors lost nothing.

With bank failures at their highest level since 1933, the FDIC's bank liquidators have been getting plenty of practice. Most often, when a bank seems close to collapse, the FDIC tries to find a healthy bank to take it over and operate it. This usually entails a type of auction in which the federal agency asks for bids on the ailing institution. Once a new owner has been found, the liquidators literally swoop down on the ailing bank, close it down, claim its books, and transfer its accounts to the new owner.

Next, the agency takes over the bad loans and attempts to collect what is owed. Often the liquidators must deal with deadbeat borrowers, who refuse to pay on their loans. When a little "arm twisting" fails, they seize the loan collateral. "Anything anyone could pledge as loan collateral we probably have one or more of," says James Davis, the head of the FDIC liquidators. Davis and his staff have seized and sold items that range "from a shrimp boat that a storm washed up on the main street in a Texas town to a coal mine that was on fire when the agency moved in. A brothel and an X-rated movie house, churches and synagogues, art objects and a collection of wild animals—the FDIC has owned them all at one time or another."*

Questions

1. The number of commercial banks on the FDIC's problem list numbers almost 1,500, or about 11 percent of the nation's banks. Why do you think there are so many problem banks?
2. In an attempt to reduce the number of bank failures, critics have suggested that banks be required to (a) maintain larger reserves to offset bad loans and (b) pay higher premiums for FDIC coverage. What effect would these two measures have on the banking system in the United States?
3. Would you deposit your money in a bank, savings and loan association, credit union, or other financial institution that did not offer federal insurance protection?

Case 17.2

Texas Billionaires Sue Their Bankers

It is very hard to resist the temptation to compare the legendary Hunt family to television's Dallas oil barons, the Ewings of South Fork. The ever-aggressive style, sometimes outdoing even J. R. Ewing himself, can readily be seen in the Hunt family's business decisions. The three Hunt brothers, Bunker, Herbert, and Lamar, have often been compared to their deceased father, famed wildcatter H. L. Hunt, who once earned his

---

* Based on information from Susan Dentzer, "The S&L Bailout Bust," *U.S. News & World Report*, June 26, 1989, pp. 20–22; Barbara Burgower, "Breaking the Banks," *Ladies' Home Journal*, June 1989, p. 24; Christine Gorman, "Cracks in the System," *Time*, August 29, 1988; and Mark Clifford, "The Liquidators," *Forbes*, October 21, 1985, p. 44.

living as a card player. Legend has it that he won his first oil lease in a poker game. Bunker and his brothers, like their father, seem to be gamblers at heart.

Now the Hunts are rolling the dice once again in the game of fortune. They are presently pitted in a bitter battle against their bankers. Volleys of charges and countercharges fly back and forth between lawyers for the Hunts' two major corporations—Placid Oil Company and Penrod Drilling Co.—and twenty-three creditor banks.

While their current problems are related to depressed oil prices, the Hunts' downfall was in the making long before the fall of oil prices. Their trouble began in the late 1970s when Bunker and Herbert amassed silver and silver securities worth $6.6 billion—more than half of the U.S. silver supply and 15 percent of the world supply. When the metals exchanges restricted trading, prices collapsed and the Hunts were unable to pay an estimated $900 million on silver-related debts to banks and brokers. Then they were forced to borrow $1.1 billion to cover losses in the silver market, and they pledged their corporate holdings in Placid Oil and Penrod Drilling as collateral. When Placid and Penrod missed their payments to the banks, both companies presented a restructuring plan that the banks rejected. A second restructuring plan was also rejected by Placid's and Penrod's banks.

Consequently, the Hunts took Placid Oil Company into bankruptcy in late 1986, filing for Chapter 11 protection under federal bankruptcy laws. The brothers hoped to reorganize the company and keep the banks from selling the company's assets to settle some $1.1 billion in defaulted bank loans. Penrod Drilling, on the other hand, did avoid bankruptcy, but is still heavily in debt.

Although Placid's Chapter 11 bankruptcy petition lists $2 billion in assets (and $979.3 million in debts), to be worth that amount, the assets must be developed. John McMullen, a Cambridge, Massachusetts-based energy consultant hired by the Hunts to assess their holdings, estimated that if the company were liquidated now, it would be worth only $180 million. With this fact in mind, the brothers tried to convince bankers that the best strategy was to reduce their loan payments and allow them to keep drilling, particularly in a risky offshore tract called Green Canyon in the Gulf of Mexico. When the banks refused, the Hunts sued their lenders for $14 billion, alleging that the banks broke promises, favored their competitors, and set out to destroy their companies. The banks countersued. Now, over three years later, both sides have tentatively agreed to drop their lawsuits as part of the Hunts' reorganization plan. Placid Oil will repay more than $800 million in cash and notes. To raise the cash, the Hunts will sell Placid's assets. Finally, the banks will also receive a 50 percent share of ownership in Penrod Drilling—the world's largest offshore oil drilling company.†

Questions

1. Do you think it is fair for the banks to foreclose on Placid Oil and Penrod Drilling when the oil market is so depressed?

2. If you were a banker, would you have let the Hunts continue to develop assets like Green Canyon in the Gulf of Mexico? Why?

3. Considering their wealth, why do you think the Hunts continued to gamble on silver and oil investments?

† Based on information from Barbara Rudolph, "Big Bill for a Bullion Binge," *Time*, August 29, 1988, p. 56; Harry Hurt III, "The Real Hunt Brothers Story," *Newsweek*, September 5, 1988, p. 50; "Their Billions Ain't What They Used to Be," *U.S. News & World Report*, September 15, 1986, pp. 49–50; Barbara Rudolph, "Down to Their Last Billion," *Time*, September 15, 1986, pp. 44–45; and Lenny Glynn, "Fall of the Silver Barons," *Maclean's*, September 22, 1986, p. 8.

FINANCIAL MANAGEMENT

18

1 Appreciate the need for financing and financial management in business

2 Understand the process of planning for financial management

3 Describe the relative advantages and disadvantages of different methods of short-term financing

4 Evaluate the advantages and disadvantages of equity financing and debt financing from the corporation's standpoint

5 Grasp the importance of using funds effectively

CHAPTER PREVIEW

In this chapter we concentrate on the acquisition and efficient use of money. Initially, we focus on two needs of business organizations: the need for money to start a business and keep it going, and the need to manage that money effectively. We also look at how firms develop financial plans and evaluate financial performance. Then we explore several approaches to borrowing money. We compare various methods of obtaining short-term financing—money that will be used for one year or less, usually to pay a firm's bills until customers pay theirs, or to cover production costs until the goods are sold. We also examine sources of long-term financing, which a firm may require for expansion, new-product development, or replacement of equipment.

Drexel Burnham Lambert, Inc.

On February 13, 1990, Drexel Burnham Lambert filed for bankruptcy. Ironically, Drexel—the securities firm that had risen to fame by providing takeover artists with billions in financing to purchase TWA, Revlon, Beatrice Foods, RJR Nabisco, and other major corporations during the 1980s—could not obtain the financing it needed to pay its current debts.

Although Drexel Burnham Lambert had been in business for 152 years, the firm was a "second tier" company on Wall Street until the early 1980s. Then, Drexel began selling junk bonds. According to financial analysts, a junk bond is a low-quality, high-yield bond issued by a company with a questionable record of sales and earnings.

The two men responsible for Drexel's early success in the junk bond market were Fred Joseph and Mike Milken. The idea (given to them by another Drexel employee) seemed inspired: The buyer, with relatively little cash, could target and take over corporate giants with money raised through Drexel's network of junk investors. At the same time, Drexel would receive a fat commission for putting the deal together. The idea—selling junk bonds—worked so well that Drexel Burnham Lambert became Wall Street's most profitable securities firm, with earnings of $545 million in 1986.

Although extremely profitable, Drexel Burnham Lambert had already run into trouble with the U.S. government. One of Drexel's brokers, Dennis B. Levine, pleaded guilty to insider trading—the buying and selling of securities based on inside information that has not been made public—in 1986. He fingered Ivan Boesky, who pleaded guilty to the same charge. Then Boesky became a government witness and in turn fingered Milken and the Drexel company for insider trading activities.

Based on Boesky's testimony and the facts uncovered in a two-year investigation, U.S. Attorney Rudolph Giuliani threatened to bring racketeering charges against Drexel. Faced with the facts, Drexel agreed to pay a $650 million fine in December 1988. As part of the settlement, the government also insisted that Drexel sever all ties with Milken. Then in March 1989, Giuliani filed a ninety-eight-count indictment against Milken. At the date of this publication, Milken has pleaded guilty to six felony counts and has agreed to pay $600 million in fines and restitution. He also faces up to twenty-eight years in prison when the final sentencing stage of his trial is completed.

Without Milken's considerable deal-making abilities, Drexel was unable to generate the necessary revenues and profits to stay in business. With almost $3 billion in liabilities, a class-action suit filed by bondholders who claim Drexel rigged the junk bond market, and intense competition from other securities firms, bankruptcy became the only alternative. Ironically, the firm's two largest creditors are the U.S. government and Michael Milken. Drexel still owes the government $150 million—the unpaid portion of the $650 million fine. The firm also owes Milken about $200 million for unpaid salary and bonuses.[1]

People on Wall Street were not particularly sorry to see Drexel Burnham Lambert file bankruptcy. Drexel had been a tough competitor. After all, it had taken a lot of business away from other securities firms: In less than seven years, Drexel had taken over the junk bond industry and had become a giant among giants. The junk bond market that Drexel helped to create was valued at more than $200 billion in 1990.

As its legacy, Drexel Burnham Lambert leaves behind a battered bond market and hundreds of corporations that must pay high interest on massive debt which itself must eventually be repaid. While the "deals" that Drexel helped finance did reshape corporate America in more ways than one, the only lasting benefit of the junk bond mania was to shake up complacent corporate managers. For some, the threat of a takeover made them realize the importance of financial management.

What Is Financial Management?

Financial management consists of all those activities that are concerned with obtaining money and using it effectively. Within a business organization, the financial manager must not only determine the best way (or ways) to raise money. She or he must also ensure that projected uses are in keeping with the organization's goals. Effective financial management thus involves careful planning. It begins with determination of the firm's financing needs.

The Need for Financing

Money is needed both to start a business and to keep it going. The original investment of the owners, along with money they may have borrowed, should be enough to get operations under way. Then, it would seem that income from sales could be used to finance the firm's continuing operations and to provide a profit as well.

This is exactly what happens in a successful firm—over the long run. But sales revenue does not generally flow evenly. Both income and expenses may vary from season to season or from year to year. Temporary funding may be needed when expenses are high or income is low. Then, too, special situations, such as the opportunity to purchase a new facility or expand an existing facility, may require more money than is available within a firm. In either case, the firm looks to outside sources of financing.

Short-Term Financing Needs   **Short-term financing** is money that will be used for a period of one year or less and then repaid. A firm might need short-term financing to pay for a new promotional campaign that is expected to increase sales revenue. Or the purchase of a computer-based inventory-control system, which will "pay for itself" within a year, might be funded with short-term money.

Although there are many short-term financing needs, two deserve special attention. First, certain necessary business practices may affect a

cash flow *the movement of money into and out of an organization*

firm's cash flow and create a need for short-term financing. **Cash flow** is the movement of money into and out of an organization. The ideal is to have sufficient money coming into the firm, in any period, to cover the firm's expenses during that period. But the ideal is not always achieved. For example, a firm that offers credit to its customers may find an imbalance in its cash flow. Such credit purchases are generally not paid until thirty or sixty days (or more) after the transaction. Short-term financing is then needed to pay the firm's bills until customers have paid theirs. An unexpectedly slow selling season or unanticipated expenses may also cause a cash-flow problem.

A second major need for short-term financing that is related to a firm's cash-flow problem is inventory. Inventory requires considerable investment for most manufacturers, wholesalers, and retailers. Moreover, most goods are manufactured four to nine months before they are actually sold to the ultimate customer. As a result, manufacturers that engage in this type of speculative production often need short-term financing. The borrowed money is used to buy materials and supplies, to pay wages and rent, and to cover inventory costs until the goods are sold. Then, the money is repaid out of sales revenue. Wholesalers and retailers may need short-term financing to build up their inventories before peak selling periods. Again the money is repaid when the merchandise is sold.

long-term financing *money that will be used for longer than one year*

Long-Term Financing Needs **Long-term financing** is money that will be used for longer than one year. Long-term financing is obviously needed to start a new business. It is also needed for executing business expansions and mergers, for developing and marketing new products, and for replacing equipment that becomes outmoded or inefficient. See Figure 18.1 for a comparison of short- and long-term financing.

The amounts of long-term financing needed by large firms can seem almost unreal. Exxon spends about $10 million to drill an exploratory offshore oil well—without knowing for sure whether oil will be found! Texas Instruments spent millions to develop and produce the TI 99/4A Personal Computer, and millions more to market it, before deciding to

FIGURE 18.1
Comparison of Short- and Long-Term Financing
Whether a business seeks short- or long-term financing depends on what the borrowed money will be used for.

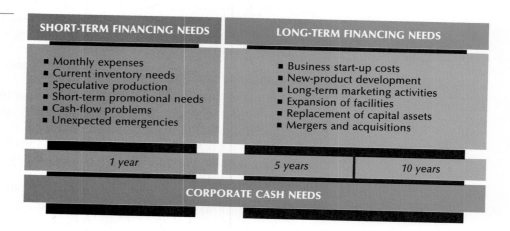

Kemper Financial Services, Inc., the asset management and financial products company, is a subsidiary of Kemper Corporation. As well as helping other companies manage their finances, Kemper, of course, also must manage its own. Kemper has a very sound investment in the PGA National, a residential and resort community in Palm Beach Gardens, Florida.

abandon the product. And R.J. Reynolds Industries borrowed $5 billion of long-term money to purchase Nabisco Brands, Inc.

The Need for Financial Management

Without financing there would be very little business. Financing gets a business started in the first place. Then financing supports the firm's production and marketing activities; pays its bills; and, when carefully managed, produces a reasonable profit.

Many firms have failed because their managers did not pay enough attention to finances. And many fairly successful firms could be highly successful if they managed their finances more carefully. For example, business people often take finances for granted. Their first focus may be on production or marketing. As long as there is sufficient financing today, they don't worry about how well it is used or whether it will be there tomorrow.

Proper financial management, on the other hand, can ensure that

▶ Financing priorities are established in line with established organizational objectives

▶ Spending is planned and controlled in accordance with established priorities

▶ Sufficient financing is available when it is needed, both now and in the future

▶ Excess cash is invested in certificates of deposit (CDs), government securities, or conservative marketable securities

These functions define effective management as applied to a particular resource: money. And, like all effective management, financial management begins with goal setting and planning.

Planning—The Basis of Sound Financial Management

financial plan   *a plan for obtaining and using the money that is needed to implement an organization's goals*

In Chapter 5, we defined a plan as an outline of the actions by which an organization intends to accomplish its goals. A **financial plan,** then, is a plan for obtaining and using the money that is needed to implement an organization's goals. Once the plan is developed and put into action, the firm's performance must be monitored and evaluated. And, like any other plan, it must be modified if necessary.

Developing the Financial Plan

Learning Objective 2
Understand the process of planning for financial management

Financial planning (like all planning) begins with the establishment of a set of valid objectives. Next, planners must assign costs to these objectives. That is, they must determine how much money is needed to accomplish each one. Finally, financial planners must identify available sources of financing and decide which to use. In the process, they must make sure that financing needs are realistic and that sufficient funding is available to meet those needs.

The three steps involved in financial planning are illustrated in Figure 18.2.

FIGURE 18.2
The Three Steps of Financial Planning
After a financial plan has been developed, it must be monitored continually to ensure that it actually fulfills the firm's objectives.

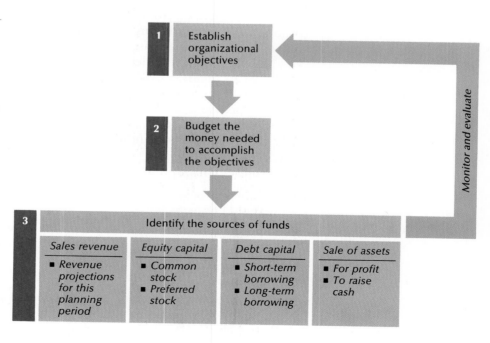

1	Establish organizational objectives
2	Budget the money needed to accomplish the objectives
3	Identify the sources of funds

Sales revenue	Equity capital	Debt capital	Sale of assets
■ Revenue projections for this planning period	■ Common stock ■ Preferred stock	■ Short-term borrowing ■ Long-term borrowing	■ For profit ■ To raise cash

Monitor and evaluate

NEWTON'S CLOTHING STORE
Sales Budget   For January 1, 199x to December 31, 199x

Department	First quarter	Second quarter	Third quarter	Fourth quarter	Totals
Infants'	$ 50,000	$ 55,000	$ 60,000	$ 70,000	$235,000
Children's	45,000	45,000	40,000	40,000	170,000
Women's	35,000	40,000	35,000	50,000	160,000
Men's	20,000	20,000	15,000	25,000	80,000
Totals	$150,000	$160,000	$150,000	$185,000	$645,000

FIGURE 18.3
Sales Budget for Newton's Clothing Store
Usually the budgeting process begins with the construction of individual budgets for sales and expenses.

Establishing Organizational Objectives As we have noted, establishing objectives is an important and ongoing management task. Objectives are *specific* statements detailing what the organization intends to accomplish within a certain period of time. If objectives are not specific, they cannot be translated into costs, and financial planning cannot proceed. They must also be realistic. Otherwise, they may be impossible to finance or achieve.

budget *a statement that projects income and/or expenditures over a specified future period of time*

Budgeting for Financial Needs A **budget** is a statement that projects income and/or expenditures over a specified future period of time. Once planners know what the firm expects to accomplish over some period of time—say, the next calendar year—they can estimate the various costs the firm will incur and the revenues it will receive. By combining these items into a companywide budget, financial planners can determine whether they must seek additional funding from sources outside the firm.

Usually the budgeting process begins with the construction of individual budgets for sales and for each of the various types of expenses: production, human resources, promotion, administration, and so on. (A typical sales budget for a retailer is shown in Figure 18.3.) Budgeting accuracy is improved when budgets are first constructed for individual departments and for shorter periods of time. These budgets can easily be combined into a companywide *cash budget*, such as that shown in Figure 18.4. In addition, they can help managers monitor and evaluate financial performance throughout the period covered by the overall cash budget.

Most firms today use one of two approaches to budgeting. In the *traditional* approach, each new budget is based on the dollar amounts

NEWTON'S CLOTHING STORE
Cash Budget

For January 1, 199x to December 31, 199x

	First quarter	Second quarter	Third quarter	Fourth quarter	Totals
Cash sales and collections	$150,000	$160,000	$150,000	$185,000	$645,000
Less payments					
Purchases	$110,000	$ 80,000	$ 90,000	$ 60,000	$340,000
Wages/salaries	25,000	20,000	25,000	30,000	100,000
Rent	10,000	10,000	12,000	12,000	44,000
Other expenses	4,000	4,000	5,000	6,000	19,000
Taxes	8,000	8,000	10,000	10,000	36,000
Total payments	$157,000	$122,000	$142,000	$118,000	$539,000
Net cash gain or (loss)	$ (7,000)	$ 38,000	$ 8,000	$ 67,000	$106,000

FIGURE 18.4
Cash Budget for Newton's Clothing Store
A companywide cash budget projects sales and expenses for a given period of time to anticipate cash surpluses and deficits.

contained in the budget for the preceding year. These amounts are modified to reflect any revised goals, and managers are required to justify only new expenditures. The problem with this approach is that it leaves room for the manipulation of budget items to protect the (sometimes selfish) interests of the budgeter or his or her department.

This problem is essentially eliminated through zero-base budgeting. **Zero-base budgeting** is a budgeting approach in which every expense must be justified in every budget. It can dramatically reduce unnecessary spending because every budget item must stand on its own merits. However, some managers feel that zero-base budgeting requires entirely too much time-consuming paperwork.

zero-base budgeting *a budgeting approach in which every expense must be justified in every budget*

Identifying Sources of Funds The four primary sources of funds, as listed in Figure 18.2, are sales revenue, equity capital, debt capital, and proceeds from the sale of assets. Future sales generally provide the greatest part of a firm's financing. Figure 18.4 shows that, for Newton's Clothing Store, sales for the year are expected to cover all expenses and to provide a cash gain of about 16 percent of sales. However, Newton's has a problem in the first quarter, when sales are expected to fall short of expenses by $7,000. In fact, one of the primary reasons for financial planning is to provide planners with adequate lead time to solve this type of problem.

A second type of funding is **equity capital,** which is money received from the sale of shares of ownership in the business. Equity capital is used almost exclusively for long-term financing. Thus it might be used to

equity capital *money received from the sale of shares of ownership in the business*

start a business and to fund expansions or mergers. It would not be considered for short-term financing needs, such as Newton's first-quarter shortfall.

debt capital *money obtained through loans of various types*

A third type of funding is **debt capital,** which is money obtained through loans of various types. Debt capital may be borrowed for either short- or long-term use—and a short-term loan seems made to order for Newton's. The firm would probably borrow the needed $7,000 (or perhaps a bit more) at some point during the first quarter and repay it from second-quarter sales revenue. In fact, Newton's might already have established a line of credit—discussed in Chapter 17—at a local bank to cover just such periodic short-term needs.

Our fourth type of funding is the proceeds from the sale of assets. A firm generally acquires assets because it needs them for its business operations. Therefore, selling assets is a drastic step. However, it may be a reasonable last resort when neither equity capital nor debt capital can be found. Assets may also be sold when they are no longer needed. When USX (formerly U.S. Steel Corp.) purchased **Marathon Oil Company,** USX was forced to pay interest and plan for eventual repayment of more than $3 billion that it borrowed to acquire Marathon. Because of depressed earnings, management realized that it could not pay off the $3-billion debt with sales revenues from the firm's steelwork operations. Management also realized that it would be impossible to sell more common or preferred stock because of the financial status of the company. Therefore, the firm resorted to selling its non-steelwork-related assets to raise the needed capital. And, as a bonus, the firm was able to dispose of unneeded assets at the same time.

In most cases, the particular funding need clearly suggests the best source of funding. (We discuss sources of equity and debt financing later in this chapter.) In all cases, though, the financial manager should identify and verify funding sources in advance to be sure they will be available when they are needed.

Toronto's Skydome baseball stadium, home of the Toronto Blue Jays, cost $360 million. The owners of the Skydome relied on presold ticket and box revenue, the sale of stock, and debt financing to raise the capital needed to construct the stadium.

Monitoring and Evaluating Financial Performance

It is important to ensure that financial plans are being implemented and to catch minor problems before they become major problems. Accordingly, the financial manager should establish a means of monitoring and evaluating financial performance. Interim budgets (weekly, monthly, or quarterly budgets) may be prepared for this purpose. Then interim reports of sales and expenses can be compared to budgeted amounts. These comparisons will point up areas that require additional or revised planning—or at least those areas where more careful investigation is called for.

Figure 18.5 shows a quarterly comparison of budgeted and actual sales for Newton's Clothing Store. Sales of children's wear are about 7 percent over budget, and sales of infants' wear are about 9 percent below budget. Although neither discrepancy is a cause for immediate alarm, the sales for both departments should be watched. The differences may be due to budgeting problems or to nonfinancial causes. In any case, such

NEWTON'S CLOTHING STORE
Sales Budget Update

First Quarter, 199x

Department	First-quarter estimate	Actual sales	Dollar difference
Infants'	$ 50,000	$ 45,600	$−4,400
Children's	45,000	48,200	+3,200
Women's	35,000	36,300	+1,300
Men's	20,000	21,100	+1,100
Totals	$150,000	$151,200	$+1,200

FIGURE 18.5
Budget Comparison for Newton's Clothing Store
Budget comparisons can point up areas that require additional planning or careful investigation.

comparisons should be routinely reported to department heads and upper-level managers. They may be used as the basis for budgeting, and they may reveal a need to take corrective action (such as promoting infants' wear more vigorously).

It is important to realize that the decision to borrow money does not mean that a firm is in financial trouble. On the contrary, astute financial management often means regular, responsible borrowing of many different kinds to meet different needs. In the next two sections we examine the sources of short- and long-term financing that are available to business firms.

Sources of Short-Term Financing

Learning Objective 3
Describe the relative advantages and disadvantages of different methods of short-term financing

Short-term financing is usually easier to obtain than long-term financing for three reasons: The shorter repayment period means there is less risk of nonpayment. The dollar amounts of short-term loans are usually smaller than those of long-term loans. And a close working relationship normally exists between the short-term borrower and the lender.

Most lenders do not require collateral for short-term financing. When they do, it is usually because they are concerned about the size of a particular loan, the borrowing firms's poor credit rating, or the general prospects of repayment. It may be the case that a financially weak firm will have difficulty securing short-term financing even when it is willing to pledge collateral to back up a loan.

BUSINESS JOURNAL

Are Takeovers Good for the Economy?

The merger and acquisition mania that dominated business headlines during the 1980s promises to continue in the 1990s. As a result, America's business leaders have had to adopt a new vocabulary—including terms such as *greenmail, spin-offs,* and *junk bonds*—and in many cases a new, more aggressive managment philisophy. Economists, financial analysts, corporate managers, and stockholders still hotly debate whether takeovers will be good for the economy—or individual companies—in the long run. But one thing is clear: There are two sides to consider when discussing the takeover question.

ARGUMENTS FOR INCREASED TAKEOVER ACTIVITY

According to Carl Icahn, head of Trans World Airlines and one of the most successful takeover artists in the United States, "The takeover boom is a treatment for a disease that is destroying American productivity: gross and widespread incompetent management."* The symptoms of this disease are corporate bureaucracy; excessive, uncontrolled spending; profits that are lackluster; and a top management team that has little to lose even if the corporation doesn't perform well. Too often, today's corporate managers are judged by the sheer size of their company, not by how profitable it is. And according to takeover advocates, it's time for a change.

Advocates argue that in almost every takeover, the purchasers have been able to make the company more profitable and productive by changing the top management team and forcing the company to concentrate on one main business. Subsidiaries and divisions that are not aligned with the company's main business are sold off, and the proceeds are used to either pay off debt or enhance the company. In short, the new management team is expected to increase sales and improve profits. And, quips one takeover advocate, the corporate manager is evaluated on the same basis as a football coach—if you don't win, you're out.

ARGUMENTS AGAINST INCREASED TAKEOVER ACTIVITY

According to the opposition, takeovers have done nothing to enhance corporate profitability or productivity. The critics argue that threats of takeovers have forced managers to devote valuable time to defending their companies from takeover attempts, thus robbing time from new product development and other vital business activities. As a result, companies in the United States are less competitive with foreign companies in Japan, West Germany, and South Korea. Opponents of takeovers are also quick to point out that takeovers rarely occur in these foreign countries.

Because cash-rich, "flabby" companies have been the most popular takeover targets, corporate managers are now working to portray their companies as lean and tough. Often, such leanness means cutting back the work force or moving plants away from areas with expensive unionized workers to locations with cheap labor—often outside the United States. Leanness also translates into managers' reluctance to invest in long-term research and development or new, more productive equipment because the profits that are realized from such investments are not immediate.

Finally, the opposition argues, companies taken over are saddled with massive debts—usually from bonds paying high interest rates—that must be paid by selling off the companies' assets, reducing divident payments to stockholders, or a combination of both. The only people who benefit from takeovers are investment bankers, brokerage firms, and the takeover artists. These people, say opponents of takeovers, receive financial rewards by manipulating America's corporations and not because they produce a tangible product or service.

---

* Carl C. Icahn, "The Case for Takeovers," *New York Times Magazine,* January 29, 1989, p. 34.

Based on information from Robert B. Reich, "American Pays the Price," *New York Times Magazine,* January 29, 1989, p. 32+ ; T. Boone Pickens, "Look What Restructuring Can Do," *Fortune,* July 3, 1989, pp. 72–73; George Russell, "Rebuilding to Survive," *Time,* February 16, 1987, p. 44; and Myron Magnet, "Restructuring Really Works," *Fortune,* March 2, 1987, p. 38.

Sources of Unsecured Short-Term Financing

unsecured financing *financing that is not backed by collateral*

Unsecured financing is financing that is not backed by collateral. A company seeking unsecured short-term capital has several options. They include trade credit, promissory notes, bank loans, commercial paper, and commercial drafts.

Trade Credit In Chapter 13 we noted that wholesalers may provide financial aid to retailers by allowing them thirty to sixty days (or more) in which to pay for merchandise. This delayed payment, which may also be granted by manufacturers, is a form of credit known as *trade credit* or the *open-book account*. More specifically, **trade credit** is a payment delay that a supplier grants to its customers.

trade credit *a payment delay that a supplier grants to its customers*

Between 80 and 90 percent of all transactions between businesses involve some trade credit. Typically, the purchased goods are delivered along with a bill (or invoice) that states the credit terms. If the amount is paid on time, no interest is generally charged. In fact, the seller may offer a cash discount to encourage prompt payment. The terms of a cash discount are specified on the invoice. For instance, "2/10, net 30" means that the customer may take a 2 percent discount if the invoice is paid within 10 days of the invoice date; if the bill is paid between 11 and 30 days, the customer must pay the entire (or net) amount.

promissory note *a written pledge by a borrower to pay a certain sum of money to a creditor at a specified future date*

Promissory Notes Issued to Suppliers A **promissory note** is a written pledge by a borrower to pay a certain sum of money to a creditor at a specified future date. Suppliers that are uneasy about extending trade credit may be less reluctant to offer credit to customers that sign promissory notes. Unlike trade credit, however, promissory notes usually provide that the borrower pay interest.

A typical promissory note is shown in Figure 18.6. Note that the customer buying on credit (or borrowing the money) is called the *maker* and is the party that issues the note. The business selling the merchandise on credit (or lending the money) is called the *payee*.

A promissory note offers two important advantages to the firm extending the credit. First, a promissory note is a legally binding and enforceable document. Second, most promissory notes are negotiable instruments that can be sold when the money is needed immediately. For example, the note shown in Figure 18.6 will be worth $820 at maturity. If it chose, the Shelton Company (the payee) could discount, or sell, the note to its own bank. The price would be slightly less than $820, because the bank charges a small fee for the service—hence the term *discount*. Shelton would have its money immediately, and the bank would collect the $820 when the note matured.

prime interest rate *the lowest rate charged by a bank for a short-term loan*

Unsecured Bank Loans Commercial banks offer unsecured short-term loans to their customers at interest rates that vary with each borrower's credit rating. The **prime interest rate** (sometimes called the *reference rate*) is the lowest rate charged by a bank for a short-term loan. This lowest rate is generally reserved for large corporations with excellent credit ratings. Organizations with good to high credit ratings may pay the prime

$ ___800.00___ ① ___Abilene___ , *Texas,* ___June 6___ ④ *A.D. 19* ___90___	

___Sixty days___ ③ *after date, without grace, for value received, I, we, or either of us, promise to*

pay to the order of ___The Shelton Company___ ⑦

① Eight hundred and no/100-------------------- *Dollars*

at ___First Bank___ *with interest from* ___June 6___ *to maturity at the rate of* ___15___ ② *per cent, per annum*

AND FROM MATURITY AT THE RATE OF FIFTEEN PER CENT, PER ANNUM, WE THE MAKERS, SURETIES, ENDORSERS AND GUARANTORS OF THIS NOTE HEREBY SEVERALLY WAIVE PRESENTATION FOR PAYMENT NOTICE OF NON-PAYMENT, PROTEST, AND NOTICE OF PROTEST AND DILIGENCE IN BRINGING SUIT AGAINST ANY PARTY HERETO, AND CONSENT THAT THE TIME OF PAYMENT MAY BE EXTENDED BY RENEWAL NOTE OR OTHERWISE ONE OR MORE TIMES FOR PERIODS DISCRETIONARY WITH THE HOLDER WITHOUT NOTICE THEREOF TO ANY OF THE SURETIES, ENDORSERS AND/OR GUARANTORS ON THIS NOTE. IT IS FURTHER EXPRESSLY AGREED THAT IF THIS NOTE IS PLACED IN THE HANDS OF AN ATTORNEY FOR COLLECTION, OR IS COLLECTED THROUGH THE PROBATE OF BANKRUPTCY COURT, OR THROUGH OTHER LEGAL PROCEEDINGS, THEN IN ANY OF SAID EVENTS, A REASONABLE AMOUNT SHALL BE ADDED AND COLLECTED AS ATTORNEY AND COLLECTION FEES

Due ___August 5, 1990___ ⑤   *Paul Robertson* ⑥

Address ___326 East Main Street___   Financial Vice-President

Phone ___555-1732___   The Richland Company

FIGURE 18.6
A Promissory Note
A promissory note is a borrower's written pledge to pay a certain sum of money to a creditor at a specified date. [Source: J. R. Kelley, J. C. McKenzie, and A. W. Evans, Business Mathematics (Boston: Houghton Mifflin, 1982), p. 242. Reprinted by permission. Odee Co. Publisher, Dallas.]

1. The principal ($800.00) is the amount of the debt. It is the amount of the credit transaction.
2. The rate (15 percent) expresses the value paid for use of the borrowed money. It is usually stated in annual or yearly terms.
3. The time (60 days) is the period for which the money is borrowed.
4. The date (June 6) is the date the note was issued.
5. The maturity date (August 5) is the day the principal and interest are due. It is often called the due date.
6. The maker (The Richland Company) is the individual or company issuing the note and borrowing the money.
7. The payee (The Shelton Company) is the individual or company extending the credit.

rate plus 2 percent. Firms with questionable credit ratings may have to pay the prime rate plus 4 percent. Of course, if the banker feels loan repayment may be a problem, the borrower's loan application may be rejected.

Banks generally offer short-term loans through promissory notes, a line of credit, or a revolving credit agreement. *Promissory notes* that are written to banks are similar to those discussed in the last section. Although repayment terms may extend to one year, most promissory notes specify repayment periods of 60 to 180 days.

The *line of credit*—in essence, a prearranged short-term loan—is discussed in Chapter 17. A bank that offers a line of credit may require that a *compensating balance* be kept on deposit at the bank. This balance may be as much as 20 percent of the line-of-credit amount. Assume that Chemical Bank in New York requires a 20 percent compensating balance on short-term loans. If you borrow $20,000, at least $4,000 of the loan amount must be kept on deposit at the bank. In this situation, the actual interest rate you must pay on the original $20,000 loan increases because you have the use of only $16,000. The bank may also require that every commercial borrower *clean up* (pay off completely) its line of credit at least once each year and not use it again for a period of 30 to 60 days. This second requirement ensures that the line of credit is used only to meet short-term needs and that it doesn't gradually become a source of long-term financing.

Even with a line of credit, a firm may not be able to borrow on short notice if the bank does not have sufficient funds available. For this reason, some firms prefer a **revolving credit agreement,** which is a guaranteed line of credit. Under this type of agreement, the bank guarantees that the money will be available when the borrower needs it. In return for the guarantee, the bank charges a commitment fee ranging from 0.25 to 1.0 percent of the *unused* portion of the revolving credit. The usual interest is charged for the portion that *is* borrowed.

revolving credit agreement *a guaranteed line of credit*

Commercial Paper   **Commercial paper** is short-term promissory notes issued by large corporations. Commercial paper is secured only by the reputation of the issuing firm; no collateral is involved. It is usually issued in large denominations, ranging from $5,000 to $100,000. Corporations issuing commercial paper pay interest rates slightly below those charged by commercial banks. Thus, issuing commercial paper is cheaper than getting short-term financing from a bank.

commercial paper   *short-term promissory notes issued by large corporations*

Large firms with excellent credit reputations can quickly raise large sums of money in this way. General Motors Acceptance Corporation (GMAC), for example, may issue commercial paper totaling millions of dollars. However, commercial paper is not without risks. If the issuing corporation later has severe financial problems, it may not be able to repay the promised amounts. The Penn Central Railroad defaulted on commercial paper worth $80 million when it filed for bankruptcy.

Commercial Drafts   A **commercial draft** is a written order requiring a customer (the *drawee*) to pay a specified sum of money to a supplier (the *drawer*) for goods or services. It is often used when the supplier is unsure about the customer's credit standing. Suppose, for example, that Martin Manufacturing sold merchandise valued at $9,800 to Barnes Wholesale Supply and required that Barnes sign a commercial draft. The draft (see Figure 18.7) would be completed as follows:

commercial draft   *a written order requiring a customer (the* drawee) *to pay a specified sum of money to a supplier (the* drawer) *for goods or services*

1. The draft form is filled out by the drawer (Martin Manufacturing). The draft contains the purchase price, interest rate, if any, and maturity date.
2. The draft is sent by the drawer to the drawee (Barnes Wholesale Supply).
3. If the information contained in the draft is correct and the merchandise has been received, the drawee marks the draft "Accepted" and signs it.
4. The customer returns the draft to the drawer. Now the drawer may (a) hold the draft until maturity, (b) discount the draft at its bank, or (c) use the draft as collateral for a loan.

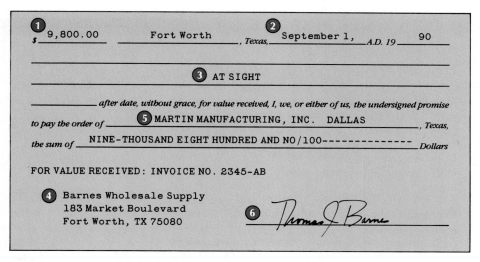

FIGURE 18.7
A Commercial Draft
A commercial draft is a written order requiring a customer to pay a specified sum of money to a supplier for goods or services.

1. The dollar amount and, in this case, the invoice amount
2. The date the draft was issued
3. This is a sight draft; no date is specified for payment
4. The customer's (or drawee's) address
5. The supplier (or drawer), the firm that sold the merchandise to Barnes Wholesale Supply
6. The signature of the drawee or of and authorized officer of the firm

In this case, the draft is similar to an ordinary check with one exception: The draft is filled out by the seller and not the buyer. A *sight draft* is a commercial draft that is payable on demand—whenever the drawer wishes to collect. A *time draft* is a commercial draft on which a payment date is specified. Like promissory notes, drafts are negotiable instruments that may be discounted or used as collateral for a loan. They are legally enforceable.

Sources of Secured Short-Term Financing

Financially secure firms prefer to save collateral for long-term borrowing needs. Yet, if a business cannot obtain enough capital via unsecured short-term financing, it must put up collateral to obtain the additional financing it needs. Almost any asset can serve as collateral. However, *inventories* and *accounts receivable* are the assets that are most commonly used for short-term financing.

Loans Secured by Inventory   Normally, *marketing intermediaries* and producers have large amounts of money invested in finished goods or merchandise inventories. In addition, producers carry raw materials and work-in-process inventories. All three types of inventory may be pledged as collateral for short-term loans. However, lenders prefer the much more salable finished goods to the other inventories.

BUSINESS JOURNAL ▰

Commercial Credit Reports

Assume that you are the owner of Mountain-Top Fashions, a small Dallas-based manufacturing company that specializes in women's sportswear. You receive an order for $12,500 worth of merchandise from a retailer in Seattle, Washington. You have never sold to this retailer before, and you have no idea if the customer will pay for the merchandise if you sell on a credit basis. How would you obtain information about the creditworthiness of the Seattle firm?

To answer this question, most business owners would turn to the Dun & Bradstreet Corp., the nation's largest source of commercial credit information. In fact, Dun & Bradstreet (known as D&B in the business community) maintains credit information on 9.5 million U.S. companies. And D&B receives over 90,000 requests each day for credit information to help business firms decide whether to lend money to another company or sell to another company on credit. With more than 90 percent of the market, D&B has a virtual monopoly in the commercial credit-information industry.

WHAT TYPE OF INFORMATION IS AVAILABLE FROM D&B?

On the basis of the information contained in a D&B credit report, a business can better judge whether a customer will pay promptly. The most easily accessible source of information is the *Dun & Bradstreet Reference Book*. Information is given on a firm's line of business, net worth, and credit rating. The current D&B credit rating system is illustrated at right. A firm with a CC2 rating has estimated financial strength, based on net worth, of $75,000 to $125,000, with an overall composite credit rating of "Good."

In addition to this type of information, it is also possible to obtain a more extensive credit report on potential commercial customers. D&B's consolidated report includes all of the above plus additional information on a firm's sales, assets, debts, bank balances, and facts relating to whether the firm is behind on its bills or not. Finally, there is a section on the company's history and background information on the officers of the company.

Composite Credit Appraisal

High	Good	Fair	Limited
1	2	3	4

Estimated Financial Strength

5A	Over	$50,000,000
4A	$10,000,000 to	50,000,000
3A	1,000,000 to	10,000,000
2A	750,000 to	1,000,000
1A	500,000 to	750,000
BA	300,000 to	500,000
BB	200,000 to	300,000
CB	125,000 to	200,000
CC	75,000 to	125,000
DC	50,000 to	75,000
DD	35,000 to	50,000
EE	20,000 to	35,000
FF	10,000 to	20,000
GG	5,000 to	10,000
HH	Up to	5,000

A WORD OF CAUTION

Users sometimes complain that the information contained in D&B reports is inaccurate, outdated, or incomplete. And since a decision to sell to a customer on credit may be based entirely on the information contained in a D&B report, inaccuracies can have serious repercussions. The company counters that some mistakes are inevitable because D&B maintains credit information on 9.5 million businesses. D&B insists that its theme is "Quality First."

Key to Dun & Bradstreet ratings used by permission. Copyright Dun & Bradstreet.

Based on information from Johnnie L. Roberts, "Dun's Credit Reports, Vital Tool of Business Can Be Off the Mark," *Wall Street Journal*, October 5, 1989, p. A1+; "Its Many Services Let D&B Influence an Array of U.S. Business Decisions," *Wall Street Journal*, October 5, 1989, p. A16; Stanley B. Block and Geoffrey A. Hirt, *Foundations of Financial Management* (Homewood, Ill.: Irwin, 1989), p. 190; and *Moody's Handbook of Common Stocks*, Fall 1989.

A lender may insist that inventory used as collateral be stored in a public warehouse. In such a case, the receipt issued by the warehouse is retained by the lender. Without this receipt, the public warehouse will not release the merchandise. The lender releases the warehouse receipt—and the merchandise—to the borrower when the borrowed money is repaid. In addition to the interest on the loan, the borrower must also pay for storage in the public warehouse. As a result, this type of loan is more expensive than an unsecured loan.

floor planning *a method of financing where the title to merchandise is given to lenders in return for short-term financing*

A special type of secured financing called *floor planning* is used by automobile, furniture, and appliance dealers. **Floor planning** is a method of financing where the title to merchandise is given to lenders in return for short-term financing. The major difference between floor planning and other types of secured short-term financing is that the borrower maintains control of the inventory. As merchandise is sold, the borrower repays the lender a portion of the loan. To ensure that the lender is repaid a portion of the loan when the merchandise is sold, the lender will occasionally check to ensure that the collateral is still in the borrower's possession.

accounts receivable *amounts that are owed to a firm by its customers*

Loans Secured by Receivables   **Accounts receivable** are amounts that are owed to a firm by its customers. They arise primarily from trade credit and are usually due in less than sixty days. It is possible for a firm to pledge its accounts receivable as collateral to obtain short-term financing. A lender may advance 70 to 80 percent of the dollar amount of the receivables. First, however, it conducts a thorough investigation to determine the *quality* of the receivables. (The quality of the receivables is the credit standing of the firm's customers.) If a favorable determination is made, the loan is approved. Then whenever the borrowing firm collects from a customer whose account has been pledged as collateral, the money must be turned over to the lender as partial repayment of the loan. An alternative approach is to notify the borrower's credit customers to make their payments directly to the lender. This approach, often called the *notification plan,* may raise questions about the borrowing firm's financial health and cause customers to take their business elsewhere.

Factoring Accounts Receivable

factor *a firm that specializes in buying other firms' accounts receivable*

Accounts receivable may be used in one other way to help raise short-term capital: They can be sold to a factoring company (or factor). **A factor** is a firm that specializes in buying other firms' accounts receivable. The factor buys the accounts receivable for less than their face value, but it collects the full dollar amount when each account is due. The factor's profit is thus the difference between the face value of the accounts receivable and what the factor has paid for them.

Even though the selling firm gets less than face value for its accounts receivable, it does receive needed cash immediately. Moreover, it has shifted both the task of collecting and the risk of nonpayment to the factor, which now owns the receivables. Generally, customers whose accounts receivable have been factored are given instructions to make their payments directly to the factor.

TABLE 18.1 *Comparison of Short-Term Financing Methods*

Type of Financing	Cost	Repayment Period	Businesses That May Use It	Comments
Trade credit	Low, if any	30 to 90 days	All businesses	Usually no finance charge
Promissory note	Moderate	1 year or less	All businesses	Usually unsecured but requires legal document; issued by borrower
Unsecured bank loan	Moderate	1 year or less	All businesses	A line of credit or revolving credit agreement may be used.
Commercial paper	Moderate	1 year or less	Large corporations with high credit ratings	Available only to large firms
Commercial draft	Moderate	1 year or less	Manufacturers and wholesalers	Issued by seller and accepted by buyer; has value and can be sold
Secured loan	High	1 year or less	Firms with questionable credit ratings	Inventory may have to be stored in a public warehouse.
Factoring	High	None	Firms that have large numbers of credit customers	Accounts receivable are sold to a factor.

Cost Comparisons

Table 18.1 compares the various types of short-term financing. As you can see, trade credit is the least expensive. Generally, the less favorable a firm's credit rating, the more likely that it will have to use a higher-cost means of financing. Factoring of accounts receivable is the highest-cost method shown.

For many purposes, short-term financing suits a firm's needs perfectly. In other cases, however, some means of long-term financing may be more appropriate.

Sources of Long-Term Financing

Sources of long-term financing vary with the size and type of business. If the business is a sole proprietorship or partnership, equity capital is acquired by the business when the owner or owners invest money in the business. For corporations, equity-financing options include the sale of stock and the use of profits not distributed to owners. The available debt-financing options are the sale of corporate bonds and long-term loans.

Learning Objective 4
Evaluate the advantages and disadvantages of equity financing and debt financing from the corporation's standpoint

Equity Financing

Some equity capital is used to start every business—sole proprietorship, partnership, or corporation. In the case of corporations, equity capital is provided by stockholders who buy shares in the company.

There are at least two reasons why equity financing is attractive to large corporations. First, the corporation need not repay money obtained from the sale of stock, and it need not repurchase the shares of stock at a later date. Thus equity financing does not have to be repaid. Occasionally a corporation buys its own stock, but only because such an investment is in its own best interest. In 1989 Mapco, Inc.—a large oil, gas, and energy company—purchased thousands of shares of its own stock with uninvested profits. The firm's top management believed the purchase was the best investment available at that particular time.

A second advantage of equity financing is that a corporation is under no legal obligation to pay dividends to stockholders. A **dividend** is a distribution of earnings to the stockholders of a corporation. Investors purchase the shares of stock of many corporations primarily for the dividends they pay. However, for any reason (if a company has a bad year, for example), the board of directors can vote to omit dividend payments. Earnings are then retained for use in funding business operations. Thus a corporation need not even pay for the use of equity capital. Of course, the corporate management may hear from unhappy stockholders if expected dividends are omitted too frequently.

There are two types of stock: common and preferred. (A common-stock certificate for Houghton Mifflin Company is shown in Figure 18.8.) Each type has advantages and drawbacks as a means of long-term financing.

dividend   *a distribution of earnings to the stockholders of a corporation*

Kohlberg Kravis Roberts arranged for financing, including $350 in equity, to purchase the Duracell company. Once acquired, KKR allowed existing Duracell management to continue to run the company. Pictured here is Duracell President C. Robert Kidder, who feels that the takeover was in the best interests of the company.

FIGURE 18.8
Common Stock
Capital is provided to the company by stockholders when they purchase shares of stock (equity) in the company. (Source: Used with permission of Houghton Mifflin Company.)

common stock   *stock whose owners may vote on corporate matters, but whose claims on profit and assets are subordinate to the claims of others*

pre-emptive rights   *the rights of current stockholders to purchase any new stock that the corporation issues before it is sold to the general public*

preferred stock   *stock whose owners usually do not have voting rights, but whose claims on profits and assets have precedence over those of common-stock owners*

Common Stock   A share of **common stock** represents the most basic form of corporate ownership: Owners may vote on corporate matters, but their claims on profits and assets are subordinate to those of preferred-stock owners. In return for the financing provided by selling common stock, management must make certain concessions to stockholders that may restrict or change corporate policies. By law, every corporation must hold an annual meeting, at which the holders of common stock may vote for directors and approve (or disapprove) major corporate actions. Among such actions are (1) amendments to the corporate charter or bylaws, (2) the sale of certain assets, (3) mergers, (4) the issuing of preferred stock or bonds, and (5) changes in the amount of common stock issued.

Many states require that a provision for pre-emptive rights be included in the charter of every corporation. **Pre-emptive rights** are the rights of current stockholders to purchase any new stock that the corporation issues before it is sold to the general public. By exercising their pre-emptive rights, stockholders are able to maintain their current proportion of ownership of the corporation. This may be important when the corporation is a small one and management control is a matter of concern to stockholders.

Money that is acquired through the sale of common stock is thus essentially cost-free, but few investors will buy common stock if they cannot foresee some return on their investment.

Preferred Stock   As noted in Chapter 3, the owners of **preferred stock** usually do not have voting rights, but their claims on profit and assets precede those of common-stock owners. Thus holders of preferred stock must receive their dividends before holders of common stock are paid, provided dividends are distributed at all. Moreover, they have first claim (after creditors) on corporate assets if the firm is dissolved or declares bankruptcy. Even so, like common stock, preferred stock does not represent a debt that must be legally repaid.

The dividend to be paid on a share of preferred stock is known before the stock is purchased. It is stated, on the stock certificate, either as a percentage of the par value of the stock or as an amount of money. The **par value** of a stock is an assigned (and often arbitrary) dollar value that is printed on the stock certificate. For example, Seaside Productions issued 8½ percent preferred stock with a par value of $50. The annual dividend amount is $4.25 per share (8.5 percent × $50 par value = $4.25 annual dividend).

A corporation usually issues one type of common stock, but it may issue many types of preferred stock with varying dividends or dividend rates. For example, Ohio Edison has one common-stock issue but four preferred-stock issues with different dividend amounts for each type of preferred stock.

On occasion, a corporation may decide to call in or buy back an issue of preferred stock when management believes it can issue new preferred stock at a lower dividend rate—or possibly common stock with no specified dividend. When this occurs, management has two options. First, they can buy shares in the market—just like another investor purchases shares of the preferred-stock issue. Second, practically all preferred stock is *callable* at the option of the corporation; that is, the corporation can buy back the stock. When the corporation exercises a call provision, the investor usually receives a call premium. A **call premium** is a dollar amount over par value that the corporation has to pay an investor for redeeming either preferred stock or a corporate bond. When considering the two options, management will naturally obtain the preferred stock in the less costly way.

Added Features for Preferred-Stock Issues

To make their preferred stock particularly attractive to investors, some corporations include cumulative, participating, and convertible features in various issues.

Cumulative preferred stock is preferred stock on which any unpaid dividends accumulate and must be paid before any cash dividend is paid to the holders of common stock. Suppose the Bartlett-Jones Corporation has issued cumulative preferred stock that pays $4 per year. In 1990 Bartlett-Jones is faced with a substantial loss, and the board of directors votes to omit dividends on both common and preferred stock. In 1991, however, the board of directors decides that profits are high enough to pay the required preferred dividend, as well as a $2-per-share dividend on its common stock. The holders of the cumulative preferred stock must first receive $8 per share ($4 for 1990 and $4 for 1991). Then and only then, holders of common stock can receive the $2-per-share dividend declared for 1991.

Participating preferred stock is preferred stock whose owners share in the corporation's earnings, along with the owners of common stock.

par value *an assigned (and often arbitrary) dollar value printed on the face of a stock certificate*

call premium *the dollar amount over par value that the corporation has to pay an investor for redeeming either preferred stock or a corporate bond*

cumulative preferred stock *preferred stock on which any unpaid dividends accumulate and must be paid before any cash dividend is paid to the holders of common stock*

participating preferred stock *preferred stock whose owners share in the corporation's earnings, along with the owners of common stock*

BUSINESS JOURNAL

Junk Bonds, Takeovers, and Mergers

Since 1980, junk bonds have returned 14 percent on the average—well above the yield on high-grade corporate bonds or U.S. Treasury bonds. As a result, large numbers of investors bought these bonds in record numbers. In 1990 the total value of outstanding junk bonds was estimated to be more than $200 billion. As the name implies, junk bonds have proved to be one of the most controversial financial investments of this era.

Most investors rely on two financial services— Standard & Poor's Reports and Moody's Investors Service, Inc.—to provide ratings for corporate bonds. Standard & Poor's bond ratings range from *AAA* (the highest) to *D* (the lowest). Moody's bond ratings range from *Aaa* (the highest) to *C* (the lowest). According to financial analysts, a junk bond is a high-yield bond issued by a corporation rated *BBB* by Standard & Poor's or *Baa* by Moody's. In both cases, the ratings stand for "Speculative." Because of the speculative nature of the junk bonds, the corporation issuing them has to increase the interest rate to attract investors.

The specific reasons for the lower bond ratings and higher interest rates vary. The corporation may have too much long-term debt, or its earnings may be low. Changing economic conditions may make payment of interest or repayment of the principal doubtful. Finally, junk bonds could have been sold to raise the necessary capital to buy out another company.

In a corporate takeover, the buyer (another company or a group of investors) with relatively little cash targets and takes over a corporate giant with money raised (with junk bonds) by investment bankers on Wall Street. The new owners are happy because they have acquired a major corporation with little, if any, cash outlay. The junk bondholders

are happy because they are able to obtain high interest rates on their investment. Finally, the investment bankers are happy because they receive a fat commission for putting the deal together. On the other side, usually the corporate managers and a large number of employees of the acquired firm are fired. (This fact may explain why the terms *unfriendly* and *hostile* are often used to portray takeovers.) And the company is forced to pay large amounts of interest on the junk bonds that were issued to acquire the company. As a result, dividends are reduced or omitted, and stockholders are left with stock in a company that is heavily in debt.

Some major corporations that have sold junk bonds—Resorts International, Federated Department Stores, Southland, and Union Carbide, to name a few of an increasing number of troubled companies—have already or are dangerously close to defaulting on interest payments to bondholders. As a result, Wall Street analysts, corporate management teams, and investors are now taking a more conservative look at junk-bond issues. While the default rate for the past three years was only 3 percent, there are predictions that it could climb to 15 percent during the 1990s. As one financial analyst points out, the future doesn't look bright for corporations that already have junk-bond financing or for companies that want to issue junk bonds in the 1990s.

Based on information from Christopher Farrell, "The Bills Are Coming Due," *Business Week*, September 11, 1989, pp. 84–87+; Susan E. Kuhn, "Junk: The Weak and the Strong," *Fortune*, October 23, 1989, p. 17; C. David Chase, *Chase Global Investment Almanac* (Homewood, Ill.: Chase Global Data & Research, Inc., 1989), pp. 199–206; and Anthony Bianco, "Power on Wall Street," *Business Week*, July 7, 1986, p. 56.

Here's how it works: First, the required dividend is paid to holders of the preferred stock. Then a stated dividend, usually equal to the dividend amount paid to preferred stockholders, is paid to the common stockholders. Finally, any remaining earnings that are available for distribution are shared by both preferred and common stockholders.

Convertible preferred stock is preferred stock that can be exchanged *at the stockholder's option* for a specified number of shares of common

convertible preferred stock *preferred stock that may be exchanged at the stockholder's option for a specified number of shares of common stock*

stock. This conversion feature provides the investor with the safety of preferred stock and the hope of greater speculative gain through conversion to common stock.

Retained Earnings Most large corporations distribute only a portion of their after-tax earnings to shareholders. The remainder, the portion of a corporation's profits that is not distributed to stockholders, is called **retained earnings.** Retained earnings are reinvested in the business. Because they are undistributed profits, they are considered a form of equity financing.

> **retained earnings** *the portion of a business's profits that is not distributed to stockholders*

Retained earnings represent a large pool of potential equity financing that does not have to be repaid. The amount of a firm's earnings that is to be retained in any year is determined by corporate management and approved by the board of directors. For a large corporation, retained earnings can amount to a hefty bit of financing. For example, in 1988 the total amount of retained earnings for General Motors was in excess of $28 billion.[2] And for Exxon Corporation, 1988 retained earnings were almost $42 billion.[3]

Most small and growing corporations pay no cash dividend—or a very small dividend—to their shareholders. All or most earnings are reinvested in the business. Stockholders don't actually lose because of this. Reinvestment tends to increase the value of their stock while it provides essentially cost-free financing. More mature corporations may distribute 40 to 60 percent of their after-tax profits as dividends. Utility companies and other corporations with very stable earnings often pay out as much as 80 to 90 percent of what they earn.

Debt Financing

For a small business, long-term debt financing is generally limited to loans. Large corporations have the additional option of issuing corporate bonds.

Corporate Bonds A **corporate bond** is a corporation's written pledge that it will repay a specified amount of money, with interest. Figure 18.9 shows a corporate bond for Baltimore Gas and Electric Company. Note that it includes the interest rate and the maturity date. The **maturity date** is the date on which the corporation is to repay the borrowed money. It also has spaces for the amount of the bond and the bond owner's name.

> **corporate bond** *a corporation's written pledge that it will repay a specified amount of money, with interest*

> **maturity date** *the date on which the corporation is to repay the borrowed money*

Large corporations issue bonds in denominations of from $1,000 to $50,000. The total face value of all the bonds in an issue usually runs into the millions of dollars. An individual or firm buys a bond generally through a securities broker. Between the time of purchase and the maturity date, the corporation pays interest to the bond owner—usually every six months—at the stated rate. The method used to pay bondholders their interest depends on whether they own registered or coupon bonds. A **registered bond** is a bond that is registered in the owner's name by the issuing company. Interest checks for registered bonds are mailed directly to the bondholder of record. When a registered bond is sold, it must be

> **registered bond** *a bond that is registered in the owner's name by the issuing company*

FIGURE 18.9
A Corporate Bond
A corporate bond is a corporation's written pledge that it will repay on the date of maturity a specified amount of money, with interest. (Source: Used with permission of Baltimore Gas and Electric Company.)

coupon bond   *a bond whose ownership is not registered by the issuing company*

endorsed by the seller before ownership can be transferred on the company books. A **coupon bond,** sometimes called a *bearer bond,* is a bond whose ownership is not registered by the issuing company. To collect interest on a coupon bond, bondholders must clip a coupon and then redeem it by following procedures outlined by the issuer. At the maturity date, the bond owner returns the bond to the corporation and receives cash equaling its face value. Coupon bonds are less secure than registered bonds. If coupon bonds are lost or stolen, interest may be collected and the bond may be redeemed by anyone who finds it. For this reason, most corporate bonds are registered.

Maturity dates for bonds generally range from fifteen to forty years after the date of issue. In the event that the interest is not paid or the firm becomes insolvent, bond owners' claims on the assets of the corporation take precedence over stockholders'. Some bonds are callable before the maturity date. For these bonds, the corporation usually pays the bond owner a call premium. The amount of the premium is specified, along with other provisions, in the bond indenture. The **bond indenture** is a legal document that details all the conditions relating to a bond issue.

bond indenture   *a legal document that details all the conditions relating to a bond issue*

From the corporation's standpoint, financing through a bond issue differs considerably from equity financing. Interest must be paid periodically, and in the eyes of the Internal Revenue Service, interest is a tax-deductible business expense. Furthermore, bonds must be redeemed for their face value at maturity. If the corporation defaults on (does not pay) either of these payments, owners of bonds could force it into bankruptcy.

A corporation may use one of three methods to ensure that it has sufficient funds available to redeem a bond issue. First, it can issue the bonds as **serial bonds,** which are bonds of a single issue that mature on different dates. For example, Seaside Productions used a twenty-five-year $50-million bond issue to finance its expansion. None of the bonds matures during the first fifteen years. Thereafter, 10 percent of the bonds mature each year, until all the bonds are retired at the end of the twenty-fifth year. Second, the corporation can establish a sinking fund. A **sinking fund** is a sum of money to which deposits are made each year for the purpose of redeeming a bond issue. Third, a corporation can pay off an old bond issue by selling new bonds. Although this may appear to perpetuate the corporation's long-term debt, a number of utility companies and railroads have used this repayment method.

A corporation that issues bonds must also appoint a **trustee,** which is an independent firm or individual that acts as the bond owners' representative. A trustee's duties are most often handled by a commercial bank or other large financial institution. The corporation must report to the trustee periodically regarding its ability to make interest payments and eventually redeem the bonds. In turn, the trustee transmits this information to the bond owners, along with its own evaluation of the corporation's ability to pay.

Most corporate bonds are debenture bonds. A **debenture bond** is a bond that is backed only by the reputation of the issuing corporation. To make its bonds more appealing to investors, however, a corporation may issue mortgage bonds. A **mortgage bond** is a corporate bond that is secured by various assets of the issuing firm. Or the corporation can issue convertible bonds. A **convertible bond** can be exchanged, at the owner's

serial bonds   *bonds of a single issue that mature on different dates*

sinking fund   *a sum of money to which deposits are made each year for the purpose of redeeming a bond issue*

trustee   *an independent firm or individual that acts as the bond owners' representative*

debenture bond   *a bond backed only by the reputation of the issuing corporation*

mortgage bond   *a corporate bond that is secured by various assets of the issuing firm*

convertible bond   *a bond that can be exchanged, at the owner's option, for a specified number of shares of the corporation's common stock*

The construction of office buildings, shopping malls, and hospitals often requires debt financing. For corporations, debt financing options include corporate bonds and long-term loans. This is the Courvoisier Center in Miami, one of many projects undertaken by the Turner Corporation in its plan of geographical expansion.

option, for a specified number of shares of the corporation's common stock. The corporation can gain in two ways by issuing convertible bonds. They usually carry a lower interest rate than nonconvertible bonds. And once a bond owner converts a bond to common stock, the corporation no longer has to redeem it.

Long-Term Loans Many businesses finance their long-range activities with loans from commercial banks, insurance companies, pension funds, and other financial institutions. Manufacturers and suppliers of heavy equipment and machinery may also provide long-term financing by granting extended credit terms to their customers.

term-loan agreement *a promissory note that requires a borrower to repay a loan in monthly, quarterly, semiannual, or annual installments*

When the loan repayment period is longer than one year, the borrower must sign a term-loan agreement. A **term-loan agreement** is a promissory note that requires a borrower to repay a loan in monthly, quarterly, semiannual, or annual installments.

Long-term business loans are normally repaid in three to seven years. Although they may occasionally be unsecured, in most cases the lender requires some type of collateral. Acceptable collateral includes real estate, machinery, and equipment. Lenders may also require that borrowers maintain a minimum amount of working capital. The interest rate and other specific terms are often based on such factors as the reasons for borrowing, the borrowing firm's credit rating, and the collateral.

Cost Comparisons

Table 18.2 compares the different types of equity and long-term debt financing. Obviously, the least expensive type of financing is through an issue of common stock. The most expensive is a long-term loan.

TABLE 18.2 *Comparison of Long-Term Financing Methods*

Type of Financing	Repayment?	Repayment Period	Interest/Dividend Rate	Businesses That May Use It
Equity				
1. Common stock	No	None	Dividends not required	All corporations that sell stock to investors
2. Preferred stock	No	None	Dividends not required but must be paid before common stockholders receive any dividends	Larger corporations that have an established investor base of common stockholders
Debt				
1. Corporate bond	Yes	Usually 15 to 40 years	Interest rates between 8% and 15%, depending on economic conditions and the risks involved	Larger corporations that investors trust
2. Long-term loan	Yes	Usually 3 to 7 years (up to 15 years)	Interest rates between 10% and 17%, depending on economic conditions and the risks involved	All firms that can meet the lender's repayment and collateral requirements

A Word About the Uses of Funds

Learning Objective 5
Grasp the importance of using funds effectively

In this chapter we have mentioned a variety of business uses of funds. They range from the payment of recurring expenses, such as rent, wages, and the cost of raw materials, to the payment of such one-time costs as plant expansions and mergers. In general, a business uses funds to pay for the resources it needs to produce and market its products. Even the interest a business pays is really the cost of a resource—money.

The effective use of finances, as we have noted, is an important function of financial management. To some extent, financial management can be viewed as a two-sided problem. On one side, the uses of funds often dictate the type or types of financing that are needed by a business. On the other side, the activities that a business can undertake are determined by the type or types of financing that are available. Financial managers must ensure that funds are available when needed, that they are obtained at the lowest possible cost, and that they are used as efficiently as possible. This responsibility may involve them in the purchasing practices of various operating departments within a firm. And, finally, financial managers must ensure that funds are available for the repayment of debts in accordance with lenders' financing terms. Prompt repayment is essential to protect the firm's credit rating and its ability to obtain financing in the future.

CHAPTER REVIEW

Summary

Financial management consists of those activities that are concerned with obtaining money and using it effectively. Short-term financing is money that will be used for one year or less. Although there are many short-term needs, cash flow and inventory are two problems that deserve special attention. Long-term financing is money that will be used for more than one year. Such financing may be required for starting a business, expansion, new-product development, or replacement of production facilities. Proper financial management can ensure that money is available when it is needed and that it is used efficiently, in keeping with organizational goals.

A financial plan begins with the organization's objectives. Next these objectives are "translated" into budgets that detail expected income and expenses. From these budgets, which may be combined into an overall cash budget, the financial manager determines what funding will be needed and where it may be obtained. The four principal sources of financing are sales revenue, equity capital (derived from the sale of

common and preferred stock), debt capital, and proceeds from the sale of assets. Once the needed funds have been obtained, the financial manager is responsible for ensuring that they are properly used. This is accomplished through a system of monitoring and evaluating the firm's financial activities.

Most short-term financing is unsecured. That is, no collateral is required. Sources of unsecured short-term financing include trade credit, promissory notes issued to suppliers, unsecured bank loans, commercial paper, and commercial drafts. Sources of secured short-term financing include loans that are secured by inventory or accounts receivable and the outright sale of receivables to factors. Trade credit is the least expensive source of short-term financing; there is no interest charge. The cost of financing through other sources generally depends on the source and on the credit rating of the firm that requires the financing. Factoring is generally the most expensive approach.

Long-term financing may be obtained as equity capital or debt capital. For a corporation, equity capital is obtained by selling either common or preferred stock. Common stock is voting stock; holders of common stock elect the corporation's directors and must approve equity funding plans. Holders of preferred stock do not vote on corporate matters, but they must be paid a specified dividend before holders of common stock are paid any dividends. Another source of equity funding is retained earnings, which are undistributed earnings that are reinvested in the corporation.

Sources of long-term debt financing are the sale of corporate bonds and long-term loans. Money that is realized from the sale of bonds must be repaid when the bonds mature. In addition, interest must be paid on that money from the time the bonds are sold until maturity. Bonds may mature in up to forty years, but long-term loans are generally repaid in three to seven years. The rate of loan interest usually depends on the financial status of the borrower, the reason for borrowing, and the kind of collateral that is pledged to back up the loan.

To a great extent, firms are financed through the investments of individuals—money that people have deposited in banks or have used to purchase stocks and bonds. In the next chapter, we look at securities markets and how they help people invest their money in business.

Key Terms

You should now be able to define and give an example relevant to each of the following terms:

financial management	accounts receivable
short-term financing	factor
cash flow	dividend
long-term financing	common stock
financial plan	pre-emptive rights
budget	preferred stock
zero-base budgeting	par value
equity capital	call premium
debt capital	cumulative preferred stock
unsecured financing	participating preferred stock
trade credit	convertible preferred stock
promissory note	retained earnings
prime interest rate	corporate bond
revolving credit agreement	maturity date
commercial paper	registered bond
commercial draft	
floor planning	

coupon bond	debenture bond
bond indenture	mortgage bond
serial bonds	convertible bond
sinking fund	term-loan agreement
trustee	

Questions and Exercises

Review Questions

1. How is short-term financing different from long-term financing? Give two business uses of each of these types of financing.
2. What is the function of budgets in financial planning?
3. What is zero-base budgeting? How does it differ from the traditional concept of budgeting?
4. How does a financial manager monitor and evaluate a firm's financing?
5. What are the four general sources of financing?
6. How is unsecured financing different from secured financing?
7. How important is trade credit as a source of short-term financing? How does trade credit differ from other kinds of short-term financing?
8. What is the difference between a line of credit and a revolving credit agreement?
9. Distinguish between a commercial draft and a promissory note. Why would a supplier require either of these?
10. Explain how factoring works. Of what benefit is factoring to a firm that sells its receivables?
11. What are the advantages of financing through the sale of stock? What are pre-emptive rights?
12. Explain each of the following features of preferred stock:
   a. The cumulative feature
   b. The participating feature
   c. The convertible feature
13. Where do a corporation's retained earnings come from? What are the advantages of this type of financing?
14. Describe the three methods used to ensure that funds are available to redeem corporate bonds at maturity.

Discussion Questions

1. Drexel Burnham Lambert helped finance many of the corporate takeovers during the 1980s. By 1986 it was the most profitable firm on Wall Street. Then in 1990 the firm filed for bankruptcy. What factors led to the decline of Drexel Burnham Lambert?

2. With regard to corporate merger activity, some experts have labeled the 1980s as a period of excess and greed. Do you agree? Justify your answer.

3. What does a financial manager do? How can she or he monitor a firm's financial success?

4. Why would a supplier offer both trade credit and cash discounts to its customers?

5. In what circumstances might a large corporation sell stock rather than bonds to obtain long-term financing? In what circumstances would it sell bonds rather than stock?

6. Why would a lender offer unsecured loans when it could demand collateral?

7. If you were the financial manager of Newton's Clothing Store, what would you do with the excess cash that the firm expects to have in the second and fourth quarters? (See Figure 18.4.)

Exercises

1. Suppose you are responsible for setting a bank's interest rates. Your prime rate is 9 percent. Determine the interest rate you would charge a new, medium-sized firm for:
   a. A six-month unsecured loan
   b. Loans on a revolving credit agreement (Also specify the commitment fee.)
   c. A three-month loan secured by the firm's accounts receivable
   d. A five-year loan secured by the firm's land and buildings
   Explain briefly how you arrived at each interest rate.

2. You want to borrow funds to finance next year's college expenses. Set up a budget showing your expected income and expenses, and determine how much money you will need to borrow. Then outline a plan for repaying the borrowed funds. Provide enough detail to convince your financing source to advance you the money.

Case 18.1

T. Boone Pickens and Mesa Limited Partnership

As head of Mesa Limited Partnership—an independent Texas oil firm—T. Boone Pickens, Jr. was often invited to join other chief executive officers from much larger firms at social and sporting events. The opinion he formed of those "Good Ol' Boys," as he called them,

was less than flattering. According to Pickens, he soon realized that "These guys really aren't that smart."* They had little invested in the companies they ran; thus, their decisions involved no personal financial risk. They were, he thought, interested mainly in themselves—in accumulating power, prestige, salaries, and perks (special benefits like company cars, yachts, and hunting lodges): "I also had gotten a look at their ballroom-size egos and saw how little they knew about their own companies. I decided that we could outthink, outwork, and outfox the big boys, and that would beat [having] all the money in the world."†

When Pickens finally did try to "outfox the big boys," however, he did it for the money, because that's what Mesa needed. In 1983, with oil prices declining, Mesa's income could not support its exploration activities. Because Pickens could not reduce exploration expenses fast enough, the firm began to lose money.

Pickens had earlier concluded that the major oil companies were undervalued; that is, the stock of these companies was selling at much less than its real value—in essence, at bargain prices. He decided to solve Mesa's financial problem by taking advantage of one of these bargains: the stock of Gulf Oil Corporation. If he could buy enough Gulf stock to control the company, then plenty of financing would become available—enough to easily see the much-smaller Mesa through its difficulties. But even if he couldn't take over Gulf Oil, Mesa would surely make a profit on the purchase and the later sale of the undervalued Gulf stock. In either case, Pickens would be solving Mesa's financial problem by taking on some of the "Good Ol' Boys."

Eventually, Pickens and Mesa were able to accumulate 13.2 percent of Gulf Oil's outstanding stock. But the "Good Ol' Boys" at Gulf fought back. Gulf Oil merged with Socal Oil & Refining Co. to form Chevron Corp. The Gulf-Socal merger cut short Pickens' attempt at a takeover of Gulf. But it nonetheless solved Mesa's financial difficulty: Mesa realized a profit of $218 million (after taxes) on its Gulf stock, more than enough to keep it in business.

Since the Gulf takeover attempt, Pickens and Mesa have tried to take over other, larger companies. In some cases, they've won and won big. Two attempted takeovers—of Phillips Petroleum and Unocal—were unsuccessful but very profitable. Together, they netted Mesa a profit of $120 million after taxes.

---

* Quoted in "Boone Speaks," *Fortune*, February 16, 1987, p. 43.

† Ibid., p. 44.

In his latest takeover attempt, Pickens and Mesa tried to take over Koito Manufacturing Company—a Tokyo-based automotive-parts manufacturer. As Koito's largest stockholder, Pickens claims that his goal is to maximize the profits and value of Koito for all stockholders. His goal is consistent with his takeover philosophy: Takeovers are good for stockholders because they force management to get more involved in their companies and become more aggressive. Koito's management, on the other hand, politely turned down Pickens' request for representation on the company's board because they felt that he was involved in a scheme designed to get the company to buy back his shares of Koito stock at an inflated price. According to Koito's management, "If such eminent U.S. companies as Gulf Oil and Phillips Petroleum can turn away Pickens' bids, Koito can snub him too."‡

Questions

1. How would you justify Mesa's attempt to take over Gulf Oil in light of Mesa's financial problems and the decline of the price of crude oil?
2. Pickens cites the separation of ownership and control as one of the basic problems in corporate management today. Do you believe that it is necessary for a corporate manager to own stock in the company for which she or he works? Why?
3. Do you agree with Pickens' philosophy that takeovers are good for stockholders?

Case 18.2

Going Public

To some people who own their own businesses, "going public" may seem like the pot of gold at the end of the rainbow. They sell off millions of tiny pieces of the company they've created, and suddenly that creation makes them very rich. It can work that way, but many business people find that turning the dream into gold is more difficult than it appears.

For one thing, timing is crucial. When the market crashed in October 1987, a number of small companies had completed all the paperwork and legal requirements necessary for going public. But, as a result of

depressed stock prices, many companies like Bytex Corporation—a communication-products firm based in Massachusetts—had to wait to sell their initial public offerings (IPOs). By waiting eighteen months, Bytex raised $10.4 million. According to Bytex's management, the wait was worth it.

Typically, companies selling stock for the first time wait for the stock market to take an upturn and for stocks in general to increase in value. If most stocks already on the market are overpriced, investors usually become hungry for IPOs.

Another factor—the expenses of going public— can keep a company's owners from cashing in on their dreams. A small company going public can expect to pay $100,000 to lawyers, accountants, and printers; the sum is closer to $300,000 for large companies. Even more important are the fees, which range from 2 to 12 percent of the total money raised, that a company must pay to an investment banker.

The investment banker plays a crucial role in taking a company public. As the underwriter, the banker agrees to buy the company's new shares or at least to do its best to find buyers. As advisor, the banker helps the company through the regulatory process and figures out how many shares to offer at what price. As marketer, the banker spreads the word about the company and rouses investors' interest.

To many company executives, the most disturbing part of going public is that they themselves must become public figures. Instead of making decisions on their own and taking responsibility for their own successes and failures, executives of a public company make decisions that are watched by government agencies and that affect thousands of shareholders. Making the company's finances public can be especially traumatic—"like getting undressed in public"—says one newly public figure.

Despite these drawbacks, hundreds of privately owned companies go public every year, raising cash to expand operations and increasing their credibility with other companies and the public at large. The success of some companies keeps the dream alive. For instance, the value of Home Shopping Network's shares rose from 18 to 42 on the day the stock was offered, and went up to 72 within a month. Liz Claiborne was originally offered at 0.75 cents a share but recently sold for $22.50 a share (eight years later).§ Although many company owners are amazed by the amount of paperwork and number of headaches in-

---

‡ Based on information from Kumiko Makihara, "T. Boone's Tokyo Campaign," *Time*, July 10, 1989, p. 45; "Look What Restructuring Can Do," *Fortune*, July 3, 1989, pp. 72–73; "A Back Burner for T. Boone Stake," *U.S. News & World Report*, July 10, 1989, p. 15; and T. Boone Pickens, *Boone* (Boston: Houghton Mifflin, 1987).

---

§ The 0.75 cent price for a share of common stock of Liz Claiborne was adjusted for stock splits.

volved in going public, one survey of executives whose companies had recently gone public found that 93 percent would go through the process again.‖

‖ Based on information from Leslie Helm, "A Wake-Up Call for Initial Public Offerings," *Business Week*, May 8, 1989, pp. 40–41; Charles M. Bartleet, Jr., "Survival of the Few," *Forbes*, June 26, 1989, pp. 266–267; Jill Wechsler, "The Nuts and Bolts of Going Public: How One Company Did It," *Working Woman*, October 1985, p. 56; Jeffrey M. Laderman, "Timing Is Everything When You Go Public," *Business Week*, November 3, 1986, p. 120; and Art Stevens, "A Plunge into the Fishbowl," *Nation's Business*, March 1985, p. 77.‖

Questions

1. A small company going public can expect to pay $100,000 to lawyers, accountants, and printers. In addition, the company will pay from 2 to 12 percent of the total money raised to an investment banker. Is going public worth the expense?
2. In your own words, describe the role of the investment banker as an underwriter, advisor, and marketer in an initial public offering (IPO).
3. Making the company's finances public can be especially traumatic—"like getting undressed in public." Why?

SECURITIES
MARKETS

1 Understand how securities are bought and sold through brokerage firms and securities exchanges

2 Appreciate the need to develop a personal investment plan and know how to draw one up

3 See how four factors—safety, income, growth, and liquidity—link investment planning to the various types of investments

4 Know the advantages and disadvantages of the traditional investment alternatives: savings accounts, stocks, bonds, mutual funds, and real estate

5 Be aware of more speculative investment techniques, including buying on margin, selling short, and trading in options and commodities

6 Be able to use the various sources of financial information, especially newspaper stock quotations and stock indexes

7 Know how federal and state authorities regulate trading in securities

CHAPTER PREVIEW

To begin with, we examine the process of buying and selling securities, noting the functions of securities exchanges and stock brokerage firms. Then we outline the reasons for developing a personal investment plan and point out several factors that should be considered in any potential investment. Next, we present several types of traditional investments. In addition, we consider more speculative investment techniques—that is, investments that can lead to large gains but are also quite risky. We also explain how to obtain and interpret financial information from newspapers, brokerage firms, and periodicals. Finally, we trace the evolution of state and federal laws governing the sale of stocks and bonds.

Merrill Lynch & Company, Inc.

Merrill Lynch & Company, Inc. was originally founded by Charles Merrill, who also founded the Safeway grocery store chain. Mr. Merrill reasoned that you could sell financial securities the same way you sold groceries, but that was fifty years ago. When William A. Schreyer became chairman in 1985, the brokerage business had changed, but Merrill Lynch had not kept up with the changes. The firm, a colossus by even Wall Street standards, generated lots of revenue, but wasn't very profitable. To change Merrill Lynch into a fine-tuned, profitable machine that could compete with any other firm, Schreyer realized that he had to solve two major problems.

First, Schreyer had to find a way to control operating costs. He immediately began to take what some employees called drastic measures. He reduced the total number of Merrill Lynch employees from 48,000 to 41,000. Salaries and bonuses were either frozen or reduced for most of the employees who kept their jobs. Unprofitable or unrelated businesses like real estate and financial information services were sold. A number of unprofitable branch offices were closed. Finally, the firm computerized clerical areas that processed the mountains of paperwork generated by daily activities.

Second, Schreyer had to find a way to make Merrill Lynch more aggressive in order to compete with Drexel Burnham Lambert, Shearson Lehman Hutton and other smaller firms. To solve this problem, Schreyer began a program to make Merrill Lynch number one in the investment banking industry. (Merrill Lynch's investment bankers are responsible for helping corporations raise money by selling new security issues.) He then used Merrill Lynch's retail division (12,000 stockbrokers working at branch offices throughout the United States) to sell the new securities generated by the investment banking division to the firm's six million individual retail customers.

In 1984 profits were $95 million. After the steps to reduce cost and increase investment banking activities were taken, the firm's profits rose dramatically. For the period 1985 to 1988, profits averaged $386 million a year. Everything seemed to be right on target, but just about the time that the firm's investment banking division began to really perform, the number of firms looking to raise money by selling new securities began to decline. As a result, the firm's investment banking revenues dropped almost overnight. At the same time, revenues from retail transactions—the firm's bread and butter—also dropped. By the end of 1989, Merrill Lynch reported a $213 million loss. While the 1989 loss was disappointing, Schreyer still believes that Merrill Lynch is on the right track. According to Schreyer, the thing that could most help improve Merrill Lynch's bottom line is a strong, healthy stock market. When that is the case, the firm will be more profitable than ever before.[1]

*T*oday, Merrill Lynch and Company, Inc. earns more than 50 percent of its annual revenues by helping the firm's six million retail customers buy and sell securities. Without the brokerage services offered by Merrill Lynch and similar, competing firms, it would be difficult, if not impossible, for the average person to buy and sell securities.

How Securities Are Bought and Sold

Learning Objective 1
Understand how securities are bought and sold through brokerage firms and securities exchanges

To purchase a sweater, you simply walk into a store that sells sweaters, choose one, and pay for it. To purchase stocks, bonds, mutual funds, and many other investments, you have to work through a representative—your stockbroker. In turn, your broker must buy or sell for you in either the primary or secondary market.

The Primary Market

primary market *a market in which an investor purchases financial securities (via an investment bank or other representative) from the issuer of those securities*

investment banking firm *an organization that assists corporations in raising funds, usually by helping sell new security issues*

The **primary market** is a market in which an investor purchases financial securities (via an investment bank or other representative) from the issuer of those securities. An **investment banking firm** is an organization that assists corporations in raising funds, usually by helping sell new security issues. An example of a financial security sold through the primary market is the common-stock issue sold by Liz Claiborne. Investors bought this stock through brokerage firms acting as agents for the investment banking firm, Merrill Lynch; and the money (almost $22 million) they paid for common stock flowed to Liz Claiborne.[2]

For a large corporation, the decision to sell securities is often complicated, time-consuming, and expensive. There are basically two methods. First, a large corporation may use an investment banking firm to sell and distribute the new security issue. This method is used by most large corporations that need a lot of financing. If this method is used, analysts for the investment bank examine the corporation's financial condition to determine whether the new issue is financially sound and how difficult it will be to sell the issue. If the analysts for the investment banking firm are satisfied that the new security issue is a good risk, the bank will buy the securities and then resell them to the bank's customers—commercial banks, insurance companies, pension funds, mutual funds, and the general public. The investment banking firm generally charges 2 to 12 percent of the gross proceeds received by the corporation issuing the securities. The size of the commission depends on the quality and financial health of the corporation issuing the new securities and the size of the new security issue. The commission allows the investment bank to make a profit while guaranteeing that the corporation will receive the needed financing.

The second method used by a corporation trying to obtain financing through the primary market is to sell directly to current stockholders. Usually, promotional materials describing the new security issue are mailed to current stockholders. These stockholders may then purchase securities directly from the corporation. Why would a corporation try to sell its own securities? The most obvious reason for doing so is to avoid the investment bank's commission. Of course, a corporation's ability to sell a new security issue without the aid of an investment banking firm is tied directly to the public's perception of the corporation's financial health.

The Secondary Market

secondary market *a market for existing financial securities that are currently traded between investors*

After securities are originally sold through the primary market, they are traded through a secondary market. The **secondary market** is a market for existing financial securities that are currently traded between investors. Usually, secondary-market transactions are completed through a securities exchange or the over-the-counter market.

securities exchange *a marketplace where member brokers meet to buy and sell securities*

Securities Exchanges   A **securities exchange** is a marketplace where member brokers meet to buy and sell securities. The securities sold at a particular exchange must first be *listed*, or accepted for trading, at that exchange. Generally, securities issued by nationwide corporations are traded at either the New York Stock Exchange or the American Stock Exchange. The securities of regional corporations are traded at smaller *regional exchanges*. These are located in Chicago, San Francisco, Philadelphia, Boston, and several other cities. The securities of very large corporations may be traded at more than one of these exchanges. Securities of American firms that do business abroad may also be listed on foreign securities exchanges—in Tokyo, London, or Paris, for example.

The largest and best-known securities exchange in the United States is the New York Stock Exchange (NYSE). It handles about 70 percent of all stock bought and sold through organized exchanges in the United States. The NYSE lists approximately 2,250 securities issued by more than 1,500 corporations, with a total market value of $3 trillion.[3] The actual trading floor of the NYSE, where listed securities are bought and sold, is approximately the size of a football field. A glass-enclosed visitors' gallery enables people to watch the proceedings below, and on a busy day the floor of the NYSE can best be described as organized confusion. Yet, the system does work and enables brokers to trade an average of more than 160 million shares per day.

Before a corporation's stock is approved for listing on the New York Stock Exchange, the firm must meet five criteria (see Figure 19.1).

The American Stock Exchange handles about 10 percent of U.S. stock transactions, and regional exchanges account for the remainder. These exchanges have generally less stringent listing requirements than the NYSE.

FIGURE 19.1
Criteria a Firm Must Meet Before Being Listed on the New York Stock Exchange
[Source: Chase, David C., Chase Global Investment Almanac *(Chase Global Data, 289 Great Road, Acton, Mass. 01720), 1990 edition, p. 70. Used by permission.]*

Annual earnings before taxes: $2.5 million

Shares of stock held publicly: 1.1 million

Market value of publicly held stock: $9 million

Number of stockholders owning at least 100 shares: 2,000

Value of tangible assets: $18 million

The Over-the-Counter Market   The **over-the-counter (OTC) market** is a network of stockbrokers who buy and sell the securities of corporations that are not listed on a securities exchange. Usually each broker specializes, or *makes a market*, in the securities of one or more specific firms. The securities of these firms are traded through its specialists, who are generally aware of their prices and of investors who are willing to buy or sell them.

over-the-counter (OTC) market *a network of stock-brokers who buy and sell the securities of corporations that are not listed on a securities exchange*

Most OTC trading is conducted by telephone. Currently, more than 5,300 stocks are traded over the counter. Since 1971, the brokers and dealers operating in the OTC market have used a computerized quotation system call *NASDAQ*—the letters stand for the *N*ational *A*ssociation of *S*ecurities *D*ealers *A*utomated *Q*uotation system. NASDAQ displays current price quotations on terminals in subscribers' offices.

The Role of the Stockbroker

account executive (or **stock broker**) *an individual who buys or sells securities for clients*

An **account executive** (or **stockbroker**) is an individual who buys or sells securities for clients. (Actually, *account executive* is the more descriptive title because account executives handle all securities—not only stocks. Most also provide securities information and advise their clients regarding investments.) Account executives are employed by stock brokerage firms, such as Merrill Lynch, Dean Witter Reynolds, and Prudential-Bache Securities. To trade at a particular exchange, a brokerage firm must be a member of that exchange. For example, the NYSE has a limited membership of 1,366 members, or "seats," as they are often called. Although seats on the NYSE are rarely sold, in 1987 a seat sold for $1 million.

market order *a request that a stock be purchased or sold at the current market price*

The Mechanics of a Transaction   Once an investor and his or her account executive have decided on a particular transaction, the investor gives the account executive an order for that transaction. A **market order** is a request that a stock be purchased or sold at the current market price. The broker's representative on the exchange's trading floor will try to get the best possible price, and the trade will be completed as soon as possible.

Stockbrokers buy and sell financial securities for their clients. Today, stockbrokers are classified as either full-service brokers (more service, higher fees) or discount brokers (less service, lower fees). Jim and Karen Cramer own their own two-person full-service brokerage business, which they run out of a small Manhattan office.

BUSINESS JOURNAL

Guidelines for Choosing an Account Executive

A good personal investment program should start before you choose an account executive. First, decide on and write down your financial goals and objectives. Then, accumulate enough money to start your investment program. Most financial experts suggest that you keep a cash reserve equal to at least three months' salary. Once you have accumulated funds beyond your cash reserve, you are ready to begin your investment program by choosing an account executive.

FACTORS THAT CAN AFFECT YOUR DECISION

All account executives, sometimes called *stockbrokers* or *registered representatives,* can buy and sell stock for you. And yet, choosing an account executive can be difficult for at least three reasons. First, you must remember to approach an account executive with a shrewd combination of trust and mistrust. While you are interested in your broker's recommendations to increase your wealth, he or she is interested in your investment trading as a means to swell commissions. Unfortunately, some account executives are guilty of churning—a practice that generates commissions by excessive buying and selling of securities.

A second factor to consider is compatibility. It is always wise to interview several potential account executives. During each interview, ask some questions to determine if you and the account executive understand each other. You must be able to communicate the types of stocks you are interested in, your expected rate of return, and the amount of risk you are willing to take to achieve your investment goals.

Finally, you must decide if you need a full-service broker or a discount broker. A *full-service broker* charges more but gives you personal investment advice. He or she can provide you with research reports from Moody's Investors Service, Standard & Poor's Corporation, and Value Line Inc.—all companies that specialize in providing investment information to investors. Also, a full-service broker should provide additional reports prepared by the brokerage firm's financial analysts. A full-service broker charges a commission of approximately 2 percent for executing an order to buy or sell stocks.

A *discount broker* simply executes buy and sell orders, usually over the phone. Generally, discount brokers do not offer investment advice; you must make your own investment decisions. Discount brokers charge commissions that average 20 to 50 percent less than those of full-service brokers.

OTHER CONCERNS

If your account executive asks you to sign a contract, read the agreement carefully. Beware of an arbitration-only clause, which prevents you from taking your claim to court if you believe that your account has been handled improperly. The growing number of arbitration cases—a 650 percent increase since 1980—is evidence of unhappy investors who feel they were victims of incompetent or unethical account executives. Also, beware of a discretionary clause in the contract that gives the broker the right to use his or her judgment in investing your money without consulting you.

A FINAL WORD OF CAUTION

After choosing your account executive, start out slowly with your first investments to "test the water." If the account executive does well with a few investments, then you will feel safer in making larger investments based on his or her advice. Once you have used an account executive for about six months, evaluate his or her performance. If you become dissatisfied with your investment program, do not hesitate to discuss your dissatisfaction with the account executive. You may even find it necessary to choose another account executive if your dissatisfaction continues. This is not at all uncommon. Remember, the final responsibility for the success of your investment program falls on your shoulders.

Based on information from "Getting the Most from a Full-Service Broker," *Fortune/1990 Investor's Guide,* Fall 1989, p. 222; Ellen Schultz, "Climbing High with Discount Brokers," *Fortune/1990 Investor's Guide,* Fall 1989, pp. 219–220+; Laura Zinn, "Battling Your Broker Just Got a Bit Easier," *Business Week,* June 5, 1989, p. 142; Wilbur Cross, *Investor Alert.* (New York: Andrews and McMeel, 1988), pp. 156–167; and Dexter Hutchins, "How to Find and Use a Stockbroker," *Fortune/1986 Investor's Guide,* Fall 1985, p. 124+.

limit order *a request that a stock be bought or sold at a price that is equal to or better than some specified price*

discretionary order *an order to buy or sell a security that lets the broker decide when to execute the transaction and at what price*

round lot *a unit of 100 shares of a particular stock*

odd lot *fewer than 100 shares of a particular stock*

A **limit order** is a request that a stock be bought or sold at the price that is equal to or better (lower for buying, higher for selling) than some specified price. Suppose you place a limit order to *sell* General Dynamics common stock at $49 per share. Then the broker's representative sells the stock only if the price is $49 per share or *more*. If you place a limit order to *buy* General Dynamics at $49, the representative buys it only if the price is $49 per share or *less*. Limit orders may or may not be transacted quickly, depending on how close the limit price is to the current market price. Usually, a limit order is good for one day, one week, one month, or good until canceled (GTC).

Finally, it is possible for investors to place a discretionary order. A **discretionary order** is an order to buy or sell a security that lets the broker decide when to execute the transaction and at what price. Financial planners advise against using a discretionary order for two reasons. First, a discretionary order gives the account executive a great deal of authority. If the account executive makes a mistake, it is the investor who suffers the loss. Second, financial planners argue that only investors (with the help of their account executive) should make investment decisions.

A typical stock transaction includes five steps, which are shown in Figure 19.2. The entire process, from receipt of the selling order to confirmation of the completed transaction, takes about twenty minutes.

Commissions   Brokerage firms are free to set their own commission charges. Like other businesses, however, they must be concerned with the fees charged by competing firms. *Full-service brokers*—those that provide information and advice as well as securities-trading services—generally charge higher fees than *discount brokers*, which buy and sell but may offer less advice and information to their clients.

On the trading floor, stocks are traded in round lots. A **round lot** is a unit of 100 shares of a particular stock. Table 19.1 shows typical commission charges for some round-lot transactions. An **odd lot** is fewer than

FIGURE 19.2
Steps in a Typical Stock Transaction

1 Account executive receives customer's order to sell stock and relays order to stock-exchange representative.

2 Firm's clerk signals transaction from booth to partner on stock-exchange floor.

3 Floor partner goes to trading post where stock is traded with a stock-exchange member with an order to buy. Generally 10 or 12 issues are traded at each trading post.

4 Floor partner signals transaction back to clerk in booth. Sale is recorded on card inserted into card reader and transmitted to ticker.

5 Sale appears on ticker, and confirmation is phoned to account executive, who notifies customer.

TABLE 19.1 *Typical Commission Charges for Round-Lot Stock Transactions*

		Commission	
	Stock Dollar Cost	Full-Service Broker	Discount Broker
100 shares @ $5 per share	$ 500	$ 37	$30
100 shares @ $25 per share	$ 2,500	$ 65	$42
100 shares @ $50 per share	$ 5,000	$ 84	$48
100 shares @ $100 per share	$10,000	$110	$55

100 shares of a particular stock. Brokerage firms generally charge higher per-share fees for trading in odd lots, primarily because several odd lots must be combined into round lots before they can actually be traded.

Commissions for trading bonds, commodities, and options are usually lower than those for trading stocks. The charge for buying or selling a $1,000 corporate bond is typically $10. No matter what kind of security is traded, the investor generally pays a commission when buying *and* when selling. Payment for the securities and for commissions is generally required within five business days of each transaction.

It is important to remember that a broker has two goals: to help investors achieve their financial objectives and to promote his or her own interests and those of the brokerage firm. (These goals do not necessarily conflict with one another, but the fact that the broker and brokerage house receive a commission on every trade may sometimes lead to recommendations to trade more frequently than necessary.) With this fact in mind, it is obvious that investors should be involved in planning their investment programs. In the next section, we discuss the steps necessary to establish a successful investment program.

The Concept of Personal Investment

personal investment *the use of one's personal funds to earn a financial return*

Personal investment is the use of one's personal funds to earn a financial return. Thus, in the most general sense, the objective of investing is to earn money with money. But that objective is completely useless for the individual, because it is so vague and so easily attained. If you place $100 in a savings account paying 5.5 percent annual interest, your money will earn 46 cents in one month. If your objective is simply to earn money with your $100, you will have attained that objective at the end of the month. Then what do you do?

Investment Objectives

Learning Objective 2
Appreciate the need to develop a personal investment plan and know how to draw one up

To be useful, an investment objective must be specific and measurable. It must be tailored to the individual so that it takes into account his or her particular financial circumstances and needs. It must also be oriented toward the future, because investing is, in general, a long-term undertak-

Today, there are more investment alternatives than ever before. Unfortunately, this increases the difficulty of determining which investment alternative is right for you. Seeking expert advice from such easily accessible sources as Business Week *articles is one helpful step toward making investment choices.*

ing. And finally, an investment goal must be realistic in terms of the economic conditions that prevail and the investment opportunities that are available.

Some counselors suggest that investment goals be stated in terms of money: "By January 1, 1999, I will have total assets of $80,000." Others believe that people are more motivated to work toward goals that are stated in terms of the particular things they desire: "By May 1, 1997, I will have accumulated enough money so that I can take a year off from work to travel around the world." Like the objectives themselves, how they are stated depends on the individual.

The following questions can be helpful in establishing valid investment objectives.

1. Why do I want to obtain some specific amount of money?
2. How much money will I need, and when?
3. What are the consequences if I don't obtain it all?
4. Is it reasonable to assume that I can obtain the amount of money I will need?
5. Do I expect my personal situation to change in a way that will affect my investment goals?
6. What economic conditions could alter my investment goals?
7. Am I willing to make the sacrifices that are necessary to ensure that my financial goals are met?

A Personal Plan of Action

Once specific goals have been formulated, an individual's investment planning is similar to planning for a business. If the goals are realistic, investment opportunities will be available to implement them. Investment planning begins with the assessment of these opportunities—including the potential return and risk involved in each. At the very least, this requires some expert advice and careful study. In many cases, investors turn to lawyers, accountants, bankers, or insurance agents. The problem of finding qualified help is compounded by the fact that many people who call themselves "financial planners" are in reality nothing more than salespersons for various financial investments, tax shelters, or insurance plans.

A true financial planner has had at least two years of training in securities, insurance, taxation, real estate, and estate planning, and has passed a rigorous examination. As evidence of training and successful completion of the qualifying examination, the College of Financial Planning in Denver allows individuals to use the designation Certified Financial Planner (CFP). Similarly, the American College in Bryn Mawr, Pennsylvania, allows individuals to use the designation Chartered Financial Consultant (ChFC) if they have completed the necessary requirements. Most CFPs and ChFCs don't sell a particular investment product or charge commissions for their investment recommendations. Instead, they charge consulting fees that range from $75 to $125 an hour.

Many investment counselors suggest that an investment program begin with the accumulation of an "emergency fund"—a certain amount of money that can be obtained quickly in case of immediate need. This money should be deposited in a savings account at the highest available interest rate. The amount of money that should be salted away in the emergency fund varies from person to person. However, most investment planners agree that an amount equal to three month's salary (after taxes) is reasonable.[4]

Once the emergency account is established, additional funds may be invested according to the individual's investment plan. Some additional funds may already be available, or money for further investing may be saved out of earnings. In either case, savings is an important part of the typical investment plan. In addition to savings, other investment alternatives are chosen by a process of evaluation and elimination and combined into a comprehensive investment program.

Once a plan has been put into operation, it must be monitored and, if necessary, modified. The most successful investors spend hours each week evaluating their own investments and investigating new investment opportunities. Both the investor's circumstances and economic conditions are subject to change. Hence all investment programs should be re-evaluated regularly.

Four Important Factors in Personal Investment

Learning Objective 3
See how four factors—safety, income, growth, and liquidity—link investment planning to the various types of investments

How can the individual (or an investment counselor) tell which investments are "right" for an investment plan and which are not? One way to do so—or at least to start doing so—is to match potential investments with investment goals in terms of four factors: safety, income, growth potential, and liquidity.

The Safety Factor   Safety in an investment means minimal risk of loss. Investment goals that require a steady increase in value or a fairly certain annual return are those that stress safety. In general, they are implemented with the more conservative investments, such as savings accounts, whose safety is guaranteed up to $100,000 by the FDIC, SAIF, or NCUA.

Other relatively safe investments include highly rated corporate and municipal bonds and the stocks of certain highly regarded corporations—sometimes called "blue-chip stocks." These corporations are generally industry leaders that have provided stable earnings and dividends over a number of years. Examples include Du Pont, Xerox, and General Electric.

To implement goals that stress a high return on their investment, investors must generally give up some safety. How much risk should they take in exchange for how much return? This question is almost impossible to answer for someone else, because the answer depends so much on the individual and his or her investment goals. However, in general, *the potential return should be directly related to the risk that is assumed.* That is, the greater the risk, the greater the potential monetary reward should be.

As we will see shortly, there are a number of risky—and potentially profitable—investments. They include some stocks, commodities, and stock options. The securities issued by new and growing corporations usually fall in this category. Not too long ago, the stock of Computer-Tabulating-Recording Company was considered a risky investment. Today the company is known as International Business Machines (IBM), and its stock is part of most conservative investment portfolios.

The Income Factor   How much income should be expected from an investment? To a certain extent, the answer to this question depends on how much risk the investor is willing to assume. Savings accounts, bonds, and certain stocks pay a predictable amount of interest or dividends each year. Such investments are generally used to implement investment goals that stress periodic income.

The investor in savings accounts and bonds knows exactly how much income he or she will receive each year. The dividends paid to stockholders can and do vary, even for the largest and most stable corporations. However, a number of corporations have built their reputations on a policy of paying dividends every three months. (The firms listed in Table 19.2 have paid dividends to their owners for at least eighty years.) The stocks of these corporations are often purchased primarily for income.

The Growth Factor   To an investor, growth means that his or her investment will increase or appreciate in value. For example, a corporation that is in the process of growing usually pays a small cash dividend or no dividend at all. Instead, profits are reinvested in the business (as retained earnings) to finance additional expansion. Such a corporation's stockholders receive little or no income from their investments. However, the value of their stock increases as the corporation grows.

TABLE 19.2   _Corporations That, Through 1989, Had Made Consecutive Dividend Payments for at Least 80 Years_

Corporation	Dividends Since	Type of Business
American Telephone and Telegraph	1881	Telephone utility
Borden, Inc.	1899	Foods
Commonwealth Edison Company	1890	Electric utility
Du Pont (E.I.) de Nemours	1904	Chemicals
Exxon Corporation	1882	Chemical & petroleum products
General Electric Company	1899	Electrical equipment
Norfolk & Southern Railway Co.	1901	Railroad
PPG Industries, Inc.	1899	Glass
Procter & Gamble Company	1891	Soap products

Source: _Standard & Poor's Stock Reports_, published by Standard & Poor's Corporation, 25 Broadway, New York, N.Y. 10004, November 1989. Reprinted with permission.

Investment goals that stress growth, or an increase in the value of the investment, can be implemented by purchasing the stocks of such "growth corporations." During the 1980s, firms in the electronics, energy, health-care, and financial-services industries showed the greatest growth. They are expected to continue growing in the 1990s. Individual firms within these industries may grow at a slower or faster rate than the industry as a whole—or they may not grow at all.

Assuming that an investor carefully chooses investments, both mutual funds and real estate may offer substantial growth possibilities. More speculative investments like strategic metals, gemstones, and collectibles (antiques and paintings) offer less predictable growth possibilities, whereas investments in commodities and stock options usually stress immediate returns as opposed to continued growth. Generally, corporate and government bonds are not purchased for growth.

liquidity   *the ease with which an asset can be converted into cash*

The Liquidity Factor   **Liquidity** is defined as the ease with which an asset can be converted into cash. Investments range from cash or cash equivalents (like investments in government securities or money-market funds) to the other extreme of frozen investments where it is impossible to get your money. Checking and savings accounts are liquid investments because they can be quickly converted into cash. Another type of bank account—a certificate of deposit—is not as liquid as a checking or savings account. There are penalties for withdrawing money from this type of account before the maturity date.

While it may be possible to sell other investments quickly, you may not be able to regain the amount of money you originally invested because of market conditions, economic conditions, or many other reasons. For example, the owner of real estate may have to lower the asking price to find a buyer for a property. It may also be difficult to find a buyer for investments in certain types of collectibles.

Different kinds of investments offer different combinations of safety, income, growth, and liquidity. Keep the nature of this important "mix" in mind as we consider various investment alternatives.

Traditional Investment Alternatives

In this section and the next, we look at some of the types of investments that are available to investors. A number of them have already been discussed. Others have only been mentioned and will be examined in more detail. Still others may be completely new to you (see Figure 19.3).

Learning Objective 4
Know the advantages and disadvantages of the traditional investment alternatives: savings accounts, stocks, bonds, mutual funds, and real estate

Bank Accounts

Bank accounts that pay interest—and are therefore investments—include passbook savings accounts, certificates of deposit, and NOW accounts. These were discussed in Chapter 17. They are the most conservative of all investments, and they provide safety and either income or growth. That

INVESTMENT ALTERNATIVES	
Traditional	**High-risk**
■ Bank accounts ■ Common stock ■ Preferred stock ■ Corporate and government bonds ■ Mutual funds ■ Real estate	■ Buying stock on margin ■ Selling short ■ Trading in commodities ■ Trading in options

FIGURE 19.3
Investment Alternatives
Traditional investments involve less risk than speculative, or high-risk, investments.

is, the interest paid on bank accounts can be withdrawn to serve as income, or it can be left on deposit to earn additional interest and increase the size of the bank account.

Figure 19.4 illustrates the concept of compound interest, which is a feature of most savings accounts and certificates of deposit. As illustrated in Figure 19.4, an initial $5,000 deposit invested at 9 percent is worth $11,839 at the end of ten years. The depositor has received $6,839 in interest over a ten-year period of time as a result of letting the interest compound and grow. A word of caution: Both the time the money is on deposit and the interest rate can affect the dollar value that a depositor receives at the end of a specified time.

Common Stock

Common stock—equity financing for a corporation—was discussed in Chapters 3 and 18. Before looking at why investors buy common stock for investment purposes, let's review why corporations sell common stock. For the corporation, the most important reason for selling common stock is that it is equity financing. The corporation is under no legal obligation to repay the money a stockholder pays for common stock. Another reason

FIGURE 19.4
Investment in a Bank Account
This chart shows how $5,000 will grow, depending on the duration of the deposit and on the rate of interest (when both the original amount—or principal—and the interest remain in the account).

FIXED SAVINGS (STARTING BALANCE = $5,000)			
	Balance at end of year		
Rate (%)	**1**	**5**	**10**
6	$5,300	$6,691	$8,954
7	5,350	7,013	9,836
8	5,400	7,347	10,795
9	5,450	7,693	11,839
10	5,500	8,053	12,969
11	5,550	8,425	14,197

to sell stock is that dividends are paid out of profits. Dividend payments are not automatic and are not guaranteed. As a result, all dividend distributions must be approved by a corporation's board of directors.

How do you make money by buying common stock? Basically, there are three ways that an investor can make money.

First, most stockholders expect to receive *dividend income*. Although the corporation's board members are under no legal obligation to pay dividends, most board members like to keep stockholders happy (and prosperous). Therefore, board members usually declare dividends if the corporation's after-tax profits are sufficient to do so. Since dividends are a distribution of profits, intelligent investors must be concerned about after-tax profits.

stock dividend *a dividend in the form of additional stock*

A corporation may pay stock dividends in place of—or in addition to—cash dividends. A **stock dividend** is a dividend in the form of additional stock. It is paid to shareholders just as cash dividends are paid: in proportion to the number of shares owned. An individual stockholder may sell the additional stock to obtain income or retain it to increase the total value of her or his stock holdings.

Second, stockholders can make money when the value of their stocks increases. In most cases, a stockholder purchases stock and then holds on to that stock for a period of time. The **market value** of a stock is the price of one share of the stock at a particular time. It is determined solely by the interaction of buyers and sellers in the various stock markets. (Note that *market value* is different from *par value*, which, as we noted in Chapter 18, is an arbitrary value that the issuing corporation assigns to a share of stock.) If the market value of the stock increases, the stockholder must decide whether he or she wants to sell the stock at the higher price or continue to hold it. If the stockholder decides to sell the stock, the monetary difference between the purchase price and the selling price represents profit or loss.

market value *the price of one share of a stock at a particular time*

bull market *a market in which average stock prices are increasing*

bear market *a market in which average stock prices are declining*

Generally, the stock market is described as either a bull market or a bear market. The term **bull market** describes a market in which average stock prices are increasing. The term **bear market** describes a market in which average stock prices are declining. Similarly, a *bull* is an investor who expects prices to go up; a *bear* is an investor who expects prices to go down.

stock split *the division of each outstanding share of a corporation's stock into a greater number of shares*

Third, stockholders can receive increased value for their stocks through *stock splits*. As a corporation prospers and grows, its stock becomes worth more. In other words, the market value of the stock tends to grow along with the company. The directors of many corporations feel that there is an optimal price range within which their firm's stock is most attractive to investors. When the market value increases beyond that range, they may declare a *stock split* to bring the price down. A **stock split** is the division of each outstanding share of a corporation's stock into a greater number of shares. A stock split, in and of itself, does not increase the value of any investor's holdings, although it is probably more likely to take place during a prosperous period for the company.

The most common stock splits result in one, two, or three new shares for each original share. For example, in 1989, the board of directors for

Honda Motor Co. approved a two-for-one stock split. After this split, a stockholder who originally owned 100 shares owned 200 shares. The value of an original share was proportionally reduced. In the case of Honda, the market value per share was reduced to approximately half of the stock's value before the two-for-one stock split. Every shareholder retained his or her proportional ownership of the firm. But, at the lower price, the stock is more attractive to the investing public because there is a greater potential for a rapid increase in dollar value.

Preferred Stock

As we noted in Chapter 18, the owners of a firm's preferred stock must receive their cash dividends before the owners of common stock are paid any dividends. Moreover, preferred-stock dividends are specified on the stock certificates. And the owners of preferred stock have first claim, after bondholders and general creditors, on the assets of the issuing corporation. These features tend to provide the holders of preferred stocks with safety and a predictable income.

In addition, holders of *cumulative* preferred stocks are assured that omitted dividends will be paid to them before holders of common stock receive any dividends. Holders of *participating* preferred stock may earn more than the specified dividend if the firm has a good year. The participating feature enables preferred stockholders to share in surplus profit, along with common stockholders, after the designated amounts have been paid to both classes of stockholders. And holders of *convertible* preferred stock may profit through growth as well as from dividends: If the value of a firm's common stock increases, the market value of its convertible preferred stock also grows. Convertibility allows the owner of convertible preferred stock to combine the lower risk of preferred stock with the possibility of greater speculative gain through conversion to common stock.

Corporate and Government Bonds

In Chapter 18 we discussed the issuing of bonds by corporations to obtain financing. The United States government and state and local governments also issue bonds, for the same reason. In addition, many government and municipal bonds are tax-free, which enables owners to earn income that is exempt from federal income taxes.

Bonds are generally considered a more conservative investment than either preferred or common stock. But they are less conservative than bank accounts. They are primarily income-producing investments. However, when overall interest rates in the economy are rising, the market value of existing bonds typically declines. They may then be purchased for less than their face value. By holding such bonds until maturity, or until interest rates decline (causing their market value to increase), bond owners can realize some profit through the growth of their investments.

Convertible bonds generally carry a lower interest rate than nonconvertible bonds—by about 1 to 2 percent. In return for accepting a lower

To increase the safety factor of some municipal housing bonds, some municipalities will purchase a form of insurance protection from the Municipal Bond Investors Assurance (MBIA) Corporation. MBIA protection guarantees that bondholders will receive interest until maturity and repayment of the principal at maturity.

mutual fund *a professionally managed investment vehicle that combines and invests the funds of many individual investors*

interest rate, holders of convertible bonds have the opportunity to benefit through investment growth. For example, assume an investor purchases a $1,000 corporate bond that is convertible to 40 shares of the company's common stock. This means that an investor could convert the bond to common stock whenever the price of the company's stock is $25 (1,000 ÷ 40 = $25) or higher. Assume that at the time the bond is purchased, the company's stock is selling for $18. In this situation, there is no reason to convert because the common stock received would be worth only $720 ($18 × 40 = $720). In reality, there is no guarantee that bondholders will convert to common stock even if the market value of the common stock does increase to $25 or higher. The reason for not exercising the conversion feature is quite simple. As the market value of the common stock increases, the price of the convertible bond also increases. By not converting to common stock, bondholders enjoy interest income from the bond in addition to increased bond value caused by the price movement of the common stock. Of course, convertible bonds, like all investments, must be carefully evaluated.

The safety of a particular bond, issued by a particular firm or government, depends very much on the financial strength of the issuer. For example, in 1983, Washington Public Power Supply could not pay off its debt on municipal bonds worth more than $2 billion, and thousands of investors lost money. Several years ago, New York City was on the verge of *defaulting* on (failing to redeem) an issue of bonds that was about to mature. Strong financial measures and new loans saved the city and the bondholders, but the experience affected the market value of all New York City bonds. In addition, the city had to pay higher-than-usual interest rates to attract investors to new issues of bonds.

Mutual Funds

A **mutual fund** combines and invests the funds of many individual investors, under the guidance of a professional manager. The major advantages of a mutual fund are its professional management and its *diversification*, or investment in a wide variety of securities. Diversification spells safety, because an occasional loss incurred with one security is usually offset by gains from other investments.

Mutual-Fund Shares and Fees A *closed-end* mutual fund sells shares (in the fund) to investors only when the fund is originally organized. And only a specified number of shares are made available at that time. Once all the shares are sold, an investor can purchase shares only from some other investor who is willing to sell them. The mutual fund itself is under no obligation to buy back shares from investors.

An *open-end* mutual fund issues and sells new shares to any investor who requests them. It also buys back shares from owners who wish to sell all or part of their holdings. For this reason, open-end funds are the more popular.

With regard to costs, there are again two types of mutual funds. An individual who invests in a *load fund* pays a sales charge every time he

BUSINESS JOURNAL

Evaluating Mutual Funds

Three years ago, Mike Mathews, a 41-year-old engineer who lives in Los Angeles, California, invested more than $15,000 in the Fidelity Select Portfolios—Electronics mutual fund because he thought all mutual funds were safe investments. After all, he reasoned, mutual funds are professionally managed, and they provide the safety of diversification. Besides, he had a friend who had made a killing with the Fidelity Magellan Fund. Two years later, after losing almost $6,000, Mathews admits that he knew nothing about Fidelity mutual funds. In fact, he didn't realize that Fidelity Investments—the nation's largest mutual-fund company—offers more than 170 different mutual funds that range from very speculative to extremely conservative investment vehicles.

A NEED FOR EVALUATION

The experience of Mike Mathews is not that uncommon. Of the more than 40 million Americans who own shares in a mutual fund, many know very little about their mutual-fund investments. Like Mathews, they assume that because a mutual fund is professionally managed and diversified, it warrants no evaluation. Nothing could be further from the truth. According to a research study conducted by Morningstar, Inc., a company that provides the data for *Business Week*'s Mutual Fund Scoreboard, only 300, or 40 percent, of the 727 mutual funds studied outperformed the stocks included in Standard & Poor's 500 Stock Index.* Investors need to realize that, like stocks and bonds, mutual funds can decrease in value.

WHAT TO LOOK FOR

When evaluating a mutual fund, consider several key factors.

1. Understand the fund's objective. Ask yourself, "Do the objectives of a specific mutual fund match my objectives?" Keep in mind that there are more than 2,700 different funds from which to choose. The Investment Company Institute—a nonprofit organization that provides information about mutual funds—classifies all funds into at least twenty-two different categories, according to risk potential. Today, mutual funds range from very speculative aggressive-growth funds to conservative funds that specialize in U.S. government bonds.

2. Evaluate the fund's past performance. While a fund's past performance doesn't guarantee success, it is still a very good predictor of what the fund will do in the future. Information on past performance is relatively easy to obtain. Information sources available at most libraries include *Donoghue's Mutual Funds Almanac, Business Week, Changing Times, Money,* and *Forbes. Business Week, Changing Times, Money,* and *Forbes* publish annual surveys that are very useful for evaluating current and potential investments in mutual funds.

You can also subscribe to any of more than fifty different mutual-fund newsletters. Many of the older newsletters have survived the test of time and provide investors with reliable advice for fees ranging from $85 to $300 a year. The most comprehensive reference reports on mutual funds are published by Wiesenberger Financial Services and Lipper Analytical Services.

3. Determine the costs involved. There are a number of different fees associated with a mutual-fund investment. You may be charged separate fees to buy shares, to sell shares, and to cover the costs of managing or marketing and distributing the fund. Be sure to ask questions related to commissions, fees, and other charges before investing in a mutual fund.

SPECIAL NOTE

These are just some of the factors to explore when evaluating a mutual fund. If other information is pertinent or available, it is your responsibility to search it out and determine how it affects your investment. Above all, take the time to do a thorough job of examining a mutual fund investment.

Based on information from Jonathan Clements, "How to Pick a Mutual Fund," *Forbes*, September 4, 1989, p. 192 + ; Gerald W. Perritt, "Hidden Costs," *Forbes*, September 4, 1989, pp. 182–183; and *1989 Mutual Fund Fact Book* (Washington, D.C.: Investment Company Institute, 1989), pp. 13–21.

---

* Jeffrey M. Laderman, "How Mutual Funds Have Battled Back," *Business Week*, September 18, 1989, pp. 100–101.

or she purchases shares. This charge is typically 7 to 8.5 percent of the investment. The purchaser of shares in a *no-load fund*, on the other hand, pays no sales charges at all. No-load funds offer the same type of investment opportunities that load funds offer, but they may have higher management fees, primarily because they assess no sales charges. Most funds (of either type) collect a management fee of about 0.5 to 1 percent of the total dollar amount invested. In addition, some funds charge a redemption fee of 1 to 5 percent of the total amount withdrawn from a mutual fund.

Mutual-Fund Investments   The managers of mutual funds tailor their investment portfolios to provide growth, income, or a combination of both. Most mutual funds are fairly conservative and relatively safe, although there are some speculative mutual funds. The major categories of mutual funds, in terms of the types of securities they invest in, are as follows:

▶ *Balanced funds*, which apportion their investments among common stocks, preferred stock, and bonds

▶ *Income funds*, which invest in stocks and bonds that pay high dividends and interest

▶ *Index funds*, which invest in common stocks that react the same way the stock market as a whole does

▶ *Industry funds*, sometimes called *specialty funds*, which invest in common stocks of companies in the same industry

▶ *Growth-income funds*, which invest in common and preferred stocks that pay good dividends *and* are expected to increase in market value

▶ *Growth funds*, which invest in the common stock of well-managed, rapidly growing corporations

▶ *Money-market funds*, which invest in short-term corporate obligations and government securities that offer high interest

▶ *Municipal-bond funds*, which invest in municipal bonds that provide investors with tax-free interest income

There are funds designed to meet just about any conceivable investment objective. Hundreds of funds trade daily under the headings "capital appreciation," "small-company growth," and "equity income." As a result, it is the investor's job to determine which is the right fund.

Real Estate

Real estate ownership represents one of the best hedges against inflation, but not all property increases in value. A poor location, for example, can result in a piece of property decreasing in value. A number of people who bought land in the Florida Everglades were taken by unscrupulous promoters. Many factors should be considered before investing in real estate. The real estate checkist presented in Figure 19.5 cites some of these factors.

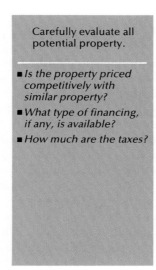

Carefully evaluate all potential property.

■ *Is the property priced competitively with similar property?*

■ *What type of financing, if any, is available?*

■ *How much are the taxes?*

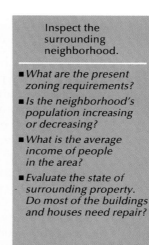

Inspect the surrounding neighborhood.

■ *What are the present zoning requirements?*

■ *Is the neighborhood's population increasing or decreasing?*

■ *What is the average income of people in the area?*

■ *Evaluate the state of surrounding property. Do most of the buildings and houses need repair?*

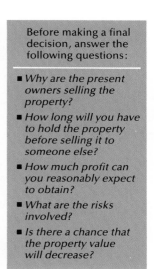

Before making a final decision, answer the following questions:

■ *Why are the present owners selling the property?*

■ *How long will you have to hold the property before selling it to someone else?*

■ *How much profit can you reasonably expect to obtain?*

■ *What are the risks involved?*

■ *Is there a chance that the property value will decrease?*

FIGURE 19.5
Real Estate Checklist
Although real estate offers one of the best hedges against inflation, not all property increases in value. Many factors should be considered before investing.

There are, of course, disadvantages to any investment, and real estate is no exception. If you want to sell your property, you must find an interested buyer with the ability to obtain enough money to complete the transaction. This can be difficult if loan money is scarce, if the real estate market is in a decline, or if you overpaid for a piece of property. If you are forced to hold your investment longer than you originally planned, taxes and installment payments must also be considered. As a rule, real estate increases in value and eventually sells at a profit, but there are no guarantees. The degree of your success depends on how well you evaluate different alternatives.

More Speculative Investment Techniques

Learning Objective 5
Be aware of more speculative investment techniques, including buying on margin, selling short, and trading in options and commodities

speculative investment *an investment that is made in the hope of earning a relatively large profit in a short time*

A **speculative investment** is an investment that is made in the hope of earning a relatively large profit in a short time. (See the high-risk investment categories in Figure 19.3.) Some securities may be speculative by their very nature; that is, they are quite risky. (In this sense, a bet on a roulette wheel in a Las Vegas casino is a speculative investment.) However, most speculative investments become so because of the methods that are used by investors to earn a quick profit. These methods can lead to large losses as well as to gains. They should not be used by anyone who does not fully understand the risks that are involved.

Buying Stock on Margin

An investor buys stock *on margin* by borrowing part of the purchase price, usually from a stock brokerage firm. As we noted in Chapter 17, the **margin requirement** is the proportion of the price of a stock that cannot be borrowed. This requirement, which is set by the Federal Reserve Board, is currently 50 percent of the value of securities purchased.

Thus, investors can presently borrow up to half the cost of a stock purchase. But why would they want to do so? Simply because they can buy twice as much stock by buying on margin. Suppose an investor expects the market price of a certain stock to increase in the next month or two. Let's say this investor has enough money to purchase 1,000 shares of the stock. But if she buys on margin, she can purchase an additional 1,000 shares. If the price of the stock increases by $5 per share, her profit will be $5 × 1,000 or $5,000, if she pays cash. But it will be $5 × 2,000 or $10,000, if she buys on margin. That is, she will earn double the profit (less the interest she pays on the borrowed money and customary commission charges) by buying her shares on margin.

The use of borrowed funds to increase the return on an investment is called **leverage.** Profit is earned by both the borrowed funds and the borrower's own money. The borrower retains all the profit and pays interest only for the temporary use of the borrowed funds. Note that the stock purchased on margin serves as collateral for the borrowed funds.

If all goes as expected, investors can increase their profits by using leverage—buying stocks on margin. However, margin buyers are subject to two problems. First, if the market price of the purchased stock does not increase as quickly as expected, interest costs mount and eventually drain the investor's profit. Second, if the price of the purchased stock falls, the leverage works against the investor. That is, because the margin buyer has purchased twice as much stock, he or she loses twice as much money.

Moreover, any decrease in the value of the stock is considered to come out of the investor's own funds, not out of the borrowed funds. If the stock's market value decreases to approximately half of the original price, the investor will receive a margin call from the brokerage firm. To satisfy the margin call, the investor must then provide additional cash or securities. If he or she cannot do so, the stock is sold and the proceeds are used to pay off the loan. Any funds remaining after the loan is paid off are returned to the investor.

Selling Short

Normally, investors buy stocks expecting that they will increase in value and can then be sold at a profit. This procedure is referred to as **buying long.** However, many securities decrease in value, for various reasons. More risk-oriented investors can use a procedure called *selling short* to make a profit when the price of an individual security is falling. **Selling short** is the process of selling stock that an investor does not actually own but has borrowed from a stockbroker and will repay at a later date. The idea is to sell at today's higher price and then buy later at a lower price.

To make a profit from a short transaction, the investor must proceed as follows:

1. Arrange to borrow a certain number of shares of a particular stock from a brokerage firm
2. Sell the borrowed stock immediately, assuming that its price will drop in a reasonably short time
3. Once the price does drop, buy the same number of shares as was sold in step 2
4. Give the newly purchased stock to the brokerage firm, in return for the borrowed stock

The investor's profit is the difference between the amount received in step 2 and the amount paid in step 3. For example, assume that you think that Sony stock is overvalued at $60 a share. You also believe that the stock will decrease in value over the next three to four months. You call your broker and arrange to borrow 100 shares of Sony stock (step 1). The broker then sells the Sony stock at the current market price of $60 a share (step 2). Also assume that three months later, the Sony stock is selling for $53 a share. You instruct your broker to purchase 100 shares of Sony stock at the lower price (step 3). The Sony stock that is purchased is used to repay the borrowed stock (step 4). In this example, you made $700 by selling short ($6,000 selling price − $5,300 purchase price = $700 profit). Naturally, the $700 profit must be reduced by commissions paid to the broker for buying and selling the Sony stock.

People often ask where the broker obtains the stock for a short transaction. The broker probably borrows the stock from other investors who have purchased Sony stock through a margin arrangement or from investors who have left stock certificates on deposit with the brokerage firm. As a result, the person who is selling short must pay any dividends declared on the borrowed stock. The mosts obvious danger, of course, is a loss resulting from an increase in the stock's market value. If the market price of the stock increases after the investor has sold it in step 2, he or she loses money.

Trading in Commodities

spot trading *the buying and selling of commodities for immediate delivery*

futures contract *an agreement to buy or sell a commodity at a guaranteed price on some specified future date*

The ownership of certain commodities (including cattle, hogs, pork bellies, various grains, sugar, coffee, frozen concentrated orange juice, cotton, gold, silver, and copper) is traded on a regular basis. The buying and selling of commodities for immediate delivery is called **spot trading.** However, most commodities transactions involve a future delivery date. A **futures contract** is an agreement to buy or sell a commodity at a guaranteed price on some specified future date.

Commodity trading is much riskier than trading in securities because prices fluctuate widely. Almost any change in economic conditions, supply and demand, or even the weather affects commodity prices. An unexpected freeze in Florida can cause the price of orange juice futures to soar. An exceptionally good harvest can have the opposite effect on grain and cattle

At 38, George Kleinman manages about two hundred accounts for clients who have at least $25,000 to invest in commodities. Although not for the average investor, commodities do offer potentially larger returns than more conservative investments.

futures. Rumors, natural disasters, and political events can also propel commodity prices upward or downward very quickly. The continual price movements and relatively low margin requirements tend to attract numbers of speculators to the commodity markets. These same characteristics make the commodity markets too risky for most investors.

Trading in Options

option   *the right to buy or sell a specified amount of stock at a specified price within a certain period of time*

An **option** is the right to buy or sell a specified amount of stock at a specified price within a certain period of time. Options are purchased and sold by investors who expect the price of a stock to change. The Chicago Board Options Exchange (CBOE) is an established exchange for the trading of options on selected stocks. The CBOE provides more liquidity and uniformity in options trading than is found in the traditional over-the-counter options market.

A *call option* gives the purchaser the right to *buy* 100 shares of a specific stock at a specified price within a specified time. Call options are sold by owners of stock. They are purchased by investors who expect the market price of the stock to increase beyond the amount specified in the call. If this occurs, the call purchaser exercises the call (buys the stock at a specified price) and then sells it on the open market for a profit. If the call purchaser does not exercise the call before it expires, she or he loses the cost of the option.

A *put option* gives the purchaser the right to *sell* 100 shares of a specific stock at a specified price within a specified time. Put options are purchased by investors who expect the market price of the stock to fall below the guaranteed price. If this occurs before the option expires, the put purchaser buys the stock at the lower market price and then sells it at the higher price guaranteed by the put. Again, if the put is not exercised before it expires, the purchaser loses the cost of the option.

Now that we know something about the traditional and the more speculative investments that are available, let's take a look at the sources of information that can help you evaluate a potential investment.

Sources of Financial Information

Learning Objective 6
Be able to use the various sources of financial information, especially newspaper stock quotations and stock indexes

A wealth of information is available to investors. Sources include newspapers and business periodicals, corporate reports, and investors' services. Most local newspapers carry several pages of business news, including reports of securities transactions. The *Wall Street Journal* (which is published on weekdays) and *Barron's* (which is published once a week) are devoted almost entirely to financial and economic news. Both include complete coverage of transactions on all major securities exchanges.

Newspaper Coverage of Securities Transactions

Securities transactions are reported as long tables of figures that tend to look somewhat forbidding. However, they are easy to decipher once you know what to look for. Because transactions involving listed stocks, OTC stocks, and bonds are reported differently, we shall examine all three types of reports.

Listed Common and Preferred Stocks   Transactions involving listed common and preferred stocks are reported together in the same table. This table usually looks like the top section of Figure 19.6. Parts of a dollar are traditionally quoted as fractions rather than as cents. Thus ⅛ means $0.125, or 12.5 cents, and ¾ means $0.75, or 75 cents. Stocks are listed alphabetically. Your first task is to move down the table to find the stock you're interested in. Then, to read the transactions report, or *stock quotation*, you simply read across the table. The last row in the table in Figure 19.6 gives detailed information about General Electric Co. (Each numbered entry in the list below the stock table refers to a numbered column of the stock table.)

If a corporation has more than one stock issue, the common stock is always listed first. Note that there are two listings for General Cinema in Figure 19.6. The first is for the company's common stock. The other is for its preferred stock, as indicated by the letter *pf* in the stock column (column 3).

52 Weeks Hi	Lo	Stock	Sym	Div	Yld %	PE	Vol 100s	Hi	Lo	Close	Net Chg
19⅛	10⅞	GenCorp	GY	.60	5.4	45	650	11⅜	11⅛	11⅛	−¼
23⅜	16⅝	Genentech	GNE	...		138	1994	20⅞	20⅛	20⅝	+¼
19⅞	14⅛	GenAmInv	GAM	1.79e	10.2	...	139	17¾	17½	17⅝	−⅛
28½	23½	GenCinema	GCN	.44	1.8	16	1185	25	24⅞	24⅞	...
27¾	23⅝	GenCinema pf		.47e	1.9	...	3	24¾	24¾	24¾	−⅛
6⅝	4	GenData	GDC	...		...	48	4⅝	4½	4⅝	+⅛
18⅞	9	GenDevlpmt	GDV	...		6	273	9½	8⅞	9⅛	−⅜
60½	41⅜	GenDynam	GD	1.00	2.4	5	728	41⅜	41	41⅜	−¼
67	43¾	GenElec	GE	1.88	3.0	15	17179	62⅞	62¼	62⅝	−½

1. Highest price paid for one share of General Electric during the past 52 weeks: $67
2. Lowest price paid for one share of General Electric during the past 52 weeks: $43¾, or $43.75
3. Abbreviated name of the company: GenElec (*pf* denotes a preferred stock.)
4. Ticker symbol or letters that identify a stock for trading: GE
5. Total dividends paid per share during the last 12 months: $1.88
6. Yield percentage, or the percentage of return based on the current dividend and current price of the stock: $1.88 ÷ $62.625 = .03, or 3%
7. Price-earnings (PE) ratio — the price of a share of stock divided by the corporation's earnings per share of stock outstanding over the last 12 months: 15 ("..." indicates that the company is operating at a loss and there are no earnings.)
8. Number of shares of General Electric traded during the day, expressed in hundreds of shares: 1,717,900
9. Highest price paid for one share of General Electric during the day: $62⅞, or $62.875
10. Lowest price paid for one share of General Electric during the day: $62¼, or $62.25
11. Price paid in the last transaction of the day: $62⅝, or $62.625
12. Difference between the price paid for the last share today and the price paid for the last share on the previous day: ½, or $0.50 (In Wall Street terms, General Electric "closed down ½" on this day.)

1	**2**	**3**	**4**	**5**	**6**	**7**	**8**	**9**	**10**	**11**	**12**
52 Weeks Hi	Lo	Stock	Sym	Div	Yld %	PE	Vol 100s	Hi	Lo	Close	Net Chg
19⅛	10⅞	GenCorp	GY	.60	5.4	45	650	11⅜	11⅛	11⅛	−¼
23⅜	16⅝	Genentech	GNE		...	138	1994	20⅞	20⅛	20⅝	+¼
19⅞	14⅛	GenAmInv	GAM	1.79e	10.2	...	139	17¾	17½	17⅝	−⅛
28½	23½	GenCinema	GCN	.44	1.8	16	1185	25	24⅞	24⅞	...
27¾	23⅝	GenCinema pf		.47e	1.9	...	3	24¾	24¾	24¾	−⅛
6⅝	4	GenData	GDC		...	...	48	4⅝	4½	4⅝	+⅛
18⅞	9	GenDevlpmt	GDV		...	6	273	9½	8⅞	9⅛	−⅜
60½	41⅜	GenDynam	GD	1.00	2.4	5	728	41⅜	41	41⅜	−¼
67	43¾	GenElec	GE	1.88	3.0	15	17179	62⅞	62¼	62⅝	−½

FIGURE 19.6
Reading Stock Quotations for Common and Preferred Stocks
(Source: Newspaper at top of figure is the Wall Street Journal, *January 16, 1990, p. C4.)*

Over-the-Counter Stocks   Today, financial information about stocks traded in the over-the-counter stock market is reported in one of two ways. First, current financial information may be reported in tables just like the one illustrated in Figure 19.6. A second method that may be used to report information about over-the-counter stocks is illustrated in Figure 19.7. When this format is used, less information about a particular stock is given, but relevent information about a stock's volume, bid price, asked

Stock & Div	Sales 100s	Bid	Asked	Net Chg.
PlexusR	35	2¹¹⁄₁₆	2¾	+¹⁄₁₆
PoeAsc .40	20	12¾	13¾	...
PlrMol	242	1⁵⁄₁₆	1⁷⁄₁₆	...
Polydex	61	1¼	1⅜	+¹⁄₁₆
PolRs un	133	2¹⁄₁₆	2³⁄₁₆	...
Polymrx	35	2⅝	2⅞	...
PortsCl	2	2	2½	...
PwSpec	230	5⅛	5¼	−¹⁄₁₆
PrabRbt	11	2¼	2¾	...
PrdHme	1199	1⅞	2¹⁄₁₆	−⅛
Prestek	92	7¾	8⅛	...
Prstk wt	55	2⅝	2⅞	...
PrvBrd	2	¹³⁄₁₆	¹⁵⁄₁₆	...
PrvB pf .32	10	2³⁄₁₆	2⅜	+¹⁄₁₆
PrfBcp	31	12	12¾	...
PrfHlt	44	3½	4¼	...
PrftTc	565	3¼	3½	...
PsvcCp	52	4¹³⁄₁₆	4⅞	...
PubcoC	138	½	¹⁷⁄₃₂	...

1. Abbreviated name of the company and dividends, if any, paid by the company during the last 12 months
2. Number of shares traded during the day, expressed in hundreds of shares
3. Amount a seller could receive for a share of stock
4. Amount for which a buyer could purchase a share of stock
5. Difference between the bid price today and the bid price on the previous day

	1	2		3	4	5

Stock & Div	Sales 100s	Bid	Asked	Net Chg.
PlexusR	35	2¹¹⁄₁₆	2¾	+¹⁄₁₆
PoeAsc .40	20	12¾	13¾	...
PlrMol	242	1⁵⁄₁₆	1⁷⁄₁₆	...
Polydex	61	1¼	1⅜	+¹⁄₁₆
PolRs un	133	2¹⁄₁₆	2³⁄₁₆	...
Polymrx	35	2⅝	2⅞	...
PortsCl	2	2	2½	...
PwSpec	230	5⅛	5¼	−¹⁄₁₆
PrabRbt	11	2¼	2¾	...
PrdHme	1199	1⅞	2¹⁄₁₆	−⅛
Prestek	92	7¾	8⅛	...
Prstk wt	55	2⅝	2⅞	...
PrvBrd	2	¹³⁄₁₆	¹⁵⁄₁₆	...
PrvB pf .32	10	2³⁄₁₆	2⅜	+¹⁄₁₆
PrfBcp	31	12	12¾	...
PrfHlt	44	3½	4¼	...
PrftTc	565	3¼	3½	...
PsvcCp	52	4¹³⁄₁₆	4⅞	...
PubcoC	138	½	¹⁷⁄₃₂	...

FIGURE 19.7
Reading Stock Quotations for Over-the-Counter Stocks
(*Source: Newspaper at top of figure is the* Wall Street Journal, *January 12, 1990, p. C6.*)

price, and net change is reported. Thus, for Polydex common stock, Figure 19.7 shows that 6,100 shares were traded on this day. The first price, or *bid price*, is the price a buyer offers to pay for one share of a particular stock. The second price, or *asked price*, is the price a seller offers to sell one share of a particular stock. Polydex had a bid price of $1¼ and an asked price of $1⅜. In addition to price, information about current dividends and net change is also included.

Bonds   Purchases and sales of bonds are reported in tables like that shown at the top of Figure 19.8. In bond quotations, prices are given as a percentage of the face value, which is usually $1,000. Thus, to find the

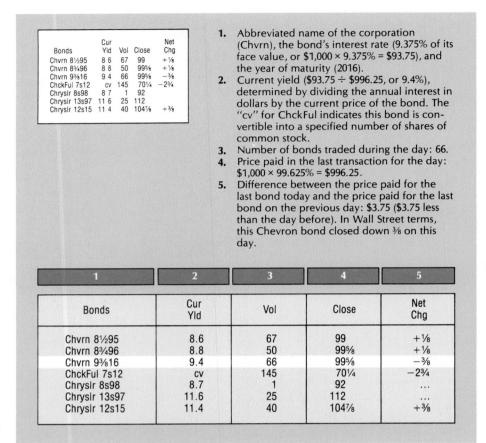

1. Abbreviated name of the corporation (Chvrn), the bond's interest rate (9.375% of its face value, or $1,000 × 9.375% = $93.75), and the year of maturity (2016).
2. Current yield ($93.75 ÷ $996.25, or 9.4%), determined by dividing the annual interest in dollars by the current price of the bond. The "cv" for ChckFul indicates this bond is convertible into a specified number of shares of common stock.
3. Number of bonds traded during the day: 66.
4. Price paid in the last transaction for the day: $1,000 × 99.625% = $996.25.
5. Difference between the price paid for the last bond today and the price paid for the last bond on the previous day: $3.75 ($3.75 less than the day before). In Wall Street terms, this Chevron bond closed down ⅜ on this day.

1	2	3	4	5
Bonds	Cur Yld	Vol	Close	Net Chg
Chvrn 8½95	8.6	67	99	+⅛
Chvrn 8¾96	8.8	50	99⅝	+⅛
Chvrn 9⅜16	9.4	66	99⅝	−⅜
ChckFul 7s12	cv	145	70¼	−2¾
Chryslr 8s98	8.7	1	92	...
Chryslr 13s97	11.6	25	112	...
Chryslr 12s15	11.4	40	104⅞	+⅜

FIGURE 19.8
Reading Bond Quotations
(Source: Newspaper at top of figure is the Wall Street Journal, *January 12, 1990, p. C14.)*

actual price paid, you must multiply the face value ($1,000) by the quotation listed in the newspaper. For example, a price that is quoted as 84 translates to a selling price of $840 ($1,000 × 84 percent = $840). The third row of Figure 19.8 gives detailed information (again, by column number) for the Chevron bond that pays 9⅜ percent interest and matures in 2016.

Other Sources of Financial Information

Brokerage-Firm Reports Brokerage firms employ financial analysts to prepare detailed reports on individual corporations and their securities. Such reports are based on the corporation's sales, earnings, management, and planning, plus other information on the company, its industry, and demand for its products. The reports may include buy or sell recommendations, and they are usually provided free to the brokerage firm's clients. Firms offering this service include E. F. Hutton, Prudential-Bache, Merrill Lynch, and most other full-service brokerage firms.

BUSINESS JOURNAL

Turn Your Computer into an Investment Tool

If you follow stock quotations and dream about the fortune you could make if only you had $10,000 to invest, sometime in the next decade you're likely to enter the relatively new world of computerized investing. Managing investments with a personal computer makes the most sense for people who already own a computer, have $10,000 to $50,000 in investments, and like to buy and sell fairly often. However, a clever investor with relatively little money can make a computer pay for itself with just one good trade.

HARDWARE REQUIREMENTS

To begin with, the home investor needs a fairly powerful personal computer (like an IBM PC, IBM clone, or Macintosh); a good printer; and a modem—a device that hooks up the computer to a telephone line. With that hardware in place, the potential investor faces the mind-boggling decisions of what software to buy and what services to subscribe to. For example, there are more than 500 on-line services and 3,300 databases that can be accessed with a computer and modem.

WHAT TYPE OF INFORMATION IS AVAILABLE?

Investors have always loved numbers, and brokerage firms have been feeding those numbers into computers for years. So it comes as no surprise that a home-computer user can access a virtually infinite amount of data. With a satellite dish, a special FM radio receiver, or a dedicated phone line and the right software, a home computer becomes a stock ticker that shows transactions as they happen while it maintains your personal investment portfolio. Typically, services that offer immediate (or *real-time*) stock quotations charge $300 to $600 for equipment and initial installation, and a monthly fee of $100 to $200. An investor with more modest means can subscribe to one of a number of services that provide stock quotations on a delayed basis—fifteen minutes after the transactions or at the end of each day. It is also possible to subscribe to one of the services that provide monthly disks full of information about selected companies in specific industries.

SOFTWARE THAT CAN HELP ANALYZE THE NUMBERS

With so much information readily available, most investors need a portfolio-analysis program to help them make sense of all the figures. Such programs can do mundane clerical chores like keeping track of the value of a portfolio, measuring that value against the Dow Jones average, and calculating current yields. They can also perform a wide variety of searches and calculations to identify trends or stocks that an investor is interested in. If, for instance, you want to know what chemical companies have price-earnings ratios of less than 15, debt-to-equity ratios of less than 50 percent, and dividends of at least 5 percent, your computer can tell you.

COMPUTERIZED TRANSACTIONS

Armed with all this information and analysis, the personal-computer user can take the ultimate step in home investing—making a stock transaction by computer. Two popular services—Charles Schwab's Equalizer ($169 plus a small monthly charge) and Fidelity's Investors Express ($13.50 a month)—enable investors with either service to buy and sell stock and other securities without ever talking to a broker. For infrequent traders, making a computerized transaction offers no great benefits. But on-line transactions are the perfect answer for the person who waits all weekend to make a trade based on Friday's late-breaking news. Such a person can input a buy or sell order on Sunday, and it will be electronically recorded the minute the market opens on Monday—before other investors can even get through to their brokers.

Based on information from Steve Kichen, "Investing by the Numbers," *Forbes,* July 27, 1988, pp. 196–198; Otis Port, "Turning Your Desktop Into a Personal Big Board," *Business Week,* March 27, 1989, p. 119; David Churbuck, "Discount Hunter," *Forbes,* June 26, 1989, pp. 252–253; Alfred Glossbrenner, "The Computer as an Investment Tool," *Working Woman,* February 1987, p. 47; Janet Bamford, "The Electronic Edge," *Forbes,* May 6, 1985, p. 102; and Bro Uttal, "Using a PC to Manage Investments," *Fortune 1986 Investor's Guide,* Fall 1985, p. 137.

Business Periodicals Most business periodicals are published weekly, twice a month, or monthly. Therefore, the financial information they contain is up to date. Business magazines like *Business Week, Fortune, Forbes,* and *Dun's Review* provide not only general economic news but also detailed financial information about individual corporations. Trade or industry publications like *Advertising Age* and *Business Insurance* may include information about the firms in a specific industry. And news magazines like *U.S. News & World Report, Time,* and *Newsweek* feature financial news regularly. These periodicals are available at libraries and are sold at newsstands and by subscription.

Corporate Reports Publicly held corporations must send their stockholders annual and quarterly reports on their operations. In addition, a corporation issuing a new security must—by law—prepare a prospectus and ensure that copies are distributed to potential investors. A **prospectus** is a detailed written description of a new security, the issuing corporation, and the corporation's top management. Both prospectuses and annual reports are usually available to the general public.

prospectus *a detailed written description of a new security, the issuing corporation, and the corporation's top management*

Investors' Services For fees ranging from $30 to $300 or more per year, various investors' services provide financial information to subscribers. Three of the most widely accepted investors' services are Standard & Poor's Stock Reports, Value Line, and Moody's Investors Service. All are fairly expensive, but their reports may be available from brokerage firms or libraries.

Stock Averages

stock average (or **stock index**) *an average of the current market prices of selected stocks*

Investors often gauge the stock market through the stock averages that are reported in newspapers and on television news programs. A **stock average** (or **stock index**) is an average of the current market prices of selected stocks. Over a period of time, these averages indicate price trends, but they cannot predict the performance of individual stocks. At best, they can give the investor a "feel" for what is happening to stock prices generally.

The *Dow Jones Industrial Average,* established in 1897, is the oldest stock index in use today. This average is composed of the prices of the common stocks of thirty leading industrial corporations. (These firms are listed in Table 19.3.) In addition, Dow Jones & Co., Inc. publishes the following averages:

▶ A *transportation average,* computed from the prices of twenty transportation-industry stocks

▶ A *utility average,* computed from the prices of fifteen utility stocks

▶ A *composite average,* computed from the prices of the sixty-five stocks included in the industrial, transportation, and utility averages

*TABLE 19.3   **The Thirty Corporations Whose Common Stocks Are Included in the Dow Jones Industrial Average**

Allied-Signal	Exxon	Philip Morris
Aluminum Co. of America	General Electric	Primerica
American Express	General Motors	Procter & Gamble
AT&T	Goodyear Tire & Rubber	Sears, Roebuck
Bethlehem Steel	IBM	Texaco
Boeing	International Paper	Union Carbide
Chevron	McDonald's	United Technologies
Coca-Cola	Merck & Co.	USX
Du Pont	3M	Westinghouse
Eastman Kodak	Navistar International	Woolworth

Source: Reprinted by permission of *Barron's*, © Dow Jones & Company, Inc., 1990. All rights reserved worldwide.

The Standard & Poor's 500 Stock Index and the New York Stock Exchange Index include more stocks than the Dow Jones averages. Thus they tend to reflect the stock market more fully. The *Standard & Poor's 500 Stock Index* is an average of the prices of 400 industrial, sixty transportation and utility, and forty financial stocks. The *New York Stock Exchange Composite Index* is computed from the prices of all stocks listed on the NYSE, weighted to reflect the number and value of outstanding shares.

It should be apparent by now that vast sums of money are involved in securities trading and that following and interpreting changes in the securities markets are complex undertakings. In an effort to protect investors from unfair treatment, both federal and state governments have acted to regulate securities trading.

Regulation of Securities Trading

Learning Objective 7
Know how federal and state authorities regulate trading in securities

Government regulation of securities trading began as a response to abusive and fraudulent practices in the sale of stocks and bonds. The states were the first to react, early in this century. Later, federal legislation was passed to regulate the interstate sale of securities.

State Regulation

The first state law regulating the sale of securities was enacted in Kansas in 1911. Within a few years, several other states had followed suit. Today, most states require that new issues be registered with a state agency and that brokers and securities dealers operating within the state be licensed.

The states also provide for the prosecution of individuals accused of the fraudulent sale of stocks and bonds.

blue-sky laws   *state laws that regulate securities trading*

The state laws that regulate securities trading are often called **blue-sky laws.** They are designed to protect investors from purchasing securities that are backed up by nothing but the "clear blue sky."

Federal Regulation

The *Securities Act of 1933,* sometimes referred to as the *Truth in Securities Act,* provides for full disclosure of important facts about corporations issuing new securities. Such corporations are required to file a *registration statement* containing specific information about the corporation's earnings, assets, and liabilities; its products or services; and the qualifications of its top management. Publication of the prospectus is also a requirement of this act.

Securities and Exchange Commission (SEC)   *the agency that enforces federal securities regulations*

The *Securities Exchange Act of 1934* created the **Securities and Exchange Commission (SEC),** which is the agency that enforces federal securities regulations. The operations of the SEC are directed by five commissioners, who are appointed by the president of the United States. The 1934 act gave the SEC the power to regulate trading on the NYSE and the American Stock Exchange. It empowered the SEC to make brokers and securities dealers pass a qualifying examination to sell securities. It also requires that corporations' registration statements be brought up to date periodically.

Seven other federal acts have been passed primarily to protect investors:

National Association of Securities Dealers (NASD)   *the organization responsible for the self-regulation of the over-the-counter securities market*

▶   The *Maloney Act of 1938* made it possible to establish the **National Association of Securities Dealers (NASD)** to oversee the self-regulation of the over-the-counter securities market.

▶   The *Investment Company Act of 1940* placed investment companies that sell mutual funds under the jurisdiction of the SEC.

▶   The *Federal Securities Act of 1964* extended the SEC's jurisdiction to include companies whose stock is sold *over the counter,* if they have total assets of at least $1 million or have more than 500 stockholders of any one class of stock.

▶   The *Securities Investor Protection Act of 1970* created the *Securities Investor Protection Corporation (SIPC).* This organization provides insurance of up to $500,000 for securities and up to $100,000 for cash left on deposit with a brokerage firm that later fails. The SIPC is, in essence, the securities-market equivalent of the FDIC and the SAIF (discussed in Chapter 17).

▶   The *Securities Amendments Act of 1975* empowered the SEC to supervise the development of a national securities market system. In addition, the law prohibited fixed commissions.

▶   The *Insider Trading Sanctions Act of 1984* strengthened the penalty provisions of the Securities Exchange Act of 1934. Under this act, people are guilty of insider trading if they use information that is available only to account executives or other brokerage-firm employees. This act also expanded the SEC's authority by empowering it to investigate such illegal acts.

▶ The *Insider Trading Act of 1988* made the top management of brokerage firms responsible for reporting to the SEC any transaction that was based on inside information. In addition, this act empowered the SEC to levy fines of up to $1 million for failure to report such trading violations.

CHAPTER REVIEW

Summary

Stocks may be purchased in either the primary or the secondary market. The primary market is a market in which an investor purchases financial securities (via an investment bank or other representative) from the issuer of those securities. Usually, an investment banking firm—an organization that assists corporations in raising funds—is involved in the marketing and distribution process. A corporation can also obtain equity financing by selling securities directly to current stockholders.

The secondary market involves transactions for existing securities that are bought and sold through a securities exchange or the over-the-counter market. Securities exchanges are marketplaces where members buy and sell securities for their clients. The New York Stock Exchange is the largest in the United States; it accounts for about 70 percent of stock traded on an organized exchange. Other securities exchanges include the American Stock Exchange and several regional exchanges. The over-the-counter market is a network of account executives (stockbrokers) who buy and sell the securities that are not traded in exchanges. If you invest in securities, chances are that you will use the services of an account executive who works for a brokerage firm. Most full-service account executives not only process your orders to buy and sell securities but also provide valuable information and advice. For these services, they are paid a commission based on the size and value of the transaction.

Personal-investment planning begins with formulating measurable and realistic investment goals. The investment plan itself is then designed to imple-

ment those goals. Many counselors suggest, as a first step, that the investor establish an emergency fund equivalent to three months' salary after taxes. Then additional funds may be invested according to the investment plan. Finally, all investments should be carefully monitored and, if necessary, the investment plan should be modified.

Depending on their particular investment goals, investors seek varying degrees of safety, income, growth, and liquidity from their investments. Safety is, in essence, freedom from the risk of loss. Generally, the greater the risk, the greater should be the potential return on an investment. Income is the periodic return from an investment. Growth is an increase in the value of the investment. Liquidity is defined as the ease with which an asset can be converted into cash.

Among the traditional investment alternatives are bank accounts, common stock, preferred stock, corporate bonds, government bonds, mutual funds, and real estate. More speculative investment techniques can provide greater returns, but they entail greater risk of loss. They include buying stock on margin, selling short, and trading in commodities and options.

Information on securities and the firms that issue them can be obtained from newspapers, business periodicals, brokerage firms, corporate reports, and investors' services. Most local newspapers report daily securities transactions and stock indexes, or averages. The averages indicate price trends but reveal nothing about the performance of individual stocks.

State and federal regulations protect investors from unscrupulous securities trading practices. Federal laws, which are enforced by the Securities and

Exchange Commission, require the registration of new securities, the publication and distribution of prospectuses, and the licensing of brokers and securities dealers. These laws apply to securities listed on the NYSE and the American Stock Exchange, to mutual funds, and to some OTC stocks.

In the next chapter we discuss the protection of finances and other assets from the hazards involved in simply existing. As you will see, these hazards include fire, theft, accident, and the legal liability for injury to others, The potential effect of hazards on firms and individuals can be minimized through effective risk management.

Key Terms

You should now be able to define and give an example relevant to each of the following terms:

primary market
investment banking firm
secondary market
securities exchange
over-the-counter (OTC) market
account executive (or stockbroker)
market order
limit order
discretionary order
round lot
odd lot
personal investment
liquidity
stock dividend
market value
bull market
bear market

stock split
mutual fund
speculative investment
margin requirement
leverage
buying long
selling short
spot trading
futures contract
option
prospectus
stock average (or stock index)
blue-sky laws
Securities and Exchange Commission (SEC)
National Association of Securities Dealers (NASD)

Questions and Exercises

Review Questions

1. What is the difference between the primary market and the secondary market?
2. When a corporation decides to sell stock, what is the role of an investment banking firm?

3. What is the difference between a securities exchange and the over-the-counter market?
4. What steps are involved in purchasing a stock listed on the NYSE?
5. What steps are involved in personal investing?
6. What is an investment "emergency fund," and why is it recommended?
7. What is meant by the safety of an investment? What is the tradeoff between safety and return on the investment?
8. In general, what kinds of investments provide income? What kinds provide growth?
9. How can the interest on savings accounts be used either as income or for growth?
10. How does a stock dividend differ from a stock split, from an investor's point of view?
11. Characterize the purchase of corporate bonds as an investment, in terms of safety, income, growth, and liquidity.
12. An individual may invest in stocks either directly or through a mutual fund. How are the two investment methods different?
13. What are the risks and rewards of purchasing stocks on margin?
14. When would a speculator sell short? buy a call option? buy a put option?
15. In what ways are newspaper stock quotations useful to investors? In what ways are stock averages useful?
16. What is the Securities and Exchange Commission? What are its principal functions?

Discussion Questions

1. According to William A. Schreyer, Chairman of Merrill Lynch, the best thing that could help improve Merrill Lynch's bottom line is a strong, healthy stock market. In what ways can a strong, healthy stock market aid a brokerage firm like Merrill Lynch?
2. Merrill Lynch uses its huge retail division to sell the new securities generated by the firm's investment banking activities. What are the advantages and disadvantages of this practice for the firm? for the firm's customers?
3. What personal circumstances might lead some investors to emphasize income rather than growth in their investment planning? What might lead them to emphasize growth rather than income?
4. Suppose you have just inherited 500 shares of IBM common stock. What would you do with or about it, if anything?

5. For what reasons might a corporation's executives be *unwilling* to have their firm's securities listed on an exchange?
6. What kinds of information would you like to have before you invest in a particular common or preferred stock? From what sources can you get that information?
7. Federal laws prohibit corporate managers from making investments that are based on "inside information"—that is, special knowledge about their firms that is not available to the general public. Why are such laws needed?

Exercises

1. Using recent newspaper stock quotations, fill in the following table for common stocks only.

   Newspaper: _____

   Date: _____

	Annual Dividend	P-E Ratio	Closing Price	Net Change
American Express (AmExp)	_____	_____	_____	_____
General Dynamics (GenDynam)	_____	_____	_____	_____
General Motors (GMot)	_____	_____	_____	_____

   a. Which of the three stocks would be the best investment for someone whose investment plan stresses income? Why?
   b. Which stock would seem to be best for an investment plan that stresses growth? (If you need more information to answer this, explain what information you need.)
   c. Can you tell from this information which stock offers the most safety? Explain.
2. Municipal bonds (those issued by cities) generally pay a lower rate of interest than corporate bonds. Through library research, determine why this is so—and why municipal bonds are still attractive to investors.

Case 19.1

What Type of Bond Is Right for You?

Are bonds safer than common or preferred stock? The answer to that question depends on a number of factors, such as who issued the bond, the likelihood of repayment at maturity, the conditions contained in the bond agreement, and the future outlook for the firm or government agency that issued the bond. Most investors rely on two financial services, Standard & Poor's Corporation and Moody's Investors Service, to provide ratings for corporate bonds. Standard & Poor's bond ratings range from *AAA* (the highest) to *D* (the lowest). Moody's bond ratings range from *Aaa* (the highest) to *C* (the lowest). For most investors, a bond rated *A* or better is probably as safe as a blue-chip stock, while a *B*-rated bond could be as risky as the most speculative stock.

Recently, a number of corporations have sold bonds to provide debt financing for expansion, research and development, debt retirement, or just about any other reason. From the investor's standpoint, these new bond issues range from very conservative to very speculative investments. Financial information about two such bond issues is provided below.

Continental Airlines	**Amoco Corporation**
Face value—$ 1,000	Face value—$1,000
Maturity date—1995	Maturity Date—2005
Interest rate—11%	Interest rate—8.38%
Current market price—$810	Current market price—$950
Current yield—13.6%	Current yield—8.8%

The Standard & Poor's rating for the Continental bond is *B* and for the Amoco bond is *AAA*.*

Questions

1. How important are the ratings issued by Moody's and Standard & Poor's? What does the Standard & Poor's *AAA* rating mean? What does the Standard & Poor's *B* rating mean?
2. The 13.6 current yield for the Continental Airlines bond is almost 5 percent higher than the current yield for the Amoco bond. Is the additional 5 percent worth the added risks involved in purchasing the lower-rated Continental bond?
3. The Continental Airlines bond matures in 1995; the Amoco bond matures in 2005. As the maturity

---

* Based on information from *Moody's Transportation Manual*, 1989, p. 619; *Moody's Industrial Manual*, Volume 1 (A–L), 1989, p. 949; John Paul Newport, Jr., "Junk Bonds Face the Big Unknown," *Fortune*, May 22, 1989, pp. 129–130; Sumner N. Levine, *The 1989 Dow Jones–Irwin Business and Investment Almanac* (Homewood, Ill.: Dow Jones–Irwin, 1989), pp. 422–423; and *Wall Street Journal*, January 12, 1990, p. C14.

MOBIL CORPORATION

LISTED	SYM.	LTPS♦	STPS♦	IND. DIV.	REC. PRICE	RANGE (52-WKS.)	YLD.	'89 YR.-END PR.
NYSE	MOB	102.5	107.9	$2.60*	59	63 - 46	4.4%	62⅝

INVESTMENT GRADE. A STRONG CHEMICAL BUSINESS PLUS HIGHER CRUDE OIL PRICE WILL MORE THAN OFF-SET LOWER PRICES AND DEMAND FOR NATURAL GAS.

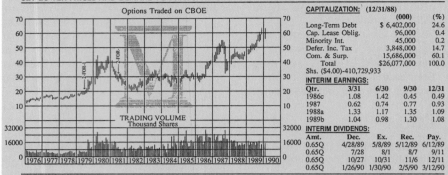

CAPITALIZATION: (12/31/88)

	(000)	(%)
Long-Term Debt	$ 6,402,000	24.6
Cap. Lease Oblig.	96,000	0.4
Minority Int.	45,000	0.2
Defer. Inc. Tax	3,848,000	14.7
Com. & Surp.	15,686,000	60.1
Total	$26,077,000	100.0

Shs. ($4.00)-410,729,933

INTERIM EARNINGS:

Qtr.	3/31	6/30	9/30	12/31
1986c	1.08	1.42	0.45	0.49
1987	0.62	0.74	0.77	0.93
1988a	1.33	1.17	1.35	1.09
1989b	1.04	0.98	1.30	1.08

INTERIM DIVIDENDS:

Amt.	Dec.	Ex.	Rec.	Pay.
0.65Q	4/28/89	5/8/89	5/12/89	6/12/89
0.65Q	7/28	8/1	8/7	9/11
0.65Q	10/27	10/31	11/6	12/11
0.65Q	1/26/90	1/30/90	2/5/90	3/12/90

BACKGROUND:

Mobil Corp. is a large vertically integrated petroleum Company, conducting its international business through three operating segments: Exploration and production, refining and marketing and Mobil Chemicals. Other operations are conducted through Mobil Credit, Mobil Land, Mining & Minerals and Research and Engineering. In 1988, geographic revenues (and earnings) were derived: U.S., 32% (40%); Canada, 2% (2%); other, 67% (58%); Eliminations, -1% (0%). Net proved crude oil reserves at the end of 1988 totaled 2,553 million barrels while net proved natural gas reserves equaled 19,637 billion cubic feet. In 1988, Mobil sold its Montgomery Ward retailing unit.

RECENT DEVELOPMENTS:

For the year ended 12/31/89, income from continuing operations fell 11% to $1.81 billion from $2.03 billion last year. Income includes a net gain of $12 million from unusual transactions. Income was limited by poor performances at the refining, marketing, and chemical businesses despite strong gains from the oil producing business. Revenues which include excise and state gasoline taxes rose 4.2% to $56.66 billion from $54.36 billion.

PROSPECTS:

Near-term results will be pressured by low prices for natural gas, which is responsible for about half of MOB's production. Downstream margins will grow as prices for oil byproducts have been increased to help offset higher production cost. Exploration and production will be tempered throughout 1990 as OPEC will continue to expand production past the 23 million barrel ceiling. Uncertain economic conditions are likely to limit capital expenditures. Extra cash on hand may augment further reductions in outstanding shares. International operations will likely lag behind domestic operation as competitive pricing pressures in most enclaves affects profit. To compensate MOB will implement an asset redeployment program to improve shareholder return.

STATISTICS:

YEAR	GROSS REVS. (Smill.)	OPER. PROFIT MARGIN %	RET. ON EQUITY %	NET INCOME (Smill.)	WORK CAP. (Smill.)	SENIOR CAPITAL (Smill.)	SHARES (000)	EARN. PER SH.$	DIV. PER SH.$	DIV. PAY. %	PRICE RANGE	P/E RATIO	AVG. YIELD %
80	62,823	23.3	25.0	f2,813	1,396	3,571	425,192	f6.62	1.73	26	44¾ - 24⅞	5.3	5.0
81	68,500	21.6	16.6	2,434	1,276	3,604	425,444	5.72	2.00	35	41¼ - 24⅛	5.7	6.1
82	63,828	19.2	9.4	1,380	538	4,717	406,146	3.31	2.00	60	28⅝ - 19½	7.3	8.3
83	58,515	20.9	10.8	1,501	1,077	5,490	406,818	3.69	2.00	54	34⅝ - 24¼	8.0	6.8
84	60,624	21.0	9.3	1,270	422	11,492	407,704	3.12	2.20	71	32⅛ - 23⅛	8.9	8.0
85	60,609	23.7	12.8	c1,040	147	9,745	408,351	c2.55	2.20	86	34⅜ - 25½	11.7	7.3
86	49,865	27.1	9.2	c1,407	437	8,286	408,732	c3.44	2.20	64	40¾ - 26¼	9.7	6.6
87	56,716	26.4	7.5	1,258	513	7,399	411,359	3.06	2.20	71	55 - 32	12.5	6.7
88	54,361	30.8	12.9	a2,031	923	6,498	410,330	a4.93	2.35	48	49⅛ - 38⅝	8.9	5.4
p89	56,656			b1,809				b4.40	2.55	58	63¼ - 45¼	12.3	4.7

♦Long-Term Price Score — Short-Term Price Score; see page 4a. STATISTICS ARE AS ORIGINALLY REPORTED. Adjusted for 2-for-1 split, 6/79 and 5/81. a-Excludes $56.0 million ($0.14 per share) gain from discontinued Montgomery Ward. b-Includes net gain of $47 million ($0.11 a share). c-Includes writedown of $508 million ($1.25 per share) from restructuring of a unit in 1985 and a charge of $150 million in 1986. f-Before $459 million ($1.08 a share) or from sale of interest on Belridge Oil Co.

INCORPORATED:
March 3, 1976 — DE
PRINCIPAL OFFICE:
150 East 42nd Street
New York, NY 10017-5666
Tel.: (212) 883-4242
ANNUAL MEETING:
Second Thurs. in May
NUMBER OF STOCKHOLDERS:
231,000

TRANSFER AGENT(S):
Chase Manhattan Bank, N.A., N.Y.
Montreal Trust Co., Calgary

REGISTRAR(S):
Chase Manhattan Bank, N.A., N.Y.
Montreal Trust Co., Calgary

INSTITUTIONAL HOLDINGS:
No. of Institutions: 972
Shares Held: 19,789,858

OFFICERS:
Chmn., Pres. & C.E.O.
   A. E. Murray
Vice Chairman
   R. F. Tucker
Vice President & C.F.O.
   L. A. Noto
Secretary
   D. T. Bartlett
Treasurer
   R. H. Gardner

FIGURE 19.9
Research Report on Mobil Corporation
(*Source:* Moody's Handbook of Common Stocks, *Spring 1990 edition, Moody's Investors Service, 99 Church Street, New York, N.Y. 10007. Tel. (212) 553-0300. Used by permission.)

dates approach, what should happen to the market price of each bond? Why?
4. What other information would you need to evaluate these two bonds? Where would you get this information?

Case 19.2

Moody's Research Information

In this chapter, we have stressed the importance of evaluating potential investments. Now, it's your turn to try your skill at evaluating a potential investment in Mobil Corporation. Assume that it is January 11, 1990, and that you have prepared a personal plan of action and established an emergency fund equal to three months' salary (after taxes). Also assume that you have saved $5,000, which can be used to purchase

Mobil's common stock. To help you evaluate your investment in Mobil Corporation, carefully examine the research report (Figure 19.9) taken from the Fall 1989 issue of *Moody's Handbook of Common Stocks*.

Questions

1. Based on the research report, would you buy Mobil common stock? Justify your answer.
2. What other investment information would you need to evaluate Mobil Corporation? Where would you obtain this information?
3. On January 11, 1990, the common stock for Mobil Corporation was selling for $58 a share. Using a recent newspaper, determine the current price for a share of Mobil's common stock. Based on this information, would your Mobil investment have been profitable if you had purchased the common stock at $58? Why?

RISK MANAGEMENT AND INSURANCE

20

1 Know what risk is, and understand the difference between a pure and a speculative risk

2 Recognize the four general techniques of risk management: avoidance, reduction, assumption, and the shifting of risk to an insurer

3 Understand the principles underlying insurance and the insurability of risks

4 Be aware of the types of insurance that can be used to protect businesses and individuals against property and casualty losses

5 Describe the types of insurance coverage that are available to individuals

6 Be able to explain the advantages and disadvantages of term, whole, endowment, and universal life insurance

CHAPTER PREVIEW

We open this chapter by defining two broad categories of risk: pure risks and speculative risks. Then we examine several methods of risk management available to individuals and businesses, and consider situations for which each method is appropriate. Next, we turn our attention to insurance companies—organizations that agree to assume responsibility for certain kinds of risk in exchange for payment of a fee. We see how insurance companies determine which risks they will cover and what prices they will charge for coverage. Then we list the major types of insurance against loss of property and losses owing to accidents. We close the chapter with a comparison of several kinds of life insurance.

First Executive Corporation

When Fred Carr became chairman and president of First Executive Corporation in 1974, the Los Angeles-based insurance company had annual sales revenues of $14 million but was losing money. Fourteen years later, the firm had increased its revenues to over $2 billion, had recorded profits in excess of $200 million, and had become the fifteenth largest life insurance company in the United States. Clearly , First Executive experienced remarkable growth in the 1980s. According to industry analysts, its success was the result of two factors.

First, the firm sold low-cost life insurance policies and annuities. (An annuity is a type of policy that guarantees payments to the policyholder at a future date.) The primary reason why First Executive was able to sell both life insurance policies and annuities at lower prices than its competitors was that the premiums the firm received were invested in junk bonds. The high interest received from its junk bond investments was then used to offset the cost of the firm's insurance business.

Second, First Executive Corporation sold most of its policies through independent agents and stockbrokers instead of establishing its own sales force. As a result, the firm was able to reduce its operational expenses to about one-half those of big competitors like Prudential Insurance and Metropolitan Life.

Ironically, the two factors that fueled First Executive's growth in the 1980s are the same factors that promise to create problems for the firm in the 1990s. In 1988, First Executive's junk bond investments totaled $5.5 billion, or 51 percent of its investment portfolio. And because a number of the companies that issued these bonds are now in financial trouble, state regulators are concerned that First Executive may be forced to declare a large number of the junk bonds in its portfolio worthless. If that happens, the value of the firm's investments—the assets that back up its policies—would

drop dramatically. To make matters worse, Fred Carr and First Executive are under federal investigation because of junk bond transactions made with Michael Milken, the former junk-bond king at the brokerage firm of Drexel Burnham Lambert.

Just at the time when First Executive needs money to build up its cash reserves, the independent agents and stockbrokers who sell First Executive's policies are also beginning to have some reservations. As a result, sales for the company's investment-oriented products are beginning to decline. Continued publicity over First Executive's junk bond investments is also affecting the firm's policyholders and stockholders. Policyholders have reacted by cashing in their policies and taking both their money and their business to other insurance companies. Stockholders, on the other hand, are concerned because any losses that result from junk bond investments will mean lower operating profits.[1]

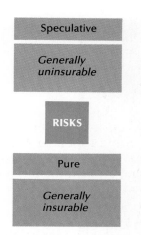

FIGURE 20.1
Classification of Risks
A speculative *risk is a risk that accompanies the possibility of earning a profit; a pure *risk is a risk that involves only the possibility of loss.*

Even with all the bad news, Fred Carr, Chairman of First Executive Corporation, is optimistic. According to Carr, the firm has built up its cash reserves in order to handle any problems that may develop. Given enough time, he thinks First Executive will be able to weather the financial storms ahead. But most insurance industry analysts are quick to point out that to stay in business, First Executive must continue to meet the needs of its customers. This means the company must continue to sell policies to customers who want to satisfy their need for safety. (You may recall from Chapter 8 that Abraham Maslow considered this a very basic human need. He placed it second only to the physiological need for food and water, clothing, shelter, and sleep.)

Today, the average American family spends more than $3,500 each year for insurance to satisfy its need for safety. The typical family purchases insurance coverage to protect its home, car, investments, and family members. Similarly, a business firm insures its resources and products against the hazards of doing business: damage, liability, theft, injury, and more. And while insurance can't guarantee safety, it can limit the financial damage of an accident or tragedy.

Firms and individuals make use of other risk-management methods as well. One example is the periodic inspection of production facilities to discover and eliminate hazards that could lead to injury. Another example is the use of smoke alarms in homes and businesses. Together, the various techniques of risk management are intended to reduce both the possibility of loss and the impact of any losses that do occur.

The Element of Risk

Learning Objective 1
Know what risk is, and understand the difference between a pure and a speculative risk

risk *the possibility that a loss or injury will occur*

speculative risk *a risk that accompanies the possibility of earning a profit*

Risk is the possibility that a loss or injury will occur. It is impossible to escape some types of risk in today's world. For individuals, driving an automobile, investing in stocks or bonds, and even jogging along a country road involve some risk. For businesses, risk is a part of every decision. In fact, the essence of business decision making is weighing the potential risks and gains involved in various courses of action.

There is obviously a difference between, say, the risk of losing money that one has invested and the risk of being hit by a car while jogging. This difference leads to the classification of risks as either speculative or pure risks (see Figure 20.1).

A **speculative risk** is a risk that accompanies the possibility of earning a profit. Most business decisions, such as the decision to market a new product, involve speculative risks. If the new product succeeds in the marketplace, there are profits; if it fails, there are losses. For example, Liquid Paper is a typewriter correction fluid that was invented and then marketed by Betty Graham. The product worked well, and the product's success eventually led Graham to form the Liquid Paper Corporation. However, in the beginning, there was a distinct possibility that office workers would reject the idea of correcting typing errors with fluid from

623

When Henry Kloss (left) and Henry Morgan decided to start a small speaker business called Cambridge SoundWorks, they could not ignore the speculative risk that all small business owners face. In fact their risk was well rewarded; in its first year, Cambridge SoundWorks sold 8,000 sets of speakers, employed 45 workers, and turned a profit on $4 million in sales.

a bottle. Hence this was one speculative risk that accompanied the chance to earn a profit with the new product.

pure risk *a risk that involves only the possibility of loss, with no potential for gain*

A **pure risk** is a risk that involves only the possibility of loss, with no potential for gain. The possibility of damage due to hurricane, fire, or auto accident is a pure risk, because there is no gain if such damage does not occur. Another pure risk is the risk of large medical bills due to a serious illness. Again, if there is no illness, there is no monetary gain.

Let us now look at the various techniques that are available for managing risk.

Risk Management

risk management *the process of evaluating the risks faced by a firm or an individual and then minimizing the costs involved with those risks*

Risk management is the process of evaluating the risks faced by a firm or an individual and then minimizing the costs involved with those risks. Any risk entails two types of costs. The first is the cost that will be incurred if a *potential* loss becomes an *actual* loss. An example is the cost of rebuilding and re-equipping an assembly plant that burns to the ground. The second type consists of the costs of reducing or eliminating the risk of potential loss. Here we would include the costs of purchasing insurance against loss by fire or the cost of not building the plant at all (this cost is equal to the profit that the plant might have earned). These two types of costs must be balanced, one against the other, if risk management is to be effective.

Most people tend to think of risk management as simply buying insurance. But, although insurance is an important part of risk management, it is not the only means of dealing with risk. Other methods may be less costly in specific situations. And some kinds of risks are uninsurable—not even an insurance company will issue a policy to protect against them. In this section, we examine the four general risk-management techniques. Then, in the following sections, we look more closely at insurance.

Risk Avoidance

An individual can avoid the risk of an automobile accident by not riding in a car. A manufacturer can avoid the risk of product failure by refusing to introduce new products. Both would be practicing risk avoidance—but at a very high cost. The person who avoids automobile accidents by foregoing cars may have to give up his or her job to do so. The business that does not take a chance on new products will probably fail when the product life cycle, discussed in Chapter 12, catches up with existing products.

There are, however, situations in which risk avoidance is a practical technique. At the personal level, individuals who stop smoking or refuse to walk through a high-crime neighborhood are avoiding risks. Jewelry stores lock their merchandise in vaults at the end of the business day to avoid losses through robbery. And, to avoid the risk of a holdup, many gasoline stations accept only credit cards or the exact amount of the purchase for sales made during after-dark hours.

Obviously, no person or business can eliminate all risks. But, by the same token, no one should assume that all risks are unavoidable.

Risk Reduction

If a risk cannot be avoided, perhaps it can be reduced. For example, an automobile passenger can reduce the risk of injury in an auto accident by wearing a seat belt. A manufacturer can reduce the risk of product failure through careful product planning and market testing. In both these situations, the cost of reducing the risk would seem to be well worth the potential saving.

Businesses face risks as a result of their operating procedures and management decision making. An analysis of operating procedures—by company personnel or outside consultants—can often point up areas where risk can be reduced. Among the techniques that can be used are:

▶ The establishment of an employee safety program to encourage awareness of safety among employees

▶ The purchase *and* use of proper safety equipment, from hand guards on machinery to goggles and safety shoes for individuals

Learning Objective 2
Recognize the four general techniques of risk management: avoidance, reduction, assumption, and the shifting of risk to an insurer

▶ Burglar alarms, security guards, and even guard dogs to protect warehouses from burglary

▶ Fire alarms, smoke alarms, and sprinkler systems to reduce the risk of fire and the losses due to fire

▶ Accurate and effective accounting and financial controls, to protect the firm's inventories and cash from pilfering

The risks involved in management decisions can be reduced only through effective decision making. These risks *increase* whenever a decision is made hastily or is based on less than sufficient information. However, the cost of reducing these risks goes up when managers take too long to make decisions. Costs also increase when managers require an overabundance of information before they are willing to decide.

Risk Assumption

An individual or firm will—and probably must—take on certain risks as part of living or doing business. Individuals who drive to work *assume* the risk of having an accident, but they wear a seat belt to reduce the risk of injury in the event of an accident. The firm that markets a new product *assumes* the risk of product failure—after first reducing that risk through market testing.

Risk assumption, then, is the act of taking responsibility for the loss or injury that may result from a risk. Generally, it makes sense to assume a risk when one or more of the following conditions exist:

As discussed in Chapter 8, the second level of Maslow's hierarchy of needs is the need for safety. This includes job security, health insurance, pension plans, and safe working conditions. These two employees must be concerned with safe working conditions as part of their jobs.

1. The potential loss is too small to worry about.
2. Effective risk management has reduced the risk.
3. Insurance coverage, if available, is too expensive.
4. There is no other way of protecting against a loss.

Large firms that own many facilities often find that a particular kind of risk assumption called self-insurance is a practical way to avoid high insurance costs. **Self-insurance** is the process of establishing a monetary fund that can be used to cover the cost of a loss. For instance, there are approximately 8,000 7-Eleven convenience stores, each worth $200,000, scattered around the country. A logical approach to self-insurance against fire losses would be to collect a certain sum—say, $200—from each store every year. The money that is collected is placed in an interest-bearing reserve fund and used as necessary to repair any fire damage that occurs to 7-Eleven stores. Money that is not used remains the property of the firm. And eventually, if the fund grows, the yearly contribution from each store can be reduced.

Self-insurance does not eliminate risks; it merely provides a means for covering losses. And it is, itself, a risky practice—at least in the beginning. 7-Eleven would suffer a considerable financial loss if more than eight stores were destroyed by fire in the first year the self-insurance program went in effect.

Shifting Risks

Perhaps the most commonly used method of dealing with risk is to shift, or transfer, the risk to an insurance company. An **insurer** (or **insurance company**) is a firm that agrees, for a fee, to assume financial responsibility for losses that may result from a specific risk. The fee charged by an insurance company is called the **premium.** A contract between an insurer and the person or firm whose risk is assumed is known as an **insurance policy.** Generally, an insurance policy is written for a period of one year. Then, if both parties are willing, it is renewed each year. It specifies exactly which risks are covered by the agreement, the dollar amounts that the insurer will pay in case of a loss, and the amount of the premium.

Insurance is thus the protection against loss that is afforded by the purchase of an insurance policy. Insurance companies will not, however, assume every kind of risk. A risk that insurance companies will assume is called an **insurable risk.** Insurable risks include the risk of loss by fire and theft, the risk of loss by automobile accidents, and the risks of sickness and death. A risk that insurance firms will not assume is called an **uninsurable risk.**

In general, pure risks are insurable, whereas speculative risks are uninsurable (see Figure 20.2). An insurance company will protect General Electric's locomotive assembly plant against losses due to fire or tornadoes. It will not, however, protect General Electric against losses due to a lack of sales orders for locomotives.

self-insurance *the process of establishing a monetary fund that can be used to cover the cost of a loss*

insurer (or **insurance company**) *a firm that agrees, for a fee, to assume financial responsibility for losses that may result from a specific risk*

premium *the fee charged by an insurance company*

insurance policy *the contract between an insurer and the person or firm whose risk is assumed*

insurance *the protection against loss that is afforded by the purchase of an insurance policy*

insurable risk *a risk that insurance companies will assume*

uninsurable risk *a risk that insurance firms will not assume*

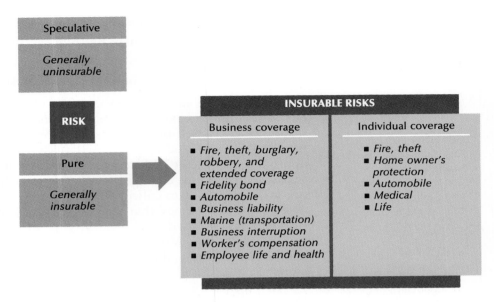

FIGURE 20.2
Insurable Risks for Businesses and Individuals
Generally, an insurance company will not protect against speculative risks such as a lack of sales.

The next section provides an overview of the basic principles of insurance and the kinds of companies that provide insurance.

Insurance and Insurance Companies

Learning Objective 3
Understand the principles underlying insurance and the insurability of risks

An insurance company is a business. Like other businesses, an insurer provides a product—protection from loss—in return for a reasonable fee. Its sales revenues are the premiums it collects from the individuals and firms that it insures. (Insurance companies typically invest the money that they have on hand at any time; thus we should include interest and dividend income as part of their revenues.) Its expenses are the costs of the various resources—salaries, rent, utilities, and so on—*plus* the amounts that the insurance company pays out to cover the losses of its clients.

Pricing and product are very important and exacting issues to an insurance company, primarily because it must set its price (its premiums) before the specific cost of its product (how much money it will have to pay out in claims) is known. For this reason, insurance companies employ mathematicians called *actuaries* to predict the likelihood of losses and to determine the premiums that should be charged. Let us look at some of the more important concepts on which insurance (and the work of actuaries) is based.

BUSINESS JOURNAL

Best Insurance Ratings

Today, the most widely recognized source of information on insurance companies that operate in the United States is A. M. Best Company. A. M. Best Company publishes *Best's Insurance Reports, Best's Key Rating Guide,* and *Best's Trend Report*—all publications that can be used to evaluate insurance companies. In fact, Best carries so much clout that companies with its A+ (superior) rating often mention it in their advertising and promotional materials.

BEST'S RATINGS CLASSIFICATIONS

The objective of Best's rating system is to evaluate the financial health of an insurance company. Factors reflected in a firm's overall rating include the company's profitability, financial leverage, liquidity, value of its assets, adequacy of cash reserves, and management. The following is a brief explanation of each rating classification.

A+ (Superior)	Superior ability to meet obligations to policy-holders
A and A− (Excellent)	Strong ability to meet obligations to policyholders
B+ (Very Good)	Very good ability to meet obligations to policy-holders
B and B− (Good)	Good ability to meet obligations to policyholders
C+ (Fairly Good)	Fairly good ability to meet obligations to policy-holders
C and C− (Fair)	Fair ability to meet obligations to policyholders

A NEED FOR EVALUATION

While most insurance companies are ethical and financially secure, there are exceptions. Because of the exceptions, consumers should evaluate insurance firms before purchasing an insurance policy. Consider the case of Sandra Coleman, the owner of Sierra, Inc.—a small New Mexico wholesale clothing firm. Ms. Coleman got a telephone call from an insurance salesperson representing New World Insurance Company. The salesperson knew that she was the owner of Sierra and asked what type of insurance coverage she had. Briefly she described her coverage and told the salesperson that she paid approximately $4,500 a year for it. Almost immediately, the salesperson told her that his company could provide the same coverage for less than $3,000 a year. The salesperson told her that his company sold most of its policies over the phone and that the company was offering coverage at a discount to small businesses that went to the trouble of switching. He told her that if she would send him a check for $1,500, he would begin processing her application. Finally, he asked her to mail the check to a Houston post-office box.

Ms. Coleman was interested in purchasing insurance coverage from New World Insurance Company, but fortunately she did some checking before mailing her $1,500 check. She looked through a copy of *Best's Insurance Reports*—available at most public libraries—but found no such company as New World Insurance. The salesperson hadn't given Ms. Coleman a telephone number, but he did call back a week later to see why he hadn't received her check. When Ms. Coleman told him that she had not been able to find any information about New World Insurance Company in *Best's Insurance Reports*, he hung up!

Information on A. M. Best Company and Best's ratings was obtained from *Best's Insurance Reports (Property—Casualty,* 90th annual edition, 1989, pp. vii–x. Courtesy of A. M. Best Company, Ambest Road, Oldwick, New Jersey 08858.)

Basic Insurance Concepts

The Principle of Indemnity   The purpose of insurance is to provide protection against loss; it is neither speculation nor gambling. This concept is expressed in the **principle of indemnity:** In the event of a loss, an insured firm or individual cannot collect, from the insurer, an amount greater than the actual dollar amount of the loss. Suppose you own a home that is valued at $100,000. However, you purchase $150,000 worth of fire insurance on your home. Even if it is totally destroyed by fire, the insurer will pay you only $100,000. That is the actual amount of your loss.

The premiums that are set by actuaries are based on the amount of risk involved and the amount to be paid in case of a loss. Generally, the greater the risk and the amount to be paid, the higher the premium.

Insurability of the Risk   As we noted earlier, insurers will accept responsibility for risks that meet at least the following conditions:

1. Losses must not be under the control of the insured. Losses due to fire, wind, or accident are generally insurable, but gambling losses are not. Moreover, an insurer will not pay a claim for damage that was intentionally caused by the insured person. For example, a person who sets fire to an insured building cannot collect on a fire insurance policy.

2. The insured hazard must be widespread. That is, the insurance company must be able to write many policies covering the same specific hazard throughout a wide geographic area. This condition allows the insurer to minimize its own risk: the risk that it will have to pay huge sums of money to clients within a particular geographic area in the event of a catastrophe caused by, say, a tornado.

3. The probability of a loss should be predictable. Insurance companies cannot tell which particular clients will suffer losses. However, their actuaries must be able to determine, statistically, what *fraction* of their clients will suffer each type of loss. They can do so, for insurable risks, by examining records of losses for past years. They can then base their premiums, at least in part, on the number and value of the losses that are expected to occur.

4. Losses must be measurable. Property that is insured must have a value that is measurable in dollars, because insurance firms reimburse losses with money. Moreover, premiums are based partly on the measured value of the insured property. As a result of this condition, insurers will not insure an item for its emotional or sentimental value, but only for its actual monetary value.

5. The policyholder must have an insurable interest. That is, the individual or firm that purchases an insurance policy must be the one that would suffer from a loss. You can purchase insurance on your own home, but you cannot insure your neighbor's home in the hope of making a profit if it should burn down! Generally, individuals are

principle of indemnity   *In the event of a loss, an insured firm or individual cannot collect, from the insurer, an amount greater than the actual dollar amount of the loss.*

considered to have an insurable interest in their family members. Therefore, a person can insure the life of a spouse, a child, or a parent. Corporations may purchase "key executive" insurance covering certain corporate officers. The proceeds from this insurance help offset the loss of the services of these key people if they die or become incapacitated.

Low-Cost, Affordable Coverage   Price is usually a marketing issue rather than a technical concept. However, the price of insurance is intimately tied to the risks and potential losses that are involved in a particular type of coverage. Insurers would like to "produce" insurance at a very low cost to their policyholders, but they must charge enough in premiums to cover their expected payouts (see Table 20.1).

Customers purchase insurance when they believe that premiums are low in relation to the possible dollar loss. For certain risks, premiums can soar so high that insurance is simply not cost-effective. A $1,000 life insurance policy for a 99-year-old man would cost about $930 per year. Clearly, a man of that age would be better off if he invested the premium amount in a bank. By this means he would use self-insurance rather than shifting the risk. Although this is an extreme example, it illustrates the fact that insurers must compete, through their prices, with alternative methods of managing risk.

TABLE 20.1   ***How U.S. Life Insurance Companies Spent Their Income—1988***

Income	
Premiums	71.1¢
Net Investment Earnings and Other Income	28.9
	100.0¢
How Used	
Benefit Payments and Additions to Funds for Policyholders and Beneficiaries	
Benefit Payments in Year	50.7¢
Additions to Policy Reserve Funds	32.7
Additions to Special Reserves and Surplus Funds	1.5
	84.9
Operating Expenses	
Commissions to Agents	5.0
Home and Field Office Expenses	7.2
	12.2
Taxes	1.8
Dividends to Stockholders of Stock Life Insurance Companies	1.1
	100.0¢

Source: 1989 Life Insurance Fact Book Update, published by the American Council of Life Insurance, 1001 Pennsylvania Avenue, N.W., Washington, D.C.   20004-2599.

With annual net investment income of over $7 billion, Metropolitan Life is one of the largest life insurance companies in the United States. Since "Met" is a mutual company, any surplus of income over expenses is distributed to policyholders as a return of part of their premiums.

Ownership of Insurance Companies

Insurance companies are owned either by stockholders or by policyholders. A **stock insurance company** is owned by stockholders and is operated to earn a profit. Like other profit-making corporations, stock insurance companies pay dividends to stockholders from surplus of income (left over after benefit payments, operating expenses, and taxes have been paid). Most of the approximately 5,000 insurance companies in the United States are stock insurance companies.

A **mutual insurance company** is an insurance company that is collectively owned by its policyholders and is thus a cooperative. Because a mutual insurance company has no stockholders, its policyholders elect the board of directors. The members of the board, in turn, choose the executives who manage the firm. Any surplus of income over expenses is distributed to policyholders as a return of part of their premiums. (This return may take the form of a reduced premium at the start of the policy year or that of a "dividend" at the end of the policy year.)

Both stock and mutual insurance companies must maintain cash reserves to cover future obligations and policyholders' claims. Cash reserves are typically invested in certificates of deposit, stocks, bonds, and real estate. As Table 20.2 shows, four of the five largest life insurance firms are mutual companies. By prudent investment of reserves, insurance firms can develop sizable incomes for their owners.

stock insurance company   *an insurance company that is owned by stockholders and is operated to earn a profit*

mutual insurance company   *an insurance company that is collectively owned by its policyholders and is thus a cooperative*

TABLE 20.2   *The Five Largest Life Insurance Companies in the United States, Ranked by Assets*

Rank	Company	Assets (millions)	Net Investment Income (millions)
1	Prudential (mutual)	$129,118.1	$8,078.1
2	Metropolitan (mutual)	98,740.3	7,380.7
3	Equitable Life (mutual)	52,511.9	2,852.7
4	Aetna Life (stock)	52,022.6	3,551.4
5	Teachers Insurance & Annuity (mutual)	44,374.1	3,979.3

Source: Fortune, "The 50 Largest Life Insurance Companies," June 4, 1990, pp. 322–323.

Careers in Insurance

Insurance companies form one of the largest industries in the United States. The industry ranks in importance with banking and finance, manufacturing, building, and electronics. Careers in insurance generally fall into two categories: sales and administration.

In the sales category, individuals can work as employees for insurance companies or as independent agents representing more than one insurance company. Recently, the insurance industry has placed increased emphasis on advanced training for sales personnel. Life insurance salespeople who

The Transamerica Life Companies are providers of individual life insurance, pension products, and reinsurance. Sig Kagawa, general agent in Honolulu, handles the insurance needs of Jim Delano, president of Lion Coffee in Kona, Hawaii.

pass examinations and meet other requirements are awarded the Chartered Life Underwriter (CLU) designation. The Chartered Property Casualty Underwriter (CPCU) designation is awarded to individuals who pass examinations and meet the requirements in all areas of insurance *except* life insurance.

Administrative employees work to meet the needs of the firm's customers. They must process policies and claims, and handle an amazing amount of paperwork. Jobs in this category include actuary, claims adjuster, claims clerk, underwriter, and a number of other essential positions. In addition to meeting the needs of customers, administrative employees are responsible for investing funds for an insurance company.

Property and Casualty Insurance

Learning Objective 4
Be aware of the types of insurance that can be used to protect businesses and individuals against property and casualty losses

In the next three sections, we examine the major types of insurance coverage offered by insurers. Here, our subject is insurance against loss of property and against losses due to accidents. In the following two sections we discuss the various kinds of health and life insurance.

Insurance is available to cover most pure risks, but specialized or customized policies can be expensive. A part of effective risk management is to ensure that, when insurance is purchased, the coverage is proper for the individual situation. Three questions can be used as guidelines in this regard: What hazards must be insured against? Is the cost of insurance coverage reasonable in this situation? What other risk-management techniques can be used to reduce insurance costs?

Fire Insurance

fire insurance *insurance that covers losses due to fire*

Fire insurance covers losses due to fire. The standard fire insurance policy provides protection against partial or complete loss of a building and/or its contents when that loss is caused by fire or lightning. Premiums depend on the construction of the building, its use and contents, whether risk-reduction devices (such as smoke and fire alarms) are installed in the building, and other factors. If a fire occurs, the insurance company reimburses the policyholder for either the actual dollar loss or the maximum amount stated in the policy, whichever is lower.

Coinsurance Clause   To reduce their insurance premiums, individuals and businesses sometimes insure property for less than its actual cash value. Their theory is that fire rarely destroys a building completely—thus they need not buy full insurance. However, if the building is partially destroyed, they expect their insurance to cover all the damage. This places an unfair burden on the insurance company, which receives less than the full premium but must cover the full loss. To avoid this problem, insurance companies include a coinsurance clause in most fire insurance policies.

coinsurance clause *a part of a fire insurance policy that requires the policyholder to purchase coverage at least equal to a specified percentage of the replacement cost of the property to obtain full reimbursement for losses*

A **coinsurance clause** is a part of a fire insurance policy that requires the policyholder to purchase coverage at least equal to a specified

BUSINESS JOURNAL

Insurance Coverage for Your Home or Apartment

It shouldn't take a tragedy to start you thinking about your insurance coverage and how well your possessions are protected, but many people wait until tragedy strikes before checking on their coverage. Exactly what should you know when buying home owner's or renter's insurance?

THE BASICS

When purchasing a home owner's or renter's policy or evaluating your current coverage, there are a number of factors to consider. First, and most important, consider whether the policy provides adequate protection for your possessions. Generally, a renter's policy covers just your possessions, whereas a home owner's policy covers both your possessions and your house. Be sure that your house is insured for at least 80 percent of its replacement value. Replacement value (not to be confused with market value) is the amount it would cost you to rebuild, using the same materials and today's labor, if your house were totally destroyed. If an insurer finds that you are insured for less than 80 percent, the company can pay claims on a depreciated basis. And it is your responsibility to pay the difference. To help you maintain adequate coverage, most policies have an inflation clause, which automatically increases coverage and premiums at each renewal.

No matter how much coverage you have, you won't collect a dime unless you can document your loss. So keep an updated inventory of the contents of your house or apartment somewhere off the premises (so that it will not be destroyed in a fire or other disaster). Insurers advise that you document your claim with close-up photos of valuables and the walls and contents of every room.

Make sure that you are well insured with liability coverage, which protects you against claims made against you by others. Typical policies offer coverage of $100,000.

ADDITIONAL COVERAGE

You may also want to add the following options to your standard home owner's or renter's policy.

1. Most policies insure belongings for their actual cash value (replacement cost minus depreciation).

But insurance experts suggest that you purchase replacement-cost coverage, which pays the actual amount required to replace an item that is destroyed or stolen. This type of coverage usually costs between 10 and 15 percent more than standard coverage.

2. For valuable personal possessions such as paintings, jewelry, furs, cameras, musical equipment, silver, coin collections, antiques, and collectibles, you may want to consider a personal-articles floater policy. This type of policy is tailored to each valuable and floats wherever the property goes. For example, if a piece of jewelry is stolen when you're in England, it is covered. When "scheduling" valuables, the item must be specifically described and values must usually be supported by a professional appraisal or bill of sale. Costs are based on the value of the insured item.

3. You can increase your liability coverage from $100,000 to $300,000 for only another $10 to $20 a year. Because of the increase in the number of lawsuits, this added coverage is advisable. A separate policy called an *umbrella* policy can be written to extend your liability coverage to $1 million.

A FINAL WORD OF CAUTION

Shop around before choosing your insurance company, and make sure that you are getting the coverage you need at a price you can afford. If you have questions about your home owner's or renter's insurance, call your agent, state insurance department, or the Insurance Information Institute's consumer hot line at 1-800-221-4954. (Financial support for the Insurance Information Institute is provided by 300 insurance companies that operate in the United States.)

Based on information from "Insuring Your Home," *Consumer Reports,* September 1989, pp. 572–578; Paul Plawin, "Get a Homeowners Insurance Checkup," *Changing Times,* June 1989, pp. 92–93; Donald H. Dunn, "Now's the Time to Ask: Am I Covered?" *Business Week,* October 21, 1985, p. 141; Peter D. Lawrence, "Insurance—Why It Pays to Appraise," *Esquire,* November 1986, p. 92; and Anne McGrath, "The Right Way to Cut Insurance Costs," *U.S. News & World Report,* September 1, 1986, p. 53.

percentage of the replacement cost of the property to obtain full reimbursement for losses. In most cases, the required percentage is 80 percent of the replacement cost. Suppose the owners of a $600,000 building decide to purchase only $300,000 worth of fire insurance. If the building is totally destroyed, the insurance company must pay the policy's face value of $300,000. However, if the building is only partially destroyed, and the damage amounts to $200,000, the insurance company will pay only $125,000. This dollar amount is calculated in the following manner:

1. The coinsurance clause requires coverage of at least 80 percent of $600,000, or $480,000.

2. The owners have purchased only $300,000 of insurance. Thus they have insured themselves for only a portion of any loss. That portion is $300,000 ÷ $480,000 = 0.625, or 62.5 percent.

3. The insurance company will therefore reimburse the owner for only 62.5 percent of any loss. In the case of a $200,000 loss, the insurance company will pay 62.5 percent of $200,000, or $125,000.

If the owners of the building had insured it for $480,000, the insurance company would have covered the entire $200,000 loss.

Extended Coverage   **Extended coverage** is insurance protection against damage caused by wind, hail, explosion, vandalism, riots or civil commotion, falling aircraft, and smoke. Extended coverage is available as an *endorsement*, or addition, to some other insurance policy—usually a fire insurance policy. The premium for extended coverage is generally quite low (much lower than the total cost of separate policies covering each individual hazard). Normally, losses caused by war, nuclear radiation or contamination, and water (other than in storms) are excluded from extended-coverage endorsements.

extended coverage *insurance protection against damage caused by wind, hail, explosion, vandalism, riots or civil commotion, falling aircraft, and smoke*

Burglary, Robbery, and Theft Insurance

Burglary is the illegal taking of property through forcible entry. A kicked-in door, a broken window pane, or pry marks on a windowsill are evidence of a burglary or attempted burglary. *Robbery* is the unlawful taking of property from an individual by force or threat of violence. A thief who uses a gun to rob a gas station is committing robbery. *Theft* (or *larceny*) is a general term that means the wrongful taking of property that belongs to another. Insurance policies are available to cover burglary only, robbery only, theft only, or all three. Premiums vary with the type and value of the property covered by the policy.

Business owners must also be concerned about crimes that employees may commit. A **fidelity bond** is an insurance policy that protects a business from theft, forgery, or embezzlement by its employees. If such a crime does occur, the insurance company reimburses the business for financial losses up to the dollar amount specified in the policy. Individual employees or specific positions within an organization may be bonded. It is also possible to purchase a "blanket" policy that covers the entire work force.

fidelity bond *an insurance policy that protects a business from theft, forgery, or embezzlement by its employees*

Fidelity bonds are most commonly purchased by banks, savings and loan associations, finance companies, and other firms whose employees handle cash on a regular basis.

While business owners are concerned about shoplifting, they often find that insurance coverage, if available, is too expensive. And, it is often difficult to collect on losses resulting from shoplifting because such losses are difficult to prove.

Motor Vehicle Insurance

Individuals and businesses purchase automobile insurance because it is required by state law, because it is required by the firm financing purchase of the vehicle, or because they want to protect their investment. Most types of automobile coverage can be broadly classified as either liability or physical damage insurance. Figure 20.3 shows the distinction.

automobile liability insurance
insurance that covers financial losses resulting from injuries or damages caused by the insured vehicle

Automobile Liability Insurance   **Automobile liability insurance** is insurance that covers financial losses resulting from injuries or damages caused by the insured vehicle. Most automobile policies have a split-liability limit that contains three numbers. For example, the liability limits stated on a typical policy are 20/50/20. The first two numbers indicate the maximum amounts the insurance company will pay for bodily injury. *Bodily injury liability coverage* pays medical bills and other costs in the event that an injury or death results from an automobile accident in which the policyholder is at fault. Bodily injury liability coverage protects the person in the other car and is usually specified as a pair of dollar amounts. In the above example, the policy limits are $20,000 for each person and $50,000 for each occurrence. This means the insurance company will pay up to $20,000 to each person injured in an accident and up to a total of $50,000 to all those injured in a single accident. Payment for additional damages above the policy limits is the responsibility of the insured. In view of the cost of medical care today, and considering the

FIGURE 20.3
Automobile Insurance Coverage
Liability insurance covers financial losses resulting from injuries or damages caused by the insured vehicle; physical damage insurance covers damage to the insured vehicle (and sometimes its passengers).

AUTOMOTIVE COVERAGE

Liability insurance	Physical damage insurance
■ *Bodily injury*	■ *Collision*
■ *Property damage*	■ *Comprehensive*
■ *Medical payments*	■ *Uninsured motorists*

size of legal settlements resulting from automobile accidents, insurance companies recommend coverage of at least $100,000 per person and $300,000 per occurrence.

Property damage liability coverage pays for the repair of damage that the insured vehicle does to the property of another person. Such damage is covered up to the amount specified in the policy. In the above example, the third number (20) indicates that the insurance company will pay up to $20,000 for property damage. Insurance companies generally recommend at least $50,000 worth of property damage liability.

Along with other automobile liability insurance, most car owners also purchase protection for the passengers in their own cars. A *medical payments endorsement* can be included in automobile coverage for a small additional premium. This endorsement provides for the payment of medical bills, up to a specified amount, for passengers (including the policyholder) injured in the policyholder's vehicle.

automobile physical damage insurance   *insurance that covers damage to the insured vehicle*

Automobile Physical Damage Insurance   Liability insurance does not pay for the repair of the insured vehicle. **Automobile physical damage insurance** is insurance that covers damage to the insured vehicle. *Collision insurance* pays for the repair of damage to the insured vehicle that is the result of an accident. Most collision coverages include a *deductible amount—* anywhere from $50 up—that the policyholder must pay. The insurance company then pays either the remaining cost of the repairs or the actual cash value of the vehicle (when the vehicle is "totaled"), whichever is less. For most automobiles, collision insurance is the most costly coverage. Premiums can, however, be reduced by increasing the deductible amount.

Automobile comprehensive coverage pays for repairs caused by fire, theft, hail, dust storm, vandalism, and almost anything else that could damage a car, except collision and normal wear and tear.

Comprehensive insurance covers damage to the insured vehicle that is caused by fire, theft, hail, dust storm, vandalism, and almost anything else that could damage a car, except collision and normal wear and tear. With the possible exception of CB radios and tape decks that are nonfactory equipment installed by the owner of the car, even the contents of the car are insured. For example, comprehensive coverage will pay for a broken windshield, stolen hubcaps, or small dents caused by a hailstorm. Like collision coverage, comprehensive coverage includes a deductible amount, usually $50 or $100.

Uninsured motorists insurance covers the insured driver and passengers from bodily injury losses (and, in some states, property damage losses) resulting from an accident caused by a driver with no liability insurance. It also covers damages caused by a hit-and-run driver. In some states and with some insurance companies, uninsured motorist coverage is not automatically included in a typical policy. And yet, it is important coverage that is quite reasonable. Often, annual premiums are $5 to $10.

No-Fault Automobile Insurance **No-fault auto insurance** is a method of paying for losses suffered in an automobile accident. It is enacted by state law and requires that those suffering injury or loss be reimbursed by their own insurance companies, without regard to who was at fault in the accident. Although there are numerous exceptions, most no-fault laws also limit the rights of involved parties to sue each other.

Massachusetts enacted the first no-fault law in 1971 in an effort to reduce both auto insurance premiums and the crushing caseload in its court system. Since then, at least twenty-seven states have followed suit. Every state with a no-fault law requires coverage for all vehicles registered in the state.

Business Liability Insurance

Business liability coverage protects the policyholder from financial losses resulting from an injury to another person or damage to another person's property. During the past ten years or so, both the number of liability claims and the size of settlements have increased dramatically. The result has been heightened awareness of the need for liability coverage—along with quickly rising premiums for this coverage.

Public liability insurance is insurance that protects the policyholder from financial losses due to injuries suffered by others as a result of negligence on the part of a business owner or employee. It covers injury or death resulting from hazards at the place of business or from the actions of employees. For example, liability claims totaling more than $2 billion were filed on behalf of the victims of the 1981 skybridge collapse in the Hyatt Regency Hotel in Kansas City, Missouri. More recent examples where damage claims totaled more than a billion dollars include the chemical accident at Union Carbide's plant in Bhopal, India, and the 1987 Du Pont Hotel fire in San Juan, Puerto Rico. *Malpractice insurance*, which is purchased by physicians, lawyers, accountants, engineers, and other professionals, is a form of public liability insurance.

no-fault auto insurance *a method of paying for losses suffered in an automobile accident; enacted by state law, requires that those suffering injury or loss be reimbursed by their own insurance companies, without regard to who was at fault in the accident*

public liability insurance *insurance that protects the policyholder from financial losses due to injuries suffered by others as a result of negligence on the part of a business owner or employee*

product liability insurance *insurance that protects the policyholder from financial losses due to injuries suffered by others as a result of using the policyholder's products*

Product liability insurance is insurance that protects the policyholder from financial losses due to injuries suffered by others as a result of using the policyholder's products. Recently, court settlements for individuals injured by defective products have been extremely large. A classic product liability case involved the Ford Motor Company and Richard Grimshaw. Grimshaw was injured when he was a passenger in a Ford Pinto that was hit from behind and burst into flames. He was so severely burned that more than fifty operations were required to treat him. He sued and was awarded $128.5 million by a jury, which decided that his injuries resulted from poor design on the part of Ford. (Later, on appeal, the award was reduced to $6 million.)

Some juries have found manufacturers and retailers guilty of negligence even when the consumer used the product incorrectly. This development and the very large awards given to injured consumers have caused management to take a hard look at potential product hazards. As part of their risk-management efforts, most manufacturers now take the following precautions.

1. Include thorough and explicit directions with their products
2. Warn customers about the hazards of using their products incorrectly
3. Remove from the market those products that are considered hazardous
4. Test their products in-house to determine whether safety problems can arise from either proper *or* improper use[2]

Such precautions can reduce both the risk of product-liability losses and the cost of liability insurance. Where the risk of death, injury, or lawsuits cannot be eliminated or at least reduced, some manufacturers have simply discontinued the product. For more information on product liability, read Case 20.1—The Manufacturer's Dilemma: Liability Insurance.

Marine (Transportation) Insurance

Marine, or transportation, coverage provides protection against the loss of goods that are being shipped from one place to another. It is the oldest type of insurance and originated with the Greeks and Romans. The term *marine insurance* was coined at a time when only goods transported by ship were insured.

ocean marine insurance *insurance that protects the policyholder against loss or damage to a ship or its cargo on the high seas*

inland marine insurance *insurance that protects against loss or damage to goods shipped by rail, truck, airplane, or inland barge*

Today marine insurance is available for goods shipped over water or land. **Ocean marine insurance** protects the policyholder against loss or damage to a ship or its cargo on the high seas. **Inland marine insurance** protects against loss or damage to goods shipped by rail, truck, airplane, or inland barge. Both types cover losses from fire, theft, and most other hazards.

Business Interruption Insurance

business interruption insurance *insurance protection for a business whose operations are interrupted because of a fire, storm, or other natural disaster*

Business interruption insurance provides protection for a business whose operations are interrupted because of a fire, storm, or other natural disaster. It is even possible to purchase coverage to protect the firm in the event that its employees go out on strike. For most businesses, interruption coverage is available as an endorsement to a fire insurance policy. Premiums are determined by the amount of coverage and the risks that are covered.

The standard business interruption policy reimburses the policyholder for both loss of profit and fixed costs in the event that it cannot operate. Profit payments are based on the profits earned by the firm during some specified period. Fixed-cost payments cover expenses that the firm incurs even when it is not operating. Employee salaries are normally not covered by the standard policy. However, they may be included for an increased premium.

Insurance Coverage for Individuals

Both the government and private insurance companies offer a number of different types of coverage for individuals in the United States. In this section, we discuss social security, unemployment insurance, worker's compensation, and medical insurance.

Public Insurance

Learning Objective 5
Describe the types of insurance that are available to individuals

Federal and state governments offer insurance programs to meet the specific needs of individuals that are eligible for coverage. For example, the social security program was established when the Social Security Act was passed by Congress in 1935. Today, it provides benefits for more than 40 million people in the United States. In reality, the Social Security program—financed by taxes paid by both employees and employers—is divided into four individual programs. First, *retirement* benefits are paid to eligible employees and self-employed individuals when they reach age 65. They can obtain reduced benefits at age 62. In 1990, the maximum retirement benefits were $975 per month. Second, *survivor* benefits are paid to a worker's spouse, dependent children, or in some cases dependent parents when a covered worker dies before retirement. Third, *disability* benefits are paid to workers who are severely disabled and unable to work. Benefits continue until it is determined that the individual is no longer disabled. When a disabled worker reaches age 65, the worker is then eligible for retirement benefits. Fourth, the *Medicare* program provides both hospital and medical coverage. Workers are eligible for coverage when they reach age 65. Persons who have received disability benefits for a period of at least twenty-four months are also eligible for Medicare coverage.

Unlike the federal Social Security program, *unemployment insurance* is a joint program between the federal and state governments. The purpose of the program is to provide benefits (employment services and money) to unemployed workers. The dollar amount and the duration of benefits are determined by state laws. The program is funded by a tax paid by employers.

Worker's Compensation

worker's compensation insurance *insurance that covers medical expenses and provides salary continuation for employees who are injured while they are at work*

Worker's compensation insurance is insurance that covers medical expenses and provides salary continuation for employees who are injured while they are at work. This insurance also pays benefits to the dependents of workers who are killed on the job. Today, every state requires that employers provide some form of worker's compensation insurance, with benefits that are established by the state. This type of insurance may be purchased from insurance companies or, in some cases, from the state. Self-insurance can also be used to meet requirements in a few states. State laws do vary; some are more stringent than others. In fact, the low cost of worker's compensation is one of many reasons for locating or moving a business to a specific state.

Salary continuation benefits are paid to employees who are unable to work because of injuries sustained on the job. These payments normally range from 60 to 75 percent of an employee's usual wage, but they may be limited to a specified number of payments. In all cases, they stop when the employee is able to return to work.

Worker's compensation premiums are paid by the employer and are generally computed as a small percentage of each employee's wages. The percentage varies with the type of job and is, in general, higher for jobs that involve greater risk of injury.

Health-Care Insurance

Today, most employers pay, as an employee benefit, part or all of the cost of health-care insurance for employees. When the employer doesn't pay for coverage, most individuals purchase their own health-care insurance when they can afford the coverage. **Health-care insurance** is insurance that covers the cost of medical attention, including hospital care, physicians' and surgeons' fees, prescription medicines, and related services. In addition, some firms also provide employees with dental and life insurance. *Major medical insurance* can also be purchased to extend medical coverage beyond the dollar limits of the standard health-care insurance policy. In all cases, the types of coverage and amounts that are paid vary according to the provisions of the specific health-care policy, regardless of whether it is paid for by the employer or the individual.

health-care insurance *insurance that covers the cost of medical attention, including hospital care, physicians' and surgeons' fees, prescription medicines, and related services*

The cost of medical care has been increasing at an alarming rate over the last twenty to thirty years. In 1965, the average American spent $181 on health care. In 1990 the Health Insurance Association of America (an industry trade association) estimated that the same individual would spend more than $2,700.[3] In an attempt to keep medical insurance premiums from rising just as quickly, insurers have developed a variety of insurance plans that are less expensive than full-coverage plans. Some plans have deductibles of $500 to $1,000. Some require that the policyholder pay 20 to 30 percent of the first $1,000 to $3,000 in medical bills. And some pay the entire hospital bill but only a percentage of other medical expenses. One additional method that can reduce the cost of health-care coverage is the use of a health maintenance organization. A

BUSINESS JOURNAL

The Increasing Costs of Health Care

Today, the average employer pays more than $2,500 a year for family health-care insurance for each employee, according to Hays/Huggins, an employee-benefits consulting firm based in Philadelphia.* This amount represents an increase of more than 180 percent since 1980. While most Americans take health-care insurance for granted, the increasing cost of health-care coverage may cause some people to wonder if they can afford to get sick.

THE COST OF COVERAGE

In addition to the $2,500 contribution made by the employer, most employees must also contribute 10 to 40 percent of the total cost of their health-care coverage. Moreover, standard health-care policies provide for a deductible, ranging from $150 to $500, that employees must pay before actual reimbursement begins. Once reimbursement does begin, most plans pay 70 to 80 percent of qualified medical expenses, and employees pay the remaining 20 to 30 percent. Usually there is a maximum dollar amount, or *cap,* of $1,000 to $2,000 on medical expenses that employees must pay in any given calendar year. Once employees have paid the cap amount, the insurance then pays 100 percent of qualified medical expenses.

COST CONTAINMENT

Faced with increasing costs that promise to rise throughout the 1990s, most employers have initiated cost-containment procedures designed to reduce their portion of employee health-care costs. Some

specific measures include: (1) increasing the portion of the premium that the employee pays; (2) contracting with independent "health management consultants" that approve both medical treatment and hospitalizations; and (3) using health maintenance organizations (HMOs) and preferred provider organizations (PPOs). HMOs are companies that agree to provide medical care for employees for a fixed fee. PPOs are groups of medical personnel who contract to furnish services for employees at discounted prices in return for prompt payment.

Still other methods are being used to lower health-care costs. J.C. Penney Company will now cover the spouse of an employee only if the employee is the primary wage earner for the family. Steelcase, Inc. gives employees "benefit dollars" that they can spend in the company's cafeteria-style benefits plan. Currently, Steelcase's plan includes eight medical options, three dental plans, and numerous forms of disability coverage. Steelcase's plan also contains a provision that the company will pay only 80 percent of future increases in the cost of health-care coverage; the remainder must be paid by the employee. Thus the company has a certain amount of protection from inflation and spiraling medical costs.

Finally, some companies adhere to the old adage that "an ounce of prevention is worth a pound of cure." For example, The Quaker Oats Co. pays cash bonuses to employees who join the firm's wellness program and stay healthy.

Based on information from "Health Costs: What, Me Worry?" *Esquire,* June 1989, p. 82; Annetta Miller, "Can You Afford to Get Sick?" *Newsweek,* January 1989, pp. 44–45+; John Schwartz, " 'Wellness' Plans: An Ounce of Prevention," *Newsweek,* January 30, 1989, p. 51; and Patti Jones, "Living Without Health Insurance," *Glamour,* April 1989, p. 158+.

* Roger Thompson, "A Checkup on Health Benefits," *Nation's Business,* March 1989, p. 48.

---

health maintenance organization (HMO) *an insurance plan that directly employs or contracts with selected physicians and hospitals to provide health-care services in exchange for a fixed, prepaid monthly premium*

health maintenance organization (HMO) is an insurance plan that directly employs or contracts with selected physicians and hospitals to provide health-care services in exchange for a fixed, prepaid monthly premium. While there have been concerns about the quality of care provided by some health maintenance organizations, they are expected to grow in the 1990s because they offer a lower-cost alternative to traditional health-care plans.

Life Insurance

Learning Objective 6
Be able to explain the advantages and disadvantages of term, whole, endowment, and universal life insurance

life insurance *insurance that pays a stated amount of money on the death of the insured individual*

beneficiary *individual or organization named in a life insurance policy as a recipient of the proceeds of that policy on the death of the insured*

Life insurance is insurance that pays a stated amount of money on the death of the insured individual. The money obviously cannot be paid to the person who is insured. Instead, it is paid to one or more beneficiaries. A **beneficiary** is a person or organization named in a life insurance policy as a recipient of the proceeds of that policy on the death of the insured.

Life insurance thus provides protection for the beneficiaries of the insured. And the amount of insurance that is needed depends very much on *their* situation. For example, a wage earner with three small children generally needs more life insurance than someone who is single. Moreover, the need for life insurance changes as a person's situation changes. Once the wage earner's children are grown and on their own, they need less protection (through their parent's life insurance) than they did when they were young. Life insurance in the United States reached a record $8.02 trillion at the end of 1988.[4] That breaks down to $32,470 per individual.

For a particular dollar amount of life insurance, premiums depend primarily on the age of the insured and on the type of insurance. The older a person is, the higher the premium. (On the average, older people are less likely to survive each year than younger people.) Finally, insurers offer several types of life insurance for customers with varying insurance needs. The price of each type depends on the benefits it provides.

Term Life Insurance

term life insurance *life insurance that provides protection to beneficiaries for a stated period of time*

Term life insurance is life insurance that provides protection to beneficiaries for a stated period of time. Because term life insurance includes no other benefits, it is the least expensive form of life insurance. It is especially attractive to young married couples who want as much protection as possible but cannot afford the higher premiums charged for other types of life insurance.

Most term life policies are in force for a period of one year. At the end of each policy year, a term life policy can be renewed at a slightly higher cost—to take into account the fact that the insured individual has aged one year. In addition, some term policies can be converted into other forms of life insurance at the option of the policyholder. This feature permits policyholders to modify their insurance protection to keep pace with changes in their personal circumstances.

Whole Life Insurance

whole life insurance *life insurance that provides both protection and savings*

cash surrender value *an amount that is payable to the holder of a whole life insurance policy if the policy is canceled*

Whole life insurance is life insurance that provides both protection and savings. In the beginning, premiums are generally higher than those for term life insurance. However, premiums for whole life insurance remain constant for as long as the policy is in force.

A whole life policy builds up savings over the years. These savings are in the form of a **cash surrender value,** which is an amount that is payable to the holder of a whole life insurance policy if the policy is

The amount of life insurance that an individual needs depends on marital status, the number of children the individual has, and the amount of income that beneficiaries will need. In a recently published book, financial analyst Glenn Daily argues that buyers of life insurance benefit from making these decisions for themselves, rather than working through an insurance agent.

canceled. In addition, the policyholder may borrow from the insurance company, at a relatively low interest rate, amounts up to the policy's cash surrender value.

Whole life insurance policies are sold in three forms:

▶ *Straight life insurance,* for which the policyholder must pay premiums as long as the insured is alive

▶ *Limited-payment life insurance,* for which premiums are paid for only a stated number of years

▶ *Single-payment life insurance,* for which one lump-sum premium is paid at the time the insurance is purchased

Which of these is best for a given individual depends, as usual, on that individual's particular situation and insurance needs.

Endowment Life Insurance

endowment life insurance *life insurance that provides protection and guarantees the payment of a stated amount to the policyholder after a specified number of years*

Endowment life insurance is life insurance that provides protection and guarantees the payment of a stated amount to the policyholder after a specified number of years. Endowment policies are generally in force for twenty years or until the insured person reaches age 65. If the insured dies while the policy is in force, the beneficiaries are paid the face amount of the policy. However, if the insured survives through the policy period, the stated amount is paid to the policyholder.

The premiums for endowment policies are generally higher than those for whole life policies. In return, the policyholder is guaranteed a future payment. Thus the endowment policy includes a sort of "enforced saving." In addition, endowment policies have cash surrender values that are usually higher than those of whole life policies.

Universal Life Insurance

universal life insurance *life insurance that combines insurance protection with an investment plan that offers a potentially greater return than that guaranteed by a whole life insurance policy*

Universal life insurance is life insurance that combines insurance protection with an investment plan that offers a potentially greater return than that guaranteed by a whole life insurance policy. Universal life insurance is the newest product available from life insurance companies. It offers policyholders several options that are not available with other types of policies. For example, policyholders may choose to make larger or smaller premium payments, to increase or decrease their insurance coverage, or even to withdraw the policy's cash value without canceling the policy. Essentially, the purchase of universal life insurance combines the purchase of annual term insurance with the buying and selling of investments.

Universal life generally offers lower premiums than whole life insurance. In fact, the premium is often called a "contribution." However, companies that offer universal life insurance may charge a fee when the policy is first purchased, each time an annual premium is paid, and when funds are withdrawn from the policy's cash value.[5] Such fees tend to decrease the return on the savings-account part of the policy.

CHAPTER REVIEW

Summary

Risk—or the possibility of loss or injury—is a part of everyday life for both businesses and individuals. Speculative risks are those that accompany the chance of earning a profit. Pure risks are those that involve only the possibility of loss, without any potential gain.

Individuals and businesses must evaluate the risks they face, and they should minimize the costs involved with those risks. Four general techniques of risk management are risk avoidance, risk reduction, risk assumption, and the shifting of risk. Usually, pure risks that cannot be avoided or reduced and that are too large to be assumed can be shifted to insurance companies.

Insurance companies, for a fee, assume risks that meet certain insurability criteria. They do so through contracts called insurance policies. An important condition in the issuing of an insurance policy is that the insured individual or firm cannot profit from the policy. That is, the payment in the event of a loss cannot exceed the actual amount of the loss. Insurance-company fees, or premiums, must be affordable. At the same time, they must be high enough to cover expected payouts and other expenses.

Stock insurance companies are profit-making corporations that are owned by stockholders. Mutual insurance companies are cooperatives that are owned by their policyholders.

Property and casualty insurance protects the policyholder against loss of property and loss due to accidents. Included in this category is insurance that protects against loss of property due to fire, theft, and various natural hazards; against liability due to injury to employees or customers; and against damage and liability resulting from automobile accidents.

Both the government and private insurance companies offer a number of different types of coverage for individuals in the United States. The federal Social Security program offers retirement, survivor, disability, and Medicare benefits to people who are eligible. Unemployment insurance—a joint program sponsored by the federal and state governments—provides both employment services and money to people who are unemployed. Employers are required to provide worker's compensation insurance to protect the worker in case of injury. And both employers and individuals purchase insurance to cover health-care costs.

All life insurance provides a stated amount of money, which is paid to beneficiaries upon the death of the insured individual. Term insurance provides this single benefit. Whole life insurance provides some savings as well—in the form of a cash surrender value. Endowment insurance also provides a guaranteed payment at the end of some specified period of time. And universal life insurance combines protection with an investment plan.

This chapter concludes our discussion of finance and risk management for firms and individuals. The next part of the book deals with the environment in which a business must operate. We begin our discussion with business law and how it affects day-to-day business operations.

Key Terms

You should now be able to define and give an example relevant to each of the following terms:

risk
speculative risk
pure risk
risk management
self-insurance
insurer (or insurance company)
premium
insurance policy
insurance
insurable risk
uninsurable risk
principle of indemnity
stock insurance company
mutual insurance company
fire insurance
coinsurance clause
extended coverage
fidelity bond
automobile liability insurance
automobile physical damage insurance
no-fault auto insurance
public liability insurance
product liability insurance
ocean marine insurance
inland marine insurance
business interruption insurance
worker's compensation insurance
health-care insurance
health maintenance organization (HMO)
life insurance
beneficiary
term life insurance
whole life insurance
cash surrender value
endowment life insurance
universal life insurance

Questions and Exercises

Review Questions

1. What is the difference between a speculative risk and a pure risk? Why are speculative risks generally uninsurable?
2. List the four general risk-handling techniques and give an example of how each is used to handle risk.
3. Under what conditions is self-insurance a practical risk-management method?
4. How does the principle of indemnity affect the following?
   a. The amount that an insurer will pay in the event of a loss
   b. The maximum amount for which property should be insured by its owner
5. What are the five principal conditions that determine whether a risk is insurable?
6. Distinguish between a stock insurance company and a mutual insurance company.
7. What is the general effect of the coinsurance clause in a fire insurance policy?
8. What is extended insurance coverage, and what does it usually "extend"?
9. What is the difference between automobile liability insurance and automobile physical damage insurance? List three liability coverages and three physical damage coverages.
10. What is the difference between public liability insurance and product liability insurance? Why would a business need these two coverages?
11. How are the premiums determined for worker's compensation insurance? Who pays them?
12. In what specific ways can an employer reduce the cost of health-care insurance?
13. What is a health maintenance organization (HMO)? How does an HMO plan differ from a more traditional health-care insurance plan?
14. List and briefly describe four different kinds of life insurance.

Discussion Questions

1. First Executive Corporation was one of the fastest-growing insurance companies in the United States during the 1980s. It achieved this level of growth by offering customers low-cost life insurance policies and annuities that were backed with junk-bond investments. Would you buy a policy or an annuity from First Executive Corporation? Why?
2. State insurance regulators require that an insurance company set aside up to 20 percent of the bonds' stated value as a cushion against possible

investment losses. For a company like First Executive Corporation, is this a reasonable requirement? Why?

3. Suppose you were the owner of a retail clothing store. To what extent could you use risk avoidance, risk reduction, and risk assumption in your risk-management program? Cite specific applications of each of these three techniques.

4. As the owner of the retail store described in Question 3, which insurance coverages would you purchase for your business? How would you determine the amount of each type of coverage to purchase?

5. The principle of indemnity does not seem to apply to life insurance because people can, within reason, purchase as much or as little of this coverage as they wish. Why should this be so?

Exercises

1. Find and read an article or two on home owner's or renter's insurance. From your reading, answer the following questions:
    a. Which hazards are generally covered by these policies?
    b. Which additional coverages are available as endorsements?

2. The owner of a $500,000 building has purchased $300,000 worth of fire insurance on the building. Assuming the insurance policy has an 80 percent coinsurance clause, how much will the owner collect from the insurance company under each of the following conditions?
    a. The building is totally destroyed by fire.
    b. A fire does $300,000 worth of damage to the building.

Case 20.1

The Manufacturer's Dilemma: Liability Insurance

American manufacturers are finding themselves increasingly burdened with rising insurance rates and expensive legal fees. They are caught in a Catch-22 because they are manufacturing products that carry an element of risk that cannot be totally eliminated. For example, in 1986, a high school football player who broke his neck in a scrimmage was awarded $12 million in a judgment against Riddell—one of the nation's largest manufacturers of football helmets. The jury ruled that the helmet should have had stickers to warn players about the danger of butting—a common practice on the football field. Riddell has appealed the verdict, but already the court case has changed

an entire industry in at least two ways. First, there were eighteen companies that manufactured football helmets in the United States in 1970. Now there are only two. Sixteen companies stopped manufacturing football helmets because of the increasing number of personal-injury lawsuits and the higher cost of product-liability coverage. Second, the two companies left have found that their insurance premiums exceed their manufacturing costs. In fact, more than $60 of a football helmet's $110 retail price is used to pay for product-liability coverage.*

Another example of the manufacturer's dilemma can be found in the field of prescription drugs and injections. Today, only one U.S. company makes the combined measles, mumps, and rubella (MMR) vaccine. Only two pharmaceutical companies make the combined diphtheria, tetanus, and pertussis (DPT) vaccine. Even more discouraging is the fact that many American pharmaceutical companies have abandoned their research and development of new drugs because of the increased risk of personal-injury lawsuits and higher liability-insurance premiums.

To help avoid liability problems, many companies are using "preventive law" to reduce their exposure to lawsuits. They've developed programs to pinpoint products, services, or manufacturing operations that could spark a lawsuit. After these danger zones have been identified, the companies either clean them up or abandon them. Companies also employ lawyers and other experts and specialists to participate in every step of developing new products and improving old ones. However, despite these programs and efforts to prevent accidents and lawsuits, preventive law can do only so much. When being judged by a jury with twenty-twenty hindsight, a company finds that it is almost impossible to prove that its product could not have been designed better.†

Questions

1. According to some insurance analysts, at least 15 percent of firms in the United States do not have product-liability coverage. Considering the dollar amounts of damage awards in product-liability

---

* Peter Brimelow and Leslie Spencer, "The Plaintiff Attorneys' Great Honey Rush," *Forbes*, October 16, 1989, p. 203.

† Based on information from Ted Gest, *U.S. News & World Report*, May 15, 1989, p. 50; "Reform the Product-Liability System to Prevent Further Economic Harm," *Nation's Business*, September 1988, p. 86; Ronald Bailey, "Legal Mayhem," *Forbes*, November 14, 1988, pp. 97–98; Brian McCombie, "The 'Catch-22' in Insurance," *Newsweek*, August 11, 1986, p. 8; and "The Manufacturer Crisis," *Consumer Reports*, August 1986, p. 544.

cases, why would a firm not obtain liability coverage?

2. What effect has the current product-liability crisis had on new-product development and the ability of U.S. firms to compete in the international marketplace?

3. Recently, a reform bill was introduced in the U.S. Senate. This legislation, if passed, would establish uniform product-liability standards throughout the United States. It would also limit the use of punitive damages and encourage quicker settlement of lawsuits. In your opinion, is there a need for this type of legislation? Justify your answer.

Case 20.2

Consumers Revolt over High Insurance Premiums

It all sounded so simple. A group of California consumer advocates led by Harvey Rosenfield proposed to roll back automobile insurance premiums by 20 percent, along with other measures designed to strengthen industry regulations and curb mismanagement in the insurance industry. And after a petition drive that resulted in more than 500,000 signatures calling for a referendum, Proposition 103 finally passed with 51 percent of the vote in November 1988.

Once the voters had approved Proposition 103, the arguments for and against insurance reform really became heated. Most consumers expected immediate premium rollbacks, while the insurance companies used legal challenges to postpone rate reductions and other major changes in California's insurance laws. Six months after the voters approved Proposition 103, a ruling by the California Supreme Court upheld the legality of Proposition 103 but qualified the law by ruling that companies must be guaranteed a reasonable profit when selling automobile coverage in the state. This ruling placed the responsibility of determining what is a fair profit on the shoulders of Roxani M. Gillespie—the current insurance commissioner of California.

On August 1, 1989, Gillespie announced plans to force seven of the state's largest insurance companies to reduce automobile rates and refund more than $300 million to consumers. The seven targeted companies, along with most of the state's remaining 800 insurance companies, requested exemptions to the premium rollback on the basis of the state's supreme court ruling. Under the court's ruling, insurance companies are required to reduce premiums *only* if they still continue to earn a fair and reasonable profit. According to insurance-industry experts, most companies don't make any profit on private passenger-automobile insurance. To make matters worse, some companies even requested approval of rate hikes to offset losses in previous years. For example, State Farm Mutual Automobile Insurance Co., which writes 14 percent of the policies in California, requested a 9.6 percent ($148.6-million) rate hike to offset the $333.2 million it lost in California in 1988‡

Realizing the magnitude of the problem, some insurance executives have suggested that a no-fault plan could offset losses and reduce expenses. Under a no-fault plan, persons suffering injury or losses are reimbursed by their own insurance companies. Although there are exceptions, most no-fault plans also limit the rights of injured parties to initiate legal action. In reality, premiums are held down because insurance companies don't have to pay large dollar settlements for legal fees or excessive court awards.

Now, over two years since the original referendum was passed, most California drivers are still waiting for low-cost, affordable automobile coverage. And, while it is still unclear how Proposition 103 will affect California drivers, state legislators in at least eighteen other states have either enacted or proposed legislation similar to the California law.§

Questions

1. The California Supreme Court upheld Proposition 103 but qualified the law by ruling that companies must be guaranteed a fair profit. Should an insurance company be guaranteed a "fair" profit? Justify your answer.

2. Assuming that most insurance companies don't earn a profit on private passenger-automobile coverage, what are the dangers of forcing insurance companies to roll back premiums?

3. Some insurance executives have suggested enacting a no-fault plan to help solve California's automobile-insurance problems. In what ways would a no-fault plan help reduce premiums?

‡ Ronald Grover, "California Insurers Won't Roll Over," *Business Week*, February 27, 1989, p. 38.

§ Based on information from Robert D. Hof, "A California Mission That May Be Impossible," *Business Week*, August 14, 1989, p. 50; Sylvia Nasar, "Hard Road Ahead for Auto Insurers," *Fortune*, May 8, 1989, p. 99; and Greg Anrig, Jr., "The Flamboyant Force Behind California's Auto Insurance Revolt," *Money*, July 1989, pp. 145–146.

CAREER PROFILE

PETER LYNCH On March 28, 1990, Peter Lynch resigned as the manager of the nation's largest and, according to many financial experts, most successful mutual fund. Retired at the age of 46, he provided us throughout his career with a basic philosophy of life that emphasizes hard work, playing by the rules, and relying on what he calls the knowledge of common sense.

When Lynch was 10 years old, his father died. From that point on, he was raised by his mother. At the age of 19, he bought stock in Flying Tiger. The stock quintupled and he was hooked on the stock market. He then worked his way through Boston College and the Wharton Business School. Later, a summer internship at Fidelity Investments led to a job in 1969. By 1974, he was director of Fidelity's research department. In May 1977, Peter Lynch began managing Fidelity's Magellan fund.

When Peter Lynch took over the Fidelity Magellan Fund, it had total assets of $20 million that were invested in 40 different stocks. Thirteen years later, the same fund had total assets of over $13 billion invested in over 1,400 different stocks, and almost one million investors. In his thirteen years as manager of the fund, investors have averaged a remarkable 28 percent return each year for a total return of 2,510 percent.

What's even more remarkable is that the Magellan fund became successful the old-fashioned way—by the hard work of Peter Lynch. Lynch is a staunch believer in gathering facts and then using those facts to make investment decisions. To gather the facts he needed, he worked at least six days a week from 6:45 A.M. to about 7:00 P.M. each day. Today, Lynch admits that managing the Magellan fund has become more difficult over the years. In fact, he had been working four hours early Sunday mornings before church for the past year in order to keep up in a business that rewards those who remain abreast of what's going on.

Lynch has also written a book, *One Up on Wall Street*. As one might suspect, his book is crammed full of "helpful hints" on how individual investors can beat the averages and become more successful. For example, he tells investors to take advantage of what he calls the knowledge of common sense. According to Lynch, "during a lifetime of buying cars or cameras, you develop a sense of what's good and what's bad, what sells and what doesn't. You know it before Wall Street knows it."* By using this knowledge to make investment decisions, investors can be years ahead of the analysts on Wall Street.

In a recent interview, Lynch said that he was leaving Fidelity and the Magellan fund because he wanted to spend more time with his family and on other personal interests. Today, he feels good about what he has accomplished. According to Lynch, "When you've made some money for a lot of people, you feel incredibly good about it, better than when you made a lot of money for a few people."†

---

* "How to Beat the Pros," *Changing Times*, May 1989, p. 32+.

† "Peter Lynch on the Meaning of Life," *Fortune* April 23, 1990, p. 197+.

Based on information from "How to Beat the Pros," *Changing Times*, May 1989, p. 32+; "Peter Lynch on the Meaning of Life," *Fortune*, April 23, 1990, p. 197+; Christopher J. Chipello, Michael Siconolfi, and Jonathan Clements, "Both Fidelity Investors and Firm Are at Sea as Magellan Boss Goes," *The Wall Street Journal*, March 29, 1990, p. A1+; Peter Lynch, "One Up on Wall Street," *Money*, January 1989, p. 128+; and Jonathan Clements, "Can Lynch Live up to His Reputation?," *Forbes*, April 3, 1989, p. 174+.

The figure in the salary column approximates the expected annual income after two or three years of service. 1 = $12,000–$15,000 2 = $16,000–$20,000 3 = $21,000–$27,000 4 = $28,000–$35,000 5 = $36,000 and up

Job Title	Educational Requirements	Salary Range	Prospects
Actuary	Bachelor's or master's degree in math, business, or statistics	3–4	Gradual growth
Bank clerk	High school diploma	1	Gradual growth
Bank officer and manager	College degree; master's degree preferred; on-the-job experience	3–4	Limited growth
Bank teller	High school diploma; some college preferred	1	Limited growth
Brokerage clerk	High school diploma; some college preferred	1–2	Limited growth
Claims adjuster	Some college preferred; on-the-job training	2	Gradual growth
Claims clerk	High school diploma	1	Gradual growth
Collection worker	High school diploma	1–2	Limited growth
Credit clerk	High school diploma; some college preferred	1–2	Greatest growth
Credit manager	College degree; on-the-job experience	2–3	Limited growth
Credit reporter	Some college preferred; on-the-job experience	2	Greatest growth
Financial analyst	College degree; on-the-job experience; master's degree helpful	4–5	Limited growth
Insurance agent	Bachelor's degree preferred	3–4	Limited growth
Insurance clerk	High school diploma; some college preferred	1–2	Gradual growth
Insurance underwriter	Bachelor's degree in insurance; on-the-job experience	2–3	Limited growth
Investment banker	College degree; master's degree helpful; on-the-job experience	5	Limited growth
Mortgage loan officer	Some college courses; bachelor's degree helpful; on-the-job experience	2–3	Limited growth
Portfolio/trust officer	College degree; on-the-job experience	3–4	Limited growth
Stockbroker	Bachelor's degree; on-the-job experience	4–5	Gradual growth
Tax preparer or consultant	College degree; on-the-job experience	3–4	Greatest growth

Part 7

THE BUSINESS ENVIRONMENT AND INTERNATIONAL ISSUES

This final part of *Business* covers two topics that affect the operations of every firm: the legal aspects of business and the relationship between business and government in the United States. It also treats a topic that is steadily increasing in importance: the benefits, problems, and methods of international trade. Included in this part are:

BUSINESS LAW

CHAPTER PREVIEW

Our initial task in this chapter is to examine the judicial, legislative, and administrative sources of law. We also describe the functions of the federal and state court systems in administering the law. Then we discuss the major categories of law that apply to business activities. These categories include (1) contract law, governing agreements between individuals or businesses; (2) property law, relating to rights of ownership; (3) laws that regulate the use of such negotiable instruments as checks, promissory notes, and commercial paper; (4) agency laws, under which agents may agree to work on behalf of individuals or organizations in a business relationship; and (5) bankruptcy laws, designed to protect both debtors and creditors.

INSIDE BUSINESS

Campeau Stores File for Bankruptcy Protection

On January 15, 1990, Campeau spokeswoman Carol Sanger announced that Campeau's Allied and Federated Department Stores were filing for protection under Chapter 11 of the U.S. bankruptcy laws. The company's bankruptcy—the largest in the history of retailing—affects 100,000 employees in more than 250 stores, hundreds of bondholders, and thousands of individual suppliers and creditors. And it may take as long as five years to work out the details of the planned reorganization. The bankruptcy petition allows Campeau to suspend interest payments on bonds and other long-term debts. Campeau can then use the cash to pay suppliers—a move that ensures continued shipments of merchandise needed by individual stores to attract customers during the firm's reorganization.

Campeau Corporation's financial problems began in 1986 when Robert Campeau—the successful Canadian real estate developer—acquired Allied Stores Corp. for $3.7 billion. The Allied stores include the Bon Marche (39 stores), Jordan Marsh (26 stores), Maas Brothers (38 stores), and Stern's (24 stores).

Two years later, Robert Campeau became involved in a bidding war with the R. H. Macy department-store chain in an attempt to purchase the Federated chain. The Federated Department Stores include Abraham & Straus (15 stores), Bloomingdale's (17 stores), Burdines (39 stores), Lazarus (46 stores), Rich's/Goldsmith (24 stores), and other stores. Although Campeau was able to purchase the Federated chain for $6.6 billion, this transaction was the beginning of the end. Faced with long-term debts that some experts have estimated to be in excess of $10 billion, Campeau immediately began to have financial problems. The stores could not generate enough cash to pay even the interest on the massive long-term debts.

Before filing Chapter 11, to ease the financial pressures, Campeau had obtained both debt and equity financing valued at $700 million from Albert, Paul, and Ralph Reichmann—three brothers who are very successful Canadian real estate developers. Campeau had also been trying to sell some retail assets including the seventeen Bloomingdale's stores—the prize jewel of the Campeau retailing empire. Although valued at $2 billion at the time of Campeau's acquisition, the Bloomingdale's stores will probably fetch only $1 billion because of today's depressed market for retail stores. Finally, the Campeau stores had been marking down merchandise to attract customers and improve the firm's cash flow position.

While the Allied and Federated chains' financial problems are huge, most financial analysts are quick to point out that they are not the result of poor management, poor merchandising practices, or operating losses. These financial problems are the result of the debt financing that was needed to purchase both chains. Simply put, Robert Campeau paid too much for the Federated and Allied stores.[1]

After Robert Campeau's Allied and Federated department-store chains filed for protection under Chapter 11 of the U.S. bankruptcy laws, the job of overseeing the firms' reorganization, sorting through a multitude of contractual obligations and financial claims, and figuring out who should get paid falls on the shoulders of Cincinnati federal bankruptcy judge J. Vincent Aug Jr. While legal experts consider this bankruptcy more complicated than most (as mentioned earlier, it is the largest in retailing history), the case involves legal questions that are fairly typical of disputes that arise out of business law.

Actually, there is no sharp distinction between business law and other kinds of law. The term *business law* simply applies to those laws that primarily affect business activities and practices. Such laws set standards of behavior for both businesses and individuals. They set forth the rights of the parties in exchanges and various types of agreements. And they provide remedies in the event that one business (or individual) believes it has been injured by another or cannot pay its debts.

For example, Pennzoil Company believed that it was monetarily injured when Texaco purchased Getty Oil Co. In 1984, Getty Oil and Pennzoil announced an agreement whereby Pennzoil would buy three-sevenths of Getty's outstanding stock for $112.50 per share. Getty's oil reserves must have excited the crude-poor Texaco because four days later Texaco offered to buy Getty shares for $125 (and, subsequently, for $128). Naturally, Getty stockholders took the higher offer, and Texaco acquired Getty to the dismay of Pennzoil management. A month later, Pennzoil sued Texaco for $15 billion in damages for interfering with its own purchase of Getty. After a lengthy court trial, a Texas jury decided that Texaco had violated Pennzoil's rights. Pennzoil was awarded a total judgment of $11.1 billion.

Three ideas are critical here. First, Pennzoil's case against Texaco was based on existing laws. Second, Pennzoil sought a remedy to its complaint within the court system, the purpose of which is to hear and decide such cases. Third, having lost its court case, Texaco sought protection from its creditors and lenders by filing for bankruptcy. All three ideas are discussed in this chapter.

Laws and the Courts

law *a rule developed by a society to govern the conduct of, and relationship among, its members*

A **law** is a rule developed by a society to govern the conduct of, and relationship among, its members. In the United States, the supreme law of the land is the U.S. Constitution. No federal, state, or local law is valid if it violates the U.S. Constitution. In addition to the U.S. Constitution, laws are developed and administered at all three levels of government (federal, state, and local). The entire group of laws dealing with a particular subject, or arising from a particular source, is often called a *body of law* or, more simply, *law*. Some examples are business law, contract law, and common law.

Sources of Laws

Each level of government derives its laws from two major sources: (1) judges' decisions, which make up common law, and (2) legislative bodies, which enact statutory laws.

Common Law   **Common law** is the body of law created by the court decisions rendered by judges. Common law began as custom and tradition in England, and it was enlarged by centuries of English court decisions. It was transported to America during the colonial period and, since then, has been further enlarged by the decisions of American judges.

This growth of common law is founded on the doctrine of *stare decisis*, a Latin term that is translated as "to stand by previous decisions." The doctrine of *stare decisis* is a practical source of law for two reasons. First, this doctrine allows the courts to be more efficient. It means that a judge's decision in a case may be used by other judges as the basis for later decisions. The earlier decision thus has the strength of law and is, in effect, a source of law. Second, the doctrine of *stare decisis* makes law more stable and predictable. If someone brings a case to court *and* the facts are the same as a case that has already been decided, then the court will make a decision based on the previous legal decision. The court may depart from the doctrine of *stare decisis* if the facts in the current case are different from those in an earlier case or if there are changes in business practices, technology, or the attitudes of society.

Statutory Law   A **statute** is a law that is passed by the U.S. Congress, a state legislature, or a local government. **Statutory law,** then, consists of all the laws that have been enacted by legislative bodies. Many aspects of common law have been incorporated into statutory law and, in the process, made more precise.

For businesses, one very important part of statutory law is the Uniform Commercial Code. The **Uniform Commercial Code (UCC)** is a set of laws designed to eliminate differences among state regulations affecting business and to simplify interstate commerce. The UCC consists of ten articles, or chapters, that cover sales, commercial paper, bank deposits and collections, transfers of title, securities, and transactions that involve collateral. It has been adopted in its entirety by all the states except Louisiana, which has adopted only part of it. The statutes that were replaced by the UCC generally varied from state to state. These variations tended to cause problems for firms that did business in more than one state.

Today, most legal experts have expanded the concept of statutory law to include administrative law. **Administrative law** consists entirely of the regulations created by government agencies that have been established by legislative bodies. The Nuclear Regulatory Commission, for example, has the power to set specific requirements for nuclear power plants. It can even halt the construction or operation of plants that do not meet such requirements. These requirements thus have the force and effect of law. Some well-known federal agencies are the Federal Communications Commission, Federal Aviation Administration, Equal Employment Opportunity Commission, and Environmental Protection Agency. State and local agencies also enact laws that both businesses and individuals must obey.

Most regulatory agencies hold hearings that are similar to court trials. Evidence is introduced, and the parties involved are represented by legal counsel. Moreover, the decisions of these agencies may be appealed in state or federal courts.

Public Law and Private Law: Crimes and Torts

public law   *the body of law that deals with the relationships between individuals or businesses and society*

Public law is the body of law that deals with the relationships between individuals or businesses and society. A violation of a public law is called a **crime.** Among the crimes that can affect a business are the following:

crime   *a violation of a public law*

▶   Burglary, robbery, and theft (discussed in Chapter 20)

▶   Embezzlement, or the unauthorized taking of money or property by an employee, agent, or trustee

▶   Forgery, or the false signing or changing of a legal document with the intent to alter the liability of another person

▶   The use of inaccurate weights, measures, or labels

▶   The use of the mails to defraud, or cheat, an individual or business

Those accused of crimes are prosecuted by a federal, state, or local government.

private law   *the body of law that governs the relationships between two or more individuals or businesses*

Private law is the body of law that governs the relationships between two or more individuals or businesses. A violation of a private law (which

Today, lawyers must determine if certain acts are a violation of public or private law. Public law deals primarily with the relationship between individuals or businesses and society. Private law, on the other hand, governs the relationship between two or more individuals or businesses.

tort *a violation of a private law*

is, in essence, a violation of another's rights) is called a **tort.** A single illegal act—shoplifting, for example—can be both a crime and a tort.

The purpose of private law is to provide a remedy for the party that is injured by a tort. In most cases, the remedy is monetary damages to compensate the injured party and punish the person committing the tort.

Generally, torts may result either from intentional acts or from negligence. Such acts as shoplifting and embezzlement are intentional torts. **Negligence** is a failure to exercise reasonable care, resulting in injury to another. Suppose the driver of a delivery truck loses control of the truck, and it damages a building. A tort has been committed, and the owner of the building may sue the driver and the driver's employer to recover the cost of the necessary repairs.

negligence *a failure to exercise reasonable care, resulting in injury to another*

An important area of tort law deals with *product liability*—the responsibility of manufacturers for negligence in designing, manufacturing, or providing operating instructions for their products. Toyota Motor Sales USA Inc. was recently slapped with a $43 million judgment in a case involving a rear-end collision of a Toyota station wagon that resulted in the deaths of three people. After a lengthy court trial, the jury decided that the car was improperly designed when originally built. Toyota Motor Sales USA has indicated that it will seek a new trial or appeal the decision.[2] In some cases, product liability has been extended to mean strict product liability. **Strict product liability** is the legal concept that holds that a manufacturer is responsible for injuries caused by its products even if it was not negligent. An injured party need only prove that the product was defective, that the defect caused the product to be unsafe, and that an injury occurred because of the defect.

strict product liability *the legal concept that holds that a manufacturer is responsible for injuries caused by its products even if it was not negligent*

The Court System

The United States has a dual court system. The federal court system consists of the Supreme Court of the United States, which was established by the Constitution, and other federal courts that were created by Congress. In addition, each of the fifty states has established its own court system. Figure 21.1 shows the makeup of both the federal court system and a typical state court system.

The Federal Court System Federal courts generally hear cases that involve

▶ Questions of constitutional law

▶ Federal crimes or violations of federal statutes

▶ Property valued at $10,000 or more between citizens of different states, or between an American citizen and a foreign nation

▶ Bankruptcy; the Internal Revenue Service; the postal laws; or copyright, patent, and trademark laws

▶ Admiralty and maritime cases

court of original jurisdiction *the first court to recognize and hear testimony in a legal action*

The United States is divided into judicial districts. Each state includes at least one district court, and more populous states have two or more. A district court is a **court of original jurisdiction,** which is the first court to

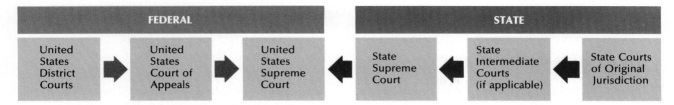

FIGURE 21.1
The Court System
The United States has a dual court system illustrated here by the federal court system and a typical state court system.

recognize and hear testimony in a legal action. The court decision is rendered by a jury, unless both parties involved in the action waive their right to a jury trial. In that case, the decision is rendered by the judge.

If the losing party is not satisfied with the decision reached in the district court, the decision may be appealed to a higher court. A court that hears cases that are appealed from lower courts is called an **appellate court.** Generally, an appellate court does not hear witnesses. Instead it examines the original trial record to decide whether some legal principle has been violated. If the appellate court finds the lower court's ruling to be in error, it may reverse that ruling, modify the decision, or return the case to the lower court for a new trial. Currently, there are thirteen U.S. courts of appeals.

The U.S. Supreme Court—the highest court in the land—consists of nine justices (the Chief Justice of the United States and eight associate justices). Like federal judges, Supreme Court justices are appointed by the president of the United States and must be confirmed by the Senate. Justices receive lifetime appointments. The Supreme Court has original jurisdiction in cases that involve ambassadors and consuls and in certain cases involving one or more states. However, its main function is to review decisions made by the U.S. courts of appeals and, in some cases, by state supreme courts.

The State Court Systems The state court systems are quite similar to the federal system in structure. All have courts of original jurisdiction and supreme courts, and most have intermediate appellate courts as well. In a state that does not have an intermediate appellate court, decisions of the court of original jurisdiction are appealed directly to the state supreme court. The decision of a state supreme court may be appealed to the U.S. Supreme Court if it involves a question of constitutional or federal law.

Other Types of Courts Other courts have been created to meet special needs at both the federal and state levels. **A court of limited jurisdiction** is a court that hears only specific types of cases. At the federal level, for example, Congress has created courts to hear cases that involve international trade, taxes and disputes with the IRS, and bankruptcy. At the state level, there are small-claims courts, which hear cases involving

appellate court *a court that hears cases that are appealed from lower courts*

court of limited jurisdiction *a court that hears only specific types of cases*

BUSINESS JOURNAL

Steps in a Court Case

In 1983, Paramount Pictures agreed to purchase a movie script written by nationally syndicated columnist Art Buchwald. The contract required Paramount to pay Buchwald and Alain Bernheim (the film's producer) $250,000 and 19 percent of the film's net profits. Later Paramount abandoned the project. Then, in 1988, Paramount introduced the film *Coming to America* starring Eddie Murphy. After viewing the film, Buchwald concluded that *Coming to America* was based on his original 1983 movie script. Buchwald then filed suit to force Paramount to honor his contract.

Like all lawsuits, a number of steps are required before a case like this can be resolved.

Step 1—Commencement of action.   In this case, Art Buchwald—the plaintiff—talks to an attorney and describes his case. The attorney then files a complaint against Paramount Pictures. The complaint contains a description of the problem and a request for damages.

Step 2—The summons.   A summons is a legal document that serves notice that a legal action has been commenced by the plaintiff. In this case, Paramount Pictures—the defendant—is notified by an officer of the court that Buchwald is initiating legal action to force Paramount to honor his original contract.

Step 3—The defendant's response.   The defendant must either appear in court or respond to the summons within fifteen to twenty days, depending on individual state requirements. Here, Paramount responds by filing an answer. An answer is a legal document that contains admissions, denials, defenses, or counterclaims. If the defendant does not reply, the court may order a default judgment in favor of the plaintiff.

Step 4—Pretrial procedures.   The purpose of pretrial procedures is to discover the facts prior to the actual trial. Each party has the right to obtain evidence—a legal procedure called *discovery*—which includes:

1. Pretrial depositions consisting of sworn testimony
2. Written interrogatories, which consist of sworn answers to questions prepared in advance by the opposing party
3. A motion for the opposing party to produce evidence

4. Demands for admission of facts by one party (under oath) at the request of the other

The evidence obtained in the discovery procedure may be so conclusive that a trial becomes unnecessary. Either party may move for a summary judgment, which means that a judge will decide the case on the basis of the evidence. Also, a pretrial conference among all lawyers and the judge is normally held in a final attempt to settle the case.

Step 5—The court trial.   If either Buchwald or Paramount is unwilling to settle out of court, and if it is impossible for the judge to decide the case on the basis of discovery-procedure evidence, the only alternative is a court trial. A jury is selected, and the attorneys make their opening statements. Witnesses are called, and all evidence relating to the case is presented. Finally, both attorneys make their summation statements. The judge then gives instructions to the jury, outlining the rules of law that are applicable to this case. The jury retires to the jury room to deliberate the case. If the jury decides in favor of the defendant, Paramount does not have to pay Buchwald. On the other hand, if the jury decides for the plaintiff, Paramount must pay Buchwald. Of course, the party who loses the case may appeal to an appellate court.

On January 8, 1990, a Los Angeles judge ruled that the 1988 Paramount film *Coming to America* was based on Buchwald's original movie script. But, for Buchwald, the battle was not over. While he was entitled to $250,000 and 19 percent of the film's net profit, Paramount argued that the film, which had grossed over $128 million, was not profitable. Even though Buchwald had won his court case, he and his lawyers still have to prove that the film was profitable.

Based on information from Jeanne McDowell, "He's Got Their Number, Almost," *Time*, January 22, 1990, p. 50; "Eddie Murphy's Testimony Disputes Buchwald's Suit," *Jet*, January 15, 1990, pp. 54–55; Jim Abramson and Amy Docker Marcus, "Buchwald Wins Battle with Paramount," *Wall Street Journal*, January 9, 1990, p. B2; and Arnold J. Goldman and William D. Sigismond, *Business Law*, 2d ed. (Boston: Houghton Mifflin Company, 1988), pp. 48–51.

claims for less than a specified dollar amount (usually $500 or $1,500, depending on the state); traffic courts; divorce courts; juvenile courts; and probate courts.

Let us now briefly discuss the major categories of business law. These are contract law, property law, laws relating to negotiable instruments, agency law, and bankruptcy law.

Contract Law

Contract law is perhaps the most important area of business law, because contracts are so much a part of doing business. Every business person should understand what a valid contract is and how it is fulfilled or violated.

contract *a legally enforceable agreement between two or more parties who promise to do, or not to do, a particular thing*

A **contract** is a legally enforceable agreement between two or more parties who promise to do, or not to do, a particular thing. The parties to a contract may be individuals or businesses. An *implied contract* is an agreement that results from the actions of the parties rather than from specific promises. For example, a person who orders dinner at a local restaurant assumes that the food will be served within a reasonable time and will be fit to eat. The restaurant owner, for his or her part, assumes that the customer will pay for the meal.

Most contracts are more explicit and formal than that between a restaurant and its customers: An *express contract* is one in which the parties involved have made oral or written promises about the terms of their agreement.

Requirements for a Valid Contract

Learning Objective 2
Recognize what constitutes a valid and enforceable contract and the principal remedies for breach of contract

To be valid and legally enforceable, an implied or express contract must meet five specific requirements, which may be characterized as follows: (1) voluntary agreement, (2) consideration, (3) legal competence of all parties, (4) lawful subject matter, and (5) proper form.

voluntary agreement *a contract requirement consisting of an offer by one party to enter into a contract with a second party and acceptance by the second party of all the terms and conditions of the offer*

Voluntary Agreement   **Voluntary agreement** consists of both an *offer* by one party to enter into a contract with a second party and *acceptance* by the second party of all the terms and conditions of the offer. If any part of the offer is not accepted, there is no contract. And, if it can be proved that coercion, undue pressure, or fraud was used to obtain a contract, it may be voided by the injured party.

Unless the method of acceptance is specified in the offer, a contract can be accepted orally or in writing. Generally, acceptance must occur within a reasonable time. If the offer calls for acceptance by a specific date, acceptance after that date does *not* result in a binding contract. Both the offer and the acceptance should be given in specific terms that would enable a reasonable person to understand the contract agreement.

Consideration   A contract is a binding agreement only when each party provides something of value to the other party. The value or benefit that

consideration *the value or benefit that one party to a contract furnishes to the other party*

one party furnishes to the other party is called **consideration.** This consideration may be money, property, a service, or the promise not to exercise a legal right. However, the consideration given by one party need not be equal in dollar value to the consideration given by the other party. As a general rule, the courts will not void a contract just because one party got a bargain.

Legal Competence   All parties to a contract must be legally competent to manage their own affairs *and* must have the authority to enter into binding agreements. In a few cases, aliens, convicts, and corporations limited by their charters may have restricted ability to enter into contracts. And the courts generally will not require minors, persons of unsound mind, or those who entered into contracts while they were intoxicated to comply with the terms of their contracts. The intent of the legal competence requirement is to protect individuals who may not have been able to protect themselves. In particular, minors can void (or nullify) contracts to which they are parties (except contracts for such necessities of life as food and shelter) at any time before they reach the age of majority. In some states, minors may void a contract even after reaching the age of majority. The business person, on the other hand, is bound by the terms and conditions of the contract.

usury *the practice of charging interest in excess of the maximum legal rate*

Lawful Subject Matter   A contract is not legally enforceable if it involves an unlawful act. Certainly, a person who contracts with an arsonist to burn down a building cannot go to court to obtain enforcement of the contract. Equally unenforceable is a contract that involves **usury,** which is the practice of charging interest in excess of the maximum legal rate. In many states, a lender who practices usury is denied the right to recover any interest at all. In a few states, such a lender may recover the maximum legal interest. Other contracts that may be unlawful include promissory notes resulting from illegal gambling activities, contracts to bribe public officials, agreements to perform services without required licenses, and contracts that restrain trade.

Proper Form of Contract   Although contracts may be oral, it is safer to commit them to writing. A written contract is visible evidence of its terms, whereas an oral contract is subject to the memories and interpretations of the parties involved. Businesses generally draw up all contractual agreements in writing so that differences can be resolved readily if a dispute develops. Figure 21.2 shows that a contract need not be complicated to be legally enforceable.

A written contract must contain the names of the parties involved and their signatures, the purpose of the contract, and all terms and conditions to which the parties have agreed. Changes to a written contract should be made in writing and should be initialed by all parties. They should be written directly on the original contract or attached to it.

The *Statute of Frauds*, which has been passed in some form by all states, requires that certain types of contracts be in writing to be enforceable. These include contracts dealing with

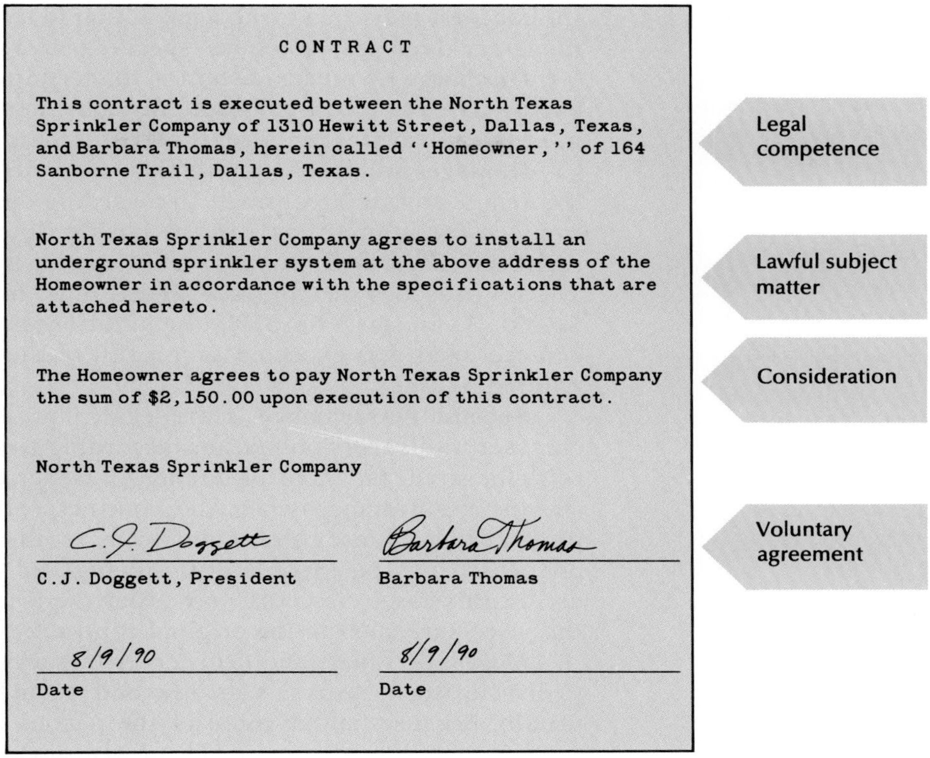

CONTRACT

This contract is executed between the North Texas Sprinkler Company of 1310 Hewitt Street, Dallas, Texas, and Barbara Thomas, herein called ''Homeowner,'' of 164 Sanborne Trail, Dallas, Texas.

North Texas Sprinkler Company agrees to install an underground sprinkler system at the above address of the Homeowner in accordance with the specifications that are attached hereto.

The Homeowner agrees to pay North Texas Sprinkler Company the sum of $2,150.00 upon execution of this contract.

North Texas Sprinkler Company

C.J. Doggett	Barbara Thomas
C.J. Doggett, President	Barbara Thomas
8/9/90	8/9/90
Date	Date

FIGURE 21.2
Contract Between a Business and a Customer
Notice that the requirements for a valid contract are satisfied and that the contract takes the proper form by containing the names of the parties involved, the purpose of the contract, and all terms and conditions.

- The exchange of land or real estate
- The sale of goods, merchandise, or personal property valued at $500 or more
- The sale of securities, regardless of the dollar amount
- Acts that will not be completed within one year after the agreement is made
- A promise to assume someone else's financial obligation
- A promise made in contemplation of marriage

Performance and Nonperformance

performance *the fulfillment of all obligations by all parties to the contract*

breach of contract *the failure of one party to fulfill the terms of a contract when there is no legal reason for that failure*

Ordinarily, a contract is terminated by **performance,** which is the fulfillment of all obligations by all parties to the contract. Occasionally, however, performance may become impossible. Death, disability, or bankruptcy, for example, may legally excuse one party from a contractual obligation. And a contract may be terminated by the mutual agreement of all parties involved. But what happens when one party simply does not perform according to a legal contract?

A **breach of contract** is the failure of one party to fulfill the terms of a contract when there is no legal reason for that failure. Other parties to the contract may then bring legal action to discharge the contract, obtain monetary damages, or require specific performance.

discharge by mutual assent *when all parties agree to void a contract*

Discharge by mutual assent is the termination of a contract when all parties agree to void a contract. Any consideration received by the parties must be returned when a contract is discharged by mutual assent.

damages *a monetary settlement awarded to a party that is injured through a breach of contract*

Damages are a monetary settlement awarded to a party that is injured through a breach of contract. In awarding damages, an attempt is made to place the injured party in the position it would be in if the contract had been performed. Suppose A contracts to paint B's house for $1,500. Then A breaches the contract, and B must hire C to paint the house for $2,000. B can sue A for $500, the additional cost she or he had to pay to achieve what was expected as a result of the original contract—a newly painted house.

specific performance *the legal requirement that the parties to a contract fulfill their obligations according to the contract (as opposed to settlement via payment of damages)*

Specific performance is the legal requirement that the parties to a contract fulfill their obligations according to the contract (as opposed to settlement via payment of damages). Generally, the courts will require specific performance when the contract calls for a unique service or product that cannot be obtained from another source. For example, only one artist may be capable of designing and creating a specific piece of art. In this case, the court may order the artist to create the artwork at the price agreed on in the original contract.

Most individuals and firms enter into a contract because they expect to live up to its terms. Very few end up in court. When they do, it is usually because one or more of the parties did not understand all the conditions of the agreement. Thus it is imperative to know what you are signing before you sign it. If there is any doubt, get legal help! Once a contract is signed, it is very difficult—and often very costly—to void.

Sales Agreements

sales agreement *a type of contract by which ownership is transferred from a seller to a buyer*

A **sales agreement** is a special (but very common) type of contract by which ownership is transferred from a seller to a buyer. Because sales agreements are contracts, they are generally subject to the conditions and requirements we have discussed.

Article 2 of the UCC (entitled "Sales") provides much of our sales law, which is derived from both common and statutory law. It covers the sale of goods only. It does not cover the sale of stocks and bonds, personal services, or real estate. Among the topics included in Article 2 are rights of the buyer and seller, acceptance and rejection of an offer, inspection of goods, delivery, transfer of ownership, and warranties.

Article 2 provides that a sales agreement may be binding even when one or more of the general contract requirements is omitted. For example, a sales agreement is legally binding when the selling price is left out of the agreement. Article 2 requires that the buyer pay the reasonable value of the goods at the time of delivery. Key considerations in resolving such issues are the actions and business history of the parties and any customery sales procedures within the particular industry.

express warranty *a written explanation of the responsibilities of the producer (or seller) in the event that a product is found to be defective or otherwise unsatisfactory*

Article 2 also deals with warranties—both express and implied. As we saw in Chapter 12, an **express warranty** is a written explanation of

BUSINESS JOURNAL

Stockbrokers, Arbitration, and Investment Contracts

Today, most brokerage firms require investors to sign contracts that include a clause that requires dissatisfied investors to submit any disputes to a three-member arbitration panel. Typically, arbitration panels include one member from the securities industry and two members from the general public. Brokerage firms prefer arbitration to lengthy court cases and the possibility of large dollar awards that a jury can grant dissatisfied customers. In addition, the arbitration clause contained in most contracts usually prohibits customers from taking disputes to either state or federal courts and from appealing the arbitration panel's decision.

Each year approximately 7,000 client-stockbroker disputes are submitted to arbitration. Despite the increased use of arbitration, the process is not without some serious flaws. In fact, a number of legislators at the federal and state level, along with consumers' advocates, argue that arbitration stacks the deck against small investors. According to a recent New York Stock Exchange study, customers win more than half of the arbitration cases, but they receive only about 15 cents for each dollar of their claims.* To date, all the investors who have challenged the arbitration clause contained in their brokerage firm contracts have lost.

Take the case of *De Quijas et al.* v. *Shearson/American Express, Inc.* According to sworn court testimony, the plaintiffs were small investors who invested their savings with Jon Grady Deaton, a stockbroker with the Shearson/American Express

brokerage firm. Deaton asked the plaintiffs to sign a standard Shearson/American Express contract. Although the plaintiffs didn't realize it, the contract contained an arbitration clause. Once the contract was signed, Deaton invested the plaintiffs' savings in risk-oriented investments and engaged in numerous illegal actions to generate commissions. After the plaintiffs lost most of their money, they filed a class action suit against Shearson/American Express. Deaton disappeared, and Shearson/American Express offered to submit the plaintiffs' dispute to arbitration. The plaintiffs then filed suit in a New Orleans federal district court to void the arbitration clause in the Shearson/American Express contract. The plaintiffs in the case wanted a jury trial instead of the arbitration process.

The federal district court in New Orleans ruled that the arbitration clause was a valid part of the contract. The plaintiffs then appealed to the United States Court of Appeals for the Fifth Circuit. The court of appeals reversed the decision and declared the arbitration clause invalid. Then Shearson/American Express appealed the case to the United States Supreme Court. On May 15, 1989, the Supreme Court ruled that arbitration clauses are binding on disputes that arise from the purchase of securities.

---

* Edward Giltenan, "Wall Street's Other Arbs," *Forbes,* March 20, 1989, p. 196.

Based on information from Geoffrey P. Miller, "Stockbrokers, Arbitration, and the Securities Act of 1933," *Preview of the United States Supreme Court Cases,* April 28, 1989, pp. 383–384; Edward Giltenan, "The Joys of Haggling," *Forbes,* June 26, 1989, p. 236; Laura Zinn, "Battling Your Broker Just Got a Bit Easier," *Business Week,* June 5, 1989, p. 142; and Stephen Wermiel, "Suing Brokers Is Now Even More Difficult," *Wall Street Journal,* May 16, 1989, p. C1.

the responsibilities of the producer (or seller) in the event that a product is found to be defective or otherwise unsatisfactory. An express warranty may also include the seller's representations concerning such product characteristics as age, durability, and quality. A *full warranty* exists when the producer or seller guarantees to fix or replace a defective product within a reasonable time without cost to the customer. A *limited warranty* exists when the producer or seller does not offer the complete protection of a full warranty. A product's limited warranty must be disclosed to the customer.

An **implied warranty** is a guarantee that is imposed or required by law. In general, the buyer is entitled to assume that

1. The merchandise offered for sale has a clear title and is not stolen.
2. The merchandise is as advertised.
3. The merchandise will serve the purpose for which it was manufactured and sold.

Any limitation to an express or implied warranty must be stated in writing.

Property Law

Property is anything that can be owned. The concept of private ownership of property is fundamental to the free-enterprise system. Our Constitution guarantees to individuals and businesses the right to own property and to use it in their own best interest.

Kinds of Property

Property is legally classified as either real property or personal property. **Real property** is land and anything that is permanently attached to it. The term also applies to water on the ground and minerals and natural resources beneath the surface. Thus, a house, a factory, a garage, and a well are all considered real property.

Learning Objective 3
Be aware of the major provisions of property law, especially those regarding the transfer of title to property

The degree to which a business is concerned with real-property law depends on the size and type of business. The owner of a small jewelry store needs only a limited knowledge of real-property law. But a national jewelry-store chain might employ several real estate experts with extensive knowledge of real-property law, property values, and real estate zoning ordinances throughout the country.

Personal property is all property other than real property. Personal property such as inventories, equipment, store fixtures, an automobile, or a book has physical or material value. It is thus referred to as *tangible personal property*. Property that derives its value from a legal right or claim is called *intangible personal property*. Examples include stocks and bonds, receivables, trademarks, patents, and copyrights.

As we noted in Chapter 12, a **trademark** is a brand that is registered with the U.S. Patent and Trademark Office. Registration guarantees the owner the exclusive use of the trademark for twenty years. At the end of that time, the registration can be renewed for additional twenty-year periods. If necessary, the owner must defend the trademark from unauthorized use—usually through legal action. McDonald's was recently forced to do exactly that, when the brand name ''Big Mac'' was used by another fast-food outlet in a foreign country.

A **patent** is the exclusive right to make, use, or sell a newly invented product or process. Patents are granted by the U.S. Patent and Trademark Office for a period of seventeen years. After that time has elapsed, the

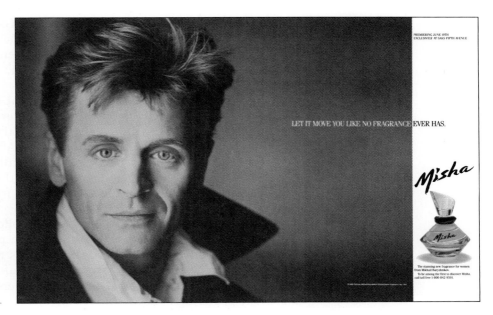

LET IT MOVE YOU LIKE NO FRAGRANCE EVER HAS.

Misha

Misha, *a new fragrance for women from Mikhail Baryshnikov, is a registered trademark of a new perfume that was introduced by Richard Barrie Fragrances in 1989.*

invention becomes available for general use. A patent holder may license others to use the patented invention, in return for a fee.

copyright *the exclusive right to publish, perform, copy, or sell an original work*

A **copyright** is the exclusive right to publish, perform, copy, or sell an original work. Copyright laws cover fiction and nonfiction, plays, poetry, musical works, photographs, films, and—nowadays—computer programs. For example, the copyright on this textbook is held by the publisher, Houghton Mifflin Company. The copyright on the television series "Dallas" is held by Lorimar Productions. A copyright is granted to the creator of the work by the U.S. Copyright Office. It generally holds for the lifetime of the creator plus fifty years.

Transfer of Ownership

deed *a written document by which the ownership of real property is transferred from one person or organization to another*

Real Property   As we noted earlier, the Statute of Frauds requires that exchanges of real estate be in writing. A **deed** is a written document by which the ownership of real property is transferred from one person or organization to another. The deed must contain the names of the previous owner and the new owner, as well as a legally acceptable description of the property being transferred. However, consideration is not required. Thus, while real estate may be given as a gift, a deed is still necessary to transfer the title.

lease *an agreement by which the right to use real property is temporarily transferred from its owner, the landlord, to a tenant*

A **lease** is an agreement by which the right to use real property is temporarily transferred from its owner, the landlord, to a tenant. In return for the use of the property, the tenant generally pays rent on a weekly, monthly, or yearly basis. A lease is granted for a specific period of time, after which a new lease may be negotiated. If the lease is terminated, the right to use the real property reverts to the landlord.

Personal Property   Suppose you go into The Gap clothing store and buy a sweater. When, exactly, do you own it? The answer depends on how you pay for it. The sale of the sweater is in essence a contract. The seller's consideration is the title to, or ownership of, the sweater. The buyer's consideration is the full price of the sweater.

When the buyer pays the *full cash price* at the time of purchase, the title to personal property passes to the buyer immediately. When the buyer purchases goods on an *installment plan*, the title passes to the buyer when he or she takes possession of the goods. Although the full cash price has not been paid, the buyer has made a legally enforceable promise to pay it. This is sufficient consideration for the transfer of ownership. Moreover, if the purchased goods are stolen from the buyer, the buyer must still pay the full purchase price.

Goods that are purchased on a *C.O.D.* (Collect On Delivery) *basis* are paid for at the time of delivery. Usually title passes to the buyer when the goods are delivered to the carrier. (In this type of sale, however, the buyer is generally allowed a reasonable time after delivery to inspect the goods and, if they are not what the buyer ordered, to reject them.)

When goods are purchased on an *F.O.B.* (Free On Board) *point of origin basis*, the buyer, rather than the seller, is responsible for shipping them. Thus, title passes to the buyer when the goods are accepted by a carrier. If the goods are damaged in transit, the buyer must attempt to collect for the damage from the carrier. On the other hand, if the merchandise is shipped on an *F.O.B. destination basis*, title passes to the buyer when the goods reach their final destination. If the goods are damaged in transit, the seller must attempt to collect from the carrier.

Laws Relating to Negotiable Instruments

Learning Objective 4
Know what a negotiable instrument is and how it is endorsed for transfer

negotiable instrument   *a written document that (1) is a promise to pay a stated sum of money and (2) can be transferred from one person or firm to another*

A **negotiable instrument** is a written document that (1) is a promise to pay a stated sum of money and (2) can be transferred from one person or firm to another. In effect, a negotiable instrument is a substitute for money. Checks are the most familiar form of negotiable instruments. However, the promissory notes, drafts, certificates of deposit, and commercial paper discussed in Chapter 18 are also negotiable. Even a warehouse receipt can qualify as a negotiable instrument if certain conditions are met.

Requirements for Negotiability

The UCC establishes the following conditions for negotiability:

▶   The credit instrument must be in writing and signed.

▶   The instrument must contain an unconditional promise or order to pay a stated sum of money.

▶   The instrument must be payable on demand or at a specified future date.

▶ The instrument must be payable to a specified person or firm or to the bearer.

If a financial document does not meet all these requirements, it is not negotiable. It may still be valid and legally enforceable, but it cannot be transferred to another business or individual.

The negotiability of financial documents helps facilitate credit transactions. A supplier who accepts, say, a promissory note, knows that if the need arises, the note can be sold to a bank in return for immediate cash. The supplier can obtain payment at any time—and so is more willing to extend credit to customers.

Endorsements

endorsement *the payee's signature on the back of a negotiable instrument*

To transfer a negotiable instrument, the payee (the person named on the face of the document) must sign it. The payee's signature on the back of a negotiable instrument is called an **endorsement.** There are four types of endorsements, as shown in Figure 21.3.

A *blank endorsement* consists only of the payee's signature. It is quick, easy, and dangerous, because it makes the instrument payable to anyone who gets possession of it—legally or otherwise. A blank endorsement should be used only when the instrument is signed in the presence of the next holder. A *restrictive endorsement* states the purpose for which the instrument is to be used. For example, the words "For Deposit Only" in Figure 21.3 mean that this check must be deposited in the specified account. This type of endorsement is probably the safest endorsement, because it renders the instrument useful only for a specified purpose.

A *special endorsement* identifies the person or firm to whom the instrument is payable. The words "Pay to the order of Robert Jones" in Figure 21.3 mean that the only person who can cash, deposit, or negotiate this check is Robert Jones. Like the restrictive endorsement, the special endorsement protects the negotiable instrument in case it is lost or stolen.

A *qualified endorsement* limits the liability of the payee in the event that the instrument is not honored. The words "without recourse" in Figure 21.3 indicate that the person who originally signed the instrument— and not the endorser Charles Hall—is responsible for payment.

FIGURE 21.3
Endorsements
The payee's signature on the back of a negotiable instrument is called an endorsement. *There are four types of endorsements.*

Blank endorsement | Restrictive endorsement | Special endorsement | Qualified endorsement

Blank endorsement	Restrictive endorsement	Special endorsement	Qualified endorsement
Charles Hall	For deposit only Acct.# 434·422·01 Charles Hall	Pay to the order of Robert Jones Charles Hall	Without recourse Charles Hall

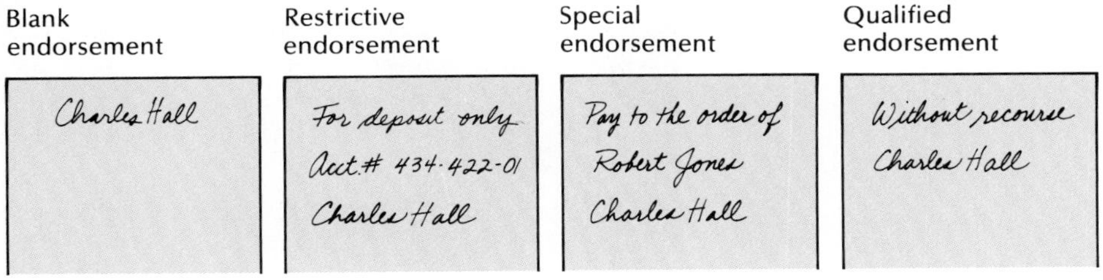

Agency Law

Learning Objective 5
Understand the agent-principal relationship

agency *a business relationship in which one party (called the* principal) *appoints a second party (called the* agent) *to act on behalf of the principal*

An **agency** is a business relationship in which one party (called the *principal*) appoints a second party (called the *agent*) to act on behalf of the principal. Most often, agents are hired to use their special knowledge for a specific purpose. For example, real estate agents are hired to sell or buy real property. Insurance agents are hired to sell insurance. And theatrical agents are hired to obtain engagements for entertainers. The officers of a firm, lawyers, accountants, and stockbrokers also act as agents.

Most agents are independent business people or firms. They are paid for their services with either set fees or commissions.

Almost any legal activity that can be accomplished by an individual can also be accomplished through an agent. (The exceptions are voting, giving sworn testimony in court, and making a will.) Moreover, under the law, the principal is bound by the actions of the agent. The principal can be held liable even if the agent acts contrary to the principal's instructions or ventures into areas not covered by a written contract of agency. However, if the agent performs an unauthorized act, he or she may be sued for damages by the principal. For this reason, a written contract describing the conditions and limits of the agency relationship is extremely important to both parties.

power of attorney *a legal document that serves as evidence that an agent has been appointed to act on behalf of a principal*

A **power of attorney** is a legal document that serves as evidence that an agent has been appointed to act on behalf of a principal. In the majority of states in the United States, a power of attorney is required in agency relationships involving the transfer of real estate, as well as in other specific situations.

Lib Hatcher is an agent for country music entertainer Randy Travis. According to industry experts, Ms. Hatcher is one of the best agents in the business and the only female to represent a major country music star in the United States.

An agent is responsible for carrying out the principal's instructions in a professional manner, for acting reasonably and with good judgment, and for keeping the principal informed of progress according to their agreement. The agent must also be careful to avoid a conflict involving the interests of two or more principals. The agency relationship is terminated when its objective is accomplished, at the end of a specified time period, or in some cases, when either party renounces the agency relationship.

Bankruptcy Law

Know how bankruptcy is initiated and resolved

bankruptcy *a legal procedure designed both to protect an individual or business that cannot meet its financial obligations and to protect the creditors involved*

voluntary bankruptcy *a bankruptcy procedure initiated by an individual or business that can no longer meet its financial obligations*

involuntary bankruptcy *a bankruptcy procedure initiated by creditors*

Bankruptcy is a legal procedure designed both to protect an individual or business that cannot meet its financial obligations and to protect the creditors involved. The Bankruptcy Reform Act was enacted in 1978 and was subsequently amended in July of 1984 and again in November of 1986. This act is divided into nine separate parts, called chapters, which explain the procedures for resolving a bankruptcy case. Under the act, bankruptcy proceedings may be initiated either by the person or business that is in financial difficulty or by the creditors.

Initiating Bankruptcy Proceedings

Voluntary bankruptcy is a bankruptcy procedure initiated by an individual or business that can no longer meet its financial obligations. To declare bankruptcy, the debtor must have debts that exceed the total value of its assets and be unable to repay the debts. Individuals, partnerships, and most corporations may file for voluntary bankruptcy.

Involuntary bankruptcy is a bankruptcy procedure initiated by creditors. The creditors must be able to prove that the individual or business has debts in excess of $5,000 and cannot pay its debts as they come due. If there are more than twelve creditors, a petition for involuntary bankruptcy must be signed by three or more creditors whose claims total at least $5,000. If there are fewer than twelve creditors, one or more creditors with claims of at least $5,000 need to sign the petition.

Today most bankruptcies are voluntary. Creditors are wary of initiating bankruptcy proceedings, because they usually end up losing most of the money that is involved. They generally feel it is better to wait and to hope the debtor will eventually be able to pay.

Resolving a Bankruptcy Case

A petition for bankruptcy is filed in a bankruptcy court. If the court declares the individual or business to be bankrupt, three means of resolution are available: liquidation, reorganization, and repayment.

Liquidation   Chapter 7 of the Bankruptcy Reform Act concerns *liquidation*, the sale of assets of a bankrupt individual or business to pay its debts (see

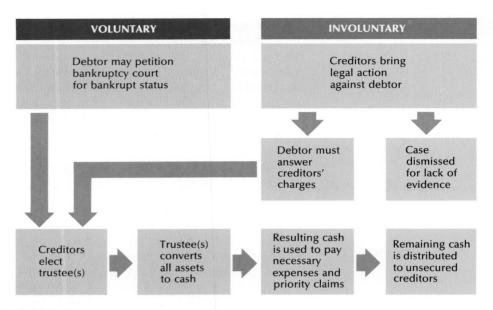

FIGURE 21.4
Steps Involved in Chapter 7 of the Bankruptcy Reform Act
Chapter 7 of the Bankruptcy Reform Act concerns liquidation of assets.

Figure 21.4). In principle, the assets of the individual or business are sold to satisfy the claims of creditors. The debtor is then relieved of all its remaining debts. Liquidation pursuant to Chapter 7 does not apply to railroads, banks, savings and loan associations, insurance companies, credit unions, or municipalities. Chapter 7 specifies the order in which claims are to be paid. First, creditors with secured claims are allowed to repossess (or assume ownership of) the collateral for their claims. Next, unsecured claims are paid in the following order:[3]

1. Costs involved in the bankruptcy case (including fees paid to trustees, attorneys, and accountants)

2. Claims that arose in the course of the debtor's business activities, after the commencement of the case

3. Claims for wages, salaries, or commissions, up to a limit of $2,000 per claimant

4. Claims for contributions to employee benefits plans

5. Claims by consumer creditors, arising from the purchase of products that have not been delivered, up to $900 per claimant

6. Federal and state taxes

The remaining cash and assets—if any—are divided among creditors with unsecured claims, in proportion to the size of their various claims.

Reorganization   Chapter 11 of the Bankruptcy Reform Act outlines the procedure for reorganizing a bankrupt business. The idea is simple: The distressed business will be preserved by correcting or eliminating the factors that got the firm into financial trouble. To implement this idea, a plan to reorganize the business is developed. Only the debtor may file a reorganization plan for the first 120 days, unless a trustee has been appointed by the court. If a trustee has been appointed, the trustee may file a reorganization plan. After 120 days, any interested party may file a reorganization plan. After the plan has been filed with the court, both the plan and a written disclosure statement are distributed to all individuals and businesses with claims against the bankrupt firm. These people and firms may testify at a hearing that is held for the purpose of confirming the plan. If the plan is confirmed, the reorganized business emerges from bankruptcy with only the financial obligations that are imposed on it by the plan. This is exactly what occurred when Campeau Stores and Texaco filed for protection under Chapter 11.

Repayment   Chapter 13 of the Bankruptcy Reform Act permits a bankrupt individual to file, with the courts, a plan for paying off specific debts. (Only individuals with a regular income, less than $100,000 in unsecured debts, and less than $350,000 in secured debts are eligible to file for repayment under Chapter 13.) The plan must provide for the repayment of specified amounts in up to three years. (In unusual circumstances, the court may extend the repayment period to five years.) If the plan is approved by the court, the individual usually pays the money to a court-appointed trustee in monthly installments. The trustee, in turn, pays the individual's creditors.

CHAPTER REVIEW

Summary

Laws are the rules that govern the conduct of, and relationships among, the members of a society. In the United States, laws originate in judicial decisions (common law) and in the enactments of legislative bodies and government agencies (statutory law). An important body of statutory law is contained in the Uniform Commercial Code, which has been adopted, in whole or in part, by all fifty states.

Public law is concerned with the relationships between a society and its members. Private law is concerned with relationships among a society's members. Private law dealing with negligence, or the failure to exercise reasonable care, is of particular interest to businesses.

The United States has a dual court system made up of the federal court system and the court systems of the fifty states. At both the federal level and the state level, court cases are first heard in courts of original jurisdiction. The decisions of these courts may be appealed to appellate courts.

A contract is a legally enforceable agreement. The conditions for a valid contract include voluntary agreement between the parties, consideration, the legal competence of all parties, subject matter that is legal, and proper contract form. Usually a contract is terminated through fulfillment of all obligations contained in the contract. If one party to a contract does not fulfill its obligations, the other party or parties may request the courts to discharge the contract, to award damages for nonperformance, or to require that the terms of the contract be fulfilled. Discharge by mutual assent occurs when all parties agree to void a contract.

A sales agreement is a contract by which ownership is transferred from a seller to a buyer. Article 2 of the Uniform Commercial Code provides much of our sales law, including the difference between an express warranty and an implied warranty. An express warranty is a written explanation of the responsibilities of the producer or seller in the event that a product is found to be defective or otherwise unsatisfactory. An implied warranty is a guarantee that is imposed or required by law. In general, the buyer is entitled to assume that the merchandise offered for sale has a clear title, the merchandise is as advertised, and the merchandise will serve the purpose for which it was manufactured and sold.

Property is anything that can be owned and is classified as either real property or personal property. Real property is land and anything that is permanently attached to it. Personal property is all property other than real property. Personal property is also classified as either tangible or intangible. Exchanges of the title to real property must be in writing. In general, the title to personal property is exchanged when the property is paid for. An exception to this rule occurs when a customer purchases goods by using an installment contract. Although the full cash price has not been paid, the buyer has made a legally enforceable promise to pay. This promise is sufficient consideration for the transfer of ownership.

A negotiable instrument is a written document that is a promise to pay a stated sum of money and can be transferred from one person or firm to another. To be negotiable, the instrument must meet certain requirements established by the UCC and must be endorsed by the payee.

An agency is a business relationship in which an agent acts on behalf of a principal. The principal is generally responsible for, and bound by, all actions of the agent. The agent is responsible for carrying out the instructions of the principal in a reasonable and professional manner.

Bankruptcy laws are designed to protect both a person or firm that cannot pay its debts and the creditors involved. Bankruptcy proceedings may be initiated by either the creditors or the person or firm that cannot cover its liabilities. Bankruptcy proceedings may be resolved through liquidation of the debtor's assets, reorganization of the bankrupt firm, or repayment of specific debts incurred by the bankrupt individual.

In this chapter we have been concerned with relationships among businesses—and, in particular, with the legal aspects of those relationships. In the next chapter we examine the relationship between business and the three levels of government in the United States. The three areas of primary concern are government assistance to, regulation of, and taxation of business.

Key Terms

You should now be able to define and give an example relevant to each of the following terms:

law	specific performance
common law	sales agreement
statute	express warranty
statutory law	implied warranty
Uniform Commercial Code (UCC)	property
	real property
administrative law	personal property
public law	trademark
crime	patent
private law	copyright
tort	deed
negligence	lease
strict product liability	negotiable instrument
court of original jurisdiction	endorsement
appellate court	agency
court of limited jurisdiction	power of attorney
contract	bankruptcy
voluntary agreement	voluntary bankruptcy
consideration	involuntary bankruptcy
usury	
performance	
breach of contract	
discharge by mutual assent	
damages	

Questions and Exercises

Review Questions

1. What are the differences between common law and statutory law?
2. What is administrative law? How does it differ from common law and the rest of statutory law?
3. What is a tort? How does the law punish those who commit torts?
4. How is the concept of strict product liability different from the concept of product liability?
5. What are the three levels of courts in the federal and state court systems? What kinds of cases are heard at each level?
6. List and describe the conditions for a legally enforceable contract.

7. When a contract is breached, what remedies are available to the injured party or parties?
8. What are the differences between an express and an implied warranty? What is implied by an implied warranty?
9. How does real property differ from personal property? Give a specific example of real property, intangible personal property, and tangible personal property, all owned by an independent service station.
10. What is the principal basis on which a court decides when the title to personal property passes from the seller to the buyer? Illustrate your answer with an example.
11. What requirements must be met for a financial instrument to be negotiable? Why is negotiability important?
12. Identify the four types of endorsements discussed in this chapter. Explain the advantages and disadvantages of each.
13. What is the relationship between an agent and a principal?
14. How is voluntary bankruptcy different from involuntary bankruptcy?
15. Briefly describe the three means of resolving a bankruptcy case under current bankruptcy law.

Discussion Questions

1. In 1986 Robert Campeau purchased the Allied Stores Corp. In 1988 he purchased the Federated Department Store chain. Then in 1990 the Campeau stores were forced to file for protection under Chapter 11 of the U.S. bankruptcy laws. Given the information presented in the opening case for this chapter, briefly describe the problems that Robert Campeau encountered since acquiring Allied Stores Corp. in 1986.
2. Most financial analysts are quick to point out that Campeau's financial problems are not the result of poor management, poor merchandising practices, or operating losses, but are the result of too much debt financing. Do you agree with the financial analysts? Why?
3. If you had been a member of the Texas jury that decided *Pennzoil* v. *Texaco*, would you have awarded Pennzoil an $11.1 billion judgment? Justify your opinion.
4. Does the United States need both federal and state court systems? What are the advantages and disadvantages of this dual court arrangement?
5. Why should the law specifically require written contracts for exchanges of real estate, sales over $500, and long-term obligations?

6. Suppose you are a party to a contract that has been breached by the other party. Under what circumstances would you sue for discharge? for damages? for specific performance?
7. In your opinion, is there a social stigma attached to bankruptcy today? Should there be?

Exercises

1. Find two or more articles describing a recent court case that involved two or more businesses.
   a. State the exact nature of the issue or issues involved in the case.
   b. Describe how these issues were resolved.
   c. State whether the resolution seems fair, and justify your answer.
2. Draw up a standard contract form for a company that sells and installs burglar alarm systems in homes. The average cost of the alarm system, including installation, is $750. Include everything required for a valid contract.
3. Obtain a check, and note on it the various items that fulfill the requirements for negotiability.

Case 21.1

Home Improvements: The Need for a Contract

The success of any remodeling project depends on two factors: (1) the choice of the right contractor and (2) a detailed, written contract that describes what the contractor is going to do. If either of these two factors are ignored, disaster can strike. Take the case of Sandra and Mike Jackson. After the arrival of their second child, the Jacksons needed more space in their two-bedroom home. Besides, they had always wanted to convert their garage into a bedroom. They looked in the home section of the *Houston Chronicle* and found the name of a contractor. The contractor came out and gave them an estimate. Because the contractor was anxious to start work immediately, the Jacksons didn't insist on a written contract. That's when their problems started. According to the Jacksons, the contractor wouldn't listen to their ideas and refused to make the changes that would turn the space into an ideal bedroom. Finally, after thirteen months, the job was finished. Six months later, the glass door the contractor had installed began to leak both air and water. The Jacksons called the contractor. To their surprise, they found that he had declared bankruptcy and was now out of the home-remodeling business.

According to consumer advocates, the Jacksons made two mistakes. First, they should have been more careful when choosing a contractor. Most experts suggest that before you talk to any contractor, you crystallize your dreams into concrete plans that a contractor can understand. Then choose a contractor who belongs to either the National Association of Home Builders (NAHB) or the National Association of the Remodeling Industry (NARI). According to the Better Business Bureau, you should always talk to more than one contractor and get more than one bid. Ask each contractor for a list of customers you can call to see if they were satisfied with the contractor's work. Above all, don't let a contractor pressure you to sign a contract prematurely.

Second, the Jacksons should have insisted on a written contract. The contract should describe exactly what the contractor is going to do, all the materials that will be used, the complete financial terms of the agreement, the starting and completion dates, and any other conditions that are relevant to the remodeling project. All special requests, oral promises, or conditions that you have should be included in the written contract. While most experts recommend including an arbitration clause in the contract to resolve any disputes, the best way to avoid problems is to get answers to questions before signing anything.*

Questions

1. The success of any remodeling project depends on two factors: (1) the choice of the right contractor and (2) a detailed written contract that describes what the contractor is going to do. Why are these two factors important?
2. Assuming the Jacksons had insisted on a written contract before the contractor began work, what type of information should have been included in the contract? Why?

Case 21.2

Polaroid v. Kodak

Because much of our law is based on previous court decisions, those decisions are carefully analyzed by

---

* Based on information from "Home Remodeling: Getting It Done Right," *Consumers' Research*, September 1989, pp. 34–36; "Hiring a Contractor," *Better Homes and Gardens*, June 1989, p. 85; "Working with a Contractor," *McCalls*, April 1989, p. 101; "Choosing a Contractor," *Better Homes and Gardens*, April 1988, p. 174; and "Working with a Contractor," *Better Homes and Gardens*, May 1988, p. 111.

both students and practicing attorneys. Here is the outline of a court case that involves two major corporations in the United States.

In 1940, Edwin Land offered to sell Eastman Kodak Co. his patented process for instant photography. Believing instant photography to be just a passing fad, Eastman Kodak rejected Land's offer. Land then founded Polaroid Corp. and continued to develop the instant-photography process. Eventually, Polaroid Corp. used its instant-photography process to capture almost 30 percent of the total camera market in the United States. Then, according to trial testimony, Eastman Kodak spent $94 million to perfect its own instant-photography process, only to scrap it after Polaroid's SX-70 camera was introduced in 1972. Four years later, in April 1976, Eastman Kodak introduced its first instant camera that was designed to compete head-on with Polaroid's SX-70 camera. Six days later, Polaroid initiated a lawsuit against Eastman Kodak, claiming that the company had violated U.S. patent laws. Eastman Kodak promptly counterclaimed that Polaroid's own designs were nothing more than new patents on Eastman Kodak's own patented processes.

After a legal battle lasting almost a decade, Eastman Kodak lost the patent case when, in October 1985, U.S. district court judge Rya W. Zoebel ruled that the company was guilty of infringing on seven Polaroid patents. In January 1986, both the U.S. circuit court of appeals and the Supreme Court of the United States upheld the 1985 decision and ordered Eastman Kodak out of the instant-photography business.

Based on the Court's ruling, Eastman Kodak's management was forced to develop a reimbursement plan for its customers who could no longer buy film for their Kodak instant cameras. Eastman Kodak offered its instant-camera owners three choices. First, they could trade in their instant equipment for a disc camera and film worth about $50. Second, they could opt to receive coupons for Kodak products valued at $50. Third, U.S. customers could exchange their instant camera for one share of Eastman Kodak common stock then selling for approximately $47.

The reimbursement plan, a public-relations triumph, soon became a logistical nightmare when the firm was besieged by phone calls from instant-camera owners. To make matters worse, Eastman Kodak's redemption plans were halted by another lawsuit. This second case, filed by dissatisfied customers, was finally resolved in 1989 when customers agreed to a combination cash-coupon settlement.

Five years after the original court decision, the U.S. district court in Boston is still trying to determine the amount of damages that Eastman Kodak will have to pay Polaroid. Legal experts are predicting that the final settlement could be as high as $1.5 billion.†

---

† Based on information from Gene G. Marcial, "Kodak and Polaroid? or GE? How About Disney?" *Business Week*, June 19, 1989, p. 84; Keith H. Hammonds, "Why Polaroid Must Remake Itself—Instantly," *Business Week*, September 19, 1988, p. 66 +; Alex Beam and William B. Glaberson, "Polaroid vs. Kodak: The Decisive Round," *Business Week*, January 13, 1989, p. 37; Janice Castro, "Instant Getaway," *Time*, January 20, 1986, p. 43; Alex Taylor III, "Kodak Scrambles to Refocus," *Fortune*, March 3, 1986, p. 34; and Michael Salter, "Paying the Patent Price," *Macleans*, January 20, 1986, p. 38.

Questions

1. Should Polaroid—as the patent holder of the instant-photography process—be allowed to monopolize the instant-camera market?
2. Based on the information in the outline at the beginning of this case, did Eastman Kodak violate U.S. patent laws?

GOVERNMENT ASSISTANCE, REGULATION, AND TAXATION

LEARNING OBJECTIVES

1 Appreciate the ways in which government can assist business firms

2 Know the reasons for—and content of—the major federal antitrust laws

3 Understand how and why the federal government regulates natural monopolies

4 Be familiar with the nature of government's response to the current deregulation movement

5 Be aware of the various taxes through which the federal, state, and local governments are financed

CHAPTER PREVIEW

We begin this chapter by describing how government supports business activities—through its information services, its funded research efforts, and its enormous purchasing power. We also examine several important laws that support business by prohibiting restraints on competition. Next, we review the definition of natural monopoly introduced in an earlier chapter. We explain how the government permits the existence of certain natural monopolies but carefully regulates their activities. Then we consider the deregulation movement, noting some of the arguments both for and against deregulation. We conclude the chapter with a discussion of federal, state, and local taxes—the primary means by which governments at all levels finance their activities.

INSIDE BUSINESS

Sematech: A Consortium Paid for by Government and Private Business

The *American Heritage Dictionary* defines a *consortium* as an association or partnership. One of the earliest and most successful consortiums was formed by the Japanese in the late 1970s. The primary purpose of the Japanese consortium was to overtake U.S. electronic firms that were producing very large scale integrated (VLSI) circuits needed for advanced computer applications. Their consortium worked so well that the Japanese dominated the VLSI market by the mid-1980s.

Then, in 1987, the Department of Defense of the U.S. federal government, state and local governments, and fourteen private companies began fighting back and formed their own consortium to outwit foreign competitors—especially the Japanese—in the semiconductor industry.* Located in Austin, Texas, the consortium was called Sematech (short for Semiconductor Manufacturing Technology).

Initial funding was a cooperative effort. First, the state of Texas, city of Austin, and University of Texas contributed between $50 million and $60 million. Second, the fourteen private companies involved in the project each committed to contribute 1 percent of their annual semiconductor sales revenues to Sematech. Finally, the Department of Defense agreed to match the funds provided by the private firms. All told, the annual operating budget for Sematech is projected at between $200 and $250 million for each of the next five years.

Each member of the consortium expects to profit from the partnership. In return for financing, the state of Texas and city of Austin will experience new jobs and economic growth. The fourteen companies will be able to use any new technology or products that result from Sematech research. Finally, the Department of Defense will no longer be dependent on foreign manufacturers for state-of-the-art semiconductors and other electronic components needed for military applications.

While Sematech is only three years old, the results look promising. Even more promising is the cooperation between the fourteen companies involved in the project. In the past, U.S. electronics companies have competed fiercely with each other. But now, given Japanese dominance in the semiconductor field and the large dollar investment required for research, former rivals have combined resources. No longer content with second place, these successful American firms intend to develop integrated circuits that will match or surpass the Japanese by the mid-1990s.[1]

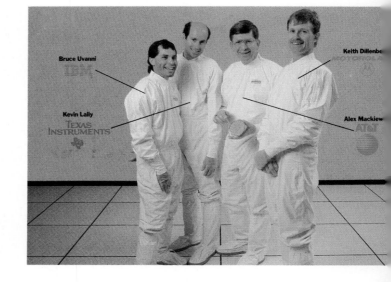

Bruce Uvanni — IBM
Kevin Lally — TEXAS INSTRUMENTS
Keith Dillenbe — MOTOROLA
Alex Mackiew — AT&T

---

* Members of the consortium include Advanced Micro Devices, Digital Equipment, Harris Corporation, Hewlett-Packard, Motorola, National Semiconductor, NCR, Rockwell International, AT&T, Intel, IBM, LSI Logic, Micron Technology, and Texas Instruments.

Faced with the erosion of U.S. technological leadership in the electronics field and the prospect of having to purchase state-of-the-art electronic components needed for sensitive military applications from foreign manufacturers, the federal government had to find some way to support American electronic firms. For this reason, the federal government got involved in the Sematech Consortium. As evidence of its support, the Department of Defense made a commitment to provide up to $500 million over five years to help finance the consortium.

The encouragement and protection of American industries—like the semiconductor industry—is, of course, a prime reason for government involvement in business. As you have seen throughout this book, there are other reasons as well. They are, in general, based on the needs of business, government, and the American public. In this chapter, we look at the ways that government is supportive of American business.

Government Support of Business

Learning Objective 1
Appreciate the ways in which government can assist business firms

Government regulations and actions that restrict certain business activities may, at the same time, support other activities. The breakup of AT&T was calculated to restrict the operations of that firm but it also opened up new markets to the firms that are now producing telephone equipment in competition with Western Electric Co. And the "equal access" portion of the consent decree directly benefited such firms as GTE, U.S. Sprint Communications, and MCI Communications. These firms are now able to compete with AT&T on a more or less equal footing.

Obviously, not all government regulations are of this nature. Many of them (and some critics say *too many* of them) are intended primarily to restrict business activities, for various reasons. We discuss government regulation and deregulation in some detail later in the chapter. Here, our main point is simply that at least some government regulations do function in support of business activities.

In addition, government supports business by providing information and assistance, by funding research, and by acting as the largest customer of American business firms.

Providing Information and Assistance to Business

The U.S. government may be the world's largest collector and user of information. Much of this information is of value to businesses and is available at minimal cost.

The U.S. Census Bureau, for example, collects and can provide a wealth of marketing data:

▶ Demographic data showing the population distribution by age, sex, race, geographic area, educational level attained, occupation, and income

▶ Housing data by type and year of construction, size, building materials, and the like

683

The Census Bureau also provides information on manufacturing and agricultural activity, government spending, and the availability of natural resources. To inform businesses about the types of data and reports that are available, the bureau publishes an annual *Catalog of U.S. Census Publications*.

Other U.S. government publications that can be valuable sources of business information include the *Survey of Current Business* from the Department of Commerce, the *Monthly Labor Review* from the Department of Labor, and the *Federal Reserve Bulletin*.

The Internal Revenue Service and the Small Business Administration provide not only information but also direct assistance. (As we saw in Chapter 4, the SBA provides management assistance and financial help to qualifying businesses.) Finally, state and local governments provide information and aid (including tax reductions and help with low-cost financing) to firms that are, or expect to be, located within their borders.

Funding Research

Every year the federal government and private business each spend about $65 billion on research. Some government-funded research is done at federal institutions such as the Centers for Disease Control in Atlanta. However, the greater portion of government-funded research is performed independently at colleges and universities under government grants.

For example, the federal government is (and has been, for some time) funding research into the causes and potential cures of cancer. This research, which is taking place at a number of institutions around the country, is simply too expensive to be funded by individual firms. Because the research is being financed with public funds, the results it yields become part of the *public domain*. That is, they become the property of

Carnegie Mellon is one of many universities in the United States that receive funding from the federal government to pursue scientific research. Government becomes involved in research because of its inherent expense and relative uncertainty of outcome. The colorful image on the cover of this graduate studies catalogue is a space-filling model of the protein T4 lysozyme, and illustrates one result of goverment-funded work ongoing in the Department of Chemistry.

TABLE 22.1   ***Budget of the United States by Department (in billions of dollars)***

Department or Other Unit	1990 Estimate	1991 Estimate
Legislative branch	2.2	2.2
Judiciary	1.5	1.5
Executive Office of the President	0.1	0.3
Funds appropriated to the president	11.5	11.1
Agriculture	42.4	45.2
Commerce	3.5	2.3
Defense—military	293.8	304.7
Defense—civilian	23.8	24.8
Education	24.5	25.1
Energy	11.0	12.5
Health and Human Services	424.3	457.2
Housing and Urban Development	22.6	24.1
Interior	3.1	5.1
Justice	6.8	7.3
Labor	23.0	23.6
State	3.9	3.9
Transportation	27.3	27.4
Treasury	235.7	238.9
Environmental Protection Agency	5.5	5.6
General Services Administration	0.1	0.4
National Aeronautics and Space Administration	12.6	14.0
Office of Personnel Management	30.5	31.8
Veterans Administration	29.8	30.5
Other agencies	14.8	18.2
Allowances	−0.4	0.9
Undistributed offsetting receipts	−102.1	−111.3
Total Outlays	1,151.8	1,207.3

Source: Executive Office of the President and Office of Management and Budget, *Budget of the United States Government: FY 1990*, p. 10-9.

all citizens—and in particular, of those who can use the results to produce cancer-fighting drugs and apparatus.

Government funding is not limited to research into diseases. In the 1940s, for example, the federal government began to finance basic research into a phenomenon called semiconduction. This research eventually led to the development of the transistor, which has become the basis of the modern electronics industry. It may well be that present government-funded research will lead to entirely new industries and jobs in the decades to come.

Buying the Products of Business

The U.S. government is the largest single purchaser of goods and services in the world. Table 22.1 shows projected federal spending for 1990 and

For Grumman Corporation, the $1.2 billion contract to build 99,150 Long Life Vehicles (LLVs) for the U.S. Postal Service is a major contract that will require over five years to complete.

1991 by department. A single purchase may range in size from a few hundred dollars for office supplies or furniture to more than a billion dollars for new aircraft. The federal government is the largest customer of many firms, and it is the only customer of some.

In addition, there are fifty state governments, 3,000 county governments, 19,000 cities, 16,000 townships, 14,000 school districts, and 30,000 special districts in this country.[2] Together, their total expenditures *exceed* the federal budget. Their needs run from paper clips to highways, from janitorial services to the construction of high-rise office buildings. And they purchase what they need from private businesses. Besides buying both products and services from private businesses, the federal and state governments help businesses by ensuring that they can operate in a competitive environment. In the next section, we examine the specific regulations that help ensure competition among business firms.

Federal Regulations to Encourage Competition

Most states have laws to encourage competition, but for the most part, these laws duplicate federal laws. We will therefore discuss only federal legislation designed to encourage competition. A substantial body of federal statutory law has been developed to guard against monopolies, price fixing, and similar restraints on competition. These laws protect consumers by ensuring that they have a choice in the marketplace. The same laws protect businesses by ensuring that they are free to compete.

trust *a business combination that is created when one firm obtains control of competing firms by purchasing their stock or their assets*

Learning Objective 2
Know the reasons for—and content of—the major federal antitrust laws

The need for such laws became apparent in the late 1800s, when monopolies or trusts were developed in the sugar, whiskey, tobacco, shoe, and oil industries, among others. A **trust** is a business combination that is created when one firm obtains control of competing firms by purchasing their stock or their assets. Eventually, the trust gains control of the entire industry and can set prices and manipulate trade to suit its own interests. As a result, there is a need for antitrust laws.

One of the most successful trusts was the Standard Oil Trust, created by John D. Rockefeller in 1882. Until 1911, the Standard Oil Trust controlled between 80 and 90 percent of the petroleum industry. The firm earned extremely high profits at the expense of smaller oil companies and consumers, primarily because it had obtained secret price concessions from the railroads that shipped its products. Very low shipping costs, in turn, enabled the firm to systematically eliminate most of its competition by deliberately holding prices down. Once this was accomplished, it quickly raised its prices.

In response to public outcry against such practices—and prices—Congress passed the Sherman Antitrust Act in 1890. Since then, Congress has enacted a number of other laws designed to protect American businesses from monopolies.

The Sherman Antitrust Act (1890)

The objectives of the *Sherman Antitrust Act* were to encourage competition and to prevent the creation of monopolies. The act specifically prohibits any contract or agreement entered into for the purpose of restraining trade. Its two most important provisions are

▶ *Section 1:* Every contract, combination in the form of trust or otherwise, or conspiracy, in restraint of trade or commerce among the several states, or with foreign nations, is hereby declared to be illegal.

▶ *Section 2:* Every person who shall monopolize or attempt to monopolize, or combine or conspire with any other person or persons to monopolize any part of the trade or commerce . . . shall be deemed guilty of a misdemeanor.[3]

price fixing *an agreement between two businesses as to the prices to be charged for goods*

market allocation *an agreement to divide a market among potential competitors*

boycott in restraint of trade *an agreement between businesses not to sell to or buy from a particular entity*

Specific business practices prohibited by the Sherman Antitrust Act include price fixing, allocation of markets among competitors, and boycotts in restraint of trade. **Price fixing** is an agreement between two businesses as to the prices to be charged for goods. A **market allocation** is an agreement to divide a market among potential competitors. A **boycott in restraint of trade** is an agreement between businesses not to sell to or buy from a particular entity.

Power to enforce the Sherman Antitrust Act was given to the Department of Justice, which may bring legal action against businesses suspected of violating its provisions. In 1911, for example, under the act, the Standard Oil Trust was broken up into thirty-nine independent companies to restore an acceptable level of competition within the oil industry. The Sherman Antitrust Act was also used to break up the Northern Securities Company in 1904 and the American Tobacco Company in 1911. It was, in fact, part of the basis for the Justice Department's 1949 and 1974 suits against AT&T.

An amendment to the Sherman Antitrust Act, the *Antitrust Procedures and Penalties Act of 1974*, made violation of the Sherman Act a felony rather than a misdemeanor. It provides for fines of up to $100,000 and prison terms of up to three years for individuals convicted of antitrust violations. The act also provides that a guilty corporation may be sued by competitors or customers for treble monetary damages.

The Clayton Act (1914)

Because the wording of the Sherman Antitrust Act is somewhat vague, it could not be used to halt specific monopolistic tactics. Congress therefore enacted the *Clayton Act* in 1914. This legislation identifies and prohibits five distinct practices that had been used to weaken trade competition:

price discrimination *the practice in which producers and wholesalers charge larger firms a lower price for goods than they charge smaller firms*

▶ **Price discrimination,** the practice in which producers and wholesalers charge larger firms a lower price for goods than they charge smaller firms. The price differential had been used by large firms to gain a competitive edge and, in many cases, to force small firms out of business. (The Clayton Act does, however, allow quantity discounts.)

tying agreement *a contract that forces an intermediary to purchase unwanted products along with the products it actually wants to buy*

▶ The **tying agreement,** which is a contract that forces an intermediary to purchase unwanted products along with the products it actually wants to buy. This practice was used to "move" a producer's slow-selling merchandise along with its more desirable merchandise. Twentieth Century-Fox Film Corp., for example, was fined under the Clayton Act for forcing theater chains to rent a less popular motion picture along with one that promised to be highly successful.[4]

binding contract *an agreement that requires an intermediary to purchase products from a particular supplier, not from the supplier's competitors*

▶ The **binding contract,** an agreement that requires an intermediary to purchase products from a particular supplier, not from the supplier's competitors. In return for signing a binding contract, the intermediary was generally given a price discount.

interlocking directorate *an arrangement in which members of the board of directors of one firm are also directors of a competing firm*

▶ The **interlocking directorate,** an arrangement in which members of the board of directors of one firm are also directors of a competing firm. This arrangement is prohibited if the combined total capital of the two firms exceeds $1 million. Thus, for example, a person may not be a director of American Airlines and Delta Air Lines at the same time. The threat to competition that such a situation creates is obvious.

community of interests *the situation in which one firm buys the stock of a competing firm to reduce competition between the two*

▶ The **community of interests,** the situation in which one firm buys the stock of a competing firm to reduce competition between the two. This is the tactic that was used to create the giant trusts of the late 1800s. Acquisition of stock may result in a horizontal or vertical merger. If it *may* substantially lessen competition or tend to create a monopoly, it is unlawful. (Remember, a horizontal merger is a merger between firms that make and sell similar products in similar markets. A vertical merger is a merger between firms that operate at different but related levels in the production and marketing of a single product.)

The Federal Trade Commission Act (1914)

In 1914 Congress also passed the *Federal Trade Commission Act,* which states that "Unfair methods of competition in commerce are hereby declared unlawful." This act also created the **Federal Trade Commission (FTC),** a five-member committee charged with the responsibility of investigating illegal trade practices and enforcing antitrust laws.

Federal Trade Commission (FTC) *a five-member committee charged with the responsibility of investigating illegal trade practices and enforcing antitrust laws*

At first, the FTC was limited to enforcement of the Sherman Antitrust, Clayton, and FTC Acts. However, in 1938, in the *Wheeler-Lea Amendment* to the FTC Act, Congress gave the FTC the power to eliminate deceptive business practices—including those that are aimed at consumers raer than competitors. This early "consumer legislation" empowered the FTC to deal with a variety of unfair business tactics without having to prove that they endanger competition.

The FTC may act on its own or on complaints lodged by businesses or individuals. The first step is to investigate the accused firm and its business practices. After its investigation, the commission can issue a **cease and desist order,** which is an order to refrain from an illegal practice. If the practice is continued, the FTC may, with the aid of the Justice Department, bring suit against the violating firm.

cease and desist order *an order to refrain from an illegal practice*

The Robinson-Patman Act (1936)

Although the Clayton Act prohibits price discrimination, it does permit quantity discounts. This provision turned out to be a major loophole in the law: It was used by large chain retailers to obtain sizable price concessions that gave them a strong competitive edge over independent stores. To correct this imbalance, the *Robinson-Patman Act* was passed by Congress in 1936. This law specifically prohibits

▶ Price differentials that "substantially" weaken competition, unless they can be justified by the actual lower selling costs associated with larger orders

▶ Advertising and promotional allowances (a form of discount), unless they are offered to small retailers as well as large retailers

The Robinson-Patman Act is more controversial than most antitrust legislation. Many economists believe that the act tends to discourage price competition rather than to eliminate monopolies. In any case, so far there have been relatively few convictions under the act because the burden of proof is on the injured party—and that is most often small business owners, who have limited time and financial resources necessary to take legal action.

The Celler-Kefauver Act (1950)

The Clayton Act prohibited building a trust by purchasing the stock of competing firms. To get around that prohibition, however, a firm could still purchase the *assets* of its competitors. The result was the same: the elimination of competition.

This gigantic loophole was closed by the *Celler-Kefauver Act*, which prohibits mergers through the purchase of assets if these mergers will tend to reduce competition. The act also requires that all mergers be approved by both the FTC and the Justice Department before they are completed.

The Antitrust Improvements Act (1976)

The laws we have discussed were enacted "after the fact"—to correct abuses. In 1976 Congress passed the *Antitrust Improvements Act* to strengthen previous legislation. This law provided additional time for the FTC and the Justice Department to evaluate proposed mergers, and it expanded the investigative powers of the Justice Department. It also authorized the attorneys general of individual states to prosecute firms accused of price fixing and to recover monetary damages for *consumers*. The major antitrust legislation is summarized in Table 22.2.

TABLE 22.2   ***Summary of Antitrust Legislation***

Government Legislation	Major Provisions	Purpose
Sherman Antitrust Act of 1890	Outlaws business monopolies	To prevent a corporation from systematically eliminating competition by forcing competing firms out of the industry
Clayton Act of 1914	Prohibits five common business practices used to reduce competition	To outlaw (1) price discrimination, (2) tying agreements, (3) binding contracts, (4) interlocking directorates, and (5) community of interests
Federal Trade Commission Act of 1914	Empowers a five-member commission to investigate illegal trade practices (strengthened by the Wheeler-Lea Act)	To outlaw unfair trade practices and deceptive advertising
Robinson-Patman Act of 1936	Provides for improved competition between small and large wholesalers and small and large retailers	To prohibit unfair pricing and to make sure promotional assistance and advertising are available to both small and large customers
Celler-Kefauver Act of 1950	Prevents one company from buying the assets of competing companies	To prevent mergers that would weaken competition; enforced by both the Federal Trade Commission and the Justice Department
Antitrust Improvements Act of 1976	Strengthens previous antitrust legislation	To provide additional time for the FTC and the Justice Department to evaluate proposed mergers

The Present Antitrust Environment

The problem with antitrust legislation and its enforcement is that it is hard to define exactly what an appropriate level of competition is. For example, a particular merger may be in the public interest because it increases the efficiency of an industry. But it may be harmful at the same time because it reduces competition. There is really no rule of law (or of economics) that can be used to determine which of these two considerations is more important in a given case.

Three factors tend to influence the enforcement and effectiveness of antitrust legislation at the present time. The first is the growing presence of foreign firms in American markets. Foreign firms have increased competition in America and thus have made it more difficult for any firm to monopolize an industry. Second, most antitrust legislation must be interpreted by the courts because it is often vague and open-ended. Thus the attitude of the courts has a lot to do with the effectiveness of these laws. And third, political considerations often determine how actively the FTC and the Justice Department pursue antitrust cases. For example, a number of large corporate mergers were allowed to take place after Ronald Reagan took office as president. At this time, the verdict is still out for the Bush administration. This political factor may very well be the primary determinant of the antitrust environment at any given time.

But what about those monopolies that our government *does* allow to exist and flourish? In the next section, we see what makes them different and how they are regulated.

Federal Regulation of Natural Monopolies

natural monopoly   *an industry requiring huge investments in capital and for which duplication of facilities would be wasteful and, thus, not in the public interest*

In Chapter 1, a **natural monopoly** is defined as an industry requiring huge investments in capital and for which duplication of facilities would be wasteful and, thus, not in the public interest. In such an industry the government may permit one or very few firms to operate. Then it carefully regulates their activities, prices, and profits. Such regulation is aimed at ensuring that the natural monopolist earns a reasonable profit but does not take advantage of its unique position. The three major regulated monopolies are the public utilities, communications, and transportation industries.

Public Utilities

Learning Objective 3
Understand how and why the federal government regulates natural monopolies

Provision of electricity to homes and businesses within an area requires the installation of expensive generating equipment, transmission lines, transformers, and protective equipment. Constant maintenance of these installations is also necessary. Moreover, electricity is most efficiently generated in large quantities. Duplication of equipment for generating and distributing electricity within a geographic area would be wasteful.

Federal Energy Regulatory Commission *the federal agency that oversees the inter-state operations of firms that sell electricity or natural gas, or op-erate gas pipelines*

Federal Communications Commission (FCC) *the federal agency responsible for the inter-state regulation of communica-tions, including television, radio, telephone, and telegraph*

Interstate Commerce Commission (ICC) *the federal agency responsible for the licen-sing and regulation of carriers*

Prices would be higher than they are at present, but profits would be lower. The quality of service would eventually deteriorate.

For these reasons, a single supplier of electricity is licensed to operate in each geographic area. Its operations are generally controlled by a city or state utilities commission that must, for example, approve any proposed rate increases. The **Federal Energy Regulatory Commission** oversees the *interstate* operations of firms that sell electricity or natural gas, or operate gas pipelines. The nuclear power plants operated by public utilities are licensed and regulated by the Nuclear Regulatory Commission.

Communications

Radio and television stations are monopolies in the sense that each has the exclusive right to broadcast on a particular frequency within a specified area. Telephone and telegraph companies both fall within our definition of a regulated monopoly. All are regulated by either state or federal agencies.

The **Federal Communications Commission (FCC)** is the federal agency responsible for the interstate regulation of communications. It was created by Congress in 1934, primarily to license radio stations and set rates for interstate telephone and telegraph services. At present, the FCC is also responsible for the licensing and regulation of television stations, cable television networks, and ham and CB radio operators.

Transportation

Various abuses in the late nineteenth century—primarily by the railroads—led to the passage of the Interstate Commerce Act in 1887. This act was really the first major piece of federal regulatory legislation. It created the **Interstate Commerce Commission (ICC),** which is responsible for licensing carriers to operate in specific geographic areas, for establishing safety standards for interstate carriers, and for approving mergers of transportation firms. Originally, its main function was to police the railroads. Since then its scope has been expanded to include all interstate carriers.

Until 1984, the Civil Aeronautics Board (CAB) set and approved airfares, licensed airlines to serve particular airports, and established standards of service for air carriers. As part of the deregulation movement (which we discuss later), the CAB was phased out of existence on December 31, 1984. Today, regulation of the airline industry is the responsibility of the Transportation Department and the Federal Aviation Administration (FAA).

Critics have argued that regulation of the transportation industry tends to benefit the carriers rather than their customers. In fact, the ICC, Transportation Department, and FAA have been criticized for not paying enough attention to the needs of consumers. As a result, each group is coming under sharp attack for ignoring pressing problems in the transportation industry.

Because of the expense re-quired to construct and op-erate plants that generate electricity, a single supplier or "natural monopoly" is licensed to operate in a specific geographic region. Natural monopolies are generally controlled by a city, state, or federal utility commission.

Other Areas of Regulation

It is impossible to manage even a small business without being affected by local, state, and federal regulations. And it is just as impossible to describe all the government regulations that affect business. In addition to the two broad areas discussed here, we have examined a variety of regulations in other chapters (and there are more in the next chapter). Chapter 2 discussed laws and regulations dealing with the physical environment and consumerism; Chapter 9, personnel and employee relations; Chapter 10, union-management relations; Chapter 19, securities; and Chapter 21, trademarks, patents, and copyrights.

By now, you are probably thinking that there must be a government regulation to govern any possible situation. Actually, government regulations began to increase in the 1930s and continued to increase until the 1970s. Then, the country went through a deregulation period that lasted almost twenty years. In the next section, we examine the effects of deregulation and the current status of the deregulation movement.

The Deregulation Movement

deregulation *the process of removing existing regulations, forgoing proposed regulations, or reducing the rate at which new regulations are enacted*

Deregulation is the process of removing existing regulations, forgoing proposed regulations, or reducing the rate at which new regulations are enacted. A movement to deregulate business began in the 1970s and continued through the 1980s. Now, politicians, federal employees, and taxpayers are wondering if the movement will continue in the 1990s.

The primary aim of the movement is to minimize the complexity of regulations that affect business and the cost of compliance. Perhaps equally important is the goal of reducing the size of the U.S. government. As of May 1989, the U.S. government

► Employed approximately 3.2 million civilian workers (in addition to 2.1 million military personnel)

► Spent more than $1 trillion, which is approximately $4,600 for every person in the United States

Learning Objective 4
Be familiar with the nature of government's response to the current deregulation movement

As the federal government has grown, the number of regulatory agencie has increased as well. In the 1970s alone, twenty new federal agenci were formed. (The average for the previous sixty years was about six n agencies per decade.) Currently, more than 100 federal agencies responsible for enforcing a staggering array of regulations. And at l fifteen federal agencies now have a direct impact on business activi These agencies are listed in Table 22.3, with the activities they regu

The Cost of Regulation

It has been estimated that federal spending for enforcing regulations the taxpayers $6 billion a year, whereas compliance with all of regulations costs businesses $100 billion each year.[5]

TABLE 22.3   Government Agencies and What They Regulate

Government Agency or Commission	Regulates
Consumer Product Safety Commission (CPSC)	Consumer protection
Environmental Protection Agency (EPA)	Pollution control
Equal Employment Opportunity Commission (EEOC)	Discrimination in employment practices
Federal Aviation Administration (FAA)	Airline industry
Federal Communications Commission (FCC)	Radio, television, telephone, and telegraph communications
Federal Energy Regulatory Commission (FERC)	Electric power and natural gas
Federal Maritime Commission (FMC)	Ocean shipping
Federal Trade Commission (FTC)	Antitrust, consumer protection
Food and Drug Administration (FDA)	Consumer protection
Interstate Commerce Commission (ICC)	Railroads, bus lines, trucking, pipelines, and waterways
Mine Safety and Health Administration (MSHA)	Worker safety and health in the mining industry
National Highway Traffic Safety Administration (NHTSA)	Vehicle safety
Nuclear Regulatory Commission (NRC)	Nuclear power and nuclear industry
Occupational Safety and Health Administration (OSHA)	Worker safety and health
Securities and Exchange Commission (SEC)	Corporate securities

The Business Roundtable is an organization of 187 of America's leading corporations. This organization completed a detailed research study to determine how much its members spend to comply with government regulations. Forty-eight corporations participated in the study. Each kept track of all costs incurred as a result of specific regulations, for a period of one year. Only costs that could be attributed to regulation were recorded. Any expense that might be incurred for sound business reasons, whether or not a regulation existed, was eliminated.

The results were staggering. Government regulations had cost the forty-eight corporations a total of $2,621,593,000. This dollar amount represented

▶   16 percent of the corporations' after-tax profits

▶   43 percent of their research-and-development costs

▶   10 percent of their capital expenditures[6]

Large corporations, such as those involved in the Business Roundtable study, can cope with government regulation. They have been doing so for some time. In essence, coping means passing the cost of regulation along to stockholders in the form of lower dividends and to consumers in the form of higher prices.

BUSINESS JOURNAL

Banks, S&Ls, and Deregulation

Deregulation has dramatically changed the banking industry over the last decade. Today, banks and savings and loan associations (S&Ls) are more than just a place to deposit money. Now, they sell insurance, stocks, mutual funds, and bonds. Some large banks also underwrite and help major corporations and municipalities sell commercial paper, mortgage-backed securities, and municipal bonds. Many banks even call themselves "financial supermarkets" or "full-service" banks to attract new customers.

Ironically, all of these activities, which are designed to make banks and S&Ls more competitive with brokerage and insurance firms, come at a time when bank failures have never been higher. So, even though the final results are still unknown, some experts are beginning to wonder if deregulation is good or bad for the customer, the banking industry, and the nation's economy.

ARGUMENTS FOR DEREGULATION

Virtually all the leading banks and financial institutions in the world are either Japanese or European. Only one American bank—Citicorp—is on the list of the world's largest financial institutions. In fact, most of the 14,000 banks and 3,000 S&Ls in the United States are small when compared to world-class financial institutions. While size is not everything, larger foreign banks are able to raise capital more cheaply and to invest more aggressively than smaller U.S. banks. Deregulation advocates blame our poor showing on our tradition of local banking and too many federal and state regulations that make it difficult for successful banks to branch out into other counties, let alone other states.

ARGUMENTS AGAINST DEREGULATION

Opponents of deregulation argue that reducing federal and state regulations creates an atmosphere that encourages banks and S&Ls to make questionable loans. To support their argument, deregulation critics cite the problems that developed when Congress enacted the Garn–St Germain Depository Institutions Act in 1982. This act enabled S&Ls to increase the total percentage of assets used to fund commercial real estate loans. Then, when the real estate market hit rock bottom in the late 1980s, a record number of S&Ls failed.

Deregulation opponents often maintain that the banking industry needs more regulations. Three specific proposals are offered to curb questionable banking activities that lead to bank and S&L failures. First, the amount of capital a bank or S&L is required to have should be directly tied to the type of loans it makes. In other words, a bank or S&L that makes speculative loans should be required to maintain larger amounts of capital to compensate for the increased risks it takes. Second, banks and S&Ls that make speculative loans should pay higher premiums for federal deposit insurance. Third, the federal government should create "supersafe" banks and S&Ls that make only certain "approved" loans. All deposits in these supersafe institutions would be federally insured, according to this far-reaching proposal. Thus, if a bank or S&L wanted to make speculative loans, it would have to use money from deposits that were not federally insured. To attract noninsured deposits, the banks and S&Ls would probably have to offer higher interest to compensate depositors for the added risk.

Based on information from John J. Curran, "Does Deregulation Make Sense?" *Fortune*, June 5, 1989, p. 181+; Mortimer B. Zuckerman, "Time to Bank on the Future," *U.S. News & World Report*, July 10, 1989, p. 64; M. S. Forbes, Jr., "A Federally Guaranteed Bank Crisis," *Forbes*, April 25, 1988, p. 39; and Vicky Cahan, "Banks Are on the Brink of Breaking Loose," *Business Week*, March 7, 1988, pp. 99–100.

Smaller firms bear a smaller regulatory burden, but they may find it harder to cope with that burden. Some are not aware of all the applicable regulations, and that can lead to legal difficulties. Others may not have the staff necessary to comply with the various documentation requirements. And, for many small businesses, stiff competition for customers requires that they pass the cost of compliance directly to their owners.

Current Attempts at Deregulation

Presidents Ford and Carter tried to control the activities of federal agencies and commissions, but they had only limited success. President Reagan began a deregulation effort almost immediately after taking office in 1981. The principal guidelines for Reagan's deregulation efforts were as follows:

► Impose regulations only if their benefits exceed their costs.

► Choose the least expensive method of achieving the goals of regulation.

► Tailor regulatory burdens to the size and nature of the affected firms.

► Reduce unnecessary paperwork and regulatory delays.[7]

During the 1980s, the deregulation movement did help many industries to post higher profits and improve financial performance. For example, the transportation industry—notably trucking, railroad, and air-transportation firms—experienced tremendous gains as a result of deregulation. One study estimates the benefits of trucking deregulation at $39 billion to $63 billion annually, while another estimates the benefits of airline deregulation at $15 billion per year. Other successful results of deregulation include (1) the widespread introduction of money-market accounts that paid consumers higher interest rates and (2) increased pricing flexibility for stock commissions that reduced the cost of buying stocks and other securities. Finally, the relaxation of restrictions on overnight mail delivery led to dramatic increases for private companies providing next-day delivery services.[8]

The deregulation drive is continuing, but there is a question as to how far it can—or should—go. Many federal agencies operate outside the immediate control of the president and Congress. If they choose, they may ignore the deregulation movement and issue regulations without answering to any government institution except the courts. Continued deregulation may even create problems for the government and for business. For example, the government has been in the process of deregulating the airline industry since 1978. Now airline officials admit that some government regulations are needed to maintain an orderly market.

Moreover, support for deregulation is mixed. Many politicians and consumers believe that deregulation has gone far enough. They argue that further deregulation could result in inferior products, dangerous working conditions, polluted air, increased bank failures, and other problems that were prevalent during the 1960s and 1970s. Even President Bush, who was President Reagan's point man for slashing government regulations, seems to have reversed course. Clearly, a number of Bush appointees who

As a result of the deregulation movement, the trucking industry has been able to post higher profits and to improve financial performance. The actual dollar savings that have resulted from deregulation of the trucking industry are estimated to range between $39 billion and $63 billion annually.

head federal agencies are expanding regulations to improve air quality, air travel, automobile regulation, and job safety.[9]

Perhaps what is needed now is not more deregulation but a fresh look at present regulation—its goals, costs, and effectiveness. Another worthwhile endeavor would be a reworking of the regulatory structure to create a "livable" environment for consumers, workers, and businesses.

Now that we have discussed both regulation and the move to deregulate, let us examine the sources of the revenues that government draws on to fund its activities, regulatory or otherwise.

Government Taxation

Whether you believe there is too much government regulation or too little, you are required to help pay for it. In one way or another, each of us helps pay for everything that government does—from regulating business to funding research into the causes and cures of cancer. We pay taxes to our local, state, and federal governments on the basis of what we earn, what we own, and even what we purchase.

Federal Taxes

It takes a lot of money to run something as big as the U.S. government. Each year vast sums are spent for human services, national defense, and interest on the national debt. In addition, the federal government must pay the salaries of its employees, cover its operating expenses, and purchase equipment and supplies that range from typewriter ribbons to aircraft carriers. Most of the money comes from taxes.

budget deficit   *an excess of
spending over income*

Taxes and Deficits   Figure 22.1 shows that the federal government had revenues of almost $909 billion in 1988. About 96 percent of that sum was obtained through taxation. However, the government actually spent more than it took in that year. In other words, there was a **budget deficit,** which is an excess of spending over income. In fact, the U.S. government has had budget deficits every year since 1960, with the exception of 1969 (see Figure 22.2).

What is disturbing about the information given in Figure 22.2 is the size of the budget deficits. Because deficits must be financed by borrowing, the outstanding debt of the U.S. government has grown to more than $3 trillion! The interest on this debt is enormous. As a result of continuing budget deficits, in 1985 politicians voted to enact the *Emergency Deficit Control Act,* common known as the Gramm-Rudman-Hollings Act, after its principal sponsors. The purpose of this act is to eventually limit federal spending to total federal revenues. Since the ultimate goal of this legislation is to eliminate deficit spending, this act will either curtail government spending or lead to an increase in taxes.

In another attempt to reduce the federal deficit and to streamline the federal income tax structure, politicians passed the *Tax Reform Act* of 1986. This act reduced tax rates, increased the standard deduction for individuals, and increased the personal exemption for individuals. It also reduced or eliminated many of the deductions that individuals had previously used to lower their taxable income. According to its advocates, the new tax law will produce enough income to cover federal expenses without unduly burdening taxpayers.

FIGURE 22.1
Federal Revenues from Taxes
*In 1988, the largest source
of federal tax revenue was
individual income taxes.*
*(Source: Office of Management
and Budget, Budget of the
United States Government:
FY 1990, p. 10-9.)*

TOTAL FEDERAL REVENUES FOR 1988 = $908.9 BILLION

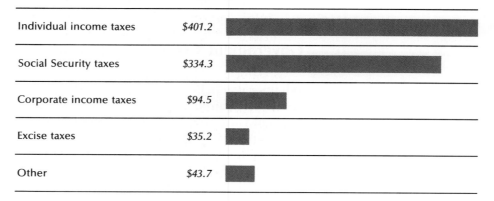

Individual income taxes	$401.2
Social Security taxes	$334.3
Corporate income taxes	$94.5
Excise taxes	$35.2
Other	$43.7

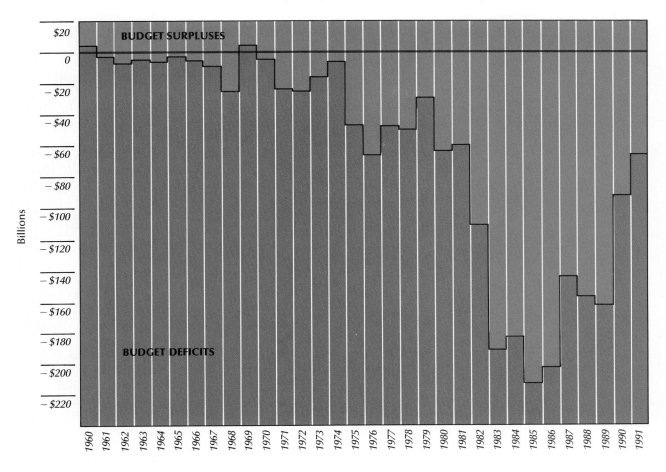

FIGURE 22.2
Federal Budgets—Surpluses and Deficits—1960 to 1991
The U.S. government has had budget deficits every year since 1960, except for
1969. Budgets are estimated for 1989, 1990, and 1991. (Source: Executive Office of the
President and Office of Management and Budget, Budget of the United States Government:
FY 1990, p. 10-9.)

While both of these legislative acts may be a step in the right direction, we appear to be left with both budget deficits and a complex federal tax structure.

Individual Income Taxes   The individual (or personal) income tax is derived from the Sixteenth Amendment to the Constitution, which was ratified in 1913. It states that "The Congress shall have the power to lay and collect taxes on incomes, from whatever source derived, without apportionment among the several states and without regard to any census or enumeration." An individual's income tax liability is computed from his or her taxable income, which is gross income less various authorized deductions from income. In 1914, the federal government collected an average of 28 cents per taxpayer. Today that average is more than $1,600 per person.

The federal income tax is a progressive tax. **A progressive tax** requires the payment of an increasing proportion of income as the individual's income increases. For example, a single individual with a taxable income of $20,000 must presently pay a federal income tax of $3,196, or 16 percent of that taxable income. A single taxpayer with a taxable income of $40,000 must pay $8,796, or 22 percent of that income.

Taxpayers who own sole proprietorships or partnerships pay their income taxes to the Internal Revenue Service in four quarterly installments. Employees pay a specified amount each pay period. That amount is withheld (deducted from the employee's paycheck) by the employer and sent to the IRS. In addition, every taxpayer must file an annual tax return by April 15 of each year, for the previous calendar year. The return shows the income, deductions, and computations on which the taxpayer's tax liability is based.

Corporate Income Taxes   Corporations pay federal income tax only on their taxable income, which is what remains after deducting *all* legal business expenses from net sales. (This is net income before taxes, discussed in Chapter 16.)

Currently, the federal corporate tax rate is 15 percent on the first $50,000 of pretax profit, 25 percent on the next $25,000, and 34 percent on profits in excess of $75,000. In the case of a corporation that has pretax profits in excess of $100,000, the amount of the tax shall be increased by the lesser of (1) 5 percent of the excess or (2) $11,750. For practical purposes, this additional tax means a 39 percent tax rate for every dollar of taxable income from $100,000 to $335,000. A corporation with a taxable income of $335,000 must pay a total of $113,900 to the federal government, as shown in Table 22.4.

Corporate income taxes provide approximately 10 percent of total federal revenues. The effectiveness and fairness of the corporate income tax are, however, the subject of continual debate. For example, President Reagan created a stir when he suggested that the corporate income tax should be eliminated because the money that corporations pay in taxes

TABLE 22.4   Federal Corporate Income Tax on an Income of $335,000

Tax on the first $50,000 @ 15%	
$50,000 × 15% =	$ 7,500
Tax on the next $25,000 @ 25%	
$25,000 × 25% =	6,250
Tax on excess over $75,000 @ 34%	
$260,000 × 34% =	88,400
Tax on excess over $100,000 @ 5%	
(not more than $11,750)	
$235,000 × 5% =	11,750
Total corporate tax	$113,900

should be reinvested in American business. Actually, many economists advocate elimination of the corporate income tax, for two reasons. First, corporate profits are subject to double taxation: The corporation pays a tax on its profits before they are distributed to stockholders. Then each stockholder pays a personal income tax on those dividends that are distributed. Second, economists consider the tax on corporate profits to be an added expense of doing business. In effect, this cost is borne by workers through lower wages, by consumers in the form of higher prices, and by stockholders through lower dividends.

The arguments against corporate taxation seem quite reasonable. However, if these taxes were abolished, the federal government would have to make up for the lost revenue somehow. The burden would probably fall on the same people who are bearing it now: workers, consumers, and stockholders.

Other Federal Taxes   Additional sources of federal revenue include Social Security, unemployment, and excise taxes, as well as customs duties. One objective of all taxes is to raise money, but excise taxes and customs duties are also designed to regulate the use of specific goods and services.

The second largest source of federal revenue is the *Social Security tax*, which is collected under the Federal Insurance Contributions Act (FICA). This tax provides funding for retirement, disability, and death benefits for contributing employees. FICA taxes are paid both by the employer and the employee. The employee's share is withheld from his or her salary by the employer and sent to the federal government with the employer's share. For 1990 the annual FICA tax was a total of 15.3 percent of the first $51,300 earned.

Under the provisions of the Federal Unemployment Tax Act (FUTA), employers must pay an *unemployment tax* equal to 6.2 percent of the first $7,000 of each employee's annual wages. Because employers are allowed credits against the 6.2 percent through participation in state unemployment programs, the actual unemployment rate paid by most employers is 0.8 percent. The tax is paid to the federal government to fund benefits for unemployed workers. Unlike the Social Security tax, the FUTA tax is levied only on employers.

excise tax   *a tax on the manufacture or sale of a particular domestic product*

An **excise tax** is a tax on the manufacture or sale of a particular domestic product. Excise taxes are used to help pay for government services directed toward the users of these products and, in some cases, to limit the use of potentially harmful products. For example, there are federal excise taxes on alcoholic beverages ($12.50 per gallon), cigarettes (8 cents per pack), and gasoline (9 cents per gallon).[10] Alcohol and tobacco products are potentially harmful to consumers: They are taxed to raise the prices of these goods and thus discourage consumption. The federal excise tax on gasoline is a source of income that can be used to build and repair highways. Although manufacturers and retailers are responsible for paying excise taxes, these taxes are usually passed on to the consumer in the form of higher retail prices.

customs (or **import**) **duty**   *a tax on a particular foreign product entering a country*

A **customs** (or **import**) **duty** is a tax on a particular foreign product entering a country. Import duties are designed to protect specific domestic

BUSINESS JOURNAL

What Happens in a Tax Audit?

Innocently, you go to the mailbox and there it is—a letter from the Internal Revenue Service (IRS). After a few moments, you catch your breath and open it, only to find that the IRS is going to audit your tax return for last year. In this situation, there are certain things you should know about the IRS's audit procedures.

WHAT ARE THE CHANCES OF GETTING AUDITED?

Your chances of getting audited are not as great as you might think. In reality, the IRS audits slightly more than one million income tax returns—an overall average of approximately 1 percent of all returns filed each year. The more money you make, the greater the chance that your return will be audited. Still, only about 2 percent of all taxpayers that report income in excess of $50,000 are audited. Also, taxpayers who itemize deductions are more likely to be audited than taxpayers that file simple returns or take the standard deductions.

All individual returns are checked for mathematical accuracy and obvious errors. Then computers score returns on their potential for an upward adjustment in taxes owed by taxpayers. The actual computer program compares specific figures on your return with "normal" amounts for all taxpayers. If, for instance, your charitable deductions are "scored" much higher than average, the IRS's computer will kick out your return for special attention and perhaps an audit.

AUDIT PROCEDURES

When you are audited, the burden of proof is on you, not the IRS. In many cases, the IRS will simply want documentation for either income or expense amounts that you claimed on your return. If you mail your documentation to the IRS, be sure to make copies of everything and use certified mail so that you can prove that you *did* respond to its request.

The most common type of IRS audit is an office audit. You may represent yourself or be represented by an attorney, CPA, or "enrolled practitioner"—a person who either is a former IRS employee or has passed the stiff IRS tax exam. For an office audit, you should bring along checks, receipts, or whatever documentation you need to substantiate your claim. If you cannot document your deduction, the IRS will throw it out.

THE APPEALS PROCESS

If you lose the first round, you may decide to appeal the decision to the auditor's supervisor. If the immediate supervisor refuses to overturn the decision, you may decide to take the IRS to court. You may choose a U.S. district court, U.S. court of claims, or U.S. tax court. Many taxpayers choose the tax court because you can petition the court for a hearing without paying the IRS. If the disputed amount is less than $5,000 for the year in question, you can go to the tax court's Small Tax Case Division. Of course, at any point you may decide to negotiate a settlement with the IRS or agree with the IRS's findings and arrange to pay the full amount.

Based on information from "How to Survive a Tax Audit," *Consumer Reports*, March 1989, pp. 172–176; Paul N. Strassels, "Sleeping Easy," *Nation's Business*, September 1989, pp. 74–75; Harry Anderson and Rich Thomas, "The Coming Tax Crackdown," *Newsweek*, April 11, 1983, pp. 54–55; Leonard Weiner, "What to Do When the IRS Comes Calling," *U.S. News & World Report*, May 2, 1983, pp. 71–72; and Julian Block, "Tax Audit Tightrope," *Vogue*, October 1982, p. 206.

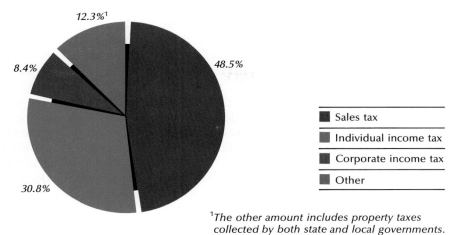

12.3%¹

8.4%

48.5%

30.8%

- Sales tax
- Individual income tax
- Corporate income tax
- Other

¹*The other amount includes property taxes collected by both state and local governments.*

FIGURE 22.3
Sources of Tax Revenues for State and Local Governments
Taxes are the primary source of revenues for both state and local governments.
(Source: Statistical Abstract of the United States, 1989, *U.S. Bureau of the Census, p. 280.)*

industries by raising the prices of competing imported products. They are first paid by the importer, but then they are passed on to consumers through higher—and less competitive—prices.

State and Local Taxes

Like the federal government, state and local governments are financed primarily through taxes. As illustrated in Figure 22.3, sales taxes provide about 50 percent of state and local tax revenues. Most states and some cities also levy taxes on the incomes of individuals and businesses. Finally, many local and county governments also tax real estate and some forms of personal property.

Sales Taxes   Sales taxes are levied by both states and cities, and are paid by the purchasers of consumer products. Retailers collect sales taxes as a specified percentage of the price of each taxed product and then forward them to the taxing authority. At present, the highest sales tax (8 percent) is paid by residents of Connecticut. Several states levy no state or city sales tax at all.

regressive tax   *a tax that takes a greater percentage of a lower income than of a higher income*

A sales tax is a regressive tax. **A regressive tax** is one that takes a greater percentage of a lower income than of a higher income. The regressiveness of the sales tax stems from the fact that lower-income households generally spend a greater proportion of their income on taxable products such as food, clothing, and other essentials. Consider the impact of a 5 percent sales tax on food items purchased by a low-income family. If this family earns $10,000 a year and spends $3,000 on food, they will pay sales taxes of $150, or 1.5 percent of their total earnings. By comparison, a family that earns $40,000 a year and spends $5,000 on food will pay sales taxes of $250, or 0.625 percent of their total earnings. Not all states collect a sales tax on all items. In fact, many states exempt food from their sales tax.

Property Taxes   Many local governments use the property taxes that are levied on real estate and personal property owned by businesses and individuals to finance their ongoing activities.

Real estate taxes are usually computed as a percentage of the assessed value of the real property. (The assessed value is determined by the local tax assessor as the fair market value of the property, a portion of its fair market value, or its replacement cost.) For example, suppose the city council has established a real estate tax rate of $2.10 per $100 of assessed valuation. Then the property tax bill for an office building with an assessed value of $200,000 will be $200,000 × $2.10/$100, or $4,200. This type of tax is called a proportional tax. A **proportional tax** is one whose percentage rate remains constant as the tax base increases. Therefore, if the tax rate remains constant at $2.10 per $100, a taxpayer who owns real estate valued at $10,000 pays $210 in taxes; a taxpayer who owns real estate valued at $100,000 pays $2,100 in taxes.

proportional tax   *a tax whose percentage rate remains constant as the tax base increases*

Certain personal property owned by businesses and individuals is also subject to local taxation. For businesses, taxable personal property normally includes machinery, equipment, raw materials, and finished inventory. In some cases, local authorities also tax the value of stocks, bonds, mortgages, and promissory notes held by businesses. For individuals, such items as trucks, automobiles, and boats may be classified as personal property and taxed as such by local authorities. Taxes on personal property are usually computed as a percentage of some assessed value.

CHAPTER REVIEW

Summary

Government's relationship with business is based on the needs of business, government, and the general public. Government supports business by enacting some of its regulations, by providing information and assistance to business, by funding much of the research that leads to new products and jobs, and by purchasing goods and services that businesses produce. At the same time, government regulates business activity in such a way as to promote competition and protect the interests of individuals.

Congress passed the Sherman Antitrust Act in 1890 as a means of restoring a reasonable level of competition within industries that had become dominated by trusts. Later antitrust legislation was intended mainly to close loopholes in previous laws and to prohibit specific practices that had been used to weaken competition. Enforcement of these laws is the responsibility of the Federal Trade Commission and the U.S. Justice Department.

Natural monopolies are industries in which the duplication of production facilities (which competition would require) would be wasteful. Government regulation of natural monopolies consists of the licensing of firms to operate in natural monopolies and the supervision of their activities. The principal natural monopolies are the public utilities, communications, and transportation industries.

Government regulation extends to a wide range of business activities, and compliance can be very costly. In response to a call for deregulation, the federal government has slowed the enactment and enforcement of some regulations and has removed others. There is, however, a question as to how much regulation—or deregulation—is most effective in maintaining orderly markets. Today, support for continued deregulation is mixed. Many politicians and consumers argue that further deregulation could result in inferior products, dangerous working conditions, polluted air, increased bank failures, and other problems that were prevalent during the 1960s and 1970s.

Federal, state, and local governments finance their activities primarily by collecting taxes. For the federal government, individual income taxes are the major source of funding. Other sources include corporate income, Social Security, unemployment, excise, and customs taxes. In spite of its huge tax revenues, however, the U.S. government continues to operate at a deficit.

Sales taxes, which are levied on purchases of consumer goods, provide about 50 percent of state and local tax revenues. Many local governments also levy property taxes, which are based on the value of the real estate and/or personal property owned by individuals and businesses.

So far in this text, we have been concerned mainly with American business within American markets. In the next chapter, we extend our discussion to business that is conducted across national borders. As we will see, international trade can be both a necessary and an exciting facet of business.

Key Terms

You should now be able to define and give an example relevant to each of the following terms:

trust

price fixing

market allocation

boycott in restraint of trade

price discrimination

tying agreement

binding contract

interlocking directorate

community of interests

Federal Trade Commission (FTC)

cease and desist order

natural monopoly

Federal Energy Regulatory Commission

Federal Communications Commission (FCC)

Interstate Commerce Commission (ICC)

deregulation

budget deficit

progressive tax

excise tax

customs (or import) duty

regressive tax

proportional tax

Questions and Exercises

Review Questions

1. In what ways does government provide assistance or support to business?
2. How do federal antitrust regulations work to support American business?

3. What situation led to passage of the Sherman Antitrust Act?
4. What was the major loophole in the Sherman Antitrust Act? How was it closed?
5. The Clayton Act specifically prohibits five practices. List these practices and briefly explain how each weakens competition.
6. Describe the process by which the FTC acts to halt an illegal business practice.
7. Why does the federal government curb monopolies like the Standard Oil Trust but readily license natural monopolies like Florida Power & Light?
8. Cite the responsibilities of the following three commissions.
   a. The Federal Communications Commission
   b. The Interstate Commerce Commission
   c. The Federal Energy Regulatory Commission
9. What are the principal reasons for the current deregulation movement? What forces may slow it down?
10. Which single tax provides the largest amount of income for the federal government? for state and local governments?
11. Why are excise taxes and customs duties sometimes referred to as regulatory taxes? What do they regulate?
12. What is "regressive" about a regressive tax?
13. What is a proportional tax? What type of property does it tax?

Discussion Questions

1. Funding for the Sematech Consortium was a cooperative effort between the federal government and fourteen large U.S. corporations. Initially, the federal government agreed to match the funds provided by the private business firms. Should the federal government contribute tax dollars to fund this type of research? Why or why not?
2. In the past, the fourteen U.S. corporations involved in the Sematech Consortium have competed fiercely with each other. Why are they now joining forces to fund semiconductor research?
3. What benefits and what problems might result from the requirement that the FTC and the Justice Department approve mergers before they take place?
4. Is there any competition at all among public utilities? Would such competition benefit or harm consumers?
5. How might legislators and regulatory agencies determine whether deregulation is needed in a

particular area? How might they determine where additional regulation is needed?

6. Are budget deficits necessary, harmful, or both? Do you believe that the Emergency Deficit Control Act will eliminate deficit spending?

Exercises

1. Outline a plan for the removal of all graduation requirements (other than the number of credit hours required) at your school over the next two years. List three advantages and three disadvantages of such deregulation.

2. Suppose a certain state levies a 4 percent sales tax on all consumer products. Develop, in detail, a method for modifying the sales tax to make it less regressive. Explain how your method would be applied, and show that your tax would actually be less regressive than the present tax.

Case 22.1

Antitrust, the FTC, and the Cola Giants

One duty of the Federal Trade Commission (FTC) is to examine proposed mergers or acquisitions, and to block any that are likely to reduce competition. During most of the 1980s, observers wondered when the commission would find a merger it didn't like. Toward the end of the decade, the commission finally found two mergers it couldn't approve. The FTC blocked the purchase of the Seven-Up Company by PepsiCo and the proposed purchase of Dr Pepper Co. by the Coca-Cola Company. The vote was 4–0 against the merger in both cases.

The mergers were part of an ongoing battle for first place in soft-drink sales. PepsiCo, with 28 percent of the soft-drink market, announced its purchase of the Seven-Up Company (with 7 percent of the market) first. If it had been permitted, the proposed acquisition would have put PepsiCo within striking distance of the Coca-Cola Company's 39 percent of the soft-drink market.

The Coca-Cola Company had never tried to purchase another soft-drink firm for fear of being turned down by the FTC or the Justice Department. But PepsiCo's attempt to buy Seven-Up gave the Coca-Cola Company the courage to try a similar move. One month after PepsiCo's announcement, the Coca-Cola Company declared that it was about to purchase the Dr Pepper Company, whose market share is also about 7 percent.

Actually, the Coca-Cola Company couldn't lose, for it was highly unlikely that the FTC would approve PepsiCo's merger but not Coke's. And whether the two mergers were permitted or blocked, the Coca-Cola Company would remain ahead of PepsiCo in the soft-drink sweepstakes. (Actually, PepsiCo would have done a bit better than the Coca-Cola Company—the asking price for Seven-Up was $380 million and that for Dr Pepper was $470 million.)

The Royal Crown Company which has 4.5 percent of the market, was not standing still in the midst of these acquisition announcements. Quickly filing an antitrust suit to block both mergers, Royal Crown pointed out that these proposed mergers would place 81 percent of the soft-drink market in the grip of two firms. And Royal Crown itself, perhaps feeling that grip, began looking for its own merger partners. One day before the FTC voted to block them, a federal judge placed a temporary restraining order on both the PepsiCo and Coca-Cola Company mergers.

With both the Coca-Cola Company and PepsiCo mergers blocked, the two cola giants began seeking new ways to expand sales revenues and increase profits. The Coca-Cola Company, the world's largest producer and distributor of soft drinks, has since expanded into foreign markets. Overseas growth in both sales and profits in the European market is expected to continue through the 1990s. PepsiCo, on the other hand, has expanded into snack foods and restaurants. PepsiCo's successful snack foods include Doritos, Ruffles, and Lay's Potato Chips; its profitable restaurants include Pizza Hut, Taco Bell, and Kentucky Fried Chicken.*

Questions

1. Should the Federal Trade Commission (FTC) have approved the mergers? Justify your answer.

2. Based on your analysis of the information presented in this case, do you think that the Coca-Cola Company's expansion into foreign markets and PepsiCo's expansion into snack foods and restaurants were sound business decisions? Why?

---

* Based on information from *Moody's Handbook of Common Stocks*, Winter 1989–1990, Moody's Investors Service, 99 Church Street, New York, N.Y. 10007; Pete Engardio, "It's Still a Free-for-All on the Soda Shelf," *Business Week*, July 7, 1986, p. 37; *U.S. News & World Report*, June 30, 1986, p. 41; Bill Powell, "Cola Mergers Lose Some Fizz," *Newsweek*, June 30, 1986, p. 48; David Pauly, "Coke Cries 'Checkmate,'" *Newsweek*, March 3, 1986, p. 53; and Scott Scredon, "Pepsi's Seven-Up Deal: Shaking up the Soft-Drink Wars," *Business Week*, February 3, 1986, p. 31.

Case 22.2

A Tax Cut for Capital Gains?

Under the Tax Reform Act of 1986—the last major revision of the Internal Revenue Code—capital gains resulting from the sale of real estate, small businesses, financial securities, and most other long-term investments are taxed as ordinary income. The 1986 tax law makes no provision for preferential treatment of capital gains; they are treated just like wages, interest, or any other income that a taxpayer might receive in a one-year period. And, depending on the amount of the taxpayer's total income (including capital gains), the tax rate is 15, 28, or 33 percent.

During his presidential campaign, George Bush promised that he would push for a reduction in the amount of taxes that Americans paid on capital gains. The overall goal of his proposal was to encourage Americans to make long-term investments because of preferential tax treatment. Once elected, he proposed the following tax rates for capital gains resulting from the sale of long-term investments:

Tax Rate	Length of Time Asset Was Held
Treated as ordinary income	Less than 1 year
25.2%	1 to 2 years
22.4%	2 to 3 years
19.6%	3 years or more

Naturally, the President's proposal received mixed reactions from both Republicans and Democrats. Advocates of the proposal argue that a reduction in the taxes paid on capital gains is good for the economy because it will lead to increased savings and investments. Advocates also point out that almost anyone who must report capital gains on a long-term invest-

ment will benefit from this tax reduction. According to the U.S. Treasury Department, 50 percent of all taxpayers will report capital gains during their lifetime.[†]

On the other hand, opponents of the President's plan argue that it is just another political giveaway program for the rich. According to opponents, more than 50 percent of all the benefits that result from the reduced tax on capital gains goes to people who make more than $200,000 a year. Opponents also maintain that the majority of Americans oppose a change in the way capital gains are taxed. A 1990 *Business Week/Harris Poll* indicates that 62 percent of those surveyed are against a big cut in capital-gains taxes.[‡] Finally, opponents argue, it doesn't make much sense to cut *any* taxes as long as the national debt is in excess of $3 trillion.[‖]

Questions

1. Advocates of the president's plan argue that a reduction in taxes on long-term capital gains is good for the economy. Do you agree? Why?
2. At the time of publication, President Bush's proposal was simply that—a proposal. Using information obtained in the library, determine how capital gains are taxed under current tax laws. Then, in your own words, describe your findings.

[†] Peter L. Spencer, "The Capital Gains Tax Cut," *Consumers' Research,* November 1989, p. 30.

[‡] "How Americans see the Tax Issue," *Business Week,* February 5, 1990, p. 27.

[‖] Based on information from Larry Martz, "A Tax-Cut Stampede," *Newsweek,* February 5, 1990, pp. 18–20; Howard Gleckman, "Congress Lines Up at the Gate for the Tax-Cut Race," *Business Week,* February 5, 1990, pp. 24–26; and Ann Reilly Dowd, "Why Your Taxes Won't Get Cut," *Fortune,* February 26, 1990, pp. 68–69+.

INTERNATIONAL BUSINESS

1 Summarize the economic basis for international business

2 Be aware of the restrictions that nations place on international trade, the objectives of these restrictions, and their results

3 Be familiar with the extent of international trade and the organizations that are working to foster it

4 Understand the methods by which a firm can organize for and enter international markets

5 Recognize the main considerations in international marketing

6 Identify the institutions that help firms and nations to finance international business

CHAPTER PREVIEW

We describe international trade in this chapter in terms of specialization, whereby each country trades the surplus goods and services it produces most efficiently for products in short supply. We also outline the restrictions that nations place on products from other countries and present some of the advantages and disadvantages of such restrictions. In addition, we discuss the social, cultural, legal, and economic factors that must be considered by firms intending to market products in other countries. Finally, we list some of the institutions that provide the complex financing necesssary for modern international trade.

INSIDE BUSINESS

International Business Pays Off

Preserved rabbits to Australia and live cockroaches to Mexico. **Carolina Biological Supply Company** of Burlington, North Carolina, has sometimes specialized in exporting the unusual. Its line of business is manufacturing and buying for resale educational supplies for science, and its method of selling to overseas markets is an unorthodox one. Carolina Biological is a mail-order company.

To locate customers, the firm purchases mailing lists of teachers all over the world. It then sends them catalog request cards, generally 100 to 200,000 cards a year. "Many people told us that mail order would not work overseas," says export manager J. Claude Harmon. But, says Harmon, after the company sent mail-order catalogs to foreign educators, it got an "astonishing response rate"—about double the rate on a domestic mailing.

Parr Instrument Co. of Moline, Illinois, sells laboratory equipment, such as calorimeters and pressure vessels, in about fifty countries. Being small can be an advantage in exporting, says Pat Malmloff, export manager for the sixty-employee company.

Parr Instrument first focused on exporting in 1973, when foreign business represented 15 percent of its sales. In eight years, it increased that percentage to 20, and by 1982, it had received the President's E Award for export achievement. The company pressed on, increasing exports in 1988 to 35 percent of sales, compared to 7 percent for U.S. scientific industries as a whole. In 1989 that achievement won the company the President's E Star Award for continued export expansion.

Bright of America of Summerville, West Virginia, hardly gave a thought to exporting during its first ten years. Then, while exhibiting the firm's plastic laminated place mats and other household novelty products at the Chi-

cago Housewares Show in 1973, the firm's sales executives were approached by an Australian who said he wanted to place an order. The salespeople at the exhibit booth were caught off guard. They didn't know how to take a foreign order, how to ship products to Australia, or how to arrange payment. Nor did anyone else in the firm.

Today, Bright of America sells its products in forty countries. In 1984 Bright was named Small Business Exporter of the Year by the U.S. Small Business Administration. In 1988 the company received the Governor's Award for Exporting. In addition, William T. Bright, the owner of the company, was named West Virginia Entrepreneur of the Year by West Virginia University in 1989.

American food giant **General Mills** is expanding distribution of its cereals worldwide. The company is currently working with a Japanese firm, Calbee Foods Company, to test-market Cheerios and Golden Grahams in Tokyo. By improving operating and organizational efficiencies, General Mills' food businesses worldwide have achieved a 46 percent increase since 1985 in sales per foods employee.[1]

Although international activities of companies like General Mills and Parr Instrument Co. receive publicity in the media, international trade is not, of course, limited to the sale of American products in foreign countries. Every nation is involved in international business to some degree.

Theoretically, international trade is every bit as logical and worthwhile as, say, trade between Indiana and Ohio. Yet, nations tend to restrict the import of certain goods for a variety of reasons, just as the United States effectively restricted the import of dried milk, sugar, textiles, steel, and automobiles to protect faltering U.S. industries.[2]

In spite of such restrictions, international trade has increased almost steadily since World War II. Many of the industrialized nations have signed trade agreements that are intended to eliminate problems in international business and to help less developed nations participate in world trade. Individual firms around the world have seized the opportunity to compete in foreign markets by exporting and increasing foreign production, as well as by other means.

The Basis for International Business

international business *all business activities that involve exchanges across national boundaries*

International business encompasses all business activities that involve exchanges across national boundaries. Thus a firm is engaged in international business when it buys some portion of its input from, or sells some portion of its output to, an organization that is located in a foreign country. (A small retail store may sell goods that were produced in some other country. However, because it purchases these goods from American distributors, it is not considered to be engaged in international trade.)

Absolute and Comparative Advantage

Learning Objective 1
Summarize the economic basis for international business

Some countries are better equipped than other countries to produce particular goods or services. The reason may be a country's natural resources, its labor supply, or even customs or a historical accident. Such a country would be best off if it could *specialize* in the production of such products, because it can produce them most efficiently. The country could use what it needed of these products and then trade the surplus for products that it could not produce efficiently.

Saudi Arabia has thus specialized in the production of crude oil and petroleum products, South Africa in diamonds, and Australia in wool. Each of these countries is said to have an absolute advantage with regard to a particular product. An **absolute advantage** is the ability to produce a specific product more efficiently than any other nation.

absolute advantage *the ability to produce a specific product more efficiently than any other nation*

One country may have an absolute advantage with regard to several products, whereas another country may have no absolute advantage at all. Yet it is still worthwhile for these two countries to specialize and trade with each other. To see why this is so, consider the following situation: You are the president of a successful manufacturing firm, and

Coca-Cola Company exports its products to many different countries, including Norway, as shown here. Norwegians are Europe's largest per capita Coca-Cola consumers. The Coca-Cola European Community Group, a new group, is charged with addressing Europe's twelve-country market. This market produces 16 percent of Coca-Cola's worldwide soft drink volume.

you can accurately type ninety words per minute. Your secretary can type eighty words per minute but would run the business poorly. You thus have an absolute advantage over your secretary in both typing and managing. But you cannot afford to type your own letters because your time is better spent in managing the business. That is, you have a comparative advantage in managing. A **comparative advantage** is the ability to produce a specific product more efficiently than any other product.

comparative advantage *the ability to produce a specific product more efficiently than any other product*

Your secretary, on the other hand, has a comparative advantage in typing because he or she can do that better than managing the business. So you spend your time managing, and you leave the typing to your secretary. Overall, the business is run as efficiently as possible, because you are each working in accordance with your own comparative advantage.

The same is true for nations: Goods and services are produced more efficiently when each country specializes in the products for which it has a comparative advantage. Moreover, by definition, every country has a comparative advantage in *some* product.

Exporting and Importing

Suppose the United States specializes in producing, say, corn. It will then produce a surplus of corn, but perhaps it will have a shortage of wine. France, on the other hand, specializes in producing wine but experiences a shortage of corn. To satisfy both needs—for corn and for wine—the two countries should trade with each other. That is, the United States should export corn and import wine. France should export wine and import corn.

exporting *selling and shipping raw materials or products to other nations*

importing *purchasing raw materials or products in other nations and bringing them into one's own country*

balance of trade *the total value of a nation's exports less the total value of its imports, over some period of time*

trade deficit *an unfavorable balance of trade*

balance of payments *the total flow of money into the country less the total flow of money out of the country, over some period of time*

Exporting is selling and shipping raw materials or products to other nations. Boeing, Co., for example, exports its airplanes to a number of countries, for use by their airlines.

Importing is purchasing raw materials or products in other nations and bringing them into one's own country. Thus, buyers for Macy's department stores may purchase rugs in India or raincoats in England and have them shipped back to the United States for resale.

Importing and exporting are the principal activities involved in international trade. They give rise to an important concept called the balance of trade. A nation's **balance of trade** is the total value of its exports *less* the total value of its imports, over some period of time. If a country imports more than it exports, its balance of trade is negative and is said to be *unfavorable*. (A negative balance of trade is unfavorable because the country must export money to pay for its excess imports.) In 1988, the United States imported $441.6 billion worth of merchandise and exported $321.8 billion worth. It thus had a trade deficit of $119.8 billion.[3] A **trade deficit** is an unfavorable balance of trade (see Figure 23.1).

On the other hand, when a country exports more than it imports, it is said to have a *favorable* balance of trade. This has consistently been the case for Japan over the last two decades or so.

A nation's **balance of payments** is the total flow of money into the country *less* the total flow of money out of the country, over some period of time. Balance of payments is thus a much broader concept than balance of trade. It includes imports and exports, of course. But it also includes investments, money spent by foreign tourists, payments by foreign governments and aid to foreign governments, and all other receipts and payments.

A continual deficit in a nation's balance of payments (a negative balance) can cause other nations to lose confidence in its economy. A continual surplus can indicate that the country encourages exports but limits imports by imposing trade restrictions.

Restrictions to International Business

Specialization and international trade can result in the efficient production of want-satisfying goods and services, on a worldwide basis. And, as we have noted, total international business is generally increasing. Yet, the nations of the world continue to erect barriers to free trade. They do so for reasons ranging from internal political and economic pressures to simple mistrust of other nations. We examine first the types of restrictions that are applied and then the arguments for and against trade restrictions.

Learning Objective 2
Be aware of the restrictions that nations place on international trade, the objectives of these restrictions, and their results

Types of Trade Restrictions

Nations are generally eager to export their products. They want to provide markets for their industries and to develop a favorable balance of trade. Hence, most trade restrictions are applied to imports from other nations.

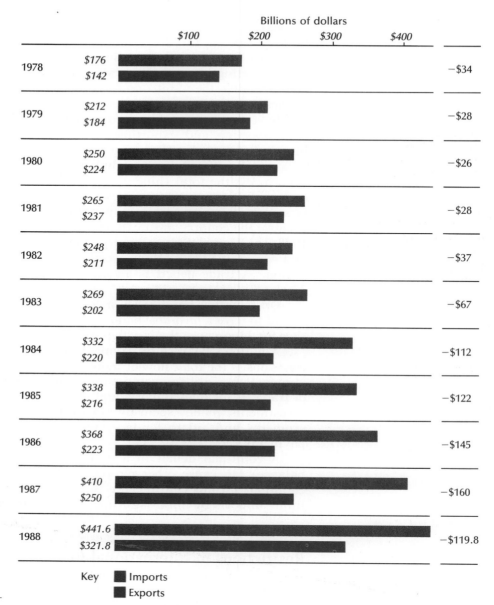

FIGURE 23.1
U.S. International Trade in Goods
If a country imports more goods than it exports, the balance of trade is said to be negative, as it was in the United States in 1988.
(Source: U.S. Department of Commerce, Bureau of Economic Analysis. National Income and Product Accounts *and* Survey of Current Business, *June 1989, p. 68.)*

import duty (or **tariff**) *a tax that is levied on a particular foreign product entering a country*

Tariffs   Perhaps the most commonly applied trade restriction is the *customs* (or *import*) *duty*, discussed in Chapter 22. As defined there, an **import duty** (also called a **tariff**) is a tax that is levied on a particular foreign product entering a country. This tax has the effect of raising the price of the product in the importing nation. Because fewer units of the product will be sold at the increased price, fewer units will be imported. Today, U.S. tariffs are the lowest in history, with average tariff rates on all imports under 4 percent.[4] (See Figure 23.2.)

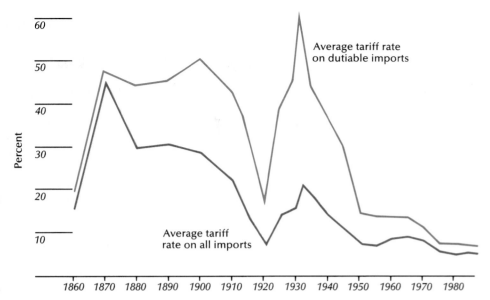

FIGURE 23.2
U.S. Tariff Rates, 1860–1987
This dramatic reduction in tariffs represents the progress achieved by steady efforts over the past fifty years to lower tariff barriers, both at home and among U.S. trading partners. (Sources: U.S. Department of Commerce and the *Economic Report of the President,* February 1989, p. 151.)

nontariff barrier *a nontax measure imposed by a government to favor domestic over foreign suppliers*

import quota *a limit on the amount of a particular good that may be imported into a country during a given period of time*

embargo *a complete halt to trading with a particular nation or in a particular product*

foreign-exchange control *a restriction on the amount of a particular foreign currency that can be purchased or sold*

Nontariff Barriers   A **nontariff barrier** is a nontax measure imposed by a government to favor domestic over foreign suppliers. Nontariff barriers create obstacles to the marketing of foreign goods in a country and increase costs for exporters. The following are a few examples of nontariff barriers.

▶   An **import quota** is a limit on the amount of a particular good that may be imported into a country during a given period of time. The limit may be set in terms of either quantity (so many pounds of beef) or value (so many dollars' worth of shoes).

Quotas may also be set on individual products imported from specific countries. For example, under a voluntary agreement with the United States, the Japanese may not ship more than 2.3 million cars annually.[5] If the Japanese had not voluntarily limited their car exports to this country, the government might have imposed an import quota on Japanese automobiles. Or the government could simply have ruled that no more than, say, 3 million automobiles per year would be imported into this country, no matter where they were manufactured.

Once an import quota has been reached, imports are halted until the specified time has elapsed.

▶   An **embargo** is a complete halt to trading with a particular nation or in a particular product. Most often the embargo is used as a political weapon. At present, the United States has import embargoes against Cuba and Vietnam—both as a result of extremely poor political relations.

▶   A **foreign-exchange control** is a restriction on the amount of a particular foreign currency that can be purchased or sold. By limiting the amount of foreign currency that importers can obtain, a government limits the amount of goods that importers can purchase with that currency. This has the effect of limiting imports from the country whose foreign exchange is being controlled.

▶ A nation can increase or decrease the value of its money relative to the currency of other nations. **Currency devaluation** is the reduction of the value of a nation's currency relative to the currencies of other countries.

currency devaluation   *the reduction of the value of a nation's currency relative to the currencies of other countries*

Devaluation increases the cost of foreign goods, while it decreases the cost of domestic goods to foreign firms. For example, suppose the English pound is worth $2. Then an American-made $2,000 computer can be purchased for £1,000. But if the pound is devalued so that it is worth only $1, that same computer will cost £2,000. The increased cost, in pounds, will reduce the import of American computers—and all foreign goods—into England.

On the other hand, before devaluation, a £500 set of English bone china costs an American $1,000. After the devaluation, the set of china will cost only $500. The decreased cost will make the china—and all English goods—much more attractive to U.S. purchasers.

Arguments for Trade Restrictions

Various reasons are advanced for trade restrictions either on the import of specific products or on trade with particular countries. We have noted that political considerations are usually involved in trade embargoes. Other frequently cited reasons for restricting trade include the following:

Under a voluntary agreement with the United States, the Japanese may not ship more than 2.3 million cars annually. The United States imports approximately 40 percent of the automobiles sold in this country, a large proportion of which are Japanese.

▶ *To equalize a nation's balance of payments:* This may be considered necessary to restore confidence in the country's monetary system and in its ability to repay its debts.

▶ *To protect new or weak industries:* A new, or *infant*, industry may not be strong enough to withstand foreign competition. Temporary trade restrictions may be used to give it a chance to grow and become self-sufficient.

▶ *To protect national security:* Restrictions in this category are generally on exports, to keep the nation's technology out of the hands of potential enemies. For example, strategic and defense-related goods cannot be exported to unfriendly nations.

▶ *To protect the health of citizens:* Products that are dangerous or unhealthy (for example, farm products that are contaminated with insecticides) may be embargoed for this reason.

▶ *To retaliate for another nation's trade restrictions:* A country whose exports are taxed by another country may respond by imposing tariffs on imports from that country.

▶ *To protect domestic jobs:* By restricting imports, a nation can protect jobs in domestic industries. However, protecting these jobs can be expensive. For example, in 1988 the cost—in higher prices to American consumers—of protecting 55,000 jobs in the automobile industry was $5.8 billion, or $105,000 per job. And to protect 9,000 jobs in the carbon-steel industry cost $6.8 billion, or $750,000 per job.[6]

Arguments Against Trade Restrictions

Trade restrictions lead to certain immediate and certain long-term economic consequences—both within the restricting nation and in world trade patterns. These include

▶ *Higher prices for consumers:* Higher prices may result from the imposition of tariffs or from the elimination of foreign competition. Recently, the consumer cost of restrictions exceeded $27 billion per year in the textile and apparel industries.[7] Large consumer costs are also associated with protection in the steel and automobile industries, as mentioned earlier.

▶ *Restriction of consumers' choices:* Again, this is a direct result of the elimination of some foreign products from the marketplace and of the artificially high prices that importers must charge for products that *are* still imported.

▶ *Misallocation of international resources:* The protection of weak industries results in the inefficient use of limited resources. The economies of both the restricting nation and other nations eventually suffer because of this waste.

▶ *Loss of jobs:* The restriction of imports by one nation must lead to cutbacks—and the loss of jobs—in the export-oriented industries of other nations. For example, recently about one out of every six U.S. manufacturing jobs was a job that produced exports.[8] The total number of jobs generated by exports reached nearly 5.6 million. This means that, on average, each $1 billion of exported merchandise supported 22,800 jobs.[9]

The Extent of International Business

Learning Objective 3
Be familiar with the extent of international trade and the organizations that are working to foster it

Restrictions or not, international business is growing. In 1988 the volume of world trade expanded by more than 9 percent, which was the highest annual rate of growth since 1976.[10] (See Figure 23.3.)

Six economies—Hong Kong, Malaysia, Singapore, South Korea, Taiwan, and Thailand—in the Asian-Pacific region are booming in world trade. This region is also experiencing a rapid rise in interregional trade. Recently, interregional trade grew 33 percent to $259 billion, making the Asian-Pacific region the fastest-growing and third-largest trading area in terms of its share of total world trade.[11]

Members of the European Community (EC) are creating a single market for goods and financial services. Tearing down trade barriers and removing other restrictions will strengthen international trade. The EC has a population of 320 million people, 33 percent more than live in the United States. The EC's gross national product is $4.6 trillion, nearly equal to that of the United States.[12]

In the United States, an export boom has revived domestic manufacturing and made a significant contribution to U.S. economic growth. After

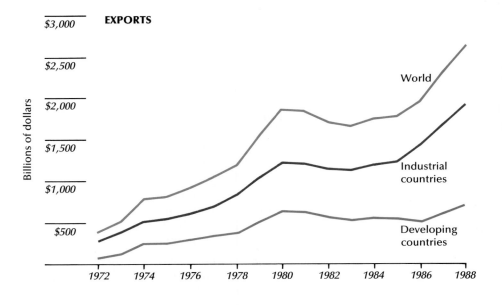

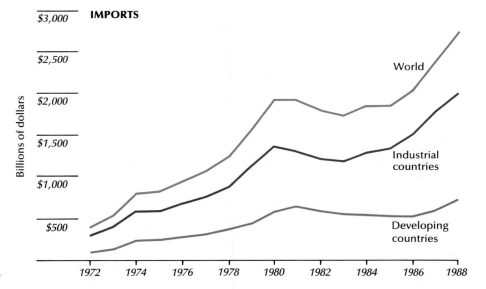

FIGURE 23.3
Volume of World Exports and Imports
World trade amounted to almost $5.5 trillion in 1988. The 1982 and 1983 declines in world trade volume resulted from a worldwide recession. (Source: Reprinted by permission from International Financial Statistics, International Monetary Fund, 1989, p. 20.)

suffering declines and sluggish growth throughout most of the 1980s, U.S. merchandise exports are accelerating rapidly (see Figure 23.4).

Table 23.1 shows the value of U.S. merchandise exports to, and imports from, each of its twenty major trading partners. Figure 23.5 categorizes American exports and imports. Its major exports are capital goods and industrial supplies and materials; its major imports are capital and consumer goods.

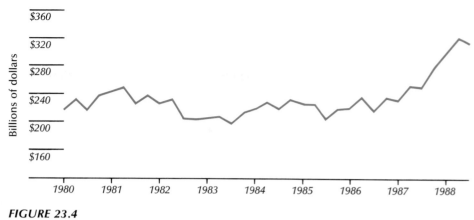

FIGURE 23.4

A Surge in U.S. Merchandise Exports
The current surge in U.S. Exports began in 1987, when they reached a record high of $250 billion. (Sources: Bureau of the Census and U.S. Industrial Outlook, 1989, p. 13.)

TABLE 23.1   Leading U.S. Markets and Suppliers—1988

	U.S. Markets			U.S. Suppliers	
Rank	Country	Merchandise Exports (billions)	Rank	Country	Merchandise Imports (billions)
	Total Exports	$321.8		Total Imports	$441.6
1	Canada	70.9	1	Japan	89.8
2	Japan	37.7	2	Canada	80.9
3	Mexico	20.6	3	West Germany	26.5
4	United Kingdom	18.4	4	Taiwan	24.8
5	West Germany	14.3	5	Mexico	23.3
6	Taiwan	12.1	6	South Korea	20.2
7	South Korea	11.3	7	United Kingdom	18.0
8	Netherlands	10.1	8	France	12.2
9	France	10.1	9	Italy	11.6
10	Belgium-Luxembourg	7.4	10	Hong Kong	10.2
11	Australia	7.0	11	Brazil	9.3
12	Italy	6.8	12	China	8.5
13	Singapore	5.8	13	Singapore	8.0
14	Hong Kong	5.7	14	Saudi Arabia	5.6
15	China	5.0	15	Venezuela	5.2
16	Venezuela	4.6	16	Sweden	5.0
17	Brazil	4.3	17	Switzerland	4.6
18	Spain	4.2	18	Netherlands	4.6
19	Switzerland	4.2	19	Belgium-Luxembourg	4.5
20	Saudi Arabia	3.8	20	Malaysia	3.7

Source: Adapted from *Business America,* April 10, 1989, p. 5.

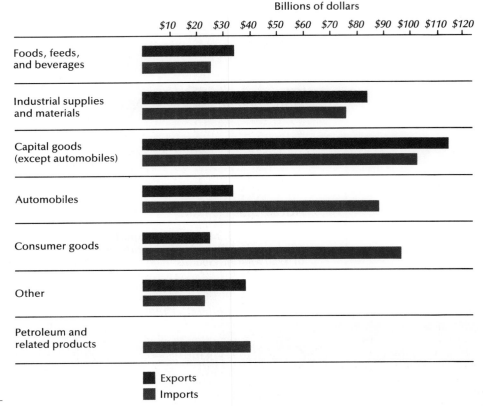

FIGURE 23.5
Selected U.S. Exports and Imports by Major Categories—1988
Our major exports are capital goods; industrial supplies and materials; and foods, feeds, and beverages. (Source: Survey of Current Business, July 1989, p. 70, Superintendent of Documents, Government Printing Office.)

The General Agreement on Tariffs and Trade (1947)

General Agreement on Tariffs and Trade (GATT) *an international organization whose goal is to reduce or eliminate tariffs and other barriers to world trade*

At the end of World War II, the United States and twenty-two other nations organized the body that came to be known as GATT. The **General Agreement on Tariffs and Trade (GATT)** is an international organization whose goal is to reduce or eliminate tariffs and other barriers to world trade. GATT is headquartered in Geneva, Switzerland. It provides a forum for tariff negotiations and a means for settling international trade disputes and problems. Since 1947 it has sponsored eight "rounds" of negotiations to reduce trade restrictions. Two of the most fruitful were the Kennedy Round and the Tokyo Round, and the third, the Uruguay Round, is under way now.

The Kennedy Round (1964–1967) In 1962 the U.S. Congress passed the *Trade Expansion Act*. This law gave President Kennedy the authority to negotiate reciprocal trade agreements that could reduce U.S. tariffs by as much as 50 percent. Armed with this authority, which was granted for a period of five years, President Kennedy called for a round of negotiations through GATT.

These negotiations, which began in 1964, have since become known as the *Kennedy Round*. They were aimed at reducing tariffs and other barriers to trade in both industrial and agricultural products. The participants were very successful in reducing tariffs—by an average of more than 35 percent. They were less successful in removing other types of trade barriers.

The Tokyo Round (1973–1979) In 1973 representatives of some 100 nations gathered in Tokyo for another round of GATT negotiations—the *Tokyo Round,* which was completed in 1979. The participants negotiated tariff cuts of 30 to 35 percent, which were to be implemented over an eight-year period. In addition, they were able to remove or ease such nontariff barriers as import quotas, unrealistic quality standards for imports, and unnecessary red tape in customs procedures.

The Uruguay Round (1986–1990) In 1986 the Uruguay Round was launched to extend trade liberalization and to widen the treaty to include textiles, agricultural products, business services, and intellectual property rights. Ninety-six countries are now GATT members.[13]

The Uruguay Round was clearly the most comprehensive and complex of all the GATT rounds. Members reached a landmark agreement on services and several other significant agreements that strengthen GATT rules and procedures.[14]

International Economic Communities

The primary objective of GATT is to remove barriers to trade on a worldwide basis. On a smaller scale, an **economic community** is an organization of nations formed to promote the free movement of resources and products among its members and to create common economic policies. A number of economic communities now exist. Table 23.2 lists the members of the four that are most familiar.

The European Community (EC), also known as the *Common Market,* was formed in 1957 by six countries—France, the Federal Republic of Germany, Italy, Belgium, the Netherlands, and Luxembourg. Its objective was freely conducted commerce among these nations and others that might later join. As shown in Table 23.2, six more nations have joined the EC. Today the twelve-member EC is closer than ever to tearing down barriers to trade and commerce within Europe so that European nations can enjoy economic freedom and prosperity. But some observers fear that the EC's current initiative, Europe 1992, might become "Fortress Europe," a community of nations bent on tearing down internal walls, only to build them externally against foreign competitors.

The *European Free Trade Association (EFTA)* was organized in 1960 in response to the formation of the European Community (EC). The original members included the United Kingdom and Denmark, both of whom later withdrew to join the EC. Like the EC, the EFTA has eliminated many restrictions on trade among its members and has developed a number of common trade policies. Unlike the EC, however, individual EFTA members determine tariffs on goods imported from and exported to nonmembers.

economic community *an organization of nations formed to promote the free movement of resources and products among its members and to create common economic policies*

As this cover of Fortune magazine proclaims, the 1990s will be a period of possibilities and opportunities for businesses, especially in the international realm. One probable area of decision making for international economic communities is the composition of their memberships.

TABLE 23.2 *Members of Major International Economic Communities*

European Community (EC)	European Free Trade Association (EFTA)	Latin American Free Trade Association (LAFTA)	Organization of Petroleum Exporting Countries (OPEC)
France	Austria	Argentina	Venezuela
Germany	Iceland	Brazil	Algeria
Italy	Norway	Chile	Libya
Belgium	Sweden	Colombia	Iraq
Netherlands	Switzerland	Ecuador	Iran
Luxembourg	Finland	Mexico	United Arab
United Kingdom	(associate member)	Paraguay	Emirates
Ireland		Peru	Ecuador
Denmark		Uruguay	Nigeria
Greece			Gabon
Portugal			Saudi Arabia
Spain			Kuwait
			Qatar
			Indonesia

The *Latin American Free Trade Association (LAFTA)* was formed in 1960. Its primary objective is completely free trade among its members, without any restrictions. This goal has not yet been achieved.

The *Organization of Petroleum Exporting Countries (OPEC)* was founded in 1960 in response to reductions in the prices that oil companies were willing to pay for crude oil. The organization was conceived as a collective-bargaining unit, to provide oil-producing nations with some control over oil prices.

Organizing for International Business

Learning Objective 4
Understand the methods by which a firm can organize for and enter international markets

A firm that has decided to enter international markets can do so in several ways. We shall discuss five different methods (or, more accurately, organizational structures): licensing, exporting, joint ventures, totally owned facilities, and multinational firms. These different approaches require varying degrees of involvement in international business. Typically, a firm begins its international operations at the simplest level. Then, depending on its goals, it may progress to higher levels of involvement.

Licensing

licensing *a contractual agreement in which one firm permits another to produce and market its product and use its brand name in return for a royalty or other compensation*

At a fairly basic level of international business is licensing. **Licensing** is a contractual agreement in which one firm permits another to produce and market its product and use its brand name in return for a royalty or other compensation. For example, an American candy manufacturer might enter into a licensing arrangement with a British firm. The British producer

BUSINESS JOURNAL

The United States and the European Community

Europe 1992 goes by many names—the European Community (EC), the Common Market, the internal market, and the single market. But it is known by only one date: 1992. That's when the trade restrictions separating the twelve-member European nations will be removed. Tearing down trade barriers and removing financial restrictions will strengthen the EC's economic power, create millions of new jobs for its citizens, and lower consumer prices.

Indeed, the European Community has made outstanding progress in the past four years toward achieving its goal of opening up its internal market to the free flow of capital, goods, products, services, and people. EC president Jacques Delors said in 1989 that the momentum toward creating the single market is irreversible.

The United States supports the European Community's 1992 program for market integration. A stronger Europe is in its best interest both commercially and strategically. U.S. exporters and investors stand to gain from a more prosperous Europe. Economists have estimated that successful implementation of the 1992 program could create 1.8 million new jobs in Europe and, over time, add $260 billion in demand for goods and services. The unified European market will be worth $4 trillion and will be composed of 320 million consumers bound by a single set of regulations and directives. This is a far different structure than the fragmented market U.S. business people have dealt with in the past.

Though not yet economically unified, the EC is the United States' largest trading partner. Their mutual stake in each market is significant, and in an increasingly global marketplace their mutual economic interests grow even closer. U.S. exports to the EC totaled $60 billion in 1987, $75.9 billion in 1988, and $87 billion in 1989.

The American trade balance with the EC has greatly improved. While only two years ago the United States ran a trade deficit with the EC of $22 billion, 1989 statistics showed the United States–European Community trade balanced (with perhaps a slight surplus for U.S. exports). In contrast, the United States' trade with Japan has only marginally improved from a $60-billion deficit in 1987 to a $50-billion deficit in 1989.

As the 1992 deadline for a single European market approaches, the link between the United States and the European Community becomes more important. The implications of Europe 1992 for U.S. firms doing business with Europe are not totally clear. If the EC keeps its doors to world trade open, U.S. firms could share in the benefits of a single European market. On the other hand, if the Europeans close their doors or put up trade barriers to foreign competitors, some U.S. firms could pay a high price. All in all, Europeans are confident that U.S. businesses will do well.

Based on information from George A. Weimer, "The West: Great Expectations," *Industry Week*, February 5, 1990, p. 15; Dan C. Taylor, "The Battle for the Global Marketplace," *The Plain Truth*, March 1990, pp. 3–8; Robert Straetz, "U.S. Exporters Should Find That Benefits of 'Europe 1992' Program Will Outweigh Problems," *Business America*, May 22, 1989, pp. 10–11; Robert A. Mosbacher, "U.S.—EC Cooperation Increases as the Single Market Takes Shape," *Business America*, January 15, 1990, p. 2 + ; Gregory O'Connor, "EC 1992: Opportunities for U.S. Manufacturing," *Business America*, January 15, 1990, pp. 1–19; Thomas Bennett and Craig S. Hakkio, "Europe 1992: Implications for U.S. Firms," *Economic Review* (Federal Reserve Bank of Kansas City), April 1989, pp. 3–17.

would be entitled to use the American firm's candy formulas, brand name, and packaging, and to advertise the product as though the candy were its own. In return, the British firm would pay the American firm a certain percentage of its income from sales of the product.

The advantage of licensing is that it provides a simple method of expanding into a foreign market with virtually no investment. On the other hand, if the licensee does not maintain the licensor's product

These tulip bulbs are ready for export from Holland to the United States. Export merchants assume all the risks of the bulb's owner-ship, distribution, and sale.

standards, the product's image may be damaged. Another disadvantage is that a licensing arrangement does not usually provide the original producer with any foreign marketing experience.

Exporting

A firm may also manufacture its products in its home country and export them for sale in foreign markets. Like licensing, exporting can be a relatively low-risk method of entering foreign markets. Unlike licensing, however, it is not a simple method; it opens up several levels of involvement to the exporting firm.

At the most basic level, the exporting firm may sell its products to an *export/import merchant*, which is essentially a merchant wholesaler. The merchant assumes all the risks of product ownership, distribution, and sale. It may even purchase the goods in the producer's home country and assume responsibility for exporting the goods.

The exporting firm may instead ship its products to an *export/import agent*, which arranges the sale of the products to foreign intermediaries for a commission or fee. The agent is an independent firm—like other agents—that sells and may perform other marketing functions for the exporter. The exporter, however, retains title to the products during shipment and until they are sold.

An exporting firm may also establish its own *sales offices*, or *branches* in foreign countries. These installations are international extensions of the firm's distribution system. They represent a deeper involvement in international business than the other exporting techniques that we have discussed—and thus they carry a greater risk. The exporting firm maintains control over sales, and it gains both experience and knowledge of foreign markets. Eventually, the firm might also develop its own sales force to operate in conjunction with foreign sales offices or branches.

Joint Ventures

As noted in Chapter 3, a joint venture is a partnership that is formed to achieve a specific goal or to operate for a specific period of time. A joint venture with an established firm in a foreign country provides immediate market knowledge and access, reduced risk, and control over product attributes. However, joint-venture agreements established across national borders can become extremely complex. As a result, such agreements generally require a very high level of commitment from all the parties involved.

A joint venture may be used to produce and market an existing product in a foreign nation or to develop an entirely new product. Kentucky Fried Chicken International has entered into a joint venture with Beijing Kentucky Company, the Beijing Animal Husbandry Bureau, and the Beijing Tourist Bureau. Of the 74,000 Kentucky Fried Chicken outlets around the world, Beijing's was the first to open in China in November 1987, and the biggest in the restaurant chain.[15]

BUSINESS JOURNAL

Ronald McDonald in Pushkin Square

Russians have been able to drink Pepsi-Cola for years, but now they can munch Big Macs—just a few blocks from Red Square. According to George A. Cohon, president of McDonald's Canadian subsidiary and organizer of a joint-venture deal that will put twenty golden-arch outlets in the USSR: "We're living all the things you hear about *perestroika*."

McDonald's has been growing rapidly, but much of that growth comes from overseas. Sales at company-owned restaurants abroad rose 19 percent in 1988, versus 4 percent in the United States. One-fourth of McDonald's restaurants are overseas, but they account for nearly one-third of the firm's sales. There are more than 11,000 pairs of golden arches in fifty-one countries, but the world's largest McDonald's is in Moscow's Pushkin Square. The restaurant seats up to 900 diners, serves as many as 15,000 customers daily, and is expected to be the highest-volume McDonald's in the world.

In 1988 McDonald's signed a joint-venture agreement with the Moscow city council to open twenty restaurants including the one in Pushkin Square. Russians will own 51 percent; McDonald's, 49 percent. The joint venture has built a 100,000-square-foot, $40-million food-processing plant in Moscow. The plant includes its own dairy and employs 630 foreigners and Russians, who test, clean, chop, and freeze potatoes, meat, buns, onions, pickles, and other essential ingredients.

To ensure its high-quality sanitary standards, McDonald's has even built a small laundry room to clean the uniforms of its employees. In addition, five Soviet managers attended a ten-week training program at McDonald's Hamburger University in Oak Brook, Illinois. "It is exciting to know we are part of history," said Alexander Egorov, the 38-year-old director of the Moscow McDonald's restaurants and one of the recipients of the Bachelor of Hamburgerology degree. Moscow customers will, of course, be served exactly the same food and drink they would get in a McDonald's anywhere else in the world.

But don't think of running to McDonald's in Moscow for a bargain. A Big Mac, French fries, and a soft drink go for 5.65 rubles ($9.32 at the official exchange rate), or the equivalent of four hours' pay for the average Russian worker. Besides, customers are limited to ten Big Macs each, to stop them from buying in bulk and reselling them at a premium to the hungry crowds waiting in line outside.

Priyatnovo appetita—enjoy your meal!

Based on information from Ronald Henkoff, "Big Mac Attacks with Pizza," *Fortune,* February 26, 1990, p. 87+; "Pushkin, Coke and Fries," *The Economist,* November 18–24, 1989, p. 34; Peter Gumbel, "Muscovites Queue Up at American Icon," *Wall Street Journal,* February 1, 1990, p. A12; "Soviets Receive 'Hamburger' Degrees," *Daily Herald* (Wheaton, Ill.), September 22, 1989, Sec. 2, p. 8; and Louis Kraar, "Top U.S. Companies Move into Russia," *Fortune,* July 31, 1989, p. 165.

Totally Owned Facilities

At a still deeper level of involvement in international business, a firm may develop its own production and marketing facilities in one or more foreign nations. This *direct investment* provides complete control over operations, but it carries a greater risk than the joint venture. The firm is really establishing a subsidiary in a foreign country. Most firms do so only after they have acquired some knowledge of the host country's markets.

Direct investment may take either of two forms. In the first, the firm builds or purchases manufacturing and other facilities in the foreign country. It uses these facilities to produce its own established products and to market them in that country and perhaps in neighboring countries.

For example, Borden, Inc. owns manufacturing facilities around the world. Recently it acquired Sooner Snacks Ltd. of the United Kingdom. Borden now sells a wide variety of potato chips, nuts, and other snacks under the Borden and Sooner Snacks brand names. These snacks are, in turn, sold in many European countries.[16]

A second form of direct investment in international business is the purchase of an existing firm in a foreign country under an arrangement that allows it to operate independently of the parent company. When Sony Corp. (a Japanese firm) decided to enter the motion-picture business in the United States, it chose to purchase Columbia Pictures Industries, Inc., rather than start a new motion-picture studio from scratch.[17]

Multinational Firms

multinational enterprise *a firm that operates on a world-wide scale, without ties to any specific nation or region*

A **multinational enterprise** is a firm that operates on a worldwide scale, without ties to any specific nation or region. The multinational firm represents the highest level of involvement in international business. It is

TABLE 23.3 *The Twenty Largest U.S. Multinational Firms*

1988 Rank	Company	Foreign Revenue (millions)	Total Revenue (millions)	Foreign Revenue as % of Total
1	Exxon	$48,192	$ 67,292	71.6%
2	Ford Motor	41,842	92,446	45.3
3	IBM	34,361	59,681	57.6
4	Mobil	33,039	49,237	67.1
5	General Motors	29,128	120,388	24.2
6	Citicorp	16,451	32,024	51.4
7	Texaco	16,325	33,544	48.7
8	E.I. du Pont de Nemours	12,896	32,917	39.2
9	ITT	10,419	24,239	43.0
10	Dow Chemical	9,185	16,682	55.1
11	Procter & Gamble	7,294	19,336	37.7
12	Eastman Kodak	7,010	17,034	41.2
13	Chase Manhattan	6,080	12,365	49.2
14	Xerox	5,739	16,441	34.9
15	Digital Equipment	5,665	11,475	49.4
16	United Technologies	5,279	18,518	28.5
17	Chevron	5,264	25,196	20.9
18	Philip Morris	5,258	25,920	20.3
19	Hewlett-Packard	5,068	9,831	51.6
20	American International Group	4,979	13,613	36.6

Source: Excerpted by permission of *Forbes* magazine, July 24, 1989. © Forbes Inc., 1989.

TABLE 23.4   *The Twenty Largest Public Companies Outside the United States*

Rank	Company	Business	Country	Sales (millions)
1	Mitsui & Co.	Trading	Japan	$130,667
2	Sumitomo Corp.	Trading	Japan	115,570
3	C. Itoh & Co.	Trading	Japan	112,327
4	Mitsubishi Corp.	Trading	Japan	104,198
5	Marubeni Corp.	Trading	Japan	99,475
6	Missho Iwai Corp.	Trading	Japan	81,371
7	Royal Dutch/Shell Group	Oil and gas	Holland	78,380
8	Banco do Brasil	Banking	Brazil	55,295
9	Toyota Motor Corp.	Automotive	Japan	53,818
10	Hitachi	Multicompany	Japan	49,897
11	British Petroleum Co.	Oil and gas	United Kingdom	46,137
12	Nippon Telephone & Telegraph	Communications	Japan	45,531
13	Matsushita Electric	Electronics	Japan	42,880
14	Daimler-Benz Group	Automotive	Germany	41,848
15	Nissan Motor Co.	Automotive	Japan	37,516
16	Toyo Menka Kaisha	Trading	Japan	36,604
17	Siemens Group	Electrical equipment	Germany	34,148
18	Fiat Group	Automotive	Italy	34,040
19	Volkswagen Group	Automotive	Germany	33,721
20	Nichimen Corp.	Trading	Japan	32,250

Source: Excerpted by permission of *Forbes* magazine, July 24, 1989. © Forbes Inc., 1989.

equally "at home" in most countries of the world. In fact, as far as the operations of the multinational enterprise are concerned, national boundaries exist only on maps. It is, however, organized under the laws of its home country.

Table 23.3 lists the twenty largest U.S. industrial, multinational corporations; Table 23.4 shows the twenty largest public companies outside the United States. Notice that thirteen of the foreign-based multinational companies are located in Japan.

According to the chairman of the board of Dow Chemical Co., a multinational firm of United States origin, "The emergence of a world economy and of the multinational corporation has been accomplished hand in hand."[18] He sees multinational enterprises moving toward what he calls the "anational company," a firm that has no nationality but belongs to all countries. In recognition of this movement, there have already been international conferences devoted to the question of how such enterprises would be controlled.

Any firm that chooses to go into business internationally beyond the licensing level encounters new challenges as well as enlarged opportunities. Many of these challenges arise in the area of marketing.

International Marketing

Learning Objective 5
Recognize the main
considerations in international
marketing

A firm's marketing program—the strategies it uses to accomplish its marketing goals—must generally be modified and adapted to foreign markets. Within each foreign nation, the firm is likely to find a combination of marketing environment and target markets that is different from those of its home country and other foreign countries. Product, pricing, distribution, and promotional strategies must be adapted accordingly. Table 23.5 shows the steps required to develop an international marketing plan.

The Marketing Environment

Cultural, social, economic, and legal forces within the host country must be clearly understood. Even so simple a feature as the color of a product or its package can present a problem. In Japan, black and white are the colors of mourning, and therefore should not be used in packaging. In Brazil, purple is the color of death. And in Egypt, green is never used on a package because it is the national color.[19]

An important economic consideration is the distribution of income (especially discretionary income), which may vary widely from nation to nation. International marketers tend to concentrate on higher-income countries, for obvious reasons. However, some producers have found that their products sell best in countries with a low income per capita. As in domestic marketing, the determining factor is how well the product satisfies its target market.

The legal and political atmosphere also varies across national borders. Giving gifts to authorities—sometimes quite large ones—is a standard business procedure in some countries. In others, including the United States, such gifts are called bribes or payoffs and are strictly illegal. Moreover, marketing activities may be regulated to varying degrees. In Japan, new brands of cigarettes must be test-marketed in sixty scattered retail outlets, and test marketing is allowed only once a year. A new brand must surpass a certain sales level before it can be mass-marketed. Furthermore, each American firm can spend no more than $660,000 per year on advertising, and a single brand can no longer be advertised after it has been on the market for three years.

Marketing information is often difficult to obtain. Consumers in some countries believe it is nobody else's business whether a new product tastes better than an old one, or which television programs they watch. And most governments don't provide population and other statistics as freely as the U.S. government does. Some may not even collect such data.

The Marketing Mix

An international marketer can adopt any of several strategies regarding its product and promotion. The possibilities include

▶ *Marketing one product via a single promotional message worldwide:* This strategy can be effective for products that have a more or less

TABLE 23.5   *Steps in International Marketing Planning*

Step	Activity	Marketing Tasks
1	Identify exportable products	Identify key selling features Identify needs that they satisfy Identify the selling constraints that are imposed
2	Identify key foreign markets for the products	Determine who the customers are Pinpoint what and when they will buy Do market research Establish priority, or "target," countries
3	Analyze how to sell in each priority market (methods will be affected by product characteristics and unique features of each country/market)	Locate available government and private-sector resources Determine service and back-up sales requirements
4	Set export prices and payment terms, methods, and techniques	Establish methods of export pricing Establish sales terms and quotations, invoices, and conditions of sale Determine methods of international payments, secured and unsecured
5	Estimate resource requirements and returns	Estimate financial requirements Estimate human resources requirements (full- or part-time export department or operation?) Estimate plant production capacity Determine necessary product adaptations
6	Establish overseas distribution network	Determine distribution agreement and other key marketing decisions (price, repair policies, returns, territory, performance, and termination) Know your customer (utilize U.S. Department of Commerce international marketing services)
7	Determine shipping, traffic, documentation procedures and requirements	Determine methods of shipments (air freight, ocean freight, truck, rail?) Finalize containerization Obtain validated export license Follow export-administration documentation procedures
8	Promote, sell, and be paid	Utilize international media, communications, advertising, trade shows, and exhibitions Determine the need for overseas travel (when, where, and how often?) Initiate customer follow-up procedures
9	Continuously analyze current marketing, economic, and political situations	Recognize changing factors influencing marketing strategies Constantly re-evaluate

Source: U.S. Department of Commerce, International Trade Administration, Washington, D.C.

As an international marketer, Procter & Gamble must adapt its product, pricing, distribution, and promotional strategies to suit each country to which it exports its products. Procter & Gamble's strategy has included a Western-style campaign in China.

standardized appeal for most people—chewing gum or soft drinks, for example. It is also the least expensive strategy.

▶ *Marketing one product but varying the promotion:* This strategy is used when it is hard to translate promotional messages or to adapt an overall promotion to local customs or social usages.

▶ *Adapting the product but using the same promotional mix:* This strategy is used when one product would not appeal to different local tastes. For example, Kraft uses slightly different formulas for the Philadelphia cream cheese it markets in different countries.

▶ *Adapting both the product and its promotion:* This is the most expensive strategy. It may be required when neither the existing product nor its promotion would appeal to foreign markets. In some cases, the international firm may develop a completely new product for a foreign market.

Distribution strategies depend on the firm's international organization—whether it is licensing, exporting, or manufacturing in the host country. For the most part, however, the international marketer uses existing distribution channels.

Cost-based pricing is more common in international marketing than in domestic marketing. The added costs of shipping, paying import duties, and complying with various regulations tend to make this the most logical pricing method. Prices are also affected by exchange rates, especially by changes in these rates. Because of these added costs and the uncertainties in the exchange rate, prices tend to be higher in foreign markets than in domestic markets.

Marketing is not the only aspect of operations that must be altered to enter the arena of international business. Another factor that is affected is financing.

Financing International Business

Learning Objective 6
Identify the institutions that help firms and nations to finance international business

International trade compounds the concerns of financial managers. Currency exchange rates, tariffs and foreign-exchange controls, and the tax structures of host nations all affect international operations and the flow of cash. In addition, financial managers must be concerned both with the financing of their international operations and with the means available to their customers to finance purchases.

Fortunately, a number of larger banks, along with business in general, have become international in scope. Many have established branches in major cities around the world. Thus, like firms in other industries, they are able to provide their services where and when they are needed. In addition, financial assistance is available from U.S. government and international sources.

The Export-Import Bank of the United States

Export-Import Bank of the United States *an independent agency of the U.S. government whose function is to assist in financing the exports of American firms*

The **Export-Import Bank of the United States** is an independent agency of the U.S. government whose function is to assist in financing the exports of American firms. *Eximbank*, as it is commonly called, extends and guarantees credit to overseas buyers of American goods and services, guarantees short-term financing for exports, and discounts negotiable instruments that arise from export transactions. It also cooperates with commercial banks in helping American exporters to offer credit to their overseas customers.

Multilateral Development Banks

multilateral development bank (MDB) *an internationally supported bank that provides loans to developing countries to help them grow*

A **multilateral development bank (MDB)** is an internationally supported bank that provides loans to developing countries to help them grow. The most familiar is the World Bank, which operates worldwide. Three other MDBs operate primarily in Africa, Asia, and Central and South America. All four are supported by the industrialized nations, including the United States.

The International Monetary Fund

International Monetary Fund (IMF) *an international bank that makes short-term loans to countries experiencing balance-of-payment deficits*

The **International Monetary Fund (IMF)** is an international bank that makes short-term loans to countries experiencing balance-of-payment deficits. This financing is contributed by member nations, and it must be repaid with interest. It is provided primarily to fund international trade.

CHAPTER REVIEW

Summary

International business encompasses all business activities that involve exchanges across national boundaries. International trade is based on specialization, whereby each country produces those goods and services that it can produce more efficiently than any other goods and services. A nation is said to have a comparative advantage relative to these goods. International trade develops when each nation trades its surplus products for those that are in short supply.

A nation's balance of trade is the difference between the value of its exports and the value of its imports. Its balance of payments is the difference between the flow of money into and out of the nation. Generally, a negative balance of trade is considered unfavorable.

In spite of the benefits of world trade, nations tend to use tariffs and nontariff barriers (import quotas, embargoes, and other restrictions) to limit trade. These restrictions are typically justified as being needed to protect a nation's economy, industries, citizens, or security. They can result in the loss of jobs, higher prices, fewer choices in the marketplace, and the misallocation of resources.

World trade totals almost $5.5 trillion annually and is generally increasing. Trade between the United States and other nations is increasing in dollar value but decreasing in terms of our share of the world market. The General Agreement on Tariffs and Trade (GATT) and various economic communities have been formed to dismantle trade barriers and provide an environment in which international business can grow even faster.

A firm may enter international markets in several ways. It may license a foreign firm to produce and market its products. It may export its products and sell them through foreign intermediaries or its own sales organization. It may enter into a joint venture with a foreign firm. It may establish its own foreign subsidiaries. Or it may develop into a multinational enterprise. Generally, each of these methods represents a deeper involvement in international business than those that precede it in this list.

A firm's marketing program must be adapted to foreign markets to account for differences in the business environments and target markets from nation to nation. Social, cultural, economic, and legal differences may require modification of elements of the marketing mix—especially the product and its promotion. Various additional costs involved in foreign marketing tend to increase the prices of exported goods.

The financing of international trade is more complex than that of domestic trade. Institutions such as Eximbank and the International Monetary Fund have been established to provide financing and ultimately increase world trade for American and international firms.

Key Terms

You should now be able to define and give an example relevant to each of the following terms:

international business	currency devaluation
absolute advantage	General Agreement on
comparative advantage	Tariffs and Trade
exporting	(GATT)
importing	economic community
balance of trade	licensing
trade deficit	multinational enterprise
balance of payments	Export-Import Bank of
import duty (or tariff)	the United States
nontariff barrier	multilateral
import quota	development bank
embargo	(MDB)
foreign-exchange control	International Monetary
	Fund (IMF)

Questions and Exercises

Review Questions

1. Why do firms engage in international trade?
2. What is the difference between an absolute and a comparative advantage in international trade? How are both types of advantages related to the concept of specialization?
3. What is a favorable balance of trade? In what way is it "favorable"?
4. List and briefly describe the principal restrictions that may be applied to a nation's imports.
5. What reasons are generally given for imposing trade restrictions?
6. What are the general effects of import restrictions on trade?
7. Define and describe the major objectives of the following:
   a. GATT
   b. Economic communities

8. Which nations are the principal trading partners of the United States? What are the major U.S. imports and exports?
9. The methods of engaging in international business may be categorized as either direct or indirect. How would you classify each of the methods described in this chapter? Why?
10. In what ways is a multinational enterprise different from a large corporation that does business in several countries?
11. List some specific environmental factors that can affect the marketing mix that a company develops for a foreign nation.
12. Under what circumstances might a firm modify the following for marketing in a foreign nation?
    a. Its product
    b. Its promotion
    c. Both its product and its promotion
13. In what ways do Eximbank, multilateral development banks, and the IMF enhance international trade?

Discussion Questions

1. What difficulties might a mail-order firm like Carolina Biological Supply Company have in breaking into markets in other countries?
2. Parr Instrument Co. of Illinois is a small company. How can smallness be an advantage in exporting?
3. What type of financial assistance might be available to companies such as Bright of America?
4. The United States restricts imports but, at the same time, supports GATT and international banks whose objective is to enhance world trade. As a member of Congress, how would you justify this contradiction to your constituents?
5. What effects might the devaluation of a nation's currency have on its business firms? on its consumers? on the debts it owes to other nations?
6. Should imports to the United States be curtailed by, say, 20 percent so as to eliminate our trade deficit? What might happen if this were done?
7. When should a firm consider expanding from strictly domestic trade to international trade? When should it consider becoming further involved in international trade? What factors might affect the firm's decisions in each case?
8. How can a firm obtain the expertise needed to produce and market its products in, say, the EC?

Exercises

1. Refer to the following table to answer these questions (assume a two-nation, two-product world economy).

    a. Which country has an absolute advantage in the production of cloth? of beef?

Country	Cloth		Beef	
	Number of Workers	Output per Hour	Number of Workers	Output per Hour
X	5	100 units	7	100 units
Y	10	100 units	8	100 units

    b. Which country has a comparative advantage in the production of cloth? of beef?
    c. How many units of cloth and how many units of beef would be produced by all thirty workers if both countries specialized? if both didn't specialize?
2. Explain how you would modify the domestic marketing mix (as you know it) to market the following products. (Use the library to obtain information you might need to know about these countries.)
    a. Wrigley's Doublemint chewing gum in China
    b. Timex watches in Algeria
    c. Hires Root Beer in France

Case 23.1

The Selling of America

Recent opinion polls reveal that Americans are concerned about increased foreign ownership of U.S. firms and real estate.

▶ A March 1988 poll by the Roper Organization (a New York firm that conducts public opinion polls) found that 84 percent of the respondents thought that foreign companies buying more American firms and real estate is not "a good idea for the United States." By a 49-to-45-percent plurality, respondents disapproved of new jobs for Americans in foreign-owned plants. At least 72 percent thought that foreign companies' investments in the United States should be restricted.

▶ In May 1988, a CBS News/New York Times survey found that 51 percent of a national sample agreed that the "increase in foreign investment poses a threat to American economic independence."

▶ A February 1989 Washington Post/ABC News poll found that 45 percent felt Japanese citizens should not be allowed to buy property in the United States, and 80 percent said there should be a limit on how many U.S. companies the Japanese should be allowed to buy.

▶ Another poll, conducted by CBS News, showed that Americans fear Japanese competition more than Soviet aggression and believe that growing Japanese investments here are a bad thing.

Ask the Ohioans. In the last few years, Ohioans have seen foreign investors acquire or increase their ownership interest in such well-known Ohio firms as Sohio Pipe Line, Libby-Owens-Ford, Hanna Mining, White Consolidated Industries, and General Motors' Terex Division. At the same time, foreign firms have established entirely new subsidiaries in Ohio, the best known of which is Honda of America Manufacturing, which produces both motorcycles and automobiles.

As shown in Figure 23.6, foreign direct investment in the United States has been increasing since 1982. Direct investment by the United Kingdom represents the largest component of foreign ownership in the United States, averaging 25 percent of total foreign direct investment since 1982. The Netherlands, at 20 percent, is the next-largest single investor. Other

European direct investment averages 22 percent. Japanese direct investment averages 11 percent, growing from 8 percent in 1982 to 13 percent in 1987. Canadian and other direct investments make up the remainder.*

Questions

1. Why are Americans concerned about increased foreign ownership of U.S. firms and real estate? Do you believe the fears are justified?
2. Which countries have heavy direct investments in the United States? What is Japan's direct investment position in the United States?

Case 23.2

United States–Canada Free Trade Agreement

January 1, 1989, marked the creation of the largest free trade area in the world. The Free Trade Agreement (FTA) between the United States and Canada phases out remaining tariffs and other trade barriers between the two countries over the next ten years, thus creating the world's largest two-way trading bloc.

The FTA will have a profound effect on American business. By offering many new trade and investment opportunities, it will fundamentally change the way U.S. and Canadian companies do business with each other and will encourage many more companies to consider exporting for the first time.

The purpose of this agreement is to stimulate economic growth and enhance consumer welfare in the two countries through more efficient resource allocation. The agreement also represents the first major reversal of a rising tide of protectionism in the United States during the last decade. Moreover, like the European Community's plan to achieve economic

---

FIGURE 23.6
Foreign Direct Investment in the United States
(Sources: Department of Commerce and the Economic Report of the President, *February 1989, p. 135.*)

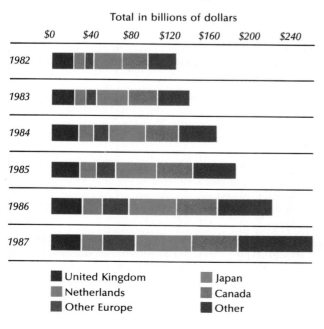

Total in billions of dollars

	United Kingdom		Japan
	Netherlands		Canada
	Other Europe		Other

---

* Based on information from *The Economic Report of the President*, February 1989, pp. 134–135; Mack Ott, "Is America Being Sold Out?" *Review*, Federal Reserve Bank of St. Louis, March–April 1989, pp. 47–52; Marcus W. Branchli, "Japanese Seek Low Profile in U.S. Deals," *Wall Street Journal*, November 10, 1989, p. A2; Gerald H. Anderson, "Three Common Misperceptions About Foreign Direct Investment," *Economic Commentary*, Federal Reserve Bank of Cleveland, July 15, 1988, pp. 1–4; Peter G. Peterson, "Japan's 'Invasion': A Matter of 'Fairness,'" *Wall Street Journal*, November 3, 1989, p. A12; Jeffrey H. Birnbaum, "Wright Angers Some with Call for Vote on More Disclosure by Foreign Investors," *Wall Street Journal*, February 17, 1989, p. A2; Malcolm S. Forbes, "Before Japan Buys Too Much of the USA," *Forbes*, January 25, 1989, p. 17; and John A. Tatom, "U.S. Investment in the 1980s: The Real Story," *Review*, Federal Reserve Bank of St. Louis, March–April 1989, pp. 3–15.

integration by 1992, this agreement sets up a concrete model for lowering barriers to international trade in services and investment.

Canada, a country of twenty-six million people, is the United States' largest trading partner. U.S. exports to Canada were recently valued at $60 billion, just slightly less than the value of U.S. exports to the twelve member countries of the European Community, with a combined population of more than 320 million. At the same time, Canada supplies about 20 percent of U.S. imports.

For Canada, the trade relationship is even more important. The United States is Canada's principal supplier and major customer, providing 70 percent of its imports and purchasing 78 percent of its exports. In 1987 the two countries exchanged goods and services totaling $166 billion, and bilateral direct investment totaled $79 billion.

In the long run, the FTA will provide the United States and Canada with more leverage to compete in a world that is rapidly moving toward regional trading blocs. The FTA moves the world a little closer to the potential of a global economy and encourages supporters of free trade throughout the world.†

Questions

1. Do you agree that the Free Trade Agreement between the United States and Canada represents a victory for both countries? Why or why not?
2. How can Canada be an ideal first foreign market for new U.S. exporters?

---

† Based on information from "Canadian Free Trade Agreement," *Illinois Economic Report,* Illinois Department of Commerce and Community Affairs, June 1989, p. 17; *The Economic Report of the President,* February 1988, pp. 128–136; "Canada–United States: Partners in Free Trade," *Canada,* Canadian Embassy, 1989; "U.S.–Canada Free Trade," *FRBSF Weekly Letter,* Federal Reserve Bank of San Francisco, February 10, 1989, pp. 1–3; "Canada—Geared for Growth," *Canada,* Department of External Affairs, 1989, pp. 1–14; Ann H. Hughes, "United States and Canada Form World's Largest Free Trade Area," *Business America,* January 30, 1989, pp. 2–3; and Karen Homolac, "Accelerated Tariff Elimination Is Possible Under Provisions of the U.S.-Canada FTA," *Business America,* January 30, 1989, p. 13.

CAREER PROFILE

RICHARD P. HUSTA A two-employee Connecticut company is doing its part to reduce the U.S. trade deficit by selling distinctive center armrests for cars to major foreign automotive manufacturers. Its customers include such foreign giants as Audi, Honda, Volkswagen, Nissan, Saab, Isuzu, and Volvo.

Richard P. Husta, founder and president of Husco Engineering Company Inc., estimates the aftermarket sales of his armrests at 50 to 60 million units. Currently, 25 percent of his sales are to overseas markets, and he expects this percentage to rise substantially in the future.

In February 1990 Husta began shipments of specially designed armrests for distribution to BMW dealers worldwide, under an exclusive agreement with BMW AG of Munich, Germany. He is exploring exclusive agreements with other foreign automotive manufacturers as well. A distinctive armrest is designed for each company.

"The key to our success is the unique design of our armrests, and I'm a bear on quality," says Husta, who designs the armrests, builds prototypes, and field tests them. He knew he had a successful product when he noticed that a Japanese company was trying to copy his armrests, although he did not think they measured up to his. He believes his efforts to make a high-quality product, to control costs, and to maintain good customer relations will pay off handsomely against international competition.

In the early stages of his business, Husta picked up some sales from individual responses to advertisements in automotive trade magazines. Later, the armrests were noticed by automotive manufacturers, who started placing substantial orders. As Husta started thinking bigger, he obtained information about foreign markets from the U.S. Department of Commerce branch office in Stamford, Connecticut.

Husta, a mechanical engineer who had worked in the corporate world for over thirty years, designed an armrest for his own car in 1980. "People saw it and wanted their own. This business began as a hobby, but I went into it full time in 1984." At the outset, Husta decided he did not want to manufacture the armrests himself. So he farms the work out to five major vendors who produce parts to his specifications and then assemble them.

How do Husta and his wife manage their enterprise alone? "We have good suppliers" says Husta. "We have excellent computers and other equipment in our home. You might say we run a mini-conglomerate. General Motors claims it needs one manager for each one hundred production employees. Considering myself and my wife as management, we have about the same ratio in our operation. Of course, my wife and I work eighty hours a week."

Based on information from *Business America*, U.S. Department of Commerce, International Trade Administration, Washington, D.C., March 26, 1990, p. 16.

The figure in the salary column approximates the expected annual income after two or three years of service. 1 = $12,000–$15,000 2 = $16,000–$20,000 3 = $21,000–$27,000 4 = $28,000–$35,000 5 = $36,000 and up

Job Title	Educational Requirements	Salary Range	Prospects
Agent/broker—imports	No college required; related training and experience essential	3–5	Gradual growth
Antitrust attorney	Bachelor's degree plus at least three years of law school; on-the-job experience	4–5	Limited growth
City manager	College degree in business or public administration; on-the-job experience	4	Limited growth
Contract lawyer	Bachelor's degree plus at least three years of law school	4–5	Limited growth
Corporate attorney	Bachelor's degree plus at least three years of law school; on-the-job experience	4–5	Gradual growth
Corporate environmental officer	College degree in business; on-the-job experience	4	Limited growth
Court clerk	High school diploma; some college preferred	1–2	No growth
Court reporter	High school diploma; technical training	2–3	Limited growth
Economist	Bachelor's degree in economics; graduate degree preferred	3–4	Gradual growth
Eligibility worker—welfare	Some college preferred	1–2	Limited growth
Foreign exchange positions clerk	High school diploma; math ability required; on-the-job experience	1	Limited growth
Health and regulatory inspector	High school diploma; some college helpful	2–3	Limited growth
Inporter, foreign buyer	High school diploma; math ability required; on-the-job experience	1–2	Limited growth
Legal assistant	Two- or four-year college degree	2–3	Greatest growth
Legal secretary	Some college preferred; on-the-job experience	2	Gradual growth
Patent attorney	Bachelor's degree plus at least three years of law school; on-the-job experience	4	Limited growth
Real estate attorney	Bachelor's degree plus at least three years of law school; on-the-job experience	4–5	Limited growth
Statistician	College degree preferred	2–3	Limited growth
Tax examiner, collector, and revenue agent	Some college preferred; on-the-job experience	2–3	No growth
Urban and regional planner	Master's degree; on-the-job experience	3–4	Gradual growth

APPENDIX
Careers in Business

Trends in Employment

As you look ahead to your own career, you should consider the effects that the trends described below will have on employment and employment opportunities.

▶ Jobs in service industries will account for an increasing proportion of total employment.

▶ Training—and retraining—will become increasingly important, as firms require their employees to understand and utilize the latest technology. Good jobs will require strong educational qualifications.

▶ Automation of factories and offices will create new types of jobs. Many of these will be computer-related. In some cases, employees will be able to complete assignments at home on remote computer terminals.

▶ The number of women in the work force, of two-income families, and of older workers will increase. There will be a greater emphasis on job sharing, flexible hours, and other innovative work practices to accommodate employees' special circumstances.

Where will the jobs be? A 1989 survey by *Monthly Labor Review* indicates that paralegals will be in greatest demand, followed closely by medical assistants. Those college graduates with majors in computer science, accounting, business, marketing, and economics will also be in high demand, according to human resources experts. There will be fewer manufacturing jobs, and those that remain will require high-tech skills.

The types of new jobs that will be created during the next decade or so will be related to technological advances. Table A.1 lists projections for the fastest-growing U.S. occupations that will provide the best opportunities for employment. Figure A.1 illustrates where job growth is most likely to occur in the United States.

Your Future in Business

It is generally agreed that competition for the better jobs will get tougher and tougher. The key to landing the job you want is planning and preparation—and planning begins with goals. In particular, it is important

A1

TABLE A.1 *Fast-Growing U.S. Occupations*

Occupations Growing Much Faster than Average	Percent Change in Employment, 1988–2000
Paralegals	75%
Medical assistants	70
Home health aides	68
Radiological technologists and technicians	66
Data processing equipment repairers	61
Medical record technicians	60
Medical secretaries	58
Physical therapists	57
Surgical technologists	56
Operations research analysts	55
Securities and financial-services sales representatives	55
Travel agents	54
Computer systems analysts	53
Physical and corrective therapy assistants	53
Social-welfare service aides	52
Occupational therapists	49
Computer programmers	48
Human services workers	45
Respiratory therapists	41
Correction officers and jailers	41

Source: *Occupational Outlook Quarterly,* Fall 1989, p. 30.

to determine your *personal* goals, to decide on the role your career will play in reaching those goals, and then to develop your career goals. Once you know where you are going, you can devise a reasonable plan for getting there.

Career Planning and Preparation

The time to begin planning is as early as possible. A good way to start is to match your interests and skills with those required by various occupations or occupational areas. The career profiles at the ends of the parts of this book can be helpful. You can obtain additional help from your school's placement office and from a variety of publications: the *College Placement Annual* and the *Occupational Outlook Handbook* published by the U.S. Department of Labor, for example. Most people find that planning to enter a general occupational area is more effective than targeting a specific job.

You must, of course, satisfy the educational requirements for the occupational area you wish to enter. Early planning will give you the opportunity to do so. But those people with whom you will be competing for the better jobs will also be fully prepared. Can you do more?

The answer is yes. Corporate recruiters say that the following factors give job candidates a definite advantage:

FIGURE A.1
Look Here for a Job
The metropolitan areas where job growth is likely to be the highest in the 1990s cluster near the nation's seacoast borders. (Source: Gurney Breckenfeld, "Where to Live—and Prosper," Fortune, February 2, 1987, p. 54. © 1987 Time Inc. All rights reserved.)

◆ Strongest growth in jobs

■ Strong growth

□ Modest growth

▼ Little growth

• Minimal growth

▶ *Work experience:* You can get valuable work experience in cooperative work/school programs, during summer vacations, or in part-time jobs during the school year. Experience in your chosen occupational area carries the most weight, but even unrelated work experience is important.

▶ *The ability to communicate well:* Verbal and written communication skills are increasingly important in all aspects of business. Yours will be tested in your letters to recruiters, in your résumé, and in interviews. You will use these same communication skills throughout your career.

▶ *Clear and realistic job and career goals:* Recruiters feel most comfortable with candidates who know where they are headed and why they are applying for a specific job.

Here again, early planning can make all the difference in defining your goals; in sharpening your communication skills (through elective courses, if necessary); and in obtaining solid work experience.

Letter and Résumé

Preparation again becomes important when it is time to apply for a position. Your college placement office and various publications (including such directories as *Standard & Poor's Register of Corporations* and *Thomas*

Register) can help you find firms to apply to for jobs. Help-wanted ads and employment agencies may also provide leads.

Your first contact with a prospective employer will probably be through the mail—in a letter expressing your interest in working for that firm. This letter should be clear and straightforward, and it should follow proper business-letter form. It (and any other letters that you write to potential employers) will be considered part of your employment credentials. See Figure A.2.

This first letter should be addressed to the personnel or human resources manager, by name if possible. You may include in this letter, very briefly, some information regarding your qualifications and your reason for writing to that particular firm. You should request an interview and, if the firm requires it, an employment application.

You may wish to include a copy of your résumé with your first letter (most applicants do). In any case, you should already have prepared the résumé, which is a summary of all your attention-getting employment achievements and capabilities. Your goal in preparing both the cover letter and the résumé is to give the potential employer the impression that you are someone who deserves an interview.

A résumé should highlight and summarize your abilities and work achievements. It should be written to grab a potential employer's interest. The employer reading your résumé should want to meet you to find out more. Your résumé needs to show that, despite your current job title, you are qualified for the higher-level position you seek. The résumé should fit on a single sheet of high-quality, white bond letter paper. It should be carefully thought out—rework it as many times as necessary to get it right and put your best foot forward. Make your résumé concise, but be sure to note everything important on it. You need not include explanations or details, because you will have an opportunity to discuss your qualifications during the interviews.

To write a résumé that sells you to a potential employer, ask former supervisors and colleagues, if necessary, to tell you what happened to work you produced. Then use action verbs to describe your major contributions. Words such as *managed* or *coordinated* sound high-powered. Passive words or phrases such as *was responsible for* or *performed* are not attention-getting. Highlight your work achievements by using percentages, numbers, or dollar amounts. Such concrete details demonstrate just how important your contributions were.

Figure A.3 shows a typical résumé. Items that should be included are your name, address, and telephone number; your work experience and major accomplishments on the job; your educational background; any awards you have won; and the principal activities you take part in outside of school or work. Avoid all extraneous information (such as weight, age, marital status, and the names and addresses of references) that could be supplied during an interview. So that the "Employment" category gets top billing, place "Education" at the bottom of the résumé, along with awards and activities entries. Reserve your employment and/or career objectives for mention in the one-page cover letters you send to potential employers with copies of your résumé.

FIGURE A.2
Letter of Application
A letter of application should give your qualifications and your reasons for applying to a given company. (Source: Adapted from Rinehard and Moncrieff, "Résumé Preparation Guide," 6th printing, p. 21. College of DuPage, Glen Ellyn, Ill.)

16 Wescott Lane
Collinsville, IL 62547

January 6, 1991

Mr. Clifford J. Ehrlich
Senior Vice President – Human Resources
Marriot Corporation
10400 Fernwood Road
Bethesda, MD 20058

Dear Mr. Ehrlich:

I am sending this letter and résumé in application for the position of Banquet Manager with your corporation. I think you will find my qualifications very compatible with those that you listed in the Hotel and Motel Journal.

For the last three years, I have been very excited about and involved in the restaurant training program at College of DuPage in Glen Ellyn, Illinois. Under the direction of George Macht, restaurant training coordinator, I became involved in both on- and off-campus educational experiences. After obtaining basic skills in the food service area, I supplemented my experience at various clubs, civic organizations, and trade shows (NRA). I feel confident that my practical experiences coupled with my educational background have well prepared me for the position you have available.

My interest in Marriot Corporation began years ago when Marriot's fine reputation was discussed in classes and has continued through my own dining experiences. I recognized your interest in cultivating good employees when I read about your six-month management training program. This program seems well designed to provide just the right exposure to the total operation of your banquet facility.

I would appreciate the opportunity to visit with you and further explain some of the information contained in the enclosed résumé. I'll be giving you a call within the next week to see if you have a few minutes to spend with me.

Sincerely yours,

Helen DeCarlis

Helen DeCarlis

Enclosure

The Job Interview

Your résumé and cover letter are, in essence, an introduction. The deciding factor in the hiring process is the interview (or several interviews) with representatives of the firm. It is through the interview that the firm gets to know you and your qualifications. At the same time, the interview provides a chance for you to learn about the firm.

JOANN CARENNA
7673 Old Ballas Road
Creve Coeur, Missouri 63128
(314) 555-0408

1987 – Present   ALLIED METALS & ALLOYS COMPANY — Manager, Chemical Procurement
St. Louis, Missouri

Manage a corporate group of 23 that purchases the major chemical raw materials for 100 consuming plants in the United States. Commodity responsibility includes pulp and paper chemicals, plastic resins, inks, waxes, coatings, solvents, and plastic film. Direct 16 professional buyers and nonexempt employees in cost-saving research and planning methods.

Designed, developed, and implemented 13 cost-reduction programs, saving more than $1 million per year since 1988. Initiated program in support of hazardous waste disposal project. Participated in strategy planning and negotiations for key materials.

1980 – 1987   Materials Manager

Designed and set up purchasing systems and procedures for M&T Chemicals, a subsidiary of AMA. Coordinated purchasing activities between corporate purchasing and M&T that improved overall raw materials quality and introduced volume discount at 31% savings annually.

1975 – 1980   CHEMICALS & PHARMACEUTICALS, LTD — Purchasing Agent
Joplin, Missouri

Negotiated for approximately $40 million of speciality and commodity raw materials. Contributed significantly to the company's cost-reduction program, with percentages on cost savings growing from 9% to 28% over 5 years. Improved reporting systems between plants and purchasing with a program now used as a model for all plant/corporate interrelations.

1972 – 1975   THIOKING CHEMICAL CORPORATION — Technical Specialist II
Canton, Ohio

Invented seven materials for which patents were awarded. Researched and developed advanced aerospace polymers.

EDUCATION: Completed management courses sponsored by Allied Metals & Alloys Company and Chemicals & Pharmaceuticals, Ltd.

B.S. in Chemistry, St. Louis, Missouri

FIGURE A.3
Résumé
A résumé presents the work experience and major accomplishments, education, and principal activities of a job applicant. (Source: Ellen Perry, "Résumé Makeover," Working Woman, *June 1985, p. 123. Reprinted with permission from* Working Woman *magazine. Copyright © 1985. WWT Partnership.)*

TABLE A.2 *Interview Questions That Job Applicants Often Find Difficult to Answer*

1. What can you tell me about yourself?
2. What are your strengths and weaknesses?
3. Have you ever been fired from a position?
4. What did you do in your last position?
5. How much did you earn in your last position?
6. How would you describe your previous supervisor?
7. Why do you want to switch jobs?
8. Are you willing to relocate?
9. What do you know about this company?
10. Why are you interested in this company?
11. Why should we hire you?
12. How long will it take you to make a contribution to this company?
13. What kind of manager would you be?
14. What are your salary requirements?
15. Why would you enjoy working for this company?

Sources: Dan Moreau, "Answers That Get You Hired," *Changing Times,* April 1989, pp. 53–55; and Thomas M. Camden and Nancy Bishop, *How to Get a Job in Dallas–Fort Worth,* Surrey Books, 1983, pp. 157–158.

Here again, preparation is the key to success. Research the firm before your first interview. Learn all you can about its products, its subsidiaries, the markets it operates in, its history, the locations of its facilities, and so on. If possible, obtain and read the firm's most recent annual report. Be prepared to ask questions about the firm and the opportunities it offers. Interviewers welcome such questions. They expect you to be interested enough to spend some time thinking about your potential relationship with their firm.

Prepare also to respond to questions that the interviewer may ask. Table A.2 is a list of typical interviewer questions that job applicants often find difficult to answer. But don't expect interviewers to stick to the list given in the table or to the items appearing in your résumé. They will be interested in anything that helps them decide what kind of person and worker you are.

Make sure you are on time for your interview and are dressed and groomed in a businesslike manner. Punctuality and appearance, like other personal qualities, are judged as part of the interviewing process. Have a copy of your résumé with you, even if you have sent one to the firm before. You may also want to bring a copy of your course transcript and letters of recommendation. If you plan to furnish interviewers with the names and addresses of references rather than with letters of recommendation, make sure you have your references' permission to do so.

Consider the interview itself as a two-way conversation, rather than as a question-and-answer session. Volunteer any information that is relevant to the interviewer's questions. If an important point is skipped in the discussion, don't hesitate to bring it up. Be yourself, but emphasize your strengths. Good eye contact and posture are important, too. They should come naturally if you take an active part in the interview.

At the conclusion of the interview, thank the recruiter for taking the time to see you. Then, a day or two later, follow up by sending him or her a short letter of thanks. In this letter, you can ask a question or two that may have occurred to you after the interview or add pertinent information that may have been overlooked.

In most cases, the first interview is used to *screen* applicants, or choose those that are best qualified. These applicants are then given a second interview, and perhaps a third—usually with one or more department heads. If the job requires relocation to a different area, applicants may be invited there for these later interviews. After the interviewing process is completed, applicants are told when to expect a hiring decision.

Accepting an Offer

"We'd like to offer you the job" may be the best news a job applicant can hear. To accept the job, you should send the firm a letter in which you express your appreciation, accept the offer, and restate the conditions of employment as you understand them. These conditions should include the starting salary and a general description of the job (responsibilities, the immediate supervisor's name, training, and such). If you have any concerns regarding the job, make sure they are cleared up before you send your letter of acceptance: The job offer and your acceptance constitute a contract between you and the firm.

Less exciting is the news that begins "We thank you for your interest in our firm, *but. . . .*" The fact is, there are many more applications for jobs than there are jobs. (This is because most people apply for several positions at the same time.) As a result, most people are turned down for some jobs during their careers. Don't be discouraged if you don't get the first position you apply for. Instead, think back over the application process, analyze it, and try to determine what might be improved. In other words, learn from your experience—and keep trying. Success will come if you persevere.

NOTES

CHAPTER 1

[1] Based on information from Christopher Knowlton, "How Disney Keeps the Magic Going," *Fortune*, December 4, 1989, pp. 111–112, 114, 116, 120, 124, 128, 132; Susan Spillman, "Animation Draws on its Storied Past," *USA Today*, November 15, 1989, pp. 1D, 2D; Richard Turner, "Kermit the Frog Jumps to Walt Disney as Company Buys Henson Associates," *Wall Street Journal*, August 29, 1989, p. 1B. [2] *Fortune*, September 29, 1986, p. 7. [3] Adapted from "The Origins of Enterprise in America," Exxon U.S.A., third quarter 1976, pp. 8–11.

CHAPTER 2

[1] Based on information from Sharon Begley, "Smothering the Waters," *Newsweek*, April 10, 1989, pp. 54–57; Geoffrey Cowley, "Dead Otters, Silent Ducks," *Newsweek*, April 24, 1989, p. 70; Claudia H. Deutsch, "The Giant with a Black Eye," *New York Times*, April 2, 1989, pp. 3–1, 3–8; Stuart Elliot, "Public Angry at Slow Action on Oil Spill," *USA Today*, pp. B1–B2; Philip Shabecoff, "Ship Runs Aground Off Alaska, Causing Largest U.S. Tanker Spill," *New York Times*, March 25, 1989, pp. 1, 19; Michael Satchell, "Tug of War Over Oil Drilling," *U.S. News & World Report*, April 10, 1989, pp. 47–48; Kenneth R. Sheets, "Would You Believe $16.67 an Hour to Scrub Rocks?" *U.S. News & World Report*, April 17, 1989, p. 48; and Rae Tyson, " 'We've Done All We Can Do' On Spill," *USA Today*, April 24, 1989, pp. 1A–2A. [2] CNN poll conducted by the Roper Center of Public Opinion Research, *U.S. News & World Report*, February 23, 1987. [3] O. C. Ferrell and Larry G. Gresham, "A Contingency Framework for Understanding Ethical Decision Making in Marketing," *Journal of Marketing*, Summer 1985, pp. 87–96. [4] "Engineers' Duty to Speak Out," The Nation, June 28, 1986, p. 880. [5] "Ozone Standards," *Environment*, March 1989, p. 24; and Merrill McLoughlin, "Our Dirty Air," *U.S. News & World Report*, June 12, 1989, pp. 48–54. [6] Merrill McLoughlin, "Our Dirty Air," *U.S. News & World Report*, June 12, 1989, pp. 48–54. [7] Dan Morse, "What's Wrong with the Superfund?," *Civil Engineering*, April 1989, pp. 40–43. [8] "Acid Rain Affects Coastal Waters Too," *Environment*, June 1988, p. 22. [9] Merrill McLoughlin, "Our Dirty Air," *U.S. News & World Report*, June 12, 1989, p. 54. [10] "A Biodegradable Recyclable Future," *The Economist*, January 7, 1989, pp. 61–62. [11] Faye Rice, "Where Will We Put All That Garbage?" *Fortune*, April 11, 1988, pp. 96–100. [12] "A Biodegradable Recyclable Future," *The Economist*, January 7, 1989, pp. 61–62. [13] "A Biodegradable Recyclable Future," *The Economist*, January 7, 1989, pp. 61–62. [14] David Landis, "Tighter Rules Put Squeeze on Firms," *USA Today*, May 26, 1989, pp. B-1, B-2.

CHAPTER 3

[1] Based on information from "The Kitchens that Don't Miss a Beat," *Business Week*, June 1989, pp. 45, 49; Erik Larson, "The Man with the Golden Touch," *Inc.*, October 1988, pp. 66–68, 70, 75–76; Stephen Michaelides, "Rich Melman Wears Gym Shoes," *Restaurant Hospitality*, May 1987, pp. 97–102. [2] "The Top 100 Industrial/Service Companies," *Black Entrepreneur*, June 1988, p. 121. [3] Cindy Skrzycki, "Why Nonprofit Businesses Are Booming," *U.S. News & World Report*, January 16, 1984, p. 65. [4] John DuMont, "Swallowing Competition," *Maclean's*, November 7, 1988, p. 42. [5] Ibid. [6] Frank Lichtenberg, "Productivity Improvements from Changes in Ownership," *Mergers and Acquisitions*, September/October 1988, pp. 48–50.

CHAPTER 4

[1] Based on information from Leslie Brokaw, Jay Finegan, and Joshua Hyatt, "Marlowe's Ghosts," *Inc.*, November 1989, pp. 66–67; Cynthia Poulos and William Hoffer, "The Business Whiz Kids," *Nation's Business*, November 1985, pp. 20–30; and Patti Watts, "Upstarts Stand Tall," *Management Review*, January 1989, pp. 25–30. [2] "Business Loans from the SBA," Small Business Administration, Washington, D.C., June 1987. [3] The State of Small Business: A Report of the President, 1989, p. 23. [4] Ibid., p. 25. [5] "Here's Help for Women," *USA Today*, May 11, 1989, p. 4B. [6] Mark Robichaux, "Teens in Business Discover Credibility Is Hard to Earn," *Wall Street Journal*, June 9, 1989, pp. B1–B2. [7] Tom McLean, "Small Companies: Failure and Success," *Accountant's Magazine*, October 1987, p. 59. [8] William P. Sommers and Aydin Koc, "Why Most New Ventures Fail (and How Others Don't)," *Management Review*, September 1987, p. 36. [9] Ibid. [10] A Report of the Committee on Small Business, House of Representatives, Ninety-Ninth Congress, January 2, 1987, p. 22. [11] Paul D. Lovett, "Meetings That Work: Plans Bosses Can Approve," *Harvard Business Review*, November–December 1988, pp. 38–41, 44. [12] Marc Leepsonn, "Building a Business: A Matter of Course," *Nation's Business*, April 1988, pp. 42–43. [13] Small Business Administration, Annual Report, 1988, p. 1. [14] *Statistical Abstract of the U.S.*, 1989, p. 527. [15] "Franchising Gets an A +," *USA Today*, October 26, 1988, p. 8B. [16] *Statistical Abstract of the U.S.*, 1989, p. 760. [17] Al Urbanski, "The Franchise Option," *Sales and Marketing Management*, February 1988, pp. 28–33.

CHAPTER 5

[1] Based on information from "Easton's $5 Million S.L. Plant the Hub of Global Sporting Goods Operation," *Deseret News*,

December 10, 1987, p. A8; Les Gould, "Building the Distribution Center of Their Dreams," *Modern Materials Handling*, July 1988, pp. 66–68; and Ronald Grover, "James Easton: Putting a 'Ping' in Baseball's Swing," *Business Week*, June 13, 1988, p. 57. [2] Briane Dumaine, "Corporate Spies Snoop to Conquer," *Fortune*, November 7, 1988, pp. 68–76. [3] Henry Mintzberg, "The Manager's Job: Folklore and Fact," *Harvard Business Review*, July–August 1975, pp. 49–61. [4] Ricky W. Griffin, *Management*, 3rd ed. (Boston: Houghton Mifflin, 1990), pp. 475–476. [5] Robert Kreitner, *Management*, 4th ed. (Boston: Houghton Mifflin, 1989), p. 511. [6] Ibid., p. 514. [7] Griffin, *Management*, p. 125. [8] Kreitner, *Management*, pp. 248–254. [9] John A. Byrne, "Business Is Bountiful for Elite Headhunters," *Business Week*, April 18, 1988, p. 28. [10] William Ouchi, *Theory Z* (Reading, Mass.: Addison-Wesley, 1981). [11] Michael Cieply, "Meanwhile, Back in Marysville," *Forbes*, March 12, 1984, p. 127. [12] Terrence Deal and Allan Kennedy, *Corporate Culture* (Reading, Mass.: Addison-Wesley, 1982). [13] Thomas Peters and Robert Waterman, *In Search of Excellence* (New York: Harper & Row, 1982).

CHAPTER 6

[1] Based on information from Mark Maremont, "Trying to Get Burger King Out of the Flames," *Business Week*, January 30, 1989, pp. 29–30; Patricia Sellers, "The Publican at Burger King," *Fortune*, March 13, 1989, p. 68; and Laurel Wentz and Liesse Erickson, "What Grand Met Plans for Pillsbury," *Advertising Age*, October 10, 1988, pp. 1, 74. [2] Joel E. Ross and Darab Unwalla, "Who Is an Intrapreneur?" *Personnel*, December 1986, pp. 45–49. [3] "Lessons From a Successful Intrapreneur," *Journal of Business Strategy*, March/April 1988, pp. 20–24.

CHAPTER 7

[1] Based on information from Joe Jancsurak, "Design for Manufacturing: The Elite Story," *Appliance Manufacturer*, June 1988, pp. 20–24; Anthony Ramirez, "Factories That Shine," *Fortune*, April 24, 1989, pp. 93, 100; and Barbara Weiss, "Hoover Design-for-Automation Program Whisks New Elites Through Production," *Metalworking News*, June 27, 1988, pp. 5, 35. [2] "Real Increase in 1988 National R&D Funds Estimated at Lowest Rate in Eleven Years," *Science Resources Studies Highlights*, February 1988, p. 3. [3] Robert Kreitner, *Management*, 4th ed. (Boston: Houghton Mifflin, 1989), p. 684. [4] The least-cost order quantity is found by applying the equation $EOQ = \sqrt{2RC/S}$, where R is the total yearly demand in units, C is the cost of processing an order, and S is the annual storage cost per unit. [5] Kreitner, *Management*, pp. 165–166. [6] Ibid., p. 122. [7] Ibid., pp. 123–124. [8] U.S. Department of Labor, *Bureau of Labor Statistics News*, July 6, 1988.

CHAPTER 8

[1] Based on information from William J. Hampton, "How Does Japan Inc. Pick Its American Workers?" *Business Week*, October 3, 1988, pp. 84, 88; Louis Kraar, "Japan's Gung-Ho U.S. Car Plants," *Fortune*, January 30, 1989, pp. 98–100, 104, 106, 108; and Marguerite Michaels, "Hands Across the Workplace," *Time*, December 26, 1988, pp. 14, 17. [2] Douglas McGregor, *The Human Side of Enterprise* (New York: McGraw-Hill, 1960). [3] Ricky W. Griffin, *Management*, 3rd ed. (Boston: Houghton Mifflin, 1990), pp. 245–246.

CHAPTER 9

[1] Based on information from "Motorola Inc.," *Business America*, December 5, 1988, pp. 8–9; John Robinson, "Beam Me Up, Scotty," *Training and Development Journal*, February 1988, pp. 46–48; and Lois Therrien, "Motorola Sends Its Work Force Back to School," *Business Week*, June 6, 1988, pp. 80–81. [2] Jeffrey J. Hallet, "Why Does Recruitment Cost So Much?" *Personnel Administrator*, December 1986, pp. 22–26. [3] Patricia A. Galagan, "IBM Gets Its Arms Around Education," *Training and Development Journal*, January 1989, pp. 35–41. [4] "Curtailing the Freedom to Fire," *Business Week*, March 19, 1984, p. 29. [5] Robert Kreitner, *Management*, 3rd ed. (Boston: Houghton Mifflin, 1989), pp. 365–366.

CHAPTER 10

[1] Based on information from "How the UAW Is Doing Its Part for GM's Parts," *Business Week*, February 13, 1989, p. 78; Michelle Krebs and Louise Kertesz, "GM, UAW Tap Talent of All Workers," *Automotive News*, October 10, 1988, pp. 1, 51; L. Jay Norman, "Mastering the Basics," *Personnel Administrator*, September 1988, pp. 70–76; and Raymond Serafin, "GM's Saturn Breaks Mold," *Advertising Age*, March 7, 1988, pp. 1, 78.

CHAPTER 11

[1] Based on information from Jean Viallet, "Vacation Corporation," *Chicago Tribune Magazine*, March 18, 1990, p. 24 +; Joshua Levine, "I Am Sorry, We Have Changed," *Forbes*, September 4, 1989, p. 136; Aimee L. Stern, "Perfect 10s Give Way to Families of Four," *Marketing Week*, March 27, 1989, p. 34; Brian Bagot, "Joining the Club," *Marketing & Media Decision*, March 1989, p. 14; Daniel Asa Rose, "No Sex, Please, We're Grown-ups," *Esquire*, November 1988, p. 45; "A Summer Romance," *Economist*, May 13, 1989, p. 79; and Brad Edmondson, "Club Med in a Family Way," *American Demographics*, January 1987, p. 24. [2] Ford Motor Company, Annual Report, 1988, p. 6. [3] General Cinema Corporation, Annual Report, 1989, pp. 6–7. [4] James F. Engel and Roger D. Blackwell, *Consumer Behavior* (Hinsdale, Ill.: Dryden Press, 1982), p. 9. [5] U.S. Department of Commerce, Bureau of Economic Analysis, 1987. [6] U.S. Department of Labor, Bureau of Economic Analysis, 1986. [7] *Wall Street Journal*, June 7, 1989, p. B1. [8] *Wall Street Journal*, August 21, 1989, p. B1. [9] "Cocktails at Tiffany," *Forbes*, February 6, 1989, p. 128. [10] Bickley Townsend, "Beyond the Boom," *American Demographics*, June 1989, p. 40. [11] *American Demographics*, March 1989, p. 15. [12] Ibid.

CHAPTER 12

[1] Based on information from James D. Sawyer, "Miata Casts a Magic Spell," *Autoweek*, May 22, 1989, p. 27; Kevin A. Wilson, "Horse Play With Mazda," *Autoweek*, March 20, 1989, p. 18; Ken Gross, "Back to the Future," *Automotive Industries*, April 1989, p. 92; Phil Berg, "The Elan of the Rising Sun," *Autoweek*, February 13, 1989, p. 18; Larry Armstrong, "Mazda Rolls Out a Poor Man's Maserati," *Business Week*, June 26, 1989, p. 66; and Kathy Barks Hoffman, "Sporty Miata Zips to Fast Start," *USA Today*, July 11, 1989, p. B1. [2] *Nielson Researcher*, no. 1, 1983, pp. 8–9. [3] Adapted from *Marketing Definitions: A Glossary of Marketing Terms* (Chicago: American

Marketing Association, 1960), p. 8. [4] Campbell Soup Company, Annual Report, 1982. [5] ConAgra, Annual Report, 1982. [6] Ford Motor Company, Annual Report, 1982, p. 3.

CHAPTER 13

[1] John Huey, "Wal-Mart: Will It Take Over the World?" *Fortune*, January 30, 1989, pp. 52–56 +. [2] Based on information from Kenneth R. Sheets, "How Wal-Mart Hits Main St.," *U.S. News & World Report*, March 13, 1989, pp. 53–55; "In Retail, Bigger Can Be Better," *Business Week*, March 27, 1989, p. 90; "The Service 500," *Fortune*, January 9, 1989, p. 189; and Wal-Mart Stores, Inc., Annual Report, 1987, pp. 8–10. [3] *U.S. Industrial Outlook 1986, Wholesale Trade* (Washington, D.C.: U.S. Government Printing Office), p. 52. [4] Barry Berman and Joel R. Evans, *Retail Management: A Strategic Approach*, 4th ed. (New York: Macmillan, 1989), pp. 68–69. [5] Ibid. [6] William M. Pride and O. C. Ferrell, *Marketing: Basic Concepts and Strategies*, 6th ed. (Boston: Houghton Mifflin, 1989), p. 362. [7] *Chain Store Age/Supermarkets*, July 1983, p. 11. [8] Stanley C. Hollander, "The Wheel of Retailing," *Journal of Marketing*, July 1960, p. 37. [9] Adapted from John F. Magee, *Physical Distribution Systems* (New York: McGraw-Hill, 1967), p. 73.

CHAPTER 14

[1] Based on information from Carlos H. Arce, "Despite Publicity, Hispanic Market is Undeveloped," *Marketing News*, January 2, 1987, p. 37; Marty Westerman, "Death of the Frito Bandito," *American Demographics*, March 1989, p. 28; Enrique Loza, "Business, Amigo? No! Amigo Business? Si!", *Public Relations Journal*, June 1988, p. 8; Brad Edmondson, "Walking Away from Dollars," *American Demographics*, November 1987, p. 21; Patricia W. Hamilton, "The $160 Billion Hispanic Market," *D&B Reports*, May–June 1989, p. 40; Brad Edmondson, "Pepsi Targets Hispanic Thirst," *American Demographics*, November 1986, p. 20; Chester A. Swenson, "Marketing to Ethnics Is a Long-Term Commitment," *Marketing News*, April 24, 1989, p. 7; George Swisshelm, "U.S. Hispanics Move to Rediscover Their Ethnic Roots," *Television-Radio Age*, July 24, 1989, p. A3; Jesse G. Wilson and Elaine G. Hartong, "Generating New Dollars for Broadcast Media," *Television-Radio Age*, July 24, 1989, p. A46; "Se Habla Espanol," *U.S. News & World Report*, March 6, 1989, p. 15. [2] *Advertising Age*, May 15, 1989, p. 24. [3] *Chicago Sun-Times*, January 25, 1984, pp. 1, 26. [4] *Wall Street Journal*, June 7, 1989, p. B1. [5] *U.S. Statistical Abstract*, 1989, p. 401. [6] Richard E. Stanley, *Promotion: Advertising, Publicity, Personal Selling, and Sales Promotion* (Englewood Cliffs, N.J.: Prentice-Hall, 1982), pp. 304–305. [7] *Advertising Age*, March 13, 1989, p. 70. [8] Ibid. [9] William M. Pride and O. C. Ferrell, *Marketing: Concepts and Strategies*, 6th ed. (Boston: Houghton Mifflin, 1989), p. 441.

CHAPTER 15

[1] Based on information from Gene Koretz, "Has High-Tech America Passed Its High-Water Mark?," *Business Week*, February 5, 1990, p. 18; Marcia Berss, "Bull in the Bear Cage," *Forbes*, March 5, 1990, pp. 78 +; *Moody's Handbook of Common Stocks*, Winter 1989–1990, Moody's Investors Service, 99 Church Street, New York, N.Y. 10007; Joel Dreyfuss, "Reinventing IBM," *Fortune*, August 14, 1989, pp. 30–35 +;

John W. Verity, "A Bold Move in Mainframes," *Business Week*, May 29, 1989, pp. 72–75 +; and Deirdre A. Depke, "Computer Makers Are Blue—But Not IBM," *Business Week*, July 24, 1989, p. 76. [2] Alicia Hills Moore and Julianne Slovak, "What Tomorrow Holds," *Fortune*, October 13, 1986, p. 43.

CHAPTER 16

[1] Kathleen A. Behof, "An Identity Crisis at Arthur Andersen," *Business Week*, October 24, 1988, p. 34. [2] Based on information from David Greising, "The New Numbers Game in Accounting," *Business Week*, July 24, 1989, pp. 20–21; "Price Andersen or Price Waterhouse," *The Economist*, September 30, 1989, p. 84; Jeffrey M. Laderman, "When One Plus One Equals No. 1," *Business Week*, June 5, 1989, p. 92 +; "Less Is More Among the Bean Counters," *U.S. News & World Report*, July 17, 1989, p. 11; "Plum Puddings," *The Economist*, December 17, 1988, pp. 90–91; Lois Therrien, "How Arthur Andersen Became a High-Tech Hotshot," *Business Week*, April 25, 1988, p. 125; and Kathleen Behof, "An Identity Crisis at Arthur Andersen," *Business Week*, October 24, 1988, p. 34. [3] Jeffrey M. Laderman, "When One Plus One Equals No. 1," *Business Week*, June 5, 1989, p. 94.

CHAPTER 17

[1] Based on information from Carol J. Loomis, "Pornography in Finance," *Fortune*, January 1, 1990, pp. 67–68; Howard Rudnitsky, "Good Timing, Charlie," *Forbes*, November 27, 1989, pp. 140–142 +; Rich Thomas and Eleanor Clift, "Asleep at the S&L Switch," *Newsweek*, December 11, 1989, p. 71; Tom Morganthau, "The S&L Scandal's Biggest Blowout," *Newsweek*, November 6, 1989, pp. 35–36; Margaret Carlson, " 'A Legal Bank Robbery,' " *Time*, November 27, 1989, p. 29; and Margaret Carlson, "Keating Takes the Fifth," *Time*, December 4, 1989, p. 46. [2] David R. Kamerschen and Eugene S. Klise, *Money and Banking* (Cincinnati: South-Western, 1976), p. 268. [3] The source of this information was Jack Climber, Vice President of Check Collection, Dallas Federal Reserve Bank, December 28, 1989.

CHAPTER 18

[1] Brett Duval Fromson, "Did Drexel Get What It Deserved?," *Fortune*, March 12, 1990, pp. 81 +; Michele Galen, "And Now, the Predator Is Preyed Upon," *Business Week*, March 5, 1990, pp. 70–71; Judith H. Dobrzynski, "After Drexel," *Business Week*, February 26, 1990, pp. 37–40; John Greenwald, "Predator's Fall," *Time*, February 26, 1990, pp. 46–50 +; Stratford P. Sherman, "Drexel Sweats the SEC Probe," *Fortune*, March 6, 1987, p. 38; Anthony Bianco, "Power on Wall Street," *Business Week*, July 7, 1986, p. 56; Chris Welles, "Did Drexel Bully Takeover Candidates?," *Business Week*, March 9, 1987, p. 43; and Stratford P. Sherman, "Travail at Drexel Burnham," *Fortune*, December 22, 1986, p. 31. [2] General Motors, Annual Report, 1988, p. 28. [3] Exxon Corporation, Annual Report, 1988, p. 26.

CHAPTER 19

[1] Based on information from Leah J. Nathans, "Merrill Scrambles for the Top of the Junk Heap," *Business Week*, March 5, 1990, p. 76; Jack Egan, "Does Your Broker Have a Hidden Agenda?," *U.S. News & World Report*, January 22, 1990,

p. 71; Jon Friedman, "The Remaking of Merrill Lynch," *Business Week*, July 17, 1989, pp. 122–125; Brett Duval Fromson, "Merrill Lynch The Stumbling Herd," *Fortune*, June 20, 1988, pp. 44–48 + ; Richard Behar, "Can Merrill Catch Up," *Forbes*, June 1, 1987, pp. 39–40; and *Moody's Handbook of Common Stocks*, Winter 1989–90 edition, Moody's Investors Service, 99 Church Street, New York, N.Y. 10007. [2] Charles M. Bartlett Jr., "Survival of the Few," *Forbes*, June 26, 1989, pp. 266–267. [3] Chase, C. David. *Chase Global Investment Almanac* (Homewood, Ill.: Chase Global Data and Research, Inc. and Dow Jones-Irwin, 1989), p. 94. [4] Robert H. Runde, "What to Do When It's Time to Invest," *Money*, October 1982, p. 83.

CHAPTER 20

[1] Gretchen Morgenson, "Dancing as Fast as He Can," *Forbes*, January 22, 1990, pp. 41–42; John Heins, "Staying in the Kitchen," *Forbes*, April 17, 1989, p. 108 + ; Kathleen Kerwin, "Milken's Shadow Hovers Over Fred Carr," *Business Week*, April 17, 1989, p. 24; Kathleen Kerwin, "This Could Be the End of a Beautiful Friendship," *Business Week*, September 4, 1989, pp. 33–34; Teresa Carson, "Fred Carr Buys Some Insurance," *Business Week*, October 26, 1987, p. 36; and Michael J. Branca, *Value Line Investment Survey*, Value Line, Inc., 711 Third Avenue, New York, N.Y., February 9, 1990, p. 1203. [2] "Proper Precautions Trim Product Liability Risks," *Inc.*, May 1980, p. 131. [3] *Source Book of Health Insurance Data: 1982–1983* (Health Insurance Association of America). [4] *The World Almanac and Book of Facts 1990* (New York: Pharos Books, 1989), p. 838. [5] Margaret Daly, "Universal Life Insurance: A Good Idea for Your Family," *Better Homes and Gardens*, April 1983, p. 25.

CHAPTER 21

[1] Based on information from John Greenwald, "How Do You Spell Relief?," *Time*, January 22, 1990, pp. 48–49; Todd Mason, "It'll Be a Hard Sell," *Business Week*, January 29, 1990, pp. 30–31; Kenneth Labich, "The Reichmanns' Rare Misstep," *Fortune*, January 29, 1990, pp. 121–122; "Bankruptcy Petition Brings Fresh Risks for Allied, Federated," *Wall Street Journal*, Tuesday, January 16, 1990, p. A1; and Nina Darnton, "Shop Till They Drop," *Newsweek*, December 11, 1989, pp. 76–78. [2] "Black Woman Wins $43 Million in Accident Suit," *Jet*, January 8, 1990, pp. 10–11. [3] Summarized from 11 *USC* 507 (1–6).

CHAPTER 22

[1] Based on information from Lee Smith, "Can Consortiums Defeat Japan?" *Fortune*, June 5, 1989, pp. 245–246 + ; Daniel Charles, "Reformers Seek Broader Military Role in Economy," *Science*, August 1988, p. 779 + ; Daniel Charles, "Can the Pentagon Fight Trade Wars?" *Science*, August 1988, p. 780; John Walsh, "Texas Wins R&D Center," *Science*, January 15,

1988, p. 248; and Otis Port, "Bob Noyce Created Silicon Valley. Can He Save It?" *Business Week*, August 15, 1988, p. 76 + . [2] *Statistical Abstract of the United States 1989*, 109th ed., U.S. Department of Commerce, p. 266. [3] See Sherman Act 15 U.S.C.A., Sec. 1-7. [4] Keith Davis, William C. Frederick, and Robert L. Blomstrom, *Business and Society*, 4th ed. (New York: McGraw-Hill, 1980), pp. 263–264. [5] *Economic Report of the President* (Washington, D.C.: U.S. Government Printing Office, 1989), pp. 188–195. [6] John L. Hysom and William J. Bolce, *Business and Its Environment* (St. Paul, Minn.: West, 1983), pp. 308–309. [7] "Deregulation: A Fast Start for the Reagan Strategy," *Business Week*, March 9, 1981, p. 63. [8] *Economic Report of the President* (Washington, D.C.: U.S. Government Printing Office, 1989), pp. 188–189. [9] Albert R. Karr and Muriel McQueen, "Adjusting Course," *Wall Street Journal*, November 27, 1989, p. 1 + . [10] Bradley R. Schiller, *The Economy Today*, 3rd ed. (New York: Random House, 1986), p. 62.

CHAPTER 23

[1] Based on information from General Mills, Inc., Annual Report, 1989, p. 12; "Exporting Pays Off," *Business America*, September 25, 1989, p. 11; "Exporting Pays Off," *Business America*, February 27, 1989, p. 14; and "Exporting Pays Off," *Business America*, February 13, 1989, p. 14. [2] Cletus C. Coughlin and Geoffrey E. Wood, "An Introduction to Non-Tariff Barriers to Trade," *Review*, Federal Reserve Bank of St. Louis, January/February 1989, p. 33. [3] *Survey of Current Business*, June 1989, p. 68. [4] U.S. Department of Commerce and the *Economic Report of the President*, February 1989, p. 151. [5] *Wall Street Journal*, October 16, 1986, p. 33. [6] "American Free Trade Policy: Rhetoric or Reality?" *Imprimis*, August 1989, p. 2. [7] *Review*, Federal Reserve Bank of St. Louis, January–February 1988, p. 17. [8] Office of the U.S. Trade Representative, Washington, D.C., 1989. [9] Lester A. Davis, "Exports Support Growing Number of U.S. Jobs," *Business America*, May 8, 1989, p. 14. [10] "International Monetary Fund: World Trade Growth Fastest in Decade," *Business America*, September 25, 1989, p. 10. [11] Steven Jones, "Imports to Asian-Pacific Nations Increase," *Wall Street Journal*, November 9, 1989, p. A2. [12] Thomas Bennett and Craig S. Hakkio, "Europe 1992: Implications for U.S. Firms," *Economic Review*, Federal Reserve Bank of Kansas City, April 1989, pp. 11–17. [13] *Wall Street Journal*, August 14, 1989, p. 1. [14] "Uruguay Round: Mid-Term Review," *Business America*, January 16, 1989, p. 2. [15] Wan Guodong, "KFC Titillates Tastebuds in Beijing," *China Reconstructs*, February 1989, p. 54. [16] Borden, Inc., Annual Report, 1988, p. 11. [17] Peter G. Peterson, "Japan's 'Invasion': A Matter of 'Fairness' " *Wall Street Journal*, November 3, 1989, p. A12. [18] Carl A. Gerstacker, *A Look at Business in 1990* (Washington, D.C.: U.S. Government Printing Office, November 1972), pp. 274–275. [19] Adapted from *Business Week*, December 6, 1976, pp. 91–92.

GLOSSARY

absolute advantage   the ability to produce a specific product more efficiently than any other nation (23)

accessory equipment   standardized equipment used in a variety of ways in a firm's production or office activities (12)

account executive (or **stock broker**)   an individual who buys or sells securities for clients (19)

accountability   the obligation of a subordinate to accomplish an assigned job or task (6)

accounting equation   the basis for the accounting process: Assets = liabilities + owners' equity (16)

accounting   the process of systematically collecting, analyzing, and reporting financial information (16)

accounts payable   short-term obligations that arise as a result of making credit purchases (16)

accounts receivable turnover   a financial ratio that is calculated by dividing net sales by accounts receivable; measures the number of times a firm collects its accounts receivable in one year (16)

accounts receivable   amounts that are owed to a firm by its customers (18)

acid-test ratio   a financial ratio that is calculated by dividing the sum of cash, marketable securities, accounts receivable, and notes receivable by current liabilities (16)

Active Corps of Executives (ACE)   a group of active managers who counsel small-business owners on a volunteer basis (4)

ad hoc committee   a committee created for a specific short-term purpose (6)

administrative law   the regulations created by government agencies that have been established by legislative bodies (21)

administrative manager   a manager who is not associated with any specific functional area but who provides overall administrative guidance and leadership (5)

advertising   a paid, nonpersonal message communi-

cated to a select audience through a mass medium (14)

advertising agency   an independent firm that plans, produces, and places advertising for its clients (14)

advertising media   the various forms of communication through which advertising reaches its audience (14)

affirmative action program   a plan designed to increase the number of minority employees at all levels within an organization (2)

agency   a business relationship in which one party (called the principal) appoints a second party (called the agent) to act on behalf of the principal (21)

agency shop   a workplace in which employees can choose not to join the union but must pay dues to the union anyway (10)

agent   a middleman that facilitates exchanges, represents a buyer or a seller, and often is hired permanently on a commission basis (13)

alien corporation   a corporation chartered by a foreign government and conducting business in the United States (3)

analytic skill   the ability to identify the relevant issues or variables in a situation, to determine how they are related, and to assess their relative importance (5)

appellate court   a court that hears cases that are appealed from lower courts (21)

arbitration   the procedure by which a neutral third party hears the two sides of a dispute and renders a decision; the decision is binding when arbitration is part of the grievance procedure, but may not be binding when arbitration is used to settle labor-contract disputes (10)

arithmetic mean   the sum of all the values of a set of data, divided by the number of items in the set (15)

arithmetic-logic unit   the part of a computer that performs mathematical operations, comparisons of data, and other types of data transformations (15)

artificial intelligence a combination of computer hardware and software that exhibits the same type of intelligence as human beings (15)

assets the things of value that a firm owns (16)

authoritarian leader one who holds all authority and responsibility, with communication usually moving from top to bottom (5)

authority the power, within the organization, to accomplish an assigned job or task (6)

automobile liability insurance insurance that covers financial losses resulting from injuries or damages caused by the insured vehicle (20)

automobile physical damage insurance insurance that covers damage to the insured vehicle (20)

balance of payments the total flow of money into the country less the total flow of money out of the country, over some period of time (23)

balance of trade the total value of a nation's exports less the total value of its imports, over some period of time (23)

balance sheet (or statement of financial position) a summary of a firm's assets, liabilities, and owners' equity accounts at a particular time, showing the various dollar amounts that enter into the accounting equation (16)

bankruptcy a legal procedure designed both to protect an individual or business that cannot meet its financial obligations and to protect the creditors involved (21)

bargaining unit the specific group of employees represented by a union (10)

barter system a system of exchange in which goods or services are traded directly for other goods and/or services—without using money (1, 17)

bear market a market in which average stock prices are declining (19)

behavior modification the use of a systematic program of reinforcement to encourage desirable organizational behavior (8)

beneficiary individual or organization named in a life insurance policy as recipient of the proceeds of that policy on the death of the insured (20)

binding contract an agreement that requires an intermediary to purchase products from a particular supplier, not from the supplier's competitors (22)

blue-sky laws state laws that regulate securities trading (19)

board of directors the top governing body of a corporation, the members of which are elected by the stockholders (3)

bond indenture a legal document that details all the conditions relating to a bond issue (18)

bonus a payment in addition to wages, salary, or commissions, usually an extra reward for outstanding performance (9)

bookkeeping the routine, day-to-day record keeping that is a necessary part of accounting (16)

boycott a refusal to do business with a particular firm (10)

boycott in restraint of trade an agreement between businesses not to sell to or buy from a particular entity (22)

brand a name, term, symbol, design, or any combination of these that identifies a seller's products and distinguishes them from competitors' products (12)

brand mark the part of a brand that is a symbol or distinctive design (12)

brand name the part of a brand that can be spoken (12)

breach of contract the failure of one party to fulfill the terms of a contract when there is no legal reason for that failure (21)

breakeven quantity the number of units that must be sold for the total revenue (from all units sold) to equal the total cost (of all units sold) (12)

broker a middleman that specializes in a particular commodity, represents either a buyer or a seller, and is likely to be hired on a temporary basis (13)

budget a statement that projects income and/or expenditures over a specified future period of time (18)

budget deficit an excess of spending over income (22)

bull market a market in which average stock prices are increasing (19)

bureaucratic structure a management system based on a formal framework of authority that is carefully outlined and precisely followed (6)

business the organized effort of individuals to produce and sell, for a profit, the goods and services that satisfy society's needs (1)

business ethics the application of moral standards to business situations (2)

business interruption insurance insurance protection for a business whose operations are interrupted because of a fire, storm, or other natural disaster (20)

business plan a carefully constructed guide for the person starting one's own business (4)

buying behavior the decisions and actions of people involved in buying and using products (11)

buying long buying stock with the expectation that it will increase in value and can then be sold at a profit (19)

call premium the dollar amount over par value that the corporation has to pay an investor for redeeming either preferred stock or a corporate bond (18)

capacity the amount of input a facility can process or output it can produce in a given time (7)

capital all the financial resources, buildings, machinery, tools, and equipment that are used in an organization's operations (1)

capital-intensive technology one in which machines and equipment do most of the work (7)

captioned photograph a picture accompanied by a brief explanation (14)

carrier a firm that offers transportation services (13)

cash flow the movement of money into and out of an organization (18)

cash surrender value an amount that is payable to the holder of a whole life insurance policy if the policy is canceled (20)

catalog discount showroom a retail outlet that displays well-known brands and sells them at discount prices through catalog sales within the store (13)

caveat emptor a Latin phrase meaning "let the buyer beware" (2)

cease and desist order an order to refrain from an illegal practice (22)

centralized organization an organization that systematically works to concentrate authority at the upper levels of the organization (6)

cents-off coupon a coupon that reduces the retail price of a particular item by a stated amount at the time of purchase (14)

certificate of deposit a document stating that the bank will pay the depositor a guaranteed interest rate for money left on deposit for a specified period of time (17)

certified public accountant (CPA) an individual who has met state requirements for accounting education and experience and has passed a rigorous three-day accounting examination (16)

chain of command the line of authority that extends from the highest to the lowest levels of an organization (6)

chain retailer a firm that operates more than one retail outlet (13)

channel of distribution (or **marketing channel**) a sequence of marketing organizations that directs a product from the producer to the ultimate user (13)

check a written order for a bank or other financial institution to pay a stated dollar amount to the business or person indicated on the face of the check (17)

close corporation a corporation whose stock is owned by relatively few people and is not traded in stock markets (3)

closed shop a workplace in which workers must join the union before they are hired, outlawed by the Taft-Hartley Act (10)

coinsurance clause a part of a fire insurance policy that requires the policyholder to purchase coverage at least equal to a specified percentage of the replacement cost of the property to obtain full reimbursement for losses (20)

collateral real or personal property that a firm or individual owns and that is pledged as security for a loan (17)

collective bargaining the process of negotiating a labor contract with management (10)

commercial bank a profit-making organization that accepts deposits, makes loans, and provides related services to its customers (17)

commercial draft a written order requiring a customer (the *drawee*) to pay a specified sum of money to a supplier (the *drawer*) for goods or services (18)

commercial paper short-term promissory notes issued by large corporations (18)

commission a payment that is some percentage of sales revenue (9)

commission merchant a middleman that carries merchandise and negotiates sales for manufacturers but does not take title to the goods it sells (13)

common law the body of law created by the court decisions rendered by judges (21)

common stock stock owned by individuals or firms who may vote on corporate matters, but whose claims on profit and assets are subordinate to the claims of others (3, 18)

community of interests the situation in which one firm buys the stock of a competing firm to reduce competition between the two (22)

community shopping center a planned shopping center that includes one or two department stores and some specialty stores, along with convenience stores (13)

comparable worth a concept that seeks equal compensation for jobs requiring about the same level of education, training, and skills (9)

comparative advantage the ability to produce a specific product more efficiently than any other products (23)

compensation the payment that employees receive in return for their labor (9)

compensation system the policies and strategies that determine employee compensation (9)

competition a rivalry among businesses for sales to potential customers (1)

component part an item that becomes part of a physical product and is either a finished item ready for assembly or a product that needs little processing before assembly (12)

compressed workweek an arrangement whereby an employee works a full forty hours per week, but in less than the standard five days (6)

computer an electronic machine that can accept, store, manipulate, and transmit data in accordance with a set of specific instructions (15)

computer network a system in which several computers can either function individually or communicate with each other (15)

computer programmer a person who develops the step-by-step instructions that are contained in a computer program (15)

conceptual skill the ability to conceptualize and think in abstract terms (5)

consideration the value or benefit that one party to a contract furnishes to the other party (21)

consumer buying behavior the purchasing of products for personal or household use, not for business purposes (11)

consumer goods products purchased by individuals for personal consumption (1)

consumer product a product purchased to satisfy personal and family needs (12)

consumer sales promotion method a sales promotion method designed to attract consumers to particular retail stores and motivate them to purchase certain new or established products (14)

consumerism all those activities intended to protect the rights of consumers in their dealings with business (2)

consumers individuals who purchase goods or services for their own personal use rather than to resell them (1)

contract a legally enforceable agreement between two or more parties who promise to do, or not to do, a particular thing (21)

control unit the part of a computer that guides the entire operation of the computer (15)

controlling the process of evaluating and regulating ongoing activities to ensure that goals are achieved (5)

convenience product a relatively inexpensive, frequently purchased item for which buyers want to exert only minimal effort (12)

convenience store a small food store that sells a limited variety of products but remains open well beyond the normal business hours (13)

convertible bond a bond that can be exchanged, at the owner's option, for a specified number of shares of the corporation's common stock (18)

convertible preferred stock preferred stock that may be exchanged *at the stockholder's option* for a specified number of shares of common stock (18)

cooperative an association of individuals or firms whose purpose is to perform some business function for all its members (3)

cooperative advertising advertising whose cost is shared by a producer and one or more local retailers (14)

copyright the exclusive right to publish, perform, copy, or sell an original work (21)

corporate bond a corporation's written pledge that it will repay a specified amount of money, with interest (18)

corporate charter a contract between the corporation and the state, in which the state recognizes the formation of the artificial person that is the corporation (3)

corporate code of ethics a guide to acceptable and ethical behavior as defined by an organization (2)

corporate culture the inner rites, rituals, heroes, and values of a firm (5)

corporate officer the chairman of the board, president, executive vice president, corporate secretary and treasurer, or any other top executive appointed by the board of directors (3)

corporation an artificial person created by law, with most of the legal rights of a real person, including the right to start and operate a business, to own or dispose of property, to borrow money, to sue or be sued, and to enter into binding contracts (3)

cost of goods sold the cost of the goods a firm has sold during an accounting period; equal to beginning inventory *plus* net purchases *less* ending inventory (16)

coupon bond a bond whose ownership is not registered by the issuing company (18)

court of limited jurisdiction a court that hears only specific types of cases (21)

court of original jurisdiction   the first court to recognize and hear testimony in a legal action (21)

craft union   an organization of skilled workers in a single craft or trade (10)

creative selling   selling products to new customers and increasing sales to present customers (14)

credit   immediate purchasing power that is exchanged for a promise to repay it, with or without interest, at a later date (17)

credit union   a financial institution that accepts deposits from, and lends money to, only those people who are its members (17)

crime   a violation of a public law (21)

cumulative preferred stock   preferred stock on which any unpaid dividends accumulate and must be paid before any cash dividend is paid to the holders of common stock (18)

currency devaluation   the reduction of the value of a nation's currency relative to the currencies of other countries (23)

current assets   cash and other assets that can be quickly converted into cash or that will be used within one year (16)

current liabilities   debts that will be repaid within one year (16)

current ratio   a financial ratio that is computed by dividing current assets by current liabilities (16)

customs (or import) duty   a tax on a particular foreign product entering a country (22)

damages   a monetary settlement awarded to a party that is injured through a breach of contract (21)

data   numerical or verbal descriptions that usually result from measurements of some sort (15)

data processing   the transformation of data into a form that is useful for a specific purpose (15)

database   a single collection of data that are stored in one place and can be used by people throughout the organization to make decisions (15)

debenture bond   a bond backed only by the reputation of the issuing corporation (18)

debt capital   money obtained through loans of various types (18)

debt-to-assets ratio   a financial ratio that is calculated by dividing total liabilities by total assets; indicates the extent to which the firm's borrowing is backed by its assets (16)

debt-to-equity ratio   a financial ratio that is calculated by dividing total liabilities by owners' equity; compares the amount of financing provided by creditors with the amount provided by owners (16)

decentralized organization   an organization in which management consciously attempts to spread authority widely in the lower levels of the organization (6)

decision making   the process of developing a set of possible alternative solutions and choosing one alternative from among that set (5)

decisional role   a role that involves various aspects of management decision making (5)

deed   a written document by which the ownership of real property is transferred from one person or organization to another (21)

delegation   the assigning of part of a manager's work and power to a subordinate (6)

demand   the quantity of a product that buyers are willing to purchase at each of various prices (1, 12)

demand deposit   an amount that is on deposit in a checking account (17)

democratic leader   one who holds final responsibility but also delegates authority to others, who help determine work assignments; communication is active upward and downward (5)

department store   a retail store that (1) employs twenty-five or more persons and (2) sells at least home furnishings, appliances, family apparel, and household linens and dry goods, each in a different part of the store (13)

departmentalization   the process of grouping jobs into manageable units according to some reasonable scheme (6)

departmentalization basis   the scheme or criterion by which jobs are grouped into units (6)

departmentalization by customer   the grouping together of all activities according to the needs of the various customer groups (6)

departmentalization by function   the grouping together of all jobs that relate to the same organizational activity (6)

departmentalization by location   the grouping together of all activities according to the geographic area in which they are performed (6)

departmentalization by product   the grouping together of all activities related to a particular product or product group (6)

depreciation   the process of apportioning the cost of a fixed asset over the period during which it will be used (16)

deregulation   the process of removing existing regulations, foregoing proposed regulations, or reducing the rate at which new regulations are enacted (22)

design planning   the development of a plan for converting a product idea into an actual commodity ready for marketing (7)

diagnostic skill the ability to assess a particular situation and identify its causes (5)

direct-mail advertising promotional material that is mailed directly to individuals (14)

directing the combined processes of leading and motivating (5)

discharge by mutual assent when all parties agree to void a contract (21)

discount a deduction from the price of an item (12)

discount rate the interest rate that the Federal Reserve System charges for loans to member banks (17)

discount store a self-service general-merchandise outlet that sells goods at lower than usual prices (13)

discretionary income disposable income less savings and expenditures on food, clothing, and housing (11)

discretionary order an order to buy or sell a security that lets the broker decide when to execute the transaction and at what price (19)

disposable income personal income less all additional personal taxes (11)

dividend a distribution of earnings to the stockholders of a corporation (18)

domestic corporation a corporation in the state in which it is incorporated (3)

domestic system a method of manufacturing in which an entrepreneur distributed raw materials to various homes, where families would process them into finished goods to be offered for sale by the merchant entrepreneur (1)

door-to-door retailer a retailer that sells directly to consumers in their homes (13)

double-entry bookkeeping a system in which each financial transaction is recorded as two separate accounting entries to maintain the balance shown in the accounting equation (16)

earnings per share a financial ratio that is calculated by dividing net income after taxes by the number of shares of common stock outstanding (16)

economic community an organization of nations formed to promote the free movement of resources and products among its members and to create common economic policies (23)

economic model of social responsibility the view that society will benefit most when business is left alone to produce and market profitable products that are needed by society (2)

economics the study of how wealth is created and distributed (1)

economy the system through which a society answers the three economic questions—what, how, and for whom (1)

electronic funds transfer (EFT) system a means for performing financial transactions through a computer terminal or telephone hookup (17)

embargo a complete halt to trading with a particular nation or in a particular product (23)

employee benefit a reward that is provided indirectly to employees—mainly a service (such as insurance) paid for by the employer or an employee expense (such as college tuition) reimbursed by the employer (9)

employee training the process of teaching operations and technical employees how to do their present jobs more effectively and efficiently (9)

endorsement the payee's signature on the back of a negotiable instrument (21)

endowment life insurance life insurance that provides protection and guarantees the payment of a stated amount to the policyholder after a specified number of years (20)

entrepreneur a person who risks time, effort, and money to start and operate a business (1)

Environmental Protection Agency (EPA) the federal agency charged with enforcing laws designed to protect the environment (2)

Equal Employment Opportunity Commission (EEOC) a government agency with the power to investigate complaints of employment discrimination and the power to sue firms that practice it (2)

equity capital money received from the sale of shares of ownership in the business (18)

equity theory a theory of motivation based on the premise that people are motivated first to achieve and then to maintain a sense of equity (8)

esteem needs the human requirements for respect, recognition, and a sense of one's own accomplishment and worth (8)

ethics the study of right and wrong and of the morality of choices made by individuals (2)

excise tax a tax on the manufacture or sale of a particular domestic product (22)

exclusive distribution the use of only a single retail outlet for a product in each geographic area (13)

expectancy theory a model of motivation based on the assumption that motivation depends on how much we want something and on how likely we think we are to get it (8)

Export-Import Bank of the United States an independent agency of the U.S. government whose function is to assist in financing the exports of American firms (23)

exporting selling and shipping raw materials or products to other nations (23)

express warranty a written explanation of the responsibilities of the producer (or seller) in the event that a product is found to be defective or otherwise unsatisfactory (12, 21)

extended coverage insurance protection against damage caused by wind, hail, explosion, vandalism, riots or civil commotion, falling aircraft, and smoke (20)

external recruiting the attempt to attract job applicants from outside the organization (9)

factor a firm that specializes in buying other firms' accounts receivable (18)

factors of production three categories of resources: land, labor, capital (1)

factory system a system of manufacturing in which all of the materials, machinery, and workers required to manufacture a product are assembled in one place (1)

family branding the strategy in which a firm uses the same brand for all or most of its products (12)

feature article a piece (of up to 3,000 words) prepared by an organization for inclusion in a particular publication (14)

Federal Communications Commission (FCC) the federal agency responsible for the interstate regulation of communications, including radio, television, telephone, and telegraph (22)

Federal Energy Regulatory Commission the federal agency that oversees the interstate operations of firms that sell electricity or natural gas, or operate gas pipelines (22)

Federal Reserve System the government agency responsible for regulating the United States banking industry (17)

Federal Trade Commission (FTC) a five-member committee charged with the responsibility of investigating illegal trade practices and enforcing antitrust laws (22)

fidelity bond an insurance policy that protects a business from theft, forgery, or embezzlement by its employees (20)

financial management all those activities that are concerned with obtaining money and using it effectively (18)

financial manager a manager who is primarily responsible for the organization's financial resources (5)

financial plan a plan for obtaining and using the money that is needed to implement an organization's goals (18)

financial ratio a number that shows the relationship between two elements of a firm's financial statements (16)

fire insurance insurance that covers losses due to fire (20)

fixed assets assets that will be held or used for a period longer than one year (16)

fixed cost a cost that is incurred no matter how many units of a product are produced or sold (12)

flexible manufacturing system (FMS) a recent development in automation that combines robotics and computer-aided manufacturing in a single system (7)

flexible workweek an arrangement in which each employee chooses the hours during which he or she will work, subject to certain limitations (6)

floor planning a method of financing where the title to merchandise is given to lenders in return for short-term financing (18)

flow chart a graphic description of the types and sequences of operations in a computer program (15)

foreign corporation a corporation in any state in which it does business except the one in which it is incorporated (3)

foreign-exchange control a restriction on the amount of a particular foreign currency that can be purchased or sold (23)

form utility utility that is created by converting production inputs into finished products (7, 11)

franchise a license to operate an individually owned business as though it were part of a chain of outlets or stores (4)

franchisee a person or organization purchasing a franchise (4)

franchising the actual granting of a franchise (4)

franchisor an individual or organization granting a franchise (4)

free enterprise the system of business in which individuals are free to decide what to produce, how to produce it, and at what price to sell it (1)

free-market economy an economic system in which individuals and firms are free to enter and leave markets at will (1)

frequency distribution a listing of the number of times each value appears in a set of data (15)

full-service wholesaler a middleman that performs the entire range of wholesaler functions (13)

functional middleman a middleman that helps in the transfer of ownership of products but does not take title to the products (13)

futures contract an agreement to buy or sell a commodity at a guaranteed price on some specified future date (19)

Gantt chart a graphic scheduling device that displays the tasks to be performed on the vertical axis and the time required for each task on the horizontal axis (7)

General Agreement on Tariffs and Trade (GATT) an international organization whose goal is to reduce or eliminate tariffs and other barriers to world trade (23)

general expenses costs that are incurred in managing a business (16)

general journal a book of original entry in which typical transactions are recorded in order of their occurrence (16)

general ledger a book of accounts that contains a separate sheet or section for each account (16)

general merchandise wholesaler a middleman that deals in a wide variety of products (13)

general partner a person who assumes full or shared operational responsibility of a business (3)

generic product (or brand) a product with no brand at all (12)

goal an end state that the organization is expected to achieve (5)

goal setting the process of developing and committing an organization to a set of goals (5)

goodwill the value of a firm's reputation, location, earning capacity, and other intangibles that make the business a profitable concern (16)

government-owned corporation a corporation owned and operated by a local, state, or federal government (3)

grapevine the informal communications network within an organization (6)

graphics program a software package that enables the user to display (and often print) data and conclusions in graphic form (15)

grievance procedure a formally established course of action for resolving employee complaints against management (10)

gross national product (GNP) the total dollar value of all goods and services produced in a country for a given time period (1)

gross profit on sales a firm's net sales *less* the cost of goods sold (16)

gross sales the total dollar amount of all goods and services sold during the accounting period (16)

hard-core unemployed workers with little education or vocational training and a long history of unemployment (2)

hardware the electronic equipment or machinery used in a computer system (15)

health maintenance organization (HMO) an insurance plan that directly employs or contracts with selected physicians and hospitals to provide healthcare services in exchange for a fixed, prepaid monthly premium (20)

health-care insurance insurance that covers the cost of medical attention, including hospital care, physicians' and surgeons' fees, prescription medicines, and related services (20)

hierarchy of needs Maslow's sequence of human needs in the order of their importance (8)

hourly wage a specific amount of money paid for each hour of work (9)

human resources management all the activities involved in acquiring, maintaining, and developing an organization's human resources (9)

human resources manager a person charged with managing the organization's formal human resources programs (5)

human resources planning the development of strategies to meet a firm's human resources needs (9)

hygiene factors job factors that reduce dissatisfaction when present to an acceptable degree, but do not necessarily result in high levels of motivation, according to the motivation-hygiene theory (8)

implied warranty a guarantee that is imposed or required by law (21)

import duty (or tariff) a tax that is levied on a particular foreign product entering a country (23)

import quota a limit on the amount of a particular good that may be imported into a country during a given period of time (23)

importing purchasing raw materials or products in other nations and bringing them into one's own country (23)

income statement a summary of a firm's revenues and expenses during a specified accounting period (16)

incorporation the process of forming a corporation (3)

independent retailer a firm that operates only one retail outlet (13)

individual branding the strategy in which a firm uses a different brand for each of its products (12)

industrial product a product bought for use in a firm's operations or to make other products (12)

industrial service an intangible product that an organization uses in its operations (12)

industrial union an organization of both skilled and unskilled workers in a single industry (10)

inflation a general rise in the level of prices (1)

informal group   a group created by the members themselves to accomplish goals that may or may not be relevant to the organization (6)

informal organization   the pattern of behavior and interaction that stems from personal rather than official relationships (6)

information   data that are presented in a form that is useful for a specific purpose

informational role   a role in which the manager either gathers or provides information (5)

injunction   a court order requiring a person or group either to perform some act or to refrain from performing some act (10)

inland marine insurance   insurance that protects against loss or damage to goods shipped by rail, truck, airplane, or inland barge (20)

input unit   the device used to enter data into a computer (15)

inspection   the examination of output to control quality (7)

institutional advertising   advertising designed to enhance a firm's image or reputation (14)

insurable risk   a risk that insurance companies will assume (20)

insurance   the protection against loss that is afforded by the purchase of an insurance policy (20)

insurance policy   the contract between an insurer and the person or firm whose risk is assumed (20)

insurer (or insurance company)   a firm that agrees, for a fee, to assume financial responsibility for losses that may result from a specific risk (20)

intangible assets   assets that do not exist physically but that have a value based on legal rights or advantages that they confer on a firm (16)

intensive distribution   the use of all available outlets for a product (13)

interlocking directorate   an arrangement in which members of the board of directors of one firm are also directors of a competing firm (22)

internal recruiting   considering present employees as applicants for available positions (9)

international business   all business activities that involve exchanges across national boundaries (23)

International Monetary Fund (IMF)   an international bank that makes short-term loans to countries experiencing balance-of-payment deficits (23)

interpersonal role   a role in which the manager deals with people (5)

interpersonal skill   the ability to deal effectively with other people (5)

Interstate Commerce Commission (ICC)   the federal agency responsible for the licensing and regulation of carriers (22)

intrapreneur   an entrepreneur working in an organizational environment who develops an idea into a product and manages the product within the firm (6)

inventory   stocks of goods and materials (7)

inventory control   the process of managing inventories in such a way as to minimize inventory costs, including both holding costs and potential stock-out costs (7, 13)

inventory turnover   a financial ratio that is calculated by dividing the cost of goods sold in one year by the average value of the inventory; measures the number of times the firm sells and replaces its merchandise inventory in one year (16)

investment banking firm   an organization that assists corporations in raising funds, usually by helping sell new security issues (19)

involuntary bankruptcy   a bankruptcy procedure initiated by creditors (21)

job analysis   a systematic procedure for studying jobs to determine their various elements and requirements (9)

job description   a list of the elements that make up a particular job (9)

job enlargement   giving a worker more things to do within the same job (6)

job enrichment   providing workers with both more tasks to do and more control over how they do their work (6)

job evaluation   the process of determining the relative worth of the various jobs within a firm (9)

job rotation   the systematic shifting of employees from one job to another (6)

job security   protection against the loss of employment (10)

job sharing   an arrangement whereby two people share one full-time position (6)

job specialization   the separation of all organizational activities into distinct tasks and the assignment of different tasks to different people (6)

job specification   a list of the qualifications required to perform a particular job (9)

joint venture   a partnership that is formed to achieve a specific goal or to operate for a specific period of time (3)

jurisdiction   the right of a particular union to organize particular workers (10)

just-in-time inventory system   a system designed to ensure that materials or supplies arrive at a facility just when they are needed (7)

labeling the presentation of information on a product or its package (12)

labor union an organization or workers acting together to negotiate their wages and working conditions with employers (10)

labor-intensive technology one in which people must do most of the work (7)

laissez-faire capitalism an economic system characterized by private ownership of property, free entry into markets, and the absence of government intervention (1)

laissez-faire leader one who waives responsibility and allows subordinates to work as they choose with a minimum of interference; communication flows horizontally among group members (5)

law a rule developed by a society to govern the conduct of, and relationship among, its members (21)

leadership the ability to influence others (5)

leading the process of influencing people to work toward a common goal (5)

lease an agreement by which the right to use real property is temporarily transferred from its owner, the landlord, to a tenant (21)

leverage the use of borrowed funds to increase the return on an investment (19)

liabilities a firm's debts and obligations—what it owes to others (16)

licensing a contractual agreement in which one firm permits another to produce and market its product and use its brand name in return for a royalty or other compensation (23)

life insurance insurance that pays a stated amount of money on the death of the insured individual (20)

limit order a request that a stock be bought or sold at a price that is equal to or better than some specified price (19)

limited liability a feature of corporate ownership that limits each owner's financial liability to the amount of money she or he has paid for the corporation's stock (3)

limited partner a person who contributes capital to a business but is not active in managing it; this partner's liability is limited to the amount that he or she has invested (3)

limited-line wholesaler a middleman that stocks only a few product lines (13)

limited-service wholesaler a middleman that assumes responsibility for a few wholesale services only (13)

line management position a position that is part of the chain of command and that includes direct responsibility for achieving the goals of the organization (6)

line of credit a loan that is approved before the money is actually needed (17)

liquidity the ease with which an asset can be converted into cash (16, 19)

lockout a firm's refusal to allow employees to enter the workplace (10)

long-term financing money that will be used for longer than one year (18)

long-term liabilities debts that need not be repaid for at least one year (16)

lower-level manager a manager who coordinates and supervises the activities of operating employees (5)

mail-order retailer a retailer that solicits orders by mailing catalogs to potential customers (13)

maintenance shop a workplace in which an employee who joins the union must remain a union member as long as he or she is employed by the firm (10)

major equipment large tools and machines used for production purposes (12)

management the process of coordinating the resources of an organization to achieve the primary goals of the organization (5)

management by objectives (MBO) a motivation technique in which a manager and his or her subordinates collaborate in setting goals (8)

management development the process of preparing managers and other professionals to assume increased responsibility in both present and future positions (9)

management excellence an approach to management that promotes feelings of excellence in employees (5)

management information system (MIS) a system that provides managers with the information they need to perform their functions as effectively as possible (15)

managerial hierarchy the arrangement that provides increasing authority at higher levels of management (6)

manufacturer (or producer) brand a brand that is owned by a manufacturer (12)

manufacturer's sales branch essentially a merchant wholesaler that is owned by a manufacturer (13)

manufacturer's sales office essentially a sales agent that is owned by a manufacturer (13)

margin requirement the proportion of the price of a stock that cannot be borrowed (19)

market a group of individuals, organizations, or both

who have needs for products in a given category and who have the ability, willingness, and authority to purchase such products (11)

market allocation   an agreement to divide a market among potential competitors (22)

market order   a request that a stock be purchased or sold at the current market price (19)

market price   in pure competition, the price at which the quantity demanded is exactly equal to the quantity supplied (1)

market segment   a group of individuals or organizations, within a market, that share one or more common characteristics (11)

market segmentation   the process of dividing a market into segments and directing a marketing mix at a particular segment or segments rather than at the total market (11)

market value   the price of one share of a stock at a particular time (19)

marketing   the process of planning and executing the conception, pricing, promotion, and distribution of ideas, goods, and services to create exchanges that satisfy individual and organizational objectives (11)

marketing concept   the business philosophy that involves the entire organization in the process of satisfying customers' needs while achieving the organization's goals (11)

marketing information system   a system for managing marketing information that is gathered continually from internal and external sources (11)

marketing manager   a manager who is responsible for facilitating the exchange of products between the organization and its customers or clients (5)

marketing mix   a combination of product, price, distribution, and promotion developed to satisfy a particular target market (11)

marketing research   the process of systematically gathering, recording, and analyzing data concerning a particular marketing problem (11)

marketing strategy   a plan that will enable an organization to make the best use of its resources and advantages to meet its objectives (11)

markup   the amount that a seller adds to the cost of a product to determine its basic price (12)

materials handling   the actual physical handling of goods, in warehousing as well as during transportation (13)

matrix structure   an organizational structure that combines vertical and horizontal lines of authority by superimposing product departmentaliza-

tion on a functionally departmentalized organization (6)

maturity date   the date on which the corporation is to repay the borrowed money (18)

measure of value   a single standard or "yardstick" that is used to assign values to, and compare the values of, products and resources (17)

median   the value that appears at the exact middle of a set of data when the data are arranged in order (15)

mediation   the use of a neutral third party to assist management and the union during their negotiations (10)

medium of exchange   anything that is accepted as payment for products and resources (17)

memory (or storage unit)   that part of a computer that stores all data entered into the computer and processed by it (15)

merchant middleman   a middleman that actually takes title to products by buying them (13)

merchant wholesaler   a middleman that purchases goods in large quantities and then sells them to other wholesalers or retailers and to institutional, farm, government, professional, or industrial users (13)

merger   the purchase of one corporation by another (3)

middle manager   a manager who implements the strategy and major policies developed by top management (5)

middleman (or marketing intermediary)   a marketing organization that links a producer and user within a marketing channel (13)

minority   a racial, religious, political, national, or other group regarded as different from the larger group of which it is a part, often singled out for unfavorable treatment (2)

mission   the means by which an organization is to fulfill its purpose (5)

missionary salesperson   a salesperson—generally employed by a manufacturer—who visits retailers to persuade them to buy the manufacturer's products (14)

mixed economy   an economy that exhibits elements of both capitalism and socialism (1)

mode   the value that appears most frequently in a set of data (15)

money   anything used by a society to purchase goods and services or resources (17)

monopolistic competition   a market situation in which there are many buyers along with relatively many sellers who differentiate their products from the products of competitors (1)

monopoly   a market (or industry) with only one seller (1)

morale   a person's attitude toward his or her job, superiors, and the firm itself (8)

mortgage bond   a corporate bond that is secured by various assets of the issuing firm (18)

motivating   the process of providing reasons for people to work in the best interests of the organization (5)

motivation   the individual, internal process that energizes, directs, and sustains behavior; the personal "force" that causes one to behave in a particular way (8)

motivation factors   job factors that increase motivation, but whose absence does not necessarily result in dissatisfaction according to the motivation-hygiene theory (8)

motivation-hygiene theory   the idea that satisfaction and dissatisfaction are distinct and separate dimensions (8)

multilateral development bank (MDB)   an internationally supported bank that provides loans to developing countries to help them grow (23)

multinational enterprise   a firm that operates on a worldwide scale, without ties to any specific nation or region (23)

multiple-unit pricing   the strategy of setting a single price for two or more units (12)

mutual fund   a professionally managed investment vehicle that combines and invests the funds of many individual investors (19)

mutual insurance company   an insurance company that is collectively owned by its policyholders and is thus a cooperative (20)

mutual savings bank   a bank that is owned by its depositors (17)

National Alliance of Businessmen (NAB)   a joint business-government program to train the hardcore unemployed (2)

National Association of Securities Dealers (NASD)   the organization responsible for the self-regulation of the over-the-counter securities market (19)

national bank   a commercial bank that is chartered by the U.S. Comptroller of the Currency (17)

National Labor Relations Board (NLRB)   the federal agency that enforces the provisions of the Wagner Act (10)

natural monopoly   an industry requiring huge investments in capital and within which duplication of facilities would be wasteful and, thus, not in the public interest (1, 22)

need   a personal requirement (8)

negligence   a failure to exercise reasonable care, resulting in injury to another (21)

negotiable instrument   a written document that (1) is a promise to pay a stated sum of money and (2) can be transferred from one person or firm to another (21)

neighborhood shopping center   a planned shopping center consisting of several small convenience and specialty stores (13)

net income   the profit earned (or the loss suffered) by a firm during an accounting period, after all expenses have been deducted from revenues (16)

net profit margin   a financial ratio that is calculated by dividing net income after taxes by net sales (16)

net sales   the actual dollar amount received by a firm for the goods and services it has sold, after adjustment for returns, allowances, and discounts (16)

news release   a typed page of generally fewer than 300 words provided by an organization to the media as a form of publicity (14)

no-fault auto insurance   a method of paying for losses suffered in an automobile accident; enacted by state law, requires that those suffering injury or loss be reimbursed by their own insurance companies, without regard to who was at fault in the accident (20)

nonprice competition   competition that is based on factors other than price (12)

nontariff barter   a nontax measure imposed by a government to favor domestic over foreign suppliers (23)

not-for-profit corporation   a corporation that is organized to provide a social, educational, religious, or other nonbusiness service rather than to earn a profit (3)

notes payable   obligations that have been secured with promissory notes (16)

NOW account   an interest-bearing checking account; NOW stands for Negotiable Order of Withdrawal (17)

objective   a specific statement detailing what an organization intends to accomplish as it goes about its mission (5)

ocean marine insurance   insurance that protects the policyholder against loss or damage to a ship or its cargo on the high seas (20)

odd lot   fewer than 100 shares of a particular stock (19)

odd pricing   the strategy of setting prices at odd amounts that are slightly below an even or whole number of dollars (12)

oligopoly   a market situation (or industry) in which there are few sellers (1)

open corporation   a corporation whose stock is traded openly in stock markets and can be purchased by any individual (3)

open-market operations   the buying and selling of U.S. government securities by the Federal Reserve System for the purpose of controlling the supply of money (17)

operating expenses   those costs that do not result directly from the purchase or manufacture of the products a firm sells (16)

operational planning   the development of plans for utilizing production facilities and resources (7)

operations management   all the activities that managers engage in for the purpose of producing goods and services (7)

operations manager   manager who creates and manages the systems that convert resources into goods and services (5)

option   the right to buy or sell a specified amount or stock at a specified price within a certain period of time (19)

order getter   a salesperson who is responsible for selling the firm's products to new customers and increasing sales to present customers (14)

order processing   those activities that are involved in receiving and filling customers' purchase orders (13)

order taker   a salesperson who handles repeat sales in ways that maintain positive relationships with customers (14)

organic structure   a management system founded on cooperation and knowledge-based authority (6)

organization   a group of two or more people working together in a predetermined fashion to achieve a common set of goals (6)

organization chart   a diagram that represents the positions and relationships within an organization (6)

organizational buying behavior   the purchasing of products by producers, governmental units, institutions, and resellers (11)

organizational height   the number of layers, or levels, of management in a firm (6)

organizational structure   a fixed pattern of (1) positions within an organization and (2) relationships among those positions (6)

organizing   the grouping of resources and activities to accomplish some end result in an efficient and effective manner (5)

orientation   the process of acquainting new employees with an organization (9)

outdoor advertising   short promotional messages on billboards, posters, and signs, and in skywriting (14)

output unit   the mechanism by which a computer transmits processed data to the user (15)

over-the-counter (OTC) market   a network of stockbrokers who buy and sell the securities of corporations that are not listed on securities exchange (19)

overtime   time worked in excess of forty hours in one week; under some union contracts, it can be time worked in excess of eight hours in a single day (10)

owners' equity   the difference between a firm's assets and its liabilities—what would be left over for the firm's owners if its assets were used to pay off its liabilities (16)

packaging   all those activities involved in developing and providing a container for a product (12)

par value   an assigned (and often arbitrary) dollar value printed on the face of a stock certificate (18)

participating preferred stock   preferred stock whose owners share in the corporation's earnings, along with the owners of common stock (18)

partnership   an association of two or more persons to act as co-owners of a business for profit (3)

patent   the exclusive right to make, use, or sell a newly invented product or process (21)

penetration pricing   the strategy of setting a low price for a new product

performance   the fulfillment of all obligations by all parties to the contract (21)

performance appraisal   the evaluation of employees' current and potential levels of performance to allow superiors to make objective human resource decisions (9)

personal income   the income an individual receives from all sources less the Social Security taxes that the individual must pay (11)

personal investment   the use of one's personal funds to earn a financial return (19)

personal property   all property other than real property (21)

personal selling   personal communication aimed at informing customers and persuading them to buy a firm's products (14)

PERT (Program Evaluation and Review Technique)   a technique for scheduling a process or project and maintaining control of the schedule (7)

physical distribution   all those activities concerned with the efficient movement of products from the producer to the ultimate user (13)

physiological needs   the things human beings require for survival (8)

picketing   marching back and forth in front of one's place of employment with signs informing the public that a strike is in progress (10)

piece-rate system   a compensation system under which employees are paid a certain amount for each unit of output they produce (8)

place utility   utility that is created by making a product available at a location where customers wish to purchase it (11)

plan   an outline of the actions by which an organization intends to accomplish its goals (5)

planned economy   an economy in which the answers to the three basic economic questions (what, how, and for whom) are determined, to some degree, through centralized government planning (1)

planning   the processes involved in developing plans (5)

planning horizon   the period during which a plan will be in effect (7)

plant layout   the arrangement of machinery, equipment, and personnel within a facility (7)

point-of-purchase display   promotional material that is placed within a retail store (14)

policy   a general guide for action in a situation that occurs repeatedly (5)

pollution   the contamination of water, air, or land through the actions of people in an industrialized society (2)

positioning   the development of a product image in buyers' minds relative to the images they have of competing products (14)

possession utility   utility that is created by transferring title (or ownership) of a product to the buyer (11)

posting   the process of transferring journal entries to the general ledger (16)

power of attorney   a legal document that serves as evidence that an agent has been appointed to act on behalf of a principal (21)

pre-emptive rights   the rights of current stockholders to purchase any new stock that the corporation issues before it is sold to the general public (18)

preferred stock   stock owned by individuals or firms who usually do not have voting rights, but whose claims on profit and assets take precedence over those of common-stock owners (3, 18)

premium   a gift that a producer offers the customer in return for using its product (14)

premium   the fee charged by an insurance company (20)

prepaid expenses   assets that have been paid for in advance but not yet used (16)

press conference   a meeting at which invited media personnel hear important news announcements and receive supplementary textual materials and photographs (14)

prestige pricing   the strategy of setting a high price to project an aura of quality and status (12)

price   the amount of money that a seller is willing to accept in exchange for a product, at a given time and under given circumstances (12)

price competition   an emphasis on setting a price equal to or lower than competitors' to gain sales or market share (12)

price discrimination   the practice in which producers and wholesalers charge larger firms a lower price for goods than they charge smaller firms (22)

price fixing   an agreement between two businesses as to the prices to be charged for goods (22)

price lining   the strategy of selling goods only at certain predetermined prices that reflect definite price breaks (12)

price skimming   the strategy of charging the highest-possible price for a product during the introduction stage of its life cycle (12)

primary market   a market in which an investor purchases financial securities (via an investment bank or other representative) from the issuer of those securities (19)

primary-demand advertising   advertising whose purpose is to increase the demand for all brands of a good or service (14)

prime interest rate   the lowest rate charged by a bank for a short-term loan (18)

principle of indemnity   In the event of a loss, an insured firm or individual cannot collect, from the insurer, an amount greater than the actual dollar amount of the loss. (20)

private accountant   an accountant who is employed by a specific organization (16)

private law   the body of law that governs the relationships between two or more individuals or businesses (21)

process material   a material that is used directly in the production of another product and is not readily identifiable in the finished product (12)

product   everything that one receives in an exchange, including all tangible and intangible attributes and expected benefits; it may be a good, service, or idea (12)

product deletion   the elimination of one or more products from a product line (12)

product design   the process of creating a set of specifications from which a product can be produced (7)

product differentiation   the process of developing and

promoting differences between one's product and all similar products (12)

product liability insurance insurance that protects the policyholder from financial losses due to injuries suffered by others as a result of using the policyholder's products (20)

product life cycle a series of stages in which a product's sales revenue and profit increase, reach a peak, and then decline (12)

product line a group of similar products that differ only in relatively minor characteristics (7)

product line a group of similar products that differ only in relatively minor characteristics (12)

product mix all the products that a firm offers for sale (12)

product modification the process of changing one or more of a product's characteristics (12)

production the process of converting resources into goods, services, or ideas (7)

productivity the average level of output per unit of time per worker (1, 7)

productivity the average output per hour for all workers in the private business sector (5)

profit what remains after all business expenses have been deducted from sales revenue (1)

profit sharing the distribution of a percentage of the firm's profit among its employees (9)

progressive tax a tax that requires the payment of an increasing proportion of income as the individual's income increases (22)

promissory note a written pledge by a borrower to pay a certain sum of money to a creditor at a specified future date (18)

promotion communication that is intended to inform, persuade, or remind an organization's target markets of the organization or its products (14)

promotion mix the particular combination of promotion methods that a firm uses in its promotional campaign to reach a target market (14)

promotional campaign a plan for combining and using the four promotion methods—advertising, personal selling, sales promotion, and publicity—in a particular promotion mix to reach one or more marketing goals (14)

property anything that can be owned (21)

proportional tax a tax whose percentage rate remains constant as the tax base increases (22)

prospectus a detailed written description of a new security, the issuing corporation, and the corporation's top management (19)

proxy a legal form that lists issues to be decided at a stockholders' meeting and requests that stock-

holders transfer their voting rights to some other individual or individuals (3)

public accountant an accountant whose services may be hired on a fee basis by individuals or firms (16)

public law the body of law that deals with the relationships between individuals or businesses and society (21)

public liability insurance insurance that protects the policyholder from financial losses due to injuries suffered by others as a result of negligence on the part of a business owner or employee (20)

public relations all activities whose objective is to create and maintain a favorable public image (14)

publicity a nonpersonal message delivered in newsstory form through a mass medium, free of charge (14)

purchasing all the activities involved in obtaining required materials, supplies, and parts from other firms (7)

pure competition the market situation in which there are many buyers and sellers of a product, and no single buyer or seller is powerful enough to affect the price of that product (1)

pure risk a risk that involves only the possibility of loss, with no potential for gain (20)

purpose the reason for an organization's existence (5)

quality circle a group of employees who meet on company time to solve problems of product quality (7)

quality control the process of ensuring that goods and services are produced in accordance with design specifications (7)

quasi-government corporation a business owned partly by the government and partly by private citizens or firms (3)

range the difference between the highest value and the lowest value in a set of data (15)

ratification approval of a labor contract by a vote of the union membership (10)

raw material a basic material that actually becomes part of a physical product; usually comes from mines, forests, oceans, recycled solid wastes (12)

real gross national product the total dollar value, adjusted for price increases, of all goods and services produced in a country during a given time period (1)

real property land and anything that is permanently attached to it (21)

recruiting the process of attracting qualified job applicants (9)

refund a return of part of the purchase price of a product (14)

regional shopping center a planned shopping center containing large department stores, numerous specialty stores, restaurants, movie theaters, and sometimes hotels (13)

registered bond a bond that is registered in the owner's name by the issuing company (18)

regressive tax a tax that takes a greater percentage of a lower income than of a higher income (22)

reinforcement theory a theory of motivation based on the premise that behavior that is rewarded is likely to be repeated, whereas behavior that has been punished is less likely to recur (8)

replacement chart a list of key personnel and their possible replacements within the firm (9)

research and development (R&D) an organized set of activities intended to identify new ideas and technical advances that have the potential to result in new goods and services (7)

reserve requirement the percentage of its deposits that a bank *must* retain, either in its own vault or on deposit with its Federal Reserve district bank (17)

responsibility the duty to do a job or perform a task (6)

retailer a middleman that buys from producers or other middlemen and sells to consumers (13)

retained earnings the portion of a business's profits that is not distributed to stockholders (18)

return on equity a financial ratio that is calculated by dividing net income after taxes by owners' equity (16)

revenues dollar amounts received by a firm (16)

revolving credit agreement a guaranteed line of credit (17, 18)

reward system the formal mechanism for defining, evaluating, and rewarding employee performance (8)

risk the possibility that a loss or injury will occur (20)

risk management the process of evaluating the risks faced by a firm or an individual and then minimizing the costs involved with those risks (20)

robotics the use of programmable machines to perform a variety of tasks by manipulating materials and tools (7)

round lot a unit of 100 shares of a particular stock (19)

S-corporation a corporation that is taxed as though it were a partnership (3)

safety needs the things human beings require for physical and emotional security (8)

salary a specific amount of money paid for an employee's work during a set calendar period, regardless of the actual number of hours worked (9)

sales agreement a type of contract by which ownership is transferred from a seller to a buyer (21)

sales forecast an estimate of the amount of a product that an organization expects to sell during a certain period of time, based on a specified level of marketing effort (11)

sales promotion the use of activities or materials as direct inducements to customers or salespersons (14)

sales support personnel employees who aid in selling but are more involved in locating prospects, educating customers, building goodwill for the firm, and providing follow-up service (14)

sample a free package or container of a product (14)

savings and loan association (S&L) a financial institution that primarily accepts savings deposits and provides home-mortgage loans (17)

scheduling the process of ensuring that materials are at the right place at the right time (7)

scientific management the application of scientific principles to management of work and workers (8)

secondary market a market for existing financial securities that are currently traded between investors (19)

Securities and Exchange Commission (SEC) the agency that enforces federal securities regulations (19)

securities exchange a marketplace where member brokers meet to buy and sell securities (19)

selection the process of gathering information about applicants for a position and then using that information to choose the most appropriate applicant (9)

selective (or brand) advertising advertising that is used to sell a particular brand of product (14)

selective distribution the use of only a portion or percentage of the available outlets for a product in each geographic area (13)

self-insurance the process of establishing a monetary fund that can be used to cover the cost of a loss (20)

self-realization needs the needs to grow and develop as people and to become all that we are capable of being (8)

selling expenses costs that are related to the firm's marketing activities (16)

selling short the process of selling stock that an

investor does not actually own but has borrowed from a stockbroker and will repay at a later date (19)

seniority   the length of time an employee has worked for the organization (10)

serial bonds   bonds of a single issue that mature on different dates (18)

Service Corps of Retired Executives (SCORE)   a group of retired business people who volunteer their services to small businesses through the SBA (4)

service economy   an economy in which the majority of the work force is involved in service industries; one in which more effort is devoted to the production of services than to the production of goods (1, 7)

shop steward   an employee who is elected by union members to serve as their representative (10)

shopping product   an item for which buyers are willing to expend considerable effort on planning and making the purchase (12)

short-term financing   money that will be used for a period of one year or less and then repaid (18)

sinking fund   a sum of money to which deposits are made each year for the purpose of redeeming a bond issue (18)

skills inventory   a computerized data bank containing information on the skills and experience of all present employees (9)

slowdown   a technique whereby workers report to their jobs but work at a slower pace than normal (10)

small business   one which is independently owned and operated for profit and is not dominant in its field (4)

Small Business Administration (SBA)   a governmental agency that assists, counsels, and protects the interests of small businesses in the United States (4)

Small Business Development Center (SBDC)   university-based group that provides individual counseling and practical training to owners of small businesses (4)

Small Business Institute (SBI)   a group of senior and graduate students in business administration who provide management counseling to small businesses (4)

Small Business Investment Company (SBIC)   privately owned firm that provides venture capital to small enterprises that meet its investment standards (4)

social audit   a comprehensive report of what an organization has done, and is doing, with regard to social issues that affect it (2)

social needs   the human requirements for love and affection and a sense of belonging (8)

social responsibility   the recognition that business activities have an impact on society, and the consideration of that impact in business decision making (2)

socioeconomic model of social responsibility   the concept that business should emphasize not only profits, but the impact of its decisions on society (2)

software   the set of instructions that tells a computer what to do (15)

sole proprietorship   a business that is owned (and usually operated) by one person (3)

span of management (or **span of control**)   the number of subordinates who report directly to one manager (6)

specialization   the separation of a manufacturing process into distinct tasks and the assignment of different tasks to different individuals (1)

specialty product   an item that possesses one or more unique characteristics for which a significant group of buyers is willing to expend considerable purchasing effort (12)

specialty store   a retail outlet that sells a single category of merchandise (13)

specialty-line wholesaler   a middleman that carries a select group of products within a single line (13)

specific performance   the legal requirement that the parties to a contract fulfill their obligations according to the contract (as opposed to settlement via payment of damages) (21)

speculative investment   an investment that is made in the hope of earning a relatively large profit in a short time (19)

speculative risk   a risk that accompanies the possibility of earning a profit (20)

spot trading   the buying and selling of commodities for immediate delivery (19)

spreadsheet program   a software package that allows the user to organize data into a grid of rows and columns (15)

staff management position   a position created to provide support, advice, and expertise within an organization (6)

standard of living   a loose, subjective measure of how well off an individual or a society is, mainly in terms of want satisfaction through goods and services (1)

standard operating procedure (SOP)   a plan that outlines the steps to be taken in a situation that arises again and again (5)

standing committee   a relatively permanent committee charged with performing some recurring task (6)

state bank   a commercial bank that is chartered by the banking authorities in the state in which it operates (17)

statistic   a measure of a particular characteristic of a group of numbers (15)

statute   a law that is passed by the U.S. Congress, a state legislature, or a local government (21)

statutory law   all the laws that have been enacted by legislative bodies (21)

stock   the shares of ownership of a corporation (3)

stock average (or **stock index**)   an average of the current market prices of selected stocks (19)

stock dividend   a dividend in the form of additional stock (19)

stock insurance company   an insurance company that is owned by stockholders and is operated to earn a profit (20)

stock split   the division of each outstanding share of a corporation's stock into a greater number of shares (19)

stockholder   a person who owns a corporation's stock (3)

store (or **private**) **brand**   a brand that is owned by an individual wholesaler or retailer (12)

store of value   a means for retaining and accumulating wealth (17)

strategy   an organization's broadest set of plans, developed as a guide for major policy setting and decision making; it defines what business the company is in or wants to be in and the kind of company it is or wants to be (5)

strict product liability   the legal concept that holds that a manufacturer is responsible for injuries caused by its products even if it was not negligent (21)

strike   a temporary work stoppage by employees, calculated to add force to their demands (10)

strikebreaker   a nonunion employee who performs the job of a striking union member (10)

supermarket   a large self-service store that sells primarily food and household products (13)

superstore   a large retail store that carries not only food and nonfood products ordinarily found in supermarkets but also additional product lines (13)

supply   an item that facilitates production and operations but does not become part of the finished product (12)

supply   the quantity of a product that producers are willing to sell at each of various prices (1, 12)

syndicate   a temporary association of individuals or firms, organized to perform a specific task that requires a large amount of capital (3)

tabular display   an array of verbal or numerical information in columns and rows (15)

tactical plan   a small-scale, short-range plan developed to implement a strategy (5)

target market   a group of persons for whom a firm develops and maintains a marketing mix suitable for the specific needs and preferences of that group (11)

task force   a committee established to investigate a major problem or pending decision (6)

technical salesperson   a salesperson who assists the company's current customers in technical matters (14)

technical skill   a specific skill needed to accomplish a specialized activity (5)

technology   the knowledge and process required to transform input resources into outputs such as specific products (7)

term life insurance   life insurance that provides protection to beneficiaries for a stated period of time (20)

term-loan agreement   a promissory note that requires a borrower to repay a loan in monthly, quarterly, semiannual, or annual installments (18)

Theory X   a concept of employee motivation generally consistent with Taylor's scientific management; assumes that employees dislike work and will function only in a highly controlled work environment (8)

Theory Y   a concept of employee motivation generally consistent with the ideas of the human relations movement; assumes that employees accept responsibility and work toward organizational goals if by so doing they also achieve personal rewards (8)

Theory Z   the belief that some middle ground between Ouchi's Type A and Type J practices is best for American business (5)

time deposit   an amount that is on deposit in an interest-bearing savings account (17)

time utility   utility that is created by making a product available when customers wish to purchase it (11)

top manager   an upper-level executive who guides and controls the overall fortunes of the organization (5)

tort   a violation of a private law (21)

total cost   the sum of the fixed costs and the variable costs attributed to a product (12)

total market approach a single marketing mix directed at the entire market for a particular product (11)

total revenue the total amount received from sales of a product (12)

trade credit a payment delay that a supplier grants to its customers (18)

trade deficit an unfavorable balance of trade (23)

trade sales promotion method a sales promotion method designed to encourage wholesalers and retailers to stock and actively promote a manufacturer's product (14)

trade salesperson a salesperson—generally employed by a food producer or processor—who assists customers in promoting products, especially in retail stores (14)

trade show an industrywide exhibit at which many sellers display their products (14)

trademark a brand that is registered with the U.S. Patent and Trademark Office and is thus legally protected from use by anyone except its owner (12, 21)

trading stamp a stamp given out by retailers in proportion to the amount spent; redeemable for a gift (14)

transportation the shipment of products to customers (13)

trial balance a summary of the balances of all general ledger accounts at the end of the accounting period (16)

trust a business combination that is created when one firm obtains control of competing firms by purchasing their stock or their assets (22)

trustee an independent firm or individual that acts as the bond owners' representative (18)

tying agreement a contract that forces an intermediary to purchase unwanted products along with the products it actually wants to buy (22)

Uniform Commercial Code (UCC) a set of laws designed to eliminate differences among state regulations affecting business and to simplify interstate commerce (21)

uninsurable risk a risk that insurance firms will not assume (20)

union security protection of the union's position as the employees' bargaining agent (10)

union shop a workplace in which new employees must join the union after a specified probationary period (10)

union-management (or labor) relations the dealings between labor unions and business management, both in the bargaining process and beyond it (10)

universal life insurance life insurance that combines insurance protection with an investment plan that offers a potentially greater return than that guaranteed by a whole life insurance policy (20)

unlimited liability a legal concept that holds a sole proprietor personally responsible for all the debts of his or her business (3)

unsecured financing financing that is not backed by collateral (18)

usury the practice of charging interest in excess of the maximum legal rate (21)

utility the ability of a good or service to satisfy a human need (7, 11)

variable cost a cost that depends on the number of units produced (12)

venture capital money that is invested in small (and sometimes struggling) firms that have the potential to become very successful (4)

vertical channel integration the combining of two or more stages of a distribution channel under a single firm's management (13)

vertical marketing system (VMS) a centrally managed distribution channel resulting from vertical channel integration (13)

visual display a diagram that represents several items of information in a manner that makes comparison easier or reflects trends among the items (15)

voluntary agreement a contract requirement consisting of an offer by one party to enter into a contract with a second party and acceptance by the second party of all the terms and conditions of the offer (21)

voluntary bankruptcy a bankruptcy procedure initiated by an individual or business that can no longer meet its financial obligations (21)

wage survey a collection of data on prevailing wage rates within an industry or a geographic area (9)

warehouse store a minimal-service retail food outlet (13)

warehousing the set of activities that are involved in receiving and storing goods and preparing them for reshipment (13)

wheel of retailing a hypothesis that suggests that new retail operations usually begin at the bottom—in price, profits, and prestige—and gradually evolve up the cost/price scale, competing with newer businesses that are evolving in the same way (13)

whistle blowing informing the press or government officials about unethical practices within one's organization (2)

whole life insurance life insurance that provides both protection and savings (20)

wholesaler a middleman that sells products to other firms (13)

wildcat strike a strike that has not been approved by the strikers' union (10)

word processing program a software package that allows the user to store documents (letters, memos, reports) in the computer memory or on a magnetic disk (15)

worker's compensation insurance insurance that covers medical expenses and provides salary continuation for employees who are injured while they are at work (20)

working capital the difference between current assets and current liabilities (16)

zero-based budgeting a budgeting approach in which every expense must be justified in every budget (18)

CREDITS

Continued from page iv.

CHAPTER 3

66 George Obremski/The Image Bank. **68** A. J. Bernstein. **70** Sunny Bak/Shooting Star. **73** Armen Kachaturian. **84** Courtesy of Marriott Corporation. **88** Courtesy Museum of Fine Arts, Boston. **91** SmithKline Beecham. **92** Courtesy of Ocean Spray Cranberries, Inc.

CHAPTER 4

98 Tony Sylvestro. **100** David Wagenaar. **102** © Peter Darley Miller/Visages. **109** Bob Sebree. **110** Francis Murphy. **112** *Inc.* Magazine, 38 Commercial Wharf, Boston, MA 02110. **117** © Cameron Mitchell.

CHAPTER 5

128 Courtesy of Marriott Corporation. **130** © Scott Frances/Esto. **132** Nancy Rica Schiff. **134** Photo by Paul Markow, Markow Southwest. **137** © Steve Liss. **145** Courtesy of Gerber Products Co. Photo: Sandi Hedrich.

CHAPTER 6

160 Steve Proehl/The Image Bank. **162** © Joyce Ravid. **166** © 1987 National Broadcasting Company, Inc. **169** Dixie Yarns, Inc.–1988 Annual Report. **176** Courtesy of Walgreen Co. **183** Steve Woit.

CHAPTER 7

190 General Instrument Corp./Franz Edson, Inc. **192** Courtesy of Hoover Company. **196** Courtesy of American Express Co. **197** Courtesy of Atari Corporation. **200** Courtesy of Intel Corporation. **208** Courtesy of Baxter Healthcare Corporation, Deerfield, IL. **213** Photo courtesy of General Motors Corporation.

CHAPTER 8

222 Photo by Jim Sims, Southdown, Inc. 1989 Annual Report. **224** Photo courtesy of Eaton Corporation. **226** Louis Psihoyos/Matrix. **227** Philadelphia Electric Company. **229** The Bettmann Archive. **230** Baker Library, Harvard Business School. **231** The Bettmann Archive. **233** The Granger Collection, New York. **239** Courtesy: Prudential Insurance Company of America. Photo: Bill Robbins. **244** Courtesy of Atlantic Richfield Company.

CHAPTER 9

250 Joseph Pobereskin/Tony Stone Worldwide. **252** Courtesy, Motorola, Inc. **254** Keith Martinson. **256** Courtesy: PacifiCorp. Photo: Bryan F. Peterson. **261** Courtesy: Rite Aid Corporation. Photo: Gary Gladstone. **269** Courtesy of Blue Cross and Blue Shield of MA. **271** Tim Brown/Tony Stone Worldwide.

CHAPTER 10

282 Courtesy of The Southern Company. Photo: © Jeff Smith. **284** General Motors Corporation. **287** The Bettmann Archive. **289** Andy Freeberg. **297** Mark Humphrey/Wide World Photos. **301** Stephen Ferry/Gamma-Liaison. **306** Rich Frishman.

CHAPTER 11

314 David J. Maenza/The Image Bank. **316** Reprinted by permission of Reebok International Ltd. **318** Courtesy of Club Med Sales, Inc. **324** Alan D. Levenson. **331** Chad Slattery. **334** Borden, Inc. **335** With permission from Scott Paper Company & Nike Inc. **340** Reproduced with permission of Kraft General Foods, Inc.

CHAPTER 12

348 Joseph McNally. **350** Mario Ruiz. **354** Courtesy of Gerber Products Co. **359** Courtesy of Friendly Ice Cream Corporation. **360** Morton International; Tom Tracy Photographer. **366** Michael O'Brien. **370** Scali, McCabe, Sloves, Inc.

CHAPTER 13

382 Courtesy of Intel Corporation. **384** Louis Psihoyos/Matrix. **387** Reprinted by permission of Dean Foods Company. **397** Courtesy of Avon Products Inc. **400** Peter Freed. **406** Union Pacific Corp. **409** Courtesy Prime Computer, Inc. © American Map Corporation, New York, No. 19384.

CHAPTER 14

414 Grafton Marshall Smith/The Image Bank. **416** Alex Webb/Magnum Photos. **421** Ad by Benetton. **423** © Gabe Palmer/Mug Shots. **426** © George Steinmetz. **431** Becton Dickinson and Company. **432** General Cinema Corporation. **435** Porsche Cars North America, Inc. **441** Produced by: Franenberry, Laughlin & Constable, Inc.; Photo: Mary Ann Holden: © 1989 OshKosh B'Gosh, Inc., Oshkosh, WI.

CHAPTER 15

448 © Gabe Palmer/Mug Shots. **450** William Taufic. **452** Photo: Gregory Heisler. © 1990 The Time Inc. Magazine Company. **455** Provided courtesy of Digital Equipment Company. **459** Photo courtesy of Hewlett-Packard Company. **462** © 1990 KnowledgeWare, Inc. Atlanta, GA. Used with permission. Advertising Agency: Alexander Marketing Services, Grand Rapids, MI. **465** Courtesy of Asea Brown Boveri Inc. **470** Photo courtesy of BT Tymet, a British Telecom Company. **475** Photo courtesy of TRW Inc. **478** Photo courtesy of Bristol-Myers Squibb Company.

CHAPTER 16

484 Flip Chalfant/The Image Bank. **486** Copyright © 1989 Andersen Consulting, AA&Co., S.C. **489** Superstock, Inc. **494** Comstock. **501** Sony Corporation of America. **509** W.W. Grainger, Inc.

CHAPTER 17

518 Photo by Paul Fusco for BP America Inc. **520** Jim Anderson/Stock Boston. **522** Scott Applewhite/AP Wide World Photos. **524** Deluxe Corporation. **528** Used by permission; The Howard Savings Bank. **534** Steve Leonard/Black Star. **541** Howard D. Simmons.

CHAPTER 18

552 Courtesy of CMS Energy. Photo: © 1990 Rob Johns. **554** Max Aguilera-Hellweg. **557** PGA National. **561** Peter Sibbald. **572** Gary Spector. **577** Courtesy of The Turner Corporation, NY, NY.

CHAPTER 19

584 COMSTOCK, Inc. **586** Claudio Edinger/Gamma-Liaison. **589** © Joyce Ravid. **593** © Business Week. Used with permission. **600** MBIA Corporation. **606** Steve Woit.

CHAPTER 20

620 © 1990 by Seth Resnick. **622** © Jacques Lowe 1990. **624** John S. Abbott. **626** Courtesy: Southern Company Services. Photo: Gary Gladstone. **632** Metropolitan Life Insurance Company. **633** Courtesy: Transamerica Corporation. Photo: Kent Barker. **638** Figgie International Inc. **645** John S. Abbott.

CHAPTER 21

652 Photo courtesy of Airbourne Express, photographer Tyler Boley. **654** Terry Ashe/TIME Magazine. **656** Alan Dorow. **659** Ethan Hoffman/Mead Corporation. **669** Courtesy of Richard Barrie Fragrances, Inc. **672** © Russell Monk.

CHAPTER 22

680 Walter Bibikow/The Image Bank. **682** Steven Pumphrey. **684** Courtesy of Carnegie Mellon University. **686** Courtesy of Grumman Corporation. **692** J. D. Duff Photography. **697** Courtesy of Sysco Corporation. Photo: Terry Vine.

CHAPTER 23

708 Greg Pease. **710** Tom Berthiaume. **712** © 1990 Arthur Meyerson. **716** Courtesy: Echlin Inc. Photo: Dana Duke. **721** Artist: Doug Johnson. © 1990 The Time Inc. Magazine Company. **724** Farrell Grehan/Photo Researchers, Inc. **730** © Mary Beth Camp/Matrix.

NAME INDEX

SUBJECT INDEX